Microsoft Word 2002

Comprehensive Concepts and Techniques

Gary B. Shelly
Thomas J. Cashman
Misty E. Vermaat

COURSE TECHNOLOGY
25 THOMSON PLACE
BOSTON MA 02210

Australia • Canada • Denmark • Japan • Mexico • New Zealand • Philippines • Puerto Rico • Singapore
South Africa • Spain • United Kingdom • United States

COPYRIGHT © 2002 Course Technology, a division of Thomson Learning.
Printed in the United States of America

Asia (excluding Japan)
Thomson Learning
5 Shenton Way #01-01
UIC Building
Singapore 068808

Latin America
Thomson Learning
Seneca, 53
Colonia Polanco
11560 Mexico D.F. Mexico

Canada
Nelson/Thomson Learning
1120 Birchmount Road
Scarborough, Ontario
Canada M1K 5G4

Japan
Thomson Learning
Nihonjisyo Brooks Bldg 3-F
1-4-1 Kudankita, Chiyoda-Ku
Tokyo 102-0073 Japan

South Africa
Thomson Learning
15 Brookwood Street
P.O. Box 1722
Soverset West 7120
South Africa

UK/Europe/Middle East
Thomson Learning
Berkshire House
168-173 High Holborn
London, WC1V 7AA United Kingdom

Australia/New Zealand
Nelson/Thomson Learning
102 Dodds Street
Southbank, Victoria 3006
Australia

Spain
Thomson Learning
Calle Magallanes, 25
28015-MADRID
ESPANA

Course Technology, the Course Technology logo, the SHELLY CASHMAN SERIES®, and **Custom Edition**® are registered trademarks used under license. All other names used herein are for identification purposes only and are trademarks of their respective owners.

For more information, contact Course Technology, 25 Thomson Place, Boston, MA 02210.

Or visit our Internet site at www.course.com

All rights reserved. No part of this work covered by the copyright hereon may be reproduced or used in any form or by any means without the written permission of the publisher.

For permission to use material from this product, contact us by
- Tel (800) 730-2214
- Fax (800) 730-2215
- www.thomsonrights.com

Course Technology reserves the right to revise this publication and make changes from time to time in its content without notice.

"Microsoft and the Microsoft Office User Specialist Logo are registered trademarks of Microsoft Corporation in the United States and other countries. Course Technology is an independent entity from Microsoft Corporation, and not affiliated with Microsoft Corporation in any manner. This textbook may be used in assisting students to prepare for a Microsoft Office User Specialist Exam. Neither Microsoft Corporation, its designated review company, nor Course Technology warrants that use of this textbook will ensure passing the relevant Exam.
"Use of the Microsoft Office User Specialist Approved Courseware Logo on this product signifies that it has been independently reviewed and approved in complying with the following standards: 'Acceptable coverage of all content related to the Microsoft Office Exam entitled "Microsoft Word 2002 Core Exam," and sufficient performance-based exercises that relate closely to all required content, based on sampling of text.'"

PHOTO CREDITS: Microsoft Word 2002 *Project 2, pages WD 2.02-03* Boy at computer, caution sign, computer, library, man biting nails, SUV, woman sleeping, Courtesy of ArtToday; *Project 3, pages WD 3.02-03* Drawing of Albert Einstein, girl working on computer, Courtesy of ArtToday; violin, hand with pen, Courtesy of Nova Development; envelopes, handshake, man working, Courtesy of PhotoDisc, Inc.; *Project 4, pages WD 4.02-03* Men shaking hands, shaking hands, offshore oil rig, Courtesy of ArtToday; Men in rooms, hand writing, leaf, eye, oil rig, and shadow, Courtesy of PhotoDisc, Inc.; *Project 5, pages WD 5.02-03* Hand writing forms, woman at computer, stack of computer paper, mail in mailbox, couple read mail at breakfast, man paying for purchase, Courtesy of PhotoDisc, Inc.; *Project 6, pages WD 6.02-03* Radio telescope, sailing ship, cowboy on horseback, message in a bottle, Courtesy of PhotoDisc, Inc.; River rocks, map, Courtesy of ArtToday.; *Project 8, pages WD 8.02-03* Young graduates, graduation cap, college graduation, Courtesy of PhotoDisc, Inc.; *Project 9, pages WD 9.02-03* Keyboard and notebook, young man at computer, hand holding pencil, woman in library, young business woman, *Courtesy of PhotoDisc, Inc.*

ISBN 0-7895-6288-X

4 5 6 7 8 9 10   BC   06 05 04 03

Microsoft Word 2002
Complete Concepts and Techniques

Contents

▮ PROJECT ONE

CREATING AND EDITING A WORD DOCUMENT

Objectives	WD 1.03
What Is Microsoft Word?	WD 1.06
Project One — Hidden Lake Announcement	WD 1.06
Starting and Customizing Word	WD 1.07
The Word Window	WD 1.12
Document Window	WD 1.12
Menu Bar and Toolbars	WD 1.14
Resetting Menus and Toolbars	WD 1.17
Speech Recognition and Handwriting Recognition	WD 1.17
Zooming Page Width	WD 1.18
Changing the Default Font Size	WD 1.19
Entering Text	WD 1.21
Entering Blank Lines into a Document	WD 1.23
Displaying Formatting Marks	WD 1.23
Entering More Text	WD 1.24
Using Wordwrap	WD 1.25
Entering Text that Scrolls the Document Window	WD 1.26
Checking Spelling as You Type	WD 1.27
Saving a Document	WD 1.29
Formatting Paragraphs and Characters in a Document	WD 1.32
Selecting and Formatting Paragraphs and Characters	WD 1.33
Selecting Multiple Paragraphs	WD 1.33
Changing the Font Size of Selected Text	WD 1.34
Changing the Font of Selected Text	WD 1.36
Right-Align a Paragraph	WD 1.36
Center a Paragraph	WD 1.38
Undoing Commands or Actions	WD 1.38
Selecting a Line and Formatting It	WD 1.39
Italicize Selected Text	WD 1.41
Scrolling	WD 1.41
Selecting a Word	WD 1.42
Underlining Selected Text	WD 1.43
Selecting a Group of Words	WD 1.44
Bold Selected Text	WD 1.44
Inserting Clip Art into a Word Document	WD 1.46
Inserting Clip Art	WD 1.46
Resizing a Graphic	WD 1.50
Saving an Existing Document with the Same File Name	WD 1.53
Printing a Document	WD 1.54
Quitting Word	WD 1.55
Opening a Document	WD 1.55
Correcting Errors	WD 1.57
Types of Changes Made to Documents	WD 1.57
Inserting Text into an Existing Document	WD 1.58
Deleting Text from an Existing Document	WD 1.58
Closing the Entire Document	WD 1.58
Word Help System	WD 1.59
Obtaining Help Using the Ask a Question Box on the Menu Bar	WD 1.59
Project Summary	WD 1.62
What You Should Know	WD 1.62
Learn It Online	WD 1.63
Apply Your Knowledge	WD 1.64
In the Lab	WD 1.66
Cases and Places	WD 1.70

▮ PROJECT TWO

CREATING A RESEARCH PAPER

Objectives	WD 2.01
Introduction	WD 2.04
Project Two — E-Retailing Research Paper	WD 2.04
MLA Documentation Style	WD 2.06
Starting Word	WD 2.06
Resetting Menus and Toolbars	WD 2.07
Displaying Formatting Marks	WD 2.07
Changing the Margins	WD 2.07
Zooming Page Width	WD 2.09
Adjusting Line Spacing	WD 2.10
Using a Header to Number Pages	WD 2.11
Headers and Footers	WD 2.11
Entering Text Using Click and Type	WD 2.13
Entering a Page Number into the Header	WD 2.14
Typing the Body of the Research Paper	WD 2.15
Applying Formatting Using Shortcut Keys	WD 2.16
Saving the Research Paper	WD 2.18
Indenting Paragraphs	WD 2.18
Using Word's AutoCorrect Feature	WD 2.20
Adding Footnotes	WD 2.24
Modifying a Style	WD 2.27
Using Word Count	WD 2.32
Automatic Page Breaks	WD 2.33
Recounting Words in a Document	WD 2.34
Creating an Alphabetical Works Cited Page	WD 2.34
Manual Page Breaks	WD 2.35
Centering the Title of the Works Cited Page	WD 2.36
Creating a Hanging Indent	WD 2.36
Inserting Arrows, Faces, and Other Symbols Automatically	WD 2.38
Creating a Hyperlink	WD 2.39
Sorting Paragraphs	WD 2.41

iii

Proofing and Revising the Research Paper	**WD 2.42**
Going to a Specific Location in a Document	WD 2.42
Moving Text	WD 2.44
Smart Tags	WD 2.47
Finding and Replacing Text	WD 2.48
Finding Text	WD 2.49
Finding a Synonym	WD 2.50
Checking Spelling and Grammar At Once	WD 2.50
Saving Again and Printing the Document	WD 2.52
Navigating to a Hyperlink	**WD 2.53**
E-Mailing a Copy of the Research Paper	**WD 2.54**
Project Summary	**WD 2.55**
What You Should Know	**WD 2.55**
Learn It Online	**WD 2.56**
Apply Your Knowledge	**WD 2.57**
In the Lab	**WD 2.58**
Cases and Places	**WD 2.64**

3 PROJECT THREE

CREATING A RESUME USING A WIZARD AND A COVER LETTER WITH A TABLE

Objectives	**WD 3.01**
Introduction	**WD 3.04**
Project Three — Resume and Cover Letter	**WD 3.05**
Starting Word	WD 3.06
Resetting Menus and Toolbars	WD 3.07
Displaying Formatting Marks	WD 3.07
Using Word's Resume Wizard to Create a Resume	**WD 3.08**
Personalizing the Resume	**WD 3.16**
Tables	WD 3.16
Zooming Text Width	WD 3.17
Styles	WD 3.18
Selecting and Replacing Text	WD 3.19
Entering a Line Break	WD 3.21
AutoFormat As You Type	WD 3.22
Viewing and Printing the Resume in Print Preview	WD 3.25
Saving the Resume	WD 3.26
Creating a Letterhead	**WD 3.27**
Opening a New Document Window	WD 3.27
Adding Color to Characters	WD 3.28
Setting Tab Stops Using the Tabs Dialog Box	WD 3.30
Collecting and Pasting	WD 3.32
Adding a Bottom Border to a Paragraph	WD 3.37
Clearing Formatting	WD 3.38
Creating a Cover Letter	**WD 3.41**
Components of a Business Letter	WD 3.41
Saving the Cover Letter with a New File Name	WD 3.41
Setting Tab Stops Using the Ruler	WD 3.42
Inserting the Current Date into a Document	WD 3.43
Creating an AutoText Entry	WD 3.44
Entering a Nonbreaking Space	WD 3.46
Inserting an AutoText Entry	WD 3.47
Creating a Table with the Insert Table Button	WD 3.49
Entering Data into a Word Table	WD 3.50
Resizing Table Columns	WD 3.51
Changing the Table Alignment	WD 3.53
Bulleting a List	WD 3.54
Saving Again and Printing the Cover Letter	WD 3.57
Addressing and Printing Envelopes and Mailing Labels	**WD 3.57**
	WD 3.58
Smart Tags	**WD 3.58**
Project Summary	**WD 3.61**
What You Should Know	**WD 3.61**
Learn It Online	**WD 3.62**
Apply Your Knowledge	**WD 3.63**
In the Lab	**WD 3.64**
Cases and Places	**WD 3.66**

■ WEB FEATURE

CREATING WEB PAGES USING WORD

Introduction	**WDW 1.01**
Saving a Word Document as a Web Page	**WDW 1.03**
Formatting the E-Mail Address as a Hyperlink	WDW 1.04
Using Word's Web Page Wizard to Create a Web Page	**WDW 1.04**
Modifying a Web Page	**WDW 1.08**
Viewing the Web Page in Your Default Browser	WDW 1.11
Editing a Web Page from Your Browser	WDW 1.12
Web Feature Summary	**WDW 1.14**
In the Lab	**WDW 1.14**

4 PROJECT FOUR

CREATING A DOCUMENT WITH A TABLE, CHART, AND WATERMARK

Objectives	**WD 4.01**
Introduction	**WD 4.04**
Project Four — Sales Proposal	**WD 4.04**
Starting Word	WD 4.06
Resetting Menus and Toolbars	WD 4.06
Displaying Formatting Marks	WD 4.06
Zooming Text Width	WD 4.07
Creating a Title Page	**WD 4.07**
Formatting and Entering Characters	WD 4.07
Adding a Border and Shading to a Paragraph	WD 4.08
Formatting Characters Using the Font Dialog Box	WD 4.12
Inserting Clip Art from the Web into a Word Document	WD 4.15
Centering the Title Page Contents Vertically on the Page	WD 4.18
Saving the Title Page	WD 4.20
Inserting an Existing Document into an Open Document	**WD 4.21**
Inserting a Section Break	WD 4.21
Inserting a Word Document into an Open Document	WD 4.24
Saving the Active Document with a New File Name	WD 4.26
Printing Specific Pages in a Document	WD 4.26
Creating Headers and Footers	**WD 4.29**
Creating a Header Different from a Previous Section Header	WD 4.29
Creating a Footer Different from a Previous Section Footer	WD 4.30
Formatting and Charting a Table	**WD 4.32**
Working with Tables	WD 4.32
Summing Table Contents	WD 4.33
Formatting a Table	WD 4.34

Formatting Nonadjacent Characters	WD 4.37
Charting a Word Table	WD 4.39
Changing the Chart in Graph	WD 4.41
Formatting the Chart in Word	WD 4.45
Formatting Paragraphs and Characters	**WD 4.46**
Keeping Lines in a Paragraph Together	WD 4.46
Customizing Bullets in a List	WD 4.48
Creating and Applying a Character Style	WD 4.50
Drawing a Table	**WD 4.53**
Drawing an Empty Table	WD 4.53
Single-Space the Table Contents	WD 4.58
Entering Data into the Table	WD 4.58
Formatting the Table	WD 4.59
Creating a Watermark	**WD 4.64**
Checking Spelling, Saving Again, and Printing the Sales Proposal	WD 4.66
Revealing Formatting	**WD 4.66**
Project Summary	**WD 4.68**
What You Should Know	**WD 4.68**
Learn It Online	**WD 4.69**
Apply Your Knowledge	**WD 4.70**
In the Lab	**WD 4.72**
Cases and Places	**WD 4.79**

5 PROJECT FIVE

GENERATING FORM LETTERS, MAILING LABELS, ENVELOPES, AND DIRECTORIES

Objectives	**WD 5.01**
Introduction	**WD 5.04**
Project Five — Form Letters, Mailing Labels, and Envelopes	**WD 5.04**
Starting Word	WD 5.06
Resetting Menus and Toolbars	WD 5.06
Displaying Formatting Marks	WD 5.07
Zooming Text Width	WD 5.07
Identifying the Main Document for Form Letters	**WD 5.07**
Identifying the Main Document	WD 5.08
Working with AutoShapes and the Drawing Canvas	**WD 5.11**
Adding an AutoShape	WD 5.11
Formatting an AutoShape	WD 5.13
Resizing and Formatting the Drawing Canvas	WD 5.16
Creating a Folder	WD 5.20
Creating a Data Source	**WD 5.21**
Editing Records in the Data Source	WD 5.29
Composing the Main Document for the Form Letters	**WD 5.30**
Modifying a Field	WD 5.30
Inserting Merge Fields into the Main Document	WD 5.32
Using an IF Field to Conditionally Print Text in a Form Letter	WD 5.35
Creating an Outline Numbered List	WD 5.38
Applying a Paragraph Style	WD 5.41
Saving the Document Again	WD 5.44
Displaying Field Codes	WD 5.45
Printing Field Codes	WD 5.46
Merging the Documents and Printing the Letters	WD 5.48
Selecting Data Records to Merge and Print	WD 5.49
Sorting Data Records to Merge and Print	WD 5.52
Viewing Merged Data	WD 5.53
Addressing and Printing Mailing Labels	**WD 5.54**
Saving the Mailing Labels	WD 5.59
Addressing and Printing Envelopes	**WD 5.59**
Saving the Envelopes	WD 5.62
Merging All Data Records to a Directory	**WD 5.63**
Saving the Directory	WD 5.69
Closing All Open Word Documents and Quitting Word	WD 5.69
Project Summary	**WD 5.71**
What You Should Know	**WD 5.71**
Learn It Online	**WD 5.72**
Apply Your Knowledge	**WD 5.73**
In the Lab	**WD 5.74**
Cases and Places	**WD 5.80**

6 PROJECT SIX

CREATING A PROFESSIONAL NEWSLETTER

Objectives	**WD 6.01**
Introduction	**WD 6.04**
Project Six — Newsletter	**WD 6.04**
Desktop Publishing Terminology	WD 6.06
Starting Word	WD 6.06
Resetting Menus and Toolbars	WD 6.06
Displaying Formatting Marks	WD 6.07
Changing All Margin Settings	WD 6.07
Zooming Text Width	WD 6.08
Creating the Nameplate	**WD 6.08**
Inserting a WordArt Drawing Object	WD 6.08
Formatting a WordArt Drawing Object	WD 6.11
Changing the WordArt Shape	WD 6.13
Adding Ruling Lines	WD 6.14
Inserting Symbols	WD 6.16
Inserting and Formatting a Floating Graphic	WD 6.18
Saving the Newsletter	WD 6.23
Formatting the First Page of the Body of the Newsletter	**WD 6.23**
Formatting a Document into Multiple Columns	WD 6.24
Justifying a Paragraph	WD 6.26
Inserting the Remainder of the Feature Article	WD 6.27
Formatting a Letter as a Drop Cap	WD 6.28
Inserting a Column Break	WD 6.29
Adding a Vertical Rule Between Columns	WD 6.33
Creating a Pull-Quote	**WD 6.36**
Inserting a Text Box	WD 6.36
Formatting the Second Page of the Newsletter	**WD 6.42**
Changing Column Formatting	WD 6.42
Using the Paste Special Command to Link Text	WD 6.45
Balancing Columns	WD 6.47
Inserting a Diagram	WD 6.49
Enhancing the Newsletter with Color and a Page Border	**WD 6.60**
Using the Format Painter Button	WD 6.61
Adding a Page Border	WD 6.62
Enhancing a Document for Online Viewing	**WD 6.64**
Highlighting Text	WD 6.65
Animating Text	WD 6.66
Collaborating with Others on a Document	**WD 6.67**
Searching for Files	WD 6.67

Inserting, Viewing, and Editing Comments	WD 6.68
Comparing and Merging Documents	WD 6.71
Project Summary	**WD 6.73**
What You Should Know	**WD 6.74**
Learn It Online	**WD 6.75**
Apply Your Knowledge	**WD 6.76**
In the Lab	**WD 6.77**
Cases and Places	**WD 6.80**

INTEGRATION FEATURE

MERGING FORM LETTERS TO E-MAIL ADDRESSES USING AN OUTLOOK CONTACTS LIST

Introduction	**WDI 1.01**
Opening an Outlook Data File	WDI 1.03
Changing the Data Source in a Form Letter	**WDI 1.04**
Merging to E-Mail Addresses	**WDI 1.09**
Integration Feature Summary	**WDI 1.12**
What You Should Know	**WDI 1.12**
In the Lab	**WDI 1.13**

7 PROJECT SEVEN

CREATING AN ONLINE FORM

Objectives	**WD 7.01**
Introduction	**WD 7.04**
Project Seven — Online Form	**WD 7.04**
Starting Word	WD 7.06
Resetting Menus and Toolbars	WD 7.06
Displaying Formatting Marks	WD 7.07
Zooming Page Width	WD 7.07
Designing an Online Form	**WD 7.07**
Creating an Online Form	**WD 7.08**
Creating a Template	WD 7.08
Highlighting Text	WD 7.13
Inserting a Table into a Form	WD 7.15
Inserting a Text Form Field that Accepts any Text	WD 7.17
Inserting a Drop-Down Form Field	WD 7.21
Inserting a Text Form Field that Requires a Number	WD 7.24
Inserting a Check Box	WD 7.25
Inserting a Text Form Field that Displays the Current Date	WD 7.29
Formatting Form Fields	WD 7.31
Using the Format Painter Button	WD 7.32
Adding Help Text to Form Fields	WD 7.34
Removing Form Field Shading	WD 7.37
Inserting and Formatting a Rectangle Drawing Object	WD 7.38
Animating Text	WD 7.45
Protecting a Form	WD 7.47
Working with an Online Form	**WD 7.49**
Saving Data on the Form	WD 7.52
Working with Templates	**WD 7.57**
Project Summary	**WD 7.59**
What You Should Know	**WD 7.60**
Learn It Online	**WD 7.61**
Apply Your Knowledge	**WD 7.62**
In the Lab	**WD 7.63**
Cases and Places	**WD 7.68**

8 PROJECT EIGHT

WORKING WITH MACROS AND VISUAL BASIC FOR APPLICATIONS (VBA)

Objectives	**WD 8.01**
Introduction	**WD 8.04**
Project Eight — Working with Macros and Visual Basic for Applications	**WD 8.04**
Starting Word and Opening an Office Document	WD 8.07
Saving the Document with a New File Name	WD 8.07
Unprotecting a Document	WD 8.08
Resetting Menus and Toolbars	WD 8.08
Displaying Formatting Marks	WD 8.09
Zooming Page Width	WD 8.09
Setting a Security Level in Word	WD 8.09
Modifying a Form	**WD 8.11**
Modifying the Graphic	WD 8.11
Inserting a Text Box and Formatting Text	WD 8.13
Creating a New Style with a Shortcut Key	WD 8.16
Filling a Drawing Object with a Gradient Effect	WD 8.19
Adding a 3-D Effect to a Drawing Object	WD 8.21
Using a Macro to Automate a Task	**WD 8.23**
Recording and Executing a Macro	WD 8.23
Assigning a Macro to a Toolbar Button	WD 8.28
Recording an Automatic Macro	WD 8.32
Editing a Recorded Macro	**WD 8.37**
Viewing a Macro's VBA Code	WD 8.38
Adding Comments to a Macro	WD 8.40
Modifying Existing Code in a Macro	WD 8.42
Entering Code Statements	WD 8.42
Creating a Macro from Scratch Using VBA	**WD 8.44**
Modifying Form Field Options	WD 8.44
Inserting a Procedure for the Macro	WD 8.46
Planning and Writing a VBA Procedure	WD 8.48
Running a Macro When a User Exits a Form Field	WD 8.50
Adding an ActiveX Control to a Form	**WD 8.51**
Inserting an ActiveX Control	WD 8.52
Setting Properties of an ActiveX Control	WD 8.53
Formatting the ActiveX Control	WD 8.56
Writing the Macro for the ActiveX Control	WD 8.57
More About Visual Basic for Applications	WD 8.61
Testing the Online Form	WD 8.61
Digital Signatures	**WD 8.64**
Attaching a Digital Signature to a File	WD 8.64
Copying, Renaming, and Deleting Macros	WD 8.67
Project Summary	**WD 8.69**
What You Should Know	**WD 8.69**
Learn It Online	**WD 8.70**
Apply Your Knowledge	**WD 8.71**
In the Lab	**WD 8.73**
Cases and Places	**WD 8.78**

9 PROJECT NINE

WORKING WITH A MASTER DOCUMENT, AN INDEX, AND A TABLE OF CONTENTS

Objectives	**WD 9.01**
Introduction	**WD 9.04**

Project Nine — Master Document, Index, and Table of Contents — WD 9.04

Starting Word	WD 9.06
Resetting Menus and Toolbars	WD 9.07
Displaying Formatting Marks	WD 9.07
Zooming Page Width	WD 9.07
Reviewing a Document	**WD 9.08**
E-Mailing a Document for Review	WD 9.08
Reviewing the Document	WD 9.09
Saving a Document with a New File Name	WD 9.11
Inserting Comments	WD 9.11
Tracking Changes	WD 9.14
Saving Multiple Versions of a Document	WD 9.16
Reviewing Tracked Changes	WD 9.17
Comparing and Merging Documents	WD 9.21
Preparing a Document to Be Included in a Longer Document	**WD 9.23**
Inserting and Formatting a Graphic	WD 9.23
Adding a Caption	WD 9.25
Creating a Cross-Reference	WD 9.28
Marking Index Entries	WD 9.30
Controlling Widows and Orphans	WD 9.32
Password-Protecting a File	WD 9.33
Working with a Master Document	**WD 9.36**
Creating an Outline	WD 9.36
Inserting a Subdocument in a Master Document	WD 9.39
Creating a Subdocument from a Master Document	WD 9.43
Modifying an Outline	WD 9.44
Entering Text and Graphics as Part of the Master Document	WD 9.46
Inserting a Diagram	WD 9.49
Creating a Table of Figures	WD 9.54
Building an Index	WD 9.56
Creating a Table of Contents	WD 9.58
Adding Bookmarks	WD 9.59
Creating Alternating Headers and Footers	WD 9.61
Setting a Gutter Margin	WD 9.63
Opening a Master Document	WD 9.65
Using the Document Map	WD 9.66
Modifying the Table of Contents and Index	WD 9.67
Project Summary	**WD 9.70**
What You Should Know	**WD 9.70**
Learn It Online	**WD 9.71**
Apply Your Knowledge	**WD 9.72**
In the Lab	**WD 9.74**
Cases and Places	**WD 9.82**

INTEGRATION FEATURE

LINKING AN EXCEL WORKSHEET AND CHARTING ITS DATA IN WORD

Introduction	**WDI 2.01**
Starting Word and Opening a Document	WDI 2.03
Saving the Document with a New File Name	WDI 2.03
Linking an Excel Worksheet	**WDI 2.03**
Creating a Chart from an Excel Worksheet	**WDI 2.06**
Editing a Linked Worksheet	**WDI 2.11**
Integration Feature Summary	**WDI 2.13**
What You Should Know	**WDI 2.13**
In the Lab	**WDI 2.14**

APPENDIX A

MICROSOFT WORD HELP SYSTEM

Using the Word Help System	**WD A.01**
Ask a Question Box	**WD A.02**
The Office Assistant	**WD A.03**
Showing and Hiding the Office Assistant	WD A.04
Turning the Office Assistant On and Off	WD A.04
Using the Office Assistant	WD A.05
The Microsoft Word Help Window	**WD A.06**
Using the Contents Sheet	WD A.07
Using the Answer Wizard Sheet	WD A.08
Using the Index Sheet	WD A.08
What's This? Command and Question Mark Button	**WD A.09**
What's This? Command	WD A.10
Question Mark Button	WD A.10
Office on the Web Command	**WD A.10**
Other Help Commands	**WD A.11**
Activate Product Command	WD A.11
WordPerfect Help Command	WD A.11
Detect and Repair Command	WD A.11
About Microsoft Word Command	WD A.11
Use Help	**WD A.12**

APPENDIX B

SPEECH AND HANDWRITING RECOGNITION

Introduction	**WD B.01**
The Language Bar	**WD B.01**
Speech Recognition	**WD B.05**
Handwriting Recognition	**WD B.09**

APPENDIX C

PUBLISHING OFFICE WEB PAGES TO A WEB SERVER — WD C.01

APPENDIX D

RESETTING THE WORD TOOLBARS AND MENUS — WD D.01

APPENDIX E

MICROSOFT OFFICE USER SPECIALIST CERTIFICATION PROGRAM

What Is MOUS Certification?	**WD E.01**
Why Should You Get Certified?	**WD E.01**
The MOUS Exams	**WD E.02**
How Can You Prepare for the MOUS Exams?	**WD E.02**
How to Find an Authorized Testing Center	**WD E.02**
Shelly Cashman Series MOUS Web Page	**WD E.02**
Microsoft Word 2002 User Specialist Certification Core and Expert Maps	**WD E.03**

Index	**I.01**
Quick Reference Summary	**QR.01**

Preface

The Shelly Cashman Series® offers the finest textbooks in computer education. We are proud of the fact that our series of Microsoft Office 4.3, Microsoft Office 95, Microsoft Office 97, and Microsoft Office 2000 textbooks have been the most widely used books in education. With each new edition of our Office books, we have made improvements based on the software and comments made by the instructors and students. The *Microsoft Office XP* books continue with the innovation, quality, and reliability that you have come to expect from the Shelly Cashman Series.

Office XP is the most significant upgrade ever to the Office suite. It provides a much smarter work experience for users. Microsoft has enhanced Office XP in the following areas: (1) streamlined user interface; (2) smart tags and task panes to help simplify the way people work; (3) speech and handwriting recognition; (4) an improved Help system; (5) enhanced Web capabilities; and (6) application-specific features. Each one of these enhancements is part of Microsoft Word 2002 and is discussed in detail.

In this *Microsoft Word 2002* book, you will find an educationally sound and easy-to-follow pedagogy that combines a step-by-step approach with corresponding screens. All projects and exercises in this book are designed to take full advantage of the Word 2002 enhancements. The popular Other Ways and More About features offer in-depth knowledge of Microsoft Word 2002. The new Learn It Online page presents a wealth of additional exercises to ensure your students have all the reinforcement they need. The project openers provide a fascinating perspective of the subject covered in the project. The project material is developed carefully to ensure that students will see the importance of learning Word for future coursework.

Objectives of This Textbook

Microsoft Word 2002: Complete Concepts and Techniques is intended for a three-unit course that presents in-depth coverage of Microsoft Word 2002. No experience with a computer is assumed, and no mathematics beyond the high school freshman level is required. The objectives of this book are:

- To teach the fundamentals of Word 2002
- To expose students to practical examples of the computer as a useful tool
- To acquaint students with the proper procedures to create documents suitable for course work, professional purposes, and personal use
- To develop an exercise-oriented approach that allows learning by doing
- To introduce students to new input technologies
- To encourage independent study, and help those who are working alone
- To assist students preparing to take the Microsoft Office User Specialist examination for both the Microsoft Word 2002 Core level and Microsoft Word 2002 Expert level.

Approved by Microsoft as Courseware for the Microsoft Office User Specialist Program Expert Level and Core Level

Microsoft Word 2002: Comprehensive Concepts and Techniques has been approved by Microsoft as courseware for the Microsoft Office User Specialist (MOUS) program. After completing the projects and exercises in this book, students will be prepared to take both the Expert-level and Core-level Microsoft Office User Specialist Exams for Microsoft Word 2002. The Word 2002 Core-level skill set is presented in the first six projects. See Appendix E for additional information on the MOUS program and for Expert-level and Core-level tables that include the Word 2002 MOUS skill set and corresponding page numbers on which a skill is discussed and practiced in the book, or visit the Web site mous.net.

By passing the certification exam for a Microsoft software program, students demonstrate their proficiency in that program to employers. This exam is offered at participating centers, participating corporations, and participating employment agencies. To purchase a Microsoft Office User Specialist certification exam, visit certiport.com.

The Shelly Cashman Series Microsoft Office User Specialist Center Web page (Figure 1) has more than fifteen Web pages you can visit to obtain additional information on the MOUS Certification program. The Web page scsite.com/offxp/cert.htm includes links to general information on certification, choosing an application for certification, preparing for the certification exam, and taking and passing the certification exam.

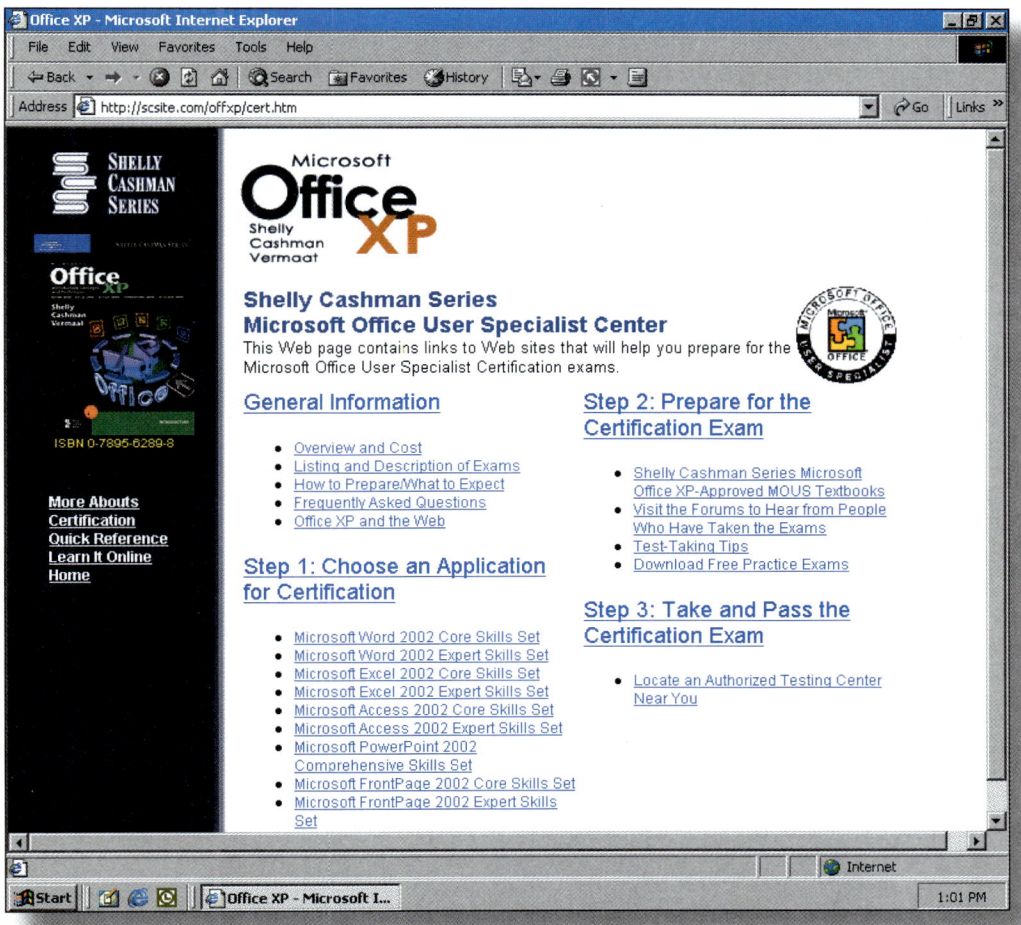

FIGURE 1 The Shelly Cashman Series Microsoft Office User Specialist Center Web Page

Other Ways

1. On Tools menu click Options, click Security tab, enter password, on File menu click Save As
2. In Voice Command mode, say "Tools, Options, Security, [type password], OK, File, Save As"

More About

Protecting Forms

If you want only authorized users to be able to unprotect a form, you should password-protect the form. To do this, click Tools on the menu bar, click Protect Document, click Forms in the Protect document for area, type the password in the Password (optional) text box, and then click the OK button. Then, reenter the password in the Confirm Password dialog box.

The Shelly Cashman Approach

Features of the Shelly Cashman Series Microsoft Word 2002 books include:

- **Project Orientation:** Each project in the book presents a practical problem and complete solution in an easy-to-understand approach.
- **Step-by-Step, Screen-by-Screen Instructions:** Each of the tasks required to complete a project is identified throughout the project. Full-color screens accompany the steps.
- **Thoroughly Tested Projects:** Every screen in the book is correct because it is produced by the author only after performing a step, resulting in unprecedented quality.
- **Other Ways Boxes and Quick Reference Summary:** The Other Ways boxes displayed at the end of most of the step-by-step sequences specify the other ways to do the task completed in the steps. Thus, the steps and the Other Ways box make a comprehensive reference unit.
- **More About Feature:** These marginal annotations provide background information and tips that complement the topics covered, adding depth and perspective.
- **Integration of the World Wide Web:** The World Wide Web is integrated into the Word 2002 learning experience by (1) More About annotations that send students to Web sites for up-to-date information and alternative approaches to tasks; (2) a MOUS information Web page so students can prepare for the MOUS Certification examinations; (3) a Word 2002 Quick Reference Summary Web page that summarizes the ways to complete tasks (mouse, menu, shortcut menu, and keyboard); and (4) the Learn It Online page at the end of each project, which has project reinforcement exercises, learning games, and other types of student activities.

Organization of This Textbook

Microsoft Word 2002: Complete Concepts and Techniques provides detailed instruction on how to use Word 2002. The material is divided into nine projects, a Web Feature, two Integration Features, five appendices, and a Quick Reference Summary.

Project 1 – Creating and Editing a Word Document In Project 1, students are introduced to Word terminology and the Word window by preparing an announcement. Topics include starting and quitting Word; entering text; checking spelling while typing; saving a document; selecting characters, words, lines, and paragraphs; changing the font and font size of text; centering, right-aligning, bolding, and italicizing text; undoing commands and actions; inserting clip art into a document; resizing a graphic; printing a document; opening a document; correcting errors; and using the Word Help System.

Project 2 – Creating a Research Paper In Project 2, students use the MLA style of documentation to create a research paper. Topics include changing margins; adjusting line spacing; using a header to number pages; entering text using Click and Type; first-line indenting paragraphs; using the AutoCorrect feature and AutoCorrect Options button; adding a footnote; modifying a style; inserting a symbol automatically; inserting a manual page break; creating a hanging indent; creating a text hyperlink; sorting paragraphs; moving text; using the Paste Options button; finding a synonym; counting and recounting words in a document; checking spelling and grammar at once; and e-mailing a document.

Project 3 – Creating a Resume Using a Wizard and a Cover Letter with a Table In Project 3, students create a resume using Word's Resume Wizard and then create a cover letter with a letterhead. Topics include personalizing the resume; using print preview; adding color to characters; setting and using tab stops; collecting and pasting; adding a bottom border; clearing formatting; inserting the current date; inserting a nonbreaking space; creating and inserting an AutoText entry; creating a bulleted list while typing; inserting a Word table; entering data into a Word table; and formatting a Word table. Finally, students prepare and print an envelope address.

Web Feature – Creating Web Pages Using Word In this Web Feature, students are introduced to creating Web pages. Topics include saving the resume created in Project 3 as a Web page; creating a Web page using the Web Page Wizard; resizing a Web page frame; editing a hyperlink; and editing a Web page from your browser.

Project 4 – Creating a Document with a Table, Chart, and Watermark In Project 4, students work with a multi-page document that has a title page. Topics include adding a border and shading to paragraphs; formatting characters using the Font dialog box; inserting clip art from the Web; centering text vertically on a page; clearing formatting; inserting a section break; inserting an existing Word document into an open document; creating headers and footers different from previous headers and footers; changing the starting page number in a section; formatting a Word table; summing columns in a table; selecting and formatting nonadjacent text; charting a Word table; modifying and formatting a chart; adding picture bullets to a list; creating and applying a character style; creating a table using the Draw Table feature; changing the direction and alignment of text in table cells; inserting a text watermark; and revealing formatting.

Project 5 – Generating Form Letters, Mailing Labels, Envelopes, and Directories In Project 5, students learn how to create and edit the main document for form letters, mailing labels, envelopes, and directories. Topics include using a letter template for the main document; creating and editing a data source; inserting and formatting an AutoShape; formatting a drawing canvas; creating a folder while saving; inserting a date field and editing its format; inserting merge fields into a main document; using an IF field; creating an outline numbered list; applying a paragraph style; displaying and printing field codes; merging and printing the documents; selecting data records to merge and print; sorting data records and table contents; inserting bar codes on the mailing labels and envelopes; and printing a document in landscape orientation.

Project 6 – Creating a Professional Newsletter In Project 6, students learn how to use Word's desktop publishing features to create a newsletter. Topics include creating and formatting a WordArt drawing object; adding ruling lines; inserting a symbol; flipping a graphic; formatting a document into multiple columns; justifying a paragraph; formatting a character as a drop cap; inserting a column break; placing a vertical rule between columns; inserting, formatting, and positioning a text box; changing character spacing; shading a paragraph; using the Paste Special command; balancing columns; inserting and formatting a diagram; using the Format Painter button; adding a page border; highlighting text; animating text; comparing and merging documents; and inserting, viewing, and editing comments.

Integration Feature – Merging Form Letters to E-Mail Addresses Using an Outlook Contacts List In this Integration Feature, students open an existing Outlook data file and use its contacts list as the data source for a main document for form letters. Then, students merge the main document for the form letters to e-mail addresses.

Project 7 – Creating an Online Form In Project 7, students learn how to create an online form and then use Word to fill in the form. Topics include creating a document template; highlighting text; inserting a table into a form; inserting text form fields, drop-down form fields, and check box form fields; formatting form fields;

using the Format Painter button; adding Help text to form fields; drawing a rectangle; filling a drawing object with a texture; formatting a drawing object; animating text; protecting a form; saving form data in a text file; opening a text file in Word; and modifying the location of workgroup templates.

Project 8 – Working with Macros and Visual Basic for Applications (VBA) In Project 8, students enhance an online form by modifying its appearance, adding macros, and inserting an ActiveX control. Topics include setting security levels in Word; creating and applying a new style; formatting a drawing object; recording and executing a macro; assigning a macro to a toolbar button; copying, renaming, and deleting macros; viewing a macro's VBA code; adding comments and VBA code statements to a macro; attaching a macro to the exit property of a form field; inserting, formatting, and setting properties of an ActiveX control; writing VBA code statements for an ActiveX control; and attaching a digital signature.

Project 9 – Working with a Master Document, an Index, and a Table of Contents In Project 9, students learn how to organize and work with a long document. Topics include e-mailing a document for review; inserting, reviewing, and deleting comments; tracking changes; accepting and rejecting tracked changes; comparing and merging documents; saving multiple versions; adding a caption; creating a cross-reference; password-protecting a document; working with a master document and subdocuments; inserting and formatting a diagram; creating a table of figures; marking index entries; building an index; creating a table of contents; adding a bookmark; creating alternating headers and footers; setting a gutter margin; and using the Document Map.

Integration Feature – Linking an Excel Worksheet and Charting Its Data in Word In this Integration Feature, students are introduced to linking Excel data to a Word document. Topics include linking an Excel worksheet to a Word document; creating a chart; linking Excel data to the chart; and editing a linked object.

Appendices The book includes five appendices. Appendix A presents an introduction to the Microsoft Word Help system. Appendix B describes how to use the speech and handwriting recognition capabilities of Word 2002. Appendix C explains how to publish Web pages to a Web server. Appendix D shows how to reset the menus and toolbars. Appendix E introduces students to the Microsoft Office User Specialist (MOUS) Certification program.

Quick Reference Summary In Microsoft Word 2002, you can accomplish a task in a number of ways, such as using the mouse, menu, shortcut menu, and keyboard. The Quick Reference Summary at the back of the book provides a quick reference to each task presented.

End-Of-Project Student Activities

A notable strength of the Shelly Cashman Series *Microsoft Word 2002* books is the extensive student activities at the end of each project. Well-structured student activities can make the difference between students merely participating in a class and students retaining the information they learn. The activities in the Shelly Cashman Series *Microsoft Word 2002* books include the following.

- **What You Should Know** A listing of the tasks completed within a project together with the pages on which the step-by-step, screen-by-screen explanations appear.

- **Learn It Online** Every project features a Learn It Online page comprised of ten exercises. These exercises include True/False, Multiple Choice, Short Answer, Flash Cards, Practice Test, Learning Games, Tips and Tricks, Newsgroup usage, Expanding Your Horizons, and Search Sleuth.
- **Apply Your Knowledge** This exercise usually requires students to open and manipulate a file on the Data Disk. To obtain a copy of the Data Disk, follow the instructions on the inside back cover of this textbook.
- **In the Lab** Three in-depth assignments per project require students to apply the knowledge gained in the project to solve problems on a computer.
- **Cases and Places** Up to seven unique real-world case-study situations.

Shelly Cashman Series Teaching Tools

The three basic ancillaries that accompany this textbook are: Teaching Tools (ISBN 0-7895-6323-1), Course Presenter (ISBN 0-7895-6466-1), and MyCourse.com. These ancillaries are available to adopters through your Course Technology representative or by calling one of the following telephone numbers: Colleges and Universities, 1-800-648-7450; High Schools, 1-800-824-5179; Private Career Colleges, 1-800-477-3692; Canada, 1-800-268-2222; and Corporations and Government Agencies, 1-800-340-7450.

Teaching Tools

The contents of the Teaching Tools CD-ROM are listed below.

- **Instructor's Manual** The Instructor's Manual includes the following for each project: project objectives; project overview; detailed lesson plans with page number references; teacher notes and activities; answers to the end-of-project exercises; a test bank of 110 questions for every project (25 multiple-choice, 50 true/false, and 35 fill-in-the-blank) with page number references; and transparency references. The transparencies are available through the Figures in the Book. The test bank questions are the same as in ExamView and Course Test Manager.
- **Figures in the Book** Illustrations for every screen and table in the textbook are available in electronic form. Use this ancillary to present a slide show in lecture or to print transparencies for use in lecture with an overhead projector.
- **ExamView** ExamView is a state-of-the-art test builder that is easy to use. With ExamView, you quickly can create printed tests, Internet tests, and computer (LAN-based) tests. You can enter your own test questions or use the test bank that accompanies ExamView. The test bank is the same as the one described in the Instructor's Manual section. Instructors who want to continue to use our earlier generation test builder, Course Test Manager, rather than ExamView, can call Customer Service at 1-800-648-7450 for a copy of the Course Test Manager database for this book.
- **Course Syllabus** Any instructor who has been assigned a course at the last minute knows how difficult it is to come up with a course syllabus. For this reason, sample syllabi are included that can be customized easily to a course.

- **Lecture Success System** Lecture Success System files are used to explain and illustrate the step-by-step, screen-by-screen development of a project in the textbook without entering large amounts of data.
- **Instructor's Lab Solutions** Solutions and required files for all the In the Lab assignments at the end of each project are available. Solutions also are available for any Cases and Places assignment that supplies data.
- **Lab Tests/Test Outs** Tests that parallel the In the Lab assignments are supplied for the purpose of testing students in the laboratory on the material covered in the project or testing students out of the course.
- **Project Reinforcement** True/false, multiple choice, and short answer questions.
- **Student Files** All the files that are required by students to complete the Apply Your Knowledge exercises are included.
- **Interactive Labs** Eighteen completely updated, hands-on Interactive Labs that take students from ten to fifteen minutes each to step through help solidify and reinforce mouse and keyboard usage and computer concepts. Student assessment is available.

Course Presenter

Course Presenter is a lecture presentation system that provides PowerPoint slides for each project. Presentations are based on the projects' objectives. Use this presentation system to present well-organized lectures that are both interesting and knowledge-based. Course Presenter provides consistent coverage at schools that use multiple lecturers in their applications courses.

MyCourse 2.0

MyCourse 2.0 offers instructors and students an opportunity to supplement classroom learning with additional course content. You can use MyCourse 2.0 to expand on traditional learning by completing readings, tests, and other assignments through the customized, comprehensive Web site. For additional information, visit mycourse.com and click the Help button.

SAM Xp

SAM XP is a powerful skills-based testing and reporting tool that measures your students' proficiency in Microsoft Office applications through real-world, performance-based questions. SAM XP is available for a minimal cost.

TOM, Training Online Manager for Microsoft Office XP

TOM is Course Technology's MOUS-approved training tool for Microsoft Office XP. Available via the World Wide Web and CD-ROM, TOM allows students to actively learn Office XP concepts and skills by delivering realistic practice through both guided and self-directed simulated instruction.

Acknowledgments

The Shelly Cashman Series would not be the leading computer education series without the contributions of outstanding publishing professionals. First, and foremost, among them is Becky Herrington, director of production and designer. She is the heart and soul of the Shelly Cashman Series, and it is only through her leadership, dedication, and tireless efforts that superior products are made possible.

Under Becky's direction, the following individuals made significant contributions to these books: Doug Cowley, production manager; Ginny Harvey, series specialist and developmental editor; Ken Russo, senior Web and graphic designer; Mike Bodnar, associate production manager; Mark Norton, Web designer; Betty Hopkins and Richard Herrera, interior design; Michelle French, Christy Otten, Kellee LaVars, Stephanie Nance, Chris Schneider, Sharon Lee Nelson, Sarah Boger, Amanda Lotter, Michael Greco, and Ryan Ung, graphic artists; Jeanne Black and Betty Hopkins, Quark layout artists; Lyn Markowicz, Nancy Lamm, Kim Kosmatka, Pam Baxter, Eva Kandarpa, Ellana Russo, and Marilyn Martin, copy editors/proofreaders; Cristina Haley, proofreader/indexer; Sarah Evertson of Image Quest, photo researcher; and Ginny Harvey, Rich Hansberger, Kim Clark, and Nancy Smith, contributing writers.

Finally, we would like to thank Richard Keaveny, associate publisher; Cheryl Ouellette, managing editor; Jim Quasney, series consulting editor; Alexandra Arnold, product manager; Erin Runyon, associate product manager; Francis Schurgot and Marc Ouellette, Web product managers; Rachel VanKirk, marketing manager; and Reed Cotter, editorial assistant.

Gary B. Shelly
Thomas J. Cashman
Misty E. Vermaat

Shelly Cashman Series – Traditionally Bound Textbooks

The Shelly Cashman Series presents the following computer subjects in a variety of traditionally bound textbooks. For more information, see your Course Technology representative or call 1-800-648-7450. For Shelly Cashman Series information, visit Shelly Cashman Online at **scseries.com**

COMPUTERS	
Computers	Discovering Computers 2002: Concepts for a Digital World, Web Enhanced, Complete Edition
	Discovering Computers 2002: Concepts for a Digital World, Web Enhanced, Introductory Edition
	Discovering Computers 2002: Concepts for a Digital World, Web Enhanced, Brief Edition
	Teachers Discovering Computers: Integrating Technology in the Classroom 2e
	Exploring Computers: A Record of Discovery 4e
	Study Guide for Discovering Computers 2002: Concepts for a Digital World, Web Enhanced
	Essential Introduction to Computers 4e (32-page)
WINDOWS APPLICATIONS	
Microsoft Office	Microsoft Office XP: Essential Concepts and Techniques (5 projects)
	Microsoft Office XP: Brief Concepts and Techniques (9 projects)
	Microsoft Office XP: Introductory Concepts and Techniques (15 projects)
	Microsoft Office XP: Advanced Concepts and Techniques (11 projects)
	Microsoft Office XP: Post Advanced Concepts and Techniques (11 projects)
	Microsoft Office 2000: Essential Concepts and Techniques (5 projects)
	Microsoft Office 2000: Brief Concepts and Techniques (9 projects)
	Microsoft Office 2000: Introductory Concepts and Techniques, Enhanced Edition (15 projects)
	Microsoft Office 2000: Advanced Concepts and Techniques (11 projects)
	Microsoft Office 2000: Post Advanced Concepts and Techniques (11 projects)
Integration	Integrating Microsoft Office XP Applications and the World Wide Web: Essential Concepts and Techniques
PIM	Microsoft Outlook 2002: Essential Concepts and Techniques
Microsoft Works	Microsoft Works 6: Complete Concepts and Techniques[1] • Microsoft Works 2000: Complete Concepts and Techniques[1] • Microsoft Works 4.5[1]
Microsoft Windows	Microsoft Windows 2000: Complete Concepts and Techniques (6 projects)[2]
	Microsoft Windows 2000: Brief Concepts and Techniques (2 projects)
	Microsoft Windows 98: Essential Concepts and Techniques (2 projects)
	Microsoft Windows 98: Complete Concepts and Techniques (6 projects)[2]
	Introduction to Microsoft Windows NT Workstation 4
	Microsoft Windows 95: Complete Concepts and Techniques[1]
Word Processing	Microsoft Word 2002[2] • Microsoft Word 2000[2] • Microsoft Word 97[1] • Microsoft Word 7[1]
Spreadsheets	Microsoft Excel 2002[2] • Microsoft Excel 2000[2] • Microsoft Excel 97[1] • Microsoft Excel 7[1] • Microsoft Excel 5[1]
Database	Microsoft Access 2002[2] • Microsoft Access 2000[2] • Microsoft Access 97[1] • Microsoft Access 7[1]
Presentation Graphics	Microsoft PowerPoint 2002[2] • Microsoft PowerPoint 2000[2] • Microsoft PowerPoint 97[1] • Microsoft PowerPoint 7[1]
Desktop Publishing	Microsoft Publisher 2002[1] • Microsoft Publisher 2000[1]
PROGRAMMING	
Programming	Microsoft Visual Basic 6: Complete Concepts and Techniques[1] • Programming in QBasic
	Java Programming: Complete Concepts and Techniques[1] • Structured COBOL Programming 2e
INTERNET	
Browser	Microsoft Internet Explorer 5: An Introduction • Microsoft Internet Explorer 4: An Introduction
	Netscape Navigator 6: An Introduction • Netscape Navigator 4: An Introduction
Web Page Creation and Design	Web Design: Introductory Concepts and Techniques • HTML: Complete Concepts and Techniques[1]
	Microsoft FrontPage 2002: Essential Concepts and Techniques • Microsoft FrontPage 2002[2]
	Microsoft FrontPage 2000[1] • JavaScript: Complete Concepts and Techniques[1]
SYSTEMS ANALYSIS	
Systems Analysis	Systems Analysis and Design 4e
DATA COMMUNICATIONS	
Data Communications	Business Data Communications: Introductory Concepts and Techniques 3e

[1]Also available as an Introductory Edition, which is a shortened version of the complete book
[2]Also available as an Introductory Edition, which is a shortened version of the complete book and also as a Comprehensive Edition, which is an extended version of the complete book

Microsoft Word 2002

PROJECT 1

Creating and Editing a Word Document

You will have mastered the material in this project when you can:

OBJECTIVES

- Start Word
- Describe the Word window
- Describe the speech and handwriting recognition capabilities of Word
- Zoom page width
- Change the default font size of all text
- Enter text into a document
- Scroll through a document
- Check spelling as you type
- Save a document
- Select text
- Change the font size of selected text
- Change the font of selected text
- Right-align a paragraph
- Center a paragraph
- Undo commands or actions
- Italicize selected text
- Underline selected text
- Bold selected text
- Insert clip art into a document
- Resize a graphic
- Print a document
- Open a document
- Correct errors in a document
- Use Word Help
- Quit Word

Mind Tools and Spell Check
Help for Writers Everywhere

"*Learning is a treasure that will follow its owner everywhere.*"
Chinese Proverb

Good spelling comes naturally to some people, but most people have difficulty remembering how to spell at least some words. For others, spelling is an arduous task. Because the sounds of words and their spellings differ so greatly, for most, spelling simply requires memorization through effort and repetition.

One study reports that 20 percent of writers do not spell well because they cannot visualize words. Even remembering simple spelling rules, such as, i before e, except after c, does not offer much assistance because of all the exceptions!

Dictionary
Mnemonics
Proofread

A spelling error in a flyer distributed on campus, a resume sent to a potential employer, or an e-mail message forwarded to an associate could lessen your credibility, cause a reader to doubt the accuracy of your statements, and leave a negative impression. In this project, Microsoft Word checks your typing for possible spelling errors in the Student Government Association announcement of a 30 percent student discount on sailboat rentals at Hidden Lake State Park.

If you type a word that does not appear in Word's dictionary, Word will flag the possible error with a wavy red underline. If the spelling is correct, you can instruct Word to ignore the flagged word. If it is misspelled, the spelling feature will offer a list of suggested corrections. Despite this assistance from the spelling checker, one study indicates college students repeatedly ignore or override the flagged words.

Word's spelling checker is a useful alternative to a dictionary, but you must not rely on it 100 percent. It will not flag commonly misused homophones, which are words that are pronounced alike but are spelled differently. For example, it is easy to confuse the homophones in the sentence, The Web site contains an incorrect cite to the reference material discussing regaining sight after experiencing blindness.

English teachers emphasize that you can learn to spell better, but not by strictly memorizing long lists or having someone mark all the errors in a paper. Instead, you need to try some strategies to improve awareness of spelling difficulties.

First, identify error patterns. For example, do you misspell the same words repeatedly? If so, write them in a list and have a friend dictate them to you. Then write the words again. If you involve your senses, hear the words spelled correctly, and then visualize the words, you increase your awareness of the problem.

Next, always consult a dictionary when you are uncertain of a word's spelling. Note the word's etymology — its origin and history. For example, the word, science, originated from the Latin word, scientia, a form of the verb to know.

Then, try a mnemonic, which is a device or code, such as an image or story that has meaning to you. Mnemonics can assist the memory and help you spell more effectively. To make a mnemonic more helpful, use positive, pleasant images that clearly relate to the word you want to remember, and are vivid enough to recall every time you see a word.

As you proofread, read from right to left. Use a pencil to point at each word as you say it aloud.

Using Microsoft Word's spelling checker, a good dictionary, and other tried-and-true approaches can enhance your spelling ability and help your writing skills.

Microsoft Word 2002

Creating and Editing a Word Document

PROJECT 1

CASE PERSPECTIVE

Tara Stellenbach is the Activities chairperson for the Student Government Association (SGA) at Green Valley Community College (GVCC). One of her responsibilities is to coordinate student discount programs with local businesses. She then prepares fliers announcing the discount programs.

Tara's favorite pastime is sailing on beautiful Hidden Lake. The large lake has crystal clear water and is located in a mountainous area just 15 miles from campus. Because no motors are allowed on Hidden Lake, it is peaceful and often scattered with sailboats. Tara decides to contact Hidden Lake State Park to inquire about student discounts for sailboat rentals. After meeting with the marketing director, Tara is elated. The marketing director agrees to give all GVCC students a 30 percent discount on sailboat rentals!

As a marketing major, Tara has learned the guidelines for designing announcements. She will use large, bold characters for the headline and title. To attract attention to the announcement, she will include a large graphic of a sailboat. When complete, she will recruit you and other members of the SGA to distribute the flier.

What Is Microsoft Word?

Microsoft Word is a full-featured word processing program that allows you to create and revise professional looking documents such as announcements, letters, resumes, and reports. You can use Word's desktop publishing features to create high-quality brochures, advertisements, and newsletters. Word also provides many tools that enable you to create Web pages with ease. From within Word, you even can place these Web pages directly on a Web server.

Word has many features designed to simplify the production of documents. With Word, you easily can include borders, shading, tables, graphics, pictures, and Web addresses in your documents. You can instruct Word to create a template, which is a form you can use and customize to meet your needs. With proper hardware, you can dictate or handwrite text instead of typing it into Word. You also can speak instructions to Word.

While you are typing, Word can perform tasks automatically. For example, Word can detect and correct spelling and grammar errors in a variety of languages. Word's thesaurus allows you to add variety and precision to your writing. Word also can format text such as headings, lists, fractions, borders, and Web addresses as you type them. Within Word, you also can e-mail a copy of your Word document to an e-mail address.

Project One — Hidden Lake Announcement

To illustrate the features of Word, this book presents a series of projects that use Word to create documents similar to those you will encounter in academic and business environments. Project 1 uses Word to produce the announcement shown in Figure 1-1.

The announcement informs students about student discounts on sailboat rentals at Hidden Lake State Park. The announcement begins with a headline that is followed by a graphic of a sailboat. Below the graphic of the sailboat is the body title, HIDDEN LAKE STATE PARK, followed by the body copy that consists of a brief paragraph about the park and another paragraph about the discount. Finally, the last line of the announcement lists the park's telephone number.

> **More About**
>
> **Word 2002**
>
> For more information on the features of Microsoft Word 2002, visit the Word 2002 More About Web page (scsite.com/wd2002/more.htm) and then click Microsoft Word 2002 Features.

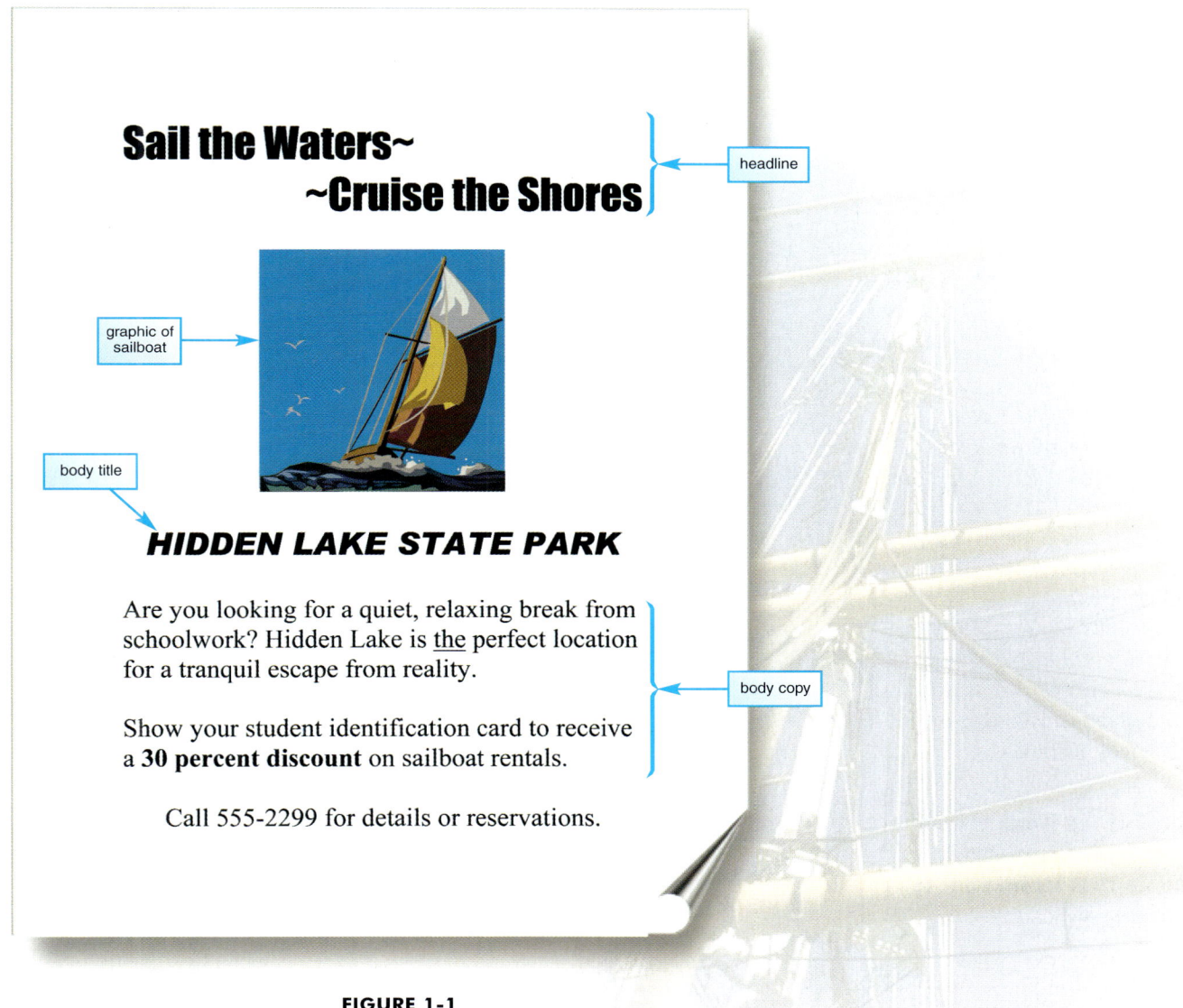

FIGURE 1-1

Starting and Customizing Word

To start Word, Windows must be running. Perform the steps on the next page to start Word, or ask your instructor how to start Word for your system.

Steps To Start Word

1 Click the Start button on the Windows taskbar, point to Programs on the Start menu, and then point to Microsoft Word on the Programs submenu.

The commands on the Start menu display above the Start button and the Programs submenu displays (Figure 1-2). If the Office Speech Recognition software is installed on your computer, the Language bar may display somewhere on the desktop.

2 Click Microsoft Word.

Office starts Word. After a few moments, an empty document titled Document1 displays in the Word window (Figure 1-3). The Windows taskbar displays the Word program button, indicating Word is running. If the Language bar displayed on the desktop when you started Word, it expands to display additional buttons.

3 If the Word window is not maximized, double-click its title bar to maximize it.

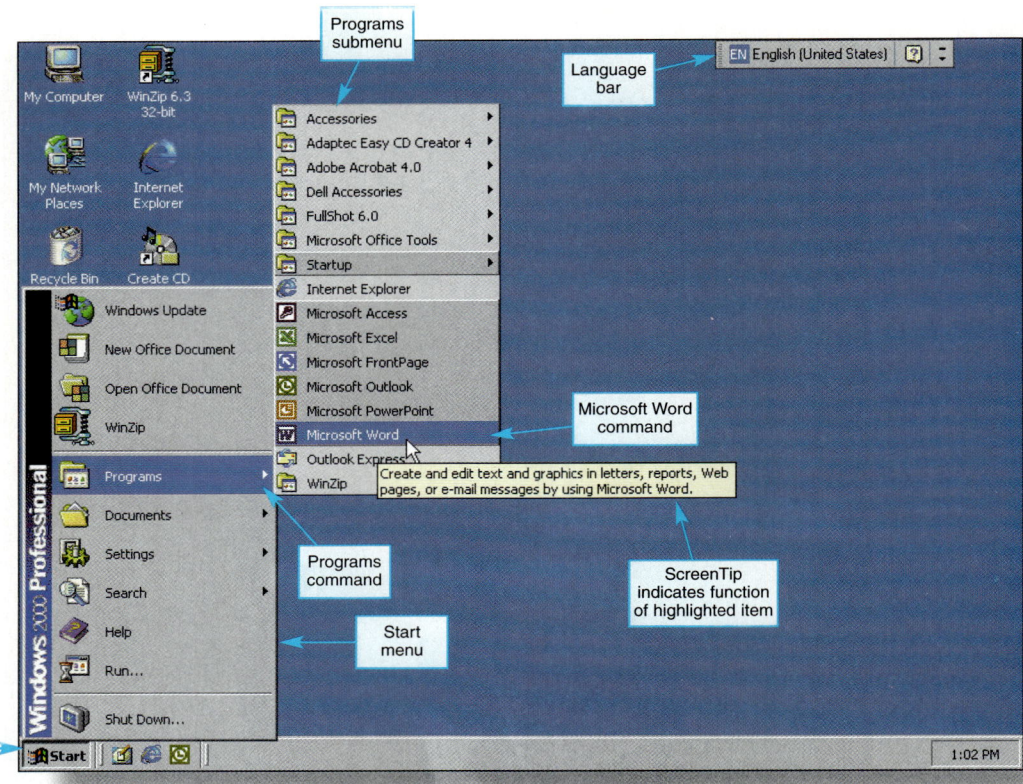

FIGURE 1-2

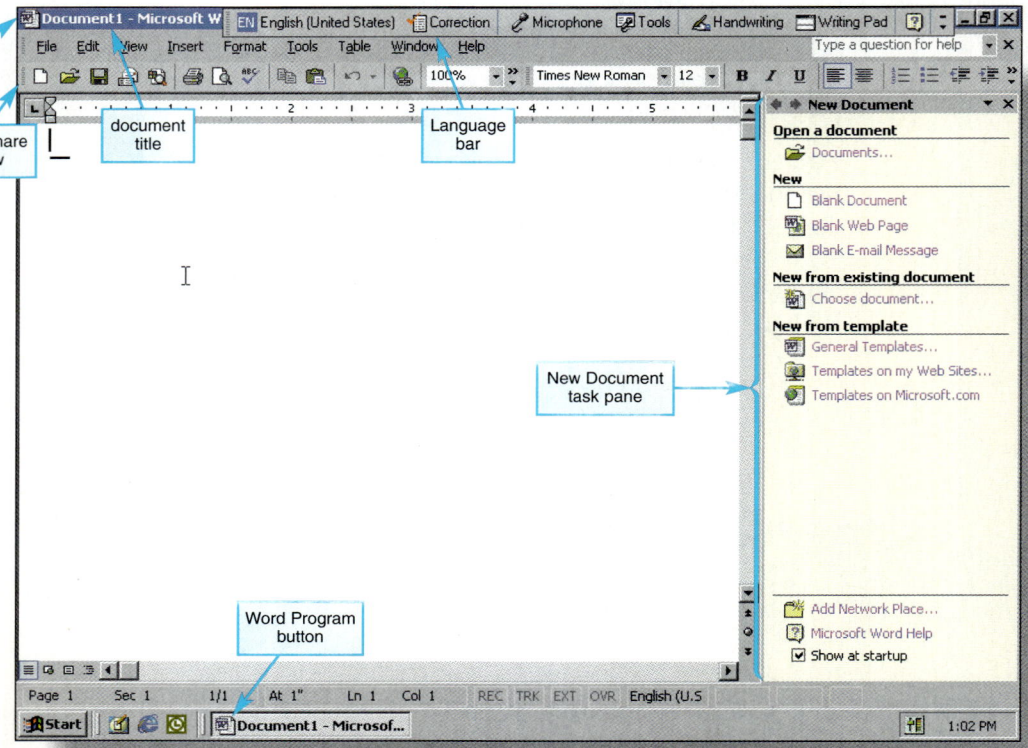

FIGURE 1-3

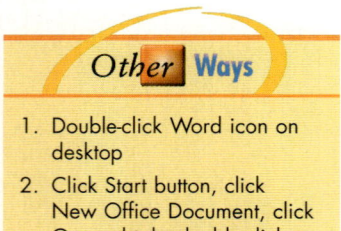

Other Ways

1. Double-click Word icon on desktop
2. Click Start button, click New Office Document, click General tab, double-click Blank Document icon

Starting and Customizing Word • WD 1.09

The screen in Figure 1-3 shows how the Word window looks the first time you start Word after installation on most computers. If the Office Speech Recognition software is installed on your computer, then when you start Word either the Language bar displays somewhere on the desktop (shown at the top of Figure 1-3) or the Language Indicator button displays on the right side of the Windows taskbar (Figure 1-5 on the next page). In this book, the Language bar will be kept minimized until it is used. For additional information about the Language bar, see page WD 1.17 and Appendix B.

Notice also that the New Document task pane displays on the screen, and that the buttons on the toolbars display on a single row. A **task pane** is a separate window that enables users to carry out some Word tasks more efficiently. In this book, to allow the maximum typing area in Word, a task pane should not display when you start Word. For more efficient use of the buttons on the toolbars, they should display on two separate rows instead of sharing a single row.

Perform the following steps to minimize the Language bar, close the New Document task pane, and display the toolbars on two separate rows.

Task Panes

When you first start Word, a small window called a task pane may display docked on the right side of the screen. You can drag a task pane title bar to float the pane in your work area or dock it on either the left or right side of a screen, depending on your personal preference.

Steps   To Customize the Word Window

 **If the Language bar displays, point to its Minimize button (Figure 1-4).**

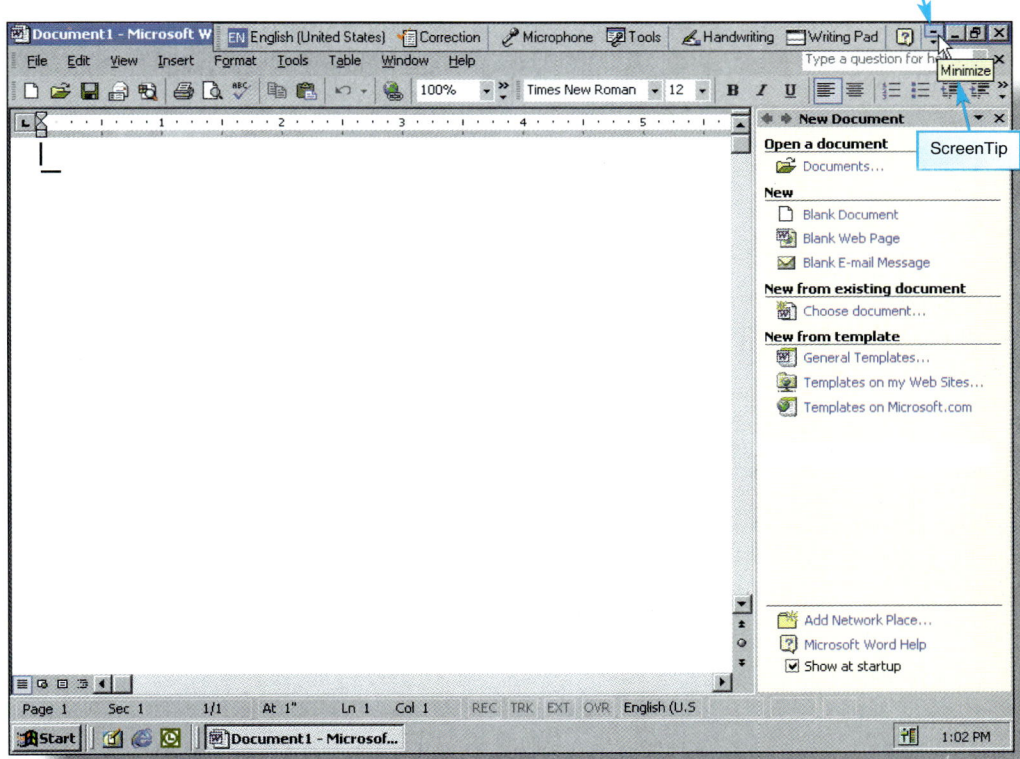

FIGURE 1-4

WD 1.10 • Project 1 • Creating and Editing a Word Document

2 **Click the Minimize button on the Language bar. If the New Document task pane displays, click the Show at startup check box to remove the check mark and then point to the Close button in the upper-right corner of the task pane title bar.**

Word minimizes the Language bar (Figure 1-5). With the check mark removed from the Show at startup check box, Word will not display the New Document task pane the next time Word starts.

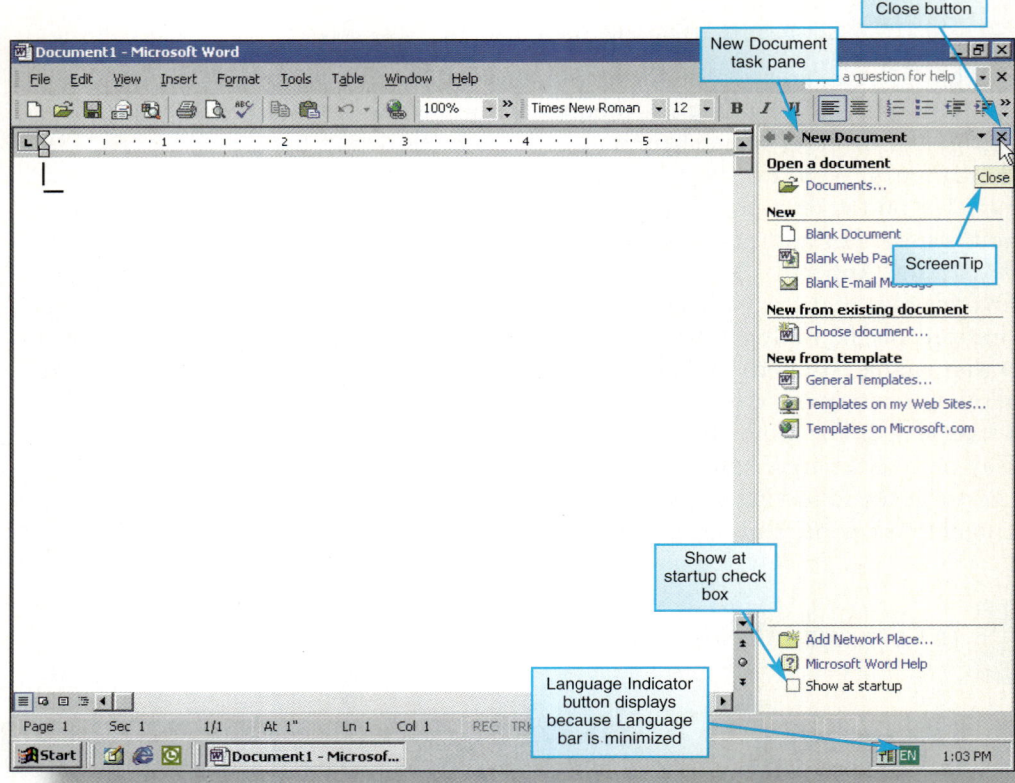

FIGURE 1-5

3 **Click the Close button on the New Document task pane. If the toolbars display positioned on the same row, point to the Toolbar Options button.**

The New Document task pane closes (Figure 1-6).

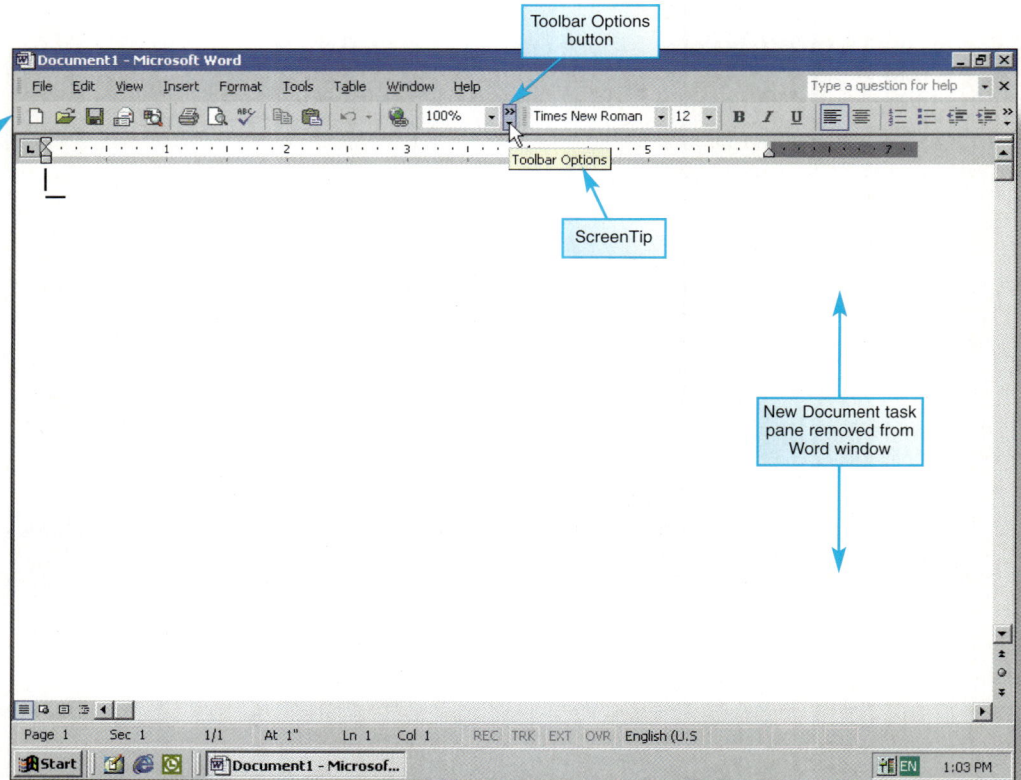

FIGURE 1-6

Starting and Customizing Word • WD 1.11

4 **Click the Toolbar Options button and then point to Show Buttons on Two Rows.**

Word displays the Toolbar Options list (Figure 1-7). The Toolbar Options list contains buttons that do not fit on the toolbars when the toolbars display on one row.

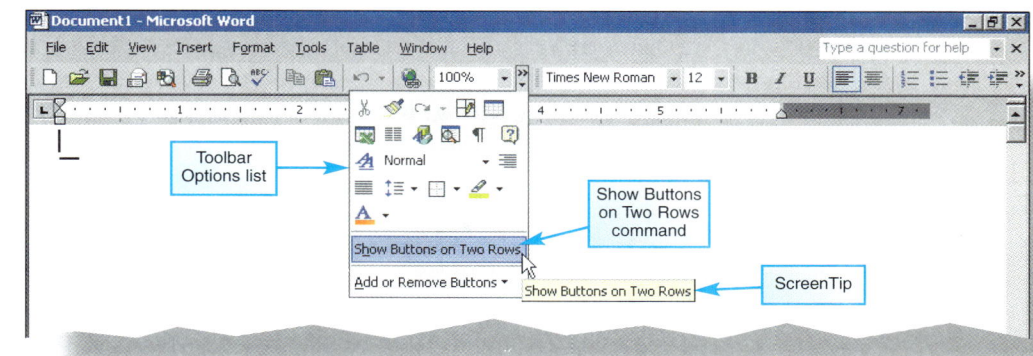

FIGURE 1-7

5 **Click Show Buttons on Two Rows. If your screen differs from Figure 1-8, click View on the menu bar and then click Normal.**

Word displays the toolbars on two separate rows (Figure 1-8). The Toolbar Options list is empty because all of the buttons fit on the toolbars when they display on two rows.

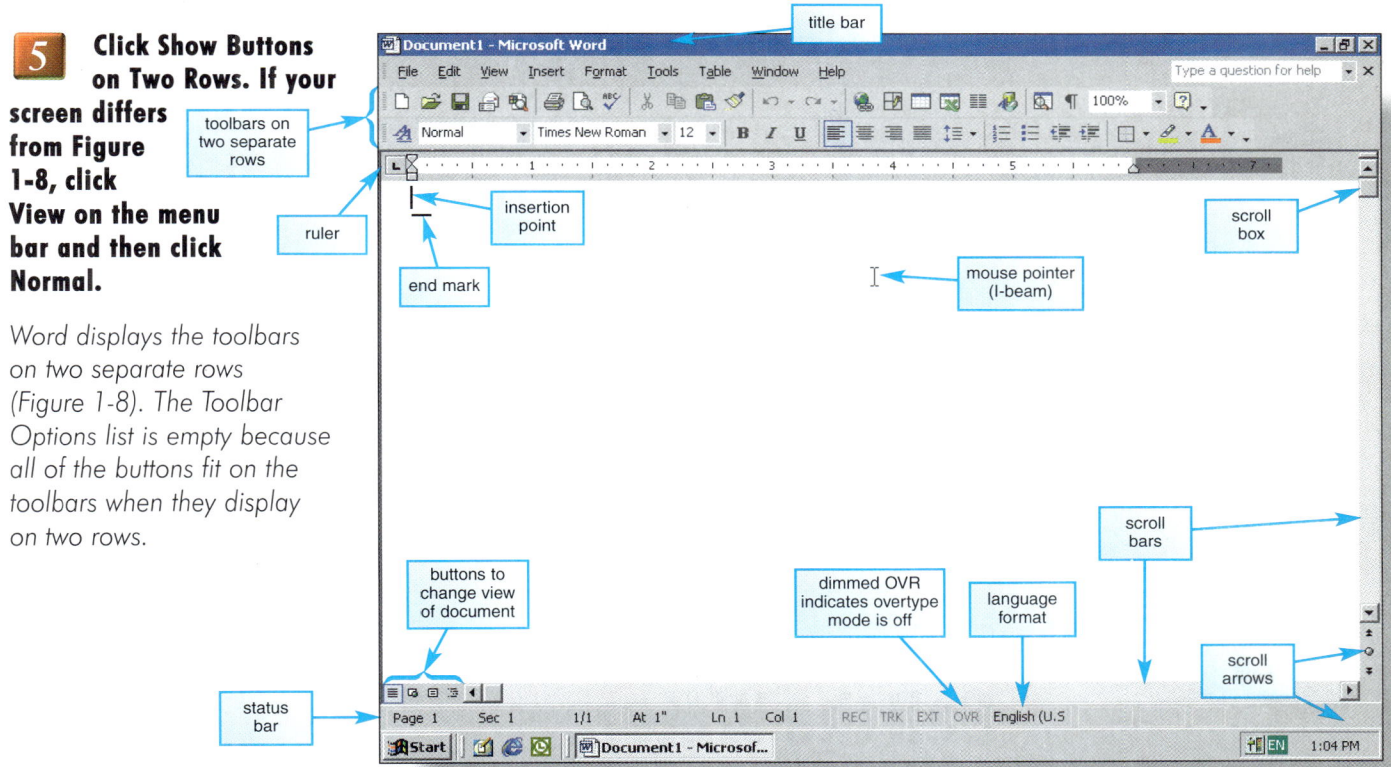

FIGURE 1-8

As an alternative to Steps 4 and 5 above, you can point to the left edge of the Formatting toolbar, and when the mouse pointer changes to a four-headed arrow, drag the toolbar down below the Standard toolbar to create two rows.

When you point to many objects in the Word window, such as a button or command, Word displays a ScreenTip. A **ScreenTip** is a short on-screen note associated with the object to which you are pointing. Examples of ScreenTips are shown in Figures 1-2, 1-4, 1-5, 1-6, and 1-7 on this and the previous pages.

Each time you start Word, the Word window displays the same way it did the last time you used Word. If the toolbars displayed on one row, then they will display on one row the next time you start Word. Similarly, if the Show at startup check box in the New Document task pane contains a check mark, then this task pane will display the next time you start Word.

The Office Assistant

The Office Assistant is an animated object that can answer questions for you. On some installations, the Office Assistant may display when Word starts. If the Office Assistant displays on your screen, right-click it and then click Hide on the shortcut menu.

As you work through creating a document, you will find that certain Word operations automatically display the task pane. In addition to the New Document task pane, Word provides seven other task panes: Clipboard, Search, Insert Clip Art, Styles and Formatting, Reveal Formatting, Mail Merge, and Translate. These task panes will be discussed as they are used in the projects.

The Word Window

The **Word window** (Figure 1-8 on the previous page) consists of a variety of components to make your work more efficient and documents more professional. The following sections discuss these components.

Document Window

The **document window** displays text, tables, graphics, and other items as you type or insert them into a document. Only a portion of your document, however, displays on the screen at one time. You view the portion of the document displayed on the screen through the document window (Figure 1-9).

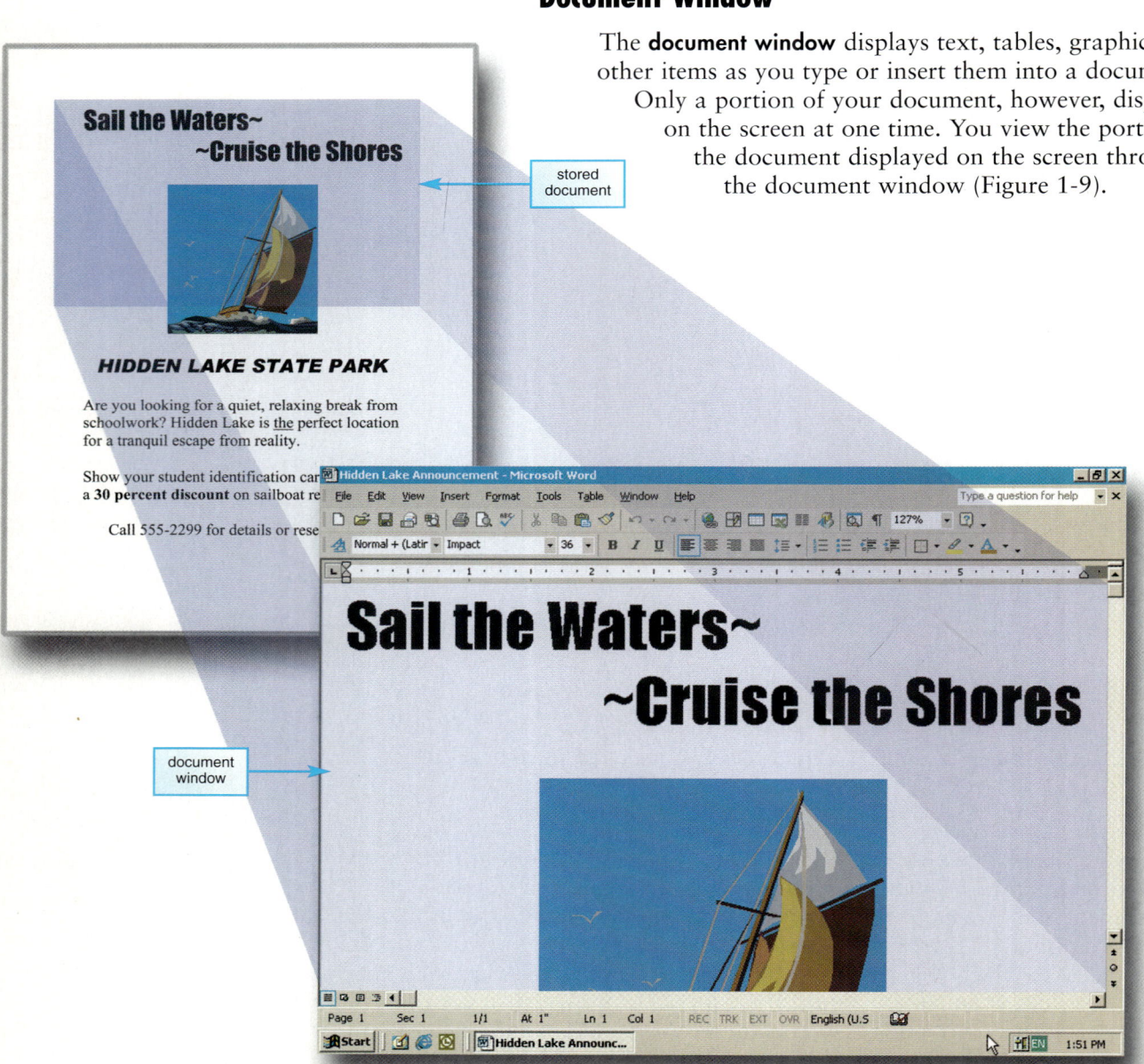

FIGURE 1-9

The document window contains several elements commonly found in other applications, as well as some elements unique to Word. The main elements of the Word document window are the insertion point, end mark, mouse pointer, rulers, scroll bars, and status bar (Figure 1-8 on page WD 1.11).

INSERTION POINT The **insertion point** is a blinking vertical bar that indicates where text will be inserted as you type. As you type, the insertion point moves to the right and, when you reach the end of a line, it moves downward to the beginning of the next line. You also can insert graphics, tables, and other items at the location of the insertion point.

END MARK The **end mark** is a short horizontal line that indicates the end of your document. Each time you begin a new line, the end mark moves downward.

MOUSE POINTER The **mouse pointer** becomes different shapes depending on the task you are performing in Word and the pointer's location on the screen. The mouse pointer in Figure 1-8 has the shape of an I-beam. Other mouse pointer shapes are described as they appear on the screen during this and subsequent projects.

RULERS At the top edge of the document window is the **horizontal ruler.** You use the horizontal ruler, usually simply called the ruler, to set tab stops, indent paragraphs, adjust column widths, and change page margins.

An additional ruler, called the vertical ruler, sometimes displays at the left edge of the Word window when you perform certain tasks. The purpose of the vertical ruler is discussed as it displays on the screen in a later project. If your screen displays a vertical ruler, click View on the menu bar and then click Normal.

SCROLL BARS By using the **scroll bars**, you can display different portions of your document in the document window. At the right edge of the document window is a vertical scroll bar. At the bottom of the document window is a horizontal scroll bar. On both the vertical and horizontal scroll bars, the position of the **scroll box** reflects the location of the portion of the document displaying in the document window.

On the left edge of the horizontal scroll bar are four buttons you can use to change the view of a document. On the bottom of the vertical scroll bar are three buttons you can use to scroll through a document. These buttons are discussed as they are used in later projects.

STATUS BAR The status bar displays at the bottom of the document window, above the Windows taskbar. The **status bar** presents information about the location of the insertion point and the progress of current tasks, as well as the status of certain commands, keys, and buttons.

From left to right, the following information displays on the status bar in Figure 1-9: the page number, the section number, the page containing the insertion point followed by the total number of pages in the document, the position of the insertion point in inches from the top of the page, the line number and column number of the insertion point, followed by several status indicators.

You use the **status indicators** to turn certain keys or modes on or off. The first four status indicators (REC, TRK, EXT, and OVR) display darkened when on and dimmed when off. For example, the dimmed OVR indicates overtype mode is off. To turn these four status indicators on or off, double-click the status indicator. These status indicators are discussed as they are used in the projects.

The Horizontal Ruler

If the horizontal ruler does not display on your screen, click View on the menu bar and then click Ruler. To hide the ruler, also click View on the menu bar and then click Ruler.

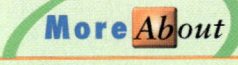

Scroll Bars

You can use the vertical scroll bar to scroll through multi-page documents. As you drag the scroll box up or down the scroll bar, Word displays a page indicator to the left of the scroll box. When you release the mouse button, the document window displays the page shown in the page indicator.

Languages

If support for multiple languages was installed on your computer, the status bar also displays the language format, which shows the name of the language you are using to create the document. You add languages through the Control Panel. Double-click the Text Services icon in the Control Panel. Click the Add button in the Installed Services area in the Text Services dialog box. Select the desired language in the Add Input Language dialog box and then click the OK button in each open dialog box.

The next status indicator displays the name of the language that appears at the location of the insertion point. In Figure 1-9 on page WD 1.12, the indicated language is English (U.S.). Word automatically detects the language as you type. Most installations of Word can detect more than 60 languages, including Chinese, Dutch, English, French, German, Italian, Japanese, and Russian. This means Word can check the spelling, grammar, and punctuation in each of these languages.

The remaining status indicators display icons as you perform certain tasks. When you begin typing in the document window, a Spelling and Grammar Status icon displays. When Word is saving your document, a Background Save icon displays. When you print a document, a Background Print icon displays. If you perform a task that requires several seconds (such as saving a document), the status bar displays a message informing you of the progress of the task.

Menu Bar and Toolbars

The menu bar and toolbars display at the top of the screen just below the title bar (Figure 1-10).

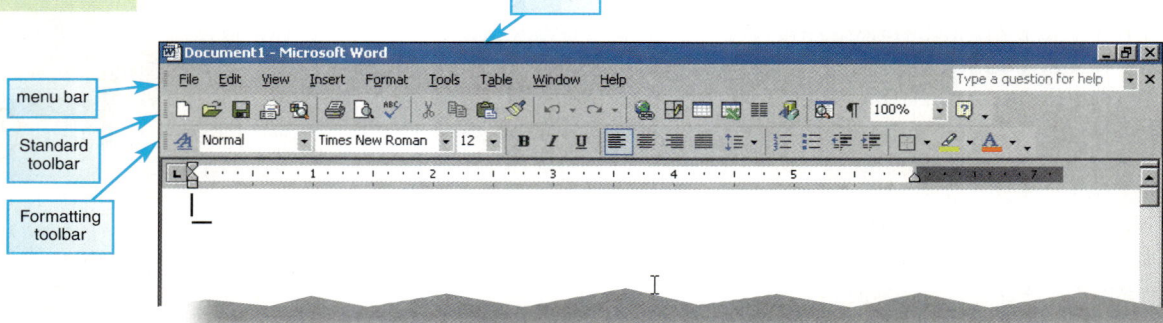

FIGURE 1-10

Menus

Right-clicking an object displays a shortcut menu (also called a context-sensitive or object menu). Depending on the object, the commands in the shortcut menu vary.

MENU BAR The **menu bar** is a special toolbar that displays the Word menu names. Each **menu** contains a list of commands you can use to perform tasks such as retrieving, storing, printing, and formatting data in your document. When you point to a menu name on the menu bar, the area of the menu bar containing the name changes to a button. To display a menu, such as the Edit menu, click the Edit menu name on the menu bar. If you point to a command on a menu that has an arrow to its right edge, a **submenu** displays another list of commands.

When you click a menu name on the menu bar, a **short menu** displays that lists your most recently used commands, as shown in Figure 1-11a.

If you wait a few seconds or click the arrows at the bottom of the short menu, it expands into a full menu. A **full menu** lists all the commands associated with a menu, as shown in Figure 1-11b. You immediately can display a full menu by double-clicking the menu name on the menu bar. In this book, when you display a menu, always display the full menu using one of these techniques:

1. Click the menu name on the menu bar and then wait a few seconds.
2. Click the menu name on the menu bar and then click the arrows at the bottom of the short menu.
3. Click the menu name on the menu bar and then point to the arrows at the bottom of the short menu.
4. Double-click the menu name on the menu bar.

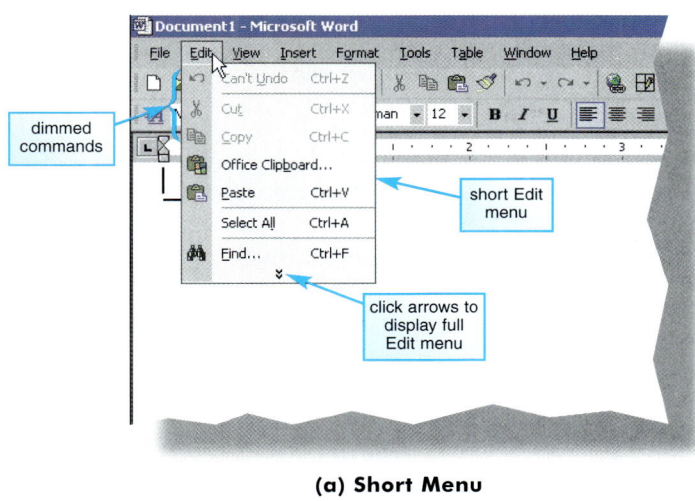

(a) Short Menu

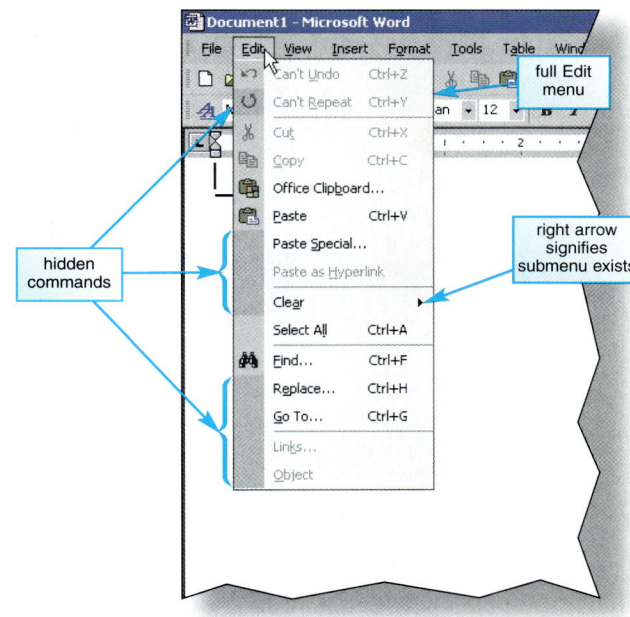

(b) Full Menu

FIGURE 1-11

Both short and full menus display some **dimmed commands** that appear gray, or dimmed, instead of black, which indicates they are not available for the current selection. A command with a dark gray shading in the rectangle to the left of it on a full menu is called a **hidden command** because it does not display on a short menu. As you use Word, it automatically personalizes the short menus for you based on how often you use commands. That is, as you use hidden commands on the full menu, Word *unhides* them and places them on the short menu.

TOOLBARS Word has many pre-defined, or built-in, toolbars. A **toolbar** contains buttons, boxes, and menus that allow you to perform tasks more quickly than using the menu bar and related menus. For example, to print a document, you click the Print button on a toolbar. Each button on a toolbar displays an image to help you remember its function. Also, when you point to a button or box on a toolbar, a ScreenTip displays below the mouse pointer (Figure 1-6 on page WD 1.10).

Two built-in toolbars are the Standard toolbar and the Formatting toolbar. Figure 1-12a illustrates the **Standard toolbar** and identifies its buttons and boxes. Figure 1-12b on the next page illustrates the **Formatting toolbar**. Each button and box is explained in detail as it is used in the projects throughout the book.

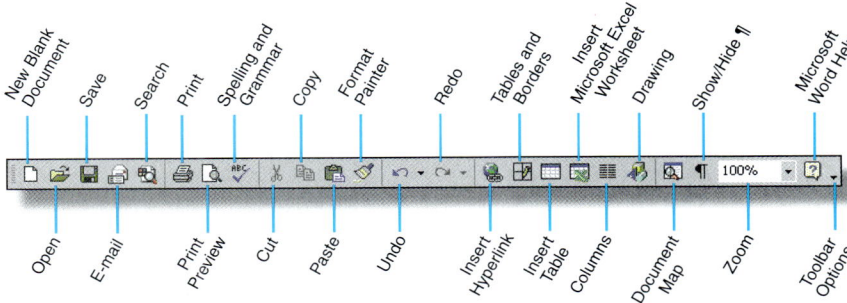

FIGURE 1-12a Standard Toolbar

More About

The Word Help System

Need Help? It is no further than the Ask a Question box in the upper-right corner of the window. Click the box that contains the text, Type a question for help (Figure 1-13a), type help, and then press the ENTER key. Word will respond with a list of items you can click to learn about obtaining help on any Word-related topic. To find out what is new in Word 2002, type what's new in Word in the Ask a Question box.

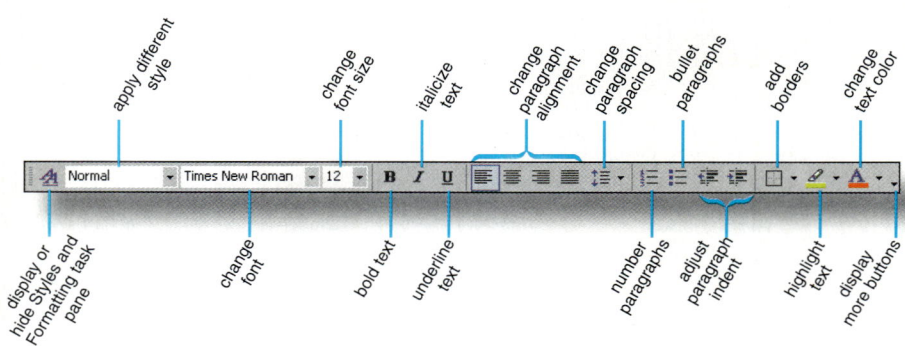

FIGURE 1-12b Formatting Toolbar

When you first install Word, the Standard and Formatting toolbars are preset to display on the same row immediately below the menu bar (Figure 1-13a). Unless the resolution of your display device is greater than 800 × 600, many of the buttons that belong to these toolbars do not display when the two toolbars share one row. The buttons that display on the toolbar are the more frequently used buttons. Hidden buttons display in the Toolbar Options list. When you click the Toolbar Options button on a toolbar, Word displays a Toolbar Options list that contains the toolbar's hidden buttons (Figure 1-13b). In this mode, you also can display all the buttons on either toolbar by double-clicking the **move handle** on the left of each toolbar.

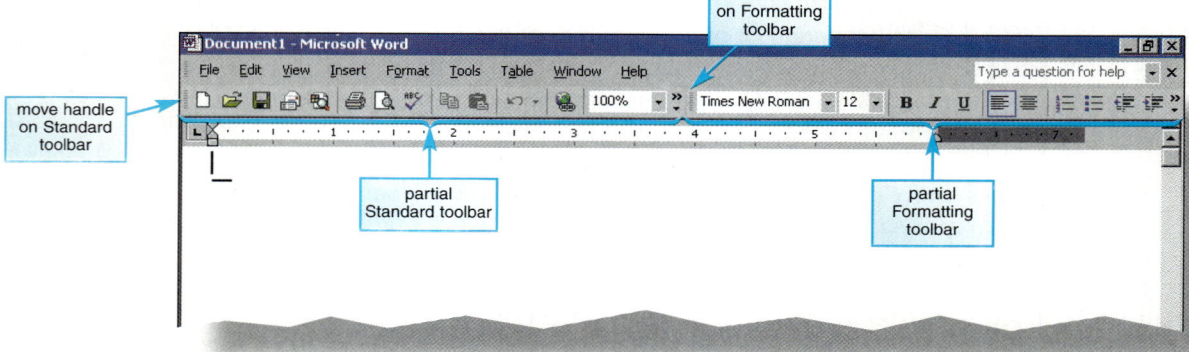

FIGURE 1-13a

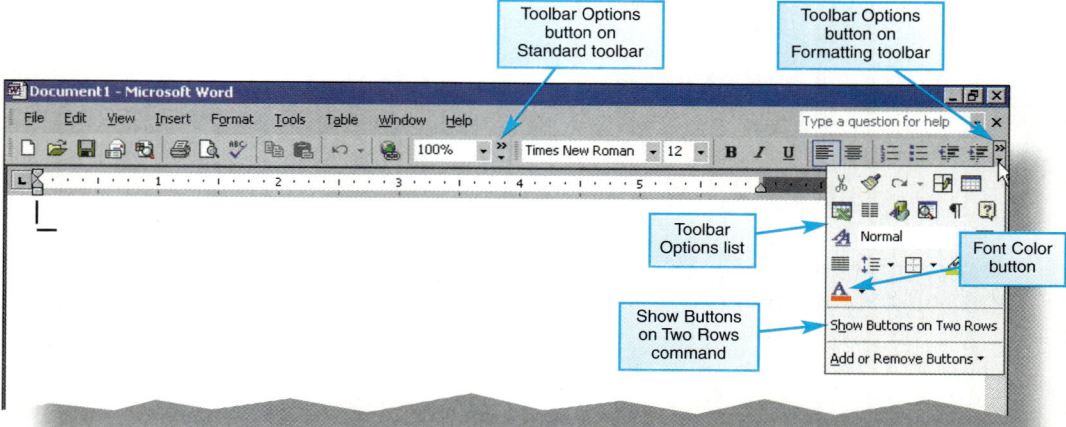

FIGURE 1-13b

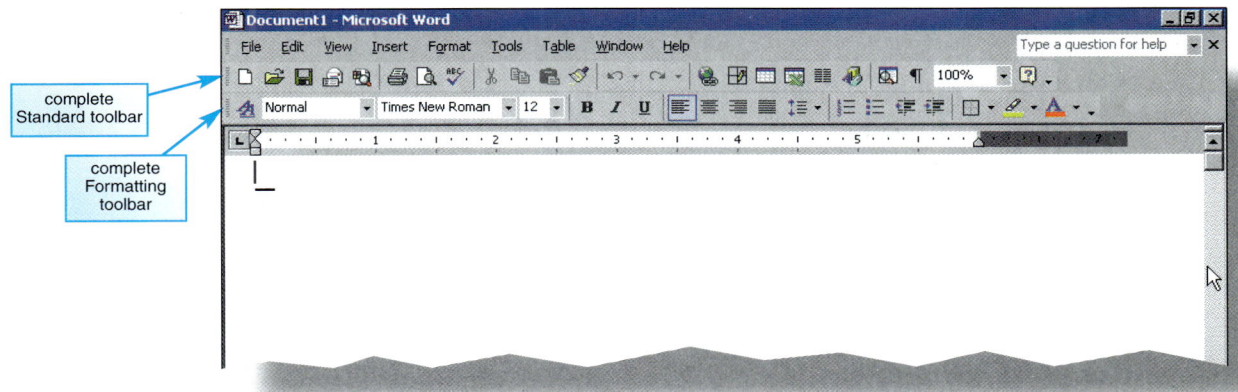

FIGURE 1-13c

In this book, the Standard and Formatting toolbars are shown on separate rows, one below the other so that all buttons display (Figure 1-13c). You show the two toolbars on two rows by clicking the Show Buttons on Two Rows command in the Toolbar Options list (Figure 1-13b).

In the previous figures, the Standard and Formatting toolbars are docked. A **docked toolbar** is one that is attached to the edge of the Word window. Depending on the task you are performing, additional toolbars may display on the Word screen. These additional toolbars display either docked or floating in the Word window. A **floating toolbar** is not attached to an edge of the Word window; that is, it displays in the middle of the Word window. You can rearrange the order of docked toolbars and can move floating toolbars anywhere in the Word window. Later in this book, steps are presented that show you how to float a docked toolbar or dock a floating toolbar.

Resetting Menus and Toolbars

Each project in this book begins with the menus and toolbars appearing as they did at the initial installation of the software. To reset your menus and toolbars so they appear exactly as shown in this book, follow the steps in Appendix D.

Speech Recognition and Handwriting Recognition

With the **Office Speech Recognition software** installed and a microphone, you can speak the names of toolbar buttons, menus, menu commands, list items, alerts, and dialog box controls, such as OK and Cancel. You also can dictate text, such as words and sentences.

To indicate whether you want to speak commands or dictate text, you use the **Language bar** (Figure 1-14a). You can display the Language bar in two ways: (1) click the Language Indicator button in the taskbar tray status area by the clock and then click Show the Language bar on the menu (Figure 1-14b on the next page), or (2) click Tools on the menu bar and then click Speech.

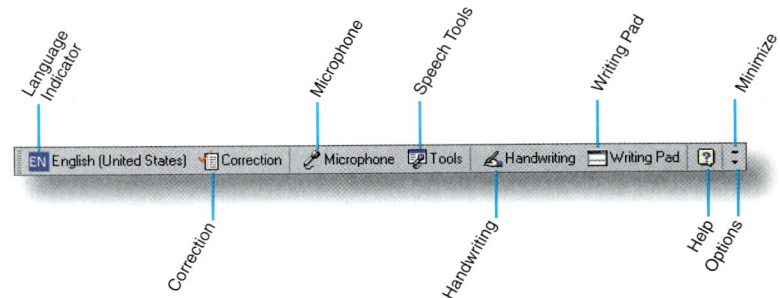

FIGURE 1-14a Language Bar

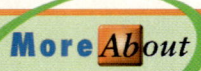

Speech Recognition

If Office Speech Recognition software is installed on your computer, you can speak instructions to Word including toolbar button names, menu names and commands, and items in dialog boxes and task panes. You also can dictate so Word writes exactly what you say. The microphone picks up others' voices and background sounds, so speech recognition is most effective when used in a quiet environment.

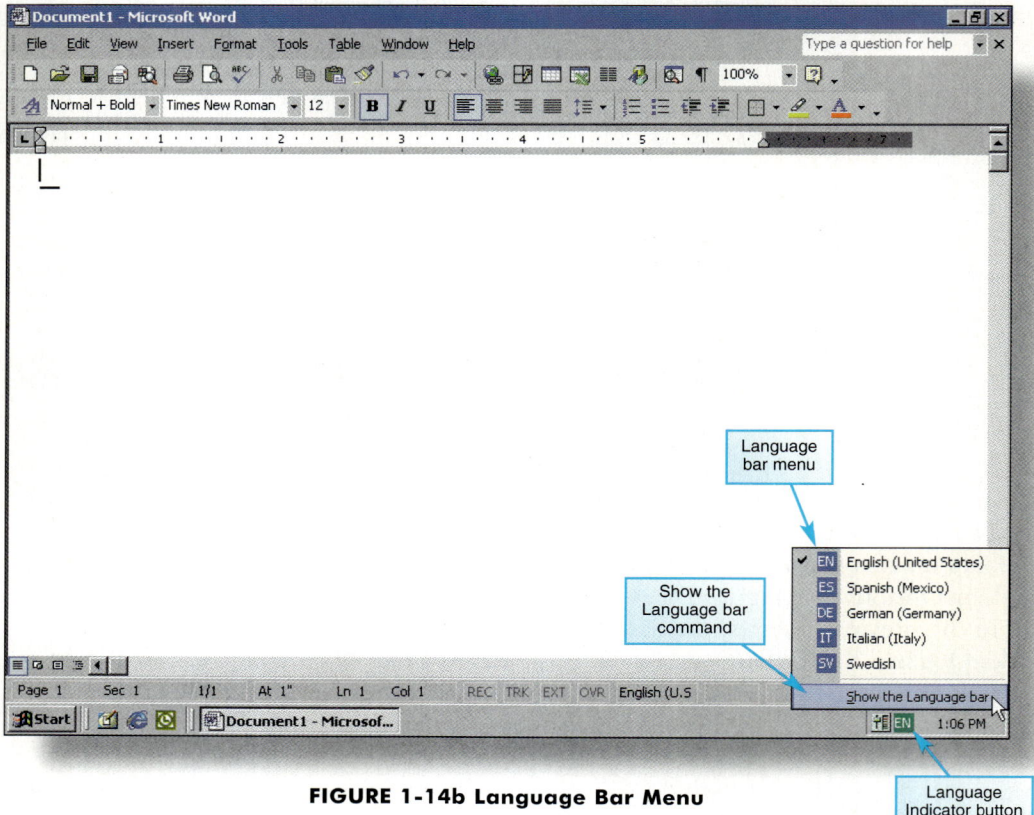

FIGURE 1-14b Language Bar Menu

If the Language Indicator button does not display in the taskbar tray status area, the Office Speech Recognition software may not be installed. To install the software, you first must start Word and then click Speech on the Tools menu.

You can use the speech recognition and handwriting recognition capabilities of Office XP to enter text into Word by speaking or writing, instead of typing. Additional information on the Office Speech Recognition, Handwriting Recognition, and other text services is available in Appendix B.

Zooming Page Width

Depending on your Windows and Word settings, the horizontal ruler at the top of the document window may show more inches or fewer inches than the ruler shown in Figure 1-15. The more inches of ruler that display, the smaller the text will be on the screen. The fewer inches of ruler that display, the larger the text will be on the screen. To minimize eyestrain, the projects in this book display the text as large as possible without extending the right margin beyond the right edge of the document window.

Two factors that affect how much of the ruler displays in the document window are the Windows screen resolution and the Word zoom percentage. The screens in this book use a resolution of 800 × 600. With this resolution, you can increase the preset zoom percentage beyond 100% so that the right margin extends to the edge of the document window. To increase or decrease the size of the displayed characters to a point where both the left and right margins are at the edges of the document window, use the **zoom page width** command as shown in the following steps.

Handwriting Recognition

If Handwriting Recognition software is installed on your computer, Word can recognize text as you write it on a handwriting input device, such as graphics tablet, or with the mouse. To use the mouse, you drag the mouse to form the cursive characters. If you have a handheld computer, or PDA, you also can convert the handheld computer's handwritten notes into text in Word.

Changing the Default Font Size • WD 1.19

Steps: To Zoom Page Width

1 **Click the Zoom box arrow on the Standard toolbar and then point to Page Width.**

Word displays a list of available zoom percentages and the Page Width option in the Zoom list (Figure 1-15).

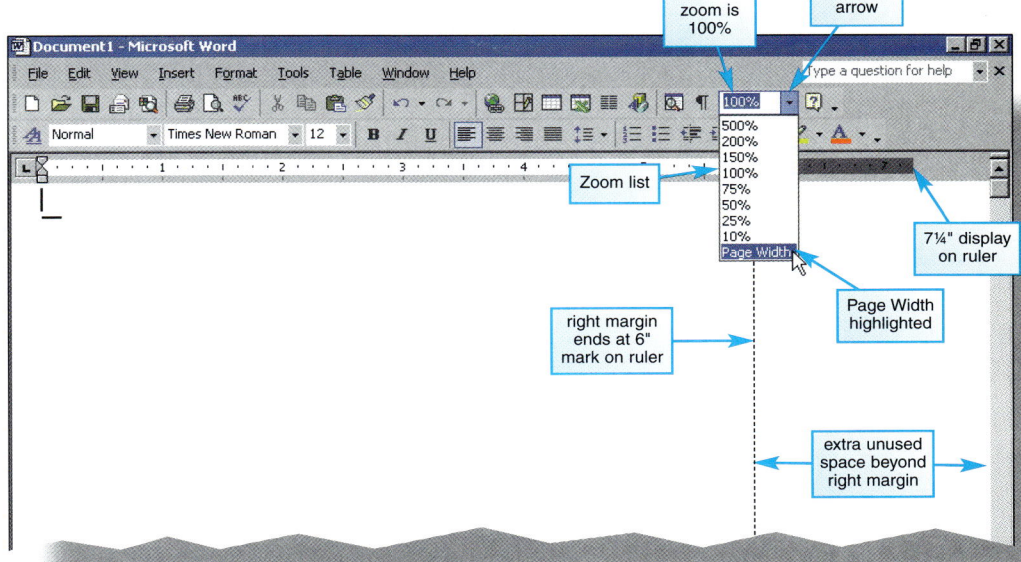

FIGURE 1-15

2 **Click Page Width.**

Word extends the right margin to the right edge of the document window (Figure 1-16).

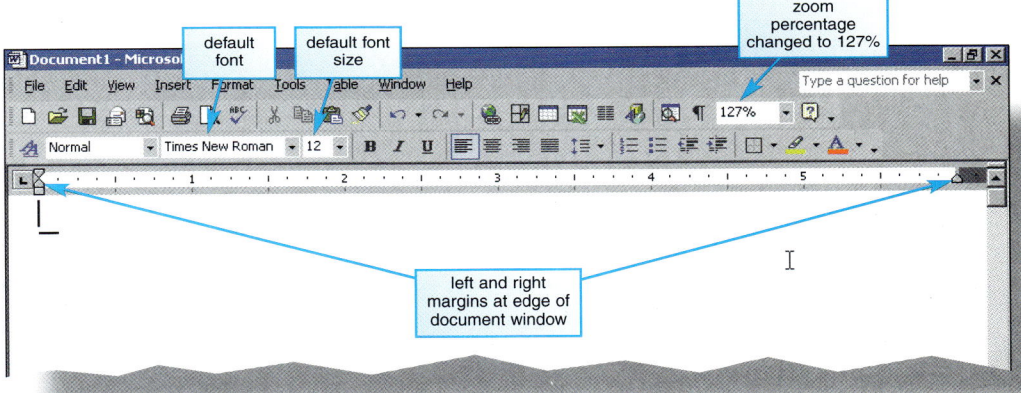

FIGURE 1-16

If your Zoom list (Figure 1-15) displayed additional options, click View on the menu bar and then click Normal.

The Zoom box in Figure 1-16 displays 127%, which Word computes based on a variety of settings. Your percentage may be different depending on your computer configuration.

Other Ways

1. On View menu click Zoom, select Page width, click OK button
2. In Voice Command mode, say "Zoom, Page Width"

Changing the Default Font Size

Characters that display on the screen are a specific shape, size, and style. The **font**, or typeface, defines the appearance and shape of the letters, numbers, and special characters. The preset, or **default**, font is Times New Roman (Figure 1-16). **Font size** specifies the size of the characters and is determined by a measurement system called

More About

Zooming

If you want to zoom to a percentage not in the Zoom list, click the Zoom box on the Standard toolbar, type the desired percentage, and then press the ENTER key.

Font Size

An announcement usually is posted on a wall. Thus, its font size should be as large as possible so that all potential readers easily can see it.

points. A single **point** is about 1/72 of one inch in height. Thus, a character with a font size of 12 is about 12/72 or 1/6 of one inch in height. On most computers, the default font size in Word is 12.

If more of the characters in your document require a larger font size than the default, you easily can change the default font size before you type. In Project 1, many of the characters in the body of the announcement are a font size of 22. Perform the following steps to increase the font size before you begin entering text.

Steps: To Increase the Default Font Size Before Typing

1 **Click the Font Size box arrow on the Formatting toolbar and then point to 22.**

A list of available font sizes displays in the Font Size list (Figure 1-17). The available font sizes depend on the current font, which is Times New Roman.

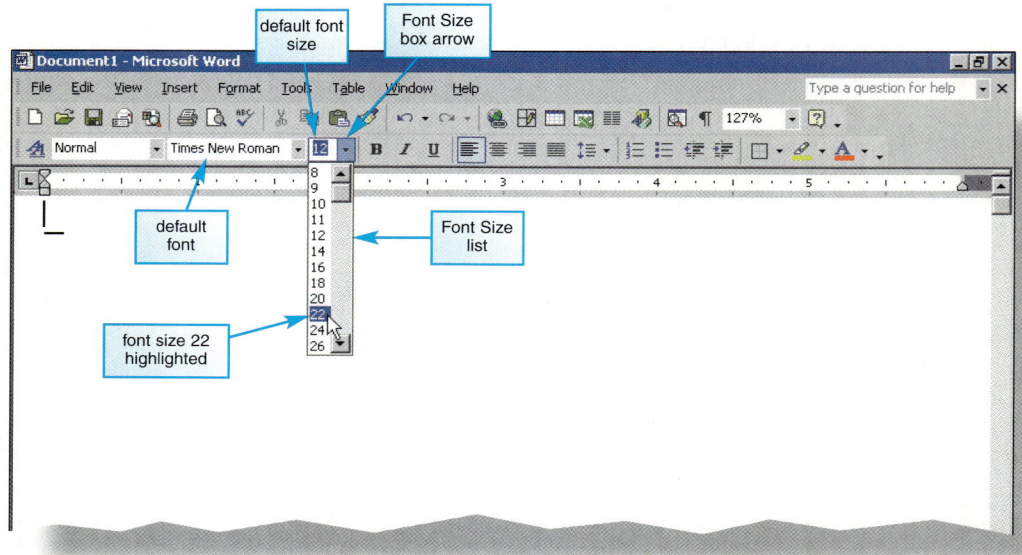

FIGURE 1-17

2 **Click 22.**

The font size for characters entered in this document changes to 22 (Figure 1-18). The size of the insertion point increases to reflect the new font size.

Other Ways

1. Right-click paragraph mark above end mark, click Font on shortcut menu, click Font tab, select desired font size in Size list, click OK button
2. On Format menu click Font, click Font tab, select desired font size in Size list, click OK button
3. Press CTRL+SHIFT+P, type desired font size, press ENTER
4. In Voice Command mode, say "Font Size, [select font size]"

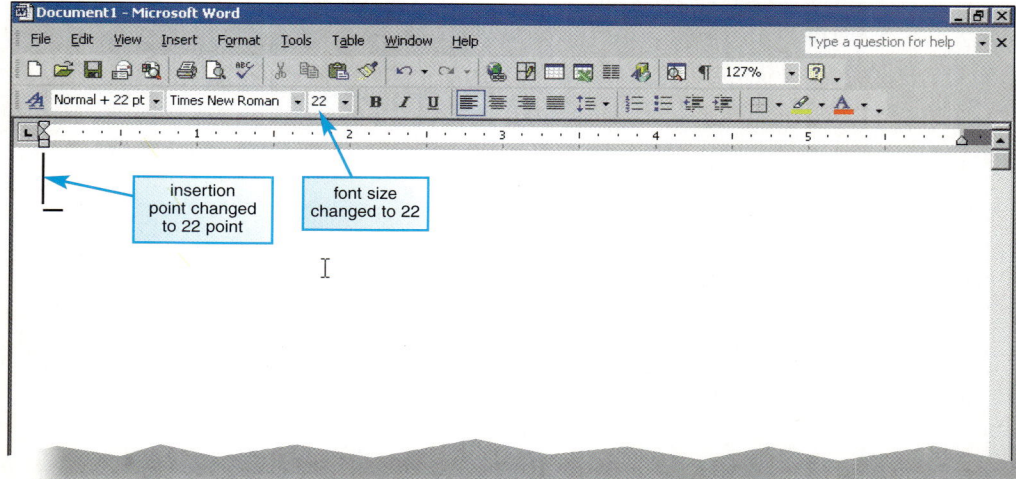

FIGURE 1-18

The new font size takes effect immediately in your document. Word uses this font size for characters you type into this announcement.

Entering Text

To enter text into a document, you type on the keyboard or speak into the microphone. The following example illustrates the steps required to type both lines in the headline of the announcement. These lines will be positioned at the left margin. Later in this project, you will format the headline so that both lines are bold and enlarged and the second line is positioned at the right margin.

Perform the following steps to begin entering the document text.

More About

The Tilde Key

On most keyboards, the TILDE (~) key is located just below the ESCAPE key and just above the TAB key. The tilde is the top character on the key. Thus, to display the tilde character on the screen, press the SHIFT key while pressing the TILDE key.

Steps: To Enter Text

1 **Type** Sail the Waters **and then press the TILDE (~) key. If you make an error while typing, press the BACKSPACE key until you have deleted the text in error and then retype the text correctly.**

As you type, the insertion point moves to the right (Figure 1-19). On most keyboards, the TILDE (~) key is immediately below the ESCAPE key.

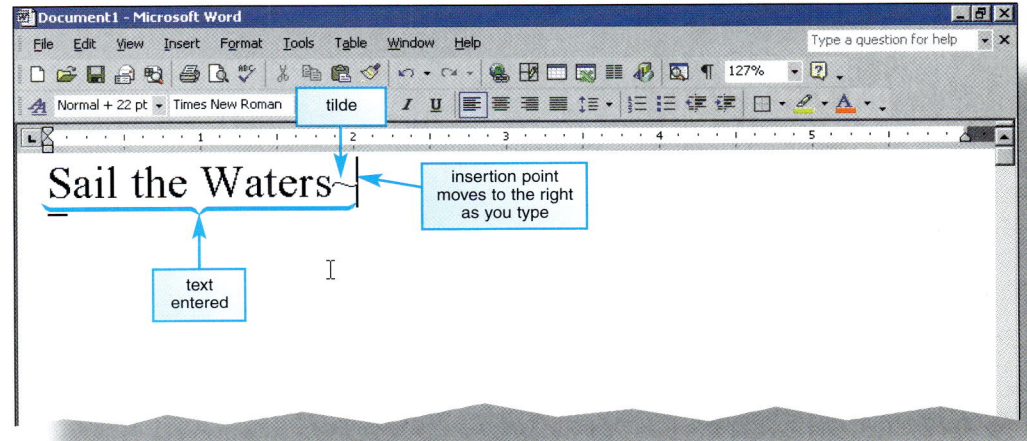

FIGURE 1-19

2 **Press the ENTER key.**

Word moves the insertion point to the beginning of the next line (Figure 1-20). Notice the status bar indicates the current position of the insertion point. That is, the insertion point currently is on line 2 column 1.

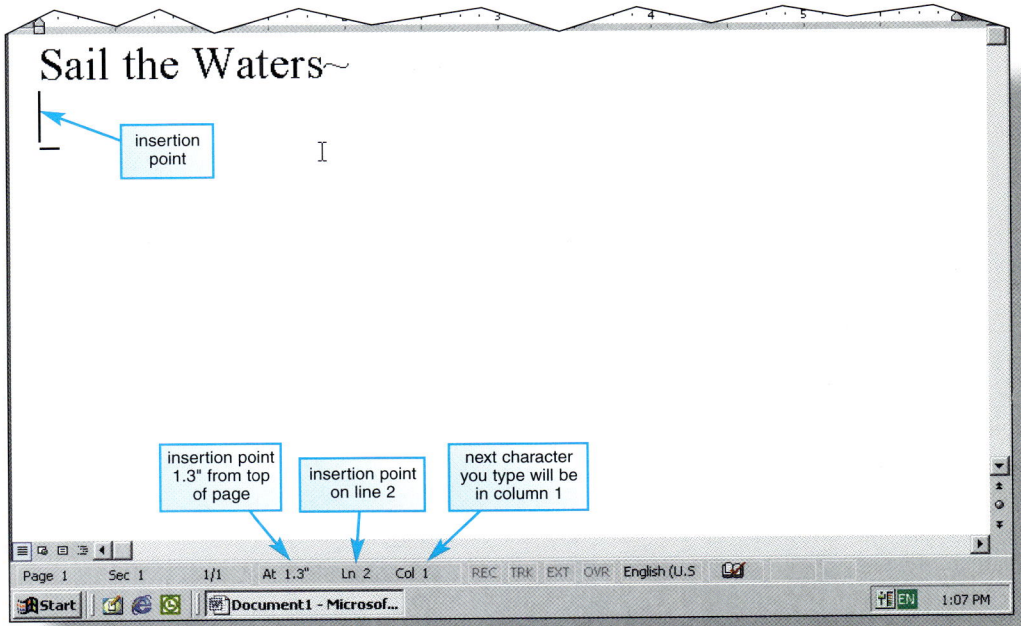

FIGURE 1-20

3 **Press the TILDE (~) key. Type** Cruise the Shores **and then press the ENTER key.**

The headline is complete (Figure 1-21). The insertion point is on line 3.

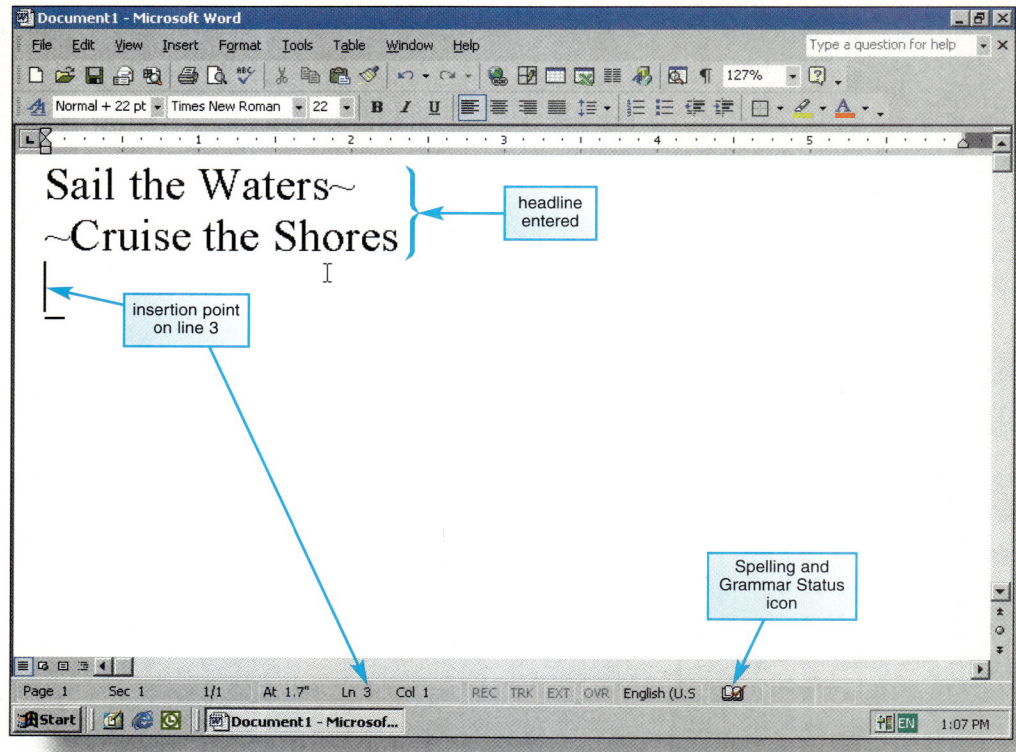

FIGURE 1-21

Other Ways

1. In Dictation mode, say "Sail the Waters, Tilde, New Line, Tilde, Cruise the Shores, New Line"

When you begin entering text into a document, the **Spelling and Grammar Status icon** displays at the right of the status bar (Figure 1-21). As you type, the Spelling and Grammar Status icon shows an animated pencil writing on paper, which indicates Word is checking for possible errors. When you stop typing, the pencil changes to either a red check mark or a red X. In Figure 1-21, the Spelling and Grammar Status icon displays a red check mark.

In general, if all of the words you have typed are in Word's dictionary and your grammar is correct, a red check mark displays on the Spelling and Grammar Status icon. If you type a word not in the dictionary (because it is a proper name or misspelled), a red wavy underline displays below the word. If you type text that may be incorrect grammatically, a green wavy underline displays below the text. When Word flags a possible spelling or grammar error, it also changes the red check mark on the Spelling and Grammar Status icon to a red X. As you enter text into the announcement, your Spelling and Grammar Status icon may show a red X instead of a red check mark. Later in this project, you will check the spelling of these words. At that time, the red X will return to a red check mark.

More About

Entering Text

In the days of typewriters, the letter l was used for both the letter l and the numeral one. Keyboards, however, have both a numeral one and the letter l. Keyboards also have both a numeral zero and the letter o. Be careful to press the correct keyboard character when creating a word processing document.

Entering Blank Lines into a Document

To enter a blank line into a document, press the ENTER key without typing any text on the line. The following example explains how to enter three blank lines below the headline.

 To Enter Blank Lines into a Document

 Press the ENTER key three times.

Word inserts three blank lines into your document below the headline (Figure 1-22).

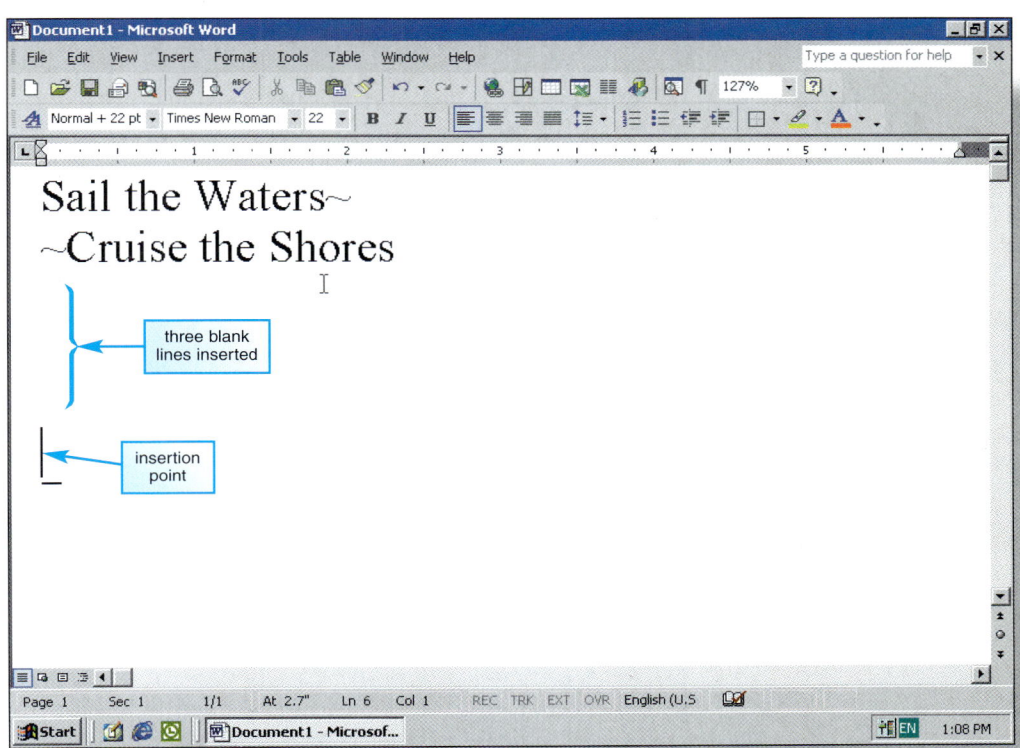

FIGURE 1-22

1. In Dictation mode, say "New Line, New Line, New Line"

Displaying Formatting Marks

To indicate where in the document you press the ENTER key or SPACEBAR, you may find it helpful to display formatting marks. A **formatting mark**, sometimes called a **nonprinting character**, is a character that displays on the screen but is not visible on a printed document. For example, the paragraph mark (¶) is a formatting mark that indicates where you pressed the ENTER key. A raised dot (•) shows where you pressed the SPACEBAR. Other formatting marks are discussed as they display on the screen.

Depending on settings made during previous Word sessions, your screen already may display formatting marks (Figure 1-23 on the next page). If the formatting marks do not display already on your screen, follow the step on the next page to display them.

Steps: To Display Formatting Marks

1 If it is not already selected, click the Show/Hide ¶ button on the Standard toolbar.

Word displays formatting marks on the screen (Figure 1-23). The Show/Hide ¶ button is selected. Selected toolbar buttons are shaded light blue and surrounded with a blue outline.

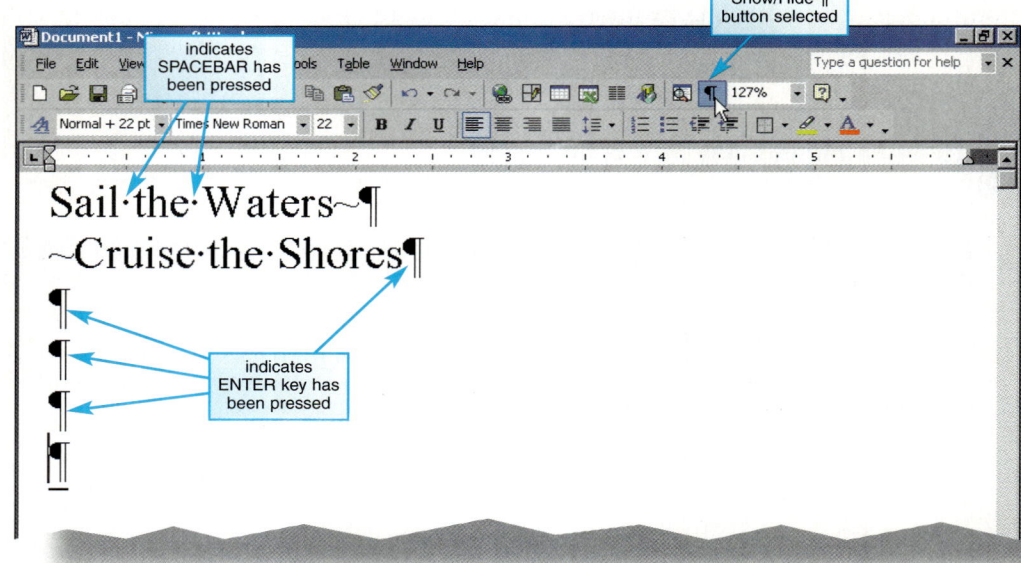

FIGURE 1-23

Other Ways

1. On Tools menu click Options, click View tab, click All, click OK button
2. Press CTRL+SHIFT+ASTERISK (*)
3. In Voice Command mode, say "Show Hide Paragraph"

Notice several changes to the Word document window (Figure 1-23). A paragraph mark displays at the end of each line to indicate you pressed the ENTER key. Each time you press the ENTER key, Word creates a new paragraph. Because you changed the font size, the paragraph marks are 22 point. Notice Word places a paragraph mark above the end mark; you cannot delete this paragraph mark. Between each word, a raised dot appears, indicating you pressed the SPACEBAR. Finally, the Show/Hide ¶ button is shaded light blue and surrounded with a blue outline to indicate it is selected.

If you feel the formatting marks clutter the screen, you can hide them by clicking the Show/Hide ¶ button again. It is recommended that you display formatting marks; therefore, the document windows presented in this book show the formatting marks.

Entering More Text

Every character of the body title (HIDDEN LAKE STATE PARK) in the announcement is capitalized. The next step is to enter this body title in all capital letters into the document window as explained below.

More About

Caps Lock

If you leave the CAPS LOCK key on and begin typing a new sentence, Word automatically may correct the problem for you, depending on its AutoCorrect settings. That is, Word may disengage the CAPS LOCK key and capitalize only the first letter of the first word in the next sentence.

TO ENTER MORE TEXT

1 Press the CAPS LOCK key on the keyboard to turn on capital letters. Verify the CAPS LOCK indicator is lit on your keyboard.

2 Type HIDDEN LAKE STATE PARK and then press the CAPS LOCK key to turn off capital letters.

3 Press the ENTER key twice.

The body title displays on line 6 as shown in Figure 1-24.

Using Wordwrap

Wordwrap allows you to type words in a paragraph continually without pressing the ENTER key at the end of each line. When the insertion point reaches the right margin, Word automatically positions it at the beginning of the next line. As you type, if a word extends beyond the right margin, Word also positions that word automatically on the next line with the insertion point.

As you enter text using Word, do not press the ENTER key when the insertion point reaches the right margin. Word creates a new paragraph each time you press the ENTER key. Thus, press the ENTER key only in these circumstances:

1. To insert blank lines into a document
2. To begin a new paragraph
3. To terminate a short line of text and advance to the next line
4. In response to certain Word commands

Perform the following step to familiarize yourself with wordwrap.

More About

Wordwrap

Your printer controls where wordwrap occurs for each line in your document. For this reason, it is possible that the same document could wordwrap differently if printed on different printers.

Steps: To Wordwrap Text as You Type

 Type Are you looking for a quiet, relaxing break from schoolwork?

Word wraps the word, schoolwork, to the beginning of line 9 because it is too long to fit on line 8 (Figure 1-24). Your document may wordwrap differently depending on the type of printer you are using.

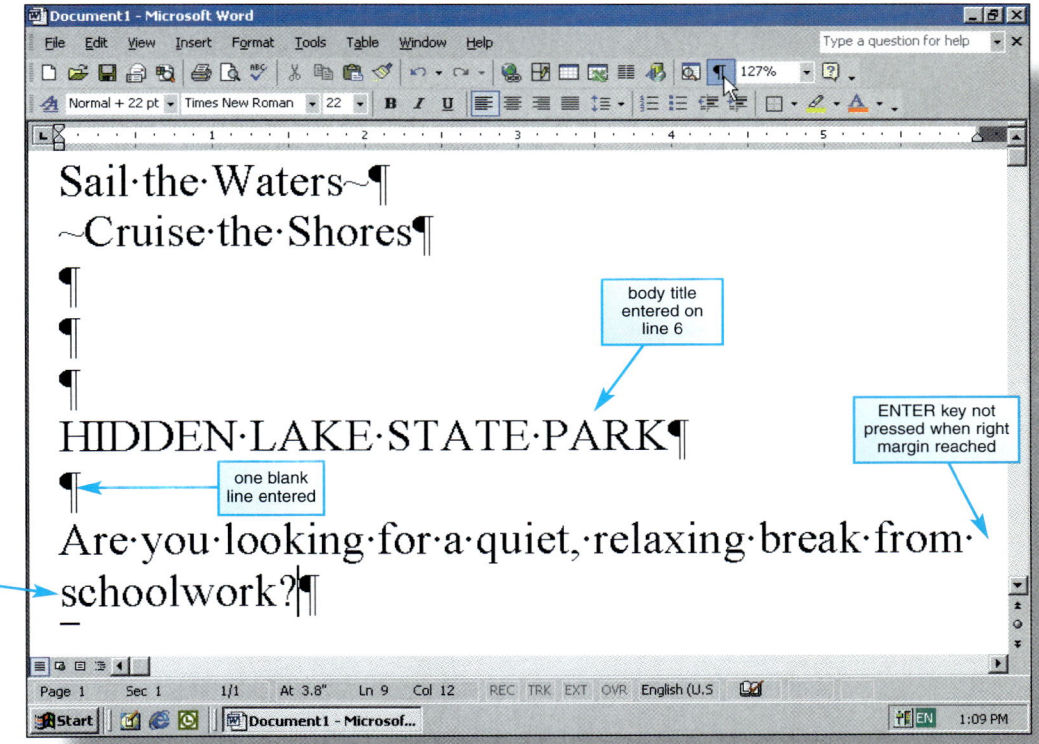

FIGURE 1-24

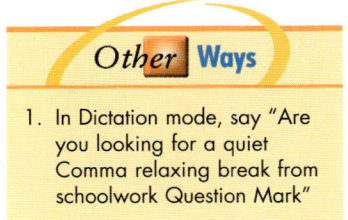

Other Ways

1. In Dictation mode, say "Are you looking for a quiet Comma relaxing break from schoolwork Question Mark"

Entering Text that Scrolls the Document Window

As you type more lines of text than Word can display in the document window, Word **scrolls** the top portion of the document upward off the screen. Although you cannot see the text once it scrolls off the screen, it remains in the document. As previously discussed, the document window allows you to view only a portion of your document at one time (Figure 1-9 on page WD 1.12).

Perform the following step to enter text that scrolls the document window.

Steps: To Enter Text that Scrolls the Document Window

1 **Press the SPACEBAR. Type** Hidden Lake is the perfect location for a tranquil escape from reality. **Press the ENTER key twice.**

Word scrolls the headline off the top of the screen (Figure 1-25). Your screen may scroll differently depending on the type of monitor you are using.

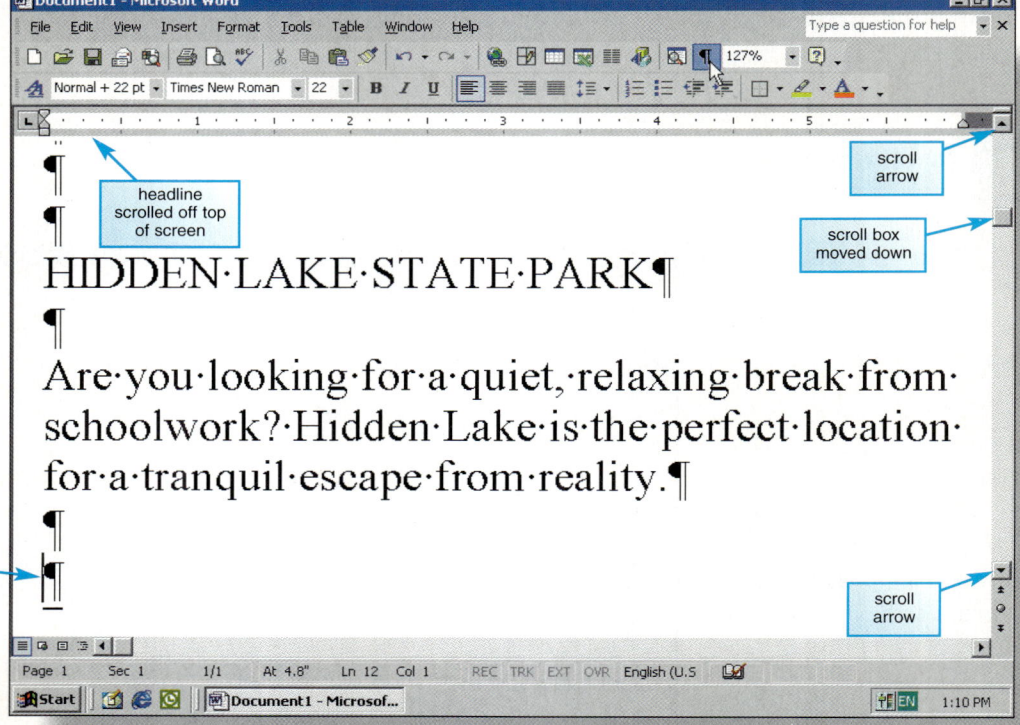

FIGURE 1-25

Other Ways

1. In Dictation mode, say "Hidden Lake is the perfect location for a tranquil escape from reality Period, New Line, New Line"

Microsoft IntelliMouse®

For more information on scrolling with the Microsoft IntelliMouse®, visit the Word 2002 More About Web page (scsite.com/wd2002/more .htm) and then click Microsoft IntelliMouse®.

When Word scrolls text off the top of the screen, the scroll box on the vertical scroll bar at the right edge of the document window moves downward (Figure 1-25). The **scroll box** indicates the current relative location of the insertion point in the document. You may use either the mouse or the keyboard to move the insertion point to a different location in a document.

With the mouse, you use the scroll arrows or the scroll box to display a different portion of the document in the document window, and then click the mouse to move the insertion point to that location. Table 1-1 explains various techniques for scrolling vertically with the mouse.

Table 1-1 Techniques for Scrolling with the Mouse

SCROLL DIRECTION	MOUSE ACTION
Up	Drag the scroll box upward.
Down	Drag the scroll box downward.
Up one screen	Click anywhere above the scroll box on the vertical scroll bar.
Down one screen	Click anywhere below the scroll box on the vertical scroll bar.
Up one line	Click the scroll arrow at the top of the vertical scroll bar.
Down one line	Click the scroll arrow at the bottom of the vertical scroll bar.

Scrolling

Computer users frequently switch between the keyboard and the mouse during a word processing session, which strains the wrist. To help prevent wrist injury, minimize switching. If your fingers are already on the keyboard, use keyboard keys to scroll. If your hand is already on the mouse, use the mouse to scroll.

When you use the keyboard to scroll, the insertion point automatically moves when you press the appropriate keys. Table 1-2 outlines various techniques to scroll through a document using the keyboard.

Table 1-2 Techniques for Scrolling with the Keyboard

SCROLL DIRECTION	KEY(S) TO PRESS	SCROLL DIRECTION	KEY(S) TO PRESS
Left one character	LEFT ARROW	Down one paragraph	CTRL+DOWN ARROW
Right one character	RIGHT ARROW	Up one screen	PAGE UP
Left one word	CTRL+LEFT ARROW	Down one screen	PAGE DOWN
Right one word	CTRL+RIGHT ARROW	To top of document window	ALT+CTRL+PAGE UP
Up one line	UP ARROW	To bottom of document window	ALT+CTRL+PAGE DOWN
Down one line	DOWN ARROW	Previous page	CTRL+PAGE UP
To end of a line	END	Next page	CTRL+PAGE DOWN
To beginning of a line	HOME	To the beginning of a document	CTRL+HOME
Up one paragraph	CTRL+UP ARROW	To the end of a document	CTRL+END

Checking Spelling as You Type

As you type text into the document window, Word checks your typing for possible spelling and grammar errors. If a word you type is not in the dictionary, a red wavy underline displays below it. Similarly, if text you type contains possible grammar errors, a green wavy underline displays below the text. In both cases, the Spelling and Grammar Status icon on the status bar displays a red X, instead of a check mark. Although you can check the entire document for spelling and grammar errors at once, you also can check these errors immediately.

To verify that the check spelling as you type feature is enabled, right-click the Spelling and Grammar Status icon on the status bar and then click Options on the shortcut menu. When the Spelling & Grammar dialog box displays, be sure Check spelling as you type has a check mark and Hide spelling errors in this document does not have a check mark.

When a word is flagged with a red wavy underline, it is not in Word's dictionary. To display a list of suggested corrections for a flagged word, you right-click it. A flagged word, however, is not necessarily misspelled. For example, many names, abbreviations, and specialized terms are not in Word's main dictionary. In these cases, you tell Word to ignore the flagged word. As you type, Word also detects duplicate words. For example, if your document contains the phrase, to the the store, Word places a red wavy underline below the second occurrence of the word, the.

Correcting Spelling

As you type, Word corrects some misspelled words automatically. For example, if you type recieve, Word automatically fixes the misspelling and displays the word, receive, when you press the SPACEBAR or type a punctuation mark. To see a complete list of automatically corrected words, click Tools on the menu bar, click AutoCorrect Options on the Tools menu, click the AutoCorrect tab, and then scroll through the list of words near the bottom of the dialog box.

In the following example, the word, identification, has been misspelled intentionally as indentification to illustrate Word's check spelling as you type feature. If you are doing this project on a personal computer, your announcement may contain different misspelled words, depending on the accuracy of your typing.

Steps: To Check Spelling as You Type

Type Show your student indentification **and then press the SPACEBAR. Position the mouse pointer in the flagged word (indentification, in this case).**

Word flags the misspelled word, indentification, by placing a red wavy underline below it (Figure 1-26). The Spelling and Grammar Status icon on the status bar now displays a red X, indicating Word has detected a possible spelling or grammar error.

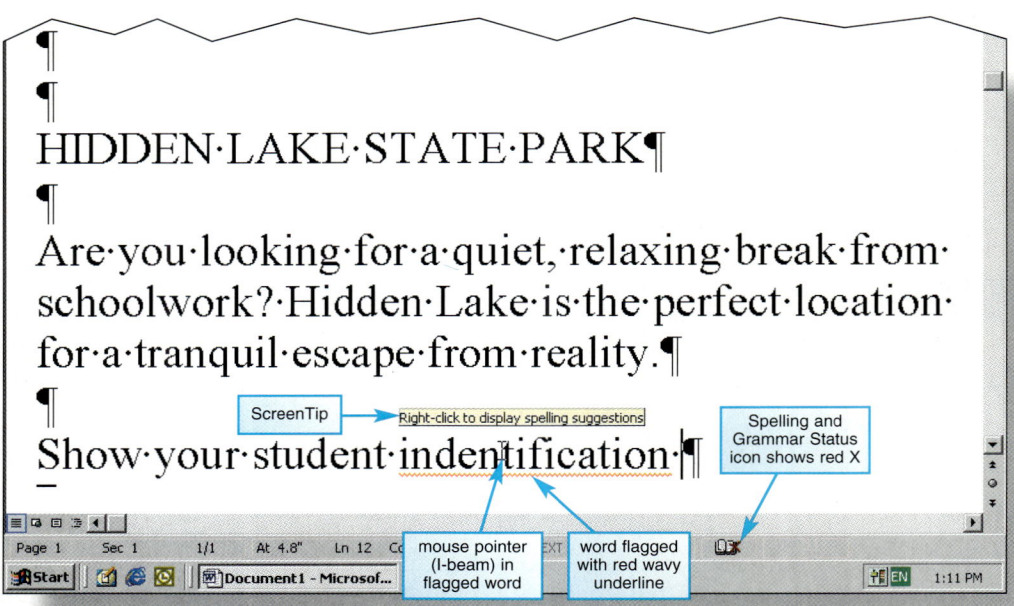

FIGURE 1-26

Right-click the flagged word, indentification. When the shortcut menu displays, point to identification.

Word displays a shortcut menu that lists suggested spelling corrections for the flagged word (Figure 1-27).

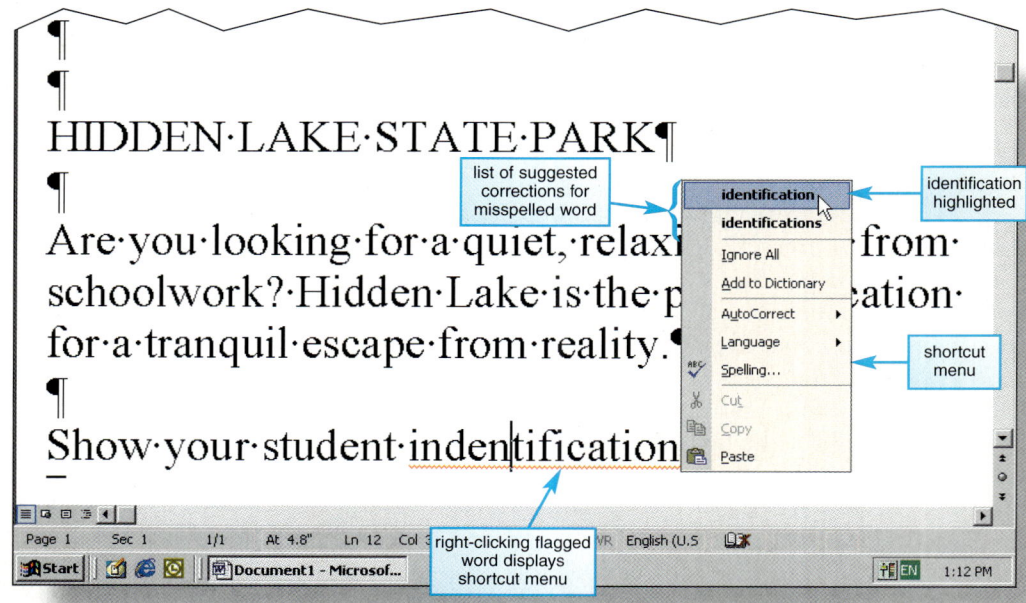

FIGURE 1-27

3 **Click identification.**

Word replaces the misspelled word with the selected word on the shortcut menu. The Spelling and Grammar Status icon once again displays a red check mark.

4 **Press the END key to move the insertion point to the end of the line and then type** card to receive a 30 percent discount on sailboat rentals. **Press the ENTER key twice. Type** Call 555-2299 for details or reservations.

The text of the announcement is complete (Figure 1-28).

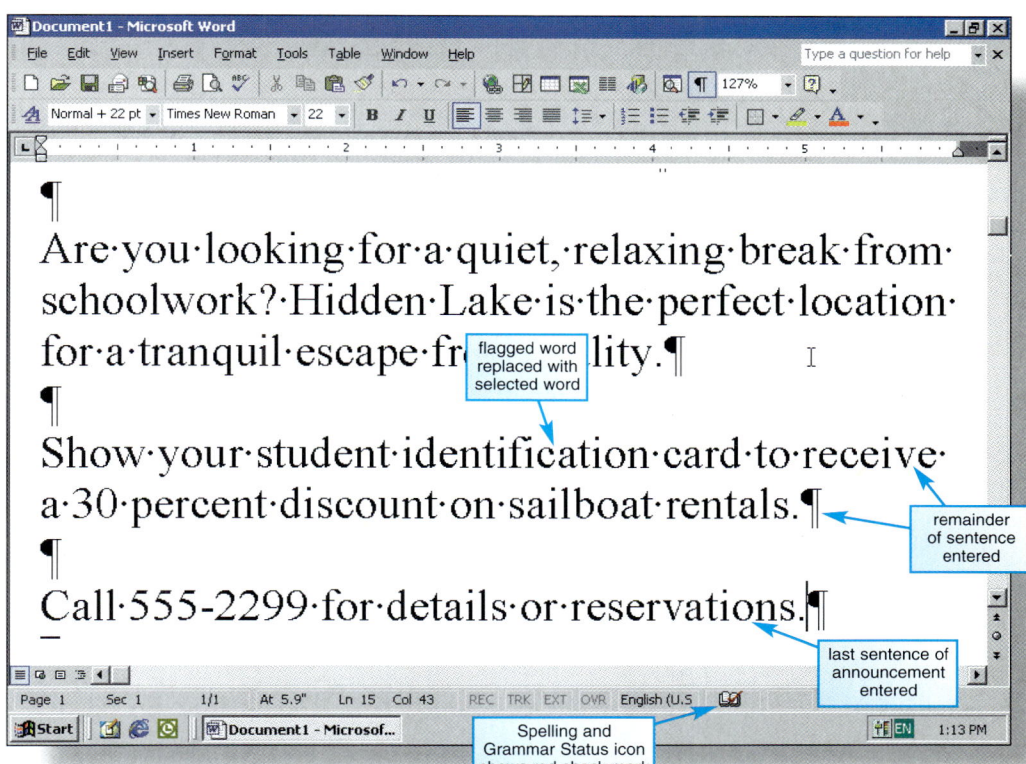

FIGURE 1-28

If a flagged word actually is spelled correctly and, for example, is a proper name, you can right-click it and then click Ignore All on the shortcut menu (Figure 1-27). If, when you right-click the misspelled word, your desired correction is not in the list on the shortcut menu, you can click outside the shortcut menu to make the menu disappear and then retype the correct word, or you can click Spelling on the shortcut menu to display the Spelling dialog box. Project 2 discusses the Spelling dialog box.

If you feel the wavy underlines clutter your document window, you can hide them temporarily until you are ready to check for spelling errors. To hide spelling errors, right-click the Spelling and Grammar Status icon on the status bar and then click Hide Spelling Errors on the shortcut menu. To hide grammar errors, right-click the Spelling and Grammar Status icon on the status bar and then click Hide Grammatical Errors on the shortcut menu.

Saving a Document

As you create a document in Word, the computer stores it in memory. If you turn off the computer or if you lose electrical power, the document in memory is lost. Hence, it is mandatory to save on disk any document that you will use later. The steps on the following pages illustrate how to save a document on a floppy disk inserted in drive A using the Save button on the Standard toolbar.

You will save the document using the file name, Hidden Lake Announcement. Depending on your Windows settings, the file type .doc may display immediately after the file name. The file type .doc indicates the file is a Word document.

Other Ways

1. Double-click Spelling and Grammar Status icon on status bar, click correct word on shortcut menu
2. In Voice Command mode, say "Spelling and Grammar"

More About

Saving

When you save a document, use meaningful file names. A file name can be up to 255 characters, including spaces. The only invalid characters are the backslash (\), slash (/), colon (:), asterisk (*), question mark (?), quotation mark ("), less than symbol (<), greater than symbol (>), and vertical bar (|).

Steps: To Save a New Document

1 **Insert a formatted floppy disk into drive A. Click the Save button on the Standard toolbar.**

Word displays the Save As dialog box (Figure 1-29). The first line from the document (Sail the Waters) displays selected in the File name text box as the default file name. With this file name selected, you can change it by immediately typing the new name.

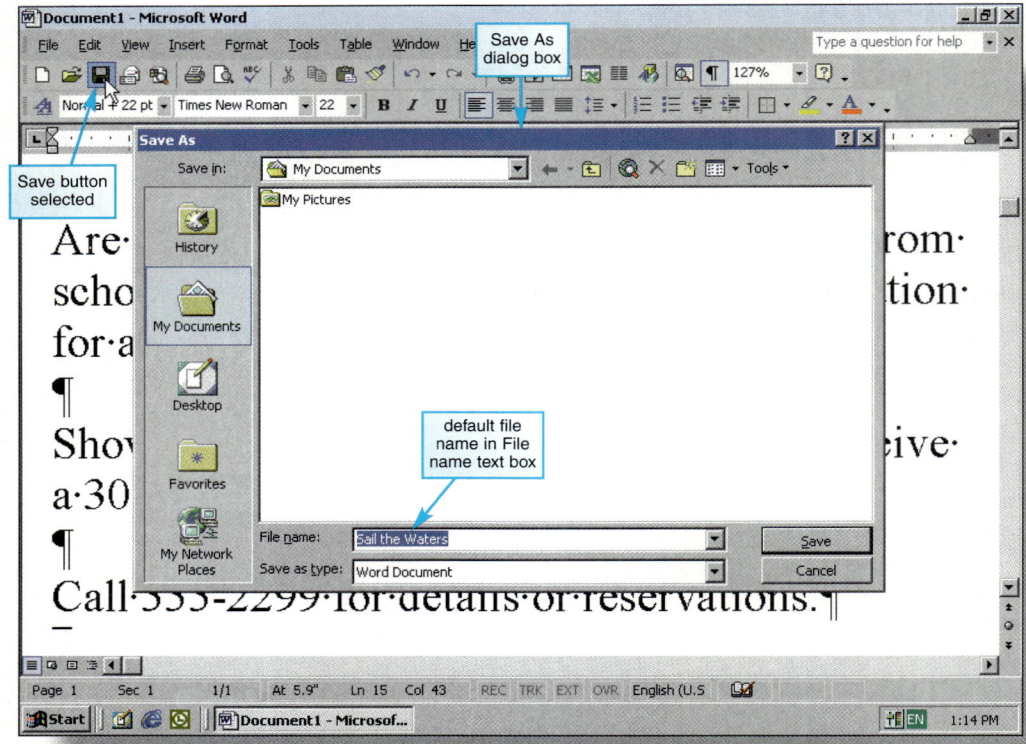

FIGURE 1-29

2 **Type** Hidden Lake Announcement **in the File name text box. Do not press the ENTER key after typing the file name.**

The file name, Hidden Lake Announcement, displays in the File name text box (Figure 1-30). Notice that the current save location is the My Documents folder. A **folder** is a specific location on a disk. To change to a different save location, use the Save in box.

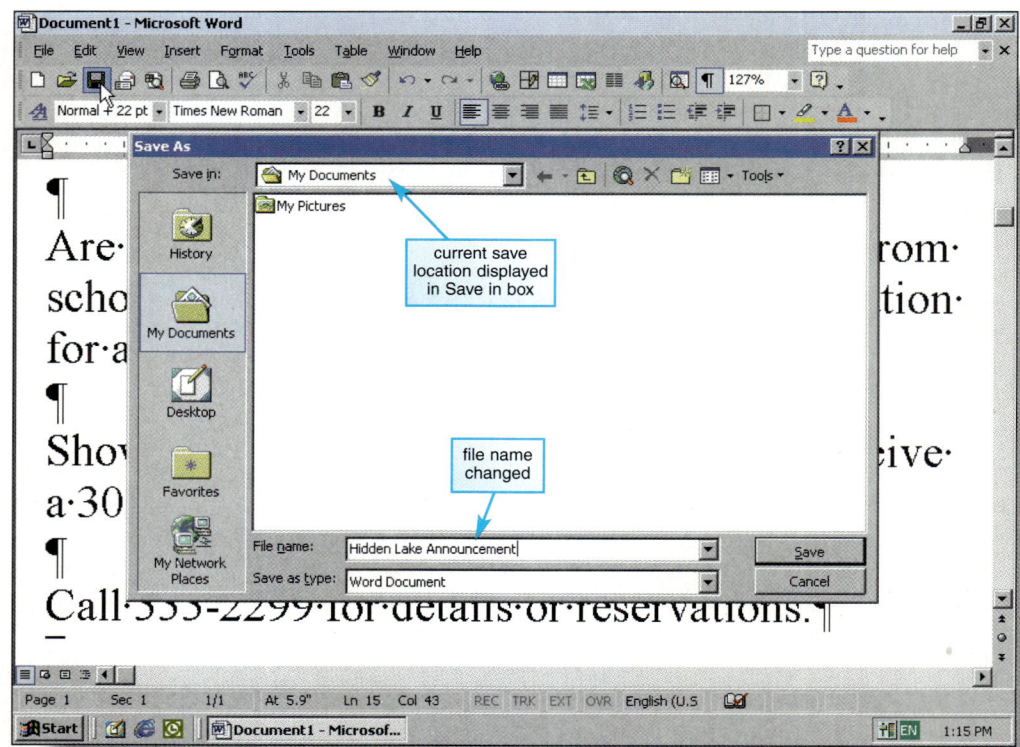

FIGURE 1-30

3 **Click the Save in box arrow and then point to 3½ Floppy (A:).**

A list of the available save locations displays (Figure 1-31). Your list may differ depending on your system configuration.

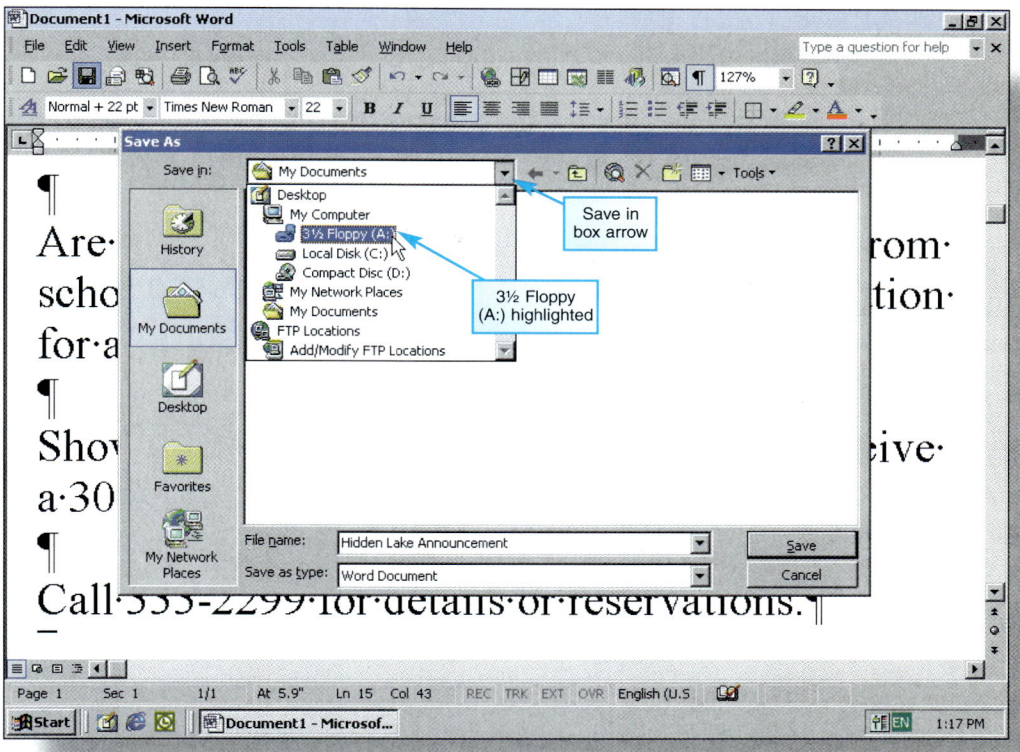

FIGURE 1-31

4 **Click 3½ Floppy (A:) and then point to the Save button in the Save As dialog box.**

The 3½ Floppy (A:) drive becomes the save location (Figure 1-32). The names of existing files stored on the floppy disk in drive A display. In Figure 1-32, the list is empty because no Word files currently are stored on the floppy disk in drive A.

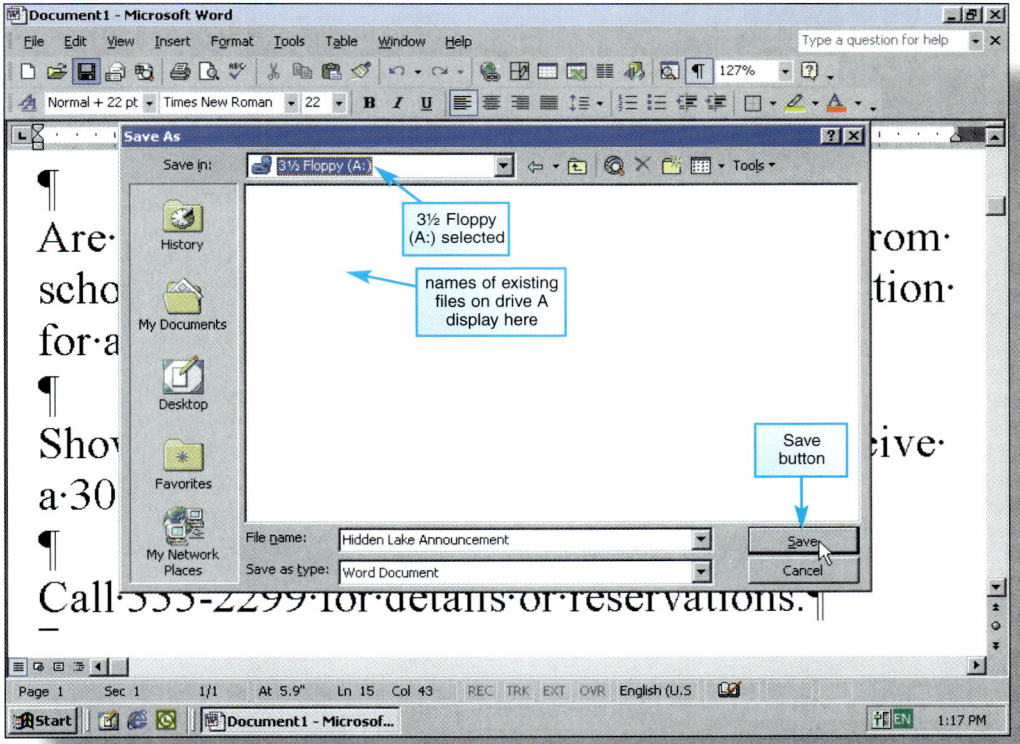

FIGURE 1-32

5 **Click the Save button in the Save As dialog box.**

Word saves the document on the floppy disk in drive A with the file name Hidden Lake Announcement (Figure 1-33). Although the announcement is saved on a floppy disk, it also remains in main memory and displays on the screen.

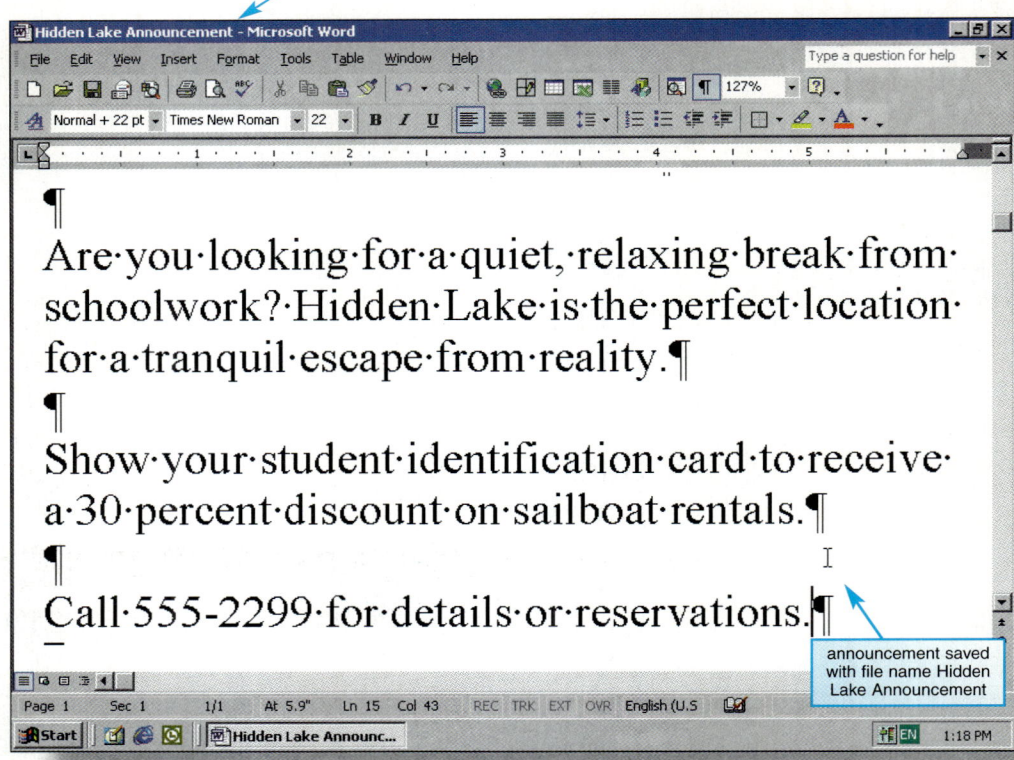

FIGURE 1-33

Other Ways

1. On File menu click Save As, type file name, select location in Save in list, click Save button in dialog box
2. Press CTRL+S, type file name, select location in Save in list, click Save button in dialog box
3. In Voice Command mode, say "File, Save As, [type file name], Save In, [select folder], Save"

More About

Formatting

Character formatting includes changing the font, font style, font size; adding an underline, color, strikethrough, or shadow; embossing; engraving; making a superscript or subscript; and changing the case of the letters. Paragraph formatting includes alignment; indentation; and spacing above, below, and between lines.

Formatting Paragraphs and Characters in a Document

The text for Project 1 now is complete. The next step is to format the characters and paragraphs in the announcement. Paragraphs encompass the text up to and including a paragraph mark (¶). **Paragraph formatting** is the process of changing the appearance of a paragraph. For example, you can center or indent a paragraph.

Characters include letters, numbers, punctuation marks, and symbols. **Character formatting** is the process of changing the way characters appear on the screen and in print. You use character formatting to emphasize certain words and improve readability of a document. For example, you can italicize or underline characters.

Very often, you apply both paragraph and character formatting to the same text. For example, you may center a paragraph (paragraph formatting) and bold the characters in a paragraph (character formatting).

With Word, you can format paragraphs and characters before you type, or you can apply new formats after you type. Earlier, you changed the font size before you typed any text, and then you entered the text. In this section, you format existing text.

Figure 1-34a shows the announcement before formatting the paragraphs and characters. Figure 1-34b shows the announcement after formatting. As you can see from the two figures, a document that is formatted not only is easier to read, but it looks more professional.

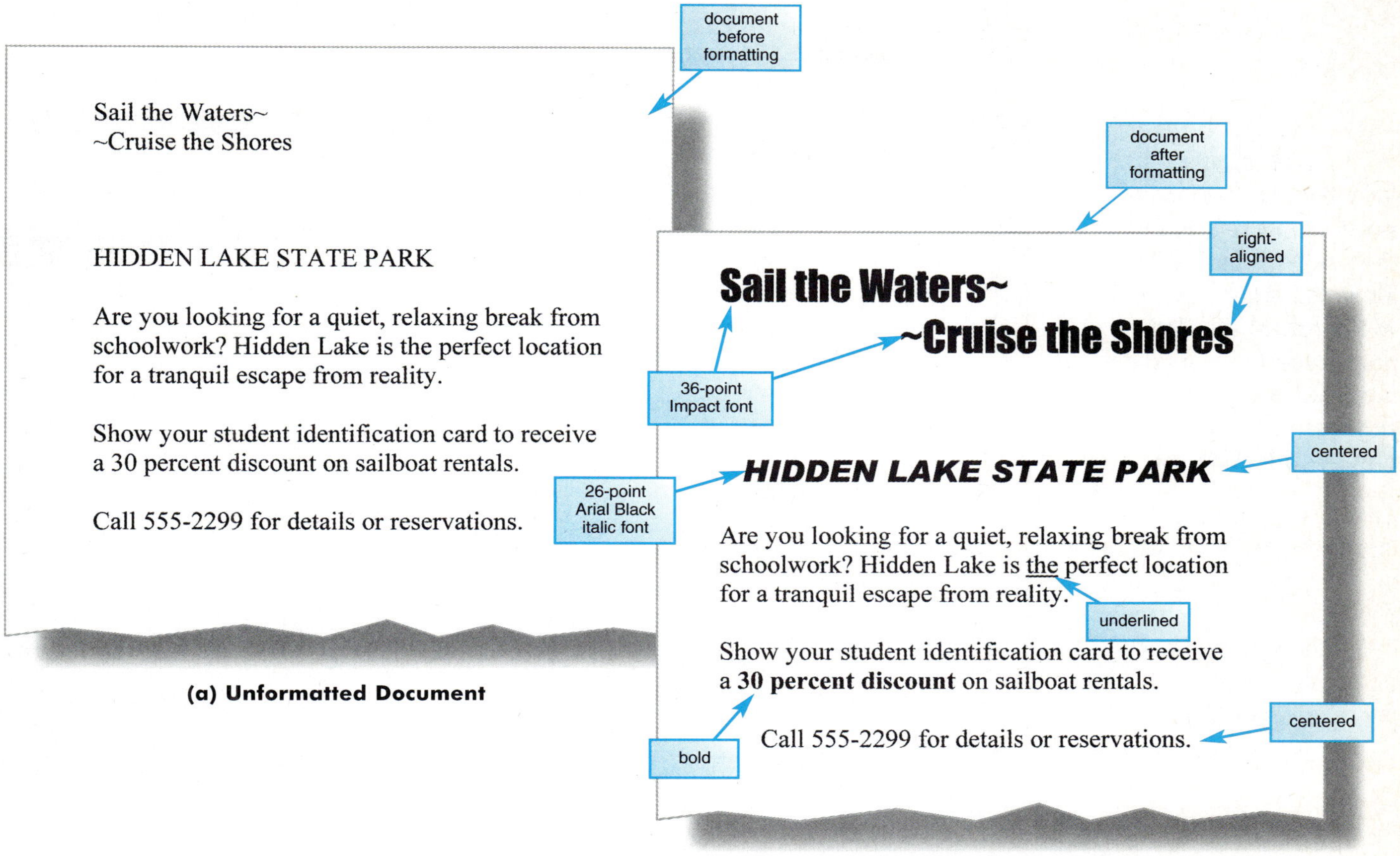

Formatting Paragraphs and Characters in a Document • WD 1.33

Sail the Waters~
~Cruise the Shores

HIDDEN LAKE STATE PARK

Are you looking for a quiet, relaxing break from schoolwork? Hidden Lake is the perfect location for a tranquil escape from reality.

Show your student identification card to receive a 30 percent discount on sailboat rentals.

Call 555-2299 for details or reservations.

(a) Unformatted Document

document before formatting

document after formatting

right-aligned

Sail the Waters~
~Cruise the Shores

36-point Impact font

HIDDEN LAKE STATE PARK ← centered

26-point Arial Black italic font

Are you looking for a quiet, relaxing break from schoolwork? Hidden Lake is <u>the</u> perfect location for a tranquil escape from reality.

underlined

Show your student identification card to receive a **30 percent discount** on sailboat rentals.

Call 555-2299 for details or reservations. ← centered

bold

(b) Formatted Document

FIGURE 1-34

Selecting and Formatting Paragraphs and Characters

To format a single paragraph, move the insertion point into the paragraph and then format the paragraph. Thus, you do not need to select a paragraph to format it. To format *multiple* paragraphs, however, you must first select the paragraphs you want to format and then format them. In the same manner, to format characters, a word, or words, you first must select the characters, word, or words to be formatted and then format your selection.

Selected text is highlighted text. That is, if your screen normally displays dark letters on a light background, then selected text displays light letters on a dark background.

Selecting Multiple Paragraphs

The first formatting step in this project is to change the font size of the characters in the headline. The headline consists of two separate lines, each ending with a paragraph mark. As previously discussed, Word creates a new paragraph each time you press the ENTER key. Thus, the headline actually is two separate paragraphs.

To change the font size of the characters in the headline, you must first **select**, or highlight, both paragraphs in the headline as shown in the steps on the next page.

Spacing

Word processing documents use variable character fonts; for example, the letter w takes up more space than the letter i. With these fonts, it often is difficult to determine how many times someone has pressed the SPACEBAR between sentences. Thus, the rule is to press the SPACEBAR only once after periods, colons, and other punctuation marks. Notice in Figure 1-34b that only one space exists between the ? and the H in Hidden.

Steps: To Select Multiple Paragraphs

1 **Press CTRL+HOME; that is, press and hold the CTRL key, then press the HOME key, and then release both keys. Move the mouse pointer to the left of the first paragraph to be selected until the mouse pointer changes to a right-pointing block arrow.**

CTRL+HOME positions the insertion point at the top of the document (Figure 1-35). The mouse pointer changes to a right-pointing block arrow when positioned to the left of a paragraph.

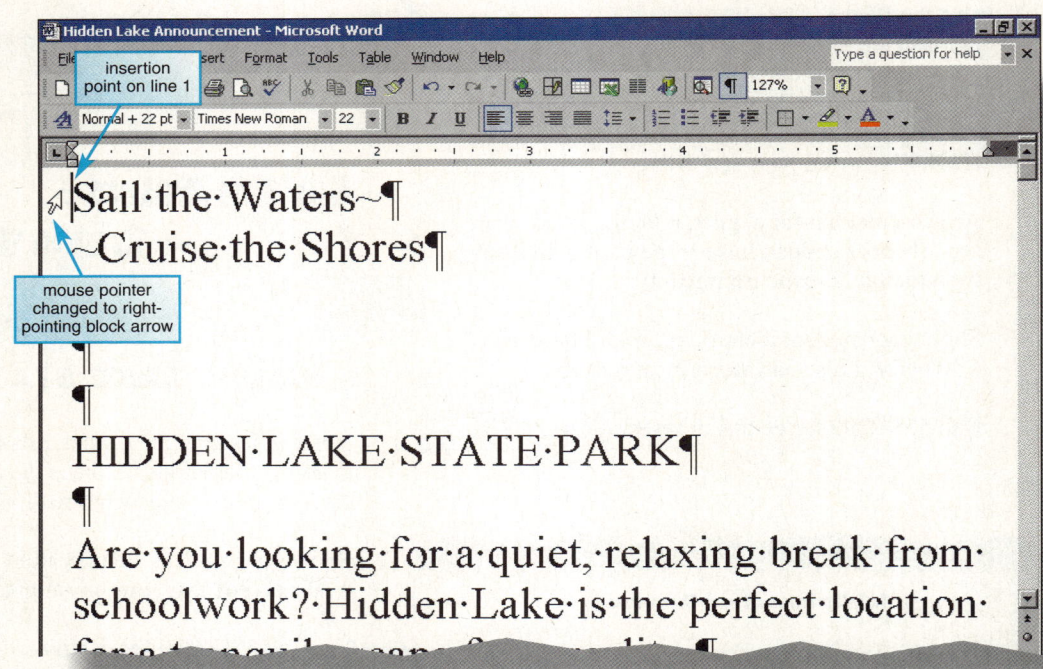

FIGURE 1-35

2 **Drag downward until both paragraphs are selected.**

Word selects (highlights) both of the paragraphs (Figure 1-36). Recall that dragging is the process of holding down the mouse button while moving the mouse and then releasing the mouse button.

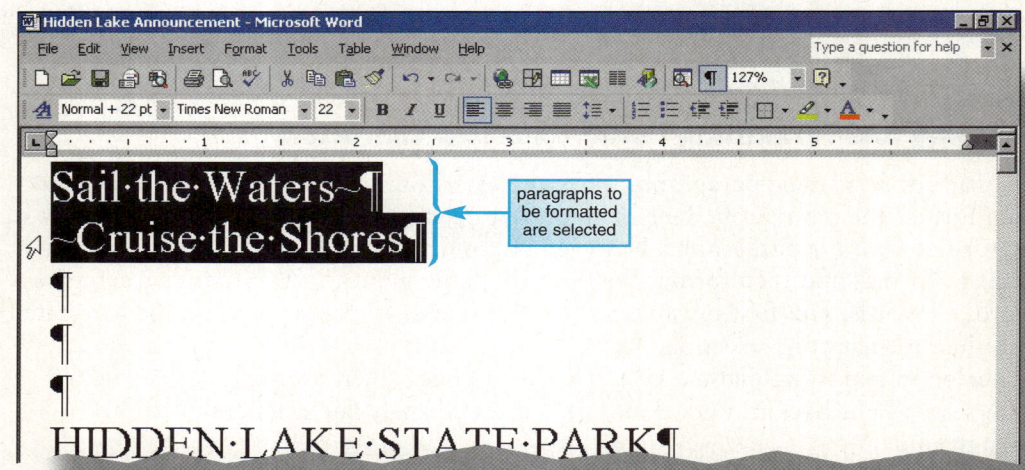

FIGURE 1-36

Other Ways

1. With insertion point at beginning of first paragraph, press CTRL+SHIFT+DOWN ARROW
2. In Voice Command mode, say "Select Paragraph"

Changing the Font Size of Selected Text

The next step is to increase the font size of the characters in the selected headline. Recall that the font size specifies the size of the characters. Earlier in this project, you changed the font size for characters in the entire announcement to 22. To give the headline more impact, it has a font size larger than the body copy. Perform the following steps to increase the font size of the headline from 22 to 36 point.

Formatting Paragraphs and Characters in a Document • WD 1.35

Steps: To Change the Font Size of Selected Text

1 While the text is selected, click the Font Size box arrow on the Formatting toolbar and then point to the down scroll arrow on the Font Size scroll bar.

Word displays a list of the available font sizes (Figure 1-37). Available font sizes vary depending on the font and printer driver.

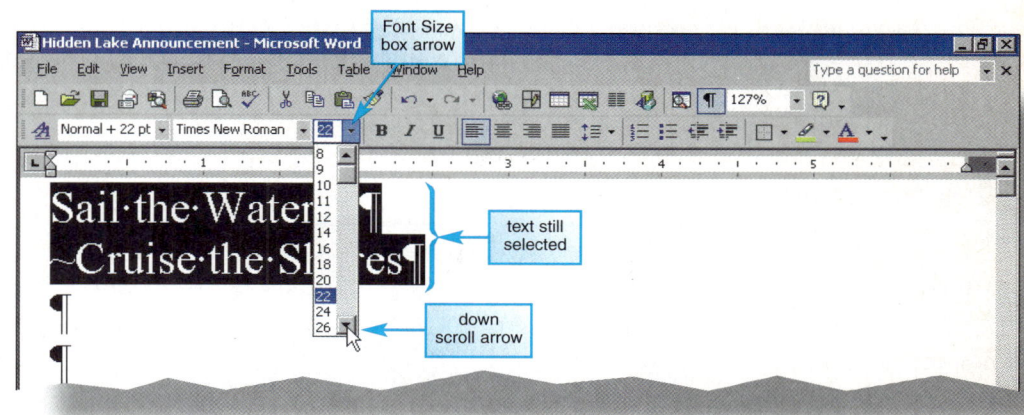

FIGURE 1-37

2 Click the down scroll arrow on the Font Size scroll bar until 36 displays in the list and then point to 36.

Word selects 36 in the list (Figure 1-38).

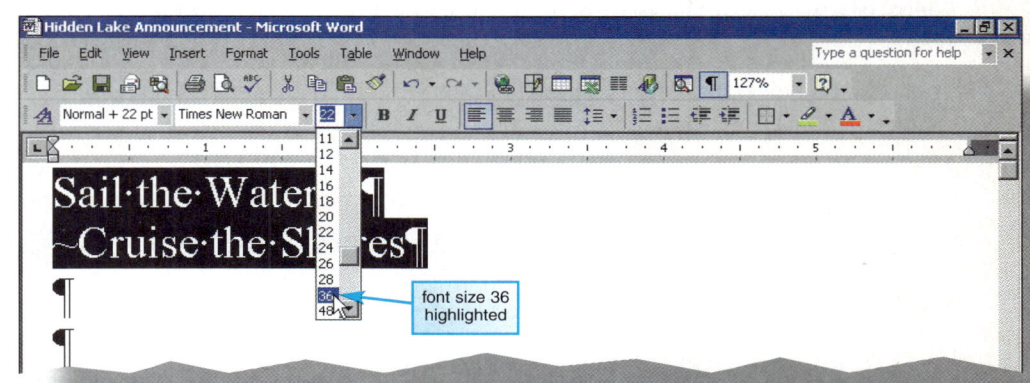

FIGURE 1-38

3 Click 36.

Word increases the font size of the headline to 36 (Figure 1-39). The Font Size box on the Formatting toolbar displays 36, indicating the selected text has a font size of 36.

FIGURE 1-39

Other Ways

1. Right-click selected text, click Font on shortcut menu, click Font tab, select font size in Size list, click OK button
2. See Other Ways 2 through 4 on page WD 1.20

Changing the Font of Selected Text

As mentioned earlier in this project, the default font in Word is Times New Roman. Word, however, provides many other fonts to add variety to your documents. Perform the following steps to change the font of the headline in the announcement from Times New Roman to Impact (or a similar font).

To Change the Font of Selected Text

1 While the text is selected, click the Font box arrow on the Formatting toolbar, scroll through the list until Impact displays, and then point to Impact (or a similar font).

Word displays a list of available fonts (Figure 1-40). Your list of available fonts may differ, depending on the type of printer you are using.

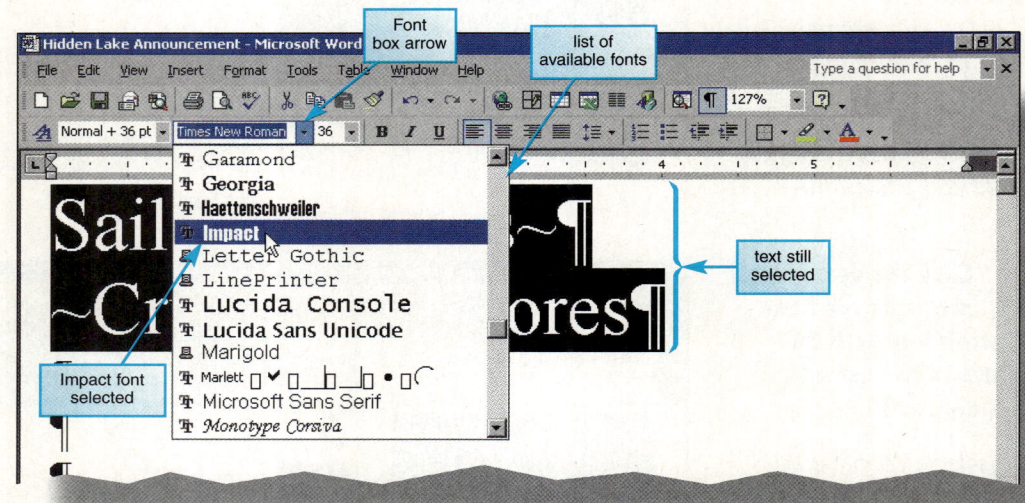

FIGURE 1-40

2 Click Impact (or a similar font).

Word changes the font of the selected text to Impact (Figure 1-41).

FIGURE 1-41

1. On Format menu click Font, click Font tab, click font name in font list, click OK button
2. Press CTRL+SHIFT+F, press DOWN ARROW to font name, press ENTER
3. In Voice Command mode, say "Font, [select font name]"

Right-Align a Paragraph

The default alignment for paragraphs is **left-aligned**, that is, flush at the left margin of the document with uneven right edges. In Figure 1-42, the Align Left button is selected to indicate the current paragraph is left-aligned.

The second line of the headline, however, is to be **right-aligned**, that is, flush at the right margin of the document with uneven left edges. Recall that the second line of the headline is a paragraph, and paragraph formatting does not require you to select the paragraph prior to formatting. Just position the insertion point in the paragraph to be formatted and then format it accordingly.

Perform the following steps to right-align the second line of the headline.

Steps: To Right-Align a Paragraph

 Click somewhere in the paragraph to be right-aligned. Point to the Align Right button on the Formatting toolbar.

Word positions the insertion point at the location you clicked (Figure 1-42).

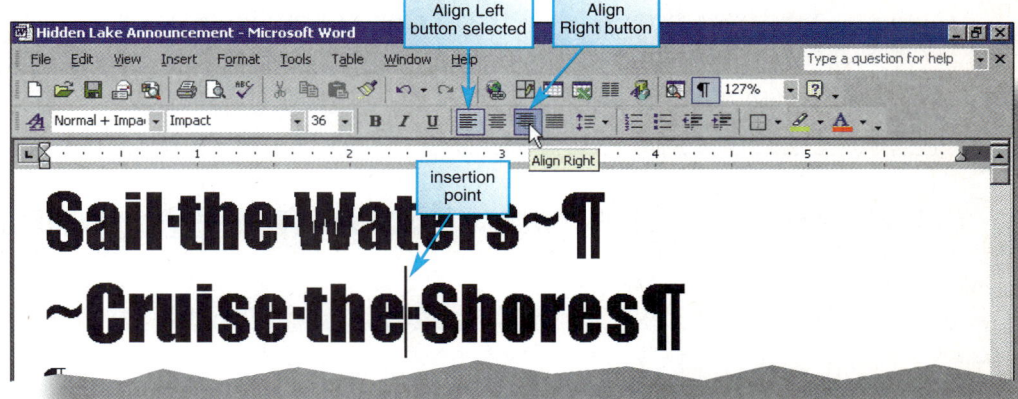

FIGURE 1-42

Click the Align Right button.

The second line of the headline is right-aligned (Figure 1-43). Notice that you did not have to select the paragraph before right-aligning it. Paragraph formatting requires only that the insertion point be positioned somewhere in the paragraph.

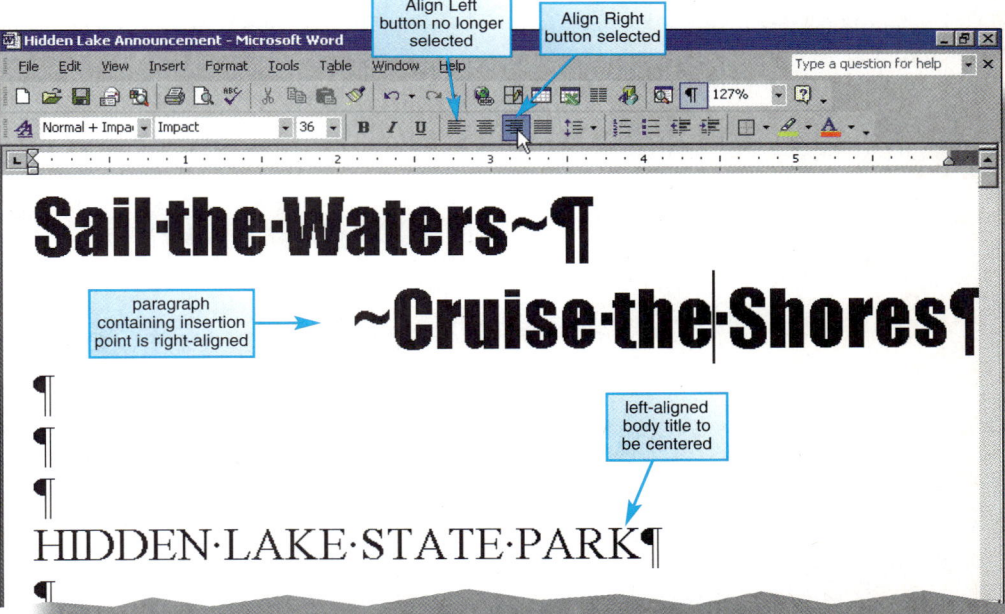

FIGURE 1-43

Other Ways

1. On Format menu click Paragraph, click Indents and Spacing tab, click Alignment box arrow, click Right, click OK button
2. Press CTRL+R
3. In Voice Command mode, say "Align Right"

When a paragraph is right-aligned, the Align Right button on the Formatting toolbar is selected. If, for some reason, you wanted to return the paragraph to left-aligned, you would click the Align Left button on the Formatting toolbar.

Center a Paragraph

The body title currently is left-aligned (Figure 1-43 on the previous page). Perform the following step to **center** it; that is, position the body title horizontally between the left and right margins on the page.

Steps To Center a Paragraph

 Click somewhere in the paragraph to be centered. Click the Center button on the Formatting toolbar.

Word centers the body title between the left and right margins (Figure 1-44). The Center button on the Formatting toolbar is selected, which indicates the paragraph containing the insertion point is centered.

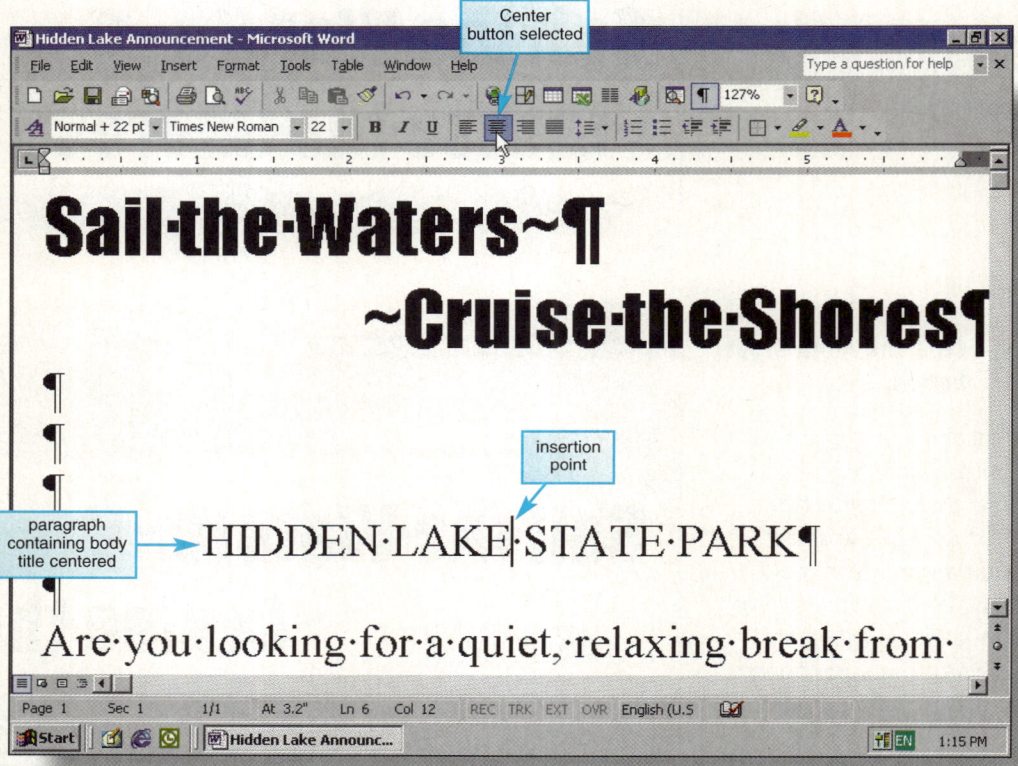

FIGURE 1-44

Other Ways

1. On Format menu click Paragraph, click Indents and Spacing tab, click Alignment box arrow, click Centered, click OK button
2. Right-click paragraph, click Paragraph on shortcut menu, click Indents and Spacing tab, click Alignment box arrow, click Centered, click OK button
3. Press CTRL+E
4. In Voice Command mode, say "Center"

When a paragraph is centered, the Center button on the Formatting toolbar is selected. If, for some reason, you wanted to return the paragraph to left-aligned, you would click the Align Left button on the Formatting toolbar.

Undoing Commands or Actions

Word provides an **Undo button** on the Standard toolbar that you can use to cancel your recent command(s) or action(s). For example, if you format text incorrectly, you can undo the format and try it again. If, after you undo an action, you decide you did not want to perform the undo, you can use the **Redo button** to undo the undo. Word prevents you from undoing or redoing some actions, such as saving or printing a document.

Perform the following steps to undo the center format to the body title using the Undo button and then re-center it using the Redo button.

To Undo an Action

1 **Click the Undo button on the Standard toolbar.**

Word returns the body title to its formatting before you issued the center command (Figure 1-45). That is, Word left-aligns the body title.

2 **Click the Redo button on the Standard toolbar.**

Word reapplies the center format to the body title (shown in Figure 1-44).

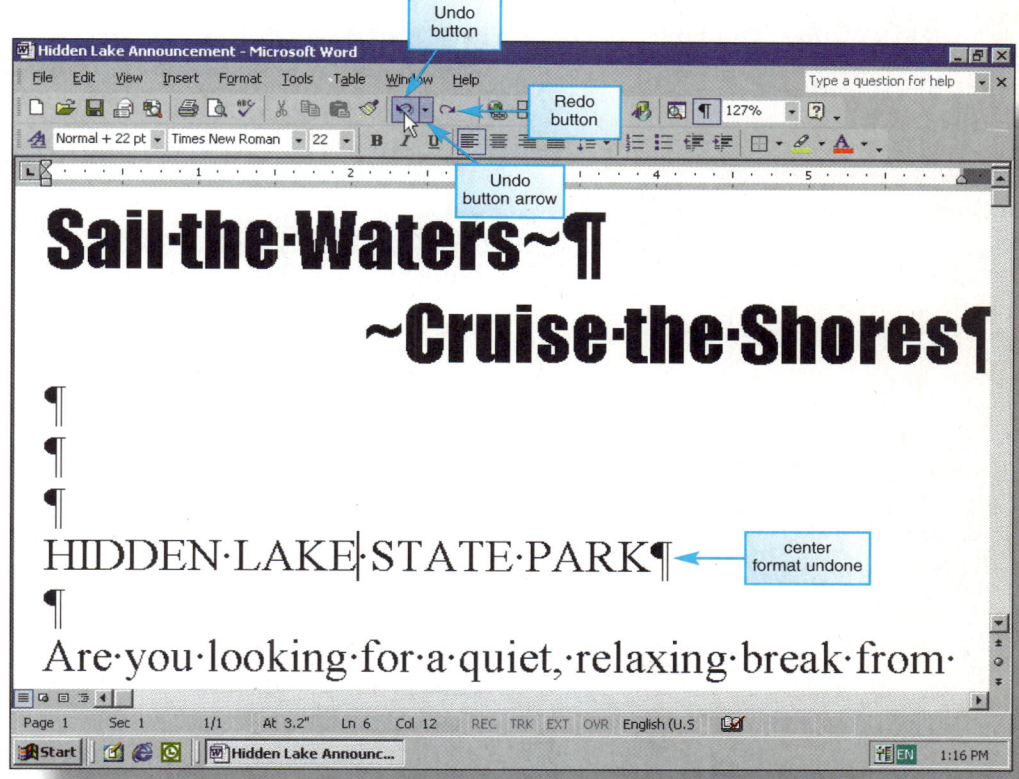

FIGURE 1-45

Other Ways

1. On Edit menu click Undo
2. Press CTRL+Z
3. In Voice Command mode, say "Undo"

You also can cancel a series of prior actions by clicking the Undo button arrow (Figure 1-45) to display the list of undo actions and then dragging through the actions you wish to undo.

Whereas the Undo command cancels an action you did not want to perform, Word also provides a **Repeat command**, which duplicates your last command so you can perform it again. The word(s) listed after Repeat vary, depending on your most recent command. For example, if you centered a paragraph and wish to format another paragraph the exact same way, you could click in the second paragraph to format and then click Repeat Paragraph Alignment on the Edit menu.

More About

Centering

The Center button on the Formatting toolbar centers text horizontally. You also can center text vertically between the top and bottom margins. To do this, click File on the menu bar, click Page Setup, click the Layout tab, click the Vertical alignment box arrow, click Center in the list, and then click the OK button.

Selecting a Line and Formatting It

The characters in the body title, HIDDEN LAKE STATE PARK, are to be a different font, larger font size, and italicized. To make these changes, you must select the line of text containing the body title. Perform the step on the next page to select the body title.

WD 1.40 • Project 1 • Creating and Editing a Word Document

 **To Select a Line**

1 **Move the mouse pointer to the left of the line to be selected (HIDDEN LAKE STATE PARK) until it changes to a right-pointing block arrow and then click.**

The entire line to the right of the mouse pointer is selected (Figure 1-46).

FIGURE 1-46

Other Ways

1. Drag through the line
2. With insertion point at beginning of desired line, press SHIFT+DOWN ARROW
3. In Voice Command, say "Select Line"

The next step is to change the font of the selected characters from Times New Roman to Arial Black and increase the font size of the selected characters from 22 to 26 point, as explained below.

TO FORMAT A LINE OF TEXT

1 While the text is selected, click the Font box arrow and then scroll to Arial Black, or a similar font, in the list. Click Arial Black, or a similar font.

2 While the text is selected, click the Font Size box arrow on the Formatting toolbar and then scroll to 26 in the list. Click 26.

The characters in the body title are 26-point Arial Black (Figure 1-47).

The Font Dialog Box

The Font dialog box has more character formatting options than the Formatting toolbar. For example, you can strikethrough, superscript, subscript, outline, emboss, engrave, and shadow characters using the Font dialog box. To display the Font dialog box, click Format on the menu bar and then click Font.

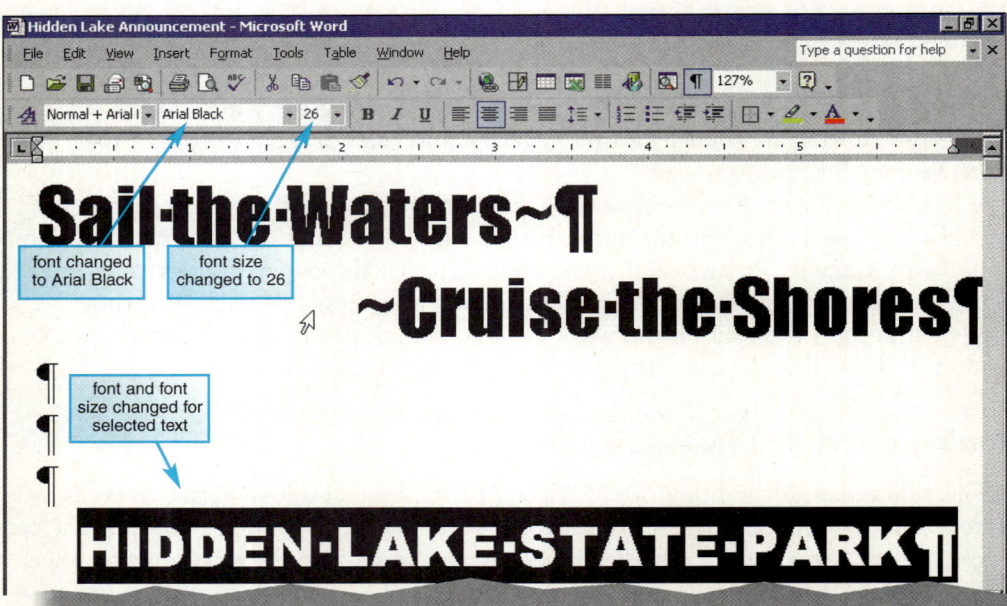

FIGURE 1-47

Italicize Selected Text

Italicized text has a slanted appearance. Perform the following step to italicize the selected characters in the body title.

 To Italicize Selected Text

1 **With the text still selected, click the Italic button on the Formatting toolbar.**

Word italicizes the text (Figure 1-48). The Italic button on the Formatting toolbar is selected.

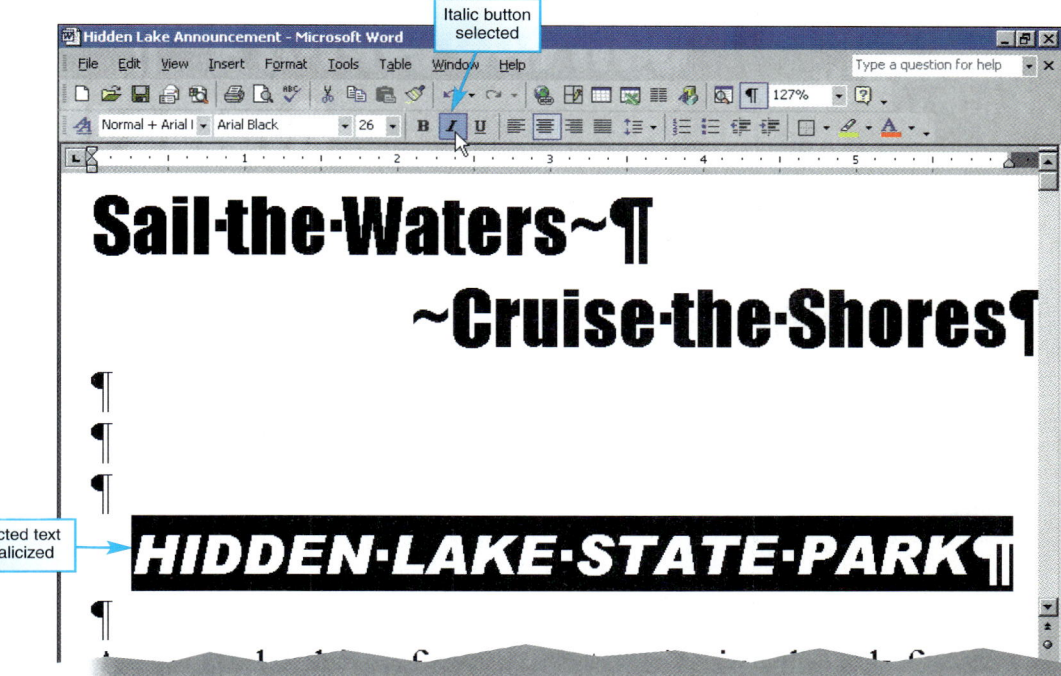

FIGURE 1-48

When the selected text is italicized, the Italic button on the Formatting toolbar is selected. If, for some reason, you wanted to remove the italics from the selected text, you would click the Italic button a second time, or you immediately could click the Undo button on the Standard toolbar.

Scrolling

The next text to format is in the lower portion of the announcement, which does not display in the document window. To continue formatting the document, perform the steps on the next page to scroll down one screen so the lower portion of the announcement displays in the document window.

Other Ways

1. On Format menu click Font, click Font tab, click Italic in Font style list, click OK button
2. Right-click selected text, click Font on shortcut menu, click Font tab, click Italic in Font style list, click OK button
3. Press CTRL+I
4. In Voice Command mode, say "Italic"

Toolbar Buttons

Many of the buttons on the toolbars are toggles; that is, click them once to format the selected text; and click them again to remove the format from the selected text.

Steps To Scroll through the Document

1 Position the mouse pointer below the scroll box on the vertical scroll bar (Figure 1-49).

2 Click below the scroll box on the vertical scroll bar.

Word scrolls down one screen in the document (shown in Figure 1-50 below). Depending on your monitor type, your screen may scroll differently.

Other Ways
1. Press PAGE DOWN or PAGE UP
2. See Tables 1-1 and 1-2 on page WD 1.27
3. In Dictation mode, say key name(s) in Table 1-2

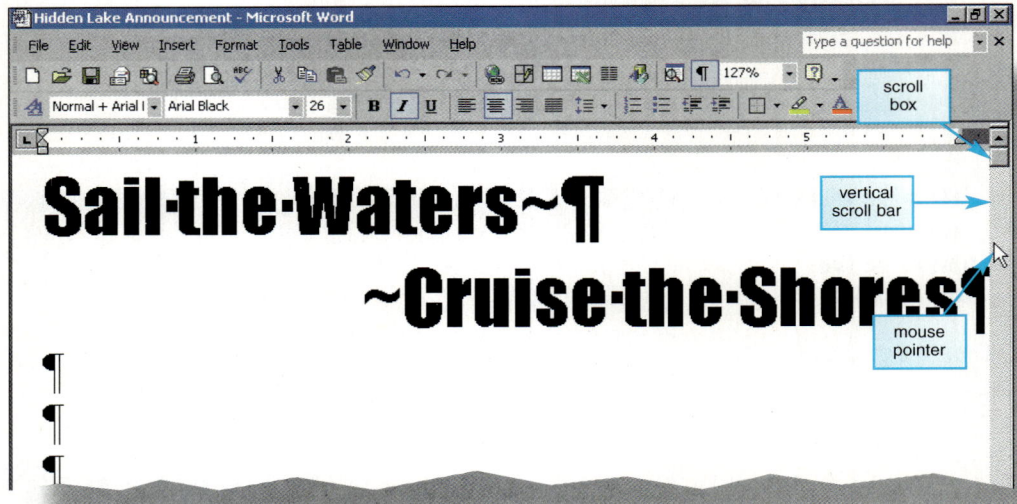

FIGURE 1-49

Selecting a Word

The next step is to underline a word in the first paragraph below the body title. To format characters in a word, you first select the entire word. Perform the following steps to select the word, the, so you can underline it.

Steps To Select a Word

1 Position the mouse pointer somewhere in the word to be formatted (the, in this case).

The mouse pointer's shape is an I-beam when you position it in unselected text in the document window (Figure 1-50).

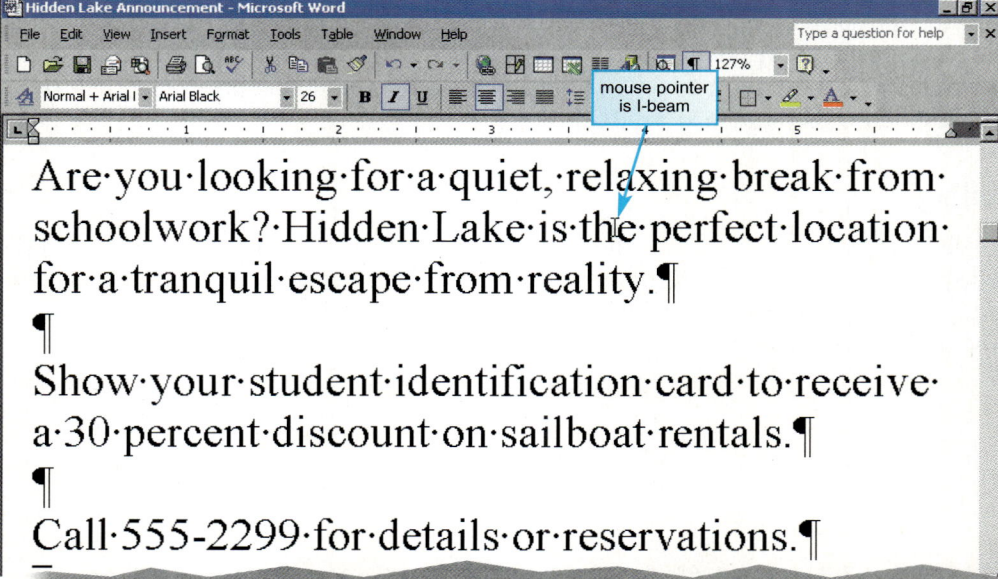

FIGURE 1-50

Formatting Paragraphs and Characters in a Document • WD 1.43

2 | **Double-click the word to be selected.**

The word, the, is selected (Figure 1-51). Notice that when the mouse pointer is positioned in a selected word, its shape is a left-pointing block arrow.

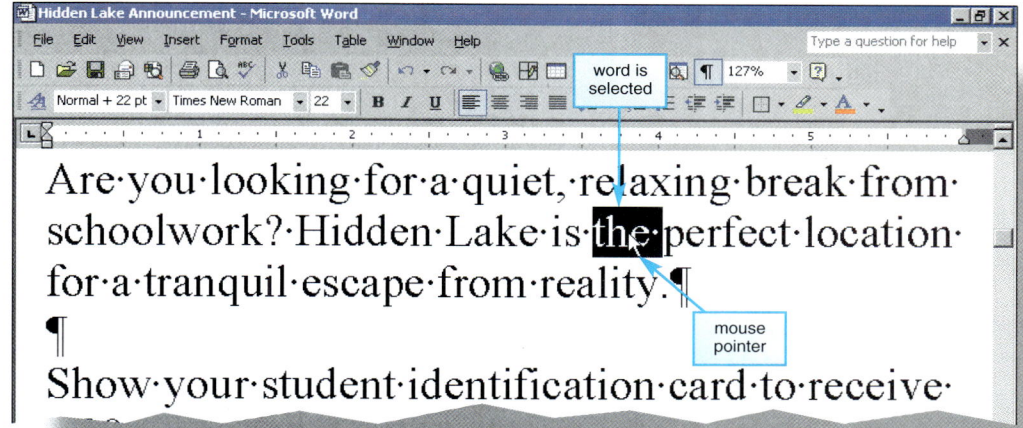

FIGURE 1-51

Other Ways

1. Drag through the word
2. With insertion point at beginning of desired word, press CTRL+SHIFT+RIGHT ARROW
3. With insertion point at beginning of desired word, in Voice Command mode, say "Select Word"

Underlining Selected Text

Underlined text prints with an underscore (_) below each character. Underlining is used to emphasize or draw attention to specific text. Follow the step below to underline the selected word.

Steps | To Underline Selected Text

1 | **With the text still selected, click the Underline button on the Formatting toolbar.**

Word underlines the text (Figure 1-52). The Underline button on the Formatting toolbar is selected.

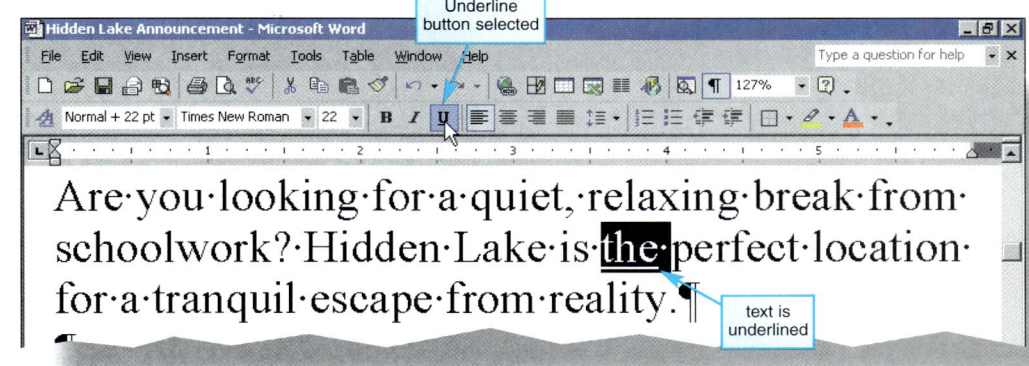

FIGURE 1-52

Other Ways

1. On Format menu click Font, click Font tab, click Underline style box arrow, click desired underline style, click OK button
2. Press CTRL+U
3. In Voice Command mode, say "Underline"

When the selected text is underlined, the Underline button on the Formatting toolbar is selected. If, for some reason, you wanted to remove the underline from the selected text, you would click the Underline button a second time, or you immediately could click the Undo button on the Standard toolbar.

In addition to the basic underline shown in Figure 1-52, Word has many decorative underlines that are available in the Font dialog box. For example, you can use double underlines, dotted underlines, and wavy underlines. In the Font dialog box, you also can change the color of an underline and instruct Word to underline only the words and not the spaces between the words. To display the Font dialog box, click Format on the menu bar and then click Font.

Selecting a Group of Words

The next step is to bold the words, 30 percent discount, in the announcement. To do this, you first must select this group of words. Perform the following steps to select a group of words.

Steps: To Select a Group of Words

1 **Position the mouse pointer immediately to the left of the first character of the text to be selected.**

The mouse pointer, an I-beam, is to the left of the 3 in 30 (Figure 1-53).

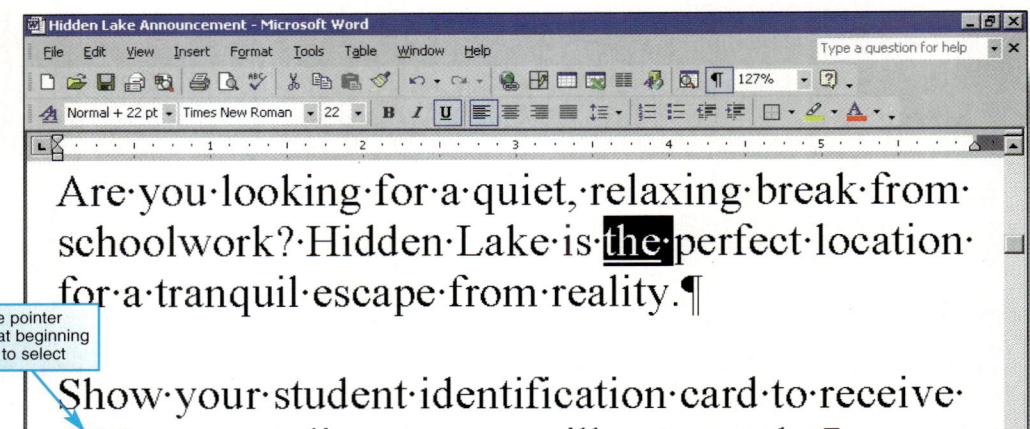

FIGURE 1-53

2 **Drag the mouse pointer through the last character of the text to be selected.**

Word selects the phrase, 30 percent discount (Figure 1-54).

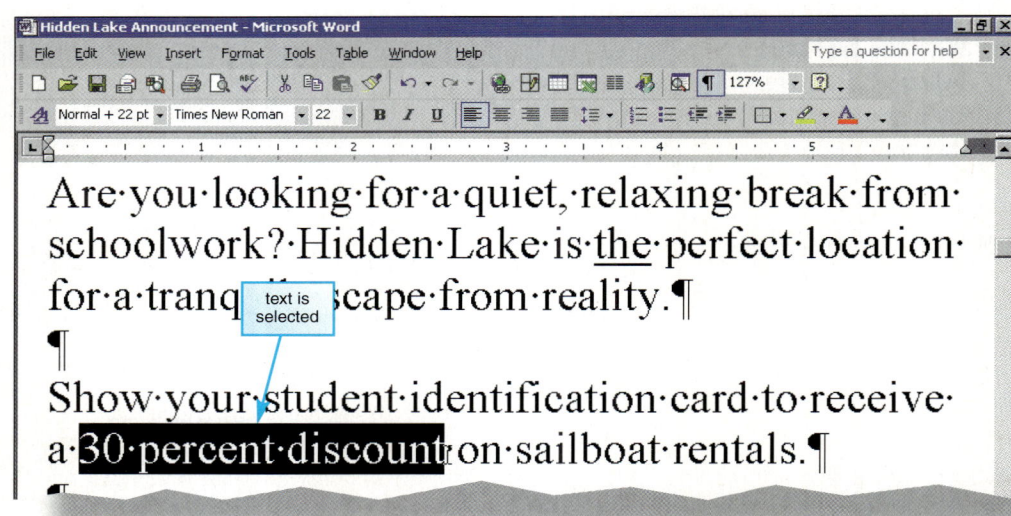

FIGURE 1-54

Other Ways

1. With insertion point at beginning of first word in the group, press CTRL+SHIFT+RIGHT ARROW until words are selected
2. In Voice Command mode, repeatedly say "Select Word"

Bold Selected Text

Bold characters display somewhat thicker and darker than those that are not bold. Perform the following step to bold the phrase, 30 percent discount.

Steps To Bold Selected Text

1 While the text is selected, click the Bold button on the Formatting toolbar. Click inside the selected text, which removes the selection (highlight) and positions the insertion point in the bold text.

Word formats the selected text in bold and positions the insertion point inside the bold text (Figure 1-55). The Bold button is selected.

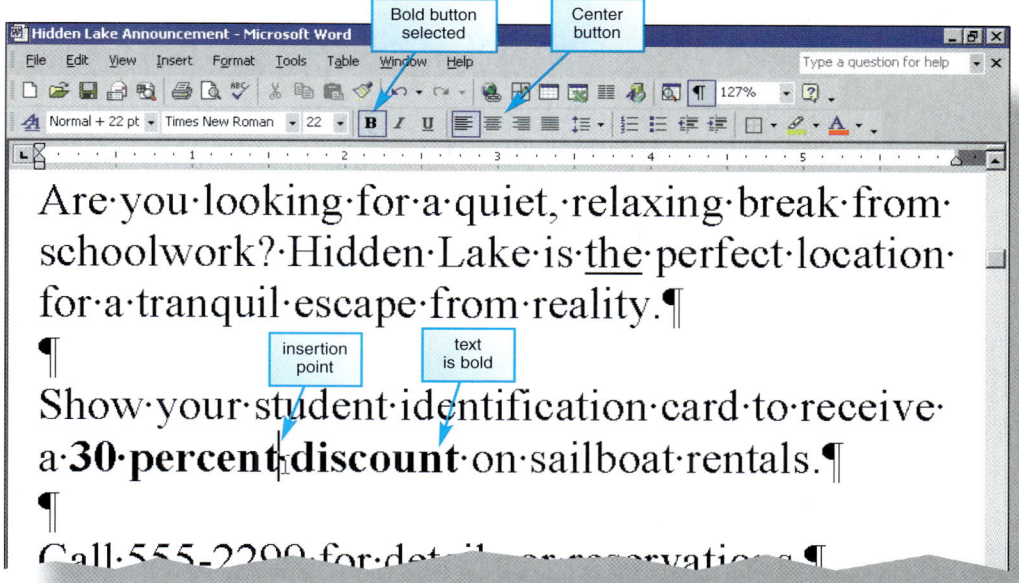

FIGURE 1-55

To remove a selection (highlight), click the mouse. If you click inside the selection, the Formatting toolbar displays the formatting characteristics of the characters and paragraphs containing the insertion point. For example, at the location of the insertion point, the characters are a 22-point Times New Roman bold font. The paragraph is left-aligned.

When the selected text is bold, the Bold button on the Formatting toolbar is selected. If, for some reason, you wanted to remove the bold format of the selected text, you would click the Bold button a second time.

The next step is to center the last line of the announcement, as described in the following steps.

Other Ways

1. On Format menu click Font, click Font tab, click Bold in Font style list, click OK button
2. Right-click selected text, click Font on shortcut menu, click Font tab, click Bold in Font style list, click OK button
3. Press CTRL+B
4. In Voice Command mode, say "Bold"

TO CENTER A PARAGRAPH

1 Click somewhere in the paragraph to be centered.

2 Click the Center button on the Formatting toolbar (shown in Figure 1-55).

Word centers the last line of the announcement (Figure 1-56).

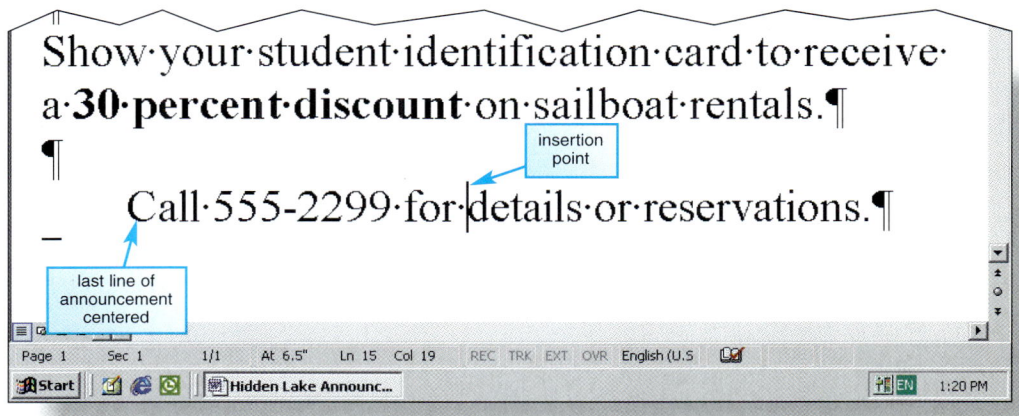

FIGURE 1-56

Clip Art

If Word displays a dialog box when you issue the command to display clip art, click the Now button to catalog all media files. If you are not connected to the Web, Word displays clip art from your hard disk. If you are connected to the Web, Word displays clip art from your hard disk and also from Microsoft's Web site. When clip art images display in the Insert Clip Art task pane, Web clips are identified by a small globe displayed in their lower-left corner.

The formatting for the announcement now is complete. The next step is to insert a graphical image into the document and then resize the image.

Inserting Clip Art into a Word Document

Files containing graphical images, also called **graphics**, are available from a variety of sources. Word 2002 includes a series of predefined graphics called **clip art** that you can insert into a Word document. Clip art is located in the **Clip Organizer**, which contains a collection of clips, including clip art, as well as photographs, sounds, and video clips. The Clip Organizer contains its own Help system to assist you in locating clips suited to your application.

Inserting Clip Art

The next step in the project is to insert a clip art image of a sailboat into the announcement between the headline and the body title. Perform the following steps to use the Insert Clip Art task pane to insert clip art into the document.

Steps   To Insert Clip Art into a Document

1 To position the insertion point where you want the clip art to be located, press CTRL+HOME and then press the DOWN ARROW key three times. Click Insert on the menu bar.

The insertion point is positioned on the second paragraph mark below the headline, and the Insert menu displays (Figure 1-57). Remember that a short menu initially displays, which expands into a full menu after a few seconds.

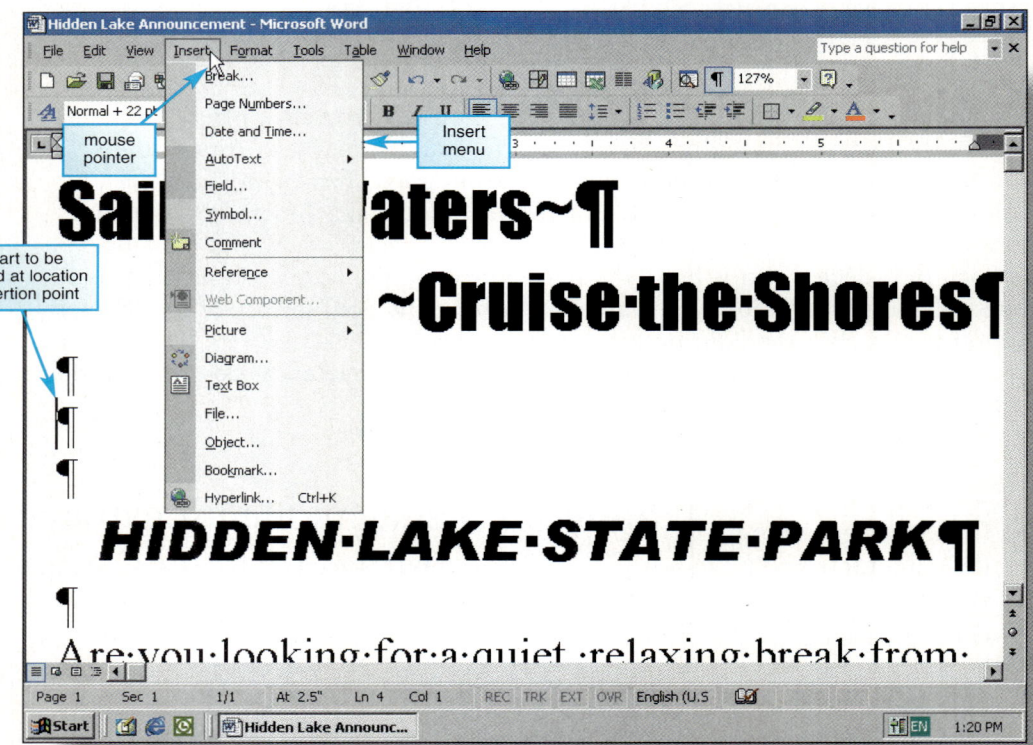

FIGURE 1-57

Inserting Clip Art into a Word Document • WD 1.47

2 **Point to Picture and then point to Clip Art.**

The Picture submenu displays (Figure 1-58). As discussed earlier, when you point to a command that has a small arrow to its right, Word displays a submenu associated with that command.

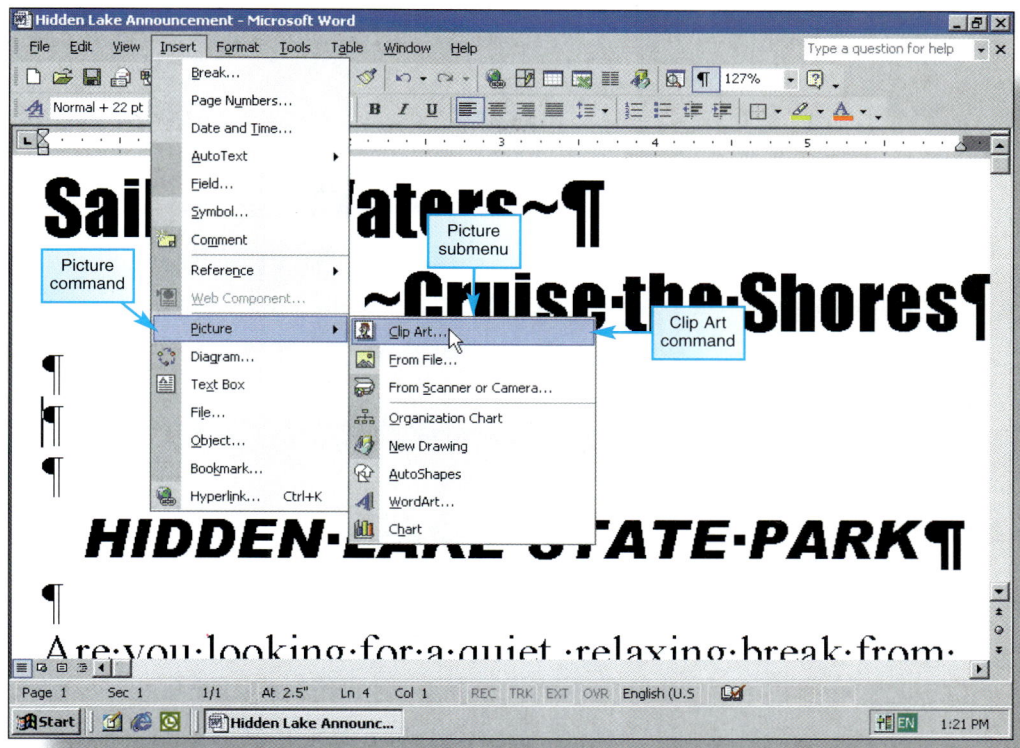

FIGURE 1-58

3 **Click Clip Art. If the Search text text box contains text, drag through the text to select it. Type** `sailboat` **and then point to the Search button.**

Word displays the Insert Clip Art task pane at the right edge of the Word window (Figure 1-59). Recall that a task pane is a separate window that enables you to carry out some Word tasks more efficiently. When you enter a description of the desired graphic in the Search text text box, Word searches the Clip Organizer for clips that match the description.

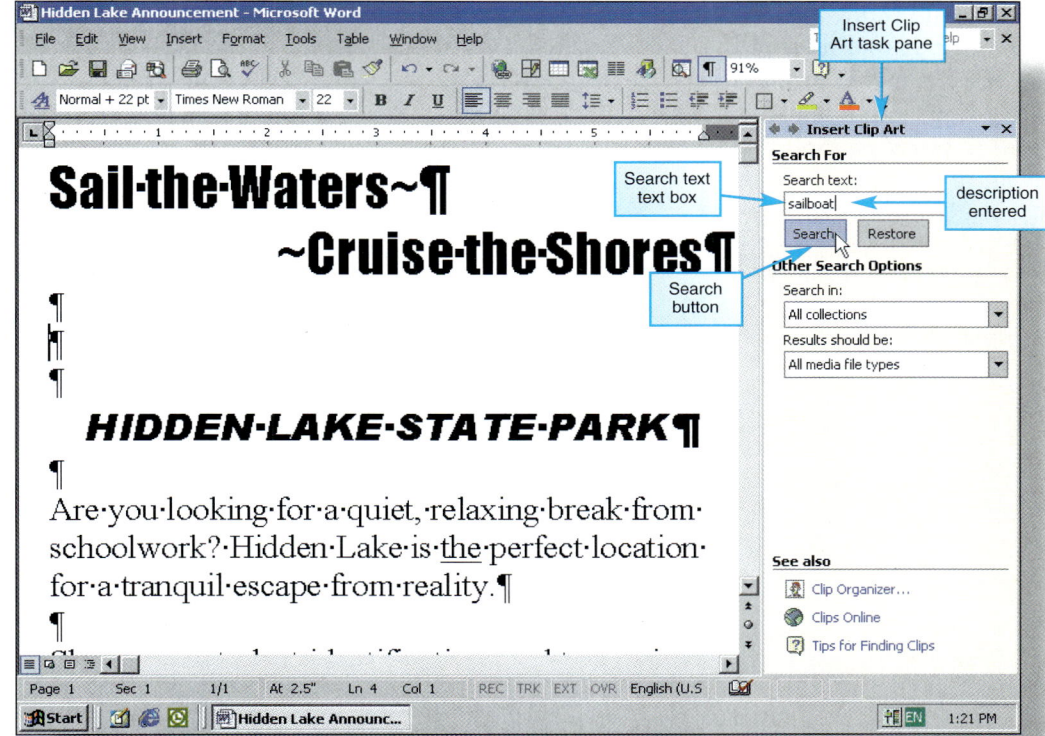

FIGURE 1-59

4 **Click the Search button.**

A list of clips that match the description, sailboat, displays (Figure 1-60). If you are connected to the Web, the Insert Clip Art task pane will display clips from the Web, as well as those installed on your hard disk.

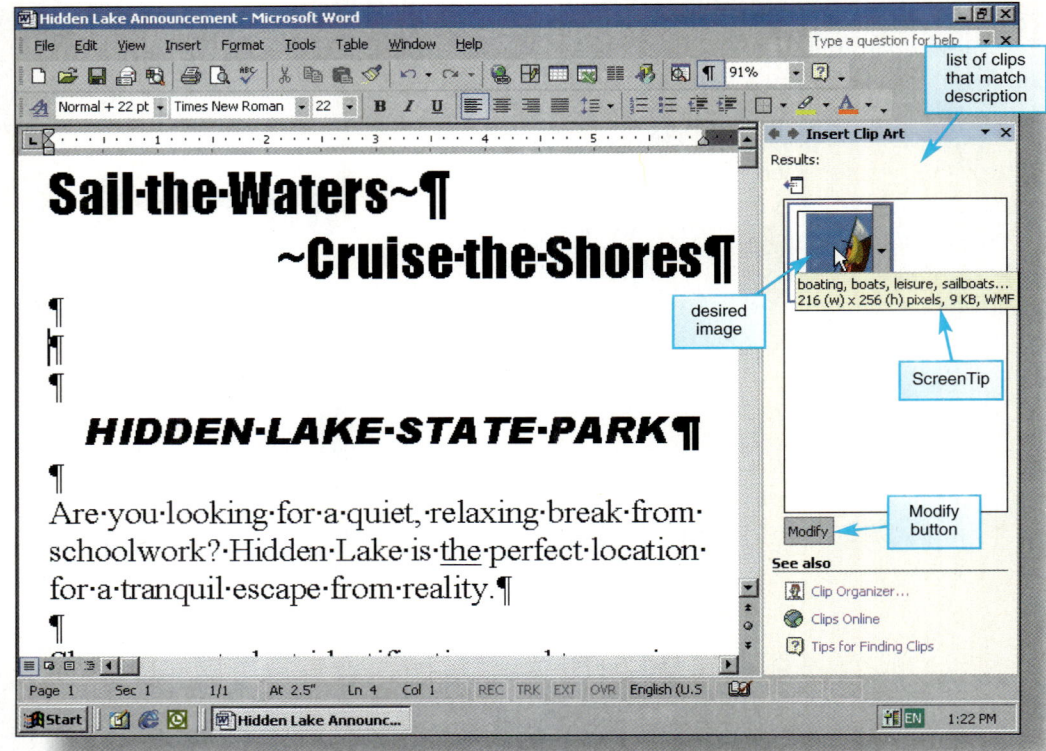

FIGURE 1-60

5 **Point to the desired image and then click the box arrow that displays to the right of the image. Point to Insert on the menu.**

When you click the box arrow, a menu displays that contains commands associated with the selected clip art image (Figure 1-61).

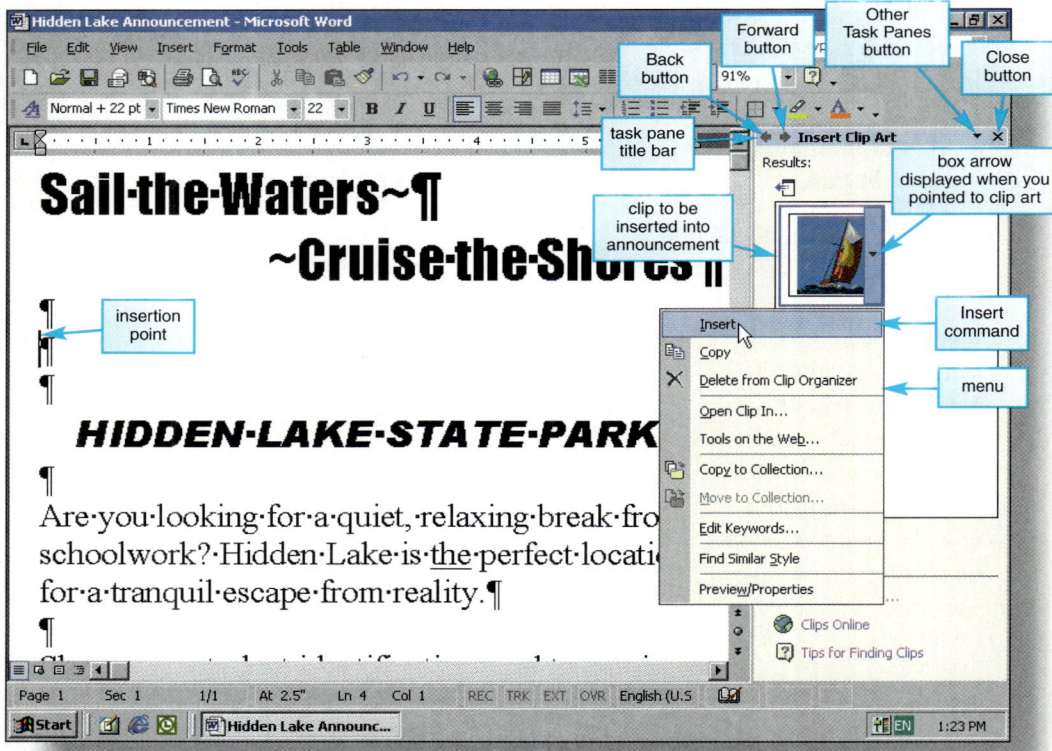

FIGURE 1-61

6 **Click Insert. Click the Close button on the Insert Clip Art task pane title bar.**

Word inserts the clip art into the document at the location of the insertion point (Figure 1-62). The image of the sailboat displays below the headline in the announcement.

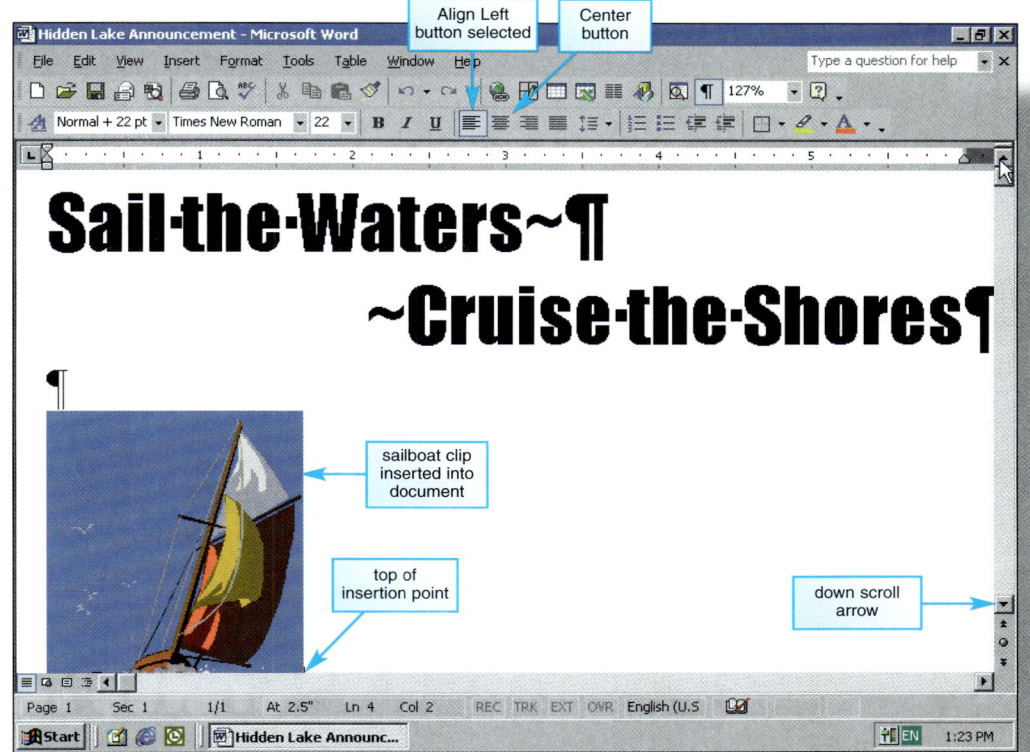

FIGURE 1-62

After you enter a description of a desired image in the Search text text box, you may want to enter a different description to locate additional or different clip art. To redisplay the Search text text box in the Insert Clip Art task pane, click the Modify button in the task pane (Figure 1-60). This will redisplay the screen shown in Figure 1-59 on page WD 1.47.

Recall that Word has eight task panes that automatically display as you perform certain operations. You also can display a task pane by clicking View on the menu bar and then clicking Task Pane. When you do this, the task pane you most recently used displays in the Word window. To display a different task pane, click the Other Task Panes button (Figure 1-61) to the left of the Close button on the task pane title bar. If you have displayed multiple task panes during a Word session, you can click the Back and Forward buttons at the left edge of the task pane title bar to scroll through the various task panes.

The clip art in the announcement is part of a paragraph. Because that paragraph is left-aligned, the clip art also is left-aligned. Notice the Align Left button on the Formatting toolbar is selected (Figure 1-62). You can use any of the paragraph alignment buttons on the Formatting toolbar to reposition the clip art. Perform the following step to center a graphic that is part of a paragraph.

TO CENTER A PARAGRAPH CONTAINING A GRAPHIC

1 If necessary, click the down scroll arrow on the scroll bar to display the entire graphic in the document window. With the insertion point on the paragraph mark containing the image, click the Center button on the Formatting toolbar.

Word centers the paragraph, which also centers the graphic in the paragraph (Figure 1-63 on the next page).

Other Ways

1. In Voice Command mode, say "Insert, Picture, Clip Art"

More About

Clip Art Packages

For more information on the clip art available for purchase, visit the Word 2002 More About Web page (scsite.com/wd2002/more.htm) and then click Clip Art.

More About

Positioning Graphics

Emphasize a graphic by placing it at the optical center of the page. To determine optical center, divide the page in half horizontally and vertically. The optical center is located one third of the way up the vertical line from the point of intersection of the two lines.

Graphics

If you have a scanner or digital camera attached to your computer, Word can insert a graphic directly from these devices. You also can scan a graphic into a file and then insert the scanned file into the Word document.

You would like the clip art in this announcement to be a little larger. Thus, the next step is to resize the graphic.

Resizing a Graphic

Once you have inserted a graphic into a document, you easily can change its size. **Resizing** includes both enlarging and reducing the size of a graphic. To resize a graphic, you first must select it.

Perform the following step to select a graphic.

To Select a Graphic

 Click anywhere in the graphic. If your screen does not display the Picture toolbar, click View on the menu bar, point to Toolbars, and then click Picture.

Word selects the graphic (Figure 1-63). A selected graphic displays surrounded by a **selection rectangle** that has small squares, called **sizing handles**, at each corner and middle location. You use the sizing handles to change the size of the graphic. When a graphic is selected, the Picture toolbar automatically displays on the screen.

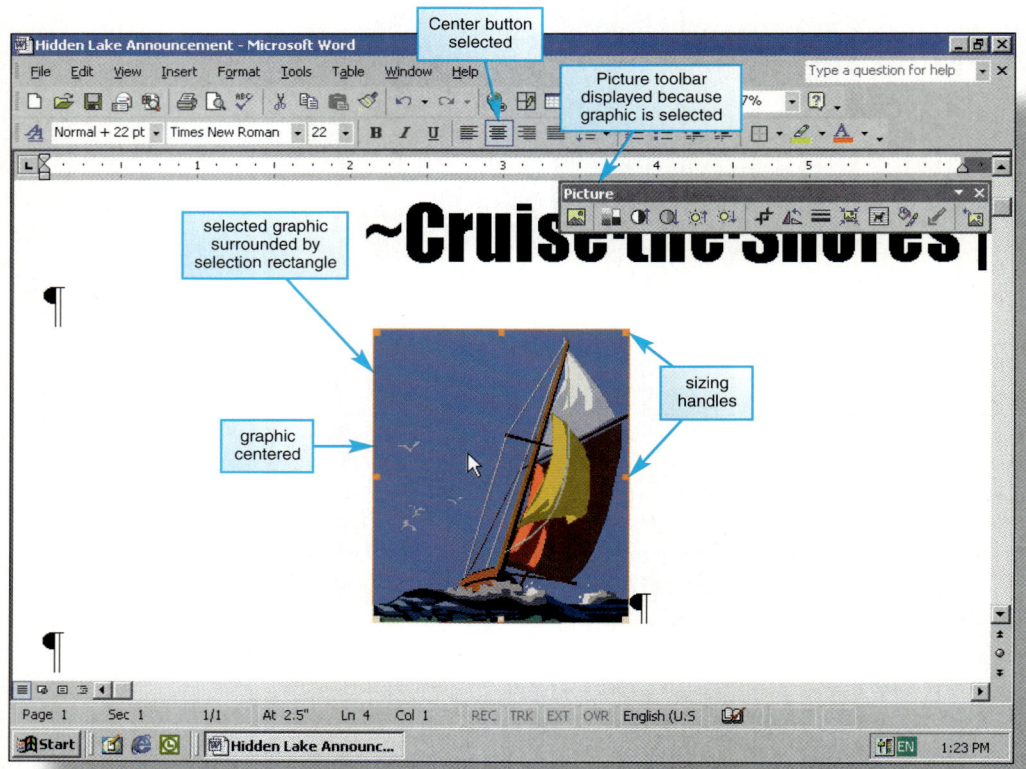

FIGURE 1-63

The Picture Toolbar

The Picture toolbar is a floating toolbar. Thus, you can drag its title bar to move the toolbar to a different location on the screen. You also can double-click the toolbar's title bar to dock the toolbar at the top of the screen.

The following steps show how to resize the graphic you just inserted and selected.

Steps To Resize a Graphic

1 **With the graphic still selected, point to the upper-left corner sizing handle.**

The mouse pointer shape changes to a two-headed arrow when it is on a sizing handle (Figure 1-64). To resize a graphic, you drag the sizing handle(s) until the graphic is the desired size.

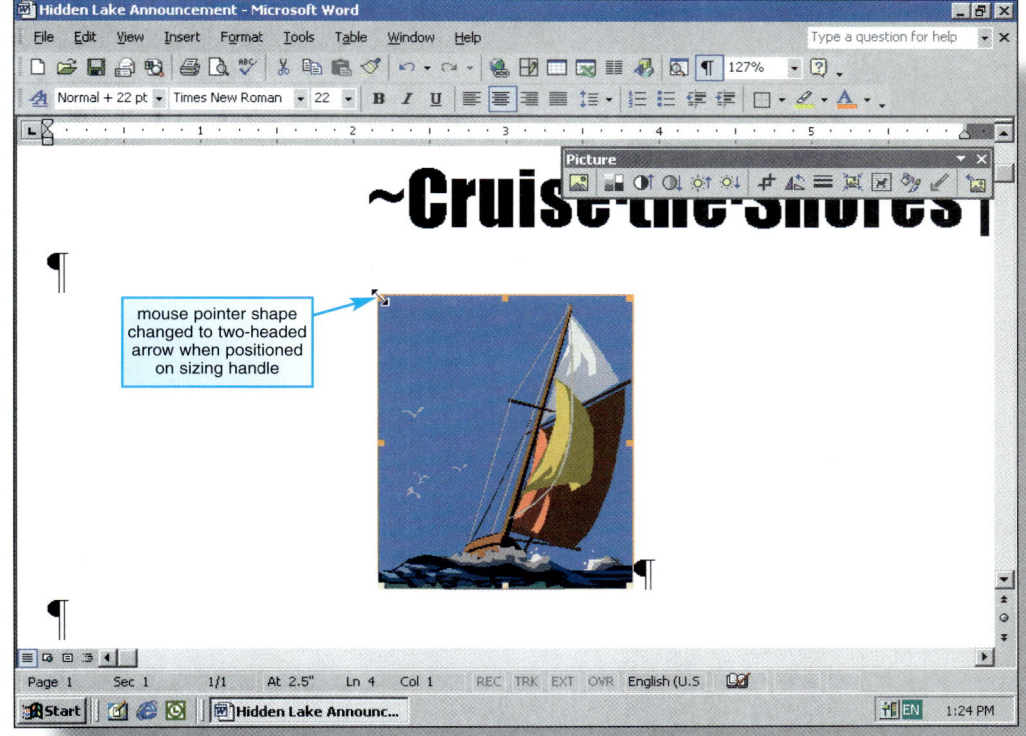

FIGURE 1-64

2 **Drag the sizing handle diagonally outward until the dotted selection rectangle is positioned approximately as shown in Figure 1-65.**

The graphic has a rectangular shape. When you drag a corner sizing handle, this shape remains intact. In this announcement, the graphic is to have a square shape.

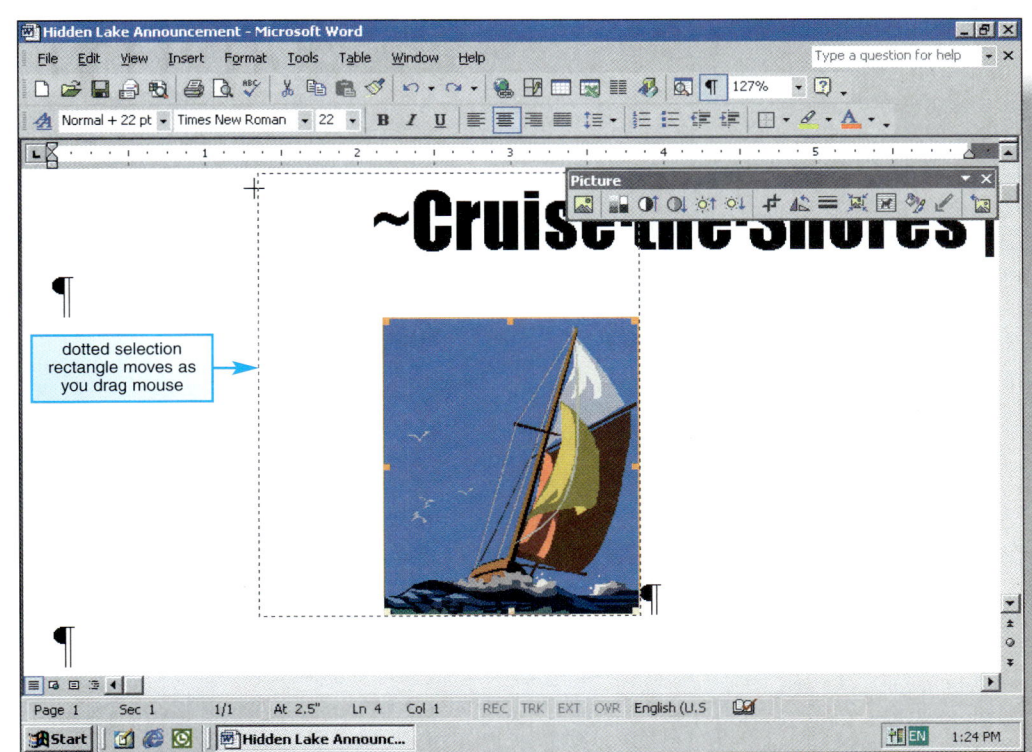

FIGURE 1-65

3 Release the mouse button. Point to the right-middle sizing handle on the graphic (Figure 1-66).

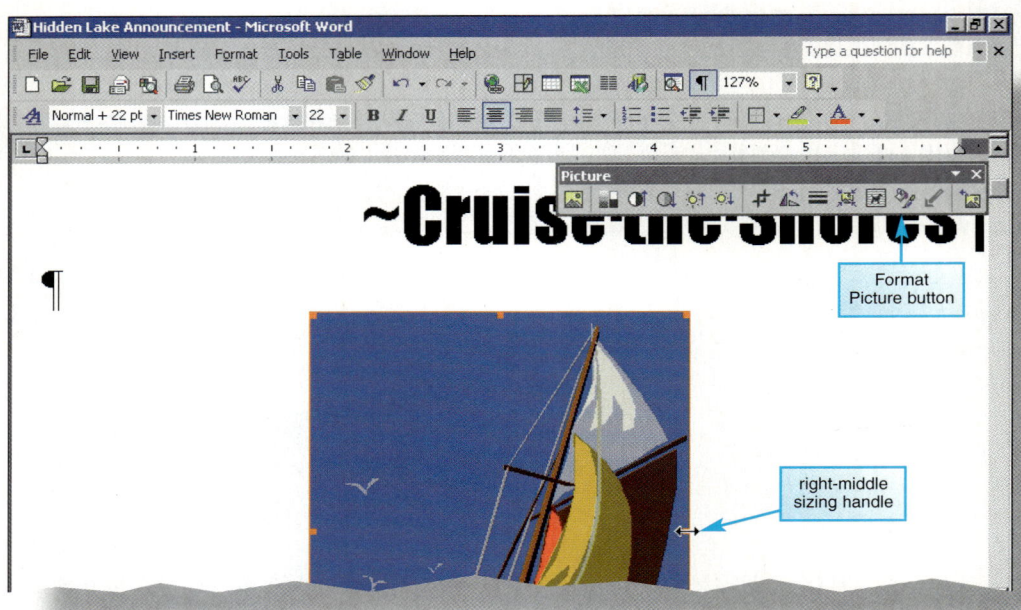

FIGURE 1-66

4 Drag the sizing handle to the right until the dotted selection rectangle is about the size of a square. Release the mouse button. Press CTRL+HOME.

Word resizes the graphic (Figure 1-67). When you click outside of a graphic or press a key to scroll through a document, Word deselects the graphic. The Picture toolbar disappears from the screen when you deselect the graphic.

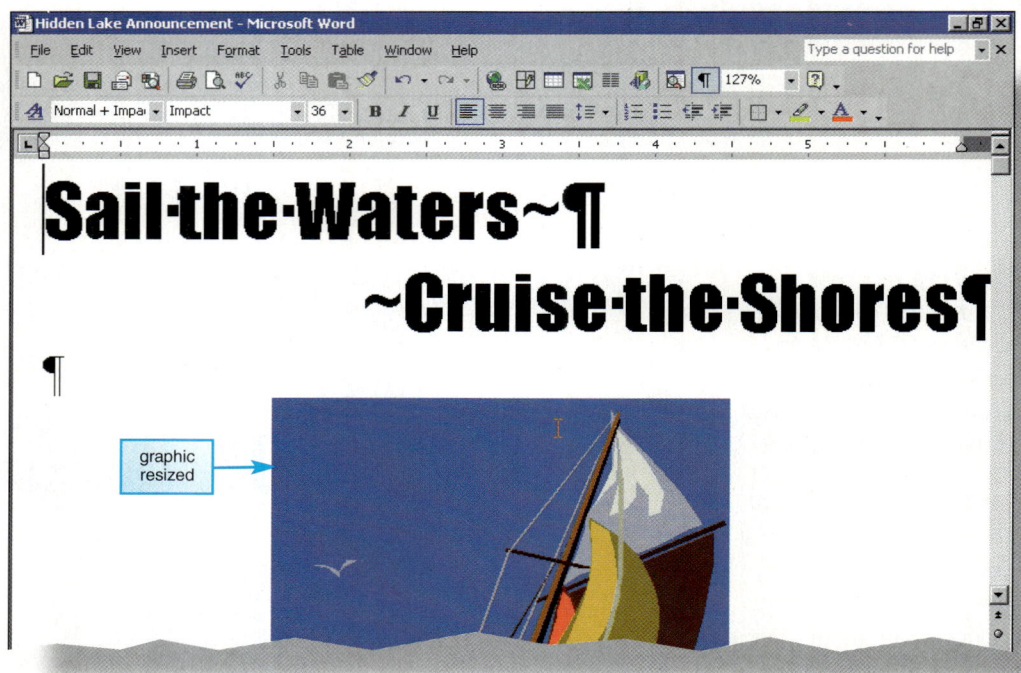

FIGURE 1-67

Other Ways

1. Click Format Picture button on Picture toolbar, click Size tab, enter desired height and width, click OK button
2. On Format menu click Picture, click Size tab, enter desired height and width, click OK button
3. In Voice Command mode, say "Format, Picture"

When you drag a middle sizing handle instead of a corner sizing handle, the proportions of the graphic change, which sometimes causes the graphic to look distorted. In this case, it gives the sail on the sailboat a windblown effect.

Instead of resizing a selected graphic by dragging with the mouse, you also can use the Format Picture dialog box to resize a graphic by clicking the Format Picture button (Figure 1-66) on the Picture toolbar and then clicking the Size tab. Using the

Size sheet, you can enter exact height and width measurements. If you have a precise measurement for a graphic, use the Format Picture dialog box; otherwise, drag the sizing handles to resize a graphic.

Sometimes, you might resize a graphic and realize it is the wrong size. In these cases, you may want to return the graphic to its original size and start again. You could drag the sizing handle until the graphic resembles its original size. To restore a resized graphic to its exact original size, click the graphic to select it and then click the Format Picture button on the Picture toolbar to display the Format Picture dialog box. Click the Size tab and then click the Reset button. Finally, click the OK button.

Resizing Graphics

To maintain the proportions of a graphic, press the SHIFT key while you drag a corner sizing handle.

Saving an Existing Document with the Same File Name

The announcement for Project 1 now is complete. To transfer the modified document with the formatting changes and graphic to your floppy disk in drive A, you must save the document again. When you saved the document the first time, you assigned a file name to it (Hidden Lake Announcement). If you use the following procedure, Word automatically assigns the same file name to the document each time you subsequently save it.

 To Save an Existing Document with the Same File Name

 **Click the Save button on the Standard toolbar.**

Word saves the document on a floppy disk inserted in drive A using the currently assigned file name, Hidden Lake Announcement (Figure 1-68).

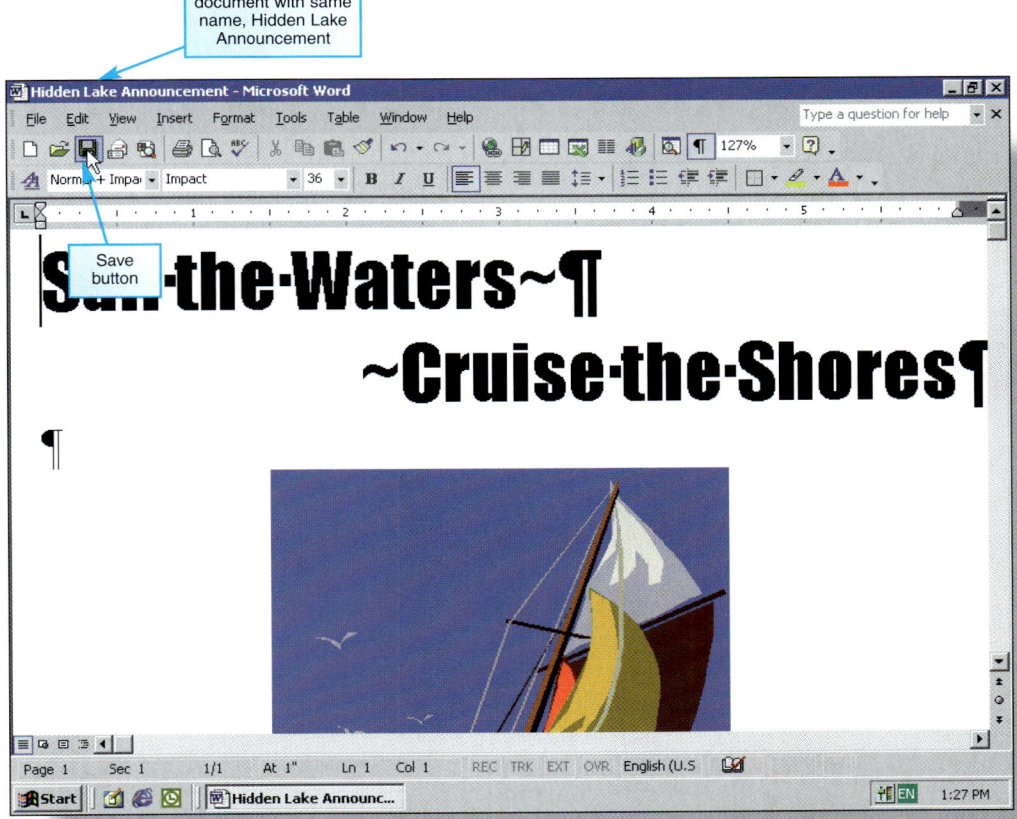

FIGURE 1-68

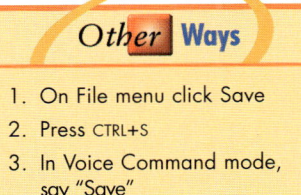

1. On File menu click Save
2. Press CTRL+S
3. In Voice Command mode, say "Save"

Printing

If you want to save ink, print faster, or decease printer over-run errors, print a draft. Click File on the menu bar and then click Print. Click the Options button, place a check mark in the Draft output check box, and then click the OK button in each dialog box.

While Word is saving the document, the Background Save icon displays near the right edge of the status bar. When the save is complete, the document remains in memory and on the screen.

If, for some reason, you want to save an existing document with a different file name, click Save As on the File menu to display the Save As dialog box. Then, fill in the Save As dialog box as discussed in Steps 2 through 5 on pages WD 1.30 through WD 1.32.

Printing a Document

The next step is to print the document you created. A printed version of the document is called a **hard copy** or **printout**. Perform the following steps to print the announcement created in Project 1.

Steps To Print a Document

 Ready the printer according to the printer instructions. Click the Print button on the Standard toolbar.

The mouse pointer briefly changes to an hourglass shape as Word prepares to print the document. While the document is printing, a printer icon displays in the tray status area on the taskbar (Figure 1-69).

2 When the printer stops, retrieve the printout, which should look like Figure 1-1 on page WD 1.07.

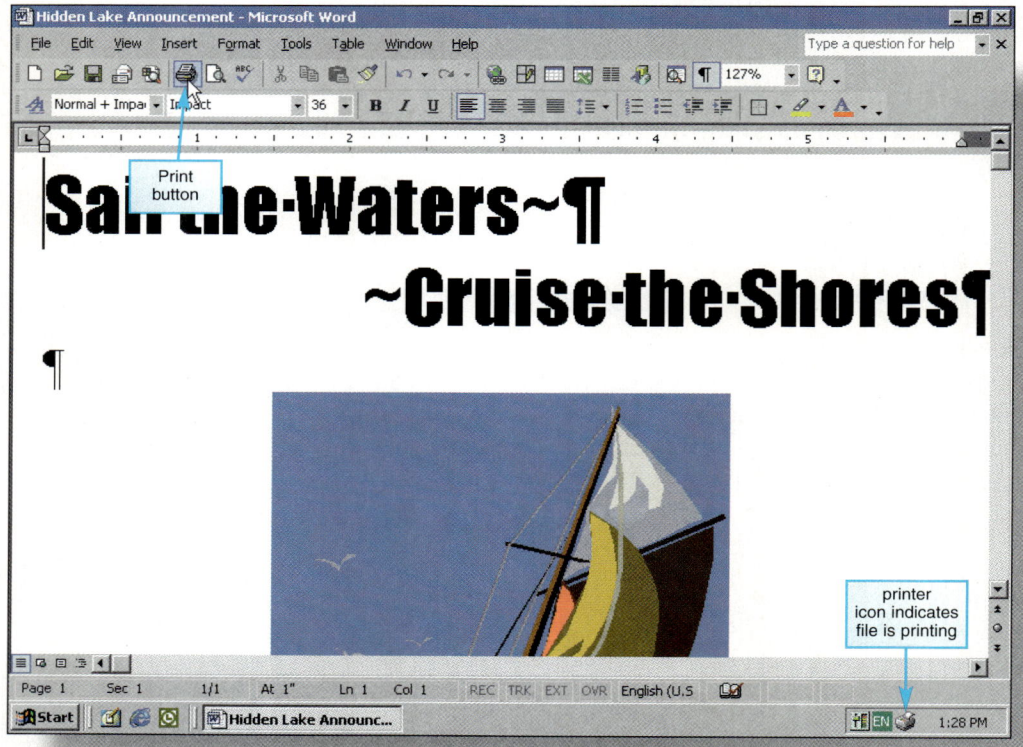

FIGURE 1-69

1. On File menu click Print, click OK button
2. Press CTRL+P, press ENTER
3. In Voice Command mode, say "Print"

When you use the Print button to print a document, Word prints the entire document automatically. You then may distribute the hard copy or keep it as a permanent record of the document.

If you wanted to print multiple copies of the document, click File on the menu bar and then click Print to display the Print dialog box. This dialog box has several printing options, including specifying the number of copies to print.

Opening a Document • WD 1.55

If you wanted to cancel your job that is printing or one you have waiting to be printed, double-click the printer icon on the taskbar (Figure 1-69). In the printer window, click the job to be canceled and then click Cancel on the Document menu.

Quitting Word

After you create, save, and print the announcement, Project 1 is complete. To quit Word and return control to Windows, perform the following steps.

Print Preview

To view a document before you print it, click the Print Preview button on the Standard toolbar. To return to the document window, click the Close Preview button on the Print Preview toolbar.

Steps To Quit Word

1 Point to the Close button in the upper-right corner of the title bar (Figure 1-70).

2 Click the Close button.

The Word window closes.

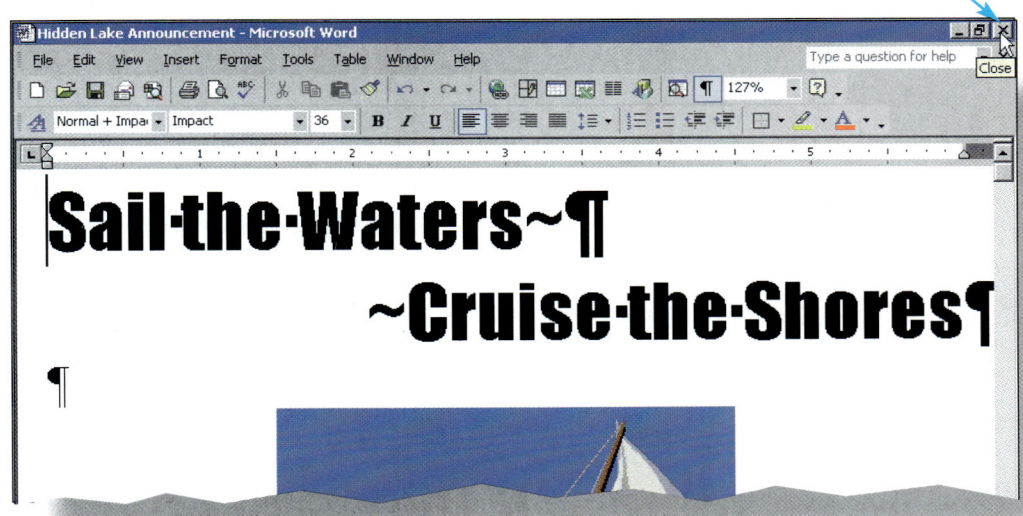

FIGURE 1-70

When you quit Word, a dialog box may display that asks if you want to save the changes. This occurs if you made changes to the document since the last save. Clicking the Yes button in the dialog box saves the changes; clicking the No button ignores the changes; and clicking the Cancel button returns to the document. If you did not make any changes since you saved the document, this dialog box usually does not display.

Other Ways

1. On File menu click Exit
2. Press ALT+F4
3. In Voice Command mode, say "File, Exit"

Opening a Document

Once you have created and saved a document, you often will have reason to retrieve it from disk. For example, you might want to revise the document or print it again. Earlier, you saved the Word document created in Project 1 on a floppy disk using the file name Hidden Lake Announcement.

The steps on the next page illustrate how to open the file Hidden Lake Announcement from a floppy disk in drive A.

Opening Files

In Word, you can open a recently used file by clicking File on the menu bar and then clicking the file name on the File menu. To instruct Word to show the recently used documents on the File menu, click Tools on the menu bar, click Options, click the General tab, click Recently used file list to place a check mark in the check box, and then click the OK button.

WD 1.56 • Project 1 • Creating and Editing a Word Document

 To Open a Document

1 **Click the Start button on the taskbar and then point to Open Office Document (Figure 1-71).**

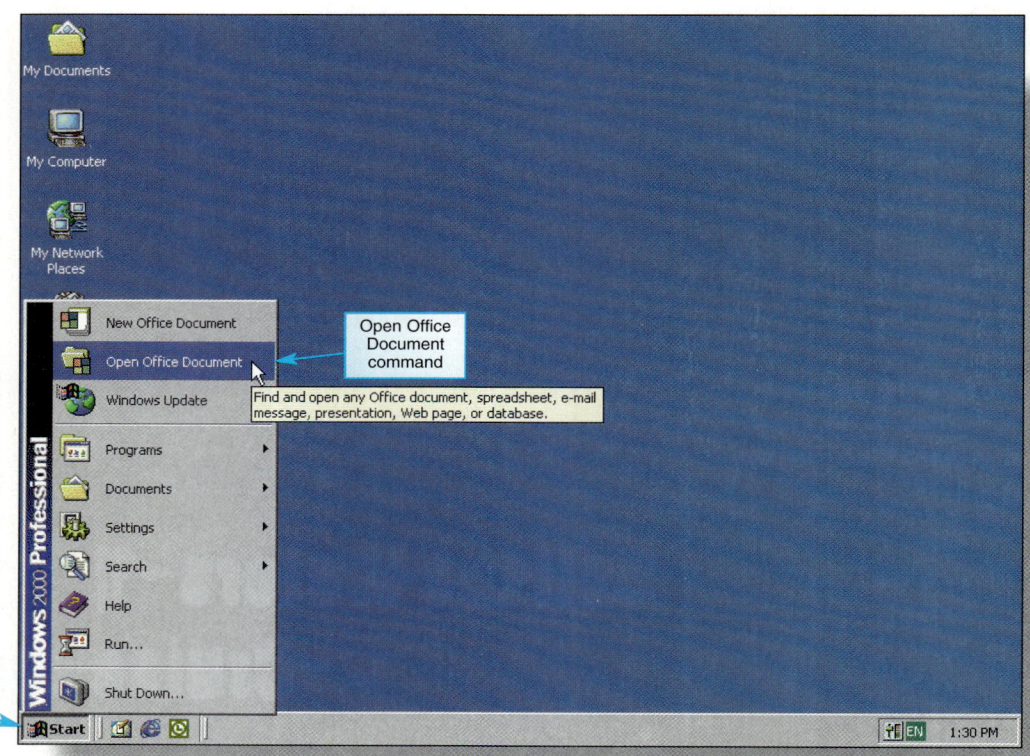

FIGURE 1-71

2 **Click Open Office Document. If necessary, click the Look in box arrow and then click 3½ Floppy (A:). If it is not selected already, click the file name Hidden Lake Announcement. Point to the Open button.**

Office displays the Open Office Document dialog box (Figure 1-72). The names of files on the floppy disk in drive A display in the dialog box.

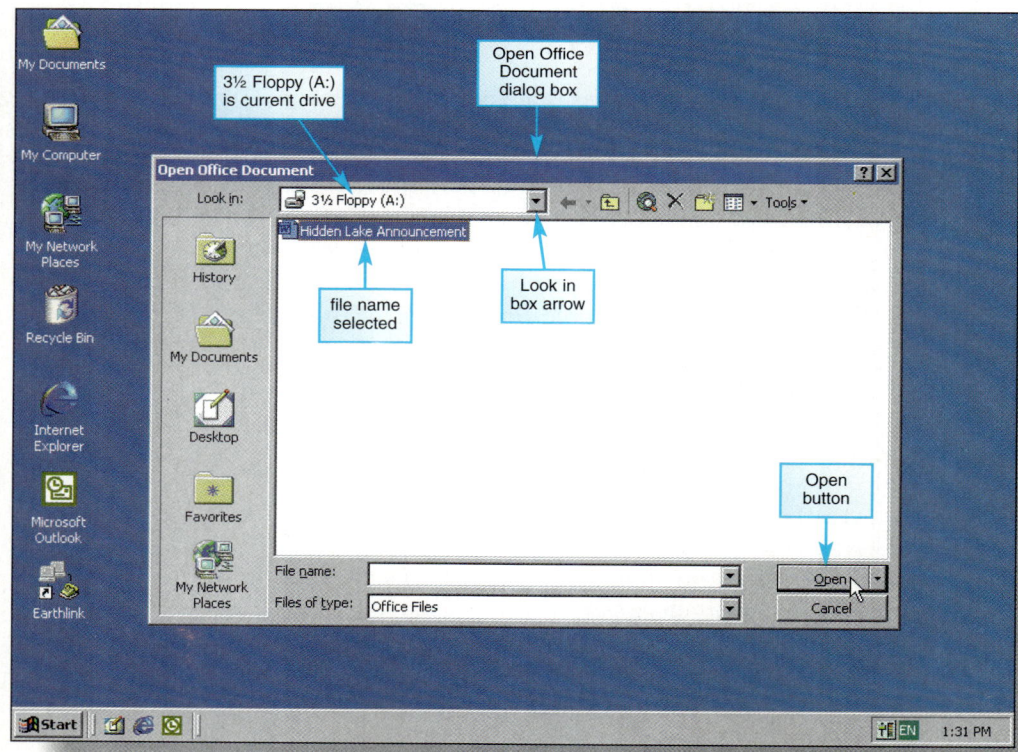

FIGURE 1-72

3 **Click the Open button.**

Office starts Word, and then Word opens the document, Hidden Lake Announcement, from the floppy disk in drive A. The document displays in the Word window (Figure 1-73).

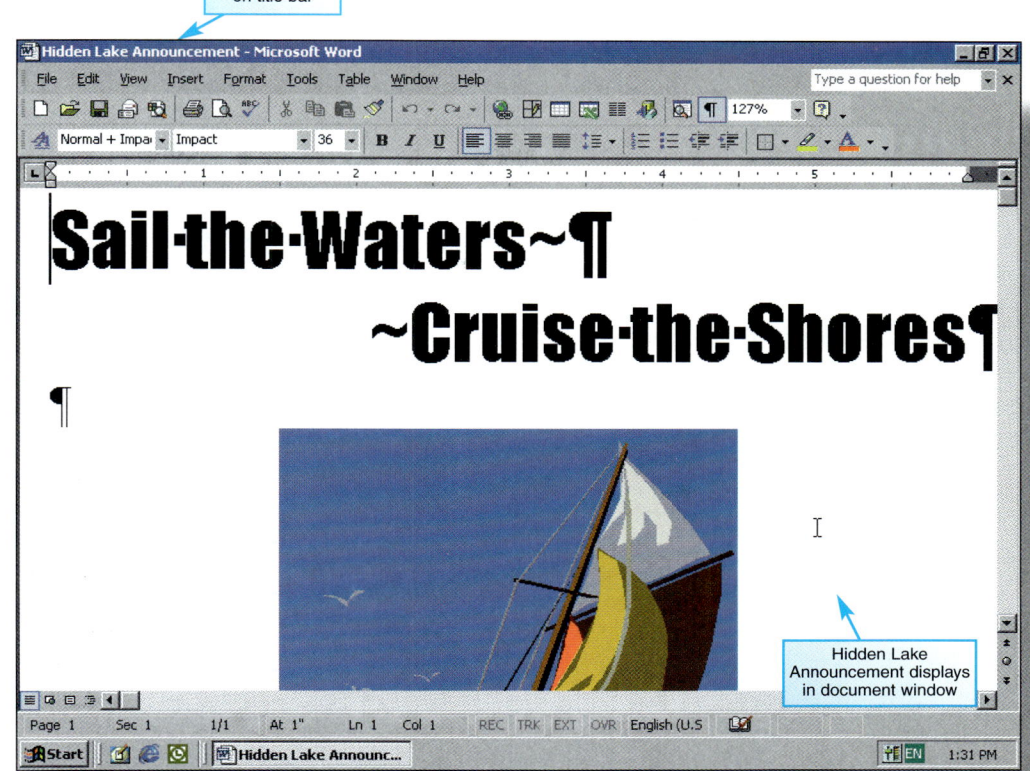

FIGURE 1-73

Other Ways

1. Right-click Start button, click Open All Users, double-click Open Office Document, select file name, click Open button in dialog box
2. Click Open button on Standard toolbar, select file name, click Open button in dialog box
3. On File menu click Open, select file name, click Open button in dialog box
4. In Voice Command mode, say "Open, [select file name], Open"

Correcting Errors

After creating a document, you often will find you must make changes to it. Changes can be required because the document contains an error or because of new circumstances.

Types of Changes Made to Documents

The types of changes made to documents normally fall into one of the three following categories: additions, deletions, or modifications.

ADDITIONS Additional words, sentences, or paragraphs may be required in a document. Additions occur when you omit text from a document and want to insert it later. For example, you may want to insert the word, all, in front of sailboat rentals in the Hidden Lake Announcement.

DELETIONS Sometimes, text in a document is incorrect or is no longer needed. For example, the state park may stop taking reservations. In this case, you would delete the words, or reservations, from the last line of the announcement.

MODIFICATIONS If an error is made in a document or changes take place that affect the document, you might have to revise the word(s) in the text. For example, the state park might change the discount from 30 to 35 percent; thus, you would change the number from 30 to 35.

Overtype

As you type, if existing text is overwritten with new text, you probably are in overtype mode. Double-click the OVR status indicator to turn overtype mode off. You also can press the INSERT key on the keyboard to turn off overtype mode.

Word provides several methods for correcting errors in a document. For each of the error correction techniques, you first must move the insertion point to the error.

Inserting Text into an Existing Document

Word inserts text to the left of the insertion point. The text to the right of the insertion point moves to the right and downward to fit the new text.

TO INSERT TEXT INTO AN EXISTING DOCUMENT

1. Click to the left of the location of text to be inserted.
2. Type the new text.

In Word, the default typing mode is insert mode. In **insert mode**, as you type a character, Word inserts the character and moves all the characters to the right of the typed character one position to the right. You can change to overtype mode by double-clicking the **OVR status indicator** on the status bar (Figure 1-8 on page WD 1.11). In **overtype mode**, Word replaces characters to the right of the insertion point. Double-clicking the OVR status indicator again returns you to insert mode.

Deleting Text from an Existing Document

It is not unusual to type incorrect characters or words in a document. As discussed earlier in this project, you can click the Undo button on the Standard toolbar to immediately undo a command or action — this includes typing. Word also provides other methods of correcting typing errors.

The Clipboard Task Pane

If you click the Cut button (or Copy button) twice in a row, Word displays the Clipboard task pane. You use the Clipboard task pane to copy and paste items within a document or from one Office document to another. To close the Clipboard task pane, click the Close button on the task pane title bar.

TO DELETE AN INCORRECT CHARACTER IN A DOCUMENT

1. Click next to the incorrect character.
2. Press the BACKSPACE key to erase to the left of the insertion point; or press the DELETE key to erase to the right of the insertion point.

TO DELETE (CUT) AN INCORRECT WORD OR PHRASE IN A DOCUMENT

1. Select the word or phrase you want to erase.
2. Right-click the selected word or phrase, and then click Cut on the shortcut menu; or click the Cut button on the Standard toolbar (Figure 1-12a on page WD 1.15); or press the DELETE key.

Closing the Entire Document

Sometimes, everything goes wrong. If this happens, you may want to close the document entirely and start over. You also may want to close a document when you are finished with it so you can begin your next document.

TO CLOSE THE ENTIRE DOCUMENT AND START OVER

1. Click File on the menu bar and then click Close. If Word displays a dialog box, click the No button to ignore the changes since the last time you saved the document.
2. Click the New Blank Document button (Figure 1-12a on page WD 1.15) on the Standard toolbar.

Word Help System • WD 1.59

You also can close the document by clicking the Close button at the right edge of the menu bar.

Word Help System

The Word Help System

The best way to become familiar with the Word Help system is to use it. Appendix A includes detailed information on the Word Help system as well as exercises that will help you gain confidence in using it.

At anytime while you are using Word, you can get answers to questions by using the **Word Help system**. Used properly, this form of online assistance can increase your productivity and reduce your frustrations by minimizing the time you spend learning how to use Word.

The following section shows how to obtain answers to your questions using the Ask a Question box. For additional information on using help, see Appendix A and Table 1-3 on page WD 1.61.

Obtaining Help Using the Ask a Question Box on the Menu Bar

The **Ask a Question box** on the right side of the menu bar lets you type free-form questions, such as *how do I save* or *how do I create a Web page*, or you can type terms, such as *copy*, *save*, or *format*. Word responds by displaying a list of topics related to the word or phrase you entered. The following steps show how to use the Ask a Question box to obtain information on handwriting recognition.

Steps **To Obtain Help Using the Ask a Question Box**

 **Click the Ask a Question box on the right side of the menu bar and then type** handwriting recognition **(Figure 1-74).**

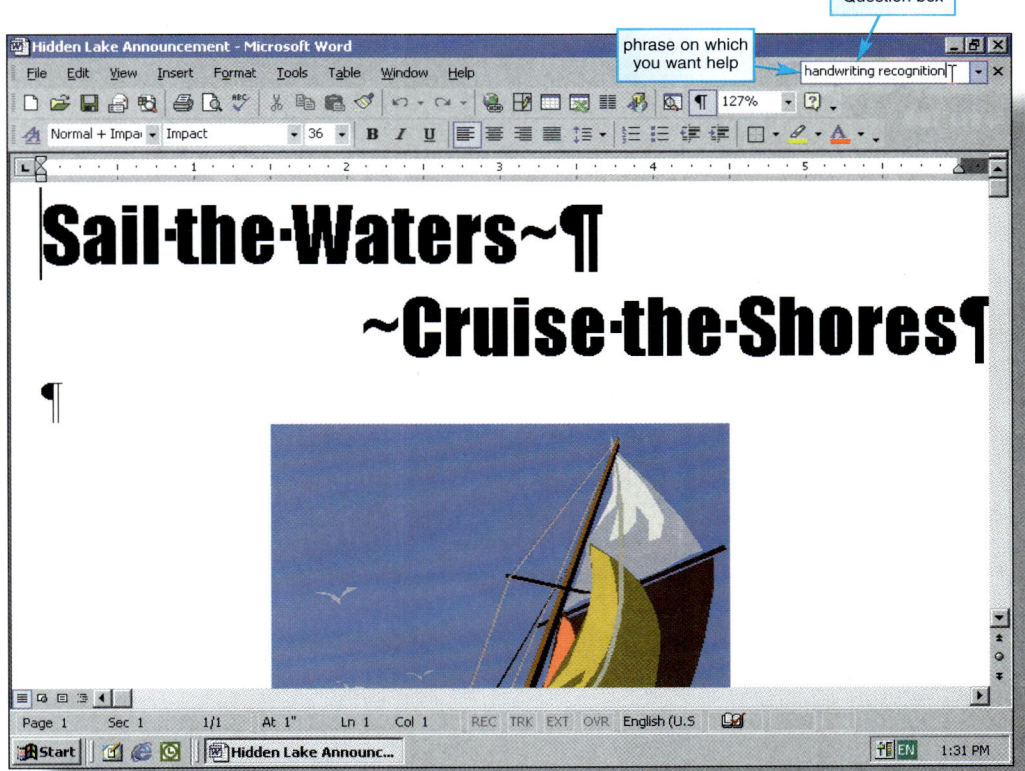

FIGURE 1-74

2 Press the ENTER key. When the list of topics displays below the Ask a Question box, point to the topic, About handwriting recognition.

A list of topics displays relating to the phrase, handwriting recognition. The shape of the mouse pointer changes to a hand, which indicates it is pointing to a link (Figure 1-75).

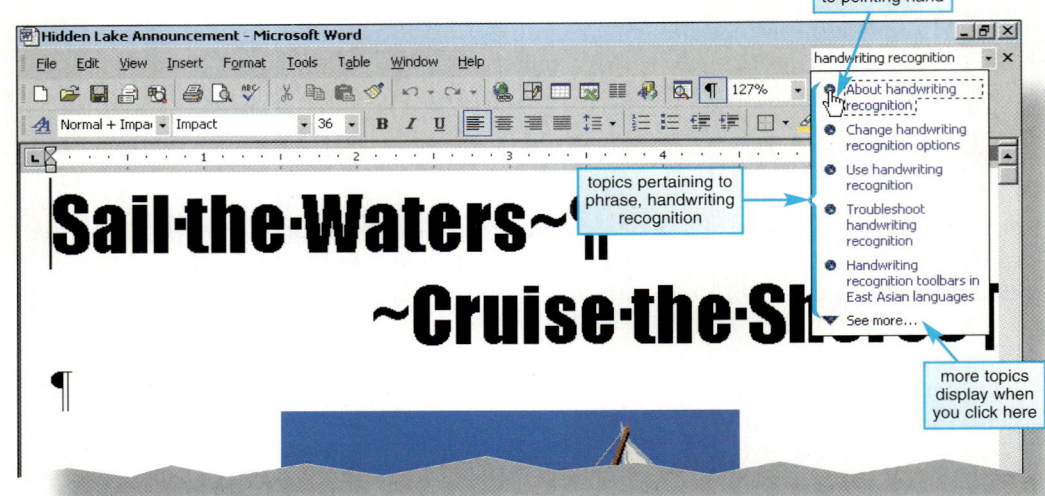

FIGURE 1-75

3 Click About handwriting recognition. When the Word Help window opens, double-click its title bar to maximize it. If necessary, click the Contents tab.

A Word Help window opens that provides Help information about handwriting recognition (Figure 1-76).

4 Click the Close button on the Word Help window title bar.

The Word Help window closes and the Word document window again is active.

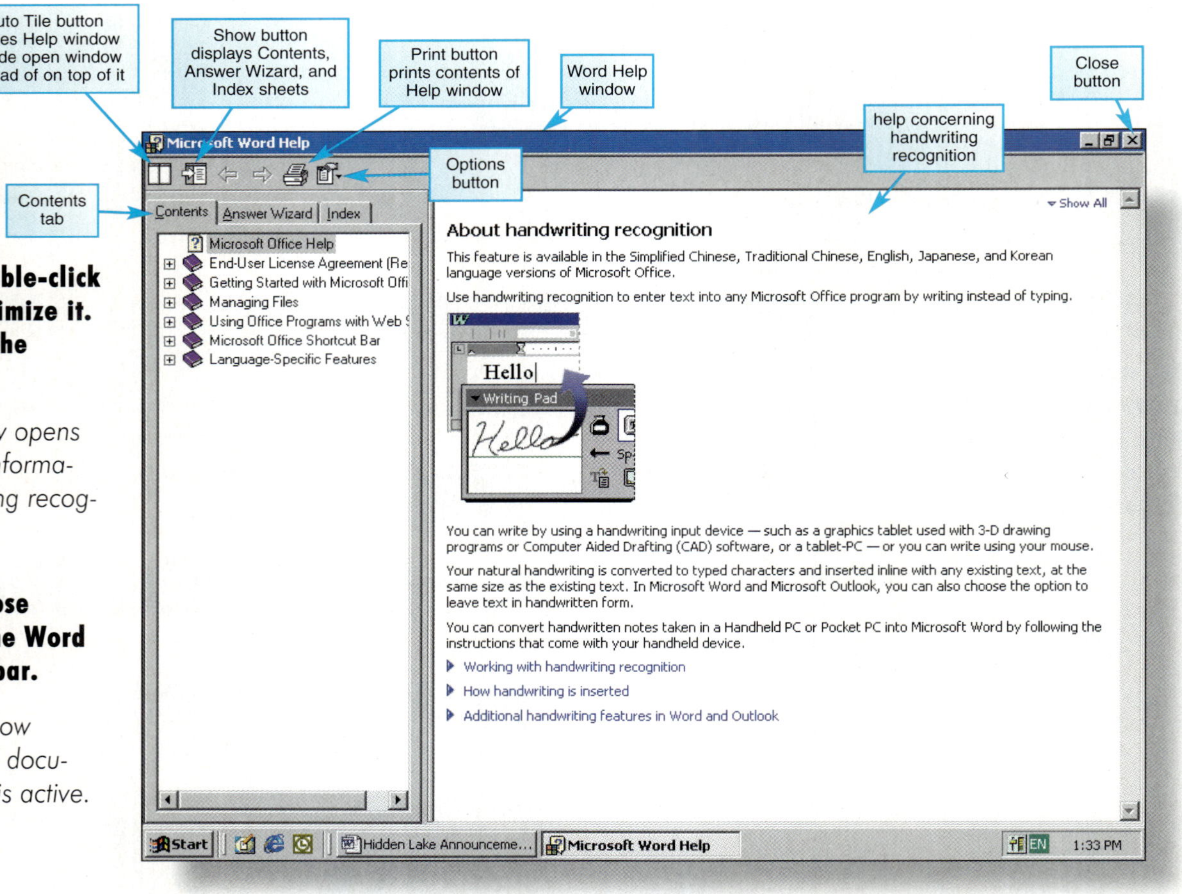

FIGURE 1-76

Use the buttons in the upper-left corner of the Word Help window (Figure 1-76) to navigate through the Help system, change the display, or print the contents of the window.

You can use the Ask a Question box to search for Help on any topic concerning Word. As you enter questions and terms in the Ask a Question box, Word adds them to the Ask a Question list. Thus, if you click the Ask a Question box arrow, a list of previously asked questions and terms will display.

Table 1-3 summarizes the eleven categories of help available to you. This table assumes the Office Assistant is off. See Appendix A for more information.

Table 1-3	Word Help System	
TYPE	**DESCRIPTION**	**HOW TO ACTIVATE**
Answer Wizard	Answers questions or searches for terms that you type in your own words.	Click the Microsoft Word Help button on the Standard toolbar. Click the Answer Wizard tab.
Ask a Question box	Answers questions or searches for terms that you type in your own words.	Type a question or term in the Ask a Question box on the menu bar and then press the ENTER key.
Contents sheet	Groups Help topics by general categories. Use when you know only the general category of the topic in question. Similar to a table of contents in a book.	Click the Microsoft Word Help button on the Standard toolbar. Click the Contents tab.
Detect and Repair	Automatically finds and fixes errors in the application.	Click Detect and Repair on the Help menu.
Hardware and Software Information	Shows product ID and allows access to system information and technical support information.	Click About Microsoft Word on the Help menu and then click the appropriate button.
Index sheet	Similar to an index in a book. Use when you know exactly what you want.	Click the Microsoft Word Help button on the Standard toolbar. Click the Index tab.
Office Assistant	Similar to the Ask a Question box in that the Office Assistant answers questions that you type in your own words, offers tips, and provides help for a variety of Word features.	Click the Office Assistant icon. If the Office Assistant does not display, click Show the Office Assistant on the Help menu.
Office on the Web	Provides access to technical resources on the Web and allows you to download free product enhancements from the Web.	Click Office on the Web on the Help menu.
Question Mark button	Identifies unfamiliar items in a dialog box.	Click the Question Mark button on the title bar of a dialog box and then click an item in the dialog box.
What's This? command	Identifies unfamiliar items on the screen.	Click What's This? on the Help menu, and then click an item on the screen.
WordPerfect Help	Assists WordPerfect users who are learning Microsoft Word.	Click WordPerfect Help on the Help menu.

The final step in this project is to quit Word.

TO QUIT WORD

1 Click the Close button in the Word window.

The Word window closes.

CASE PERSPECTIVE SUMMARY

Tara is thrilled with the completed announcement. The characters in the headline and body title are large enough so students can read them from a distance, and the image of the sailboat is quite eye-catching. She takes the announcement to the school's Promotions Department and receives approval to post it in several locations around campus, mail it to each student's home, print it in the school newspaper, and publish it on the Web. As a member of the SGA, you assist Tara with these activities.

Project Summary

Project 1 introduced you to starting Word and creating a document. Before entering any text in the document, you learned how to change the font size. You also learned how to save and print a document. You used Word's check spelling as you type feature. Once you saved the document, you learned how to format its paragraphs and characters. Then, you inserted and resized a clip art image. You learned how to insert, delete, and modify text. Finally, you learned one way to use the Word Help system.

What You Should Know

Having completed this project, you now should be able to perform the following tasks:

- Bold Selected Text *(WD 1.45)*
- Center a Paragraph *(WD 1.38, WD 1.45)*
- Center a Paragraph Graphic Containing a Graphic *(WD 1.49)*
- Change the Font of Selected Text *(WD 1.36)*
- Change the Font Size of Selected Text *(WD 1.35)*
- Check Spelling as You Type *(WD 1.28)*
- Close the Entire Document and Start Over *(WD 1.58)*
- Customize the Word Window *(WD 1.9)*
- Delete an Incorrect Character in a Document *(WD 1.58)*
- Delete (Cut) an Incorrect Word or Phrase in a Document *(WD 1.58)*
- Display Formatting Marks *(WD 1.24)*
- Enter Blank Lines into a Document *(WD 1.23)*
- Enter More Text *(WD 1.24)*
- Enter Text *(WD 1.21)*
- Enter Text that Scrolls the Document Window *(WD 1.26)*
- Format a Line of Text *(WD 1.40)*
- Increase the Default Font Size Before Typing *(WD 1.20)*
- Insert Clip Art into a Document *(WD 1.46)*
- Insert Text into an Existing Document *(WD 1.58)*
- Italicize Selected Text *(WD 1.41)*
- Obtain Help Using the Ask a Question Box *(WD 1.59)*
- Open a Document *(WD 1.56)*
- Print a Document *(WD 1.54)*
- Quit Word *(WD 1.55, WD 1.61)*
- Resize a Graphic *(WD 1.51)*
- Right-Align a Paragraph *(WD 1.37)*
- Save a New Document *(WD 1.30)*
- Save an Existing Document with the Same File Name *(WD 1.53)*
- Scroll through the Document *(WD 1.42)*
- Select a Graphic *(WD 1.50)*
- Select a Group of Words *(WD 1.44)*
- Select a Line *(WD 1.40)*
- Select a Word *(WD 1.42)*
- Select Multiple Paragraphs *(WD 1.34)*
- Start Word *(WD 1.08)*
- Underline Selected Text *(WD 1.43)*
- Undo an Action *(WD 1.39)*
- Wordwrap Text as You Type *(WD 1.25)*
- Zoom Page Width *(WD 1.19)*

More About

Microsoft Certification

The Microsoft Office Specialist Certification program provides an opportunity for you to obtain a valuable industry credential — proof that you have the Word 2002 skills required by employers. For more information, see Appendix E or visit the Shelly Cashman Series Microsoft Office Specialist Web page at scsite.com/offxp/cert.htm.

More About

Quick Reference

For a table that lists how to complete tasks covered in this book using the mouse, menu, shortcut menu, and keyboard, see the Quick Reference Summary at the back of this book or visit the Shelly Cashman Series Office XP Web page (scsite.com/offxp/qr.htm) and then click Microsoft Word 2002.

Learn It Online • WD 1.63

Learn It Online

Instructions: To complete the Learn It Online exercises, start your browser, click the Address bar, and then enter scsite.com/offxp/exs.htm. When the Office XP Learn It Online page displays, follow the instructions in the exercises below.

1 Project Reinforcement – TF, MC, and SA

Below Word Project 1, click the Project Reinforcement link. Print the quiz by clicking Print on the File menu. Answer each question. Write your first and last name at the top of each page, and then hand in the printout to your instructor.

2 Flash Cards

Below Word Project 1, click the Flash Cards link. When Flash Cards displays, read the instructions. Type 20 (or a number specified by your instructor) in the Number of Playing Cards text box, type your name in the Name text box, and then click the Flip Card button. When the flash card displays, read the question and then click the Answer box arrow to select an answer. Flip through Flash Cards. Click Print on the File menu to print the last Flash Card if your score is 15 (75%) correct or greater and then hand it in to your instructor. If your score is less than 15 (75%) correct, then redo this exercise by clicking the Replay button.

3 Practice Test

Below Word Project 1, click the Practice Test link. Answer each question, enter your first and last name at the bottom of the page, and then click the Grade Test button. When the graded practice test displays on your screen, click Print on the File menu to print a hard copy. Continue to take practice tests until you score 80% or better. Hand in a printout of the final practice test to your instructor.

4 Who Wants to Be a Computer Genius?

Below Word Project 1, click the Computer Genius link. Read the instructions, enter your first and last name at the bottom of the page, and then click the Play button. Hand in your score to your instructor.

5 Wheel of Terms

Below Word Project 1, click the Wheel of Terms link. Read the instructions, and then enter your first and last name and your school name. Click the Play button. Hand in your score to your instructor.

6 Crossword Puzzle Challenge

Below Word Project 1, click the Crossword Puzzle Challenge link. Read the instructions, and then enter your first and last name. Click the Play button. Work the crossword puzzle. When you are finished, click the Submit button. When the crossword puzzle redisplays, click the Print button. Hand in the printout.

7 Tips and Tricks

Below Word Project 1, click the Tips and Tricks link. Click a topic that pertains to Project 1. Right-click the information and then click Print on the shortcut menu. Construct a brief example of what the information relates to in Word to confirm you understand how to use the tip or trick. Hand in the example and printed information.

8 Newsgroups

Below Word Project 1, click the Newsgroups link. Click a topic that pertains to Project 1. Print three comments. Hand in the comments to your instructor.

9 Expanding Your Horizons

Below Word Project 1, click the Articles for Microsoft Word link. Click a topic that pertains to Project 1. Print the information. Construct a brief example of what the information relates to in Word to confirm you understand the contents of the article. Hand in the example and printed information to your instructor.

10 Search Sleuth

Below Word Project 1, click the Search Sleuth link. To search for a term that pertains to this project, select a term below the Project 1 title and then use the Google search engine at google.com (or any major search engine) to display and print two Web pages that present information on the term. Hand in the printouts to your instructor.

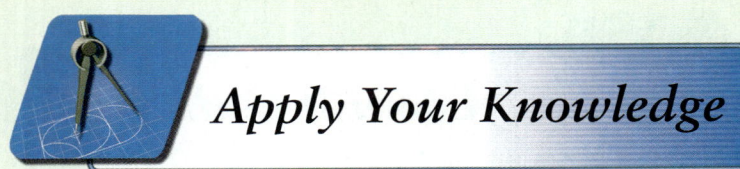

Apply Your Knowledge

1 Checking Spelling and Grammar and Modifying a Document

Instructions: Start Word. Open the document, Volleyball Tournament, on the Data Disk. See the inside back cover of this book for instructions for downloading the Data Disk or see your instructor for information on accessing files in this book.

As shown in Figure 1-77, the document is a volleyball tournament announcement that contains many spelling and grammar errors. You are to right-click each of the errors and then click the appropriate correction on the shortcut menu. You also modify some formats in the announcement.

spelling and grammar errors are flagged on printout to help you identify them

Bring a Freind~
~Bring a Team

Sand Volleyball Tournament

Join us at Central Field on on Saturday, June 21, and Sunday, June 22, for a coed sand volleyball tournament. Teams is limited to 10 plyers.

Games begin at 9:00 a.m. and end st dusk. Complimentary refreshments served aal day.

cash prize for first place! Trophies will be given to the second and third place team's.

Call 555-5583 for entry information.

FIGURE 1-77

Apply Your Knowledge

As discussed in this project, Word flags potential spelling errors with a red wavy underline. A green wavy underline indicates that Word detected a possible grammar error. ***Hint:*** If your screen does not display the grammar errors, use the Word Help system to determine how to enable the check grammar feature. Perform the following tasks:

1. Position the insertion point at the beginning of the document. Right-click the flagged word, Freind. Change the flagged word to the word, Friend, by clicking Friend on the shortcut menu.
2. Right-click the flagged word, on. Click Delete Repeated Word on the shortcut menu to remove the duplicate occurrence of the word, on.
3. Right-click the flagged words, Teams is. Change the flagged words to the words, Teams are, by clicking Teams are on the shortcut menu.
4. Right-click the flagged word, plyers. Change the flagged word to the word, players, by clicking players on the shortcut menu.
5. Right-click the flagged word, st. Because the shortcut menu does not display the correct word, at, click outside the shortcut menu to remove it from the screen. Correct the misspelled word, st, to the correct word, at, by removing the letter s and replacing it with the letter a.
6. Right-click the flagged word, aal. Change the flagged word to the word, all, by clicking all on the shortcut menu.
7. Right-click the flagged word, cash. Capitalize the word, cash, by clicking Cash on the shortcut menu.
8. Right-click the flagged word, team's. Change the flagged word to its correct plural by clicking teams on the shortcut menu.
9. Scroll to the top of the document. Position the insertion point after the word Team in the second line of the headline and then press the EXCLAMATION POINT (!) key. The second line of the headline now should read: Bring a Team!
10. Select the body title line below the graphic by pointing to the left of the line (Sand Volleyball Tournament) then clicking.
11. With the body text selected, click the Font Size box arrow on the Formatting toolbar and then click 24 to change the font size from 28 to 24 point.
12. With the body text selected, click the Font box arrow in the Formatting toolbar and then click Verdana to change the font to Verdana.
13. Double-click the word entry in the last line of the announcement. Click Edit on the menu bar and then click Cut to delete the word, entry.
14. Position the insertion point immediately to the left of the telephone number in the last line of the announcement. Type (708) and then press the SPACEBAR. The last line of the announcement now should read: Call (708) 555-5583 for information.
15. Click File on the menu bar and then click Save As. Save the document using Corrected Volleyball Tournament as the file name.
16. Print the revised document.

WD 1.66 • Project 1 • Creating and Editing a Word Document

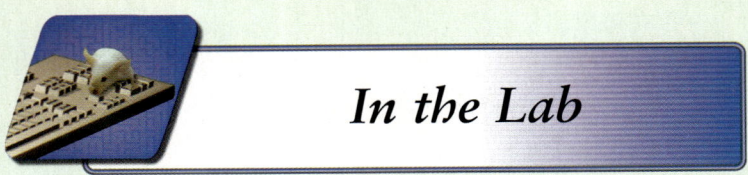

In the Lab

1 Creating an Announcement with Clip Art

Problem: Your neighbor is a member of the Prestwick Heights Garden Club. She has asked you to assist her in preparing an announcement for the upcoming club-sponsored garden walk. You prepare the announcement shown in Figure 1-78. *Hint*: Remember, if you make a mistake while formatting the announcement, you can click the Undo button on the Standard toolbar to undo your last action.

Instructions:

1. Change the font size from 12 to 20 by clicking the Font Size box arrow on the Formatting toolbar and then clicking 20.
2. If necessary, click the Show/Hide ¶ button on the Standard toolbar to display formatting marks.
3. Create the announcement shown in Figure 1-78. Enter the document first without clip art and unformatted; that is without any bold, underlined, italicized, right-aligned, or centered text. If Word flags any misspelled words as you type, check the spelling of these words and correct them.
4. Save the document on a floppy disk with Garden Club Announcement as the file name.
5. Select the two lines of the headline. Change their font to Albertus Extra Bold, or a similar font. Change their font size from 20 to 36.
6. Click somewhere in the second line of the headline. Right-align it.
7. Click somewhere in the body title line. Center it.
8. Select the body title line. Increase its font size from 20 to 28. Bold it.
9. In the second paragraph of the body copy, select the restaurant name: The Botanic Cafeteria. Italicize the name.

FIGURE 1-78

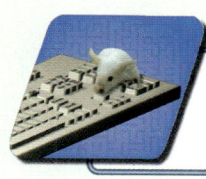

In the Lab

10. In the same paragraph, select the number 20. Underline it.
11. Click somewhere in the last line of the announcement. Center it.
12. Insert the graphic of the child holding daffodils between the headline and the body title line. Search for the text, daffodils, in the Insert Clip Art task pane to locate the graphic.
13. Center the selected graphic by centering the paragraph.
14. Save the announcement again with the same file name.
15. Print the announcement.

2 Creating an Announcement with Resized Clip Art

Problem: The owner of Wallace House Bed & Breakfast has requested that each student in your class prepare an announcement advertising the inn. The student that creates the winning announcement will receive a complimentary dinner. You prepare the announcement shown in Figure 1-79. *Hint:* Remember, if you make a mistake while formatting the announcement, you can click the Undo button on the Standard toolbar to undo your last action.

Instructions:

1. Change the font size from 12 to 22 by clicking the Font Size box arrow on the Formatting toolbar and then clicking 22.
2. If it is not already selected, click the Show/Hide ¶ button on the Standard toolbar to display formatting marks.

FIGURE 1-79

(continued)

In the Lab

Creating an Announcement with Resized Clip Art *(continued)*

3. Create the announcement shown in Figure 1-79 on the previous page. Enter the document first without the clip art and unformatted; that is, without any bold, underlined, italicized, right-aligned, or centered text. If Word flags any misspelled words as you type, check the spelling of these words and correct them.
4. Save the document on a floppy disk with Wallace House Announcement as the file name.
5. Select the two lines of the headline. Change their font to Monotype Corsiva, or a similar font. Change their font size from 20 to 36. Bold both lines.
6. Click somewhere in the second line of the headline. Right-align it.
7. Click somewhere in the body title line. Center it.
8. Select the body title line. Increase its font size from 20 to 28. Bold it.
9. Select the word, complimentary, in the second paragraph of the body copy. Underline it.
10. In the same paragraph, select the words, Dinner by reservation only. Italicize the words.
11. Click somewhere in the last line of the announcement. Center it.
12. Insert the graphic of the house by the lake between the headline and the body title line. Search for the text, house, in the Insert Clip Art task pane to locate the graphic. Center the graphic.
13. Enlarge the graphic of the house by the lake. If you make the graphic too large, the announcement may flow onto two pages. If this occurs, reduce the size of the graphic so the announcement fits on a single page. *Hint:* Use Help to learn about print preview, which is a way to see the page before you print it. To exit print preview and return to the document window, click the Close button on the Print Preview toolbar.
14. Save the announcement again with the same file name.
15. Print the announcement.

3 Creating an Announcement with Resized Clip Art and a Bulleted List

Problem: As assistant to the events planner for your park district, you design announcements of community activities. Next month, the park district is sponsoring a trip to Hannah Village Zoo. You prepare the announcement shown in Figure 1-80. *Hint:* Remember, if you make a mistake while formatting the announcement, you can click the Undo button on the Standard toolbar to undo your last action.

Instructions:

1. Change the font size from 12 to 18.
2. If they are not already showing, display formatting marks.
3. Create the announcement shown in Figure 1-80. Enter the document first without the clip art and unformatted; that is, without any bulleted, bold, underlined, italicized, right-aligned, or centered text. Check spelling as you type.
4. Save the document on a floppy disk with Hannah Village Announcement as the file name.
5. Format the first line of the headline to 36-point Clarendon Condensed or a similar font. Format the second line of the headline to 36-point Comic Sans MS bold or a similar font.
6. Center both lines of the headline.
7. Center the body title line. Format the body title line to 36-point Verdana bold, or a similar font.
8. Add bullets to the three paragraphs of body copy. A **bullet** is a symbol positioned at the beginning of a paragraph. In Word, the default bullet symbol is a small darkened circle. A list of paragraphs with bullets is called a **bulleted list**. *Hint:* Use Help to learn how to add bullets to a list of paragraphs.

In the Lab

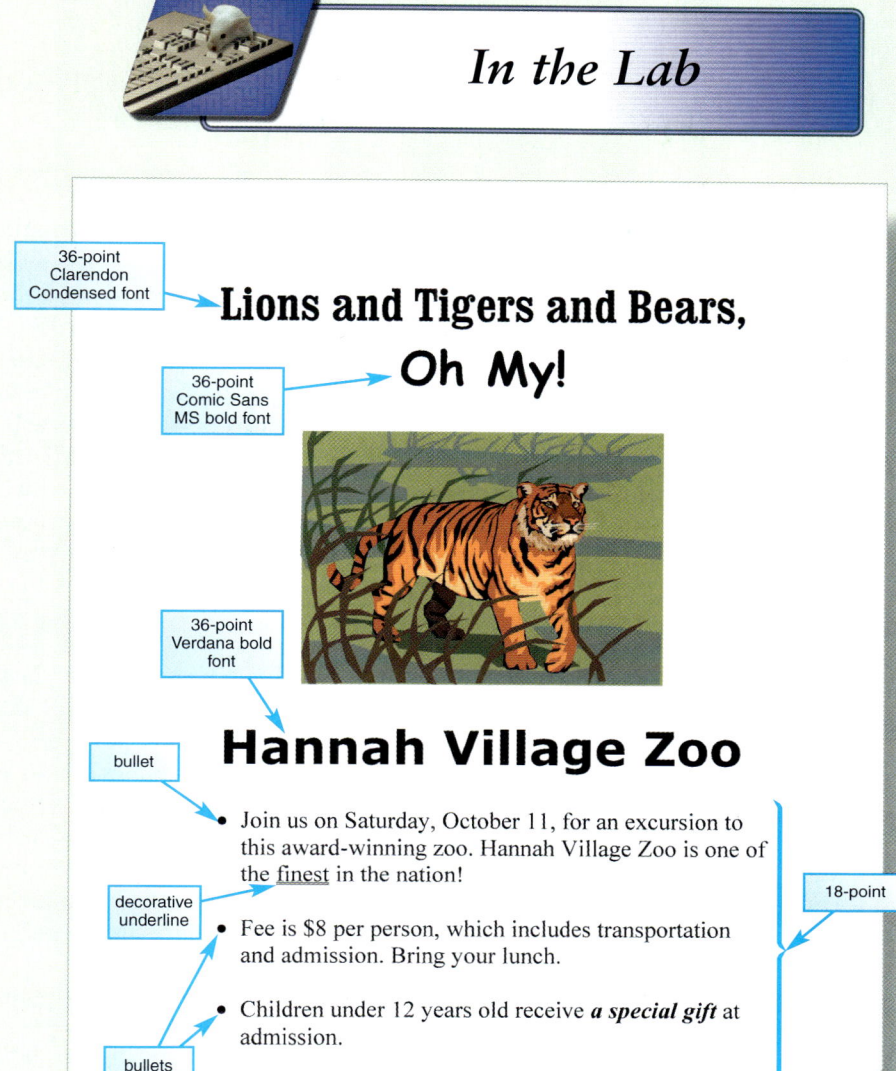

FIGURE 1-80

9. Underline the word, finest, in the first paragraph of the body copy using a decorative underline. *Hint:* Use Help to learn how to add a decorative underline to text.
10. Bold and italicize the phrase, a special gift, in the third paragraph of the body copy.
11. Center the last line of the announcement.
12. Insert the graphic of the tiger between the headline and the body title line. Search for the text, tiger, in the Insert Clip Art task pane to locate the graphic. Center the graphic.
13. Enlarge the graphic of the tiger. If you make the graphic too large, the announcement may flow onto two pages. If this occurs, reduce the size of the graphic so the announcement fits on a single page. *Hint:* Use Help to learn about print preview, which is a way to see the page before you print it. To exit print preview and return to the document window, click the Close button on the Print Preview toolbar.
14. Save the announcement again with the same file name.
15. Print the announcement.

Cases and Places

The difficulty of these case studies varies:
▶ are the least difficult; ▶▶ are more difficult; and ▶▶▶ are the most difficult.

1 ▶ You have been assigned the task of preparing an announcement for Agway Foods, Inc. The announcement is to contain a clip art image of farm equipment. Use the following text: first line of headline – Need Some $$?; second line of headline – Need a Summer Job?; body title – Agway Foods, Inc.; first paragraph of body copy – Are you looking for extra income this summer? We will show you how to work the fields. No experience necessary for this full-time seasonal employment.; second paragraph of body copy – Work to be performed at various locations in Herndon county. Must have own transportation.; last line – For details, call 555-9000. Use the concepts and techniques presented in this project to create and format this announcement. Ask your instructor if you should bullet the paragraphs of the body copy. Be sure to check spelling in the announcement.

2 ▶ You have been assigned the task of preparing an announcement for a new welding class at the College of Westerville. The announcement contains a clip art image of a welder. Use the following text: first line of headline – Welding Class~; second line of headline – ~Sign up Today; body title – College of Westerville; first paragraph of body copy – For fun or for credit, learn the fundamentals of welding. Our certified welding instructors use a hands-on technique to teach the fine art of welding.; second paragraph of body copy – Class will be taught in the automotive shop at the North Campus on Route 64.; last line – Call 555-3350 for a schedule or to register. Use the concepts and techniques presented in this project to create and format this announcement. Use a decorative underline in the announcement. Ask your instructor if you should bullet the paragraphs of the body copy. Be sure to check spelling in the announcement.

3 ▶▶ Your school district is looking for bus drivers. As an assistant in the transportation department, you have been asked to prepare an announcement that will be sent home with each child in the district. You are to include a graphic of a school bus. The school district's name is Allegheny and number is 314. Bus drivers are needed for the 2003-2004 school year. No experience is necessary. Training will be provided on Friday, August 22, in the transportation lot on Keswick Road. Point out that bus drivers enjoy flexible hours and good pay. More information can be obtained by calling John Stevens at 555-8850. Use the concepts and techniques presented in this project to create the announcement. Use a decorative underline in the announcement. Ask your instructor if you should bullet the paragraphs of the body copy. Be sure to check spelling and grammar in the announcement.

Cases and Places

4 ▶▶ Your neighbor has asked you to prepare an announcement that recruits employees for his business. He provides you with these details. The job openings are for telephone sales representatives. Employees have flexible work hours, day or night. Employees also can earn money while working from home or from the office. The only requirements are a telephone and a pleasant personality. It is a great employment opportunity and has an excellent salary. This job allows you to earn extra cash and unlock the secret to entrepreneurial freedom. Call 555-6879 for more information. Use the concepts and techniques presented in this project to create the announcement. Include a clip art image from the Web by connecting to the Web before searching for clip art in the Insert Clip Art task pane. Use a decorative underline in the announcement. Ask your instructor if you should bullet the list of paragraphs of the body copy. Be sure to check spelling and grammar in the announcement.

5 ▶▶ The owner of your apartment building has asked you to prepare an announcement about an apartment she has for rent. The name of the apartment complex is Country Walker Apartments. The available apartment is a one-bedroom unit with an eat-in kitchen. Air conditioning, heat, and water are included in the rent, which is $600 per month. Pets are allowed. The unit has a one-car garage. The complex has laundry facilities on site. The apartment is located near a large shopping mall, community college, and train station. For more information, call 555-9878. Use the concepts and techniques presented in this project to create the announcement. Include a clip art image from the Web by connecting to the Web before searching for clip art in the Insert Clip Art task pane. Use a decorative underline in the announcement. Ask your instructor if you should bullet the list of paragraphs of the body copy. Be sure to check spelling and grammar in the announcement.

6 ▶▶▶ Schools, churches, libraries, grocery stores, and other public places have bulletin boards for announcements and other postings. Often, these bulletin boards have so many announcements that some go unnoticed. At one of the above-mentioned organizations, find a posted announcement that you think might be overlooked. Copy the text from the announcement. Using this text, together with the techniques presented in this project, create an announcement that would be more likely to catch a reader's eye. Format the announcement effectively and include a bulleted list and suitable clip art image. Use a decorative underline in the announcement. Change the color of the characters. *Hint:* Use Help to learn about changing the color of text. Be sure to check spelling and grammar in the announcement.

7 ▶▶▶ Advertisements are a company's way of announcing products or services to the public. You can find advertisements in printed media such as newspapers and magazines. Many companies also advertise on the World Wide Web. Find a printed advertisement or one on the Web that you feel lacks luster. Copy the text from the announcement. Using this text, together with the techniques presented in this project, create an announcement that would be more likely to catch a reader's eye. Format the announcement effectively and include a bulleted list and suitable clip art image. Change the color of the characters. *Hint:* Use Help to learn about changing the color of text. Be sure to check spelling and grammar in the announcement.

Microsoft **Word 2002**

Microsoft Word 2002

PROJECT 2

Creating a Research Paper

You will have mastered the material in this project when you can:

OBJECTIVES

- Describe the MLA documentation style for research papers
- Change the margin settings in a document
- Adjust line spacing in a document
- Use a header to number pages of a document
- Enter text using Click and Type
- Apply formatting using shortcut keys
- Indent paragraphs
- Use Word's AutoCorrect feature
- Add a footnote to a research paper
- Modify a style
- Count the words in a document
- Insert a manual page break
- Create a hanging indent
- Insert a symbol automatically
- Create a hyperlink
- Sort selected paragraphs
- Go to a specific location in a document
- Move text
- Find and replace text
- Use the Paste Options button
- Understand how smart tags work
- Find a synonym for a word
- Check spelling and grammar at once
- Display the Web page associated with a hyperlink
- E-mail a copy of a document

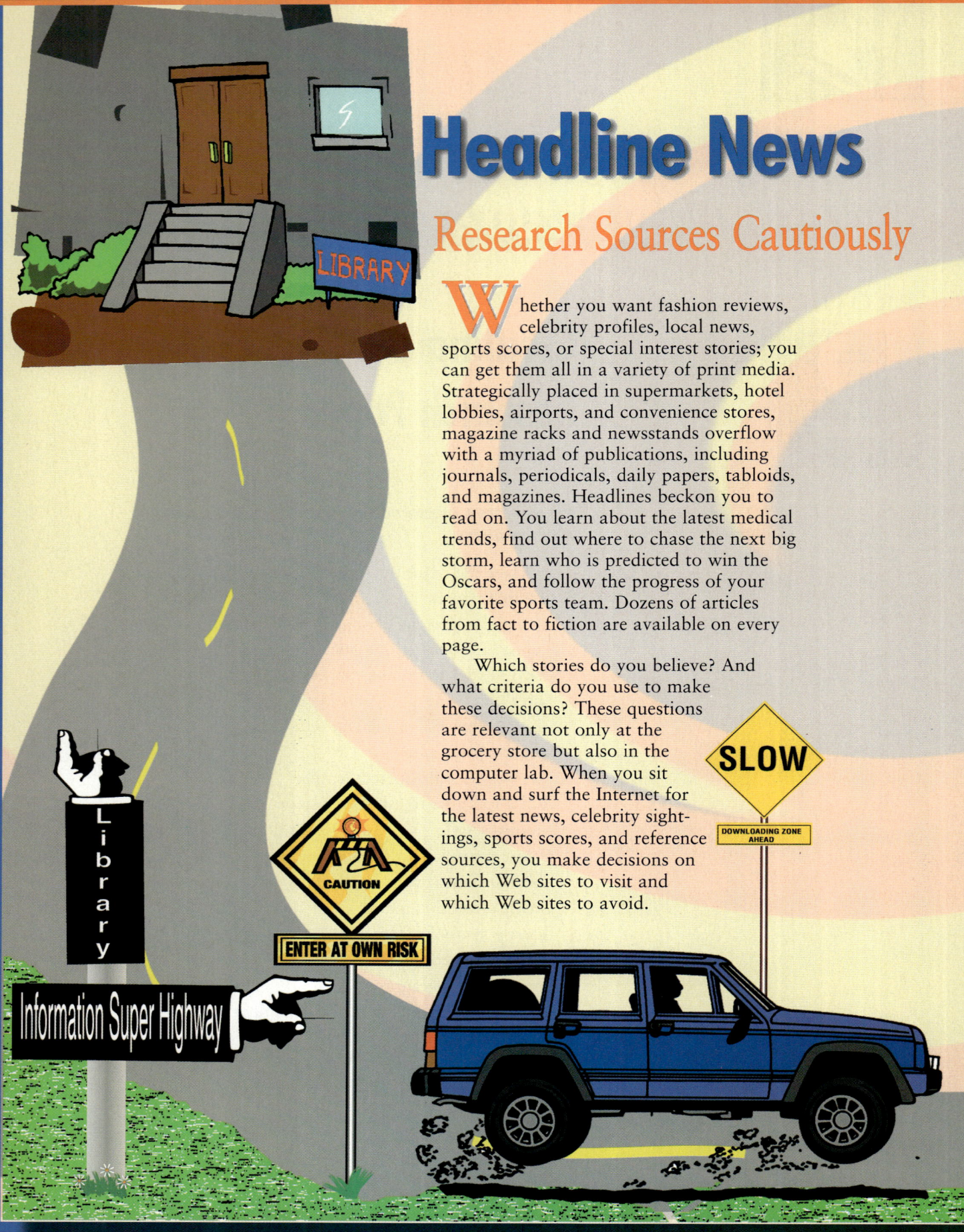

Headline News

Research Sources Cautiously

Whether you want fashion reviews, celebrity profiles, local news, sports scores, or special interest stories; you can get them all in a variety of print media. Strategically placed in supermarkets, hotel lobbies, airports, and convenience stores, magazine racks and newsstands overflow with a myriad of publications, including journals, periodicals, daily papers, tabloids, and magazines. Headlines beckon you to read on. You learn about the latest medical trends, find out where to chase the next big storm, learn who is predicted to win the Oscars, and follow the progress of your favorite sports team. Dozens of articles from fact to fiction are available on every page.

Which stories do you believe? And what criteria do you use to make these decisions? These questions are relevant not only at the grocery store but also in the computer lab. When you sit down and surf the Internet for the latest news, celebrity sightings, sports scores, and reference sources, you make decisions on which Web sites to visit and which Web sites to avoid.

Microsoft **Word 2002**

Not so long ago, students relied on only books and magazines in the library for the bulk of their research material. These permanent sources were professionally evaluated and edited. Not so with the Internet, where you will find everything from reliable research to fictitious opinions. No one performs quality control checks to verify accuracy and reliability. Anyone can build a Web site and fill it with any content imaginable. And this content can be updated before your eyes.

In this project, you will create a research paper on the topic of electronic retailing (e-retailing), which is the process of selling products and services using the Web. You will create a hyperlink in the document that allows navigation to a specific Web page when the research paper displays on the screen and the computer is connected to the Internet. The Works Cited page lists the sources used to obtain information for the research report. The sources include material from a book, a report in a periodical, and an article available on the Shelly Cashman Series Web site (scsite.com). How can you judge the reliability of these materials, particularly the article posted on the Web? Just remember the three S's: structure, source, and style.

Structure — Does the information seem objective or biased? Are authorities used as sources? When was the Web site created or updated? Is a contact person listed so you can verify information? Are working hyperlinks provided that refer you to additional sources?

Source — Examine the Web address to find out the Web site's sponsor. Is it a nonprofit organization (.org), a school (.edu), the government (.gov), or a commercial business (.com)? Is the purpose of the Web site to provide information or to make a profit?

Style — Does the Web site look organized and professional? Can you navigate easily with a minimum of mouse clicks? Does it contain an index and the capability of searching for specific information?

William Miller, a former president of the Association of College and Research Libraries, says that on the Web, "Much of what purports to be serious information is simply junk — not current, objective, or trustworthy." By following the three S's, you will be able to determine when you have valuable information.

Microsoft Word 2002

Creating a Research Paper

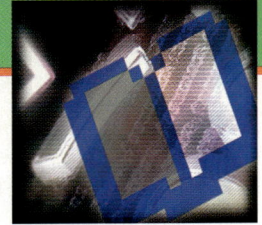

PROJECT 2

CASE PERSPECTIVE

Jordan Marcott is a full-time college student, majoring in Marketing. Ms. Blythe, the instructor in her introductory computer class, has assigned a short research paper that requires a minimum of 375 words. The paper must discuss some aspect of computers and be written according to the MLA documentation style, which specifies guidelines for report preparation. The paper is to contain one footnote and three references — one of which must be obtained from the World Wide Web. Finally, all students are to submit their papers electronically via e-mail to Ms. Blythe.

When Jordan graduates from college, she plans to work in retail management. She is very interested in retailing on the Web, so she decides to write the research paper on electronic retailing (e-retailing). Jordan intends to review computer magazines at the school's library, surf the Internet, and e-mail a couple of e-retailers for information on their businesses. She also plans to use the Internet to obtain the guidelines for the MLA style of documentation. Jordan has asked you to assist her with the Web searches because you are very familiar with the Internet.

Introduction

In both academic and business environments, you will be asked to write reports. Business reports range from proposals to cost justifications to five-year plans to research findings. Academic reports focus mostly on research findings. Whether you are writing a business report or an academic report, you should follow a standard style when preparing it.

Many different styles of documentation exist for report preparation, depending on the nature of the report. Each style requires the same basic information; the differences among styles appear in the manner of presenting the information. For example, one documentation style may use the term bibliography, whereas another uses references, and yet a third prefers works cited. Two popular documentation styles for research papers are the **MLA** (**Modern Language Association of America**) and **APA** (**American Psychological Association**) styles. This project uses the MLA documentation style.

Project Two — E-Retailing Research Paper

Project 2 illustrates the creation of a short research paper describing e-retailing. As shown in Figure 2-1, the paper follows the MLA documentation style. The first two pages present the research paper and the third page alphabetically lists the works cited.

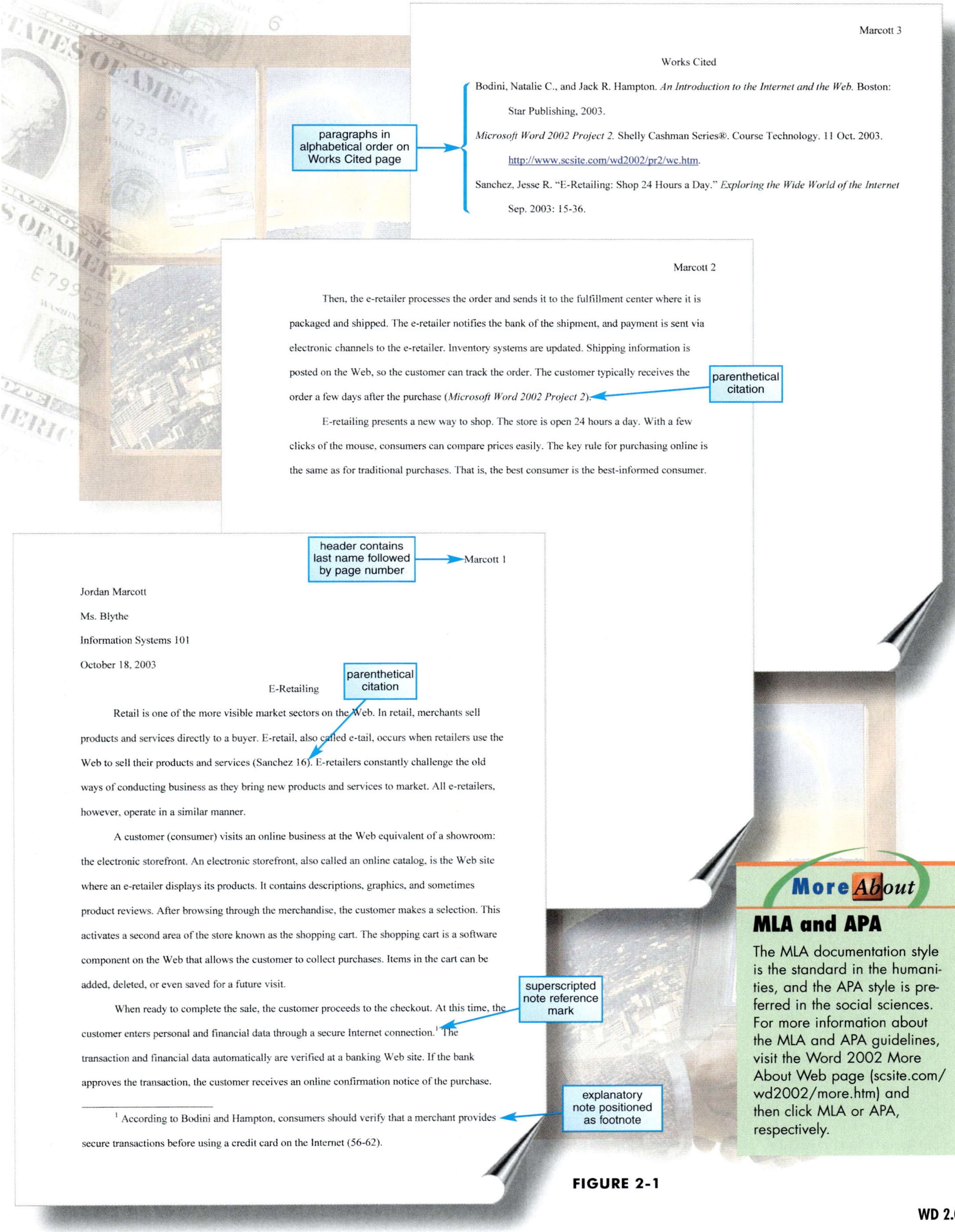

Marcott 3

Works Cited

Bodini, Natalie C., and Jack R. Hampton. *An Introduction to the Internet and the Web.* Boston: Star Publishing, 2003.

Microsoft Word 2002 Project 2. Shelly Cashman Series®. Course Technology. 11 Oct. 2003. http://www.scsite.com/wd2002/pr2/wc.htm.

Sanchez, Jesse R. "E-Retailing: Shop 24 Hours a Day." *Exploring the Wide World of the Internet* Sep. 2003: 15-36.

Marcott 2

Then, the e-retailer processes the order and sends it to the fulfillment center where it is packaged and shipped. The e-retailer notifies the bank of the shipment, and payment is sent via electronic channels to the e-retailer. Inventory systems are updated. Shipping information is posted on the Web, so the customer can track the order. The customer typically receives the order a few days after the purchase (*Microsoft Word 2002 Project 2*).

E-retailing presents a new way to shop. The store is open 24 hours a day. With a few clicks of the mouse, consumers can compare prices easily. The key rule for purchasing online is the same as for traditional purchases. That is, the best consumer is the best-informed consumer.

Marcott 1

Jordan Marcott

Ms. Blythe

Information Systems 101

October 18, 2003

E-Retailing

Retail is one of the more visible market sectors on the Web. In retail, merchants sell products and services directly to a buyer. E-retail, also called e-tail, occurs when retailers use the Web to sell their products and services (Sanchez 16). E-retailers constantly challenge the old ways of conducting business as they bring new products and services to market. All e-retailers, however, operate in a similar manner.

A customer (consumer) visits an online business at the Web equivalent of a showroom: the electronic storefront. An electronic storefront, also called an online catalog, is the Web site where an e-retailer displays its products. It contains descriptions, graphics, and sometimes product reviews. After browsing through the merchandise, the customer makes a selection. This activates a second area of the store known as the shopping cart. The shopping cart is a software component on the Web that allows the customer to collect purchases. Items in the cart can be added, deleted, or even saved for a future visit.

When ready to complete the sale, the customer proceeds to the checkout. At this time, the customer enters personal and financial data through a secure Internet connection.[1] The transaction and financial data automatically are verified at a banking Web site. If the bank approves the transaction, the customer receives an online confirmation notice of the purchase.

---
[1] According to Bodini and Hampton, consumers should verify that a merchant provides secure transactions before using a credit card on the Internet (56-62).

FIGURE 2-1

More About

MLA and APA

The MLA documentation style is the standard in the humanities, and the APA style is preferred in the social sciences. For more information about the MLA and APA guidelines, visit the Word 2002 More About Web page (scsite.com/wd2002/more.htm) and then click MLA or APA, respectively.

MLA Documentation Style

When writing papers, you should adhere to some style of documentation. The research paper in this project follows the guidelines presented by the MLA. To follow the MLA style, double-space text on all pages of the paper with one-inch top, bottom, left, and right margins. Indent the first word of each paragraph one-half inch from the left margin. At the right margin of each page, place a page number one-half inch from the top margin. On each page, precede the page number by your last name.

The MLA style does not require a title page. Instead, place your name and course information in a block at the left margin beginning one inch from the top of the page. Center the title one double-space below your name and course information.

In the body of the paper, place author references in parentheses with the page number(s) of the referenced information. The MLA style uses in-text **parenthetical citations** instead of noting each source at the bottom of the page or at the end of the paper. In the MLA style, notes are used only for optional explanatory notes.

If used, explanatory notes elaborate on points discussed in the body of the paper. Use superscripts (raised numbers) for **note reference marks**, which signal that an explanatory note exists, and also sequence the notes. Position explanatory notes either at the bottom of the page as footnotes or at the end of the paper as endnotes. Indent the first line of each explanatory note one-half inch from the left margin. Place one space following the note reference mark before beginning the note text. Double-space the note text. At the end of the note text, you may list bibliographic information for further reference.

The MLA style uses the term **works cited** for the bibliographical references. The works cited page alphabetically lists works that are referenced directly in the paper. List works by each author's last name, or, if the author's name is not available, by the title of the work. Italicize or underline the title of the work. Place the works cited on a separate numbered page. Center the title, Works Cited, one inch from the top margin. Double-space all lines. Begin the first line of each entry at the left margin, indenting subsequent lines of the same entry one-half inch from the left margin.

Starting Word

Perform the following steps to start Word, or ask your instructor how to start Word for your system.

TO START AND CUSTOMIZE WORD

1. Click the Start button on the Windows taskbar, point to Programs on the Start menu, and then click Microsoft Word on the Programs submenu.
2. If the Word window is not maximized, double-click its title bar to maximize it.
3. If the Language bar displays on the screen, click its Minimize button.
4. If the New Document task pane displays in the Word window, click the Show at startup check box to remove the check mark and then click the Close button in the upper-right corner of the task pane title bar.
5. If the toolbars display positioned on the same row, click the Toolbar Options button and then click Show Buttons on Two Rows.
6. If your screen differs from Figure 2-2 on page WD 2.08, click View on the menu bar and then click Normal.

Word starts. After a few moments, an empty document titled Document1 displays in the Word window (shown in Figure 2-2).

More About

Citing Sources

Information that commonly is known or accessible to the audience constitutes common knowledge and does not need to be listed as a parenthetical citation or in a bibliography. If, however, you question whether certain information is common knowledge, you should document it — just to be safe.

More About

Titles of Works

Titles of books, periodicals, and Web sites typically are underlined when a research paper is submitted in printed form. Some instructors require that Web addresses be hyperlinks for online access. Word formats hyperlinks with an underline. To distinguish hyperlinks from titles, the MLA allows titles to be italicized, if approved by the instructor.

More About

APA Style

In the APA style, double-space all pages of the paper with 1.5" top, bottom, left, and right margins. Indent the first word of each paragraph .5" from the left margin. In the upper-right margin of each page, place a running head that consists of the page number double-spaced below a summary of the paper title.

Resetting Menus and Toolbars

To set the menus and toolbars so they appear exactly as shown in this book, you should reset your menus and toolbars as outlined in Appendix D or follow these steps.

TO RESET MENUS AND TOOLBARS

1. Click the Toolbar Options button on the Standard toolbar and then point to Add or Remove Buttons. Point to Standard on the Add or Remove Buttons submenu. Scroll to and then click Reset Toolbar on the Standard submenu.
2. Click the Toolbar Options button on the Formatting toolbar and then point to Add or Remove Buttons. Point to Formatting on the Add or Remove Buttons submenu. Scroll to and then click Reset Toolbar on the Formatting submenu.
3. Click the Toolbar Options button on the Standard toolbar and then point to Add or Remove Buttons. Click Customize on the Add or Remove Buttons submenu.
4. When the Customize dialog box displays, if necessary, click the Options tab. Click the Reset my usage data button. When the Microsoft Word dialog box displays, click the Yes button. Click the Close button in the Customize dialog box.

Word resets the menus and toolbars.

Displaying Formatting Marks

As discussed in Project 1, it is helpful to display formatting marks that indicate where in the document you pressed the ENTER key, SPACEBAR, and other keys. Perform the following step to display formatting marks.

TO DISPLAY FORMATTING MARKS

1. If the Show/Hide ¶ button on the Standard toolbar is not already selected, click it.

Word displays formatting marks in the document window, and the Show/Hide ¶ button on the Standard toolbar is selected (shown in Figure 2-2 on the next page).

Changing the Margins

Word is preset to use standard 8.5-by-11-inch paper, with 1.25-inch left and right margins and 1-inch top and bottom margins. These margin settings affect every page in the document. Often, you may want to change these default margin settings. For example, the MLA documentation style requires one-inch top, bottom, left, and right margins throughout the paper. Thus, the steps on the next page illustrate how to change the margin settings for a document when the window is in normal view. To verify the document window is in normal view, click View on the menu bar and then click Normal.

Writing Papers

The Web contains numerous sites with information, tips, and suggestions on writing research papers. College professors and fellow students develop many of these Web sites. For a list of links to Web sites on writing research papers, visit the Word 2002 More About Web page (scsite.com/wd2002/more.htm) and then click Links to Sites on Writing Research Papers.

Changing Margins

In print layout view, you can change margin settings using the horizontal and vertical rulers. Current margin settings are shaded in gray. The margin boundary is located where the gray meets the white. To change a margin setting, drag the margin boundary on the ruler. To see the numeric margin settings, hold down the ALT key while dragging the margin boundary on the ruler.

Steps: To Change the Margin Settings

1 Click File on the menu bar and then point to Page Setup (Figure 2-2).

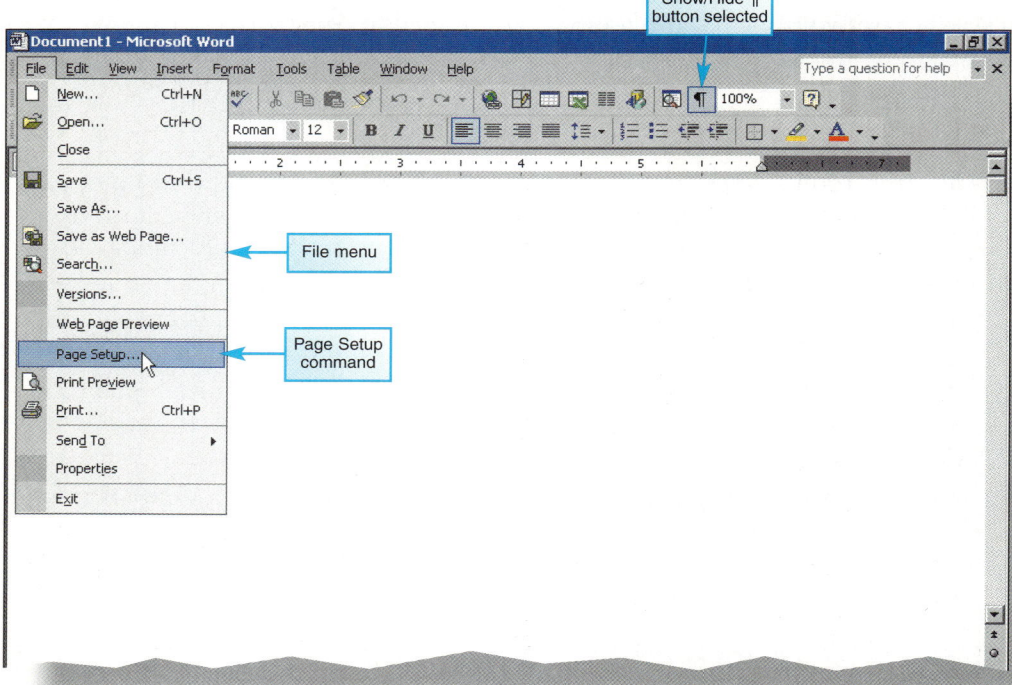

FIGURE 2-2

2 Click Page Setup. If necessary, click the Margins tab when the Page Setup dialog box displays.

Word displays the Page Setup dialog box (Figure 2-3). The current margin settings display in the text boxes.

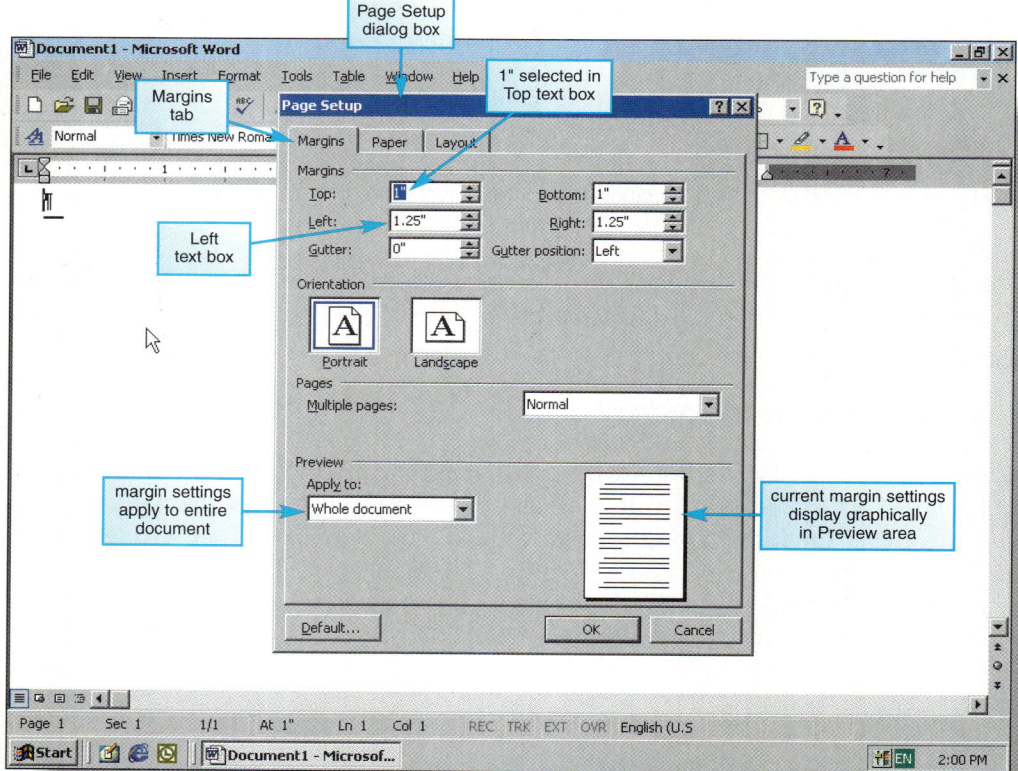

FIGURE 2-3

3 **With 1" selected in the Top text box, press the TAB key twice to select 1.25" in the Left text box. Type 1 and then press the TAB key. Type 1 and then point to the OK button.**

The new left and right margin settings are 1 inch (Figure 2-4). Instead of typing margin values, you can click the text box arrows to increment or decrement the number in the text box.

4 **Click the OK button.**

Word changes the left and right margins.

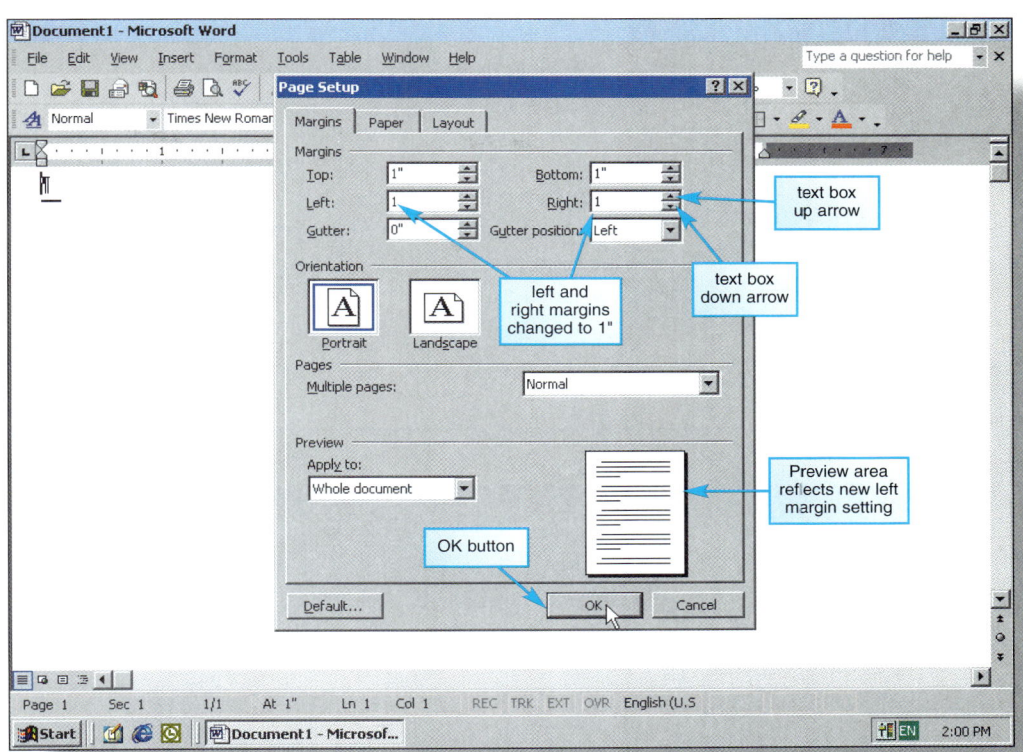

FIGURE 2-4

The new margin settings take effect in the document immediately. Word uses these margins for the entire document.

When you change the margin settings in the text boxes in the Page Setup dialog box, the Preview area (Figure 2-4) does not adjust to reflect a changed margin setting until the insertion point leaves the respective text box. That is, you must press the TAB or ENTER key or click another text box if you want to view a changed margin setting in the Preview area.

Zooming Page Width

As discussed in Project 1, when you **zoom page width**, Word displays text on the screen as large as possible without extending the right margin beyond the right edge of the document window. Perform the following steps to zoom page width.

TO ZOOM PAGE WIDTH

1 Click the Zoom box arrow on the Standard toolbar.

2 Click Page Width in the Zoom list.

Word extends the right margin to the right edge of the document window (shown in Figure 2-5 on the next page). Word computes the zoom percentage based on a variety of settings. Your percentage may be different depending on your computer configuration.

Other Ways

1. In print layout view, drag margin boundary(s) on ruler
2. In Voice Command mode, say "File, Page Setup, Margins, Left, [type left margin setting], Right, [type right margin setting], OK"

More About

The Page Setup Dialog Box

A document printed in portrait orientation is taller than it is wide. A document printed in landscape orientation is wider than it is tall. If you want to change the orientation of a printout from portrait to landscape, click the Landscape box in the Orientation area in the Page Setup dialog box (Figure 2-4).

Adjusting Line Spacing

Line spacing is the amount of vertical space between lines of text in a document. By default, Word single-spaces between lines of text and automatically adjusts line height to accommodate various font sizes and graphics. The MLA documentation style requires that you **double-space** the entire paper; that is, one blank line should display between each line of text. Perform the following steps to adjust the line spacing from single to double.

Steps: To Double-Space Text

 **Point to the Line Spacing button arrow on the Formatting toolbar (Figure 2-5).**

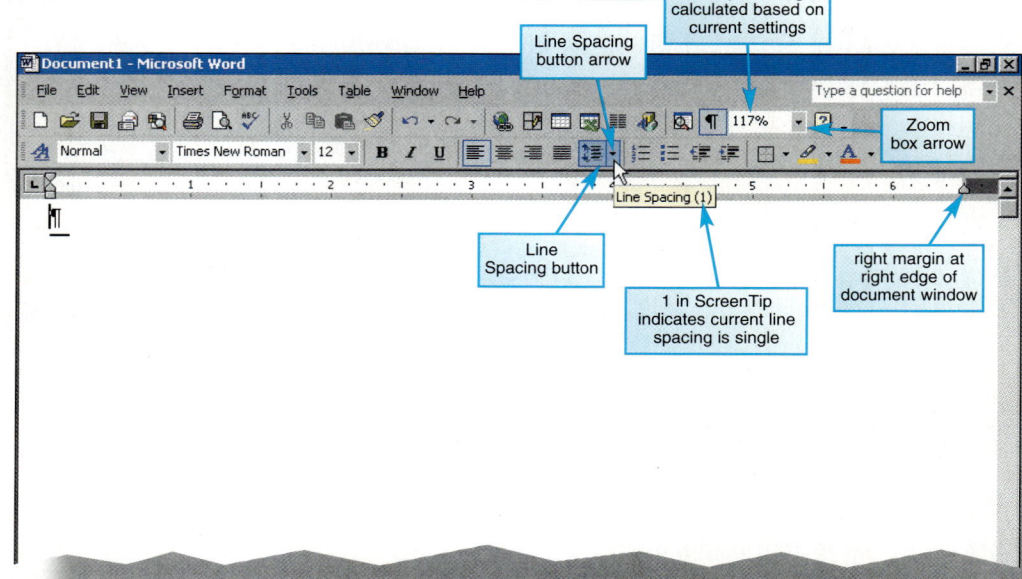

FIGURE 2-5

Click the Line Spacing button arrow and then point to 2.0.

Word displays a list of line spacing options (Figure 2-6).

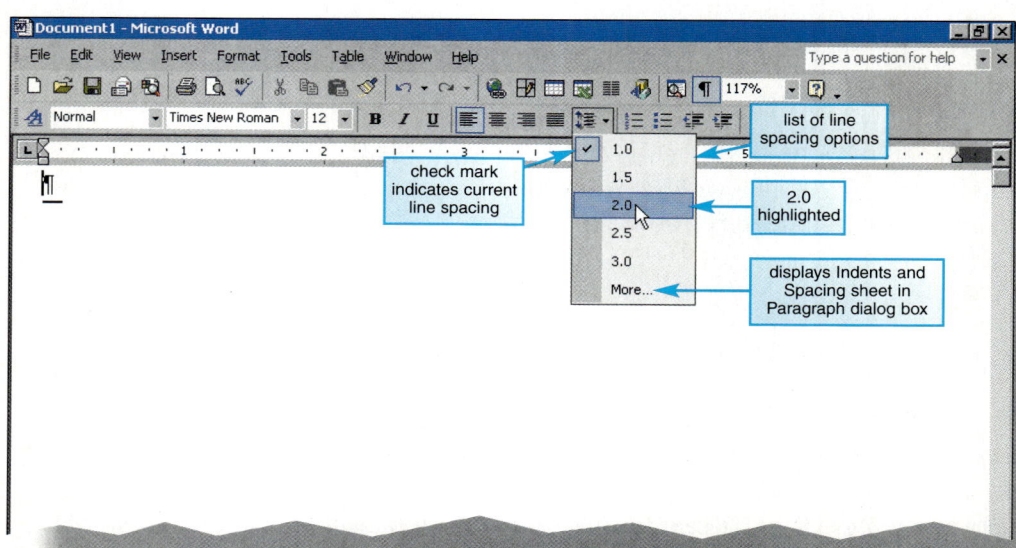

FIGURE 2-6

3 **Click 2.0.**

Word changes the line spacing to double at the location of the insertion point (Figure 2-7).

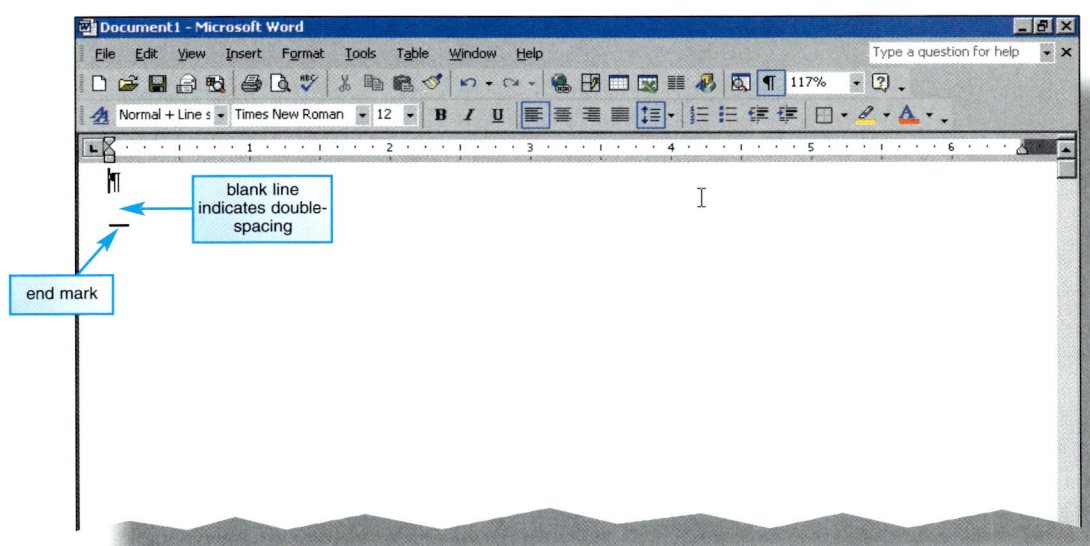

FIGURE 2-7

Notice when line spacing is double (Figure 2-7), the end mark displays one blank line below the insertion point.

The Line Spacing list (Figure 2-6) contains a variety of settings for the line spacing. The default, 1 (for single), and the options 1.5, 2 (for double), 2.5, and 3 (for triple) instruct Word to adjust line spacing automatically to accommodate the largest font or graphic on a line. For additional line spacing options, click More in the Line Spacing list and then click the Line Spacing box arrow in the Indents and Spacing sheet in the Paragraph dialog box.

If you wanted to apply the most recently set line spacing to the current or selected paragraphs, you would click the Line Spacing button instead of the Line Spacing button arrow.

Using a Header to Number Pages

In Word, you easily can number pages by clicking Insert on the menu bar and then clicking Page Numbers. Using the Page Numbers command, you can specify the location (top or bottom of page) and alignment (right, left, or centered) of the page numbers.

The MLA style requires that your last name display to the left of the page number on each page. The Page Numbers command does not allow you to enter text along with the page number. Thus, to place your name to the left of the page number, you must create a header that contains the page number.

Headers and Footers

A **header** is text you want printed at the top of each page in the document. A **footer** is text you want printed at the bottom of every page. In Word, headers print in the top margin one-half inch from the top of every page, and footers print in the bottom margin one-half inch from the bottom of each page, which meets the MLA style. Headers and footers can include text and graphics, as well as the page number, total number of pages, current date, and current time.

Other Ways

1. On Format menu click Paragraph, click Indents and Spacing tab, click Line spacing box arrow, click Double, click OK button
2. Right-click paragraph, click Paragraph on shortcut menu, click Indents and Spacing tab, click Line Spacing box arrow, click Double, click OK button
3. Press CTRL+2
4. In Voice Command mode, say "Line Spacing, [select 2]"

More About

Line Spacing

If the top of characters or a graphic is chopped off, then line spacing probably was set to Exactly in the Paragraph dialog box. To remedy the problem, change the line spacing to Single (1.0), 1.5, Double (2.0), 2.5, 3.0, or At least, all of which accommodate the largest font or graphic. To display the Paragraph dialog box, click Format on the menu bar and then click Paragraph.

In this project, you are to precede the page number with your last name placed one-half inch from the top of each page. Your last name and the page number should print **right-aligned**; that is, at the right margin.

To create the header, first you display the header area in the document window. Then, you can enter the header text into the header area. Use the procedures on the following pages to create the header with page numbers according to the MLA documentation style.

Steps: To Display the Header Area

1 Click View on the menu bar and then point to Header and Footer (Figure 2-8).

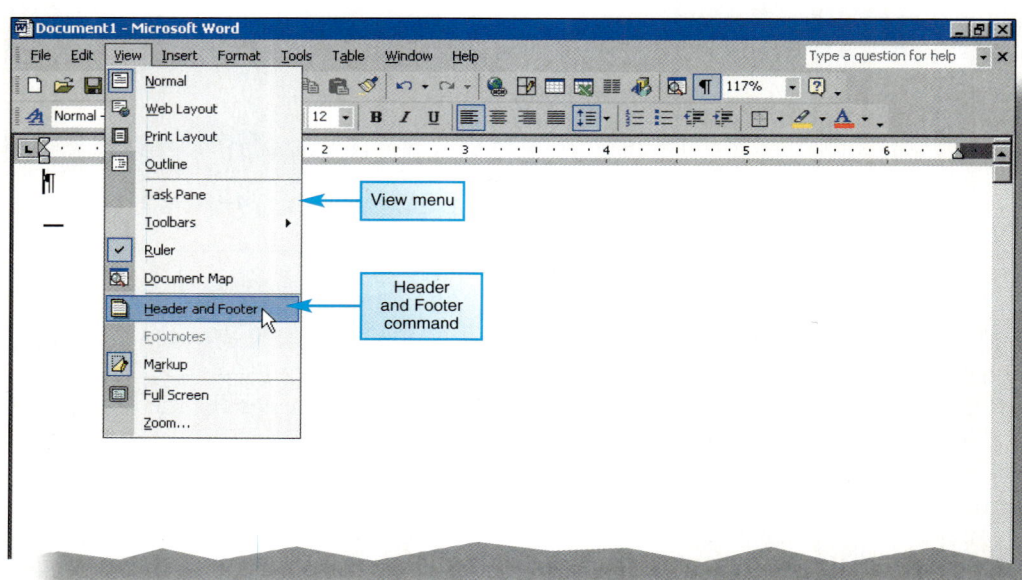

FIGURE 2-8

2 Click Header and Footer.

Word switches from normal view to print layout view and displays the Header and Footer toolbar (Figure 2-9). You type header text in the header area.

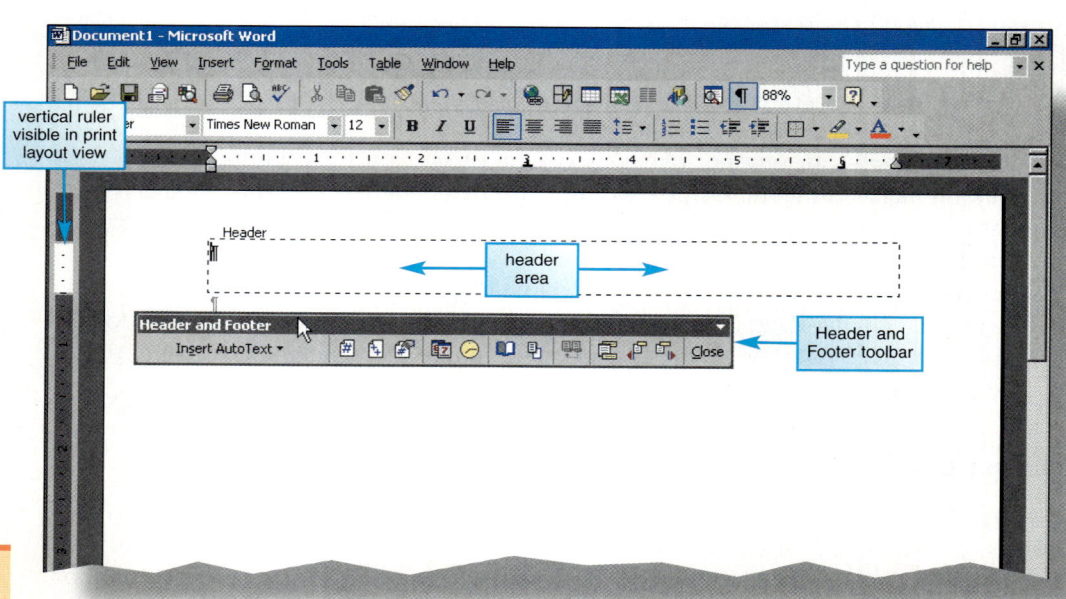

FIGURE 2-9

1. In Voice Command mode, say "View, Header and Footer"

Using a Header to Number Pages • WD 2.13

The Header and Footer toolbar initially floats in the document window. To move a floating toolbar, drag its title bar. You can **dock**, or attach, a floating toolbar above or below the Standard and Formatting toolbars by double-clicking the floating toolbar's title bar. To move a docked toolbar, drag its move handle. Recall that the move handle is the vertical bar to the left of the first button on a docked toolbar. If you drag a floating toolbar to an edge of the window, the toolbar snaps to the edge of the window. If you drag a docked toolbar to the middle of the window, the toolbar floats in the Word window. If you double-click between two buttons or boxes on a docked toolbar, it returns to its original floating position.

The header area does not display on the screen when the document window is in normal view because it tends to clutter the screen. To see the header in the document window with the rest of the text, you must display the document in print preview, which is discussed in a later project, or switch to print layout view. When you click the Header and Footer command on the View menu, Word automatically switches to **print layout view**, which displays the document exactly as it will print. In print layout view, the Print Layout View button on the horizontal scroll bar is selected (Figure 2-10 below).

Print Layout View

You also can click the Print Layout View button on the horizontal scroll bar to switch to print layout view, which shows the positioning of headers, footers, and footnotes. In print layout view, click the Select Browse Object button on the vertical scroll bar and then click Browse by Page on the Select Browse Object menu. With this setting, you can click the double arrows on the bottom of the vertical scroll bar to move forward or backward an entire page.

Entering Text Using Click and Type

When in print layout view, you can use **Click and Type** to format and enter text, graphics, and other items. To use Click and Type, you double-click a blank area of the document window. Word automatically formats the item you enter according to the location where you double-click. Perform the following steps to use Click and Type to right-align and then enter the last name into the header area.

Click and Type

Click and Type is not available in normal view, in a bulleted or numbered list, or in a document formatted into multiple columns.

 **To Click and Type**

1 Point to the right edge of the header area to display a right-align icon next to the I-beam.

As you move the Click and Type pointer around the window, the icon changes to represent formatting that will be applied if you double-click at that location (Figure 2-10).

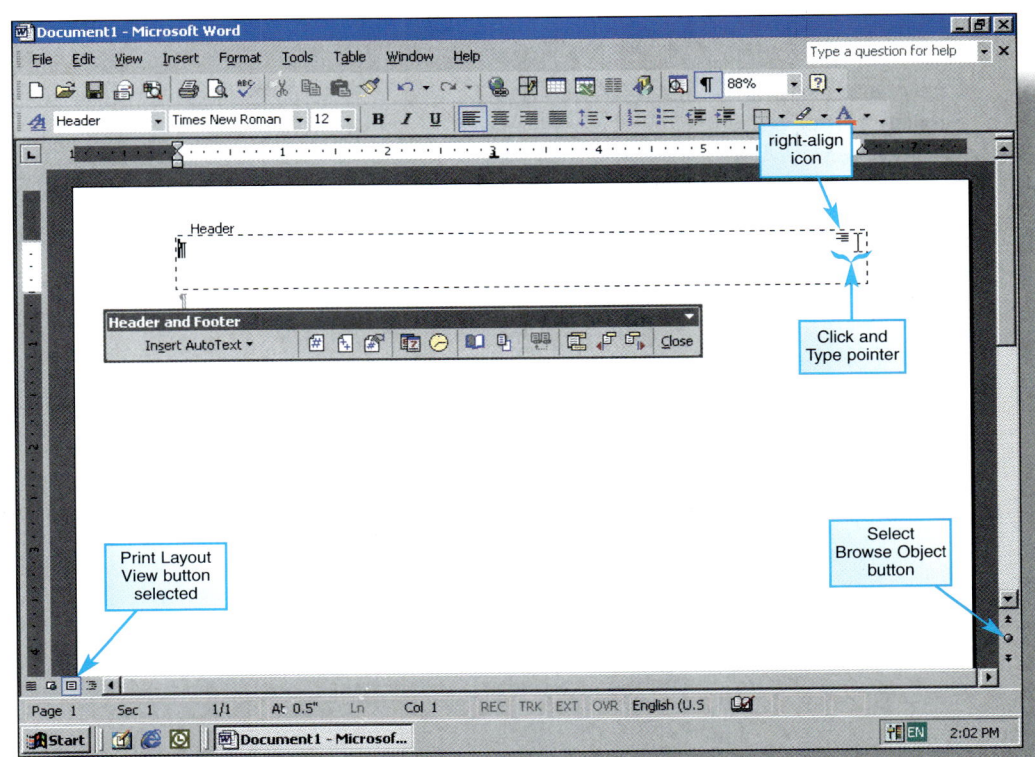

FIGURE 2-10

2 **Double-click. Type** `Marcott` **and then press the SPACEBAR.**

Word displays the last name, Marcott, right-aligned in the header area (Figure 2-11).

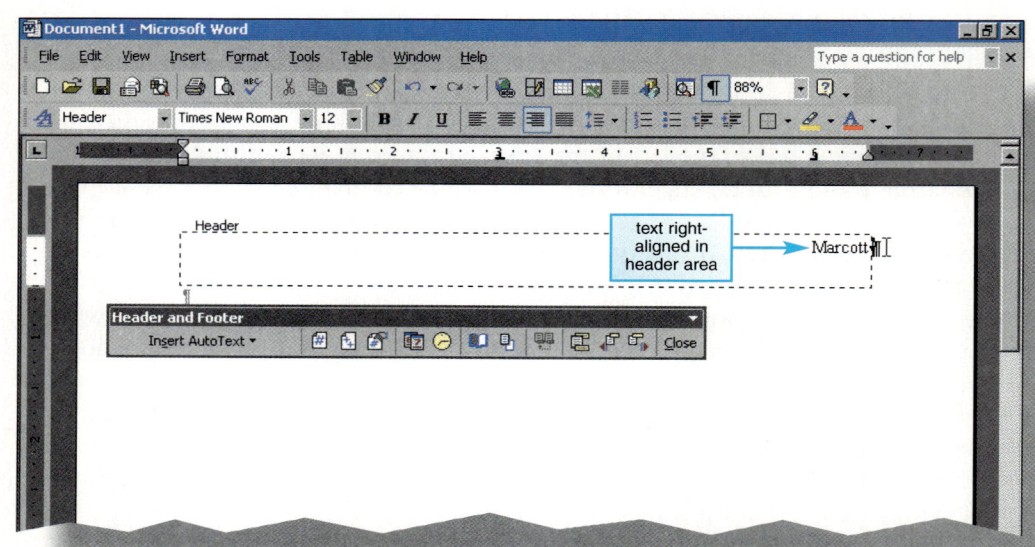

FIGURE 2-11

The next step is to enter the page number into the header area.

Entering a Page Number into the Header

Perform the following steps to enter a page number into the header area.

 To Enter a Page Number

1 **Click the Insert Page Number button on the Header and Footer toolbar.**

Word displays the page number 1 in the header area (Figure 2-12).

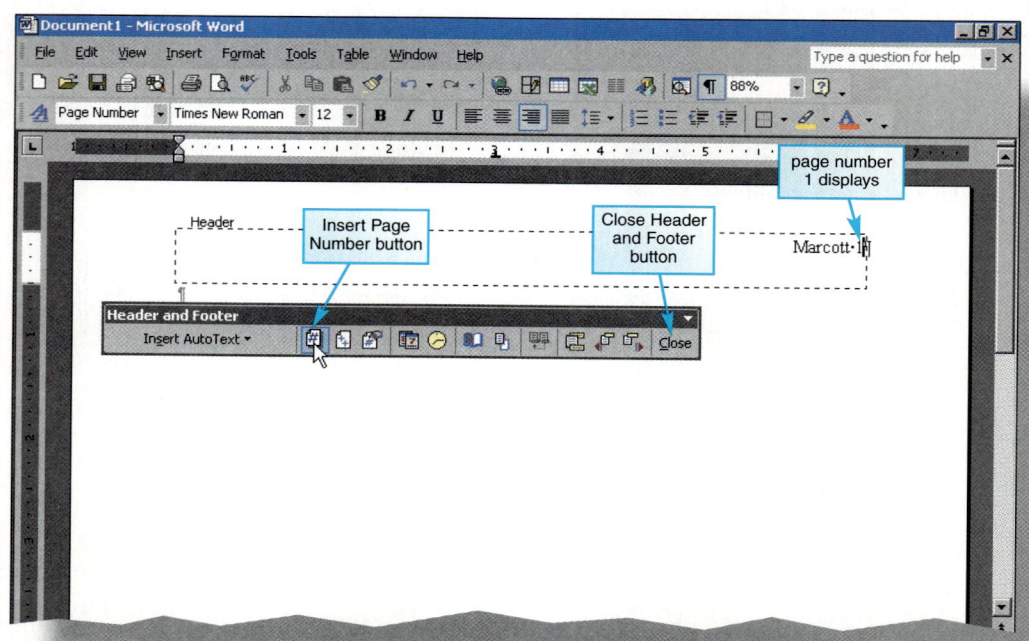

FIGURE 2-12

2 **Click the Close Header and Footer button on the Header and Footer toolbar.**

Word closes the Header and Footer toolbar and returns the screen to normal view (Figure 2-13).

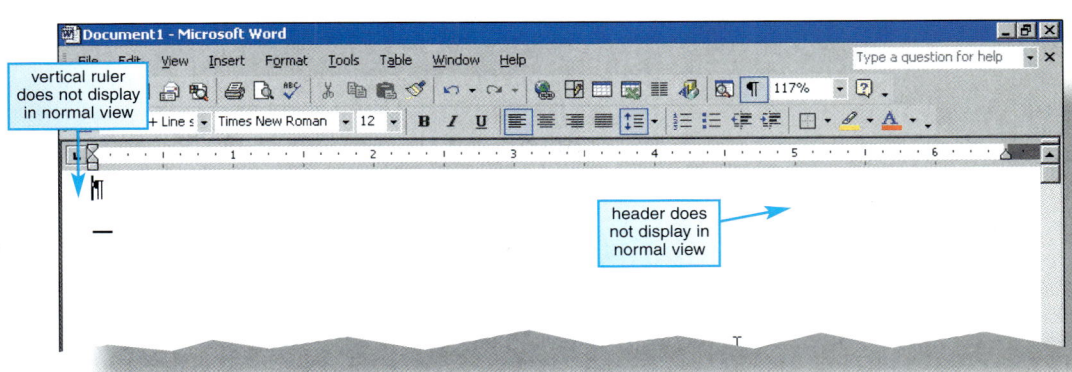

FIGURE 2-13

Other Ways

1. On Insert menu click Page Numbers, click OK button
2. In Voice Command mode, say "Insert Page Number"

The header does not display on the screen in normal view. Although it disappears from the screen, the header still is part of the document. To view the header, you can click View on the menu bar and then click Header and Footer; you can switch to print layout view; or you can display the document in print preview. Project 3 discusses print layout view and print preview in more depth.

Figure 2-14 illustrates the buttons on the Header and Footer toolbar. Just as the Insert Page Number button on the Header and Footer toolbar inserts the page number into the document, three other buttons on the Header and Footer toolbar insert items into the document. The Insert Number of Pages button inserts the total number of pages in the document; the Insert Date button inserts the current date; and the Insert Time button inserts the current time.

To edit an existing header, you can follow the same procedure that you use to create a new header. That is, you can click View on the menu bar and then click Header and Footer to display the header area. If you have multiple headers, click the Show Next button on the Header and Footer toolbar until the appropriate header displays in the header area. Edit the header as you would any Word text and then click the Close Header and Footer button on the Header and Footer toolbar.

To create a footer, click View on the menu bar, click Header and Footer, click the Switch Between Header and Footer button on the Header and Footer toolbar, and then follow the same procedure as you would to create a header.

Other buttons on the Header and Footer toolbar are explained as they are used in later projects.

FIGURE 2-14

Typing the Body of the Research Paper

The body of the research paper encompasses the first two pages of the research paper. You will enter the paper and then modify it later in the project so it matches Figure 2-1 on page WD 2.05. The steps on the following pages illustrate how to type the body of the research paper.

As discussed earlier in this project, the MLA style does not require a separate title page for research papers. Instead, place your name and course information in a block at the top of the page at the left margin. Perform the step on the next page to begin typing the body of the research paper.

More About

Writing Papers

When preparing to write a paper, many students take notes to keep track of information. One method is to summarize the information. Another is to paraphrase, or rewrite the information in your own words. A third method is to quote the exact words of the original. Be sure to use quotation marks when directly quoting a source.

APA Title Page

APA guidelines require a title page as a separate page of a research paper, instead of placing name and course information on the paper's first page. The running head (header), which contains a brief summary of the title and the page number, also is on the title page.

Smart Tags

Word notifies you of a smart tag by displaying a smart tag indicator, such as the purple dotted underline shown in Figure 2-15. You can use smart tags to perform certain actions. For example, you can schedule an appointment on the underlined date in Outlook Calendar. If your screen does not display smart tag indicators, click Tools on the menu bar, click AutoCorrect Options, click the Smart Tags tab, place a check mark in the Label text with smart tags check box, be sure a check mark is in the Dates check box, and then click the OK button.

Shortcut Keys

To print a complete list of shortcut keys in Word, search for keyboard shortcuts in Help. In the upper-right corner of the Help window, click Show All. Click the Print button and then click the Print button in the dialog box.

TO ENTER NAME AND COURSE INFORMATION

1. Type Jordan Marcott and then press the ENTER key. Type Ms. Blythe and then press the ENTER key. Type Information Systems 101 and then press the ENTER key. Type October 18, 2003 and then press the ENTER key.

The student name displays on line 1, the instructor name on line 2, the course name on line 3, and the paper due date on line 4 (Figure 2-15).

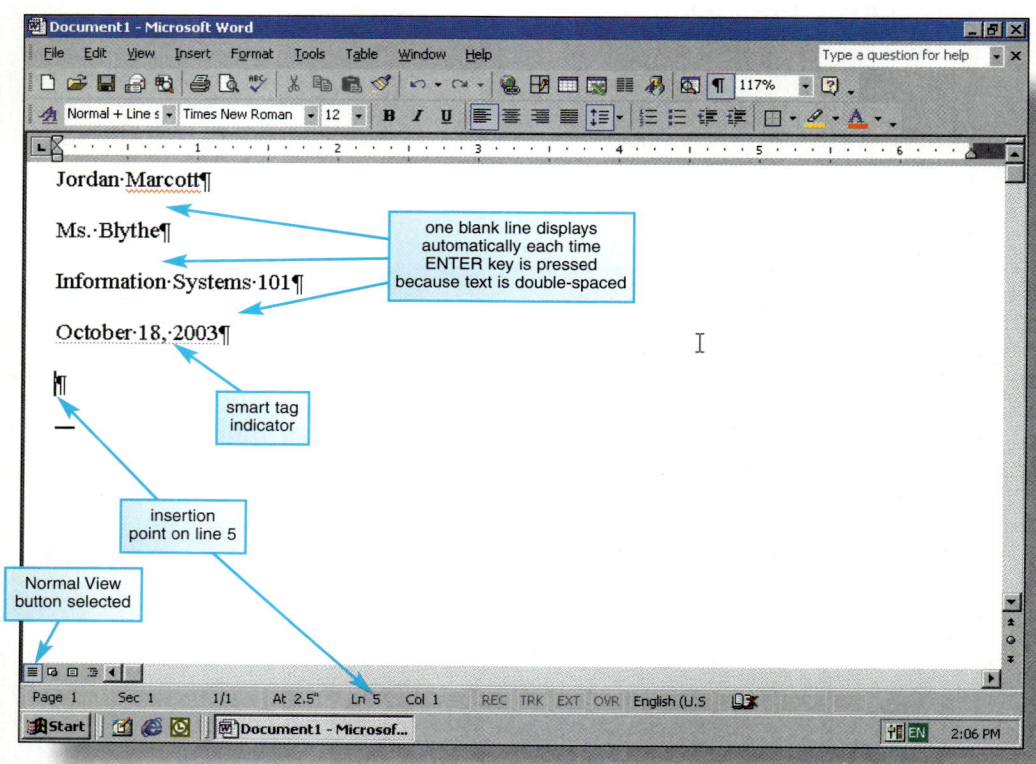

FIGURE 2-15

Notice in Figure 2-15 that the insertion point currently is on line 5. Each time you press the ENTER key, Word advances two lines on the screen. The line counter on the status bar is incremented by only one, however, because earlier you set line spacing to double.

If you watch the screen as you type, you may have noticed that as you typed the first few characters in the month, Octo, Word displayed the **AutoComplete tip**, October, above the characters. To save typing, you could press the ENTER key while the AutoComplete tip displays, which instructs Word to place the text of the AutoComplete tip at the location of your typing.

Applying Formatting Using Shortcut Keys

The next step is to enter the title of the research paper centered between the page margins. As you type text, you may want to format paragraphs and characters as you type them, instead of entering them and then formatting them later. In Project 1, you typed the characters in the document and then selected the ones to be formatted and applied the desired formatting using toolbar buttons. When your fingers are already on the keyboard, it sometimes is more efficient to use **shortcut keys**, or keyboard key combinations, to format text as you type it.

Perform the following steps to center a paragraph with the shortcut keys CTRL+E and then left-align a paragraph with the shortcut keys CTRL+L. (Recall from Project 1 that a notation such as CTRL–E means to press the letter e while holding the CTRL key.)

Steps: To Use Shortcut Keys to Format Text

 **Press CTRL+E. Type E-Retailing and then press the ENTER key.**

Word centers the title between the left and right margins (Figure 2-16). The paragraph mark and insertion point are centered because the formatting specified in the previous paragraph is carried forward to the next paragraph.

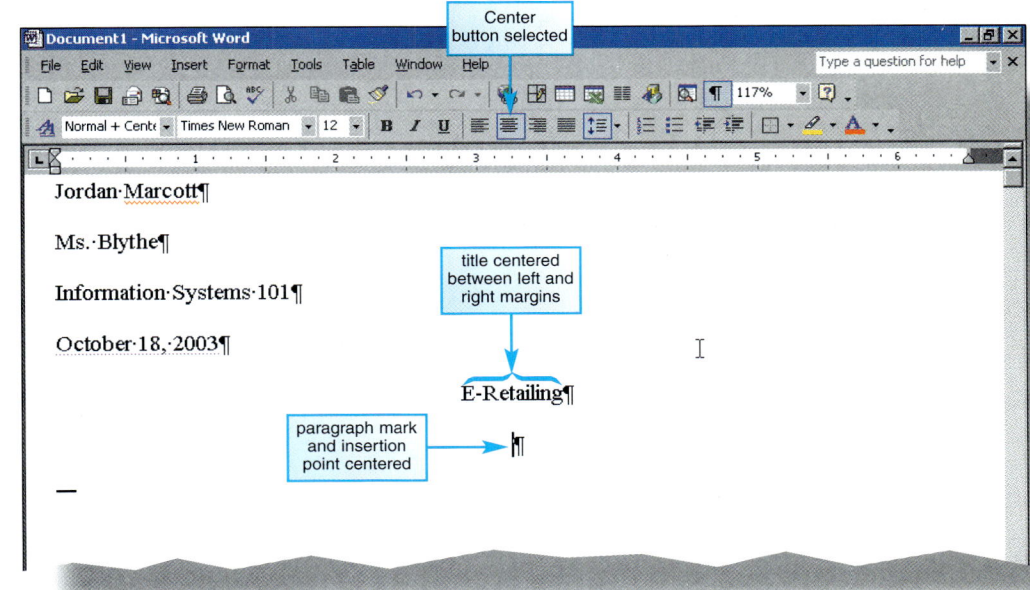

FIGURE 2-16

Press CTRL+L.

Word positions the paragraph mark and the insertion point at the left margin (Figure 2-17). The next text you type will be left-aligned.

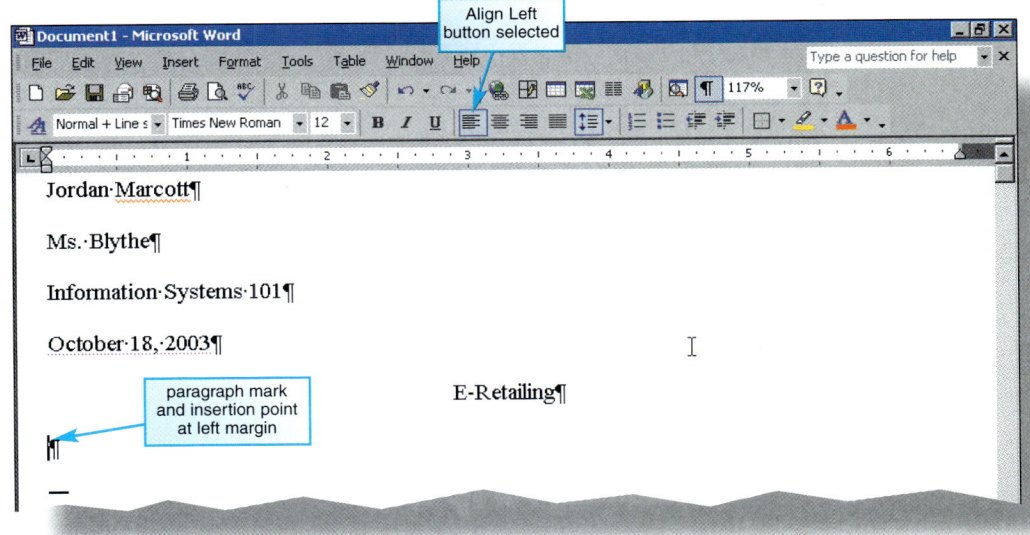

FIGURE 2-17

Word has many shortcut keys for your convenience while typing. Table 2-1 on the next page lists the common shortcut keys for formatting characters. Table 2-2 on the next page lists common shortcut keys for formatting paragraphs.

Table 2-1 Shortcut Keys for Formatting Characters	
CHARACTER FORMATTING TASK	**SHORTCUT KEYS**
All capital letters	CTRL+SHIFT+A
Bold	CTRL+B
Case of letters	SHIFT+F3
Decrease font size	CTRL+SHIFT+<
Decrease font size 1 point	CTRL+[
Double-underline	CTRL+SHIFT+D
Increase font size	CTRL+SHIFT+>
Increase font size 1 point	CTRL+]
Italic	CTRL+I
Remove character formatting (plain text)	CTRL+SPACEBAR
Small uppercase letters	CTRL+SHIFT+K
Subscript	CTRL+=
Superscript	CTRL+SHIFT+PLUS SIGN
Underline	CTRL+U
Underline words, not spaces	CTRL+SHIFT+W

Table 2-2 Shortcut Keys for Formatting Paragraphs	
PARAGRAPH FORMATTING TASK	**SHORTCUT KEYS**
1.5 line spacing	CTRL+5
Add/remove one line above	CTRL+0
Center paragraph	CTRL+E
Decrease paragraph indent	CTRL+SHIFT+M
Double-space lines	CTRL+2
Hanging indent	CTRL+T
Increase paragraph indent	CTRL+M
Justify paragraph	CTRL+J
Left-align paragraph	CTRL+L
Remove hanging indent	CTRL+SHIFT+T
Remove paragraph formatting	CTRL+Q
Right-align paragraph	CTRL+R
Single-space lines	CTRL+1

Saving the Research Paper

You now should save your research paper. For a detailed example of the procedure summarized below, refer to pages WD 1.30 through WD 1.32 in Project 1.

TO SAVE A DOCUMENT

1. Insert a floppy disk into drive A.
2. Click the Save button on the Standard toolbar.
3. Type E-Retailing Paper in the File name text box.
4. Click the Save in box arrow and then click 3½ Floppy (A:).
5. Click the Save button in the Save As dialog box.

Word saves your document with the file name, E-Retailing Paper (shown in Figure 2-18).

The Ruler

If the horizontal ruler does not display on your screen, click View on the menu bar and then click Ruler.

Indenting Paragraphs

According to the MLA style, the first line of each paragraph in the research paper is to be indented one-half inch from the left margin. This procedure, called **first-line indent**, can be accomplished using the horizontal ruler. The **First Line Indent marker** is the top triangle at the 0" mark on the ruler (Figure 2-18). The small square at the 0" mark is the **Left Indent marker**. The Left Indent marker is used to change the entire left margin, whereas the First Line Indent marker affects only the first line of the paragraph.

Perform the following steps to first-line indent the paragraphs in the research paper.

Steps — To First-Line Indent Paragraphs

1 With the insertion point on the paragraph mark in line 6, point to the First Line Indent marker on the ruler (Figure 2-18).

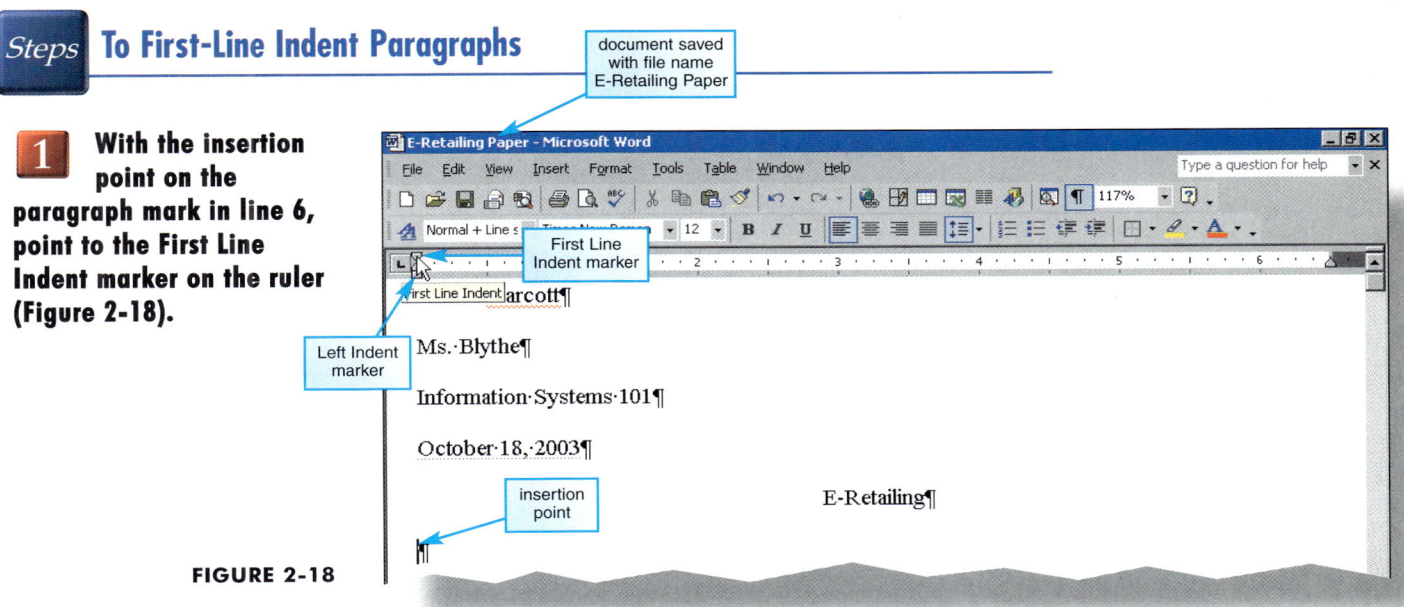

FIGURE 2-18

2 Drag the First Line Indent marker to the .5" mark on the ruler.

As you drag the mouse, a vertical dotted line displays in the document window, indicating the proposed location of the first line of the paragraph (Figure 2-19).

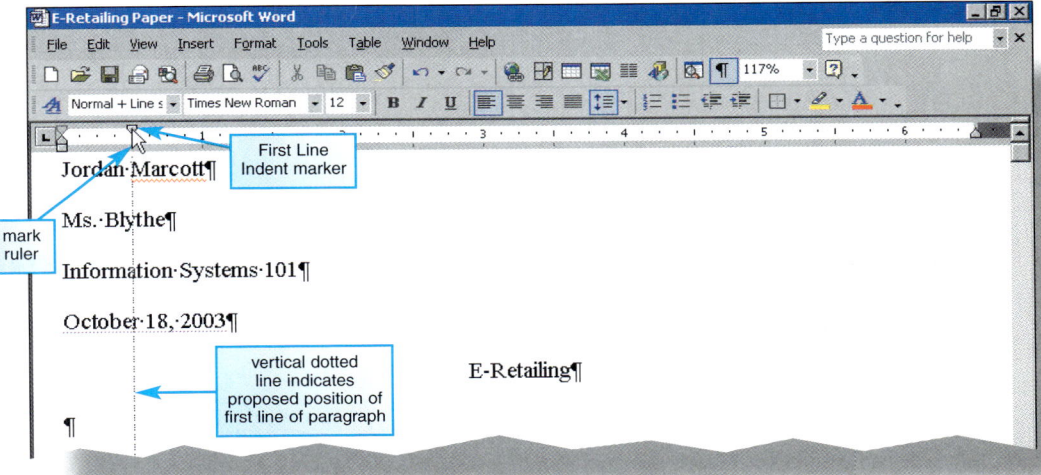

FIGURE 2-19

3 Release the mouse button.

The First Line Indent marker displays at the .5" mark on the ruler, or one-half inch from the left margin (Figure 2-20). The paragraph mark containing the insertion point in the document window also moves one-half inch to the right.

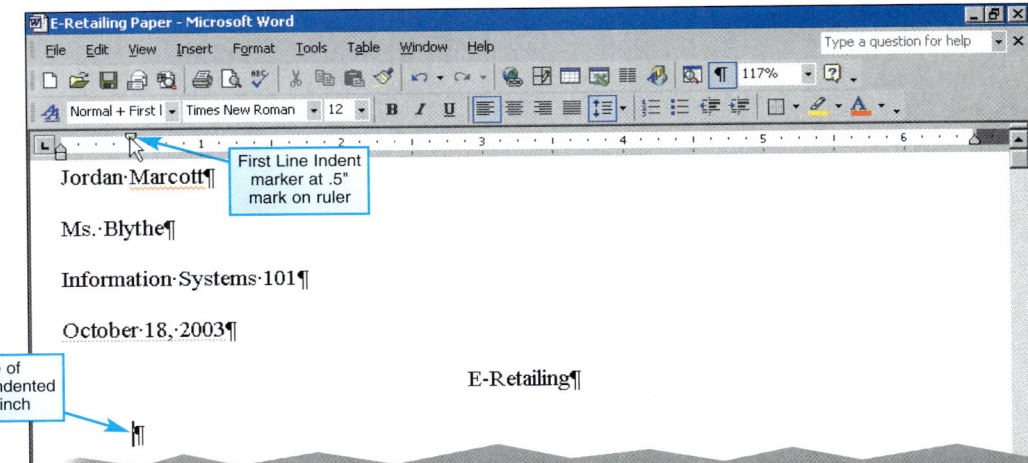

FIGURE 2-20

4 **Type the first paragraph of the research paper body as shown in Figure 2-21. Press the ENTER key. Type** A customer (consumer) visits an online business at the Web equivalent of a showroom: the electronic storefront.

Word automatically indents the first line of the second paragraph by one-half inch (Figure 2-21).

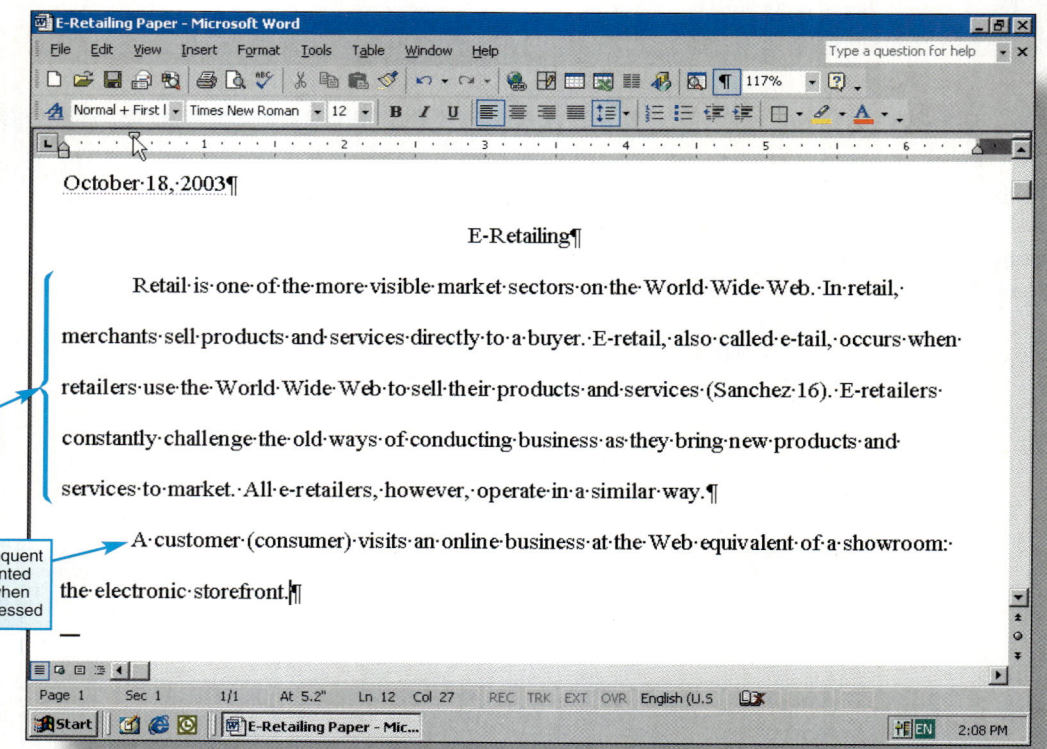

FIGURE 2-21

Other Ways

1. On Format menu click Paragraph, click Indents and Spacing tab, click Special box arrow, click First line, click OK button
2. Right-click paragraph, click Paragraph on shortcut menu, click Indents and Spacing tab, click Special box arrow, click First line, click OK button
3. Press TAB key at beginning of paragraph
4. In Voice Command mode, say "Format, Paragraph, Indents and Spacing, Special, First line, OK"

Recall that each time you press the ENTER key, the paragraph formatting in the previous paragraph is carried forward to the next paragraph. Thus, once you set the first-line indent, its format carries forward automatically to each subsequent paragraph you type.

Using Word's AutoCorrect Feature

As you type, you may make typing, spelling, capitalization, or grammar errors. For this reason, Word provides an **AutoCorrect** feature that automatically corrects these kinds of errors as you type them in the document. For example, if you type the text, ahve, Word automatically changes it to the word, have, when you press the SPACEBAR or a punctuation mark key such as a period or comma.

Word has predefined many commonly misspelled words, which it automatically corrects for you. In the following steps the word, catalog, is misspelled intentionally as catelog to illustrate the AutoCorrect as you type feature.

More About

AutoCorrect

You can add entries to the AutoCorrect list while checking spelling. Right-click the word flagged with the red wavy underline. Point to AutoCorrect on the shortcut menu and then click the correction you want added to the AutoCorrect list.

Steps: To AutoCorrect as You Type

1 **Press the SPACEBAR. Type the beginning of the next sentence and misspell the word, catalog, as follows:** An electronic storefront, also called an online catelog **as shown in Figure 2-22.**

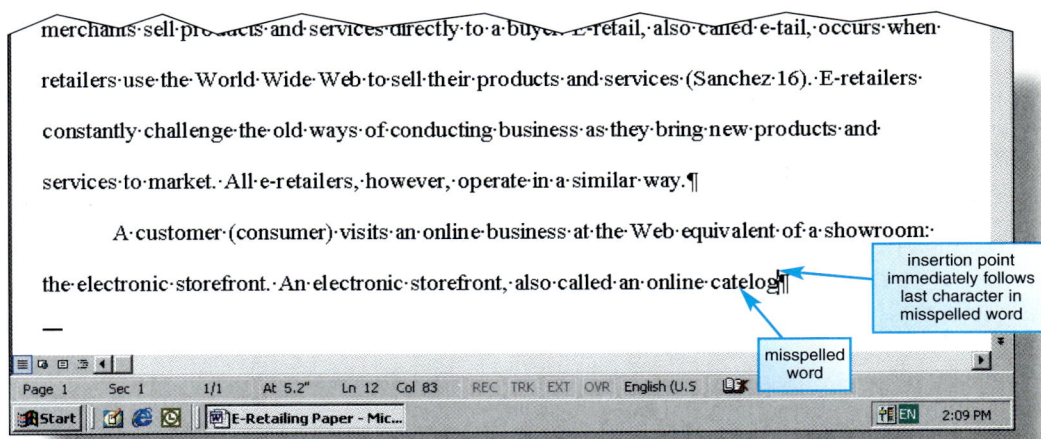

FIGURE 2-22

2 **Press the COMMA key. Press the SPACEBAR. Type the rest of the sentence:** is the Web site where an e-retailer displays its products.

As soon as you press the COMMA key, Word's AutoCorrect feature detects the misspelling and corrects the misspelled word (Figure 2-23).

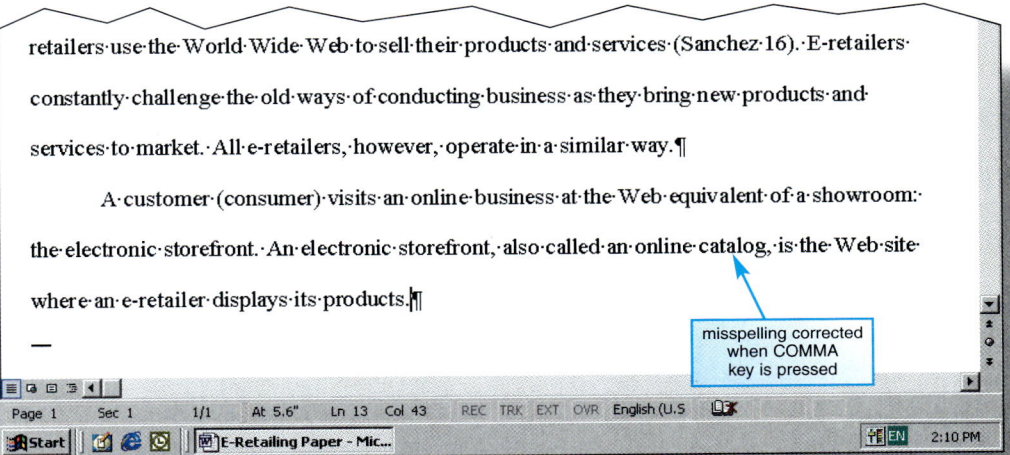

FIGURE 2-23

Word has a list of predefined typing, spelling, capitalization, and grammar errors that AutoCorrect can detect and correct. If you do not like a change that Word automatically makes in a document and you immediately notice the automatic correction, you can undo the change by clicking the Undo button on the Standard toolbar; clicking Edit on the menu bar and then clicking Undo; or pressing CTRL+Z.

If you do not immediately notice the change, you still can undo a correction automatically made by Word through the AutoCorrect Options button. When you point near text that automatically was corrected, Word displays a small blue box below the text. If you click the small blue box, Word displays the AutoCorrect Options button. When you click the **AutoCorrect Options button**, a menu displays that allows you to undo a correction or change how Word handles future automatic corrections of this type. The steps on the next page show how to use the AutoCorrect Options button and menu.

More About

AutoCorrect Options

The AutoCorrect Options is a type of smart tag. The small blue box that displays below the automatically corrected text (Figure 2-24 on the next page) is one type of smart tag indicator. If the smart tag indicator or AutoCorrect Options button do not display on your screen, click Tools on the menu bar, click AutoCorrect Options, click the AutoCorrect tab, place a check mark in the Show AutoCorrect Options buttons check box, and then click the OK button.

Steps To Use the AutoCorrect Options Button

1 **Position the mouse pointer at the beginning of the text automatically corrected by Word (in this case, the c in catalog).**

Word displays a small blue box below the automatically corrected text (Figure 2-24).

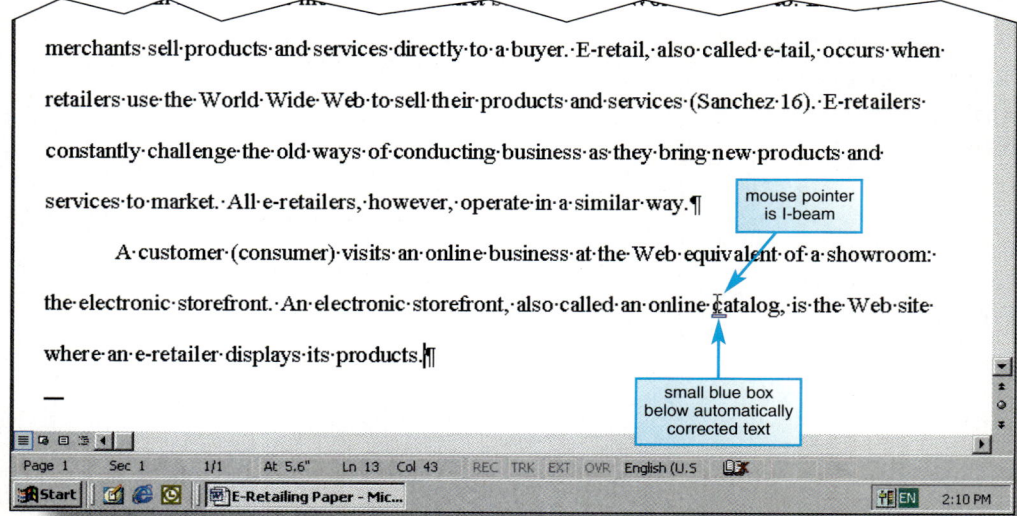

FIGURE 2-24

2 **Point to the small blue box to display the AutoCorrect Options button and then click the AutoCorrect Options button.**

Word displays the AutoCorrect Options menu (Figure 2-25).

3 **Press the ESCAPE key to remove the AutoCorrect Options menu from the window.**

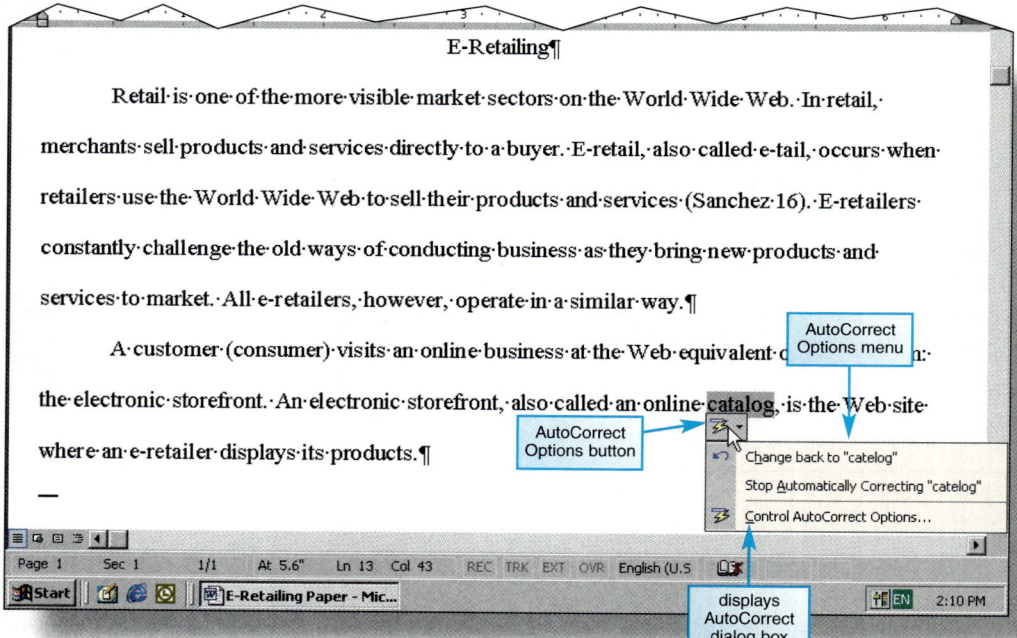

FIGURE 2-25

When you move the mouse pointer, the AutoCorrect Options button disappears from the screen.

In addition to the predefined list of AutoCorrect spelling, capitalization, and grammar errors, you can create your own AutoCorrect entries to add to the list. For example, if you often misspell the word, software, as softare, you should create an AutoCorrect entry for it as shown in these steps.

Typing the Body of the Research Paper • WD 2.23

Steps: To Create an AutoCorrect Entry

1 Click Tools on the menu bar and then point to AutoCorrect Options (Figure 2-26).

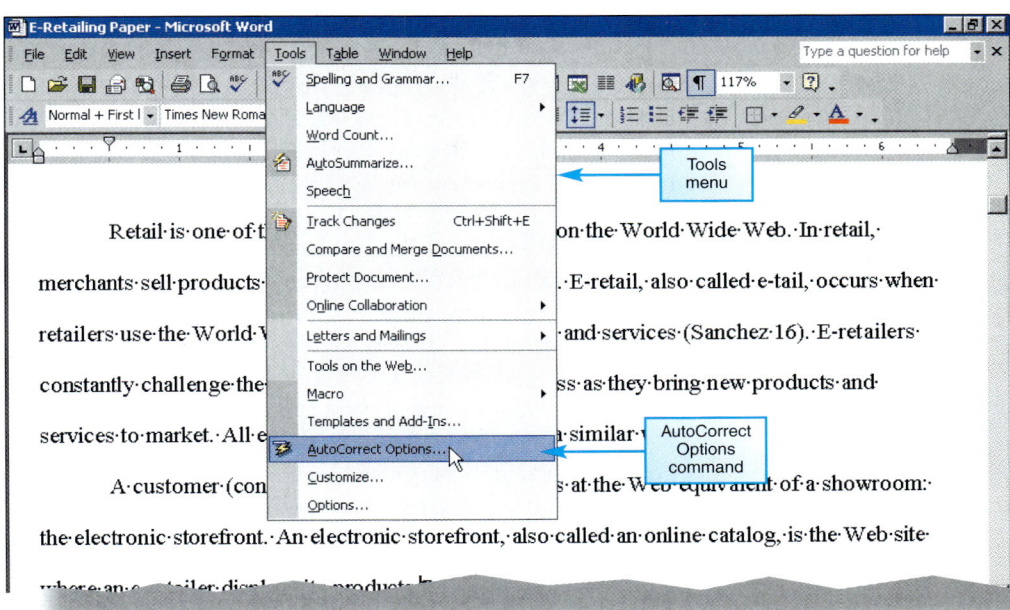

FIGURE 2-26

2 Click AutoCorrect Options. When the AutoCorrect dialog box displays, type `softare` in the Replace text box. Press the TAB key and then type `software` in the With text box. Point to the Add button.

Word displays the AutoCorrect dialog box. The Replace text box contains the misspelled word, and the With text box contains its correct spelling (Figure 2-27).

3 Click the Add button. (If your dialog box displays a Replace button instead, click it and then click the Yes button in the Microsoft Word dialog box.) Click the OK button.

Word adds the entry alphabetically to the list of words to correct automatically as you type.

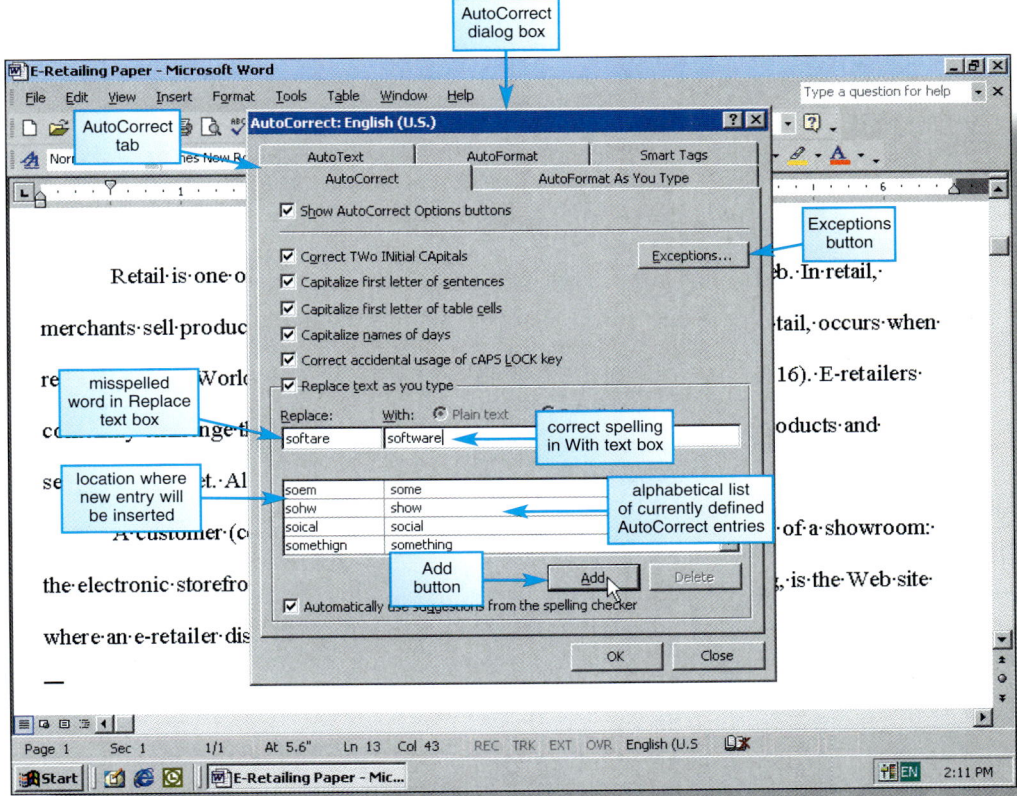

FIGURE 2-27

More About

Quick Reference

For a table that lists how to complete tasks covered in this book using the mouse, menu, shortcut menu, and keyboard, see the Quick Reference Summary at the back of this book or visit the Shelly Cashman Series Office XP Web page (scsite.com/offxp/qr.htm) and then click Microsoft Word 2002.

In addition to creating AutoCorrect entries for words you commonly misspell, you can create entries for abbreviations, codes, and so on. For example, you could create an AutoCorrect entry for asap, indicating that Word should replace this text with the phrase, as soon as possible.

If, for some reason, you do not want Word to correct automatically as you type, you can turn off the replace as you type feature by clicking Tools on the menu bar, clicking AutoCorrect Options, clicking the AutoCorrect tab (Figure 2-27 on the previous page), clicking the Replace text as you type check box to remove the check mark, and then clicking the OK button.

The AutoCorrect sheet (Figure 2-27) contains other check boxes that correct capitalization errors if the check boxes are selected. If you type two capital letters in a row, such as TH, Word makes the second letter lowercase, Th. If you begin a sentence with a lowercase letter, Word capitalizes the first letter of the sentence. If you type the name of a day in lowercase, such as tuesday, Word capitalizes the first letter of the day, Tuesday. If you leave the CAPS LOCK key on and begin a new sentence such as aFTER, Word corrects the typing, After, and turns off the CAPS LOCK key.

Sometimes you do not want Word to AutoCorrect a particular word or phrase. For example, you may use the code WD. in your documents. Because Word automatically capitalizes the first letter of a sentence, the character you enter following the period will be capitalized (in the previous sentence, it would capitalize the letter i in the word, in). To allow the code WD. to be entered into a document and still leave the AutoCorrect feature turned on, you need to set an exception. To set an exception to an AutoCorrect rule, click Tools on the menu bar, click AutoCorrect Options, click the AutoCorrect tab, click the Exceptions button in the AutoCorrect sheet (Figure 2-27), click the appropriate tab in the AutoCorrect Exceptions dialog box, type the exception entry in the text box, click the Add button, click the Close button in the AutoCorrect Exceptions dialog box, and then click the OK button in the AutoCorrect dialog box.

Perform the following steps to continue adding text to the body of the paper.

TO ENTER MORE TEXT

1. Press the SPACEBAR. Type the remainder of the second paragraph of the paper as shown in Figure 2-28.

2. Press the ENTER key. Type the first two sentences of the third paragraph of the paper as shown in Figure 2-28.

The second paragraph and first two sentences of the third paragraph are entered (Figure 2-28).

More About

Citing Sources

Both the MLA and APA guidelines suggest the use of in-text parenthetical citations, as opposed to footnoting each source of material in a paper. These parenthetical acknowledgments guide the reader to the end of the paper for complete information on the source.

Adding Footnotes

As discussed earlier in this project, explanatory notes are optional in the MLA documentation style. They are used primarily to elaborate on points discussed in the body of the paper. The style specifies that a **superscript** (raised number) be used for a note reference mark to signal that an explanatory note exists either at the bottom of the page as a **footnote** or at the end of the document as an **endnote**.

Word, by default, places notes at the bottom of each page. In Word, **note text** can be any length and format. Word automatically numbers notes sequentially by placing a **note reference mark** in the body of the document and also in front of the note text. If you insert, rearrange, or remove notes, Word renumbers any subsequent note reference marks according to their new sequence in the document.

Typing the Body of the Research Paper • WD 2.25

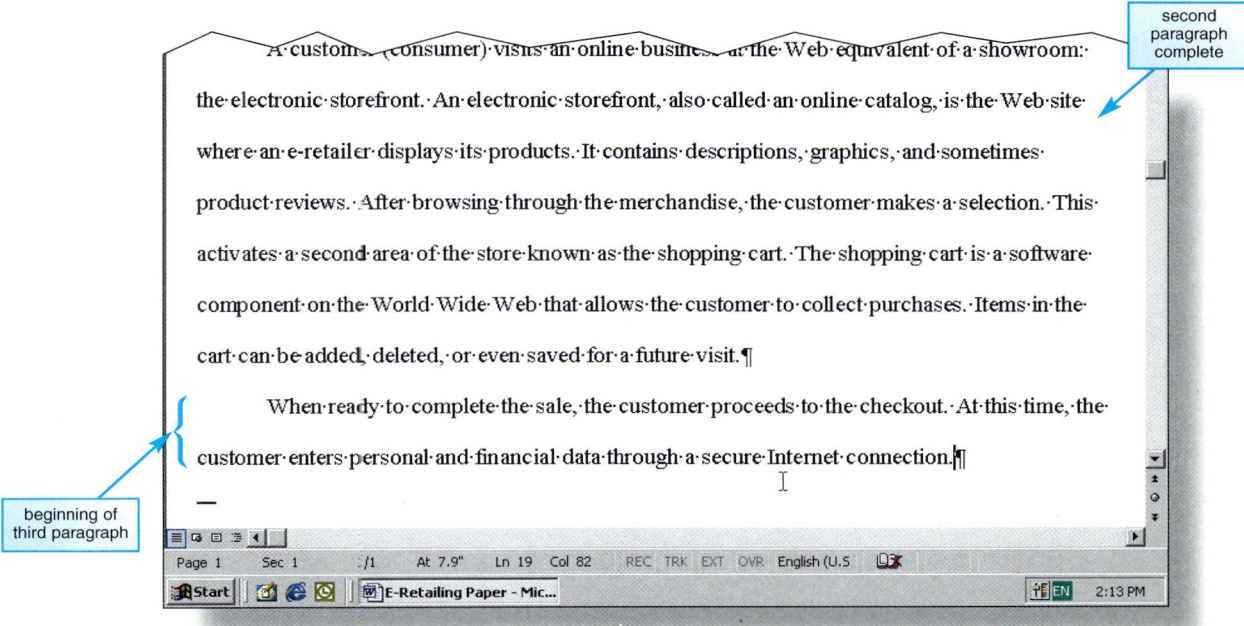

FIGURE 2-28

Perform the following steps to add a footnote to the research paper.

 **To Add a Footnote**

1 **Click Insert on the menu bar, point to Reference, and then point to Footnote.**

The insertion point is positioned immediately after the period following the end of the second sentence in the third paragraph of the research paper (Figure 2-29).

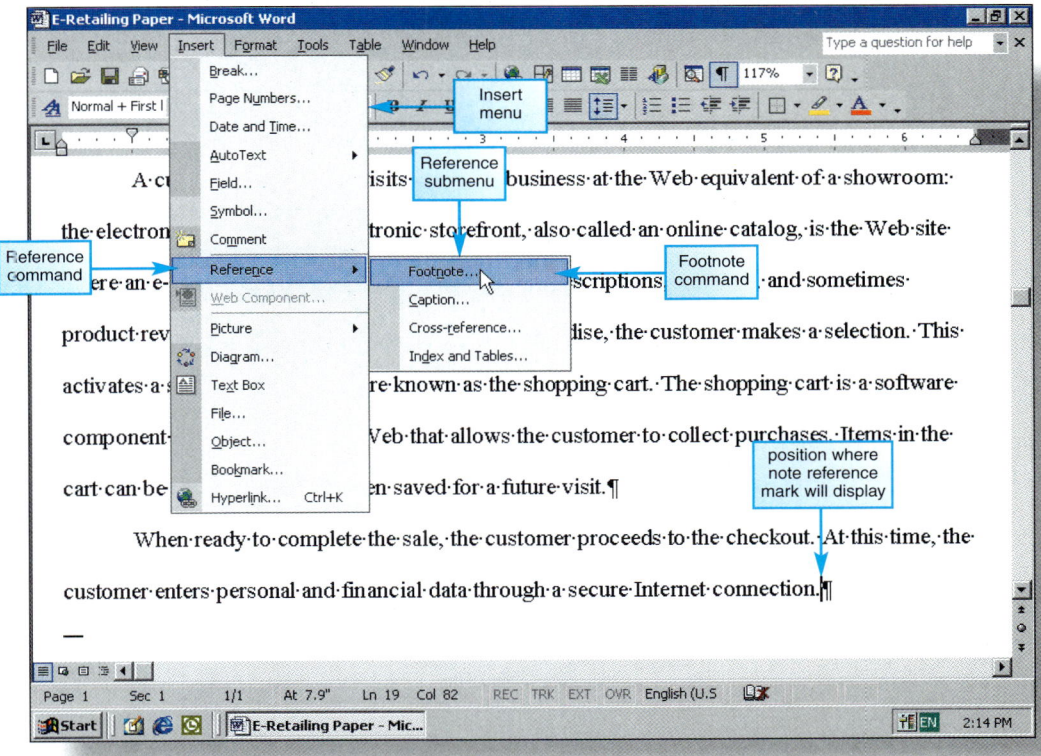

FIGURE 2-29

2 **Click Footnote. When the Footnote and Endnote dialog box displays, point to the Insert button.**

Word displays the Footnote and Endnote dialog box (Figure 2-30). If you wanted to create endnotes instead of footnotes, you would click Endnotes in the Footnote and Endnote dialog box.

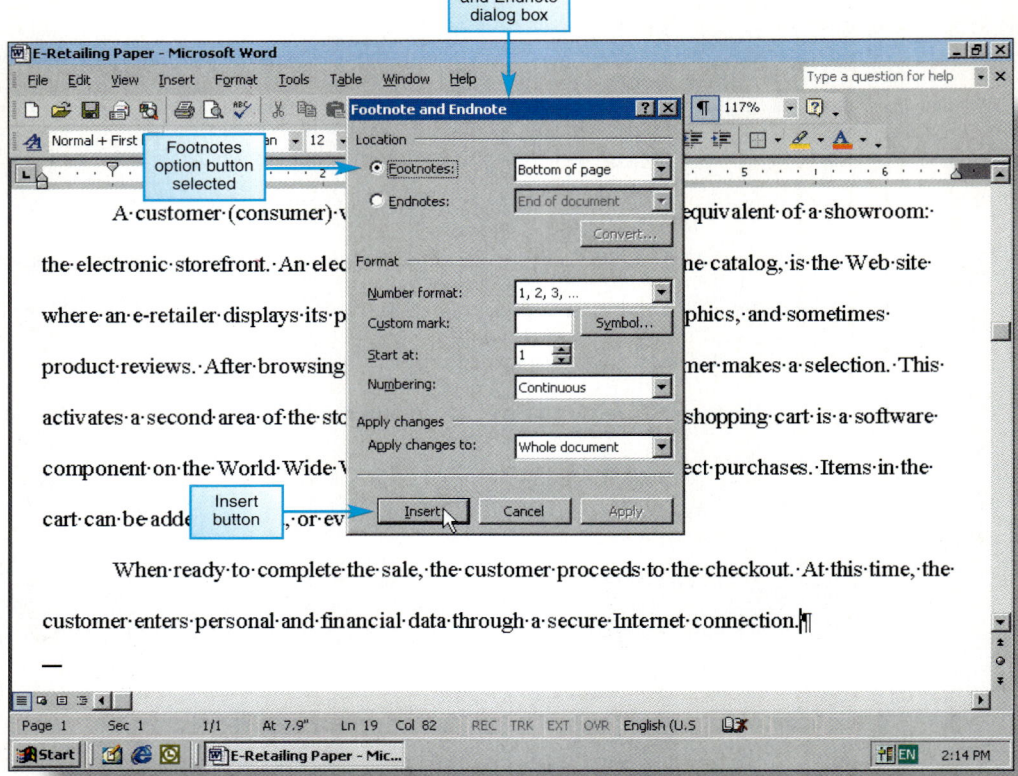

FIGURE 2-30

3 **Click the Insert button.**

Word opens a *note pane* in the lower portion of the Word window with the note reference mark (a superscripted 1) positioned at the left margin of the note pane (Figure 2-31). The note reference mark also displays in the document window at the location of the insertion point. Note reference marks are, by default, superscripted; that is, raised above other letters.

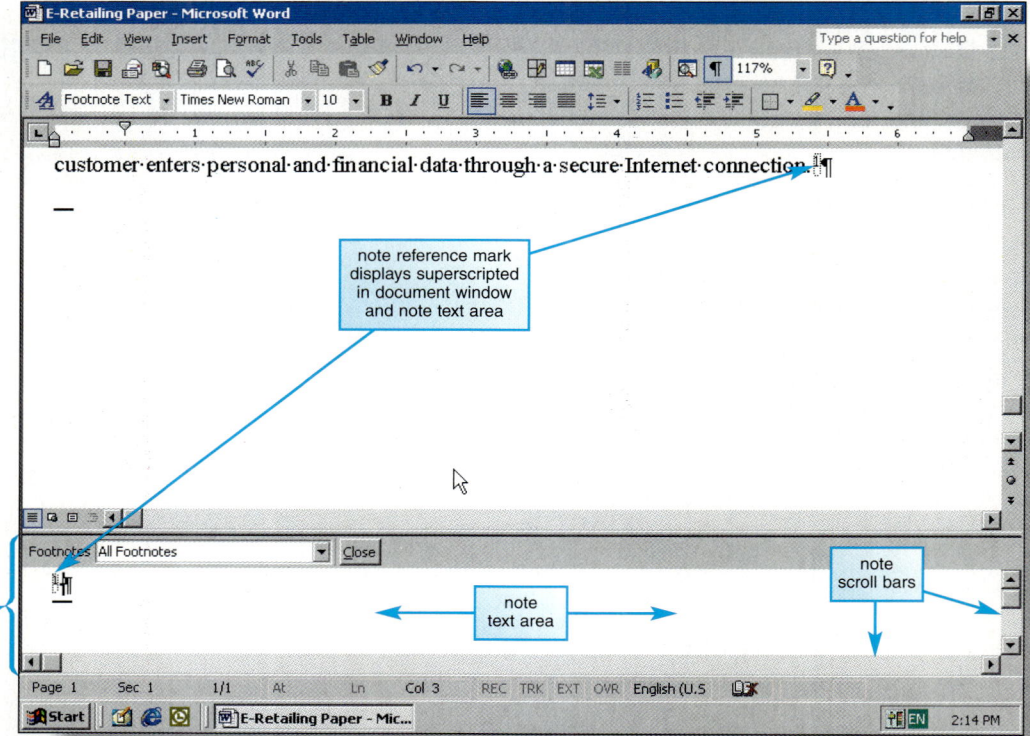

FIGURE 2-31

4 **Type** According to Bodini and Hampton, consumers should verify that a merchant provides secure transactions before using a credit card on the Internet (56-62).

The note text displays in the note pane (Figure 2-32).

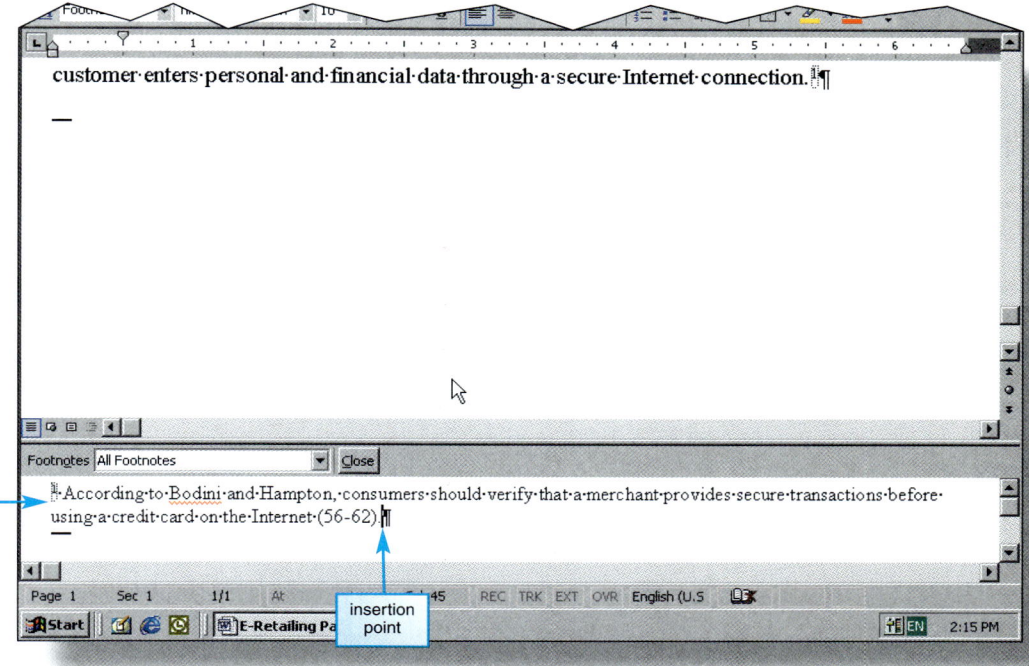

FIGURE 2-32

The footnote is not formatted according to the MLA requirements. Thus, the next step is to modify the style of the footnote.

Modifying a Style

A **style** is a named group of formatting characteristics that you can apply to text. Word has many built-in, or predefined, styles that you may use to format text. The formats defined by these styles include character formatting, such as the font and font size; paragraph formatting, such as line spacing and text alignment; table formatting; and list formatting.

Whenever you create a document, Word formats the text using a particular style. The base style for a new Word document is the **Normal style**, which for a new installation of Word 2002 most likely uses 12-point Times New Roman font for characters and single-spaced, left-aligned paragraphs. As you type, you can apply different styles to the text. You also can create your own styles. A later project discusses applying and creating styles.

When the insertion point is in the note text area, the entered note text is formatted using the Footnote Text style. The Footnote Text style defines characters as 10-point Times New Roman and paragraphs as single-spaced and left-aligned.

You could change the paragraph formatting of the footnote text to first-line indent and double-spacing as you did for the text in the body of the document. Then, you would change the font size from 10 to 12 point. If you use this technique, however, you will need to change the format of the footnote text for each footnote you enter into the document. A more efficient technique is to modify the format of the Footnote Text style to first-line indent and double-spaced paragraphs and a 12-point font size. By changing the formatting of the Footnote Text style, every footnote you enter will use the formats defined in this style.

Other Ways

1. In Voice Command mode, say "Insert, Reference, Footnote, Insert, Dictation, [note text]"

More About

Styles

The Style box on the Formatting toolbar displays the name of the style applied to the location of the insertion point. To view the list of styles associated with the current document, click the Style box arrow on the Formatting toolbar or display the Styles and Formatting task pane by clicking the Styles and Formatting button on the Formatting toolbar. To apply a style, select the text to format, click the Style box arrow on the Formatting toolbar, and then click the desired style name; or select the desired style name in the Styles and Formatting task pane.

Perform the following steps to modify the Footnote Text style.

Steps: To Modify a Style

1 **Right-click the note text in the note pane and then point to Style on the shortcut menu (Figure 2-33).**

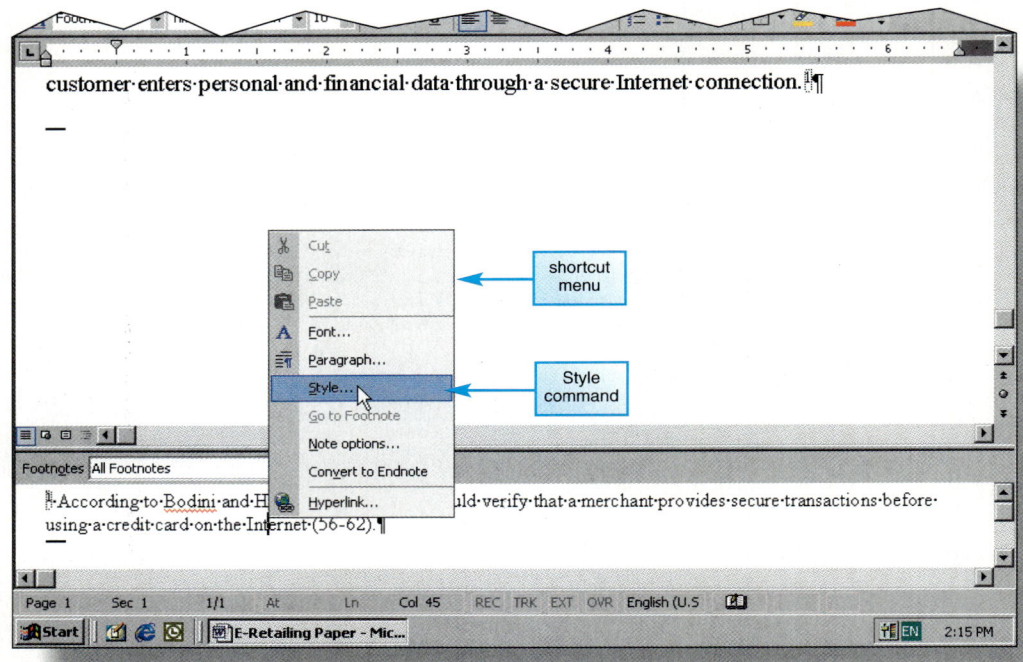

FIGURE 2-33

2 **Click Style. When the Style dialog box displays, if necessary, click Footnote Text in the Styles list. Point to the Modify button.**

Word displays the Style dialog box (Figure 2-34). Footnote Text is selected in the Styles list. The Preview area shows the formatting associated with the selected style.

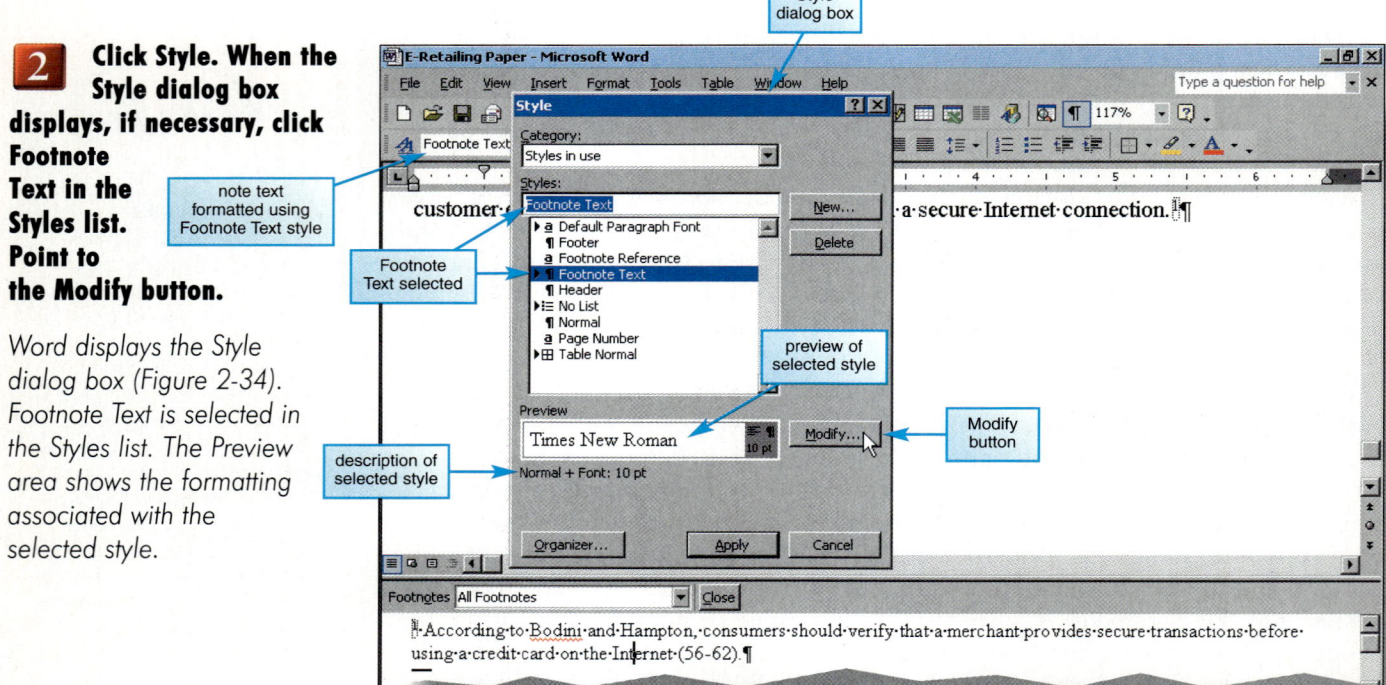

FIGURE 2-34

Typing the Body of the Research Paper • WD 2.29

3 **Click the Modify button. When the Modify Style dialog box displays, click the Font Size box arrow in the Formatting area and then click 12 in the Font Size list. Click the Double Space button.**

Word displays the Modify Style dialog box (Figure 2-35). The font size for the Footnote Text style is changed to 12, and paragraph spacing is changed to double. The first-line indent still must be set.

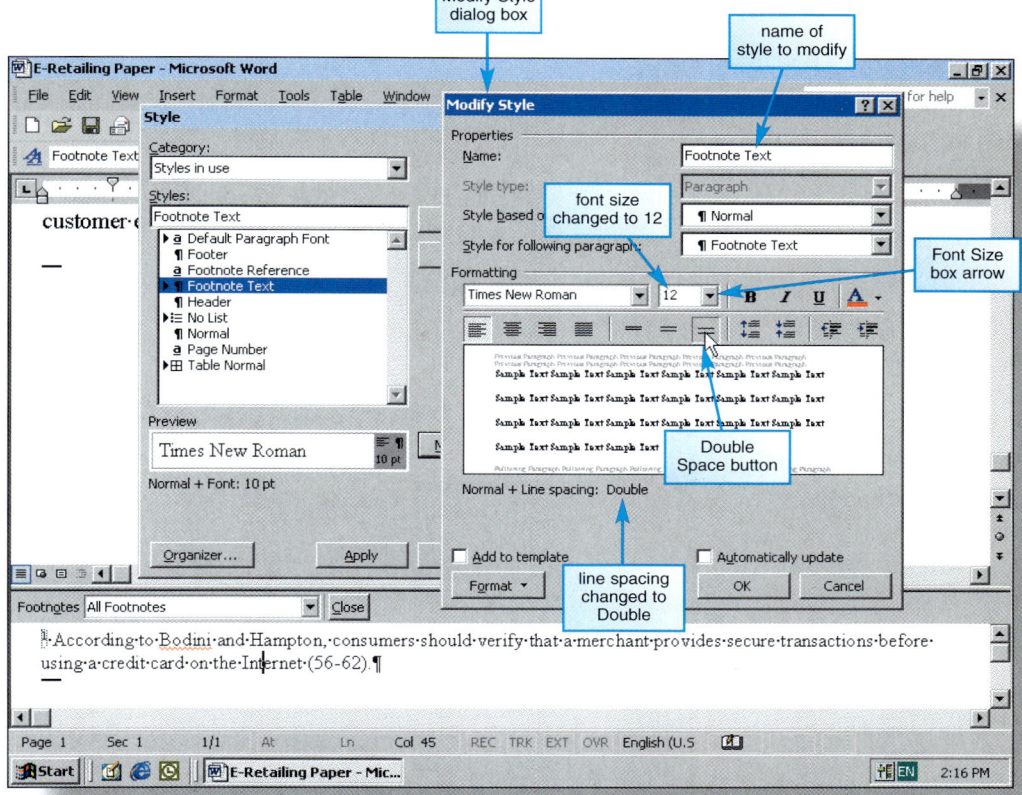

FIGURE 2-35

4 **Click the Format button and then point to Paragraph.**

A menu of formatting commands displays above the Format button (Figure 2-36).

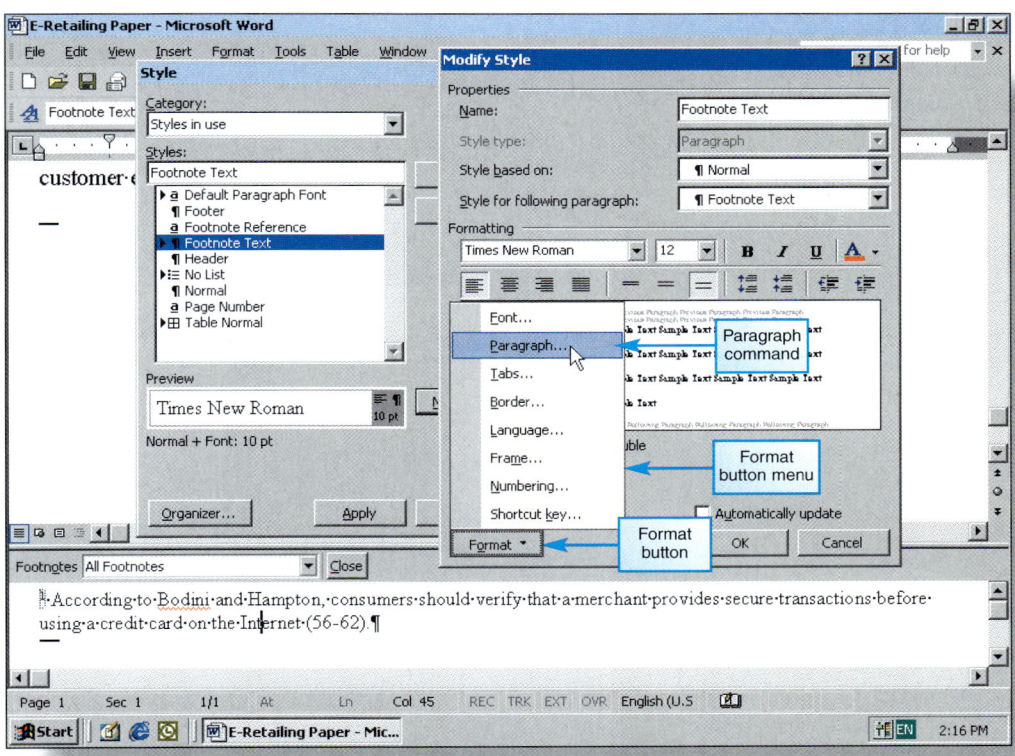

FIGURE 2-36

WD 2.30 • Project 2 • Creating a Research Paper

5 **Click Paragraph. When the Paragraph dialog box displays, click the Special box arrow and then click First line. Point to the OK button.**

Word displays First line in the Special box (Figure 2-37). Notice the default first-line indent is 0.5".

6 **Click the OK button. When the Modify Style dialog box is visible again, point to the OK button.**

Word modifies the Footnote Text style to first-line indented paragraphs (Figure 2-38).

7 **Click the OK button. When the Style dialog box is visible again, click the Apply button. If necessary, click the up scroll arrow in the note pane to display the entire note text.**

Word indents the first line of the note by one-half inch, sets the line spacing for the note to double, and changes the font size of the note text to 12 (shown in Figure 2-39).

Other Ways

1. Click Styles and Formatting button on Formatting toolbar, point to style name in Pick formatting to apply list and click style name box arrow, click Modify
2. In Voice Command mode, say "Context menu, Style, Modify, Font Size, [select font size], Double Space, Format, Paragraph, Special, First line, OK, OK, Apply"

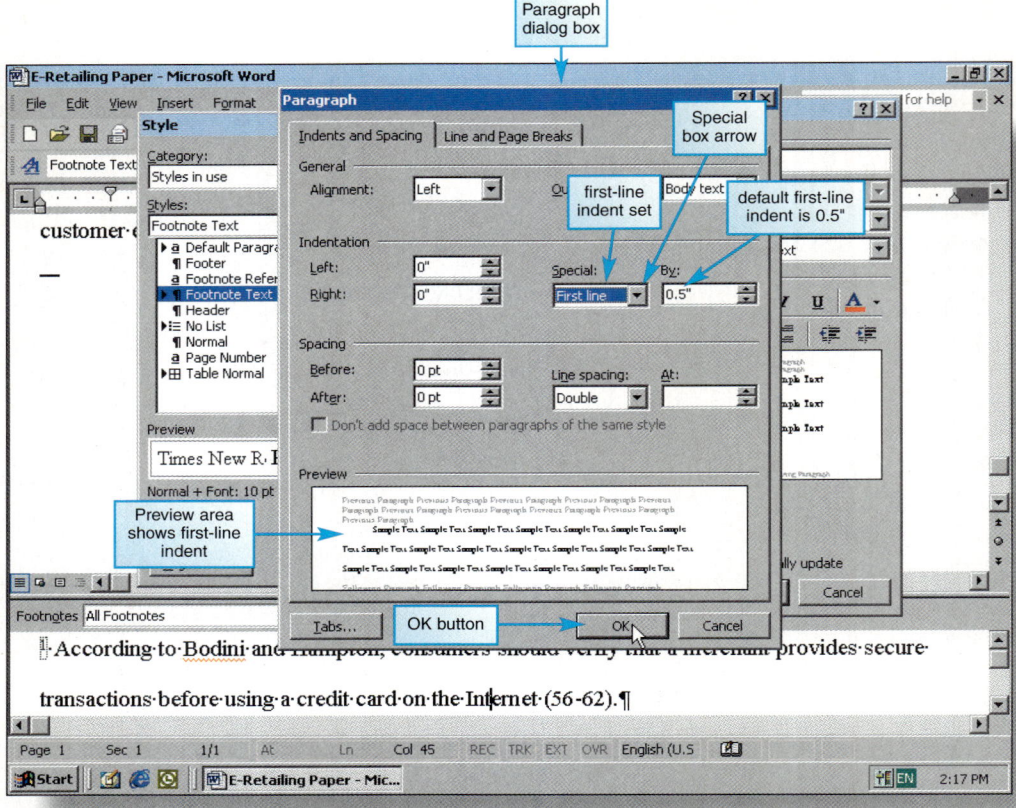

FIGURE 2-37

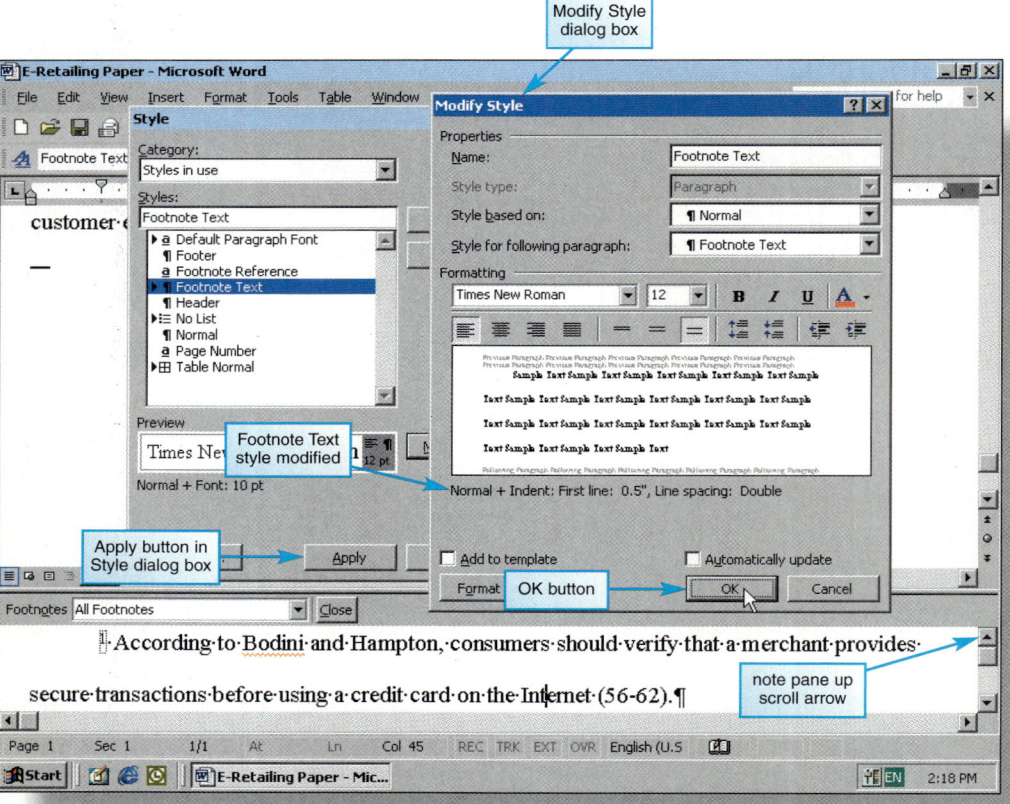

FIGURE 2-38

Any future footnotes entered into the document will use a 12-point font with the paragraphs first-line indented and double-spaced. The footnote is complete. The next step is to close the note pane.

To Close the Note Pane

1 Point to the Close button in the note pane (Figure 2-39).

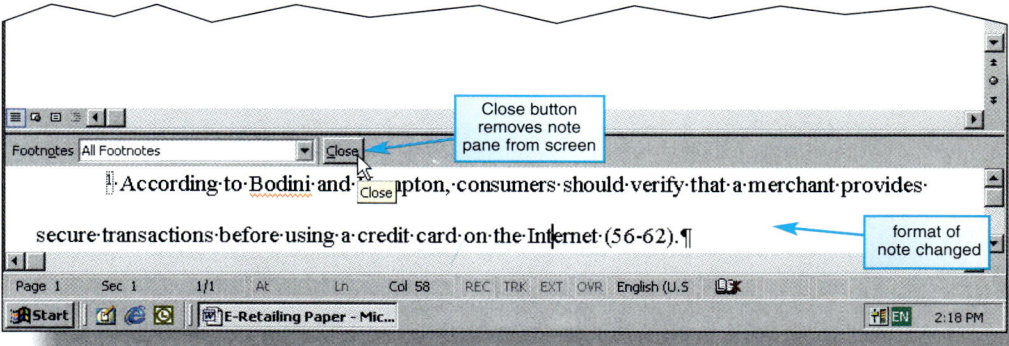

FIGURE 2-39

2 Click the Close button. If you want to see the note text while in normal view, point to the note reference mark in the document window.

Word closes the note pane (Figure 2-40).

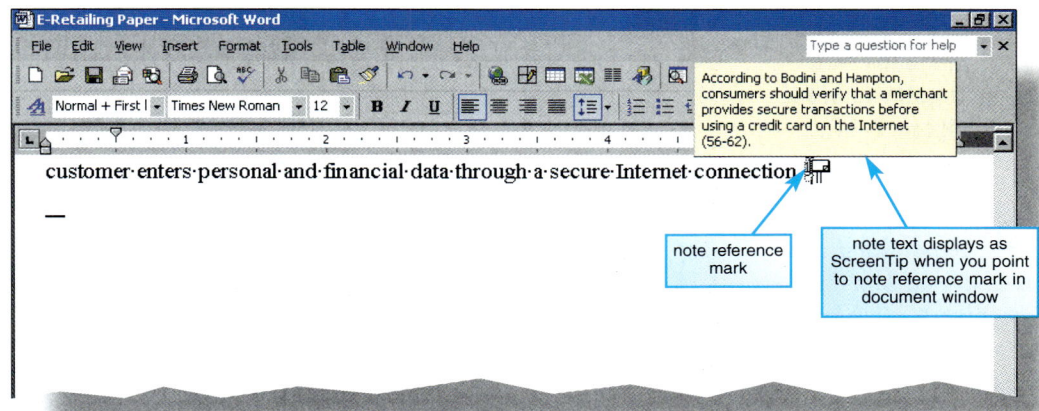

FIGURE 2-40

When Word closes the note pane and returns to the document window, the note text disappears from the screen. Although the note text still exists, it usually is not visible as a footnote in normal view. If, however, you point to the note reference mark, the note text displays above the note reference mark as a ScreenTip (Figure 2-40). To remove the ScreenTip, move the mouse pointer.

If you want to verify that the note text is positioned correctly on the page, you must switch to print layout view or display the document in print preview. Project 3 discusses print preview and print layout view.

To delete a note, you select the note reference mark in the document window (not in the note pane) by dragging through the note reference mark and then clicking the Cut button on the Standard toolbar. Another way to delete a note is to click immediately to the right of the note reference mark in the document window and then press the BACKSPACE key twice, or click immediately to the left of the note reference mark in the document window and then press the DELETE key twice.

Other Ways

1. Press ALT+C
2. In Voice Command mode, say "Close"

More About

Note Numbering

To change the number format of footnotes or endnotes (e.g., from 1, 2, 3, to i, ii, iii), click the Number format box arrow in the Footnote and Endnote dialog box (Figure 2-30 on page WD 2.26) and then click the desired format.

More About

Notes

To convert current footnotes to endnotes, click Insert on the menu bar, point to Reference, and then click Footnote. Click the Convert button in the Footnote and Endnote dialog box. Click Convert all footnotes to endnotes and then click the OK button. Click the Close button in the Footnote and Endnote dialog box.

To move a note to a different location in a document, select the note reference mark in the document window (not in the note pane), click the Cut button on the Standard toolbar, click the location where you want to move the note, and then click the Paste button on the Standard toolbar. When you move or delete notes, Word automatically renumbers any remaining notes in the correct sequence.

You edit note text using the note pane at the bottom of the Word window. To display the note text in the note pane, double-click the note reference mark in the document window or click View on the menu bar and then click Footnotes. Edit the note as you would any Word text and then click the Close button in the note pane.

Using Word Count

Often when you write papers, you are required to compose a paper with a minimum number of words. The requirement for the research paper in this project was a minimum of 375 words. Word provides a command that displays the number of words, as well as the number of pages, characters, paragraphs, and lines in your document. The following steps show how to use word count and display the Word Count toolbar, which allows you easily to recount words as you type more text.

To Count Words

1 Click Tools on the menu bar and then point to Word Count (Figure 2-41).

2 Click Word Count. When the Word Count dialog box displays, if necessary, click Include footnotes and endnotes to place a check mark in the check box. Click the Show Toolbar button.

Word displays the Word Count dialog box (Figure 2-42). The Word Count toolbar displays floating in the Word window.

3 Click the Close button in the Word Count dialog box.

Word removes the Word Count dialog box from the screen, but the Word Count toolbar remains on the screen (shown in Figure 2-43).

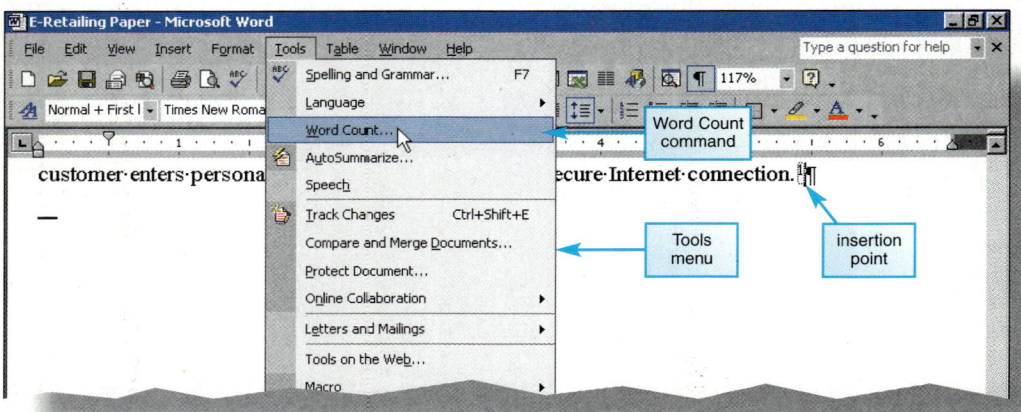

FIGURE 2-41

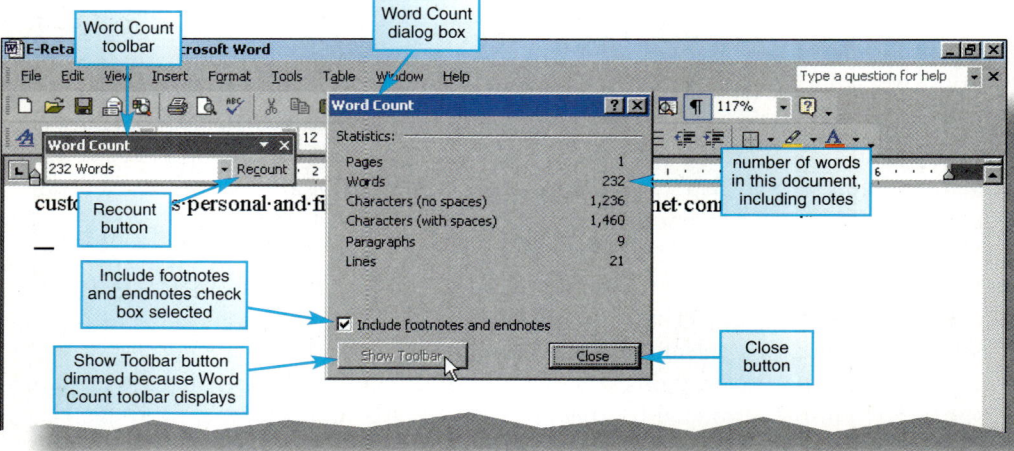

FIGURE 2-42

The Word Count dialog box presents a variety of statistics about the current document, including number of pages, words, characters, paragraphs, and lines (Figure 2-42). You can choose to have note text included or not included in these statistics. If you want statistics on only a section of the document, select the section and then issue the Word Count command.

At anytime, you can recount the number of words in a document by clicking the Recount button on the Word Count toolbar. The Word Count toolbar floats on the screen. As discussed earlier in this project, you can move a floating toolbar by dragging its title bar.

Word Count

You also can display statistics about a document by clicking File on the menu bar, clicking Properties, and then clicking the Statistics tab. The information in this tabbed sheet, however, does not include words and characters in the footnotes or endnotes.

Automatic Page Breaks

As you type documents that exceed one page, Word automatically inserts page breaks, called **automatic page breaks** or **soft page breaks**, when it determines the text has filled one page according to paper size, margin settings, line spacing, and other settings. If you add text, delete text, or modify text on a page, Word recomputes the position of automatic page breaks and adjusts them accordingly.

Word performs page recomputation between the keystrokes, that is, in between the pauses in your typing. Thus, Word refers to the automatic page break task as **background repagination**. In normal view, automatic page breaks display on the Word screen as a single dotted horizontal line. The following step illustrates Word's automatic page break feature.

Steps To Page Break Automatically

1 **With the insertion point positioned as shown in Figure 2-41, press the SPACEBAR and then type the last two sentences of the third paragraph of the paper. Press the ENTER key and then type the fourth paragraph. Italicize the text in the parenthetical citation.**

As you type, Word places an automatic page break between the third and fourth paragraphs in the paper (Figure 2-43). The status bar now displays Page 2 as the current page.

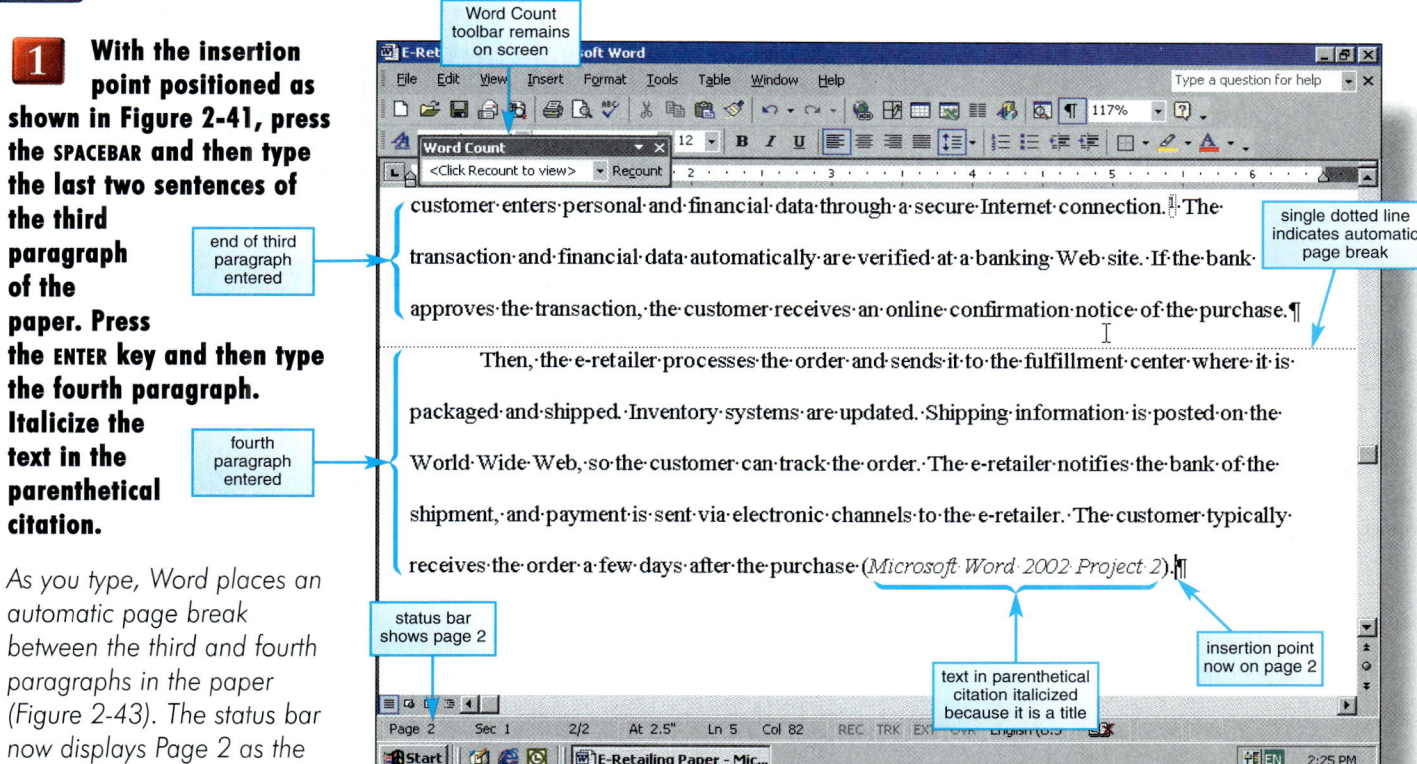

FIGURE 2-43

More About

Word Count Toolbar

You can move the Word Count toolbar anywhere on the screen by dragging its title bar.

Your page break may occur at a different location, depending on the type of printer connected to the computer.

The header, although not shown in normal view, contains the name Marcott and the page number 2. If you wanted to view the header, click View on the menu bar and then click Header and Footer. Then, click the Close Header and Footer button on the Header and Footer toolbar to return to normal view.

Recounting Words in a Document

As soon as you type the last paragraph of the body of the paper, you want to recount the number of words to see if you have met the minimum number of words requirement. Perform the following steps to use the Word Count toolbar to recount words in a document.

Steps To Recount Words

1 Press the ENTER key. Type the last paragraph of the research paper as shown in Figure 2-44. Click the Recount button on the Word Count toolbar.

The Word Count toolbar displays the number of words in the document. You can close the Word Count toolbar because the research paper contains the required minimum number of words.

2 Click the Close button on the Word Count toolbar.

Word removes the Word Count toolbar from the screen.

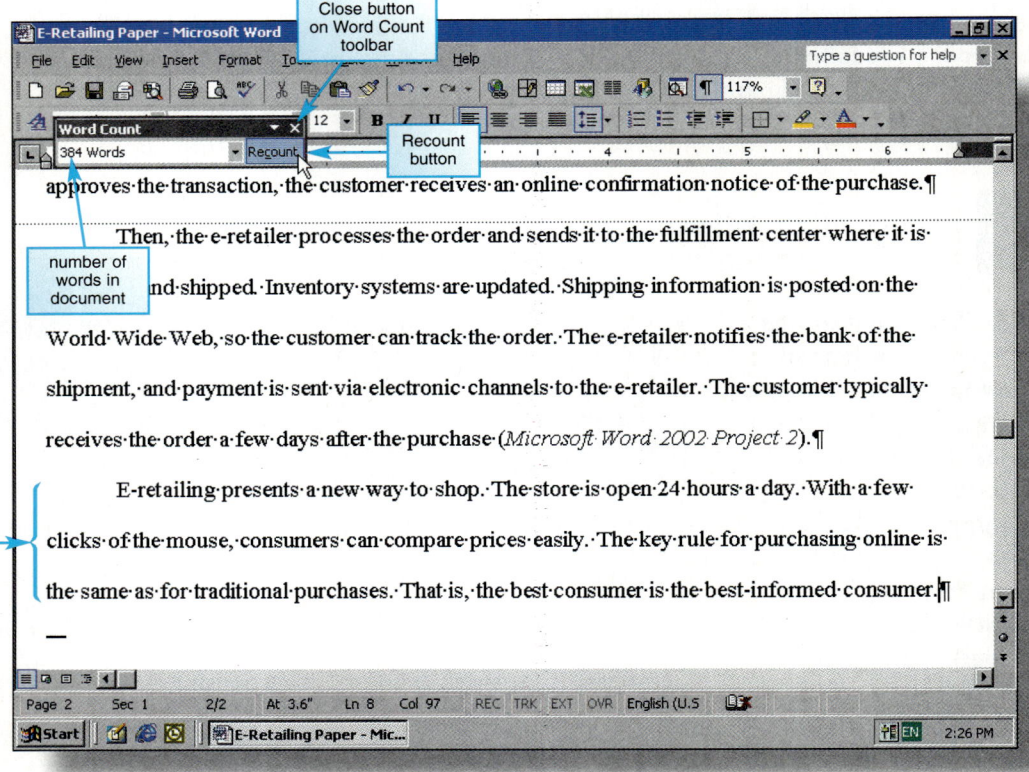

FIGURE 2-44

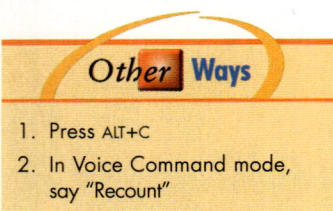

Other Ways

1. Press ALT+C
2. In Voice Command mode, say "Recount"

Creating an Alphabetical Works Cited Page

According to the MLA style, the **works cited page** is a bibliographical list of works that are referenced directly in the research paper. Place the list on a separate numbered page with the title, Works Cited, centered one inch from the top margin.

Creating an Alphabetical Works Cited Page • WD 2.35

The works are to be alphabetized by the author's last name or, if the work has no author, by the work's title. The first line of each entry begins at the left margin. Indent subsequent lines of the same entry one-half inch from the left margin.

The first step in creating the works cited page is to force a page break so the works cited display on a separate page.

Manual Page Breaks

The works cited are to display on a separate numbered page. Thus, you must insert a manual page break following the body of the research paper. A **manual page break**, or **hard page break**, is one that you force into the document at a specific location. Manual page breaks display on the screen as a horizontal dotted line, separated by the words, Page Break. Word never moves or adjusts manual page breaks; however, Word does adjust any automatic page breaks that follow a manual page break. Word inserts manual page breaks just before the location of the insertion point.

Perform the following step to insert a manual page break after the body of the research paper.

Bibliographical References

The MLA documentation style uses the title, Works Cited, for the page containing bibliographical references, whereas the APA style uses the title, References. APA guidelines for preparing the reference list entries differ significantly from the MLA style. Refer to an APA handbook or the Web for specifics.

Steps: To Page Break Manually

 **With the insertion point at the end of the research paper, press the ENTER key. Then, press CTRL+ENTER.**

The shortcut keys, CTRL+ENTER, instruct Word to insert a manual page break immediately above the insertion point and position the insertion point immediately below the manual page break (Figure 2-45). The status bar indicates the insertion point now is located on page 3.

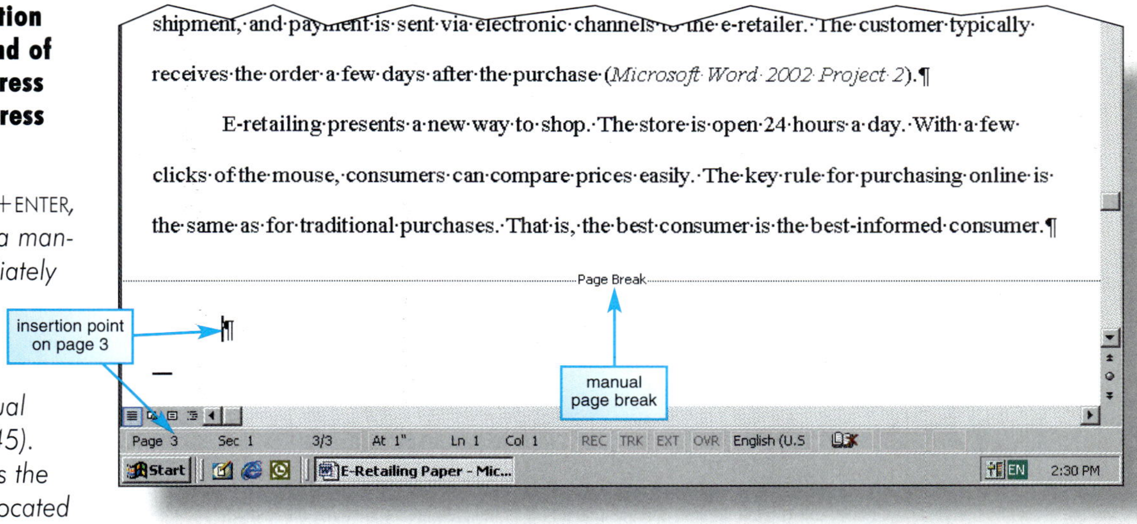

FIGURE 2-45

The manual page break displays as a horizontal dotted line with the words, Page Break, in the middle of the line. The header, although not shown in normal view, contains the name Marcott and the page number 3. If you wanted to view the header, click View on the menu bar and then click Header and Footer. Then, click the Close Header and Footer button on the Header and Footer toolbar to return to normal view.

If, for some reason, you wanted to remove a manual page break from your document, you must first select it by double-clicking it. Then, press the DELETE key; or click the Cut button on the Standard toolbar; or right-click the selection and then click Cut on the shortcut menu.

Other Ways

1. On Insert menu click Break, click Page break, click OK button
2. In Voice Command mode, say "Insert, Break, OK"

Centering the Title of the Works Cited Page

The works cited title is to be centered between the margins. If you simply click the Center button on the Formatting toolbar, the title will not be centered properly. Instead, it will be one-half inch to the right of the center point because earlier you set first-line indent at one-half inch. That is, Word indents the first line of every paragraph one-half inch. To properly center the title of the works cited page, you must move the First Line Indent marker back to the left margin before clicking the Center button as described in the following steps.

TO CENTER THE TITLE OF THE WORKS CITED PAGE

1. Drag the First Line Indent marker to the 0" mark on the ruler.
2. Click the Center button on the Formatting toolbar.
3. Type Works Cited as the title.
4. Press the ENTER key.
5. Because your fingers already are on the keyboard, press CTRL+L to left-align the paragraph mark.

The title displays centered properly, and the insertion point is left-aligned (Figure 2-46).

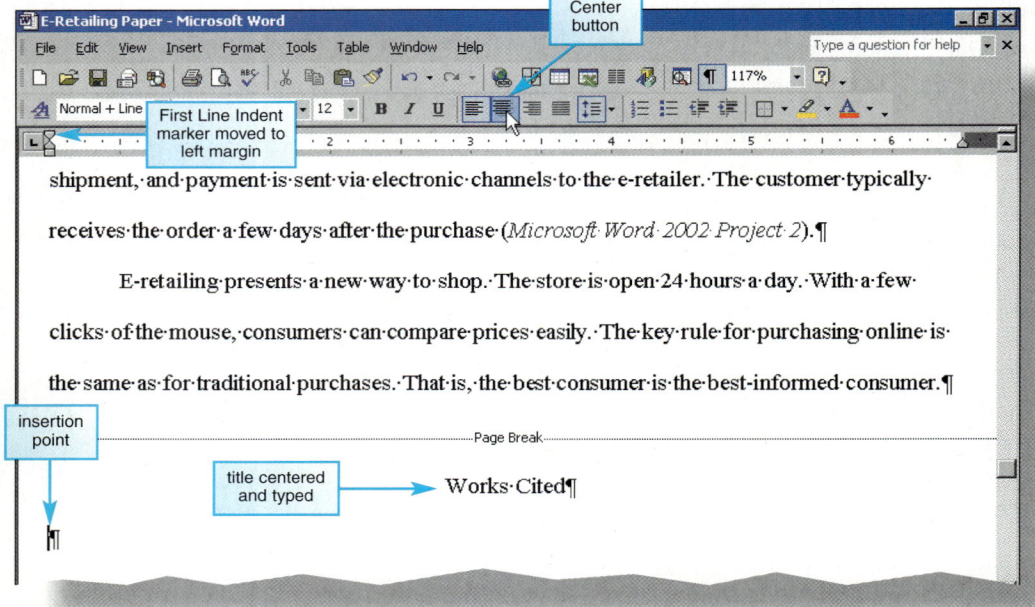

FIGURE 2-46

More About

Reveal Formatting

To see a list of formatting that has been applied to text in a document, select the text, click Format on the menu bar, and then click Reveal Formatting to display the Reveal Formatting task pane. To change a format applied to the selected text, click the blue link in the Reveal Formatting task pane and then change the format in the dialog box that displays.

More About

Crediting Sources

When writing a research paper, you must acknowledge sources of information. Citing sources is a matter of ethics and honesty. Use caution when summarizing or paraphrasing a source. Do not plagiarize, which includes using someone else's words or ideas and claiming them as your own.

Creating a Hanging Indent

On the works cited page, the first line of each entry begins at the left margin. Subsequent lines in the same paragraph are indented one-half inch from the left margin. In essence, the first line hangs to the left of the rest of the paragraph; thus, this type of paragraph formatting is called a **hanging indent**.

One method of creating a hanging indent is to use the horizontal ruler. The **Hanging Indent marker** is the bottom triangle at the 0" mark on the ruler (Figure 2-47). As discussed earlier in this project, the small square at the 0" mark is called the Left Indent marker. Perform the following steps to create a hanging indent.

Steps To Create a Hanging Indent

1 With the insertion point in the paragraph to format (Figure 2-46), point to the Hanging Indent marker on the ruler (Figure 2-47).

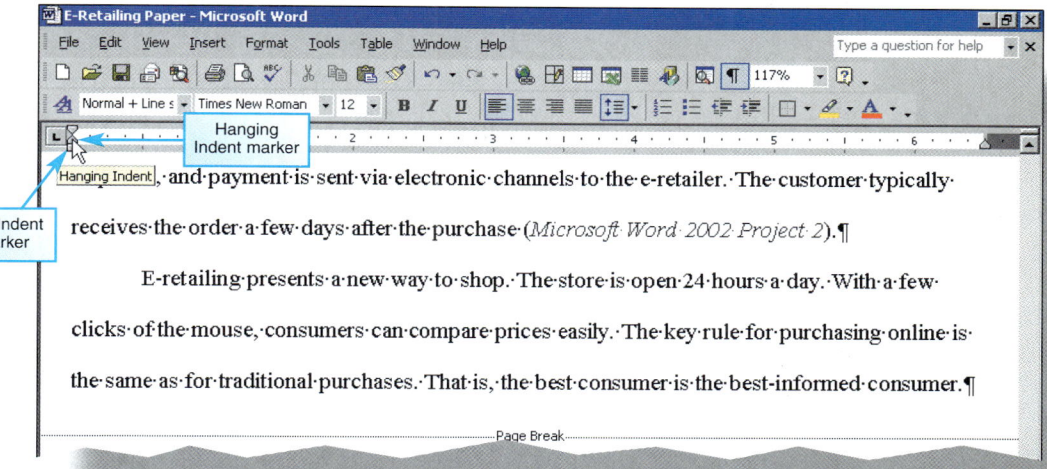

FIGURE 2-47

2 Drag the Hanging Indent marker to the .5" mark on the ruler.

The Hanging Indent marker and Left Indent marker display one-half inch from the left margin (Figure 2-48). When you drag the Hanging Indent marker, the Left Indent marker moves with it. The insertion point in the document window remains at the left margin because only subsequent lines in the paragraph are to be indented.

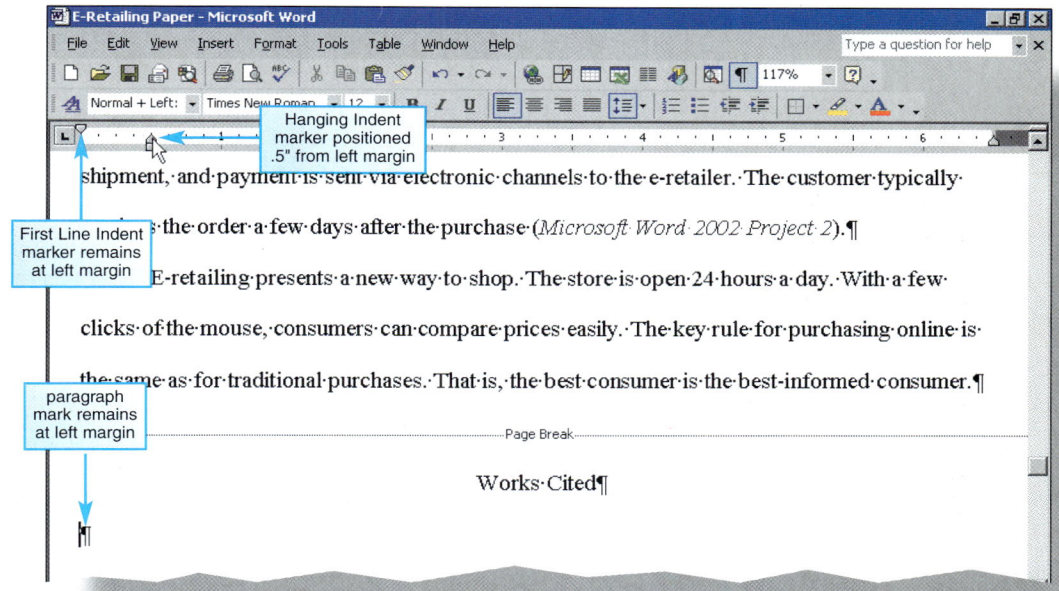

FIGURE 2-48

To drag both the First Line Indent and Hanging Indent markers at the same time, you drag the Left Indent marker on the ruler.

Enter two of the works in the works cited as explained in the following steps.

TO ENTER WORKS CITED PARAGRAPHS

1 Type Sanchez, Jesse R. "E-Retailing: Shop 24 Hours a Day." Press the SPACEBAR. Press CTRL+I to turn on italics. Type Exploring the Wide World of the Internet and then press CTRL+I to turn off italics. Press the SPACEBAR. Type Sep. 2003: 15-36. Press the ENTER key.

Other Ways

1. On Format menu click Paragraph, click Indents and Spacing tab, click Special box arrow, click Hanging, click OK button
2. Press CTRL+T
3. In Voice Command mode, say "Format, Paragraph, Indents and Spacing, Special, Hanging, OK"

2. Type Bodini, Natalie C., and Jack R. Hampton. Press the SPACEBAR. Press CTRL+I to turn on italics. Type An Introduction to the Internet and the Web. Press CTRL+I to turn off italics. Press the SPACEBAR. Type Boston: Star Publishing, 2003. Press the ENTER key.

Two of the works cited paragraphs are entered (Figure 2-49).

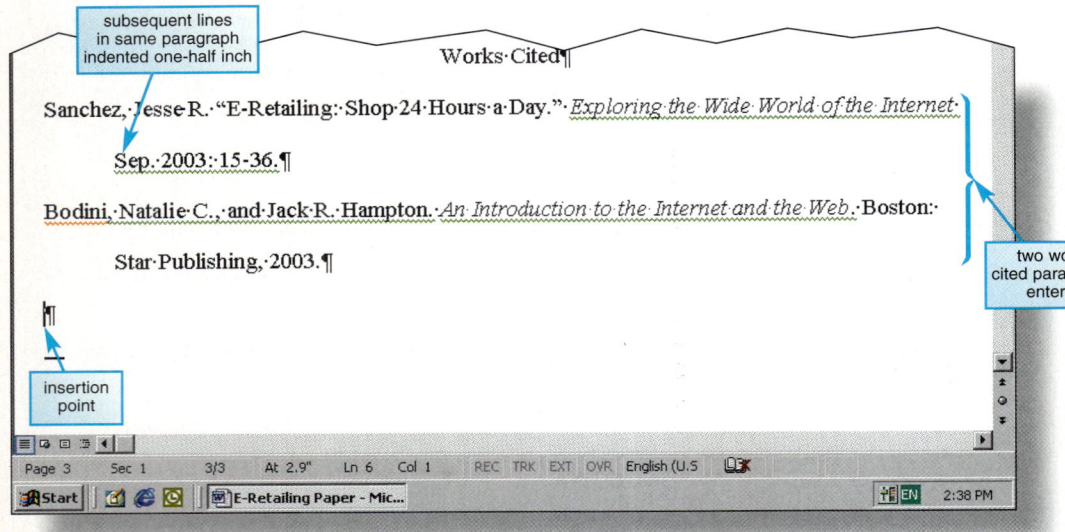

FIGURE 2-49

When Word wraps the text in each works cited paragraph, it automatically indents the second line of the paragraph by one-half inch. When you press the ENTER key at the end of the first paragraph of text, the insertion point returns automatically to the left margin for the next paragraph. Recall that each time you press the ENTER key, Word carries forward the paragraph formatting from the previous paragraph to the next paragraph.

Inserting Arrows, Faces, and Other Symbols Automatically

As discussed earlier in this project, Word has predefined many commonly misspelled words, which it automatically corrects for you as you type. In addition to words, this built-in list of **AutoCorrect entries** also contains some commonly used symbols. For example, to insert a smiling face into a document, you type :) and Word automatically changes it to ☺. Table 2-3 lists the characters you type to insert arrows, faces, and other symbols into a Word document.

You also can enter the first four symbols in Table 2-3 and other symbols by clicking Insert on the menu bar, clicking Symbol, clicking the Special Characters tab, clicking the desired symbol in the Character list, clicking the Insert button, and then clicking the Close button in the Symbol dialog box.

As discussed earlier in this project, if you do not like a change that Word automatically makes in a document and you immediately notice the automatic correction, you can undo the change by clicking the Undo button on the Standard toolbar; clicking Edit on the menu bar and then clicking Undo; or pressing CTRL+Z.

If you do not immediately notice the change, you can undo a correction automatically made by Word through the AutoCorrect Options button. Figures 2-24 and 2-25 on page WD 2.22 illustrated how to display and use the AutoCorrect Options button.

The next step in the research paper is to enter text that uses the registered trademark symbol. Perform the following steps to insert automatically the registered trademark symbol into the research paper.

Table 2-3	Word's Automatic Symbols	
TO DISPLAY	DESCRIPTION	TYPE
©	copyright symbol	(c)
®	registered trademark symbol	(r)
™	trademark symbol	(tm)
…	ellipsis	...
☺	smiling face	:) or :-)
😐	indifferent face	:| or :-|
☹	frowning face	:(or :-(
→	thin right arrow	-->
←	thin left arrow	<--
⇒	thick right arrow	==>
⇐	thick left arrow	<==
⇔	double arrow	<=>

Creating an Alphabetical Works Cited Page • WD 2.39

Steps To Insert a Symbol Automatically

1 **With the insertion point positioned as shown in Figure 2-49, press CTRL+I to turn on italics. Type** Microsoft Word 2002 Project 2. **Press CTRL+I to turn off italics. Press the SPACEBAR. Type** Shelly Cashman Series(r **as shown in Figure 2-50.**

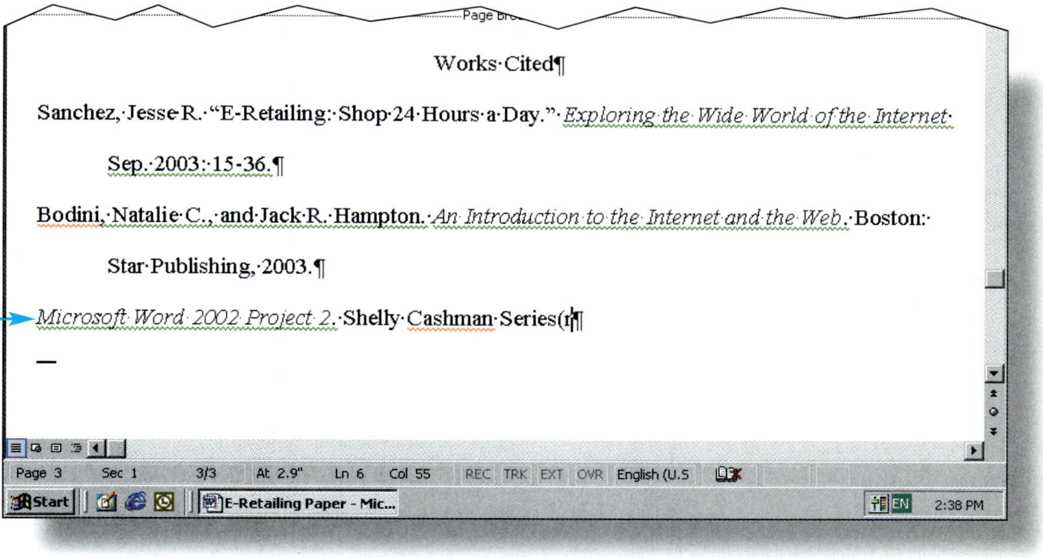

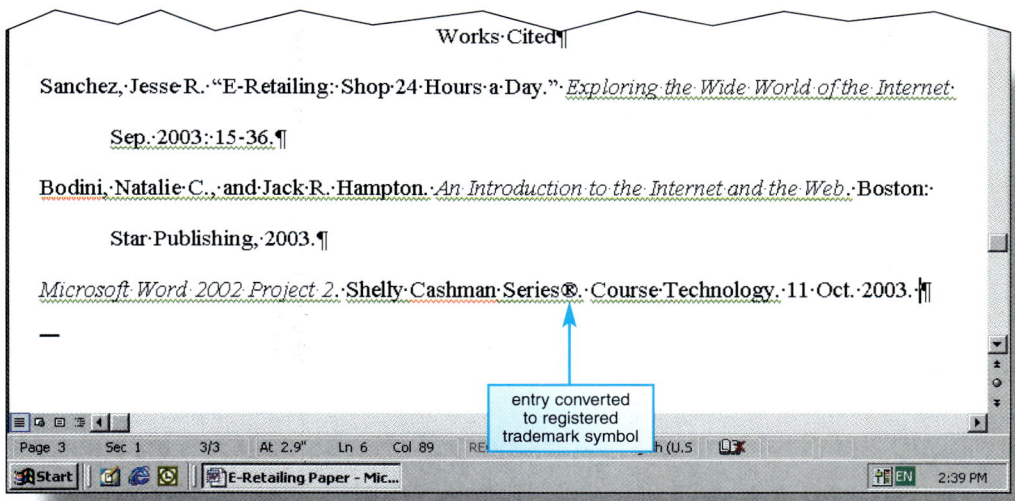

FIGURE 2-50

2 **Press the RIGHT PARENTHESIS key.**

Word automatically converts the (r) to ®, the registered trademark symbol (Figure 2-51).

3 **Press the PERIOD key. Press the SPACEBAR. Type** Course Technology. 11 Oct. 2003. **Press the SPACEBAR.**

FIGURE 2-51

Creating a Hyperlink

In Word, you can create a hyperlink simply by typing the address of the file or Web page to which you want to link and then pressing the SPACEBAR or the ENTER key. A **hyperlink** is a shortcut that allows a user to jump easily and quickly to another location in the same document or to other documents or Web pages. **Jumping** is the process of following a hyperlink to its destination. For example, by clicking a hyperlink in the document window while pressing the CTRL key (called CTRL+clicking), you jump to another document on your computer, on your network, or on the World Wide Web. When you close the hyperlink destination page or document, you return to the original location in your Word document.

More About

Hyperlinks

If Word does not automatically convert your Web addresses to hyperlinks, click Tools on the menu bar, click AutoCorrect Options, click the AutoFormat As You Type tab, place a check mark in the Internet and network paths with hyperlinks check box, and then click the OK button.

In this project, one of the works cited is from a Web page on the Internet. When someone displays your research paper on the screen, you want him or her to be able to CTRL+click the Web address in the work and jump to the associated Web page for more information. If you wish to create a hyperlink to a Web page from a Word document, you do not have to be connected to the Internet. Perform the following steps to create a hyperlink as you type.

Steps To Create a Hyperlink as You Type

1 **With the insertion point positioned as shown in Figure 2-51 on the previous page, type** `http://www.scsite.com/wd2002/pr2/wc.htm.` **as shown in Figure 2-52.**

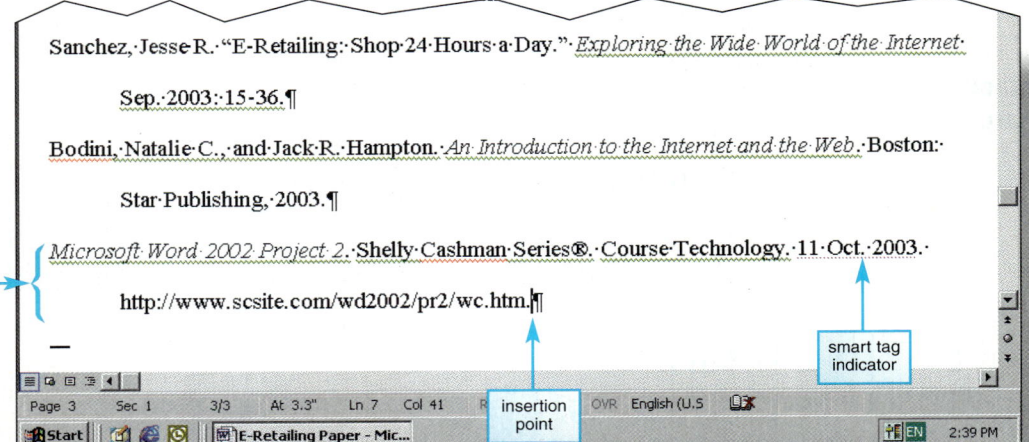

FIGURE 2-52

2 **Press the ENTER key.**

As soon as you press the ENTER key after typing the Web address, Word formats it as a hyperlink (Figure 2-53). That is, the Web address is underlined and colored blue.

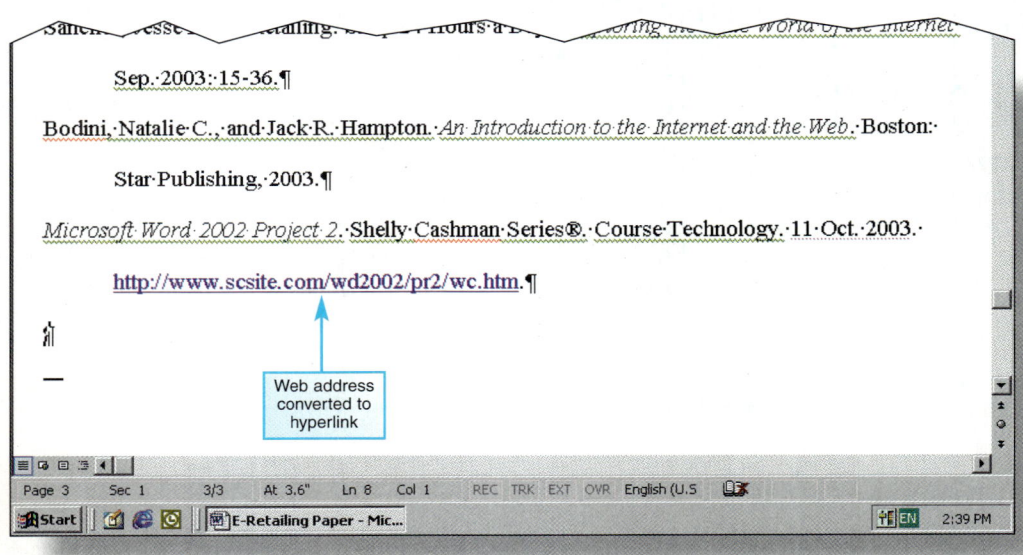

FIGURE 2-53

Other Ways

1. Select text, click Insert Hyperlink button on Standard toolbar, click Existing File or Web Page in the Link to bar, type Web address in Address text box, click OK button
2. Right-click selected text, click Hyperlink on shortcut menu, click Existing File or Web Page in the Link to bar, type Web address in Address text box, click OK button

Later in this project, you will jump to the hyperlink just created.

Sorting Paragraphs

The MLA style requires that the works cited be listed in alphabetical order by the first character in each work. In Word, you can arrange paragraphs in alphabetic, numeric, or date order based on the first character in each paragraph. Ordering characters in this manner is called **sorting**. Perform the following steps to sort the works cited paragraphs.

Steps: To Sort Paragraphs

1 Select all the works cited paragraphs by pointing to the left of the first paragraph and dragging down. Click Table on the menu bar and then point to Sort.

Word displays the Table menu (Figure 2-54). All of the paragraphs to be sorted are selected.

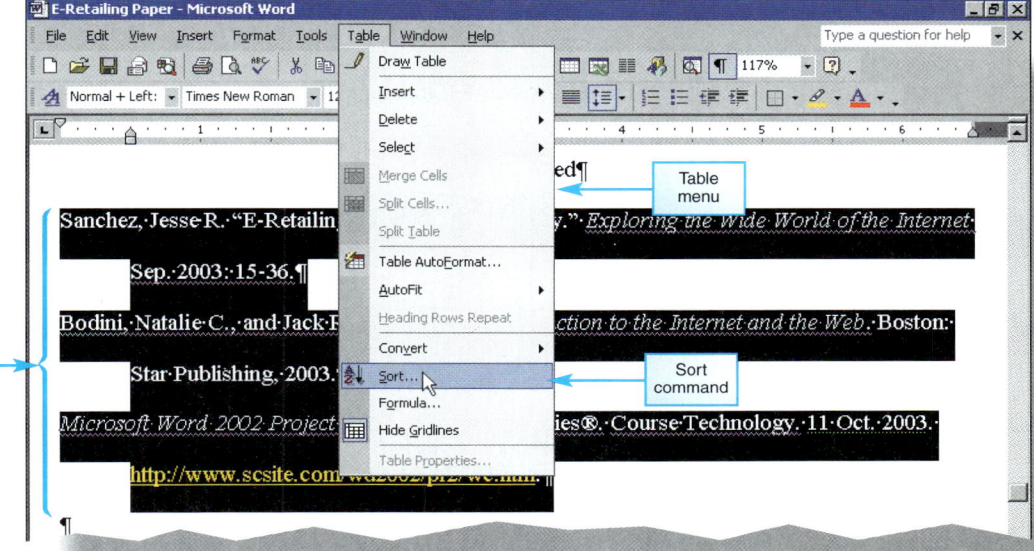

FIGURE 2-54

2 Click Sort. When the Sort Text dialog box displays, point to the OK button.

Word displays the Sort Text dialog box (Figure 2-55). In the Sort by area, Ascending, the default, is selected. Ascending sorts in alphabetic, numeric, or earliest to latest date order.

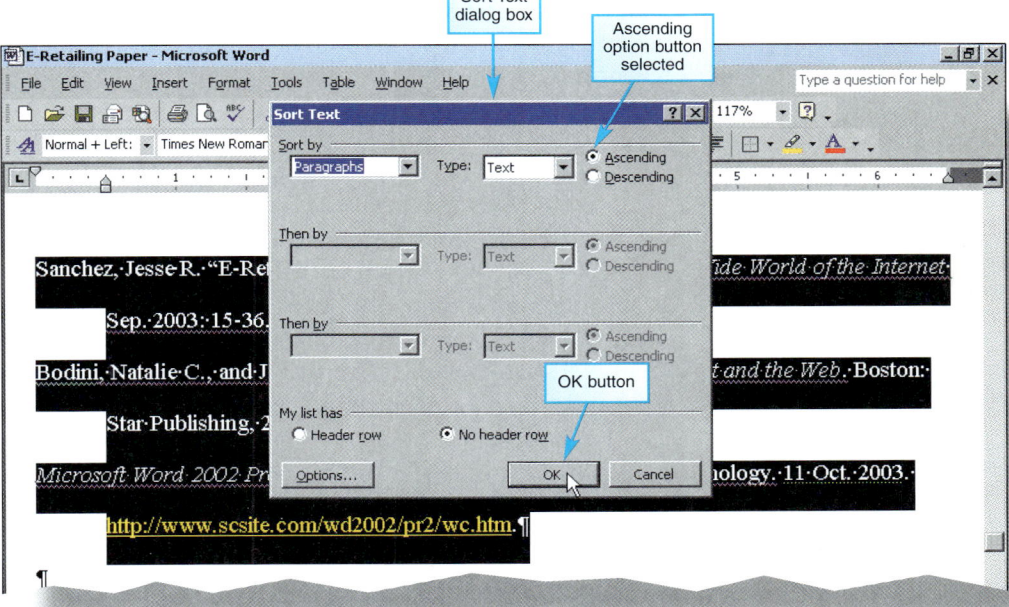

FIGURE 2-55

3 **Click the OK button. Click inside the selected text to remove the selection.**

Word sorts the works cited paragraphs alphabetically (Figure 2-56).

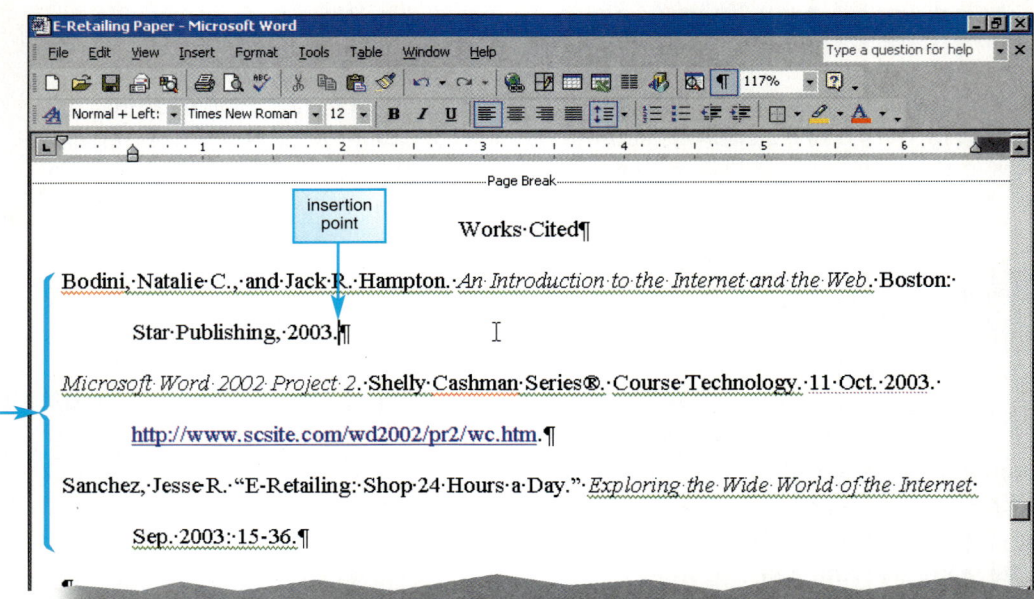

FIGURE 2-56

Other Ways

1. In Voice Command mode, say "Table, Sort, OK"

If you accidentally sort the wrong paragraphs, you can undo a sort by clicking the Undo button on the Standard toolbar.

In the Sort Text dialog box (Figure 2-55 on the previous page), the default sort order is Ascending. By default, Word orders in **ascending sort order**, which means from the beginning of the alphabet to the end of the alphabet, smallest number to the largest number, or earliest date to the most recent date. For example, if the first character of each paragraph to be sorted is a letter, Word sorts the selected paragraphs alphabetically.

You also can sort in descending order by clicking Descending in the Sort Text dialog box. **Descending sort order** means sorting from the end of the alphabet to the beginning of the alphabet, the largest number to the smallest number, or the most recent date to the earliest date.

More About

Proofreading

When proofreading a paper, ask yourself these questions: Is the purpose clear? Does the title suggest the topic? Does the paper have an introduction, body, and conclusion? Is the thesis clear? Does each paragraph in the body relate to the thesis? Is the conclusion effective? Are all sources acknowledged?

Proofing and Revising the Research Paper

As discussed in Project 1, once you complete a document, you might find it necessary to make changes to it. Before submitting a paper to be graded, you should proofread it. While **proofreading**, you look for grammatical errors and spelling errors. You want to be sure the transitions between sentences flow smoothly and the sentences themselves make sense. To assist you in this proofreading effort, Word provides several tools. The following pages discuss these tools.

Going to a Specific Location in a Document

Often, you would like to bring a certain page, footnote, or other object into view in the document window. To accomplish this, you could scroll through the document to find a desired page, footnote, or item. Instead of scrolling through the document, Word provides an easier method of going to a specific location via the Select Browse Object menu. Perform the following steps to go to the top of page two in the research paper.

Steps: To Browse by Page

1 **Click the Select Browse Object button on the vertical scroll bar. When the Select Browse Object menu displays, point to Browse by Page.**

Word displays the Select Browse Object menu (Figure 2-57). As you point to various commands on the Select Browse Object menu, Word displays the command name at the bottom of the menu.

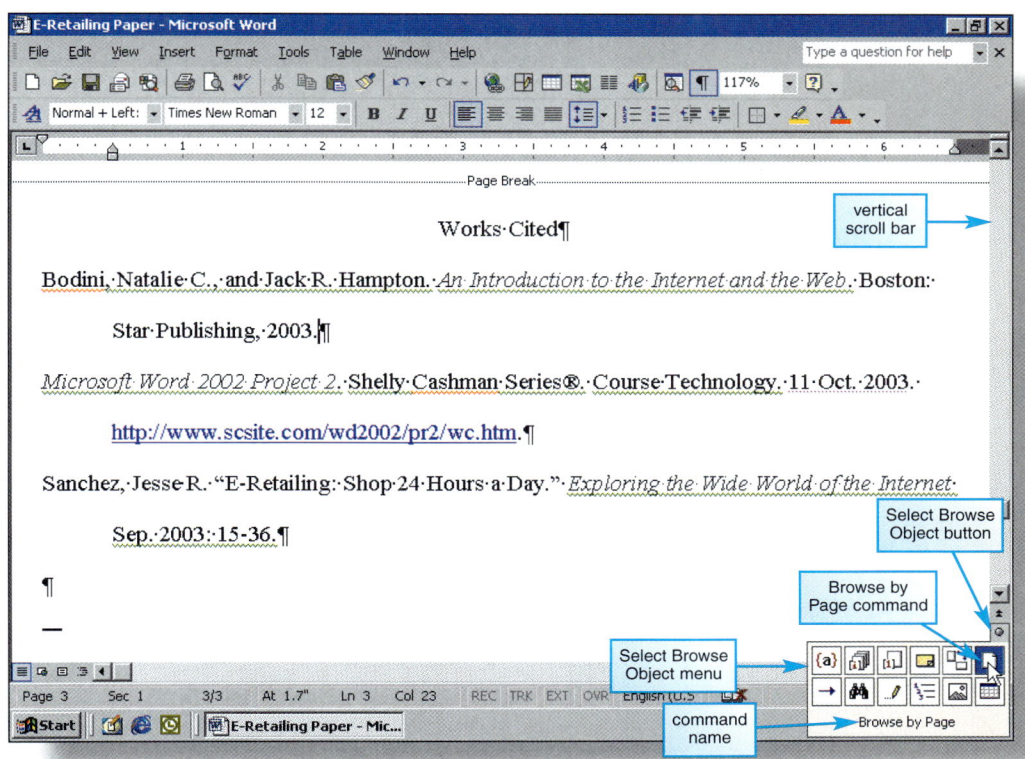

FIGURE 2-57

2 **Click Browse by Page. Point to the Previous Page button on the vertical scroll bar.**

Word closes the Select Browse Object menu and displays the top of page 3 at the top of the document window (Figure 2-58).

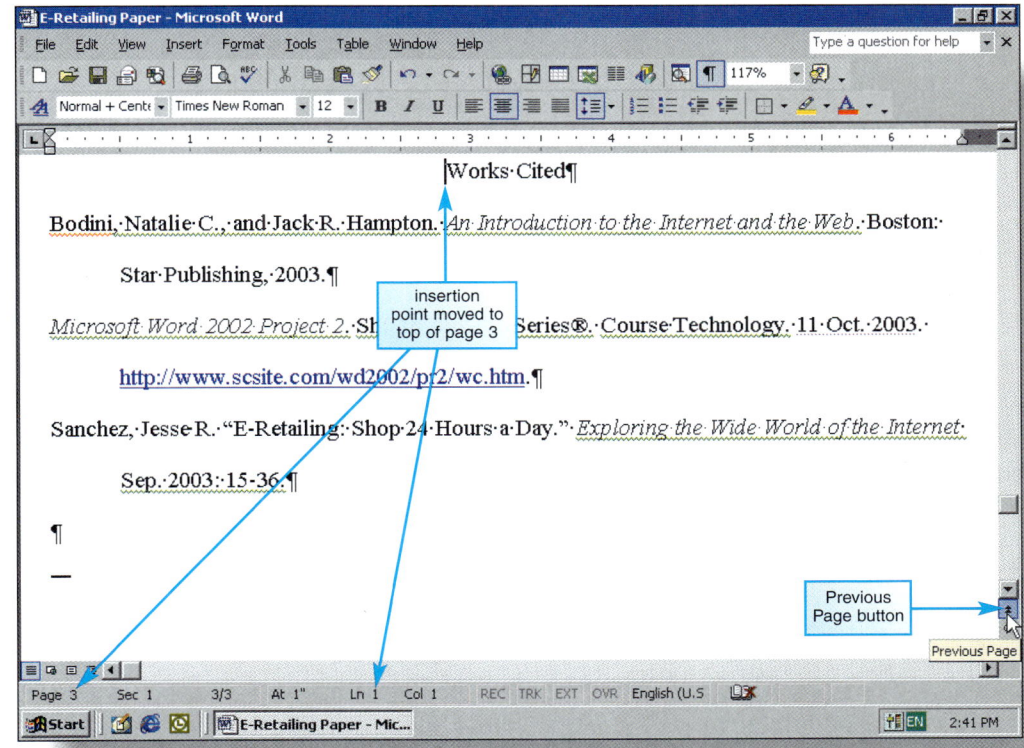

FIGURE 2-58

Click the Previous Page button.

Word places the top of page 2 (the previous page) at the top of the document window (Figure 2-59).

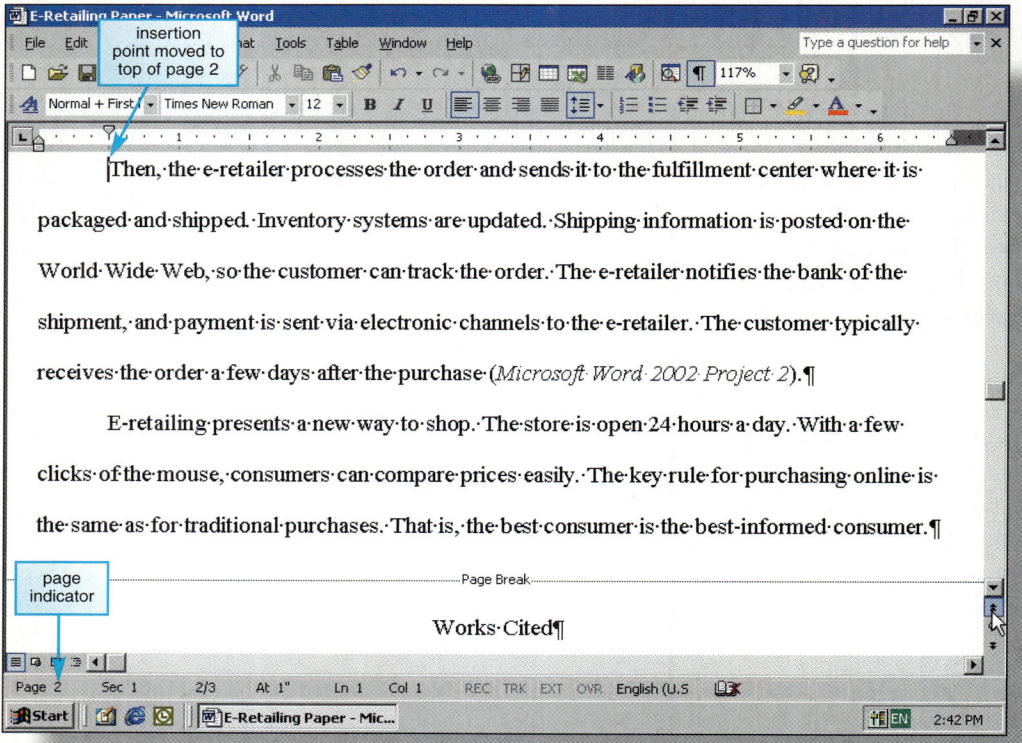

FIGURE 2-59

1. Double-click page indicator on status bar (Figure 2-59), click Page in Go to what list, type page number in Enter page number text box, click Go To button, click Close button
2. On Edit menu click Go To, and then proceed as described in 1 above starting with click Page in Go to what list
3. Press CTRL+G, and then proceed as described in 1 above starting with click Page in Go to what list
4. In Voice Command mode, click "Select Browse Object, Go To, Page, [type page number], Go To, Close"

Depending on the command you click in the Select Browse Object menu, the function of the buttons above and below the Select Browse Object button on the vertical scroll bar changes. When you select Browse by Page, the buttons become Previous Page and Next Page buttons; when you select Browse by Footnote, the buttons become Previous Footnote and Next Footnote buttons, and so on.

Moving Text

While proofreading the research paper, you realize that text in the fourth paragraph would flow better if the fourth sentence was moved so it followed the first sentence. That is, you want to move the fourth sentence so it is the second sentence in the fourth paragraph.

To move text, such as words, characters, sentences, or paragraphs, you first select the text to be moved and then use drag-and-drop editing or the cut-and-paste technique to move the selected text. With **drag-and-drop editing**, you drag the selected item to the new location and then insert, or *drop*, it there. **Cutting** involves removing the selected item from the document and then placing it on the **Clipboard**, which is a temporary Windows storage area. **Pasting** is the process of copying an item from the Clipboard into the document at the location of the insertion point. Project 3 demonstrates cutting and pasting. This project demonstrates using drag-and-drop editing.

To drag-and-drop a sentence in the research paper, first select a sentence as shown in the next step.

Moving Text

When moving text a long distance or between applications, use the Clipboard task pane to cut and paste. (To display the Clipboard task pane, click Edit on the menu bar and then click Office Clipboard.) When moving text a short distance, the drag-and-drop technique is more efficient.

Steps: To Select a Sentence

1 Position the mouse pointer (an I-beam) in the sentence to be moved. Press and hold the CTRL key. While holding the CTRL key, click the sentence. Release the CTRL key.

Word selects the entire sentence (Figure 2-60). Notice that Word includes the space following the period in the selection.

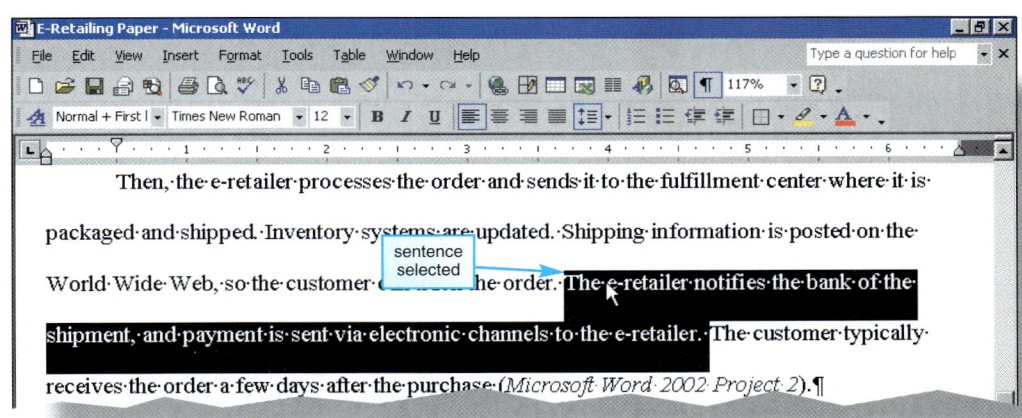

FIGURE 2-60

Other Ways

1. Drag through the sentence
2. With insertion point at beginning of sentence, press CTRL+SHIFT+RIGHT ARROW until sentence is selected
3. In Voice Command mode, say "Select sentence"

In the previous steps and throughout Projects 1 and 2, you have selected text and then formatted it. Table 2-4 summarizes the techniques used to select various items with the mouse.

Table 2-4	Techniques for Selecting Items with the Mouse
ITEM TO SELECT	**MOUSE ACTION**
Block of text	Click at beginning of selection, scroll to end of selection, position mouse pointer at end of selection, hold down SHIFT key and then click; or drag through the text
Character(s)	Drag through character(s)
Document	Move mouse to left of text until mouse pointer changes to a right-pointing block arrow and then triple-click
Graphic	Click the graphic
Line	Move mouse to left of line until mouse pointer changes to a right-pointing block arrow and then click
Lines	Move mouse to left of first line until mouse pointer changes to a right-pointing block arrow and then drag up or down
Paragraph	Triple-click paragraph; or move mouse to left of paragraph until mouse pointer changes to a right-pointing block arrow and then double-click
Paragraphs	Move mouse to left of paragraph until mouse pointer changes to a right-pointing block arrow, double-click and then drag up or down
Sentence	Press and hold CTRL key and then click sentence
Word	Double-click the word
Words	Drag through words

More About

Selecting Text

In Word, you can select non-adjacent text. This is helpful if you want to format multiple items the same way. To select items that are not next to each other (nonadjacent), do the following. Select the first item, such as a word or paragraph, as usual. Press and hold down the CTRL key. While holding down the CTRL key, select any additional items. All selected items display highlighted on the screen.

With the sentence to be moved selected, you can use drag-and-drop editing to move it. You should be sure that drag-and-drop editing is enabled by clicking Tools on the menu bar, clicking Options, clicking the Edit tab, verifying a check mark is next to Drag-and-drop text editing, and then clicking the OK button.

Perform the steps on the next page to move the selected sentence so it becomes the second sentence in the paragraph.

Steps: To Move Text

1 **With the mouse pointer in the selected text, press and hold the mouse button.**

When you begin to drag the selected text, the insertion point changes to a dotted insertion point (Figure 2-61).

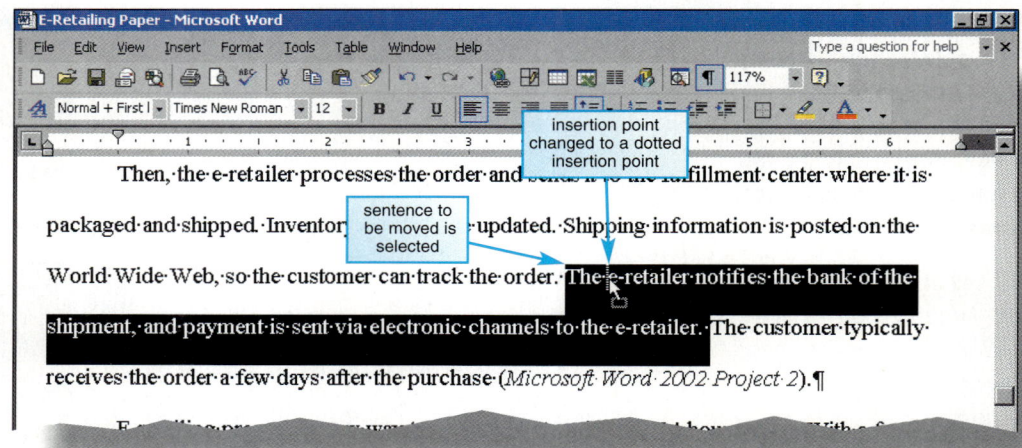

FIGURE 2-61

2 **Drag the dotted insertion point to the location where the selected text is to be moved.**

The dotted insertion point follows the space after the first sentence in the paragraph (Figure 2-62).

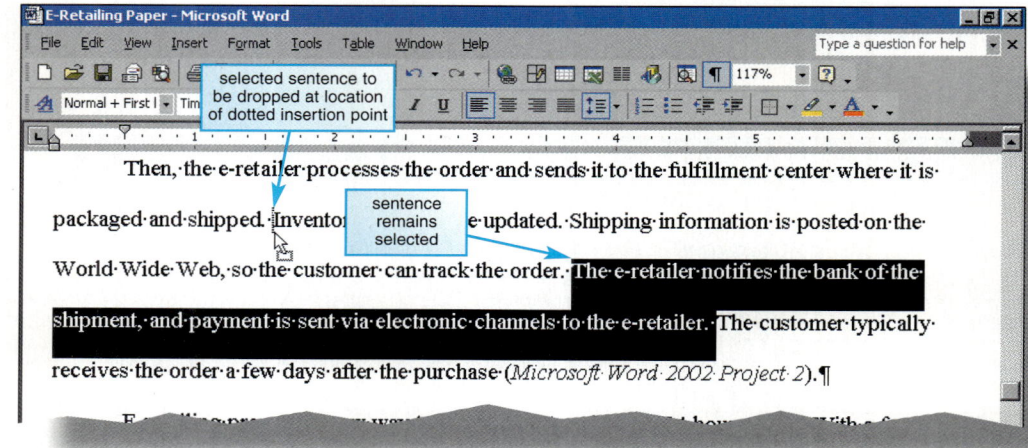

FIGURE 2-62

3 **Release the mouse button. Click outside the selected text to remove the selection.**

Word moves the selected text to the location of the dotted insertion point (Figure 2-63).

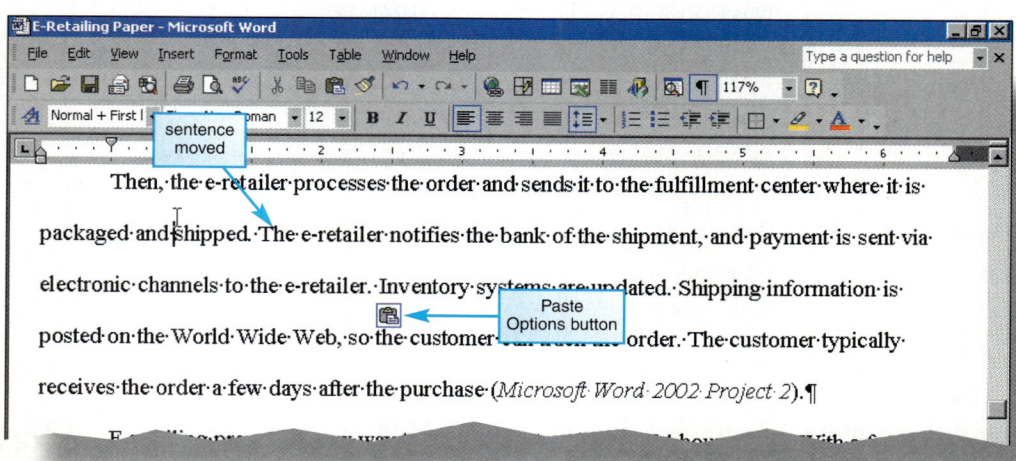

FIGURE 2-63

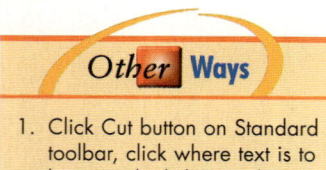

Other Ways

1. Click Cut button on Standard toolbar, click where text is to be pasted, click Paste button on Standard toolbar

If you accidentally drag text to the wrong location, you can click the Undo button on the Standard toolbar.

You can use drag-and-drop editing to move any selected item. That is, you can select words, sentences, phrases, and graphics and then use drag-and-drop editing to move them.

When you drag-and-drop text, Word automatically displays a Paste Options button near the location of the dropped text (Figure 2-63). If you click the **Paste Options button**, a menu displays that allows you to change the format of the text that was moved. The following steps show how to display the Paste Options menu.

More About

Drag-and-Drop

If you hold down the CTRL key while dragging a selected item, Word copies the item instead of moving it.

Steps: To Display the Paste Options Menu

 Click the Paste Options button.

Word displays the Paste Options menu (Figure 2-64).

 Press the ESCAPE key to remove the Paste Options menu from the window.

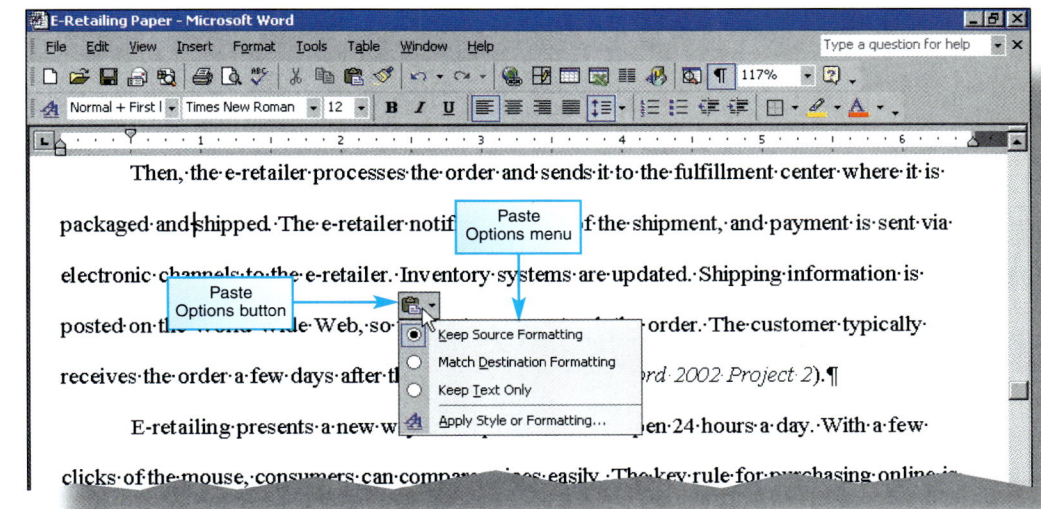

FIGURE 2-64

Smart Tags

A **smart tag** is a button that automatically appears on the screen when Word performs a certain action. In this project, you used two smart tags: AutoCorrect Options (Figures 2-24 and 2-25 on page WD 2.22) and Paste Options (Figure 2-64). In addition to AutoCorrect Options and Paste Options, Word provides other smart tags. Table 2-5 summarizes the smart tags available in Word.

With the AutoCorrect Options and Smart Tag Actions, Word notifies you that the smart tag is available by displaying a **smart tag indicator** on the screen. The smart tag indicator for AutoCorrect Options smart tag is a small blue box. The smart tag

Table 2-5	Smart Tags in Word	
BUTTON	NAME	MENU FUNCTION
	AutoCorrect Options	Undoes an automatic correction, stops future automatic corrections of this type, or displays the AutoCorrect Options dialog box
	Paste Options	Specifies how moved or pasted items should display, e.g., with original formatting, without formatting, or with different formatting
	Smart Tag Actions • Person name	Adds this name to Outlook Contacts folder, sends an e-mail, or schedules a meeting in Outlook Calendar with this person
	• Date or time	Schedules a meeting in Outlook Calendar at this date or time or displays your calendar
	• Address	Adds this address to Outlook Contacts folder or displays a a map or driving directions
	• Place	Adds this place to Outlook Contacts folder or schedules a meeting in Outlook Calendar at this location

Smart Tag Actions

The commands in the Smart Tag Actions menu vary depending on the smart tag. For example, the Smart Tag Actions menu for a date includes commands that allow you to schedule a meeting in Outlook Calendar or display your Outlook Calendar. The Smart Tag Actions menu for an address includes commands for displaying a map of the address or driving directions to or from the address.

indicator for Smart Tag Actions is a purple dotted line, as shown in Figure 2-15 on page WD 2.16. If you want to display a smart tag button, point to the smart tag indicator.

Clicking a smart tag button displays a menu that contains commands relative to the action performed at the location of the smart tag. For example, if you want to add a name in your Word document to the Outlook Contacts folder, point to the purple dotted line below the name to display the Smart Tag Actions button, click the Smart Tag Actions button to display the Smart Tag Actions menu, and then click Add to Contacts on the Smart Tag Actions menu to display the Contacts dialog box in Outlook.

Finding and Replacing Text

While proofreading the paper, you notice that it contains the phrase, World Wide Web, more than once in the document (Figure 2-65). You prefer to use the word, Web. Therefore, you wish to change all occurrences of World Wide Web to just the word, Web. To do this, you can use Word's find and replace feature, which automatically locates each occurrence of a word or phrase and then replaces it with specified text, as shown in these steps.

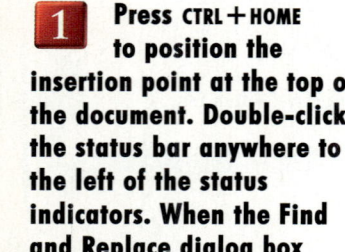

To Find and Replace Text

1 Press CTRL+HOME to position the insertion point at the top of the document. Double-click the status bar anywhere to the left of the status indicators. When the Find and Replace dialog box displays, click the Replace tab. Type World Wide Web in the Find what text box. Press the TAB key. Type Web in the Replace with text box. Point to the Replace All button.

Word displays the Find and Replace dialog box (Figure 2-65). The Replace All button replaces all occurrences of the Find what text with the Replace with text.

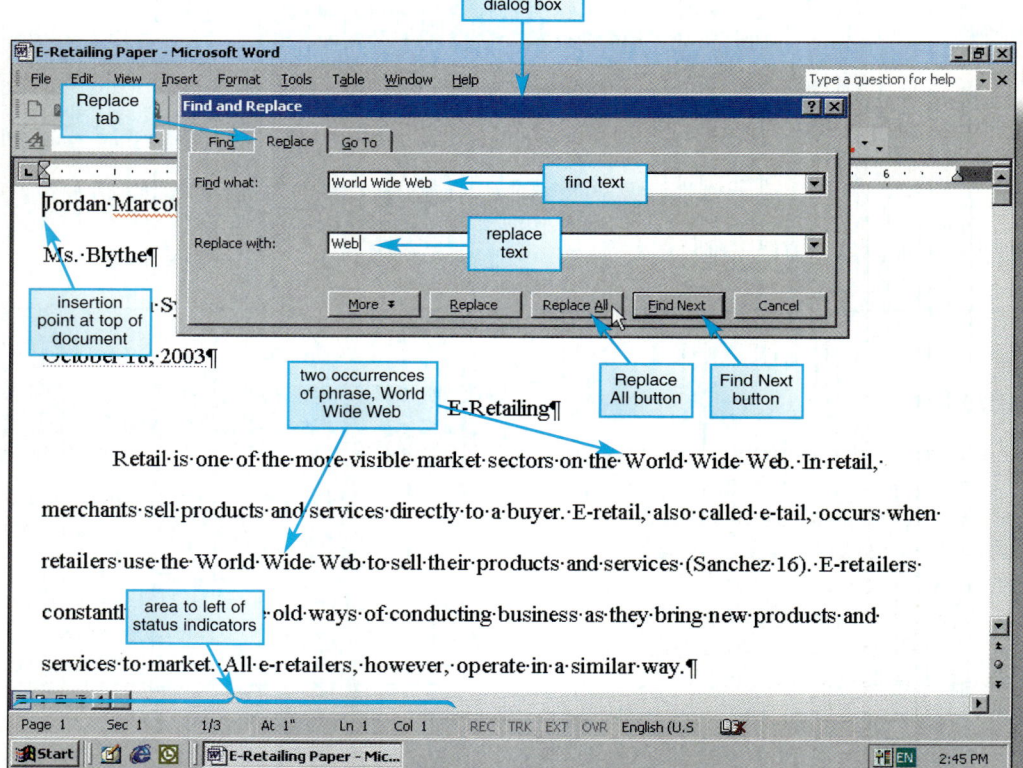

FIGURE 2-65

2 **Click the Replace All button.**

A Microsoft Word dialog box displays indicating the total number of replacements made (Figure 2-66). The word, Web, displays in the document instead of the phrase, World Wide Web.

3 **Click the OK button. Click the Close button in the Find and Replace dialog box.**

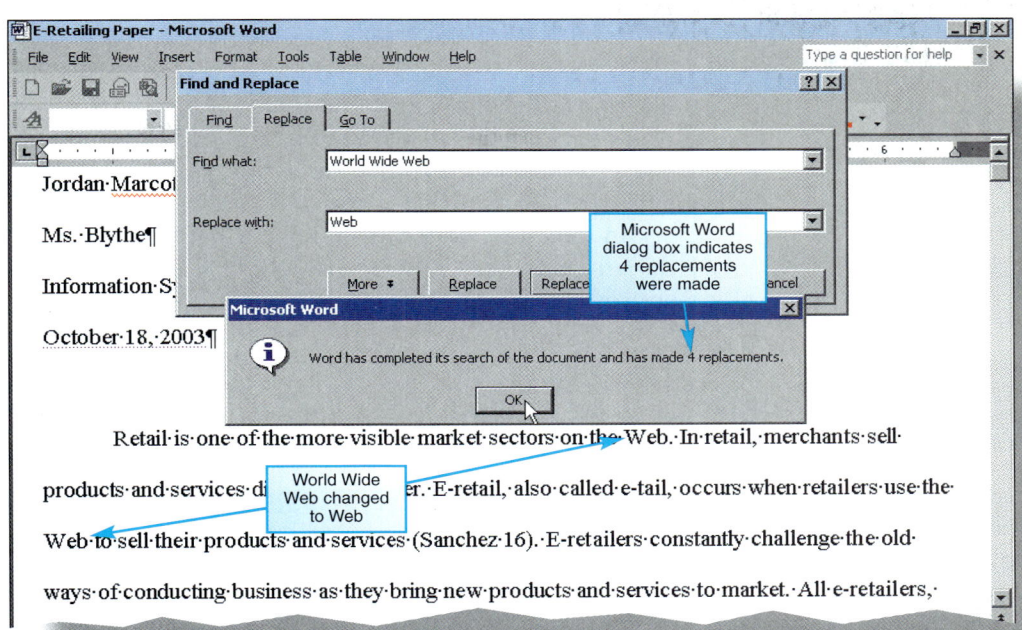

FIGURE 2-66

In some cases, you may want to replace only certain occurrences of the text, not all of them. To instruct Word to confirm each change, click the Find Next button in the Find and Replace dialog box (Figure 2-65), instead of the Replace All button. When Word locates an occurrence of the text, it pauses and waits for you to click either the Replace button or the Find Next button. Clicking the Replace button changes the text; clicking the Find Next button instructs Word to disregard the replacement and look for the next occurrence of the Find what text.

If you accidentally replace the wrong text, you can undo a replacement by clicking the Undo button on the Standard toolbar. If you used the Replace All button, Word undoes all replacements. If you used the Replace button, Word undoes only the most recent replacement.

Finding Text

Sometimes, you may want only to find text, instead of finding *and* replacing text. To search for just a single occurrence of text, you would follow these steps.

TO FIND TEXT

1 Click the Select Browse Object button on the vertical scroll bar and then click Find on the Select Browse Object menu.

2 Type the text to locate in the Find what text box and then click the Find Next button. To edit the text, click the Cancel button in the Find and Replace dialog box; to find the next occurrence of the text, click the Find Next button.

Other Ways

1. Click Select Browse Object button on vertical scroll bar, click Find, click Replace tab, type Find what text, type Replace with text, click Replace All button, click Close button
2. On Edit menu click Replace, and then proceed as described in 1 above starting with type Find what text
3. Press CTRL+H, and then proceed as described in 1 above starting with type Find what text
4. In Voice Command mode, say "Select Browse Object, Find, Replace, [type text to find], Tab, [type text to replace], OK, OK, Close"

More About

Finding

To search for formatting or special characters, click the More button in the Find dialog box. To find formatting, use the Format button in the Find dialog box. To find a special character, use the Special button.

Synonyms

For access to an online thesaurus, visit the Word 2002 More About Web page (scsite.com/wd2002/more.htm) and then click Online Thesaurus.

Finding a Synonym

When writing, you may discover that you used the same word in multiple locations or that a word you used was not quite appropriate. In these instances, you will want to look up a **synonym**, or word similar in meaning, to the duplicate or inappropriate word. A **thesaurus** is a book of synonyms. Word provides synonyms and a thesaurus for your convenience.

In this project, you would like a synonym for the word, way, at the end of the first paragraph of the research paper. Perform the following steps to find an appropriate synonym.

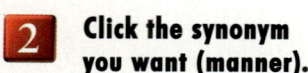

To Find a Synonym

1 **Right-click the word for which you want to find a synonym (way, in this case). Point to Synonyms on the shortcut menu and then point to the appropriate synonym (manner) on the Synonyms submenu.**

Word displays a list of synonyms for the word containing the insertion point (Figure 2-67).

2 **Click the synonym you want (manner).**

Word replaces the word, way, in the document with the selected word, manner (shown in Figure 2-68).

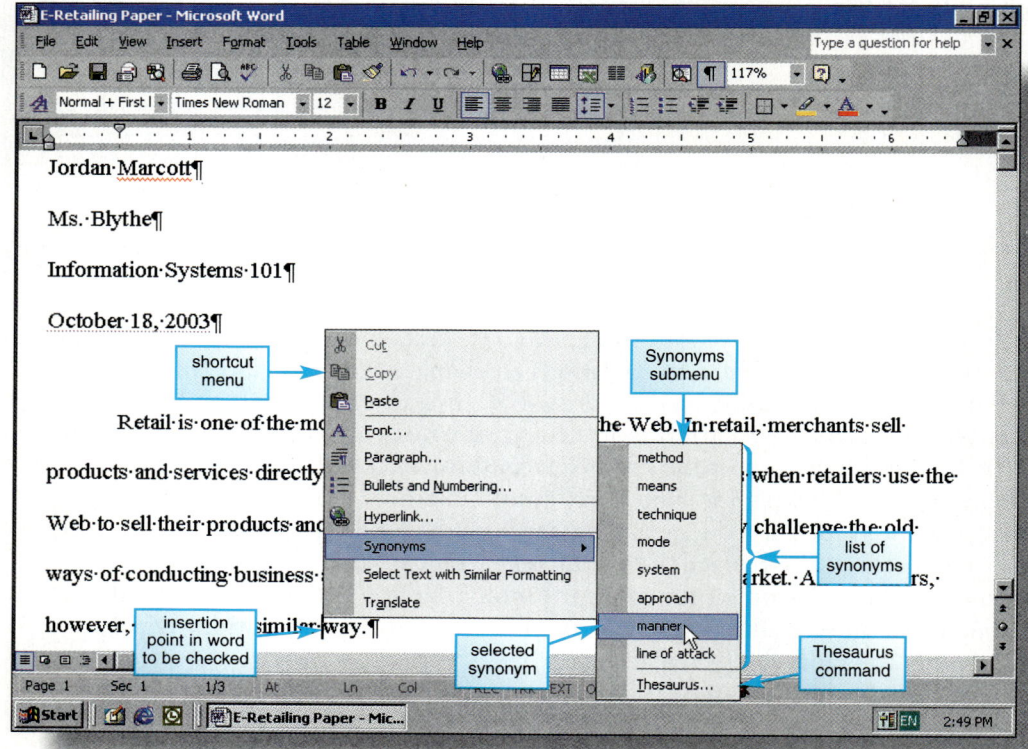

FIGURE 2-67

Other Ways

1. Click word, press SHIFT+F7, click appropriate meaning in Meanings list, click desired synonym in Replace with Synonym list, click Replace button
2. In Voice Command mode, with insertion point in word, say "Right Click, Synonyms, [select synonym]"

If the synonyms list does not display an appropriate word, you can display the Thesaurus dialog box by clicking Thesaurus on the Synonyms submenu (Figure 2-67). In the Thesaurus dialog box, you can look up synonyms for a different meaning of the word. You also can look up an **antonym**, or word with an opposite meaning.

Checking Spelling and Grammar At Once

As discussed in Project 1, Word checks your spelling and grammar as you type and places a wavy underline below possible spelling or grammar errors. Project 1 illustrated how to check these flagged words immediately. As an alternative, you can wait and check the entire document for spelling and grammar errors at once.

Proofing and Revising the Research Paper • WD 2.51

The following steps illustrate how to check spelling and grammar in the E-Retailing Paper at once. In the following example the word, constantly, has been misspelled intentionally as constenty to illustrate the use of Word's check spelling and grammar at once feature. If you are completing this project on a personal computer, your research paper may contain different misspelled words, depending on the accuracy of your typing.

> **More About**
>
> **Flagged Words**
>
> If you right-click a word, a shortcut menu displays. Commands in a shortcut menu vary depending on the object you right-click. If you right-click a word flagged with a red or green wavy underline, the shortcut menu displays spelling or grammar corrections for the flagged word.

Steps: To Check Spelling and Grammar At Once

1 Press CTRL+HOME to move the insertion point to the beginning of the document. Point to the Spelling and Grammar button on the Standard toolbar.

When you click the Spelling and Grammar button, Word will begin the spelling and grammar check at the location of the insertion point, which is at the beginning of the document (Figure 2-68).

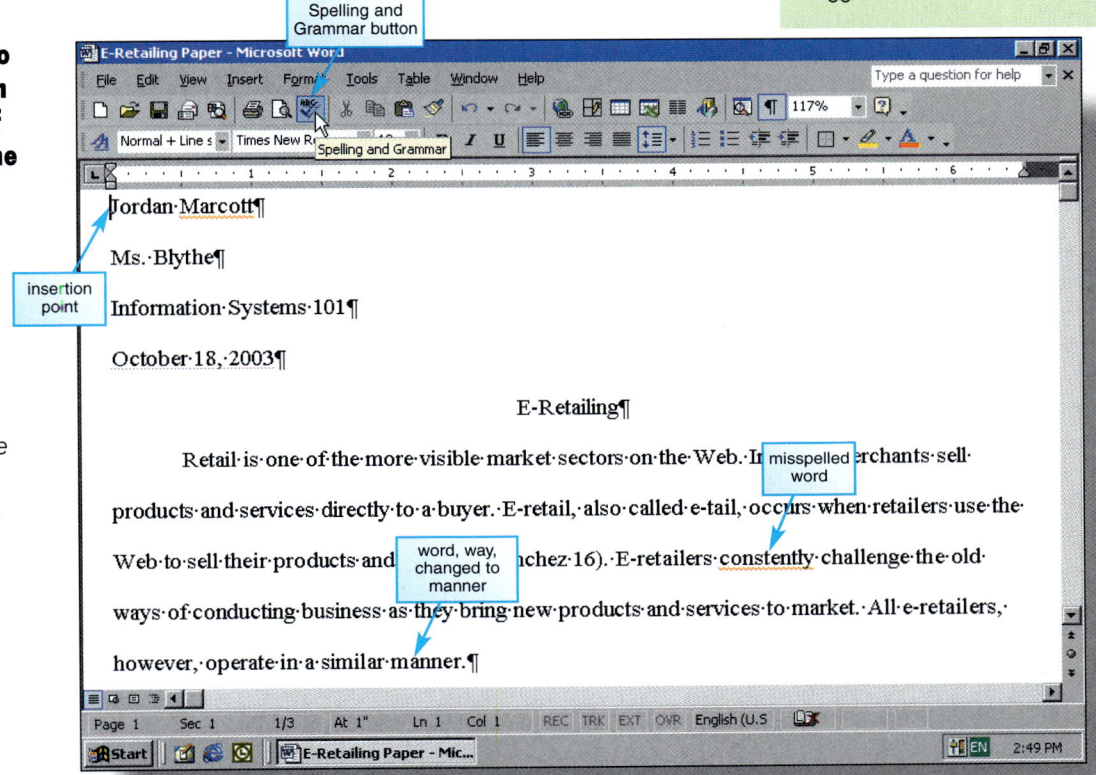

FIGURE 2-68

2 Click the Spelling and Grammar button. When the Spelling and Grammar dialog box displays, point to the Ignore All button.

Word displays the Spelling and Grammar dialog box (Figure 2-69). Word did not find Marcott in its dictionary because Marcott is a proper name. Marcott is spelled correctly.

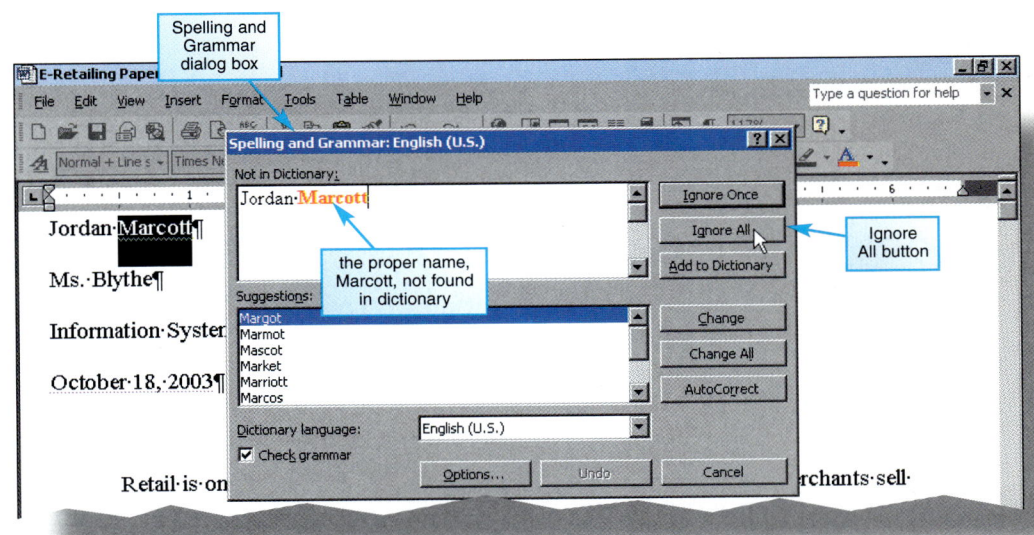

FIGURE 2-69

 **Click the Ignore All button. When Word flags the misspelled word, constently, point to the Change button.**

Word continues the spelling and grammar check until it finds the next error or reaches the end of the document (Figure 2-70). Word did not find the misspelled word, constently, in its dictionary. The Suggestions list displays suggested corrections for the flagged word.

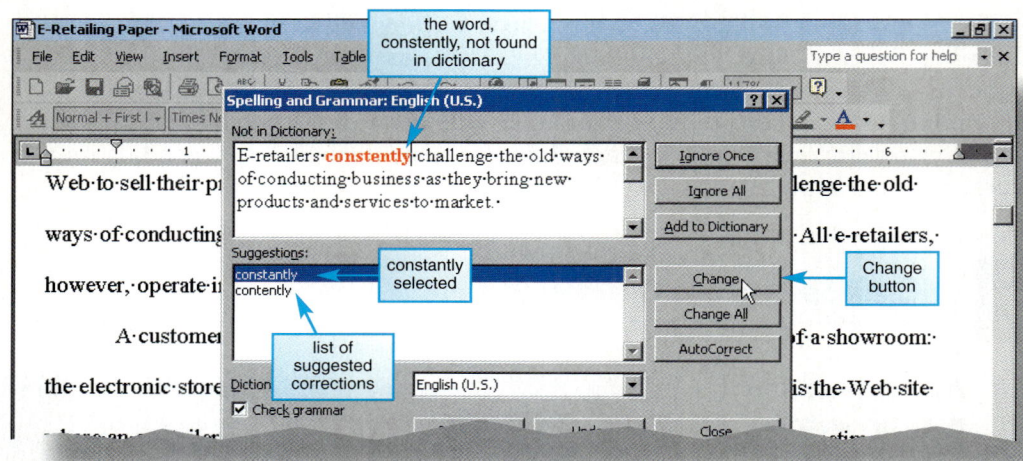

FIGURE 2-70

 **Click the Change button.**

Word corrects the misspelled word and then flags an error on the Works Cited page (Figure 2-71).

Click the Ignore Once button for each grammar error that Word flags on the Works Cited page. When Word has completed the spelling and grammar check, click the OK button to close the dialog box.

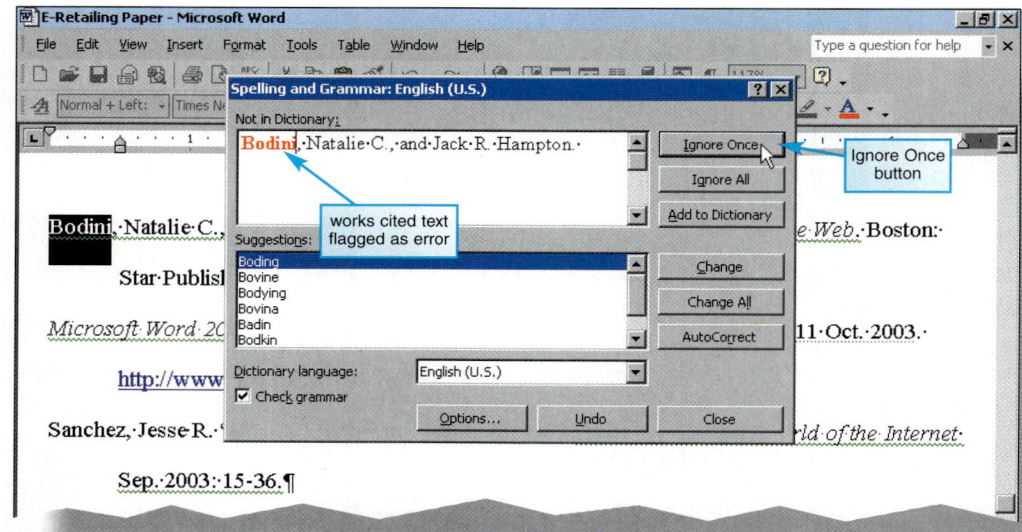

FIGURE 2-71

Other Ways

1. On Tools menu click Spelling and Grammar
2. Right-click flagged word, click Spelling on shortcut menu
3. Press F7
4. In Voice Command mode, say "Spelling and Grammar"

Your document no longer displays red and green wavy underlines below words and phrases. In addition, the red X on the Spelling and Grammar Status icon has returned to a red check mark.

Saving Again and Printing the Document

The document now is complete. You should save the research paper again and print it, as described in the following steps.

TO SAVE A DOCUMENT AGAIN AND PRINT IT

1 Click the Save button on the Standard toolbar and then click the Print button.

Word saves the research paper with the same file name, E-Retailing Paper. The completed research paper prints as shown in Figure 2-1 on page WD 2.05.

Navigating to a Hyperlink

Recall that a requirement of this research paper is that one of the works be a Web page and be formatted as a hyperlink. Perform the following steps to check your hyperlink.

Steps: To Navigate to a Hyperlink

1 **Display the third page of the research paper in the document window and then point to the hyperlink.**

When you point to a hyperlink in a Word document, a ScreenTip displays above the hyperlink (Figure 2-72).

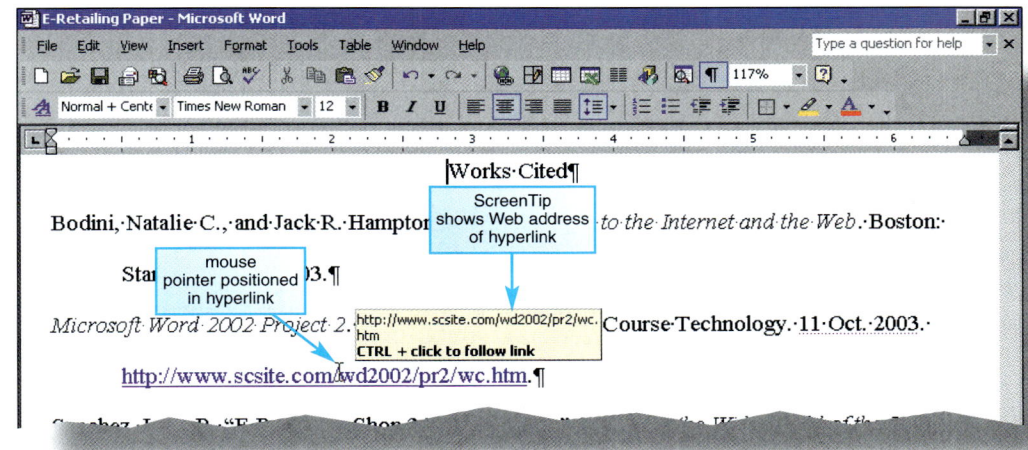

FIGURE 2-72

2 **While holding the CTRL key, click the hyperlink. Release the CTRL key.**

If you currently are not connected to the Web, Word connects you using your default browser. The www.scsite.com/wd2002/pr2/wc.htm Web page displays (Figure 2-73).

3 **Close the browser window. If necessary, click the Microsoft Word program button on the taskbar to redisplay the Word window. Press CTRL+HOME.**

The first page of the research paper displays in the Word window.

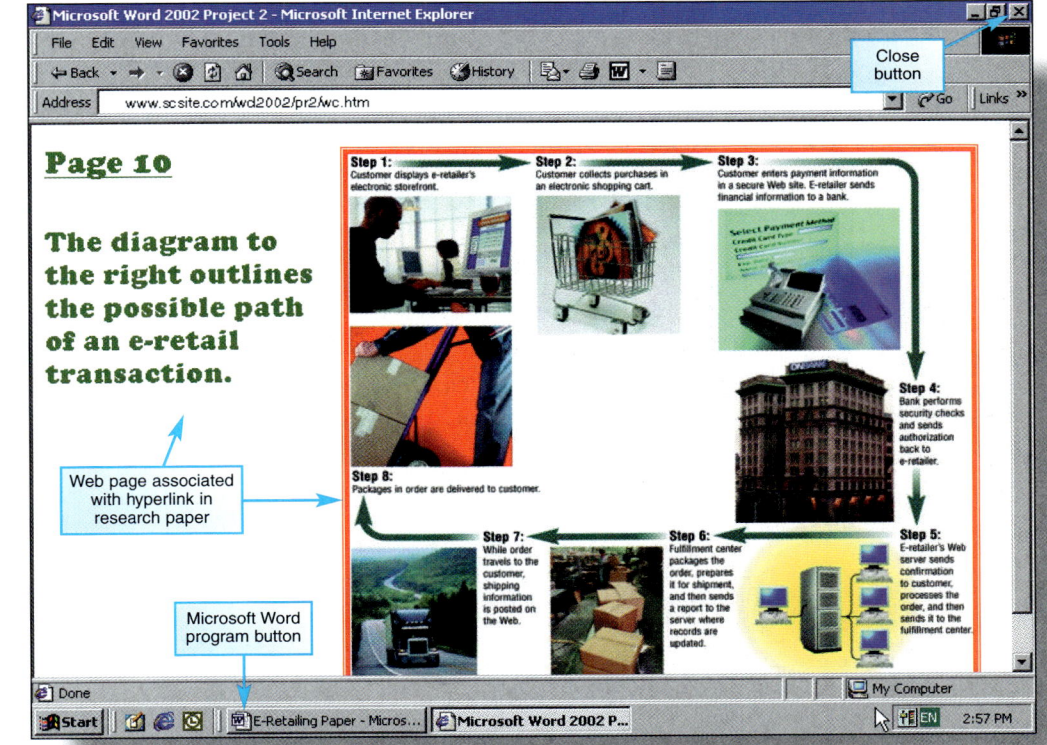

FIGURE 2-73

WD 2.54 • Project 2 • Creating a Research Paper

E-Mailing

To e-mail a document as an attachment, click File on the menu bar, point to Send To, and then click Mail Recipient (as Attachment).

E-Mailing a Copy of the Research Paper

Your instructor, Ms. Blythe, has requested you e-mail her a copy of your research paper so she can verify your hyperlink. Perform the following step to e-mail the document from within Word.

Steps — To E-Mail a Document

1 Click the E-mail button on the Standard toolbar. Fill in the To text box with Ms. Blythe's e-mail address, the Subject text box with the name of the paper, and the Introduction text box as shown in Figure 2-74.

Word displays certain buttons and boxes from your e-mail editor inside the Word window.

2 Click the Send a Copy button.

The document is e-mailed to the recipient named in the To text box.

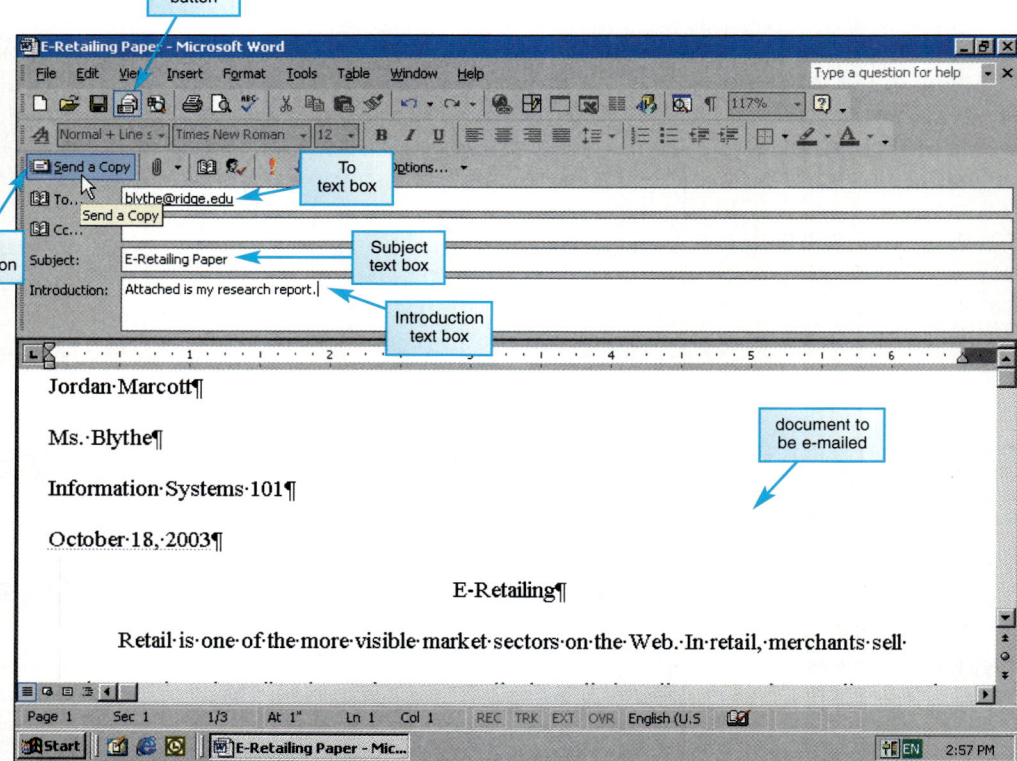

FIGURE 2-74

Other Ways

1. On File menu point to Send To, on Send To submenu click Mail Recipient
2. In Voice Command mode, say "E-mail"

If you want to cancel the e-mail operation, click the E-mail button again. The final step in this project is to quit Word, as described in the following step.

TO QUIT WORD

1 Click the Close button in the Word window.

The Word window closes.

CASE PERSPECTIVE SUMMARY

Jordan accomplished her goal — learning about e-retailing while completing Ms. Blythe's research paper assignment. Based on her findings, she has decided to pursue a career in retail management for a Web-based merchant. She decides to create a resume, listing this goal as the objective on her resume. Jordan decides to use Word's Resume Wizard to create her resume. She also contacts the Office of Career Development at her school to assist her with wording on the resume. After finishing the resume, she shows Ms. Blythe. Jordan cannot wait to begin her new career!

Project Summary

Project 2 introduced you to creating a research paper using the MLA documentation style. You learned how to change margin settings, adjust line spacing, create headers with page numbers, and indent paragraphs. You learned how to use Word's AutoCorrect feature. Then, you added a footnote in the research paper. You alphabetized the works cited page by sorting its paragraphs and included a hyperlink to a Web page in one of the works. You learned how to count words, browse through a Word document, move text, and find and replace text. You looked up a synonym and checked spelling and grammar in the entire document. Finally, you navigated to a hyperlink and e-mailed a copy of a document.

What You Should Know

Having completed this project, you now should be able to perform the following tasks:

- Add a Footnote *(WD 2.25)*
- AutoCorrect as You Type *(WD 2.21)*
- Browse by Page *(WD 2.43)*
- Center the Title of the Works Cited Page *(WD 2.36)*
- Change the Margin Settings *(WD 2.08)*
- Check Spelling and Grammar At Once *(WD 2.51)*
- Click and Type *(WD 2.13)*
- Close the Note Pane *(WD 2.31)*
- Count Words *(WD 2.32)*
- Create a Hanging Indent *(WD 2.37)*
- Create a Hyperlink as You Type *(WD 2.40)*
- Create an AutoCorrect Entry *(WD 2.23)*
- Display Formatting Marks *(WD 2.07)*
- Display the Header Area *(WD 2.12)*
- Display the Paste Options Menu *(WD 2.47)*
- Double-Space Text *(WD 2.10)*
- E-Mail a Document *(WD 2.54)*
- Enter a Page Number *(WD 2.14)*
- Enter More Text *(WD 2.24)*
- Enter Name and Course Information *(WD 2.16)*
- Enter Works Cited Paragraphs *(WD 2.37)*
- Find a Synonym *(WD 2.50)*
- Find and Replace Text *(WD 2.48)*
- Find Text *(WD 2.49)*
- First-Line Indent Paragraphs *(WD 2.19)*
- Insert a Symbol Automatically *(WD 2.39)*
- Modify a Style *(WD 2.28)*
- Move Text *(WD 2.46)*
- Navigate to a Hyperlink *(WD 2.53)*
- Page Break Automatically *(WD 2.33)*
- Page Break Manually *(WD 2.35)*
- Quit Word *(WD 2.54)*
- Recount Words *(WD 2.34)*
- Reset Menus and Toolbars *(WD 2.07)*
- Save a Document *(WD 2.18)*
- Save a Document Again and Print It *(WD 2.52)*
- Select a Sentence *(WD 2.45)*
- Sort Paragraphs *(WD 2.41)*
- Start and Customize Word *(WD 2.06)*
- Use Shortcut Keys to Format Text *(WD 2.17)*
- Use the AutoCorrect Options Button *(WD 2.22)*
- Zoom Page Width *(WD 2.09)*

Microsoft Certification

The Microsoft Office Specialist Certification program provides an opportunity for you to obtain a valuable industry credential — proof that you have the Word 2002 skills required by employers. For more information, see Appendix E or visit the Shelly Cashman Series Microsoft Office Specialist Web page at scsite.com/offxp/cert.htm.

Learn It Online

Instructions: To complete the Learn It Online exercises, start your browser, click the Address bar, and then enter scsite.com/offxp/exs.htm. When the Office XP Learn It Online page displays, follow the instructions in the exercises below.

1 Project Reinforcement TF, MC, and SA

Below Word Project 2, click the Project Reinforcement link. Print the quiz by clicking Print on the File menu. Answer each question. Write your first and last name at the top of each page, and then hand in the printout to your instructor.

2 Flash Cards

Below Word Project 2, click the Flash Cards link. When Flash Cards displays, read the instructions. Type 20 (or a number specified by your instructor) in the Number of Playing Cards text box, type your name in the Name text box, and then click the Flip Card button. When the flash card displays, read the question and then click the Answer box arrow to select an answer. Flip through Flash Cards. Click Print on the File menu to print the last flash card if your score is 15 (75%) correct or greater and then hand it in to your instructor. If your score is less than 15 (75%) correct, then redo this exercise by clicking the Replay button.

3 Practice Test

Below Word Project 2, click the Practice Test link. Answer each question, enter your first and last name at the bottom of the page, and then click the Grade Test button. When the graded practice test displays on your screen, click Print on the File menu to print a hard copy. Continue to take practice tests until you score 80% or better. Hand in a printout of the final practice test to your instructor.

4 Who Wants to Be a Computer Genius?

Below Word Project 2, click the Computer Genius link. Read the instructions, enter your first and last name at the bottom of the page, and then click the Play button. Hand in your score to your instructor.

5 Wheel of Terms

Below Word Project 2, click the Wheel of Terms link. Read the instructions, and then enter your first and last name and your school name. Click the Play button. Hand in your score to your instructor.

6 Crossword Puzzle Challenge

Below Word Project 2, click the Crossword Puzzle Challenge link. Read the instructions, and then enter your first and last name. Click the Play button. Work the crossword puzzle. When you are finished, click the Submit button. When the crossword puzzle redisplays, click the Print button. Hand in the printout.

7 Tips and Tricks

Below Word Project 2, click the Tips and Tricks link. Click a topic that pertains to Project 2. Right-click the information and then click Print on the shortcut menu. Construct a brief example of what the information relates to in Word to confirm you understand how to use the tip or trick. Hand in the example and printed information.

8 Newsgroups

Below Word Project 2, click the Newsgroups link. Click a topic that pertains to Project 2. Print three comments. Hand in the comments to your instructor.

9 Expanding Your Horizons

Below Word Project 2, click the Articles for Microsoft Word link. Click a topic that pertains to Project 2. Print the information. Construct a brief example of what the information relates to in Word to confirm you understand the contents of the article. Hand in the example and printed information to your instructor.

10 Search Sleuth

Below Word Project 2, click the Search Sleuth link. To search for a term that pertains to this project, select a term below the Project 2 title and then use the Google search engine at google.com (or any major search engine) to display and print two Web pages that present information on the term. Hand in the printouts to your instructor.

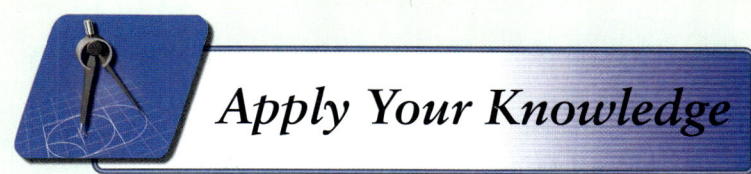

Apply Your Knowledge

1 Revising a Document

Instructions: Start Word. Open the document, Picture CD Paragraph, on the Data Disk. See the inside back cover of this book for instructions for downloading the Data Disk or see your instructor for information on accessing the files in this book.

The document is a paragraph of text. You are to revise the paragraph as follows: move a sentence; change the format of the moved sentence; replace all occurrences of the word, electronic, with the word, digital; and remove an automatic hyperlink format. The revised paragraph is shown in Figure 2-75. Perform the following tasks:

1. Press and hold the CTRL key. While holding the CTRL key, click in the sentence that is italicized to select the sentence. Release the CTRL key.
2. Press and hold down the left mouse button. Drag the dotted insertion point to the end of the paragraph and then release the mouse button to move the sentence. Click outside the selection to remove the highlight.
3. Click the Paste Options button that displays to the right of the moved sentence. To remove the italic format from the moved sentence, click Keep Text Only on the shortcut menu.
4. Press CTRL+HOME to position the insertion point at the top of the document. Double-click the status bar anywhere to the left of the status indicators. When the Find and Replace dialog box displays, click the Replace tab.
5. Type electronic in the Find what text box, press the TAB key, and then type digital in the Replace with text box. Click the Replace All button. Click the OK button in the Microsoft Word dialog box. Click the Close button in the Find and Replace dialog box.
6. At the end of the paragraph, press the SPACEBAR and then type this sentence: For more information on Picture CDs, enter the Web address of www.scsite.com/dc2002/ch7/weblink.htm and click Picture CDs.
7. To remove the hyperlink automatic format from the Web address, point to the beginning of the Web address (that is, the w in www). Click the small blue box below the w and then click the AutoCorrect Options button. Click Undo Hyperlink on the shortcut menu.
8. Click File on the menu bar and then click Save As. Use the file name, Revised Picture CD Paragraph, and then save the document on your floppy disk.
9. Print the revised paragraph.

> Internet evangelists have predicted the move to digital and online photograph storage. These predictions now are becoming reality. Picture CD is a new film digitation service from Kodak. This technology bridges the film to digital gap by providing a solution that gives people the benefit of both film and digital pictures. Picture CDs allow you to view pictures on the computer. With a Picture CD, you can print, modify, improve, and enhance photographs, and send e-mail postcards. To purchase a Picture CD, just check the box for Kodak Picture CD on your processing envelope when you drop off film for processing. For more information on Picture CDs, enter the Web address of www.scsite.com/dc2002/ch7/weblink.htm and click Picture CDs.

FIGURE 2-75

In the Lab

1 Preparing a Research Paper

Problem: You are a college student currently enrolled in a business data systems class. Your assignment is to prepare a short research paper (400-425 words) about a global positioning system (GPS). The requirements are that the paper be presented according to the MLA documentation style and have three references (Figures 2-76a through 2-76c). One of the three references must be from the Web and formatted as a hyperlink on the Works Cited page.

Hazelwood 1

Terry Hazelwood

Mr. Winkler

Business Data Systems 110

November 11, 2003

Global Positioning System

A global positioning system (GPS) consists of one or more earth-based receivers that accept and analyze signals sent by satellites in order to determine the receiver's geographic location. A GPS receiver is a handheld or mountable device, which can be secured to an automobile, boat, airplane, farm and construction equipment, or a computer. Some GPS receivers send location information to a base station, where humans can give you personal directions.

GPS has a variety of uses: to locate a person or object; ascertain the best route between two points; monitor the movement of a person or object; or create a map (Slifka 16-19). GPSs help scientists, farmers, pilots, dispatchers, and rescue workers operate more productively and safely. A rescue worker, for example, might use a GPS to locate a motorist stranded in a blizzard. A surveyor might use a GPS to create design maps for construction projects.

GPSs also are popular in consumer products for travel and recreational activities (*Microsoft Word 2002 Project 2*). Many cars use GPSs to provide drivers with directions or other information, automatically call for help if the airbag deploys, dispatch roadside assistance, unlock the driver's side door if keys are locked in the car, and track the vehicle if it is stolen. For cars not equipped with a GPS, drivers can mount or place one in the glove compartment. Hikers and remote campers also carry GPS receivers in case they need emergency help or directions.

A new use of GPS places the device on a computer chip. The chip, called Digital Angel™, is worn as a bracelet or chain or woven into fabric and has an antenna that

FIGURE 2-76a

In the Lab

Hazelwood 2

communicates with a GPS satellite (Dugan and Rosen 42-50). The chip measures and sends biological information to the GPS satellite. If information relayed indicates a person needs medical attention, dispatchers can send emergency medical help immediately. Other possible uses of Digital Angel™ include locating a missing person or pet, tracking parolees, and protecting valuables. Retailers take advantage of this technology, too. For example, a coffee shop could send a coupon into a handheld computer as the people walk by their store.

FIGURE 2-76b

Hazelwood 3

Works Cited

Dugan, Richard D., and Betty Ann Rosen. *Digital Concepts for the New Age*. San Francisco: Webster Clark Publishing, 2003.

Microsoft Word 2002 Project 2. Shelly Cashman Series® Course Technology. 6 Nov. 2003. http://www.scsite.com/wd2002/pr2/wc1.htm.

Slifka, Henry R. "An Introduction to GPS." *Modern Computing* Oct. 2003: 10-35.

FIGURE 2-76c

Instructions:

1. If necessary, click the Show/Hide ¶ button on the Standard toolbar. Change all margins to one inch. Adjust line spacing to double. Create a header to number pages. Type the name and course information at the left margin. Center and type the title. First-line indent all paragraphs in the paper.
2. Type the body of the paper as shown in Figure 2-76a and Figure 2-76b. To enter the trademark symbol (™), type (tm). At the end of the body of the research paper, press the ENTER key and then insert a manual page break.
3. Create the works cited page (Figure 2-76c).
4. Check the spelling of the paper at once.
5. Save the document on a floppy disk using GPS Paper as the file name.
6. If you have access to the Web, CTRL+click the hyperlink to test it.
7. Print the research paper. Handwrite the number of words in the research paper above the title of your printed research paper.

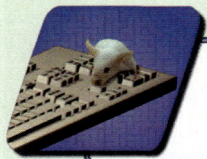

In the Lab

2 Preparing a Research Report with Footnotes

Problem: You are a college student currently enrolled in a data communications class. Your assignment is to prepare a short research paper in any area of interest to you. The requirements are that the paper be presented according to the MLA documentation style and have three references. One of the three references must be from the Internet and formatted as a hyperlink on the works cited page. You decide to prepare a paper on computers and entertainment (Figures 2-77a and 2-77b).

Frey 1

Holly Frey

Ms. Robinson

Data Communications 100

November 5, 2003

Computers and Entertainment

    In the past, you played board games with friends and family members, viewed fine art in an art gallery, listened to music on your stereo, watched a movie at a theater or on television, and inserted pictures into sleeves of photo albums. Today, you can have a much more fulfilling experience in each of these areas of entertainment.

    In addition to playing exciting, action-packed, 3-D multiplayer games, you can find hours of entertainment on the computer. For example, you can make a family tree, read a book or magazine online, listen to music on the computer, compose a video, edit pictures, or plan a vacation. These forms of entertainment are available on CD-ROM, DVD-ROM, and also on the Web. On the Web, you can view images of fine art in online museums, galleries, and centers.[1] Some artists sell their works online. Others display them for your viewing pleasure.

    You have several options if you wish to listen to music while working on the computer. Insert your favorite music CD into the CD or DVD drive on your computer and listen while you work. Visit an online radio station to hear music, news, and sporting events (Peyton 25). At some of these sites, you even can watch videos of artists as they sing or play their songs.

    Instead of driving to the music store or video store to purchase music or movies, you can buy them on the Web. After paying for the music or movie online, you download it to your hard

---

    [1] Simms and Foster list many Web addresses of fine art galleries, such as the Louvre, that display works online for your enjoyment (78-93).

FIGURE 2-77a

# In the Lab

> Frey 2
>
> disk. Once on your hard disk, you listen to the music or watch the movie on the computer. Or, you can transfer it to a CD using a CD-RW and play the music on any audio CD player or the movie on a DVD player (*Microsoft Word 2002 Project 2*).
>
> Some people prefer to create their own music or movies. You can compose music and other sound effects using external devices such as an electric piano keyboard or synthesizer. You also can transfer or create movies by connecting a video camera to the computer. Once on the computer, the music or movies are ready for editing, e-mailing, or posting to a Web page.

FIGURE 2-77b

Part 1 Instructions: Perform the following tasks to create the research paper:

1. If necessary, click the Show/Hide ¶ button on the Standard toolbar. Change all margin settings to one inch. Adjust line spacing to double. Create a header to number pages. Type the name and course information at the left margin. Center and type the title. First-line indent all paragraphs in the paper.
2. Type the body of the paper as shown in Figure 2-77a and Figure 2-77b. At the end of the body of the research paper, press the ENTER key once and insert a manual page break.
3. Create the works cited page. Enter the works cited shown below as separate paragraphs. Format the works properly and then sort the paragraphs.
   (a) Simms, Jeffrey K., and Laura C. Foster. Technological Entertainment. Chicago: Clark Davidson Press, 2003.
   (b) Peyton, Bonnie R. "World Music: A Multitude of Radio Waves Now Online." Technology April 2003: 25-29.
   (c) Microsoft Word 2002 Project 2. Shelly Cashman Series®. Course Technology. 30 Oct. 2003. http://www.scsite.com/wd2002/pr2/wc2.htm.
4. Check the spelling of the paper.
5. Save the document on a floppy disk using Computers and Entertainment Paper as the file name.
6. If you have access to the Web, CTRL+click the hyperlink to test it.
7. Print the research paper. Handwrite the number of words, including the footnotes, in the research paper above the title of your printed research paper.

Part 2 Instructions: Perform the following tasks to modify the research paper:

1. Use Word to find a synonym of your choice for the word, find, in the first sentence of the second paragraph.
2. Change all occurrences of the word, pictures, to the word, photographs.
3. Insert a second footnote at the end of the third sentence in the last paragraph of the research paper. Use the following footnote text: Many digital video cameras allow you also to take digital still photographs.

(continued)

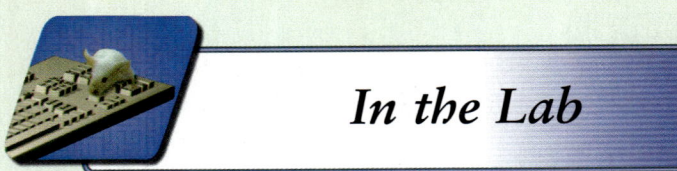

In the Lab

Preparing a Research Report with Footnotes *(continued)*

4. In the first footnote, find the word, display, and change it to the word, exhibit.
5. Save the document on a floppy disk using Computers and Entertainment Paper - Part 2a as the file name.
6. Print the revised research paper with the notes positioned as footnotes.
7. Convert the footnotes to endnotes. Recall that endnotes display at the end of a document. (***Hint***: Use Help to learn about converting footnotes to endnotes.)
8. Modify the Endnote text style to 12-point font, double-spaced text with a first-line indent. Insert a page break so the endnotes are placed on a separate, numbered page. Center the title, Endnotes, double-spaced above the notes.
9. Change the format of the note reference marks to capital letters (A, B, etc.). ***Hint***: Use Help to learn about changing the number format of note reference marks.
10. Save the document on a floppy disk using Computers and Entertainment Paper - Part 2b as the file name.
11. Print the revised research paper with notes positioned as endnotes. Handwrite the number of words, including the footnotes, in the research paper above the title of the printed research paper.

3 Composing a Research Paper from Notes

Problem: You have drafted the notes shown in Figure 2-78. Your assignment is to prepare a short research paper from these notes. Review the notes and then rearrange and reword them. Embellish the paper as you deem necessary. Add a footnote that refers the reader to the Web for more information. Present the paper according to the MLA documentation style.

Instructions: Perform the following tasks:

1. Change all margin settings to one inch. Adjust line spacing to double. Create a header to number pages. Type the name and course information at the left margin. Center and type the title. First-line indent all paragraphs in the paper.
2. Create an AutoCorrect entry that automatically corrects the spelling of the misspelled word, moniters, to the correct spelling, monitors.
3. Compose the body of the paper from the notes in Figure 2-78. Be sure to include a footnote as specified. At the end of the body of the research paper, press the ENTER key once and insert a manual page break. Create the works cited page from the listed sources. Be sure to sort the works.
4. Check the spelling and grammar of the paper. Save the document on a floppy disk using Green Computing Research Paper as the file name. Print the research paper. Handwrite the number of words, including the footnotes, in the research paper above the title of the printed research paper.
5. E-mail the research paper to your instructor, if your instructor gives you permission to do so.

In the Lab

Green computing involves reducing the electricity and environmental waste while using a computer. Computers use, and often waste, resources such as electricity and paper. Society has become aware of this waste and is taking measures to combat it.

ENERGY STAR program (source: "What's New in Computing Today," an article on pages 9-24 in the September 2003 issue of High Tech, author Roger R. Mobley):
- ENERGY STAR program encourages manufacturers to create energy-efficient devices that require little power when they are not in use. For example, many devices switch to standby mode after a specified number of inactive minutes.
- Computers and devices that meet ENERGY STAR guidelines display an ENERGY STAR® label.
- Personal computers, monitors, and printers should comply with the ENERGY STAR program, which was developed by the United States Department of Energy (DOE) and the United States Environmental Protection Agency (EPA).

Obsolete computers and devices (source: Computer Learning for the New Professional, a book published by Gulf Publishing Company in Houston, Texas, 2003, pages 56-64, authors James D. Holmes and Katie A. Marsden.):
- Do not store obsolete computers and devices in your basement, storage room, attic, warehouse, or any other location.
- Computers, monitors, and other equipment contain toxic materials and potentially dangerous elements including lead, mercury, and flame retardants. In a landfill, these materials release into the environment.
- Experts recommend refurbishing or recycling the equipment. For this reason, local governments are working on methods to make it easy for the consumer to recycle this type of equipment. Manufacturers can use the millions of pounds of recycled raw material in products such as outdoor furniture and automotive parts.

To reduce further the environmental impact of computing, simply alter a few habits (source: a Web site titled Microsoft Word 2002 Project 2 sponsored by the Shelly Cashman Series® at Course Technology; site visited on 1 Oct. 2003; Web address is http://www.scsite.com/wd2002/pr2/wc3.htm.):
- Use computers and devices that comply with the ENERGY STAR program.
- Recycle toner cartridges. Recycle old computers and printers.
- Telecommute (saves gas).
- Do not leave the computer and devices running overnight.
- Use paperless methods to communicate.
- Recycle paper. Buy recycled paper.
- Turn off your monitor, printer, and other devices when not in use.
- Shop online (saves gas).

FIGURE 2-78

Cases and Places

The difficulty of these case studies varies:
▸ are the least difficult; ▸▸ are more difficult; and ▸▸▸ are the most difficult.

1 ▸ Project 1 of this book discussed the components of the Word window (pages WD 1.12 through WD 1.17). Using the material presented on these pages, write a short research paper (350-400 words) that describes the purpose and functionality of one or more of these components: the document window, insertion point, end mark, mouse pointer, rulers, scroll bars, status bar, menu bar, or toolbars. Use your textbook, Word Help, and any other resources available. Include at least two references and one explanatory note. Use the concepts and techniques presented in this project to format the paper.

2 ▸▸ A smart card, which is similar in size to a credit card or ATM card, stores data on a thin microprocessor embedded in the card. Using the school library, other textbooks, magazines, the Internet, or other resources, research the types of smart cards, popular uses of smart cards, or the role of e-money with smart cards. Then, prepare a brief research paper (400-450 words) that discusses your findings. Include at least one explanatory note and two references, one of which must be a Web site on the Internet. Use the concepts and techniques presented in this project to format the paper.

3 ▸▸ A handheld computer, sometimes called a PDA, is a lightweight, palm-sized or pocket-sized computer. Using the school library, other textbooks, the Internet, magazines, or other resources, research the points to consider when purchasing a handheld computer. Then, prepare a brief research paper (400-450 words) that discusses features, applications, price, and accessories of current handheld computers. Include at least one explanatory note and two references, one of which must be a Web site on the Internet. Use the concepts and techniques presented in this project to format the paper.

4 ▸▸ An electronic book is a digital text that gives a user access to information through links, which often are bold or underlined words. Using the school library, other textbooks, the Internet, magazines, or other resources, research electronic books on the market today. Then, prepare a brief research paper (400-450 words) that discusses the features of these books and the methods publishers use to distribute these electronic books. Include at least one explanatory note and two references, one of which must be a Web site on the Internet. Use the concepts and techniques presented in this project to format the paper.

5 ▸▸▸ The options available for obtaining software have grown considerably in the past few years. You can shop in-person at a bricks-and-mortar retail store or purchase online through a retailer on the Web. On the Web, you can subscribe to software, download software, or have it delivered to your doorstep. Select a software application, such as word processing, spreadsheets, accounting, or graphics. Investigate the various means available for obtaining this software. Visit or call a bricks-and-mortar computer store. Look through newspapers or magazines for retailers. Search the Web for an online store. Then, prepare a brief research paper (500-550 words) on the various options for the software application and recommend the one you believe is the best choice. Include at least two explanatory notes and three references, one of which must be a Web site on the Internet. Use the concepts and techniques presented in this project to format the paper.

Microsoft Word 2002

PROJECT 3

Creating a Resume Using a Wizard and a Cover Letter with a Table

You will have mastered the material in this project when you can:

O B J E C T I V E S

- Create a resume using Word's Resume Wizard
- Identify the Word screen in print layout view
- Zoom text width
- Identify styles in a document
- Replace selected text with new text
- Insert a line break
- AutoFormat text as you type
- Use print preview to view and print a document
- Open a new document window
- Add color to characters
- Set and use tab stops
- Switch from one open Word document to another
- Collect and paste using the Clipboard task pane
- Add a bottom border to a paragraph
- Clear formatting
- Convert a hyperlink to regular text
- Identify the components of a business letter
- Insert the current date
- Create an AutoText entry
- Insert a nonbreaking space
- Insert an AutoText entry
- Insert a Word table
- Enter data into a Word table
- Format a Word table
- Create a bulleted list as you type
- Address and print an envelope

Present Your Image

A Great Resume Makes Your Words Count

In 1905, a young physicist sought a teaching position at the university level. His handwritten resume included his educational background, his qualifications, and his personal interests. At that time, he had submitted his Ph.D thesis, which was awaiting acceptance. His works included papers on particle theory, quantum theory, and the special theory of relativity. He played the violin and sailed, and was a family man. Who was this young physicist?

Yes, he was Albert Einstein, who wrote by hand literally dozens of letters seeking employment as a teacher while he labored in relative obscurity at the Swiss patent office. The same year, he published three studies that set the world of science on its ear. Fame eventually helped, but persistence in his search paid off when he finally landed a teaching appointment at the University of Zurich after years as a patent clerk.

No one can tell whether Einstein might have met his goals more quickly if he would have had the benefit of modern word processing software, but certainly Microsoft Word would have made his life easier.

As you embark on your professional life, you have the advantage of using Word to prepare a resume and a personalized cover letter. In this project, you will learn these skills. Resume writing is important in directing the image you present to a potential employer. The stronger the skill and experience descriptions in your resume, the more likely you are to obtain interviews and salary offers. With employers receiving hundreds of resumes, it is vital to capture their attention quickly with a well-written document that matches your skills with the job you seek. Providing a personalized cover letter with each resume enables you to elaborate on positive points in your resume and gives you an opportunity to show a potential employer your written communications skills.

Using the Résumé Wizard creates a resume that is tailored to your preferences. The Wizard provides the style, formats the resume with appropriate headings and spacing, and makes it easy for you to present your best qualities.

If good guidelines exist for doing something, then why not use them? This same practicality is built into the Résumé Wizard. Word provides the tools that eliminate the need to start from scratch every time, while you provide responses and supply the substance.

To understand the importance of using these guidelines, consider the meaning of the word represent: to bring clearly before the mind. When creating letters and resumes, which are two elements of business life that are fundamental to success, it is critical to bring a favorable image to mind. These documents must be crisp, to the point, and good-looking, because usually they are the first glimpse a prospective employer gets of a job-seeker.

As you contemplate a career or a career move, present your image by identifying and promoting your top skills, and use a design that gets attention and content that sells. Then, think about the words of Oliver Wendell Holmes: "Every calling is great when greatly pursued."

Microsoft Word 2002

Creating a Resume Using a Wizard and a Cover Letter with a Table

PROJECT 3

CASE PERSPECTIVE

Tyrone James Carter recently graduated from North Carolina State with a bachelor's degree in social studies teaching. He plans to continue toward a master's degree in education and also obtain his North Carolina teaching certificate, so he can teach social studies at the high-school level. While continuing his education, he wants to work as a teacher's assistant. In the classified section of the *Herald Times*, Tyrone locates a social studies teacher's assistant position at Peterson High School. The ad requests a resume and an accompanying cover letter from all applicants. Tyrone has neither. Because you work in the school's Office of Career Development, Tyrone has asked you to help him create a professional resume and cover letter.

Based on your suggestion, Tyrone will use Word's Resume Wizard to create his resume. He will address the cover letter to Ms. Mae Li, personnel director at Peterson High School and include all essential business letter components. With Tyrone's solid background and your resume writing expertise, you create an effective package that should ensure his success in obtaining the position.

Introduction

At some time in your professional life, you will prepare a resume along with a personalized cover letter to send to a prospective employer(s). In addition to some personal information, a **resume** usually contains the applicant's educational background and job experience. Employers review many resumes for each vacant position. Thus, you should design your resume carefully so it presents you as the best candidate for the job. You also should attach a personalized cover letter to each resume you send. A **cover letter** enables you to elaborate on positive points in your resume; it also provides you with an opportunity to show a potential employer your written communication skills. Accordingly, it is important that your cover letter is written well and follows proper business letter rules.

Composing documents from scratch can be a difficult process for many people. To assist with this task, Word provides wizards and templates. A **wizard** asks you several basic questions and then uses a template to prepare and format a document for you based on your responses. A **template** is similar to a form with prewritten text; that is, Word prepares the requested document with text and/or formatting common to all documents of this nature. Once Word creates a document from a template, you then fill in the blanks or replace prewritten words in the document. In addition to wizards using templates, Word also provides many templates you can use to create documents. This project discusses how to use a wizard. Project 5 discusses creating a document directly from a template.

Project Three — Resume and Cover Letter

Tyrone James Carter, a recent college graduate, is seeking a full-time position as a teacher's assistant at a high school. Project 3 uses Word to produce his resume, shown in Figure 3-1, and a personalized cover letter and envelope, shown in Figure 3-2 on the next page.

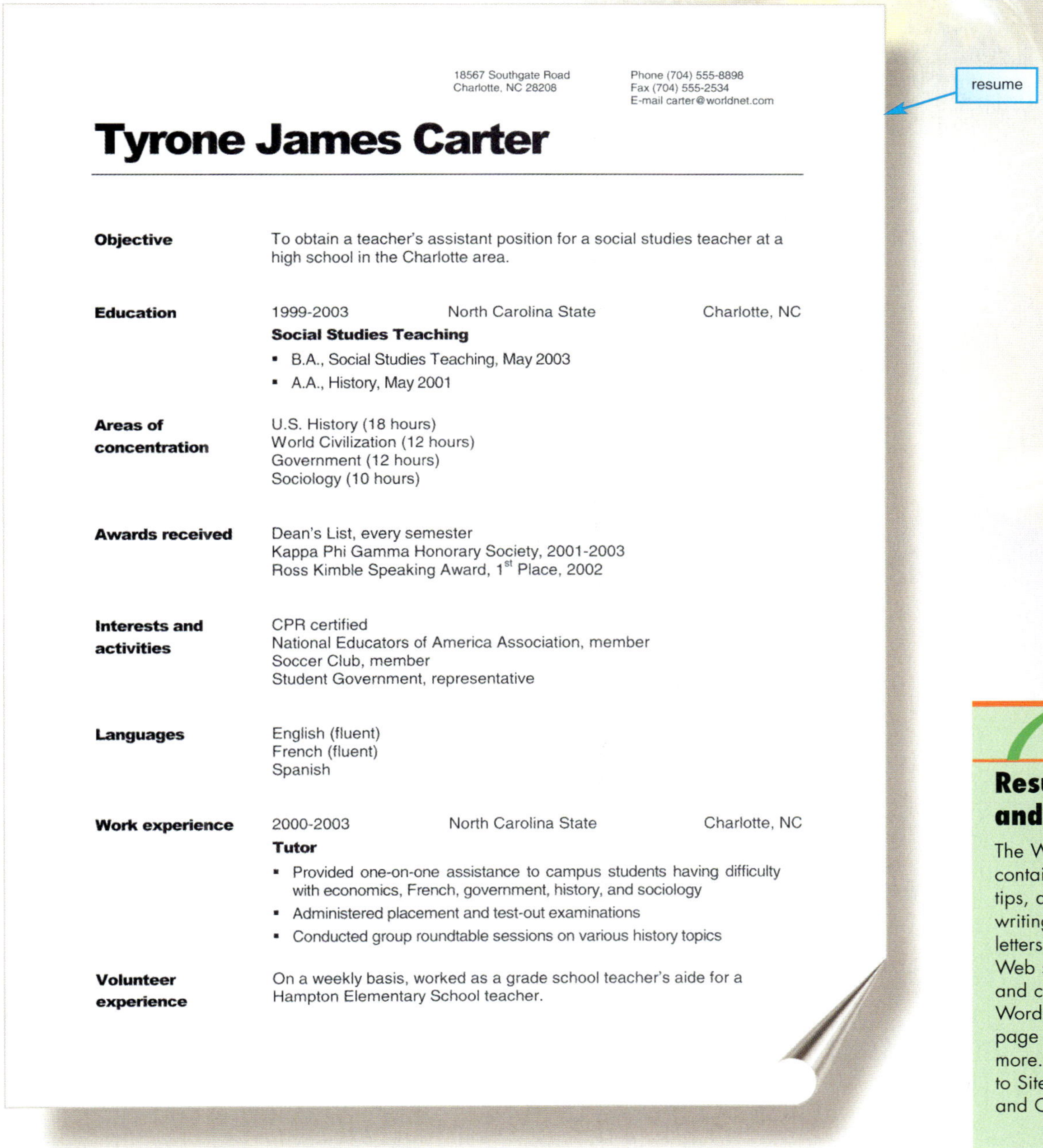

18567 Southgate Road
Charlotte, NC 28208

Phone (704) 555-8898
Fax (704) 555-2534
E-mail carter@worldnet.com

resume

Tyrone James Carter

Objective   To obtain a teacher's assistant position for a social studies teacher at a high school in the Charlotte area.

Education   1999-2003   North Carolina State   Charlotte, NC
Social Studies Teaching
- B.A., Social Studies Teaching, May 2003
- A.A., History, May 2001

Areas of concentration
U.S. History (18 hours)
World Civilization (12 hours)
Government (12 hours)
Sociology (10 hours)

Awards received
Dean's List, every semester
Kappa Phi Gamma Honorary Society, 2001-2003
Ross Kimble Speaking Award, 1st Place, 2002

Interests and activities
CPR certified
National Educators of America Association, member
Soccer Club, member
Student Government, representative

Languages
English (fluent)
French (fluent)
Spanish

Work experience   2000-2003   North Carolina State   Charlotte, NC
Tutor
- Provided one-on-one assistance to campus students having difficulty with economics, French, government, history, and sociology
- Administered placement and test-out examinations
- Conducted group roundtable sessions on various history topics

Volunteer experience
On a weekly basis, worked as a grade school teacher's aide for a Hampton Elementary School teacher.

FIGURE 3-1

More About

Resumes and Cover Letters

The World Wide Web contains a host of information, tips, and suggestions on writing resumes and cover letters. For a list of links to Web sites on writing resumes and cover letters, visit the Word 2002 More About Web page (scsite.com/wd2002/more.htm) and then click Links to Sites on Writing Resumes and Cover Letters.

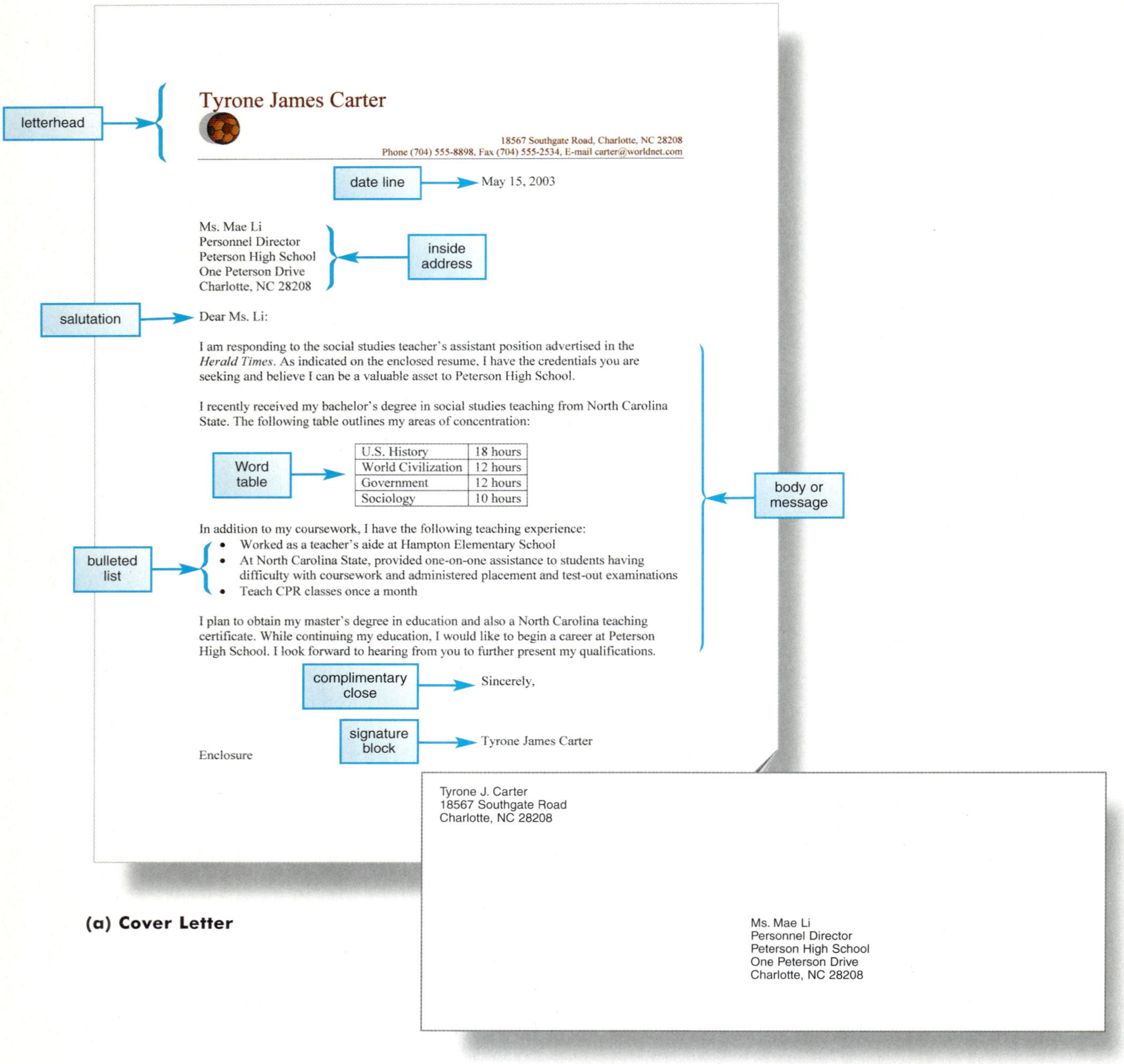

WD 3.06 • **Project 3** • Creating a Resume Using a Wizard and a Cover Letter with a Table

Microsoft Word 2002

Tyrone James Carter
18567 Southgate Road, Charlotte, NC 28208
Phone (704) 555-8898, Fax (704) 555-2534, E-mail carter@worldnet.com

- letterhead

May 15, 2003 — date line

Ms. Mae Li
Personnel Director
Peterson High School
One Peterson Drive
Charlotte, NC 28208 — inside address

Dear Ms. Li: — salutation

I am responding to the social studies teacher's assistant position advertised in the *Herald Times*. As indicated on the enclosed resume, I have the credentials you are seeking and believe I can be a valuable asset to Peterson High School.

I recently received my bachelor's degree in social studies teaching from North Carolina State. The following table outlines my areas of concentration:

U.S. History	18 hours
World Civilization	12 hours
Government	12 hours
Sociology	10 hours

— Word table

— body or message

In addition to my coursework, I have the following teaching experience:
- Worked as a teacher's aide at Hampton Elementary School
- At North Carolina State, provided one-on-one assistance to students having difficulty with coursework and administered placement and test-out examinations
- Teach CPR classes once a month

— bulleted list

I plan to obtain my master's degree in education and also a North Carolina teaching certificate. While continuing my education, I would like to begin a career at Peterson High School. I look forward to hearing from you to further present my qualifications.

Sincerely, — complimentary close

Tyrone James Carter — signature block

Enclosure

(a) Cover Letter

Tyrone J. Carter
18567 Southgate Road
Charlotte, NC 28208

Ms. Mae Li
Personnel Director
Peterson High School
One Peterson Drive
Charlotte, NC 28208

(b) Envelope

FIGURE 3-2

More About

Business Letters

A finished business letter should look like a symmetrically framed picture with evenly-spaced margins, all balanced below an attractive letterhead. In addition, the contents of the letter should contain proper grammar, correct spelling, logically constructed sentences, flowing paragraphs, and sound ideas.

Starting Word

Perform the following steps to start Word, or ask your instructor how to start Word for your system.

TO START AND CUSTOMIZE WORD

1. Click the Start button on the Windows taskbar, point to Programs on the Start menu, and then click Microsoft Word on the Programs submenu.
2. If the Word window is not maximized, double-click its title bar to maximize it.
3. If the Language bar displays on the screen, click its Minimize button.
4. If the New Document task pane displays in the Word window, click the Show at startup check box to remove the check mark and then click the Close button in the upper-right corner of the task pane title bar.
5. If the toolbars display positioned on the same row, click the Toolbar Options button and then click Show Buttons on Two Rows.
6. If your screen differs from Figure 3-3 on the next page, click View on the menu bar and then click Normal.

More About

Job Searches

The World Wide Web has several sites that assist you in locating a job. For a list of links to Web sites on job searches, visit the Word 2002 More About Web page (scsite.com/wd2002/more.htm) and then click Links to Sites on Job Searches.

Office starts Word. After a few moments, an empty document displays in the Word window (shown in Figure 3-3 on the next page).

Resetting Menus and Toolbars

To set the menus and toolbars so they appear exactly as shown in this book, you should reset your menus and toolbars as outlined in Appendix D or follow these steps.

TO RESET MENUS AND TOOLBARS

1. Click the Toolbar Options button on the Standard toolbar and then point to Add or Remove Buttons. Point to Standard on the Add or Remove Buttons submenu. Scroll to and then click Reset Toolbar on the Standard submenu.
2. Click the Toolbar Options button on the Formatting toolbar and then point to Add or Remove Buttons. Point to Formatting on the Add or Remove Buttons submenu. Scroll to and then click Reset Toolbar on the Formatting submenu.
3. Click the Toolbar Options button on the Standard toolbar and then point to Add or Remove Buttons. Click Customize on the Add or Remove Buttons submenu.
4. When the Customize dialog box displays, if necessary, click the Options tab and then click the Reset my usage data button. When the Microsoft Word dialog box displays, click the Yes button. Click the Close button in the Customize dialog box.

Word resets the menus and toolbars.

Displaying Formatting Marks

As discussed in Project 1, it is helpful to display formatting marks that indicate where in the document you pressed the ENTER key, SPACEBAR, and other keys. Perform the following step to display formatting marks.

TO DISPLAY FORMATTING MARKS

1. If the Show/Hide ¶ button on the Standard toolbar is not already selected, click it.

Word displays formatting marks in the document window, and the Show/Hide ¶ button on the Standard toolbar is selected (shown in Figure 3-3 on the next page).

WD 3.08 • Project 3 • Creating a Resume Using a Wizard and a Cover Letter with a Table

Microsoft **Word 2002**

Wizards and Templates

Once you have created a document using a wizard or template, Word displays the wizard or template name in the New from template area in the New Document task pane. Thus, your Figure 3-4 may differ from the one shown below. In addition to those installed on your hard disk, Microsoft has more wizards and templates available on the Web that you can download. To do this, click Templates on Microsoft.com in the New from template area in the New Document task pane.

Using Word's Resume Wizard to Create a Resume

You can type a resume from scratch into a blank document window, or you can use the **Resume Wizard** and let Word format the resume with appropriate headings and spacing. Then, you can customize the resulting resume by filling in the blanks or selecting and replacing text.

When you use a wizard, Word displays a dialog box with the wizard's name on its title bar. A wizard's dialog box displays a list of **panel names** along its left side with the currently selected panel displaying on the right side of the dialog box (Figure 3-6). Each panel presents a different set of options, in which you select preferences or enter text. To move from one panel to the next within the wizard's dialog box, you click the Next button or click the panel name on the left side of the dialog box.

Perform the following steps to create a resume using the Resume Wizard. A wizard retains the settings selected by the last person who used the wizard. Thus, some selections on your screen initially may display differently from the figures shown here. Be sure to verify that your settings match the screens shown in the following steps before clicking the Next button in each dialog box.

Steps   To Create a Resume Using Word's Resume Wizard

1 Click File on the menu bar and then point to New (Figure 3-3).

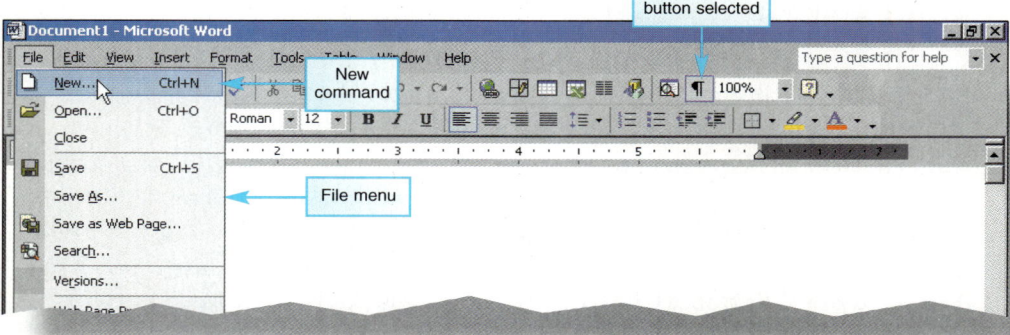

FIGURE 3-3

2 Click New. When the New Document task pane displays, point to General Templates in the New from template area.

Word displays the New Document task pane (Figure 3-4). You access wizards through the General Templates dialog box.

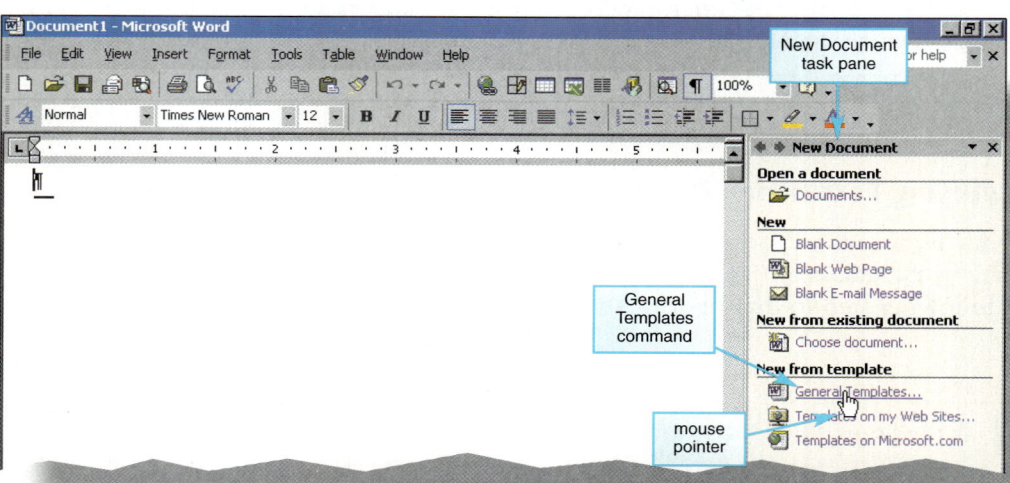

FIGURE 3-4

Using Word's Resume Wizard to Create a Resume • WD 3.09

3 **Click General Templates. If necessary, click the Other Documents tab when the Templates dialog box displays. Click the Resume Wizard icon.**

Office displays several wizard and template icons in the Other Documents sheet in the Templates dialog box (Figure 3-5). Icons without the word, wizard, are templates. If you click an icon, a sample of the resulting document displays in the Preview area.

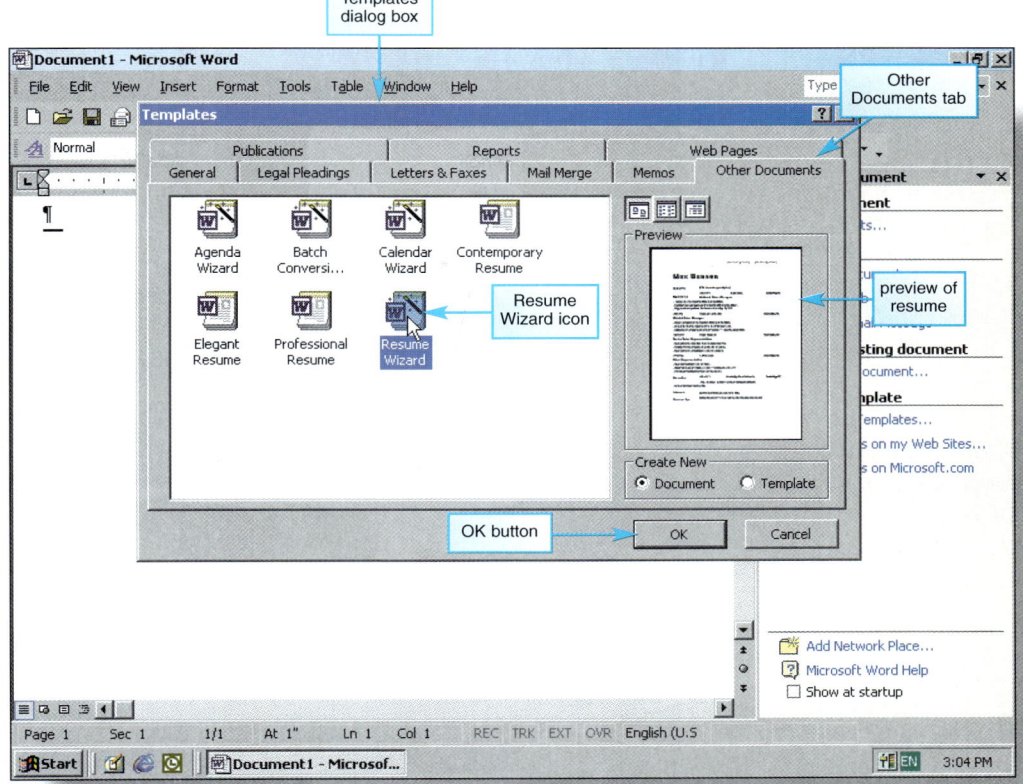

FIGURE 3-5

4 **Click the OK button. When the Resume Wizard dialog box displays, point to the Next button.**

After a few seconds, Word displays the *Start panel* of the Resume Wizard dialog box, informing you the Resume Wizard has started (Figure 3-6). This dialog box has a *Microsoft Word Help button* you can click to obtain help while using this wizard. When you create a document based on a wizard, Word creates a new document window, which is called Document2 in this figure.

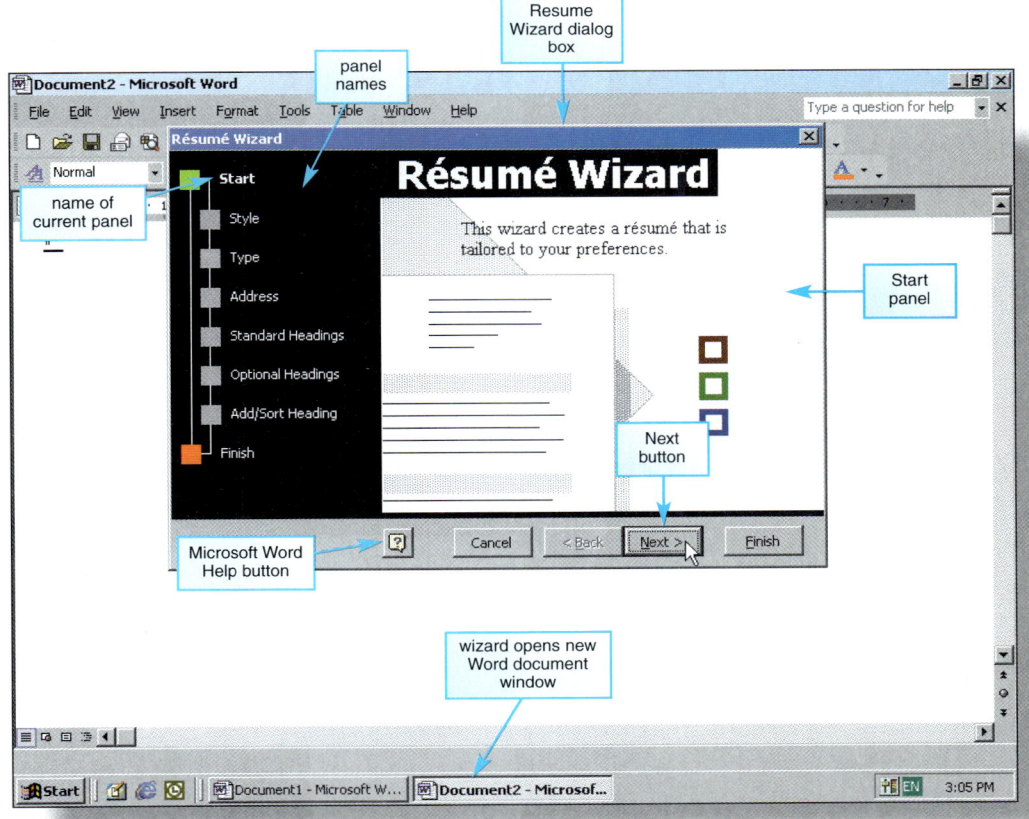

FIGURE 3-6

5 **Click the Next button. When the Style panel displays, if necessary, click Professional. Point to the Next button.**

Word displays the *Style panel* in the Resume Wizard dialog box, requesting the style of your resume (Figure 3-7). Word provides three styles of wizards and templates: Professional, Contemporary, and Elegant. A sample of each resume style displays in this panel.

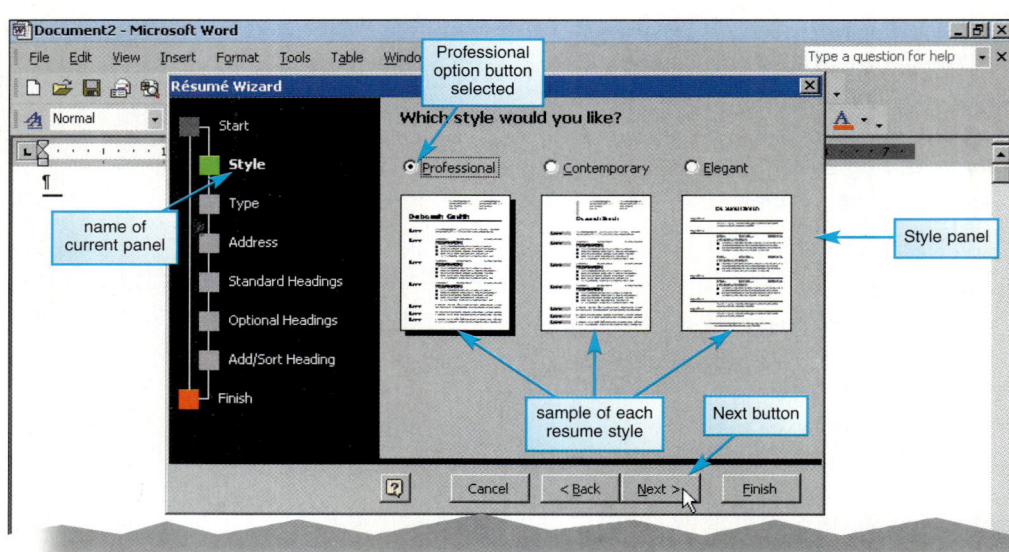

FIGURE 3-7

6 **Click the Next button. When the Type panel displays, if necessary, click Entry-level resume. Point to the Next button.**

Word displays the *Type panel* in the Resume Wizard dialog box, asking for the type of resume that you want to create (Figure 3-8).

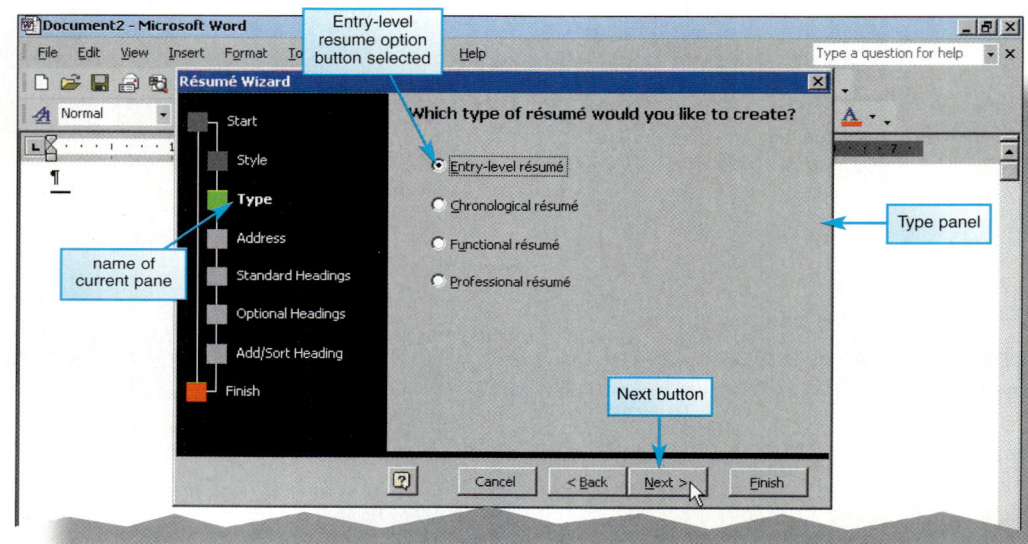

FIGURE 3-8

7 **Click the Next button.**

Word displays the *Address panel* in the Resume Wizard dialog box, with the name selected (Figure 3-9). The name displayed and selected in your Name text box will be different, depending on the name of the last person who used the Resume Wizard.

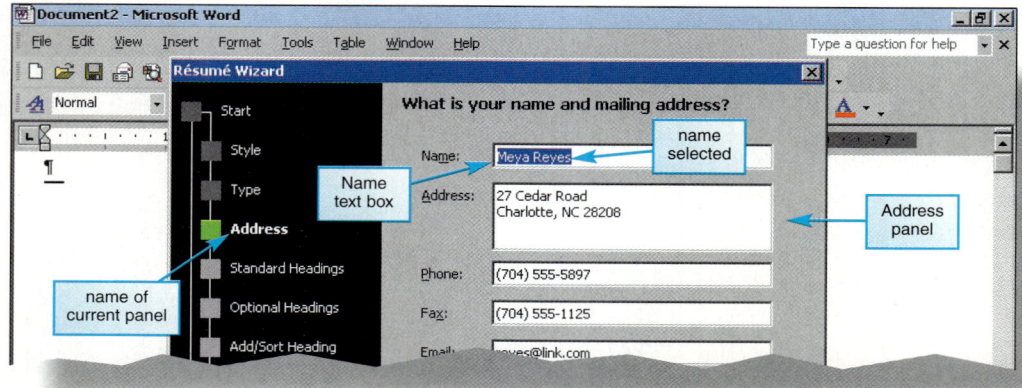

FIGURE 3-9

Using Word's Resume Wizard to Create a Resume • WD 3.11

8 **With the name in the Name text box selected, type** Tyrone James Carter **and then press the TAB key. Type** 18567 Southgate Road **and then press the ENTER key. Type** Charlotte, NC 28208 **and then press the TAB key. Type** (704) 555-8898 **and then press the TAB key. Type** (704) 555-2534 **and then press the TAB key. Type** carter@worldnet.com **and then point to the Next button.**

As you type the new text, it automatically replaces the selected text (Figure 3-10).

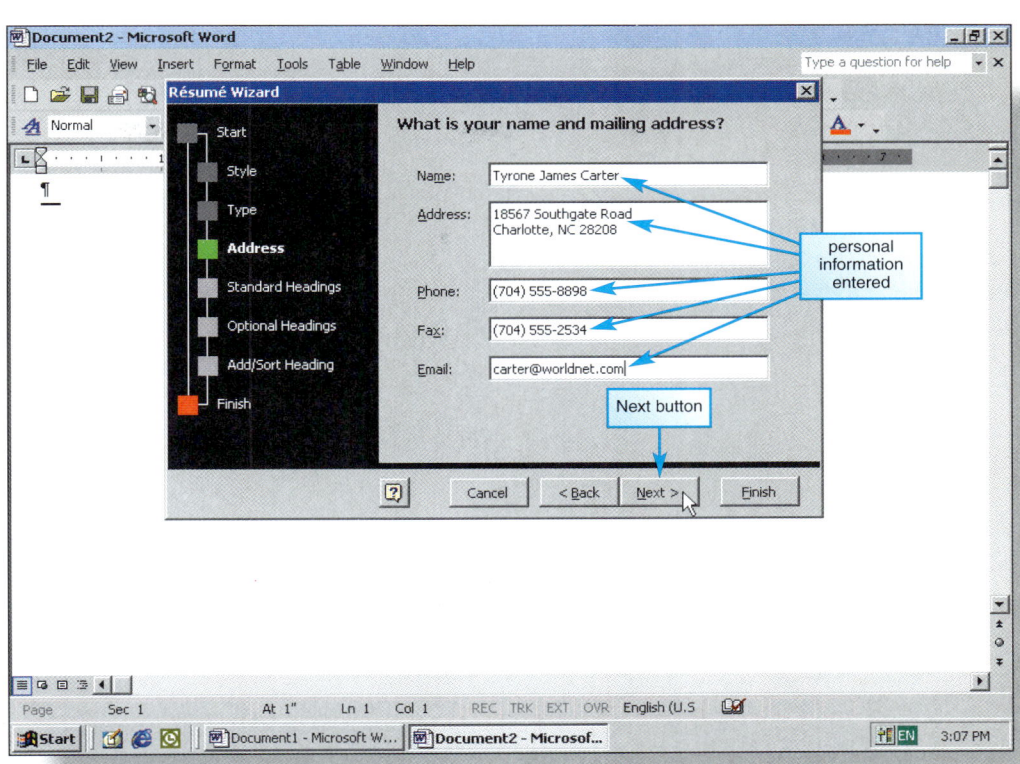

FIGURE 3-10

9 **Click the Next button. When the Standard Headings panel displays, if necessary, click Hobbies and References to remove the check marks. All other check boxes should have check marks. If any do not, place a check mark in the check box by clicking it. Point to the Next button.**

*Word displays the **Standard Headings panel** in the Resume Wizard dialog box, which requests the headings you want on your resume (Figure 3-11). You want all headings, except for these two: Hobbies and References.*

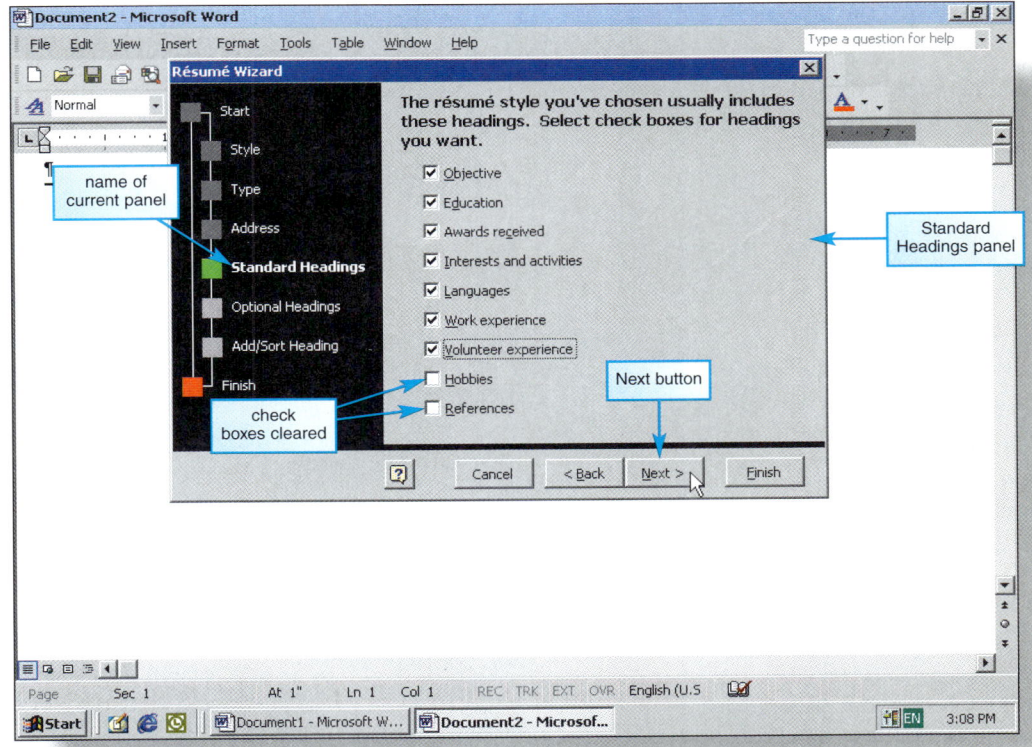

FIGURE 3-11

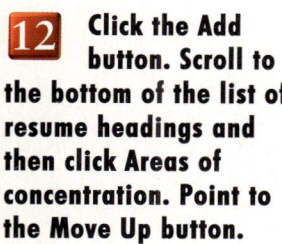 **Click the Next button. If necessary, remove any check marks from the check boxes. Point to the Next button in the Optional Headings panel.**

Word displays the Optional Headings panel in the Resume Wizard dialog box, which allows you to choose additional headings for your resume (Figure 3-12). All of these check boxes should be empty because none of these headings is required on the resume.

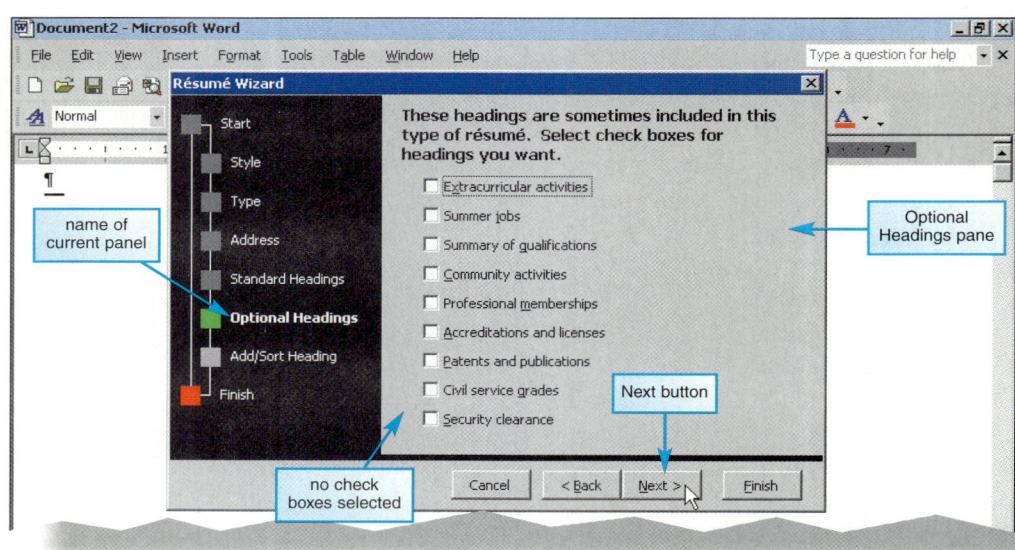

FIGURE 3-12

Click the Next button. When the Add/Sort Heading panel displays, type Areas of concentration **in the additional headings text box. Point to the Add button.**

Word displays the Add/Sort Heading panel in the Resume Wizard dialog box, which allows you to enter any additional headings you want on the resume (Figure 3-13).

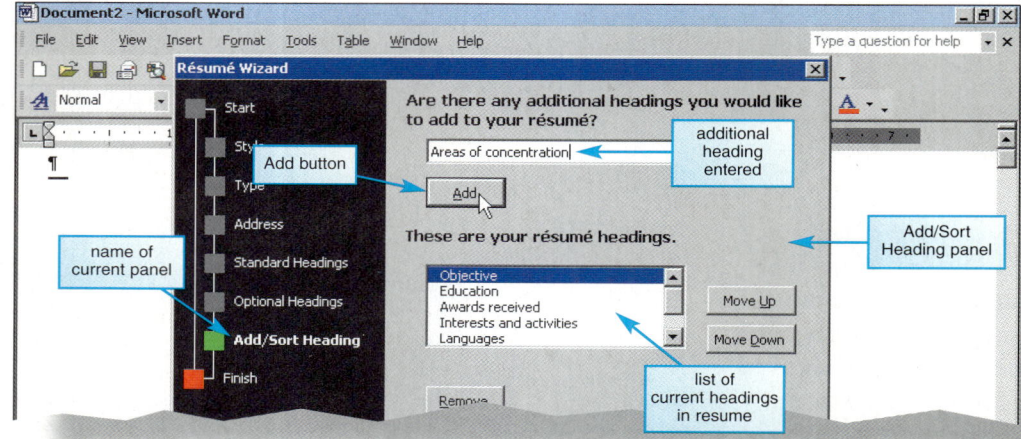

FIGURE 3-13

Click the Add button. Scroll to the bottom of the list of resume headings and then click Areas of concentration. Point to the Move Up button.

Word selects the Areas of concentration heading (Figure 3-14). You can rearrange the order of the headings on your resume by selecting a heading and then clicking the appropriate button (Move Up button or Move Down button).

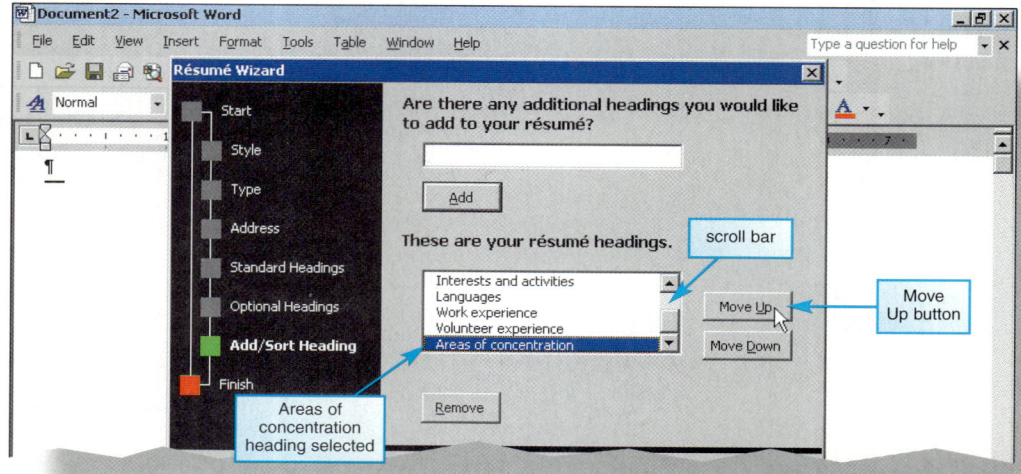

FIGURE 3-14

13 **Click the Move Up button five times.**

Word moves the heading, Areas of concentration, above the Awards received heading (Figure 3-15).

14 **If the last person using the Resume Wizard included additional headings, you may have some unwanted headings. Your heading list should be as follows: Objective, Education, Areas of concentration, Awards received, Interests and activities, Languages, Work experience, and Volunteer experience. If you have an additional heading(s), click the unwanted heading and then click the Remove button.**

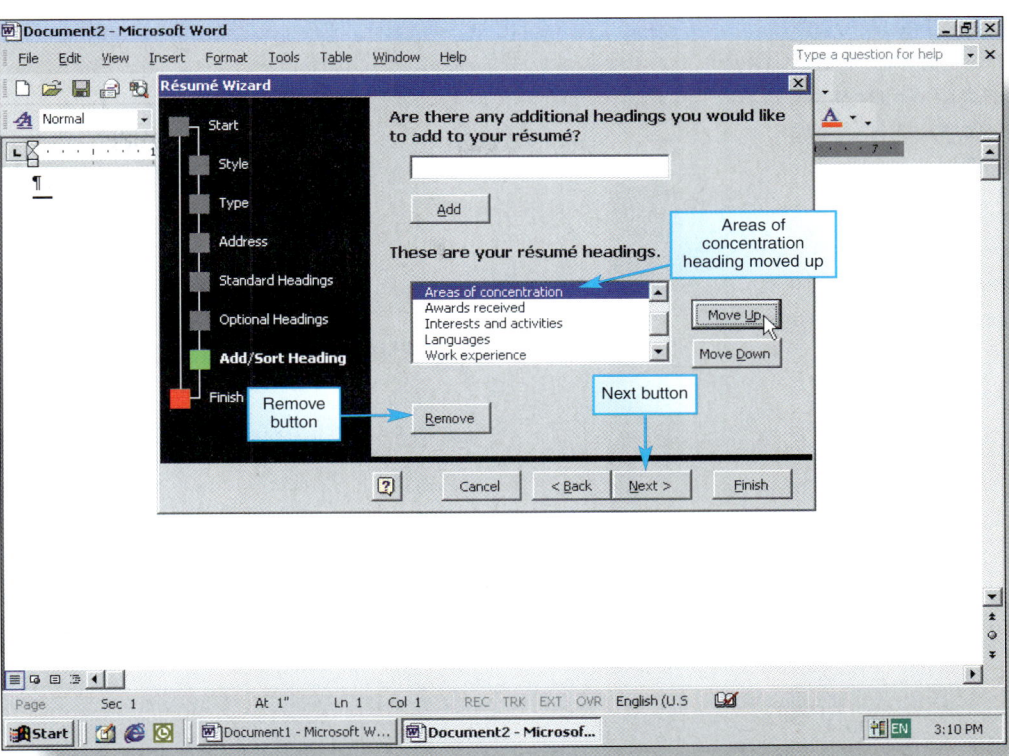

FIGURE 3-15

15 **Click the Next button. When the Finish panel displays, point to the Finish button.**

Word displays the *Finish panel* in the Resume Wizard dialog box, which indicates the wizard is ready to create your document (Figure 3-16).

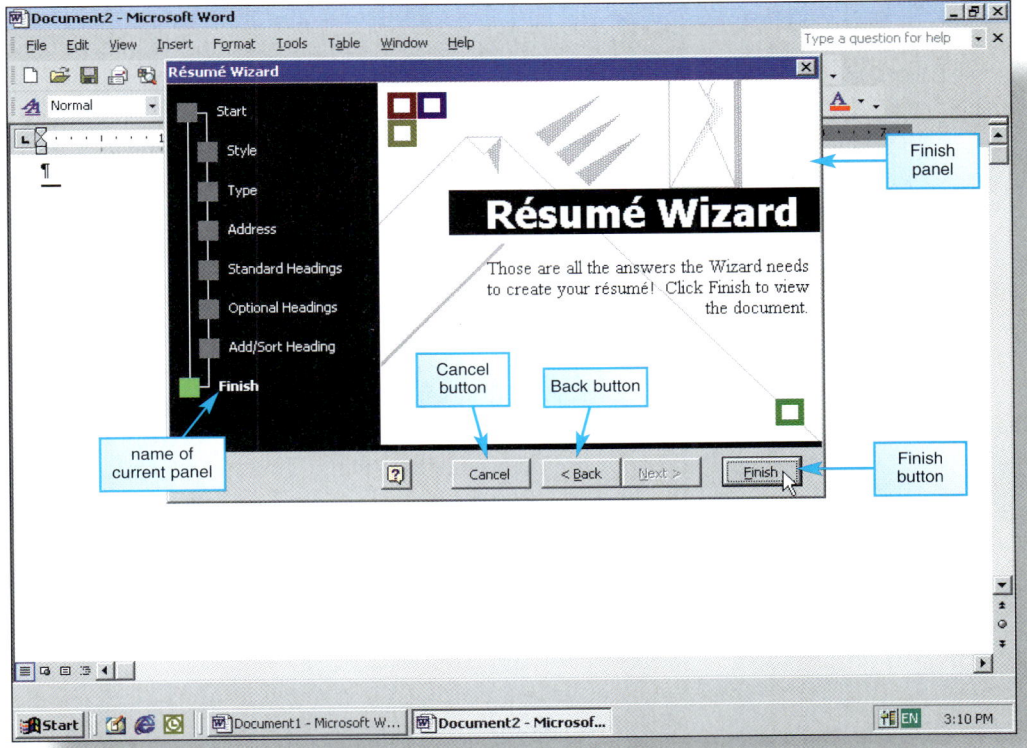

FIGURE 3-16

 **Click the Finish button. If the Office Assistant displays on the screen, click its Cancel button.**

Word creates an entry-level professional style resume layout (Figure 3-17). You are to personalize the resume as indicated.

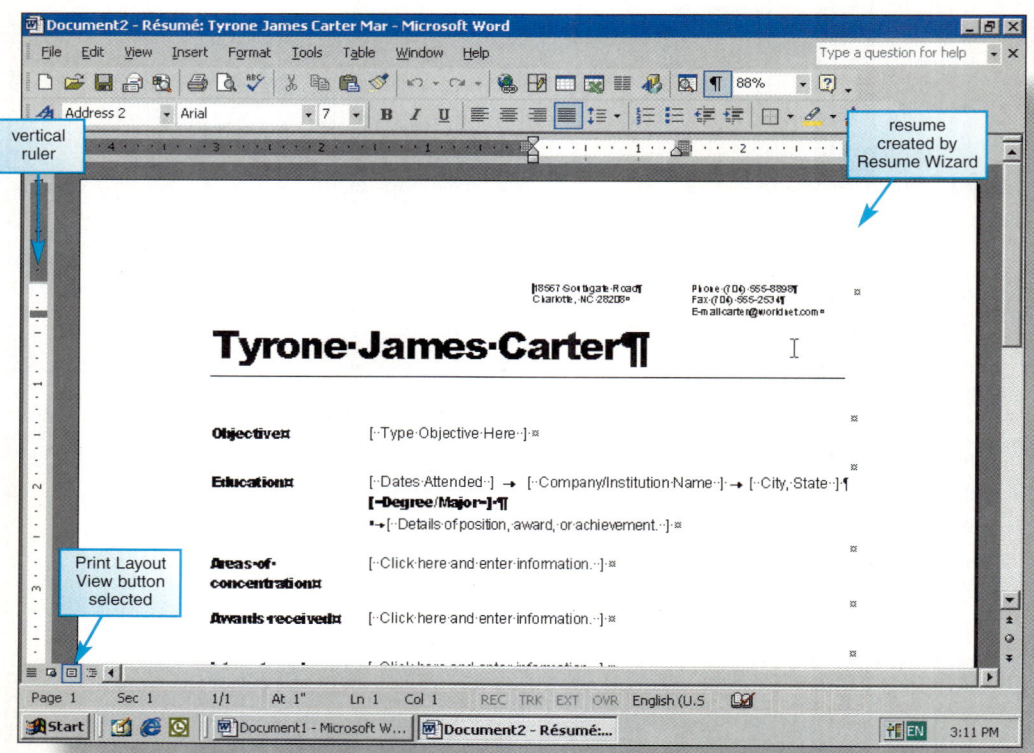

FIGURE 3-17

Other Ways

1. On View menu click Task Pane, click Other Task Panes button on task pane title bar and then click New Document, click General Templates, click Other Documents tab, double-click Resume Wizard icon
2. Click Start button on Windows taskbar, click New Office Document, click Other Documents tab, double-click Resume Wizard icon
3. Right-click Start button on Windows taskbar, click Open All Users, double-click New Office Document, click Other Documents tab, double-click Resume Wizard icon
4. With task pane displaying, in Voice Command mode, say "General Templates, Other Documents, [select Resume Wizard], OK"

Program Buttons

If the Windows taskbar does not display a separate program button for each open Word document, click Tools on the menu bar, click Options, click the View tab, place a check mark in the Windows in Taskbar check box, and then click the OK button.

When you create a resume using the Resume Wizard (Figure 3-16 on the previous page), you can click the panel name or the Back button in any panel of the Resume Wizard dialog box to change the previous options you selected. To exit from the Resume Wizard and return to the document window without creating the resume, click the Cancel button in any panel of the Resume Wizard dialog box.

In addition to the Resume Wizard, Word provides many other wizards to assist you in creating documents: agenda for a meeting, calendar, envelope, fax cover sheet, legal pleading, letter, mailing label, memorandum, and Web page.

Word displays the resume in the document window in print layout view. You can tell that the document window is in print layout view by looking at the screen (Figure 3-17 above). In print layout view, the **Print Layout View button** on the horizontal scroll bar is selected. Also, a **vertical ruler** displays at the left edge of the document window, in addition to the horizontal ruler at the top of the window.

Your screen was in normal view when you created documents in Project 1 and for most of Project 2. In Project 2, when you created the header, the window switched to print layout view. In both normal view and print layout view, you can type and edit text. The difference is that **print layout view** shows you an exact view of the printed page. That is, in print layout view, Word places the entire piece of paper in the document window, showing precisely the positioning of the text, margins, headers, footers, and footnotes.

To display more of the document on the screen in print layout view, you can hide the white space at the top and bottom of the pages and the gray space between pages. Perform the following steps to hide the white space, if your screen displays it.

Using Word's Resume Wizard to Create a Resume • WD 3.15

Steps: To Hide White Space

1 **Point to the top of the page in the document window until the Hide White Space button displays.**

The mouse pointer changes to the Hide White Space button when positioned at the top of the page (Figure 3-18).

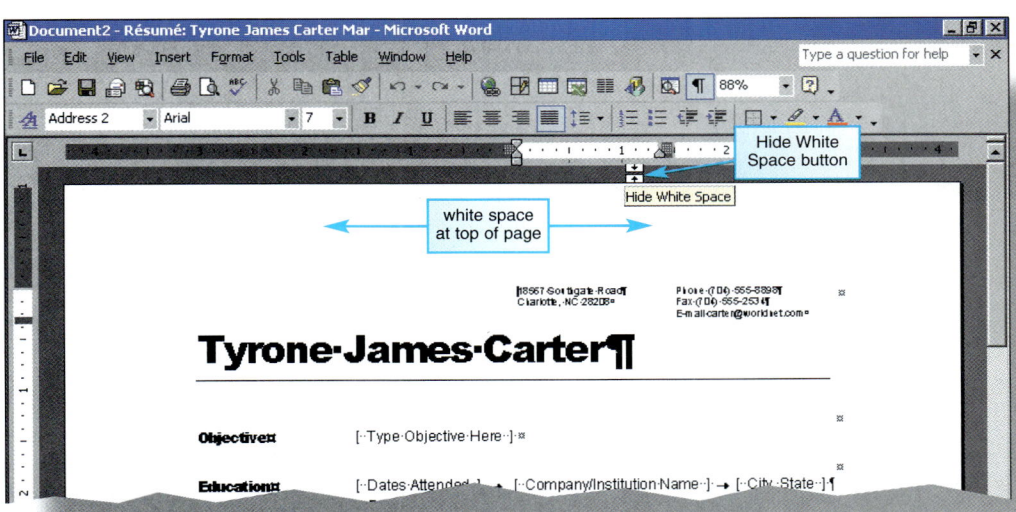

FIGURE 3-18

2 **Click the Hide White Space button.**

Word moves the page up in the document window (Figure 3-19).

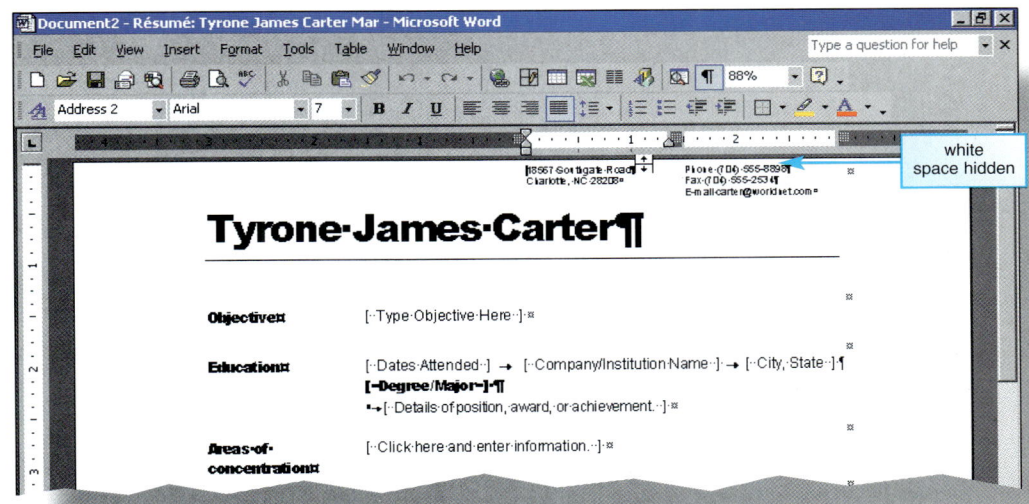

FIGURE 3-19

To see the entire resume created by the Resume Wizard, you should print the document that displays in the Word window, as described in the following steps.

TO PRINT THE RESUME CREATED BY THE RESUME WIZARD

1 Ready the printer and then click the Print button on the Standard toolbar.

2 When the printer stops, retrieve the hard copy resume from the printer.

The printed resume is shown in Figure 3-20 on the next page.

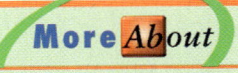

Hiding White Space

If you want Word always to hide white space, click Tools on the menu bar, click Options, click the View tab, remove the check mark from the White space between pages check box, and then click the OK button. This command is available only when the Word screen is in print layout view.

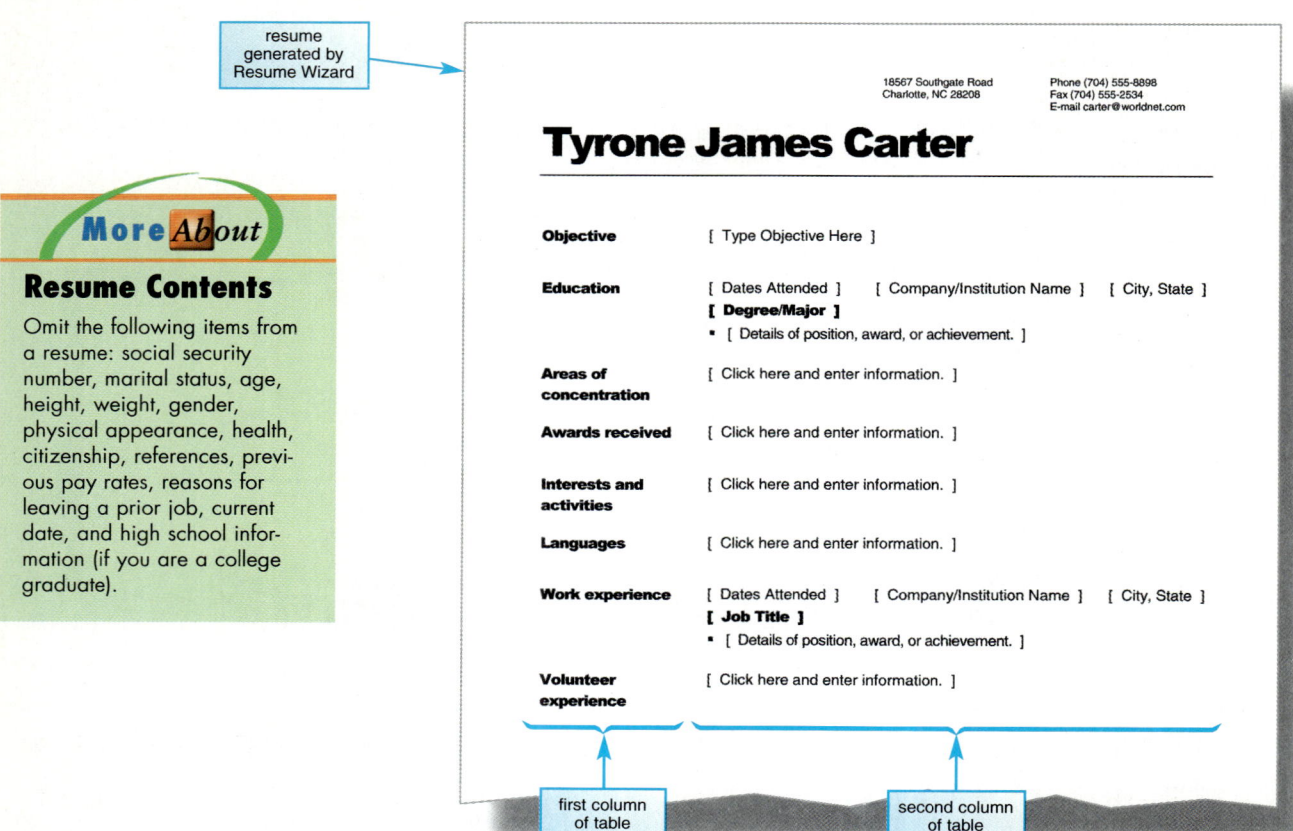

FIGURE 3-20

More About

Resume Contents

Omit the following items from a resume: social security number, marital status, age, height, weight, gender, physical appearance, health, citizenship, references, previous pay rates, reasons for leaving a prior job, current date, and high school information (if you are a college graduate).

Personalizing the Resume

The next step is to personalize the resume. Where Word has indicated, you type the objective, education, areas of concentration, awards received, interests and activities, languages, work experience, and volunteer experience next to the respective headings. The following pages show how to personalize the resume generated by the Resume Wizard.

Tables

More About

Tables

To select a single cell in a table, click to the left of the cell. To select an entire row, click to the left of the row. To select an entire column, click the column's top border. To add a row or column to the middle of a table, click where you want to insert the row or column, click Table on the menu bar, point to Insert, and then click the appropriate command.

When the Resume Wizard prepares a resume, it arranges the body of the resume as a table. A Word **table** is a collection of rows and columns. As shown in Figure 3-21, the first column of the table in the resume contains the section headings (Objective, Education, Areas of concentration, Awards received, Interests and activities, Languages, Work experience, and Volunteer experience). The second column of the table contains the details for each of these sections. Thus, this table contains two columns. It also contains eight rows — one row for each section of the resume.

The intersection of a row and a column is called a **cell**, and cells are filled with text. Each cell has an **end-of-cell mark**, which is a formatting mark that assists you with selecting and formatting cells. Recall that formatting marks do not print on a hard copy.

To see clearly the rows, columns, and cells in a Word table, some users prefer to show gridlines. As illustrated in Figure 3-21, **gridlines** help identify the rows and columns in a table. If you want to display gridlines in a table, position the insertion point somewhere in the table, click Table on the menu bar, and then click **Show Gridlines**. If you want to hide the gridlines, click somewhere in the table, click Table on the menu bar, and then click **Hide Gridlines**.

The Ruler

When the insertion point is in a table, the ruler shows the boundaries of each column in the table. For example, in Figure 3-21, the address information at the top of the resume is a separate table of one row and two columns. The ruler shows the width of each column.

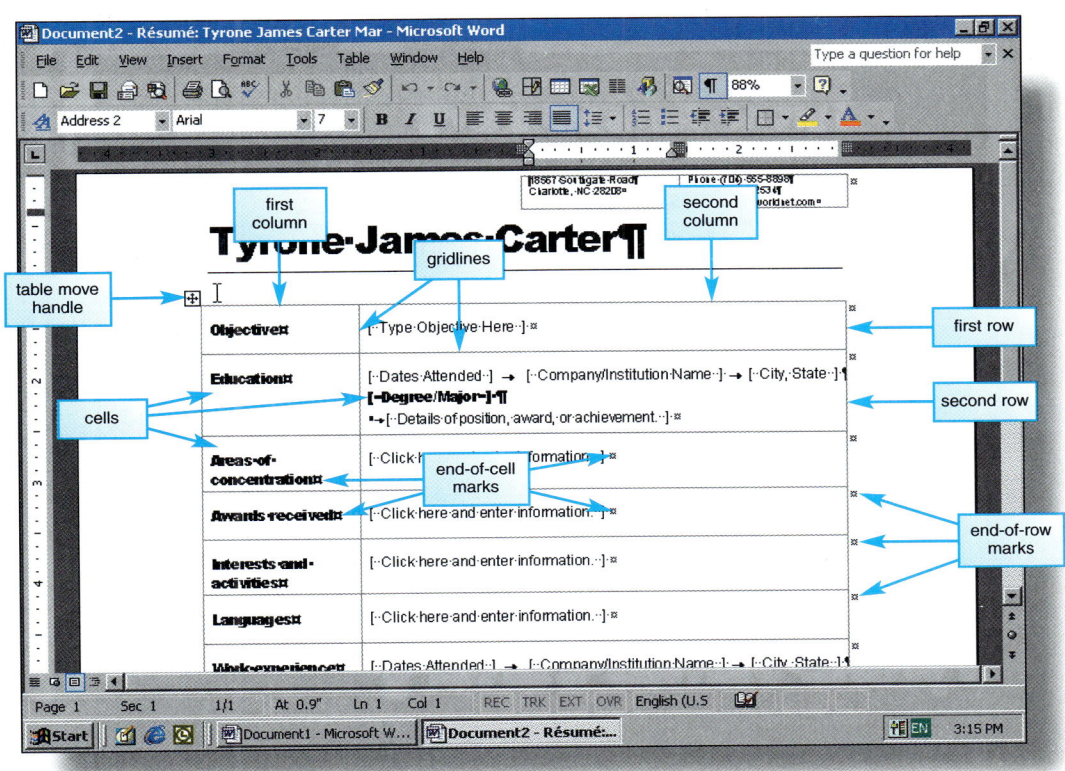

FIGURE 3-21

When you point to the upper-left corner of the table, the table move handle displays. You drag the **table move handle** to move the table to a new location. You also can resize a table, add or delete rows or columns in a table, and format a table. These and other features of tables are discussed in more depth when you create the cover letter later in this project.

Zooming Text Width

In Projects 1 and 2, your screen was in normal view and you used the zoom page width command to display text on the screen as large as possible without extending the right margin beyond the right edge of the document window. In print layout view, the zoom page width command places the edges of the paper at the margins — making the text smaller on the screen. To make the text as large as possible on the screen in print layout view, you should **zoom text width** as shown in the steps on the next page.

Zooming

If you have a Microsoft IntelliMouse®, you can zoom in and out of a document by holding the CTRL key while rotating the wheel forward or backward. To learn other features of the IntelliMouse®, click the Start button on the taskbar, point to Programs, point to Microsoft Hardware, point to Mouse, and then click Online User's Guide.

Steps To Zoom Text Width

1 Click the Zoom box arrow on the Standard toolbar and then point to Text Width in the Zoom list (Figure 3-22).

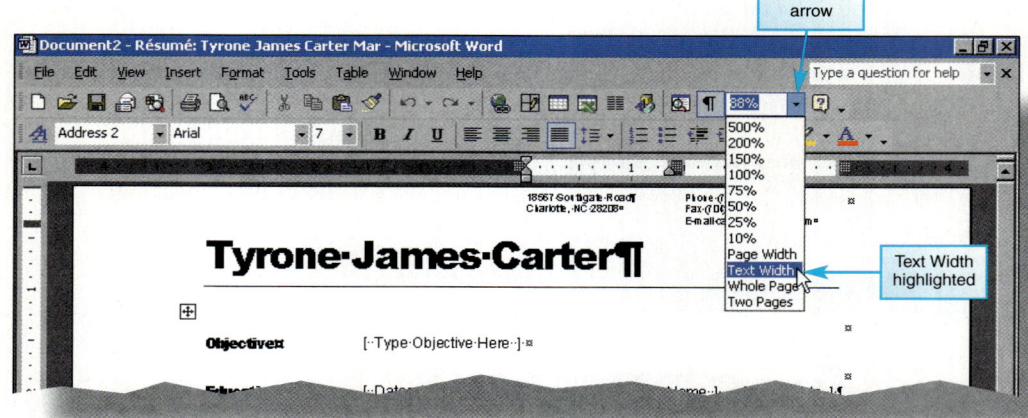

FIGURE 3-22

2 Click Text Width.

Word extends the text to the edges of the document window (Figure 3-23).

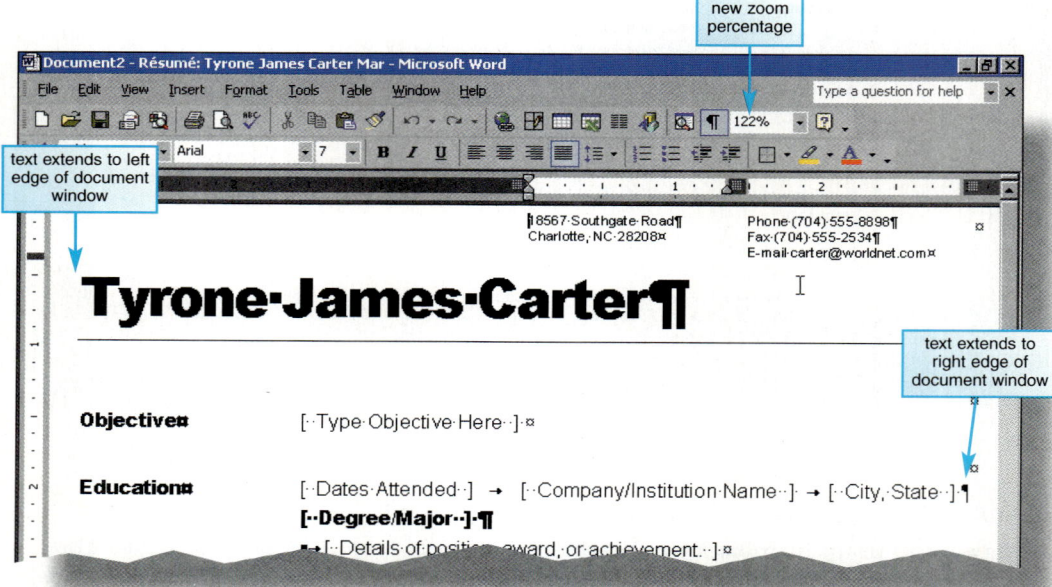

FIGURE 3-23

1. On View menu click Zoom, select Text Width, click OK button
2. In Voice Command mode, say "Zoom, Text Width"

Word computes a zoom percentage based on a variety of settings. The percentage that displays in your Zoom box may be different, depending on your system configuration. Notice in Figure 3-22 above that the Zoom list contains more options when the document window is in print layout view than when it is in normal view.

Styles

When you use a wizard to create a document, Word formats the document using styles. As discussed in Project 2, a **style** is a named group of formatting characteristics that you can apply to text. Recall that the formats defined by a style include character formatting, such as the font and font size; paragraph formatting, such as line spacing and text alignment; table formatting; and list formatting. In Project 2, you changed the formats assigned to the Footnote Text style.

The Style box on the Formatting toolbar displays the name of the style associated with the location of the insertion point or selection. You can identify many of the characteristics assigned to a style by looking at the Formatting toolbar. For example, in Figure 3-24 below, the characters in the selected paragraph are formatted with the Objective style, which uses 10-point Arial font.

If you click the Style box arrow on the Formatting toolbar, the list of styles associated with the current document displays. You also may select the appropriate style from the Style list before typing the text so that the text you type will be formatted according to the selected style.

Another way to work with styles is by clicking the Styles and Formatting button on the Formatting toolbar, which displays the Styles and Formatting task pane. Through the **Styles and Formatting task pane** you can view, create, and apply styles. The Styles and Formatting task pane is shown later when it is used.

In Word, four basic styles exist: paragraph styles, character styles, list styles, and table styles. **Paragraph styles** affect formatting of an entire paragraph, whereas **character styles** affect formats of only selected characters. **List styles** affect alignment and fonts in a numbered or bulleted list, and **table styles** affect the borders, shading, alignment, and fonts in a Word table. In the Style list and Styles and Formatting task pane, paragraph style names usually are followed by a proofreader's paragraph mark (¶); character style names usually are followed by an underlined letter a (a); list styles usually are followed by a bulleted list icon; and table styles usually are followed by a table icon.

> **More About**
>
> **Styles**
>
> Another way to see the formatting is to display the Styles and Formatting task pane by clicking the Styles and Formatting button on the Formatting toolbar. This task pane displays the formats applied to text at the location of the insertion point. To apply a different style, click the desired style in the Pick formatting to apply list in the Styles and Formatting task pane. Or, click the Style box arrow on the Formatting toolbar and then click the desired style.

Selecting and Replacing Text

The next step in personalizing the resume is to select text that the Resume Wizard inserted into the resume and replace it with personal information. The first heading on the resume is the objective. You enter the objective where the Resume Wizard inserted the words, Type Objective Here, which is called **placeholder text**.

To replace text in Word, select the text to be removed and then type the desired text. To select the placeholder text, Type Objective Here, you click it. Then, type the objective. As soon as you begin typing, Word deletes the selected placeholder text. Thus, you do not need to delete the selection before you begin typing.

Perform the following steps to enter the objective into the resume.

Steps — To Select and Replace Placeholder Text

1 **Click the placeholder text, Type Objective Here.**

Word selects the placeholder text in the resume (Figure 3-24). Notice the style is Objective in the Style box on the Formatting toolbar.

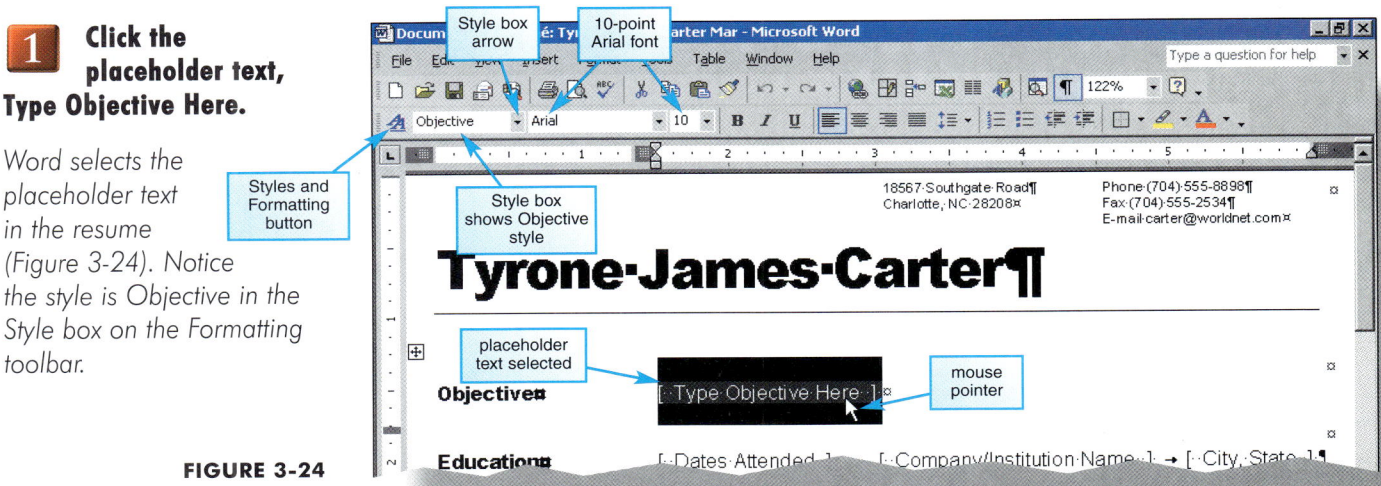

FIGURE 3-24

2 **Type** To obtain a teacher's assistant position for a social studies teacher at a high school in the Charlotte area.

Word replaces the selected placeholder text, Type Objective Here, with the objective you type (Figure 3-25). Your document may wordwrap on a different word depending on the type of printer you are using.

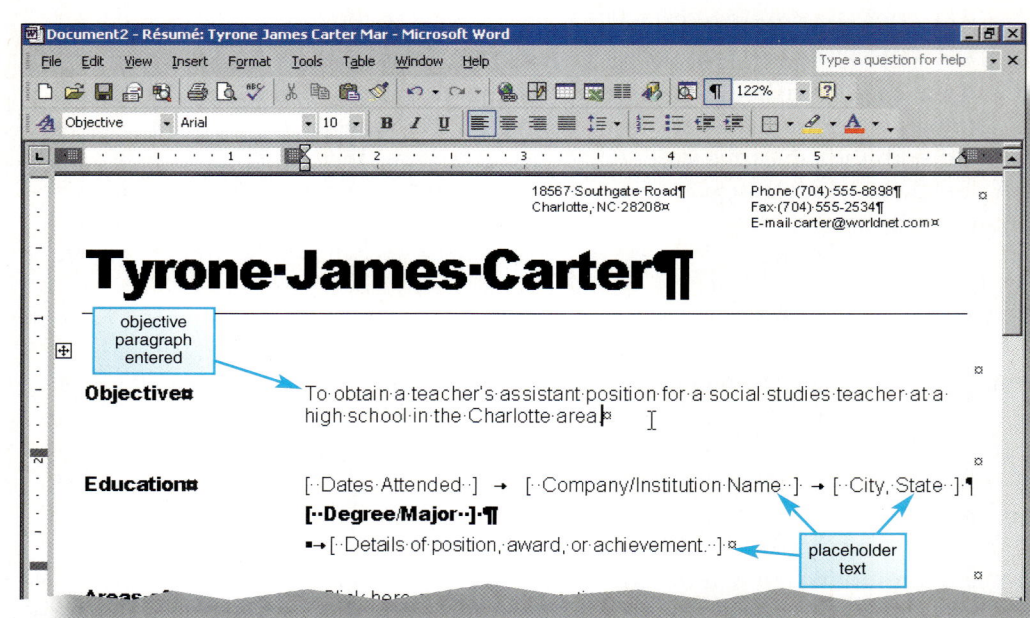

FIGURE 3-25

The next step in personalizing the resume is to replace the placeholder text in the education section of the resume with your own words and phrases as described in the following steps.

TO SELECT AND REPLACE MORE PLACEHOLDER TEXT

1 If necessary, scroll down to display the entire education section of the resume. Click, or if necessary drag through, the placeholder text, Dates Attended. Type 1999-2003 and then click the placeholder text, Company/Institution Name.

2 Type North Carolina State and then click the placeholder text, City, State. Type Charlotte, NC and then click the placeholder text, Degree/Major. Type Social Studies Teaching and then click the placeholder text, Details of position, award, or achievement.

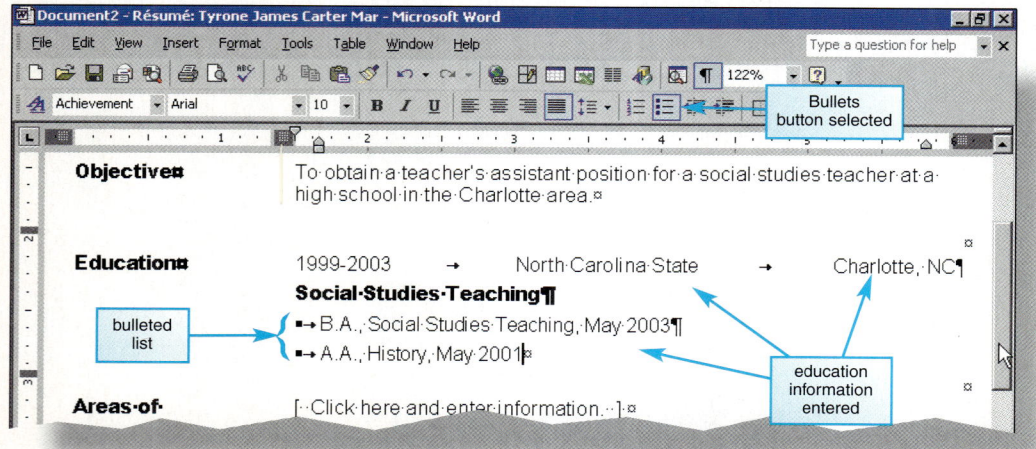

3 Type B.A., Social Studies Teaching, May 2003 and then press the ENTER key. Type A.A., History, May 2001 as the last item in the list.

The education section is entered (Figure 3-26).

FIGURE 3-26

A **bullet** is a dot or other symbol positioned at the beginning of a paragraph. A **bulleted list** is a list of paragraphs that each begin with a bullet character. For example, the list of degrees in the education section of the resume is a bulleted list (Figure 3-26). When the insertion point is in a paragraph containing a bullet, the Bullets button on the Formatting toolbar is selected. In a bulleted list, each time you press the ENTER key, a bullet displays at the beginning of the new paragraph. This is because Word carries forward paragraph formatting when you press the ENTER key.

Entering a Line Break

The next step in personalizing the resume is to enter text in the areas of concentration section. The style used for the characters in the areas of concentration section of the resume is the Objective style. A paragraph formatting characteristic of the Objective style is that when you press the ENTER key, the insertion point advances downward at least 11 points, which leaves nearly an entire blank line between each paragraph.

You want the lines within the areas of concentration section to be close to each other (Figure 3-1 on page WD 3.05). Thus, you will not press the ENTER key between each area of concentration. Instead, you press SHIFT+ENTER to create a **line break**, which advances the insertion point to the beginning of the next physical line — ignoring any paragraph formatting instructions.

Perform the following steps to enter text in the areas of concentration section using a line break, instead of a paragraph break, between each line.

> **More About**
>
> **Bullets**
>
> To apply a different bullet character to selected paragraphs, click Format on the menu bar, click Bullets and Numbering, click the desired bullet style, and then click the OK button. For additional bullet styles, click the Customize button in the Bullets and Numbering dialog box.

Steps To Enter a Line Break

1 If necessary, scroll down to display the areas of concentration section of the resume. In the areas of concentration section, click the placeholder text, Click here and enter information. Type U.S. History (18 hours) and then press SHIFT+ENTER.

Word inserts a **line break character**, which is a formatting mark, at the end of the line and moves the insertion point to the beginning of the next physical line (Figure 3-27).

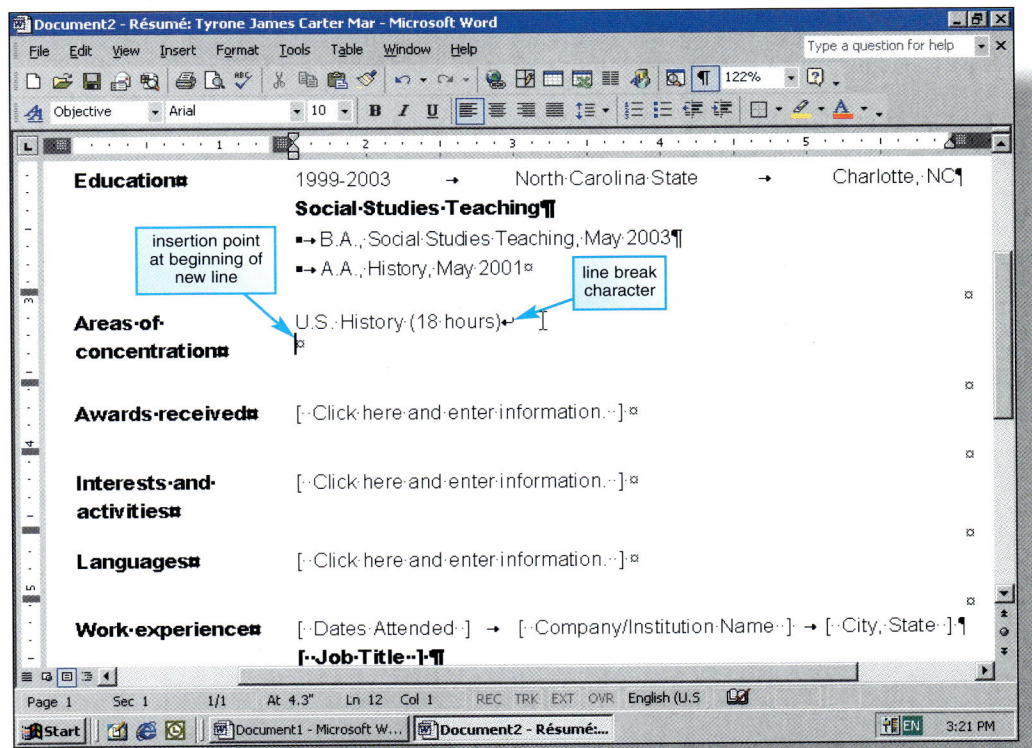

FIGURE 3-27

2 **Type** World Civilization (12 hours) **and then press** SHIFT+ENTER. **Type** Government (12 hours) **and then press** SHIFT+ENTER. **Type** Sociology (10 hours) **as the last entry. Do not press** SHIFT+ENTER **at the end of this line.**

The areas of concentration section is entered (Figure 3-28).

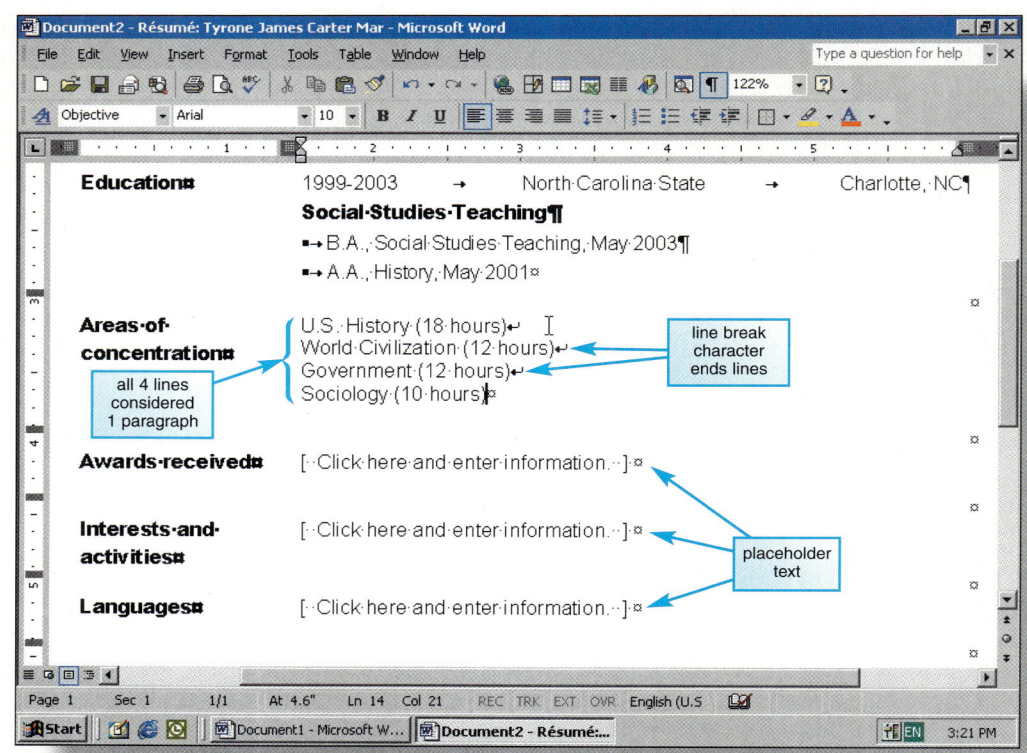

FIGURE 3-28

The next step is to enter the first two awards in the awards received section of the resume.

TO ENTER MORE TEXT WITH LINE BREAKS

1 If necessary, scroll down to display the awards received section of the resume. In the awards received section, click the placeholder text, Click here and enter information. Type Dean's List, every semester and then press SHIFT+ENTER.

2 Type Kappa Phi Gamma Honorary Society, 2001-2003 and then press SHIFT+ENTER.

The first two awards are entered in the awards received section (shown in Figure 3-29).

AutoFormat As You Type

As you type text into a document, Word automatically formats it for you. Table 3-1 outlines commonly used AutoFormat As You Type options and their results.

AutoFormat

For an AutoFormat option to work as expected, it must be turned on. To check if an AutoFormat option is enabled, click Tools on the menu bar, click AutoCorrect Options, click the AutoFormat As You Type tab, select the appropriate check boxes, and then click the OK button. For example, Format beginning of list item like the one before it and Automatic bulleted lists both should contain check marks if you want Word to add bullets automatically as you type.

Table 3-1 Commonly Used AutoFormat As You Type Options

TYPED TEXT	AUTOFORMAT FEATURE	EXAMPLE
Quotation marks or apostrophes	Changes straight quotation marks or apostrophes to curly ones	"the" becomes "the"
Text, a space, one hyphen, one or no spaces, text, space	Changes the hyphen to an en dash	ages 20 - 45 becomes ages 20 – 45
Text, two hyphens, text, space	Changes the two hyphens to an em dash	Two types--yellow and red becomes Two types—yellow and red
Web or e-mail address followed by space or ENTER key	Formats Web or e-mail address as a hyperlink	www.scsite.com becomes www.scsite.com
Three hyphens, underscores, equal signs, asterisks, tildes, or number signs and then ENTER key	Places a border above a paragraph	--- This line becomes _____ This line
Number followed by a period, hyphen, right parenthesis, or greater than sign and then a space or tab followed by text	Creates a numbered list when you press the ENTER key	1. Word 2. Excel becomes 1. Word 2. Excel
Asterisk, hyphen, or greater than sign and then a space or tab followed by text	Creates a bulleted list when you press the ENTER key	* Standard toolbar * Formatting toolbar becomes • Standard toolbar • Formatting toolbar
Fraction and then a space or hyphen	Converts the entry to a fraction-like notation	1/2 becomes ½
Ordinal and then a space or hyphen	Makes the original a superscript	3rd becomes 3rd

Steps: To AutoFormat as You Type

1 **Type** Ross Kimble Speaking Award, 1st **(Figure 3-29).**

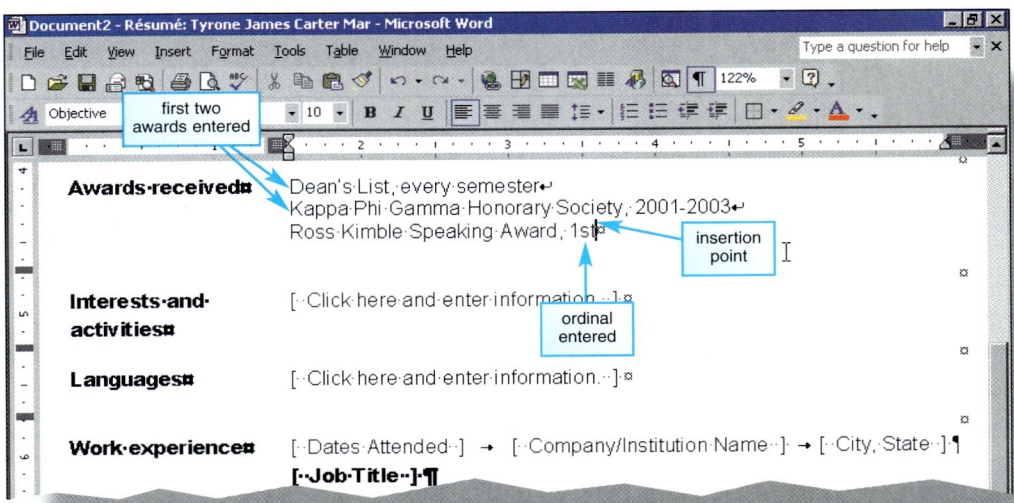

FIGURE 3-29

2 **Press the SPACEBAR. Type** `Place, 2002` **as the end of the award.**

Word automatically converts the st in 1st to a superscript (Figure 3-30).

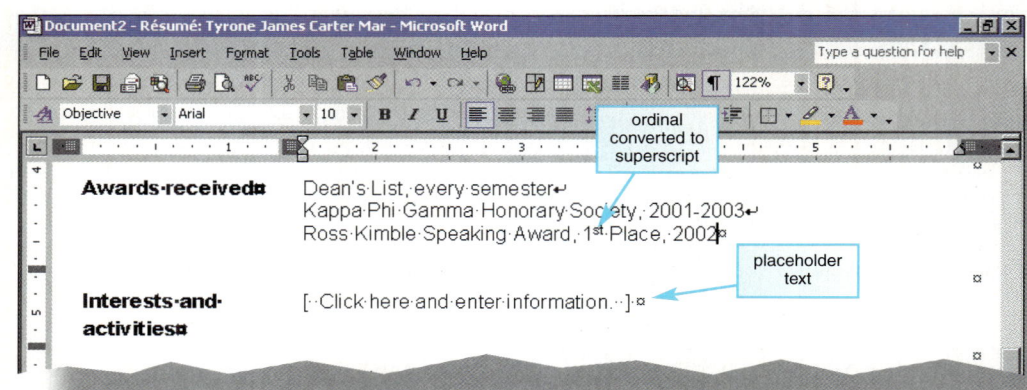

FIGURE 3-30

Enter the remaining text for the resume as described in the following steps.

TO ENTER THE REMAINING SECTIONS OF THE RESUME

1 If necessary, scroll down to display the interests and activities section of the resume. Click the placeholder text, Click here and enter information. Type `CPR certified` and then press SHIFT+ENTER.

2 Type `National Educators of America Association, member` and then press SHIFT+ENTER. Type `Soccer Club, member` and then press SHIFT+ENTER. Type `Student Government, representative` as the last activity. Do not press SHIFT+ENTER at the end of this line.

3 If necessary, scroll down to display the languages section of the resume. Click the placeholder text, Click here and enter information. Type `English (fluent)` and then press SHIFT+ENTER. Type `French (fluent)` and then press SHIFT+ENTER. Type `Spanish` as the last language. Do not press SHIFT+ENTER at the end of this line.

4 If necessary, scroll down to display the work experience section of the resume. Click, or if necessary drag through, the placeholder text, Dates Attended. Type `2000-2003` as the years. Click the placeholder text, Company/Institution Name. Type `North Carolina State` and then click the placeholder text, City, State. Type `Charlotte, NC` and then click the placeholder text, Job Title. Type `Tutor` as the title.

5 Click the placeholder text, Details of position, award, or achievement. Type `Provided one-on-one assistance to campus students having difficulty with economics, French, government, history, and sociology` and then press the ENTER key. Type `Administered placement and test-out examinations` and then press the ENTER key. Type `Conducted group roundtable sessions on various history topics` as the last item in the list.

6 If necessary, scroll down to display the volunteer experience section of the resume. Click the placeholder text, Click here and enter information. Type `On a weekly basis, worked as a grade school teacher's aide for a Hampton Elementary School teacher`. Do not press the ENTER key at the end of this line.

References

Do not list references on your resume, and do not state "References Available Upon Request." Employers assume you will give references, if asked, and this information simply clutters a resume. Often you are asked to list references on your application. Be sure to give your references a copy of your resume.

The interests and activities, languages, work experience, and volunteer experience sections of the resume are complete (Figure 3-31).

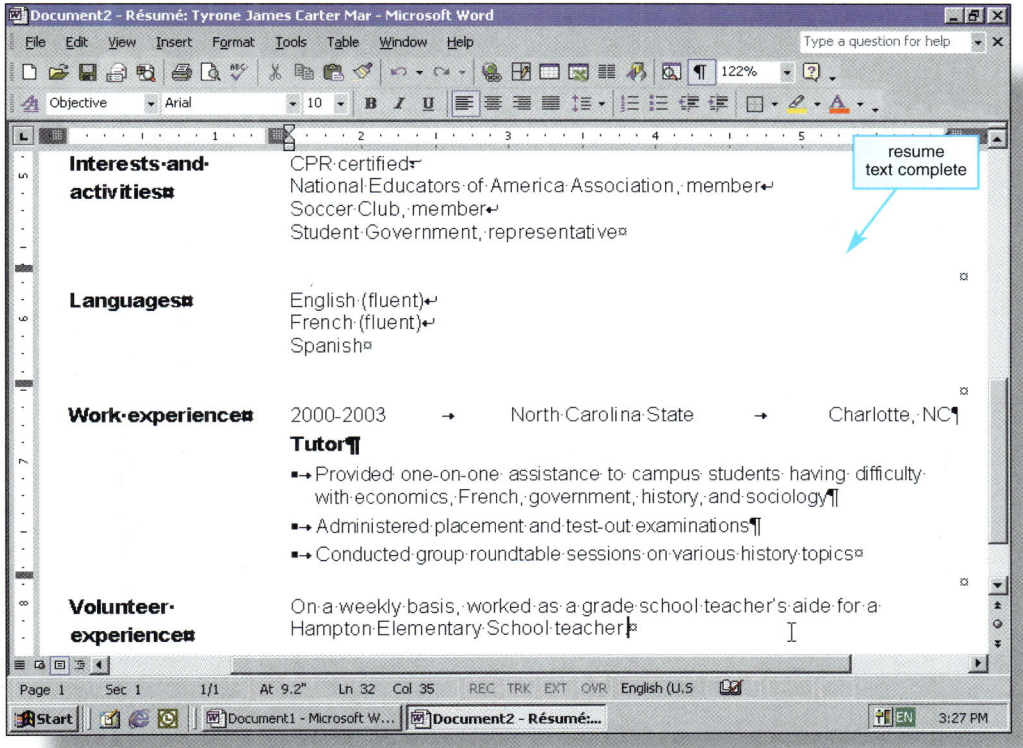

FIGURE 3-31

Viewing and Printing the Resume in Print Preview

To see exactly how a document will look when you print it, you should display it in **print preview**. Print preview displays the entire document in reduced size on the Word screen. In print preview, you can edit and format text, adjust margins, view multiple pages, reduce the document to fit on a single page, and print the document.

Perform the following steps to view and print the resume in print preview.

Steps: To Print Preview a Document

 Point to the Print Preview button on the Standard toolbar (Figure 3-32).

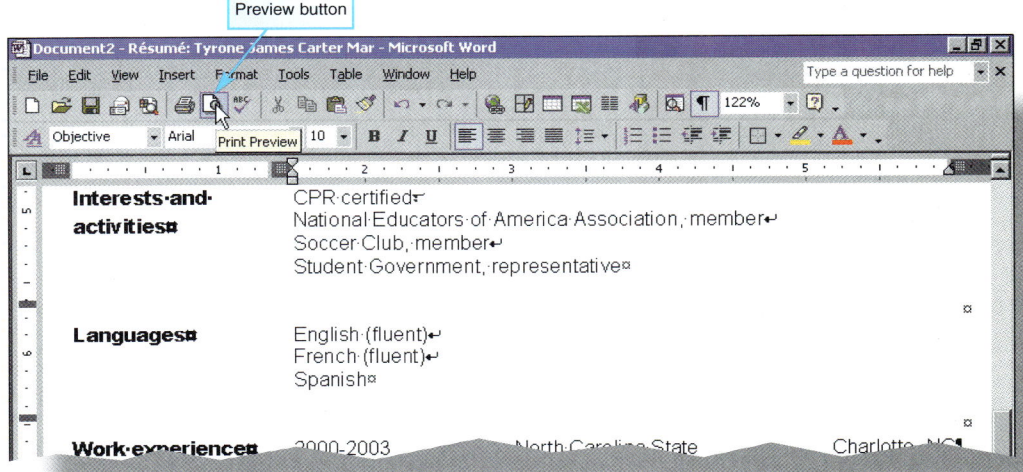

FIGURE 3-32

Printing

If you want to save ink, print faster, or decrease printer overrun errors, print a draft. Click File on the menu bar, click Print, click the Options button, place a check mark in the Draft output check box, and then click the OK button in both dialog boxes.

2 **Click the Print Preview button. Point to the Print button on the Print Preview toolbar.**

Word displays the document in print preview (Figure 3-33). The *Print Preview toolbar* displays below the menu bar; the Standard and Formatting toolbars disappear from the screen.

3 **Click the Print button on the Print Preview toolbar. When the printer stops, retrieve the printout (shown in Figure 3-1 on page WD 3.05). Click the Close Preview button on the Print Preview toolbar.**

Word returns to the document window, displaying the resume (shown in Figure 3-34).

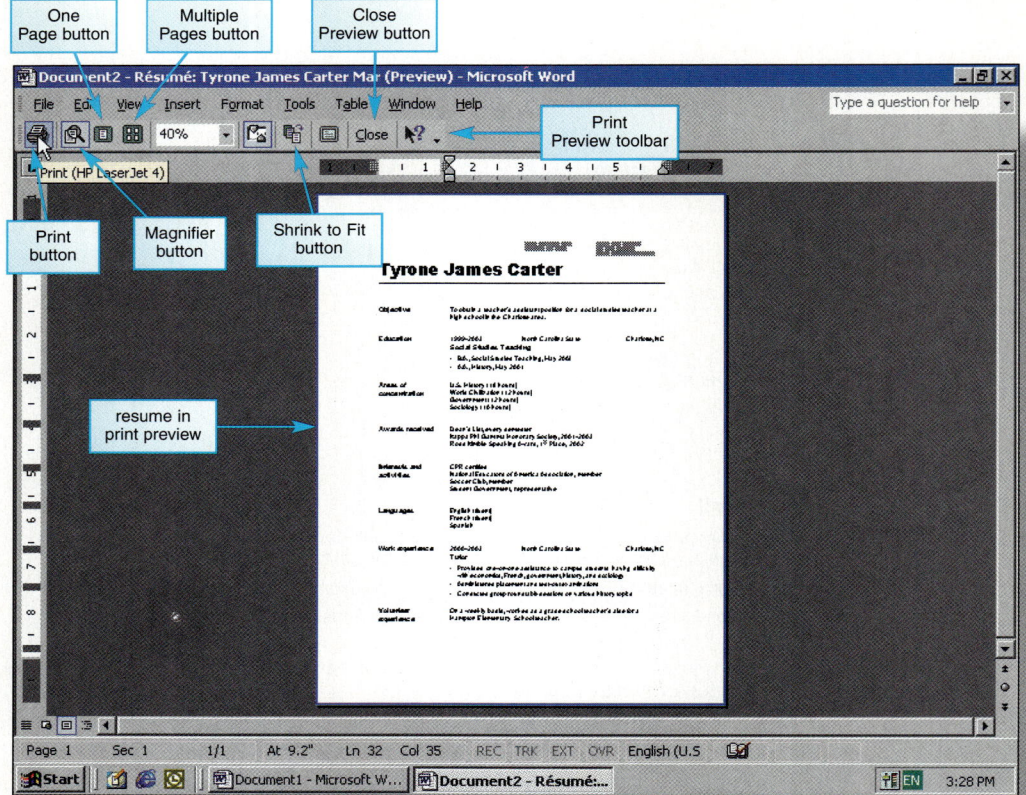

FIGURE 3-33

Other Ways

1. On File menu click Print Preview
2. Press CTRL+F2
3. In Voice Command mode, say "Print Preview"

Print Preview

If the page is not centered in the Print Preview window, click the One Page button. With the Magnifier button on the Print Preview toolbar selected, you can click in the document to zoom in or out. Magnifying a page does not affect the printed document. To edit a document, click the Magnifier button to deselect it and then edit the text. If a document spills onto a second page by a line or two, click the Shrink to Fit button and Word will try to fit it all on a single page.

Saving the Resume

The resume now is complete. Thus, you should save it. For a detailed example of the procedure summarized below, refer to pages WD 1.30 through WD 1.32 in Project 1.

TO SAVE A DOCUMENT

1 Insert your floppy disk into drive A.

2 Click the Save button on the Standard toolbar.

3 Type Carter Resume in the File name text box. Do not press the ENTER key.

4 Click the Save in box arrow and then click 3½ Floppy (A:).

5 Click the Save button in the Save As dialog box.

Word saves the document on a floppy disk in drive A with the file name, Carter Resume (shown in Figure 3-34).

The next step in Project 3 is to create a cover letter to send with the resume to a potential employer. Do not close the Carter Resume. You will use it again later in this project to copy the address, telephone, fax, and e-mail information.

Creating a Letterhead

You have created a resume to send to prospective employers. Along with the resume, you will enclose a personalized cover letter. You would like the cover letter to have a professional looking letterhead (Figure 3-2a on page WD 3.06). The following pages describe how to use Word to create a letterhead.

In many businesses, letterhead is preprinted on stationery that everyone in a company uses for correspondence. For personal letters, the expense of preprinted letterhead can be costly. Thus, you can create your own letterhead and save it in a file. When you want to create a letter with the letterhead, you simply open the letterhead file and then save the file with a new name, preserving the original letterhead file.

The steps on the following pages illustrate how to create a personal letterhead file.

Opening a New Document Window

The resume currently displays in the document window. You want the resume document to remain open because you intend to use it again during this Word session. That is, you will be working with two documents at the same time: the resume and the letterhead. Word will display each of these documents in a separate document window.

Perform the following steps to open a new document window for the letterhead file.

Steps To Open a New Document Window

1 Point to the New Blank Document button on the Standard toolbar (Figure 3-34).

2 Click the New Blank Document button.

Word opens a new document window (shown in Figure 3-35 on the next page).

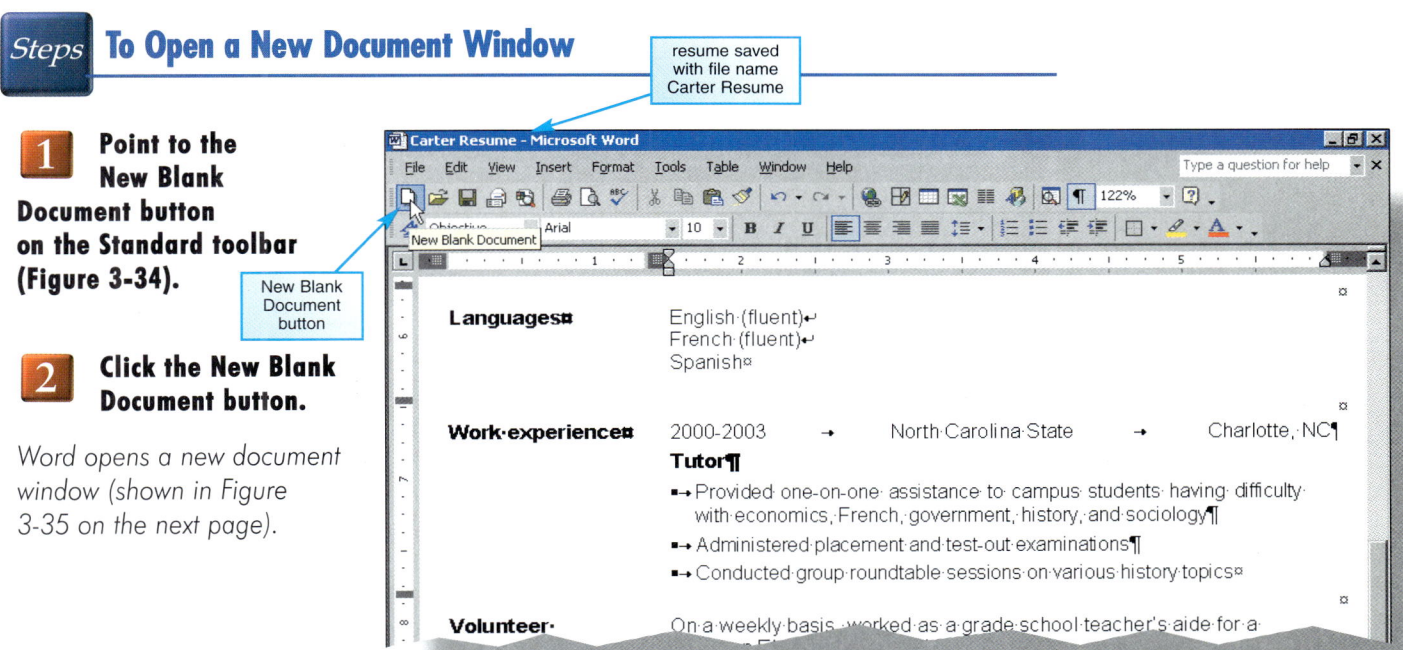

FIGURE 3-34

> **More About**
>
> **Letterhead Design**
>
> Letterhead designs vary. Some are centered at the top of the page, while others have text or graphics aligned with the left and right margins. Another style places the company's name and logo at the top of the page with the address and other information at the bottom. A well-designed letterhead adds professionalism to correspondence.

> **Other Ways**
>
> 1. On File menu click New, click Blank Document in New area in New Document task pane
> 2. Press CTRL+N
> 3. In Voice Command mode, say "New Blank Document"

Program Buttons

If the Windows taskbar does not display a separate program button for each open Word document, click Tools on the menu bar, click Options, click the View tab, place a check mark in the Windows in Taskbar check box, and then click the OK button.

The Carter Resume document still is open. The program buttons on the taskbar display the names of the open Word document windows. The Document3 button on the taskbar is recessed, indicating that it is the active document currently displaying in the Word document window.

The name in the letterhead is to be a font size of 20. Perform the following steps to change the font size.

TO CHANGE THE FONT SIZE

1. Click the Font Size box arrow on the Formatting toolbar.
2. Click 20 in the Font Size list.

Word changes the displayed font size to 20 (shown in Figure 3-35 below).

Adding Color to Characters

The characters in the letterhead are to be dark red. Perform the following steps to change the color of the characters before you type them.

Steps: To Color Characters

1 **Point to the Font Color button arrow on the Formatting toolbar.**

The color that displays below the letter A on the Font Color button is the most recently used color for characters (Figure 3-35). The color on your button may differ from this figure.

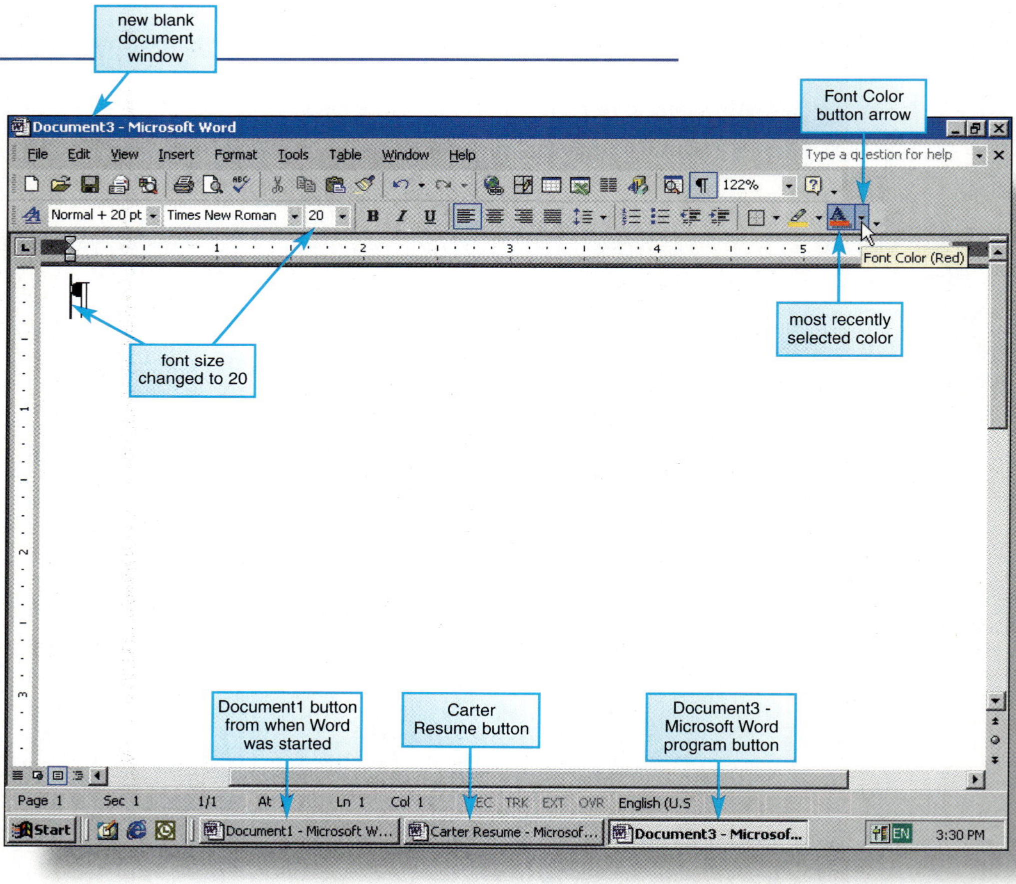

FIGURE 3-35

2 **Click the Font Color button arrow. Point to Dark Red, which is the first color on the second row on the color palette.**

Word displays a list of available colors on the color palette (Figure 3-36). Automatic is the default color, which usually is black.

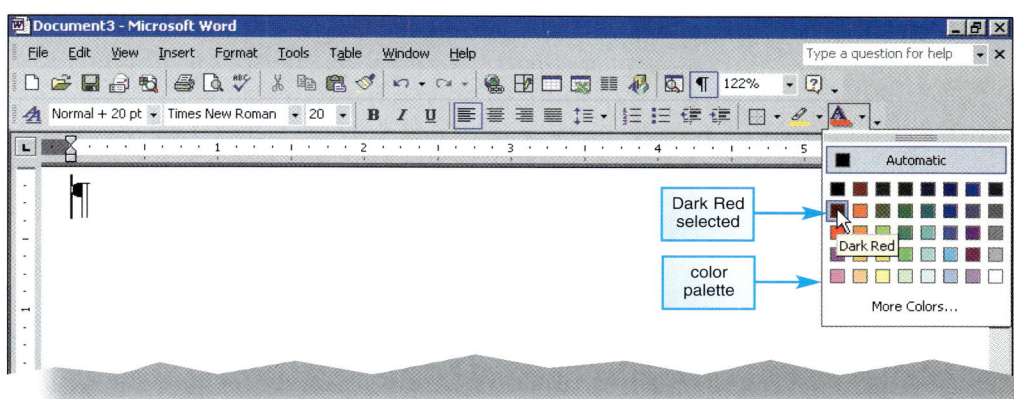

FIGURE 3-36

3 **Click Dark Red. Type** Tyrone James Carter **and then press the ENTER key.**

Word displays the first line of the letterhead in dark red (Figure 3-37).

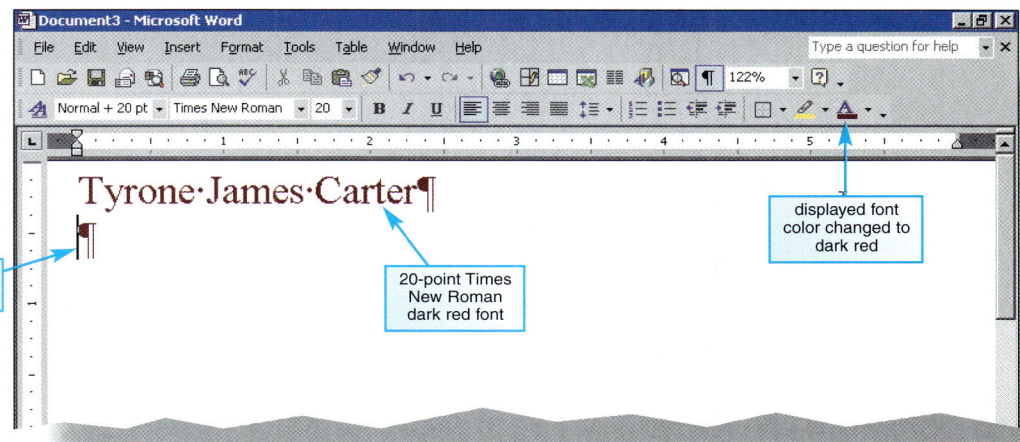

FIGURE 3-37

Notice the paragraph mark on line 2 is dark red. Recall that each time you press the ENTER key, Word carries forward formatting to the next paragraph. If, for some reason, you wanted to change the text back to black at this point, you would click the Font Color button arrow on the Formatting toolbar and then click Automatic on the color palette.

The next step is to insert a graphic of a soccer ball and resize it as described in the following steps.

TO INSERT AND RESIZE A GRAPHIC

1. With the insertion point below the name as shown in Figure 3-37, click Insert on the menu bar, point to Picture, and then click Clip Art on the Picture submenu.

2. When the Insert Clip Art task pane displays, if necessary, drag through any text in the Search text text box to select the text. Type soccer and then press the ENTER key.

3. Point to the clip of the soccer ball that matches the one shown in Figure 3-38 on the next page. Click the button arrow that displays to the right of the clip and then click Insert on the menu. Click the Close button on the Insert Clip Art task pane title bar.

Other Ways

1. On Format menu click Font, click Font tab, click Font color box arrow, click desired color, click OK button
2. Right-click paragraph mark or selected text, click Font on shortcut menu, click Font tab, click Font color box arrow, click desired color, click OK button
3. In Voice Command mode, say "Font Color, Dark Red"

4. Click the graphic to select it. Drag the upper-right corner sizing handle diagonally toward the center of the graphic until the selection rectangle is positioned approximately as shown in Figure 3-38.

5. Click the paragraph mark to the right of the graphic to position the insertion point to the right of the graphic (shown in Figure 3-39).

Word inserts the graphic of the soccer ball (Figure 3-38). You resize the graphic to approximately one-eighth of its original size (shown in Figure 3-39).

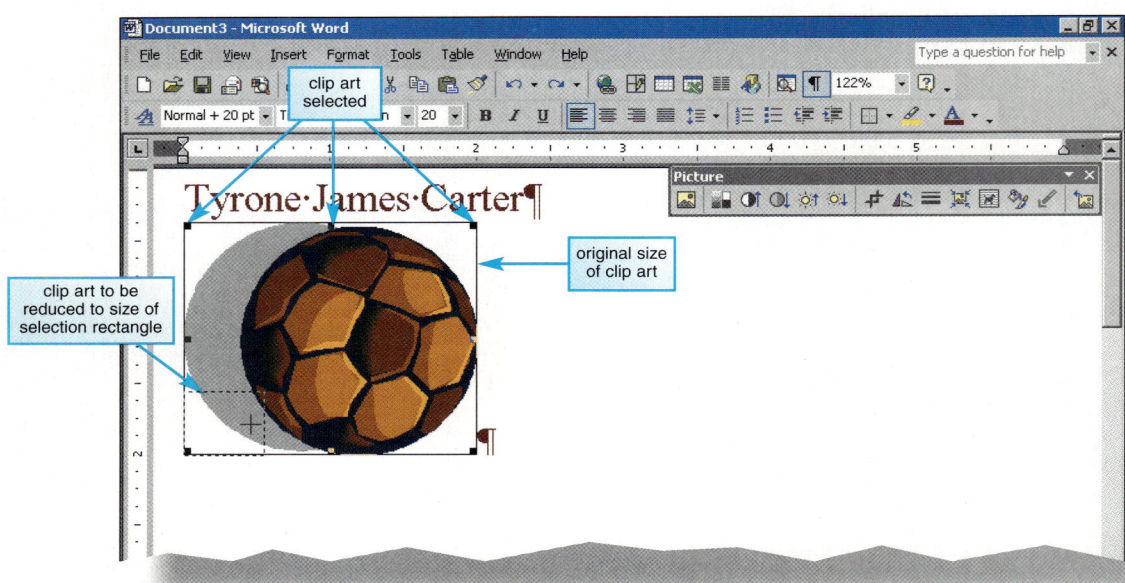

FIGURE 3-38

The Tabs Dialog Box

You can use the Tabs dialog box to change an existing tab stop's alignment or position. You also can place leader characters in the empty space occupied by the tab. Leader characters, such as a series of dots, often are used in a table of contents to precede the page number. Simply click the desired type of leader in the Leader area in the Tabs dialog box.

Setting Tab Stops Using the Tabs Dialog Box

The graphic of the soccer ball is left-aligned (Figure 3-38). The address is to be positioned at the right margin of the same line. If you click the Align Right button, the graphic will be right-aligned. In Word, a paragraph cannot be both left-aligned and right-aligned. To place text at the right margin of a left-aligned paragraph, you set a tab stop at the right margin.

A **tab stop** is a location on the horizontal ruler that tells Word where to position the insertion point when you press the TAB key on the keyboard. A tab stop is useful for indenting text or aligning columns.

Word, by default, places a tab stop at every .5" mark on the ruler (Figure 3-40). These default tabs are indicated on the horizontal ruler by small **tick marks**. You also can set your own custom tab stops. When you set a **custom tab stop**, Word clears all default tab stops to the left of the custom tab stop. You can specify how the text will align at a tab stop: left, centered, right, or decimal. Word stores tab settings in the paragraph mark at the end of each paragraph. Thus, each time you press the ENTER key, any custom tab stops are carried forward to the next paragraph.

In the letterhead for this project, you want the tab stop to be right-aligned with the right margin, that is, at the 6" mark on the ruler. One method of setting custom tab stops is to click the ruler at the desired location of the tab stop. You cannot click, however, at the right margin location. Thus, use the Tabs dialog box to set a custom tab stop at the 6" mark, as shown in the following steps.

Creating a Letterhead • WD 3.31

 To Set Custom Tab Stops Using the Tabs Dialog Box

1 With the insertion point positioned between the paragraph mark and the graphic, click Format on the menu bar and then point to Tabs (Figure 3-39).

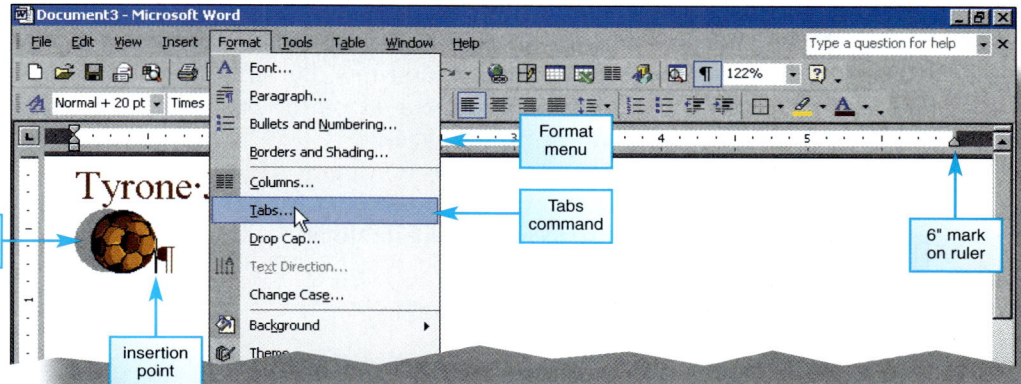

FIGURE 3-39

2 Click Tabs. When the Tabs dialog box displays, type 6 in the Tab stop position text box and then click Right in the Alignment area. Point to the Set button.

Word displays the Tabs dialog box (Figure 3-40).

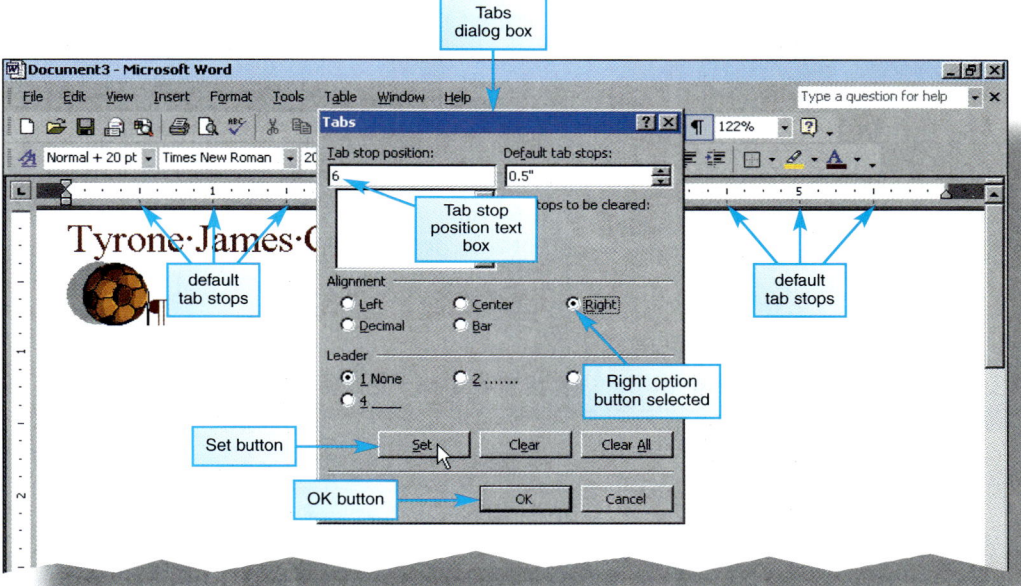

FIGURE 3-40

3 Click the Set button and then click the OK button.

Word places a right tab marker at the 6" mark on the ruler and removes all default tab stops that display to the left of the tab marker (Figure 3-41).

Other Ways

1. Click button on left of ruler until desired tab stop alignment displays and then click ruler
2. In Voice Command mode, say "Format, Tabs"

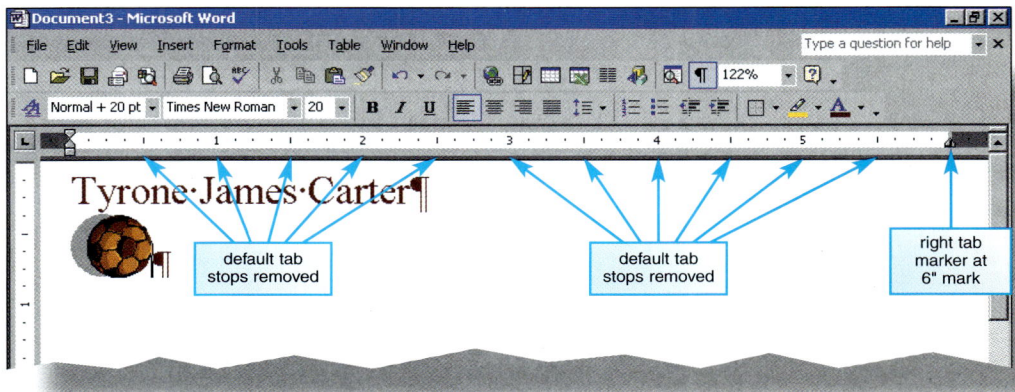

FIGURE 3-41

Tab Alignment

If you have a series of numbers that you want aligned on the decimal point, such as dollar amounts, use a decimal-aligned tab stop for the data.

Clipboards

The Windows Clipboard, which can hold only one item at a time, is separate from the Office Clipboard. When you collect multiple items on the Office Clipboard, the last copied item also is copied to the Windows Clipboard. When you clear the Office Clipboard, the Windows Clipboard also is cleared.

When you set a custom tab stop, the tab marker on the ruler reflects the alignment of the characters at the location of the tab stop. A capital letter L (◣) indicates a left-aligned tab stop. A mirror image of a capital letter L (◢) indicates a right-aligned tab stop. An upside down T (◥) indicates a centered tab stop. An upside down T with a dot next to it (◥) indicates a decimal-aligned tab stop. The tab markers are discussed as they are presented in these projects. The tab marker on the ruler in Figure 3-41 on the previous page indicates text entered at that tab stop will be right-aligned.

To move the insertion point from one tab stop to another, you press the TAB key. When you press the TAB key, a formatting mark, called a **tab character**, displays in the empty space between tab stops.

Collecting and Pasting

The next step in creating the letterhead is to copy the address, telephone, fax, and e-mail information from the resume to the letterhead. To copy multiple items from one Office document to another, you use the Office Clipboard. The **Office Clipboard** is a temporary storage area that can hold up to 24 items (text or graphics) copied from any Office application. You copy, or **collect**, items and then paste them in a new location. **Pasting** is the process of copying an item from the Office Clipboard into the document at the location of the insertion point. When you paste an item into a document, the contents of the Office Clipboard are not erased.

To copy the address, telephone, fax, and e-mail information from the resume to the letterhead, you first switch to the resume, copy the items to the Office Clipboard, switch back to the letterhead, and then paste the information from the Office Clipboard into the letterhead. The following pages illustrate this process.

Follow these steps to switch from the letterhead to the resume.

Steps: To Switch from One Open Document to Another

1 **Point to the Carter Resume - Microsoft Word button on the Windows taskbar (Figure 3-42).**

2 **Click the Carter Resume - Microsoft Word button.**

Word switches from the cover letter to the resume (shown in Figure 3-43).

Other Ways

1. On Window menu click document name
2. Press ALT+TAB
3. In Voice Command mode, say "Window [document number]"

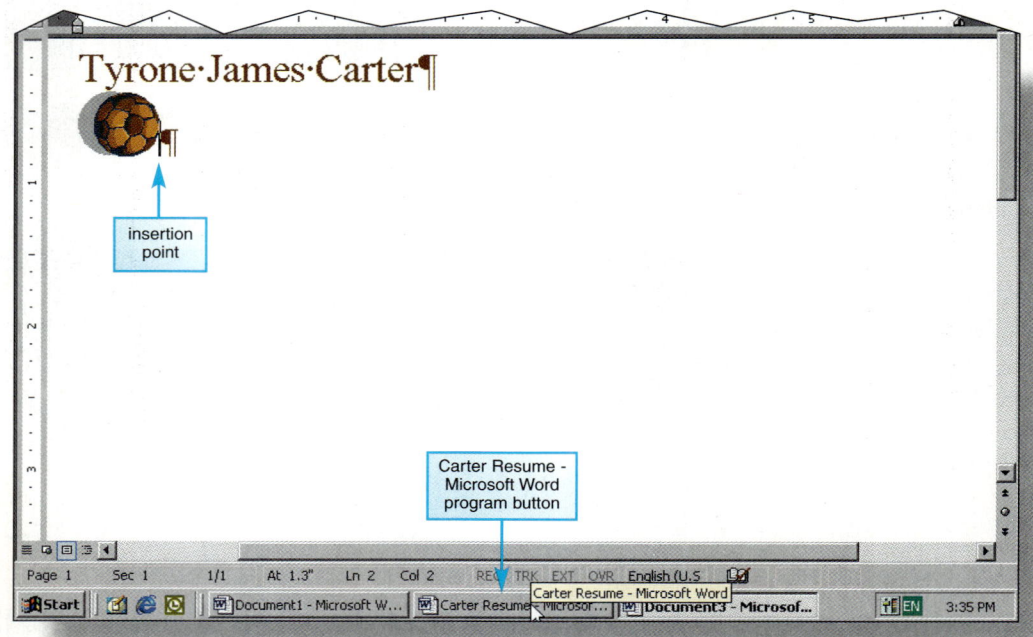

FIGURE 3-42

Creating a Letterhead • WD 3.33

You can copy multiple items to the Office Clipboard and then can paste them later. Each copied item displays as an entry in the Office Clipboard gallery of the Clipboard task pane. The entry displays an icon that indicates the Office program from which the item was copied. The entry also displays a portion of text that was copied or a thumbnail of a graphic that was copied. The most recently copied item displays at the top of the gallery.

Perform the following steps to copy five items to the Office Clipboard.

The Office Clipboard

The Office Clipboard may display automatically on the Word screen if you click the Copy button or the Cut button on the Standard toolbar twice in succession, or if you copy and paste an item and then copy another item.

 **To Collect Items**

1 Press CTRL+HOME to display the top of the resume. Click Edit on the menu bar then point to Office Clipboard (Figure 3-43).

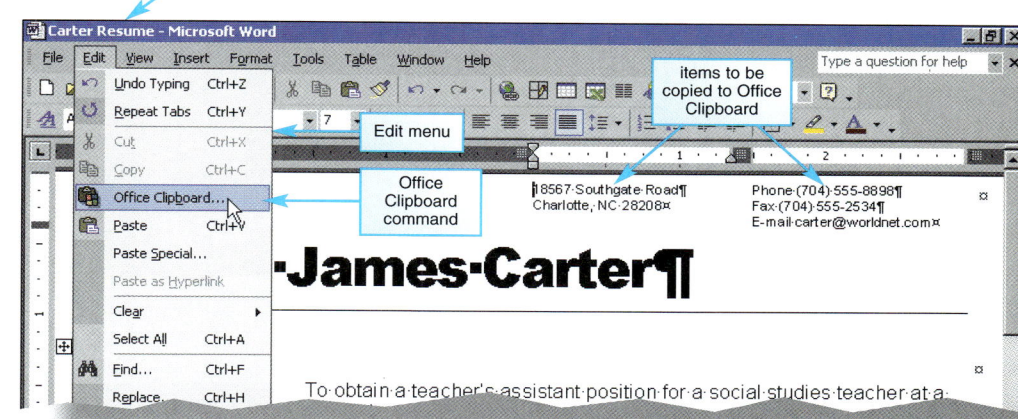

FIGURE 3-43

2 Click Office Clipboard. If the Office Clipboard gallery in the Clipboard task pane is not empty, click the Clear All button in the Clipboard task pane. In the resume, drag through the street address, 18567 Southgate Road (do not select the paragraph mark after the address). Point to the Copy button on the Standard toolbar.

The Clipboard task pane displays on the screen (Figure 3-44). The Office Clipboard icon displays in the tray status area of the Windows taskbar, indicating the Office Clipboard displays in at least one open Office program.

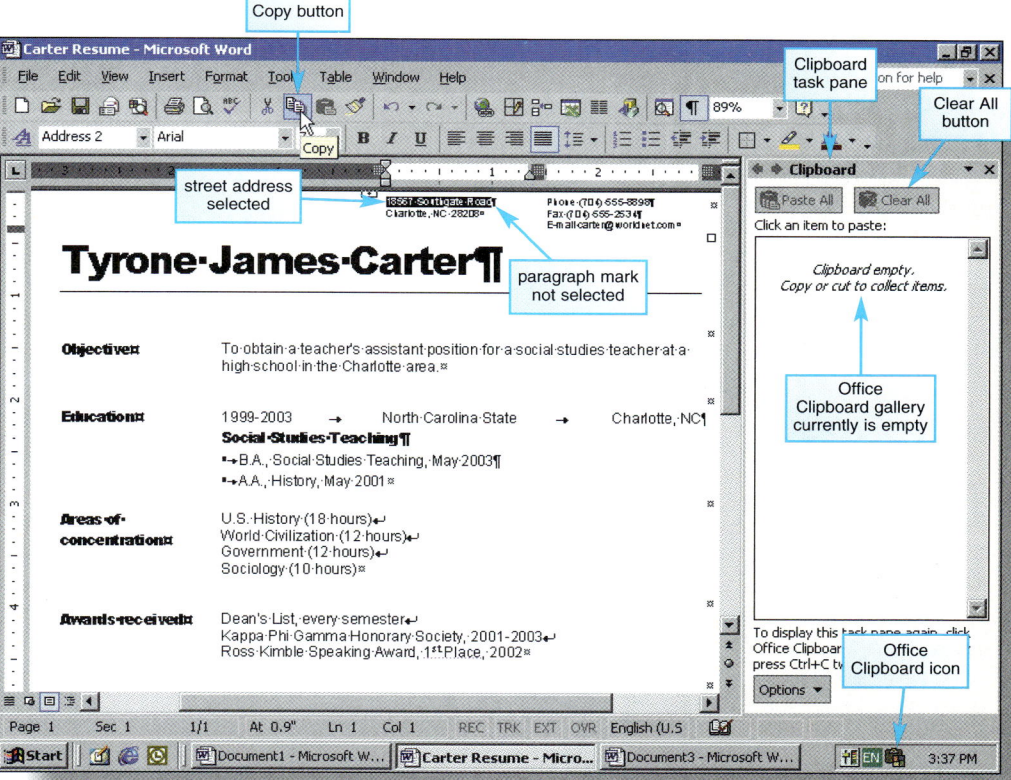

FIGURE 3-44

3 **Click the Copy button.**

Word copies the selection to the Office Clipboard and places an entry in the Office Clipboard gallery in the Clipboard task pane (Figure 3-45).

4 **Drag through the city, state, and postal code information. Click the Copy button on the Standard toolbar. Drag through the telephone information. Click the Copy button on the Standard toolbar. Drag through the fax information. Click the Copy button on the Standard toolbar. Drag through the e-mail information. Click the Copy button on the Standard toolbar (Figure 3-46).**

1. With Clipboard task pane displaying and item to copy selected, on Edit menu click Copy
2. With Clipboard task pane displaying, right-click selected item, click Copy on shortcut menu
3. With Clipboard task pane displaying and item to copy selected, press CTRL+C
4. With Clipboard task pane displaying, in Voice Command mode, say "Copy"

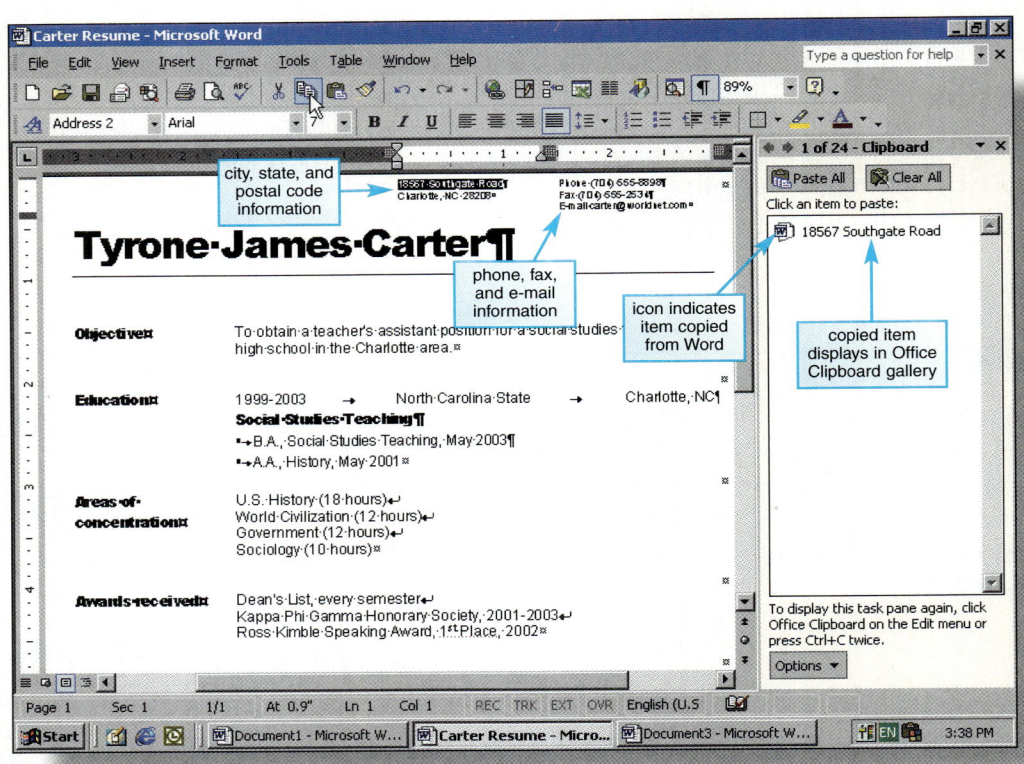

FIGURE 3-45

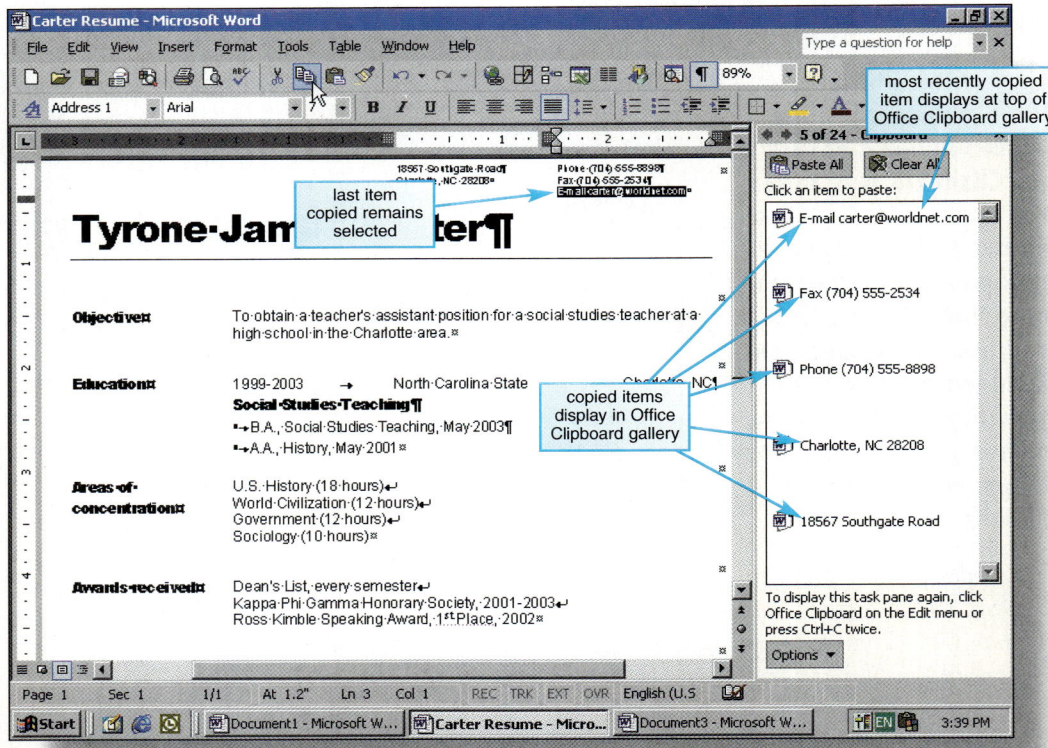

FIGURE 3-46

Each time you copy an item to the Office Clipboard, a ScreenTip displays above the Office Clipboard icon in the tray status area of the Windows taskbar, indicating the number of entries currently in the Office Clipboard. The Office Clipboard can store up to 24 items at one time. When you copy a 25th item, Word deletes the first item to make room for the new item. When you point to a text entry in the Office Clipboard gallery of the Office task pane, the first several characters of text in the item display as a ScreenTip.

The next step is to paste the copied items into the letterhead. When you switch to another document, the Clipboard task pane might not display on the screen. You could display it by clicking Edit on the menu bar and then clicking Office Clipboard. If the Office Clipboard icon displays in the tray status area, however, you can double-click the icon to display the Clipboard task pane.

Perform the following steps to paste the items from the Office Clipboard into the letterhead.

The Office Clipboard Icon

If the Office Clipboard icon does not display on the Windows taskbar (Figure 3-47), click the Options button at the bottom of the Clipboard task pane and then click Show Office Clipboard icon on Taskbar.

Steps To Paste from the Office Clipboard

1 **Click the Document3 - Microsoft Word button on the Windows taskbar to display the letterhead document window. Double-click the Office Clipboard icon in the tray status area of the Windows task bar to display the Clipboard task pane.**

2 **With the insertion point between the paragraph mark and the soccer ball graphic (shown in Figure 3-42 on page WD 3.32), press the TAB key.**

The insertion point is positioned at the 6" mark on the ruler, the location of the right-aligned tab stop (Figure 3-47). The right-pointing arrow is a formatting mark that displays each time you press the TAB key.

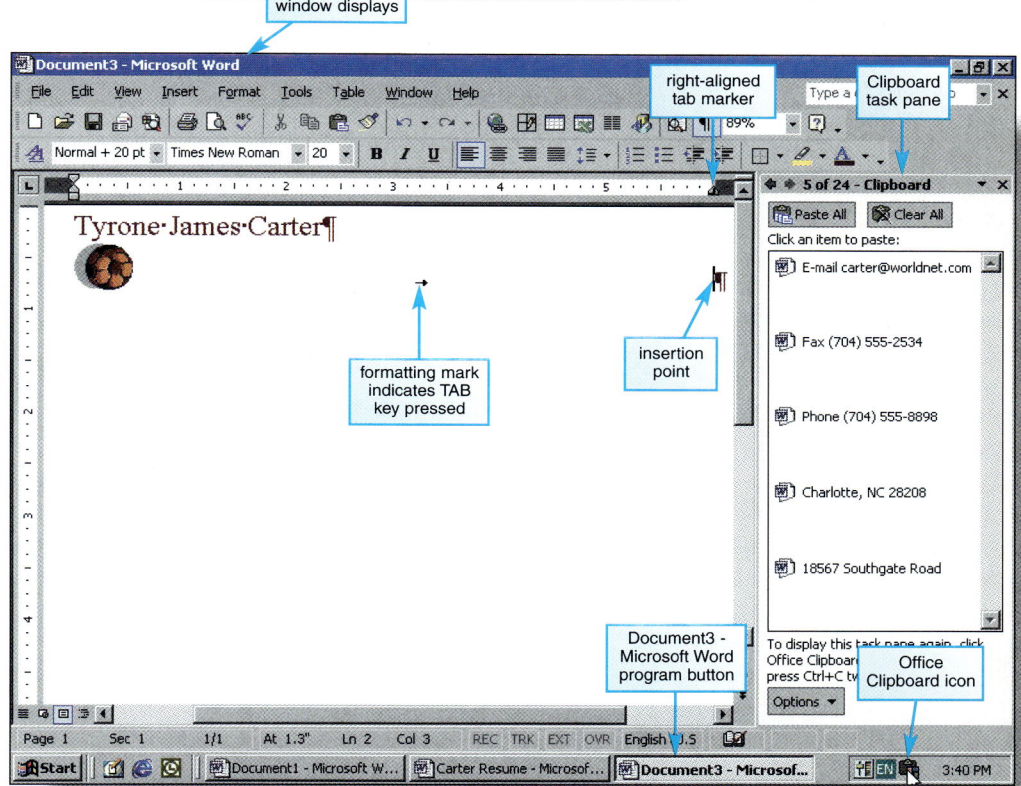

FIGURE 3-47

3 **Point to the bottom (first) entry in the Office Clipboard gallery to select it and then click.**

Word pastes the contents of the clicked item at the location of the insertion point (Figure 3-48). Notice the text is aligned with the right margin because the tab stop is right-aligned.

4 **Press the COMMA key and then the SPACEBAR. Click the second entry (city, state, postal code) in the Office Clipboard gallery. Press the ENTER key. Press the TAB key. Click the third entry (phone) in the Office Clipboard gallery. Press the COMMA key and then the SPACEBAR. Click the fourth entry (fax) in the Office Clipboard gallery. Press the COMMA key and then the SPACEBAR. Click the fifth entry (e-mail) in the Office Clipboard gallery.**

Items from the Office Clipboard are pasted into the letterhead (Figure 3-49).

5 **Click the Close button in the upper-right corner of the Clipboard task pane title bar to close the task pane.**

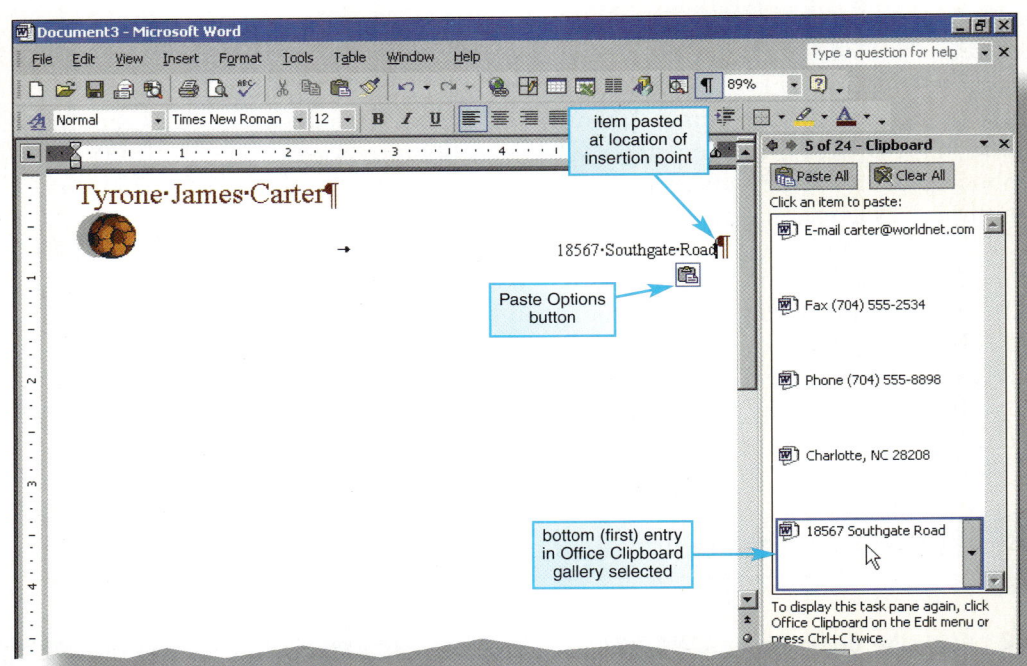

FIGURE 3-48

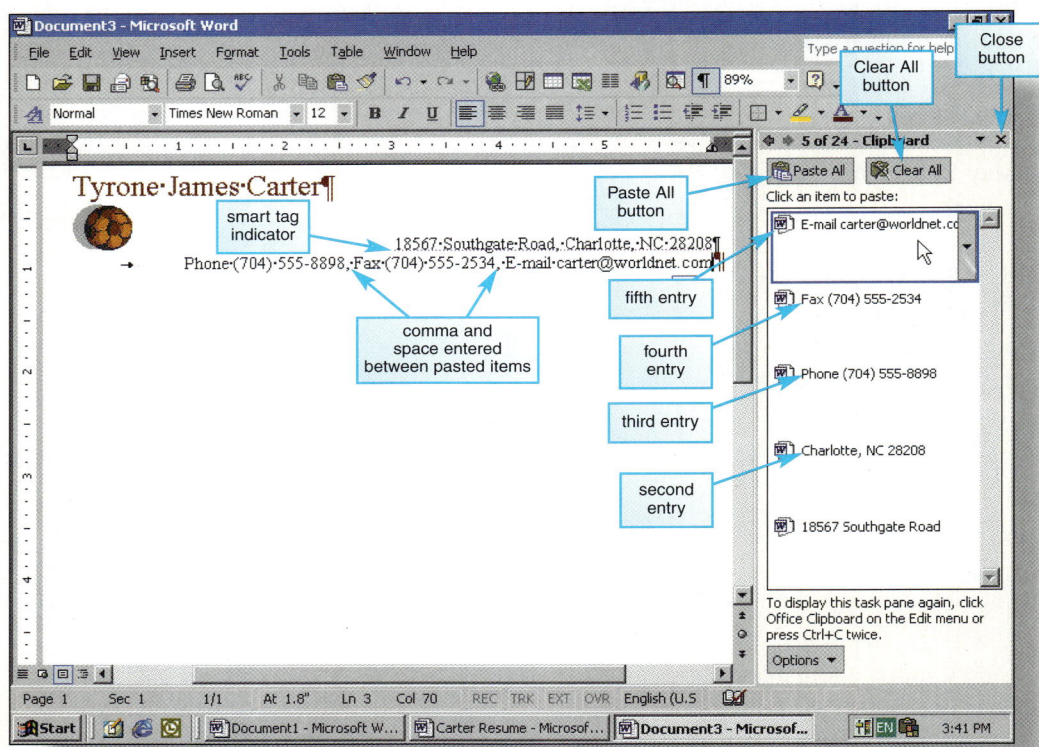

FIGURE 3-49

Other Ways

1. With Clipboard task pane displaying, on Edit menu click Paste
2. With Clipboard task pane displaying, press CTRL+V
3. With Clipboard task pane displaying, in Voice Command mode, say "Paste"

If you wanted to paste all items in a row without any characters in between them, you would click the Paste All button in the Clipboard task pane. If you wanted to erase all items on the Office Clipboard, you would click the Clear All button in the Clipboard task pane.

The next step is to change the font size to 9 and the color of the characters to dark red in the address, telephone, fax, and e-mail information in the letterhead.

TO CHANGE THE FONT SIZE

1. Drag through the address, telephone, fax, and e-mail information in the letterhead, including both paragraph marks at the end of the lines.
2. Click the Font Size box arrow on the Formatting toolbar and then click 9 in the Font Size list.

Word changes the font size to 9 (shown in Figure 3-50 below).

Recall that the Font Color button displays the most recently used color, which is dark red, in this case. When the color you want to use displays on the Font Color button, you simply click the button as shown in the following steps.

More About

Paste Options

To change the format of a pasted item, click the Paste Options button (Figure 3-48) and then click the desired format. For example, to remove all formats such as extra paragraph marks, click Keep Text Only on the Paste Options menu.

More About

The Clipboard Gallery

To delete an item from the Office Clipboard gallery, point to the item in the gallery, click the box arrow to the right of the item, and then click Delete.

Steps: To Color Characters the Same Color

1. **With the address, telephone, fax, and e-mail information still selected, point to the Font Color button on the Formatting toolbar (Figure 3-50).**

2. **Click the Font Color button. Click inside the selected text to remove the highlight.**

Word changes the color of the selected characters to dark red (shown in Figure 3-51 on the next page).

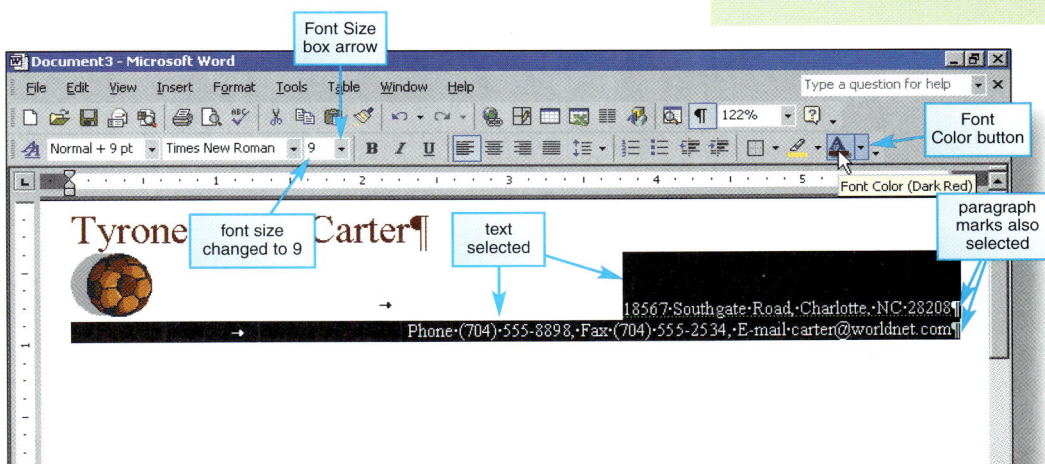

FIGURE 3-50

Adding a Bottom Border to a Paragraph

To add professionalism to the letterhead, you would like to draw a horizontal line from the left margin to the right margin immediately below the telephone, fax, and e-mail information. In Word, you can draw a solid line, called a **border**, at any edge of a paragraph. That is, borders may be added above or below a paragraph, to the left or right of a paragraph, or any combination of these sides.

Perform the steps on the next page to add a bottom border to the paragraph containing telephone, fax, and e-mail information.

Other Ways

1. On Format menu click Font, click Font tab, click Font color box arrow, click desired color, click OK button
2. Right-click paragraph mark or selected text, click Font on shortcut menu, click Font tab, click Font color box arrow, click desired color, click OK button
3. In Voice Command mode, say "Font Color, Dark Red"

Steps: To Bottom Border a Paragraph

 Position the insertion point in the paragraph to border, click the Border button arrow on the Formatting toolbar, and then point to Bottom Border on the border palette.

Word displays the border palette either horizontally or vertically below the Border button (Figure 3-51). Using the border palette, you can add a border to any edge of a paragraph.

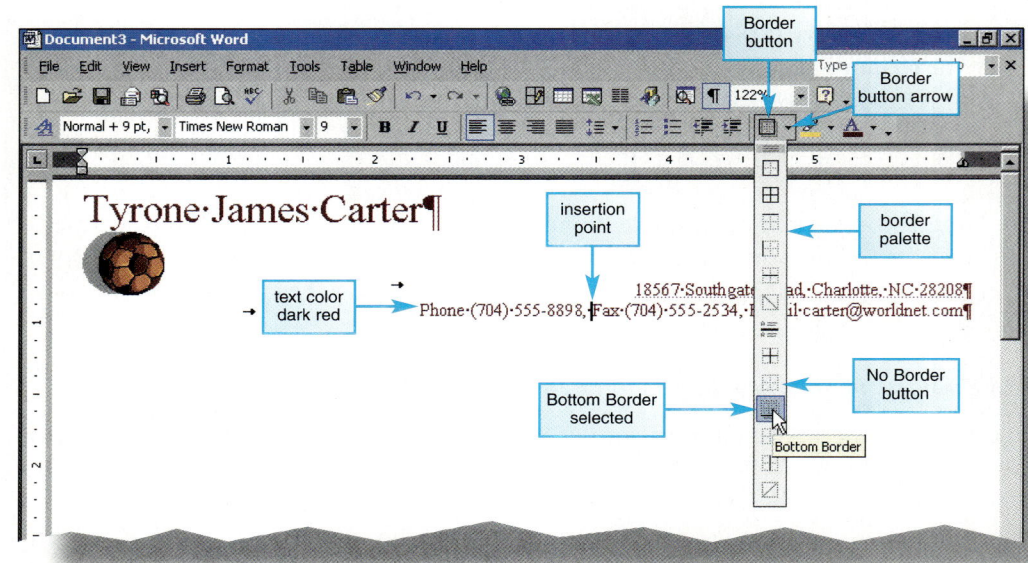

FIGURE 3-51

 Click Bottom Border.

Word places a bottom border below the paragraph containing the insertion point (Figure 3-52). The Border button on the Formatting toolbar now displays the icon for a bottom border.

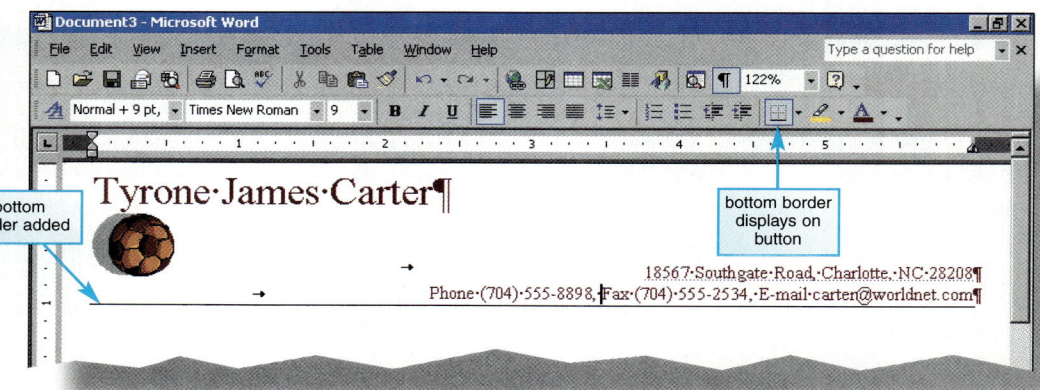

FIGURE 3-52

1. Click Border button arrow on Tables and Borders toolbar, click Bottom Border
2. On Format menu click Borders and Shading, click Borders tab, click Bottom button in Preview area, click OK button
3. In Voice Command mode, say "Borders, Outside Border"

If, for some reason, you wanted to remove a border from a paragraph, you would position the insertion point in the paragraph, click the Border button arrow on the Formatting toolbar, and then click the No Border button (Figure 3-51) on the border palette.

Clearing Formatting

The next step is to position the insertion point below the letterhead, so that you can type the content of the letter. When you press the ENTER key at the end of a paragraph containing a border, Word moves the border forward to the next paragraph. It also retains all current settings. That is, the paragraph will be a dark red font with a bottom border. Instead, you want the paragraph and characters on the new line to use the Normal style: black font with no border. In Word the term, **clear formatting**, refers to returning the formatting to the Normal style.

Perform the following steps to clear formatting at the location of the insertion point.

Steps: To Clear Formatting

1 Press the END key to position the insertion point at the end of line 3 and then press the ENTER key. Click the Styles and Formatting button on the Formatting toolbar.

Word displays the Styles and Formatting task pane (Figure 3-53). The insertion point is on line 4. Formatting at the insertion point consists of a bottom border and a dark red font. You want to clear this formatting.

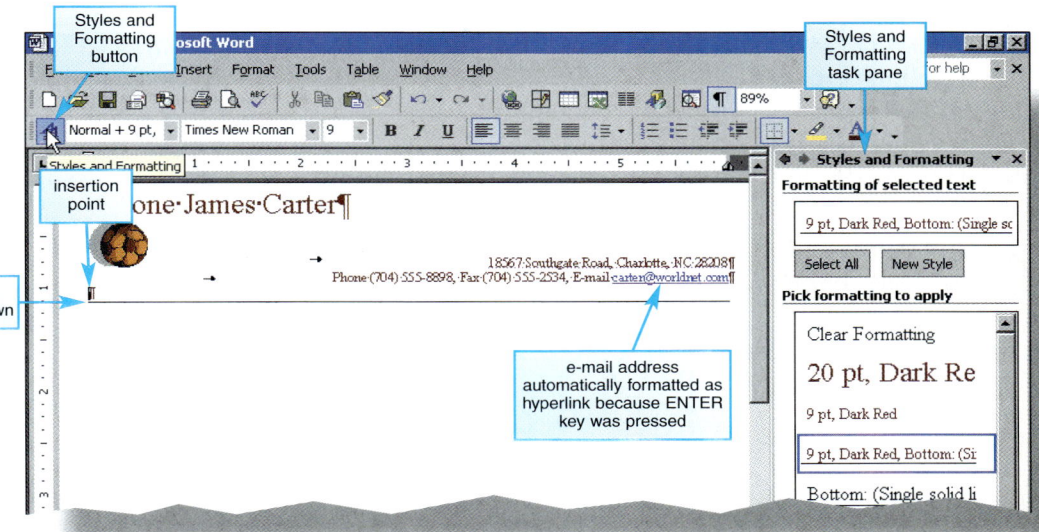

FIGURE 3-53

2 Click Clear Formatting in the Pick formatting to apply area in the Styles and Formatting task pane.

Word applies the Normal style to the location of the insertion point (Figure 3-54).

3 Click the Close button in the upper-right corner of the task pane title bar to close the task pane.

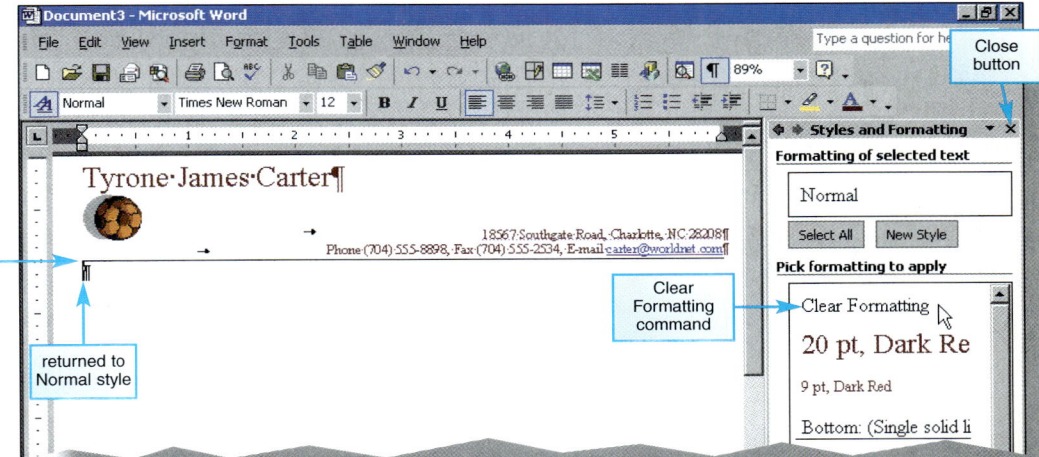

FIGURE 3-54

Other Ways

1. Click Style box arrow on Formatting toolbar, scroll to and click Clear Formatting
2. Press CTRL+SPACEBAR, press CTRL+Q
3. In Voice Command mode, say "Styles and Formatting, Clear Formatting, Styles and Formatting"

The next step is to remove the hyperlink autoformat from the e-mail address in the letterhead. As discussed earlier in this project, Word automatically formats text as you type. When you press the ENTER key or SPACEBAR after entering an e-mail address or Web address, Word automatically formats the address as a hyperlink, that is, colored blue and underlined (shown in Figure 3-53). You do not want this format applied to the e-mail address.

Perform the following steps to convert the e-mail address from a hyperlink to regular text.

Steps: To Convert a Hyperlink to Regular Text

 Right-click the e-mail address and then point to Remove Hyperlink on the shortcut menu (Figure 3-55).

 Click Remove Hyperlink. Position the insertion point on the paragraph mark below the border.

Word removes the hyperlink format from the e-mail address (shown in Figure 3-56 on page WD 3.42).

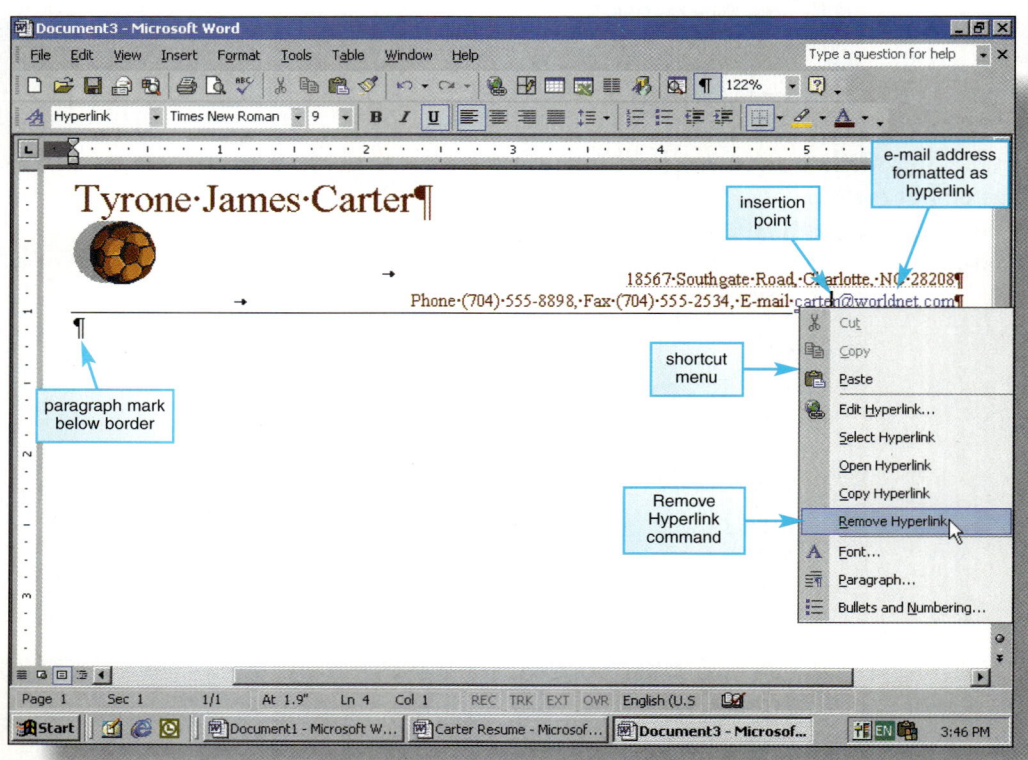

FIGURE 3-55

Other Ways

1. With insertion point in hyperlink, click Insert Hyperlink button on Standard toolbar, click Remove Link button
2. With insertion point in hyperlink, on Insert menu click Hyperlink, click Remove Link button
3. With insertion point in hyperlink, press CTRL+K, press ALT+R
4. With insertion point in hyperlink, in Voice Command mode, say "Right Click, Remove Hyperlink"

Letterhead

Letterhead should contain the complete legal name of the company, group, or individual; full street address including building, room, suite number, or post office box; city; state; and postal code. Some also include a logo, telephone and fax number, Web and e-mail address.

Now that you have created your letterhead, you should save it in a file.

TO SAVE THE LETTERHEAD

1. Insert your floppy disk into drive A.
2. Click the Save button on the Standard toolbar.
3. Type the file name `Carter Letterhead` in the File name text box.
4. If necessary, click the Save in box arrow and then click 3½ Floppy (A:).
5. Click the Save button in the Save As dialog box.

Word saves the document on a floppy disk in drive A with the file name, Carter Letterhead.

Each time you wish to create a letter, you would open your letterhead file (Carter Letterhead) and then immediately save it with a new file name. By doing this, your letterhead file will remain unchanged for future use.

Creating a Cover Letter

You have created a letterhead for the cover letter. The next step is to compose the cover letter. The following pages outline how to use Word to compose a cover letter that contains a table and a bulleted list.

Components of a Business Letter

During your professional career, you most likely will create many business letters. A **cover letter** is one type of business letter. All business letters contain the same basic components.

When preparing business letters, you should include all essential elements. **Essential business letter elements** include the date line, inside address, message, and signature block (Figure 3-2a on the page WD 3.06). The **date line**, which consists of the month, day, and year, is positioned two to six lines below the letterhead. The **inside address**, placed three to eight lines below the date line, usually contains the addressee's courtesy title plus full name, business affiliation, and full geographical address. The **salutation**, if present, begins two lines below the last line of the inside address. The body of the letter, the message, begins two lines below the salutation. Within the **message**, paragraphs are single-spaced with double-spacing between paragraphs. Two lines below the last line of the message, the **complimentary close** displays. Capitalize only the first word in a complimentary close. Type the **signature block** at least four lines below the complimentary close, allowing room for the author to sign his or her name.

You can follow many different styles when you create business letters. The cover letter in this project follows the **modified block style**. Table 3-2 outlines the differences between three common styles of business letters.

> **More About**
>
> **Cover Letters**
>
> You always should send a personalized cover letter with a resume. The cover letter should highlight aspects of your background relevant to the position. To help you recall past achievements and activities, keep a personal file containing documents that outline your accomplishments.

Table 3-2 Common Business Styles

LETTER STYLES	FEATURES
Block	All components of the letter begin flush with the left margin.
Modified Block	The date, complimentary close, and signature block are centered, positioned approximately ½" to the right of center, or at the right margin. All other components of the letter begin flush with the left margin.
Modified Semi-Block	The date, complimentary close, and signature block are centered, positioned approximately ½" to the right of center, or at the right margin. The first line of each paragraph in the body of the letter is indented ½" to 1" from the left margin. All other components of the letter begin flush with the left margin.

Saving the Cover Letter with a New File Name

The document in the document window currently has the name Carter Letterhead, the name of the personal letterhead. You want the letterhead to remain intact. Thus, you should save the document with a new file name, as described in these steps.

TO SAVE THE DOCUMENT WITH A NEW FILE NAME

1. If necessary, insert your floppy disk into drive A.
2. Click File on the menu bar and then click Save As.
3. Type the file name `Carter Cover Letter` in the File name text box.
4. If necessary, click the Save in box arrow and then click 3½ Floppy (A:).
5. Click the Save button in the Save As dialog box.

Word saves the document on a floppy disk in drive A with the file name, Carter Cover Letter (shown in Figure 3-56 on the next page).

> **More About**
>
> **Saving**
>
> As an alternative to saving the letterhead as a Word document, you could save it as a template by clicking the Save as type box arrow in the Save As dialog box and then clicking Document Template. To use the template, click File on the menu bar, click New, click General Templates in the New Document task pane, and then double-click the template icon or name.

Tabs

To insert a vertical line at a tab stop, click the button at the left edge of the horizontal ruler until its icon changes to a Bar Tab icon (a vertical bar) and then click the location on the ruler.

Setting Tab Stops Using the Ruler

The first required element of the cover letter is the date line, which in this letter is to be positioned two lines below the letterhead. The date line, which contains the month, day, and year, begins 3.5 inches from the left margin, or one-half inch to the right of center. Thus, you should set a custom tab stop at the 3.5" mark on the ruler.

Earlier you used the Tabs dialog box to set a tab stop because you could not use the ruler to set a tab stop at the right margin. In the following steps, you set a left-aligned tab stop using the ruler.

Steps: To Set Custom Tab Stops Using the Ruler

1 With the insertion point on the paragraph mark below the border, press the ENTER key. If necessary, click the button at the left edge of the horizontal ruler until it displays the Left Tab icon. Point to the 3.5" mark on the ruler.

Each time you click the button at the left of the horizontal ruler, its icon changes (Figure 3-56). The left tab icon looks like a capital letter L (□).

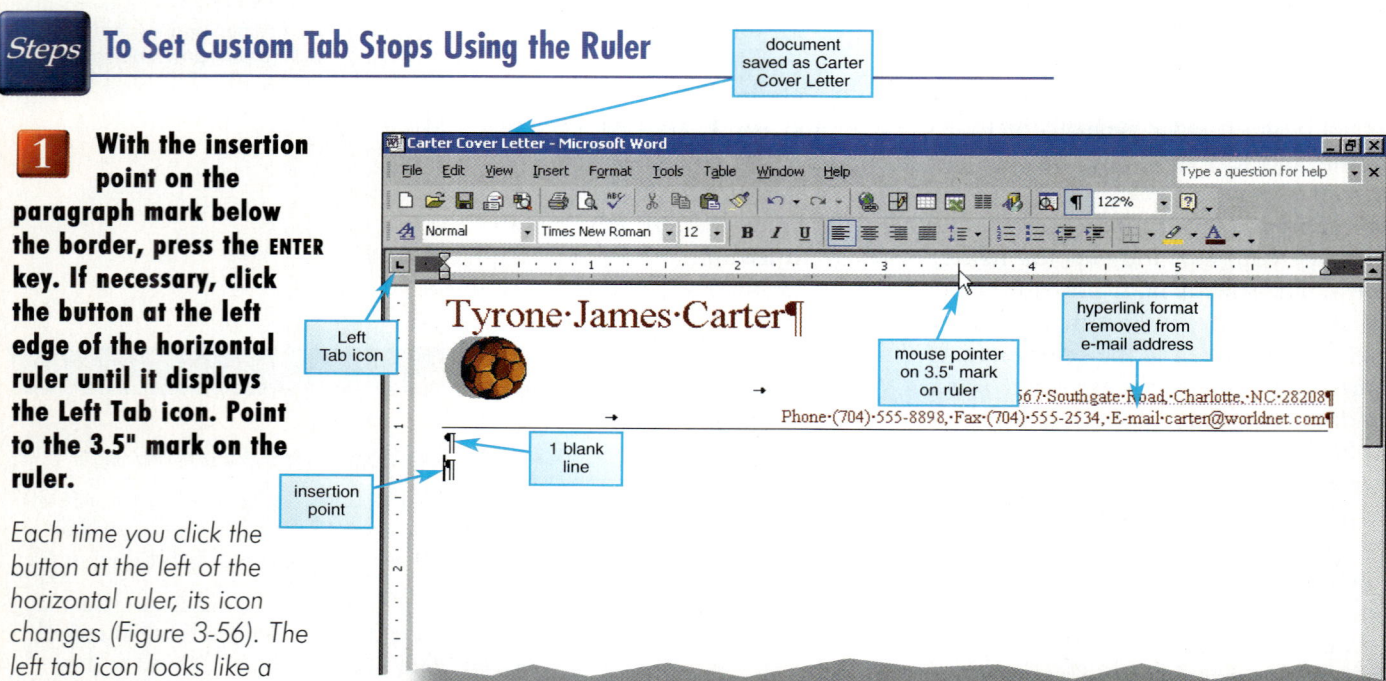

FIGURE 3-56

2 Click the 3.5" mark on the ruler.

Word places a left tab marker at the 3.5" mark on the ruler (Figure 3-57). The text you type at this tab stop will be left-aligned.

Other Ways

1. On Format menu click Tabs, enter tab stop position, click appropriate alignment, click OK button
2. In Voice Command mode, say "Format, Tabs"

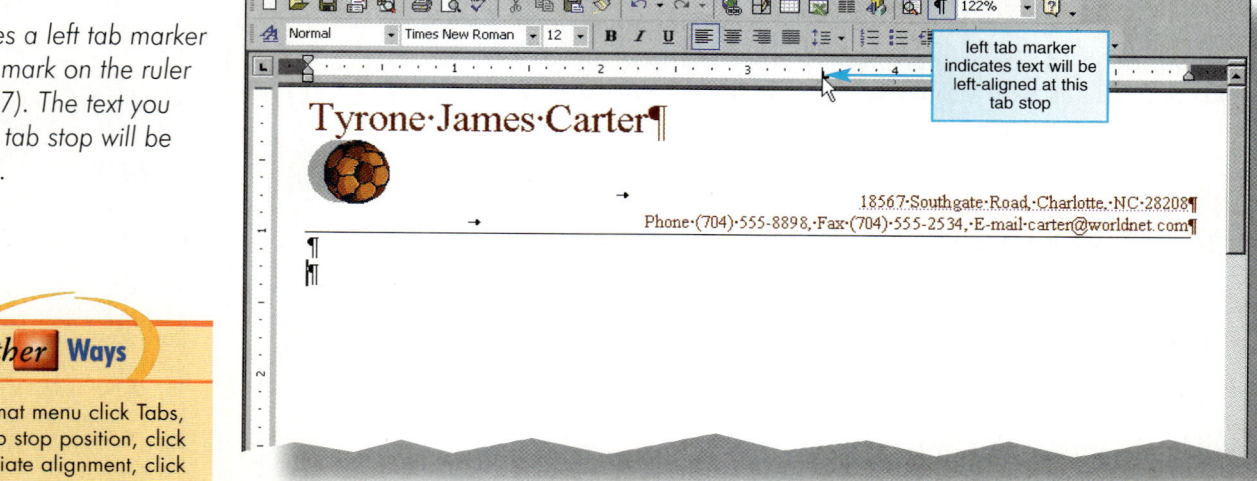

FIGURE 3-57

If, for some reason, you wanted to move a custom tab stop, drag the tab marker to the desired location on the ruler.

If you wanted to change the alignment of a custom tab stop, you could remove the existing tab stop and then insert a new one as described in the steps above. To remove a custom tab stop, point to the tab marker on the ruler and then drag the tab marker down and out of the ruler. You also could use the Tabs dialog box to change an existing tab stop's alignment or position. As discussed earlier in this project, you click Format on the menu bar and then click Tabs to display the Tabs dialog box.

Dates

A field is a set of codes that instructs Word to perform a certain action. If you want Word to display the current date or time when you print a document, make it a field. That is, place a check mark in the Update automatically check box in the Date and Time dialog box (Figure 3-59 on the next page) when you insert the current date or time.

Inserting the Current Date into a Document

The next step is to enter the current date at the 3.5" tab stop in the document. Word provides a method of inserting a computer's system date into a document. Perform the following steps to insert the current date into the cover letter.

 **To Insert the Current Date into a Document**

1 Press the TAB key. Click Insert on the menu bar and then point to Date and Time (Figure 3-58).

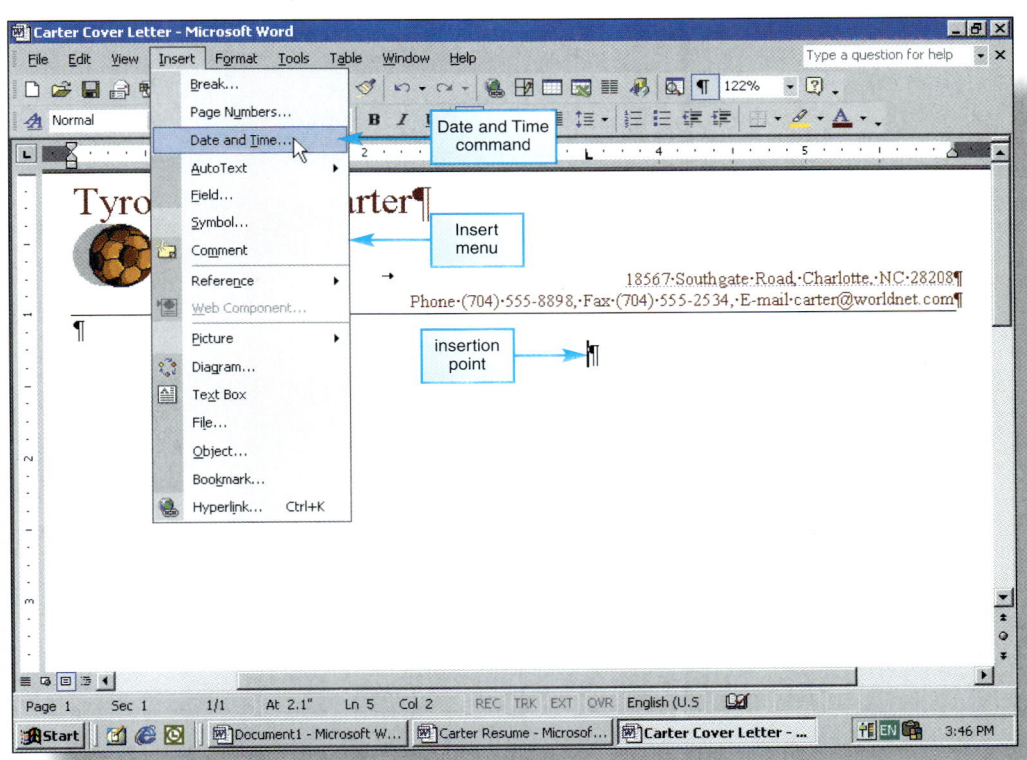

FIGURE 3-58

 **Click Date and Time. When the Date and Time dialog box displays, click the desired format (in this case, May 15, 2003). If a check mark displays in the Update automatically check box, click the check box to remove the check mark. Point to the OK button.**

Word displays a list of available dates and times in the Date and Time dialog box (Figure 3-59). Your dialog box will differ, showing the current system date stored in your computer.

 **Click the OK button.**

Word displays the current date at the location of the insertion point (shown in Figure 3-60).

Other Ways

1. In Voice Command mode, say "Insert, Date and Time, [select format], OK"

More About

Inside Addresses

Pay close attention to the spelling, punctuation, and official abbreviations of company names. For example, does the company name spell out the word, and, or does it use the ampersand character (&)? Is the word, Company, spelled out or abbreviated?

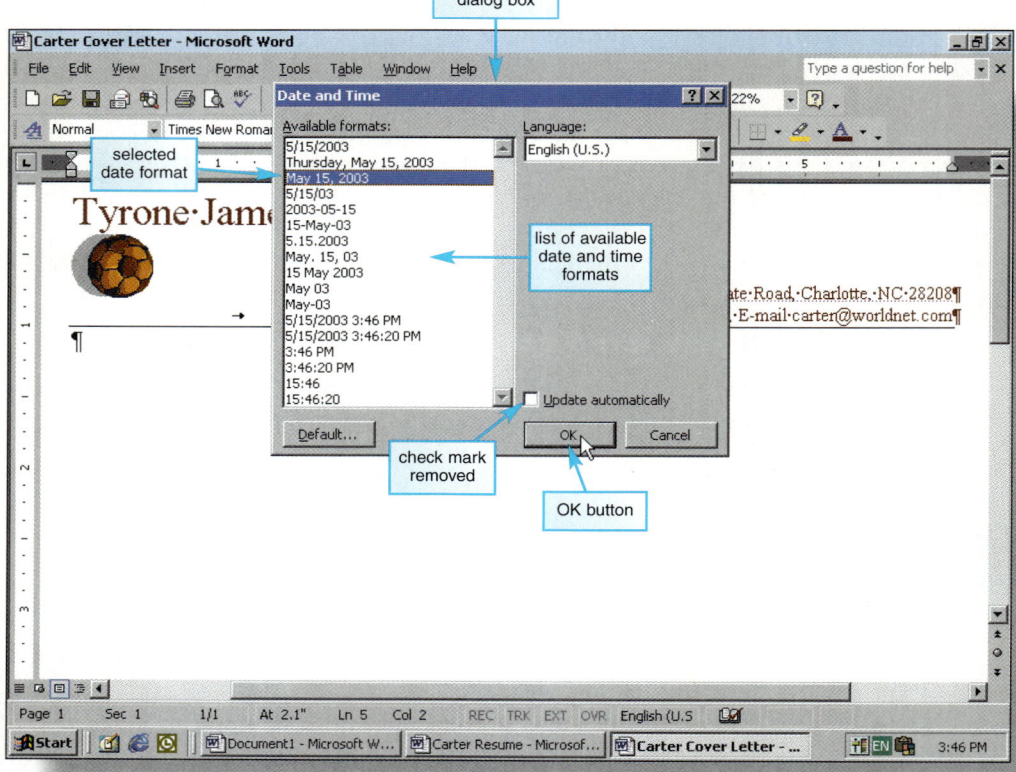

FIGURE 3-59

The next step is to type the inside address and salutation in the cover letter as described in the following steps.

TO ENTER THE INSIDE ADDRESS AND SALUTATION

1. With the insertion point at the end of the date, press the ENTER key three times.
2. Type `Ms. Mae Li` and then press the ENTER key. Type `Personnel Director` and then press the ENTER key. Type `Peterson High School` and then press the ENTER key. Type `One Peterson Drive` and then press the ENTER key. Type `Charlotte, NC 28208` and then press the ENTER key twice.
3. Type `Dear Ms. Li` and then press the COLON key (:).

The inside address and salutation are entered (Figure 3-60).

Creating an AutoText Entry

If you use the same text frequently, you can store the text in an **AutoText entry** and then use the stored entry throughout the open document, as well as future documents. That is, you type the entry only once, and for all future occurrences of the text, you access the stored entry as you need it. In this way, you avoid entering the text inconsistently or incorrectly in different locations throughout the same document.

Creating a Cover Letter • WD 3.45

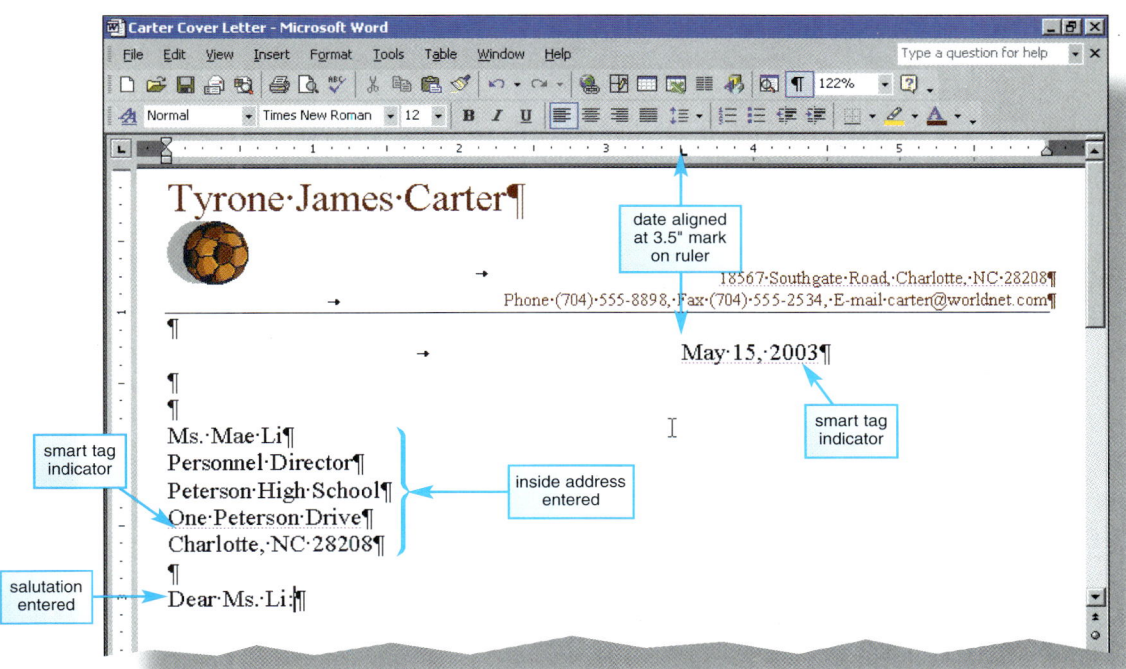

FIGURE 3-60

Perform the following steps to create an AutoText entry for the prospective employer's name.

Steps: To Create an AutoText Entry

1 **Drag through the text to be stored, in this case, Peterson High School. If the Smart Tag Actions button displays when you try to drag, move the mouse pointer up and then try dragging again. Be sure not to select the paragraph mark at the end of the text. Click Insert on the menu bar and then point to AutoText. Point to New on the AutoText submenu.**

The employer name, Peterson High School, in the inside address is selected (Figure 3-61). Notice the paragraph mark is not part of the selection.

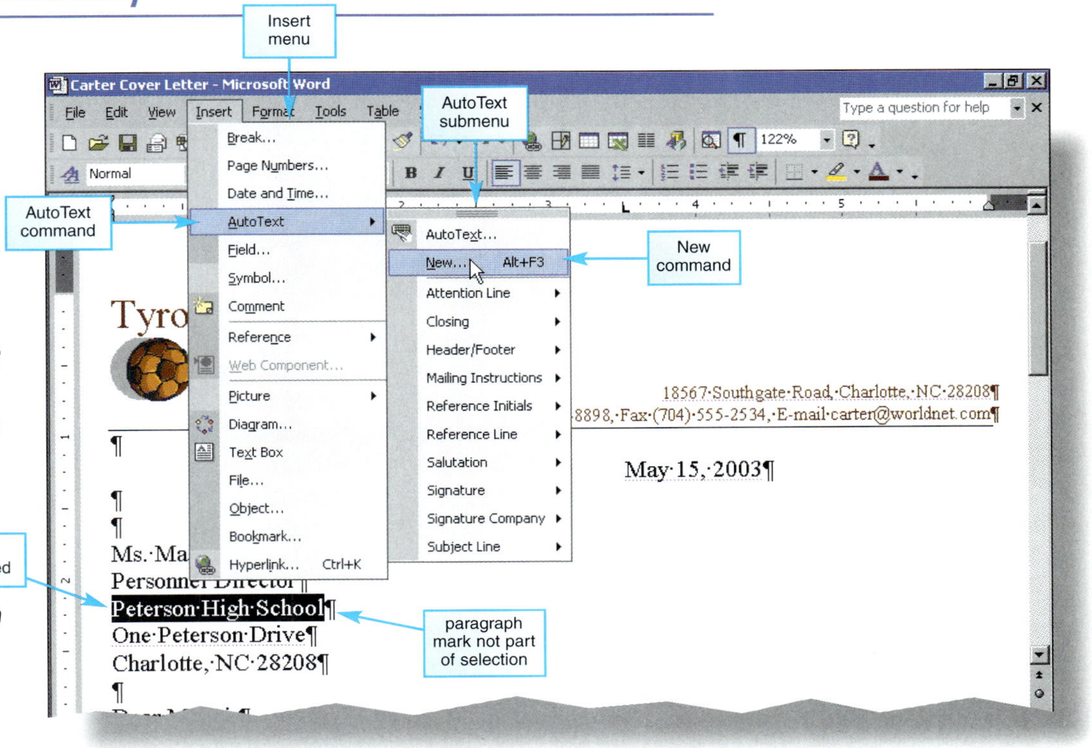

FIGURE 3-61

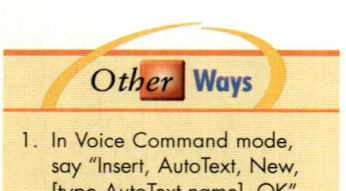

Click New. When the Create AutoText dialog box displays, type phs **and then point to the OK button.**

Word displays the Create AutoText dialog box (Figure 3-62). In this dialog box, Word proposes a name for the AutoText entry. You change it to a shorter name, phs.

Click the OK button. If Word displays a dialog box, click the Yes button.

Word stores the AutoText entry and closes the AutoText dialog box.

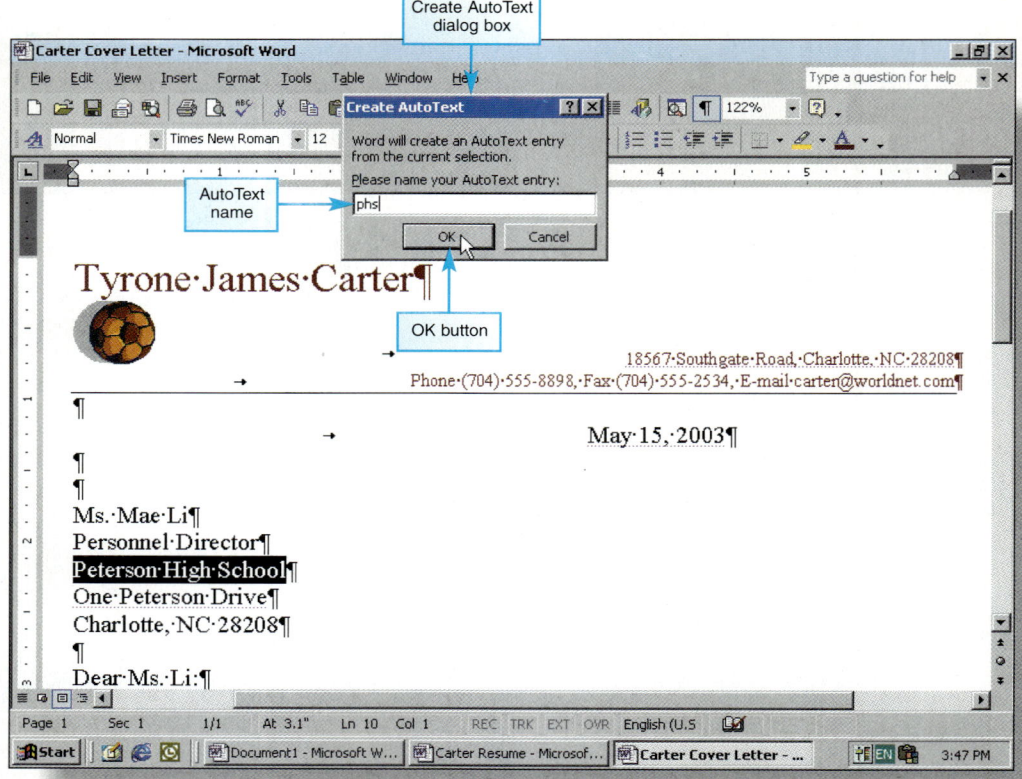

FIGURE 3-62

Other Ways

1. In Voice Command mode, say "Insert, AutoText, New, [type AutoText name], OK"

The name, phs, has been stored as an AutoText entry. Later in the project, you will use the AutoText entry, phs, instead of typing the employer name, Peterson High School.

Entering a Nonbreaking Space

Some compound words, such as proper names, dates, units of time and measure, abbreviations, and geographic destinations, should not be divided at the end of a line. These words either should fit as a unit at the end of a line or be wrapped together to the next line.

Word provides two special characters to assist with this task: nonbreaking space and nonbreaking hyphen. You press CTRL+SHIFT+SPACEBAR to enter a **nonbreaking space**, which is a special space character that prevents two words from splitting if the first word falls at the end of a line. Similarly, you press CTRL+SHIFT+HYPHEN to enter a **nonbreaking hyphen**, which is a special type of hyphen that prevents two words separated by a hyphen from splitting at the end of a line. When you enter these characters into a document, a formatting mark displays on the screen.

Perform the following steps to enter a nonbreaking space between the words in the newspaper name.

Salutations

The salutation "To whom it may concern" should be avoided — it is extremely impersonal. If you cannot obtain the name and gender of the company officer to whom you are addressing the letter, then use the recipient's title in the salutation, e.g., Dear Personnel Supervisor.

Steps To Insert a Nonbreaking Space

1 **Scroll the salutation to the top of the document window. Click after the colon in the salutation and then press the ENTER key twice. If the Office Assistant displays, click Just type the letter without help. Type** I am responding to the social studies teacher's assistant position advertised in the **and then press the SPACEBAR. Press CTRL+I to turn on italics. Type** Herald **and then press CTRL+SHIFT+SPACEBAR.**

Word enters a nonbreaking space after the word, Herald (Figure 3-63).

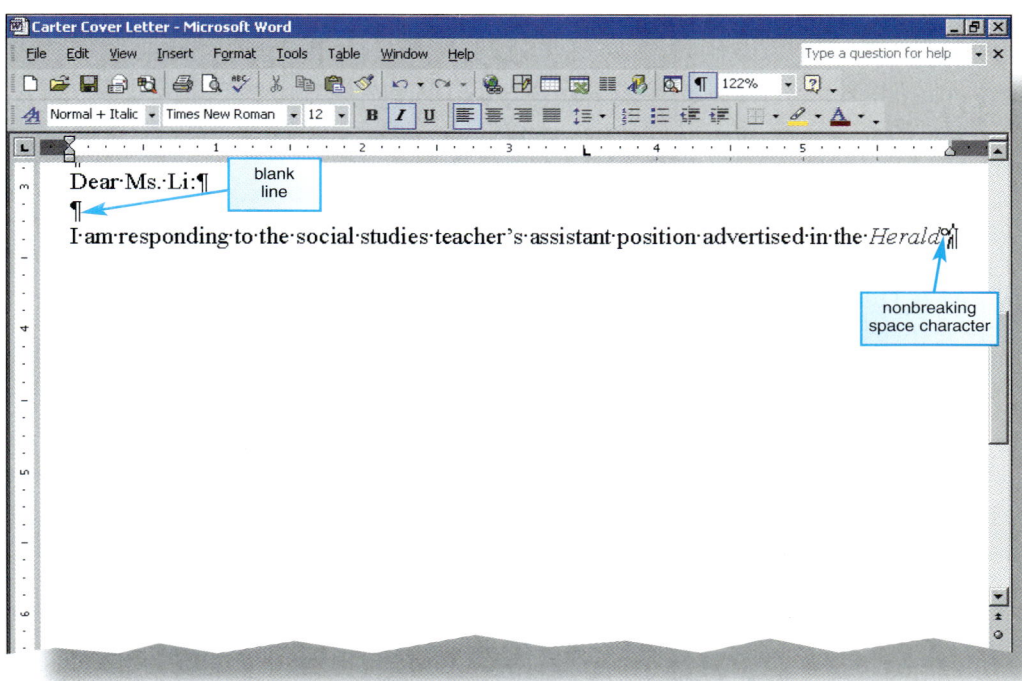

FIGURE 3-63

2 **Type** Times **and then press CTRL+I to turn off italics. Press the PERIOD key.**

Word wraps the two words in the newspaper title, Herald Times, to the next line (Figure 3-64).

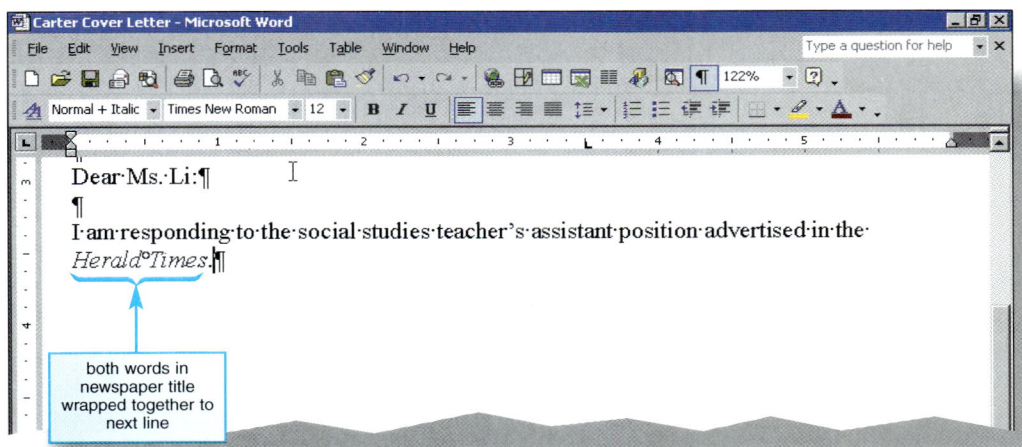

FIGURE 3-64

Inserting an AutoText Entry

At the end of the next sentence in the body of the cover letter, you want to put the prospective employer name, Peterson High School. Recall that earlier in this project, you stored an AutoText entry name of phs for Peterson High School. Thus, you will type the AutoText entry's name and then instruct Word to replace the AutoText entry's name with the stored entry of Peterson High School.

Perform the steps on the next page to insert an AutoText entry.

Other Ways

1. On Insert menu click Symbol, click Special Characters tab, click Nonbreaking Space in Character list, click Insert button, click Close button
2. In Dictation mode, say "Control Shift Spacebar"

Steps: To Insert an AutoText Entry

1 **Press the SPACEBAR. Type** As indicated on the enclosed resume, I have the credentials you are seeking and believe I can be a valuable asset to phs **as shown in Figure 3-65.**

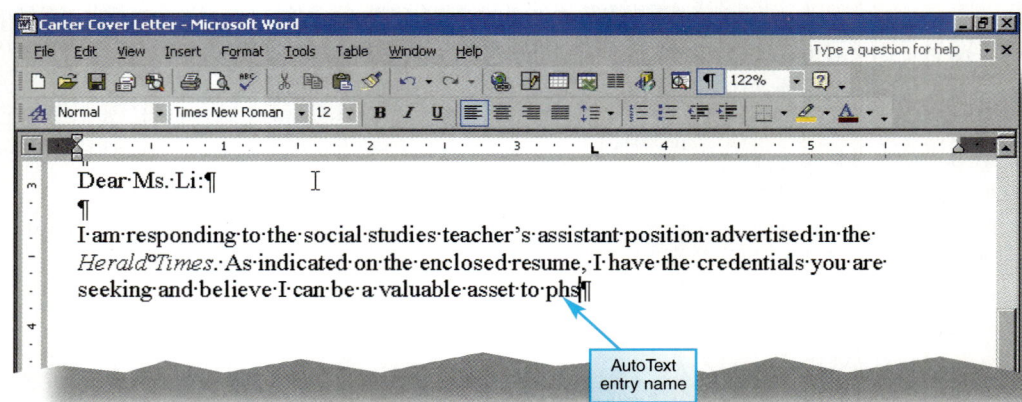

FIGURE 3-65

2 **Press the F3 key. Press the PERIOD key.**

Word replaces the characters, phs, with the stored AutoText entry, Peterson High School, when you press the F3 key (Figure 3-66).

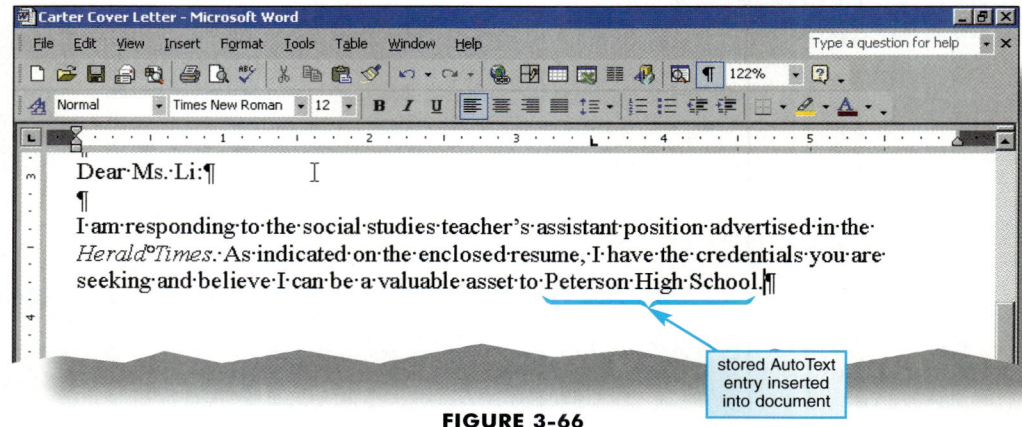

FIGURE 3-66

Other Ways

1. Type first few characters to display AutoComplete tip, press ENTER
2. On Insert menu point to AutoText, point to appropriate AutoText entry, click desired AutoText entry on submenu
3. On Insert menu point to AutoText, click AutoText, select desired AutoText entry name, click OK button

Pressing the F3 key instructs Word to replace the AutoText entry name with the stored AutoText entry. In Project 2, you learned how to use the AutoCorrect feature, which enables you to insert and also create AutoCorrect entries (just as you did for this AutoText entry). The difference between an AutoCorrect entry and an AutoText entry is that the AutoCorrect feature makes corrections for you automatically as soon as you press the SPACEBAR or a punctuation mark key, whereas you must press the F3 key or click the AutoText command to instruct Word to make an AutoText correction.

If you watch the screen as you type, you may discover that AutoComplete tips display on the screen. As you type, Word searches the list of AutoText entry names and if one matches your typing, Word displays its complete name above your typing as an **AutoComplete tip**. In addition to AutoText entries, Word proposes AutoComplete tips for the current date, a day of the week, a month, and so on. If your screen does not display AutoComplete tips, click Tools on the menu bar, click AutoCorrect Options, click the AutoText tab, click Show AutoComplete suggestions, and then click the OK button. To view the complete list of entries, click Tools on the menu bar, click AutoCorrect, click the AutoText tab, and then scroll through the list of entries. To ignore an AutoComplete tip proposed by Word, simply continue typing to remove the AutoComplete tip from the screen.

Perform the following steps to enter the next paragraph into the cover letter.

TO ENTER A PARAGRAPH

1. Press the ENTER key twice.
2. Type I recently received my bachelor's degree in social studies teaching from North Carolina State. The following table outlines my areas of concentration and then press the COLON key.
3. Press the ENTER key twice.

The paragraph is entered (shown in Figure 3-67 below).

The next step is to enter a table into the cover letter.

Creating a Table with the Insert Table Button

The next step in composing the cover letter is to place a table listing your areas of concentration (Figure 3-2a on page WD 3.06). You create this table using Word's table feature. As discussed earlier in this project, a Word table is a collection of rows and columns, and the intersection of a row and a column is called a cell.

Within a Word table, you easily can rearrange rows and columns, change column widths, sort rows and columns, and sum the contents of rows and columns. You also can format and chart table data.

The first step in creating a table is to insert an empty table into the document. When inserting a table, you must specify the total number of rows and columns required, which is called the **dimension** of the table. The table in this project has two columns. You often do not know the total number of rows in a table. Thus, many Word users create one row initially and then add rows as they need them. The first number in a dimension is the number of rows, and the second is the number of columns.

Perform the following steps to insert a 1 × 2 table; that is, a table with one row and two columns.

More About

Word Tables

Although you can use the TAB key to create a table, many Word users prefer to use the table feature. With a Word table, you can arrange numbers and text in columns. For emphasis, tables can be shaded and have borders. The contents of Word tables can be sorted, and you can have Word sum the contents of an entire row or column.

Steps To Insert an Empty Table

1. **Click the Insert Table button on the Standard toolbar. Point to the cell in the first row and second column of the grid to select the first two cells in the first row of the grid.**

Word displays a grid to define the dimension of the desired table (Figure 3-67). Word will insert the table immediately above the insertion point.

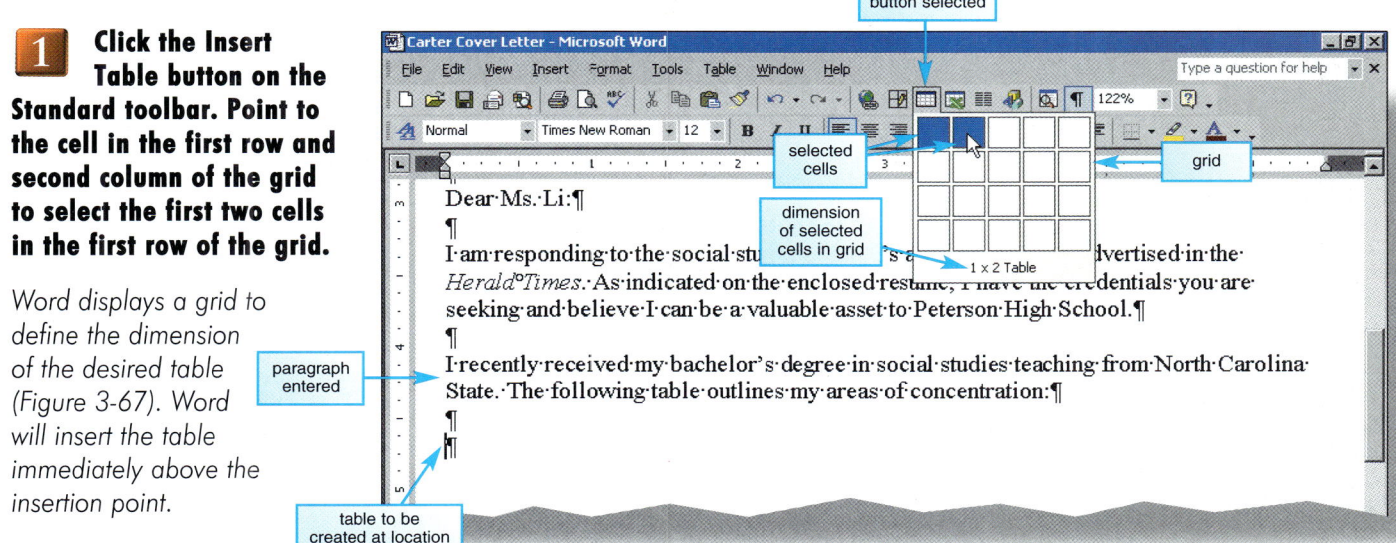

FIGURE 3-67

2 **Click the cell in the first row and second column of the grid.**

Word inserts an empty 1 × 2 table into the document (Figure 3-68). The insertion point is in the first cell (row 1 and column 1) of the table.

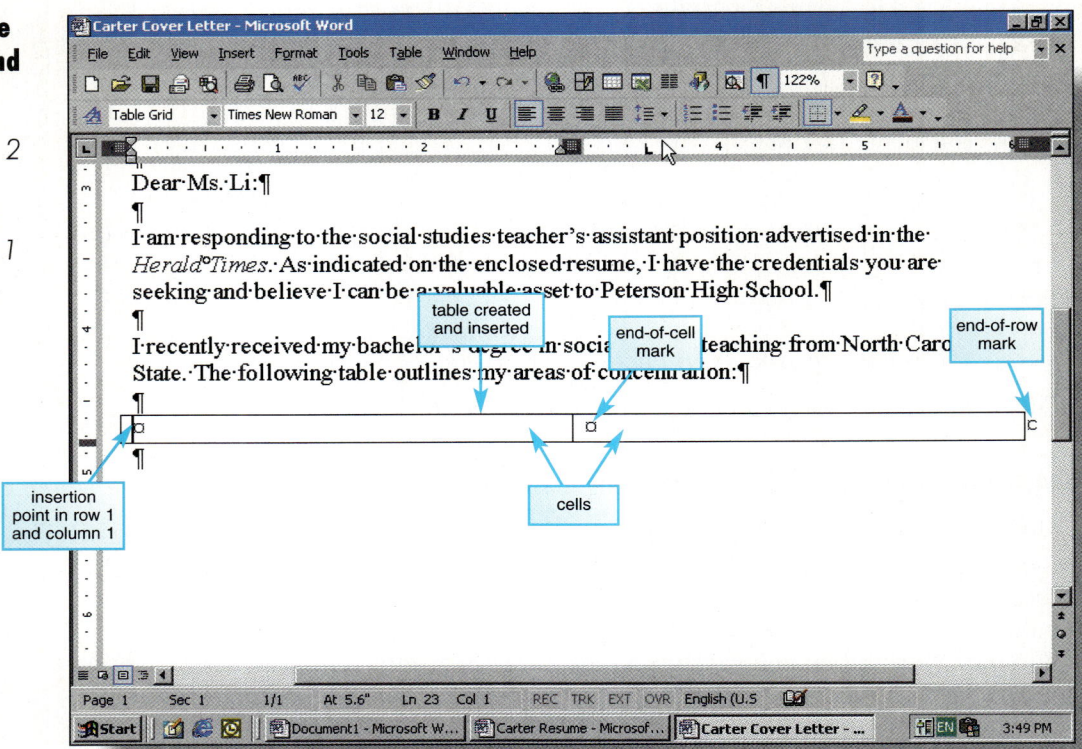

FIGURE 3-68

1. On Table menu point to Insert, click Table on Insert submenu, enter number of columns, enter number of rows, click OK button
2. In Voice Command mode, say "Insert Table, [select table dimension]"

Draw Table

To use Draw Table, click the Tables and Borders button on the Standard toolbar to change the mouse pointer to a pencil. Use the pencil to draw from one corner to the opposite diagonal corner to define the perimeter of the table. Then, draw the column and row lines inside the perimeter. To remove a line, use the Eraser button on the Tables and Borders toolbar.

As discussed earlier in this project, each row of a table has an end-of-row mark, which you can use to add columns to the right of a table. Each cell has an end-of-cell mark, which you can use to select a cell. The end-of-cell mark currently is left-aligned; thus it is positioned at the left edge of each cell. You can use any of the paragraph formatting buttons on the Formatting toolbar to change the alignment of the text within the cells. For example, if you click the Align Right button on the Formatting toolbar, the end-of-cell mark and any entered text will display at the right edge of the cell.

For simple tables, such as the one just created, Word users click the Insert Table button to create a table. For more complex tables, such as one with a varying number of columns per row, Word has a Draw Table feature that allows you to use a pencil pointer to draw a table on the screen. Project 4 discusses the Draw Table feature.

Entering Data into a Word Table

The next step is to enter data into the empty table. Cells are filled with data. The data you enter within a cell wordwraps just as text does between the margins of a document. To place data into a cell, you click the cell and then type. To advance rightward from one cell to the next, press the TAB key. When you are at the rightmost cell in a row, also press the TAB key to move to the first cell in the next row; do not press the ENTER key. The ENTER key is used to begin a new paragraph within a cell.

To add new rows to a table, press the TAB key with the insertion point positioned in the bottom right corner cell of the table.

Perform the following steps to enter data into the table.

To Enter Data into a Table

1 **If necessary, scroll the table up in the document window. With the insertion point in the left cell of the table, type** U.S. History **and then press the TAB key. Type** 18 hours **and then press the TAB key.**

Word enters the table data into the first row of the table and adds a second row to the table (Figure 3-69). The insertion point is positioned in the first cell of the second row.

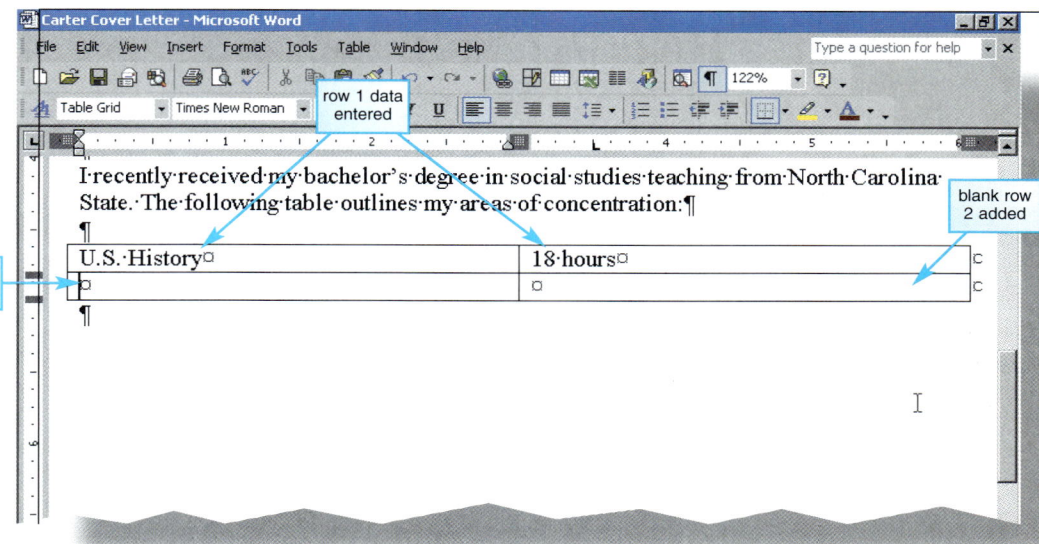

FIGURE 3-69

2 **Type** World Civilization **and then press the TAB key. Type** 12 hours **and then press the TAB key. Type** Government **and then press the TAB key. Type** 12 hours **and then press the TAB key. Type** Sociology **and then press the TAB key. Type** 10 hours **as shown in Figure 3-70.**

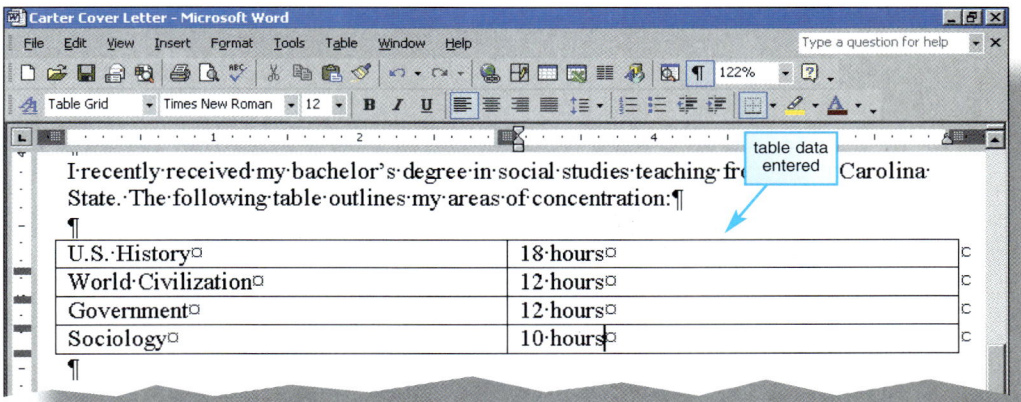

FIGURE 3-70

1. In Dictation mode, say "U.S. History, Tab, 18 hours, Tab"

You modify the contents of cells just as you modify text in a document. To delete the contents of a cell, select the cell contents by pointing to the left edge of a cell and clicking when the mouse pointer changes direction, and then press the DELETE key. To modify text in a cell, click in the cell and then correct the entry. You can double-click the OVR indicator on the status bar to toggle between insert and overtype modes. You also can drag and drop or cut and paste the contents of cells.

Resizing Table Columns

The table in this project currently extends from the left margin to the right margin of the document. You want each column only to be as wide as the longest entry in the table. That is, the first column must be wide enough to accommodate the words, World Civilization; and the second column must be wide enough for the phrase, 18 hours.

Table Commands

If a Table command is dimmed on the Table menu, the insertion point might not be in the table.

Perform the following steps to instruct Word to fit automatically the width of the columns to the contents of the table.

Steps: To Fit Columns to Table Contents

1 **With the insertion point in the table, click Table on the menu bar, point to AutoFit, and then point to AutoFit to Contents (Figure 3-71).**

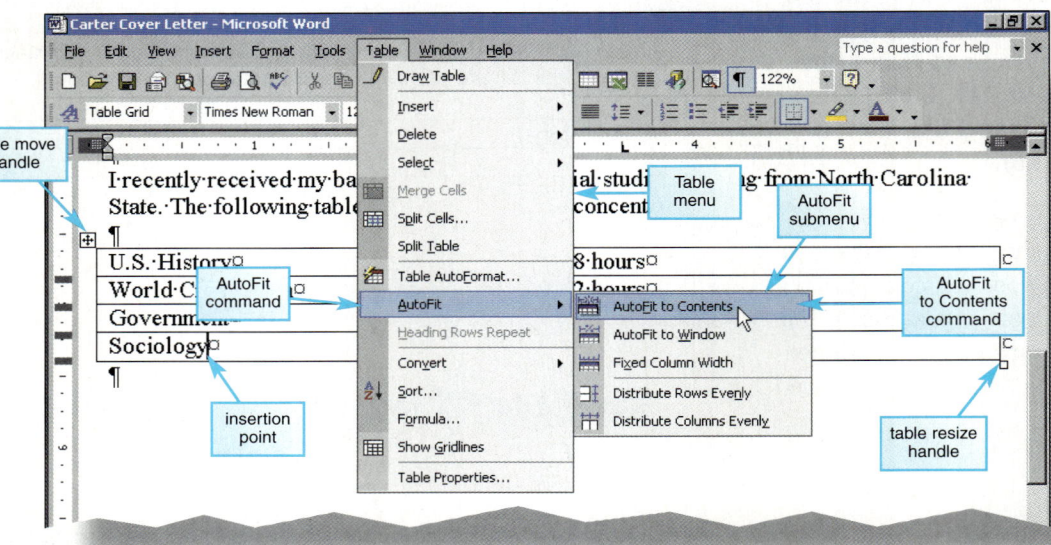

FIGURE 3-71

2 **Click AutoFit to Contents.**

Word automatically adjusts the widths of the columns based on the amount of text in the table (Figure 3-72). In this case, Word reduces the widths of the columns.

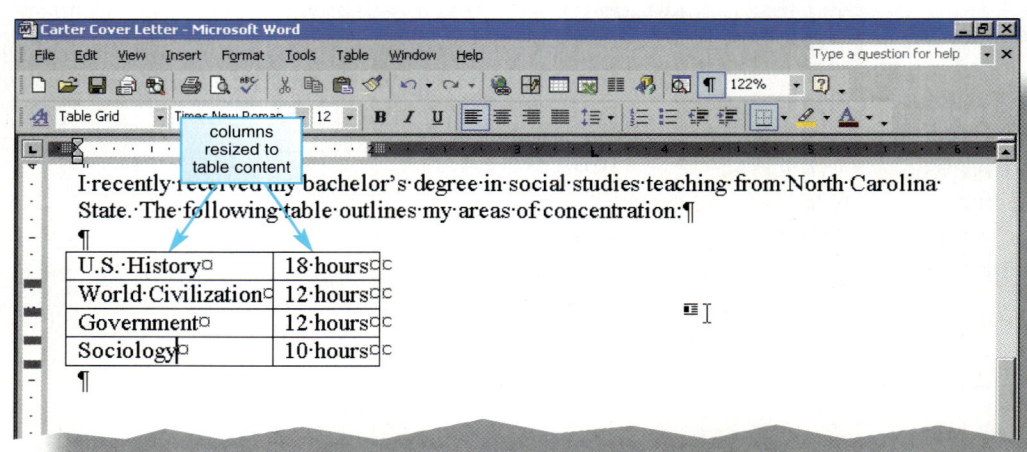

FIGURE 3-72

1. Double-click column boundary
2. Right-click table, point to AutoFit on shortcut menu, click AutoFit to Contents
3. In Voice Command mode, say "Table, AutoFit, AutoFit to Contents"

If you do not want to resize the columns to the table widths, Word provides other options. You can drag a **column boundary**, the border to the right of a column, until the column is the desired width. Similarly, you can resize a row by dragging the **row boundary**, the border at the top of a row, until the row is the desired height. You also can resize the entire table by dragging the **table resize handle**, which is a small square that will display when you point to the bottom right corner of the table (Figure 3-71).

Creating a Cover Letter • WD 3.53

Changing the Table Alignment

When you first create a table, it is left-aligned; that is, flush with the left margin. In this cover letter, the table should be centered. To center a table, you first must select the entire table and then center it using the Center button on the Formatting toolbar, as shown in the following series of steps.

AutoFormat

Word has many predefined table formats that you can apply to tables. With the insertion point in the table, click Table on the menu bar, click Table AutoFormat (Figure 3-71), click the desired format, and then click the OK button.

 **To Select a Table**

1 **Position the mouse pointer in the table so the table move handle displays. Position the mouse pointer on the table move handle and then click.**

Word selects the entire table (Figure 3-73).

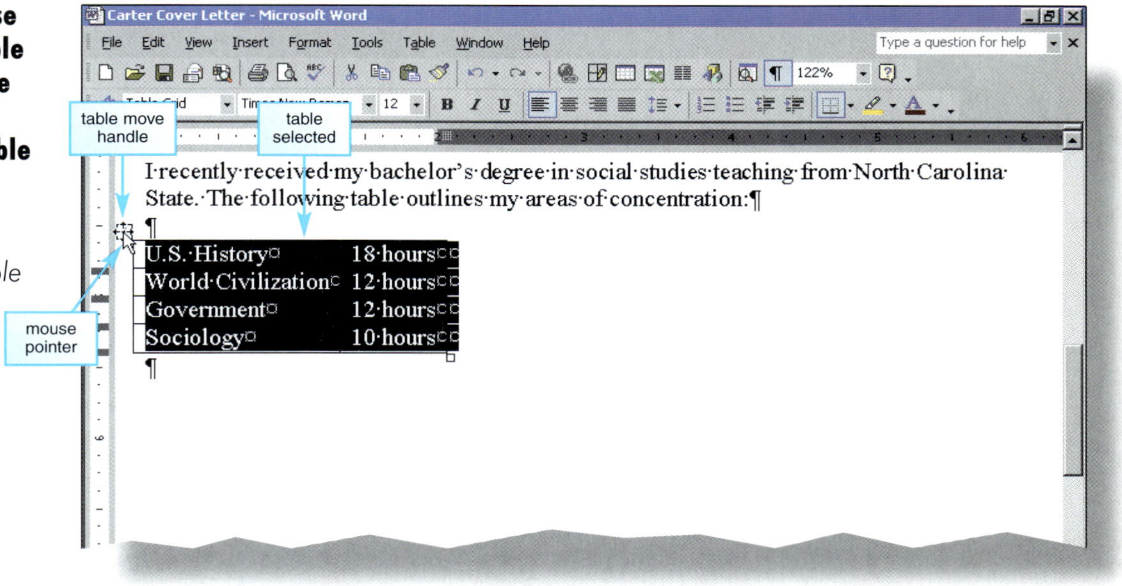

FIGURE 3-73

When working with tables, you may need to select the contents of cells, rows, columns, or the entire table. Table 3-3 identifies how to select various items in a table.

Table 3-3 Selecting Items in a Table	
ITEM TO SELECT	ACTION
Cell	Click left edge of cell
Column	Click border at top of column
Multiple cells, rows, or columns adjacent to one another	Drag through cells, rows, or columns
Multiple cells, rows, or columns not adjacent to one another	Select first cell, row, or column and then hold down CTRL key while selecting next cell, row, or column
Next cell	Press TAB key
Previous cell	Press SHIFT+TAB
Row	Click to left of row
Table	Click table move handle

Other Ways

1. On Table menu point to Select, click Table
2. With insertion point in table, press ALT+5 (using the 5 on the numeric keypad with NUM LOCK off)
3. In Voice Command mode, say "Table, Select, Table"

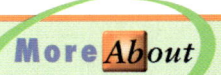

Tabs

The TAB key advances the insertion point from one cell to the next in a table. Thus, press CTRL+TAB to insert a tab character into a cell.

Table Formats

You can change the width of a column to an exact measurement. Hold down the ALT key while dragging markers on the ruler. Or, click Table on the menu bar, click Table Properties, click the Column tab, enter desired measurements, and then click the OK button. Similarly, to change the row height to an exact measurement, click the Row tab in the Table Properties dialog box, enter desired measurements, and then click the OK button.

Perform the following step to center the selected table between the margins.

TO CENTER A SELECTED TABLE

1. Click the Center button on the Formatting toolbar.

Word centers the selected table between the left and right margins (shown in Figure 3-73 on the previous page).

When an entire table is selected and you click the Center button on the Formatting toolbar, Word centers the entire table. If you wanted to center the contents of the cells, you would select the cells by dragging through them and then click the Center button.

Perform the following steps to add more text below the table.

TO ADD MORE TEXT

1. If necessary, scroll up. Click the paragraph mark below the table.

2. Press the ENTER key. Type In addition to my coursework, I have the following teaching experience and then press the COLON key. Press the ENTER key.

The text is entered (shown in Figure 3-74 below).

The next step is to enter a bulleted list into the cover letter.

Bulleting a List

You can type a list and then place the bullets on the paragraphs at a later time, or you can use Word's AutoFormat As You Type feature to bullet the paragraphs as you type them (Table 3-1 on page WD 3.23).

Perform the following steps to add bullets automatically to a list as you type.

Steps To Bullet a List as You Type

1. **Press the ASTERISK key (*). Press the SPACEBAR. Type** Worked as a teacher's aide at Hampton Elementary School **as the first list item (Figure 3-74).**

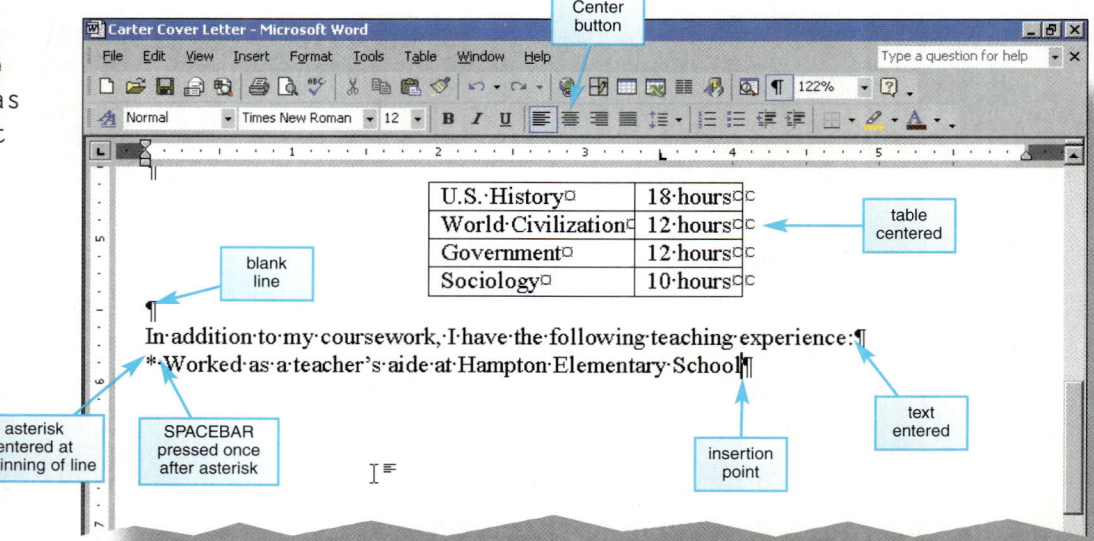

FIGURE 3-74

2 **Press the ENTER key.**

Word converts the asterisk to a bullet character, places another bullet on the second list item, and indents the two bulleted paragraphs.

3 **Type** At North Carolina State, provided one-on-one assistance to students having difficulty with coursework and administered placement and test-out examinations **and then press the ENTER key. Type** Teach CPR classes once a month **and then press the ENTER key.**

Word places a bullet on the next line (Figure 3-75).

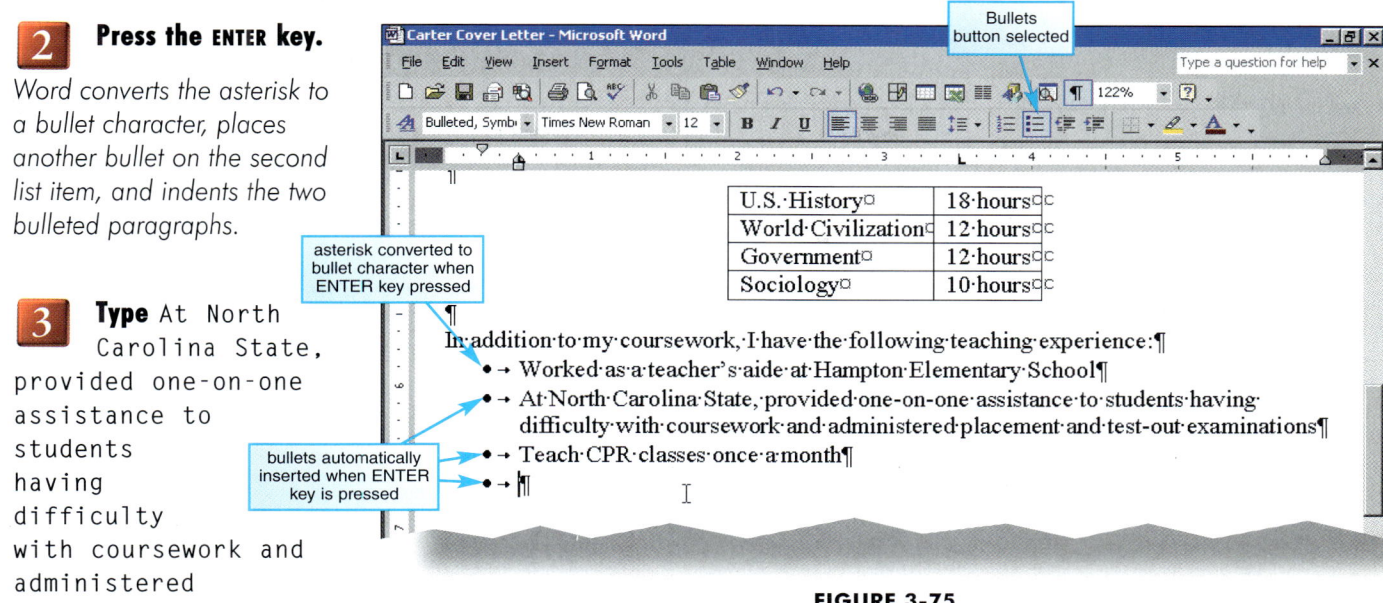

FIGURE 3-75

4 **Press the ENTER key.**

Word removes the lone bullet because you pressed the ENTER key twice (Figure 3-76). The Bullets button no longer is selected.

Other Ways

1. Select list, click Bullets button on Formatting toolbar
2. Select list, right-click selection, click Bullets and Numbering on shortcut menu, click Bulleted tab, click desired bullet type, click OK button
3. Select list, on Format menu click Bullets and Numbering, click Bulleted tab, click desired bullet type, click OK button
4. With list selected, in Voice Command mode, say "Bullets"

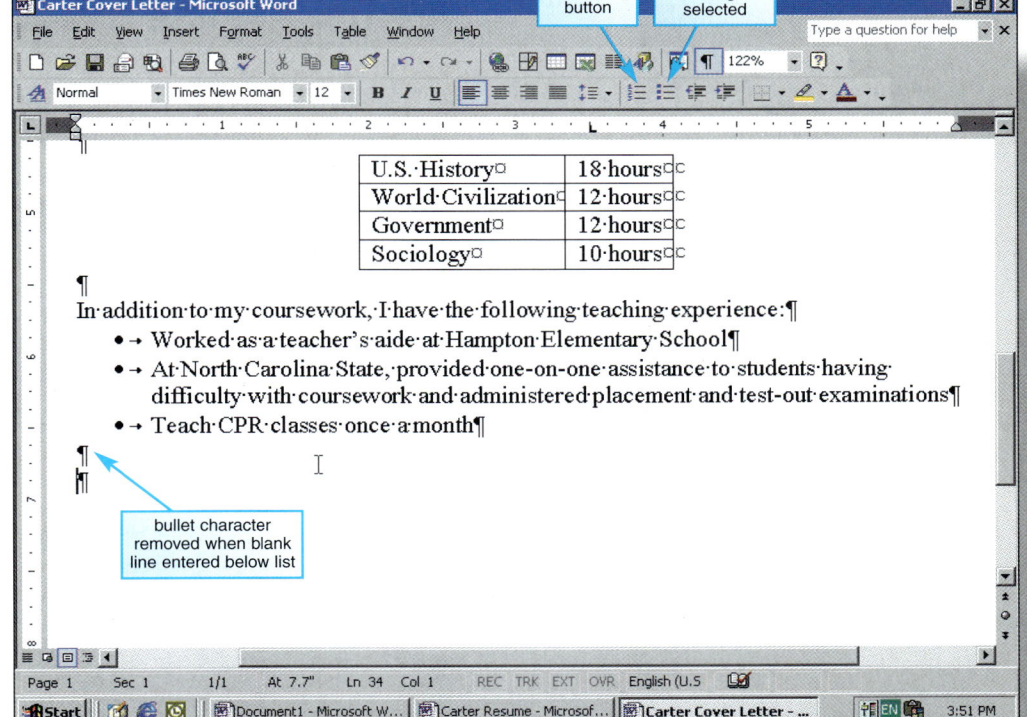

FIGURE 3-76

Numbered Lists

To apply a different numbering style to a list (e.g., a, b, c, instead of 1, 2, 3), select the list, click Format on the menu bar, click Bullets and Numbering, click the Numbered tab, click the desired numbering scheme, and then click the OK button.

When the insertion point is in a bulleted list, the Bullets button on the Formatting toolbar is selected (Figure 3-75 on the previous page). To instruct Word to stop bulleting paragraphs, you press the ENTER key twice or click the Bullets button.

You may have noticed that Word displayed the AutoCorrect Options button when it formatted the list automatically to a bulleted list. If you did not want the list to be a bulleted list, you could click the AutoCorrect Options button and then click Undo Automatic Bullets on the shortcut menu.

You can add numbers as you type, just as you can add bullets as you type. To number a list, type the number one followed by a period and then a space (1.) at the beginning of the first item and then type your text. When you press the ENTER key, Word places the number two (2.) at the beginning of the next line automatically. As with bullets, press the ENTER key twice at the end of the list or click the Numbering button (Figure 3-76 on the previous page) on the Formatting toolbar to stop numbering.

Perform the following steps to enter the remainder of the cover letter.

TO ENTER THE REMAINDER OF THE COVER LETTER

1. Type the paragraph shown in Figure 3-77, making certain you use the AutoText entry, phs, to insert the school name.

2. Press the ENTER key twice. Press the TAB key. Type Sincerely and then press the COMMA key.

3. Press the ENTER key four times. Press the TAB key. Type Tyrone James Carter and then press the ENTER key.

4. Type Enclosure as the final text.

The cover letter text is complete (Figure 3-77).

AutoText

Word provides many AutoText categories of entries for business letters. Categories include attention line, closing, mailing instructions, salutation, and subject line. To insert an AutoText entry, click Insert on the menu bar, point to AutoText, point to the desired category, and then click the desired entry. Or, click the All Entries button on the AutoText toolbar, point to the desired category, and then click the desired entry.

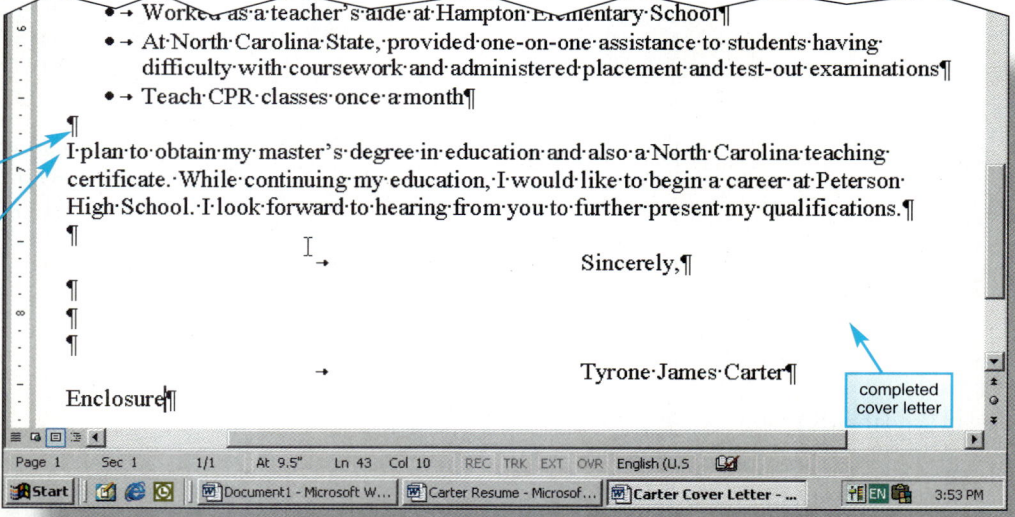

FIGURE 3-77

Proofreading

You should be absolutely certain that your resume and accompanying cover letter are error free. Check spelling and grammar using Word. Proofread for errors. Set the resume and cover letter aside for a couple of days, and then proofread them again. Ask others, such as a friend or teacher, to proofread them also.

Addressing and Printing Envelopes and Mailing Labels • WD 3.57

Saving Again and Printing the Cover Letter

The cover letter for the resume now is complete. You should save the cover letter again and then print it as described in the following steps.

TO SAVE A DOCUMENT AGAIN

1. Click the Save button on the Standard toolbar.

Word saves the cover letter with the same file name, Carter Cover Letter.

TO PRINT A DOCUMENT

1. Click the Print button on the Standard toolbar.

The completed cover letter prints as shown in Figure 3-2a on page WD 3.06.

Addressing and Printing Envelopes and Mailing Labels

The final step in this project is to address and print an envelope, as shown in the following steps.

> **More About**
>
> **Printing**
>
> Use a laser printer to print the resume and cover letter on standard letter-size white or ivory paper. Be sure to print a copy for yourself, and read it — especially before the interview. Most likely, the interviewer will have copies in hand, ready to ask you questions about the contents of both the resume and cover letter.

Steps To Address and Print an Envelope

1. **Scroll through the cover letter to display the inside address in the document window. Drag through the inside address to select it. Click Tools on the menu bar, point to Letters and Mailings, and then point to Envelopes and Labels on the Letters and Mailings submenu (Figure 3-78).**

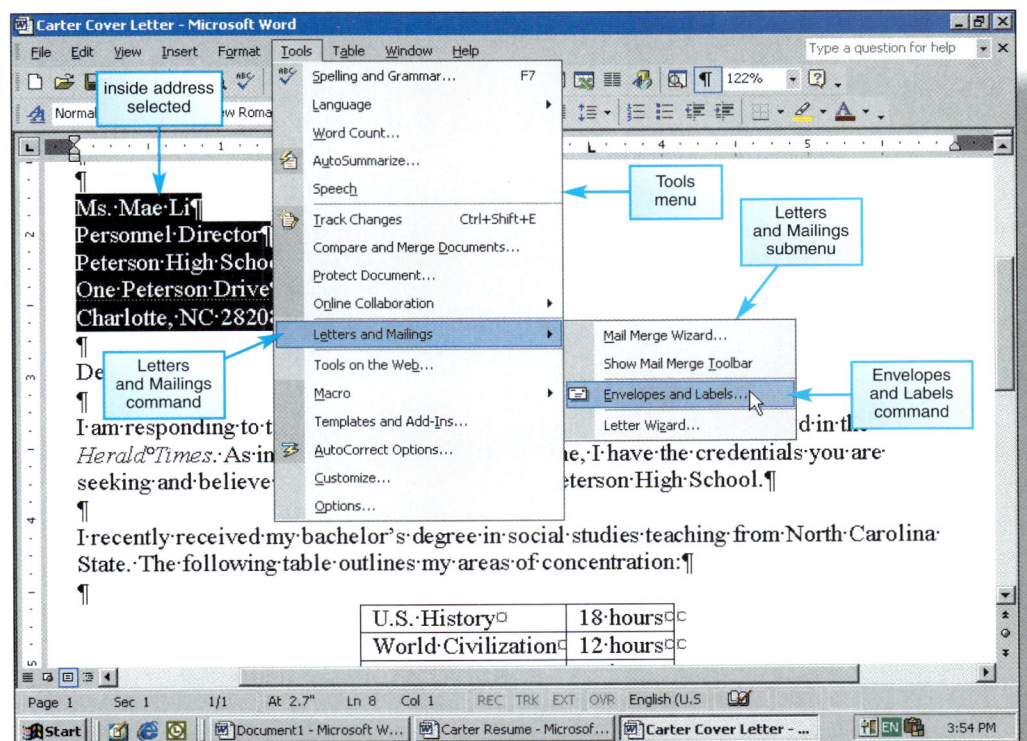

FIGURE 3-78

2 Click Envelopes and Labels. When the Envelopes and Labels dialog box displays, if necessary, click the Envelopes tab. Click the Return address text box. Type `Tyrone J. Carter` and then press the ENTER key. Type `18567 Southgate Road` and then press the ENTER key. Type `Charlotte, NC 28208` and then point to the Print button in the Envelopes and Labels dialog box.

Word displays the Envelopes and Labels dialog box (Figure 3-79).

3 Insert an envelope into your printer, as shown in the Feed area of the dialog box. Click the Print button in the dialog box. If a Microsoft Word dialog box displays, click the No button.

Word prints the envelope (shown in Figure 3-2b on page WD 3.06).

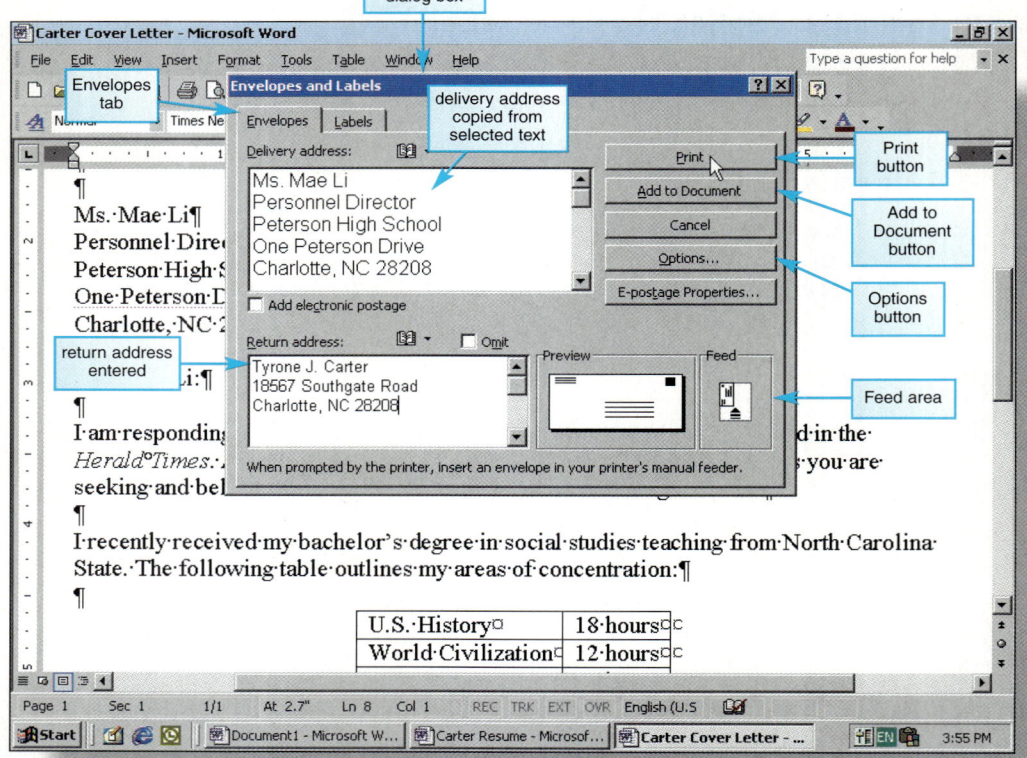

FIGURE 3-79

Instead of printing the envelope immediately, you can add it to the document by clicking the Add to Document button in the Envelopes and Labels dialog box. To specify a different envelope or label type (identified by a number on the box of envelopes or labels), click the Options button in the Envelopes and Labels dialog box.

Instead of printing an envelope, you can print a mailing label. To do this, click the Labels tab in the Envelopes and Labels dialog box. Type the delivery address in the Address box. To print the same address on all labels on the page, click Full page of the same label. Click the Print button.

More About

Office Supplies

For more information on where to obtain supplies for printing documents, visit the Word 2002 More About Web page (scsite.com/wd2002/more.htm) and then click Online Office Supplies.

Smart Tags

A **smart tag** is a button that automatically appears on the screen when Word performs a certain action. In Project 2, you worked with the AutoCorrect Options and Paste Options smart tags. This section discusses the third type of smart tag, called **Smart Tag Actions**, which performs various functions depending on the object identified by the smart tag indicator.

The smart tag indicator for Smart Tag Actions is a purple dotted underline. As shown throughout this project, a smart tag indicator displays below addresses and dates. A smart tag indicator also may display below names, places, times, and financial symbols. To view or change the list of objects recognized as smart tags, click Tools on the menu bar, click AutoCorrect Options, and then click the Smart Tags tab.

Smart Tags • WD 3.59

When you point to a smart tag indicator, the Smart Tag Actions button displays on the screen. Clicking the Smart Tag Actions button displays a Smart Tag Actions menu. The commands in the Smart Tag Actions menu vary depending on the smart tag. For example, the Smart Tag Actions menu for a date includes commands that allow you to schedule a meeting in Outlook Calendar or display your Outlook Calendar. The Smart Tag Actions menu for an address includes commands for displaying a map of the address or driving directions to or from the address.

Perform the following steps to use a smart tag to display a map showing the location of the employer's address in the cover letter. In order for the following steps to work properly, your computer must have an Internet connection.

More About

Quick Reference

For a table that lists how to complete tasks covered in this book using the mouse, menu, shortcut menu, and keyboard, see the Quick Reference Summary at the back of this book or visit the Shelly Cashman Series Office XP Web page (scsite.com/offxp/qr.htm) and then click Microsoft Word 2002.

Steps: To Use the Smart Tag Actions Button

1 Click anywhere to remove the highlight. Position the mouse pointer on the smart tag indicator below the street address, One Peterson Drive, in the inside address of the cover letter.

Word displays the Smart Tag Actions button (Figure 3-80).

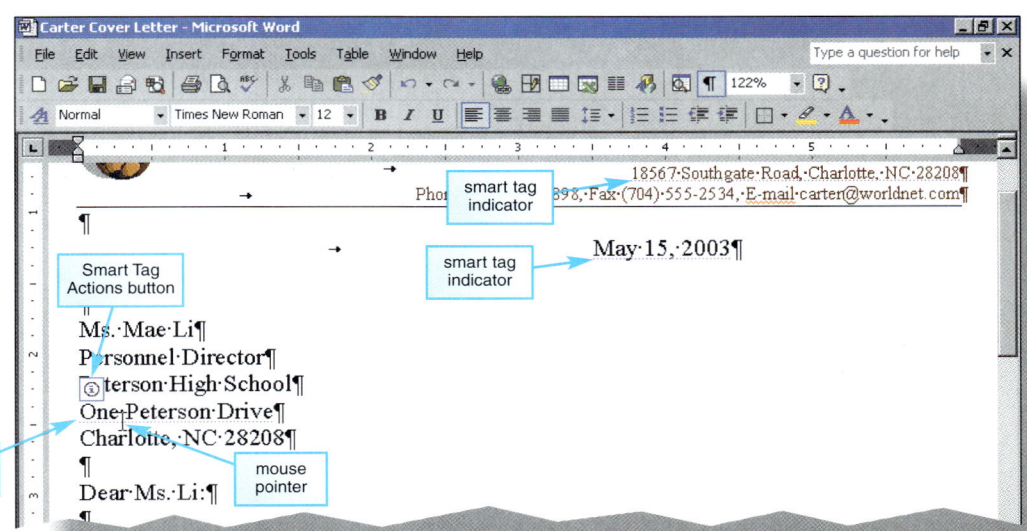

FIGURE 3-80

2 Click the Smart Tag Actions button. Point to Display Map on the Smart Tag Actions menu (Figure 3-81).

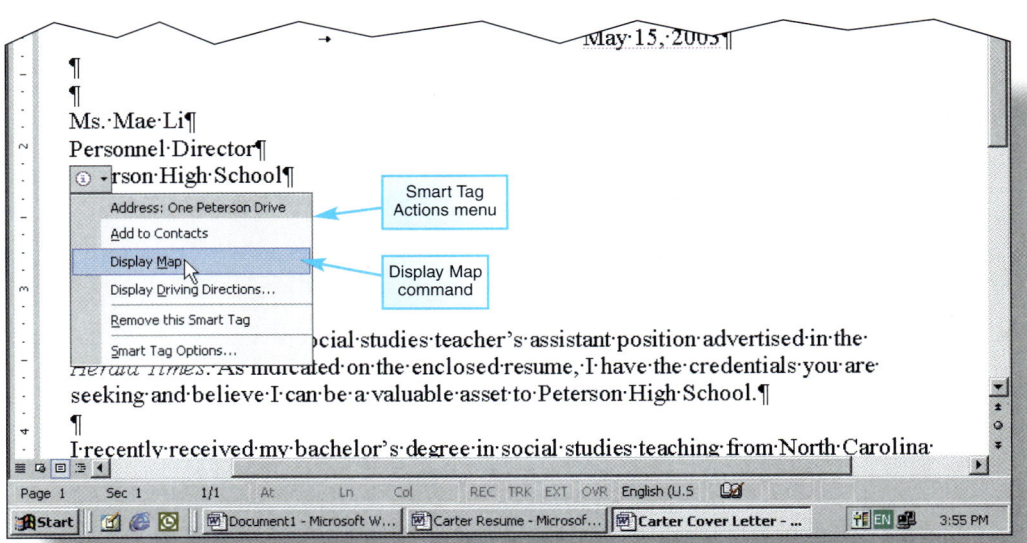

FIGURE 3-81

3 **Click Display Map. If the browser asks you to select a specific address from a list, do so and then click Find a map at the bottom of the window.**

Word starts your browser program. If necessary, your computer connects to the Web. The browser window displays a map of the address in the Word document (Figure 3-82). You can print, save, or e-mail the map.

4 **Close the browser window.**

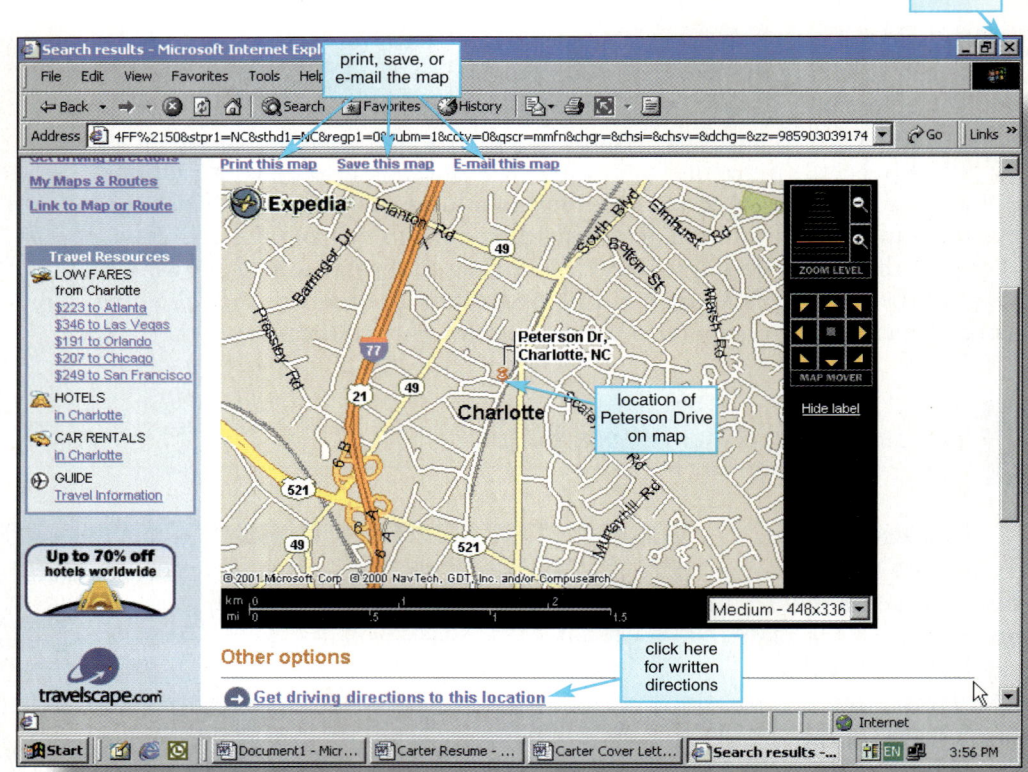

FIGURE 3-82

The final step in this project is to quit Word as described in the step below.

TO QUIT WORD

1 Click the Close button in the Word window.

The Word window closes.

CASE PERSPECTIVE SUMMARY

With your resume writing expertise and Tyrone's solid background, you have created an effective resume and cover letter. Tyrone immediately staples the two documents together, places them in the envelope, adds necessary postage, and delivers the envelope to the post office. As he places his cover letter and resume in the mail, Tyrone dreams about starting a career at Peterson High School. He plans to wait one week to hear from Ms. Li, the personnel director at Peterson High School. If she has not contacted him in that time, Tyrone plans to follow up with a telephone call to her.

Project Summary

Project 3 introduced you to creating a resume using a wizard and creating a cover letter with a letterhead, a bulleted list, and a table. You used the Resume Wizard to create a resume and then used several formatting techniques to personalize the resume. You viewed and printed the resume in print preview. You created a letterhead and then the cover letter. While creating the letterhead, you learned how to add color to characters, set custom tab stops, collect and paste between documents, and add a border to a paragraph. You created an AutoText entry, which you used when you personalized the cover letter. Finally, you addressed and printed an envelope.

What You Should Know

Having completed this project, you now should be able to perform the following tasks:

- Add More Text *(WD 3.54)*
- Address and Print an Envelope *(WD 3.57)*
- AutoFormat as You Type *(WD 3.23)*
- Bottom Border a Paragraph *(WD 3.38)*
- Bullet a List as You Type *(WD 3.54)*
- Center a Selected Table *(WD 3.54)*
- Change the Font Size *(WD 3.28, WD 3.37)*
- Clear Formatting *(WD 3.39)*
- Collect Items *(WD 3.33)*
- Color Characters *(WD 3.28)*
- Color Characters the Same Color *(WD 3.37)*
- Convert a Hyperlink to Regular Text *(WD 3.40)*
- Create a Resume Using Word's Resume Wizard *(WD 3.08)*
- Create an AutoText Entry *(WD 3.45)*
- Display Formatting Marks *(WD 3.07)*
- Enter a Line Break *(WD 3.21)*
- Enter a Paragraph *(WD 3.49)*
- Enter Data into a Table *(WD 3.51)*
- Enter More Text with Line Breaks *(WD 3.22)*
- Enter the Inside Address and Salutation *(WD 3.44)*
- Enter the Remainder of the Cover Letter *(WD 3.56)*
- Enter the Remaining Sections of the Resume *(WD 3.24)*
- Fit Columns to Table Contents *(WD 3.52)*
- Hide White Space *(WD 3.15)*
- Insert a Nonbreaking Space *(WD 3.47)*
- Insert an AutoText Entry *(WD 3.48)*
- Insert an Empty Table *(WD 3.49)*
- Insert and Resize a Graphic *(WD 3.29)*
- Insert the Current Date into a Document *(WD 3.43)*
- Open a New Document Window *(WD 3.27)*
- Paste from the Office Clipboard *(WD 3.35)*
- Print a Document *(WD 3.57)*
- Print Preview a Document *(WD 3.25)*
- Print the Resume Created by the Resume Wizard *(WD 3.15)*
- Quit Word *(WD 3.60)*
- Reset Menus and Toolbars *(WD 3.07)*
- Save a Document *(WD 3.26)*
- Save a Document Again *(WD 3.57)*
- Save the Document with a New File Name *(WD 3.41)*
- Save the Letterhead *(WD 3.40)*
- Select a Table *(WD 3.53)*
- Select and Replace Placeholder Text *(WD 3.19)*
- Select and Replace More Placeholder Text *(WD 3.20)*
- Set Custom Tab Stops Using the Ruler *(WD 3.42)*
- Set Custom Tab Stops Using the Tabs Dialog Box *(WD 3.31)*
- Start and Customize Word *(WD 3.07)*
- Switch From One Open Document to Another *(WD 3.32)*
- Use the Smart Tags Actions Button *(WD 3.59)*
- Zoom Text Width *(WD 3.18)*

Microsoft Certification

The Microsoft Office Specialist Certification program provides an opportunity for you to obtain a valuable industry credential — proof that you have the Word 2002 skills required by employers. For more information, see Appendix E or visit the Shelly Cashman Series Microsoft Office Specialist Web page at scsite.com/offxp/cert.htm.

Learn It Online

Instructions: To complete the Learn It Online exercises, start your browser, click the Address bar, and then enter scsite.com/offxp/exs.htm. When the Office XP Learn It Online page displays, follow the instructions in the exercises below.

1 Project Reinforcement TF, MC, and SA

Below Word Project 3, click the Project Reinforcement link. Print the quiz by clicking Print on the File menu. Answer each question. Write your first and last name at the top of each page, and then hand in the printout to your instructor.

2 Flash Cards

Below Word Project 3, click the Flash Cards link. When Flash Cards displays, read the instructions. Type 20 (or a number specified by your instructor) in the Number of Playing Cards text box, type your name in the Name text box, and then click the Flip Card button. When the flash card displays, read the question and then click the Answer box arrow to select an answer. Flip through Flash Cards. Click Print on the File menu to print the last flash card if your score is 15 (75%) correct or greater and then hand it in to your instructor. If your score is less than 15 (75%) correct, then redo this exercise by clicking the Replay button.

3 Practice Test

Below Word Project 3, click the Practice Test link. Answer each question, enter your first and last name at the bottom of the page, and then click the Grade Test button. When the graded practice test displays on your screen, click Print on the File menu to print a hard copy. Continue to take practice tests until you score 80% or better. Hand in a printout of the final practice test to your instructor.

4 Who Wants to Be a Computer Genius?

Below Word Project 3, click the Computer Genius link. Read the instructions, enter your first and last name at the bottom of the page, and then click the Play button. Hand in your score to your instructor.

5 Wheel of Terms

Below Word Project 3, click the Wheel of Terms link. Read the instructions, and then enter your first and last name and your school name. Click the Play button. Hand in your score to your instructor.

6 Crossword Puzzle Challenge

Below Word Project 3, click the Crossword Puzzle Challenge link. Read the instructions, and then enter your first and last name. Click the Play button. Work the crossword puzzle. When you are finished, click the Submit button. When the crossword puzzle redisplays, click the Print button. Hand in the printout.

7 Tips and Tricks

Below Word Project 3, click the Tips and Tricks link. Click a topic that pertains to Project 3. Right-click the information and then click Print on the shortcut menu. Construct a brief example of what the information relates to in Word to confirm you understand how to use the tip or trick. Hand in the example and printed information.

8 Newsgroups

Below Word Project 3, click the Newsgroups link. Click a topic that pertains to Project 3. Print three comments. Hand in the comments to your instructor.

9 Expanding Your Horizons

Below Word Project 3, click the Articles for Microsoft Word link. Click a topic that pertains to Project 3. Print the information. Construct a brief example of what the information relates to in Word to confirm you understand the contents of the article. Hand in the example and printed information to your instructor.

10 Search Sleuth

Below Word Project 3, click the Search Sleuth link. To search for a term that pertains to this project, select a term below the Project 3 title and then use the Google search engine at google.com (or any major search engine) to display and print two Web pages that present information on the term. Hand in the printouts to your instructor.

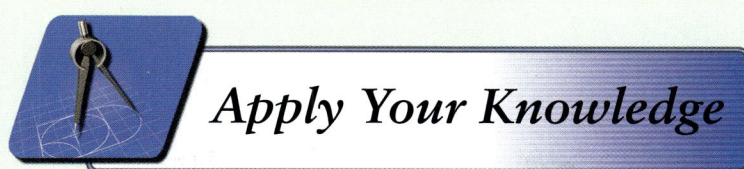

Apply Your Knowledge

1 Working with a Table

Instructions: Start Word. Open the document, College Expenses Table, on the Data Disk. See the inside back cover of this book for instructions for downloading the Data Disk or see your instructor for information on accessing the files in this book.

The document is a Word table that you are to edit and format. The revised table is shown in Figure 3-83. Perform the following tasks:

1. Select the Phone row by pointing to the left of the row until the mouse pointer changes to a right pointing arrow and then clicking. Right-click in the selected row and then click Delete Rows on the shortcut menu to delete the Phone row.
2. Add a new row to the bottom of the table. In the first cell of the new row, type Total as the entry.
3. Point to the top of the Senior column until the mouse pointer changes to a downward pointing arrow and then click to select the column. Right-click the selected column and then click Insert Columns on the shortcut menu to insert a column. Fill in the column as follows: Column Title – Junior; Room & Board - $3,627.58; Tuition & Books – 5,347.99; Clothing – 540.23; Entertainment – 700.05; Miscellaneous – 358.38.
4. Click the Tables and Borders button on the Standard toolbar to display the Tables and Borders toolbar. If necessary, click the Draw Table button on the Tables and Borders toolbar to deselect the button. Position the insertion point in the Freshman Total cell (second column, last row). Click the AutoSum button on the Tables and Borders toolbar to sum the contents of the column. Repeat for Sophomore, Junior, and Senior totals. Click the Close button on the Tables and Borders toolbar to remove the toolbar from the screen. Leave the screen in print layout view.
5. Select all cells containing numbers and then click the Align Right button on the Formatting toolbar.
6. Click somewhere in the table. Click Table on the menu bar and then click Table AutoFormat. In the Table AutoFormat dialog box, scroll to and then click Table Elegant in the Table styles list. If necessary, remove the check mark from the Heading rows check box. Click the Apply button.
7. Point to the upper-left corner of the table to display the table move handle. Click the table move handle to select the table. Click the Center button on the Formatting toolbar to center the table. Click anywhere to remove the selection.
8. Point to the column border between the first and second columns and then double-click to increase the width of the first column.
9. Click File on the menu bar and then click Save As. Use the file name, Revised College Expenses Table, to save the document on your floppy disk.
10. Print the revised table.

FIGURE 3-83

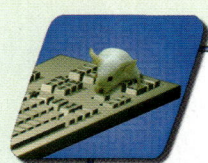

In the Lab

1 Using Word's Resume Wizard to Create a Resume

Problem: You are a student at Wooster State College expecting to receive your Bachelor of Science degree in Mechanical Engineering this May. As the semester end is approaching quickly, you are beginning a search for full-time employment upon graduation. You prepare the resume shown in Figure 3-84 using Word's Resume Wizard.

Instructions:

1. Use the Resume Wizard to create a resume. Select the Professional style for the resume. Use the name and address information in Figure 3-84 when the Resume Wizard requests it.
2. Personalize the resume as shown in Figure 3-84. When entering multiple lines in the Awards received, Certificates, Languages, and Extracurricular activities sections, be sure to enter a line break at the end of each line, instead of a paragraph break.
3. Check the spelling of the resume.
4. Save the resume on a floppy disk with Duke Resume as the file name.
5. View and print the resume from within print preview.

FIGURE 3-84

In the Lab

2 Creating a Cover Letter with a Table

Problem: You prepared the resume shown in Figure 3-84 and now are ready to create a cover letter to send to a prospective employer (Figure 3-85).

Instructions:

1. Create the letterhead shown at the top of Figure 3-85. If you completed In the Lab 1, use the Office Clipboard to copy and paste the address information from the resume to the letterhead. Save the letterhead with the file name, Duke Letterhead.

2. Create the letter shown in Figure 3-85 using the modified block style. Set a tab stop at the 3.5" mark on the ruler for the date line, complimentary close, and signature block. Insert the current date. After entering the inside address, create an AutoText entry for Thermal Power Plant #424, and insert the AutoText entry whenever you have to enter the company name. Remove the hyperlink format from the e-mail address. Center the table.

3. Save the letter on a floppy disk with Duke Cover Letter as the file name.

4. Check the spelling of the cover letter. Save the cover letter again with the same file name.

5. View and print the cover letter from within print preview.

6. Address and print an envelope and a mailing label using the inside and return addresses in the cover letter.

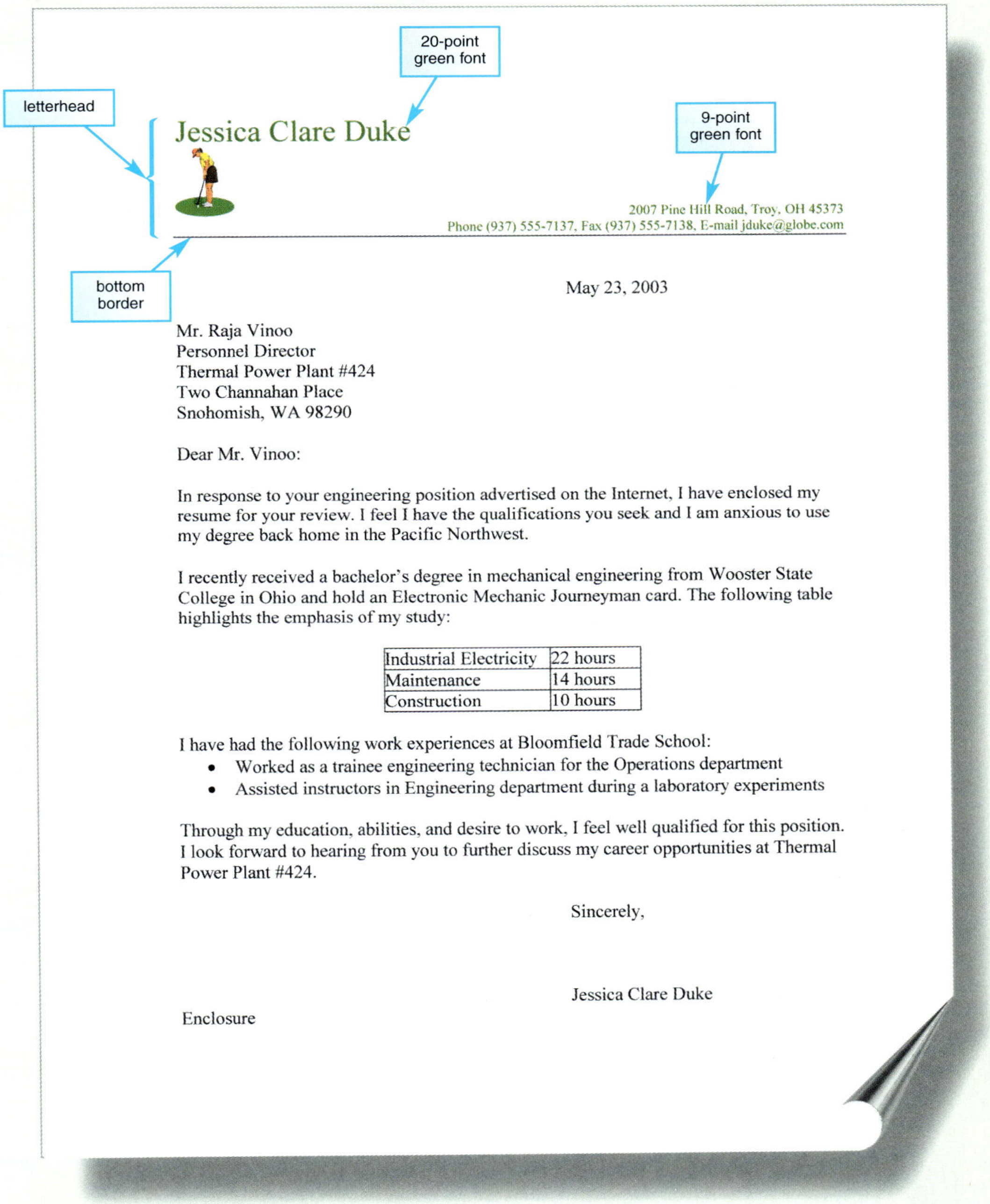

FIGURE 3-85

Cases and Places

The difficulty of these case studies varies:
► are the least difficult; ►► are more difficult; and ►►► are the most difficult.

1 ► Your boss has asked you to create a calendar for January so he can post it on the office bulletin board. Use the Calendar Wizard in the Other Documents sheet in the Templates dialog box. Use the following settings in the wizard: banner style, portrait print direction, leave room for a picture, January 2003 for both the start and end date. With the calendar on the screen, click the current graphic and delete it. Insert a clip art image of a snowflake or a similar seasonal graphic and then resize the image so it fits in the entire space for the graphic.

2 ► You have been asked to prepare the agenda for the next morning meeting. Use the Agenda Wizard in the Other Documents sheet in the Templates dialog box. Use the following settings in the wizard: style – standard; meeting date – 10/21/2003; meeting time – 8:00 a.m. to 8:45 a.m.; title – Morning Meeting; meeting location – Oak Room; include all headings in Headings panel; names on agenda – Meeting called by, Facilitator, Note taker, and Attendees; Topics, People, and Minutes – Monthly goals, Jim Johnson, 30; Safety, Bob Ayala, 15; add a form for recording the minutes. On the agenda created by the wizard, add the following names in the appropriate spaces: G. Esteban called the meeting and is the facilitator, R. Wasilowski will be the note taker; all people listed in this assignment will be attending – along with T. Brooks, D. Lopez, M. Cartright, and you. The meeting is an informational meeting. Also, attendees should read the minutes from the last meeting and bring their own coffee. As a special note, remind the attendees to please be on time.

3 ►► A potential employer has asked you to fax your cover letter and resume so she may review it immediately. Use the Fax Wizard and the following settings: create the fax cover sheet with a note and print the fax so you can send it on a separate fax machine. It must be faxed to William O'Brien at Linkland Materials (1972 Elwood Drive, Snohomish, Washington 98290; telephone 555-2346; fax 555-2347). Each is one page in length. Fax a copy to Craig Ziemba at the same number. In the fax, write a message informing William O'Brien that your cover letter and resume are attached and that he can contact you if he has any questions. Use your own name, address, and telephone information in the fax.

4 ►► As chairperson of the annual company outing, you look for volunteers to assist with various activities. You have compiled a list of jobs for the picnic: publicity, plan meal and order food, activities, setup, and cleanup. A tent has been reserved on the grounds of the Hannah Nature Center. You prepare a memorandum that informs fellow employees of the event location and asks for their assistance with the event. A copy of the memo should be sent to Barbara Lindahl. Use the Memo Wizard, together with the concepts and techniques presented in this project, to create and format the interoffice memorandum.

5 ►►► Obtain a copy of last Sunday's newspaper. Look through the classified section and cut out a want ad in an area of interest. Assume you are in the market for the position being advertised. Use the Resume Wizard to create a resume. Include a table and a numbered list in the cover letter. After setting tabs at the 3.5" mark, change them to the 3" mark. Use the want ad for the inside address and your personal information for the return address. Try to be as accurate as possible when personalizing the resume and cover letter. Submit the want ad with your cover letter and resume. Address and print an envelope. Then, print an entire page of mailing labels using your home address.

Microsoft Word 2002

Creating Web Pages Using Word

CASE PERSPECTIVE

In Project 3, Tyrone James Carter created his resume with your assistance (Figure 3-1 on page WD 3.05). Recently, Tyrone has been surfing the Internet and has discovered that many people have their own personal Web pages with links to other Web sites and Web pages such as resumes and schedules. These personal Web pages are very impressive. To make himself more marketable to a potential employer, Tyrone has asked you to help him create a personal Web page that contains a hyperlink to his resume. To do this, he must save his resume as a Web page. Tyrone also wants his Web page to contain two more hyperlinks: one to his favorite Web site (www.scsite.com) and another to his e-mail address. This way, potential employers easily can send him an e-mail message.

To complete this Web Feature, you will need the resume created in Project 3 so you can save it as a Web page and then use the resulting Web page as a hyperlink destination. (If you did not create the resume, see your instructor for a copy of it.)

Introduction

Word provides three techniques for creating Web pages. If you have an existing Word document, you can save it as a Web page. If you do not have an existing Word document, you can create a Web page by using a Web page template or the Web Page Wizard, which provides customized templates you can modify easily. In addition to these Web tools, Word has many other **Web page authoring** features. For example, you can include frames, hyperlinks, sounds, videos, pictures, scrolling text, bullets, horizontal lines, check boxes, option buttons, list boxes, text boxes, and scripts on Web pages.

In this Web Feature, you save the resume created in Project 3 as a Web page. Then, you use Word's Web Page Wizard to create another Web page that contains two frames (Figure 1a on the next page). A **frame** is a rectangular section of a Web page that can display another separate Web page. Thus, a Web page that contains multiple frames can display multiple Web pages simultaneously. Word stores all frames associated with a Web page in a single file called the **frames page**. The frames page is not visible on the screen; it simply is a container for all frames associated with a Web page. When you open the frames page in Word or a Web browser, all frames associated with the Web page display on the screen.

In this Web Feature, the file name of the frames page is Carter Personal Web Page. When you initially open this frames page, the left frame contains the title Tyrone James Carter and two hyperlinks — My Resume and My Favorite Site; the right frame displays Tyrone's resume (Figure 1a). As discussed in Project 3, a hyperlink is a shortcut that allows a user to jump easily and quickly to another location in the same document or to other documents or Web pages. In the left frame, the My Resume hyperlink is a link to the resume Web page, and the My Favorite Site hyperlink is a link to www.scsite.com.

When you click the My Favorite Site hyperlink in the left frame, the www.scsite.com Web site displays in the right frame (Figure 1b). When you click the My Resume hyperlink in the left frame, the resume Web page displays in the right frame. The resume itself contains a hyperlink to an e-mail address. When you click the e-mail address, Word opens your e-mail program automatically with the recipient's address (carter@worldnet.com) already filled in (Figure 1c). You simply type a message and then click the Send button, which places the message in the Outbox or sends it if you are connected to an e-mail server.

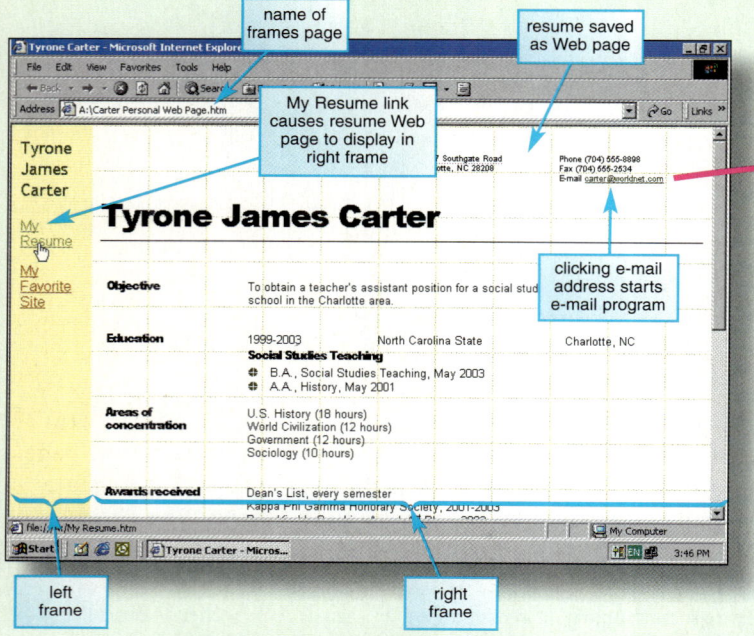

(a) Web Page Displaying Resume

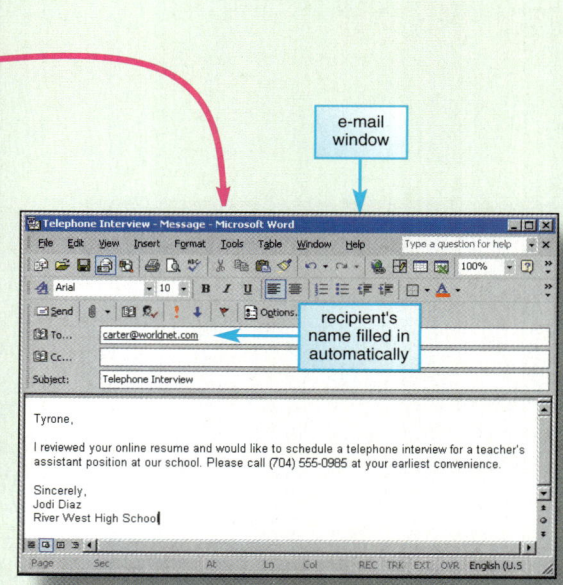

(c) E-mail Program

Once you have created Web pages, you can publish them. **Publishing** is the process of making Web pages available to others, for example on the World Wide Web or on a company's intranet. In Word, you can publish Web pages by saving them to a Web folder or to an FTP location. The procedures for publishing Web pages in Microsoft Office are discussed in Appendix C.

This Web Feature is for instructional purposes. Thus, you create and save your frames page and associated Web pages on a floppy disk rather than to the Web. Saving these pages to the floppy disk may be a slow process because writing to a floppy disk takes more time than writing to a hard disk — please be patient.

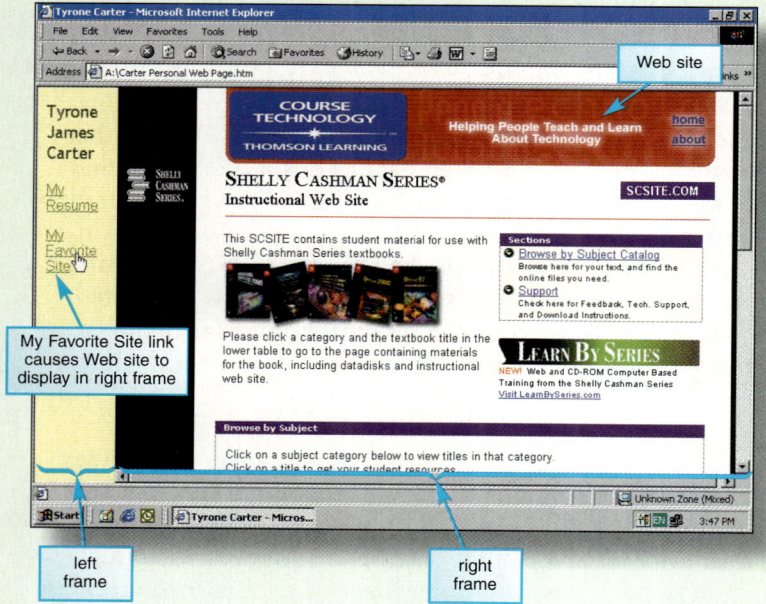

(b) Web Page Displaying Web Site

FIGURE 1

Saving a Word Document as a Web Page • WDW 1.03

Saving a Word Document as a Web Page

Once you have created a Word document, you can save it as a Web page so that it can be published and then viewed by a Web browser, such as Internet Explorer. Perform the following steps to save the resume created in Project 3 as a Web page.

Web Page Titles

To change the title that displays on the title bar of a Web page, click the Change Title button in the Save As dialog box (see Figure 3).

Steps To Save a Word Document as a Web Page

1 Start Word and then open the file named Carter Resume created in Project 3. Click File on the menu bar and then point to Save as Web Page (Figure 2).

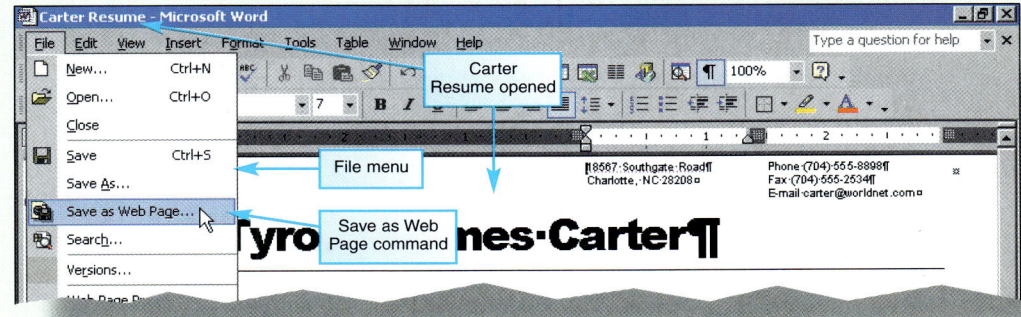

FIGURE 2

2 Click Save as Web Page. When the Save As dialog box displays, type `Carter Resume Web Page` in the File name text box and then, if necessary, change the Save in location to 3½ Floppy (A:) as shown in Figure 3. Point to the Save button in the Save As dialog box.

3 Click the Save button in the Save As dialog box.

Word saves the resume as a Web page and displays it in the Word window (shown in Figure 4 on the next page).

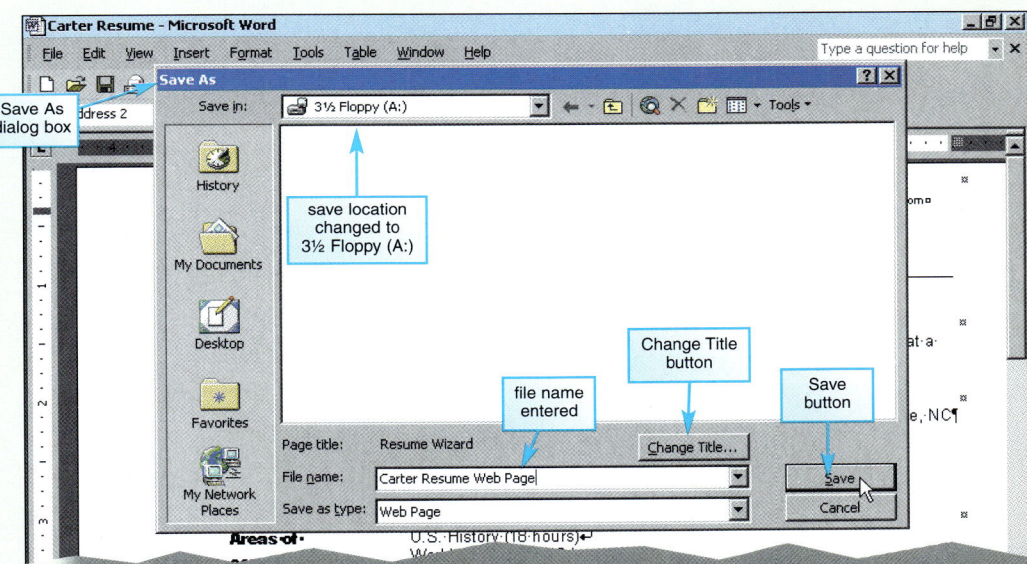

FIGURE 3

Web Page Design

For information on guidelines for designing Web pages, visit the Word 2002 More About Web page (scsite.com/wd2002/more.htm) and then click Web Page Design.

Word switches to Web layout view and also changes some of the toolbar buttons and menu commands to provide Web page authoring features. For example, the Standard toolbar now displays a New Web Page button (Figure 4). The Web Layout View button on the horizontal scroll bar is selected.

The resume displays in the Word window much like it will display in a Web browser. Some of Word's formatting features are not supported by Web pages. Thus, your Web page may display slightly different from the original Word document.

Formatting the E-Mail Address as a Hyperlink

You want the e-mail address in your resume to be formatted as a hyperlink so that when someone clicks the e-mail address on the Web page, his or her e-mail program starts automatically and displays an e-mail window with your e-mail address already filled in.

As described in Project 3, when you press the SPACEBAR or ENTER key after a Web or e-mail address, Word automatically formats it as a hyperlink. Perform the following steps to format the e-mail address as a hyperlink.

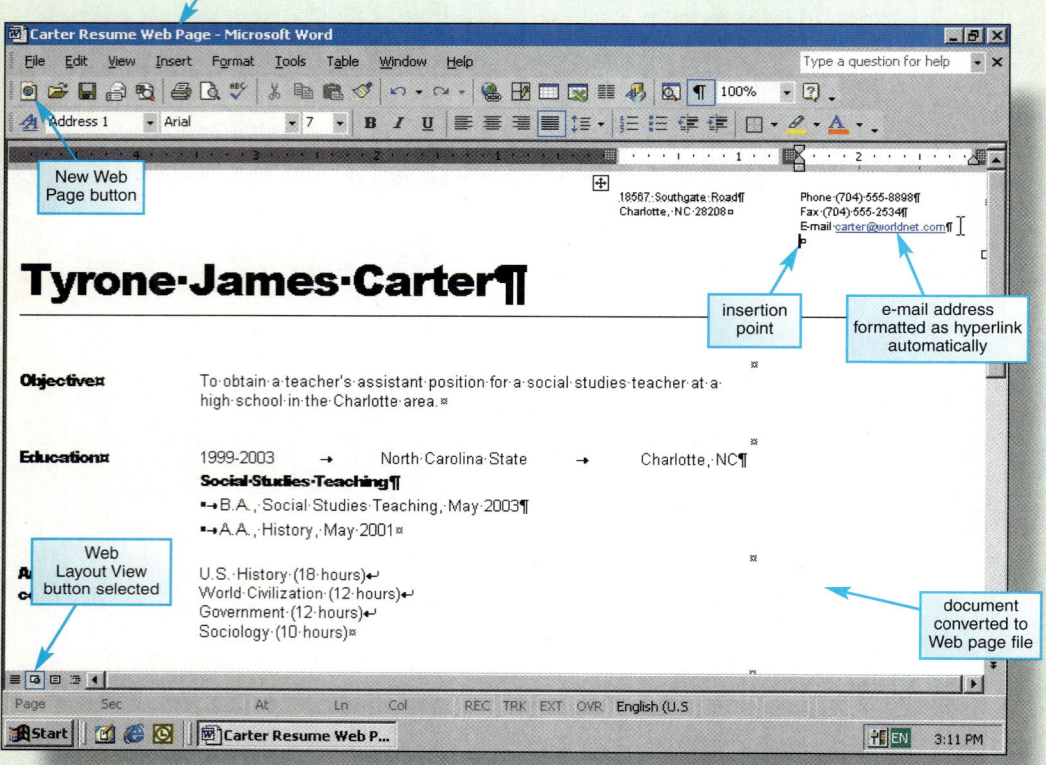

FIGURE 4

TO FORMAT A HYPERLINK AUTOMATICALLY

1 Position the insertion point immediately after the e-mail address; that is, after the m in com.

2 Press the ENTER key. If Word displays a dialog box about installing an AutoCorrections feature, click the No button.

Word automatically formats the e-mail address as a hyperlink; that is, it is colored blue and underlined (Figure 4).

You now are finished modifying the Carter Resume Web Page file. Perform the following steps to save the file again and then close it.

TO SAVE AND CLOSE A WEB PAGE

1 Click the Save button on the Standard toolbar.

2 Click File on the menu bar and then click Close.

Word saves the file and closes it. The Word window is empty.

Using Word's Web Page Wizard to Create a Web Page

In the previous section, you saved an existing Word document as a Web page. Next, you want to create a Web page that contains a link to the Web page just created. You can create a Web page from scratch using a Web page template or you can use the **Web Page Wizard**. Because this is your first experience creating a new Web page with frames, you should use the Web Page Wizard as shown in the following steps.

More About

AutoFormat

If Word does not automatically convert an e-mail or Web address to a hyperlink as you type, click Tools on the menu bar, click AutoCorrect Options, click the AutoFormat As You Type tab, place a check mark in the Internet and network paths with hyperlinks check box, and then click the OK button.

Steps To Create a Web Page Using the Web Page Wizard

1 Click File on the menu bar and then click New. When the New Document task pane displays, click General Templates. When the Templates dialog box displays, if necessary, click the Web Pages tab. Point to the Web Page Wizard icon.

Word displays several Web page template icons and the Web Page Wizard icon in the Web Pages sheet of the Templates dialog box (Figure 5).

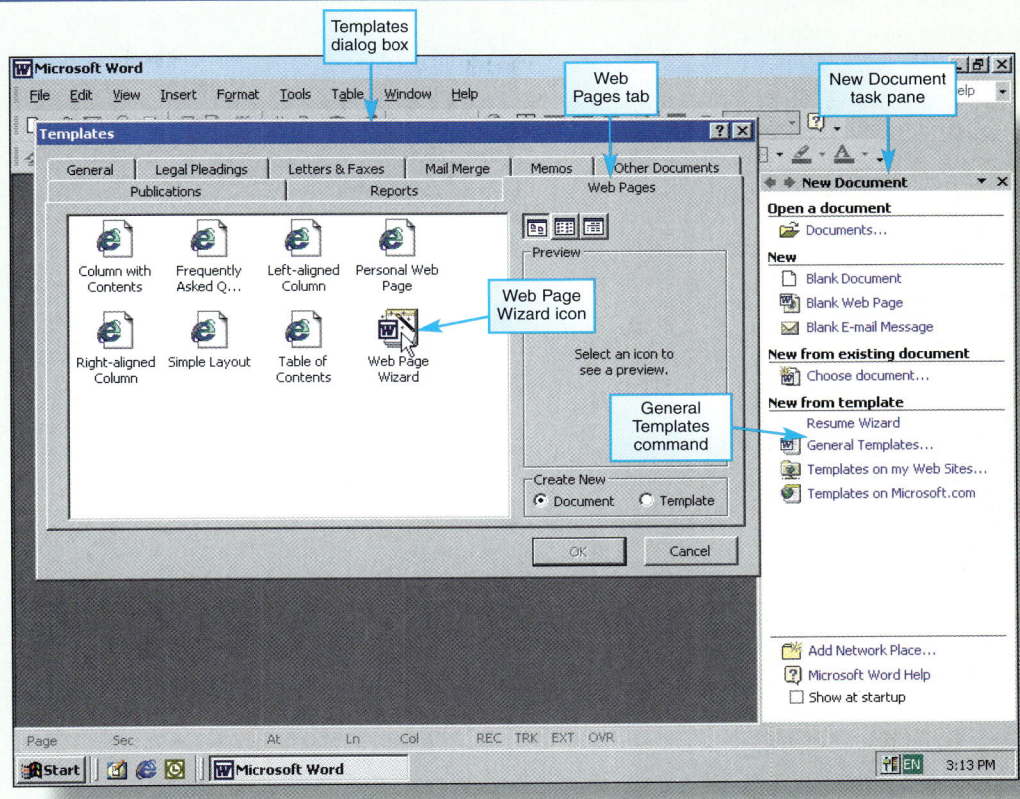

FIGURE 5

2 Double-click the Web Page Wizard icon. When the Start panel displays in the Web Page Wizard dialog box, click the Next button. When the Title and Location panel displays, type `Tyrone Carter` in the Web site title text box. Press the TAB key and then type `a:` in the Web site location text box. Point to the Next button.

Word displays the Title and Location panel in the Web Page Wizard dialog box (Figure 6). The title you enter in this dialog box displays in the Web browser's title bar.

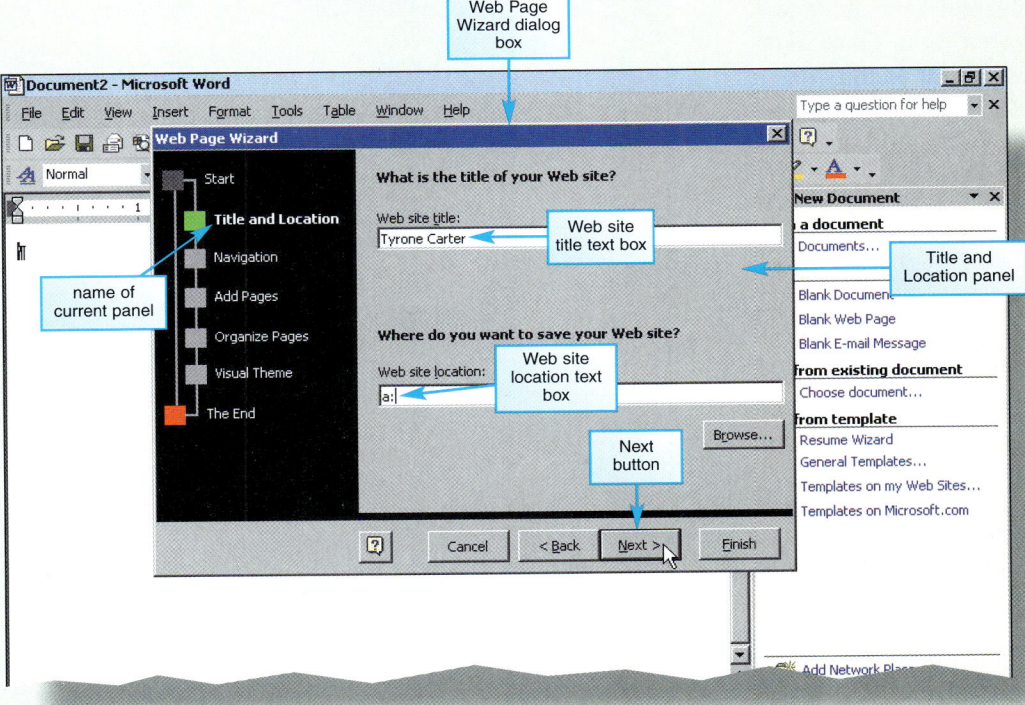

FIGURE 6

3 **Click the Next button. When the Navigation panel displays, if necessary, click Vertical frame. Point to the Next button.**

Word displays the *Navigation panel* in the Web Page Wizard dialog box (Figure 7). In this dialog box, you select the placement of hyperlinks on your Web page(s).

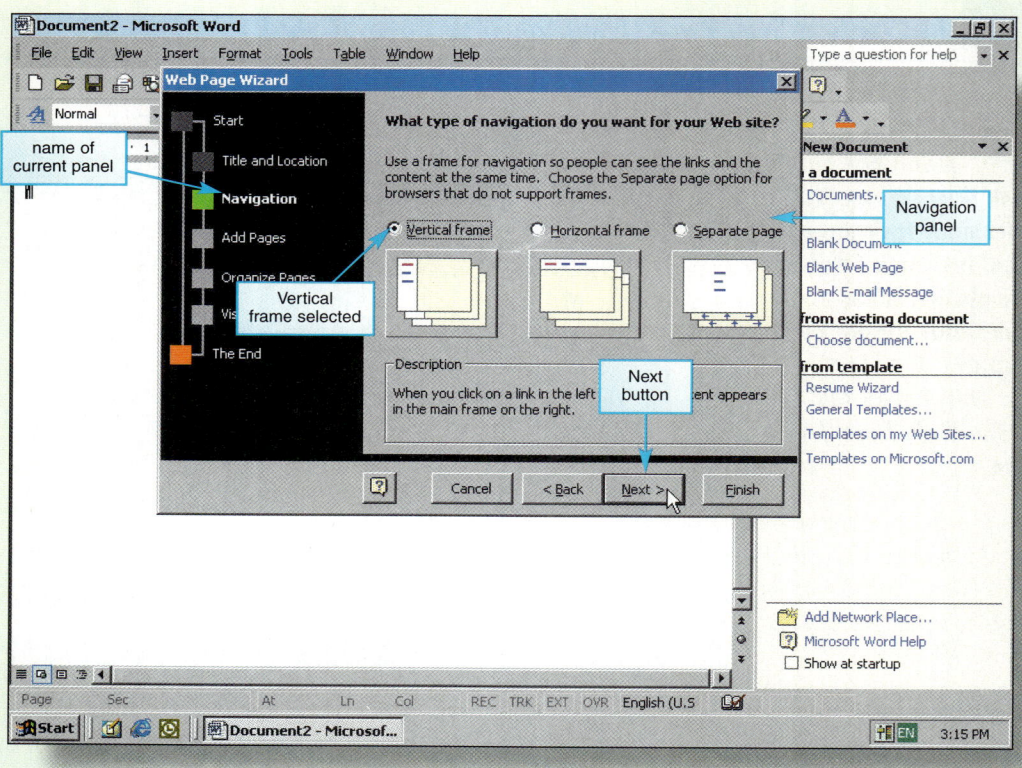

FIGURE 7

4 **Click the Next button. When the Add Pages panel displays, click the Remove Page button three times and then point to the Add Existing File button.**

Word displays the *Add Pages panel* that initially lists three Web page names: Personal Web Page, Blank Page 1, and Blank Page 2. You do not want any of these Web page names on your Web page; thus, you remove them (Figure 8). You will add Carter Resume Web Page to the list by clicking the Add Existing File button.

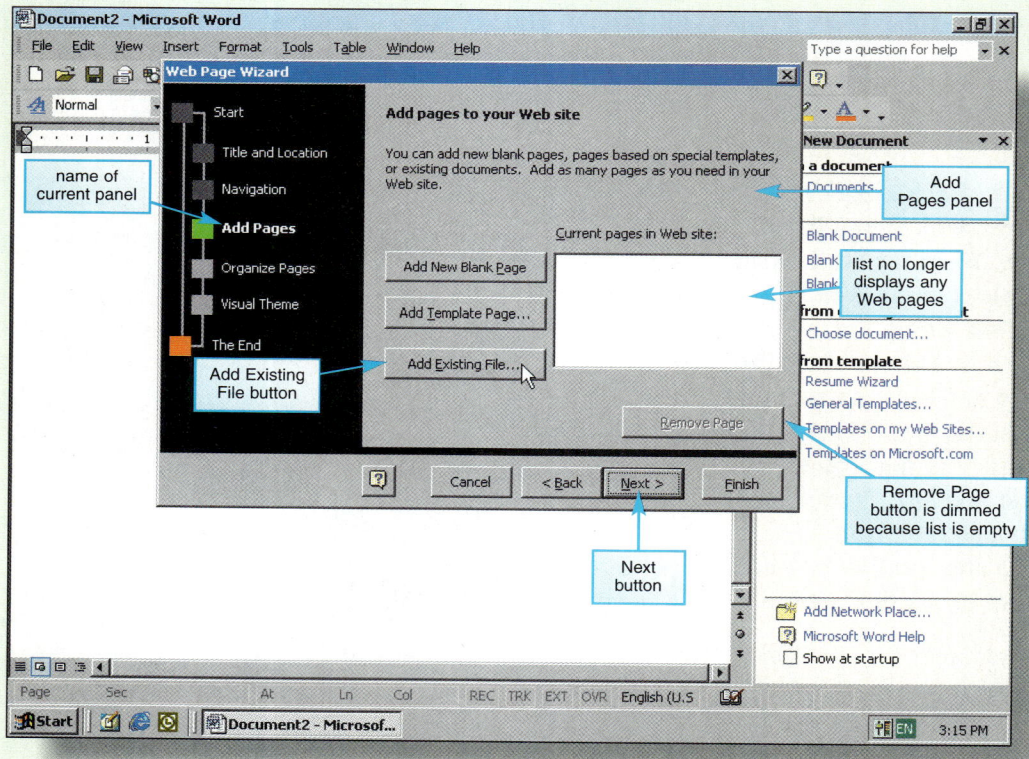

FIGURE 8

5 **Click the Add Existing File button to display the Open dialog box. If necessary, change the Look in location to 3½ Floppy (A:). Click Carter Resume Web Page and then point to the Open button in the Open dialog box (Figure 9).**

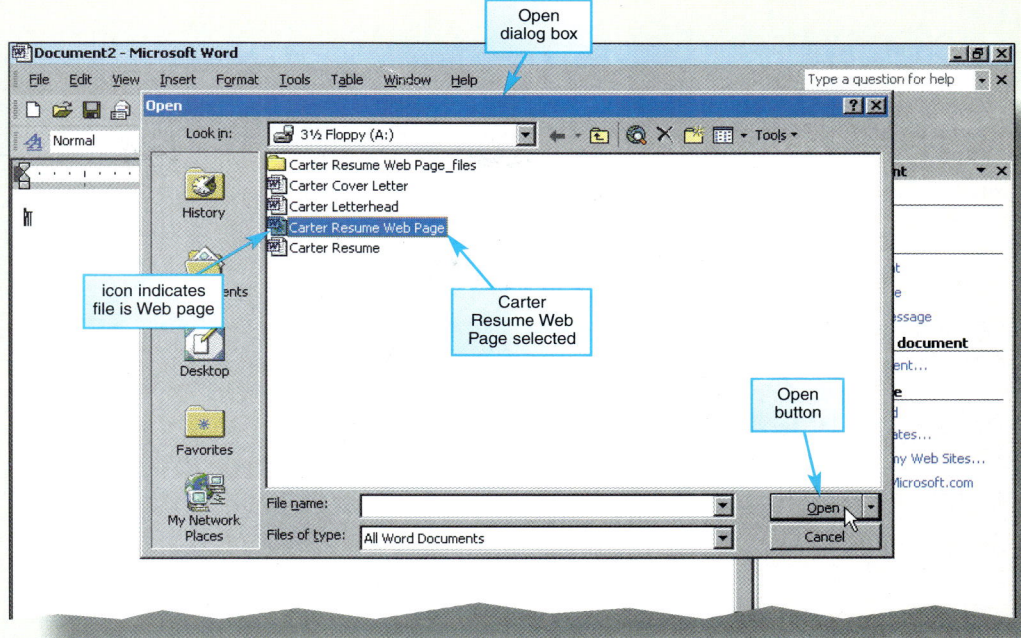

FIGURE 9

6 **Click the Open button in the Open dialog box. When the Add Pages panel is visible again, click the Next button.**

The wizard adds Carter Resume Web Page to the list in the Add Pages panel.

7 **When the Organize Pages panel displays, click the Rename button. When the Rename Hyperlink dialog box displays, type My Resume in the text box. Point to the OK button.**

In the Organize Pages panel in the Web Page Wizard, you specify the sequence and names of the hyperlinks that will display in the left frame of the Web page (Figure 10).

8 **Click the OK button.**

Word renames the hyperlink to My Resume.

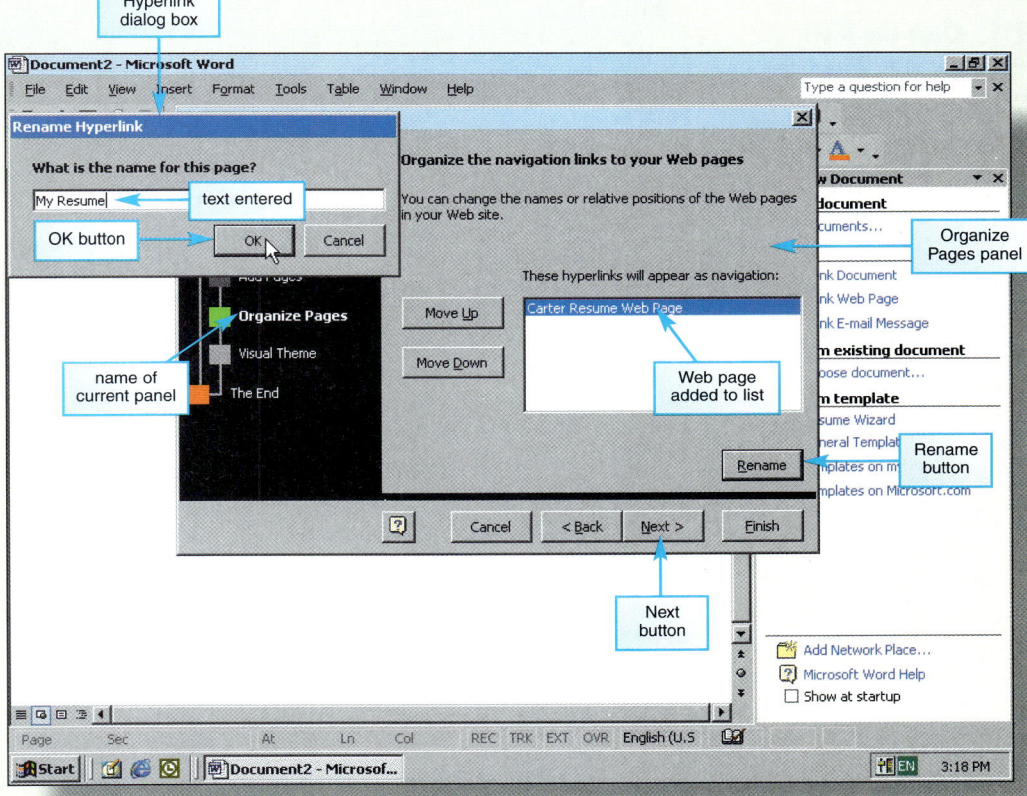

FIGURE 10

WDW 1.08 • Web Feature • Creating Web Pages Using Word

9 **Click the Next button. If the displayed theme in the Visual Theme panel is not Global Marketing, click the Browse Themes button. When the Theme dialog box displays, scroll to and then click Global Marketing (or a similar theme) in the Choose a Theme list. Click the OK button. Point to the Next button in the Visual Theme panel.**

Word displays the *Visual Theme panel* in the Web Page Wizard dialog box (Figure 11). A *theme* is a collection of defined design elements and color schemes.

10 **Click the Next button. When the The End panel displays, click the Finish button. If the Office Assistant or a dialog box displays a message about navigation features, click the Yes button. If a Frames toolbar displays in your document window, click its Close button to remove it from the screen.**

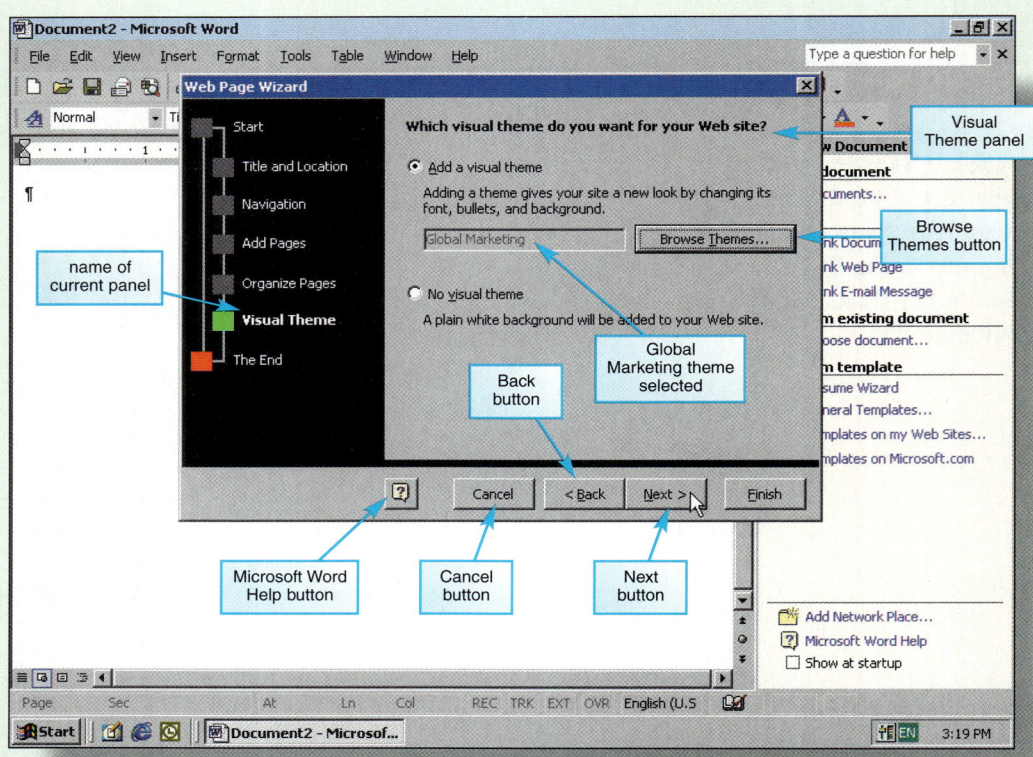

FIGURE 11

After about a minute, Word displays a layout of the Web pages (shown in Figure 12). The My Resume hyperlink displays in a frame on the left, and the resume displays in a frame on the right.

Other Ways

1. On View menu click Task Pane, click Other Task Panes button on task pane title bar and then click New Document, click General Templates, click Web Pages tab, double-click Web Page Wizard icon
2. Click Start button on Windows taskbar, click New Office Document, click Web Pages tab, double-click Web Page Wizard icon
3. With task pane displaying, in Voice Command mode, say "General Templates, Other Documents, [select Web Page Wizard], OK"

When creating a Web page using the Web Page Wizard, you can click the Back button (Figure 11) in any panel of the Web Page Wizard dialog box to change any previously entered information. For help with entering information into the Web Page Wizard, click the Microsoft Word Help button in the appropriate panel. To exit from the Web Page Wizard and return to the document window without creating the Web page, click the Cancel button in any of the Web Page Wizard dialog boxes.

Modifying a Web Page

The next step is to modify the Web pages. First, you make the left frame smaller, and then you add the My Favorite Site hyperlink to the left frame.

The Web page is divided into two frames, one on the left and one on the right. A **frame border** separates the frames. When you point to the frame border, the mouse pointer shape changes to a double-headed arrow.

You want to make the left frame narrower. To do this, you drag the frame border as illustrated in the following steps.

Modifying a Web Page • WDW 1.09

Steps To Resize a Web Page Frame

 Point to the frame border.

The mouse pointer shape changes to a double-headed arrow, and Word displays the ScreenTip, Resize (Figure 12).

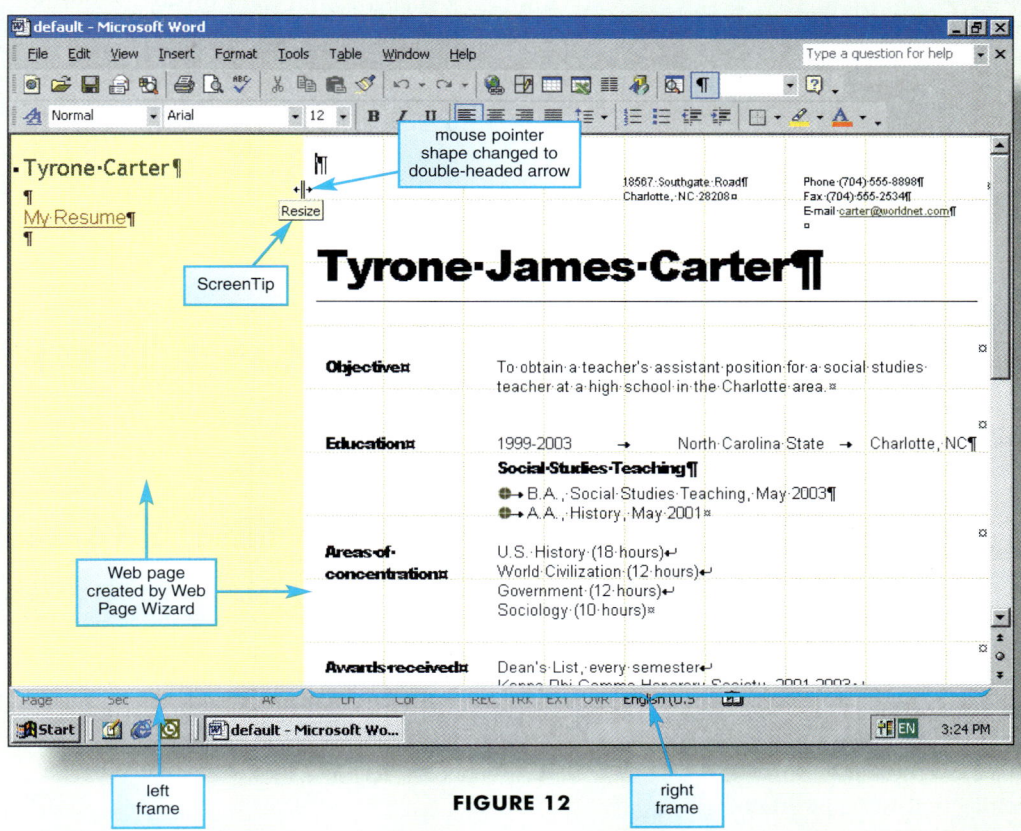

FIGURE 12

Drag the frame border to the left until it is positioned on the letter a in Carter (Figure 13).

Word narrows the left frame and widens the right frame (shown in Figure 14 on the next page).

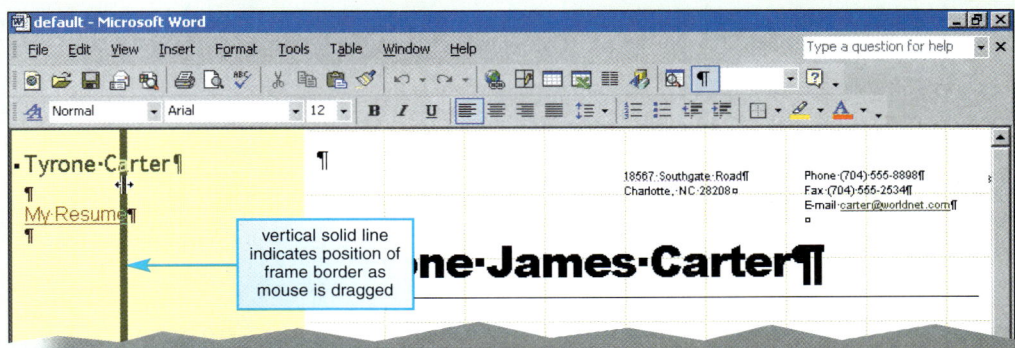

FIGURE 13

In the left frame, you want to add a My Favorite Site hyperlink. You used the Web Page Wizard to link the My Resume hyperlink to the Web page file called Carter Resume Web Page, which means when you click the My Resume link in the left frame, the Carter Resume Web Page file displays in the right frame. Similarly, when you click the My Favorite Site hyperlink, you want a Web site to display in the right frame.

The first step is to enter the hyperlink text, My Favorite Site, into the left frame as described in the steps on the next page.

Highlights

Highlighting alerts the reader to the text's importance, much like a highlight marker does on a printed document. To highlight text, select it, click the Highlight button arrow on the Formatting toolbar, and then click the desired highlight color.

Linking

Instead of linking to a file, you can link to objects in a document, such as bookmarks. To link text to an object, click Place in This Document in the Link to area in the Insert Hyperlink dialog box and then click the object name in the Look in area.

TO ENTER AND FORMAT TEXT

1. Click in the left frame of the Web page. Click the paragraph mark below the My Resume hyperlink and then press the ENTER key.
2. Click the Font Size box arrow and then click 12.
3. Type My Favorite Site as the text.

Word enters the text, My Favorite Site, in the left frame using a font size of 12 (shown in Figure 14).

Perform the following steps to link the My Favorite Site text to a Web site.

 **To Add a Hyperlink**

1. **Drag through the text, My Favorite Site. Click the Insert Hyperlink button on the Standard toolbar. When the Insert Hyperlink dialog box displays, if necessary, click Existing File or Web Page in the Link to bar. Type** www.scsite.com **in the Address text box and then point to the OK button (Figure 14).**

2. **Click the OK button.**

Word formats the text, My Favorite Site, as a hyperlink that when clicked displays the associated Web site in the right frame (shown in Figure 1b on page WDW 1.02).

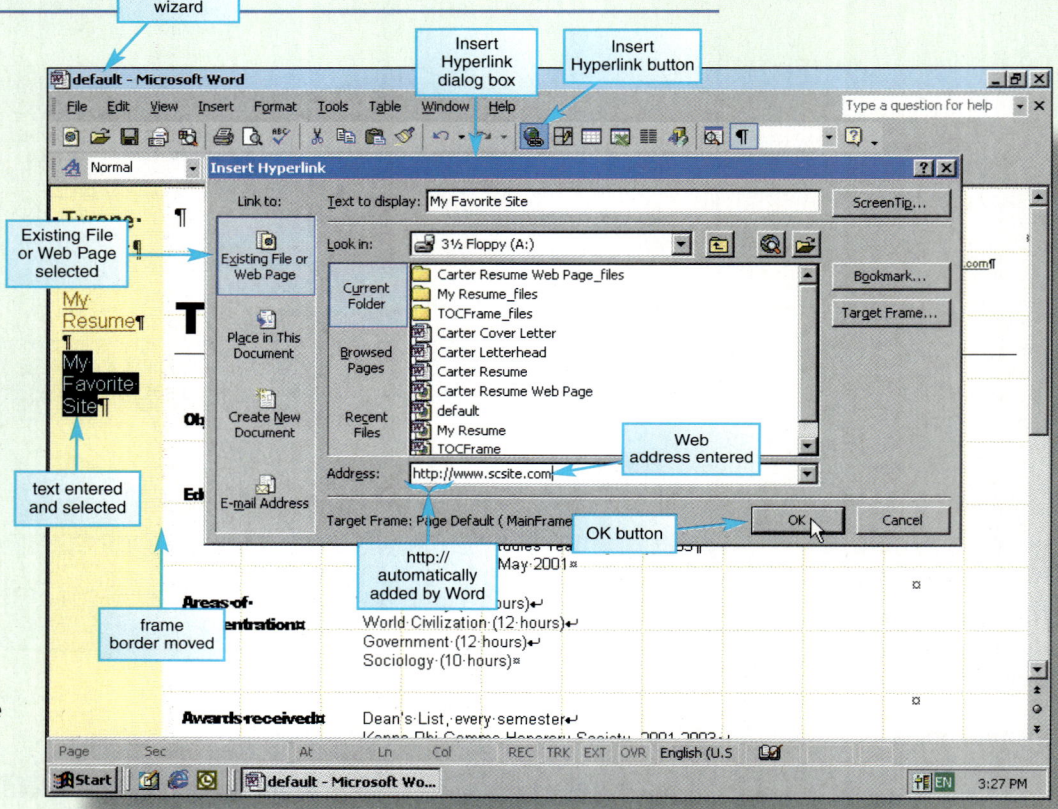

FIGURE 14

Quick Reference

For a table that lists how to complete tasks covered in this book using the mouse, menu, shortcut menu, and keyboard, see the Quick Reference Summary at the back of this book or visit the Shelly Cashman Series Office XP Web page (scsite.com/offxp/qr.htm) and then click Microsoft Word 2002.

If you wanted to edit an existing hyperlink, you right-click the hyperlink text and then click Edit Hyperlink on the shortcut menu. Word will display the Edit Hyperlink dialog box instead of the Insert Hyperlink dialog box. Other than the title bar, these two dialog boxes are the same.

The Resume Wizard assigned the file name, default, to this frames page (Figure 14). The next step is to save the frames page with a new file name, as described in the following steps.

Modifying a Web Page • WDW 1.11

TO SAVE THE FRAMES PAGE WITH A NEW FILE NAME

1. Insert your floppy disk into drive A. Click File on the menu bar and then click Save As.
2. Type the file name `Carter Personal Web Page` in the File name text box. Do not press the ENTER key.
3. If necessary, click the Save in box arrow and then click 3½ Floppy (A:). Click the Save button in the Save As dialog box.

Word saves the frames page and associated frames on a floppy disk in drive A with the file name, Carter Personal Web Page.

Viewing the Web Page in Your Default Browser

To see how the Web page looks in your default browser without actually connecting to the Internet, use the **Web Page Preview command**, which displays on the File menu when Word is in Web layout view, as shown in these steps.

HTML

If you wish to view the HTML source code associated with the Web page you have created, click View on the menu bar and then click HTML Source, which starts the Script Editor. To quit the Script Editor, click File on the menu bar and then click Exit.

Steps To View a Web Page in the Browser Window

1. **Click File on the menu bar and then point to Web Page Preview (Figure 15).**

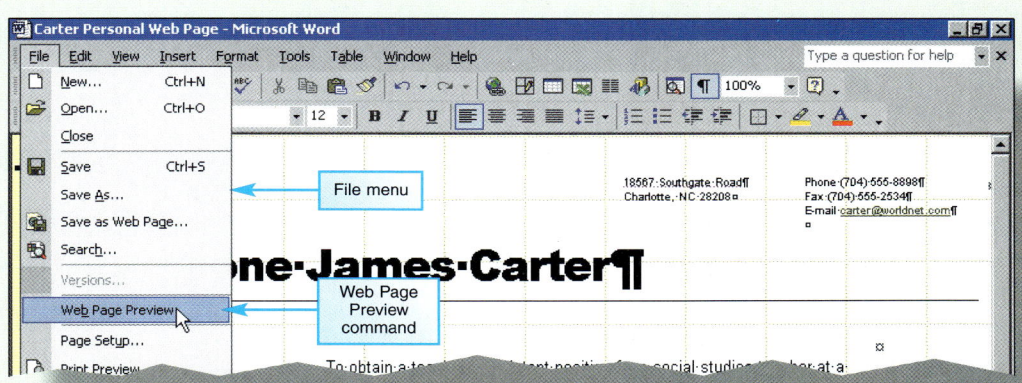

FIGURE 15

2. **Click Web Page Preview. If necessary, maximize the browser window.**

Word opens the Web browser in a separate window and displays the open Web page file in the browser window (Figure 16).

3. **Click the Close button on the browser title bar to close the browser window.**

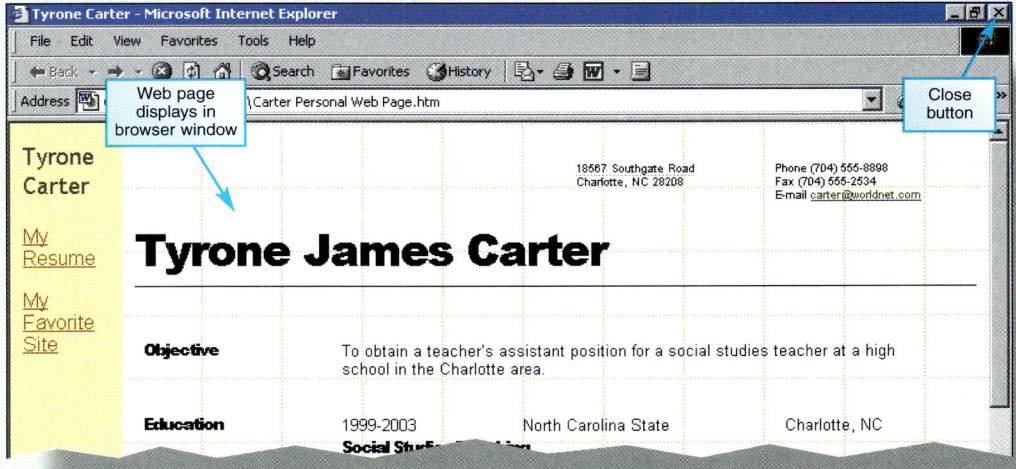

FIGURE 16

More About

Opening Web Pages

To open the Web page directly from Word, click the Open button on the Standard toolbar. If necessary, click the Files of type box arrow and then click Web Pages (or All Files). Click the file name of the Web page (which has an extension of .htm or .html) and then click the Open button in the dialog box.

From the browser window (Figure 16 on the previous page), you can test your hyperlinks to be sure they work — before you publish them to the Web. For example, in the left frame, click the My Favorite Site link to display the Web site www.scsite.com in the right frame. (If you are not connected to the Internet, your browser will connect you and then display the Web site.) Click the My Resume link to display the Carter Resume Web Page in the right frame. Click the e-mail address to open your e-mail program with the address, carter@worldnet.com, entered in the recipient's address box.

The next step is to quit Word.

TO QUIT WORD

1. Click the Close button on the Word title bar.

The Word window closes.

Editing a Web Page from Your Browser

One of the powerful features of Office XP is the ability to edit a Web page directly from Internet Explorer. The following steps illustrate how to open your Web page in Internet Explorer and then edit it from Internet Explorer.

Steps: To Edit a Web Page from Your Browser

1. **Click the Start button on the taskbar, point to Programs, and then click Internet Explorer. When the Internet Explorer window opens, click the Address box. Type a: and then press the ENTER key. Double-click Carter Personal Web Page in the list. When the resume Web page displays, if necessary, maximize the window. Point to the Edit with Microsoft Word button on the toolbar.**

Internet Explorer opens the Carter Personal Web Page and displays it in the browser window (Figure 17). Internet Explorer determines the Office program you used to create the Web page and associates that program with the Edit button.

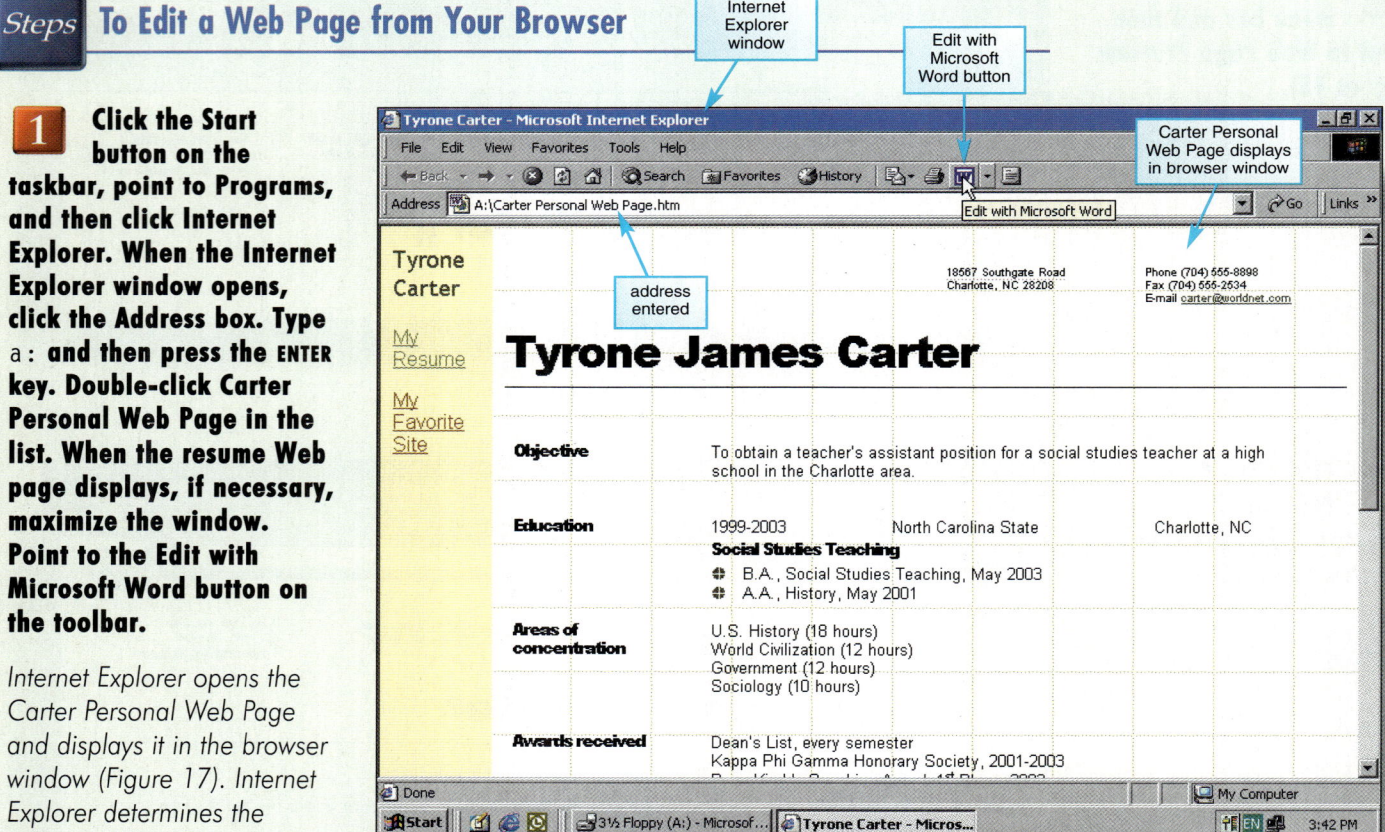

FIGURE 17

2 **Click the Edit with Microsoft Word button.**

Internet Explorer starts Microsoft Word and displays the Carter Personal Web Page in the Word window.

3 **In the left frame, click to the left of the C in Carter. Type** James **and then press the SPACEBAR.**

Tyrone's middle name displays in the left frame of the Web page (Figure 18).

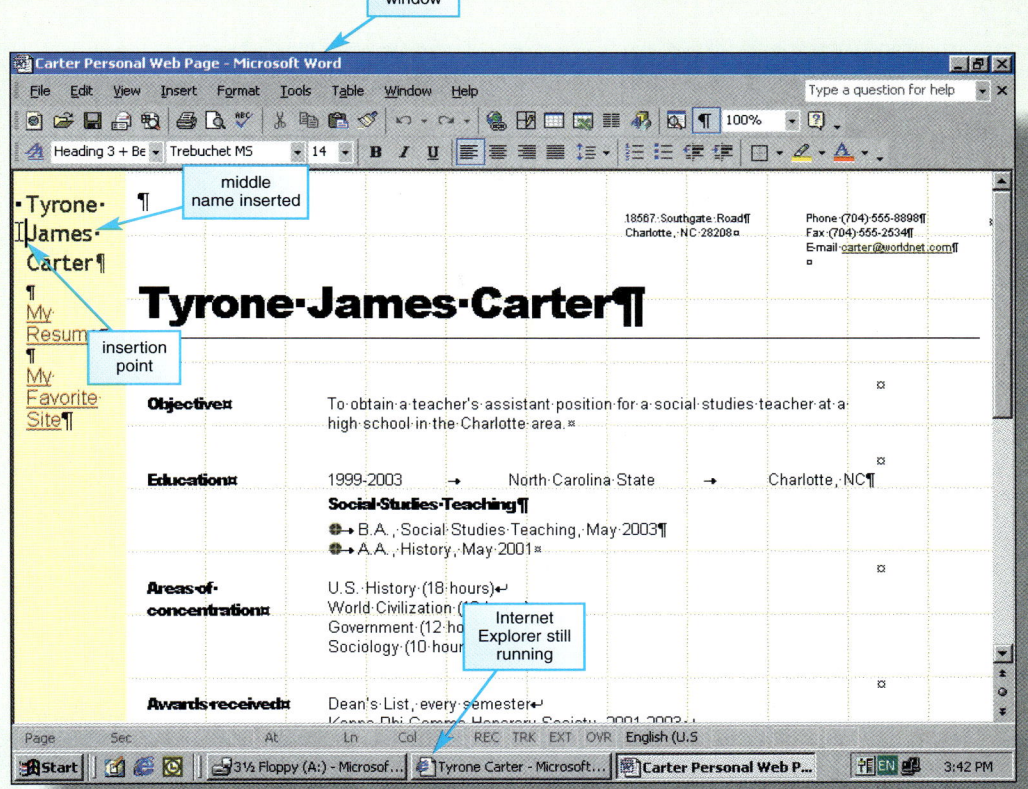

FIGURE 18

4 **Click the Save button on the Standard toolbar. Click the Close button on the Word title bar to close the Word window. When the Internet Explorer window redisplays, click the Refresh button on the toolbar.**

Internet Explorer displays the revised Web page (Figure 19).

5 **Click the Close button on the Internet Explorer window title bar to close the browser window.**

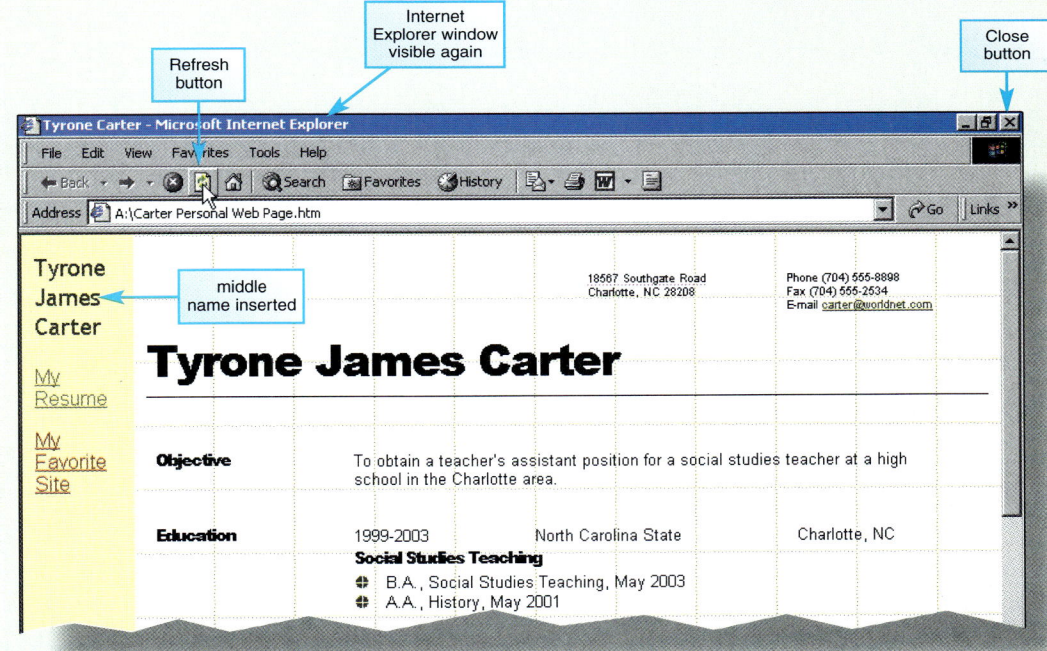

FIGURE 19

The final step is to make your Web pages and associated files available to others on a network, on an intranet, or on the World Wide Web. See Appendix C and then talk to your instructor about how you should do this for your system.

CASE PERSPECTIVE SUMMARY

Tyrone is thrilled with his personal Web pages. They look so professional! Tyrone now is ready to publish the Web pages and associated files to the World Wide Web. After talking with his ISP's technical support staff, he learns he can use Word to save a copy of his Web page files directly on his ISP's Web server. You are familiar with this feature of Word and assist Tyrone with this task. Next, he connects to the Web and displays his personal Web pages from his browser. Tyrone is quite impressed with himself!

Web Feature Summary

This Web Feature introduced you to creating a Web page by saving an existing Word document as a Web page file. You also created a new Web page with frames using the Web Page Wizard and then modified this Web page. You created a hyperlink to an e-mail address, one to a Web page file, and another to a Web site. Finally, you viewed and edited a Web page from the browser window.

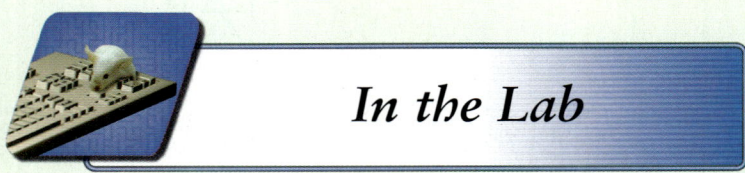

In the Lab

1 Saving a Word Document as a Web Page

Problem: You created the research paper shown in Figure 2-76 on pages WD 2.58 and WD 2.59 in Project 2. You decide to save this research paper as a Web page.

Instructions: Open the GPS Paper shown in Figure 2-76. (If you did not create the research paper, see your instructor for a copy.) Then, save the paper as a Web page using the file name, GPS Paper Web Page. Print the Web page. Use the Web Page Preview command to view the Web page in your browser. Close the browser window. If you have access to a Web server or ftp site, save the Web page to the server or site (see Appendix C for instructions).

2 Creating a Web Page with a Hyperlink to a Web Site

Problem: You created the resume shown in Figure 3-84 on page WD 3.63 in Project 3. You decide to create a personal Web page with a link to this resume. Thus, you also must save the resume as a Web page.

Instructions: Open the Duke Resume shown in Figure 3-84. (If you did not create the resume, see your instructor for a copy.) Then, save the resume as a Web page using the file name, Duke Resume Web Page. Convert the e-mail address to a hyperlink. Save the Web page again. Create a personal Web page with frames using the Web Page Wizard. Use the following settings as the wizard requests them: apply vertical frame navigation; create a hyperlink to the Duke Resume Web Page; change the name of the hyperlink to My Resume; and select a visual theme you like best. Insert a hyperlink called My Favorite Site and link it to your favorite Web address. Resize the left frame. Save the Web page. Test your Web page links. Print the Web page. Use the Web Page Preview command to view the Web page in your browser. Close the browser window. Quit Word. Start Internet Explorer and display the Web page in the browser window. Click the Edit with Microsoft Word button. In Word, change the name on the resume to your name. Save the change and quit Word. Refresh the Internet Explorer window.

Microsoft Word 2002

PROJECT 4

Creating a Document with a Table, Chart, and Watermark

OBJECTIVES

You will have mastered the material in this project when you can:

- Add a border and shading to a paragraph
- Format characters using the Font dialog box
- Insert clip art from the Web
- Center text vertically on a page
- Insert a section break
- Insert a Word document into an open document
- Create a header different from a previous header
- Change the starting page number in a section
- Create a footer different from a previous footer
- Format an existing Word table
- Sum columns in a table using the AutoSum button
- Select and format nonadjacent text
- Create a chart from a Word table
- Modify a chart in Microsoft Graph
- Format a chart in Word
- Keep paragraph lines together
- Add picture bullets to a list
- Create and apply a character style
- Use the Draw Table feature to create a table
- Change the direction of text in table cells
- Change alignment of text in table cells
- Insert a text watermark
- Reveal formatting

Career Hunt
Evaluate Prospective Employers Carefully

Planning for a career requires commitment to your goals. After graduation, your skills are fresh and you are ready to search for the perfect job. Where do you start? Campus placement centers, executive search and employment agencies, and the Internet all are viable methods for seeking employment. Many companies advertise their job opportunities and market their businesses on corporate Web sites. Likewise, job seekers prepare electronic resumes and send them to prospective employers or search for jobs on employment Web sites. Regardless of the method you use to start the process, to be successful at finding the right employment, research potential companies to determine their financial situation, hiring plans, and growth strategies. Look for established companies with solid assets.

An easy way to locate such relevant information is through the corporation's annual report. This document contains narratives explaining the corporation's mission, vision for expansion, and significant developments. These features are supplemented by the use of charts and graphs reflecting the company's activities during the year compared with previous years.

An annual report is similar to the business proposal you will create in Project 4 for the To Your Health Society. Both documents are tailored to specific audiences. Each publication contains an attractive title page, tables, charts, and a variety of design elements. The proposal in this project contains a graphic watermark that displays behind the first and second pages of the proposal. Companies sometimes use their logos or other graphics as watermarks on documents to add visual appeal.

Say you are a graduate with an engineering degree seeking a career with an international corporation known for research and development. Your college placement center provides a variety of sources from which you can obtain information about qualified businesses, including facts about BP, which is one of the world's larger petroleum and chemical companies. You acquire a copy of BP's annual report and are directed to its Web site for additional details.

As you peruse the annual report, you find that the BP parent company name changed to BP from BP Amoco (named after the merger between BP and Amoco in December, 1998). You locate BP financial highlights, which reflect the latest acquisitions, joint ventures, and the addition of new business streams. All these categories are of interest to you, the results are favorable, and the data is depicted in an organized manner using charts and graphs.

In addition to the charts and graphs comprising the annual report, the document contains features on environmental and social issues and highlights the company's worldwide exploration. You conclude that this is a successful company.

Although the report is distributed to shareholders once a year, production takes nearly six months and requires a team approach involving personnel throughout the corporation. Managers write reports, photographers capture images of oil fields and personnel throughout the world, accountants gather financial data, and design team members plan the document's organization. As press time nears, personnel review manuscripts for accuracy and legality, produce charts and graphs, scan photos, and design pages. Computers allow last-minute changes to be made so the document is as accurate as possible.

The report is printed and distributed, and next, the meticulous task of posting all the information to the Web begins.

Then, when a company contacts you for an interview, learn as much as you can about it by reviewing its annual report, whether printed or online. Being well informed about the company dynamics just might get you the job!

Microsoft Word 2002

Creating a Document with a Table, Chart, and Watermark

PROJECT

CASE PERSPECTIVE

You have been a member of the To Your Health Society for seven years. For the past four years, this society has sponsored a To Your Health Auction, where all proceeds reach a health-related charity. The society will auction any item that is new or in like-new condition or an antique. Sample items auctioned include art, computers, electronics, books, movies, music, clothing, appliances, clocks, tools, and outdoor equipment. For each item sold at the auction, the donor and the buyer each specify a charity to which they want the proceeds directed. The To Your Health Society has raised a tremendous amount of funds at past auctions.

To announce the auction and persuade the public to donate items, members of the society prepare and mail a proposal to businesses and homes in the surrounding community. The proposal also requests the assistance of volunteers for the time before and during the auction. The vice president of the To Your Health Society has asked you to design this year's proposal because he knows you are a marketing major with a minor in computer technology. You are thrilled to participate in this assignment. You will complete the proposal for his review within a week.

Introduction

Sometime during your professional life, you most likely will find yourself placed in a sales role. You might be selling a tangible product, such as vehicles or books, or a service, such as Web page design or interior decorating. Within an organization, you might be selling an idea, such as a benefits package to company employees or a budget plan to upper management. Instead of selling a product, you might be trying to persuade people to take an action such as signing a petition, joining a club, or donating to a cause. To sell an item or persuade the public, you may find yourself writing a proposal. Proposals vary in length, style, and formality, but all are designed to elicit acceptance from the reader.

A proposal generally is one of three types: planning, research, or sales. A **planning proposal** offers solutions to a problem or improvement to a situation. A **research proposal** usually requests funding for a research project. A **sales proposal** sells an idea, a product, or a service.

Project Four — Sales Proposal

Project 4 uses Word to produce the sales proposal shown in Figure 4-1. The sales proposal is designed to persuade readers to donate an item(s) or volunteer their time to the To Your Health auction, a charity event. The proposal has a colorful title page to attract the readers' attention. To add impact, the body of the sales proposal has a watermark containing the words, Great Cause, behind the text and uses tables and a chart to summarize data.

(a) Title Page

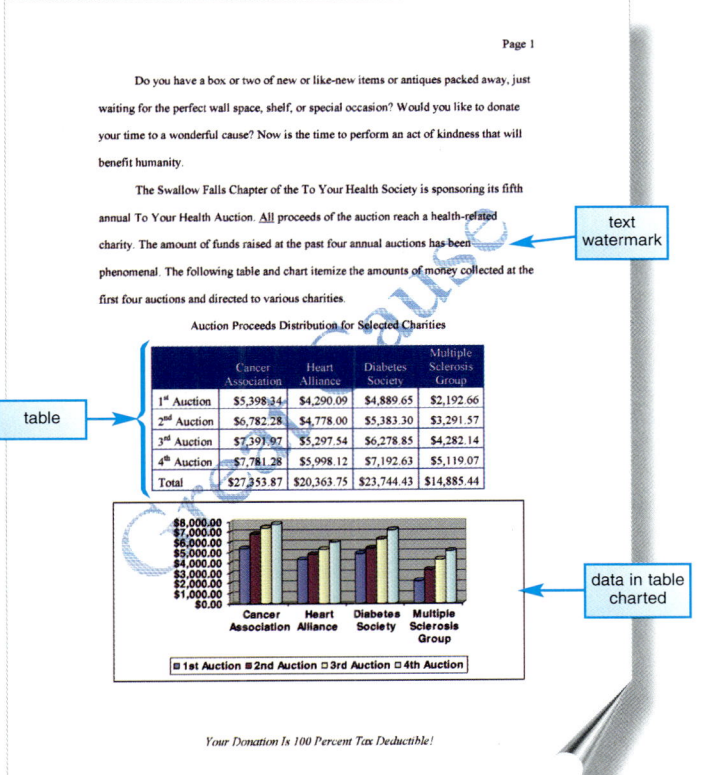

(b) First Page of Body of Sales Proposal

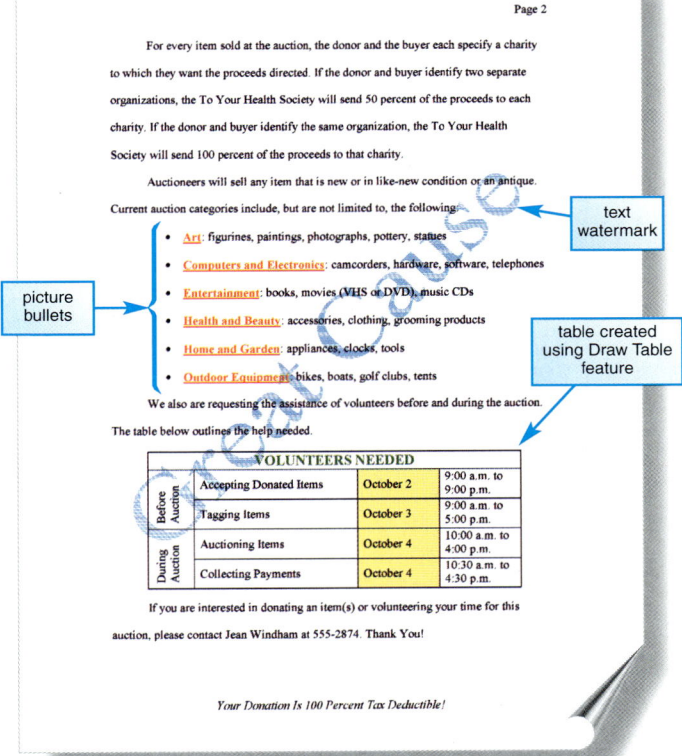

(c) Second Page of Body of Sales Proposal

FIGURE 4-1

Writing Proposals

For more information on writing proposals, visit the Word 2002 More About Web page (www.scsite.com/wd2002/more.htm) and then click Writing Proposals.

Starting Word

Perform the following steps to start Word, or ask your instructor how to start Word for your system.

TO START AND CUSTOMIZE WORD

1. Click the Start button on the Windows taskbar, point to Programs on the Start menu, and then click Microsoft Word on the Programs submenu.
2. If the Word window is not maximized, double-click its title bar to maximize it.
3. If the Language bar displays on the screen, click its Minimize button.
4. If the New Document task pane displays in the Word window, click the Show at startup check box to remove the check mark and then click the Close button in the upper-right corner of the task pane title bar.
5. If the toolbars display positioned on the same row, click the Toolbar Options button and then click Show Buttons on Two Rows.
6. Click View on the menu bar and then click Print Layout.

Word starts. After a few moments, an empty document titled Document1 displays in the Word window. You will use print layout view in this project because the proposal contains tables. Thus, the Print Layout View button on the horizontal scroll bar is selected (shown in Figure 4-2 on page WD 4.08).

Resetting Menus and Toolbars

To set the menus and toolbars so they appear exactly as shown in this book, you should reset your menus and toolbars as outlined in Appendix D or follow these steps.

TO RESET MENUS AND TOOLBARS

1. Click the Toolbar Options button on the Standard toolbar and then point to Add or Remove Buttons. Point to Standard on the Add or Remove Buttons submenu. Scroll to and then click Reset Toolbar on the Standard submenu.
2. Click the Toolbar Options button on the Formatting toolbar and then point to Add or Remove Buttons. Point to Formatting on the Add or Remove Buttons submenu. Scroll to and then click Reset Toolbar on the Formatting submenu.
3. Click the Toolbar Options button on the Standard toolbar and then point to Add or Remove Buttons. Click Customize on the Add or Remove Buttons submenu.
4. When the Customize dialog box displays, if necessary, click the Options tab and then click the Reset my usage data button. When the Microsoft Word dialog box displays, click the Yes button. Click the Close button in the Customize dialog box.

Word resets the menus and toolbars.

Sales Proposals

A sales proposal may be solicited or unsolicited. If someone else requests that you develop the proposal, it is solicited. If you write the proposal because you recognize a need, the proposal is unsolicited. A sales proposal is successful if it addresses how its product or service meets the reader's needs better than the competition does.

Displaying Formatting Marks

As discussed Project 1, it is helpful to display formatting marks that indicate where in the document you pressed the ENTER key, SPACEBAR, and other keys. Perform the following step to display formatting marks.

TO DISPLAY FORMATTING MARKS

1 If the Show/Hide ¶ button on the Standard toolbar is not selected already, click it.

Word displays formatting marks in the document window, and the Show/Hide ¶ button on the Standard toolbar is selected (shown in Figure 4-2 on the next page).

Zooming Text Width

As discussed in previous projects, when you **zoom text width** in print layout view, Word displays the text on the screen as large as possible without extending the right margin beyond the right edge of the document window. Perform these steps to zoom text width.

TO ZOOM TEXT WIDTH

1 Click the Zoom box arrow on the Standard toolbar.

2 Click Text Width.

Word computes the zoom percentage and displays it in the Zoom box (shown in Figure 4-2). Your percentage may be different depending on your computer.

Creating a Title Page

A **title page** should be designed to attract the readers' attention. The title page of the sales proposal in Project 4 (Figure 4-1a on page WD 4.05) contains color, shading, an outside border, shadowed text, clip art, and a variety of fonts and font sizes. The steps on the following pages discuss how to create this title page. The text watermark, which displays on all pages of the sales proposal, is created at the end of this project.

Formatting and Entering Characters

The first step in creating the title page is to enter the phrase, Auction It!, centered and using 72-point Bookman Old Style bold blue font, as described below.

TO FORMAT CHARACTERS

1 Click the Center button on the Formatting toolbar.

2 Click the Font box arrow on the Formatting toolbar. Scroll to and then click Bookman Old Style (or a similar font) in the list of available fonts.

3 Click the Font Size box arrow on the Formatting toolbar. Scroll to and then click 72.

4 Click the Bold button on the Formatting toolbar.

5 Click the Font Color button arrow on the Formatting toolbar. Click Blue on the color palette.

6 Type `Auction It!`

Word enters the phrase, Auction It!, centered and using 72-point Bookman Old Style bold blue font (shown in Figure 4-2).

Title Pages

Formal proposals often require a specific format for the title page. Beginning about three to four inches from the top margin, the following components are each centered and on a separate line: title; the word, For; reader's name, job title, organization, and address; the word, by; your name, job title, and organization; and the date the proposal was written.

More About

Borders

You can add a border to any edge of a paragraph. That is, borders may be added above or below a paragraph, to the left or right of a paragraph, or any combination of these sides. To add the most recently defined border, click the Border button on the Formatting toolbar. To change border specifications, use the Tables and Borders toolbar.

Adding a Border and Shading to a Paragraph

The next step is to surround the phrase, Auction It!, with a 4½-point red outside border. You also want light yellow shading inside the border.

In Project 2, you added a bottom border to a paragraph using the Border button on the Formatting toolbar. When you click this button, Word applies the most recently defined border or the default border to the current paragraph. One method of specifying a different point size, color, shading, and placement of a border is to use the **Tables and Borders toolbar**.

To display the Tables and Borders toolbar, click the **Tables and Borders button** on the Standard toolbar. When you click the Tables and Borders button, the Tables and Borders toolbar displays in the Word window. Also, if your Word window is not already in print layout view, Word automatically switches to print layout view. The Tables and Borders button on the Standard toolbar remains selected until you close the Tables and Borders toolbar.

Perform the following steps to add a 4½-point red outside border around a paragraph using the Tables and Borders toolbar.

Steps: To Border a Paragraph

1 With the insertion point on line 1, point to the Tables and Borders button on the Standard toolbar (Figure 4-2).

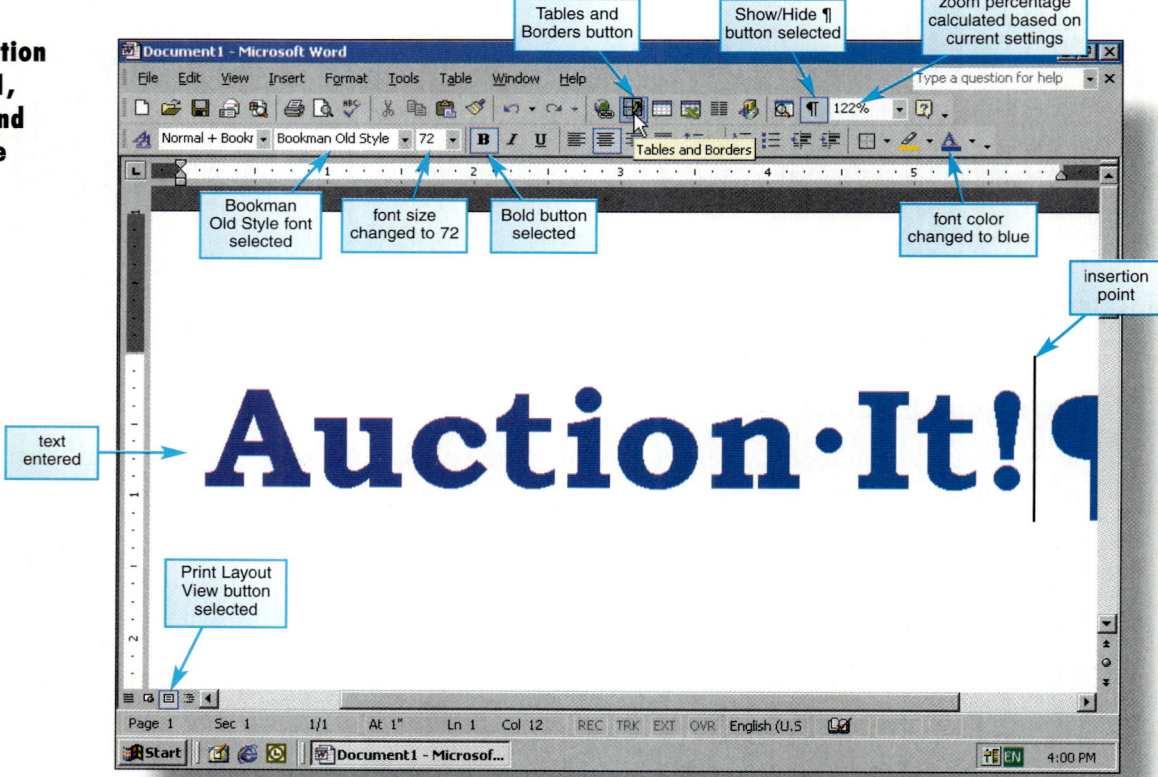

FIGURE 4-2

Creating a Title Page • WD 4.09

2 Click the Tables and Borders button. If the Tables and Borders toolbar is floating in the Word window, point to its title bar.

The Tables and Borders toolbar displays (Figure 4-3). Depending on the last position of this toolbar, it may be floating or it may be docked.

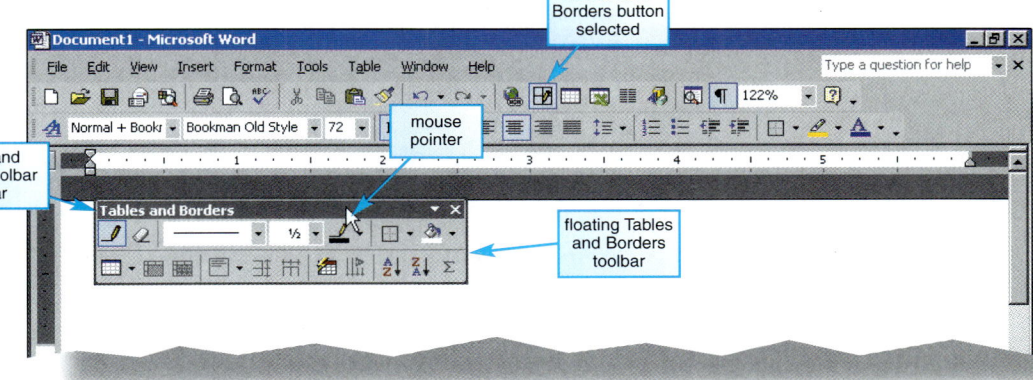

FIGURE 4-3

3 If the Tables and Borders toolbar is floating in the Word window, double-click the title bar of the Tables and Borders toolbar.

Word docks the Tables and Borders toolbar above or below the Formatting toolbar.

4 Click the Line Weight box arrow on the Tables and Borders toolbar and then point to 4 ½ pt.

Word displays a list of available line weights (Figure 4-4).

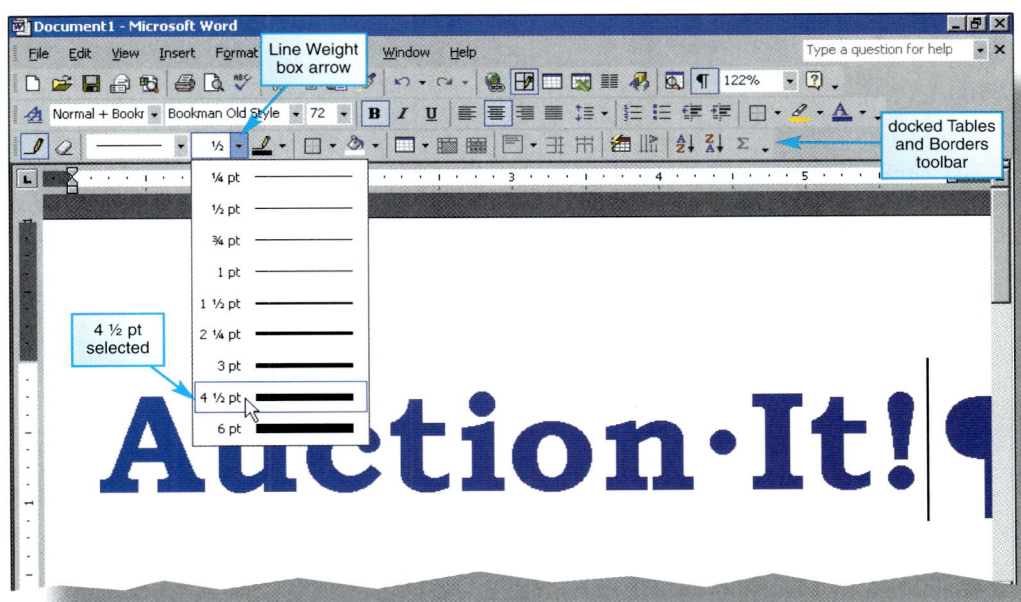

FIGURE 4-4

5 Click 4 ½ pt.

Word changes the line weight to 4 ½ point.

6 Click the Border Color button arrow on the Tables and Borders toolbar. Point to Red on the color palette.

Word displays a color palette for border colors (Figure 4-5).

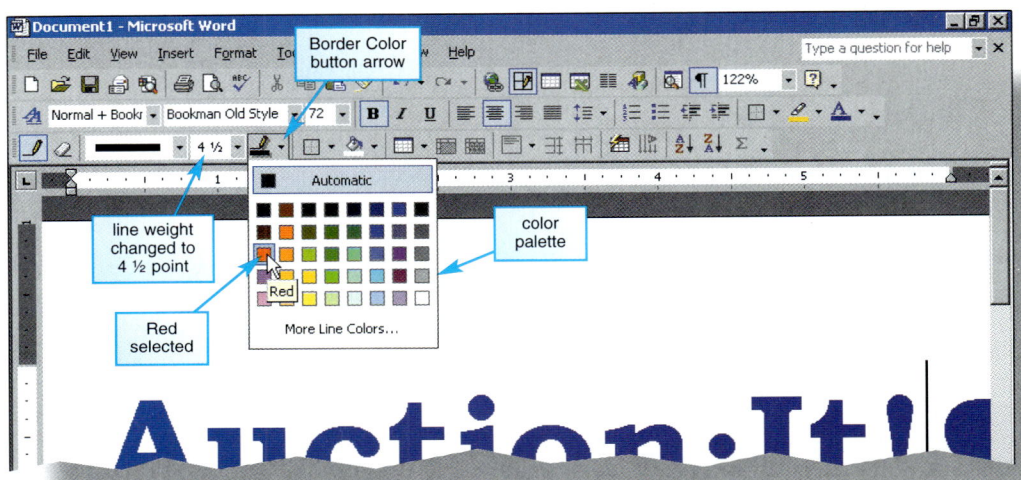

FIGURE 4-5

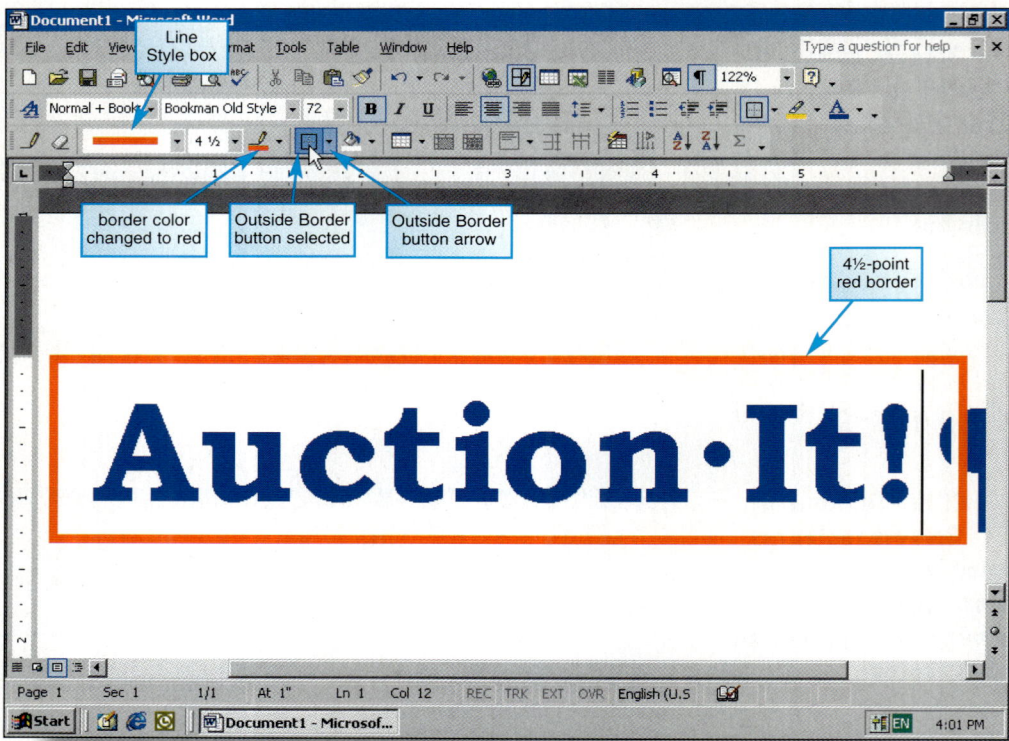

FIGURE 4-6

7 Click Red.

Word changes the color of the border to red, as shown in the Line Style box and on the Border Color button.

8 Click the Outside Border button on the Tables and Borders toolbar. (If your Border button does not show an outside border, click the Border button arrow on the Tables and Borders toolbar and then click Outside Border.)

Word places a 4½-point red outside border around the phrase, Auction It! (Figure 4-6).

1. On Format menu click Borders and Shading, click Borders tab, click Box in Setting area, click desired style, color, and width, click OK button
2. With Tables and Borders toolbar displaying, in Voice Command mode, say "Line Weight, [select line weight], Border Color, [select color]"

Removing Borders

If you wanted to remove a border from a paragraph, position the insertion point somewhere in the paragraph containing the border, click the Border button arrow on either the Formatting toolbar or on the Tables and Borders toolbar, and then click No Border on the border palette.

As previously discussed, Word provides two Border buttons: one on the Formatting toolbar and one on the Tables and Borders toolbar. To place a border using the same settings as the most recently defined border, simply click the Border button on the Formatting toolbar. To change the size, color, or other settings of a border, use the Tables and Borders toolbar or the Borders and Shading dialog box.

The next step is to shade the paragraph containing the words, Auction It!, in light yellow. When you shade a paragraph, Word shades the rectangular area containing the paragraph from the left margin to the right margin. If the paragraph is surrounded by a border, Word shades inside the border.

Perform the following steps to shade a paragraph.

Creating a Title Page • WD 4.11

Steps: To Shade a Paragraph

1 With the insertion point on line 1, click the Shading Color button arrow on the Tables and Borders toolbar. Point to Light Yellow on the color palette.

Word displays a color palette for shading (Figure 4-7).

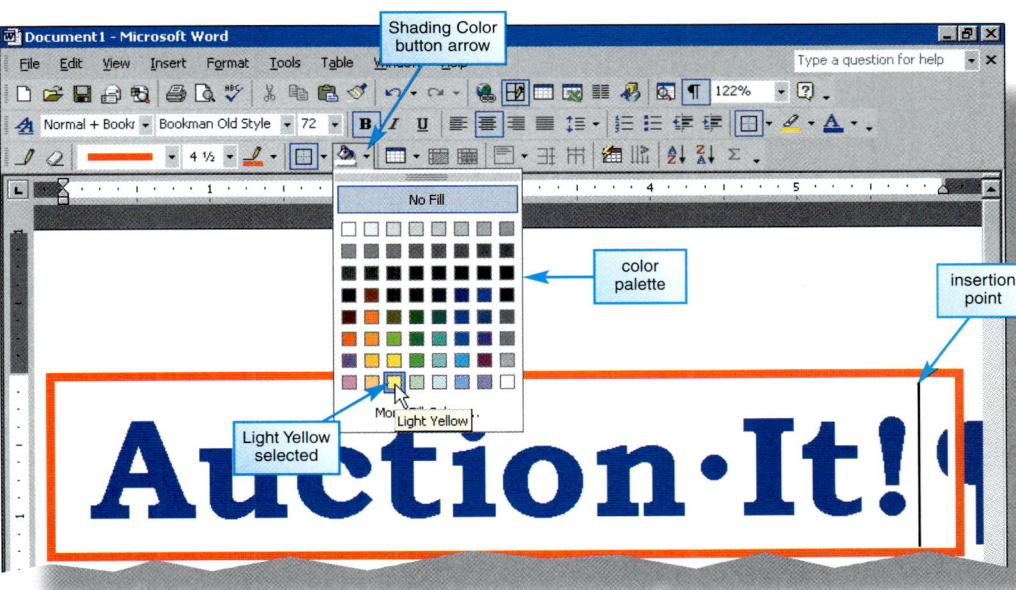

FIGURE 4-7

2 Click Light Yellow. Click the Tables and Borders button on the Standard toolbar to remove the Tables and Borders toolbar from the Word screen.

Word shades the current paragraph light yellow (Figure 4-8). The Tables and Borders toolbar no longer displays on the screen.

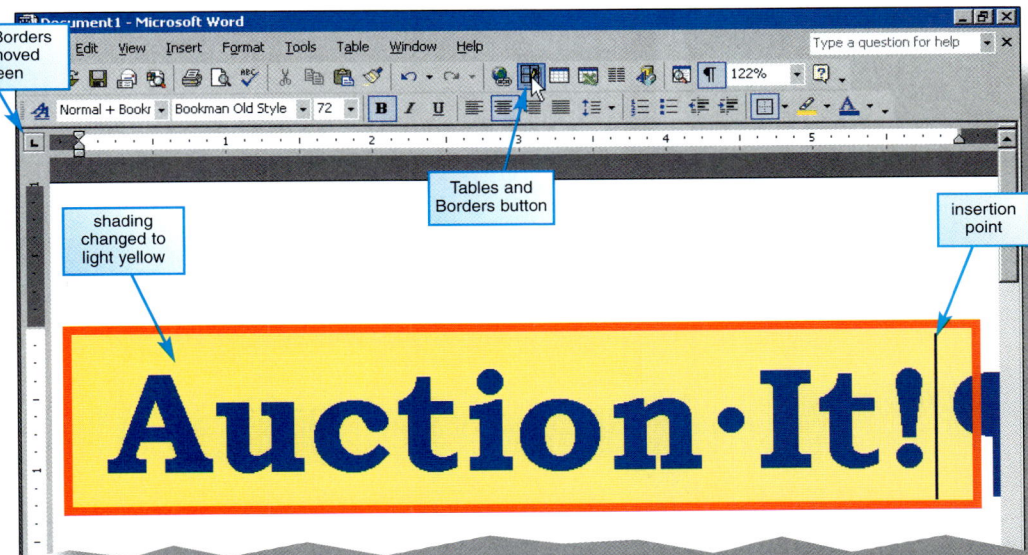

FIGURE 4-8

Other Ways

1. On Format menu click Borders and Shading, click Shading tab, click desired color in Fill area, click OK button
2. With Tables and Borders toolbar displaying, in Voice Command mode, say "Shading Color, [select color]"

The first line of the title page is entered and formatted. When you press the ENTER key to advance the insertion point to the next line on the title page, the border and shading also will display on line 2 and the characters will be 72-point Bookman Old Style font because Word carries forward formatting each time you press the ENTER key. You do not want the paragraphs and characters on line 2 to have the same formatting as line 1. Instead, you want them to use the Normal style.

Shading

You can make paragraph shading narrower than the margin width by dragging the markers on the ruler. To adjust the left edge of the shading inward, drag the Left Indent marker to the right. To adjust the right edge of the shading inward, drag the Right Indent marker to the left.

Clearing Formatting

The Clear Formatting command applies the Normal style to the location of the insertion point. Thus, instead of clicking the Clear Formatting command in the Style list or in the Styles and Formatting task pane, you can click Normal in the Style list.

Recall from Project 2 that the base style for a new Word document is the Normal style, which for a new installation of Word 2002 usually uses 12-point Times New Roman font for characters and single-spaced, left-aligned paragraphs. In a previous project, you used the Styles and Formatting task pane to clear formatting, which returns the current paragraph to the Normal style. Perform the following steps to clear formatting using the Style box on the Formatting toolbar.

TO CLEAR FORMATTING

1. With the insertion point positioned at the end of line 1 (shown in Figure 4-8 on the previous page), press the ENTER key.
2. Click the Style box arrow on the Formatting toolbar and then point to Clear Formatting (Figure 4-9).
3. Click Clear Formatting.

Word applies the Normal style to the location of the insertion point (shown in Figure 4-10).

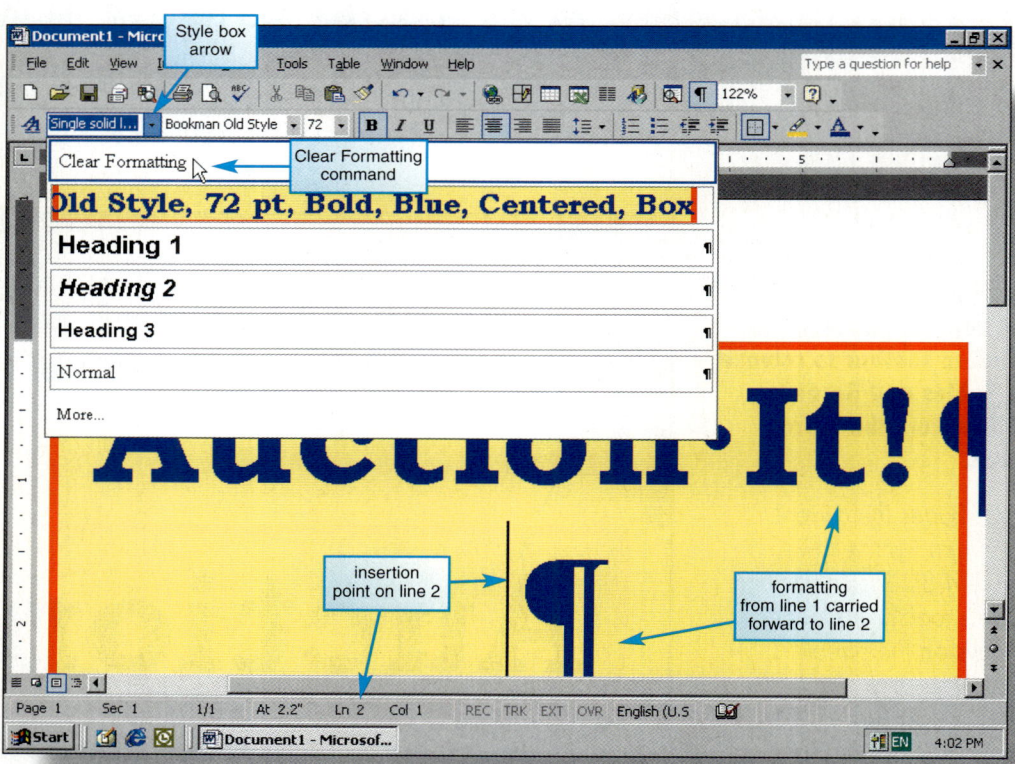

FIGURE 4-9

Depending on your installation of Word, the Normal style might be a different font or font size.

Formatting Characters Using the Font Dialog Box

The next step is to enter the phrase, All Proceeds Go to Charity, on the title page. This phrase is to be 48-point Century Gothic bold italic red font. Each letter in this phrase is to display a shadow. A **shadow** is a light gray duplicate image that displays on the lower-right edge of a character or object. Also, you want extra space between each character so the phrase spans across the width of the page.

You could use buttons on the Formatting toolbar to format much of the phrase. The shadow effect and expanded spacing, however, are applied using the Font dialog box. Thus, you will apply all formats to the phrase using the Font dialog box, as shown in the following steps.

Steps: To Format Characters Using the Font Dialog Box

 With the insertion point positioned on line 2, press the ENTER key three times. Press CTRL+E to center the paragraph on line 5. Type All Proceeds **and then press the ENTER key. Type** Go to Charity **and the drag through the two lines of text on lines 5 and 6 to select them. Right-click the selected text and then point to Font on the shortcut menu.**

Word displays a shortcut menu (Figure 4-10). The text in lines 5 and 6 of the document is selected.

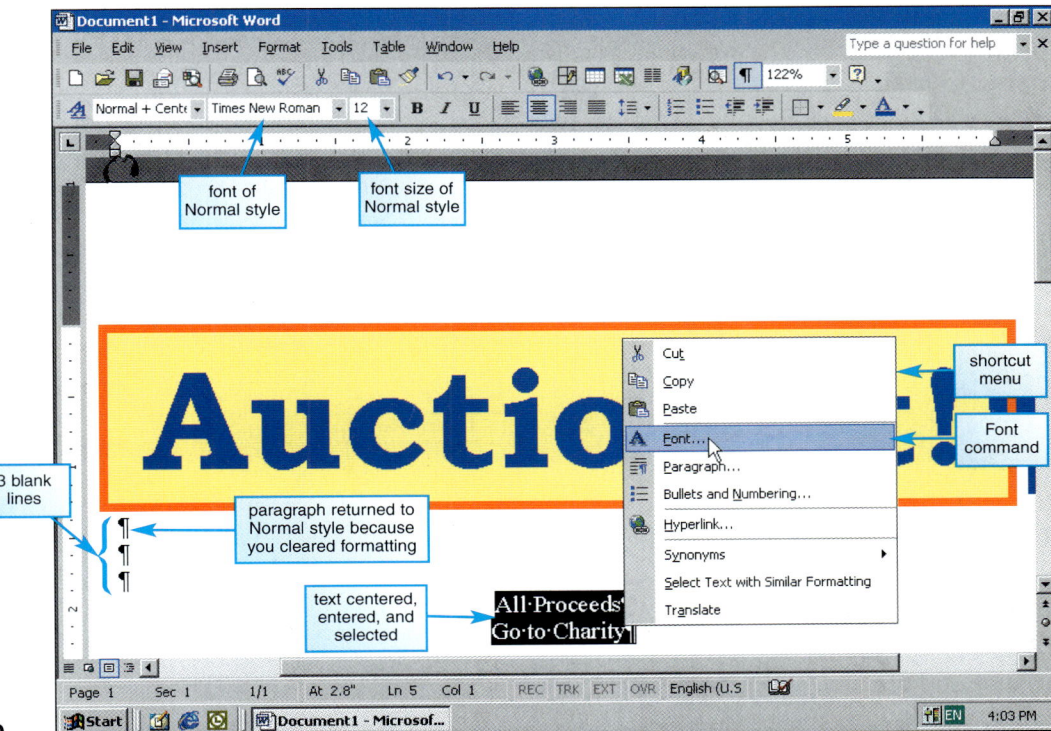

FIGURE 4-10

2 Click Font. If necessary, click the Font tab when the Font dialog box displays. Scroll through the Font list and then click Century Gothic (or a similar font). Click Bold Italic in the Font style list. Scroll through the Size list and then click 48. Click the Font color box arrow and then click Red. Click Shadow in the Effects area. Point to the Character Spacing tab.

Word displays the Font dialog box (Figure 4-11). The Preview area reflects the current selections.

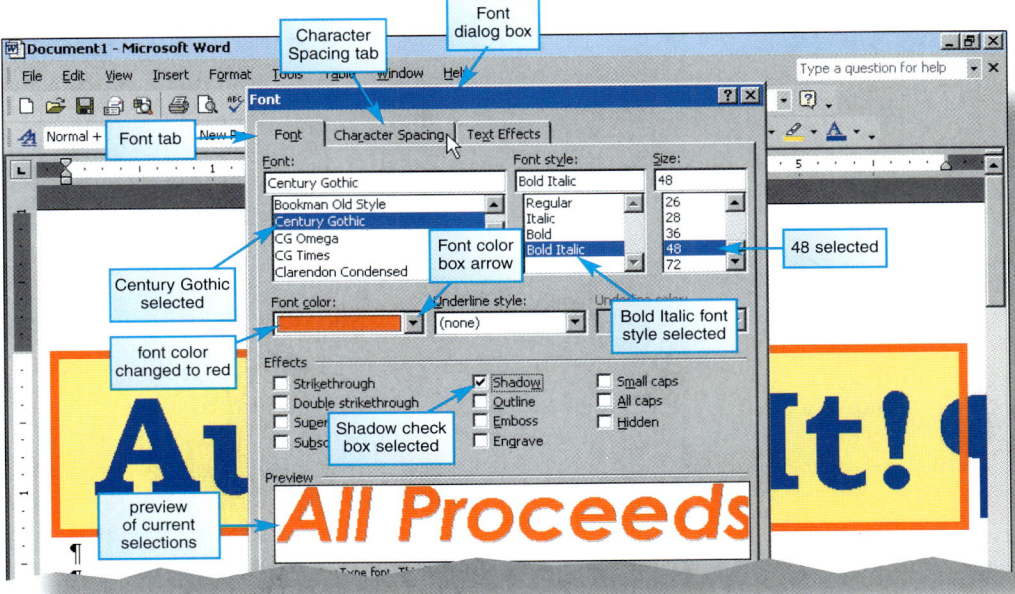

FIGURE 4-11

3 **Click the Character Spacing tab. Click the Spacing box arrow and then click Expanded. Press the TAB key to select the text in the Spacing By box. Type 5 and then point to the OK button.**

Word displays the Character Spacing sheet in the Font dialog box (Figure 4-12). The Preview area displays the text with five points between each character.

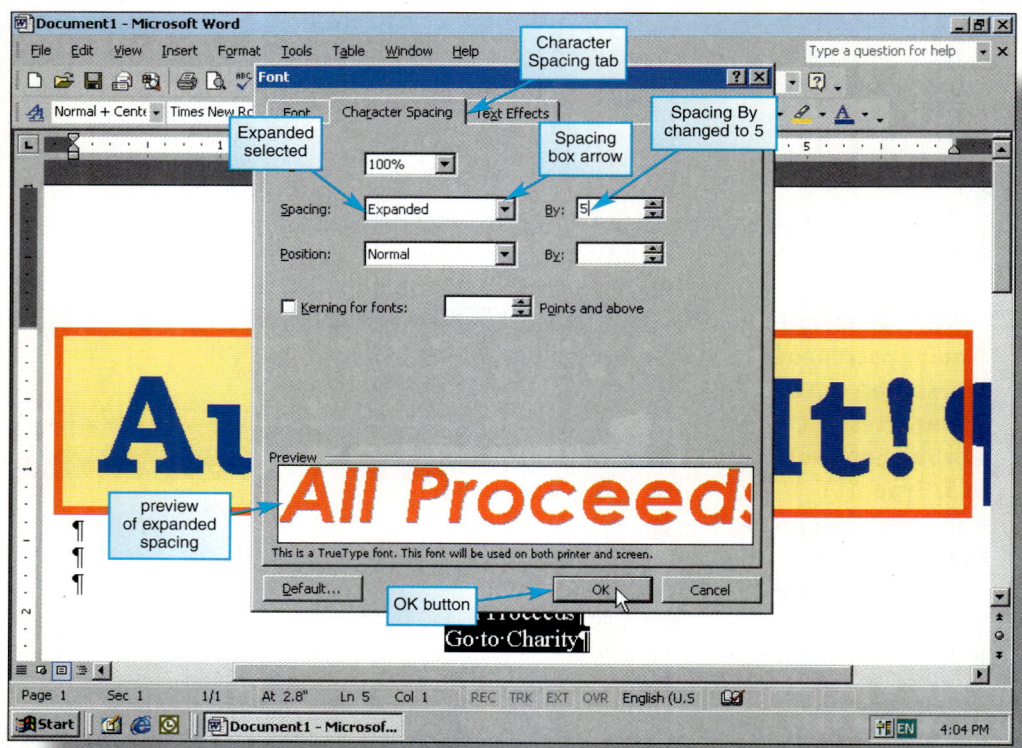

FIGURE 4-12

4 **Click the OK button. Click at the end of line 6 to position the insertion point after the word, Charity.**

Word displays the characters in the phrase, All Proceeds Go to Charity, formatted to 48-point Century Gothic bold italic red font with a shadow and expanded by 5 points (Figure 4-13).

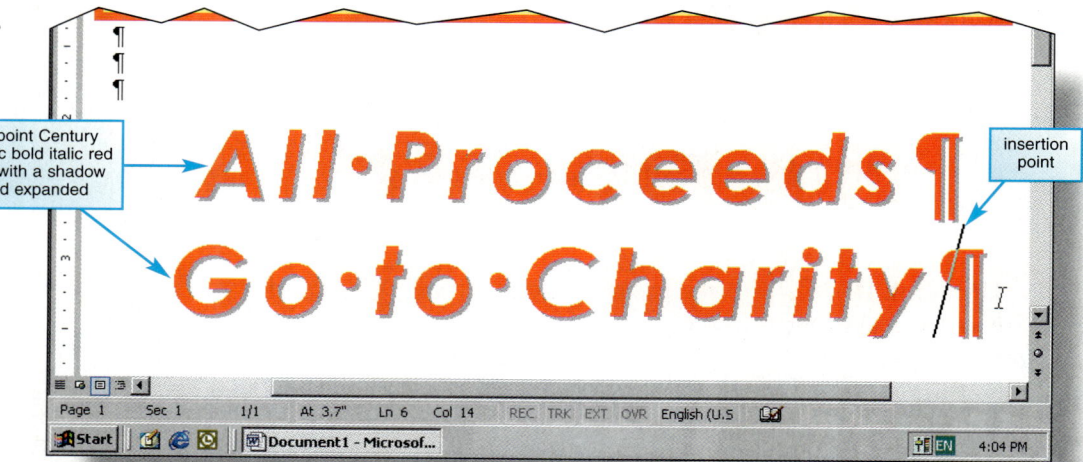

FIGURE 4-13

1. On Format menu click Font, [select formats], click OK button
2. In Voice Command mode, say "Format, Font, [select formats], OK"

In addition to a shadow, the Font sheet in the Font dialog box (Figure 4-11 on the previous page) contains many other character effects you can add to text in a document. Table 4-1 illustrates the result of each of these effects.

The insertion point currently is at the end of line 6 in the document window (Figure 4-13). When you press the ENTER key, the paragraph and character formatting will carry forward to line 7. You want to return formatting on line 7 to the Normal style. Perform the following steps to clear formatting below line 6.

TO CLEAR FORMATTING

1. With the insertion point positioned at the end of line 6 (shown in Figure 4-13), press the ENTER key.
2. Click the Style box arrow on the Formatting toolbar and then click Clear Formatting (shown in Figure 4-9 on page WD 4.12).

Word applies the Normal style to the location of the insertion point, which is on line 7.

Table 4-1	Character Effects Available in the Font Dialog Box	
TYPE OF EFFECT	PLAIN TEXT	FORMATTED TEXT
Strikethrough	Auction	~~Auction~~
Double strikethrough	Charity	~~Charity~~
Superscript	1st	1st
Subscript	H20	H$_2$0
Shadow	To Your Health	To Your Health
Outline	To Your Health	To Your Health
Emboss	To Your Health	To Your Health
Engrave	To Your Health	To Your Health
Small caps	To Your Health	TO YOUR HEALTH
All caps	To Your Health	TO YOUR HEALTH
Hidden	To Your Health	

Text Effects

For documents to be viewed online, you can apply animated effects to text such as moving rectangles or blinking lights. To do this, select the text, click Format on the menu bar, click Font, click the Text Effects tab, click the desired animation, and then click the OK button.

Inserting Clip Art from the Web into a Word Document

As discussed in Project 1, Word 2002 includes a series of predefined graphics called **clip art** that you can insert into a Word document. This clip art is located in the Clip Organizer, which contains a collection of clips, including clip art, as well as photographs, sounds, and video clips.

To insert clip art, you use the Insert Clip Art task pane. Word displays miniature clip art images, called **thumbnails**, in the Insert Clip Art task pane. When the thumbnails display in the Insert Clip Art task pane, some display a small icon in their lower-left corner. Thumbnails with these icons are linked to clip art images not installed on your computer. For example, if you are connected to the Web while searching for clip art images, thumbnails from the Web also display in the Insert Clip Art task pane. In this case, the icon that displays on the thumbnail is a small globe. Table 4-2 illustrates various icons that may display on a thumbnail in the Insert Clip Art task pane.

If a thumbnail displays a small icon of a star (⭐) in its lower-right corner, the clip art contains animation. These clip art images have the appearance of motion when displayed in some Web browsers.

The steps on the next page illustrate how to insert a clip art image from the Web into the Word document.

Clip Art

For more information on clip art, visit the Word 2002 More About Web page (www.scsite.com/wd2002/more.htm) and then click Clip Art.

Table 4-2	Icons on Thumbnails in Insert Clip Art Task Pane
ICON	LOCATION OF CLIP
	CD-ROM or DVD-ROM
	Microsoft's Web site
	Web site partnering with Microsoft (free clip)
	Web site partnering with Microsoft (clip available for a fee)
	Unavailable clip

Note: The following steps assume your computer is connected to the Internet. If it is not, go directly to the shaded steps at the top of page WD 4.17.

Steps To Insert Clip Art from the Web

1 With the insertion point on line 7, press the ENTER key. Press CTRL+E to center the insertion point. Click Insert on the menu bar, point to Picture, and then click Clip Art. If necessary, scroll up to display the title page in the document window. In the Insert Clip Art task pane, drag through any text in the Search text text box to select the text. Type `auction` and then press the ENTER key.

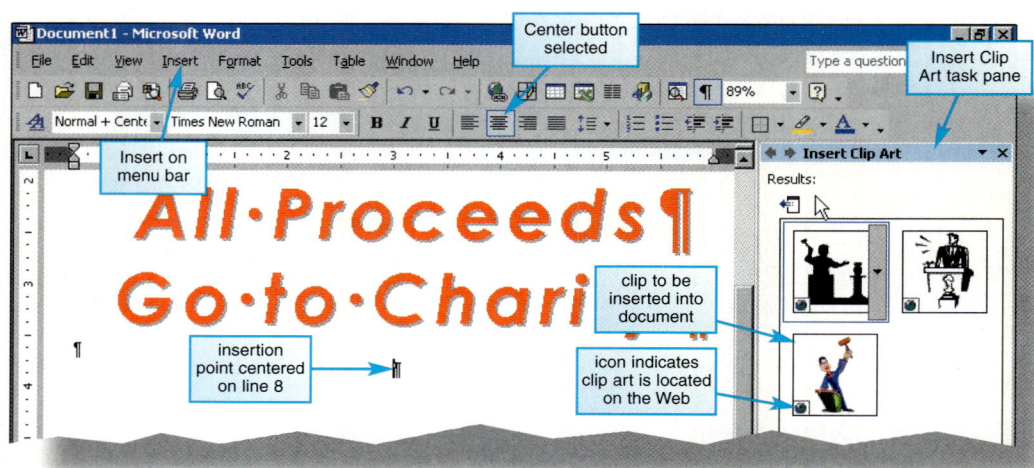

FIGURE 4-14

Word displays thumbnails of clips that match the description (Figure 4-14). The globe icon in the lower-left corner of a thumbnail indicates the clip art is located on the Web.

2 Point to the clip to be inserted (shown in Figure 4-14) and then click the box arrow that displays to the right of the clip. Click Insert on the menu and then click the Close button on the Insert Clip Art task pane title bar. If necessary, scroll to display the image in the document window.

Word inserts the clip into your document at the location of the insertion point (Figure 4-15).

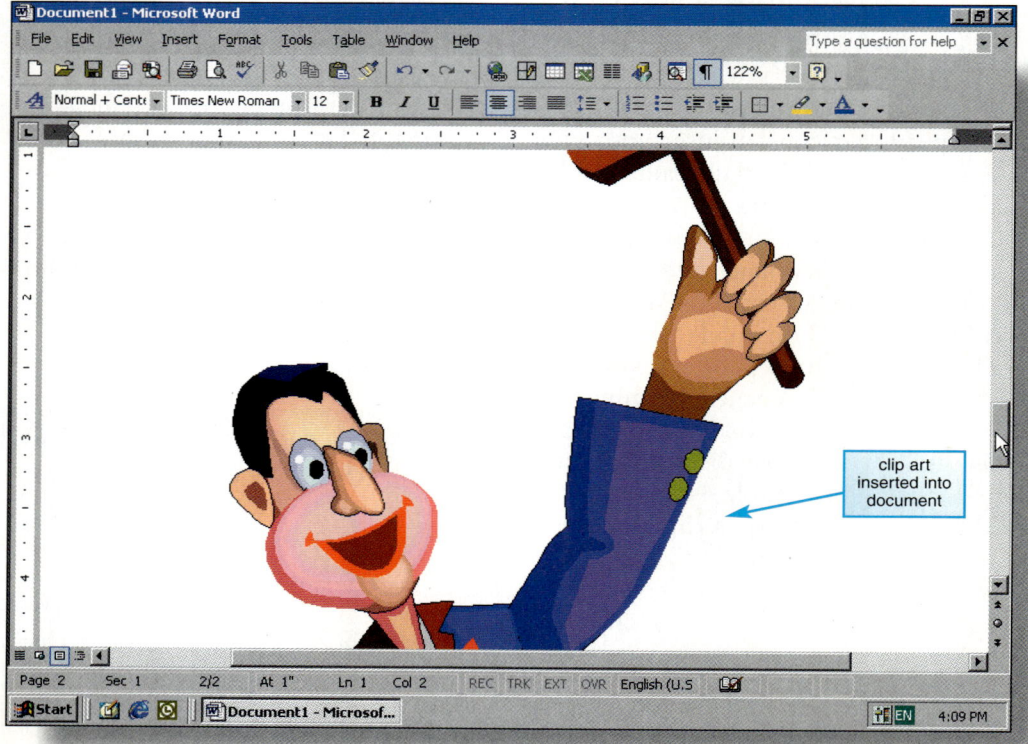

FIGURE 4-15

1. In Voice Command mode, say "Insert, Picture, Clip Art"

Creating a Title Page • WD 4.17

If you do not have access to the Web, you can insert the clip art file into the Word document from the Data Disk, as described in the following steps. If you did not download the Data Disk, see the inside back cover for instructions for downloading the Data Disk or see your instructor.

TO INSERT A GRAPHIC FILE FROM THE DATA DISK

1. With the insertion point on line 7, press the ENTER key. Press CTRL+E to center the insertion point.
2. Click Insert on the menu bar, point to Picture, and then click From File.
3. Insert the Data Disk into drive A. When the Insert Picture dialog box displays, click the Look in box arrow and then click 3½ Floppy (A:). Click the file name j0087094 and then click the Insert button.

Word inserts the clip into your document at the location of the insertion point (shown in Figure 4-15).

> **More About**
>
> **Opening Graphics**
>
> If you have a file containing a graphic image, you can open the file by following the shaded steps to the left. Graphic files Word can open include those with extensions or file types of .gif, .jpg, .png, .bmp, .wmf, .tif, and .eps. When you scan a photograph or other image and save it as a graphic file, you can select the file type for the saved graphic through the photo editing or illustration software.

The graphic of the auctioneer is too large for the title page. You need to reduce its size by about 60 percent. In previous projects, you dragged the sizing handles on the graphic to resize it. In the following steps, you will use the Format Picture dialog box to resize the graphic.

Steps To Resize a Graphic Using the Format Picture Dialog Box

1 **Double-click the graphic. When the Format Picture dialog box displays, click the Size tab. In the Scale area, double-click the number in the Height text box. Type** 40 **and then press the TAB key. Point to the OK button.**

Word displays the Format Picture dialog box (Figure 4-16). When you press the TAB key in the Height text box, Word automatically enters the same percentage (40) in the Width text box.

2 **Click the OK button.**

Word resizes the graphic to 40 percent of its original size (shown in Figure 4-17 on the next page).

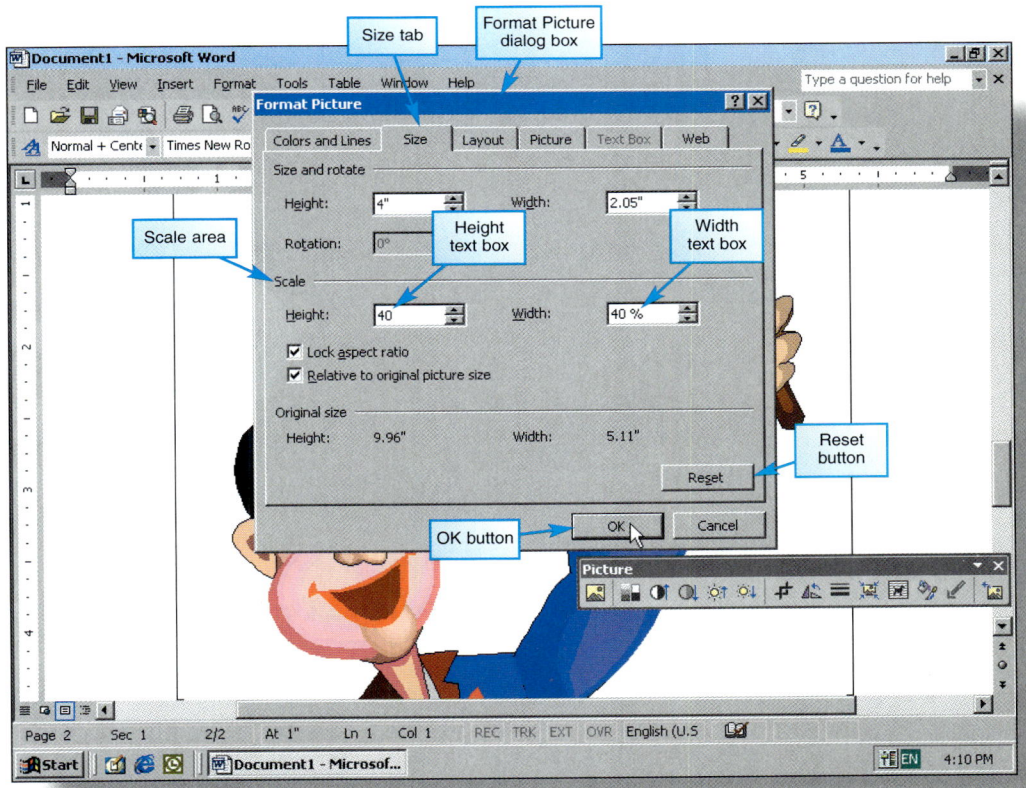

FIGURE 4-16

Positioning Graphics

To specify exactly where Word should position a graphic, click the Advanced button in the Layout sheet in the Format Picture dialog box. For example, to position a graphic exactly one inch from the top of the page, click the Picture Position tab in the Advanced Layout sheet. In the Vertical area, type 1 in the Absolute position text box, click the below box arrow, and then click Page.

If you want a graphic to be an exact height and width, you can type the measurements in the Height and Width text boxes in the Size and rotate area in the Size sheet in the Format Picture dialog box. If you want to return a graphic to its original size and start resizing it again, click the Reset button (Figure 4-16 on the previous page) in the Size sheet in the Format Picture dialog box.

Perform the following steps to display the entire title page in the document window so you can see the layout of the page.

TO ZOOM WHOLE PAGE

1. Click the Zoom box arrow on the Standard toolbar and then point to Whole Page (Figure 4-17).

2. Click Whole Page (shown in Figure 4-18).

Word displays the title page in reduced form so that the entire page displays in the document window (shown in Figure 4-18).

Graphics

In addition to clip art, you can insert drawing objects such as shapes, lines, curves, arrows, flowchart symbols, stars, and diagrams into Word documents. To do this, display the Drawing toolbar by clicking the Drawing button on the Standard toolbar. Then, click the appropriate button on the Drawing toolbar and use the mouse to draw the object in the document window.

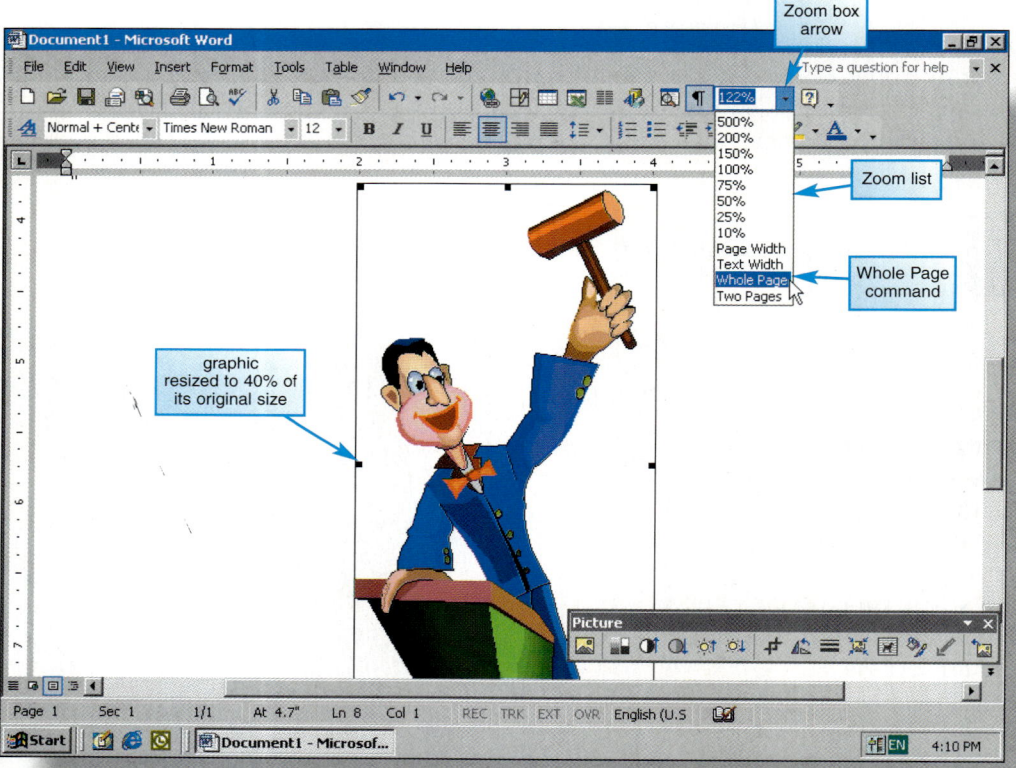

FIGURE 4-17

Centering the Title Page Contents Vertically on the Page

For visual appeal, you would like to center the contents of the title page vertically, that is, between the top and bottom margins. As discussed in previous projects, the default top margin in Word is one inch, which includes a one-half inch header. Notice in Figure 4-18 that the insertion point, which is at the top of the title page text, is 1" from the top of the page.

Perform the following steps to center the contents of a page vertically.

Centering Vertically

When you center a page vertically, Word does not change the size of the top and bottom margins. Instead, it changes the size of the header and footer areas to accommodate the extra spacing.

Steps: To Center Text Vertically

1 Press CTRL+HOME to position the insertion point at the top of the document. Click File on the menu bar and then point to Page Setup (Figure 4-18).

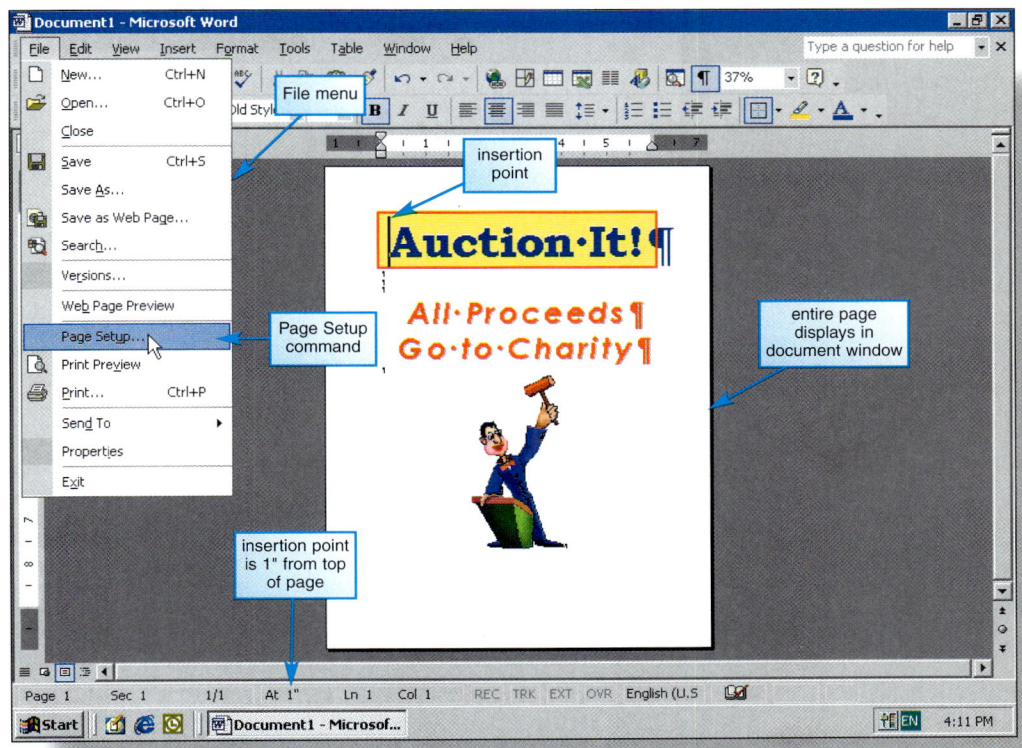

FIGURE 4-18

2 Click Page Setup. If necessary, click the Layout tab when the Page Setup dialog box displays. Click the Vertical alignment box arrow and then click Center. Point to the OK button.

Word displays the Page Setup dialog box (Figure 4-19). The vertical alignment is changed to Center.

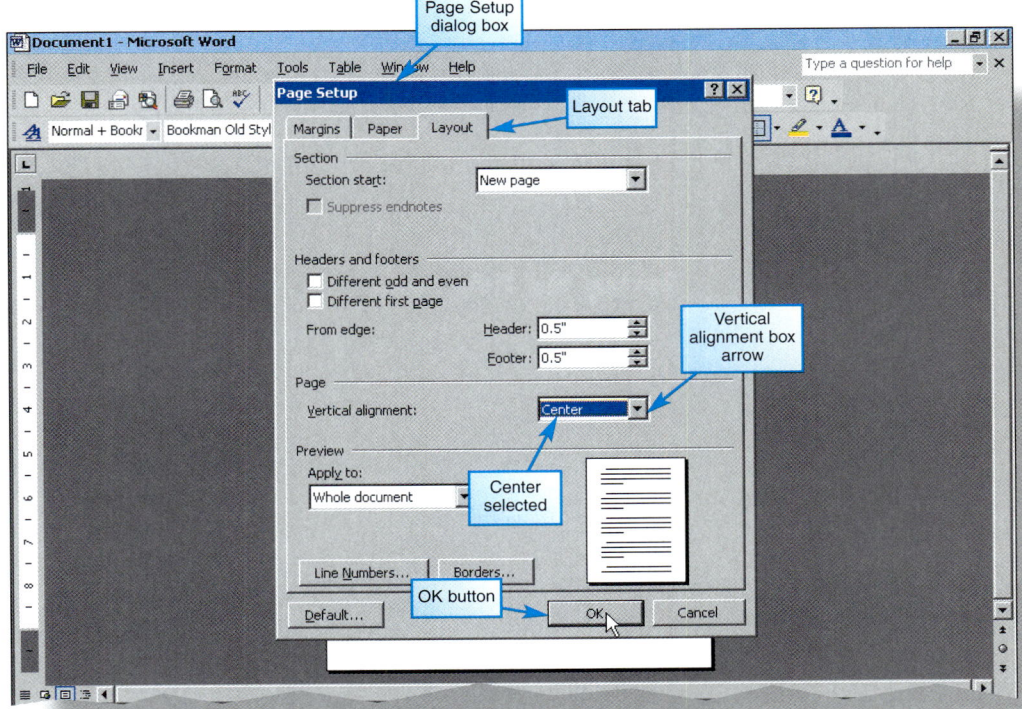

FIGURE 4-19

3 **Click the OK button.**

Word centers the contents of the title page vertically (Figure 4-20). The status bar shows the insertion point now is 1.6" from the top of the document, which means the empty space above and below the text totals approximately 3.2".

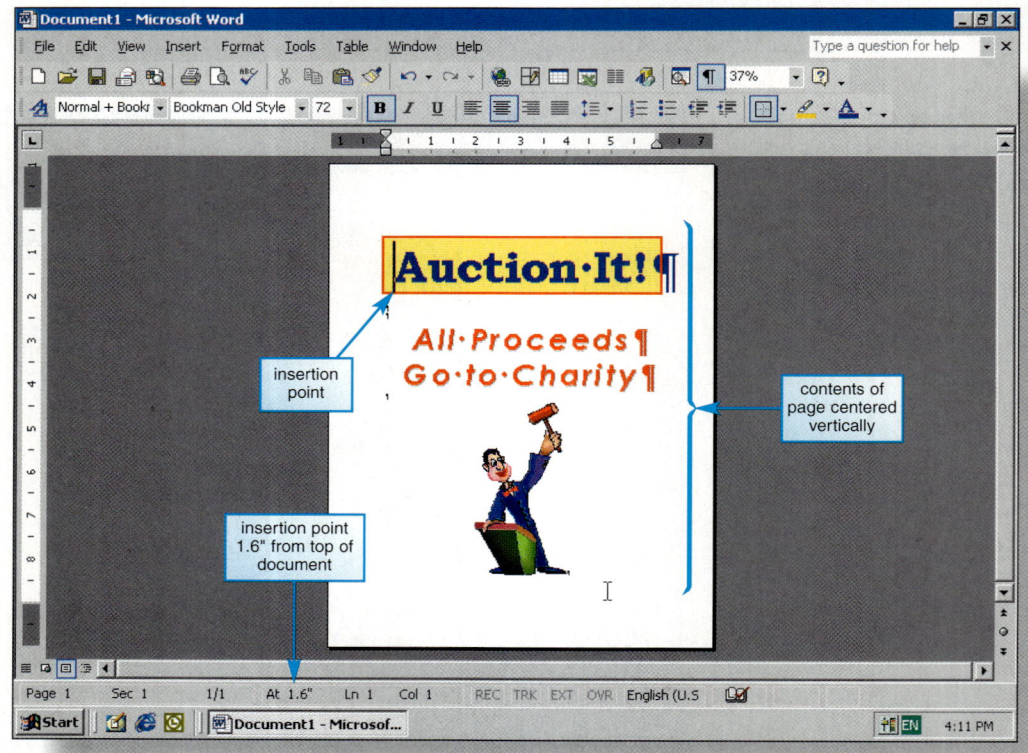

FIGURE 4-20

1. In Voice Command mode, say "File, Page Setup, Layout, Vertical alignment, Center, OK"

Perform the following steps to change the zoom back to text width.

TO ZOOM TEXT WIDTH

1 Click the Zoom box arrow on the Standard toolbar and then click Text Width.

Word computes the zoom percentage and displays it in the Zoom box (shown in Figure 4-21 on page WD 4.22). Your percentage may be different depending on your computer.

Saving the Title Page

Save the title page by performing the following steps.

TO SAVE A DOCUMENT

1 Insert a floppy disk into drive A. Click the Save button on the Standard toolbar.

2 Type `Auction Title Page` in the File name text box.

3 Click the Save in box arrow and then click 3½ Floppy (A:).

4 Click the Save button in the Save As dialog box.

Word saves the document on a floppy disk in drive A with the file name, Auction Title Page (shown in Figure 4-21).

The title page for the sales proposal is complete. The next step is to insert a draft of the proposal following the title page.

Inserting an Existing Document into an Open Document

Assume you already have prepared a draft of the body of the proposal and saved it with the file name Auction Draft. You would like the draft to display on a separate page following the title page. Once the two documents display on the screen together as one document, you save this active document with a new name so each of the original documents remains intact.

The inserted pages of the sales proposal are to use the Times New Roman font and be left-aligned. When you press the ENTER key at the bottom of the title page, the paragraph and character formatting will carry forward to the next line. You want to return formatting on the new line to the Normal style. Perform the following steps to clear formatting so the inserted pages use the Normal style.

TO CLEAR FORMATTING

1. Press CTRL+END to move the insertion point to the end of the title page. If necessary, scroll down to display the insertion point in the document window. Press the ENTER key.
2. Click the Style box arrow on the Formatting toolbar and then click Clear Formatting (shown in Figure 4-9 on page WD 4.12).

Word applies the Normal style to the location of the insertion point, which now is on line 9 (shown in Figure 4-21 on the next page).

Inserting a Section Break

The body of the sales proposal requires page formatting different from that of the title page. Earlier in this project, you vertically centered the contents of the title page. The body of the proposal should have top alignment; that is, it should begin one inch from the top of the page.

Whenever you want to change page formatting for a portion of a document, you must create a new **section** in the document. Each section then may be formatted differently from the others. Thus, the title page formatted with centered vertical alignment must be in one section, and the body of the proposal formatted with top alignment must be in another section.

A Word document can be divided into any number of sections. All Word documents have at least one section. During the course of creating a document, if you need to change the top margin, bottom margin, page alignment, paper size, page orientation, page number position, or contents or position of headers, footers, or footnotes, you must create a new section.

When you create a new section, a **section break** displays on the screen as a double dotted line separated by the words, Section Break. Section breaks do not print. When you create a section break, you specify whether or not the new section should begin on a new page.

The body of the sales proposal is to be on a separate page following the title page. Perform the steps on the next page to insert a section break that instructs Word to begin the new section on a new page in the document.

More About

Drafting a Proposal

All proposals should have an introduction, body, and conclusion. The introduction could contain the subject, purpose, statement of problem, need, background, or scope. The body may include available or required facilities, cost, feasibility, methods, timetable, materials, or equipment. The conclusion summarizes key points or requests some action.

More About

Section Breaks

To see formatting associated with a section, double-click the section break notation to display the Layout sheet in the Page Setup dialog box. In this dialog box, you can click the Borders button to add a border to a section.

Steps To Insert a Next Page Section Break

1 Be sure the insertion point is positioned on the paragraph mark on line 9. Click Insert on the menu bar and then point to Break (Figure 4-21).

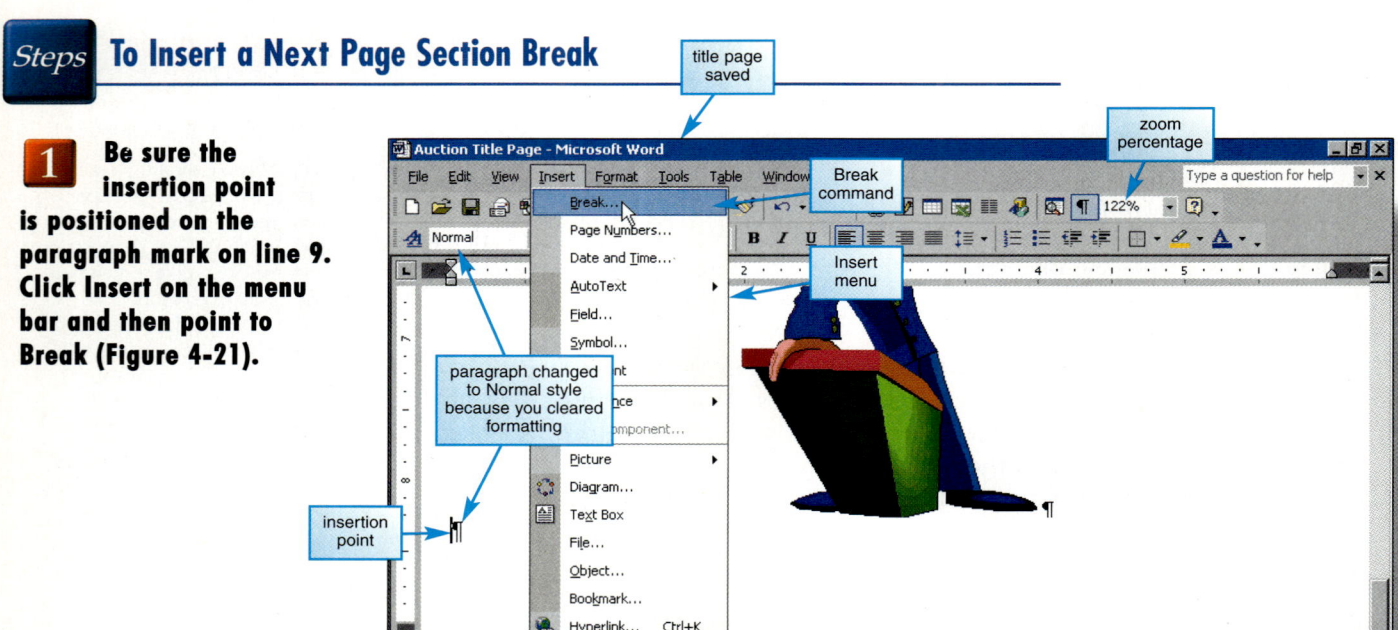

FIGURE 4-21

2 Click Break. When the Break dialog box displays, click Next page in the Section break types area. Point to the OK button.

Word displays the Break dialog box (Figure 4-22). The Next page option instructs Word to place the new section on the next page.

3 Click the OK button.

Word inserts a next page section break in the document (shown in Figure 4-24).

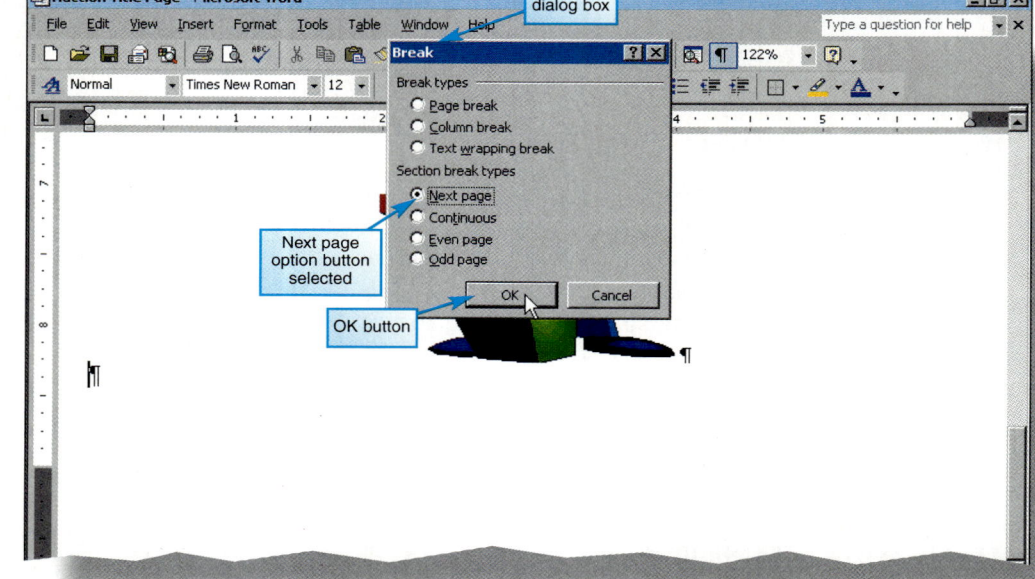

FIGURE 4-22

1. In Voice Command mode, say "Insert, Break, Next page, OK"

Word places the insertion point and paragraph mark in the new section, which is on a new page. Notice in Figure 4-23 that the status bar indicates the insertion point is on page 2 in section 2. Also, the insertion point is positioned 5.4" from the top of the page because earlier you changed the page formatting to centered vertical alignment. You want the body of the proposal to have top alignment; that is, the insertion point should be one inch from the top of the page. Perform the following the steps to change the alignment of section two from center to top.

Steps: To Change Page Alignment of a Section

1 Be sure the insertion point is in section 2. Click File on the menu bar and then click Page Setup. If necessary, click the Layout tab when the Page Setup dialog box displays. Click the Vertical alignment box arrow and then click Top. Point to the OK button.

Word displays the Page Setup dialog box (Figure 4-23).

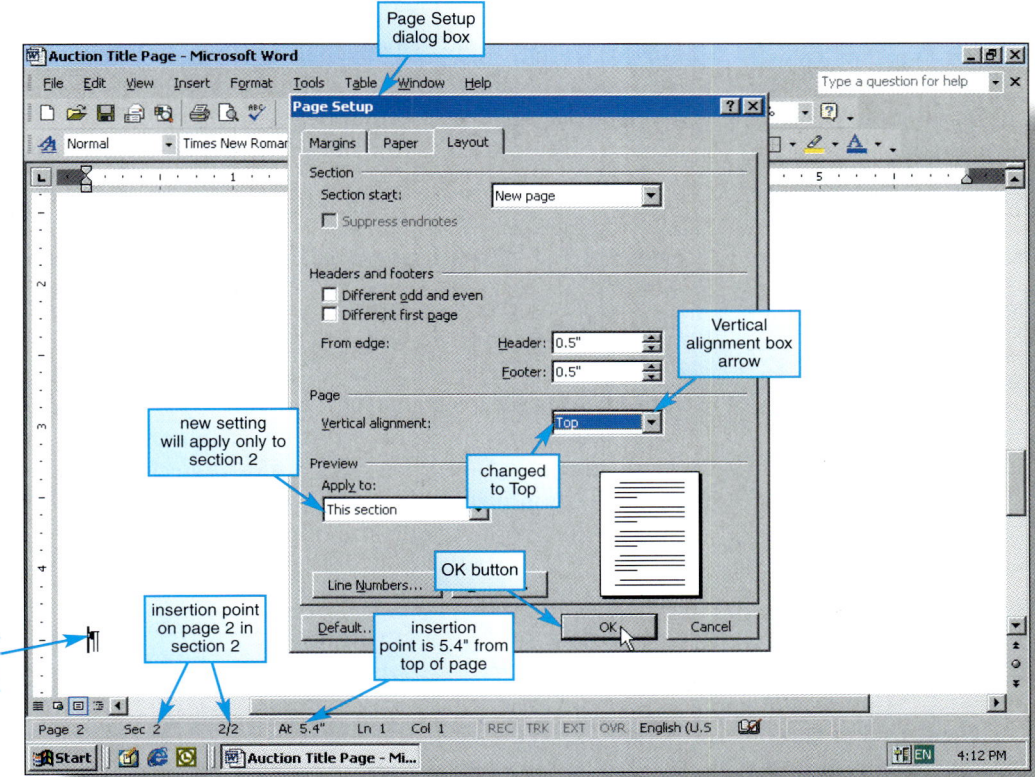

FIGURE 4-23

2 Click the OK button. Scroll up so the bottom of page 1 and the top of page 2 display in the document window.

Word changes the vertical alignment of section 2 to top (Figure 4-24). Notice the status bar indicates the insertion point now is positioned 1" from the top of the page, which is the top margin setting for section 2.

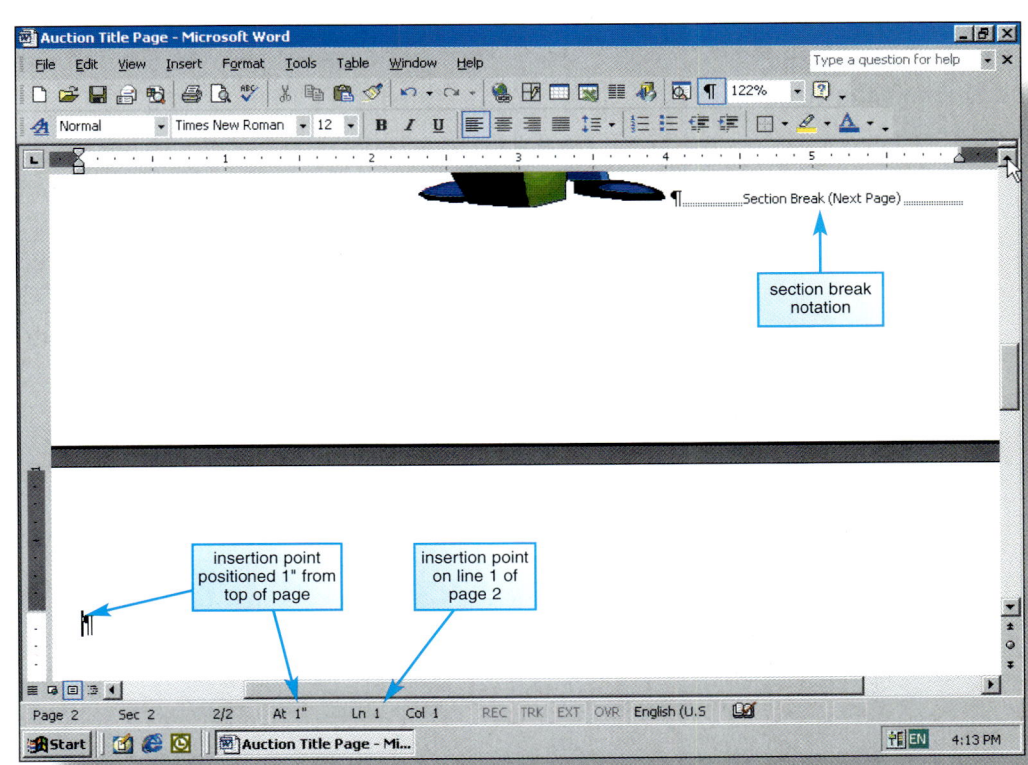

FIGURE 4-24

Opening Files

If you do not remember the exact file name you wish to open, you can substitute a special character, called a wildcard, for the character(s) you have forgotten. The asterisk (*) character is a substitute for zero to multiple characters, and the question mark (?) character is a substitute for one character. For example, typing cat* in the File name text box will display file names such as catcher, cathedral, and cats at play. Typing cat? in the File name text box will display file names that only are four characters in length, such as cats or cat1.

Word stores all section formatting in the section break. Notice in Figure 4-24 on the previous page that the section break notation displays on the screen as the words, Section Break (Next Page). You can delete a section break and all associated section formatting by selecting the section break notation, right-clicking the selection, and then clicking Cut on the shortcut menu. To select a section break, point to its left until the mouse pointer changes direction and then click. If you accidentally delete a section break, you can restore it by clicking the Undo button on the Standard toolbar.

Inserting a Word Document into an Open Document

The next step is to insert the draft of the sales proposal at the top of the second page of the document. The draft is located on the Data Disk. If you did not download the Data Disk, see the inside back cover for instructions for downloading the Data Disk or see your instructor.

If you created a Word file at an earlier time, you may have forgotten its name. For this reason, Word provides a means to display the contents of, or **preview**, any file before you insert it. Perform the following steps to preview and then insert the draft of the proposal into the open document.

 To Insert a Word Document into an Open Document

1 If necessary, insert the Data Disk into drive A. Be sure the insertion point is positioned on the paragraph mark at the top of section 2. Click Insert on the menu bar and then point to File (Figure 4-25).

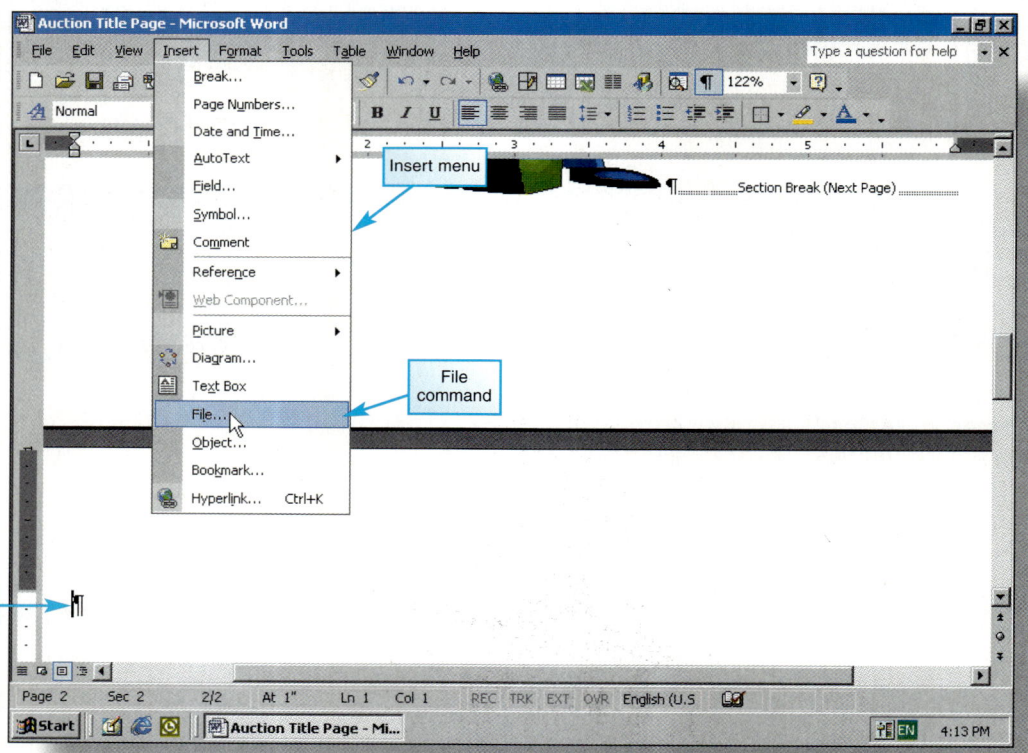

FIGURE 4-25

2 **Click File. When the Insert File dialog box displays, click the Look in box arrow and then click 3½ Floppy (A:). Click the Views button arrow and then click Preview. Click Auction Draft and then point to the Insert button.**

Word displays the Insert File dialog box (Figure 4-26). A list of Word documents on the Data Disk displays. The contents of the selected file (Auction Draft) display on the right side of the dialog box.

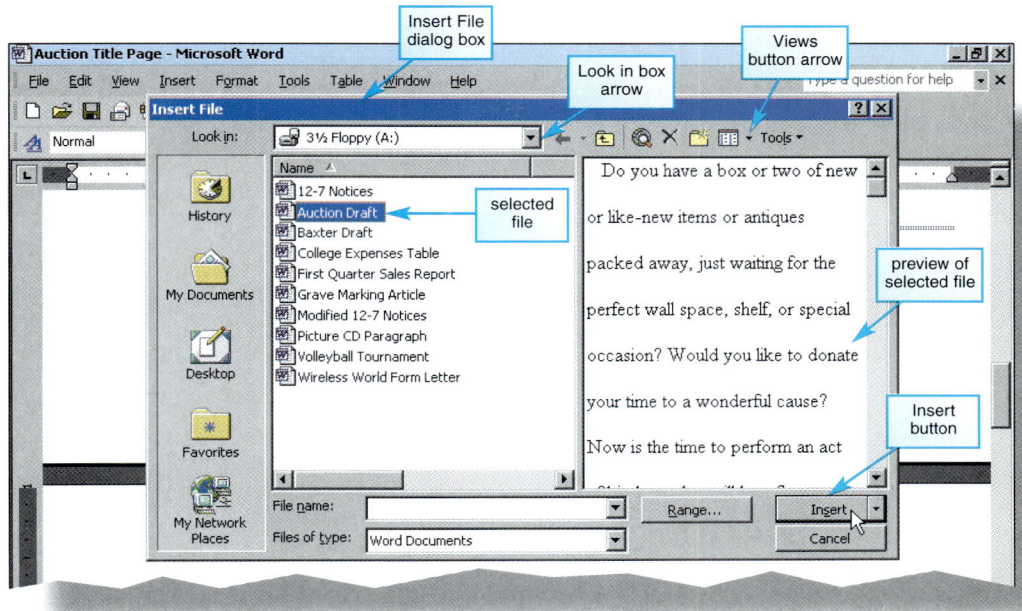

FIGURE 4-26

3 **Click the Insert button.**

Word inserts the file, Auction Draft, into the open document at the location of the insertion point. The insertion point is at the end of the inserted document.

4 **Press SHIFT+F5.**

Word positions the insertion point on line 1 of page 2, which was its location prior to inserting the new Word document (Figure 4-27). Pressing SHIFT+F5 instructs Word to place the insertion point at your last editing location.

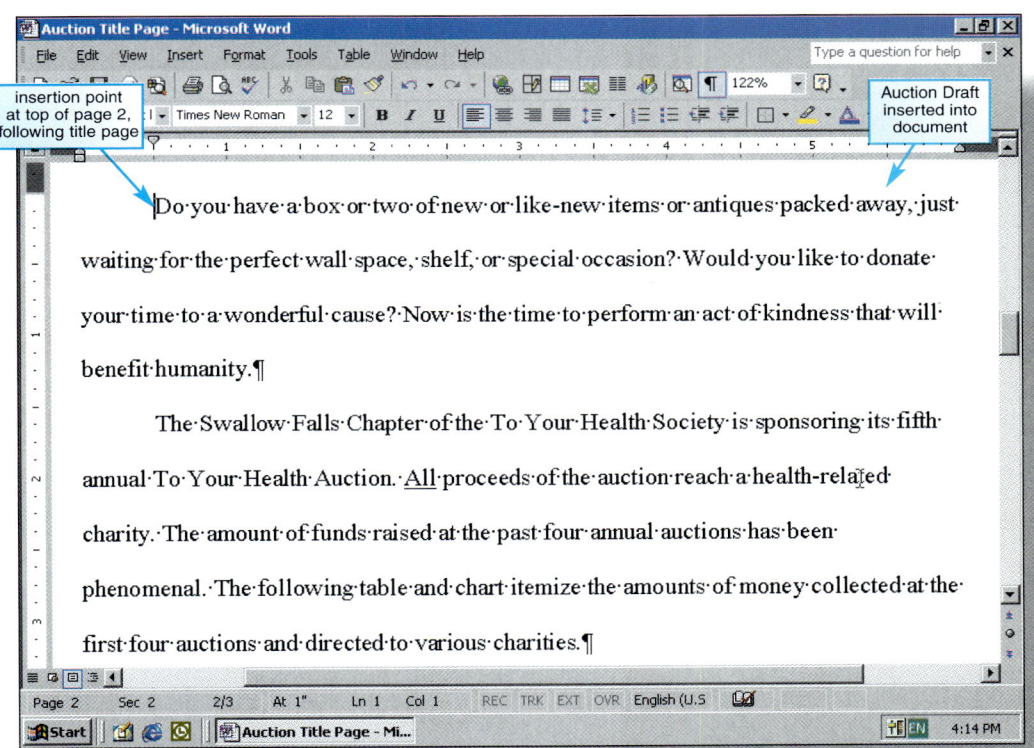

FIGURE 4-27

Word inserts the entire document at the location of the insertion point. If the insertion point, therefore, is positioned in the middle of the open document when you insert another Word document, the open document continues after the last character of the inserted document.

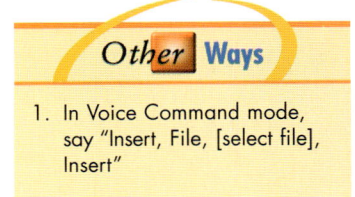

Other Ways

1. In Voice Command mode, say "Insert, File, [select file], Insert"

Files

In the Insert File and Open dialog boxes, click the Views button arrow to change how the files display in the dialog box. Click the Tools button arrow and then click Delete to delete the selected file. Click the Tools button arrow and then click Properties to display a variety of information about the selected file.

As illustrated in Figure 4-26 on the previous page, previewing files before opening them is very useful if you have forgotten the name of a file. For this reason, both the Open and Insert File dialog boxes allow you to preview files by clicking the Views button arrow.

Saving the Active Document with a New File Name

The current file name on the title bar is Auction Title Page, yet the active document contains both the title page and the draft of the sales proposal. You want to keep the title page as a separate document called Auction Title Page. Thus, you should save the active document with a new file name. If you save the active document by clicking the Save button on the Standard toolbar, Word will assign it the current file name. You want the active document to have a new file name. Perform the following steps to save the active document with a new file name.

TO SAVE AN ACTIVE DOCUMENT WITH A NEW FILE NAME

1. If necessary, insert the floppy disk containing your title page into drive A.
2. Click File on the menu bar and then click Save As.
3. Type Auction Proposal in the File name text box. Do not press the ENTER key.
4. If necessary, click the Save in box arrow and then click 3½ Floppy (A:).
5. Click the Save button in the Save As dialog box.

Word saves the document on a floppy disk in drive A with the file name, Auction Proposal (shown in Figure 4-29 on page WD 4.29).

Saving

Through the Save As dialog box, you also can change the file type. The default file type is a Word document, which is a Word 2002 format. Other file types to which you can save include Web page, rich text format, Works, earlier versions of Word, and several versions of WordPerfect. Use the File menu or press the F12 key to display the Save As dialog box.

Printing Specific Pages in a Document

The title page is the first page of the proposal. The body of the proposal is the second and third pages. To see a hard copy of the body of the proposal, perform the following steps.

TO PRINT SPECIFIC PAGES IN A DOCUMENT

1. Ready the printer.
2. Click File on the menu bar and then click Print.
3. When the Print dialog box displays, click Pages in the Page range area. Type 2-3 in the Pages text box and then click the OK button.

Word prints the inserted draft of the sales proposal (Figure 4-28a).

When you remove the document from the printer, review it carefully. Depending on your printer, wordwrap may occur in different locations from those shown in Figure 4-28a.

By adding a header and a footer, formatting and charting the table, changing the bullets to picture bullets, inserting another table into the document, and adding a watermark, you can make the body of the proposal more attention-grabbing. These enhancements to the body of the sales proposal are shown in Figure 4-28b on page WD 4.28. The following pages illustrate how to change the document in Figure 4-28a so it looks like Figure 4-28b.

Printing Colors

If you have a black-and-white printer and print a document with colors, the colors other than black or white will print in shades of gray.

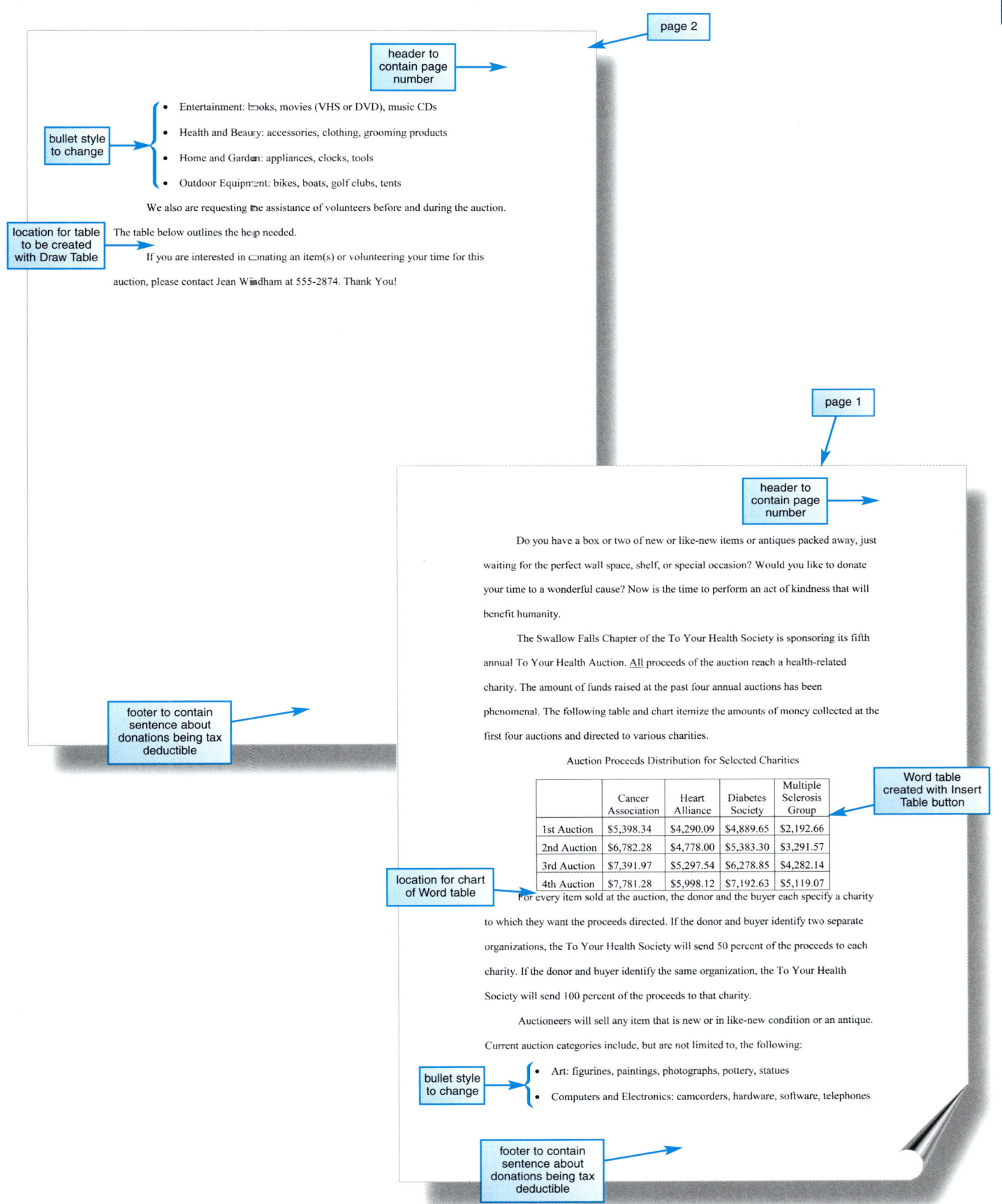

FIGURE 4-28a Auction Draft

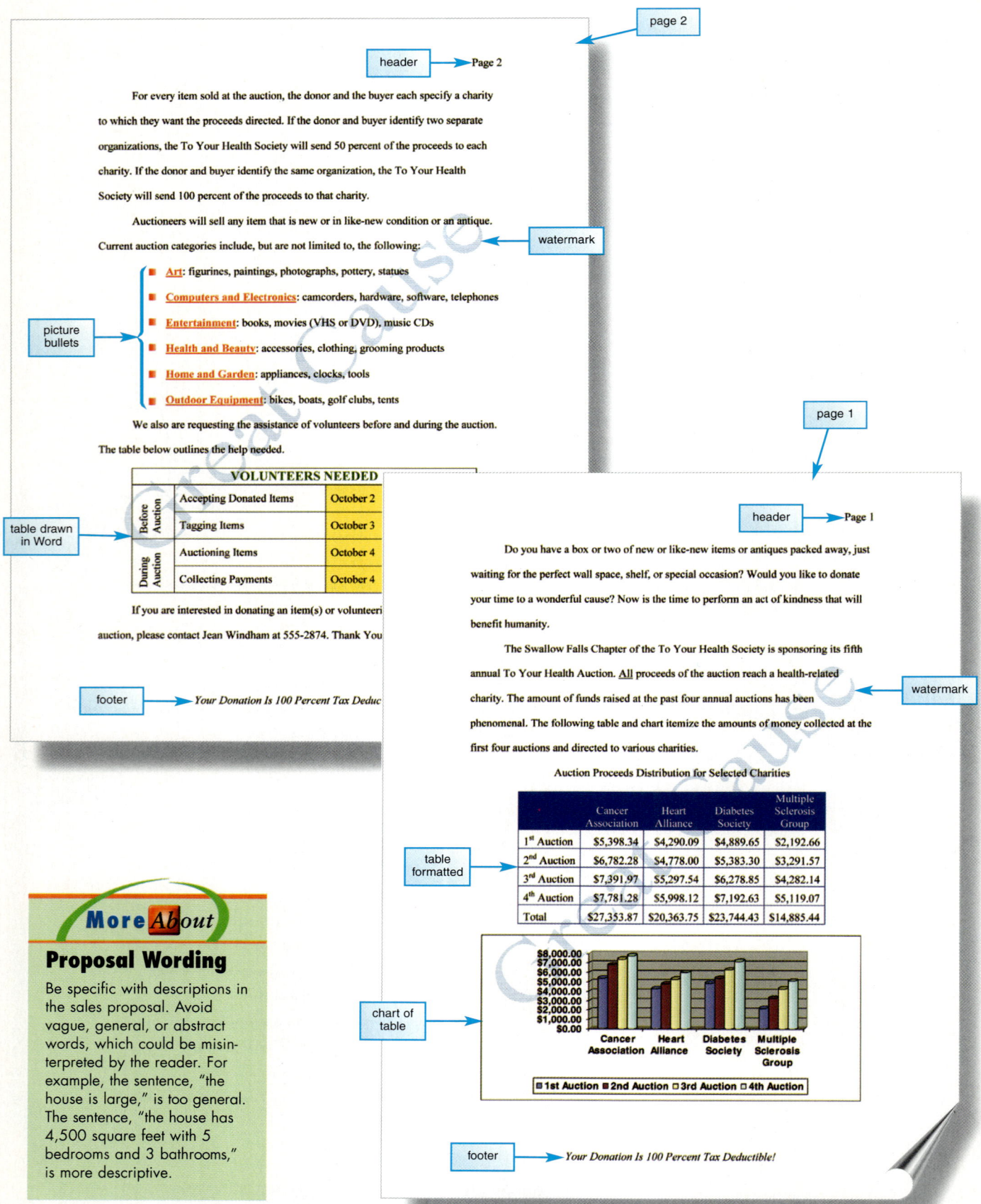

FIGURE 4-28b Body of Sales Proposal with Enhancements

Creating Headers and Footers

As discussed in Project 2, a **header** is text that prints at the top of each page in the document. A **footer** is text that prints at the bottom of every page. In this proposal, you want the header and footer to display on each page in the body of the sales proposal. You do not want the header and footer on the title page. Recall that the title page and the body of the sales proposal are in two separate sections. Thus, the header and footer should not display in section 1, but they should display in section 2.

Creating a Header Different from a Previous Section Header

In this proposal, the header consists of the word, Page, followed by the page number. This header should display only on the pages in section 2 of the document. Thus, be sure the insertion point is in section 2 when you create the header.

Perform the following steps to add a header only to the second section of the document.

TO CREATE A HEADER DIFFERENT FROM THE PREVIOUS SECTION HEADER

1. Be sure the insertion point is on line 1 of page 2, as shown in Figure 4-27 on page WD 4.25.
2. Click View on the menu bar and then click Header and Footer.
3. Click the Align Right button on the Formatting toolbar. Type `Page` and then press the SPACEBAR.
4. Click the Insert Page Number button on the Header and Footer toolbar.

Word displays the Header and Footer toolbar (Figure 4-29). Notice the header area title displays, Header -Section 2-.

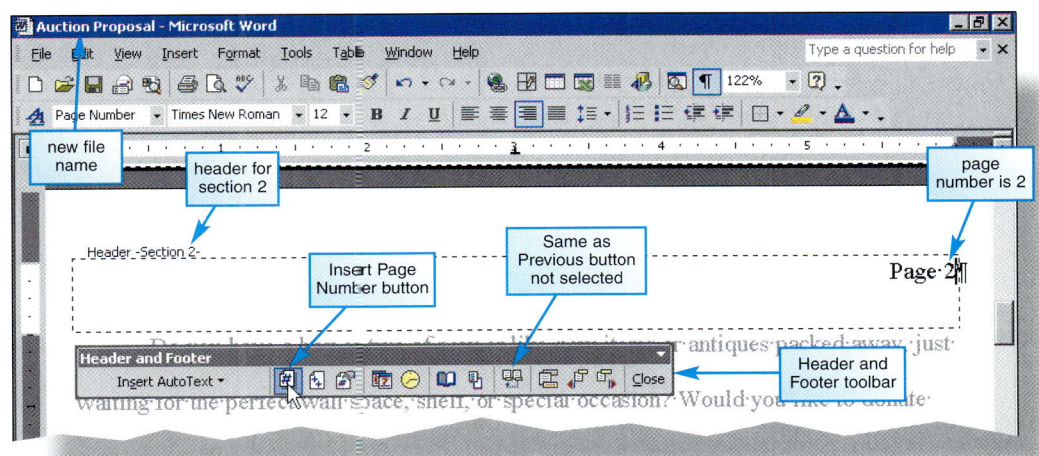

FIGURE 4-29

Notice the Same as Previous button on the Header and Footer toolbar is not selected. When this button is not selected, Word does not copy the typed header into the previous section. If you wanted the header typed in section 2 also to display in section 1, you would have clicked the Same as Previous button on the Header and Footer toolbar.

Headers and Footers

If a portion of the header or footer does not display when you print the document, the header or footer may be in a nonprintable area of the printer. Check the printer manual for specifications on how close it can print to the edge of the paper. Then, click File on the menu bar, click Page Setup, click the Layout tab, adjust the From edge text box to a value that is larger than the printer's minimum margin setting, and then click the OK button.

Page Numbers

If Word displays {PAGE} instead of the actual page number, then field codes are displaying. To turn off field codes, press ALT+F9. If Word prints {PAGE} instead of the actual page number, click File on the menu bar, click Print, click the Options button, remove the check mark from the Field codes check box, and then click the OK button in each dialog box.

In Figure 4-29 on the previous page, the page number is a 2 because Word begins numbering pages from the beginning of the document. You want to begin numbering the body of the sales proposal with a number 1. Thus, you need to instruct Word to begin numbering the pages in section 2 with the number 1.

Perform the following steps to page number differently in a section.

To Page Number Differently in a Section

 Click the Format Page Number button on the Header and Footer toolbar. When the Page Number Format dialog box displays, click Start at in the Page numbering area and then point to the OK button.

Word displays the Page Number Format dialog box (Figure 4-30). By default, the number 1 displays in the Start at box.

 Click the OK button.

Word changes the starting page number for section 2 to the number 1 (shown in Figure 4-31).

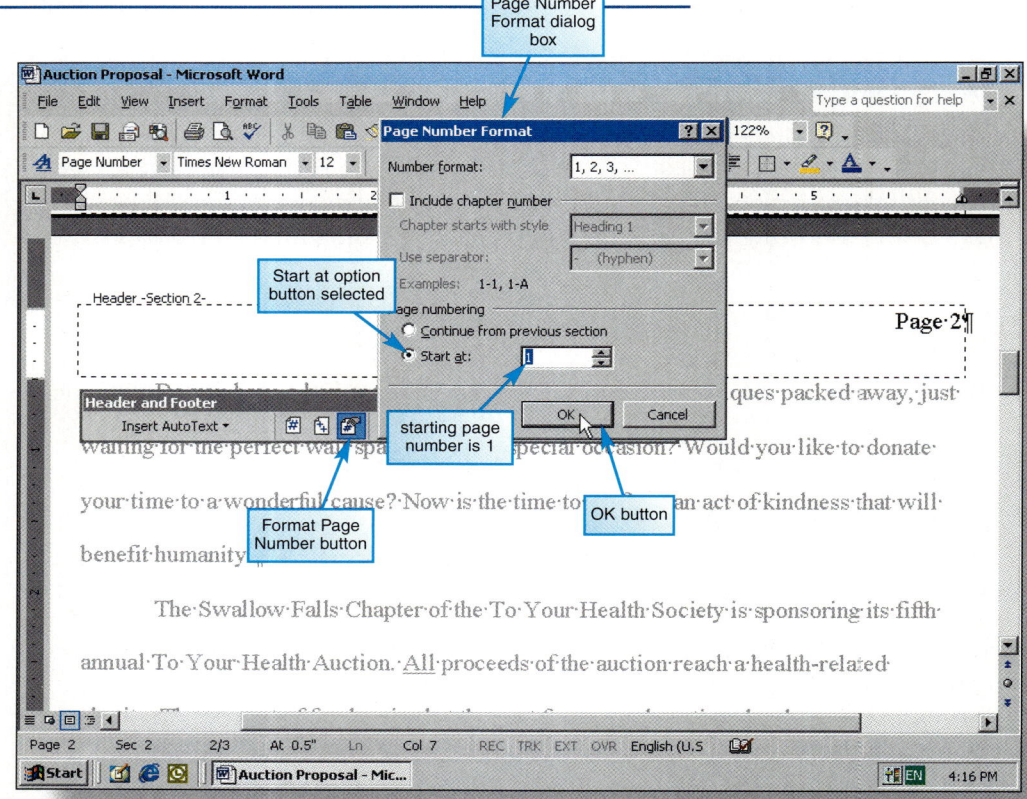

FIGURE 4-30

1. On Insert menu click Page Numbers, click Format button, click Start at in Page numbering area, click OK button
2. With Header and Footer toolbar displaying, in Voice Command mode, say "Format Page Number, Start at, OK"

The next step is to create the footer.

Creating a Footer Different from a Previous Section Footer

In this proposal, the footer consists of the following sentence: Your Donation Is 100 Percent Tax Deductible! This footer should display only on the pages in section 2 of the document. Thus, be sure the insertion point is in section 2 when you create the footer.

Perform the following steps to add a footer only to the second section of the document.

Creating Headers and Footers • WD 4.31

 **To Create a Footer Different from the Previous Section Footer**

1 Point to the Switch Between Header and Footer button on the Header and Footer toolbar (Figure 4-31).

2 Click the Switch Between Header and Footer button.

Word displays the footer area in the document window. The footer area title displays, Footer -Section 2-.

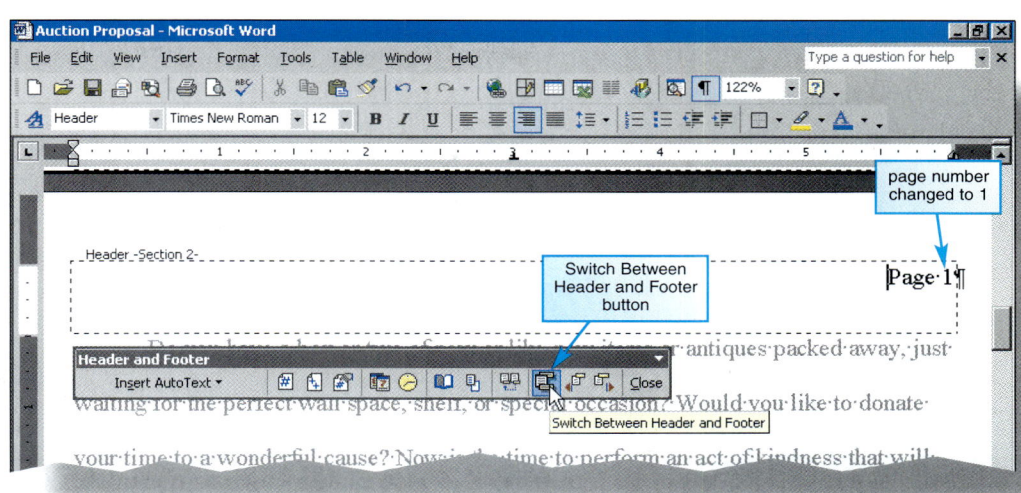

FIGURE 4-31

3 Click the Center button on the Formatting toolbar. Click the Italic button on the Formatting toolbar. Type `Your Donation Is 100 Percent Tax Deductible!` and then point to the Close Header and Footer button on the Header and Footer toolbar (Figure 4-32).

4 Click the Close Header and Footer button to remove the Header and Footer toolbar from the screen.

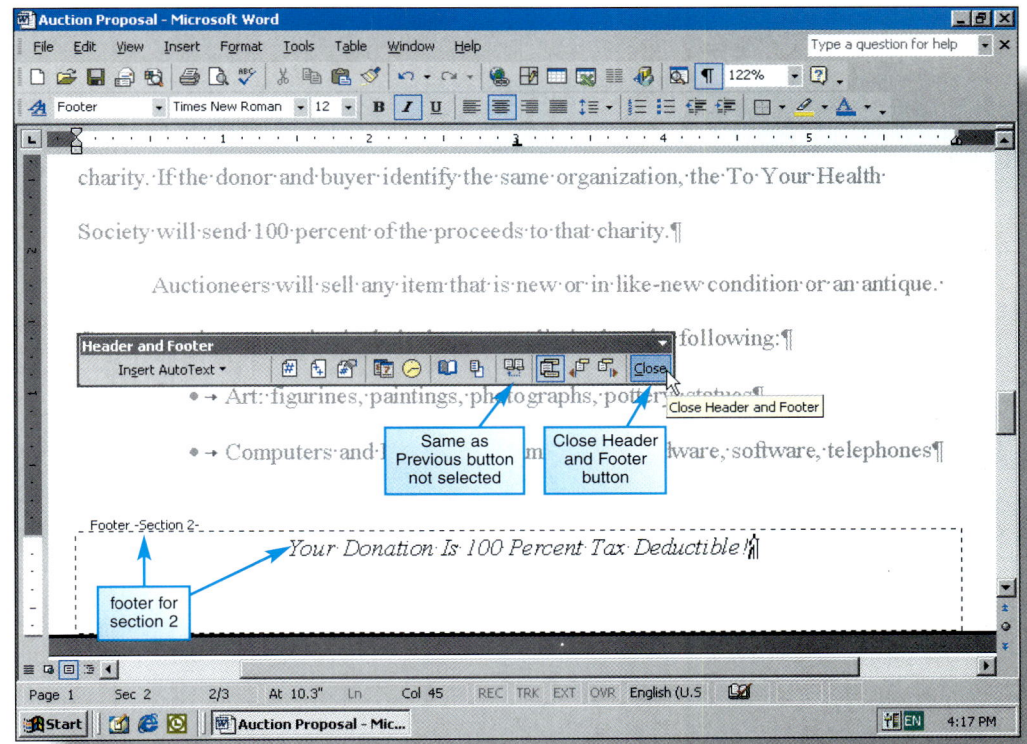

FIGURE 4-32

Other Ways

1. With Header and Footer toolbar displaying, in Voice Command mode, say "Switch Between Header and Footer, [type text], Close Header and Footer"

Fields

To add a field such as a file name into a header or footer, click the Insert AutoText button on the Header and Footer toolbar, and then click the desired field name.

Moving Tables

To move a table to a new location, point to the upper-left corner of the table until the table move handle displays (a small box containing a four-headed arrow). Point to the table move handle and then drag it to move the table to a new location.

Notice you used the same technique as for the header. That is, the Same as Previous button on the Header and Footer toolbar is not selected (Figure 4-32 on the previous page). When this button is not selected, Word does not copy the typed footer into the previous section. If you wanted the footer typed in section 2 also to display in section 1, you would have clicked the Same as Previous button on the Header and Footer toolbar.

Formatting and Charting a Table

The sales proposal draft contains a Word table (shown in Figure 4-28a on page WD 4.27) that was created using the Insert Table button on the Standard toolbar. This table contains five rows and five columns. The first row identifies the charity; the remaining rows show the donated proceeds for each of the previous auctions. The first column identifies the auction, and the remaining columns show the proceeds donated to each charity.

You want to add a row to the table that shows total dollar amounts contributed to each charity. You also plan to format the table and data within the table so it looks more appealing. Then, you will create a chart of this table (shown in Figure 4-28b on page WD 4.28) to show graphically the proceeds donated to each charity for each auction. The following pages explain how to sum the contents of the table, format the table, chart its contents, modify the chart, and then format the chart.

Working with Tables

The next step is to add a row to the bottom of the table that shows total dollar amounts contributed to each charity. To add a row to the end of a table, position the insertion point in the bottom-right corner cell and then press the TAB key, as shown in the following steps.

 To Add a Row to a Table

1 Scroll to display the table in the document window. Position the insertion point at the end of the lower-right corner cell of the table (Figure 4-33).

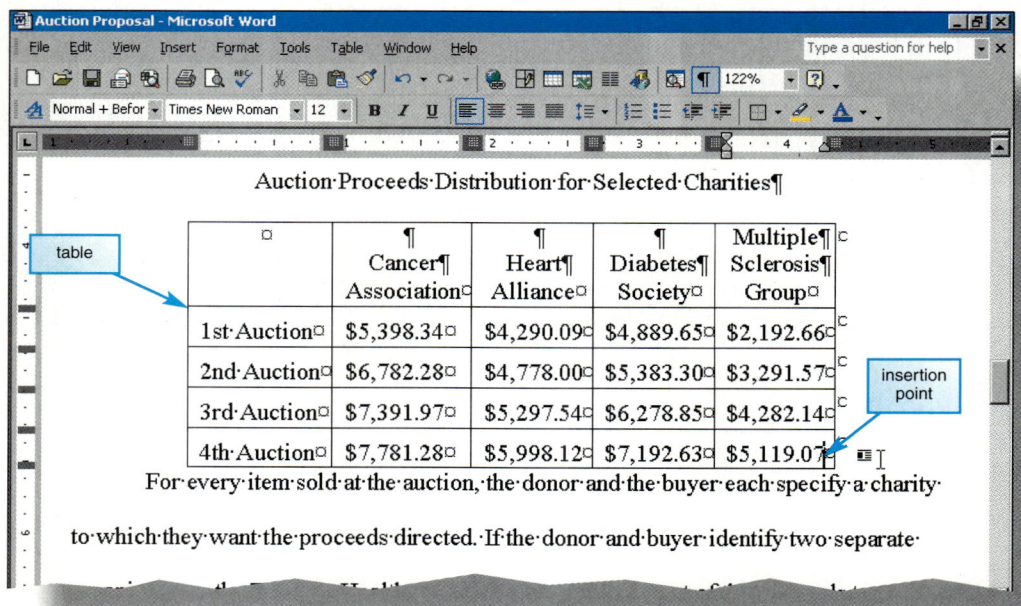

FIGURE 4-33

2 **Press the TAB key. Type** Total **and then press the TAB key.**

Word adds a row to the bottom of the table (Figure 4-34). The first cell in the new row contains the word, Total. The remaining cells in the new row are empty.

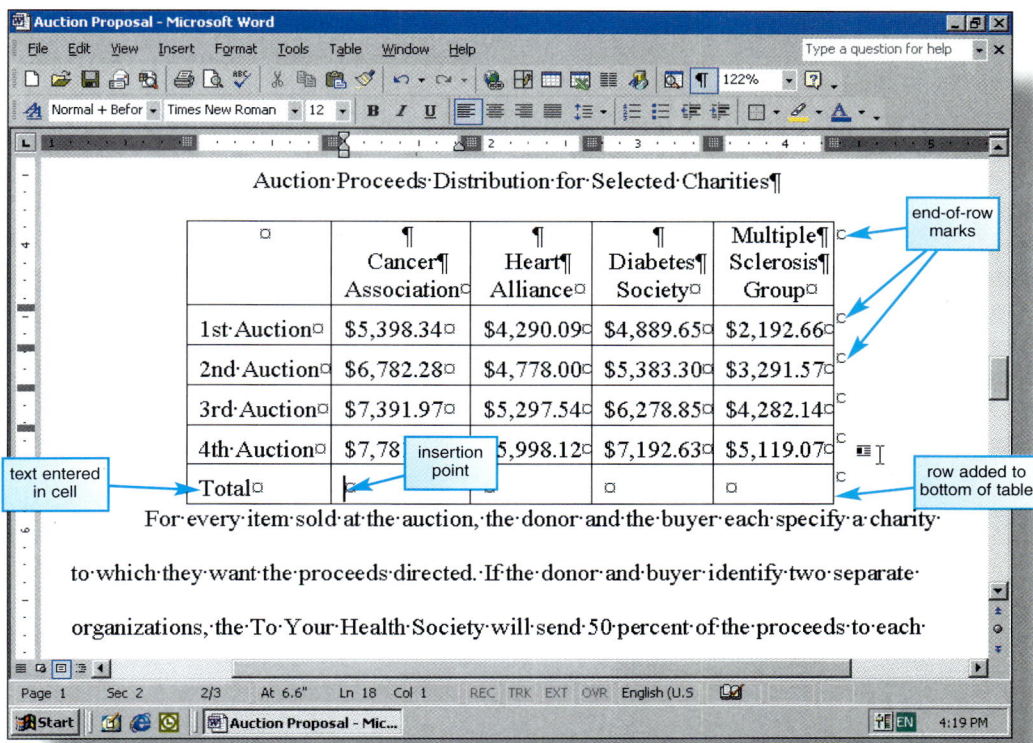

FIGURE 4-34

Depending on the task you want to perform in a table, the function of the Table button on the Standard toolbar changes, and the commands on the Table menu and associated shortcut menu change. To **add rows** in the middle of a table, select the row below where the new row is to be inserted, then click the Insert Rows button on the Standard toolbar (the same button you clicked to insert a table); or click Insert Rows on the shortcut menu; or click Table on the menu bar, point to Insert, and then click Rows Above. To **add a column** in the middle of a table, select the column to the right of where the new column is to be inserted and then click the Insert Columns button on the Standard toolbar (the same button you clicked to insert a table); or click Insert Columns on the shortcut menu; or click Table on the menu bar, point to Insert, and then click Columns to the Left. To add a column to the right of a table, select the end-of-row marks at the right edge of the table, then click the Insert Columns button; or click Insert Columns on the shortcut menu; or click Table on the menu bar, point to Insert, and then click Columns to the Right.

If you want to **delete row(s)** or **delete column(s)** from a table, select the row(s) or column(s) to delete and then click Delete Rows or Delete Columns on the shortcut menu, or click Table on the menu bar, click Delete, and then click the appropriate item to delete.

Summing Table Contents

To quickly total a column or a row, Word provides an **AutoSum button** on the Tables and Borders toolbar. Perform the step on the next page to sum a column in the table.

Other Ways

1. Click Insert Table button arrow on Tables and Borders toolbar, click Insert Rows Above or Insert Rows Below
2. On Table menu point to Insert, click Rows Above or Rows Below
3. In Voice Command mode, say "Table, Insert, [Select Rows Above or Rows Below]"

More About

Table Columns

When the insertion point is in a table, the ruler displays column markers that indicate the beginning and ending of columns. A column boundary is the vertical gridline immediately to the right of a column in the table itself. To resize a column width, drag the column boundary in the table or the column marker on the ruler. Holding down the ALT key while dragging markers displays column width measurements.

Steps To Sum a Column in a Table

  Click the Tables and Borders button on the Standard toolbar to display the Tables and Borders toolbar. With the insertion point in the cell to place the sum (shown in Figure 4-34 on the previous page), click the AutoSum button on the Tables and Borders toolbar.

Word places the sum of the numbers in the column in the current cell (Figure 4-35).

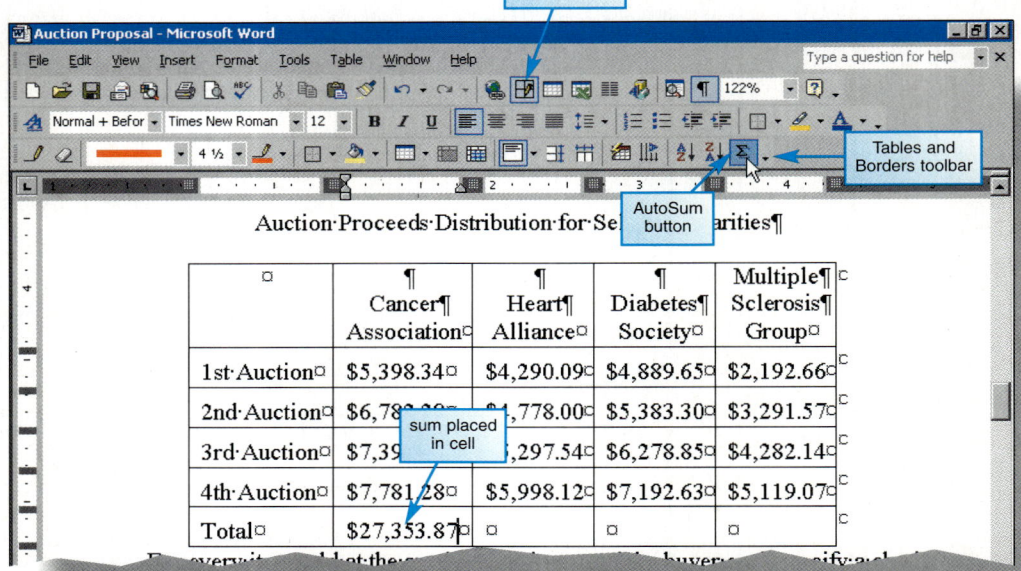

FIGURE 4-35

Other Ways

1. On Table menu click Formula, if necessary type =SUM(ABOVE) in Formula text box, click OK button
2. In Voice Command mode, say "AutoSum"

If you wanted to sum the contents of a row instead of a column, you would place the insertion point in the empty cell at the right of the row and then click the AutoSum button. Depending on the location of the insertion point, Word determines if it should sum a row or a column. If Word uses the wrong formula, you can change it. The formula for summing a column is =SUM(ABOVE) and the formula for summing a row is =SUM(LEFT). To change an existing formula, click Table on the menu bar and then click Formula. Make the change in the Formula dialog box and then click the OK button. You also use the Formula dialog box if you want to enter a formula into a cell other than summing a row or column.

Perform the following steps to place sums in the remaining cells in the last row of the table.

More About

Copying Tables

If you have two similar tables in a document, you can copy the first table and then modify the second one. To copy a table, point to the table move handle, press and hold the CTRL key, drag a copy of the table to a new location, and then release the CTRL key.

TO SUM COLUMNS IN A TABLE

 Press the TAB key. Click the AutoSum button on the Tables and Borders toolbar.

 Press the TAB key. Click the AutoSum button on the Tables and Borders toolbar.

3 Press the TAB key. Click the AutoSum button on the Tables and Borders toolbar.

Word computes and enters sums into cells in the last row of the table (shown in Figure 4-36).

Formatting a Table

The table in the document looks dull. You would like to add some color and other formats to it. Although you can format each row, column, and cell of a table individually, Word provides a Table AutoFormat feature that contains predefined formats for tables. Perform the following steps to format the entire table using Table AutoFormat.

Formatting and Charting a Table • WD 4.35

Steps To AutoFormat a Table

1 **With the insertion point in the table, click the Table AutoFormat button on the Tables and Borders toolbar. When the Table AutoFormat dialog box displays, scroll through the Table styles list and then click Table Grid 8. Be sure all check boxes at the bottom of the dialog box contain check marks. Point to the Apply button.**

Word displays the Table AutoFormat dialog box (Figure 4-36).

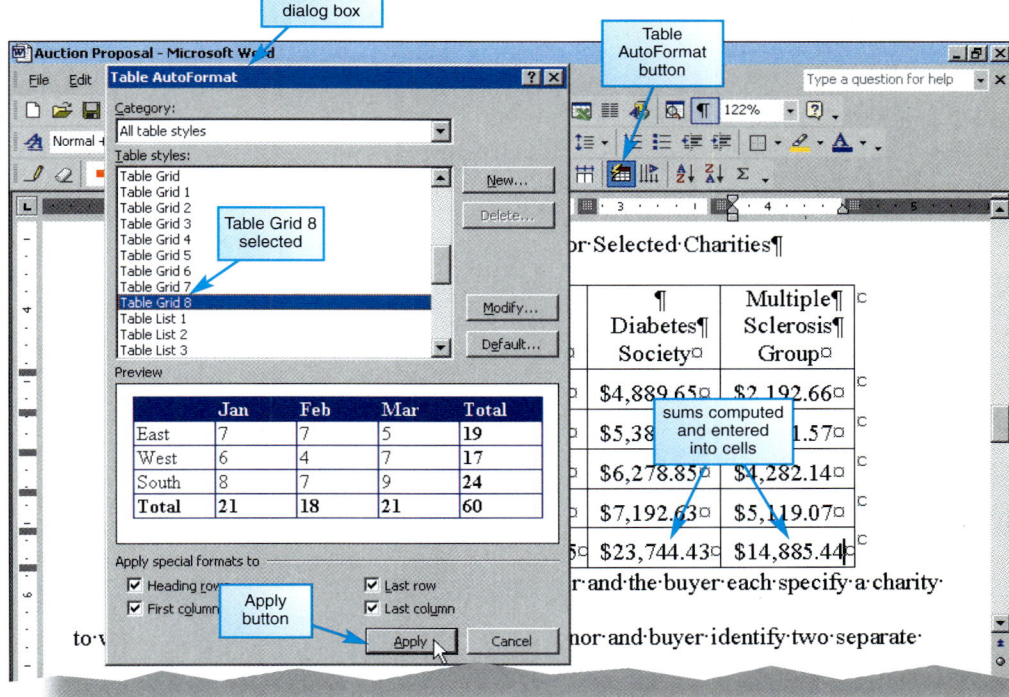

FIGURE 4-36

2 **Click the Apply button. Click the Tables and Borders button on the Standard toolbar to remove the Tables and Borders toolbar from the screen.**

Word formats the table according to the Table Grid 8 style (Figure 4-37).

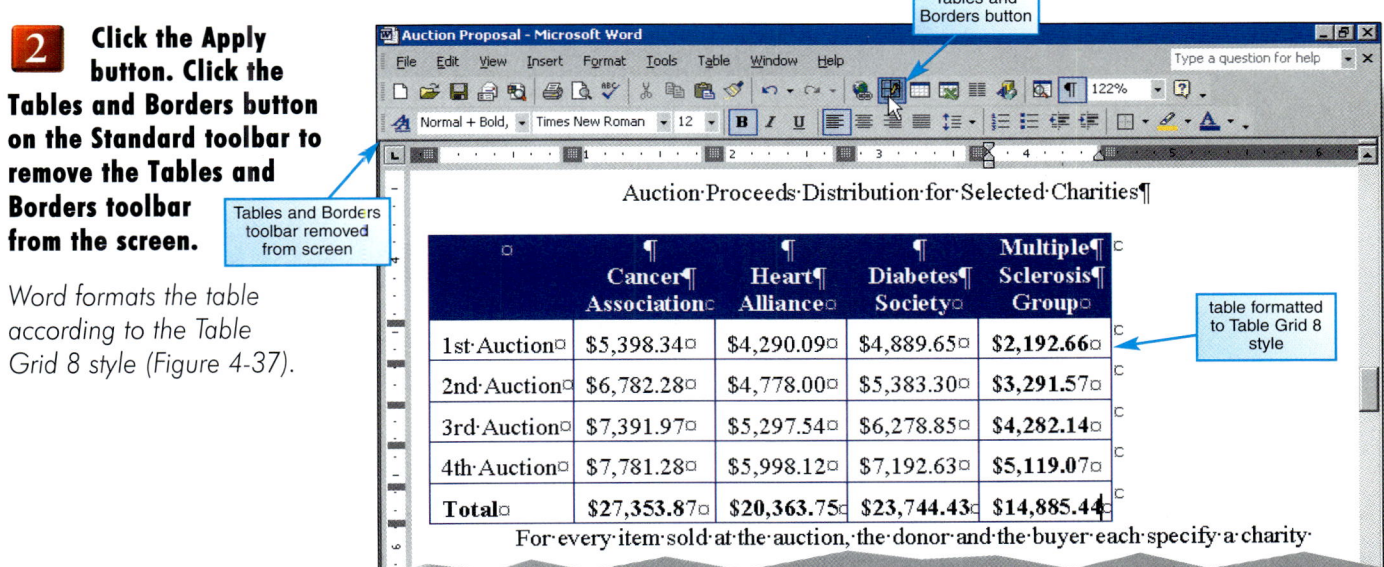

FIGURE 4-37

Perform the steps on the next page to center the table horizontally between the page margins.

Other Ways

1. On Table menu click Table AutoFormat, click desired table style, click Apply button
2. In Voice Command mode, say "Table AutoFormat, [select table style], Apply"

Deleting Table Contents

To delete the contents of a table and leave an empty table on the screen, select the table contents and then press the DELETE key.

TO CENTER A TABLE

1. Position the mouse pointer in the table to display the table move handle in the upper-left corner of the table. Position the mouse pointer on the table move handle and click to select the table.

2. With the entire table selected, click the Center button on the Formatting toolbar.

3. Click anywhere to remove the selection in the table.

Word centers the selected table (shown in Figure 4-38).

Just as with paragraphs, you can left-align, center, or right-align data in table cells. By default, the data you enter into the cells is left-aligned. You can change the alignment just as you would for a paragraph. If you want to change the alignment of multiple cells, you must select the cells. Perform the following steps to right-align the contents of all the cells that contain dollar amounts.

 To Right-Align Cell Contents

1. **Drag through the cells to right-align, as shown in Figure 4-38. Point to the Align Right button on the Formatting toolbar.**

The cells containing the dollar amounts are to be right-aligned and thus are selected (Figure 4-38).

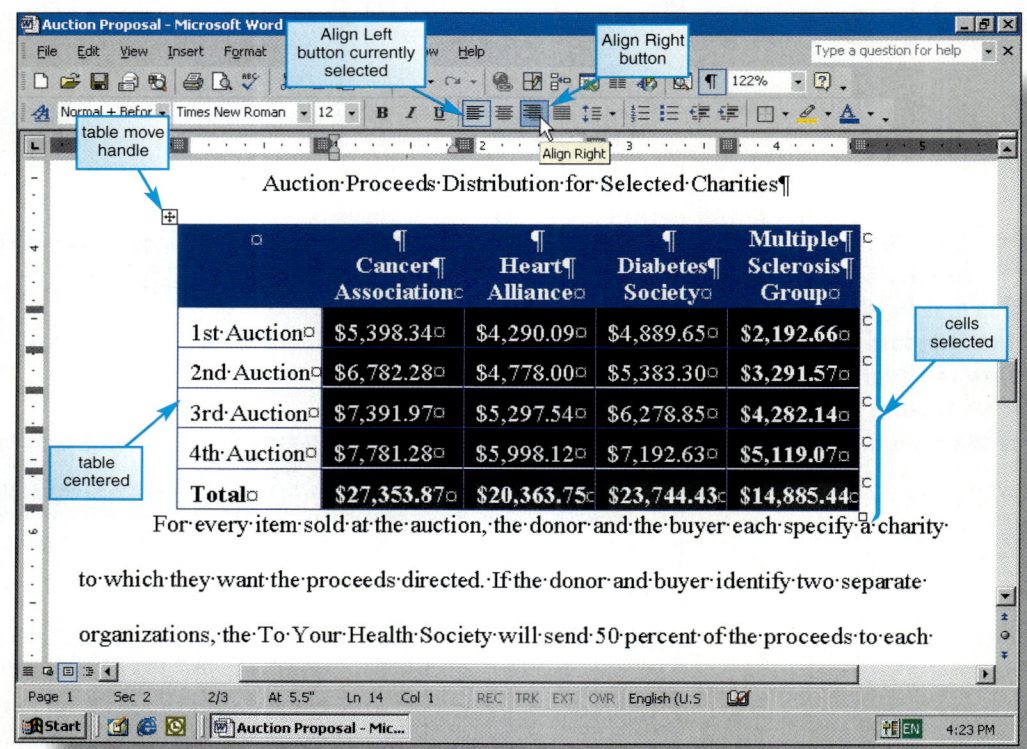

FIGURE 4-38

Formatting and Charting a Table • WD 4.37

2 **Click the Align Right button. Click in the selected cells to remove the selection.**

Word right-aligns the data in the selected cells (Figure 4-39).

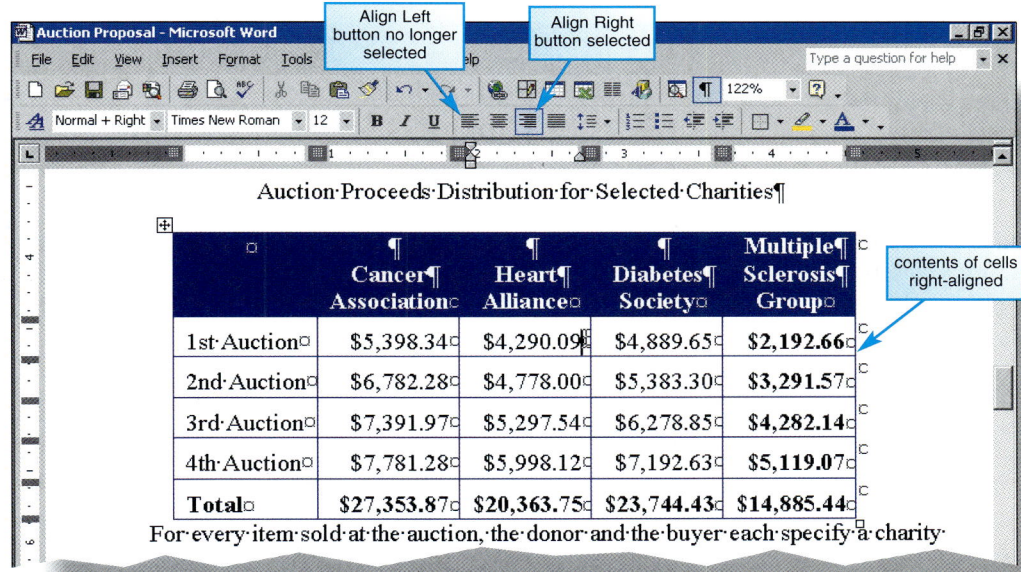

FIGURE 4-39

Formatting Nonadjacent Characters

The next step is to change the ordinals in the first column of the table to be superscripts. That is, the 1st should display as 1st, the 2nd as 2nd, and so on. To do this, you select the characters to be superscripted and then use the Font dialog box to apply this character effect to the selected text.

You want to select the st in 1st, the nd in 2nd, the rd in 3rd, and the th in 4th. In Word, you can select several segments of text that are not next to each other, called nonadjacent text or noncontiguous text. Select the first segment of text. To select additional nonadjacent text, press and hold the CTRL key while selecting each additional segment of text.

Perform the following steps to select nonadjacent text.

Other Ways

1. On Format menu click Paragraph, click Indents and Spacing tab, click Alignment box arrow, click Right, click OK button
2. Press CTRL+R
3. In Voice Command mode, say "Align Right"

 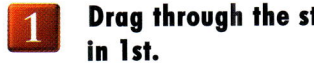

1 **Drag through the st in 1st.**

Word selects the st (Figure 4-40).

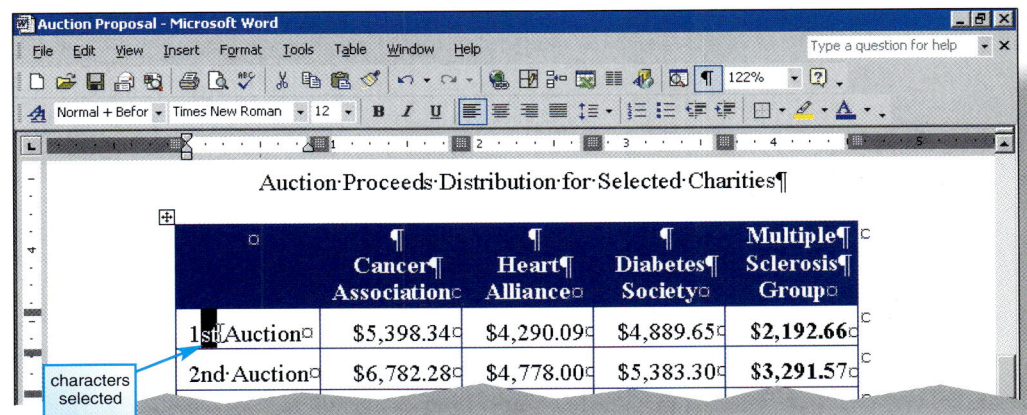

FIGURE 4-40

2 **Press and hold the CTRL key. While holding down the CTRL key, drag through the nd in 2nd. While holding down the CTRL key, drag through the rd in 3rd. While holding down the CTRL key, drag through the th in 4th. Release the CTRL key.**

Word selects the nonadjacent text (Figure 4-41).

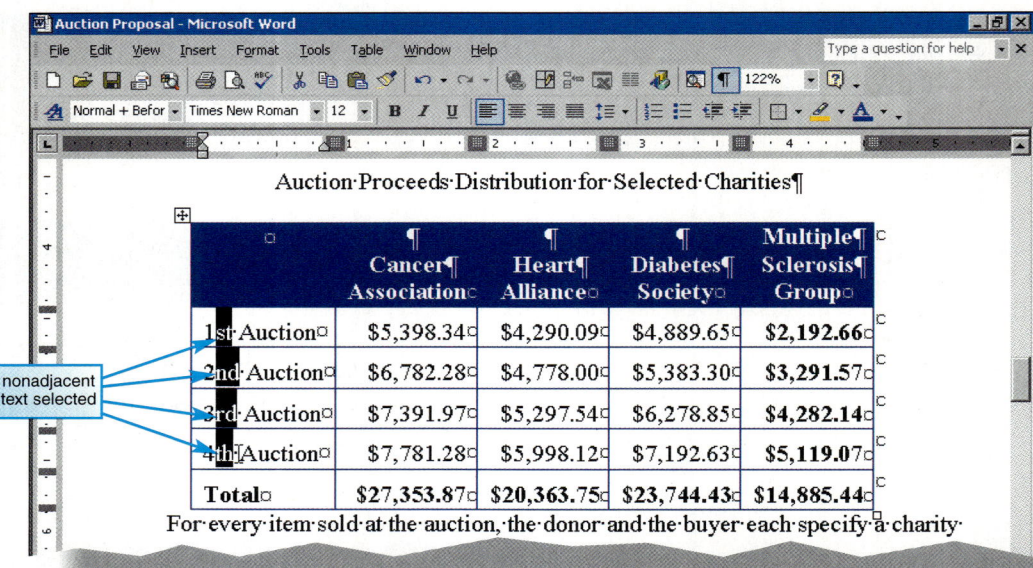

FIGURE 4-41

The next step is to apply the superscript character effect to the selected text.

Steps To Superscript Selected Characters

1 **Click Format on the menu bar and then click Font. When the Font dialog box displays, if necessary, click the Font tab. Click Superscript in the Effects area to place a check mark in the check box. Point to the OK button.**

Word displays the Font dialog box (Figure 4-42). The Preview area shows the superscript effect applied to the text.

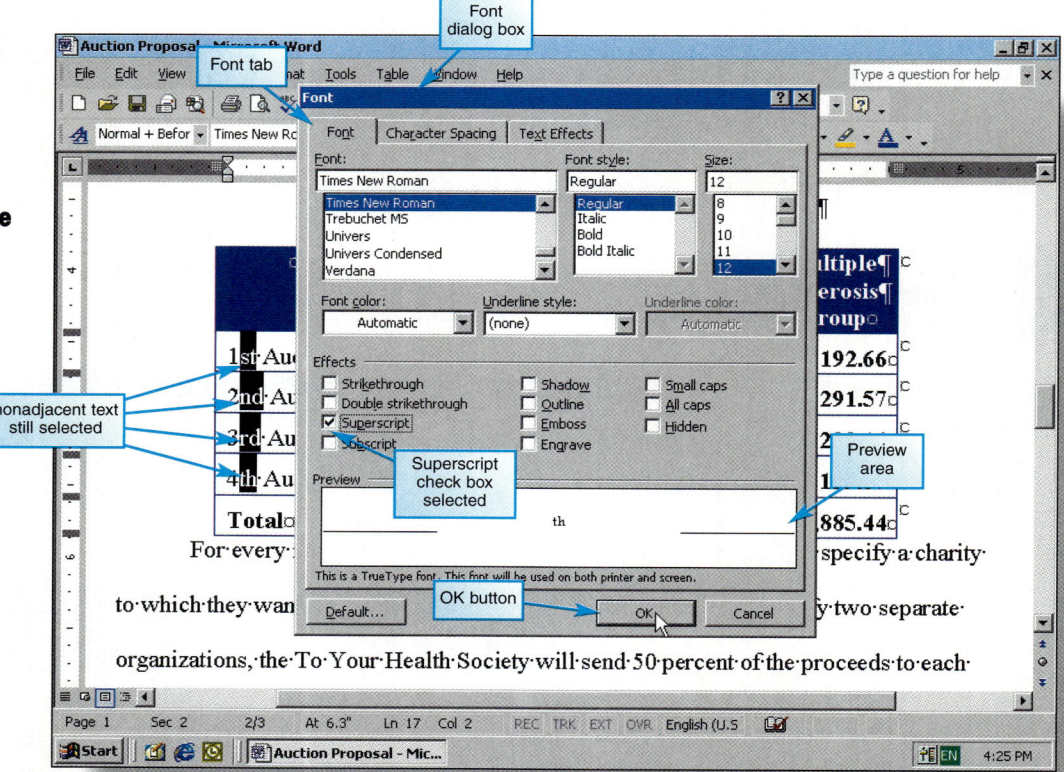

FIGURE 4-42

2 **Click the OK button. Click anywhere to remove the selections.**

Word superscripts the selected text (Figure 4-43).

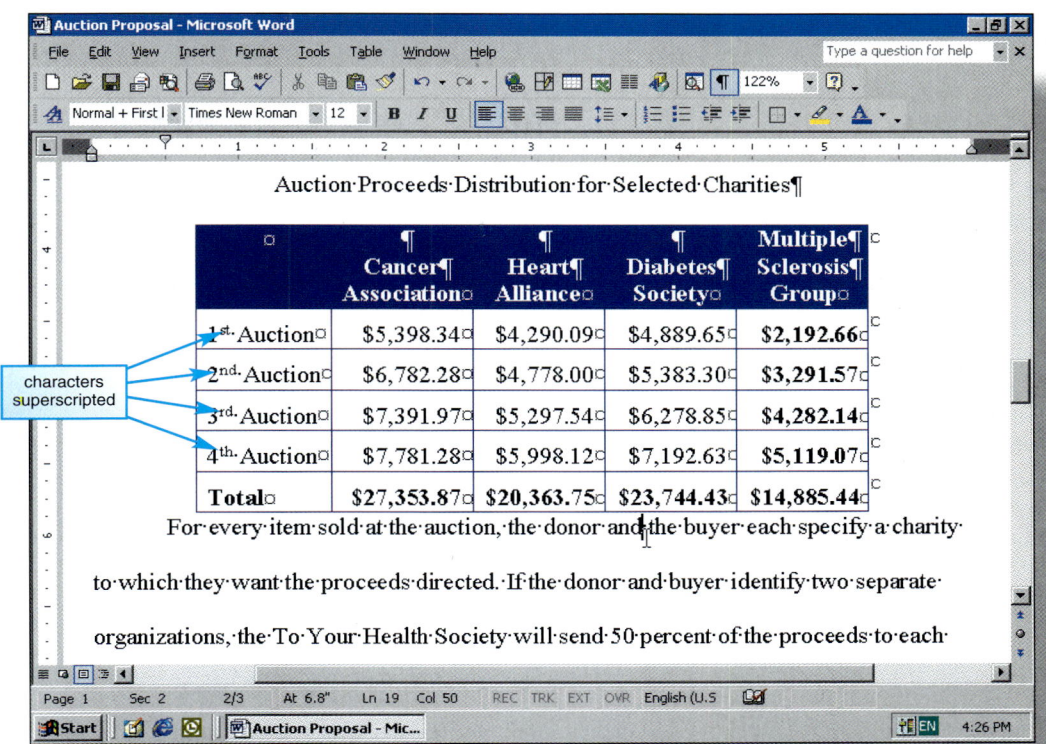

FIGURE 4-43

As discussed earlier in this project and shown in Figure 4-42, the Font sheet in the Font dialog box contains many other character effects you can add to text in a document. Table 4-1 on page WD 4.15 identified all of the available character effects.

Charting a Word Table

When you create a Word table, you easily can chart its data using an embedded charting application called **Microsoft Graph 2002**. Graph has its own menus and commands because it is an application embedded in the Word program. Using Graph commands, you can modify the appearance of the chart once you create it.

To create a chart from a Word table, the top row and left column of the table must contain text labels, and the other cells in the table must contain numbers. The table in the Auction Proposal meets these criteria.

To chart a Word table, first select the rows and columns in the table to be charted. In this project, you do not want to chart the last row in the table that contains the totals. Thus, you will select the first five rows in the table and then chart the table. Perform the steps on the next page to chart a Word table.

Other Ways

1. On Format menu click Font, click Font tab, click Superscript, click OK button
2. In Voice Command mode, say "Format, Font, Font, Superscript, OK"

Word 2002 Features

For more information on features and capabilities of Word 2002, visit the Word 2002 More About Web page (www.scsite.com/wd2002/more.htm) and then click Features and Capabilities of Word 2002.

Steps: To Chart a Table

1 Point to the left of (outside) the first row in the table (the row headings) until the mouse pointer changes to a right-pointing arrow and then drag downward until the first five rows in the table are selected.

Word selects the rows to be charted (Figure 4-44). Notice the last row of the table is not selected.

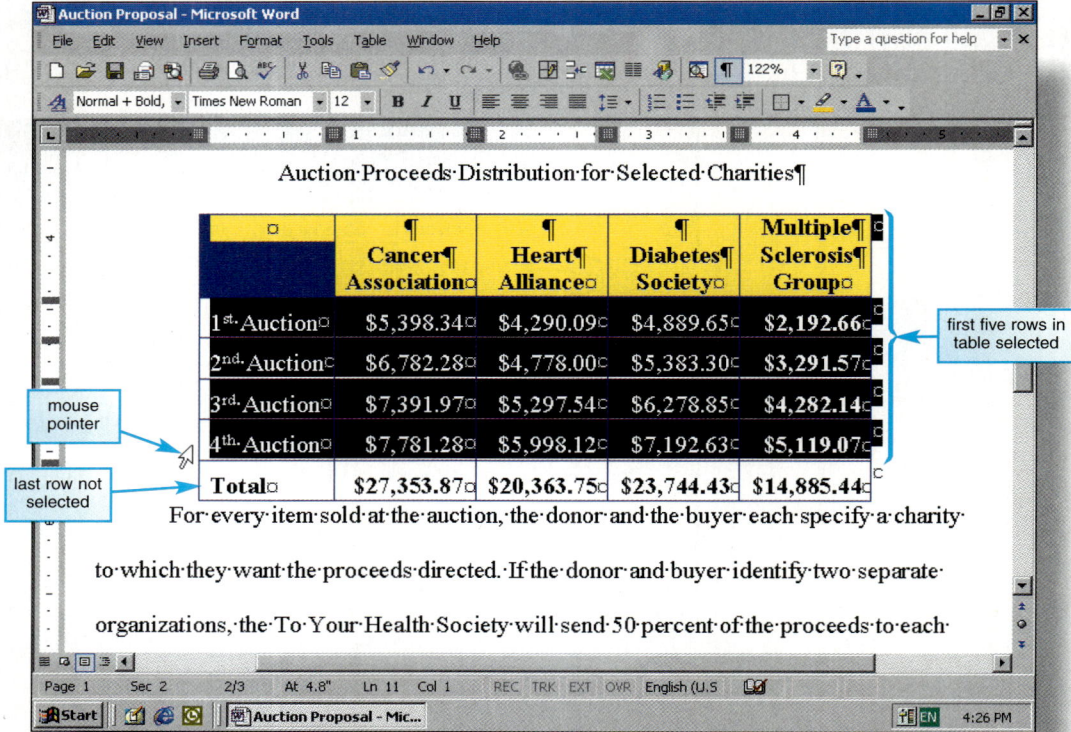

FIGURE 4-44

2 Click Insert on the menu bar, point to Picture, and then point to Chart (Figure 4-45).

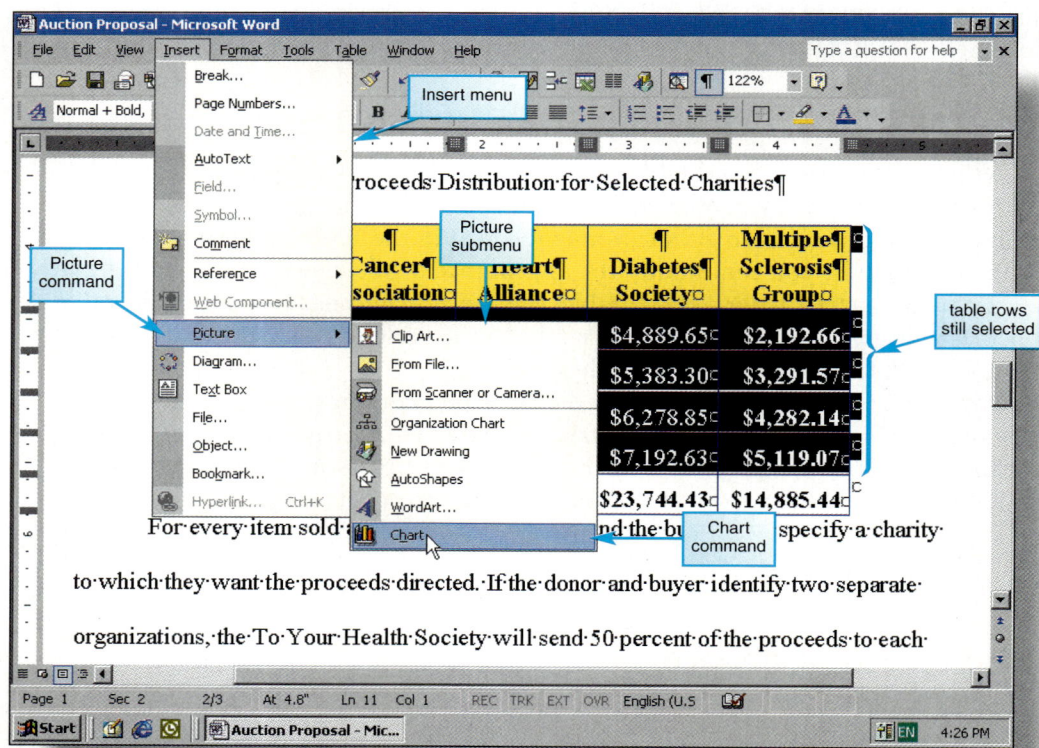

FIGURE 4-45

3 **Click Chart.**

Word starts the Microsoft Graph 2002 application (Figure 4-46). Graph creates a chart of the selected rows in the table.

4 **If Graph displays a Datasheet window, click the Close button in the upper-right corner of the Datasheet window to remove the Datasheet window from the screen.**

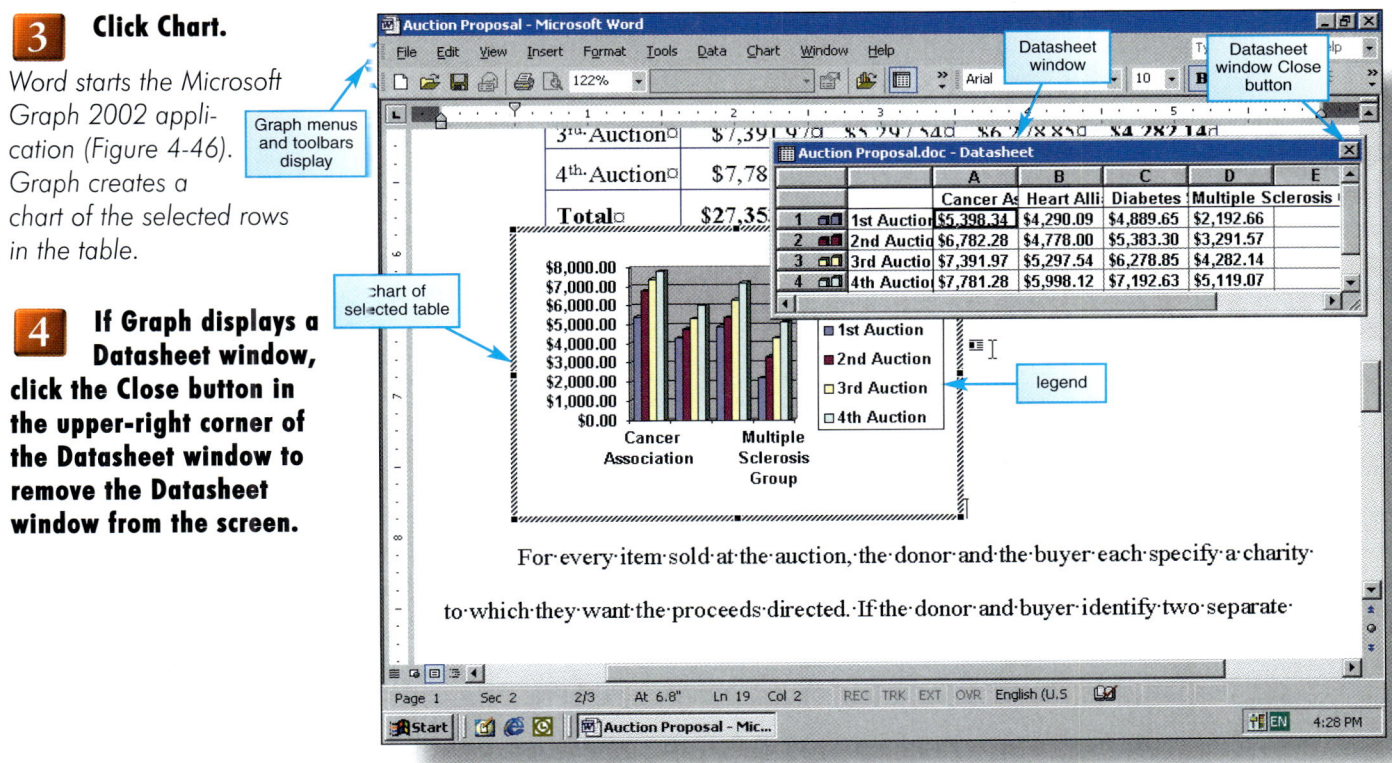

FIGURE 4-46

The menus on the menu bar and buttons on the toolbars change to Graph menus and toolbars because the Graph program is running inside your Word program. During the course of the steps on the following pages, you may inadvertently click somewhere outside the chart, which exits Graph and returns to Word menus and toolbars. If this occurs, simply double-click in the chart to return to Graph.

Graph places the contents of the table into a **Datasheet window**, also called a **datasheet** (shown in Figure 4-46). Graph then charts the contents of the datasheet. Although you can modify the contents of the datasheet, it is not necessary in this project. Thus, you close the Datasheet window.

Changing the Chart in Graph

You would like to move the legend so it displays below the chart, resize the chart, and change the shape of the bars in the chart. The following pages illustrate each of these changes.

The first step in changing the chart is to move the legend so it displays below the chart instead of to the right of the chart. The **legend** is a box on the right side of the chart that identifies the colors assigned to categories in the chart. Perform the steps on the next page to move the legend in the chart.

Other Ways

1. On Insert menu click Object, click Create New tab, click Microsoft Graph Chart in Object type list, click OK button
2. In Voice Command mode, say "Insert, Picture, Chart"

More About

Datasheets

A datasheet can contain up to 4,000 rows and 4,000 columns. Working in a datasheet is very similar to working in an Excel worksheet. To insert a row or column, right-click a row heading or column heading and then click Insert on the shortcut menu. To enter data in a cell, click in the cell and then enter the data or text.

Steps: To Move Legend Placement in a Chart

1 If necessary, scroll to display the chart in the document window. Point to the legend in the chart and then right-click. Point to Format Legend on the shortcut menu (Figure 4-47).

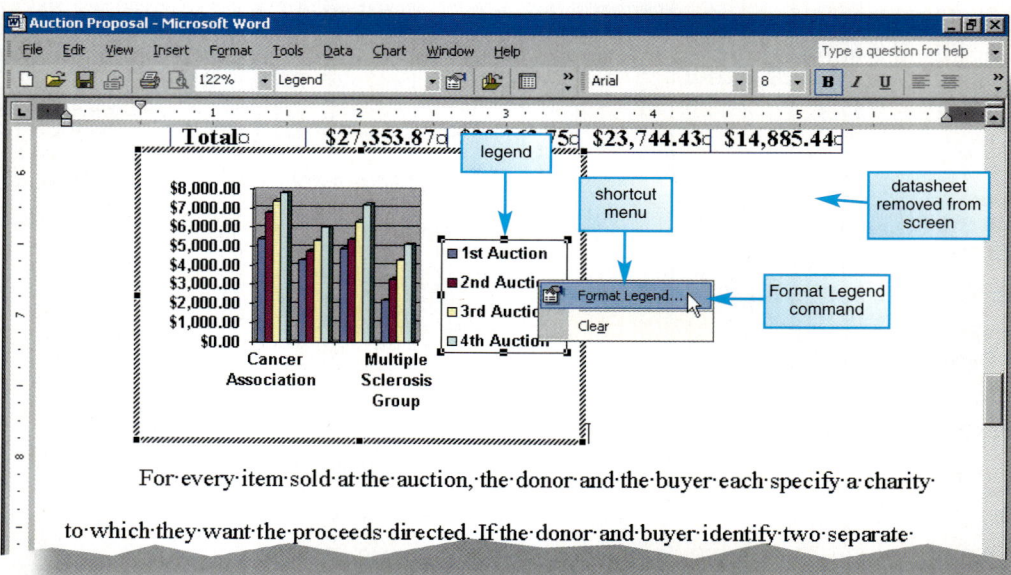

FIGURE 4-47

2 Click Format Legend. If necessary, click the Placement tab when the Format Legend dialog box displays. Click Bottom in the Placement area and then point to the OK button.

Graph displays the Format Legend dialog box (Figure 4-48).

3 Click the OK button.

Graph places the legend below the chart (shown in Figure 4-49).

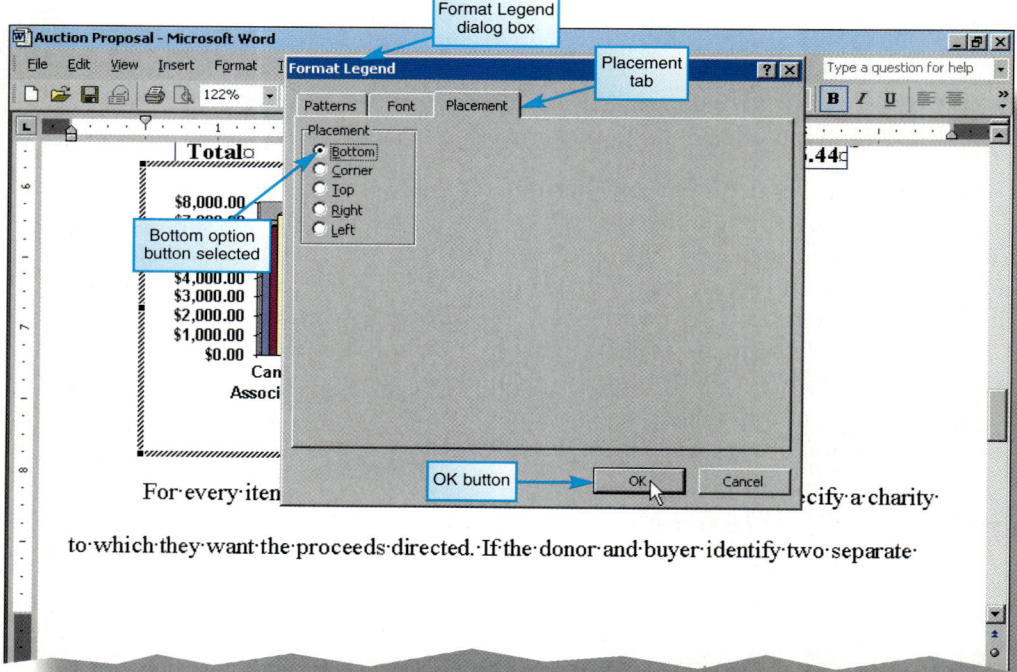

FIGURE 4-48

Notice that not all charity labels show on the category axis (the horizontal axis) because the chart is too narrow. Thus, the next step is to resize the chart so it is wider.

You resize a chart the same way you do any other graphical object. That is, you drag the chart's sizing handles, as shown in the following steps.

Steps: To Resize a Chart

1 Point to the bottom-right sizing handle on the chart and drag downward and to the right as shown in Figure 4-49.

2 Release the mouse button. If the chart does not display properly, click above the scroll box on the scroll bar and then click below the scroll box on the scroll bar to redisplay the chart.

Graph resizes the chart (shown in Figure 4-50).

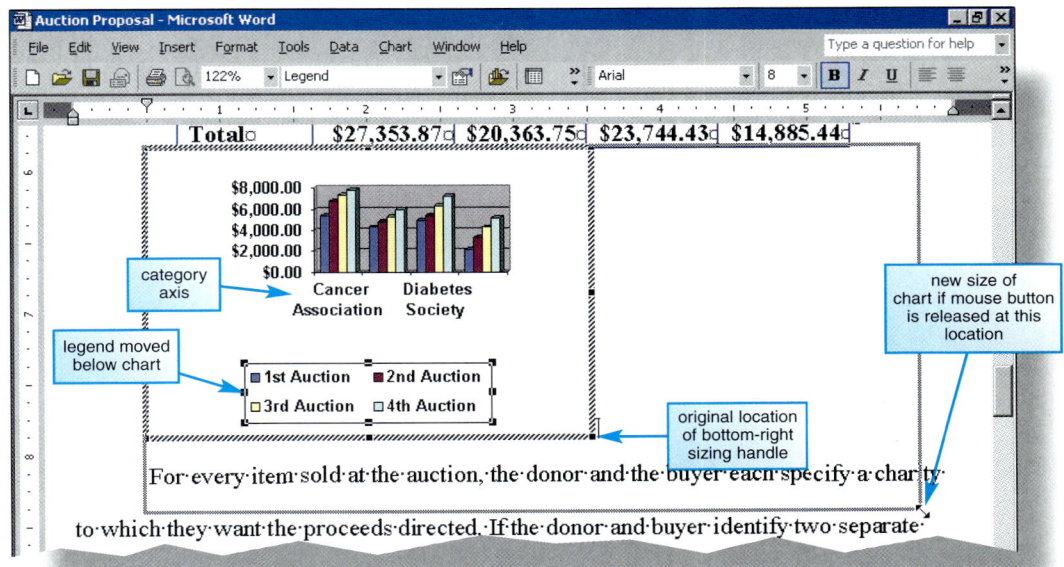

FIGURE 4-49

The next step is to change the chart type so the columns display with a cylindrical shape instead of a rectangular shape. Perform the following steps to change the chart type.

Steps: To Change the Chart Type

1 Point to the right of the columns in the chart and then right-click when the words, Plot Area, display as the ScreenTip. Point to Chart Type on the shortcut menu (Figure 4-50).

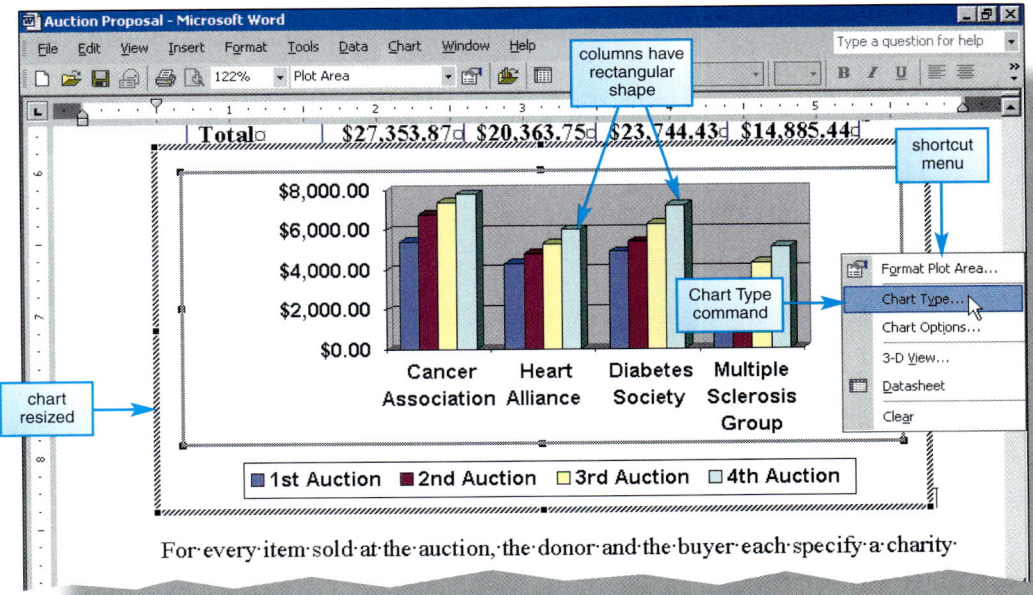

FIGURE 4-50

2 Click Chart Type. If necessary, click the Standard Types tab when the Chart Type dialog box displays. Scroll to and then click Cylinder in the Chart type list. Point to the OK button.

Graph displays the Chart Type dialog box (Figure 4-51).

3 Click the OK button.

Graph changes the shape of the columns to a cylindrical shape (shown in Figure 4-52).

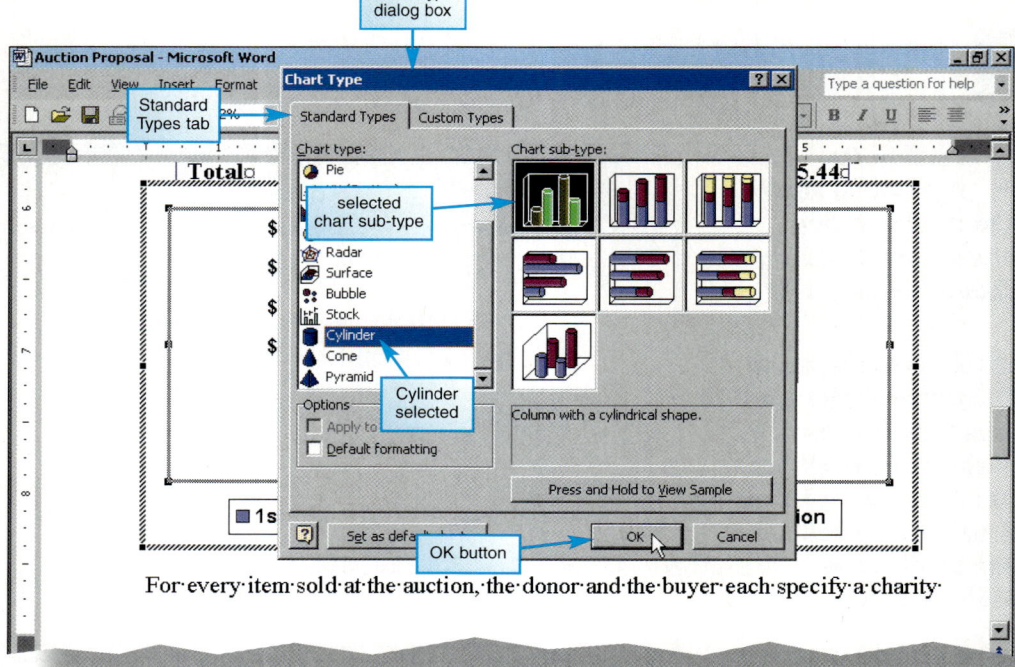

FIGURE 4-51

You are finished modifying the chart. The next step is to exit Graph and return to Word.

To Exit Graph and Return to Word

1 Click somewhere outside the chart. If necessary, scroll to display the chart in the document window. If all of the labels do not display on the category axis, double-click the chart, drag the right-middle sizing handle to make the chart wider, and then click somewhere outside the chart again.

Word closes the Graph application (Figure 4-52). Word's menus and toolbars redisplay below the title bar.

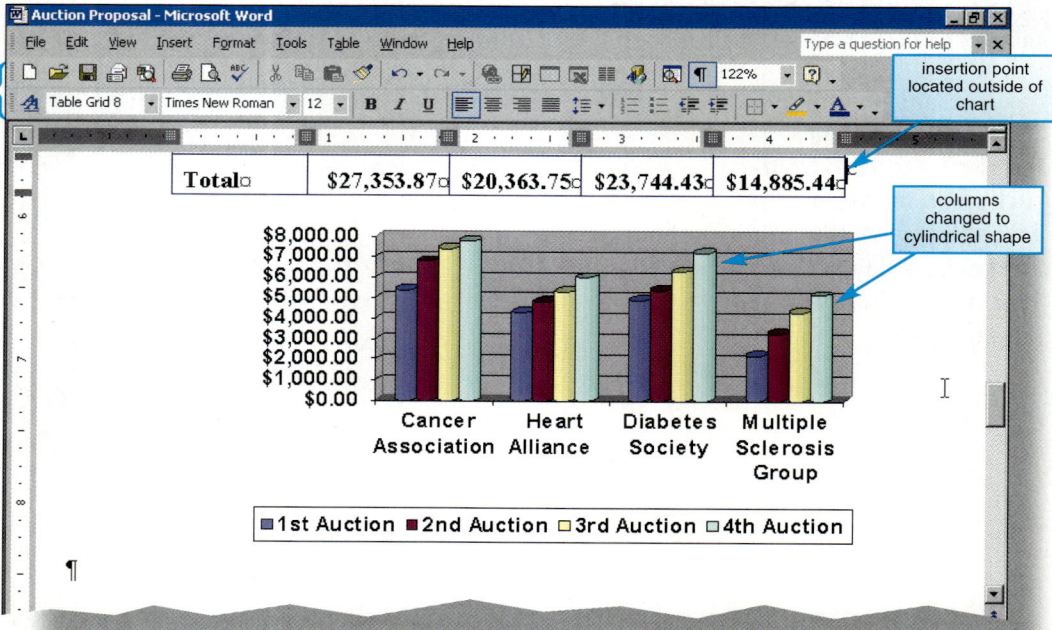

FIGURE 4-52

Formatting and Charting a Table • WD 4.45

If you wanted to modify an existing chart in a document, you would double-click the chart to reopen the Microsoft Graph 2002 application. Then, you can make changes to the chart. When you are finished making changes to the chart, click anywhere outside the chart to return to Word.

Formatting the Chart in Word

The chart now is part of the paragraph below the table. Thus, you can apply any paragraph alignment settings to the chart. The chart should be centered. If you select the chart and then click the Center button on the Formatting toolbar, the chart will not be centered properly. Instead, it will be one-half inch to the right of the center point because first-line indent is set at one-half inch (shown in Figure 4-53). Thus, you need to remove the first-line indent setting in order to center the paragraph properly.

You also want to add an outside border to the chart and insert a blank line between the chart and the table. Earlier in this project, you added an outside border to a paragraph on the title page. Its line weight was 4½ point and its color was red. You do not want this same border definition for the chart. Instead, you want a ½-point border in black.

The chart is part of the paragraph. To insert a blank line above a paragraph, position the insertion point in the paragraph and then press **CTRL+0** (the numeral zero).

Perform the following steps to center, outline, and insert a blank line above the chart.

Chart Titles

To add a title to a chart, double-click the chart to open Microsoft Graph, click Chart on the menu bar, click Chart Options, type the desired chart title in the Chart title text box, and then click the OK button. Click anywhere outside the chart to exit Microsoft Graph and return to Word.

Steps To Format a Chart

 Click anywhere in the chart.

Word selects the chart (Figure 4-53). A selected chart displays surrounded by a selection rectangle that has sizing handles at each corner and middle location.

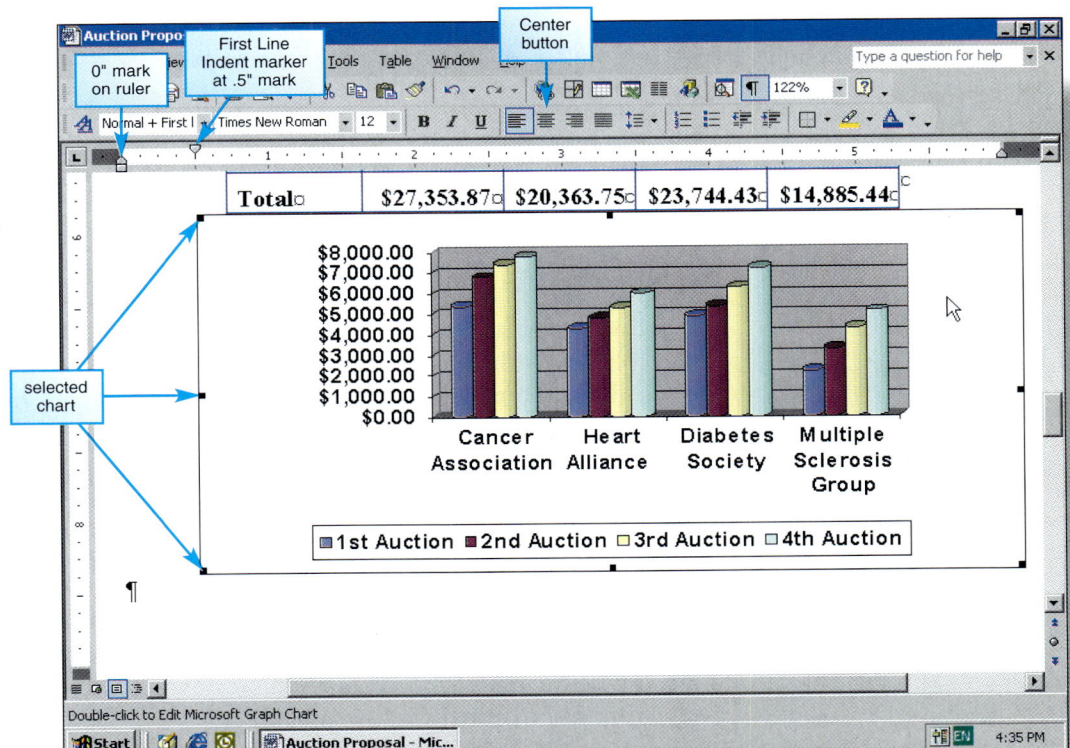

FIGURE 4-53

2 Drag the First Line Indent marker to the 0" mark on the ruler. Click the Center button on the Formatting toolbar. Click the Tables and Borders button on the Standard toolbar. If necessary, click the Line Weight box arrow on the Tables and Borders toolbar and then click ½ pt. Click the Border Color button arrow on the Tables and Borders toolbar and then click Automatic on the color palette. Click the Outside Border button on the Tables and Borders toolbar. Click the Tables and Borders button on the Standard toolbar to close the Tables and Borders toolbar. Press CTRL+0 (the numeral zero). Click outside the chart to deselect it.

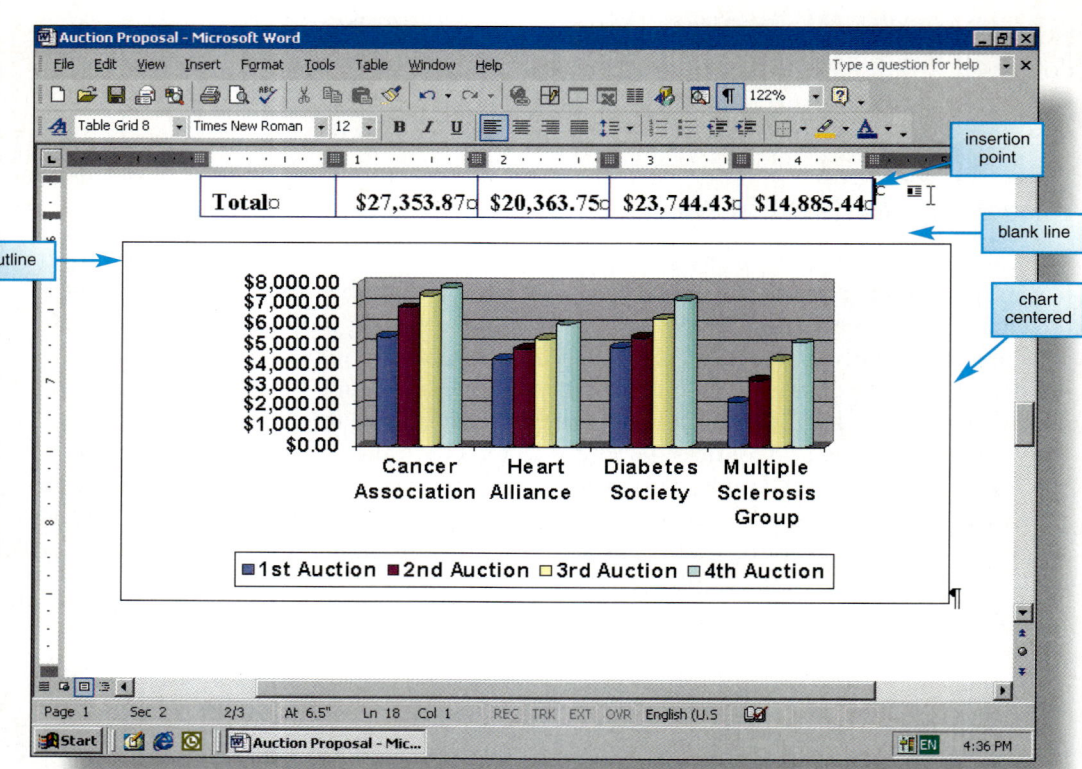

FIGURE 4-54

Word centers the chart between the left and right margins, places an outside border around the chart, and inserts a blank line above the chart (Figure 4-54).

Formatting Paragraphs and Characters

In this document, you want to ensure that a page break does not occur in the paragraph below the chart. You also want to change the bullet character in the bulleted list and emphasize the characters in the category names at the beginning of each bulleted item. The following pages illustrate each of these formatting changes.

Keeping Lines in a Paragraph Together

You want the entire paragraph of text that follows the chart to display together on the same page. That is, a page break should not occur in the middle of the paragraph. Although the paragraph already may display together in your document, if you change printers or other settings, the first few lines of the paragraph may move to display below the chart. Perform the following steps to ensure that the paragraph always displays together on the same page.

Keeping Tables Together

If you do not want a page break to occur in the middle of a table, position the insertion point in the table, click Table on the menu bar, click Table Properties, click the Row tab, remove the check mark from the Allow row to break across pages check box, and then click the OK button.

Steps: To Keep Lines Together

1 **Right-click the paragraph below the chart and then point to Paragraph on the shortcut menu.**

Word displays a shortcut menu (Figure 4-55).

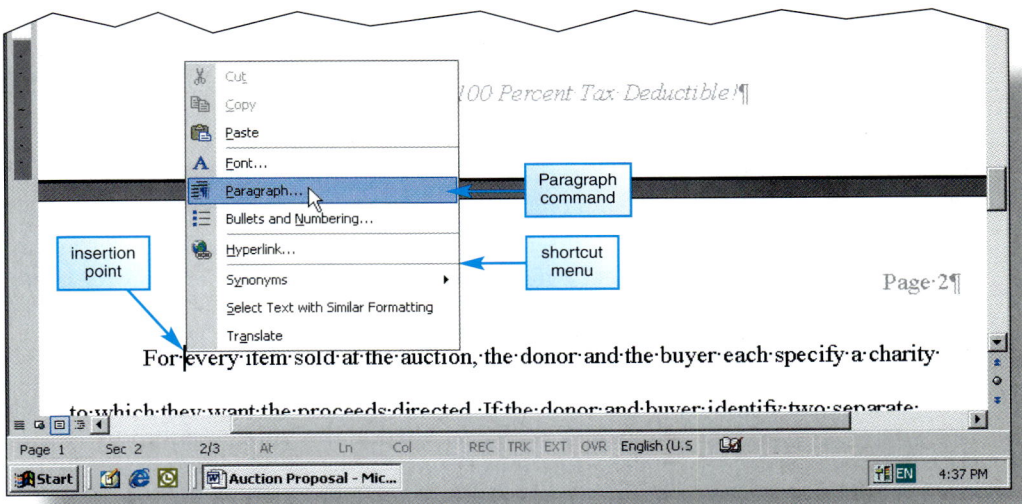

FIGURE 4-55

2 **Click Paragraph. When the Paragraph dialog box displays, if necessary, click the Line and Page Breaks tab. Place a check mark in the Keep lines together check box. Point to the OK button.**

Word displays the Paragraph dialog box (Figure 4-56). The Keep lines together check box ensures a page break does not occur within a paragraph.

3 **Click the OK button.**

Word ensures a page break does not occur in the current paragraph.

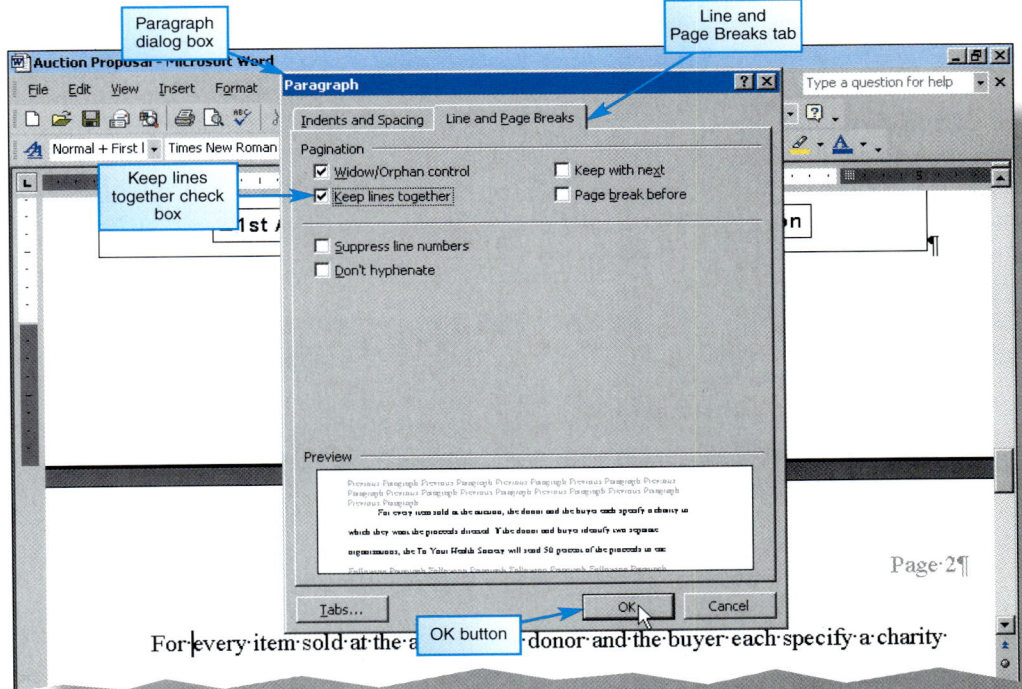

FIGURE 4-56

The options in the Line and Page Breaks tab of the Paragraph dialog box (Figure 4-56) are designed to provide you with options in how paragraphs print. The Keep lines together check box that was illustrated in the previous steps also can be used to ensure that a page break does not occur within multiple paragraphs. That is, select the paragraphs and then follow the steps shown above.

Other Ways

1. On Format menu click Paragraph, click Line and Page Breaks tab, place a check mark in Keep lines together check box, click OK button
2. In Voice Command mode, say "Format, Paragraph, Line and Page Breaks, Keep lines together, OK"

If you do not want a page break to occur between two consecutive paragraphs, you would click in the first paragraph and then place a check mark in the Keep with next check box in the Line and Page Breaks dialog box in the Paragraph dialog box. Similarly, if you want a page break to occur immediately before a paragraph, place a check mark in the Page break before check box.

A **widow** occurs when the last line of a paragraph displays by itself at the top of a page, and an **orphan** occurs when the first line of a paragraph displays by itself at the bottom of a page. Word, by default, prevents widows and orphans from occurring in a document. If, for some reason, you wanted to allow a widow or an orphan in a document, you would position the insertion point in the appropriate paragraph, display the Line and Page Breaks sheet in the Paragraph dialog box, and then remove the check mark from the Widow/Orphan control check box.

Customizing Bullets in a List

The draft of the sales proposal contains a bulleted list (shown in Figure 4-28a on page WD 4.27). To change the bullet symbol from a small, solid circle to the picture bullets shown in Figure 4-28b on page WD 4.28, use the Bullets and Numbering dialog box. Perform the following steps to change the bullets in the list to picture bullets.

Bullet Symbols

For additional bullet symbols, click Bullets and Numbering on the Format menu, click the Bulleted tab, click a bullet style, click the Customize button, click the Character button, select the desired bullet symbol, and then click the OK button.

To Add Picture Bullets to a List

1. Scroll down and then select the paragraphs in the bulleted list. Right-click the selection. Point to Bullets and Numbering on the shortcut menu (Figure 4-57).

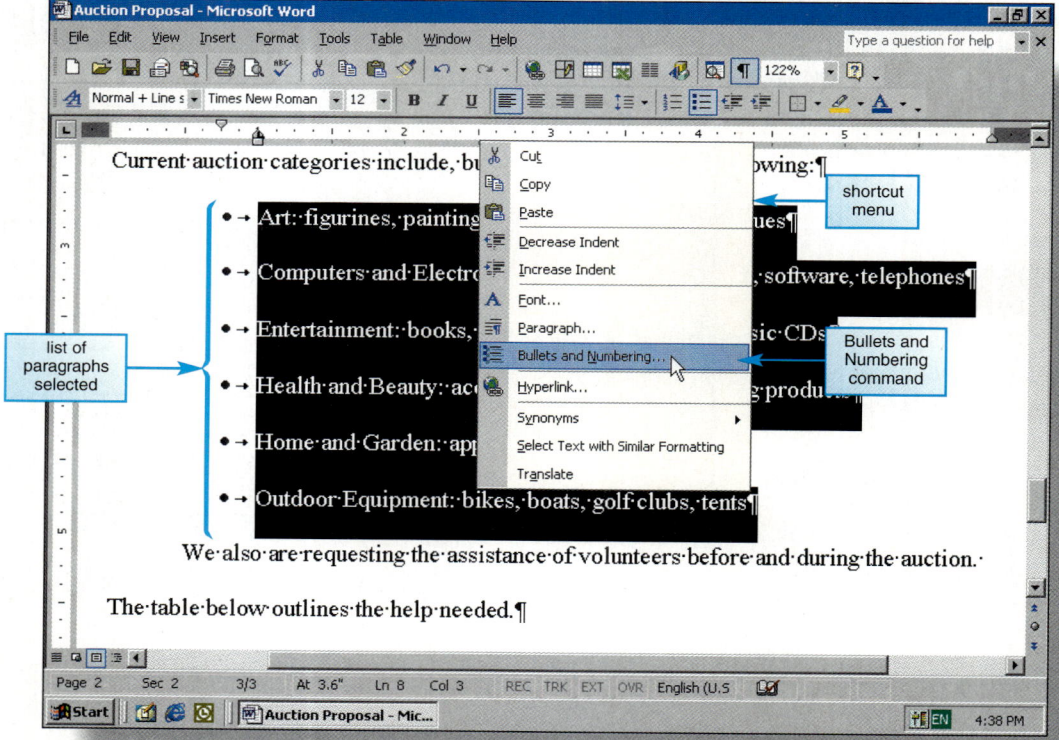

FIGURE 4-57

2 **Click Bullets and Numbering. If necessary, click the Bulleted tab when the Bullets and Numbering dialog box displays. Point to the Customize button.**

Word displays the Bullets and Numbering dialog box (Figure 4-58).

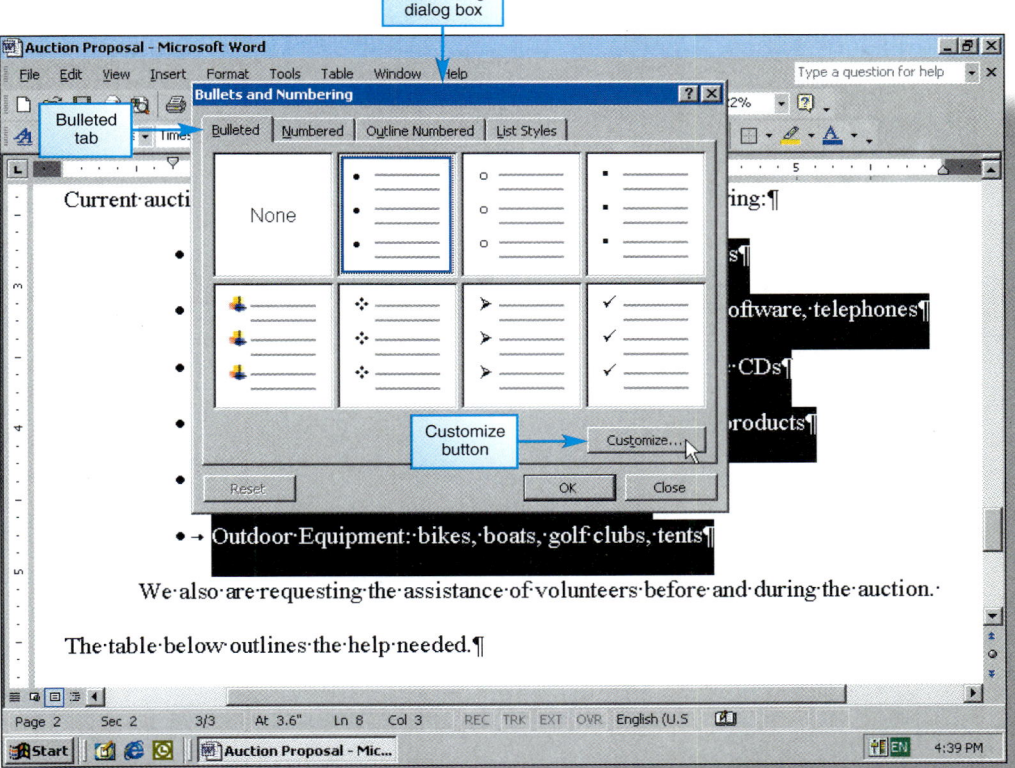

FIGURE 4-58

3 **Click the Customize button. When the Customize Bulleted List dialog box displays, click the Picture button. When the Picture Bullet dialog box displays, click the desired picture bullet (second row, third column) and then point to the OK button.**

Word displays the Picture Bullet dialog box (Figure 4-59). The selected picture bullet has a box around it, indicating it is selected.

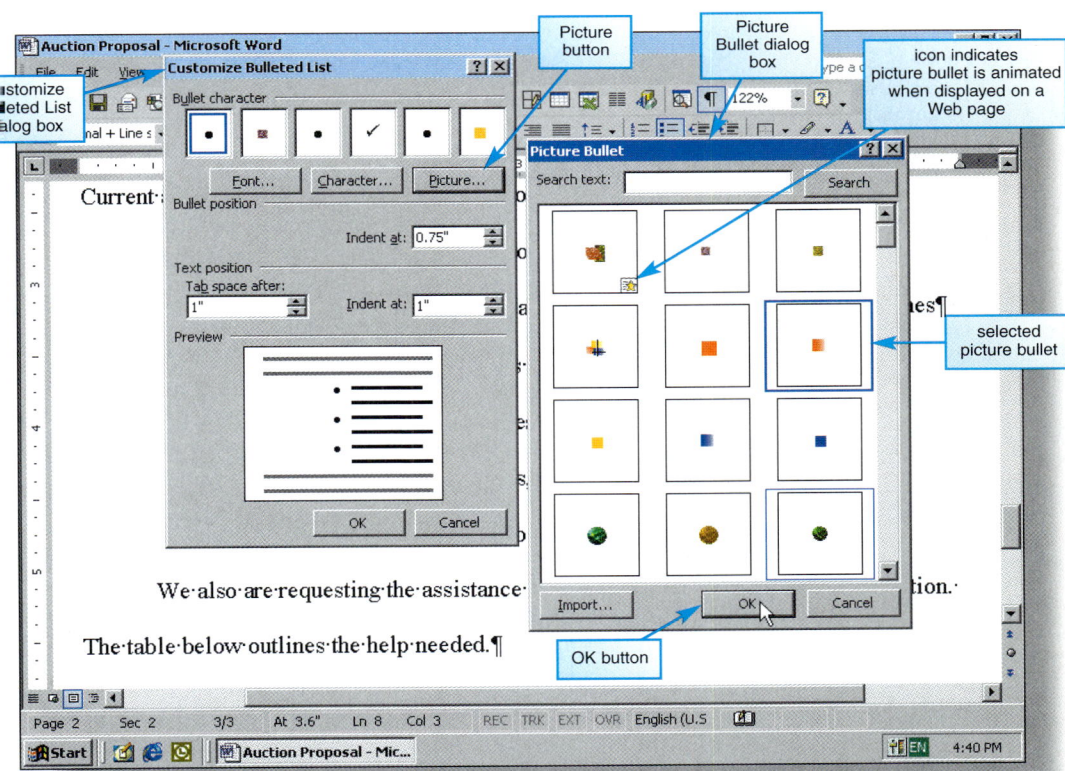

FIGURE 4-59

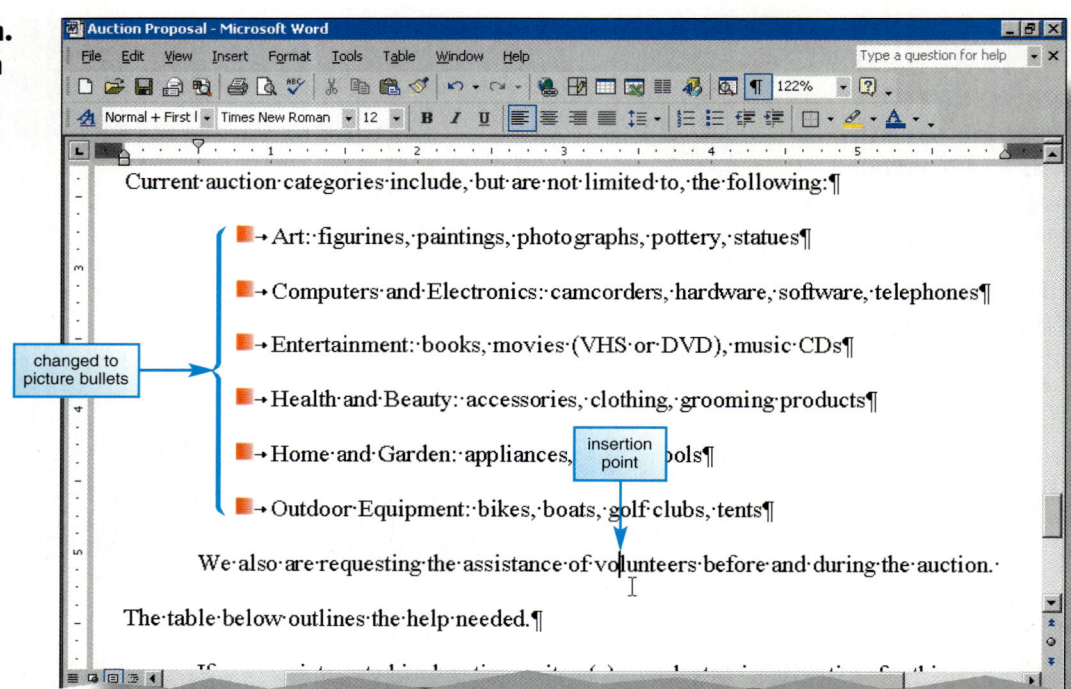

4 Click the OK button. Click the OK button in the Customize Bulleted List dialog box. When the Word window is visible again, click outside the selected list to remove the selection.

Word changes the default bullets to picture bullets (Figure 4-60).

FIGURE 4-60

1. Select list, on Format menu click Bullets and Numbering, click Bullets tab, click Customize button, click Picture button, click desired bullet style, click OK button, click OK button.
2. Select list, in Voice Command mode, say "Format, Bullets and Numbering, Bullets, Customize, Picture, [select desired bullet style], OK, OK"

Styles

If you want to create a new style that is based on text that you already have formatted, select the text and then display the Styles and Formatting task pane. When you click the New Style button, the formats of the selected text will display in the New Style dialog box.

In addition to picture bullets, the Bullets and Numbering dialog box (Figure 4-58 on the previous page) provides a number of other bullet styles. To use one of these styles, simply click the desired style in the dialog box and then click the OK button.

Creating and Applying a Character Style

The first word or phrase in each bulleted item identifies an auction category. You want these categories to be noticed by the reader. Thus, you will format them to bold, underlined, and red. These formatting changes are all character formats. As discussed in Project 1, **character formats** affect the way characters appear on the screen and in print. Character formats emphasize certain characters, words, and phrases to improve readability of a document.

You want the same character formats (bold, underlined, and red) applied to each of the category names in the bulleted list. You could select each of the category names and then format them.

A more efficient technique is to create a character style. If you decide to modify the formats of the category names at a later time, you simply change the formats assigned to the style. All characters in the document based on that style will be changed automatically. Without a style, you would have to select all the category names again and then change their format. Thus, creating a style saves time in the long run.

Recall that a **style** is a named group of formatting characteristics that you can apply to text. Whenever you create a document, Word formats the text using a particular style. The base style for a new Word document is the Normal style, which for a new installation of Word 2002 mostly likely uses 12-point Times New Roman font for characters. For the bulleted list, you also want the categories to be bold, underlined, and red.

Perform the following steps to create a character style called Auction Categories.

Steps To Create a Character Style

1 **Click the Styles and Formatting** button on the Formatting toolbar. If necessary, scroll to display the bulleted list in the document window. Click the New Style button in the Styles and Formatting task pane. When the New Style dialog box displays, **type** `Auction Categories` in the Name text box. Click the Style type box arrow and then click Character. In the New Style dialog box, click the Bold button, click the Underline button, click the Font Color button arrow, and then, if necessary, click Red. Point to the OK button.

Word displays the New Style dialog box (Figure 4-61).

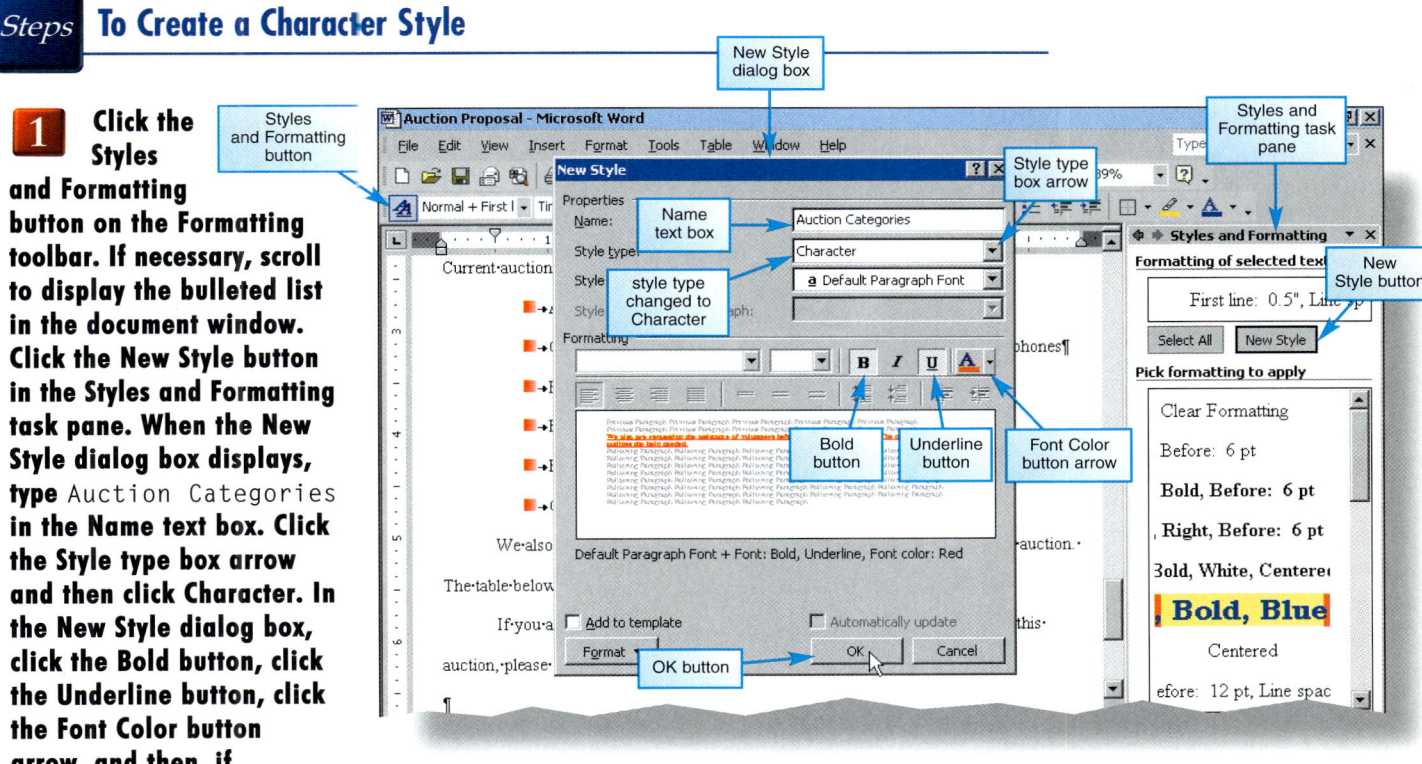

FIGURE 4-61

2 **Click the OK button.**

Word inserts the new style, Auction Categories, alphabetically in the Pick formatting to apply area in the Styles and Formatting task pane (Figure 4-62).

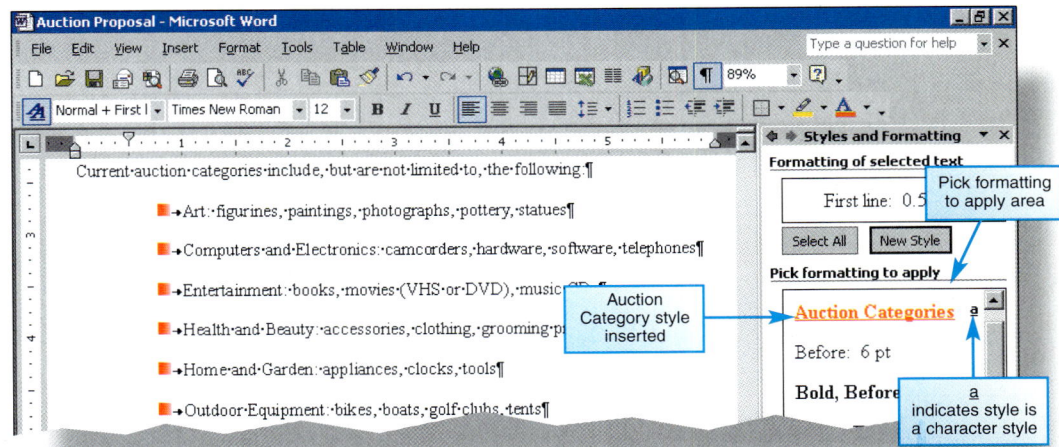

FIGURE 4-62

The next step is to apply the style to the auction category names in the bulleted list. Perform the steps on the next page to apply a style.

Other Ways

1. On Format menu click Styles and Formatting, click New Style button, define style, click OK button
2. In Voice Command mode, say "Styles and Formatting, New Style, [define style], OK"

Steps To Apply a Character Style

1 Double-click the category name, Art, to select it. Press and hold the CTRL key. Drag through the category name, Computers and Electronics; double-click the category name, Entertainment; drag through the category name, Health and Beauty; drag through the category name, Home and Garden; drag through the category name, Outdoor Equipment; and then release the CTRL key.

Word selects the nonadjacent text that is to be based on the Auction Categories style (Figure 4-63).

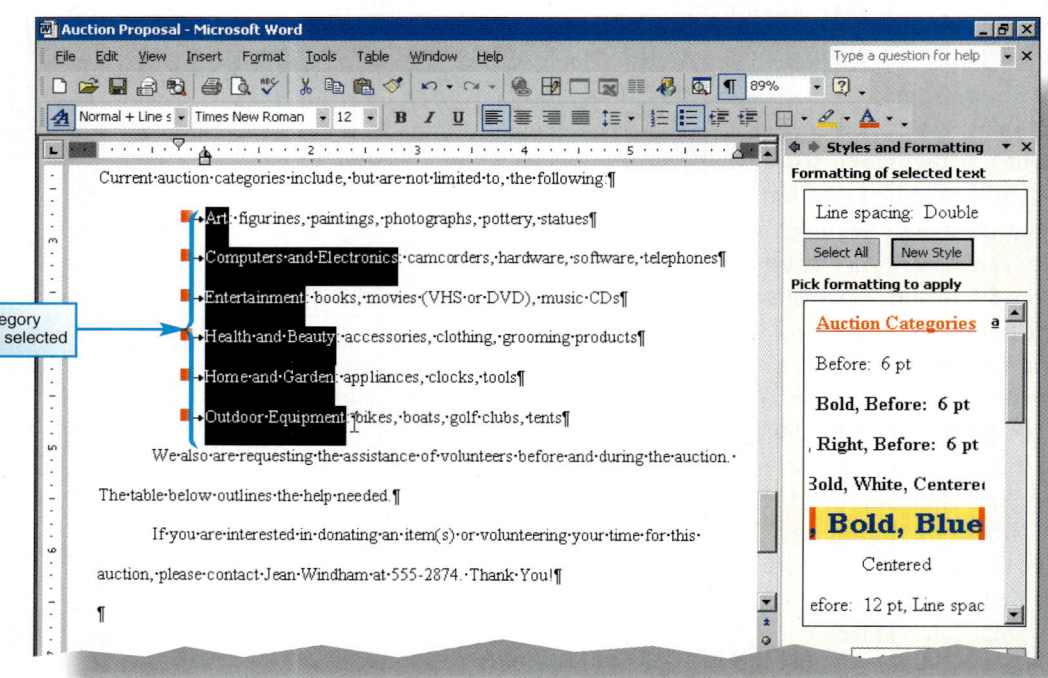

FIGURE 4-63

2 With the Styles and Formatting task pane displaying in the Word window, click Auction Categories in the Pick formatting to apply area. Click in the bulleted list to remove the selection.

Word applies the character format, Auction Categories, to the category names in the bulleted list (Figure 4-64).

3 Close the Styles and Formatting task pane by clicking its Close button.

1. Click Style box arrow on Formatting toolbar and then click style name
2. In Voice Command mode, say "Style, [select style name]"

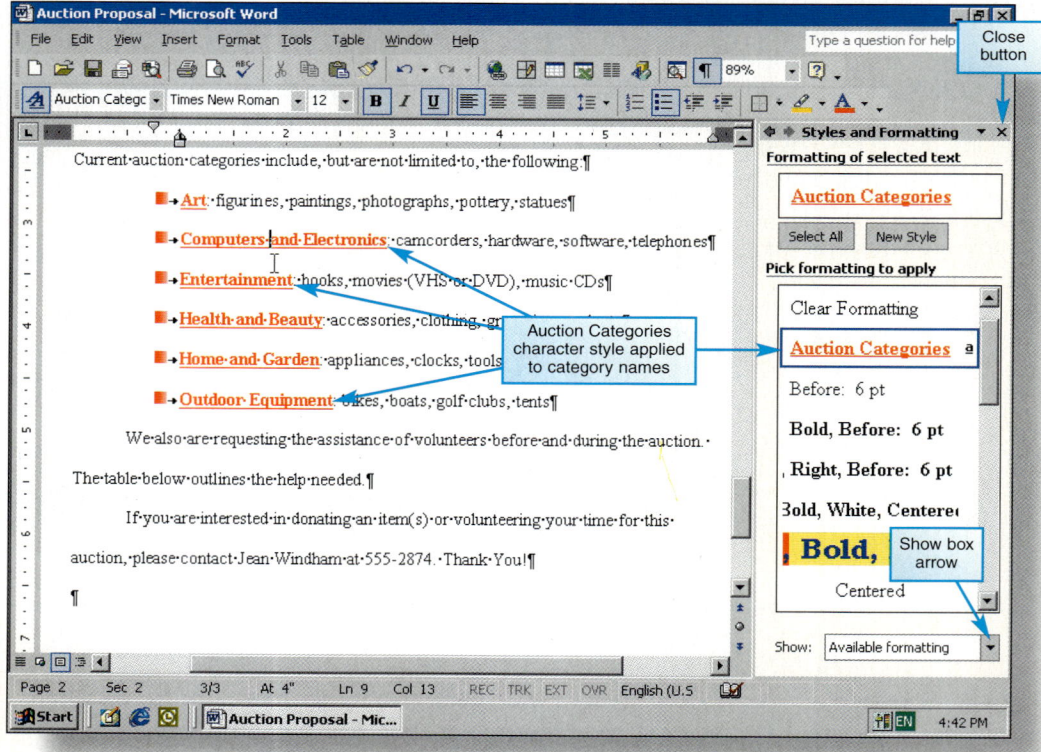

FIGURE 4-64

If a style you wish to use does not display in the Pick formatting to apply area of the Styles and Formatting task pane and you know the style was defined, click the Show box arrow in the Styles and Formatting task pane and then click All styles.

Drawing a Table

You are to insert a table to precede the last paragraph of the proposal (Figure 4-28b on page WD 4.28). As previously discussed, a Word table is a collection of rows and columns; the intersection of a row and a column is called a cell. Cells are filled with data.

When you want to create a simple table, one with the same number of rows and columns, use the Insert Table button on the Standard toolbar to create the table. To create a more complex table, use Word's **Draw Table feature**.

The table to be created at this point in the project is a complex table. It contains a varying number of columns per row. The following pages discuss how to draw the table shown in Figure 4-65.

Changing Styles

To change all text in a document from one style to another, click inside the text formatted using style you want to change. Click the Select All button in the Styles and Formatting task pane to instruct Word to select all text in the document formatted using that style. In the Pick formatting to apply list in the Styles and Formatting task pane, click the new style to apply to all the selected text.

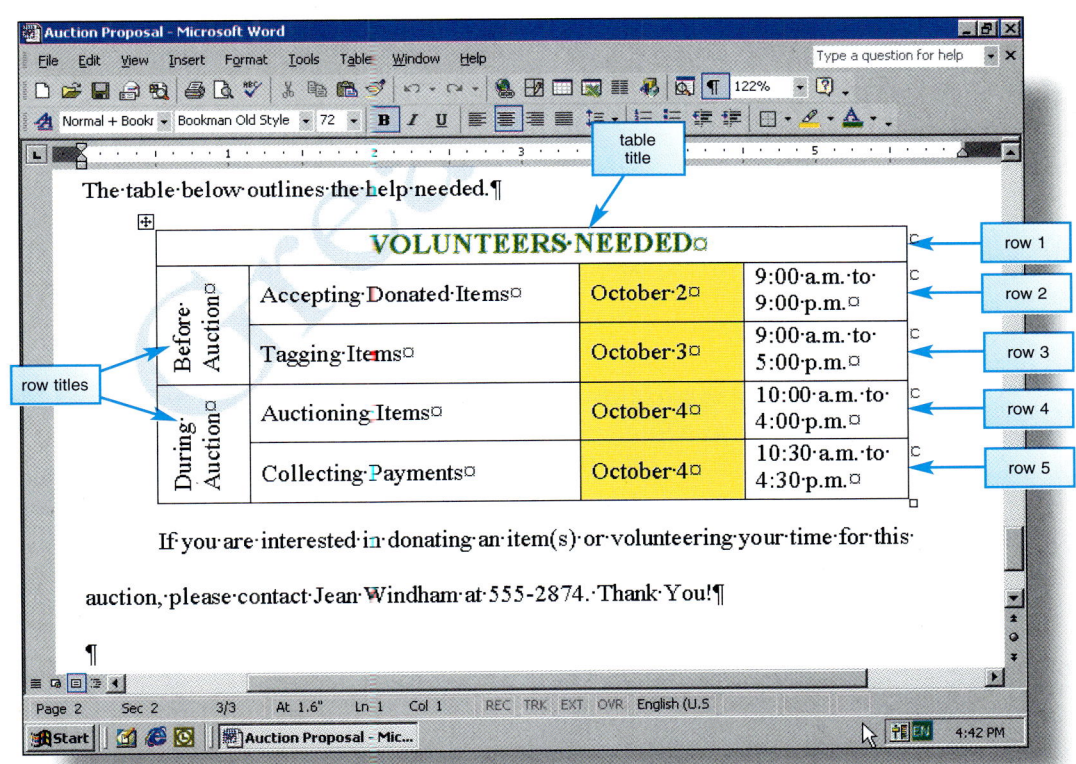

FIGURE 4-65

Draw Table

If you make a mistake while drawing a table, remember you always can click the Undo button to undo your most recent action.

Drawing an Empty Table

The first step is to draw an empty table in the document. To draw a table, you use the **Draw Table button** on the Tables and Borders toolbar. When the Draw Table button is selected, the mouse pointer shape changes to a pencil. To draw the boundary, rows, and columns of the table, you drag the pencil pointer on the screen.

Perform the steps on the next page to draw the table shown in Figure 4-65. If you make a mistake while drawing the table, remember that you can click the Undo button on the Standard toolbar to undo your most recent action.

Drawing Tables

To draw a table, the Draw Table button on the Tables and Borders toolbar must be selected (Figure 4-66 on the next page). If it is not selected, click it.

Steps: To Draw a Table

1 Scroll to and then position the insertion point at the beginning of the last paragraph (to the left of the word, If). Click the Tables and Borders button on the Standard toolbar to display the Tables and Borders toolbar. If it is not selected already, click the Draw Table button on the Tables and Borders toolbar. Move the mouse pointer, which is the shape of a pencil, into the document window to the location shown in Figure 4-66.

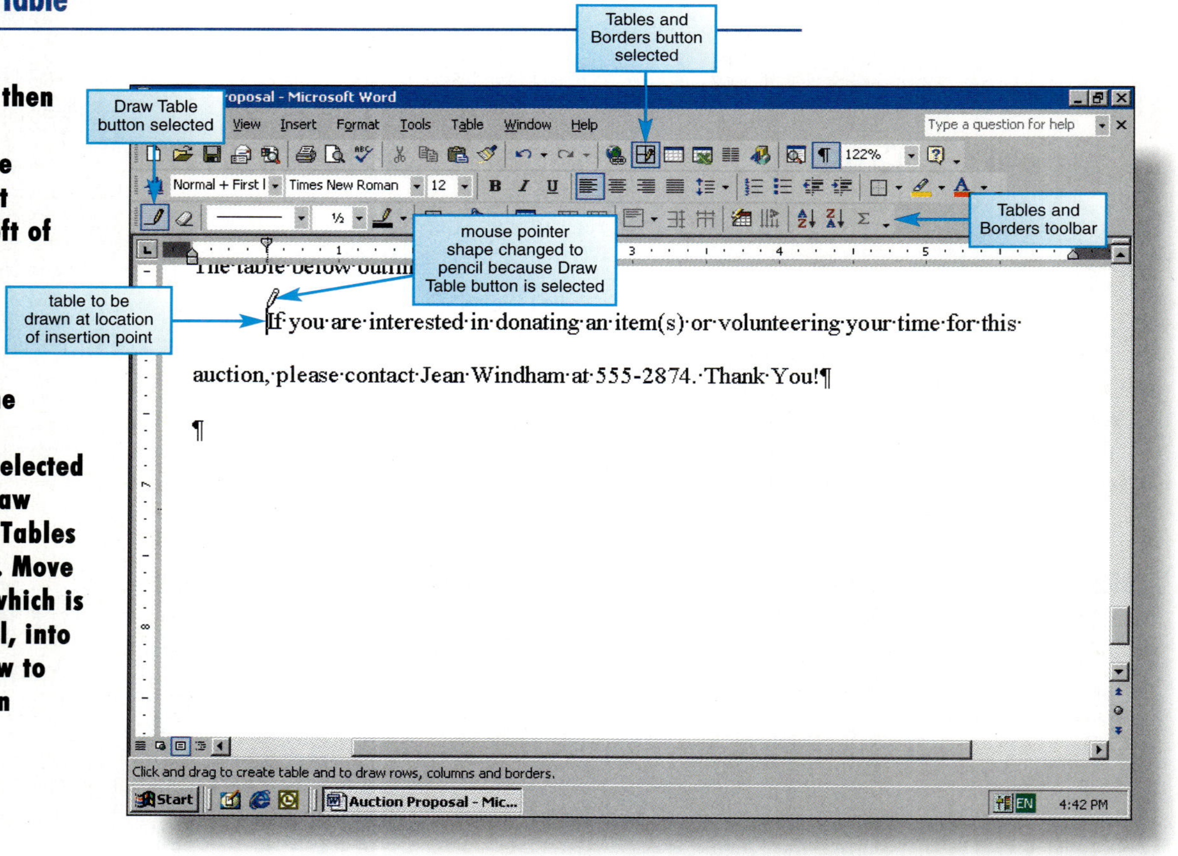

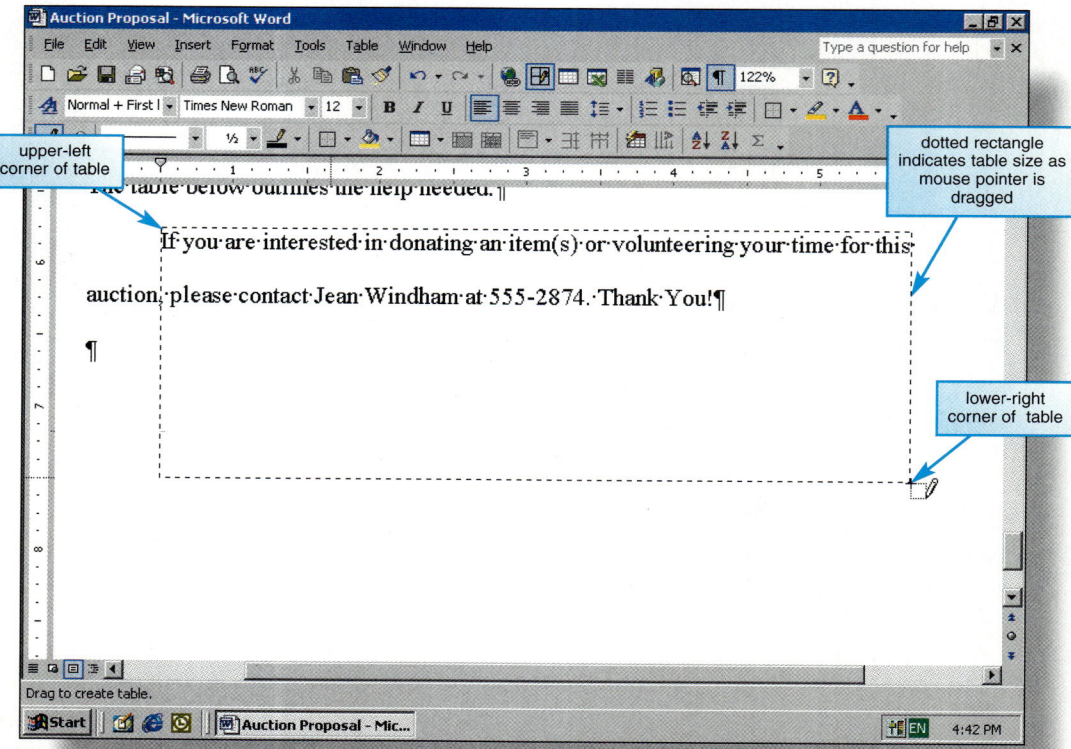

FIGURE 4-66

2 Drag the pencil pointer downward and to the right until the dotted rectangle is positioned similarly to the one shown in Figure 4-67.

Word displays a dotted rectangle that indicates the table's size (Figure 4-67).

FIGURE 4-67

Drawing a Table • WD 4.55

3 Release the mouse button. If Word wraps the text around the table, right-click the table, click Table Properties on the shortcut menu, click the Table tab, click None in the Text wrapping area, and then click the OK button.

Word draws the table border. The Outside Border button on the Tables and Borders toolbar is selected.

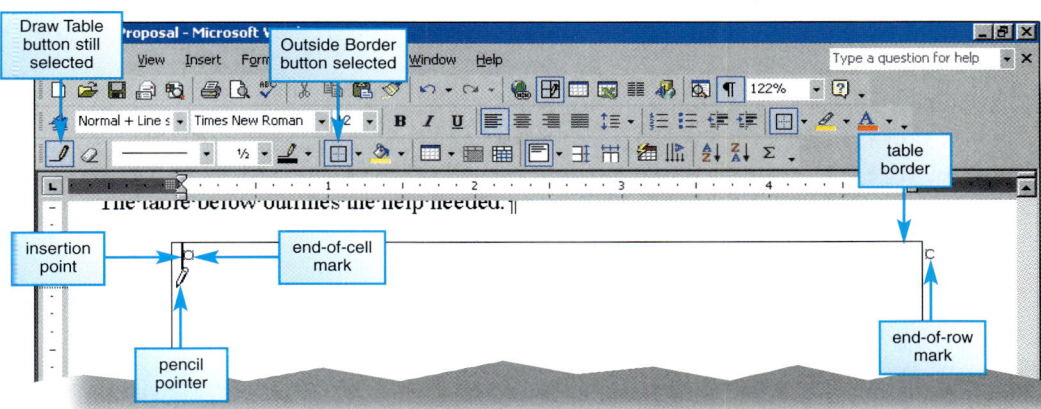

FIGURE 4-68

4 Position the pencil pointer in the table as shown in Figure 4-68.

5 Drag the pencil pointer to the right to draw a horizontal line. Position the pencil pointer as shown in Figure 4-69.

Word draws a horizontal line, which forms the bottom border of the first row in the table (Figure 4-69).

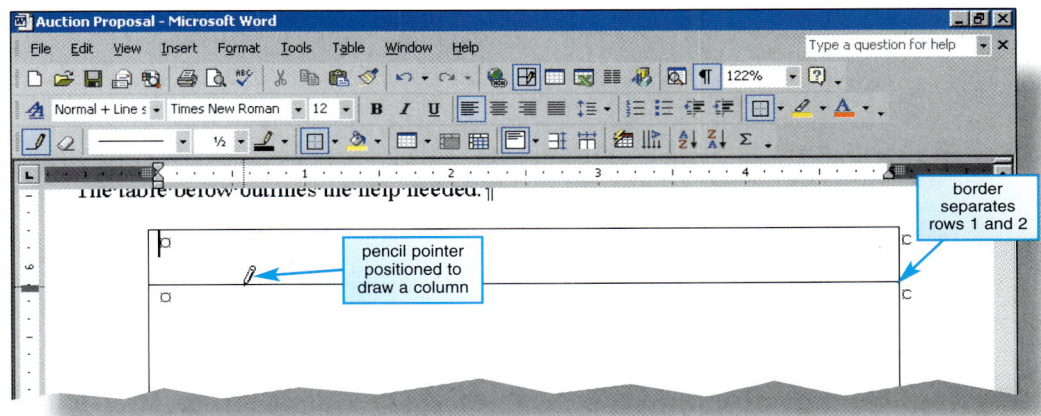

FIGURE 4-69

6 Draw three vertical lines to form the column borders, similarly to those shown in Figure 4-70.

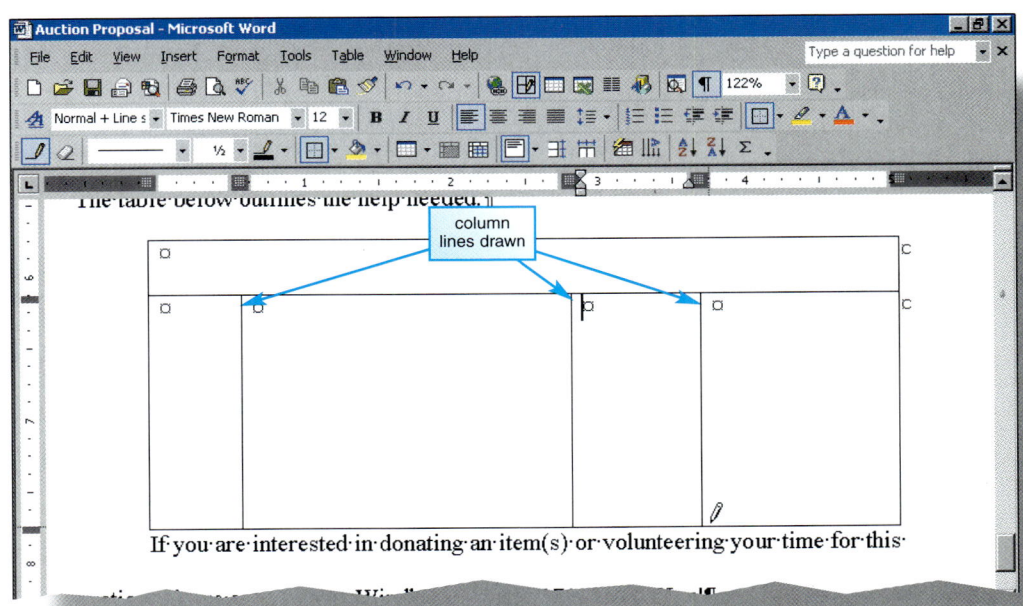

FIGURE 4-70

7 **Draw three horizontal lines to form the row borders, similarly to those shown in Figure 4-71.**

The empty table displays as shown in Figure 4-71.

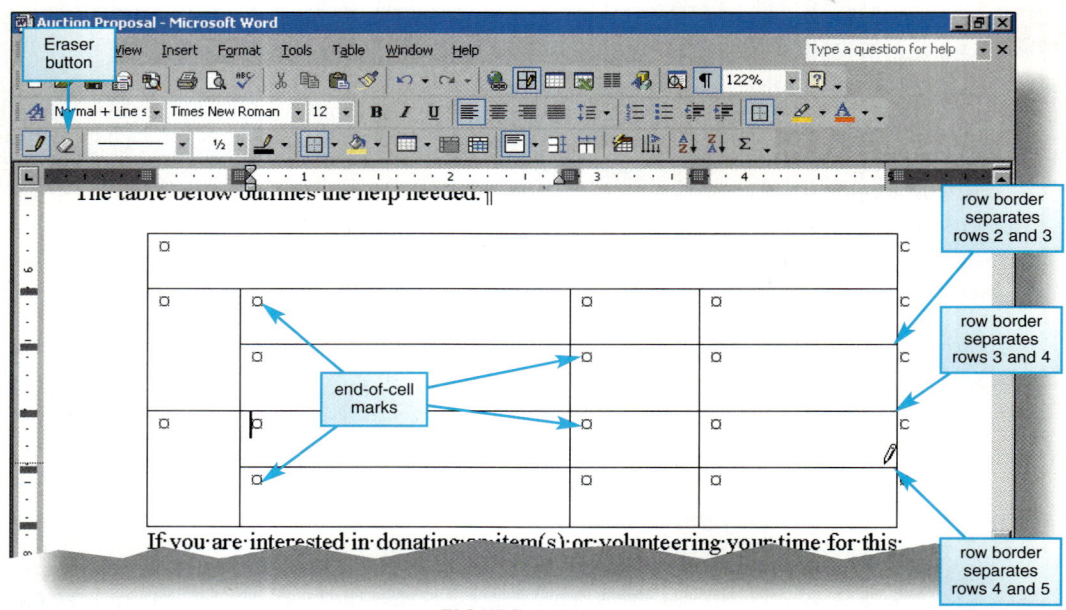

FIGURE 4-71

Other Ways

1. On Table menu click Draw Table, use pencil pointer to draw table
2. In Voice Command mode, say "Tables and Borders, [use pencil pointer to draw table]"

Table Wrapping

When you draw a table, Word may wrap the text of the document around the table. To remove the text wrapping, right-click the table, click Table Properties, click the Table tab, click None in Text wrapping area, and then click the OK button. To have Word automatically wrap text around the table, hold down the CTRL key while you draw the table.

After drawing rows and columns in the table, if you want to remove and redraw a line, click the **Eraser button** on the Tables and Borders toolbar (Figure 4-71) and then drag the mouse pointer (an eraser shape) through the line to erase. Click the Eraser button again to turn the eraser pointer off.

All Word tables that you draw have a one-half-point border, by default. To change this border, you can use the Tables and Borders toolbar, as described earlier in this project.

Notice the end-of-cell marks currently are left-aligned in each cell (Figure 4-71), which indicates the data will be left-aligned in the cells.

To format a table or data in a table, first you must select the cell(s) and then apply the appropriate formats. Selecting table text is an important function of working with Word tables. Thus, techniques to select table items are summarized in Table 4-3.

Table 4-3	Techniques for Selecting Items in a Table
ITEM TO SELECT	**ACTION**
Cell	Click the left edge of the cell.
Row	Click to the left of the row.
Column	Click the column's top gridline or border.
Cells, rows, or columns	Drag through the cells, rows, or columns.
Text in next cell	Press the TAB key.
Text in previous cell	Press SHIFT+TAB.
Entire table	Position the mouse pointer in the table and then click the table move handle.

Because you drew the table borders with the mouse, some of the rows may be varying heights. Perform the following step to make the row spacing in the table even.

Drawing a Table • WD 4.57

Steps: To Distribute Rows Evenly

1 **With the insertion point somewhere in the table, click the Distribute Rows Evenly button on the Tables and Borders toolbar.**

Word makes the height of the selected rows uniform (Figure 4-72).

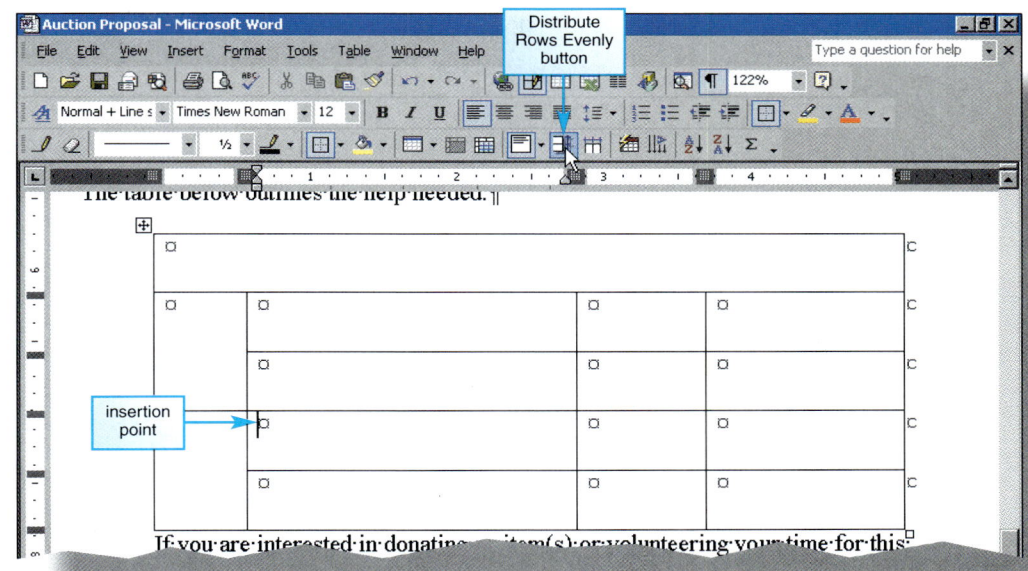

FIGURE 4-72

Other Ways

1. Select cells, on Table menu point to AutoFit, click Distribute Rows Evenly on AutoFit submenu
2. Drag row boundaries (borders) on table or Table Row markers on vertical ruler
3. In Voice Command mode, say "Distribute Rows Evenly"

You want the last two columns in the table to be the same width. Because you drew the borders of these columns, they may be varying widths. Perform the following steps to evenly size these columns.

Steps: To Distribute Columns Evenly

1 **Point to the left of the cell shown in Figure 4-73 until the mouse pointer changes to a right-pointing solid arrow.**

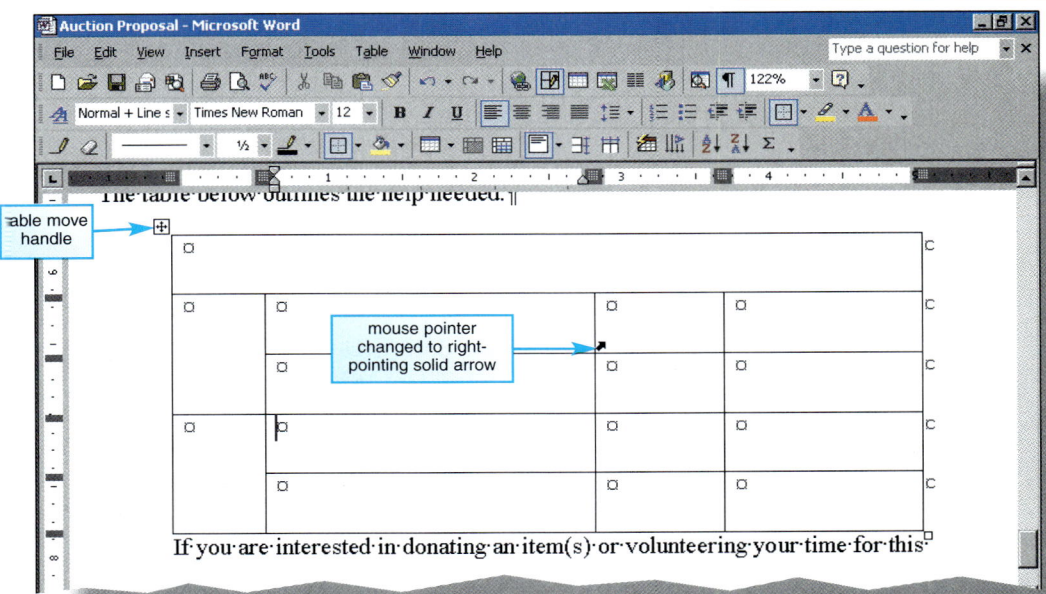

FIGURE 4-73

2 Drag through the eight cells shown in Figure 4-74 and then click the Distribute Columns Evenly button on the Tables and Borders toolbar.

Word applies uniform widths to the selected columns (Figure 4-74).

3 Click inside the table to remove the selection.

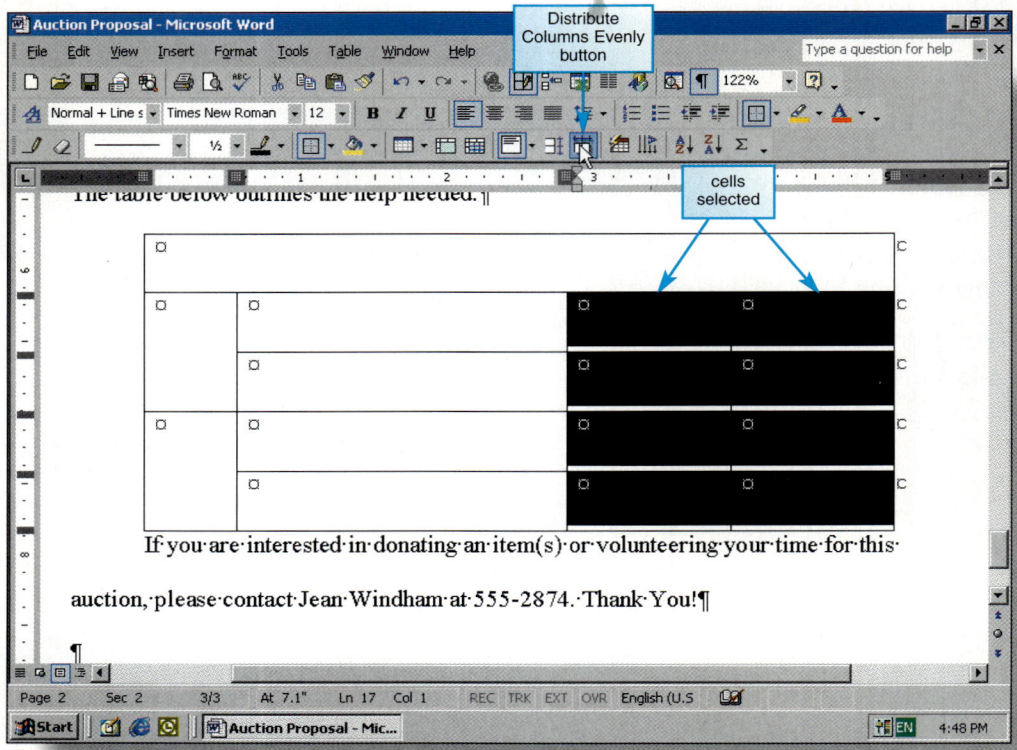

FIGURE 4-74

Other Ways

1. Select cells, on Table menu point to AutoFit, click Distribute Columns Evenly on AutoFit submenu
2. Drag row boundaries (borders) on table
3. Drag Table Column markers on horizontal ruler
4. In Voice Command mode, say "Distribute Columns Evenly"

More About

Line Widths and Borders

To change the thickness of table borders, click the Line Weight box arrow on the Tables and Borders toolbar and then click the desired weight. To display both an outside border, as well as a border between rows and columns, click the Outside Border button arrow and then click All Borders.

Single-Space the Table Contents

You want the data you type within the cells to be single-spaced, instead of double-spaced. Perform the following steps to single-space the table cells.

TO SINGLE-SPACE TABLE CONTENTS

1 Position the mouse pointer in the table to display the table move handle in the upper-left corner of the table (shown in Figure 4-73 on the previous page). Position the mouse pointer on the table move handle and then click to select the table.

2 With the entire table selected, press CTRL+1.

3 Click anywhere to remove the selection in the table.

Word single-spaces the cells in the table. The size of the table does not change.

When you enter data that wraps within a cell, it will be single-spaced instead of double-spaced.

Entering Data into the Table

The next step is to enter the data into the table. To advance from one column to the next, press the TAB key. To advance from one row to the next, also press the TAB key; do not press the ENTER key. Use the ENTER key to begin a new paragraph within a cell.

Perform the following steps to enter the data into the table.

TO ENTER DATA INTO A TABLE

1. Click in the first cell of the table. Click the Center button on the Formatting toolbar.
2. Type VOLUNTEERS NEEDED and then press the TAB key.
3. Type Before Auction and then press the TAB key. Type Accepting Donated Items and then press the TAB key. Type October 2 and then press the TAB key. Type 9:00 a.m. to 9:00 p.m. and then press the TAB key twice. Type Tagging Items and then press the TAB key. Type October 3 and then press the TAB key. Type 9:00 a.m. to 5:00 p.m. and then press the TAB key.
4. Type During Auction and then press the TAB key. Type Auctioning Items and then press the TAB key. Type October 4 and then press the TAB key. Type 10:00 a.m. to 4:00 p.m. and then press the TAB key twice. Type Collecting Payments and then press the TAB key. Type October 4 and then press the TAB key. Type 10:30 a.m. to 4:30 p.m.

The table data is entered (Figure 4-75).

Nested Tables

You can create a table within a table, or a nested table, using the Drawing toolbar. To do this click the Draw Table button on the Tables and Borders toolbar to display the pencil pointer. Draw the new table inside the current table. When you are finished, click the Draw Table button to turn off the pencil pointer.

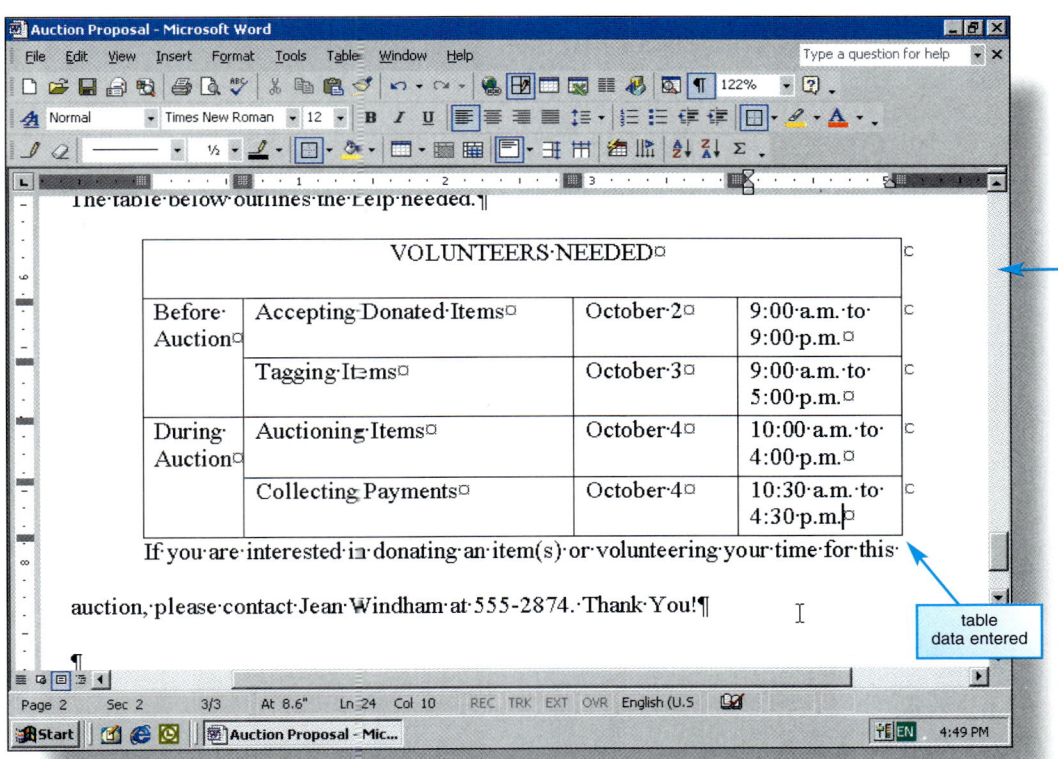

FIGURE 4-75

The next step is to rotate the row heading text, Before Auction and During Auction, so it displays vertically instead of horizontally.

Formatting the Table

The data you enter in cells displays horizontally. You can change the text so it displays vertically. Changing the direction of text adds variety to your tables.

Perform the steps on the next page to display the row heading text vertically.

Quick Reference

For a table that lists how to complete tasks covered in this book using the mouse, menu, shortcut menu, and keyboard, see the Quick Reference Summary at the back of this book or visit the Shelly Cashman Series Office XP Web page (scsite.com/offxp/qr.htm) and then click Microsoft Word 2002.

Steps To Vertically Display Text in a Cell

1 Select the row heading text cells containing the words, Before Auction and During Auction by dragging through them. Point to the Change Text Direction button on the Tables and Borders toolbar.

The cells to be formatted are selected (Figure 4-76).

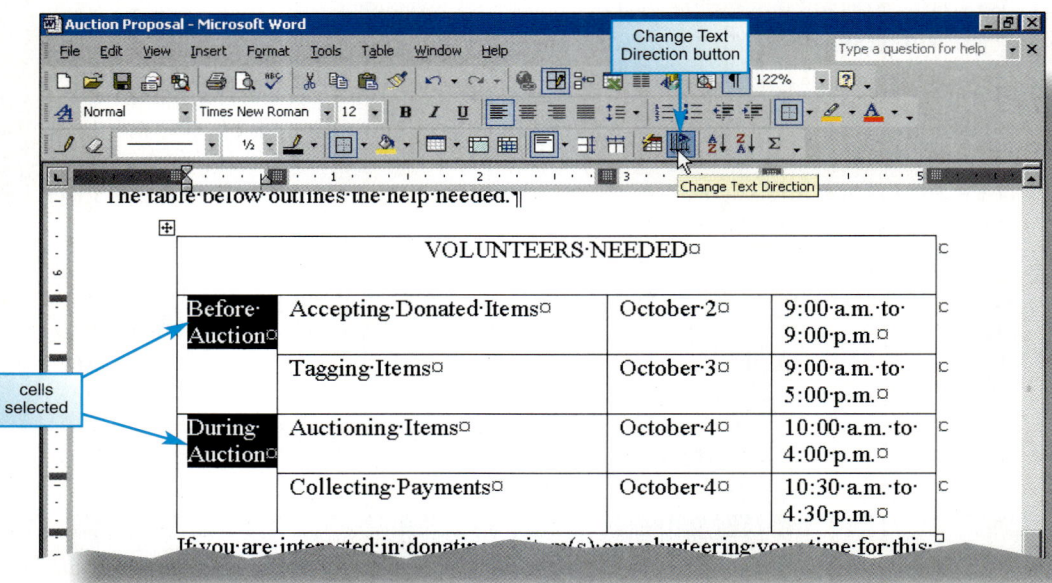

FIGURE 4-76

2 Click the Change Text Direction button twice.

Word displays the text vertically so that it reads from bottom to top (Figure 4-77).

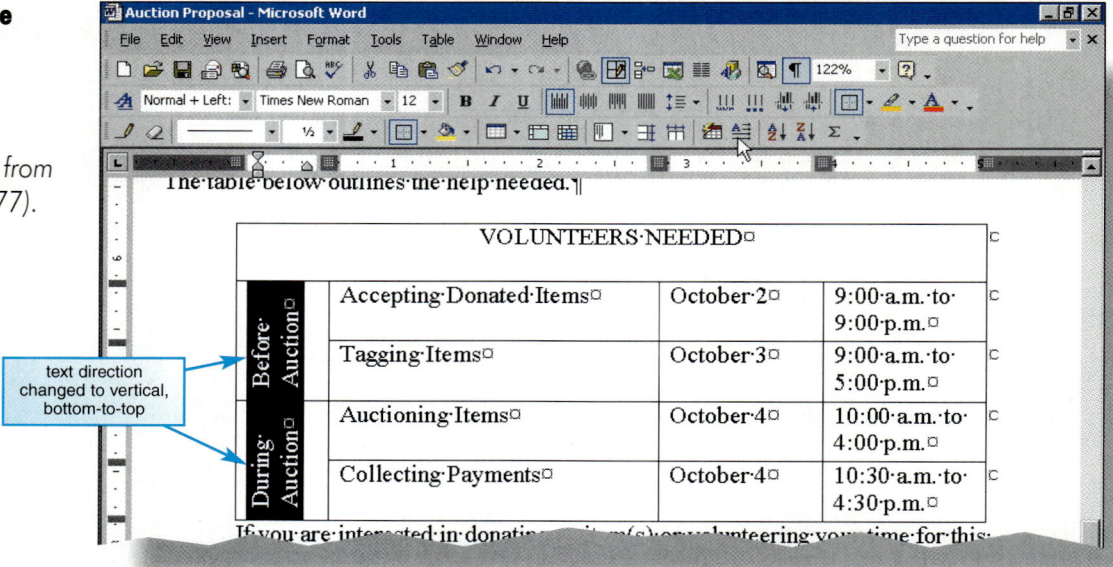

FIGURE 4-77

The first time you click the Change Text Direction button, Word displays the text vertically so it reads from top to bottom. The second time you click the Change Text Direction button, Word displays the text vertically so it reads from bottom to top (Figure 4-77). If you click the button a third time, the text would display horizontally again.

The title of the table should be 14-point Times New Roman bold green font. Perform the following steps to format the table title.

TO FORMAT THE TABLE TITLE

1. Drag through the table title, VOLUNTEERS NEEDED.
2. Click the Font Size button arrow on the Formatting toolbar and then click 14. Click the Bold button on the Formatting toolbar. Click the Font Color button arrow and then click Green.
3. Click in the first row to remove the selection.

Word formats the table title (shown in Figure 4-78).

You also want to narrow the height of the row containing the table title. Perform the following steps to change a row's height.

Steps: To Change Row Height

1 **Point to the bottom border of the first row. When the mouse pointer changes to a double two-headed arrow, drag up until the proposed row border looks like Figure 4-78.**

When you release the mouse button, Word will resize the row according to the location to which you dragged the row border.

2 **Release the mouse button.**

Word resizes the row (shown in Figure 4-79 on the next page).

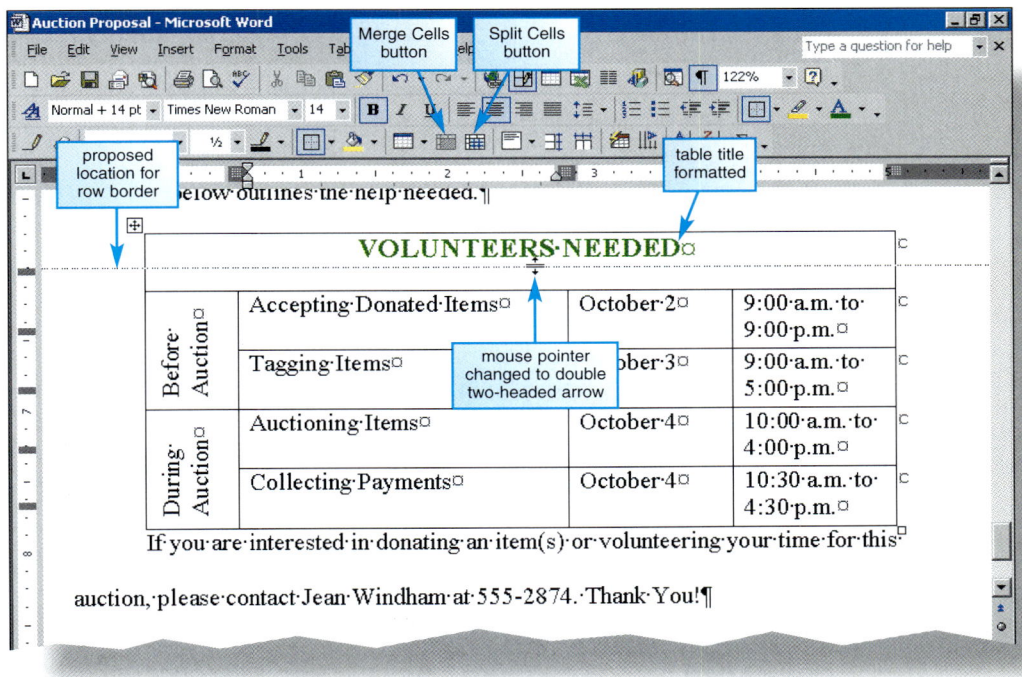

FIGURE 4-78

Microsoft Certification

The Microsoft Office User Specialist (MOUS) Certification program provides an opportunity for you to obtain a valuable industry credential — proof that you have the Word 2002 skills required by employers. For more information, see Appendix E or visit the Shelly Cashman Series MOUS Web page at scsite.com/offxp/cert.htm.

Other Ways

1. On Table menu click Table Properties, click Row tab, enter row height in Specify height text box, click OK button
2. Right-click row, click Table Properties on shortcut menu, click Row tab, enter row height in Specify height text box, click OK button
3. In Voice Command mode, say "Table, Table Properties, Row, OK"

If you wanted to change the width of a column, you would drag the column border similarly to the way you dragged the row border in the previous steps.

If you wanted to merge two or more cells into a single cell, you would select the cells and then click the Merge Cells button on the Tables and Borders toolbar. By contrast, you can split a single cell into one or more cells by clicking the cell and then clicking the Split Cells button on the Tables and Borders toolbar. When the Split Cells dialog box displays, enter the number of columns and rows you want the cell to split and then click the OK button.

The next step is to change the alignment of the data in the second and third columns. In addition to aligning text horizontally in a cell (left, centered, or right) by clicking the appropriate button on the Formatting toolbar, you can center it vertically within a cell using the Align button arrow on the Tables and Borders toolbar. Perform the steps on the next page to align data in cells.

Steps To Align Data in Cells

1 Select the cells in the second and third columns of the table by dragging through them. Click the Align button arrow on the Tables and Borders toolbar. Point to Align Center Left.

Word displays a list of cell alignment options (Figure 4-79). Align Center Left is selected.

2 Click Align Center Left.

Word changes the alignment of the selected cells to center left (shown in Figure 4-80).

Other Ways

1. In Voice Command mode, say "Align, Center Left"

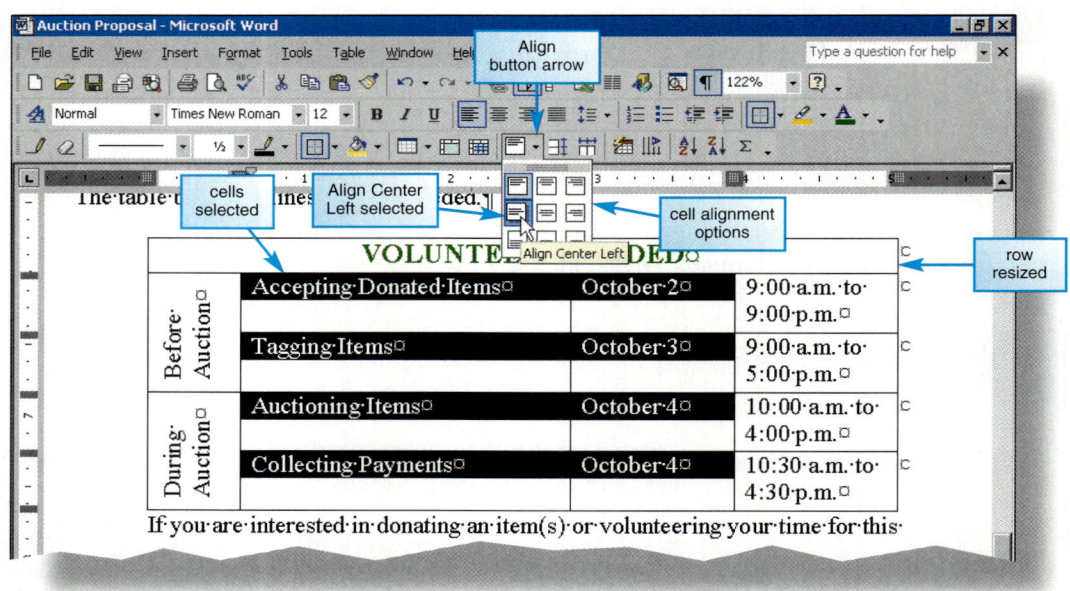

FIGURE 4-79

Notice in Figure 4-79 that when you click the Align button arrow on the Tables and Borders toolbar, Word provides several cell alignment options. Table 4-4 illustrates the various alignment options.

The next step is to shade cells in the third column in the table light yellow. Earlier in this project, you shaded some characters on the title page in light yellow. Thus, the Shading Color button already displays light yellow on its face. To shade the cells the same color, select the cells and then click the Shading Color button, as described in these steps.

TO SHADE TABLE CELLS

1 Select the four cells in the third column that contain the October date.

2 Point to the Shading Color button on the Tables and Borders toolbar (Figure 4-80).

3 Click the Shading Color button. (If necessary, click the Shading Color button arrow and then click Light Yellow.)

4 Click in the selected cells to remove the selection.

5 Click the Tables and Borders button on the Standard toolbar to remove the Tables and Borders toolbar from the screen.

Word shades the cells in light yellow (shown in Figure 4-81).

Table 4-4 Cell Alignment Options

Align Top Left	October 2		
Align Top Center		October 2	
Align Top Right			October 2
Align Center Left	October 2		
Align Center		October 2	
Align Center Right			October 2
Align Bottom Left	October 2		
Align Bottom Center		October 2	
Align Bottom Right			October 2

Drawing a Table • WD 4.63

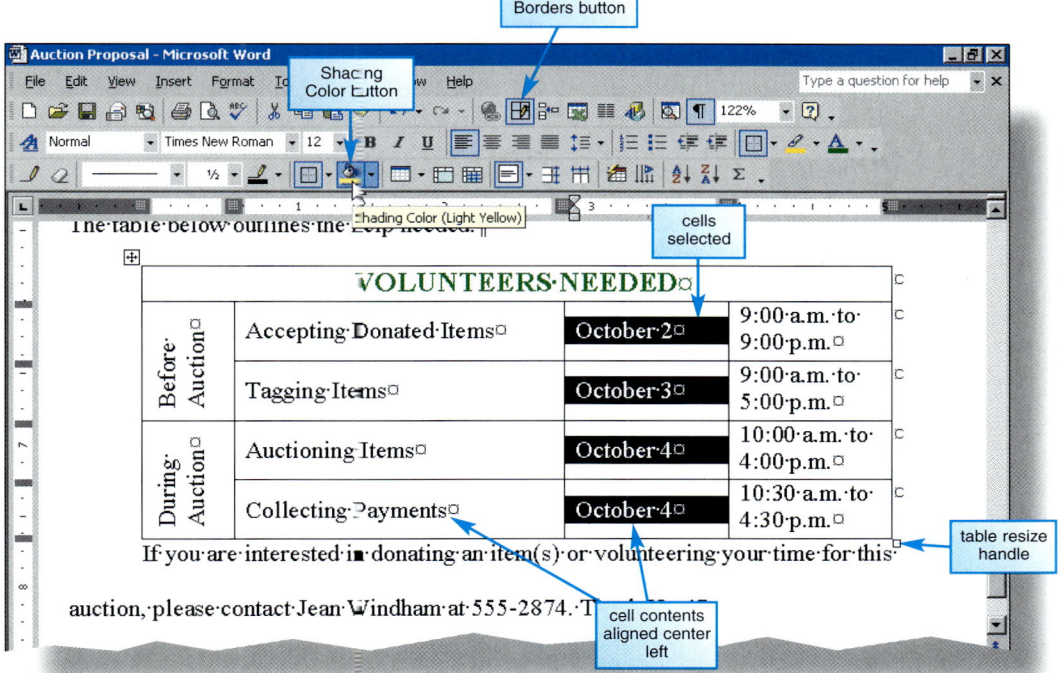

FIGURE 4-80

The final step in formatting the table is to add a blank line between the table and the paragraph below it, as described in the following step.

TO ADD A BLANK LINE ABOVE A PARAGRAPH

1. Position the insertion point in the last paragraph of the proposal and then press CTRL+0 (the numeral zero).

Word adds a blank line above the paragraph (Figure 4-81).

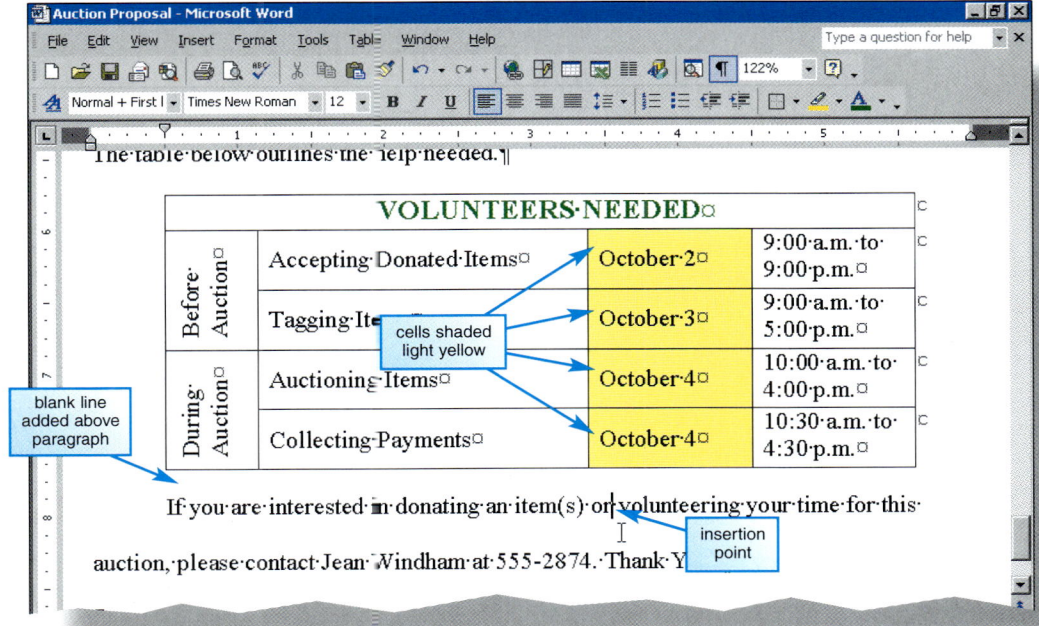

FIGURE 4-81

More About

Shading

To remove shading from a cell(s), select the cell(s), click the Shading Color button arrow on the Tables and Borders toolbar, and then click No Fill on the palette.

More About

Blank Lines

You can use menus instead of using shortcut keys to add a blank line above a paragraph. Click Format on the menu bar, click Paragraph, click the Indents and Spacing tab, change the Before text box in the Spacing area to 12 pt, and then click the OK button. To add a blank line after a paragraph, change the After text box in the Spacing area to 12 pt.

If the last paragraph spills onto the next page, then make the table smaller so the paragraph fits at the bottom of page. To do this, drag the table resize handle (shown in Figure 4-80 on the previous page) that displays in the lower-right corner of the table inward.

More About

Watermarks

To create a picture watermark, click Picture watermark in the Printed Watermark dialog box, click the Select Picture button, locate the picture, and then click the OK button in the Printed Watermark dialog box.

Creating a Watermark

A **watermark** is text or a graphic that displays on top of or behind the text in a document. For example, a catalog may print the words, Sold Out, on top of sold-out items. A product manager may want the word, Draft, to print behind his or her first draft of a five-year plan. Some companies use their logos or other graphics as watermarks on documents to add visual appeal to the document.

In this project, you would like the words, Great Cause, to display on the pages of the proposal. Perform the following steps to create this watermark.

Steps To Create a Text Watermark

1. **Click Format on the menu bar, point to Background, and then point to Printed Watermark (Figure 4-82).**

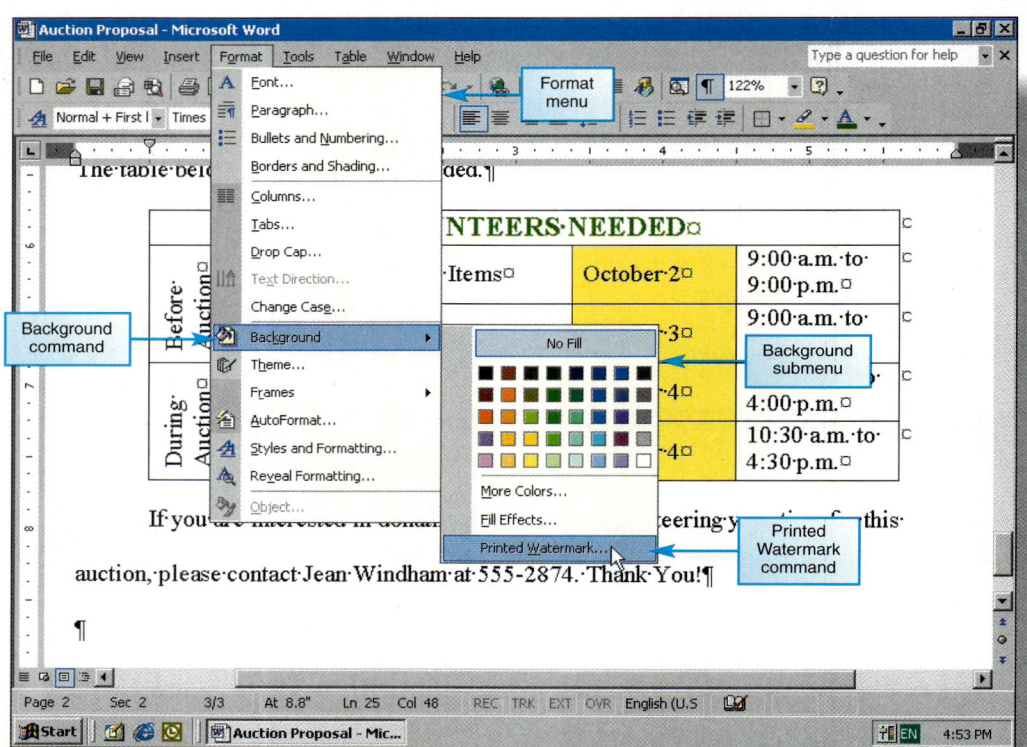

FIGURE 4-82

2 **Click Printed Watermark. When the Printed Watermark dialog box displays, click Text watermark. Drag through the text in the Text text box to select it. Type** Great Cause **in the Text text box. Click the Color box arrow and then click Pale Blue. If necessary, click Diagonal. Point to the OK button.**

Word displays the Printed Watermark dialog box (Figure 4-83). The Semitransparent setting adjusts the brightness and contrast so the text displays faded.

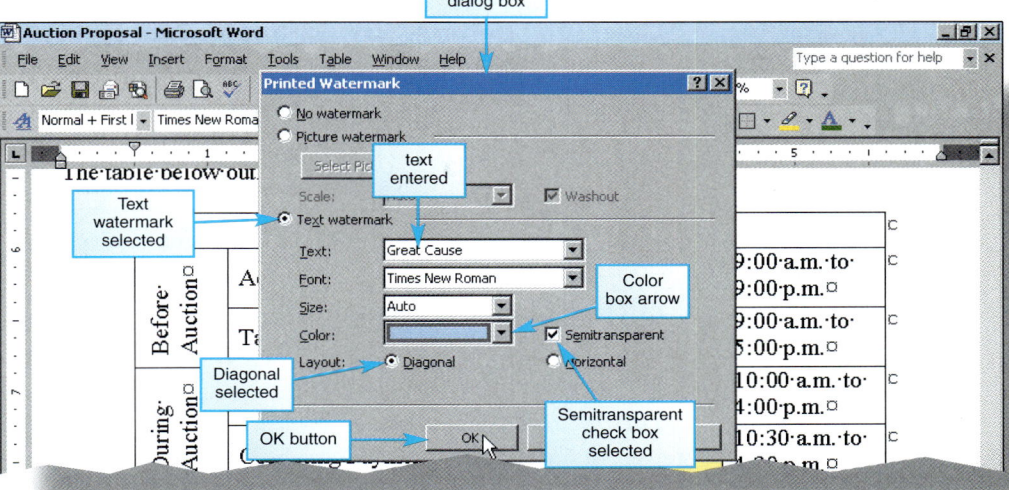

FIGURE 4-83

3 **Click the OK button.**

The watermark displays faded behind the text of the proposal (shown in Figure 4-84).

If you want to remove a watermark, click No watermark in the Printed Watermark dialog box (Figure 4-83). To see how the watermark looks in the entire document, view the document in print preview, as described in the following steps.

> **Other Ways**
>
> 1. In Voice Command mode, say "Format, Background, Printed Watermark, [enter settings], OK"

TO PRINT PREVIEW A DOCUMENT

1 Click the Print Preview button on the Standard toolbar. If necessary, click the Multiple Pages button on the Print Preview toolbar and then click the third icon in the first row of the grid (1 × 3 Pages) to display all three pages of the proposal as shown in Figure 4-84.

2 When finished viewing the document, click the Close Preview button on the Print Preview toolbar.

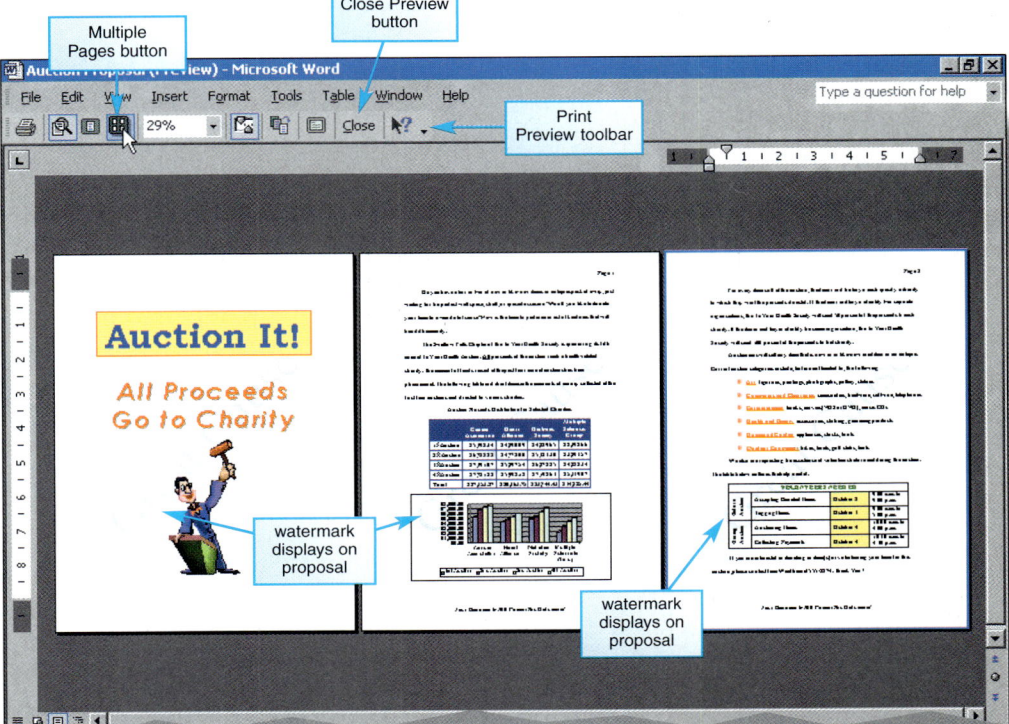

FIGURE 4-84

Printing

If you want to save ink, print faster, or decrease printer overrun errors, print a draft. Click File on the menu bar and then click Print. Click the Options button, place a check mark in the Draft output check box, and then click the OK button in each dialog box.

Checking Spelling, Saving Again, and Printing the Sales Proposal

Perform the following steps to check the spelling of the document, save the document, and then print the document.

TO CHECK SPELLING, SAVE, AND PRINT THE DOCUMENT

1. Click the Spelling and Grammar button on the Standard toolbar. Correct any misspelled words.
2. Click the Save button on the Standard toolbar.
3. Click the Print button on the Standard toolbar.

The document prints as shown in Figure 4-1 on page 4.05.

Reveal Formatting

To format selected text similarly to the text that surrounds it, select the text and then display the Reveal Formatting task pane. Point in the Selected text text box, click the box arrow to its right, and then click Apply Formatting of Surrounding Text.

Revealing Formatting

Sometimes, when you review a document, you want to know what formats were applied to certain text items. For example, you may wonder what font, font size, font color, border size, border color, or shading color you used on the first line of the title page. To display formatting applied to text, use the **Reveal Formatting task pane**. Perform the following steps to reveal formatting.

 To Reveal Formatting

1. **Press CTRL+HOME to position the insertion point in the first line of the document, Auction It! Click Format on the menu bar and then point to Reveal Formatting (Figure 4-85).**

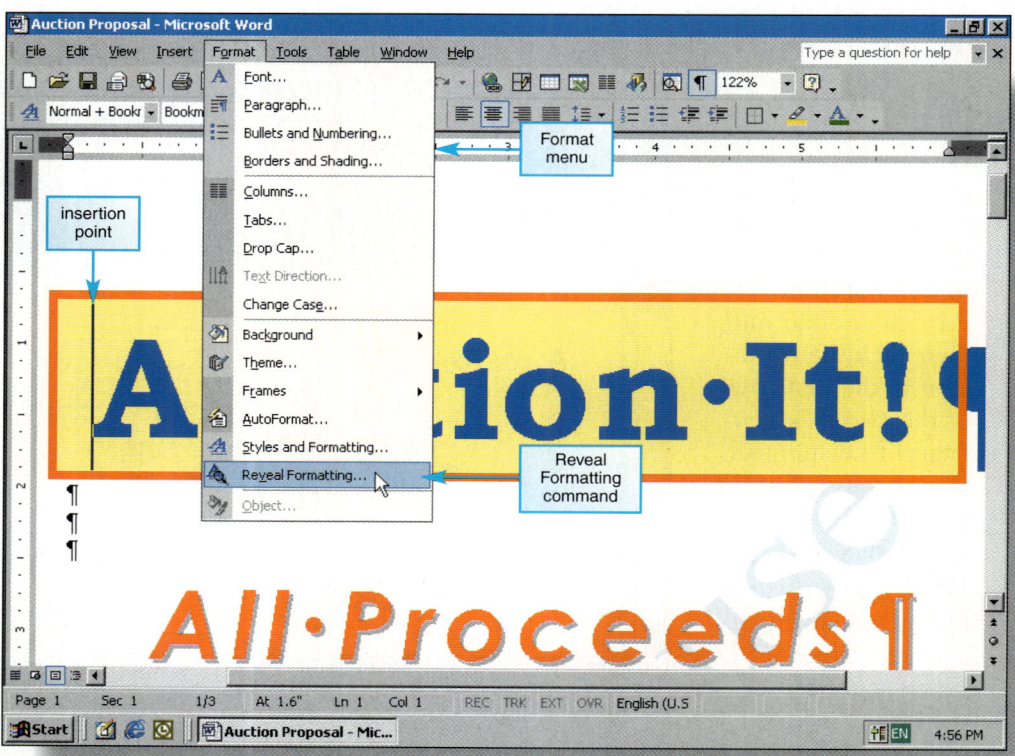

FIGURE 4-85

2 **Click Reveal Formatting.**

Word displays the Reveal Formatting task pane (Figure 4-86). The Reveal Formatting task pane shows formatting applied to the location of the insertion point.

3 **Click the Close button on the Reveal Formatting task pane to close the task pane.**

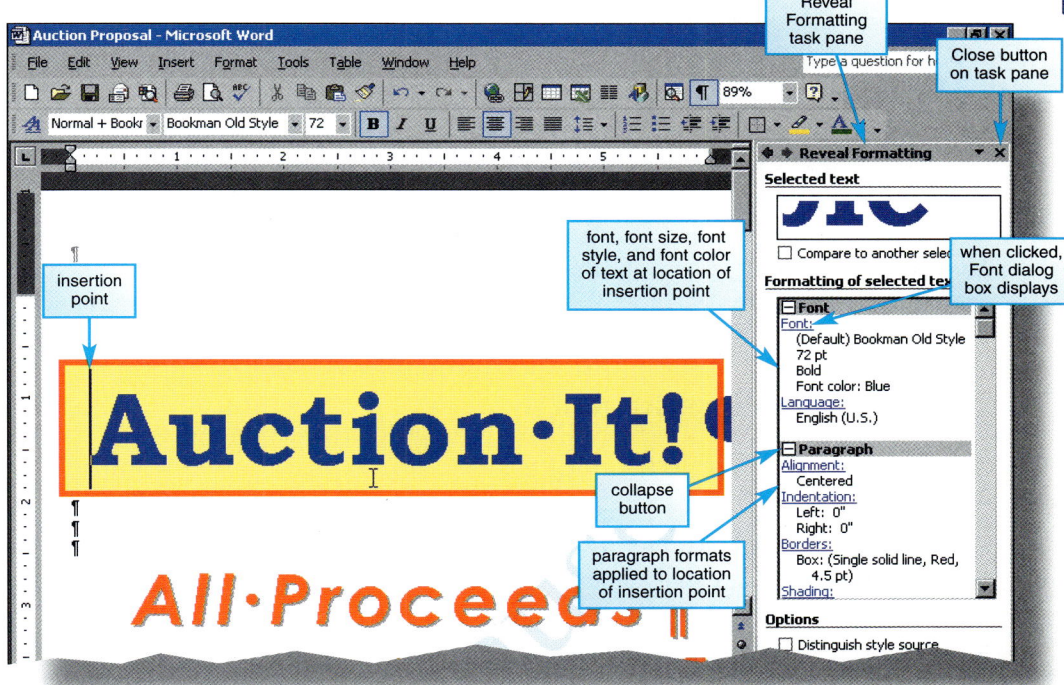

FIGURE 4-86

When the Reveal Formatting task pane displays, you can click any text in the document window and the contents of the Reveal Formatting task pane changes to show formatting applied to the location of the insertion point. To display or hide items in the Formatting of selected text area of the Reveal Formatting task pane, click the expand (+) or collapse (-) buttons. For example, clicking the collapse button to the left of Font hides the character formats applied to the text.

If you want to change the format of text through the Reveal Formatting task pane, select the text and then click the blue underlined word in the Formatting of selected text area to display the linked dialog box. For example, clicking Font in the Reveal Formatting task pane displays the Font dialog box. As soon as you click the OK button in the dialog box, Word changes the format of the selected text.

Project 4 now is complete. Follow this step to quit Word.

TO QUIT WORD

1 Click the Close button in the Word window.

The Word window closes.

Other Ways

1. In Voice Command mode, say "Format, Reveal Formatting"

More About

Proofreading

Ask yourself these questions when proofreading the proposal: Is the subject original and specific? Is its purpose clear? Does the proposal provide specifics, rather than generalizations? Is the product or service beneficial? Is the length appropriate for the subject? Is the wording appropriate for the reader's background?

CASE PERSPECTIVE SUMMARY

As promised, you finish the sales proposal for the vice president of the To Your Health Society within a week and set up an appointment to meet with him. He is quite impressed with the proposal. He mentions that your creativity with colors and graphics makes this proposal much more appealing than any other he has seen. In fact, he would like to incorporate your work into the Web site. You point out that you have experience developing Web pages and would be willing to update the society's Web page, if he would like. Without hesitation, he offers you the job.

Project Summary

Project 4 introduced you to creating a proposal with a title page, table, chart, and a watermark. First, you created a title page that contained a graphic from the Web. You learned how to insert an existing Word document into the active document. You inserted a header and also a footer in the body of the proposal that was different from the title page header. Next, you formatted an existing Word table and charted it using the embedded program, Microsoft Graph. You added picture bullets to a list. Then, you used the Draw Table feature to create a complex table. Finally, you added a text watermark to the document.

What You Should Know

Having completed this project, you now should be able to perform the following tasks:

- Add a Blank Line Above a Paragraph *(WD 4.63)*
- Add a Row to a Table *(WD 4.32)*
- Add Picture Bullets to a List *(WD 4.48)*
- Align Data in Cells *(WD 4.62)*
- Apply a Character Style *(WD 4.52)*
- AutoFormat a Table *(WD 4.35)*
- Border a Paragraph *(WD 4.08)*
- Center a Table *(WD 4.36)*
- Center Text Vertically *(WD 4.19)*
- Change Page Alignment of a Section *(WD 4.23)*
- Change Row Height *(WD 4.61)*
- Change the Chart Type *(WD 4.43)*
- Chart a Table *(WD 4.40)*
- Check Spelling, Save, and Print the Document *(WD 4.66)*
- Clear Formatting *(WD 4.21, WD 4.12, WD 4.15)*
- Create a Character Style *(WD 4.51)*
- Create a Footer Different from the Previous Section Footer *(WD 4.31)*
- Create a Header Different from the Previous Section Header *(WD 4.29)*
- Create a Text Watermark *(WD 4.64)*
- Display Formatting Marks *(WD 4.07)*
- Distribute Columns Evenly *(WD 4.57)*
- Distribute Rows Evenly *(WD 4.57)*
- Draw a Table *(WD 4.54)*
- Enter Data into a Table *(WD 4.59)*
- Exit Graph and Return to Word *(WD 4.44)*
- Format a Chart *(WD 4.45)*
- Format Characters *(WD 4.07)*
- Format Characters Using the Font Dialog Box *(WD 4.13)*
- Format the Table Title *(WD 4.61)*
- Insert a Graphic File from the Data Disk *(WD 4.17)*
- Insert a Next Page Section Break *(WD 4.22)*
- Insert a Word Document into an Open Document *(WD 4.23)*
- Insert Clip Art from the Web *(WD 4.16)*
- Keep Lines Together *(WD 4.47)*
- Move Legend Placement in a Chart *(WD 4.42)*
- Page Number Differently in a Section *(WD 4.30)*
- Print Specific Pages in a Document *(WD 4.26)*
- Print Preview a Document *(WD 4.65)*
- Quit Word *(WD 4.67)*
- Reset Menus and Toolbars *(WD 4.06)*
- Resize a Chart *(WD 4.43)*
- Resize a Graphic Using the Format Picture Dialog Box *(WD 4.17)*
- Reveal Formatting *(WD 4.66)*
- Right-Align Cell Contents *(WD 4.36)*
- Save a Document *(WD 4.20)*
- Save an Active Document with a New File Name *(WD 4.26)*
- Select Nonadjacent Text *(WD 4.37)*
- Shade a Paragraph *(WD 4.09)*
- Shade Table Cells *(WD 4.62)*
- Single-Space the Table Contents *(WD 4.58)*
- Start and Customize Word *(WD 4.06)*
- Sum a Column in a Table *(WD 4.34)*
- Sum Columns in a Table *(WD 4.34)*
- Superscript Selected Characters *(WD 4.38)*
- Vertically Display Text in a Cell *(WD 4.60)*
- Zoom Text Width *(WD 4.07, WD 4.20)*
- Zoom Whole Page *(WD 4.18)*

Learn It Online • WD 4.69

PROJECT 4

Learn It Online

Instructions: To complete the Learn It Online exercises, start your browser, click the Address bar, and then enter scsite.com/offxp/exs.htm. When the Office XP Learn It Online page displays, follow the instructions in the exercises below.

1 Project Reinforcement TF, MC, and SA

Below Word Project 4, click the Project Reinforcement link. Print the quiz by clicking Print on the File menu. Answer each question. Write your first and last name at the top of each page, and then hand in the printout to your instructor.

2 Flash Cards

Below Word Project 4, click the Flash Cards link. When Flash Cards displays, read the instructions. Type 20 (or a number specified by your instructor) in the Number of Playing Cards text box, type your name in the Name text box, and then click the Flip Card button. When the flash card displays, read the question and then click the Answer box arrow to select an answer. Flip through Flash Cards. Click Print on the File menu to print the last flash card if your score is 15 (75%) correct or greater and then hand it in to your instructor. If your score is less than 15 (75%) correct, then redo this exercise by clicking the Replay button.

3 Practice Test

Below Word Project 4, click the Practice Test link. Answer each question, enter your first and last name at the bottom of the page, and then click the Grade Test button. When the graded practice test displays on your screen, click Print on the File menu to print a hard copy. Continue to take practice tests until you score 80% or better. Hand in a printout of the final practice test to your instructor.

4 Who Wants to Be a Computer Genius?

Below Word Project 4, click the Computer Genius link. Read the instructions, enter your first and last name at the bottom of the page, and then click the Play button. Hand in your score to your instructor.

5 Wheel of Terms

Below Word Project 4, click the Wheel of Terms link. Read the instructions, and then enter your first and last name and your school name. Click the Play button. Hand in your score to your instructor.

6 Crossword Puzzle Challenge

Below Word Project 4, click the Crossword Puzzle Challenge link. Read the instructions, and then enter your first and last name. Click the Play button. Work the crossword puzzle. When you are finished, click the Submit button. When the crossword puzzle redisplays, click the Print button. Hand in the printout.

7 Tips and Tricks

Below Word Project 4, click the Tips and Tricks link. Click a topic that pertains to Project 4. Right-click the information and then click Print on the shortcut menu. Construct a brief example of what the information relates to in Word to confirm you understand how to use the tip or trick. Hand in the example and printed information.

8 Newsgroups

Below Word Project 4, click the Newsgroups link. Click a topic that pertains to Project 4. Print three comments. Hand in the comments to your instructor.

9 Expanding Your Horizons

Below Word Project 4, click the Articles for Microsoft Word link. Click a topic that pertains to Project 4. Print the information. Construct a brief example of what the information relates to in Word to confirm you understand the contents of the article. Hand in the example and printed information to your instructor.

10 Search Sleuth

Below Word Project 4, click the Search Sleuth link. To search for a term that pertains to this project, select a term below the Project 4 title and then use the Google search engine at google.com (or any major search engine) to display and print two Web pages that present information on the term. Hand in the printouts to your instructor.

Apply Your Knowledge

1 Working with Tables

Instructions: Start Word. Open the document, First Quarter Sales Report, on the Data Disk. If you did not download the Data Disk, see the inside back cover for instructions for downloading the Data Disk or see your instructor.

The document contains a table created with the Draw Table feature. You are to modify the table so it looks like Figure 4-87.

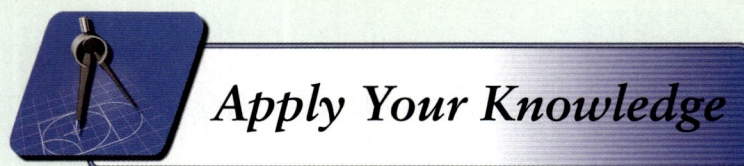

Kipper Electronics					
First Quarter Sales Report					
		January	February	March	Total
Dist. 1	Chicago	45,443	34,221	41,202	**120,866**
	Dallas	67,203	52,202	39,668	**159,073**
	San Francisco	68,778	60,980	49,127	**178,885**
Dist. 2	Boston	79,985	68,993	45,024	**194,002**
	Detroit	45,494	41,220	22,101	**108,815**
	Miami	57,925	56,898	49,056	**163,879**
Total First Quarter Sales		**364,828**	**314,514**	**246,178**	**925,520**

FIGURE 4-87

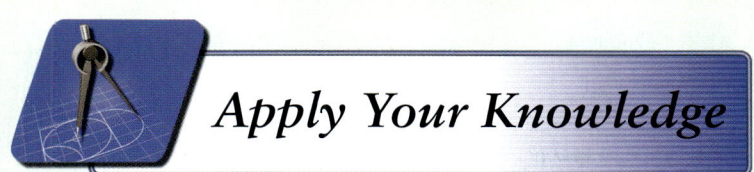

Apply Your Knowledge

Perform the following tasks.

1. Position the insertion point in the cell containing the title, Kipper Electronics. If necessary, click the Tables and Borders button on the Standard toolbar to display the Tables and Borders toolbar. Click the Split Cells button on the Tables and Borders toolbar. When the Split Cells dialog box displays, type 1 in the Number of columns text box. Press the TAB key and then type 2 in the Number of rows text box. Click the OK button to split the cell containing the company name into two cells. Click in the cell below the company title. Type First Quarter Sales Report as the subtitle.
2. Select the cell containing the title, Kipper Electronics. Center it, bold it, and change its font size to 28. Click the Shading Color button arrow on the Tables and Borders toolbar and then click Teal. Click the Font Color button arrow on the Formatting toolbar and then click White.
3. Select the row containing the subtitle, First Quarter Sales Report. Center and bold the subtitle. Click the Font Color button arrow on the Formatting toolbar and then click Teal.
4. Select the cell containing the label, Total First Quarter Sales, and the cell immediately to its right. Click the Merge Cells button on the Tables and Borders toolbar.
5. Select the cells containing the row headings, Dist. 1 and Dist. 2. Click the Change Text Direction button on the Tables and Borders toolbar twice. Click the Align button arrow on the Tables and Borders toolbar and then click Align Center.
6. Click in the table to remove the selection. Drag the left edge of the table rightward to make the cells containing Dist. 1 and Dist. 2 narrower. The cell containing the words, Total First Quarter Sales, should fit on one line (that is, it should not wrap).
7. Select the last four columns containing January, February, March, and Total. Click the Distribute Columns Evenly button on the Tables and Borders toolbar.
8. Click the table move handle in the upper-left corner of the table to select the entire table. Click the Center button on the Formatting toolbar to center the entire table.
9. Click the cell in the last row to contain the total quarterly cells for January and then click the AutoSum button on the Tables and Borders toolbar. Repeat this process for February and March totals.
10. Click the cell to contain the Total Sales for Miami. Click the AutoSum button on the Tables and Borders toolbar. Repeat this process for each cell in the rightmost column of the table — working your way up the table. If your totals are incorrect, click Table on the menu bar, click Formula, be sure the formula is =SUM(LEFT), and then click the OK button. Click the cell in the bottom right corner of the table and then click the AutoSum button on the Tables and Borders toolbar.
11. Center the cells containing the column headings, January, February, March, and Total.
12. Right-align the cells containing numbers.
13. Select the rows below the subtitle, First Quarter Sales Report, and then click the Distribute Rows Evenly button on the Tables and Borders toolbar.
14. Bold the numbers in the last row and also in the rightmost column.
15. Click File on the menu bar and then click Save As. Use the file name, Revised First Quarter Sales Report.
16. Print the revised document.
17. Position the insertion point in the first row of the table. Click Format on the menu bar and then click Reveal Formatting. On your printout, write down all the formatting assigned to this row.

In the Lab

1 Creating a Proposal that Uses the Draw Table Feature

Problem: The owner of Rocky Grove Animal Hospital has hired you to prepare a sales proposal describing the facility (Figures 4-88a and 4-88b), which will be mailed to all community residents.

Instructions:

1. Create the title page as shown in Figure 4-88a. Use the keyword, veterinarian, to locate the clip art image in the Clip Organizer. Resize the graphic to 183% of the original size (approximately 2.9" wide and 3.6" high). *Hint:* Double-click the graphic and then click the Size tab.

2. Center the contents of the title page vertically using the Page Setup dialog box. Insert a next page section break. Clear formatting. Change the vertical alignment for the second section to top. Adjust line spacing to double.

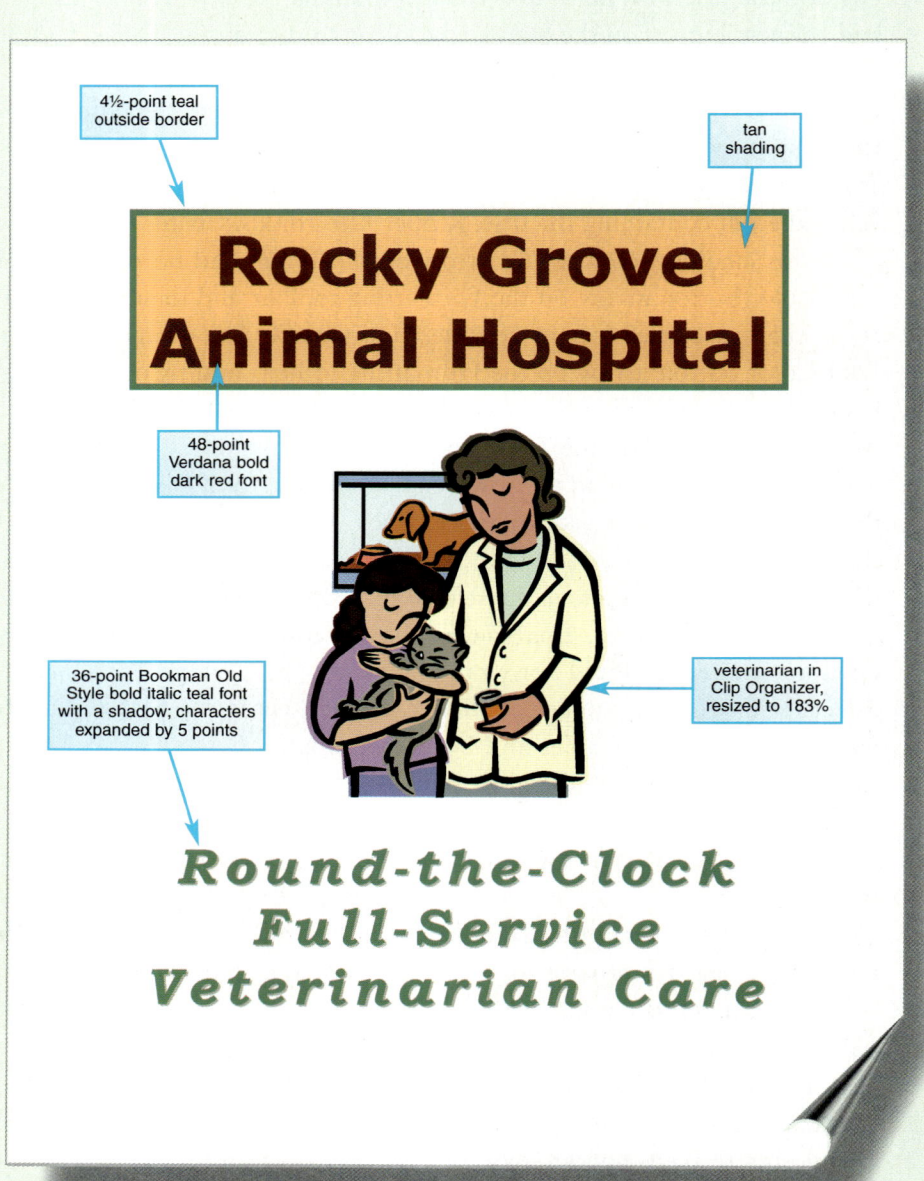

FIGURE 4-88a

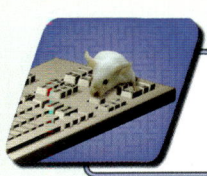

In the Lab

3. Type the body of the proposal as shown in Figure 4-88b.
   a. The body of the proposal has a list with blue diamond-shaped picture bullets. Create a character style of bold, dark red characters with a shadow. Apply the character style to the text in the bulleted list.
   b. Create the table with the Draw Table feature. Distribute rows evenly in the table. Center the table. Single-space the contents of the table. Bold all text in the table. Change the direction of the row titles, General Practice and Treatment and Surgery, and then center the titles. Change the alignment of the second column to Align Center. Shade the General Practice services light yellow; shade the Treatment and Surgery services light green.
4. Check the spelling. Save the document with Animal Hospital Proposal as the file name. View and print the document in print preview.

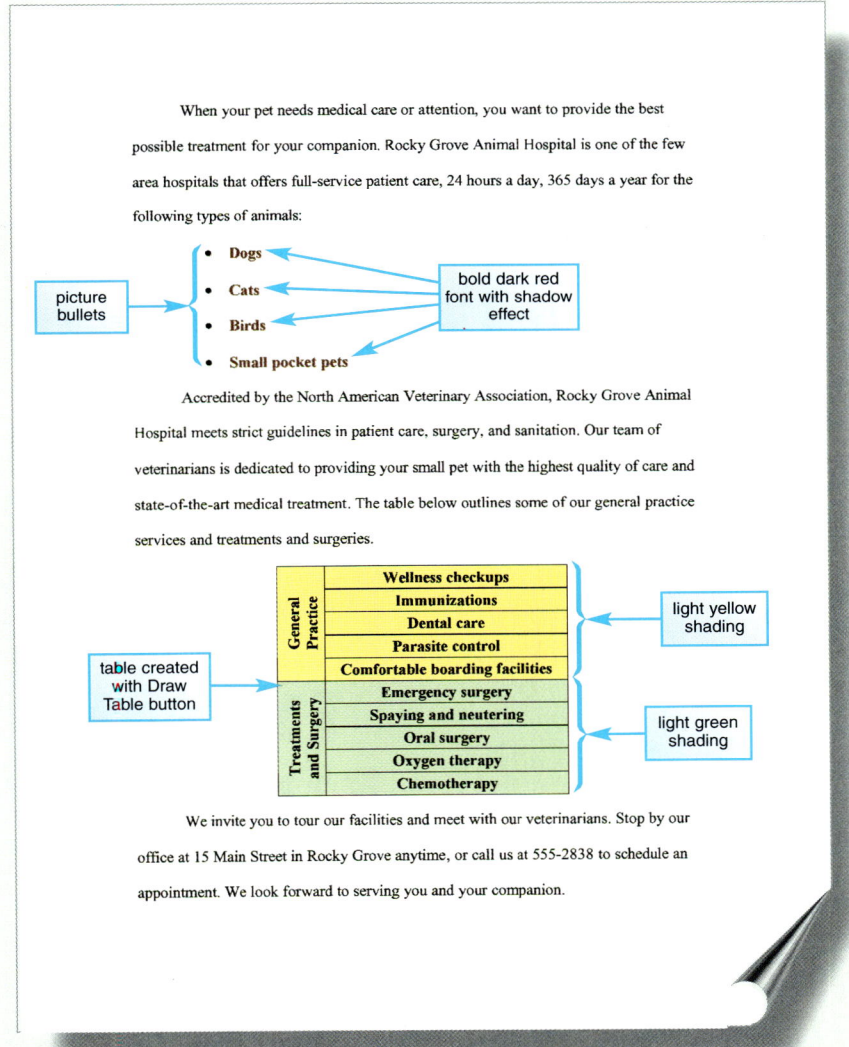

FIGURE 4-88b

In the Lab

2 Creating a Proposal that Contains Clip Art from the Web and a Chart

Problem: Your neighbor owns Katy's Deli and has hired you to create a sales proposal for the party subs she makes at her delicatessen. You develop the proposal shown in Figures 4-89a and 4-89b.

Instructions:

1. Create the title page as shown in Figure 4-89a. Use the keyword, subs, to locate the image of the submarine sandwich, which is located on the Web. If you do not have access to the Web, you can insert the file (file name j0264396.wmf) from the Data Disk. If you did not download the Data Disk, see the inside back cover for instructions for downloading the Data Disk or see your instructor.

2. Center the contents of the title page vertically using the Page Setup dialog box. Insert a next page section break. Clear formatting. Change the vertical alignment for the second section to top. Adjust line spacing to double.

3. Create the body of the proposal as shown in Figure 4-89b. The body of the proposal has picture bullets and a table created using the Insert Table button. The table contains four columns and four rows and is formatted using the Table Grid 8 AutoFormat option (be sure the Last column and Last row check boxes do not contain check marks). Center the column headings. Center the table between the page margins. Distribute the last three columns evenly. Chart the table. Resize the chart so it is wider. Change the chart type to clustered bar with 3-D visual effect. Add a ½ point dark blue outline around the chart. Insert a blank line above the chart.

4. Check the spelling. Save the document with Deli Proposal as the file name. View and print the document in print preview.

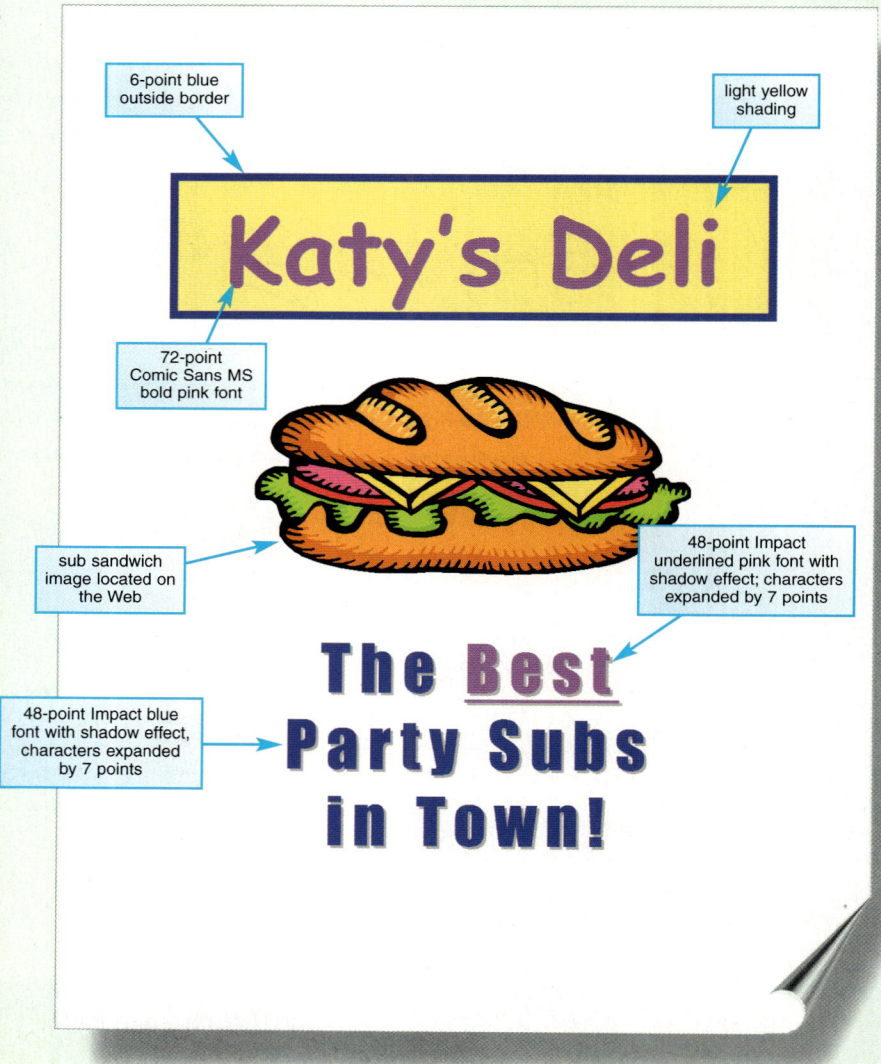

FIGURE 4-89a

In the Lab

Are you planning a party for a birthday, graduation, or a retirement? Do you need to feed a lot of people at a picnic or luncheon at school or work? Let Katy's Deli cater your event. We will prepare and deliver the following items for your guests:

- **3- to 12-foot-long submarine sandwich**
- **Cole slaw and potato salad**
- **Chips and dip**
- **Canned beverages**

(picture bullets; blue font)

Not only are our sandwiches delicious, they are nutritious. The following table and chart compare a 6-inch submarine sandwich made at Katy's Deli with those made at two other local delicatessens. The sandwiches compared were on Italian bread and contained ham, turkey, cheese, lettuce, tomatoes, onions, green peppers, pickles, oil, and vinegar. As shown in the chart, Katy's Deli provides the lowest cholesterol, total fat, and calories.

	Katy's Deli	Subs n Suds	Towne Subs
Calories	240	380	315
Total Fat (g)	35	51	46
Cholesterol (mg)	20	35	30

(Word table formatted to Table Grid 8 style)

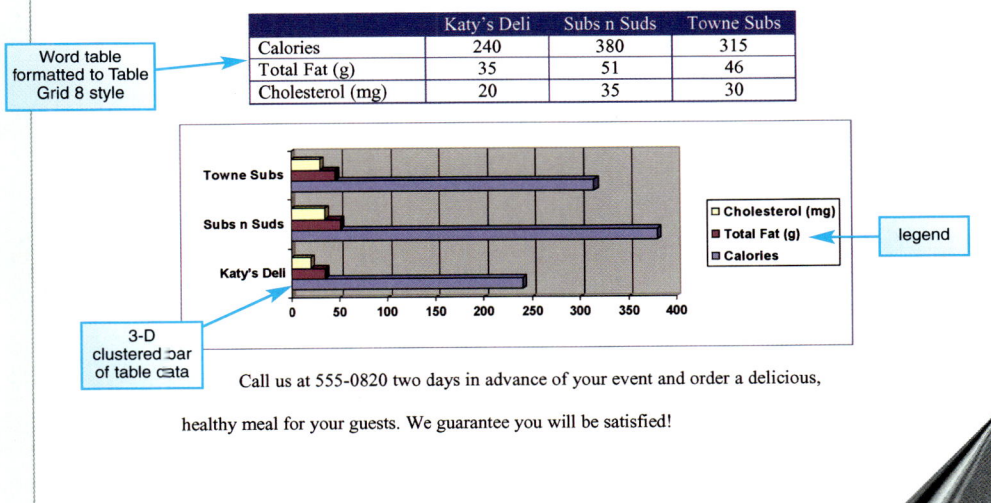

(3-D clustered bar of table data; legend)

Call us at 555-0820 two days in advance of your event and order a delicious, healthy meal for your guests. We guarantee you will be satisfied!

FIGURE 4-89b

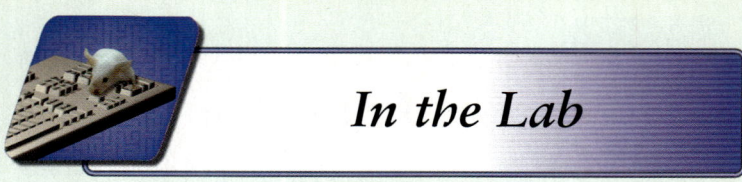

In the Lab

3 Enhancing a Draft of a Proposal

Problem: You work for the marketing director at Baxter College Alumni Association. You create a title page (Figure 4-90a) for an informal sales proposal that your boss has drafted (Figures 4-90b and 4-90c) to be sent to recent college graduates. You decide to add picture bullets, another table, a chart, and a watermark to the proposal.

This lab uses the Data Disk. If you did not download the Data Disk, see the inside back cover for instructions for downloading the Data Disk or see your instructor.

Instructions:

1. Create the title page as shown in Figure 4-90a. *Hint:* Use the Font dialog box to apply the underline in color and the engrave effect. Use the keywords, graduate owl, to locate the image of the owl in the graduation cap, which is located on the Web. If you do not have access to the Web, you can insert the file (file name ED00073_.wmf) from the Data Disk.

2. Center the contents of the title page vertically. Insert a next page section break. Clear formatting. Insert the draft of the body of the proposal below the title page using the File command on the Insert menu. The draft is called Baxter Draft on the Data Disk. The draft of the body of the proposal is shown in Figures 4-90b and 4-90c. Be sure to change the vertical alignment to top for section 2.

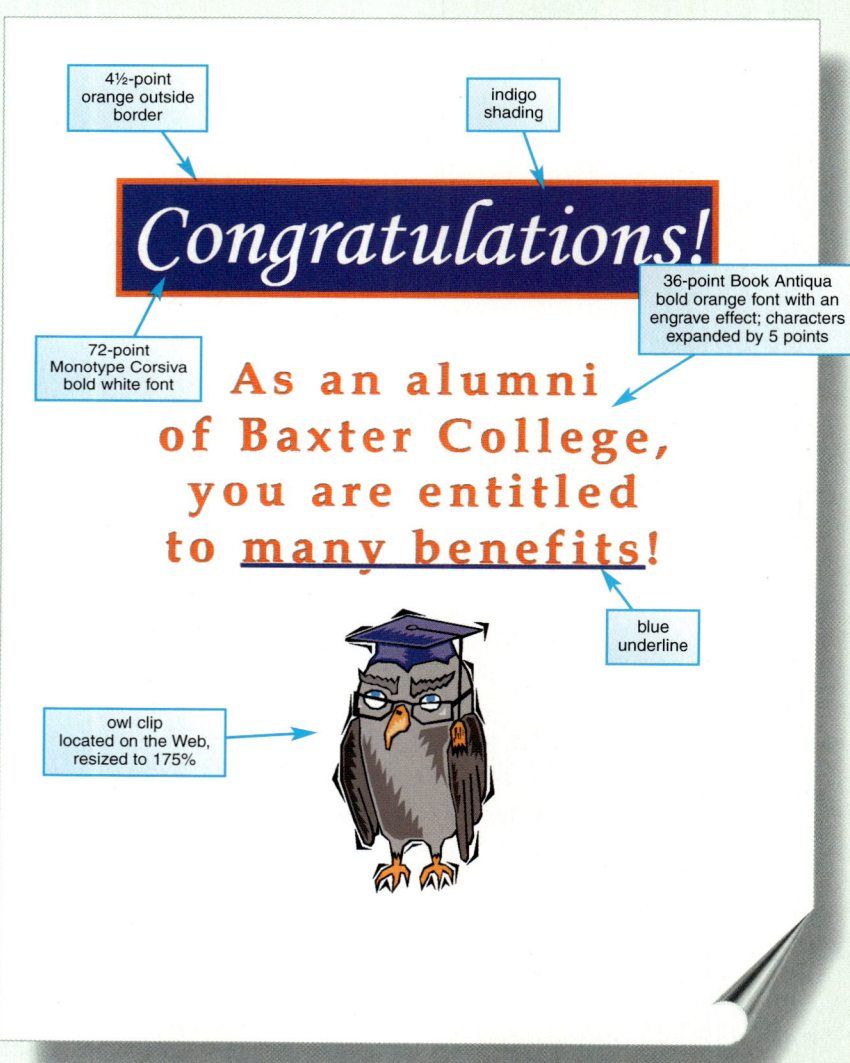

FIGURE 4-90a

In the Lab

Congratulations on your recent graduation from Baxter College. As you join the ranks of thousands of other alumni, the Baxter College Alumni Association (BCAA) is proud to present you with a complimentary one-year membership into the alumni club. Members of the BCAA are entitled to the following benefits:

- Receive the Baxter Alumnus magazine (monthly)
- Join a local alumni club
- Stay in touch with other alumni
- Exclusive access to the Career Opportunity Center
- Automobile, life, and health insurance plans
- Members-only, no annual fee, credit card
- Discounts on airfare, car rentals, and hotel room rates
- Club sponsored outings and discounted event tickets

BCAA also has a Web site designed to meet many of your alumni needs. At the site, you can renew your membership, look up alumni, visit the alumni store, or register for outings. Visit us at www.bcaa.org today.

An exciting year is in store for members of BCAA. The table below outlines some of our upcoming events.

The Baxter College Alumni Association currently has more than 30,000 members. Any family member of an alumnus is welcome to join. We also have a Mini-Baxter Club for children of members. The table and chart below illustrate the diversity in our club.

FIGURE 4-90b

Age/Gender Breakdown of BCAA Members

	Male	Female
Mini-Baxter Club	1,500	1,756
20 to 29 years old	2,098	2,837
30 to 39 years old	3,208	3,998
40 to 49 years old	3,108	3,828
50 to 59 years old	4,927	4,298
60 years and older	2,038	2,009

Your first year into the BCAA is free. Every year thereafter is $30. For each adult family member, the fee is $15 per year. Children under 18 years of age may join the Mini-Baxter Club for $10 per child per year.

If you have any questions, please call Marilyn Stevens at 555-2828 or e-mail her at stevens@bcaa.org. We look forward to meeting you soon!

FIGURE 4-90c

(continued)

In the Lab

Enhancing a Draft of a Proposal *(continued)*

3. On the first page of the body of the proposal, change the style of bullet characters in the list to picture bullets.
4. On the first page of the body of the proposal below the third paragraph in the proposal, use the Draw Table button to create a table that is similar to the one below. Format the table with shading and a colorful border.
5. Change the formatting of the paragraph that follows the table in Step 4 to Keep lines together and Page break before.
6. Set all paragraph formatting in the entire document so that no widows or orphans occur.
7. On the second page of the body of the proposal, add a row to the table that totals the values in the two right columns. Then, chart the first seven rows of the table (all but the total row). Enlarge the chart so it is wider. Move the legend to the left of the chart. Change the chart type to cylinder.

June	New Graduates' Party	Benton Street Cafe
	10th Annual Golf Outing	Greenwood Country Club
July	Trimble Mill Shopping Center (bus trip)	
	Alumni Night at Arlington Stadium (bus trip)	
	15th Annual Family Picnic	Haywood Park

8. Add a header containing the page number to section 2 of the proposal.
9. Add a footer containing the words, Congratulations Graduate!, to section 2 of the proposal.
10. Change the header so it includes the word, Page, to the left of the page number.
11. Create a text watermark on the proposal that contains the words, Baxter Alumnus.
12. Save the active document with the file name, Baxter Proposal, using the Save As command on the File menu.
13. View the document in print preview. Print the document from within print preview.
14. Position the insertion point in the first line of the title page. Click Format on the menu bar and then click Reveal Formatting. On your printout, write down all formatting assigned to this paragraph.

Cases and Places

The difficulty of these case studies varies:
▸ are the least difficult; ▸▸ are more difficult; and ▸▸▸ are the most difficult.

1 ▸ As assistant to the promotions director, you have been assigned the task of preparing a sales proposal that recruits new members to the Vintage Auto Club. The title page is to contain the name, Vintage Auto Club, followed by an appropriate graphic, and then the slogan, Tooling the Countryside with Friends. The body of the proposal should contain the following: first paragraph — Would you like to show your antique automobile? Want to meet new friends? Do you like Sunday afternoon drives? The Vintage Auto Club always is looking for new members. As a member you are entitled to a variety of benefits., list with picture bullets — Monthly issue of Vintage Auto Club, Reduced rates at hotels and motels across the country, Discounts on Auto America orders, Low-rate antique automobile insurance protection, Listings of Vintage Auto Club Chapter members in your area, Participation in Vintage Auto Club Chapter outings; next paragraph — The Vintage Auto Club currently has more than 75,000 members nationwide. Upon membership, you will be sent a current catalog of all members across the nation; the data for the table is shown in the table to the right; last paragraph — A membership costs just $30 per year. Mention this article when you join and receive a 30 percent discount on your first year's membership. Call 708-555-3982, e-mail us at vintageautoclub@hill.com, or visit our Web site at www.vintageautoclub.com to join today!

Sample Chapter Breakdowns

		ADULT	TEEN	CHILD
Northern California	Male	345	178	98
	Female	341	198	89
Southern California	Male	492	120	59
	Female	467	101	75

2 ▸▸ Assume you are running for an office in your school's Student Government Association. You plan to design a sales proposal to post around campus that sells you; that is, it explains why you are the best candidate for the job. Create a proposal that outlines your interests, summarizes your activities, and highlights your accomplishments. It also may present your background, education, and other pertinent experiences. Use whatever personal information you believe is relevant to the office being sought. Place your name, an appropriate graphic, and a slogan on the title page. Be sure the body of the proposal includes the following items: a list with picture bullets, a table, a chart, and a watermark. Set all paragraph formatting in the entire document so that no widows or orphans occur.

3 ▸▸ During the course of a semester, you utilize several facilities on campus. These may include registration, advising, cafeteria, day care, computer facilities, career development, fitness center, library, bookstore, student government, and/or the tutoring center. Select an item from this list, or one of your own, that you feel needs improvement at your school. Visit the library or surf the Internet for guidelines on preparing a planning proposal. Develop a planning proposal you could submit to the Dean of Students that recommends some action the school could take to improve the situation. Design an appropriate title page. Be sure the body of the proposal includes the following items: a list with picture bullets, a table, a chart, and a watermark. Set all paragraph formatting in the entire document so that no widows or orphans occur.

Cases and Places

4 ▶▶ Assume your school is creating or modifying a core curriculum, which is a list of courses that every enrolled student must complete prior to graduation — regardless of major. Much discussion/controversy centers on the list of essential courses. As an active member of the Student Government Association, you have been asked for your recommendations on which classes you feel should be in the core curriculum and why. Visit the library or surf the Internet for guidelines on preparing a planning proposal. Develop a planning proposal that recommends a core curriculum to your school's Curriculum Committee. Design an appropriate title page. Be sure the body of the proposal includes the following items: a list with picture bullets, a table, a chart, and a watermark. Set all paragraph formatting in the entire document so that no widows or orphans occur.

5 ▶▶▶ You have been assigned the task of writing a proposal to request funds to landscape or enhance the landscape on the grounds at your school. The proposal should describe the current condition of the grounds, as well as the proposed landscaping designs (e.g., trees, grass, sod, flowers, shrubs, etc.). Provide a minimum of two alternative cost quotations, with sources of the quotations cited. Visit the library or surf the Internet for guidelines on preparing a research proposal. Draft a research proposal that presents your findings, suggests two alternatives, and then recommends your suggested design to your school's decision-making body. Design an appropriate title page. Be sure the body of the proposal includes the following items: a list with picture bullets, a table, a chart, a header with a page number, a footer, and a watermark. Set all paragraph formatting in the entire document so that no widows or orphans occur.

6 ▶▶▶ Your school has a budget for student trips. You have been assigned the task of writing a proposal to request funds for your entire class to attend an out-of-town conference. Locate a conference that appeals to you. The proposal should describe the conference, its relevance, and all associated costs (e.g., travel, conference, meals, lodging, supplies, etc.). For travel and lodging, provide a minimum of two alternative cost quotations, with sources of the quotations cited. Visit the library or surf the Internet for guidelines on preparing a research proposal. Draft a research proposal that presents your findings, suggests the cost alternatives, and then recommends the best package to your school's decision-making body. Design an appropriate title page. Be sure the body of the proposal includes the following items: a list with picture bullets, a table, a chart, a header with a page number, a footer, and a watermark. Set all paragraph formatting in the entire document so that no widows or orphans occur.

Microsoft Word 2002

PROJECT 5

Generating Form Letters, Mailing Labels, Envelopes, and Directories

You will have mastered the material in this project when you can:

O B J E C T I V E S

- Explain the merge process
- Use the Mail Merge Wizard and the Mail Merge toolbar
- Use a letter template for the main document in a mail merge
- Insert and format an AutoShape
- Format a drawing canvas
- Create a folder while saving
- Create and edit a data source
- Explain the terms, data record and data field
- Edit a field format
- Insert and edit merge fields in a main document
- Use an IF field in a main document
- Create an outline numbered list
- Apply a paragraph style
- Turn field codes on and off
- Merge and print form letters
- Selectively merge and print form letters
- Sort data records
- Address and print mailing labels
- Address and print envelopes
- Merge all data records to a directory
- Change page orientation
- Close all open Word documents

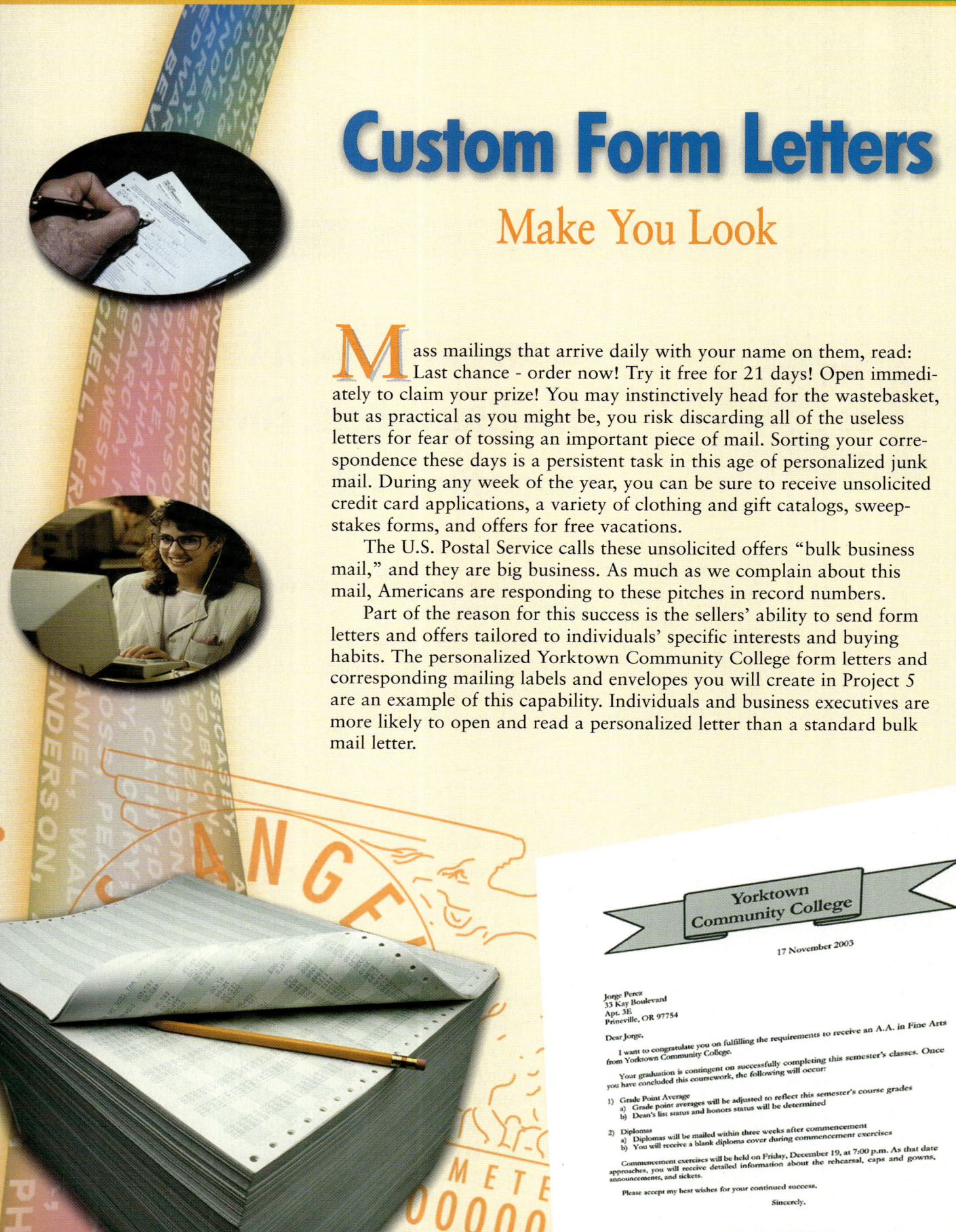

Custom Form Letters
Make You Look

Mass mailings that arrive daily with your name on them, read: Last chance - order now! Try it free for 21 days! Open immediately to claim your prize! You may instinctively head for the wastebasket, but as practical as you might be, you risk discarding all of the useless letters for fear of tossing an important piece of mail. Sorting your correspondence these days is a persistent task in this age of personalized junk mail. During any week of the year, you can be sure to receive unsolicited credit card applications, a variety of clothing and gift catalogs, sweepstakes forms, and offers for free vacations.

The U.S. Postal Service calls these unsolicited offers "bulk business mail," and they are big business. As much as we complain about this mail, Americans are responding to these pitches in record numbers.

Part of the reason for this success is the sellers' ability to send form letters and offers tailored to individuals' specific interests and buying habits. The personalized Yorktown Community College form letters and corresponding mailing labels and envelopes you will create in Project 5 are an example of this capability. Individuals and business executives are more likely to open and read a personalized letter than a standard bulk mail letter.

Where do these marketers get your name? How do they know you just bought a house, had a baby, or like to golf? Whether you like it or not, specific details of all phases of your life are fields in highly specialized databases used to churn out four million tons of personalized letters every year.

Much of the data in these databases comes from public records in local governmental offices: birth certificates, business licenses, and marriage certificates. Real estate records contain the owner, price, and date sold of every parcel of land. State and federal tax lien information, civil lawsuits, and bankruptcy filings are easily obtainable. Records are generated each time you use or apply for a credit card. Consumers volunteer information when they describe their family size, income, and hobbies on product warranty cards. Telephone books and U.S. Postal Service address change forms also are major sources of profitable data.

Companies research, compile, and rent this data to marketers at the average rate of $100 to $300 per 1,000 names. Listmakers boast they have more than 10,000 customized lists for rent. As a result, about 70 billion pieces of bulk business mail lands in U.S. mailboxes each year, with the average American receiving more than 20 pieces each week.

Companies can rent several lists and search for the same names appearing on each one. For example, a financial institution marketing credit cards to affluent homeowners with good credit histories can merge lists with Census Bureau records of people living in specific areas, the buying habits of people in these neighborhoods, and credit reports showing good credit risks. Some companies may use up to 100 lists to fine-tune the names in an attempt to find appropriate mail prospects.

With their targeted mailings reaching nearly 100 times as many consumers as compared with television advertisements, it is no surprise that direct marketers utilize the U.S. Postal Service. This successful type of solicitation means that consumers can expect to receive even more bulk business mail in the future.

Microsoft Word 2002

Generating Form Letters, Mailing Labels, Envelopes, and Directories

PROJECT 5

CASE PERSPECTIVE

Elizabeth Pulaski, registrar at Yorktown Community College, has hired you as a part-time student assistant. Your responsibilities include administrative tasks such as posting details about admissions, courses, and degrees; filing applications; and correspondence. Elizabeth has asked you to send a letter to all upcoming graduates, informing them of general graduation procedures.

Instead of typing a separate letter to each student on the mailing list, you use Word to create a form letter because much of the information in each letter is identical. You will create a separate file containing the names and addresses of each student on the mailing list; this file is called a data source. Then, you will merge the student data in the data source with the form letter so that an individual letter prints for each student on the mailing list. Each form letter also should print the type of degree the student is receiving and specify whether the student is graduating with honors. To graduate with honors requires a GPA of 3.8 or higher. Thus, the data source must include each student's degree and GPA. Using Word, you also plan to address and print mailing labels or envelopes for each student on the mailing list.

Introduction

Individuals and business people are more likely to open and read a personalized letter than a letter addressed as Dear Sir, Dear Madam, or To Whom It May Concern. Typing individual personalized letters, though, can be a time-consuming task. Thus, Word provides the capability of creating a form letter, which is an easy way to generate mass mailings of personalized letters. The basic content of a group of form letters is similar. Items such as name, address, city, state, and ZIP code, however, vary from one letter to the next. With Word, you easily can address and print mailing labels or envelopes for the form letters.

Both business and personal correspondence regularly uses form letters to communicate via the postal service or e-mail with groups of people. **Business form letters** include announcements of sales to customers or notices of benefits to employees. **Personal form letters** include letters of application for a job or invitations to participate in a sweepstakes giveaway.

Project Five — Form Letters, Mailing Labels, and Envelopes

Project 5 illustrates how to create a business form letter and address and print corresponding mailing labels or envelopes. The form letter is sent to graduating students, informing them of upcoming graduation procedures. Each form letter also identifies the type of degree the student will be receiving and specifies whether the student is graduating with honors. The student's GPA determines whether he or she graduates with honors.

The process of generating form letters involves creating a main document for the form letter and a data source, and then merging, or *blending*, the two together into a series of individual letters as shown in Figure 5-1.

(a) Main Document for the Form Letter

placeholder for address fields

Yorktown Community College

17 November

merge field → «AddressBlock»

«GreetingLine» ← *placeholder for salutation fields*

I want to congratulate you on fulfilling the requirements to receive an «Degree» in «Major» { IF GPA >= 3.8 " with honors" "" } from Yorktown Community College. ← *IF field* / *merge field*

Your graduation is contingent on successfully completing this semester's classes. Once you have concluded this coursework, the following will occur:

1) Grade Point Average
   a) Grade point averages will be adjusted to reflect this semester's course grades
   b) Dean's list status and honors status will be determined
2) Diplomas
   a) Diplomas will be mailed within three weeks after commencement
   b) You will receive a blank diploma cover during commencement exercises

outline numbered list

Commencement exercises will be held on Friday, December 19, at 7:00 p.m. As that date approaches, you will receive detailed information about the rehearsal, caps announcements, and tickets.

Please accept my best wishes for your continued success.

Sincerely,

Elizabeth Pulaski
Registrar

(b) Data Source

First Name	Last Name	Address Line 1	Address Line 2	City	State	ZIP Code	Degree	Major	GPA
Caitlin	Callaghan	45 Bridge Street		Bend	OR	97708	A.S.	Computer Technology	3.9
Jorge	Perez	33 Kay Boulevard	Apt. 3E	Prineville	OR	97754	A.A.	Fine Arts	3.7
Krishna	Singh	P.O. Box 45	Route 2 West	Bend	OR	97702	A.A.	Political Science	3.75
Leilani	Kahale	14 Central Avenue		Redmond	OR	97756	A.S.	Supervision	3.6
Alex	Kasoulos	9888 Lock Road		Prineville	OR	97754	A.S.	Food Service	3.8

(c) Form Letters

form letter 1 — *school name in banner shape*

Yorktown Community College

17 November 2003

student name and address in first data record

Caitlin Callaghan
45 Bridge Street
Bend, OR 97708

Dear Caitlin, ← *first name in first data record*

I want to congratulate you on fulfilling the requirements to receive an A.S. in Computer Technology with honors from Yorktown Community College. ← *phrase, with honors, present because first data record's GPA is greater than 3.8*

Your graduation is contingent on successfully completing this semester's classes. Once you have concluded this coursework, the following will occur:

1) Grade Point Average
   a) Grade point averages will be adjusted to reflect this semester's course grades
   b) Dean's list status and honors status will be determined
2) Diplomas
   a) Diplomas will be mailed within three weeks after commencement
   b) You will receive a blank diploma cover during commencement exercises

Commencement exercises will be held on Friday, December 19, at 7:00 p.m. As that date approaches, you will receive detailed information about the rehearsal, caps and gowns, announcements, and tickets.

Please accept my best wishes for your continued success.

Sincerely,

Elizabeth Pulaski
Registrar

44 BROADWAY STREET • REDMOND, OREGON • 97756
PHONE: 541-555-0088 • FAX: 541-555-0089

Yorktown Community College

17 November 20

student name and address in second data record

Jorge Perez
33 Kay Boulevard
Apt. 3E
Prineville, OR 97754

Dear Jorge, ← *first name in second data record*

I want to congratulate you on fulfilling the requirements to receive an A.A. in Fi from Yorktown Community College.

Your graduation is contingent on successfully completing this semester's classes you have concluded this coursework, the following will occur:

phrase, with honors, not present because second data record's GPA is less than 3.8

e point averages will be adjusted to reflect this semester's course grades
's list status and honors status will be determined

a) Diplomas will be mailed within three weeks after commencement
b) You will receive a blank diploma cover during commencement exercises

Commencement exercises will be held on Friday, December 19, at 7:00 p.m. As th approaches, you will receive detailed information about the rehearsal, caps and announcements, and tickets.

Please accept my best wishes for your continued success.

Sincerely,

form letter 2, *form letter 3*, *form letter 4*, *form letter 5*

FIGURE 5-1

Writing Letters

For more information on writing letters, visit the Word 2002 More About Web page (www.scsite.com/wd2002/more.htm) and then click Writing Letters.

Merging is the process of combining the contents of a data source with a main document. A **main document** contains the constant, or unchanging, text, punctuation, spaces, and graphics. In Figure 5-1a on the previous page, the main document represents the portion of the form letter that repeats from one merged letter to the next. Conversely, the **data source** contains the variable, or changing, values for each letter. In Figure 5-1b, the data source contains five different students. Thus, one form letter is generated for each student listed in the data source.

Starting Word

Perform the following steps to start Word, or ask your instructor how to start Word for your system.

TO START AND CUSTOMIZE WORD

1. Click the Start button on the Windows taskbar, point to Programs on the Start menu, and then click Microsoft Word on the Programs submenu.
2. If the Word window is not maximized, double-click its title bar to maximize it.
3. If the Language bar displays on the screen, click its Minimize button.
4. If the New Document task pane displays in the Word window, click the Show at startup check box to remove the check mark and then click the Close button in the upper-right corner of the task pane title bar.
5. If the toolbars display positioned on the same row, click the Toolbar Options button and then click Show Buttons on Two Rows.
6. Click View on the menu bar and then click Print Layout.

Word starts. After a few moments, an empty document titled Document1 displays in the Word window. You use print layout view in this project because the letterhead contains a shape, and shapes display properly only in print layout view. The Print Layout View button on the horizontal scroll bar is selected (shown in Figure 5-3 on page WD 5.09).

Resetting Menus and Toolbars

To set the menus and toolbars so they appear exactly as shown in this book, reset your menus and toolbars as outlined in Appendix D or follow these steps.

TO RESET MENUS AND TOOLBARS

1. Click the Toolbar Options button on the Standard toolbar and then point to Add or Remove Buttons. Point to Standard on the Add or Remove Buttons submenu. Scroll to and then click Reset Toolbar on the Standard submenu.
2. Click the Toolbar Options button on the Formatting toolbar and then point to Add or Remove Buttons. Point to Formatting on the Add or Remove Buttons submenu. Scroll to and then click Reset Toolbar on the Formatting submenu.
3. Click the Toolbar Options button on the Standard toolbar and then point to Add or Remove Buttons. Click Customize on the Add or Remove Buttons submenu.

4 When the Customize dialog box displays, if necessary, click the Options tab and then click the Reset my usage data button. When the Microsoft Word dialog box displays, click the Yes button. Click the Close button in the Customize dialog box.

Word resets the menus and toolbars.

Displaying Formatting Marks

It is helpful to display formatting marks that indicate where in the document you pressed the ENTER key, SPACEBAR, and other keys. Perform the following step to display formatting marks.

TO DISPLAY FORMATTING MARKS

1 If the Show/Hide ¶ button on the Standard toolbar is not selected already, click it.

Word displays formatting marks in the document window, and the Show/Hide ¶ button on the Standard toolbar is selected (shown in Figure 5-2 on the next page).

Zooming Text Width

When you **zoom text width** in print layout view, Word displays the text on the screen as large as possible without extending the right margin beyond the right edge of the document window. Perform these steps to zoom text width.

TO ZOOM TEXT WIDTH

1 Click the Zoom box arrow on the Standard toolbar.

2 Click Text Width.

Word computes the zoom percentage and displays it in the Zoom box (shown in Figure 5-2). Your percentage may be different depending on your computer.

Identifying the Main Document for Form Letters

Creating form letters requires merging a main document with a data source. To create form letters using Word's mail merge, you perform these tasks: (1) identify the main document, (2) create or specify the data source, (3) enter text, graphics, and fields into the main document for the form letter, and (4) merge the data source with the main document to generate and print the form letters. The following pages illustrate these tasks.

Word provides two methods of merging documents: the Mail Merge Wizard and the Mail Merge toolbar. The **Mail Merge Wizard** uses a task pane to guide you through the process of merging. The **Mail Merge toolbar** provides buttons and boxes you use to merge documents. This project first illustrates the Mail Merge Wizard and then later uses the Mail Merge toolbar.

More About

Business Letter Software

For more information on business letter software, visit the Word 2002 More About Web page (www.scsite.com/wd2002/more.htm) and then click Business Letter Software.

Main Document Types

In addition to form letters, mailing labels, envelopes, directories, and e-mail mass mailings, you can merge a main document to faxes. In order to create and distribute merged faxes, you must have a fax modem installed and also have the necessary fax software, such as Microsoft Fax, and a compatible e-mail program, such as Microsoft Outlook. Otherwise, the fax option will be unavailable (dimmed).

Identifying the Main Document

The first step in the mail merge process is to identify the type of document you are creating for the main document. Basic installations of Word support five types of main documents: letters, e-mail messages, envelopes, labels, and directory. In this section, you are creating letters as the main document. Later in this project, you will specify labels, envelopes, and a directory as the main document. The Integration Feature that follows Project 6 shows how to specify e-mail messages as the main document.

When creating letters, such as the form letter in this project, you have three basic options: type the letter from scratch into a blank document window, as you did with the cover letter in Project 3, use the letter wizard and let Word format the letter based on your responses to the wizard, or use a letter template. As discussed in Project 3, a **template** is similar to a form with prewritten text. In the case of the letter template, Word prepares a letter with text and/or formatting common to all letters. Then, you customize the resulting letter by selecting and replacing prewritten text.

Word provides three styles of wizards and templates: Professional, Contemporary, and Elegant. The form letter in this project uses the Elegant Merge Letter template. Perform the following steps to use a template as the main document for a form letter.

To Use a Template as the Main Document in a Mail Merge

1 Click Tools on the menu bar, point to Letters and Mailings, and then point to Mail Merge Wizard (Figure 5-2).

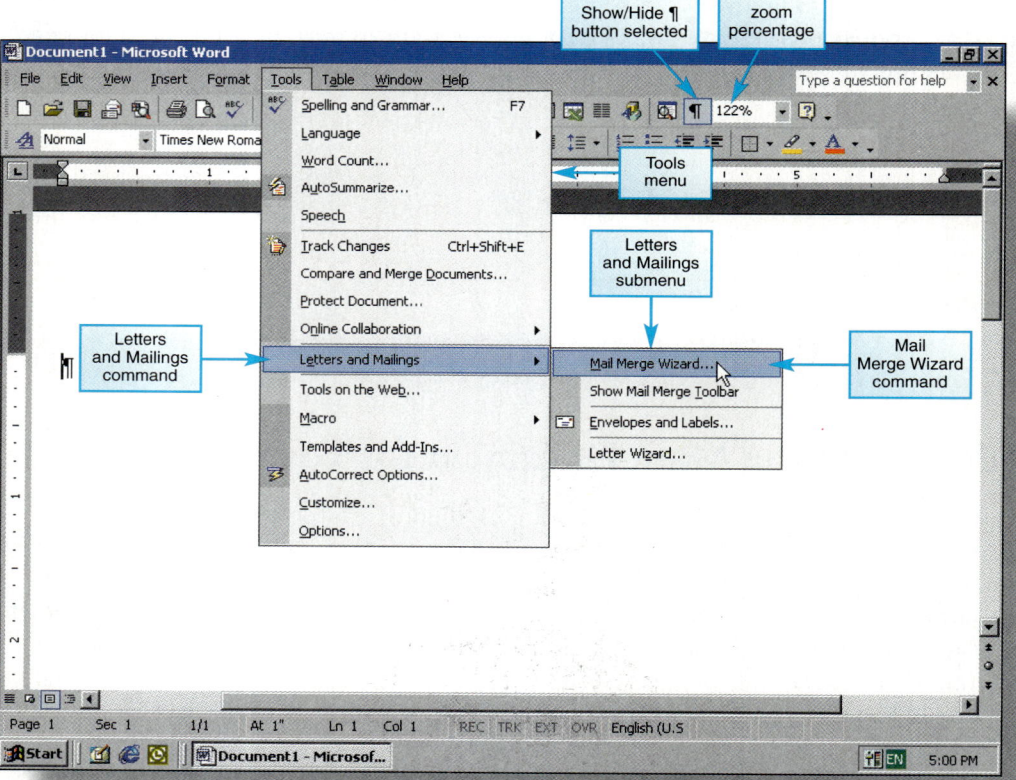

FIGURE 5-2

2 **Click Mail Merge Wizard. If necessary, click Letters in the Select document type area in the Mail Merge task pane. At the bottom of the task pane, point to Next: Starting document.**

Word displays Step 1 of the Mail Merge Wizard in the Mail Merge task pane (Figure 5-3). Step 1 of the Mail Merge Wizard displays the available types of main documents.

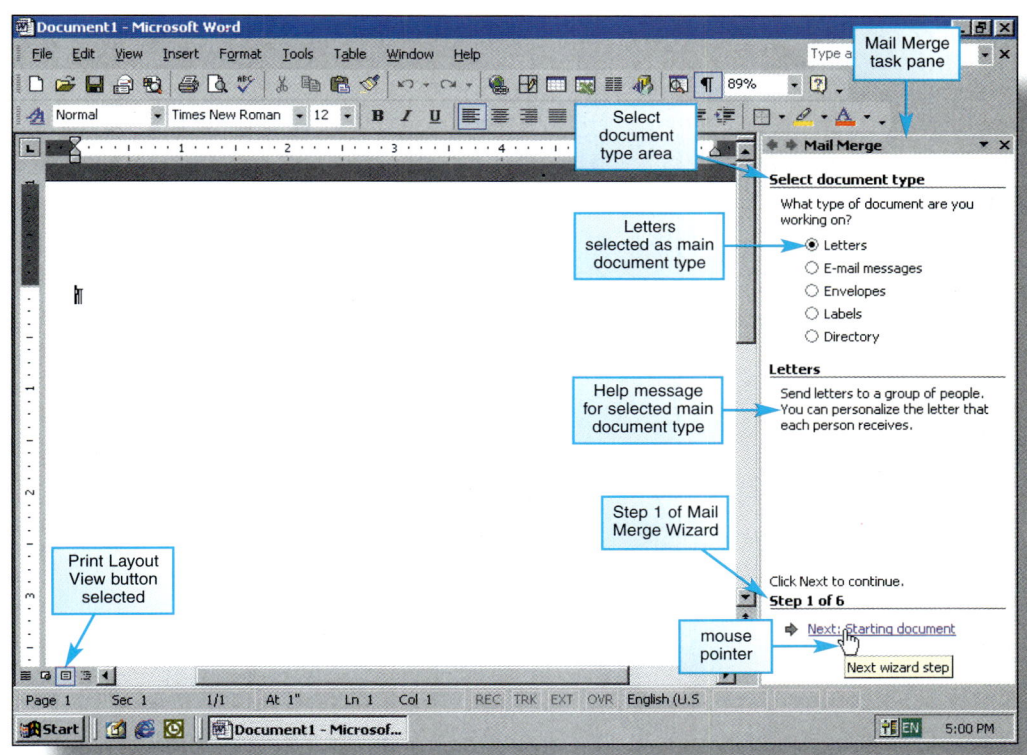

FIGURE 5-3

3 **Click Next: Starting document. Click Start from a template in the Select starting document area in the Mail Merge task pane. When the Start from a template area displays, click Select template. When the Select Template dialog box displays, click the Elegant Merge Letter icon and then point to the OK button.**

Step 2 of the Mail Merge Wizard allows you to specify how to begin creating your main document: from the current document in the document window, from a template, or from an existing document not displaying in

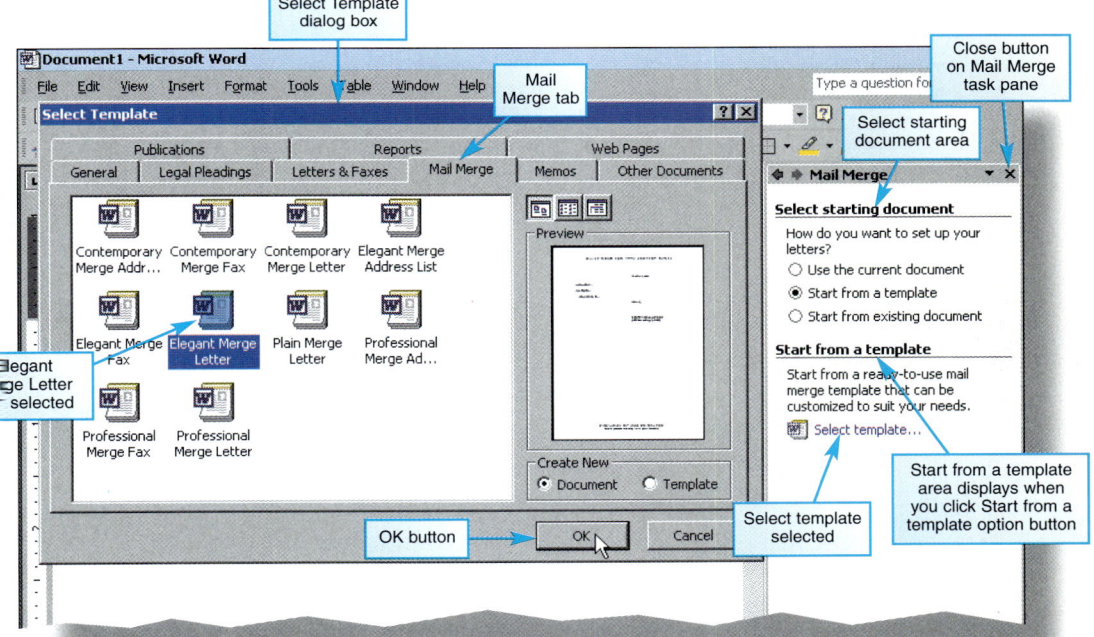

FIGURE 5-4

the document window. When you click Select template, Word displays several template icons in the Mail Merge sheet in the Select Template dialog box (Figure 5-4).

4 **Click the OK button. Click the Close button in the upper-right corner of the Mail Merge task pane title bar to close the task pane.**

In the document window, Word displays a document that is based on the Elegant Merge Letter template (Figure 5-5). The letter template instructs Word to display the current date in the letter. Thus, your date line more than likely will display a different date.

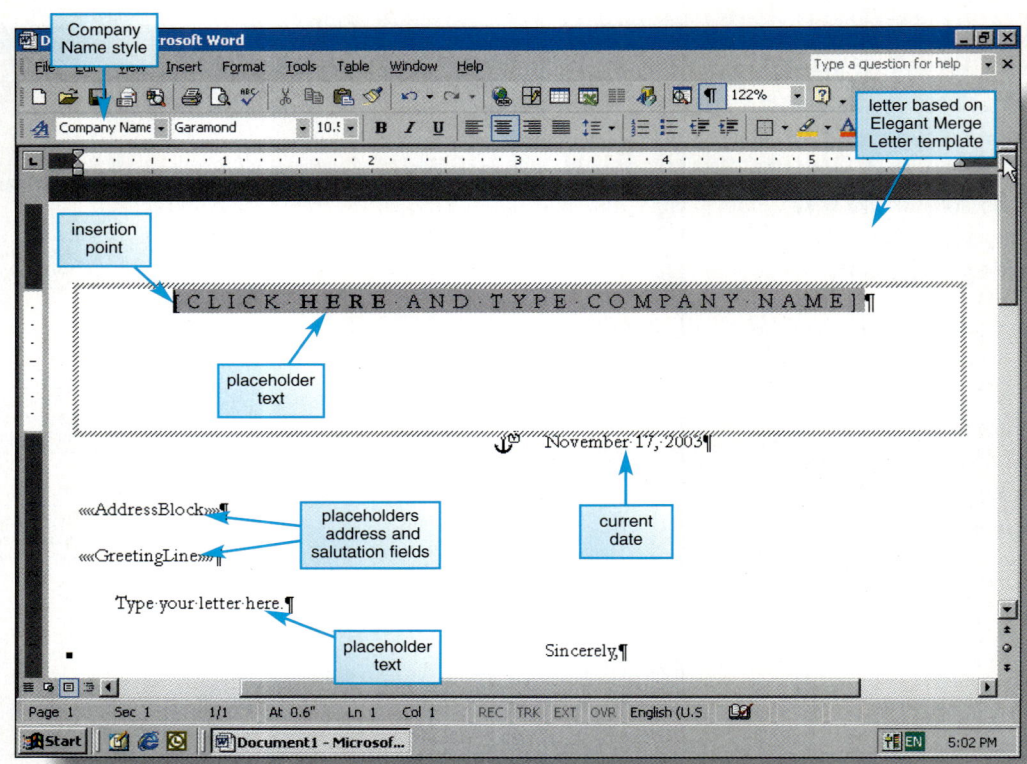

FIGURE 5-5

Other Ways

1. On File menu click New, click General Templates, click Mail Merge tab, click template name, click OK button
2. In Voice Command mode, say "File, New, General Templates, Mail Merge, [select template name], OK"

Recall that a template displays prewritten text, called **placeholder text**, that you select and replace to personalize the document. Figure 5-5 identifies some of the placeholder text created by the Elegant Merge Letter template.

In Project 3, you learned that all business letters have common elements such as a date line, inside address, message, and signature block. The Elegant Merge Letter template uses formatting for a **modified block style** letter; that is, the date line, complimentary close, and signature block are slightly to the right of the center point, and all other letter components begin flush with the left margin.

In creating a letter from a template, Word uses styles to represent various elements of the letter. As discussed in previous projects, a style is a named group of formatting characteristics that you can apply to text. Figure 5-6 identifies the styles used by the Elegant Merge Letter template.

The Style box on the Formatting toolbar displays the name of the style associated with the location of the insertion point or the current selection (shown in Figure 5-5). When you modify the form letter, the style associated with the location of the insertion point will be applied to the text you type.

At this point, you close the Mail Merge task pane because you want to create the letterhead for the letter. With the Mail Merge task pane closed, the document window displays larger on the screen. Later in this project, you will redisplay the Mail Merge task pane to continue working with the Mail Merge Wizard.

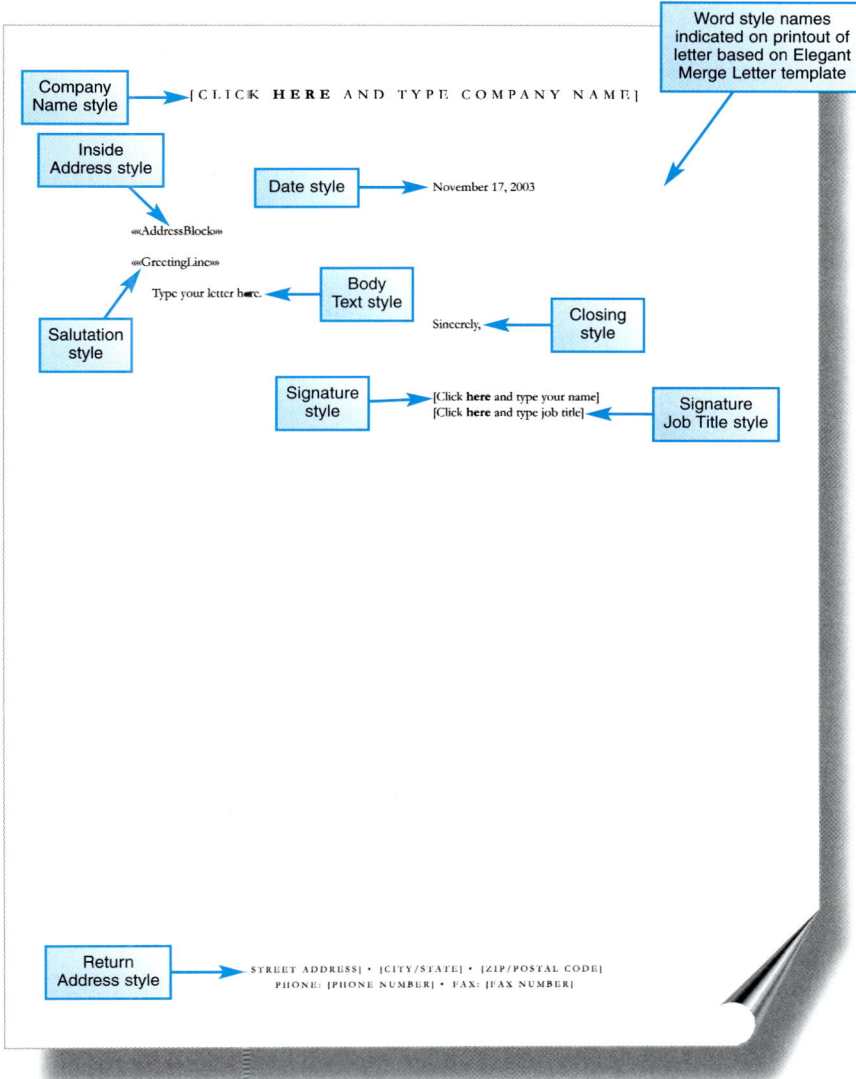

FIGURE 5-6

> **More About**
>
> **Letters**
>
> Business letters should contain the following items from top to bottom: date line, inside address, body or message, and signature block. Many business letters contain additional items such as a special mailing notation(s), attention line, salutation, subject line, complimentary close, reference initials, and enclosure notation.

Working with AutoShapes and the Drawing Canvas

You can insert two types of graphics into a Word document: a picture and a drawing object. A **picture** is a graphic that was created in another program. Examples of pictures include scanned images, photographs, and clip art. A **drawing object** is a graphic that you create using Word. When you add a drawing object to a document, Word automatically places a drawing canvas around the drawing object. A **drawing canvas** is a container that helps you to resize and arrange shapes on the page.

Adding an AutoShape

The top of the form letter in this project is to display a banner that contains the school name. A banner is a type of drawing object. In Word, you can add a banner to a document using the AutoShapes button on the Drawing toolbar. An **AutoShape** is a shape that Word has predefined. Examples of AutoShapes include rectangles, circles, triangles, arrows, flowcharting symbols, stars, banners, and callouts.

Perform the steps on the next page to insert a banner AutoShape into a document.

> **More About**
>
> **Drawing Canvas**
>
> The drawing canvas automatically displays when you add an AutoShape. To display the drawing canvas without adding an AutoShape, click Insert on the menu bar, point to Picture, and then click New Drawing on the Picture submenu.

Steps To Insert an AutoShape

1 **Click the placeholder text, CLICK HERE AND TYPE COMPANY NAME, to select it. If the Drawing toolbar does not display on your screen, click the Drawing button on the Standard toolbar to display the Drawing toolbar. Click the AutoShapes button on the Drawing toolbar, point to Stars and Banners, and then point to the Up Ribbon.**

The placeholder text displays surrounded by a frame (Figure 5-7). Word frames the company name to provide flexibility in its location. The next project discusses frames in more depth.

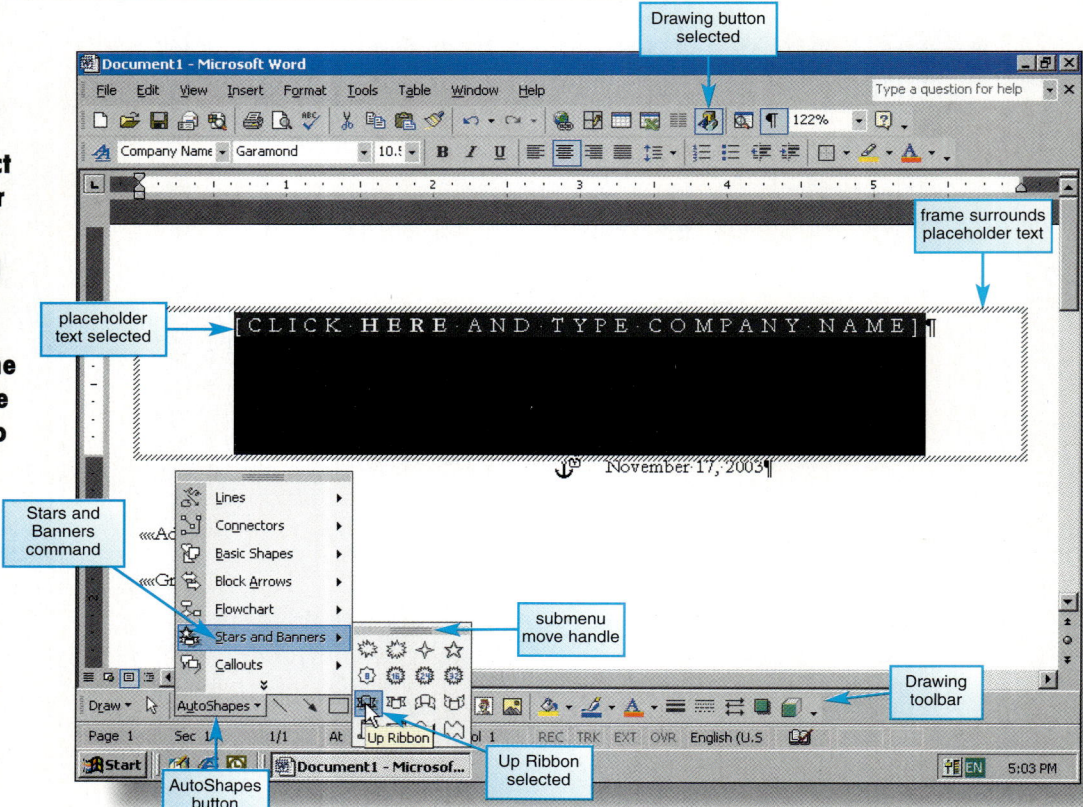

FIGURE 5-7

2 **Click the Up Ribbon. When the drawing canvas displays, position the mouse pointer as shown in Figure 5-8.**

Word displays the drawing canvas (Figure 5-8). The Drawing Canvas toolbar also may display on the screen. The drawing canvas is surrounded by a patterned rectangle. This rectangle does not print; you use it to resize or move the drawing canvas and its contents.

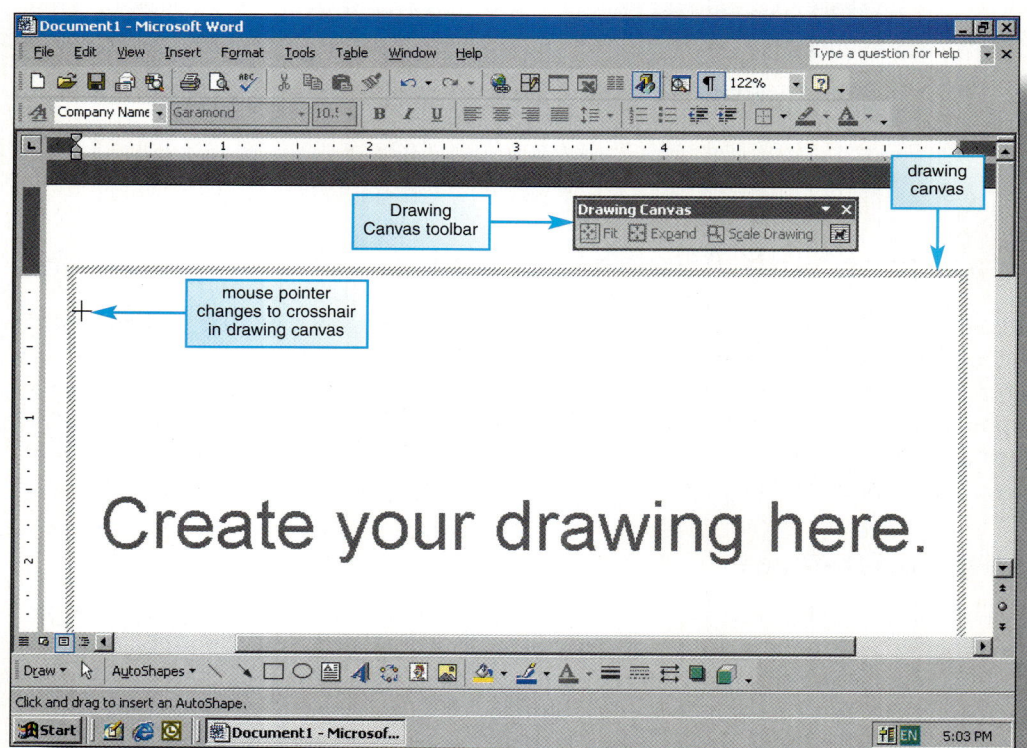

FIGURE 5-8

3 **Drag the mouse to the right and downward to form a banner as shown in Figure 5-9.**

4 **Release the mouse button. Once the shape is drawn, if you need to resize it, simply drag the sizing handles.**

Word replaces the placeholder text with the banner AutoShape (shown in Figure 5-10 on the next page). Word surrounds the AutoShape with a patterned rectangle, which you can use to resize or move the AutoShape.

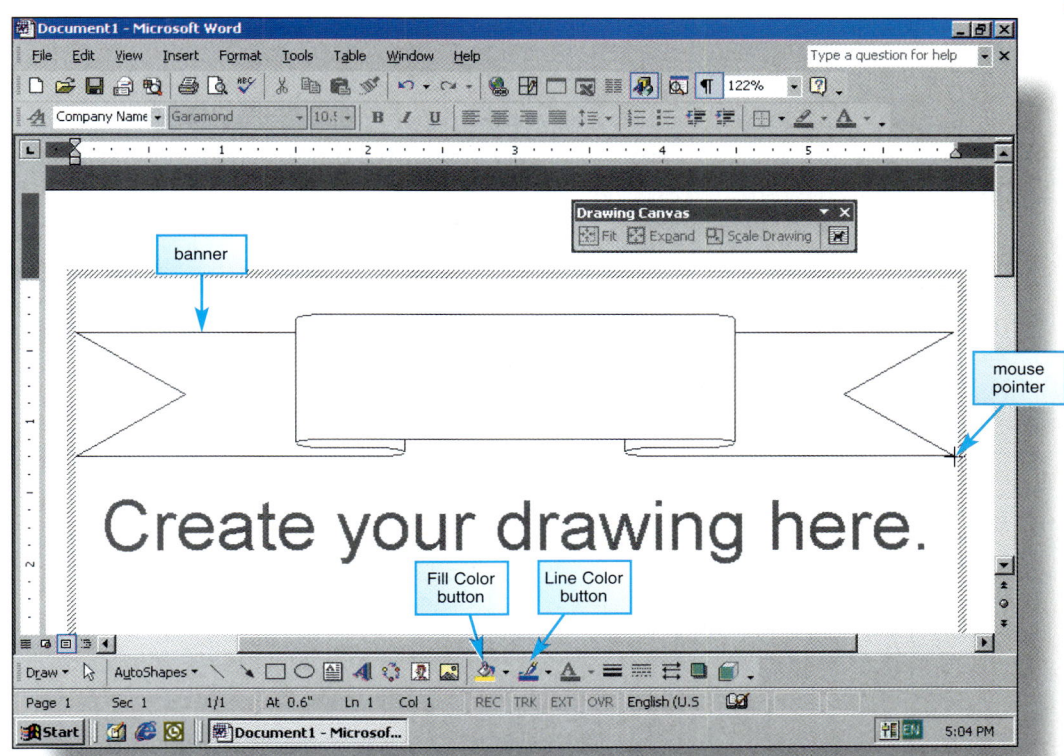

FIGURE 5-9

If, for some reason, you wanted to delete an AutoShape, click it to select it and then press the DELETE key or click the Cut button on the Standard toolbar.

Formatting an AutoShape

The next step is to format the banner AutoShape to match the school's colors: gold and violet. The inside of the banner should be filled with gold. The line around the edge of the banner should be violet and a little thicker. You could use the Fill Color and Line Color buttons on the Drawing toolbar to change the fill color to gold and line color to violet. To increase the thickness of the line, however, you must use the Format AutoShape dialog box. Thus, you will use the Format AutoShape dialog box for all formatting changes to the banner.

In the Format AutoShape dialog box, you also can check the size of the banner. To fit the school name properly in the banner, the width of the banner should be six inches, and the height should be one inch.

Perform the steps on the next page to format an AutoShape.

Other Ways

1. With Drawing toolbar displaying, in Voice Command mode, say "AutoShapes, Stars and Banners, [AutoShape name], [draw shape]"

Submenus

Some submenus display a move handle at their top (shown in Figure 5-7). When you point to a submenu's move handle, the mouse pointer has a four-headed arrow attached to it. If you drag the move handle, Word converts the submenu to a floating toolbar. You later can close the floating toolbar by clicking its Close button.

Steps: To Format an AutoShape

 Position the mouse pointer inside the banner.

The mouse pointer has a four-headed arrow attached to it when positioned in an AutoShape (Figure 5-10).

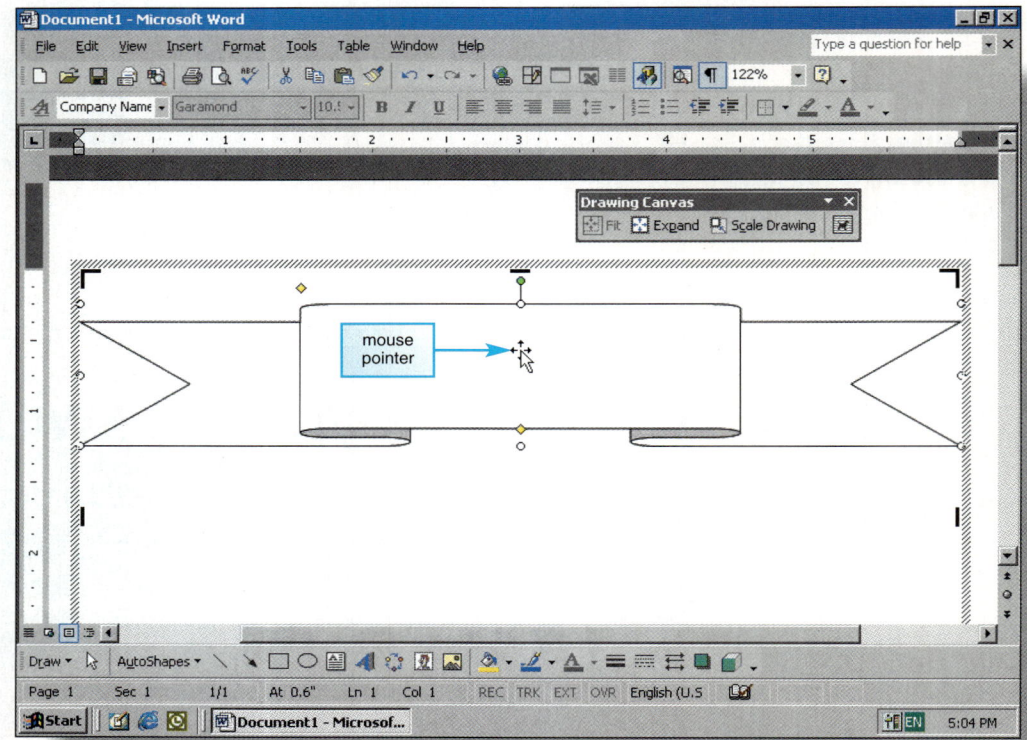

FIGURE 5-10

2 **Double-click inside the banner. When the Format AutoShape dialog box displays, if necessary, click the Size tab. If necessary, change the Height to 1" and the Width to 6" in the Size and rotate area. Point to the Colors and Lines tab.**

Word displays the Format AutoShape dialog box (Figure 5-11). In the Size and rotate area, the Height text box displays 1" and the Width text box displays 6".

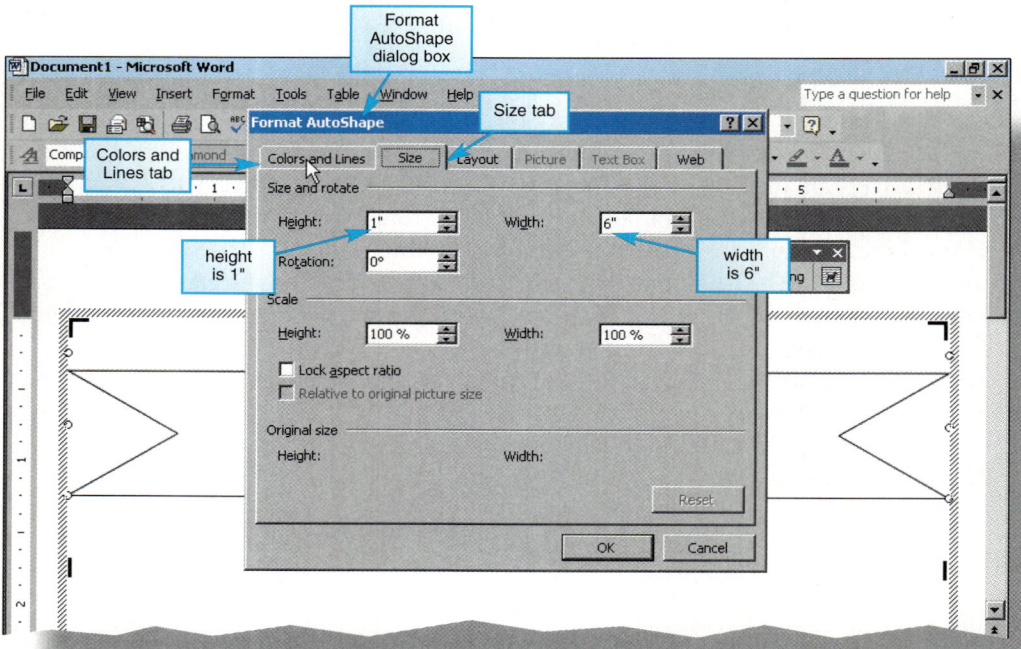

FIGURE 5-11

3 **Click the Colors and Lines tab. In the Fill area, click the Color box arrow and then click Gold. In the Line area, click the Color box arrow and then click Violet. Click the Weight text box up arrow repeatedly until the Weight text box displays 2 pt. Point to the OK button.**

Word displays the Colors and Lines sheet in the Format AutoShape dialog box (Figure 5-12).

4 **Click the OK button.**

Word fills the banner with gold, changes the line color to violet, and increases the thickness of the line (shown in Figure 5-13).

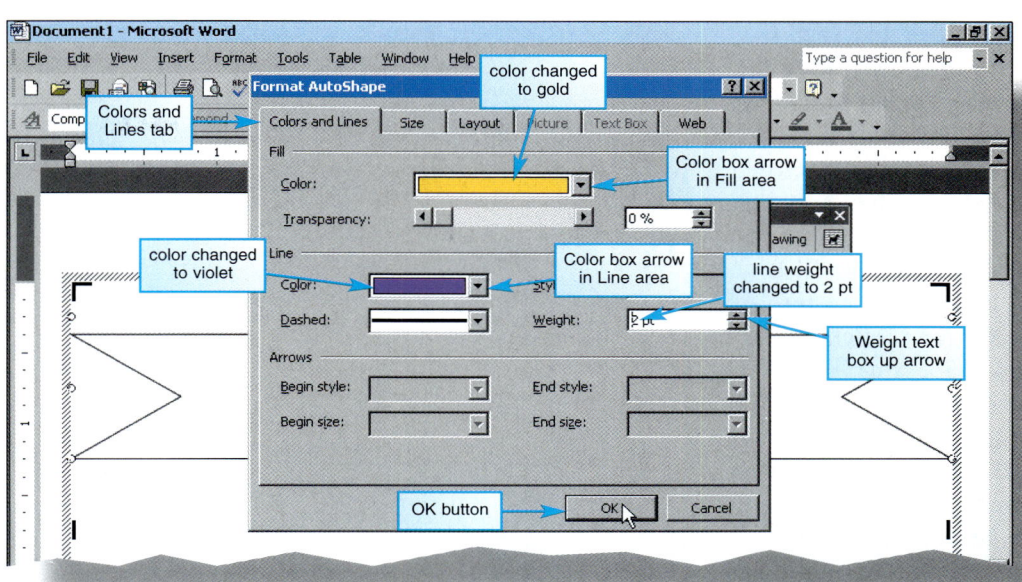

FIGURE 5-12

Other Ways

1. On Format menu click AutoShape
2. Right-click AutoShape, click Format AutoShape on shortcut menu
3. In Voice Command mode, say "Format, AutoShape"

Steps: To Add Text to an AutoShape

1 **Right-click the AutoShape and then point to Add Text on the shortcut menu (Figure 5-13).**

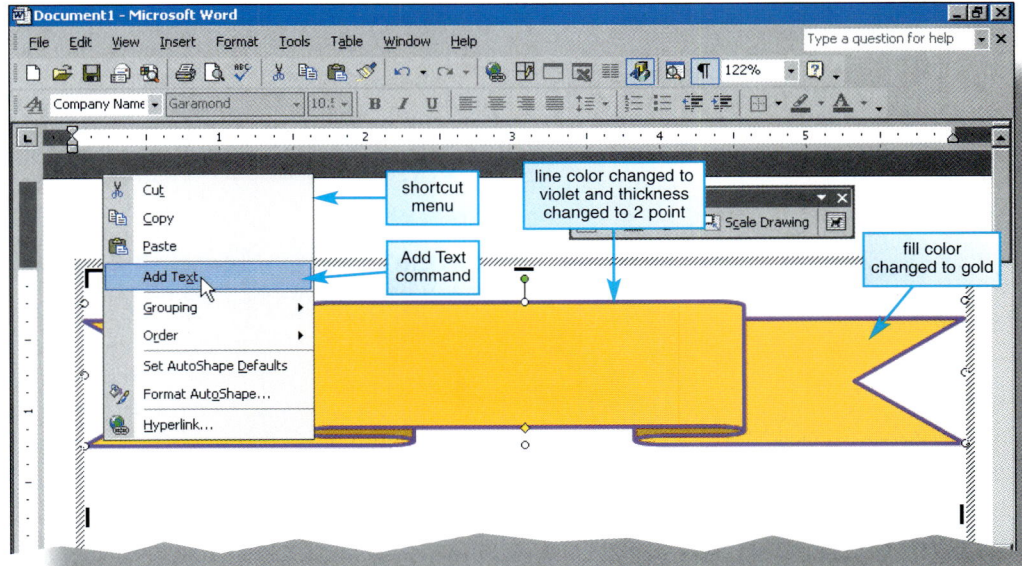

FIGURE 5-13

 2 Click Add Text. If necessary, drag the Drawing Canvas toolbar so it does not cover the Formatting toolbar. Click the Font Size box arrow on the Formatting toolbar and then click 24. Click the Bold button on the Formatting toolbar. Click the Center button on the Formatting toolbar. Click the Font Color button arrow on the Formatting toolbar and then click Violet. Type Yorktown and then press the ENTER key. Type Community College and then click outside the AutoShape but inside the drawing canvas to deselect the AutoShape.

The school name displays in the banner AutoShape (Figure 5-14). The drawing canvas remains selected. The Text Box toolbar also may display on your screen.

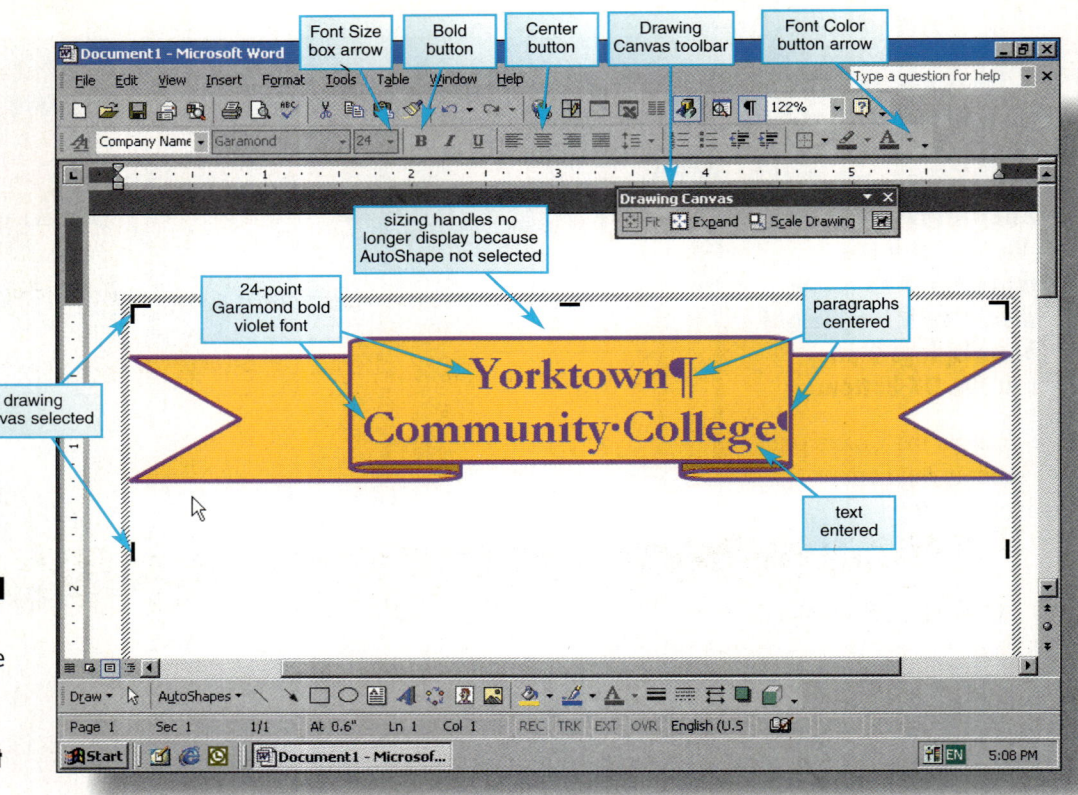

FIGURE 5-14

Other Ways

1. In Voice Command mode, say "Right Click, Add Text, [enter text]"

AutoShape Text

You can resize a text box to be as wide as the text it contains. Point to the edge of the AutoShape and then double-click when the mouse pointer has a four-headed arrow attached to it. When the Format AutoShape dialog box displays, click the Text Box tab and then place a check mark in the Resize AutoShape to fit text check box. Click the OK button.

If the drawing canvas becomes deselected, click in the drawing canvas in an area outside the AutoShape to select the drawing canvas again. A selected drawing canvas displays the angled sizing handles at its corners and straight sizing handles at its middle locations.

Resizing and Formatting the Drawing Canvas

Recall that Word placed a drawing canvas around the banner AutoShape. The height of the drawing canvas is about 3.5 inches, which is too big for this letter. You want the drawing canvas to extend about .25 inches above and below the banner AutoShape. Thus, you must resize the drawing canvas by dragging its bottom border up.

Perform the following steps to resize the drawing canvas.

Working with AutoShapes and the Drawing Canvas • WD 5.17

Steps: To Resize the Drawing Canvas

1 **Scroll down until the bottom of the drawing canvas displays in the document window. Position the mouse pointer on the bottom-middle sizing handle until the mouse pointer changes to a T. Drag the bottom-middle sizing handle upward until the dotted line is positioned as shown in Figure 5-15.**

Word displays a dotted line as you drag the mouse (Figure 5-15). When you release the mouse, the bottom of the drawing canvas will be resized to the location of the dotted line.

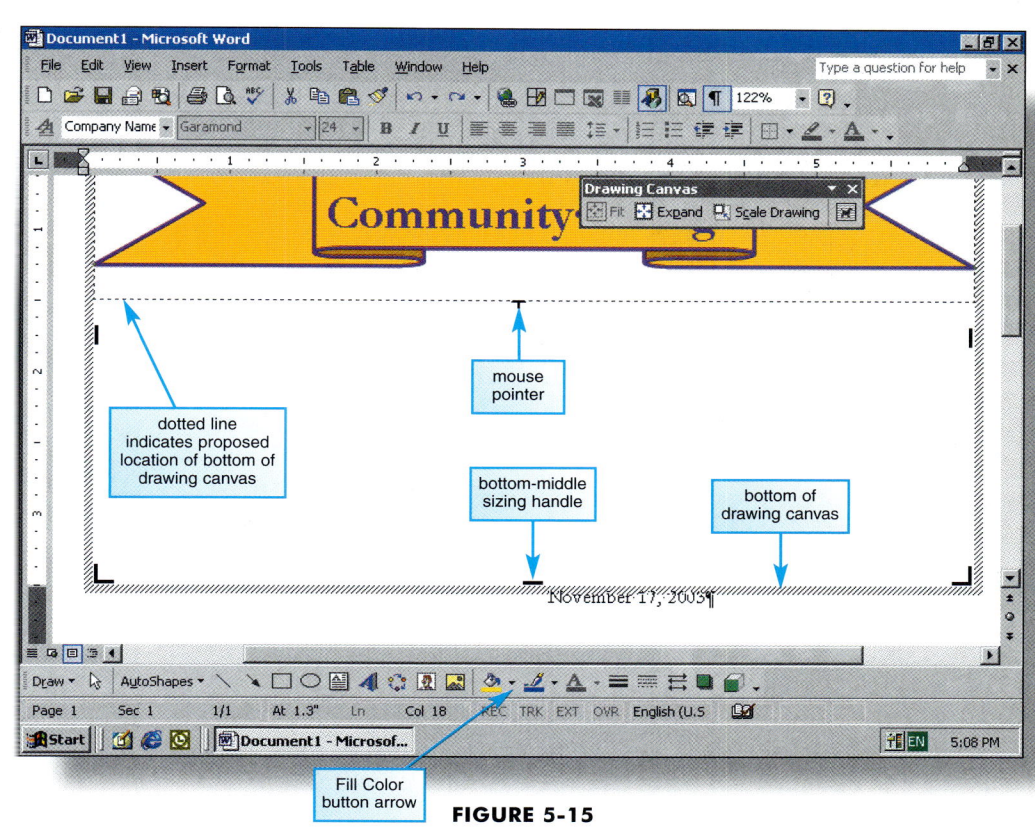

FIGURE 5-15

2 **Release the mouse button.**

Word resizes the drawing canvas (shown in Figure 5-16 on the next page).

The next step is to fill the drawing canvas with a transparent shade of gray. If you simply wanted to fill the drawing canvas, you would select it and then click the Fill Color button arrow on the Drawing toolbar. To make the fill color transparent, however, you must use the Format Drawing Canvas dialog box, as shown in the steps on the next page.

Other Ways

1. On Format menu click Drawing Canvas, click Size tab, enter height and width values in the Size and rotate area, click OK button
2. Right-click drawing canvas in area outside AutoShape, click Format Drawing Canvas on shortcut menu, click Size tab, enter height and width values in the Size and rotate area, click OK button
3. In Voice Command mode, say "Format, Drawing Canvas, Size, [enter height and width values], OK"

Steps: To Format a Drawing Canvas

1 Scroll up to display the entire drawing canvas in the document window. Point to an edge of the drawing canvas and double-click when the mouse pointer has a four-headed arrow attached to it. When the Format Drawing Canvas dialog box displays, if necessary, click the Colors and Lines tab. In the Fill area, click the Color box arrow and then click Gray-25%. Drag the Transparency slider until the Transparency text box displays 50%. Point to the OK button.

Word displays the Format Drawing Canvas dialog box (Figure 5-16). As you drag the slider to the right, the fill color becomes more transparent.

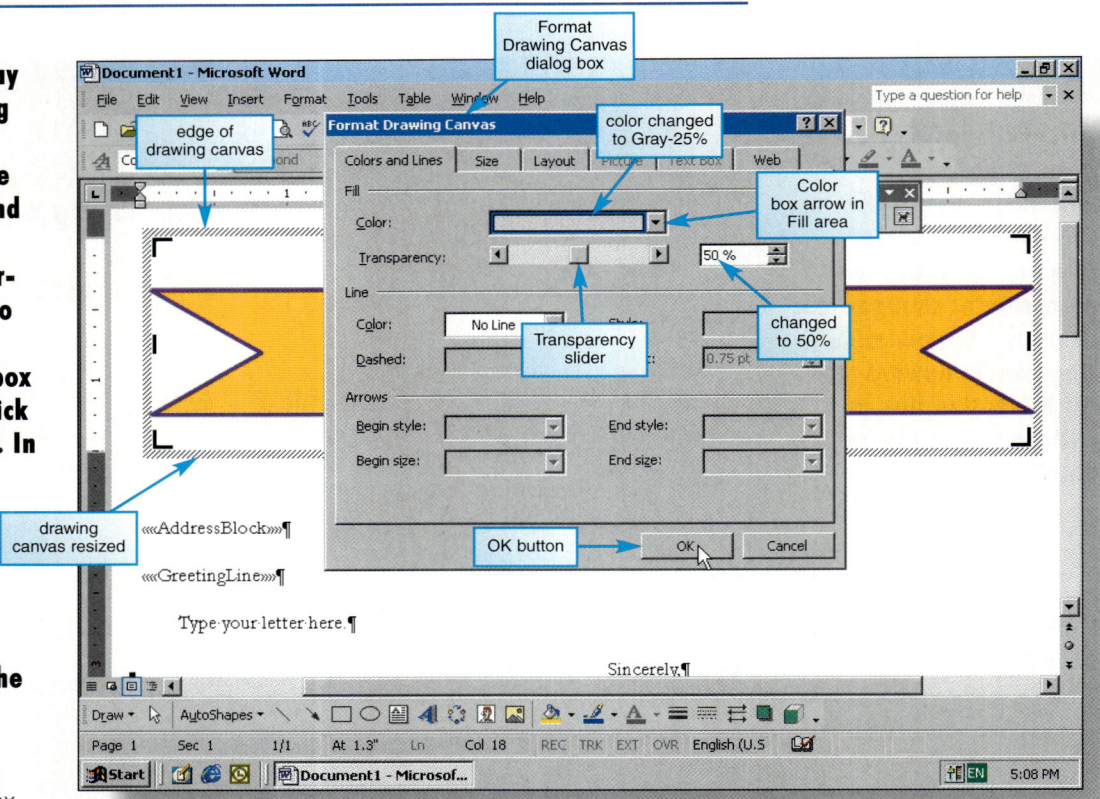

FIGURE 5-16

2 Click the OK button. Click the Drawing button on the Standard toolbar to remove the Drawing toolbar from the screen.

Word fills the drawing canvas with a transparent shade of gray (Figure 5-17).

Other Ways

1. On Format menu click Drawing Canvas
2. Right-click edge of drawing canvas in area outside AutoShape, click Format Drawing Canvas on shortcut menu
3. In Voice Command mode, say "Format, Drawing Canvas"

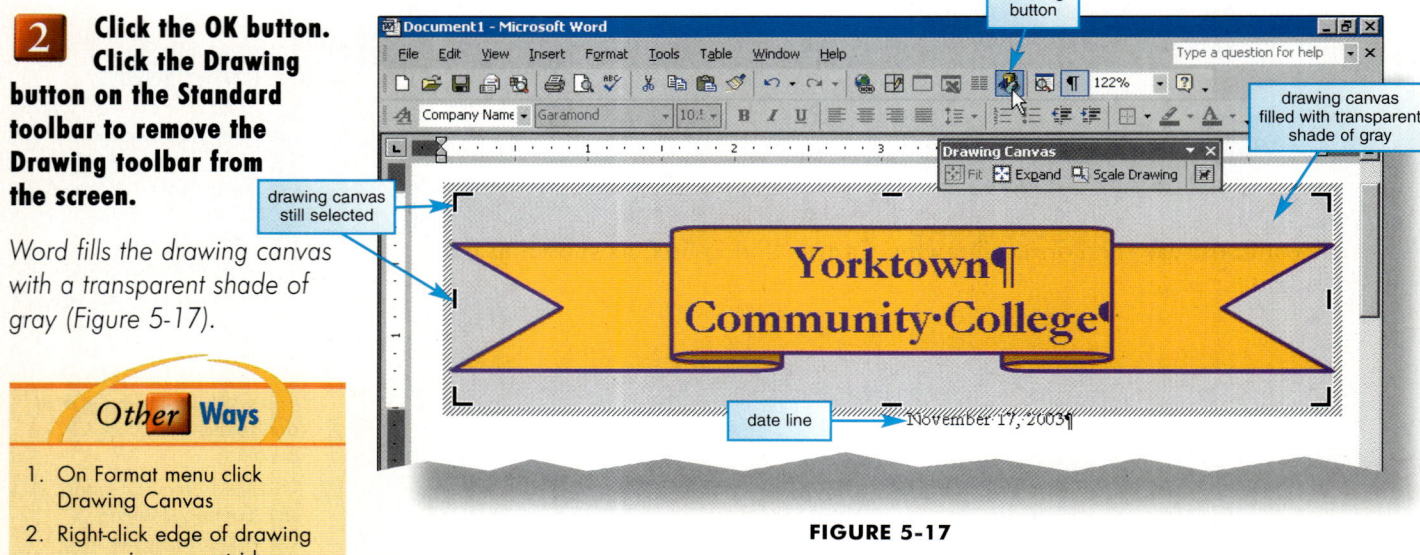

FIGURE 5-17

Notice in Figure 5-17 that the bottom of the drawing canvas touches the top of the date. This is apparent because you filled the drawing canvas with gray. Thus, you want some white space between the drawing canvas (the gray fill) and the date. In a previous project, you pressed CTRL+0 (the numeral zero) to add one blank line, which is equal to 12 points, above a paragraph. In this project, you want 24 points, or the equivalent of two blank lines above the date. Perform the following steps to change paragraph formatting.

Steps: To Change Paragraph Formatting

1 **Position the insertion point in the date line in the letter. Click Format on the menu bar and then click Reveal Formatting. In the Reveal Formatting task pane, scroll to display all the paragraph settings in the Formatting of selected text area and then point to Spacing.**

Word displays the Reveal Formatting task pane (Figure 5-18).

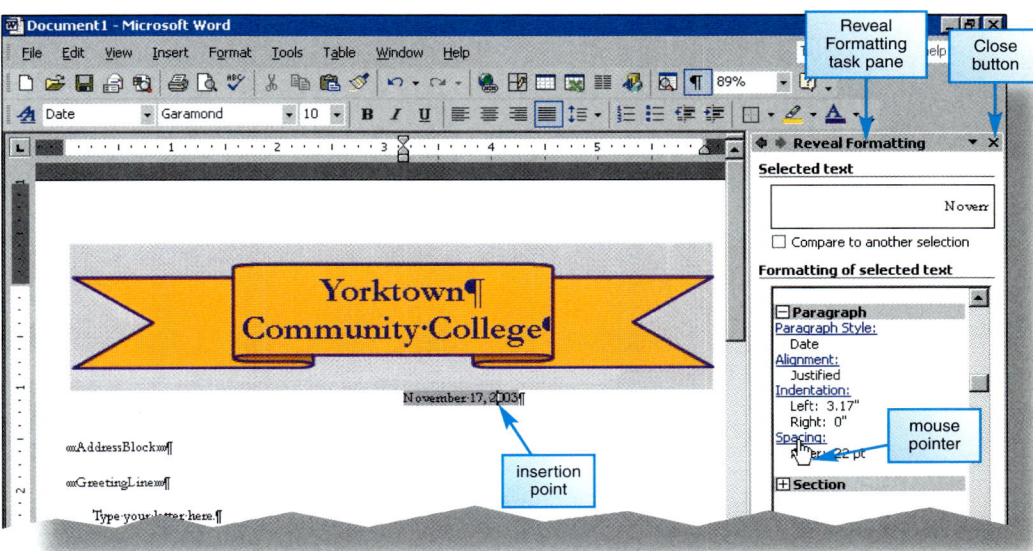

FIGURE 5-18

2 **Click Spacing. In the Spacing area in the Paragraph dialog box, click the Before text box up arrow repeatedly until the text box displays 24 pt. Point to the OK button.**

Word displays the Paragraph dialog box (Figure 5-19).

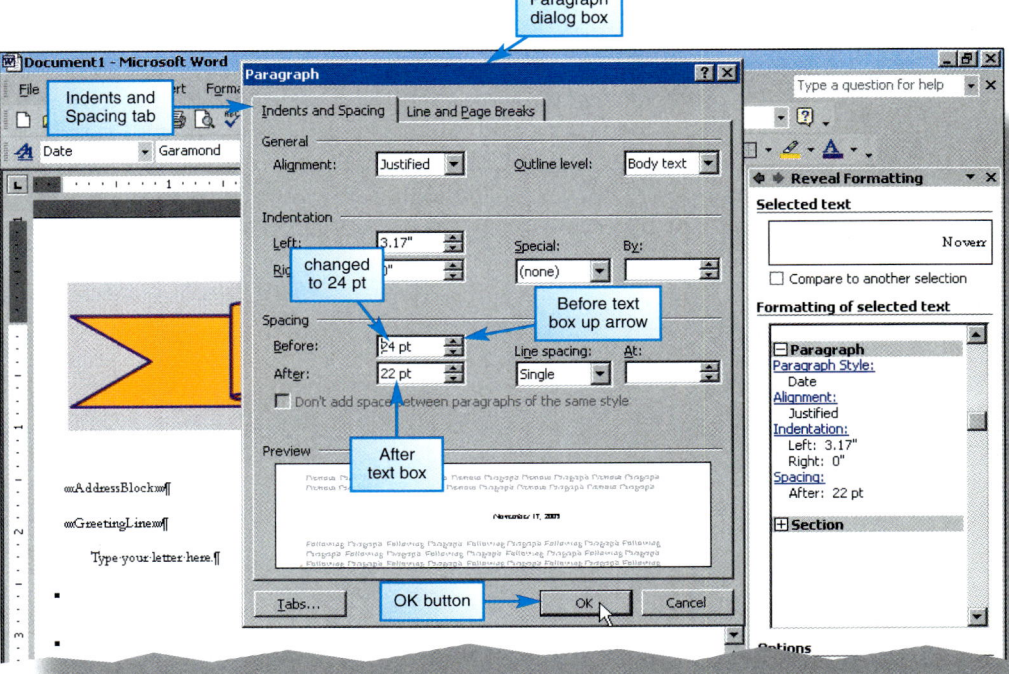

FIGURE 5-19

 **3** **Click the OK button. Click the Close button on the Reveal Formatting task pane title bar to close the task pane.**

Word adds 24 points above the paragraph containing the date (Figure 5-20).

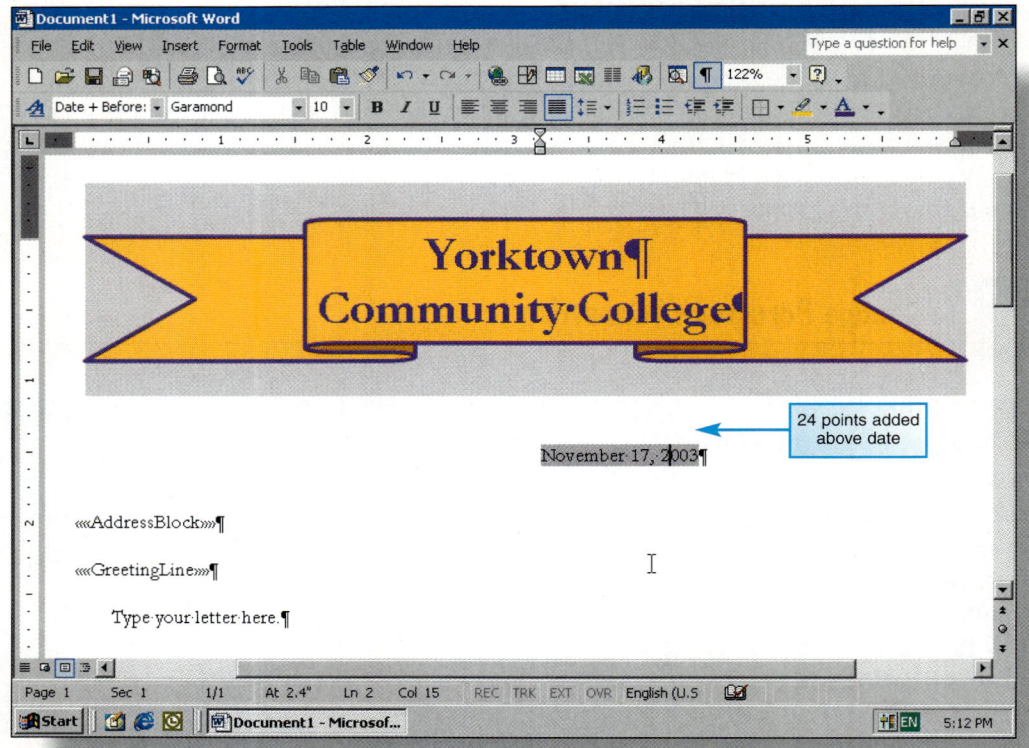

FIGURE 5-20

Other Ways

1. On Format menu click Paragraph
2. Click Paragraph on shortcut menu
3. In Voice Command mode, say "Format, Paragraph"

Through the Paragraph dialog box, you also can adjust the amount of space that displays after a paragraph by changing the value in the After text box in the Spacing area (Figure 5-19 on the previous page).

Creating a Folder

You have performed several tasks to the form letter and should save it. You want to save this and all other documents created in this project in a folder called Graduation. This folder does not exist so you must create it. Rather than creating the folder in Windows, you can create folders in Word, which saves you time.

Perform the following steps to create a folder during the process of saving a document.

More About

Dialog Boxes

You can resize some dialog boxes, such as the Save As dialog box and the Open dialog box. Simply point to the edge of the dialog box and drag when the mouse pointer shape changes to a double-headed arrow.

Steps | To Create a Folder while Saving

1 Insert your floppy disk into drive A. Click the Save button on the Standard toolbar. When the Save As dialog box displays, type Graduation Form Letter in the File name text box. Do not press the ENTER key after typing the file name. If necessary, click the Save in box arrow and then click 3½ Floppy (A:). Click the Create New Folder button. Type Graduation in the New Folder dialog box and then point to the OK button.

Word displays the New Folder dialog box inside the Save As dialog box (Figure 5-21).

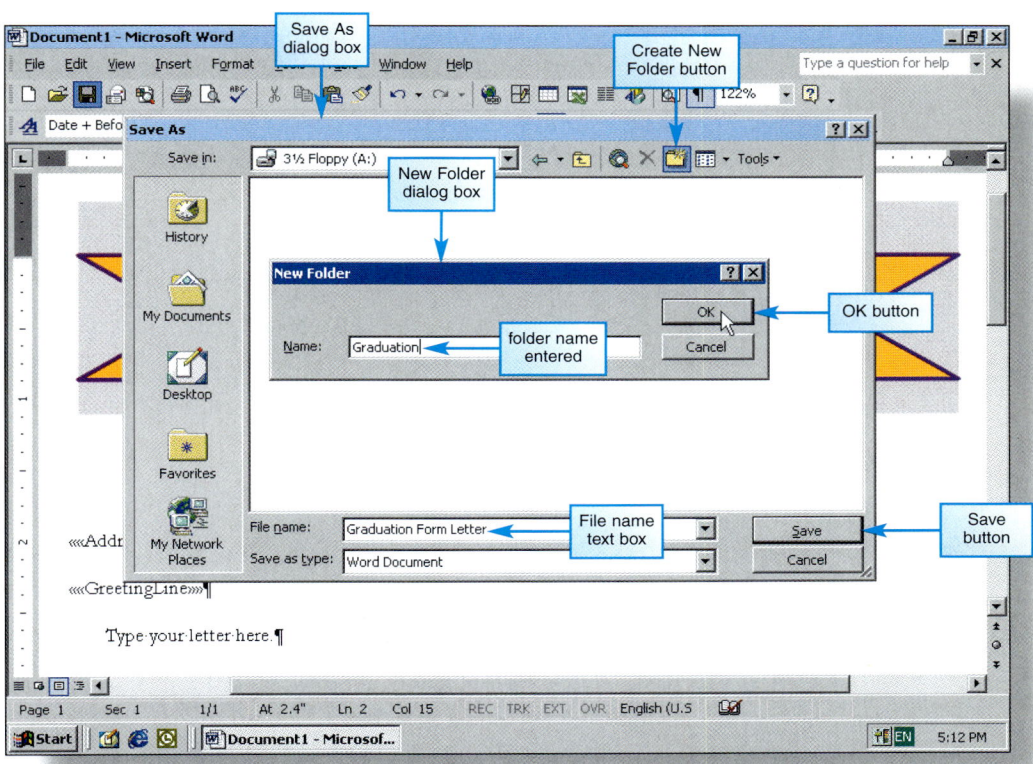

FIGURE 5-21

2 Click the OK button. Click the Save button in the Save As dialog box.

Word creates the Graduation folder on a floppy disk in drive A and then saves the document in the folder with the file name, Graduation Form Letter (shown in Figure 5-23 on page WD 5.23).

Other dialog boxes, such as the Open and Insert File dialog boxes, also have a Create New Folder button, saving you the time of using Windows to create a new folder for document storage.

1. On File menu click Save As
2. Press CTRL+F12
3. In Voice Command mode, say "File, Save As"

Creating a Data Source

A data source is a file that contains the data that changes from one merged document to the next. As shown in Figure 5-22 on the next page, a data source often is organized as a table that consists of a series of rows and columns. Each row is called a **record**. The first row of a data source is called the **header record** because it identifies the name of each column. Each row below the header row is called a **data record**. Data records contain the text that varies in each copy of the merged document. The data source for this project contains five data records. In this project, each data record identifies a different student. Thus, five form letters will be generated from this data source.

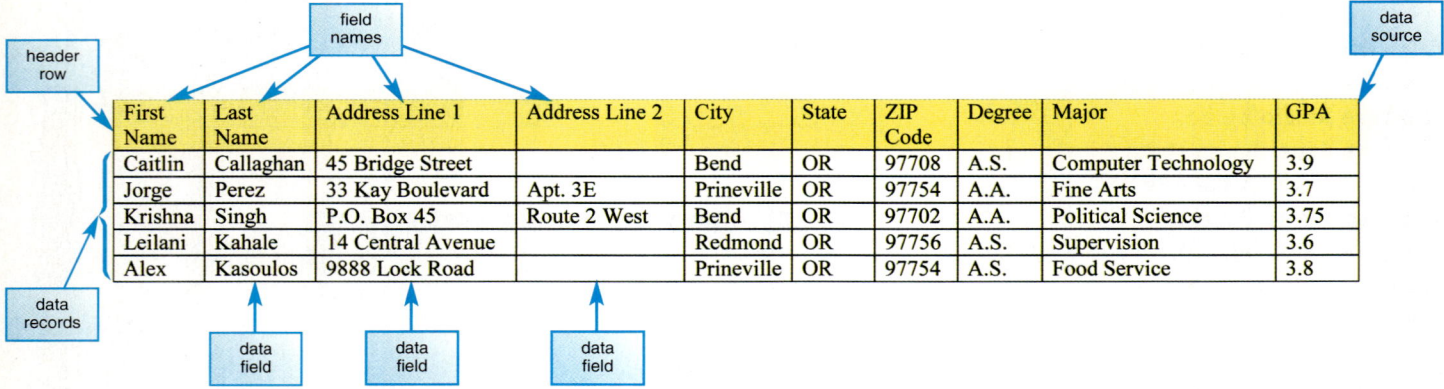

FIGURE 5-22

Terminology

The terms field and record originate from the computer programming field. Don't be intimidated by these terms. A field is simply a column in a table, and a record is a row. Instead of the term field, some programmers use the terms variable or attribute to identify a column of data.

Data Sources

A data source can be an Access database table, an Outlook contacts list, an Excel worksheet, or a Word table. If the necessary records already exist in one of these Office applications, you can instruct Word to use the existing file as the data source for the mail merge.

Each column in the data source is called a **data field**. A data field represents a group of similar data. Each data field must be identified uniquely with a name, called a **field name**. For example, First Name is the name of the field (column) that contains the first names of students. In this project, the data source contains ten data fields with the following field names: First Name, Last Name, Address Line 1, Address Line 2, City, State, ZIP Code, Degree, Major, and GPA.

The first step in creating a data source is to decide which fields it will contain. That is, you must identify the data that will vary from one merged document to the next. For each field, you must decide on a field name. Field names must be unique; that is, no two field names may be the same.

Data sources often contain the same fields. For this reason, Word provides you with a list of 13 commonly used field names. You will use seven of the 13 field names supplied by Word: First Name, Last Name, Address Line 1, Address Line 2, City, State, and ZIP Code. You will delete the other six field names from the list supplied by Word. That is, you will delete Title, Company Name, Country, Home Phone, Work Phone, and E-mail Address. Then, you will add three new field names, Degree, Major, and GPA, because you want to store student degree types, majors, and GPAs in the data source.

Fields may be listed in any order in the data source. That is, the order of fields has no effect on the order in which they will print in the main document.

Earlier, you closed the Mail Merge Wizard, which displayed in the Mail Merge toolbar. At this time, you wish to continue with the Mail Merge Wizard to create the new data source. Perform the following steps to restart the Mail Merge Wizard and type a new data source.

Steps To Type a New Data Source

1 **Click Tools on the menu bar, point to Letters and Mailings, and then click Mail Merge Wizard. Click Type a new list in the Select recipients area in the Mail Merge task pane. When the Type a new list area displays, point to Create.**

Word restarts the Mail Merge Wizard, which remembers where you left off in the merge process (Figure 5-23). You have three choices for working with a data source: use an existing list, select from Outlook contacts, or type a new list.

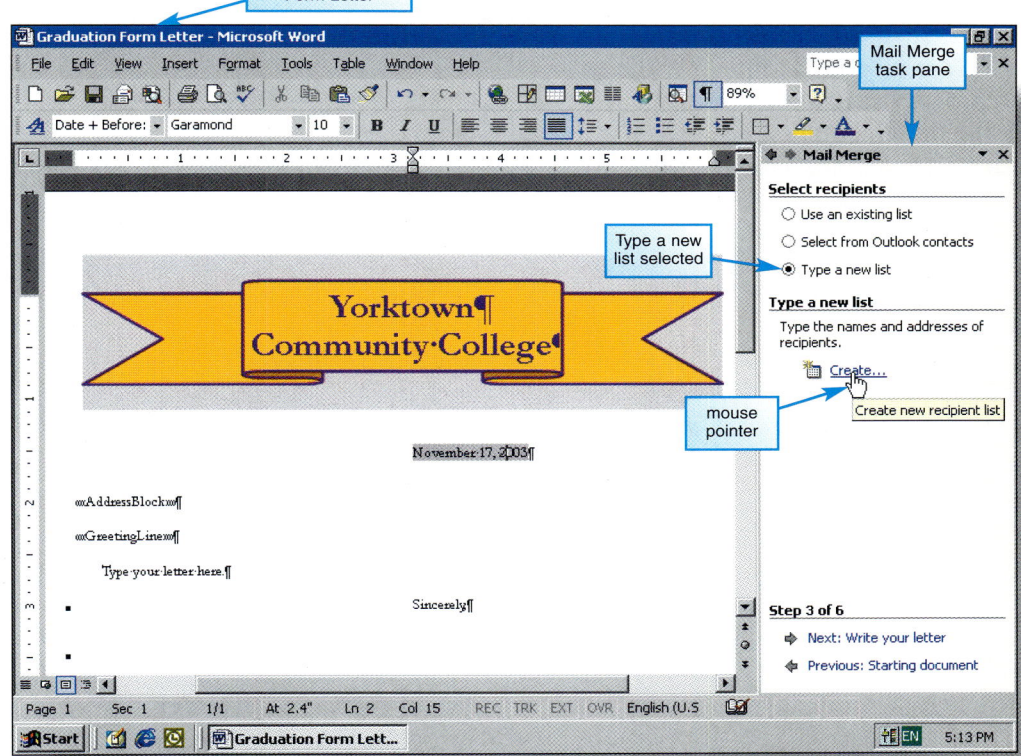

FIGURE 5-23

2 **Click Create. When the New Address List dialog box displays, point to the Customize button.**

Word displays the New Address List dialog box (Figure 5-24). You enter data records into the data source through this dialog box. In the Enter Address information list, Word displays a list of 13 commonly used field names. You can modify this list by clicking the Customize button.

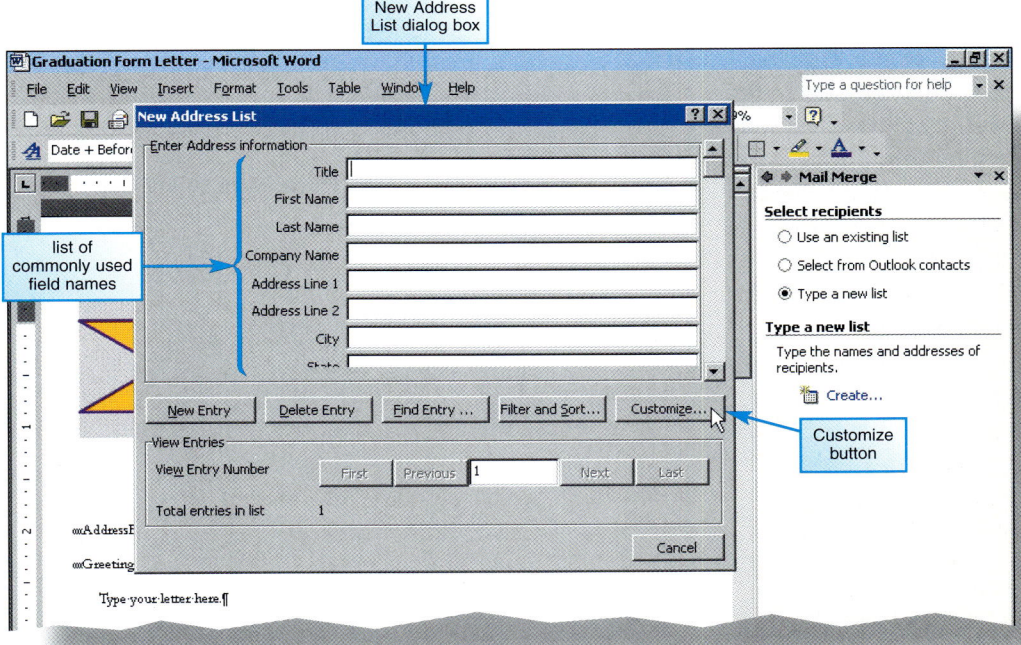

FIGURE 5-24

3 **Click the Customize button. When Word displays the Customize Address List dialog box, be sure Title is selected in the Field Names list and then click the Delete button. When the Microsoft Word dialog box displays, point to the Yes button.**

Word displays a dialog box asking if you are sure you want to delete the selected field (Figure 5-25). The field name, Title, is selected for removal.

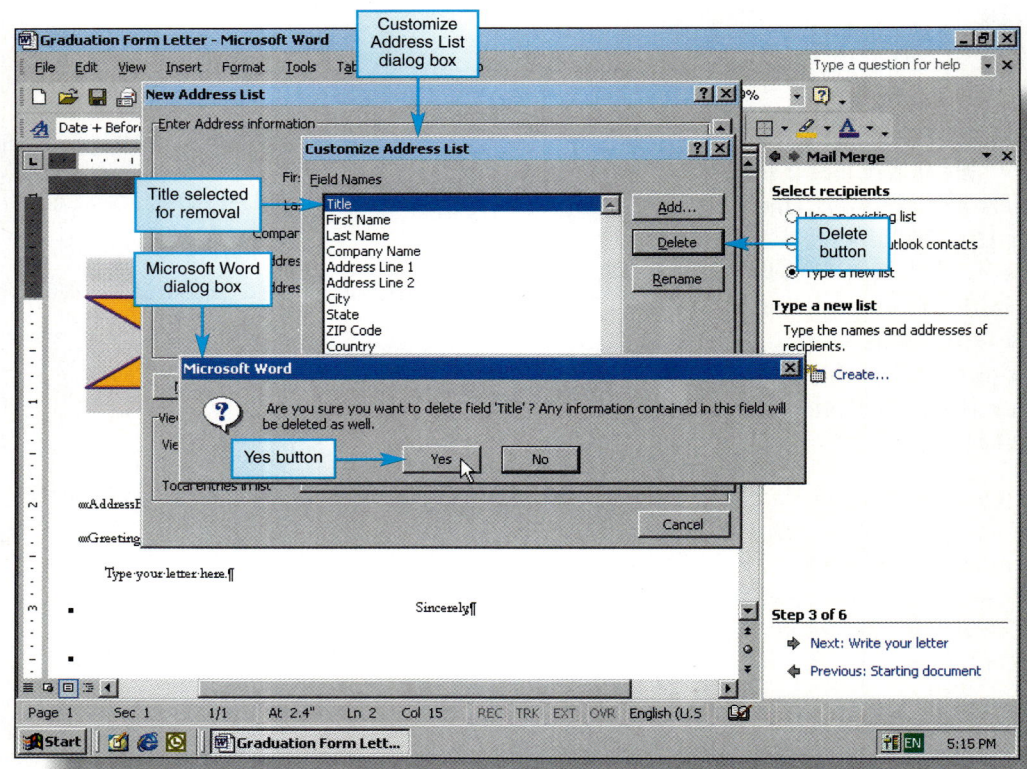

FIGURE 5-25

4 **Click the Yes button. Click Company Name in the Field Names list. Click the Delete button. Click the Yes button. Click Country in the Field Names list. Click the Delete button. Click the Yes button. Click Home Phone in the Field Names list. Click the Delete button. Click the Yes button. Click Work Phone in the Field Names list. Click the Delete button. Click the Yes button. Click E-mail Address in the Field Names list. Click the Delete button. Click the Yes button.**

Word removes six field names from the list (Figure 5-26). The next step is to add the Degree, Major, and GPA field names to the list.

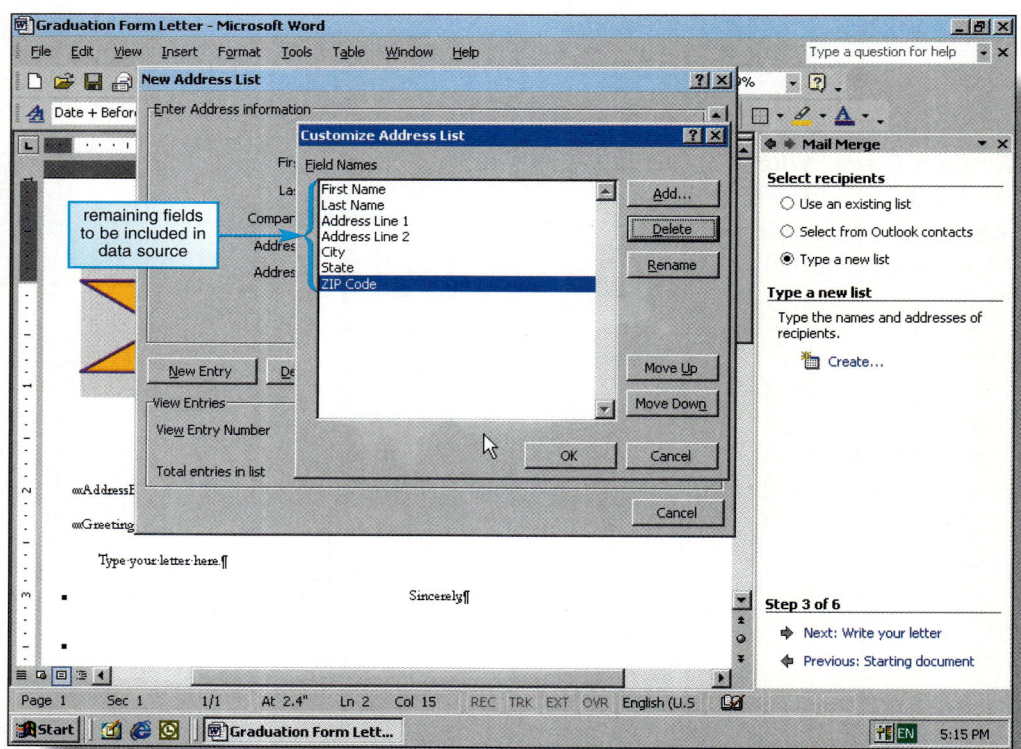

FIGURE 5-26

Creating a Data Source • WD 5.25

5 Click the Add button. When Word displays the Add Field dialog box, type Degree in the text box and then point to the OK button.

Word displays the Add Field dialog box (Figure 5-27).

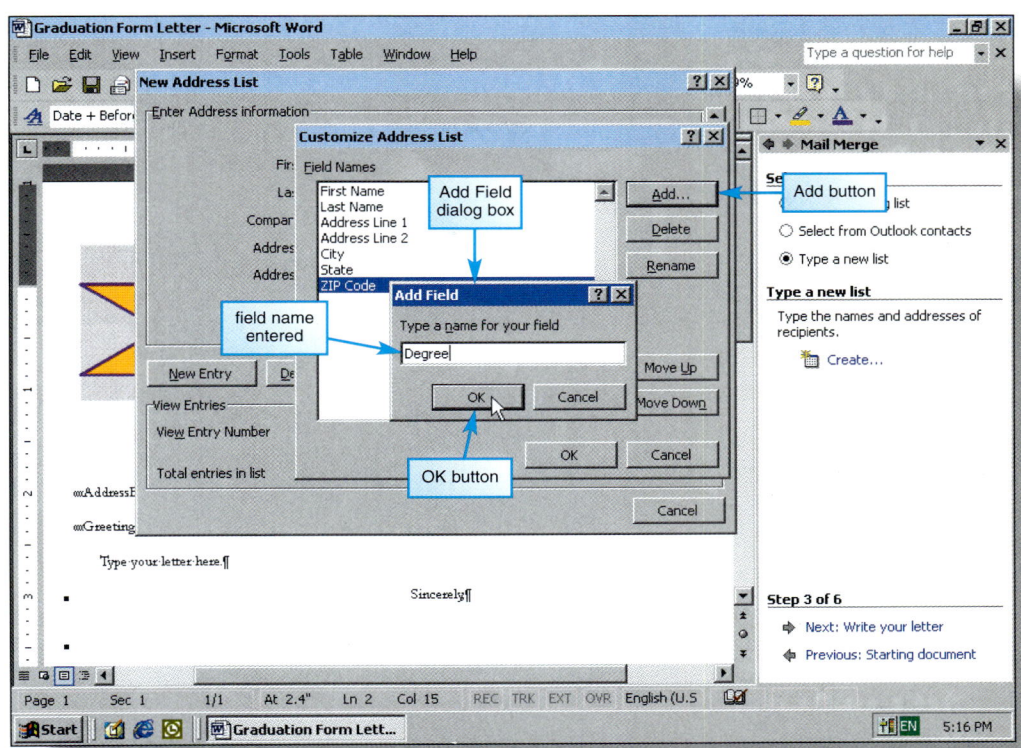

FIGURE 5-27

6 Click the OK button.

Word adds the Degree field name to the bottom of the Field Names list.

7 Click the Add button. When Word displays the Add Field dialog box, type Major in the text box and then click the OK button. Click the Add button. When Word displays the Add Field dialog box, type GPA in the text box and then click the OK button. Point to the OK button in the Customize Address List dialog box.

Word adds the Major and GPA field names to the bottom of the Field Names list (Figure 5-28).

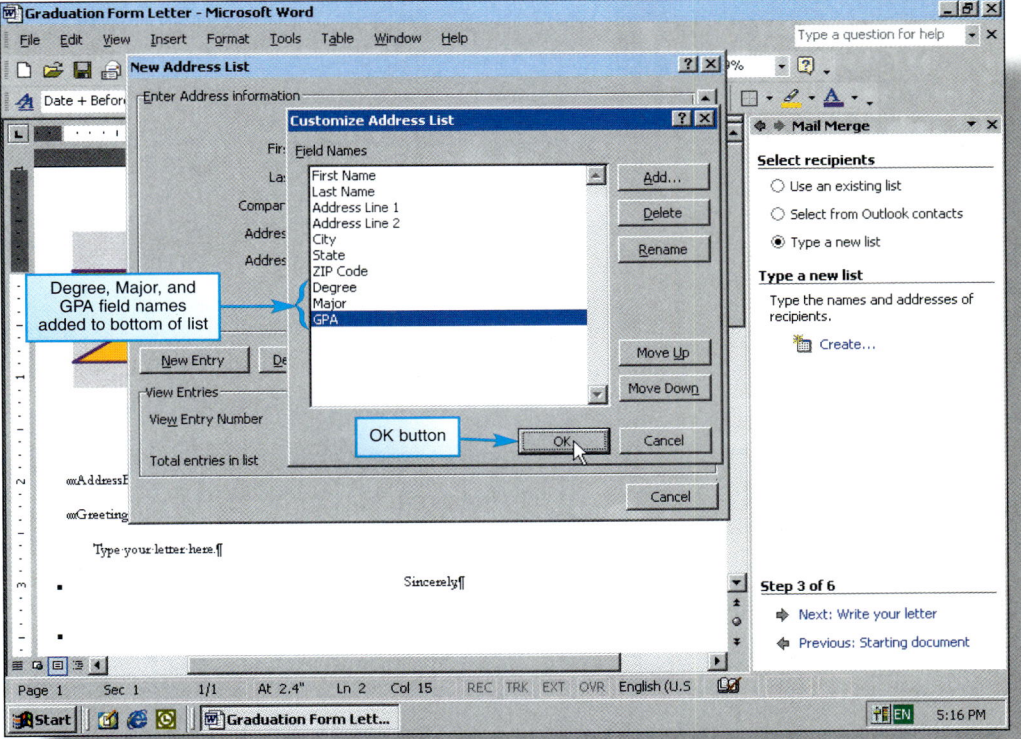

FIGURE 5-28

WD 5.26 • Project 5 • Generating Form Letters, Mailing Labels, Envelopes, and Directories

8 Click the OK button. When the Customize Address List dialog box closes, click the First Name text box in the New Address List dialog box.

Word displays the new list of field names in the Enter Address information area in the New Address dialog box (Figure 5-29). The insertion point displays in the First Name text box, ready for your first data record entry. Text you enter in this dialog box becomes records in the data source.

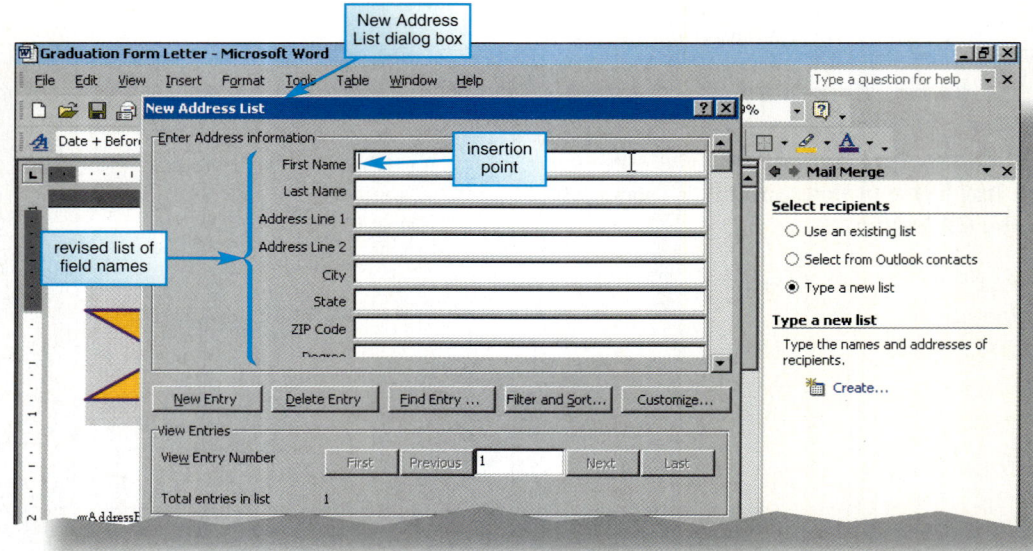

FIGURE 5-29

9 Type Caitlin and then press the ENTER key. Type Callaghan and then press the ENTER key. Type 45 Bridge Street and then press the ENTER key twice. Type Bend and then press the ENTER key. Type OR and then press the ENTER key. Type 97708 as the ZIP Code (Figure 5-30).

If you notice an error in a text box, click the text box and then correct the error as you would in the document window.

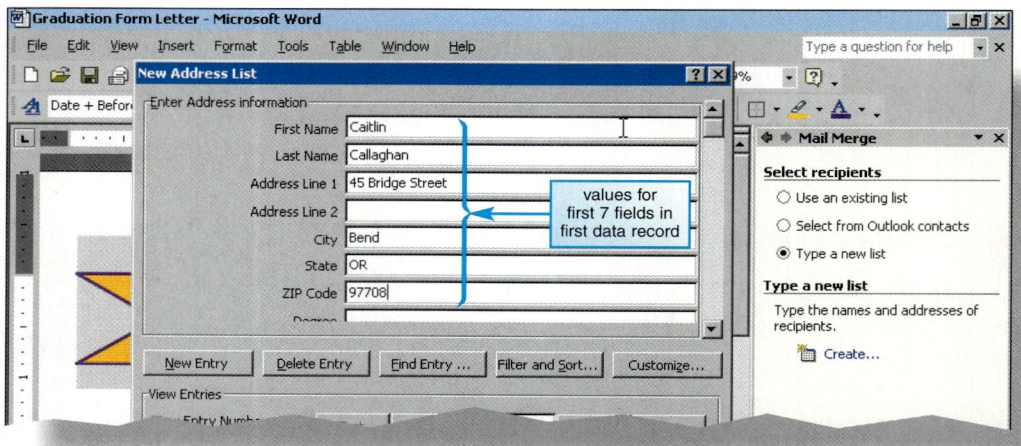

FIGURE 5-30

10 Press the ENTER key. Type A.S. and then press the ENTER key. Type Computer Technology and then press the ENTER key. Type 3.9 and then point to the New Entry button.

The first three fields scroll off the top of the dialog box to make room for the last three fields (Figure 5-31).

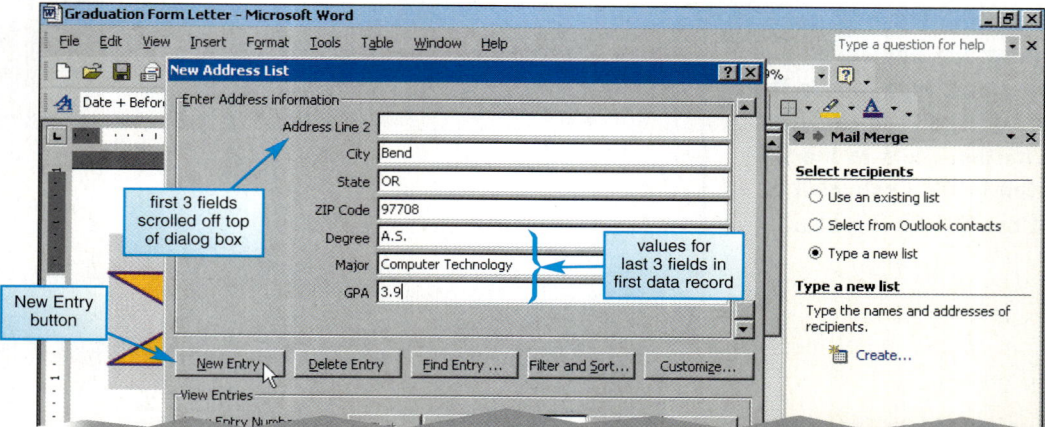

FIGURE 5-31

11 **Click the New Entry button.**

Word adds the entered data to the data source and clears the text boxes in the Enter Address information area in preparation for the next data record to be entered (Figure 5-32).

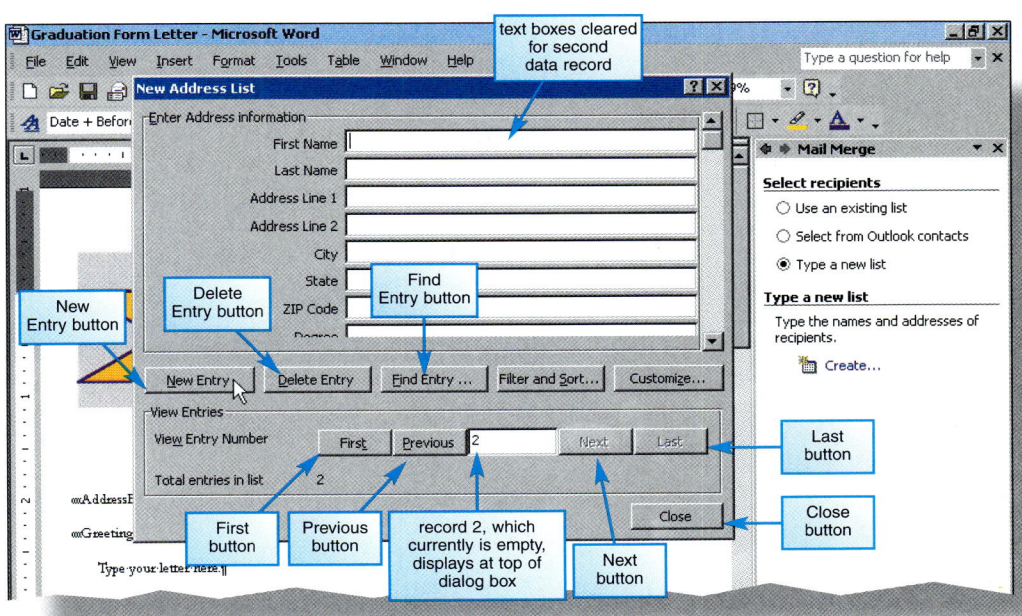

FIGURE 5-32

The next step is to enter the remaining four records into the New Address List dialog box, as described in the steps below.

TO ENTER MORE RECORDS

1. Type Jorge and then press the ENTER key. Type Perez and then press the ENTER key. Type 33 Kay Boulevard and then press the ENTER key. Type Apt. 3E and then press the ENTER key. Type Prineville and then press the ENTER key. Type OR and then press the ENTER key. Type 97754 and then press the ENTER key. Type A.A. and then press the ENTER key. Type Fine Arts and then press the ENTER key. Type 3.7 and then click the New Entry button.

2. Type Krishna and then press the ENTER key. Type Singh and then press the ENTER key. Type P.O. Box 45 and then press the ENTER key. Type Route 2 West and then press the ENTER key. Type Bend and then press the ENTER key. Type OR and then press the ENTER key. Type 97702 and then press the ENTER key. Type A.A. and then press the ENTER key. Type Political Science and then press the ENTER key. Type 3.75 and then click the New Entry button.

3. Type Leilani and then press the ENTER key. Type Kahale and then press the ENTER key. Type 14 Central Avenue and then press the ENTER key twice. Type Redmond and then press the ENTER key. Type OR and then press the ENTER key. Type 97756 and then press the ENTER key. Type A.S. and then press the ENTER key. Type Supervisior and then press the ENTER key. Type 3.6 and then click the New Entry button.

4. Type Alex and then press the ENTER key. Type Kasoulos and then press the ENTER key. Type 9888 Lock Road and then press the ENTER key twice. Type Prineville and then press the ENTER key. Type OR and then press the ENTER key. Type 97754 and then press the ENTER key. Type A.S. and then press the ENTER key. Type Food Service and then press the ENTER key. Type 3.8 and then click the Close button (shown in Figure 5-32).

The data records are entered in the data source.

Organizing Data

Organize the information in a data source so it is reusable. For example, you may want to print a person's title, first, middle, and last name (e.g., Mr. Roger A. Bannerman) in the inside address but only the title and last name in the salutation (Dear Mr. Bannerman). Thus, you should break the name into separate fields: title, first name, middle initial, and last name.

When you click the Close button in the New Address List dialog box, the Mail Merge Wizard instructs you to save the data source. Perform the following steps to save the data source in the Graduation folder you created earlier in this project.

Steps: To Save the Data Source when Prompted by the Mail Merge Wizard

1 When the Save Address List dialog box displays, type `Graduate List` in the File name box. If necessary, change the drive to 3½ Floppy (A:) and then double-click the Graduation folder. Point to the Save button in the Save As dialog box.

The data source for this project will be saved with the file name, Graduate List (Figure 5-33). Word saves the data source as a Microsoft Office Address List, which is a Microsoft Access database file.

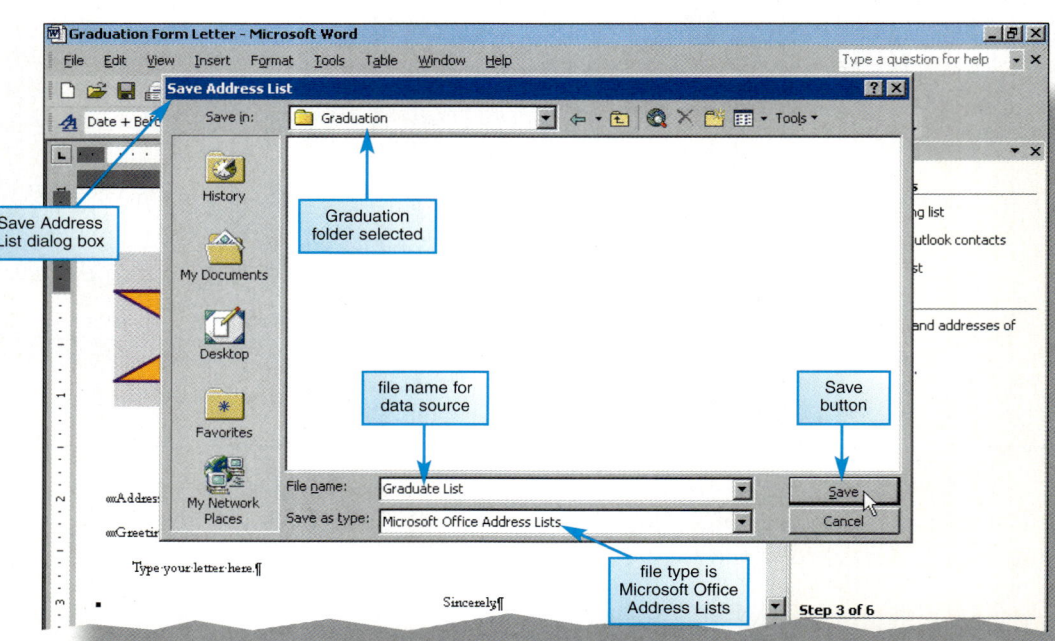

FIGURE 5-33

2 Click the Save button in the Save Address List dialog box. When the Mail Merge Recipients dialog box displays, point to the OK button.

Word saves the data source in the Graduation folder on the disk in drive A using the file name, Graduate List, and then displays the Mail Merge Recipients dialog box (Figure 5-34).

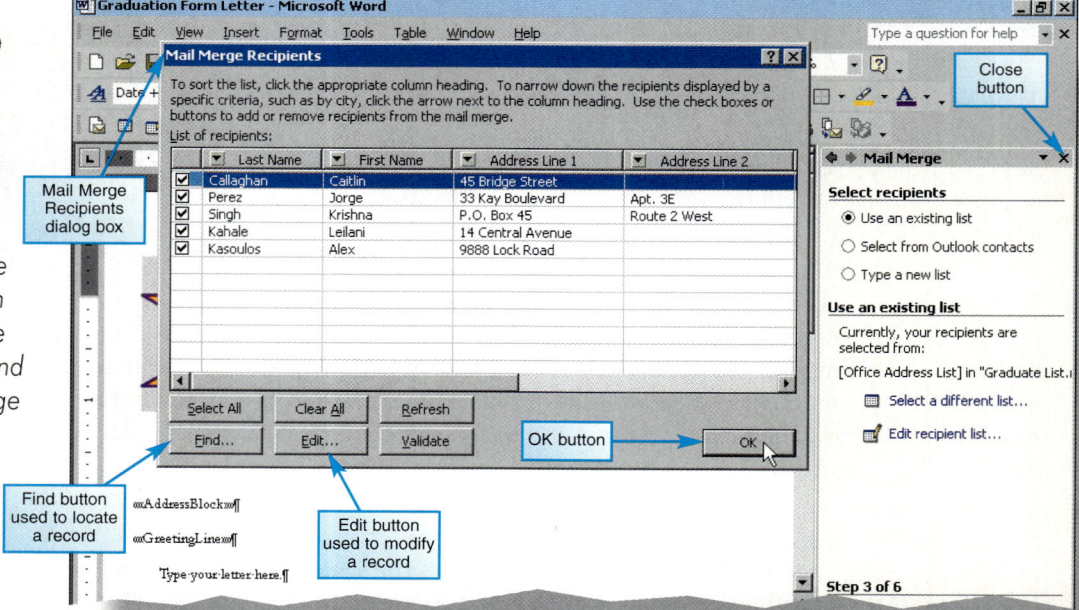

FIGURE 5-34

3 Click the OK button. Click the Close button on the right edge of the Mail Merge task pane title bar. If the Mail Merge toolbar does not display on the screen, click Tools on the menu bar, point to Letters and Mailings, and then click Show Mail Merge Toolbar.

Word displays the Mail Merge toolbar docked at the top of the screen (Figure 5-35). You close the Mail Merge task pane because you want to enter the contents of the form letter next.

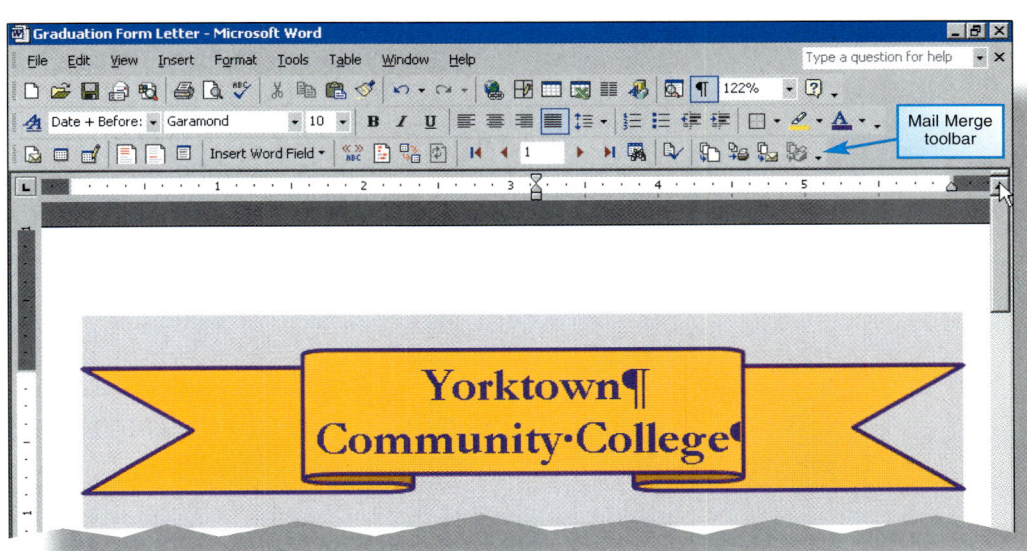

FIGURE 5-35

If you are familiar with Microsoft Access, you can open the Graduate List file in Access. You do not have to be familiar with Access, however, to continue with the mail merge. Word simply stores a data source as an Access table because it is an efficient method of storing a data source.

Editing Records in the Data Source

The Mail Merge toolbar displays on the screen because you have identified a main document and a data source. Figure 5-36 identifies the buttons and boxes on the Mail Merge toolbar. These buttons and boxes are explained as they are used.

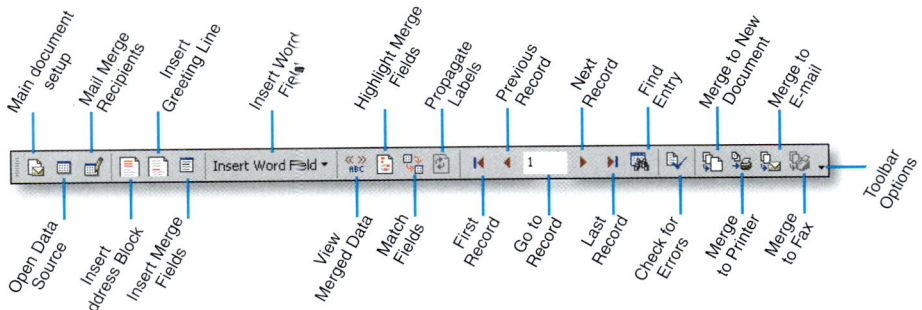

FIGURE 5-36

All of the data records have been entered into the data source and saved with the file name, Graduate List. To add more data records to the data source, click the Mail Merge Recipients button on the Mail Merge toolbar to display the Mail Merge Recipients dialog box (shown in Figure 5-34). Click the Edit button in the Mail Merge Recipients dialog box to display the data records in a dialog box similar to the one shown in Figure 5-32 on page WD 5.27. Then add records as described in the previous steps.

Saving Data Sources

Word, by default, saves a data source in the My Data Sources folder on your hard disk. Likewise, when you open a data source, Word initially looks in the My Data Sources folder for the file. The default file type for a new data source created in Word is called a Microsoft Address List. If you are familiar with Microsoft Access, you can open and view a Microsoft Address List file type in Access.

Docked Toolbars

Word docks the Mail Merge toolbar at the top of the Word window. If you want to move the docked toolbar above or below the Standard and Formatting toolbars, drag the move handle on the Mail Merge toolbar to position the toolbar in a new location.

To change an existing data record in the data source, display the data record by clicking the Mail Merge Recipients button on the Mail Merge toolbar to display the Mail Merge Recipients dialog box (shown in Figure 5-34 on page WD 5.28). Click the data record to change in the Mail Merge Recipients dialog box. If the list of data records is long, you can click the Find button to locate an item, such as the first name, quickly in the list. With the record to change selected, click the Edit button in the Mail Merge Recipients dialog box to display the selected data record in a dialog box similar to the one shown in Figure 5-32 on page WD 5.27.

To delete a record, display it using the same procedure described in the previous paragraph. Then, click the Delete Entry button in the dialog box (Figure 5-32).

Composing the Main Document for the Form Letters

The next step is to enter and format the text, graphics, and fields in the main document, which in this case is the form letter (see Figure 5-1a on page WD 5.05). The steps on the following pages illustrate how to compose the main document for the form letter.

Modifying a Field

The date line at the top of the form letter displays the date November 17, 2003 in the form: month day, year. You want the date to display as 17 November 2003 in the form: day month year. In this letter, Word automatically displays the current computer date in the date line because the date actually is a field.

Earlier in this project, you worked with data fields. A field, however, does not have to be associated with a data source. A **field** can be any placeholder for a value that changes. For example, when you print a document that contains a date field, Word prints the current date on the document. If you want to update a field on the screen, for example if the date displayed is not the current computer date, click the date field and then press the F9 key.

To change the date from displaying as November 17, 2003 to display as 17 November 2003, edit the field. Perform the following steps to edit a field.

Date Formats

Most business letters use the following date format: month day, year (November 17, 2003). Thus, Word uses this format as its default date format. Some people, however, prefer other date formats. This project demonstrates how to change the date format from this standard to another format.

Date Fields

To insert a date field into a Word document, click Insert on the menu bar, click Date and Time, select the desired date format, place a check mark in Automatically update check box, and then click the OK button.

Steps: To Edit a Field

1 Right-click the field (in this case, the date) and then point to Edit Field on the shortcut menu (Figure 5-37).

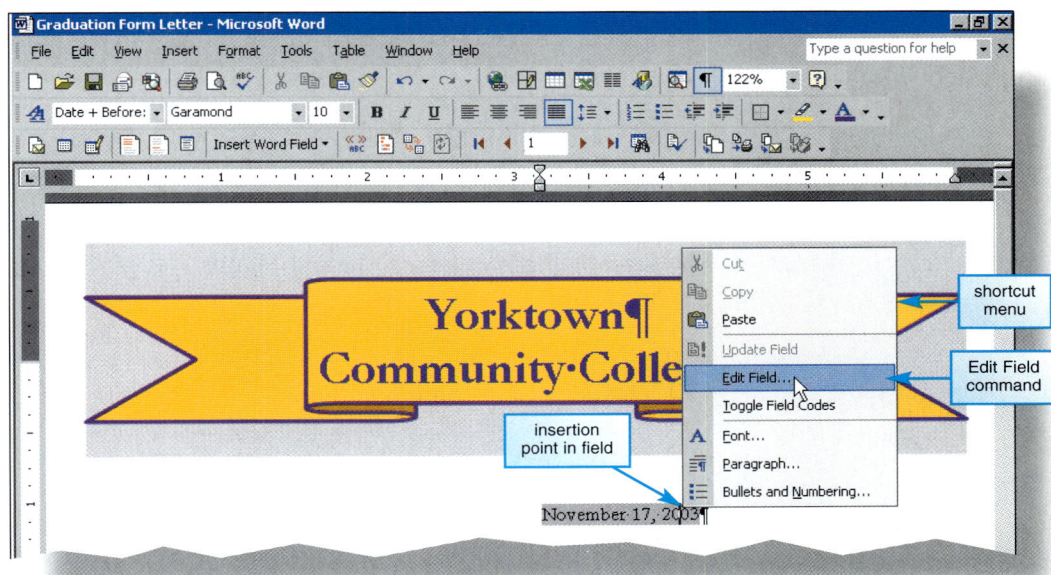

FIGURE 5-37

2 Click Edit Field. When the Field dialog box displays, click the desired format in the Date formats list (in this case, 17 November 2003). Point to the OK button.

Word displays the Field dialog box, which shows a list of available formats for dates and times (Figure 5-38). The format d MMMM yyyy displays in the Date formats text box. Your screen will not show 17 November 2003; instead, it will display the current system date stored in your computer.

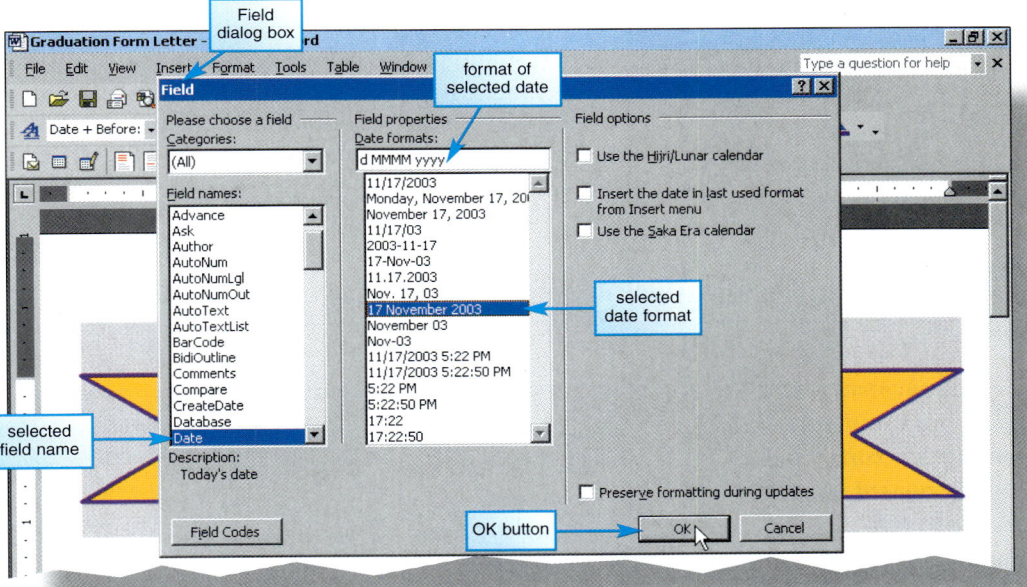

FIGURE 5-38

3 Click the OK button.

Word displays the current date in the format, d MMM yyyy, in the form letter (Figure 5-39).

FIGURE 5-39

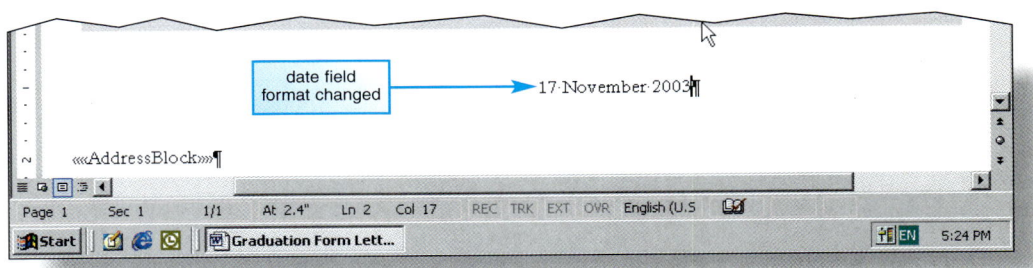

Inserting Merge Fields into the Main Document

In a letter, the inside address displays below the date line, and the salutation displays below the inside address. The contents of the inside address are located in the data source. That is, data in the data source is to display in the main document.

Earlier in this project, you created the data source for this form letter. Recall that each field in the data source is assigned a field name. To link the data source to the main document, you must insert these field names into the main document.

In the main document, these field names are called **merge fields** because they merge, or combine, the main document with the contents of the data source. When a merge field is inserted into the main document, Word surrounds the field name with **merge field characters** (shown in Figure 5-40). The merge field characters, which are chevrons, mark the beginning and ending of a merge field. Merge field characters are not on the keyboard; therefore, you cannot type them directly into the document. They automatically display when a merge field is inserted into the main document.

Most letters contain an address and salutation. For this reason, Word provides an AddressBlock merge field and a GreetingLine merge field. The **AddressBlock merge field** contains several fields related to an address: title, first name, middle name, last name, suffix, company, street address 1, street address 2, city, state, and postal code. When Word is instructed to use the AddressBlock merge field, it automatically looks for any fields in the associated data source that are related to an address and then formats the address block properly when you merge the data source with the main document. For example, if your inside address does not use a title, middle name, suffix, or company, Word omits these items from the inside address and adjusts the spacing so the address prints correctly.

The **GreetingLine merge field** contains text and fields related to a salutation. The default greeting for the salutation is in the format: Dear Mr. Randall. In this letter, you want a less formal salutation that displays the student's first name following the word, Dear. Then, you want a comma after the first name. Perform the following steps to edit the GreetingLine merge field.

More About

Salutations

Formal business letters typically use a more formal salutation (e.g., Dear Ms. Cartright:). Less formal business letters may use a less formal salutation. Less formal salutations may address the reader by his or her first name. In this case, the salutation also may end with a comma instead of a colon (e.g., Dear Beth,).

Steps: To Edit the GreetingLine Merge Field

1 If necessary, scroll down to display the GreetingLine merge field in the document window. Right-click the GreetingLine merge field and then point to Edit Greeting Line on the shortcut menu.

The merge field may display shaded in gray (Figure 5-40).

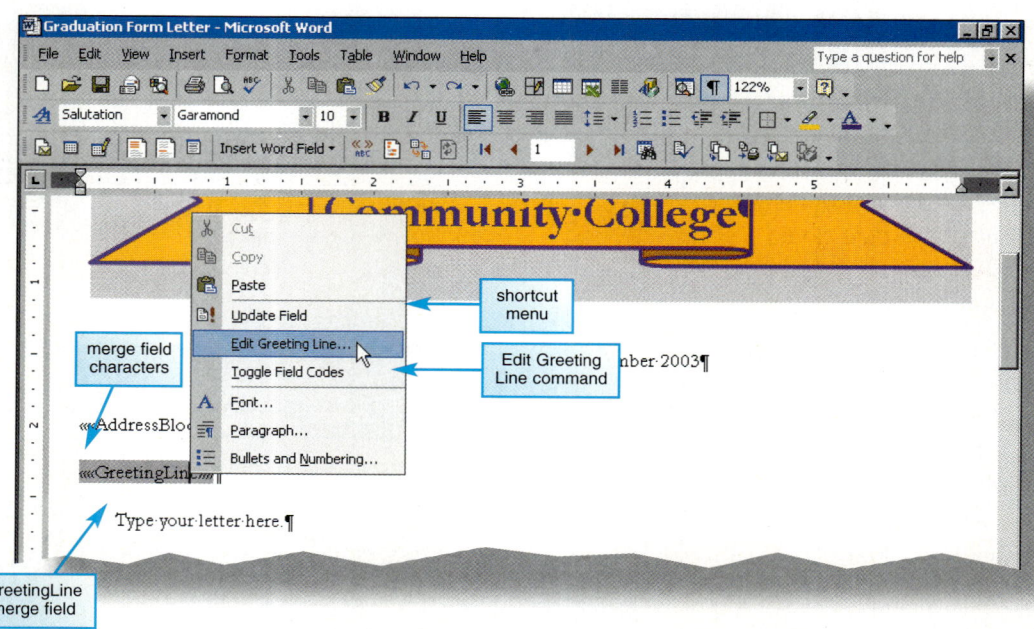

FIGURE 5-40

2 **Click Edit Greeting Line. When the Greeting Line dialog box displays, click the middle box arrow in the Greeting line format area, scroll to and then click Joshua. Point to the OK button.**

Word displays the Greeting Line dialog box (Figure 5-41). The first box arrow displays a list of initial phrases in the greeting line; the second box arrow displays a list of formats for the name; the third box arrow displays a list of punctuation formats to end the salutation.

3 **Click the OK button.**

Word modifies the format of the greeting line.

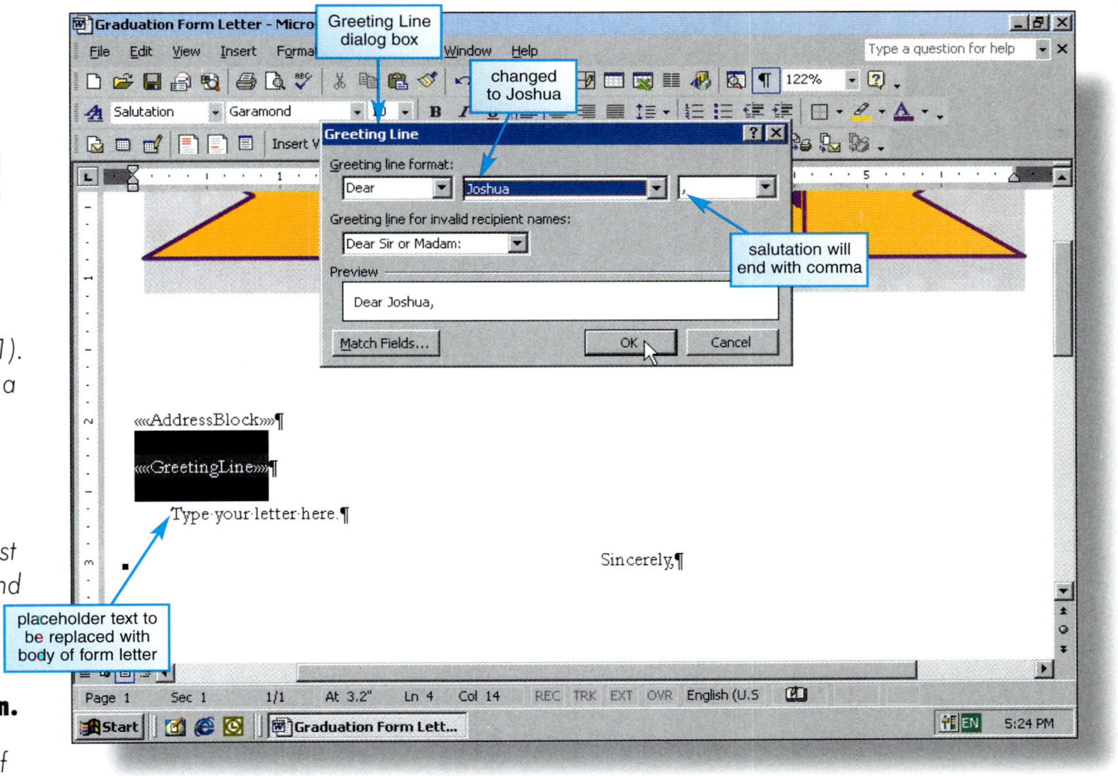

FIGURE 5-41

You will not notice a change in the GreetingLine merge field at this time. The new format will display when you merge the form letter to the data source later in this project.

The next step is to begin typing the body of the letter, which is to be located where Word has the placeholder text, Type your letter here. Perform the following steps to begin typing the body of the form letter.

TO BEGIN TYPING THE BODY OF THE FORM LETTER

1. Triple-click the placeholder text containing the sentence, Type your letter here., to select it.
2. With the sentence selected, type `I want to congratulate you on fulfilling the requirements to receive an` and then press the SPACEBAR.

The beginning of the first sentence below the GreetingLine merge field is entered (shown in Figure 5-42 on the next page).

The first sentence in the first paragraph of the letter identifies the type of degree the student is receiving and the major, for example, A.S. in Computer Technology. Both the degree and major are data fields in the data source. To instruct Word to use data fields from the data source, you insert merge fields in the main document for the form letter, as shown in the steps on the next page.

Fields

When you position the insertion point in a field, the entire field usually is shaded gray. The shading displays on the screen to help you identify fields; the shading does not print on a hard copy. Thus, the merge fields display shaded when you click them. To select an entire field, double-click it.

Steps: To Insert Merge Fields into the Main Document

1 With the insertion point positioned as shown in Figure 5-42, click the Insert Merge Fields button on the Mail Merge toolbar. When the Insert Merge Field dialog box displays, click Degree in the Fields list and then point to the Insert button.

Word displays a list of field names in the data source file associated with this main document (Figure 5-42). The field you select will be inserted in the main document at the location of the insertion point.

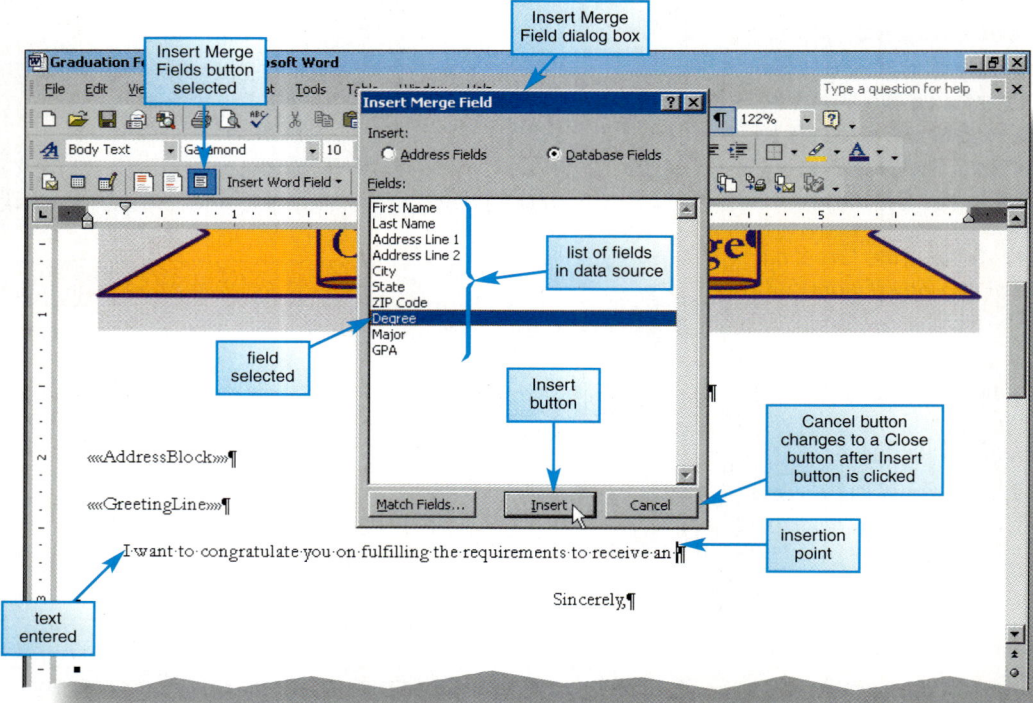

FIGURE 5-42

2 Click the Insert button. Click the Close button in the dialog box. Press the SPACEBAR. Type in and then press the SPACEBAR. Click the Insert Merge Fields button on the Mail Merge toolbar and then click Major in the Fields list. Click the Insert button and then the Close button in the dialog box.

Word displays the merge fields, Degree and Major, surrounded by merge field characters in the main document (Figure 5-43). When you merge the data source with the main document, the student's degree (e.g., A.S.) and major (e.g., Computer Technology) will print at the location of the merge fields, Degree and Major, respectively.

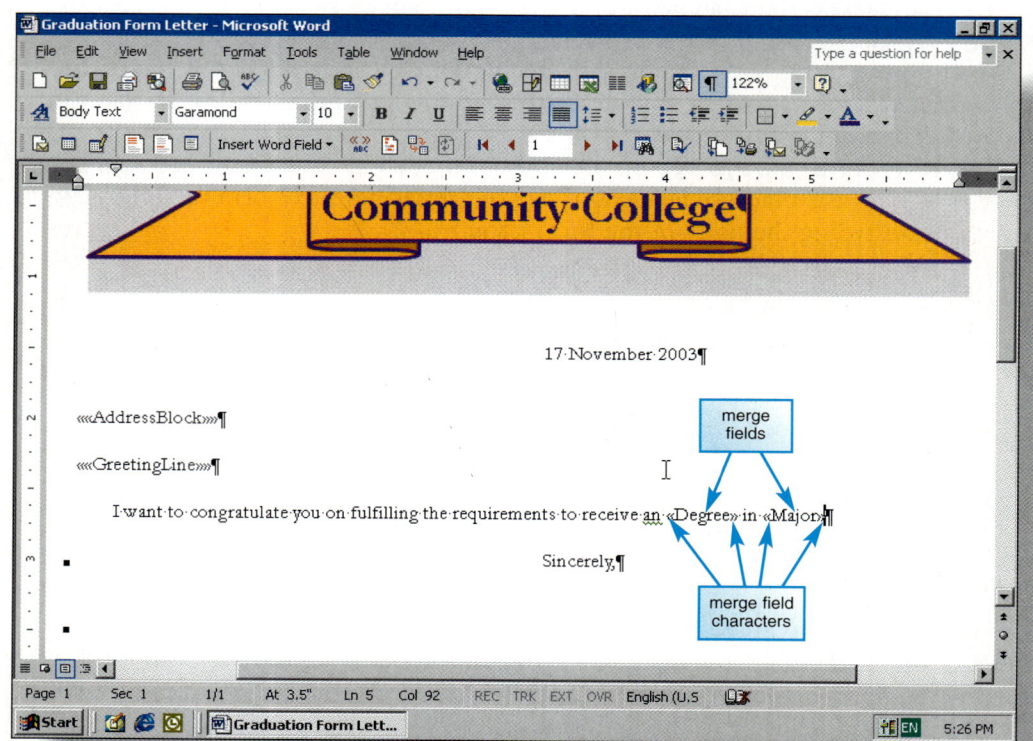

FIGURE 5-43

To change the format of merge fields, select the merge field in the main document and then apply the desired formatting. Later in this project, you increase the font size of all characters in the body of the letter.

Using an IF Field to Conditionally Print Text in a Form Letter

In addition to merge fields, you can insert Word fields that are designed specifically for a mail merge. An **IF field** is an example of a Word field. One form of the IF field is called an **If...Then**: If a condition is true, then perform an action. For example, If Mary owns a house, then send her information on homeowner's insurance. Another form of the IF field is called an **If...Then...Else**: If a condition is true, then perform an action; else perform a different action. For example, If John has an e-mail address, then send him an e-mail message; else send him the message via the postal service.

In this project, the form letter checks the student's GPA. If the GPA is greater than or equal to 3.8, then the student is graduating with honors. Thus, you will use an If...Then: If the GPA is greater than or equal to 3.8, then print the words, with honors, on the form letter.

The phrase that appears after the word If is called a condition. A **condition** consists of an expression, followed by a comparison operator, followed by a final expression.

EXPRESSION The expression in a condition can be a merge field, a number, a series of characters, or a mathematical formula. Word surrounds a series of characters with quotation marks ("). To indicate an empty, or null, expression, Word places two quotation marks together ("").

COMPARISON OPERATOR The comparison operator in a condition must be one of six characters: = (equal to or matches the text), <> (not equal to or does not match text), < (less than), <= (less than or equal to), > (greater than), >= (greater than or equal to).

If the result of a condition is true, then Word evaluates the **true text**. If the result of the condition is false, Word evaluates the **false text** if it exists. In this project, the first expression in the condition is a merge field (GPA); the comparison operator is greater than or equal to (>=); and the second expression is the number 3.8. The true text is " with honors". The false text is a null expression because this is an If...Then, instead of an If...Then...Else. The complete IF field is as follows:

If GPA >= 3.8 " with honors" ""

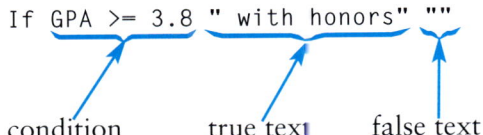

condition   true text   false text

Perform the steps on the next page to insert the IF field into the form letter.

Field Codes

When you insert fields into a document, if the fields display surrounded by braces instead of chevrons and extra instructions appear between the braces, then field codes have been turned on. To turn off field codes, press ALT+F9.

IF Fields

The term, IF field, originates from computer programming. Don't be intimidated by the terminology. An IF field simply specifies a decision. Some programmers refer to it as an IF statement. An IF field can be simple or complex. Complex IF fields include one or more nested IF fields, which is a second IF field inside true or false text of the first IF field.

Word Fields

In addition to the IF field, Word provides other fields that may be used in form letters. For example, the ASK and FILLIN fields prompt the user to enter data for each record in the data source. The SKIP RECORD IF field instructs the mail merge to not generate a form letter for a data record if a specific condition is met.

Steps: To Insert an IF Field into the Main Document

1 With the insertion point positioned as shown in Figure 5-44, click the Insert Word Field button on the Mail Merge toolbar. When the list of Word fields displays, point to If...Then...Else.

A list of Word fields that may be inserted into the main document displays (Figure 5-44).

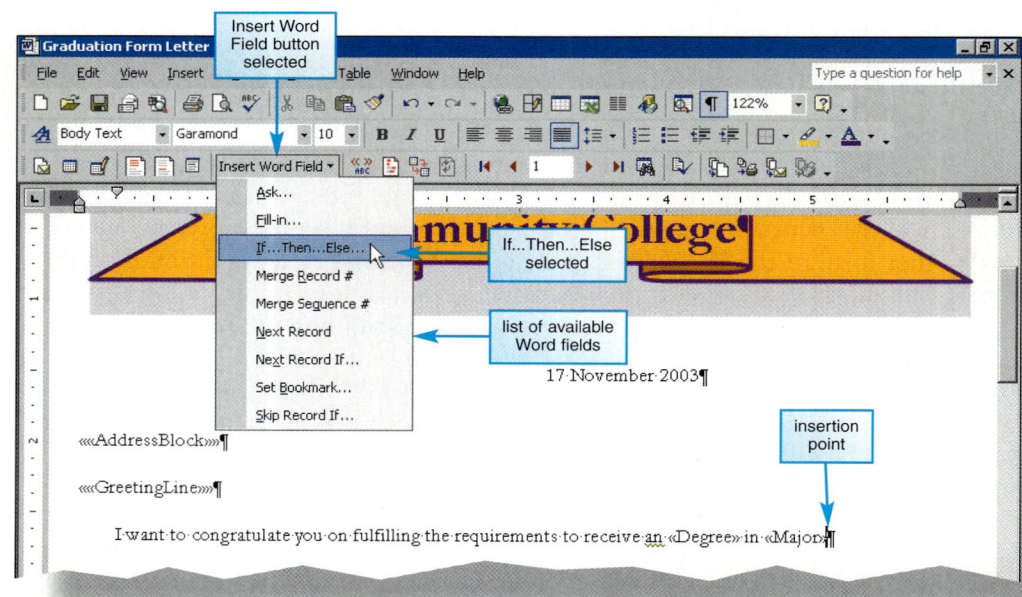

FIGURE 5-44

2 Click If...Then...Else. When the Insert Word Field: IF dialog box displays, point to the Field name box arrow.

Word displays the Insert Word Field: IF dialog box (Figure 5-45). You can specify the IF condition in the IF area of this dialog box.

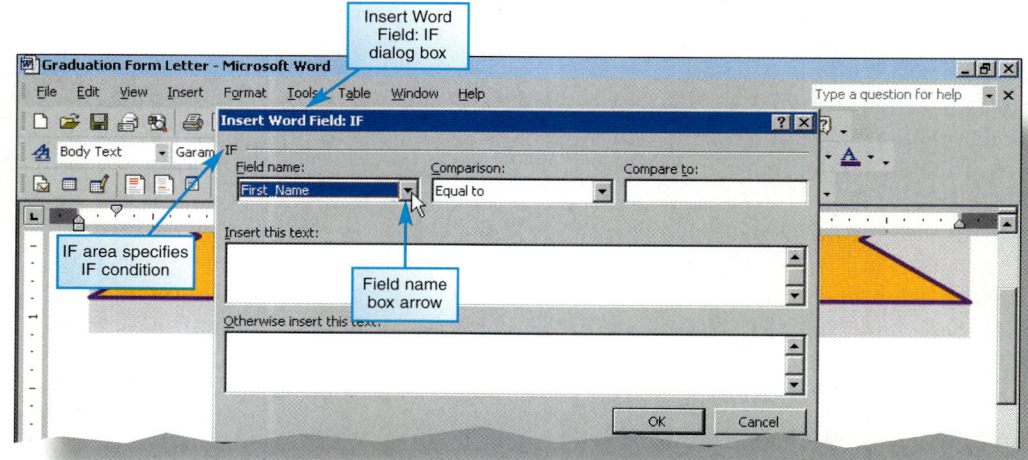

FIGURE 5-45

3 Click the Field name box arrow. Scroll through the list of fields and then point to GPA.

Word displays a list of fields in the data source (Figure 5-46).

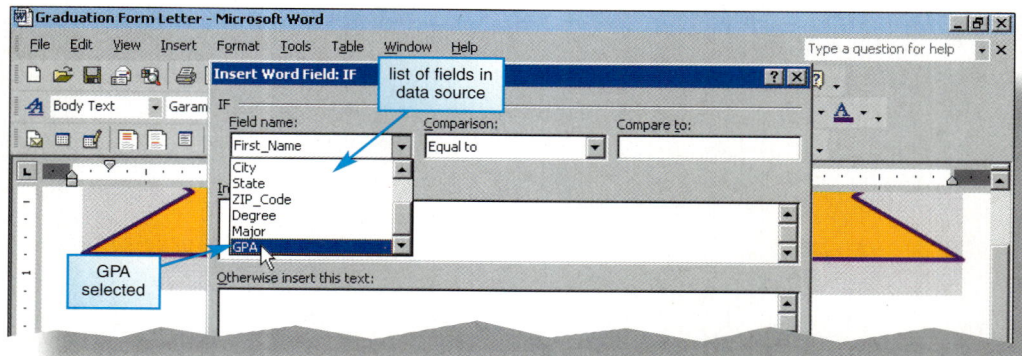

FIGURE 5-46

Composing the Main Document for the Form Letters • WD 5.37

4 **Click GPA. Click the Comparison box arrow and then click Greater than or equal. Click the Compare to text box. Type** `3.8` **and then press the TAB key. Press the SPACEBAR. Type** `with honors` **and then point to the OK button.**

The entries in the Insert Word Field: IF dialog box are complete (Figure 5-47).

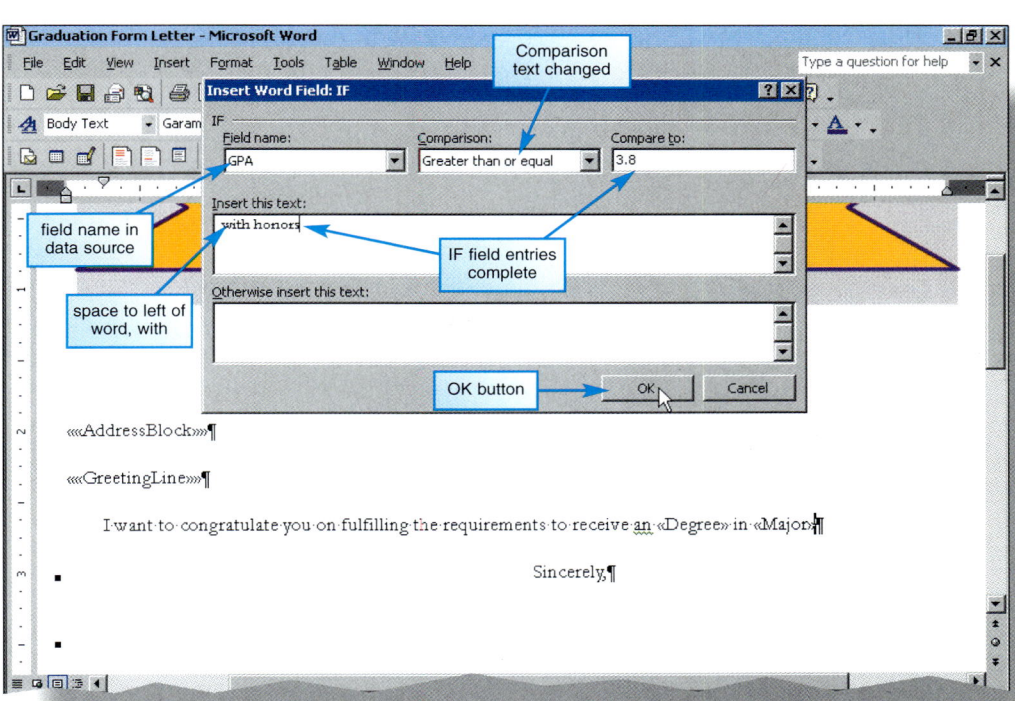

FIGURE 5-47

5 **Click the OK button.**

The words, with honors, display at the location of the insertion point in the main document because the first record in the data source has a GPA value that is greater than 3.8.

6 **Press the SPACEBAR. Type** `from Yorktown Community College.` **Press the ENTER key.**

Word positions the insertion point one blank line below the paragraph (Figure 5-48).

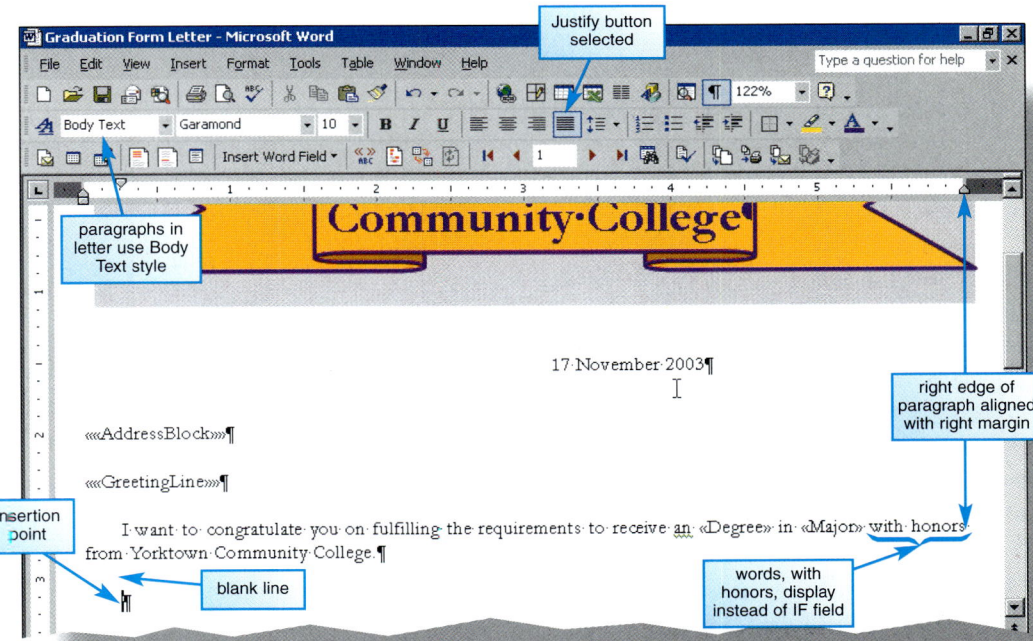

FIGURE 5-48

1. With Mail Merge toolbar displaying, in Voice Command mode, say "Insert Word Field, [enter condition], OK"

The paragraphs of the body of the Elegant Merge Letter template use the Body Text style. This style specifies single-spacing within paragraphs and double-spacing between paragraphs. Thus, each time you press the ENTER key, Word places a blank line between paragraphs.

The Body Text style also specifies to **justify** paragraphs, which means the left and right edges of the paragraphs are aligned with the left and right margins, respectively, like the edges of newspaper columns. Thus, the Justify button on the Formatting toolbar is selected (Figure 5-48 on the previous page).

Perform the following step to enter another paragraph of text into the form letter.

TO ENTER A PARAGRAPH OF TEXT

1. With the insertion point positioned as shown in Figure 5-48, type `Your graduation is contingent on successfully completing this semester's classes. Once you have concluded this coursework, the following will occur:` and then press the ENTER key.

The paragraph is entered (shown in Figure 5-51).

Creating an Outline Numbered List

The next step is to enter an outline numbered list in the form letter (shown in Figure 5-1a on page WD 5.05). An **outline numbered list** is a list that contains several levels of items, with each level displaying a different numeric, alphabetic, or bullet symbol.

To ensure that no existing formatting will affect the outline numbered list, the first step in creating the list is to clear formatting, which changes the paragraph from the Body Text style to the Normal style. Perform the following steps to create an outline numbered list.

Steps | To Create an Outline Numbered List

1. **If necessary, scroll down to display the insertion point in the document window. With the insertion point positioned below the paragraph just entered, click the Style box arrow on the Formatting toolbar and then click Clear Formatting. Click Format on the menu bar and then point to Bullets and Numbering.**

    Word clears formatting of the paragraph at the location of the insertion point (Figure 5-49). The Style box now displays Normal, instead of Body Text.

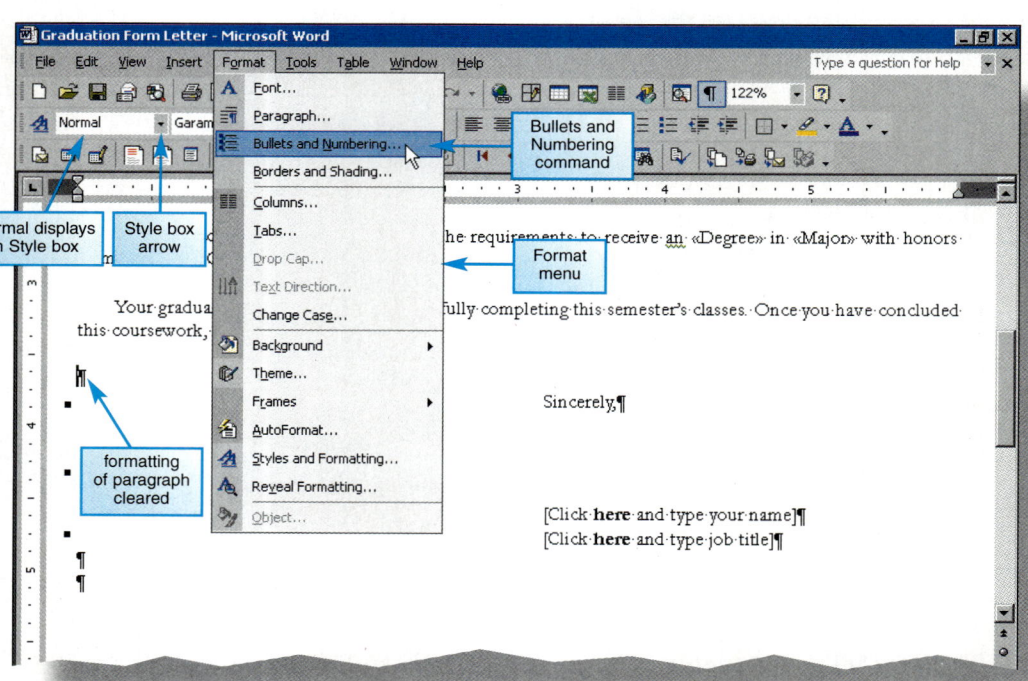

FIGURE 5-49

2 **Click Bullets and Numbering. When the Bullets and Numbering dialog box displays, if necessary, click the Outline Numbered tab. Click the desired number or bullet style in the list and then point to the OK button.**

Word displays the Bullets and Numbering dialog box (Figure 5-50).

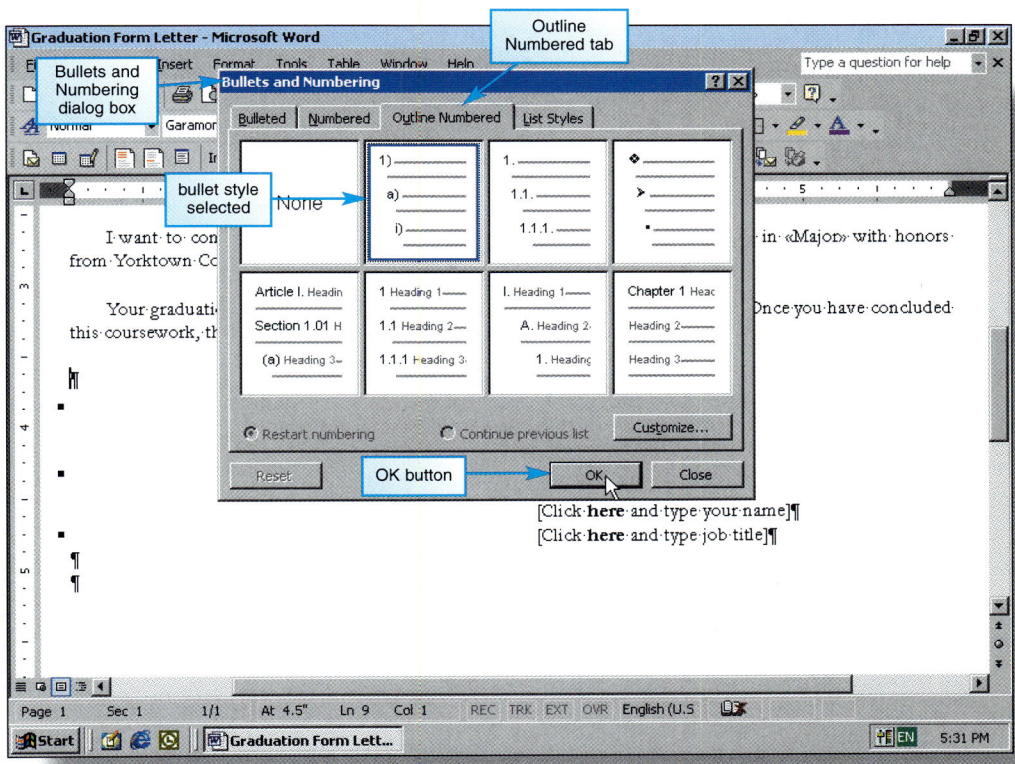

FIGURE 5-50

3 **Click the OK button. Type** Grade Point Average **and then press the ENTER key.**

Word places the number one, 1), on the first item in the list (Figure 5-51). The number two, 2), displays on the next line. This list item needs to be demoted to a second-level list item, indented below the first list item.

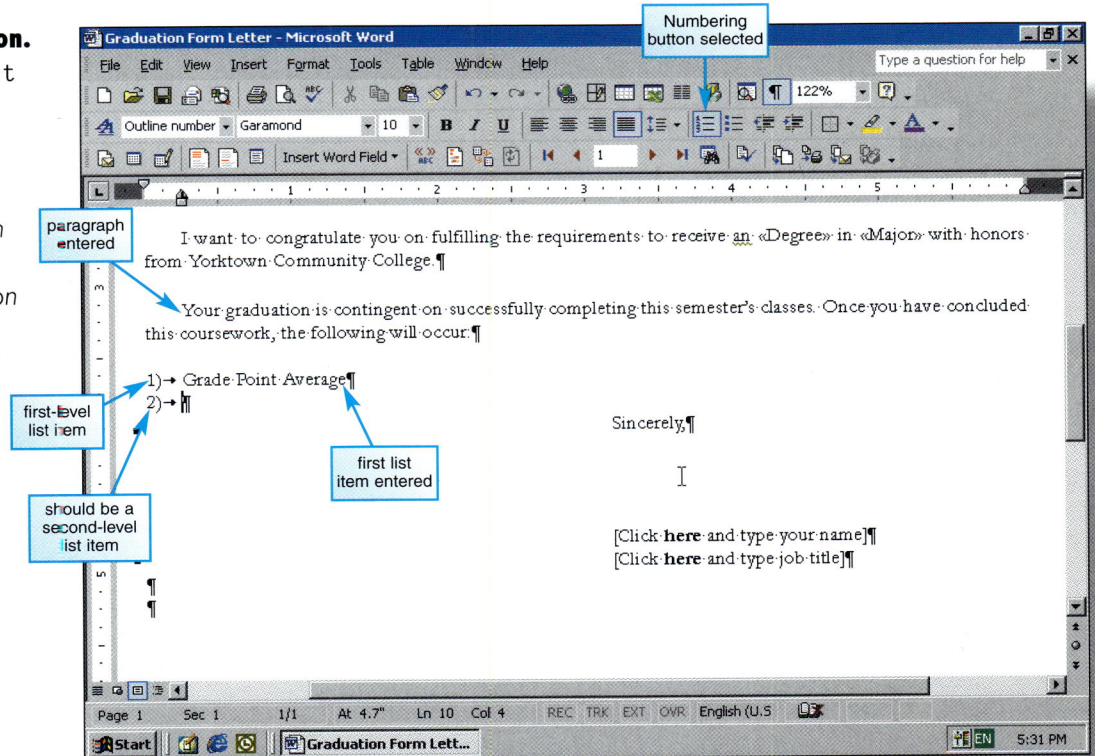

FIGURE 5-51

4 **Press the TAB key to demote the current list item. Type** Grade point averages will be adjusted to reflect this semester's course grades **and then press the ENTER key. Type** Dean's list status and honors status will be determined **and then press the ENTER key.**

The second level list items are entered (Figure 5-52). The letter c displays on the next line. This list item needs to be promoted to a first-level list item, aligned below the number one.

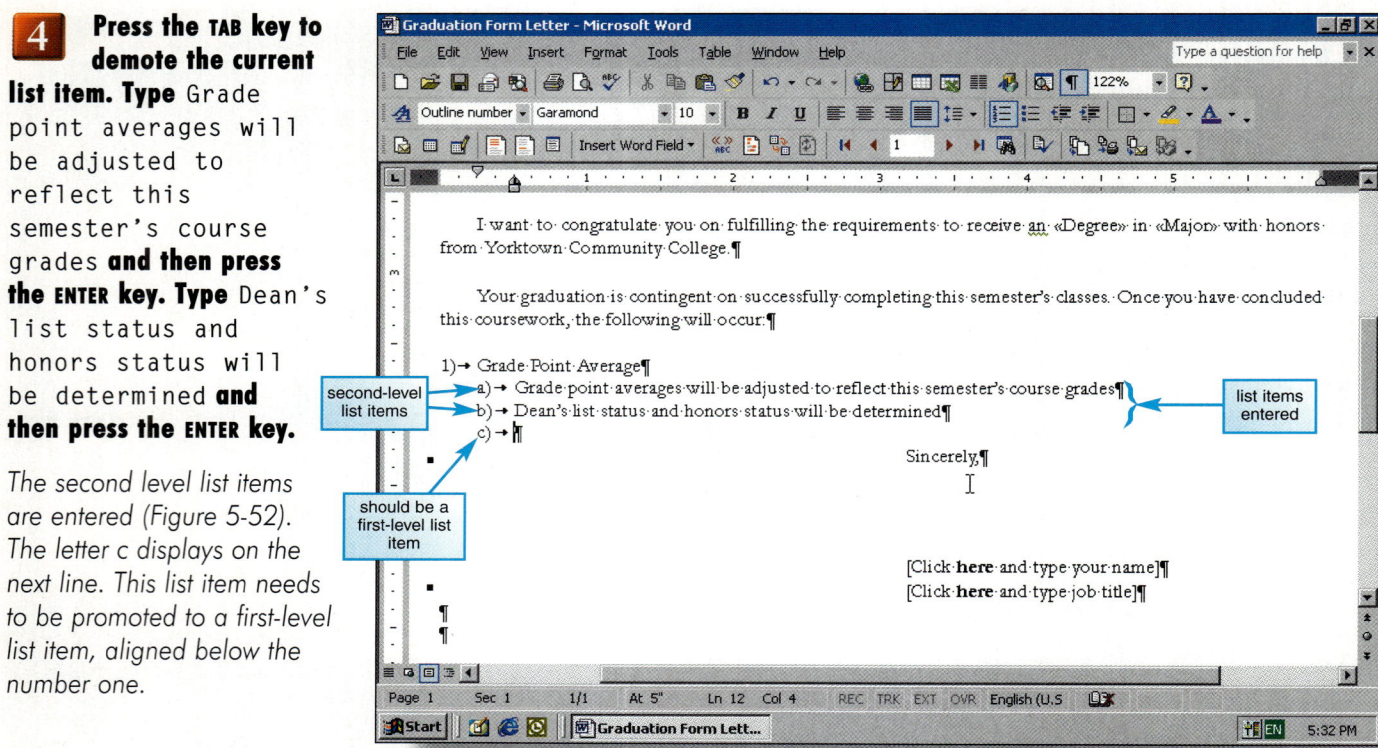

FIGURE 5-52

5 **Press SHIFT+TAB to promote the current list item. Press CTRL+0 (the numeral zero) to add a blank line above the paragraph containing the number two list item. Type** Diplomas **and then press the ENTER key. Press the TAB key to demote the current list item. Press CTRL+0 (the numeral zero) to remove the blank line above the paragraph containing the letter a) list item.**

Pressing CTRL+0 is a toggle that adds or removes a blank line above a paragraph (Figure 5-53).

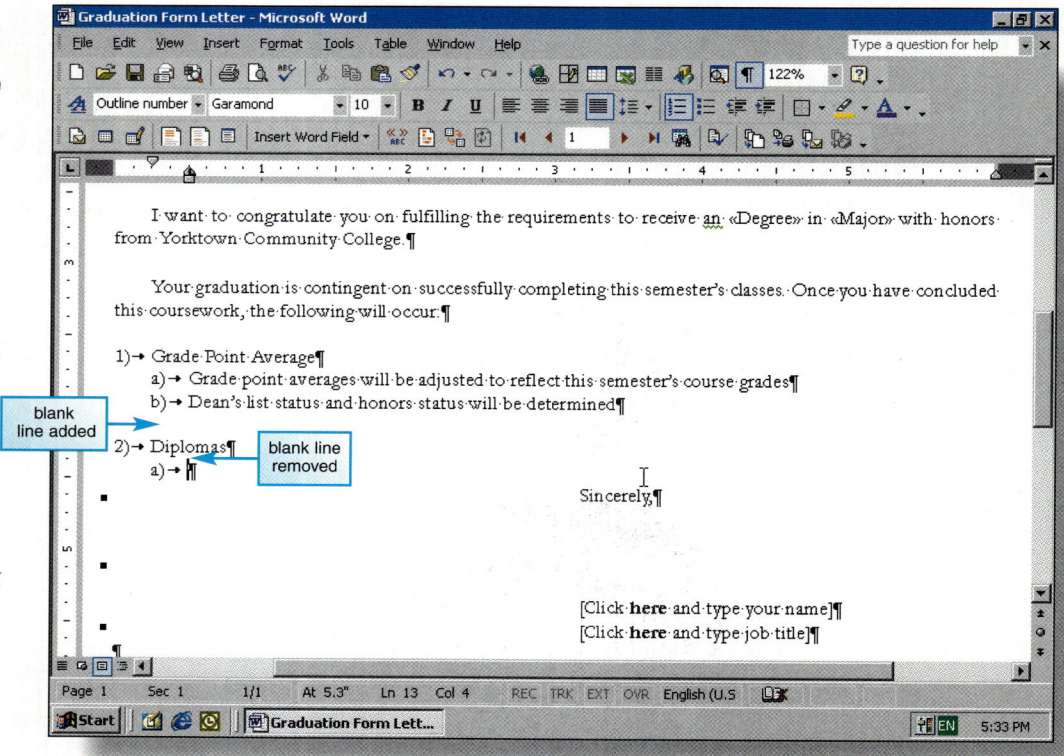

FIGURE 5-53

6. **Type** Diplomas will be mailed within three weeks after commencement **and then press the ENTER key. Type** You will receive a blank diploma cover during commencement exercises **and then press the ENTER key twice.**

The items in the list are entered (Figure 5-54). Word removes the numbered list bullet symbol from the current paragraph when you press the ENTER key twice at the end of a numbered or bulleted list.

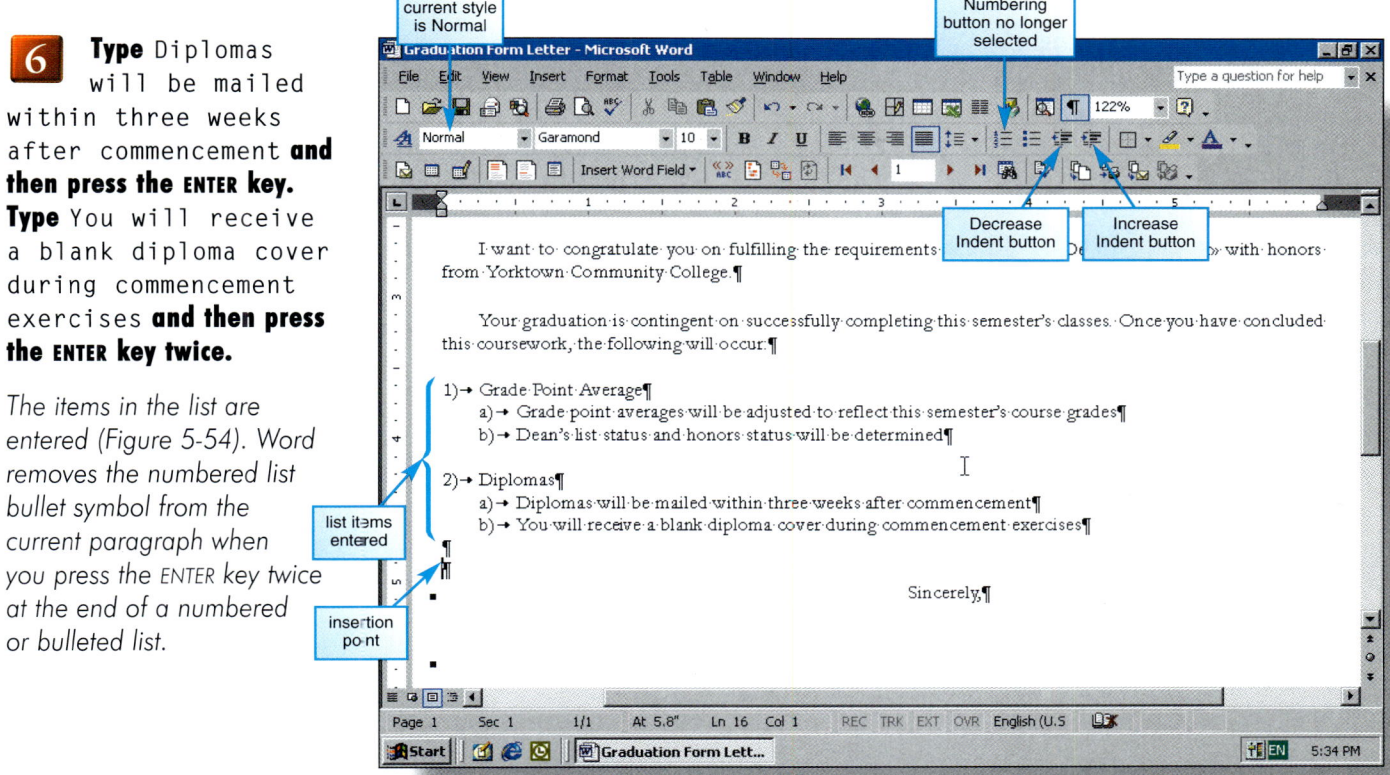

FIGURE 5-54

You also can click the Increase Indent button (Figure 5-54) on the Formatting toolbar to demote a list item in an outline numbered list. Likewise, you can click the Decrease Indent button on the Formatting toolbar to promote a list item.

Instead of pressing the ENTER key twice at the bottom of a list to stop Word from automatically numbering, you can click the Numbering button on the Formatting toolbar (Figure 5-54) to remove a number from a list item.

Applying a Paragraph Style

The next step is to enter the last paragraph of text into the body of the cover letter. The paragraphs in the cover letter use the Body Text style, which sets spacing above and below the paragraph, first-line indents the paragraph, and justifies the text in the paragraph. The current paragraph is set to the Normal style because you cleared formatting before creating the outline numbered list.

Perform the steps on the next page to apply the Body Text paragraph style to the current paragraph.

Other Ways

1. Right-click paragraph, click Bullets and Numbering on shortcut menu, click Outline Numbered tab, click numbering style, click OK button
2. In Voice Command mode, say "Format, Bullets and Numbering, Outline Numbered, [select numbering style], OK"

Steps: To Apply a Paragraph Style

 **1** With the insertion point positioned two lines below the outline numbered list, click the Style box arrow on the Formatting toolbar, scroll to and then point to Body Text.

Word displays a list of styles associated with the current document (Figure 5-55).

2 Click Body Text.

The entered paragraphs will be formatted according to the Body Text paragraph style (shown in Figure 5-56).

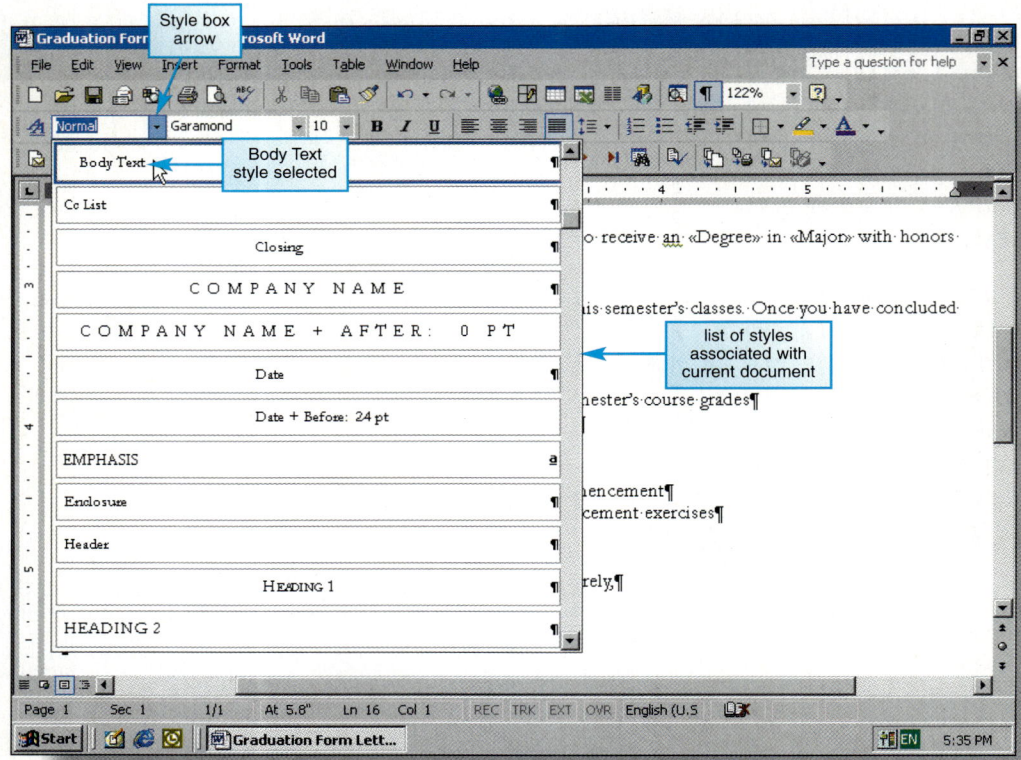

FIGURE 5-55

Other Ways

1. On Format menu click Styles and Formatting, click style name in Pick formatting to apply area
2. Click Styles and Formatting button on Formatting toolbar, click style name in Pick formatting to apply area
3. In Voice Command mode, say "Style, [select style]"

Many different styles are associated with a document. To view the complete list, click the Style box arrow on the Formatting toolbar or click the Styles and Formatting button on the Formatting toolbar (Figure 5-56) to display the Styles and Formatting task pane.

Perform the following steps to enter the text in the remainder of the letter.

TO ENTER MORE TEXT

1 Type Commencement exercises will be held on Friday, December 19, at 7:00 p.m. As that date approaches, you will receive detailed information about the rehearsal, caps and gowns, announcements, and tickets. Press the ENTER key.

2 Type Please accept my best wishes for your continued success.

3 If necessary, scroll down to display the signature block. Click the placeholder text in the signature block, Click **here** and type your name, and then type Elizabeth Pulaski as the name.

4 Click the placeholder text in the signature block, Click **here** and type your job title, and then type Registrar as the title.

The body and signature block portions of the letter are complete (Figure 5-56).

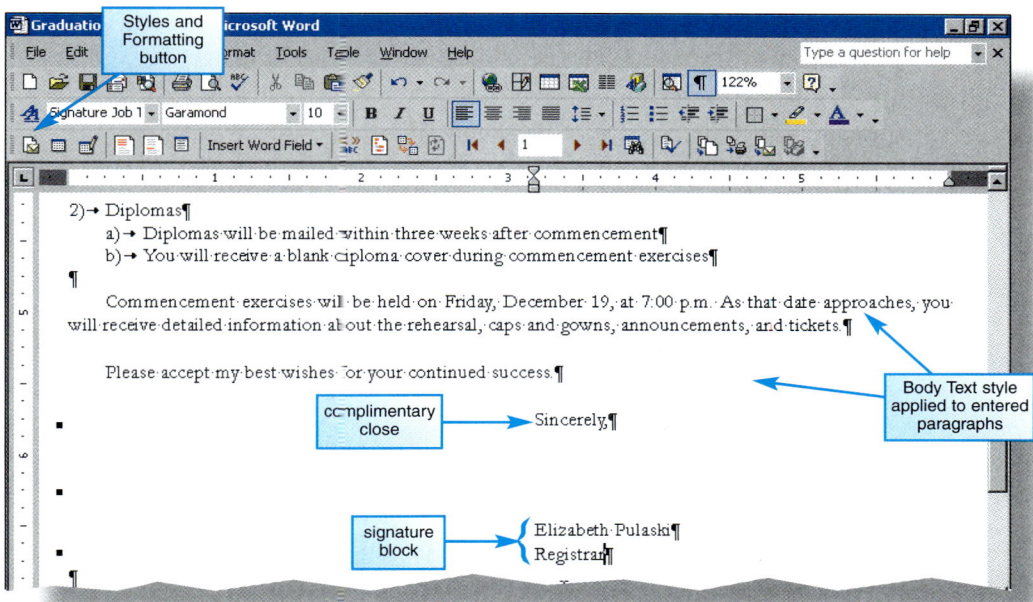

FIGURE 5-56

The return address at the bottom of the letter is formatted using the All Caps character effect (shown in Figure 5-6 on page 5.11). Thus, as you type characters, Word automatically converts them to capital letters. Perform the following steps to enter the return address at the bottom of the letter.

TO SELECT AND REPLACE MORE PLACEHOLDER TEXT

1. Scroll to the bottom of the letter to display the return address in the document window. Click the placeholder text, STREET ADDRESS. Type 44 BROADWAY STREET and then click the placeholder text, CITY/STATE.
2. Type REDMOND, OREGON and then click the placeholder text, ZIP/POSTAL CODE.
3. Type 97756 and then click the placeholder text, PHONE NUMBER.
4. Type 541-555-0088 and then click the placeholder text, FAX NUMBER.
5. Type 541-555-0089 as the fax number.

Word displays the return address at the bottom of the letter (Figure 5-57).

More About

Character Effects

To apply other character effects, click Format on the menu bar, click Font, click the Font tab, click the desired effect in the Effects area, and then click the OK button.

More About

Frames

A frame is a container for text that allows you to position the text anywhere on the page. In the Elegant Merge Letter template, the return address is contained in a text frame. To move a frame, simply point to it and drag it to the desired location.

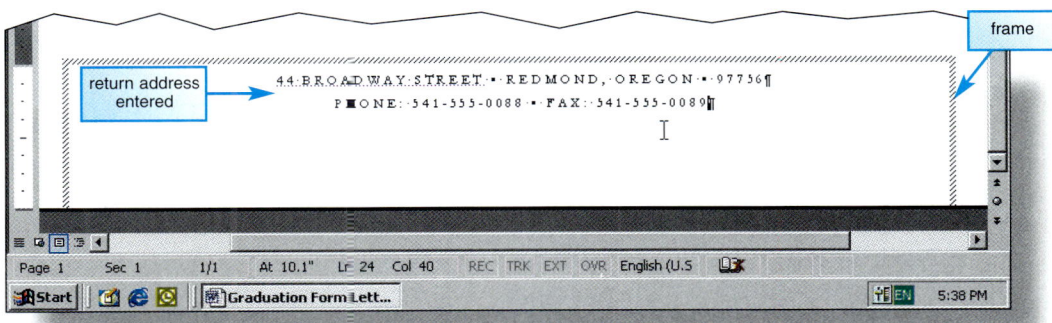

FIGURE 5-57

The next step is to change the font size of characters below the letterhead and above the return address to 12 point. Perform the following steps to change the font size of characters in the form letter.

TO CHANGE THE FONT SIZE OF TEXT

1. Click the Zoom box arrow on the Standard toolbar and then click 50%. Scroll up or down to position the entire body of the letter in the document window.
2. Drag from the date line down through the signature block to select the text in the letter.
3. Click the Font Size box arrow on the Formatting toolbar and then click 12 (Figure 5-58).
4. Click anywhere in the document to remove the selection.
5. Click the Zoom box arrow on the Standard toolbar and then click Text Width to redisplay the text as large as possible on the screen.

Word changes the font size to 12 (shown in Figure 5-59).

Locking Fields

If you wanted to lock a field so that its field results cannot be changed, click the field and then press CTRL+F11. To subsequently unlock a field so that it may be updated, click the field and then press CTRL+SHIFT+F11.

Electronic Signatures

For more information on electronic signatures, visit the Word 2002 More About Web page (www.scsite.com/wd2002/more.htm) and then click Electronic Signatures.

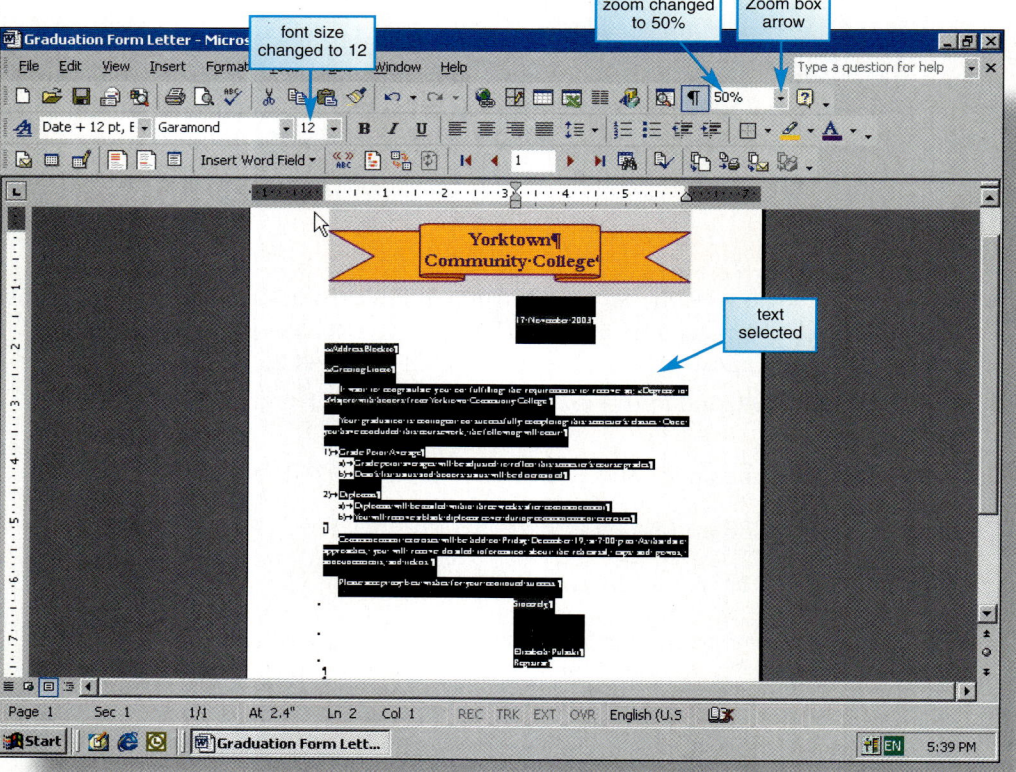

FIGURE 5-58

Saving the Document Again

The main document for the form letter now is complete. Thus, you should save it again, as described in the following step.

TO SAVE A DOCUMENT AGAIN

1 Click the Save button on the Standard toolbar.

Word saves the main document for the form letter with the same name, Graduation Form Letter, in the Graduation folder.

Displaying Field Codes

The instructions in the IF field do not display in the document; instead, the field results display. **Field results** represent the value to display after Word evaluates the instructions of the IF field. For example, the words, with honors, display in the document window (Figure 5-59) because the GPA in first data record is greater than 3.8.

The instructions of the IF field are referred to as **field codes**, and the default for Word is field codes off. Thus, field codes do not print or display unless you turn them on. You use one procedure to display field codes on the screen and a different procedure to print them on a hard copy.

The following steps illustrate how to turn on a field code so you can see it on the screen. Most Word users only turn on a field code to verify its accuracy or to modify it. Field codes tend to clutter the screen. Thus, you should turn them off after viewing them.

Perform the following steps to display the field codes for the IF field.

Main Documents

When you open a main document, Word attempts to open the associated data source file, too. If the data source is not in exactly the same location (i.e., drive and folder) as when it originally was saved, Word displays a dialog box indicating that it could not find the data source. When this occurs, click the Find Data Source button to display the Open Data Source dialog box, where you can locate the data source file.

Steps: To Display a Field Code

1 Scroll to and then right-click the text, with honors. Point to Toggle Field Codes on the shortcut menu (Figure 5-59).

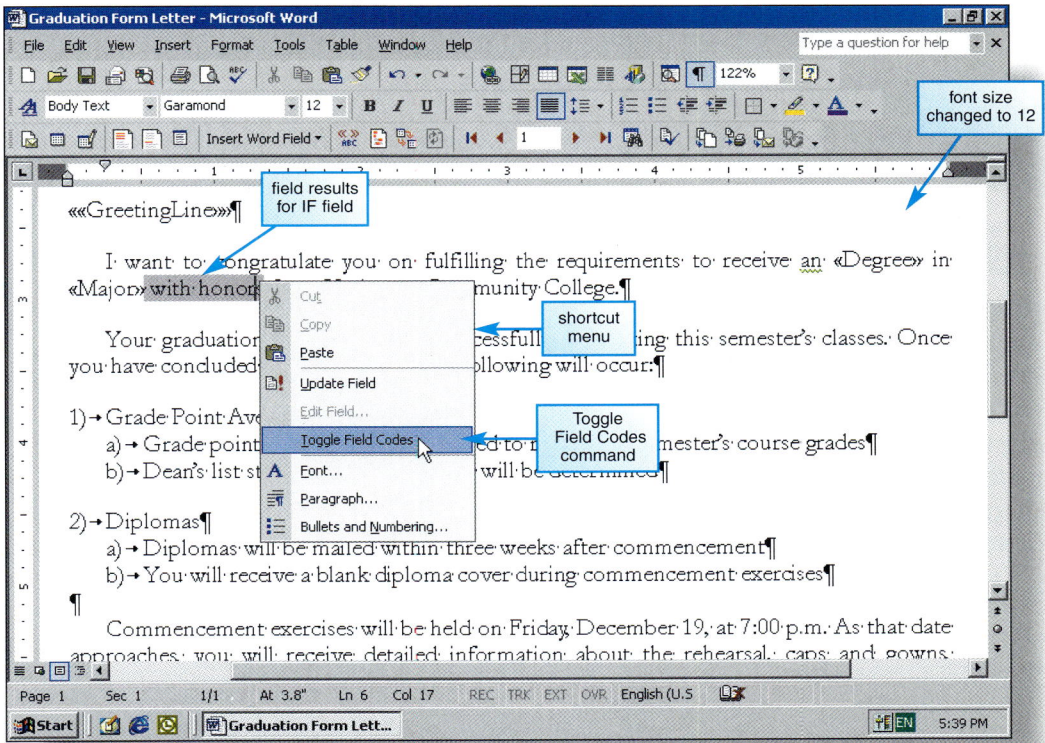

FIGURE 5-59

2 **Click Toggle Field Codes.**

Word displays the field code instead of the field results (Figure 5-60). The instructions in the IF field display. With field codes on, braces surround a field instead of chevrons.

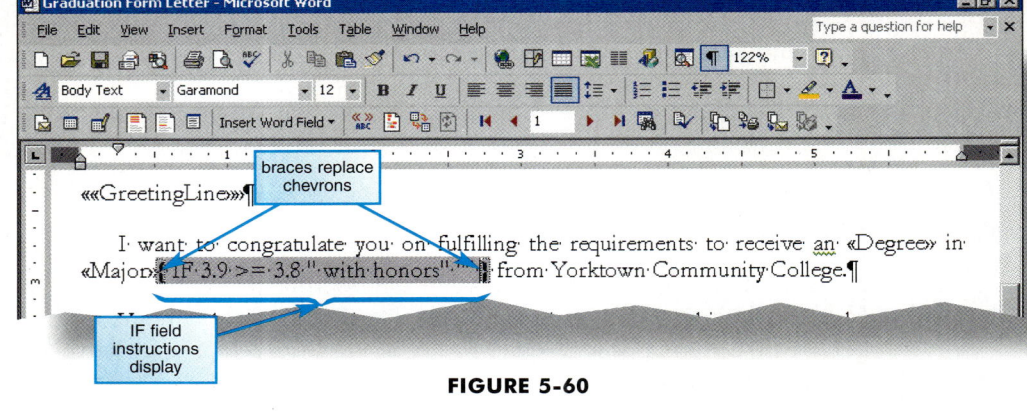

FIGURE 5-60

Other Ways

1. With insertion point in field, press SHIFT+F9
2. With insertion point in field, in Voice Command mode, say "Right Click, Toggle Field Codes"

If you wanted all field codes in a document to display on the screen, you would press ALT+F9. Then, to hide all the field codes, press ALT+F9 again.

Whether field codes are on or off on your screen has no effect on the merge process.

Printing Field Codes

When you merge or print a document, Word automatically hides any field codes that show on the screen. You may want to print the field codes version of the form letter, however, so you have a hard copy of the field codes for future reference. When you print field codes, you must remember to turn off the field codes option so that future documents print field results instead of field codes. For example, with field codes on, merged form letters will display field codes instead of data.

Perform the following steps to print the field codes in the main document and then turn off the field codes print option for future printing.

 To Print Field Codes in the Main Document

1 **Click File on the menu bar and then click Print. When the Print dialog box displays, click the Options button. When the next Print dialog box displays, place a check mark in the Field codes check box. Point to the OK button.**

Word displays a Print dialog box within another Print dialog box (Figure 5-61). The Field codes check box is selected.

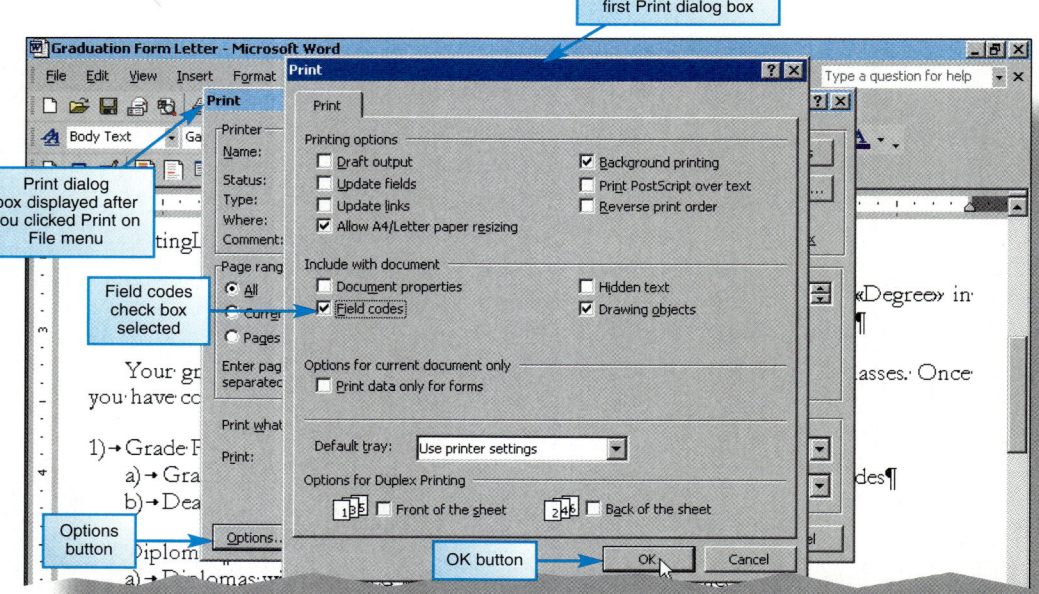

FIGURE 5-61

Composing the Main Document for the Form Letters • WD 5.47

2 **Click the OK button. Click the OK button in the remaining Print dialog box.**

Word prints the main document with all field codes showing (Figure 5-62). Notice the contents of the letter are cluttered with many fields.

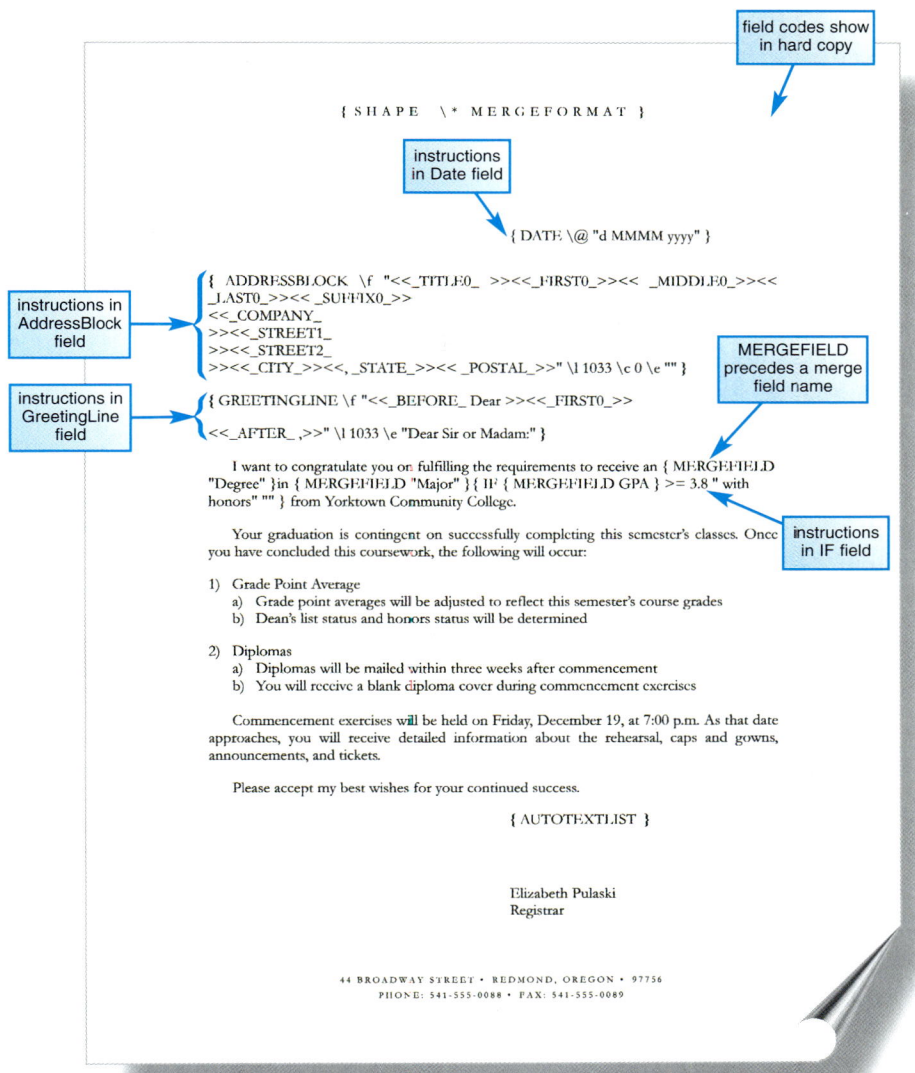

FIGURE 5-62

You should turn off printed field codes so that future documents do not print field codes. Perform the following steps to turn off field codes for printing.

TO TURN FIELD CODES OFF FOR PRINTING

1 Click Tools on the menu bar and then click Options.

2 When the Options dialog box displays, if necessary, click the Print tab. Click Field codes in the Include with document area to remove the check mark.

3 Click the OK button.

Word turns off field codes for printed documents.

Other Ways

1. On Tools menu click Options, click Print tab, click Field codes, click OK button, click Print button on Standard toolbar
2. In Voice Command mode, say "File, Print, Options, Field codes, OK, OK"

Merging the Documents and Printing the Letters

The data source and main document for the form letter are complete. The next step is to merge them to generate the individual form letters. Perform the following steps to merge form letters, sending the merged letters to the printer.

Steps: To Merge the Form Letters to the Printer

1 Click the Merge to Printer button on the Mail Merge toolbar. When the Merge to Printer dialog box displays, if necessary, click All. Point to the OK button.

Word displays the Merge to Printer dialog box (Figure 5-63). In this dialog box, you indicate which data records should be merged.

2 Click the OK button. When the Print dialog box displays, click the OK button. If Word displays a message about locked fields, click the OK button.

Word prints five separate letters, one for each student in the data source (shown in Figure 5-1c on page WD 5.05).

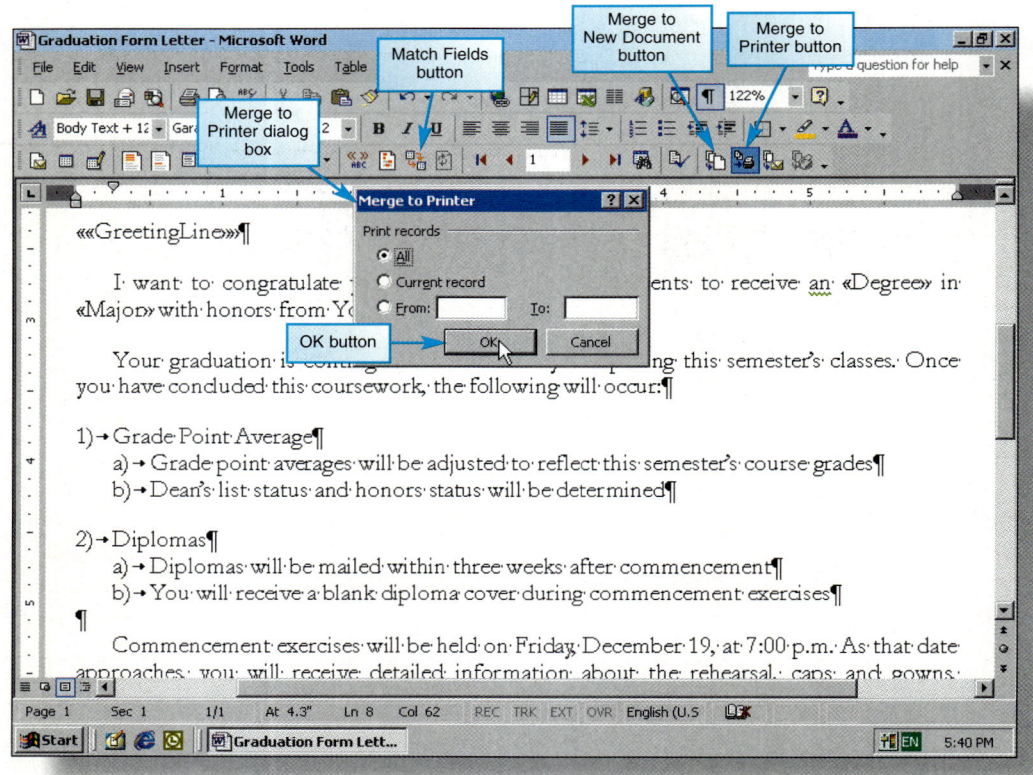

FIGURE 5-63

Other Ways

1. With Mail Merge toolbar displaying, in Voice Command mode, say "Merge to Printer, All, OK"

The contents of the data source merge with the merge fields in the main document to generate the form letters. Word prints five form letters because the data source contains five records. The address lines suppress blanks. That is, students without a second address line begin the city on the line immediately below the first address line. In addition, the words, with honors, print only if the student's GPA is greater than or equal to 3.8.

If you notice errors in the printed form letters, edit the main document the same way you edit any other document. Then, save the changes and merge again. If the wrong field results display, Word may be mapping the fields incorrectly. To view fields, click the Match Fields button on the Mail Merge toolbar (Figure 5-63). Then, review the list of fields in the list. For example, the Last Name should map to the Last Name field in the data source. If it does not, click the box arrow to change the name of the data source field.

Instead of immediately printing the merged form letters, you could send them into a new document window by clicking the Merge to New Document button on the Mail Merge toolbar (see Figure 5-63). With this button, you view the merged form letters in a new document window on the screen to verify their accuracy before printing the letters. When you are finished viewing the merged form letters, you can print them by clicking the Print button on the Standard toolbar. In addition, you can save these merged form letters in a file. If you do not want to save the merged form letters, close the document window by clicking the Close button at the right edge of the menu bar. When the Microsoft Word dialog box displays asking if you want to save the document, click the No button.

Printing

If you want to save ink, print faster, or decrease printer overrun errors, print a draft. Click File on the menu bar, click Print, click the Options button, place a check mark in the Draft output check box, and then click the OK button in each dialog box.

Selecting Data Records to Merge and Print

Instead of merging and printing all of the records in the data source, you can choose which records will merge, based on a condition you specify. The dialog box in Figure 5-63 allows you to specify by record number which records to merge. Often you merge based on the contents of a specific field. For example, you may want to merge and print only those students in the mailing list who are receiving an A.A. degree.

Perform the following steps to select records for a merge.

Steps: To Select Records to Merge

1 Click the Mail Merge Recipients button on the Mail Merge toolbar.

Word displays the Mail Merge Recipients dialog box (Figure 5-64). You must scroll to the right to display the Degree field in this dialog box.

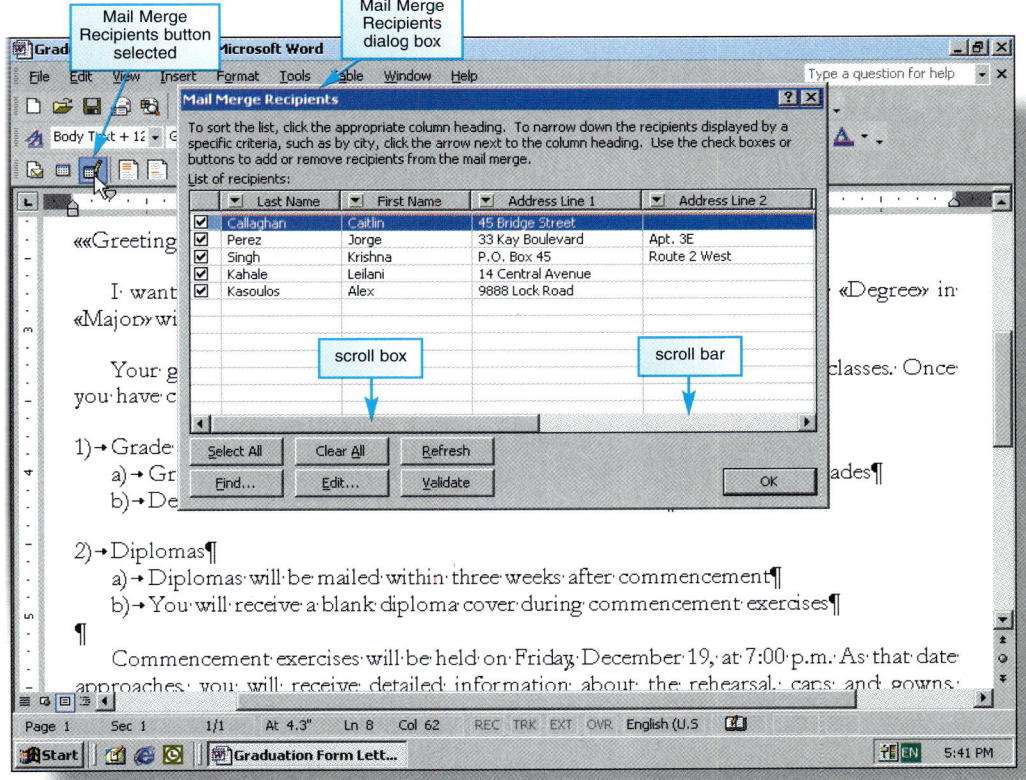

FIGURE 5-64

2 Drag the scroll box to the right edge of the Mail Merge Recipients dialog box. Click the arrow to the left of the field name, Degree. Point to A.A. in the list.

Word displays a list of selection criteria for the Degree field (Figure 5-65).

3 Click A.A.

Word reduces the number of data records that display in the Mail Merge Recipients dialog box to two because two students are receiving an A.A. degree.

4 Click the OK button in the Mail Merge Recipients dialog box. Click the Merge to Printer button on the Mail Merge toolbar. When the Merge to Printer dialog box displays, if necessary, click All. Click the OK button. When the Print dialog box displays, click the OK button. If Word displays a message about locked fields, click the OK button.

Word prints the form letters that match the specified condition: Degree is equal to A.A. (Figure 5-66). Two form letters print because two students are receiving A.A. degrees.

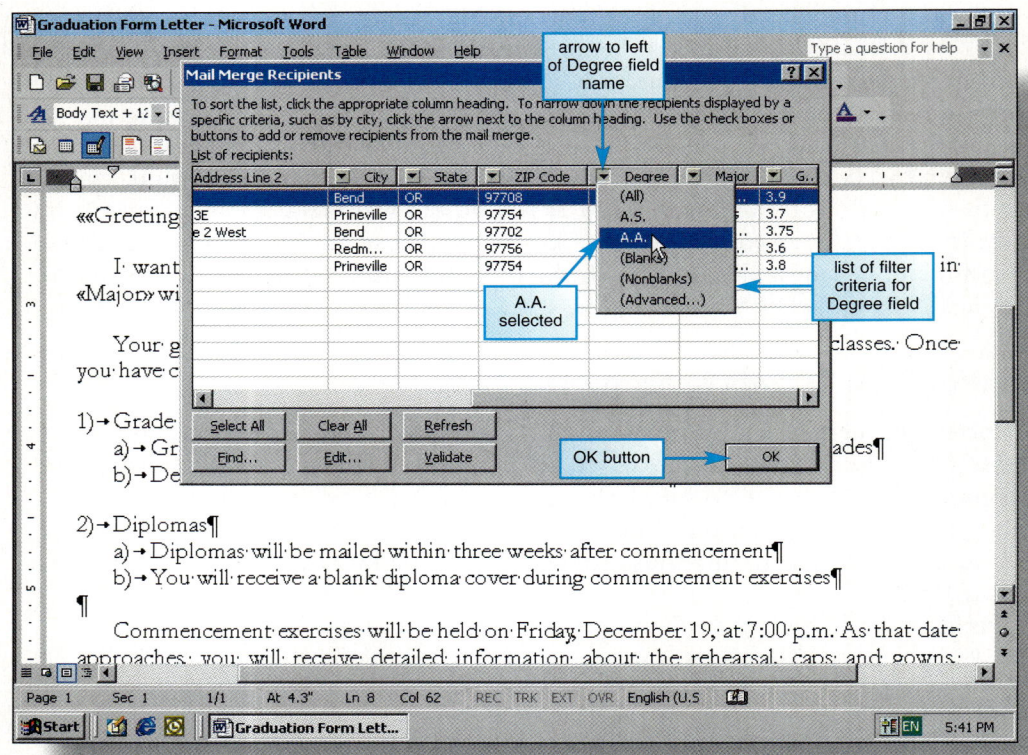

FIGURE 5-65

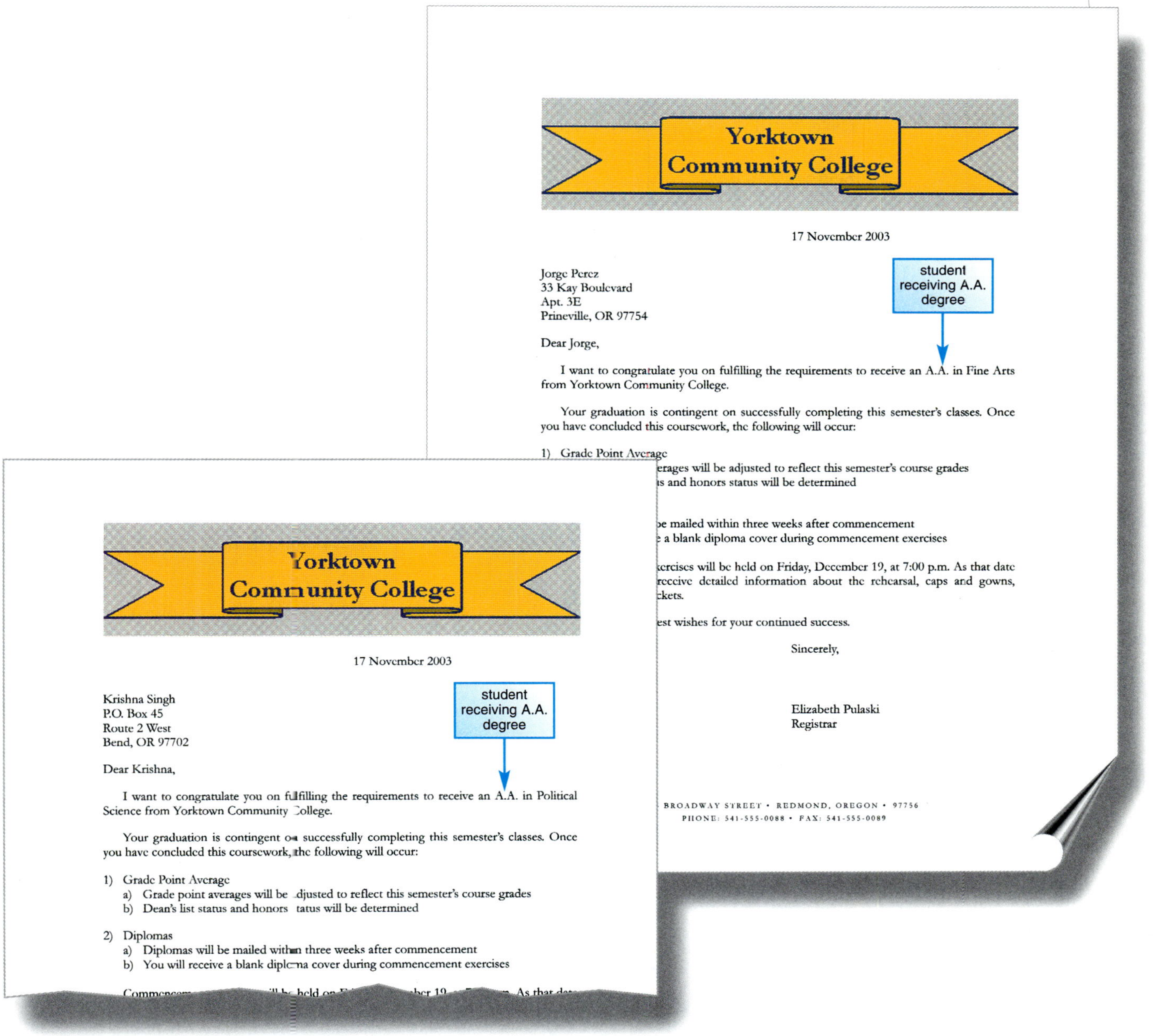

FIGURE 5-66

You should remove the merge condition so that future merges will not be restricted to students receiving A.A. degrees.

TO REMOVE A MERGE CONDITION

1. Click the Mail Merge Recipients button on the Mail Merge toolbar.
2. Scroll to the right of the dialog box and then click the arrow to the left of the field name, Degree. Click (All) in the list.
3. Click the OK button.

Word removes the specified condition.

Merge Conditions

When a field has a merge condition set, Word colors the arrow in blue that displays to the left of the field name. Thus, the arrow to the left of the Degree field will be blue when you perform Step 2 in the steps to the left.

In addition to selecting records based on values in a field, Word provides other choices by which you can select the data records (Figure 5-65 on page WD 5.50). The (Blanks) option selects records that contain blanks in that field, and the (Nonblanks) option selects records that do not contain blanks in that field. The (Advanced) option displays the Filter and Sort dialog box, which allows you to perform more advanced record selection operations.

Sorting Data Records to Merge and Print

If you mail the form letters using the U.S. Postal Service's bulk rate mailing service, the post office requires you to sort and group the form letters by ZIP code. Thus, follow these steps to sort the data records by ZIP code.

Steps: To Sort the Data Records

1 Click the Mail Merge Recipients button on the Mail Merge toolbar. When Word displays the Mail Merge Recipients dialog box, scroll to the right until the ZIP Code field displays in the dialog box and then point to the ZIP Code field name (Figure 5-67).

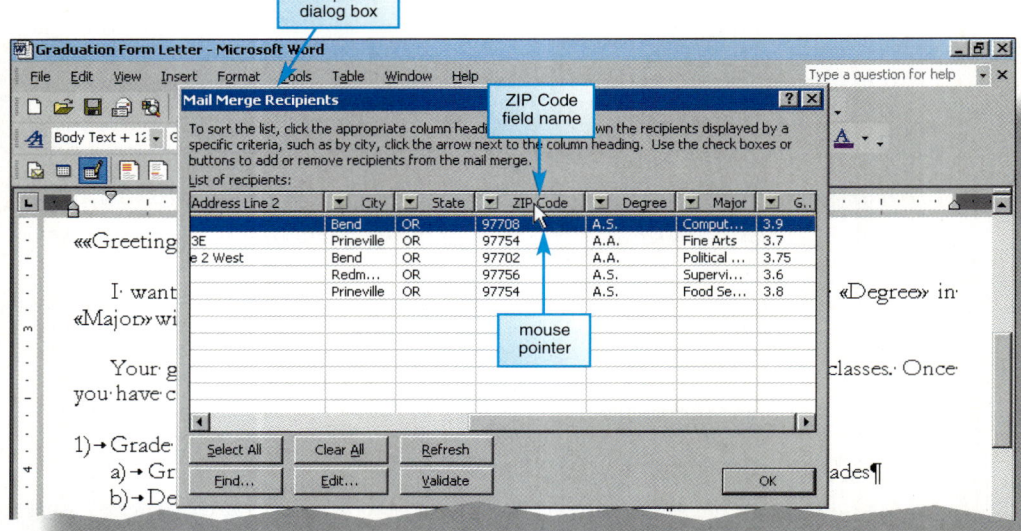

FIGURE 5-67

2 Click the ZIP Code field name. If necessary, scroll to the right to display the ZIP Code field again.

The data records are sorted by ZIP code (Figure 5-68). Future merged documents will print in ZIP code order.

3 Click the OK button in the Mail Merge Recipients dialog box.

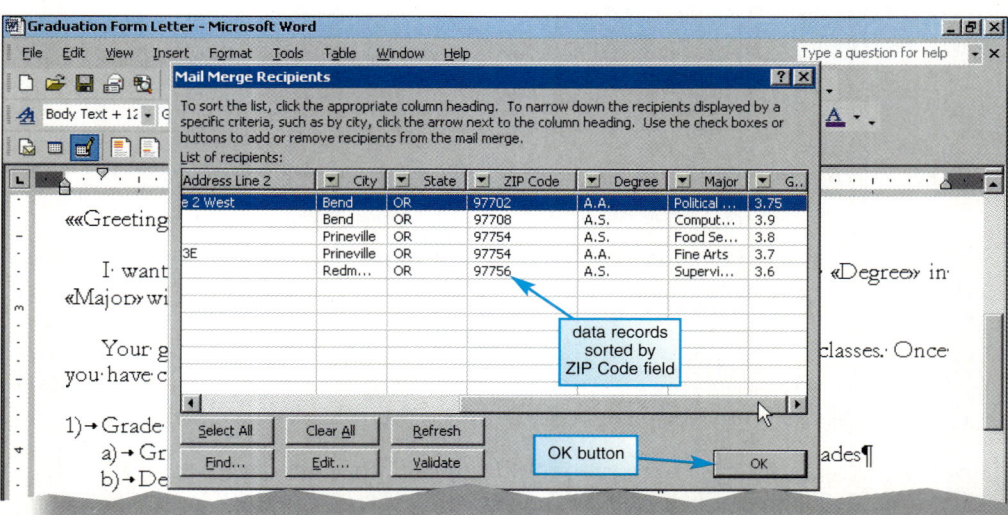

FIGURE 5-68

If you chose to merge the form letters again at this point, Word would print them in postal code order; that is, Krishna Singh's letter would print first and Leilani Kahale's letter would print last.

Viewing Merged Data

You can verify the order of the data records without printing them by using the **View Merged Data button** on the Mail Merge toolbar, as shown in the following steps.

To View Merged Data in the Main Document

 If necessary, scroll up to display the AddressBlock merge field in the document window. Click the View Merged Data button on the Mail Merge toolbar.

Word displays the contents of the first data record in the main document, instead of the merge fields (Figure 5-69). The View Merged Data button is selected.

Click the View Merged Data button on the Mail Merge toolbar again.

Word displays the merge fields in the main document, instead of the field values.

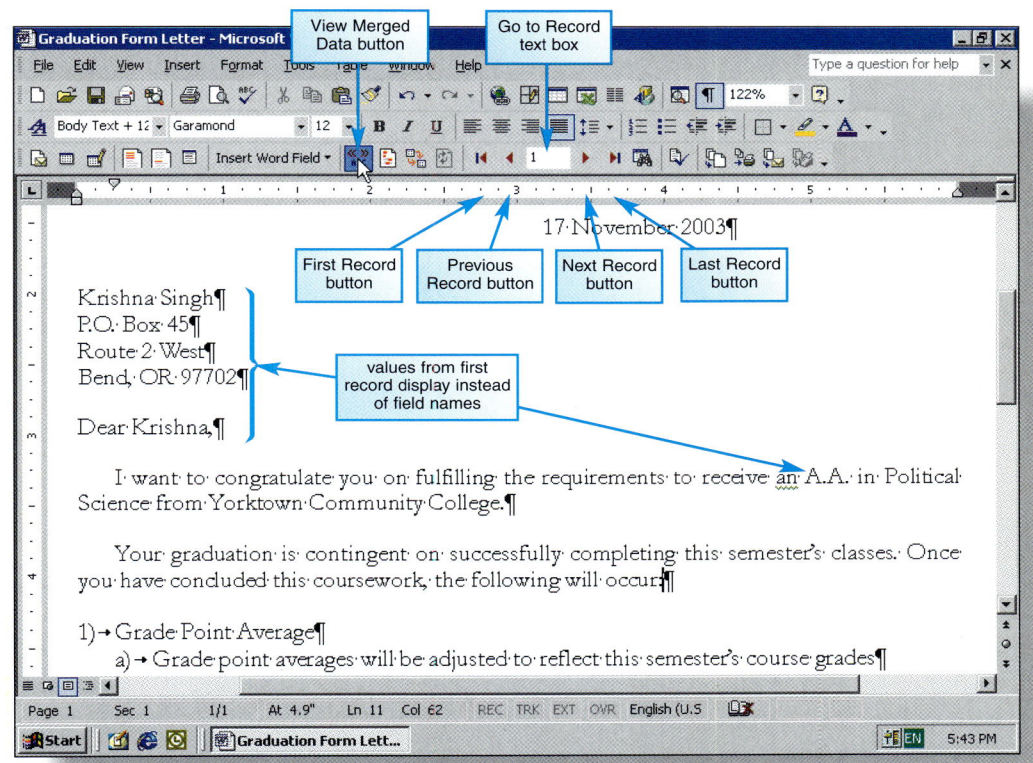

FIGURE 5-69

1. With Mail Merge toolbar displaying, in Voice Command mode, say "View Merged Data"

When you are viewing merged data in the main document (the View Merged Data button is selected), you can click the **Last Record button** (Figure 5-69) on the Mail Merge toolbar to display the values from the last record in the data source, the **First Record button** to display the values in record one, the **Next Record button** to display the values in the next consecutive record number, or the **Previous Record button** to display the values from the previous record number. You also can display a particular record by clicking the **Go to Record text box**, typing the record number you would like to display in the main document, and then pressing the ENTER key.

Mailing Labels

Instead of addressing mailing labels from a data source, you can print a label(s) for a single address. Click Tools on the menu bar, point to Letters and Mailings, click Envelopes and Labels, click the Labels tab, type the name and address in the Address text box, click the Options button and select the label type, click the OK button, and then click the Print button in the Envelopes and Labels dialog box.

Addressing and Printing Mailing Labels

Now that you have merged and printed the form letters, the next step is to print addresses on mailing labels to be affixed to envelopes for the form letters. The mailing labels will use the same data source as the form letter, Graduate List. The format and content of the mailing labels will be exactly the same as the inside address in the main document for the form letter. That is, the first line will contain the student's first name followed by the last name. The second line will contain his or her street address, and so on. Thus, you will use the AddressBlock merge field in the mailing labels.

If your printer can print graphics, you can add a **POSTNET** (**POS**Tal **N**umeric **E**ncoding **T**echnique) **delivery-point bar code**, usually referred to simply as a **bar code**, below the address on each mailing label. Using a bar code speeds up delivery by the U.S. Postal Service. The POSTNET bar code represents the addressee's ZIP code and first street address.

You follow the same basic steps to create the main document for the mailing labels as you did to create the main document for the form letters. The major difference is that the data source already exists because you created it earlier in this project.

To address mailing labels, you specify the type of labels you intend to use. Word will request the manufacturer's name, as well as a product number and name. You can obtain this information from the box of labels. For illustration purposes in addressing these labels, the manufacturer is Avery, and the product name is address labels, which has a product number of 5160.

The following pages illustrate how to address and print these mailing labels using an existing data source.

Steps: To Address and Print Mailing Labels Using an Existing Data Source

1 **Click the New Blank Document button on the Standard toolbar. Click Tools on the menu bar, point to Letters and Mailings, and then click Mail Merge Wizard. Click Labels in the Select document type area in the Mail Merge task pane. Point to Next: Starting document.**

Word displays Step 1 of the Mail Merge Wizard in the Mail Merge task pane (Figure 5-70). Step 1 of the Mail Merge Wizard displays the available types of main documents.

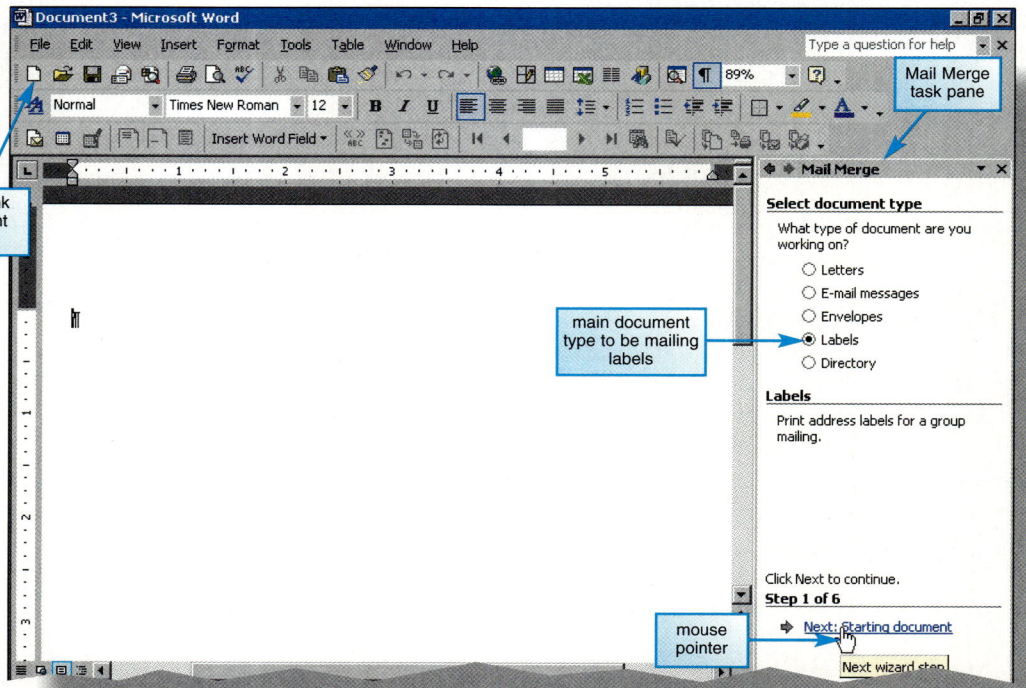

FIGURE 5-70

Addressing and Printing Mailing Labels • WD 5.55

2 **Click Next: Starting document.** If necessary, click Change document layout in the Select starting document area in the Mail Merge task pane. When the Change document layout area displays, click Label options. When the Label Options dialog box displays, click the desired Avery product number in the Product number list (in this case, 5160 - Address). Point to the OK button.

Step 2 of the Mail Merge Wizard allows you to specify the label product information (Figure 5-71). If you have a dot matrix printer, your printer information will differ from this figure. The Product number list displays the product numbers for all possible Avery mailing label sheets compatible with your printer.

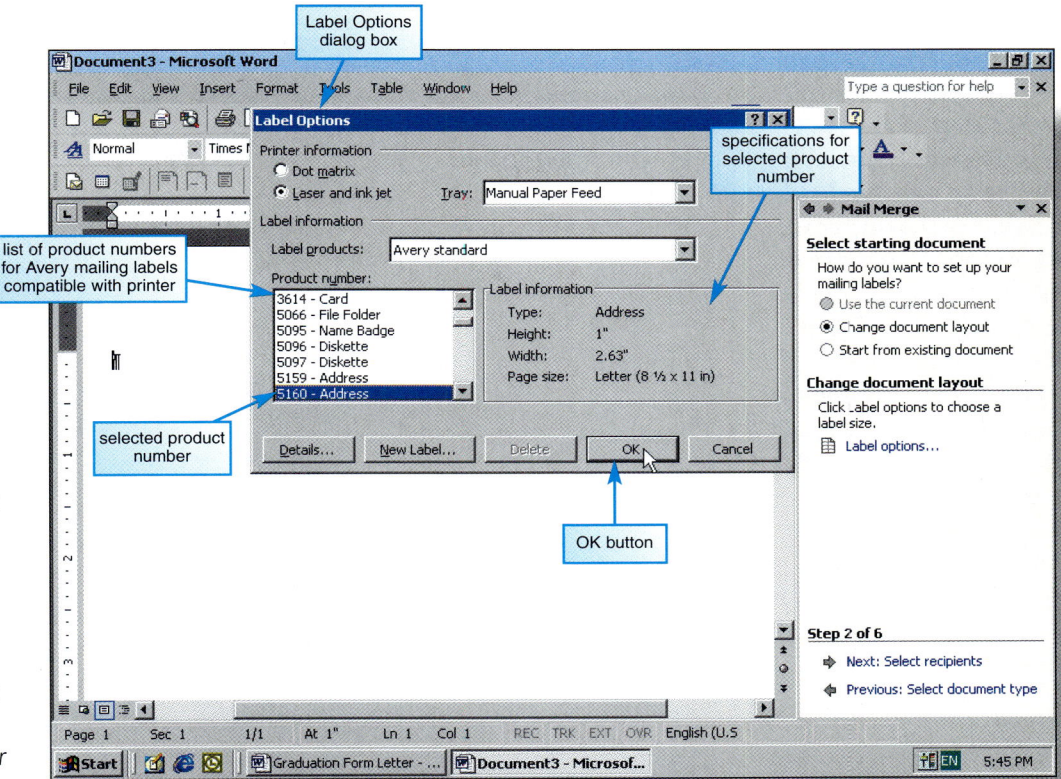

FIGURE 5-71

3 **Click the OK button. In the Mail Merge task pane, point to Next: Select recipients.**

Word displays the selected label layout in the main document (Figure 5-72). The next step is to select the data source. You will open and use the same data source you created for the form letters.

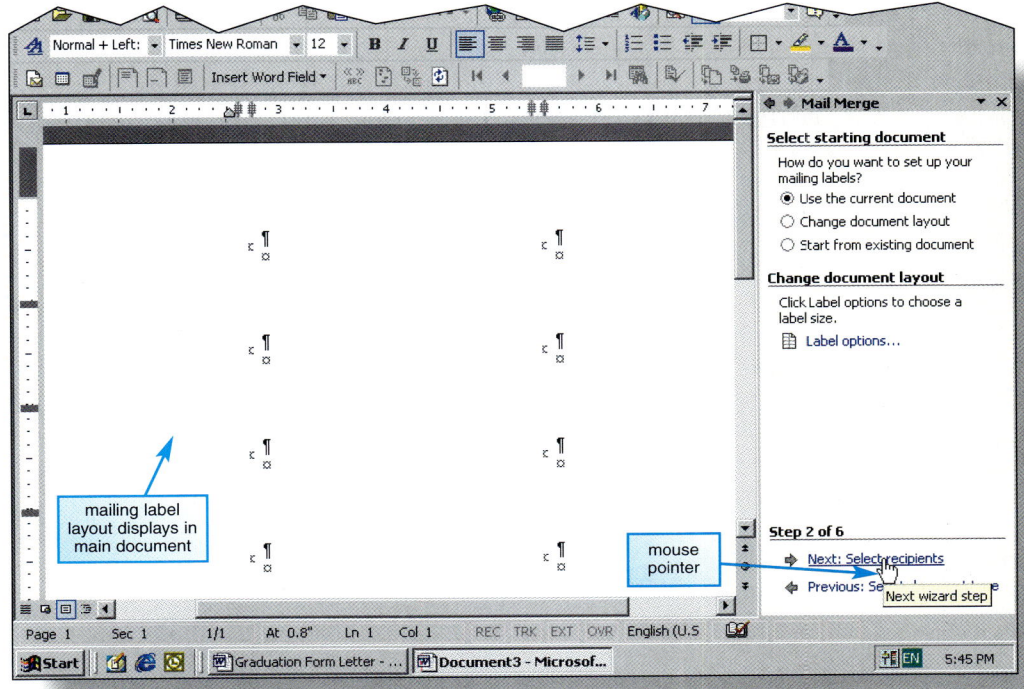

FIGURE 5-72

4. **Click Next: Select recipients to display the next step of the Mail Merge Wizard. If necessary, click Use an existing list in the Select recipients area. Click Browse in the Use an existing list area. When Word displays the Select Data Source dialog box, if necessary, click the Look in box arrow, click 3½ Floppy (A:), and then double-click the Graduation folder. Click the file name, Graduate List, and then point to the Open button in the Select Data Source dialog box.**

Word displays the Select Data Source dialog box (Figure 5-73). You use the existing data source, Graduate List, to address the mailing labels.

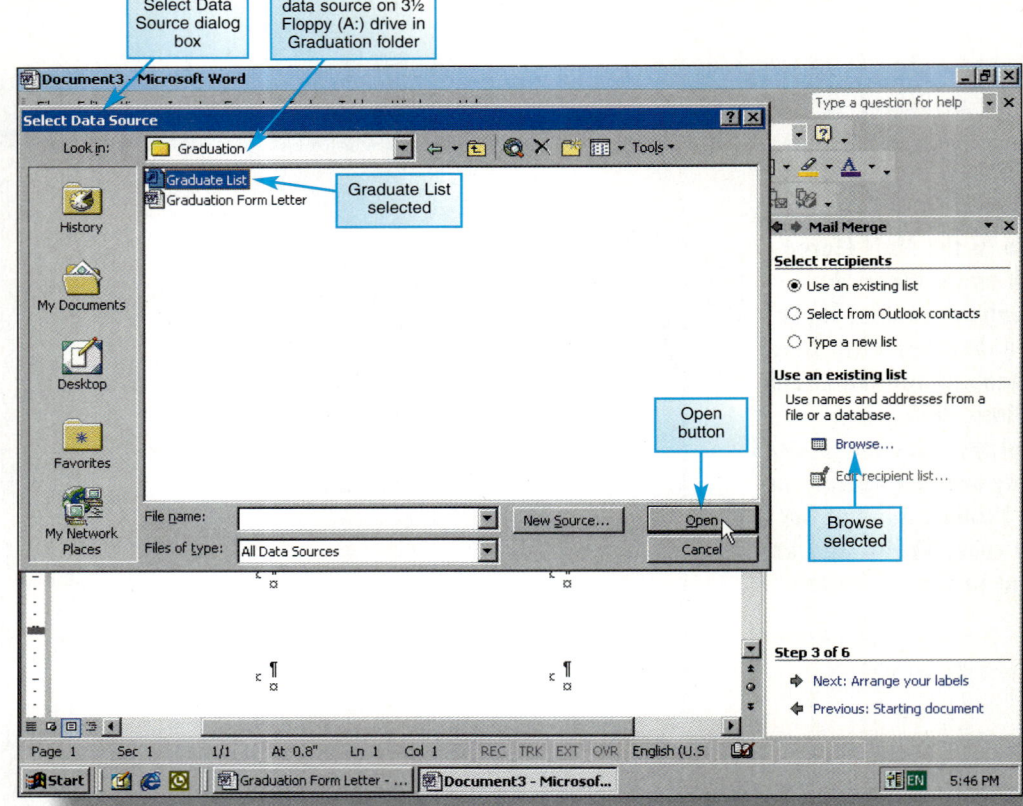

FIGURE 5-73

5. **Click the Open button in the Open Data Source dialog box. When the Mail Merge Recipients dialog box displays, scroll to the right until the ZIP Code field displays in the dialog box and then click the ZIP Code field name. Point to the OK button.**

The Mail Merge Recipients dialog box displays (Figure 5-74). The students are listed in ZIP code order.

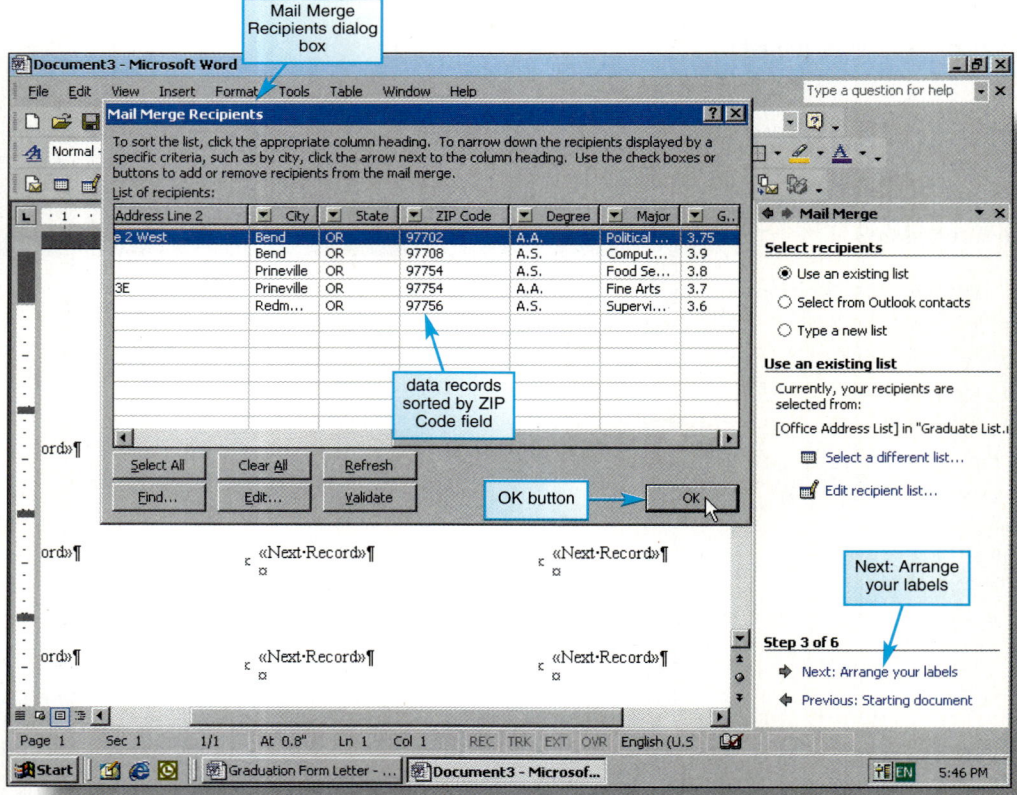

FIGURE 5-74

Click the OK button. At the bottom of the Mail Merge task pane, click Next: Arrange your labels. In the Arrange your labels area, click Address block. When the Insert Address Block dialog box displays, point to the OK button.

Word displays the Insert Address Block dialog box (Figure 5-75). Word automatically matches fields and suppresses blank lines. Thus, the address information will print according to the data in the data source.

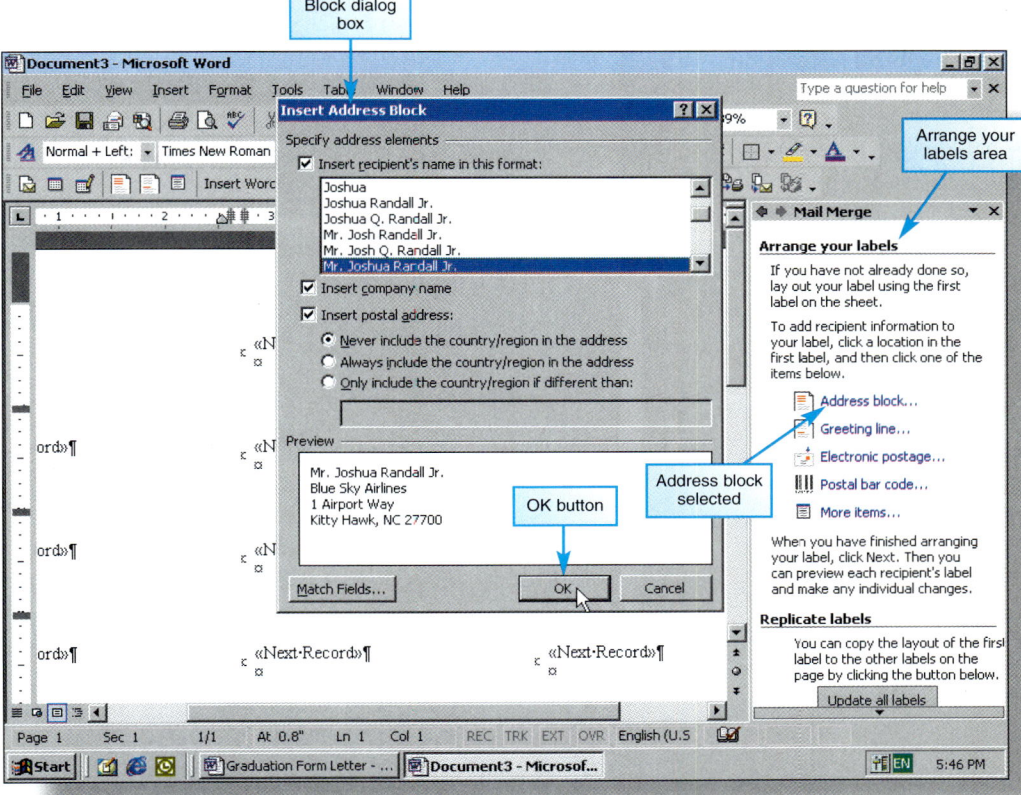

FIGURE 5-75

7 Click the OK button. If necessary, scroll to the left to display the first label in the document window. In the Arrange your labels area, click Postal bar code. When the Insert Postal Bar Code dialog box displays, be sure the Merge field with ZIP code box displays ZIP_Code and the Merge field with street address box displays Address_Line_1. Point to the OK button.

Word inserts the AddressBlock field into the first mailing label and then displays the Insert Postal Bar Code dialog box (Figure 5-76). Notice that Word places an underscore character (_) wherever a field contains a space.

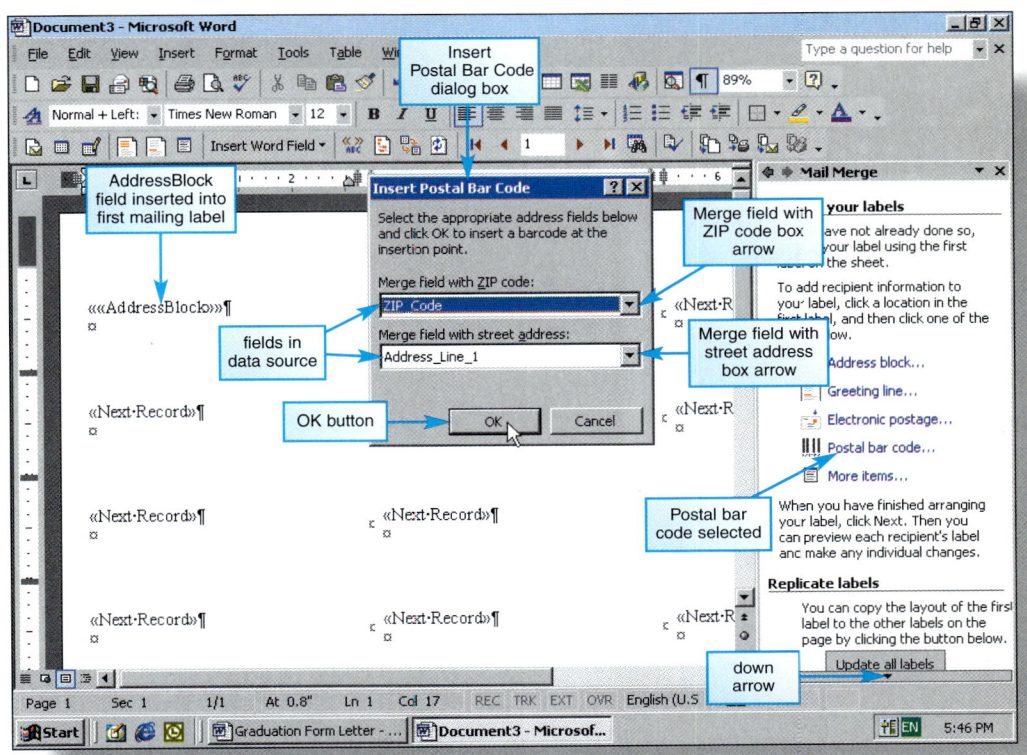

FIGURE 5-76

8 **Click the OK button.**

Word places a bar code on the first mailing label. The next step is to copy the layout of the first label to the rest of the labels in the main document.

9 **Point to the down arrow at the bottom of the Mail Merge task pane to scroll to the bottom of the task pane. Click the Update all labels button.**

Word copies the layout of the first label to the remaining label layouts in the main document (Figure 5-77).

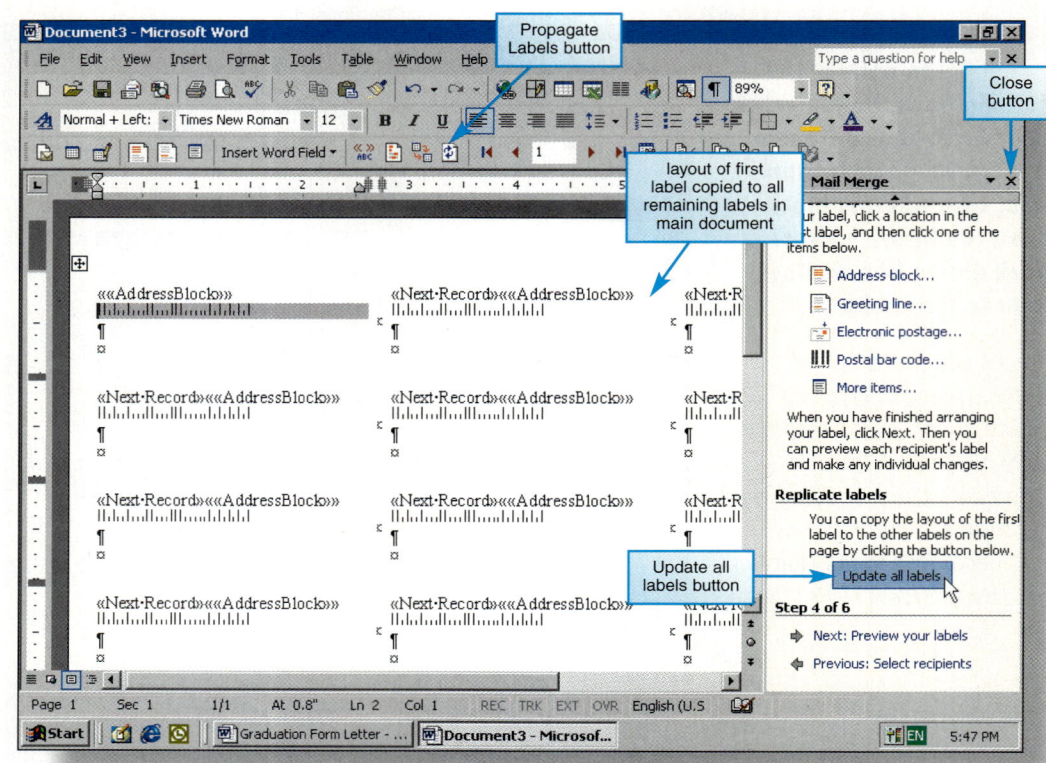

FIGURE 5-77

10 **Click the Close button in the upper-right corner of the Mail Merge task pane. Click the View Merged Data button on the Mail Merge toolbar to display the data records on the label layout in the document window.**

Word displays the addresses in ZIP code order in the mailing label layout of the main document (Figure 5-78).

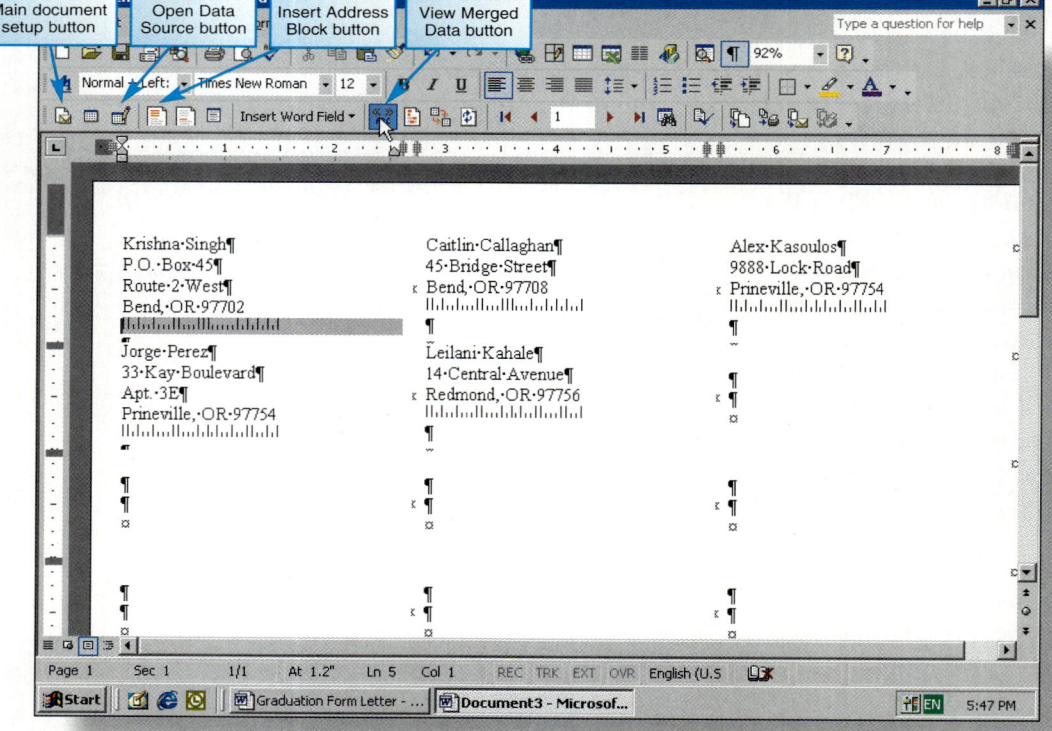

FIGURE 5-78

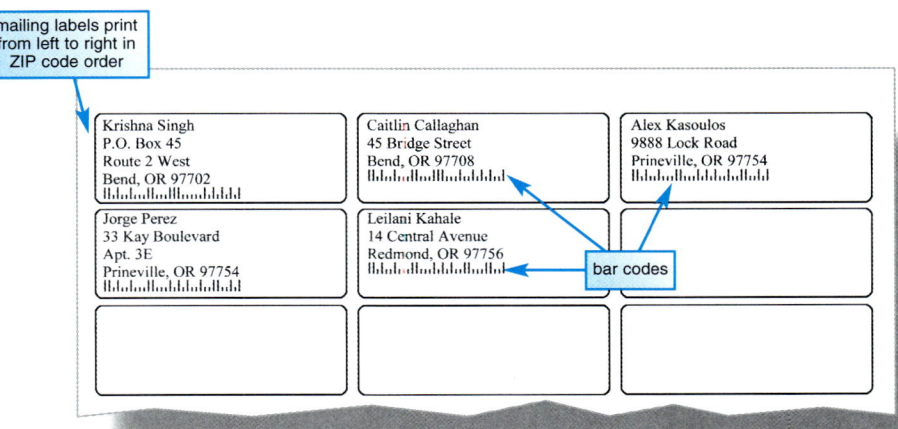

11 If necessary, insert blank mailing label paper into the printer. Click the Merge to Printer button on the Mail Merge toolbar. When the Merge to Printer dialog box displays, if necessary, click All. Click the OK button. When the Print dialog box displays, click the OK button. Retrieve the mailing labels from the printer.

FIGURE 5-79

The mailing labels print as shown in Figure 5-79.

If you do not wish to print bar codes on the labels, then you can use the buttons on the Mail Merge toolbar for the entire mailing label mail merge. Click the Main document setup button (Figure 5-78) and then click Labels in the dialog box. Click the Open Data Source button to display the Select Data Source dialog box. Click the Insert Address Block button to display the Insert Address Block dialog box. Click the Propagate Labels button to copy the layout of the first label to the remaining labels in the main document.

Saving the Mailing Labels

Perform the following steps to save the mailing label main document.

TO SAVE THE MAILING LABEL MAIN DOCUMENT

1. Insert your floppy disk into drive A.
2. Click the Save button on the Standard toolbar.
3. Type the file name Graduation Labels in the File name text box. Do not press the ENTER key after typing the file name.
4. If necessary, click the Save in box arrow, click 3½ Floppy (A:), and then double-click the Graduation folder.
5. Click the Save button in the Save As dialog box.

Word saves the document with the file name, Graduation Labels, in the Graduation folder on the floppy disk in drive A.

More About

Data Sources

Word initially looks in the My Data Sources folder for a data source when it displays the Select Data Source dialog box. To find a data source in a different location, click the Look in box arrow, locate the file, and then click the Open button in the dialog box.

Addressing and Printing Envelopes

Instead of addressing mailing labels to affix to envelopes, your printer may have the capability of printing directly onto envelopes. To print the label information directly on envelopes, follow the same basic steps as you did to address the mailing labels. Perform the steps on the next page to address envelopes using an existing data source.

Steps: To Address and Print Envelopes Using an Existing Data Source

  Click the New Blank Document button on the Standard toolbar. Click Tools on the menu bar, point to Letters and Mailings, and then click Mail Merge Wizard. Click Envelopes in the Select document type area in the Mail Merge task pane. Point to Next: Starting document.

Word displays Step 1 of the Mail Merge Wizard in the Mail Merge task pane (Figure 5-80). Step 1 of the Mail Merge Wizard displays the available types of main documents.

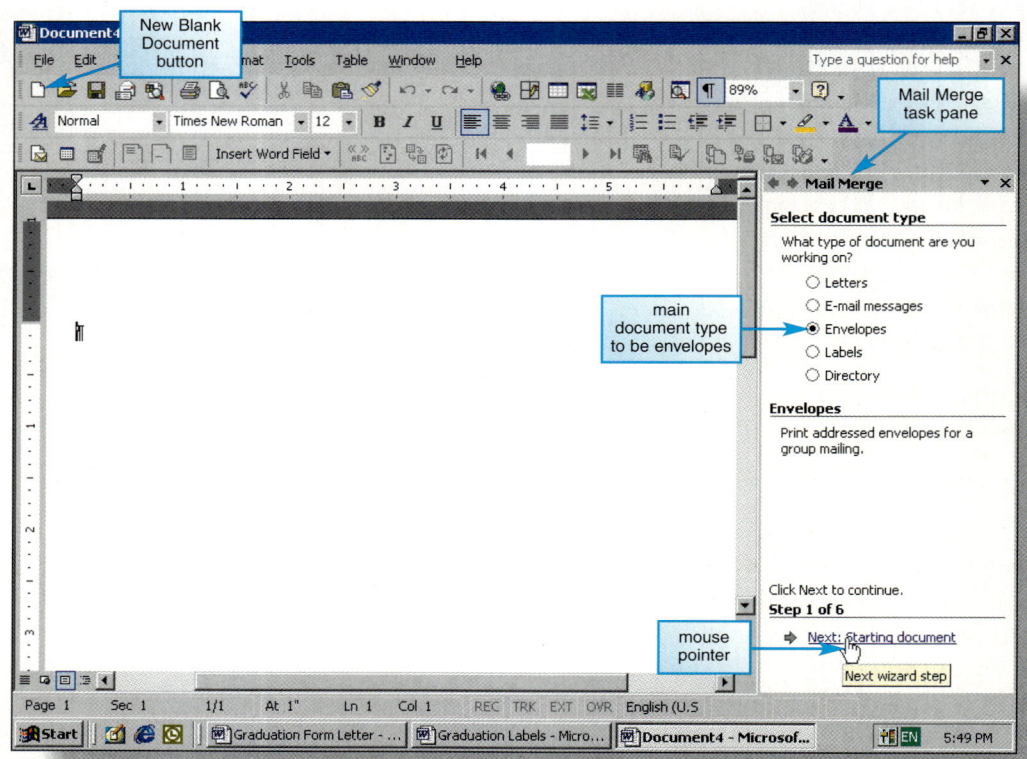

FIGURE 5-80

Click Next: Starting document. If necessary, click Change document layout in the Select starting document area in the Mail Merge task pane. When the Change document layout area displays, click Envelope options. When the Envelope Options dialog box displays, select the envelope size and then point to the OK button.

Step 2 of the Mail Merge Wizard allows you to specify the envelope size (Figure 5-81). Depending on your printer, the contents of the Envelope Options sheet may differ.

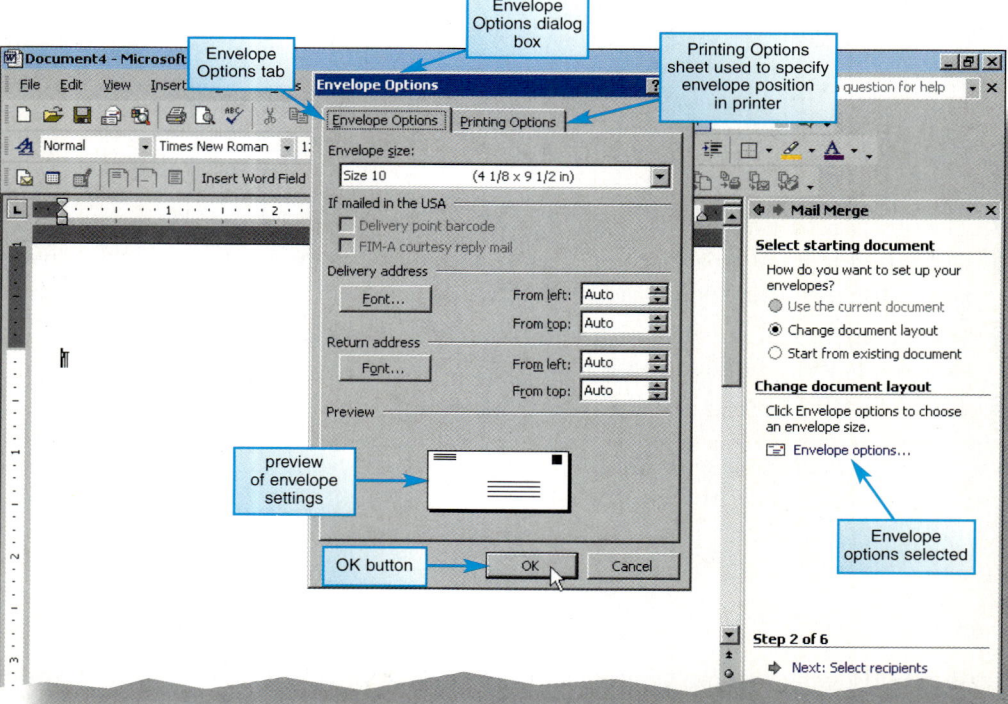

FIGURE 5-81

3 Click the OK button. With the insertion point in the upper-left corner of the envelope layout, click the Font Size box arrow and then click 12. Type Yorktown Community College and then press the ENTER key. Type 44 Broadway Street and then press the ENTER key. Type Redmond, OR 97756 and then click the paragraph mark in the middle of the envelope layout. Point to Next: Select recipients at the bottom of the Mail Merge task pane.

Word displays the envelope layout as the main document (Figure 5-82). The return address displays in the upper-left corner. The next step is to open the data source and insert the AddressBlock field and postal bar code in the middle of the envelope layout, which is surrounded by a frame.

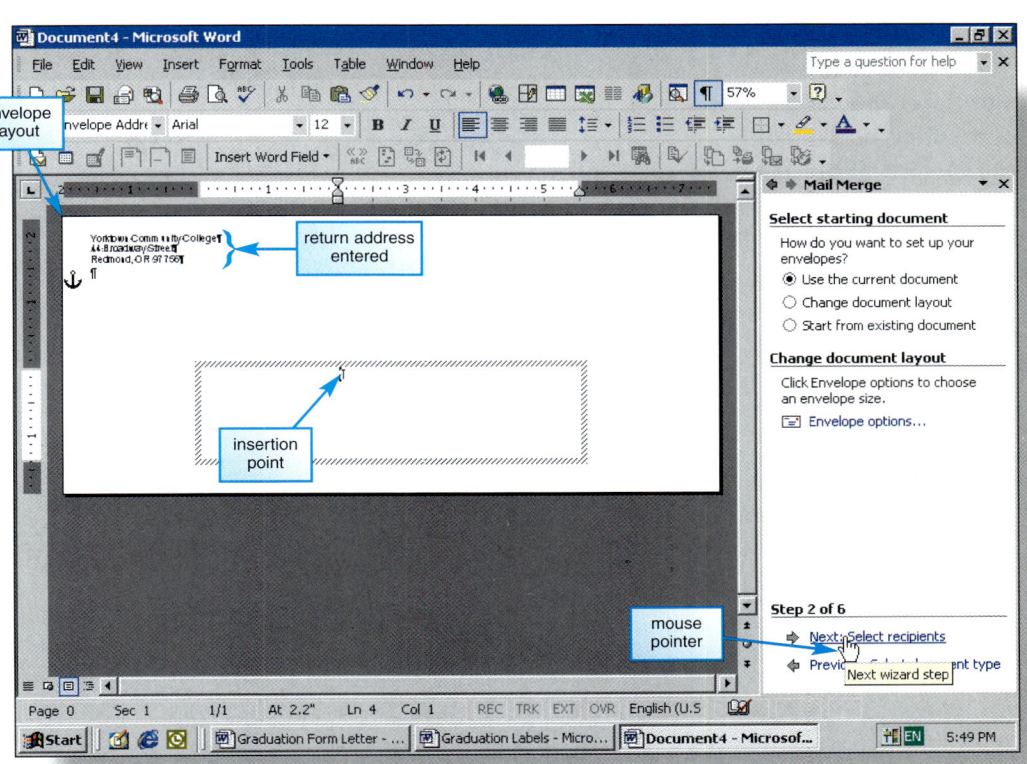

FIGURE 5-82

4 Follow Steps 4 through 8 on pages WD 5.56 through WD 5.58, substituting references to labels with envelopes. Click the Close button in the upper-right corner of the Mail Merge task pane.

Word opens the data source, inserts the AddressBlock field and the postal bar code onto the envelope layout (Figure 5-83).

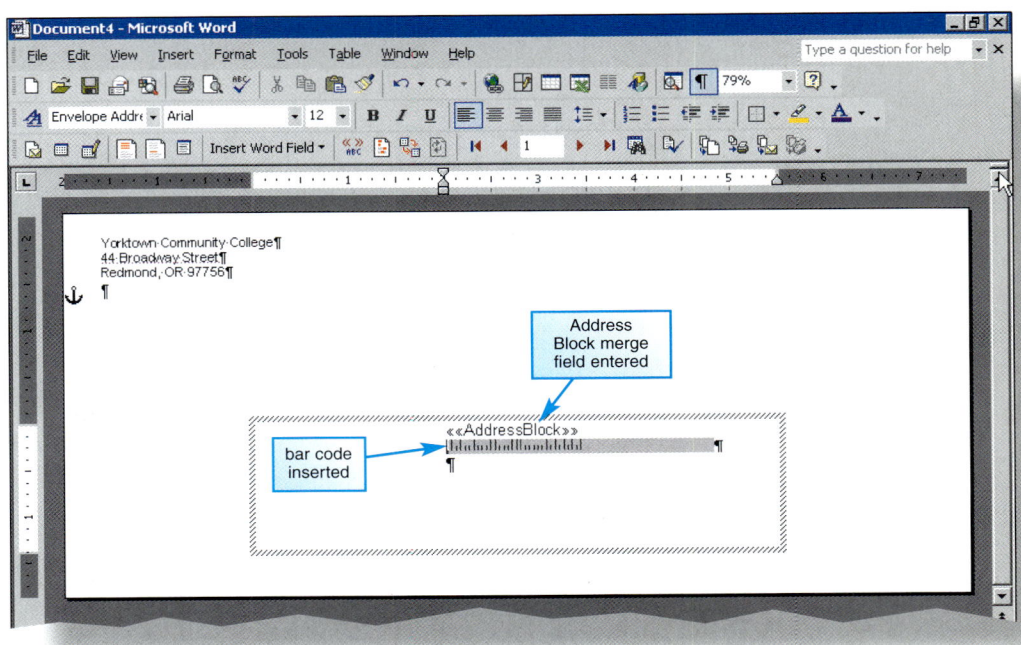

FIGURE 5-83

5. **If necessary, insert envelopes into the printer. Click the Merge to Printer button on the Mail Merge toolbar. When the Merge to Printer dialog box displays, if necessary, click All. Click the OK button. When the Print dialog box displays, click the OK button. Retrieve the envelopes from the printer.**

The envelopes print as shown in Figure 5-84.

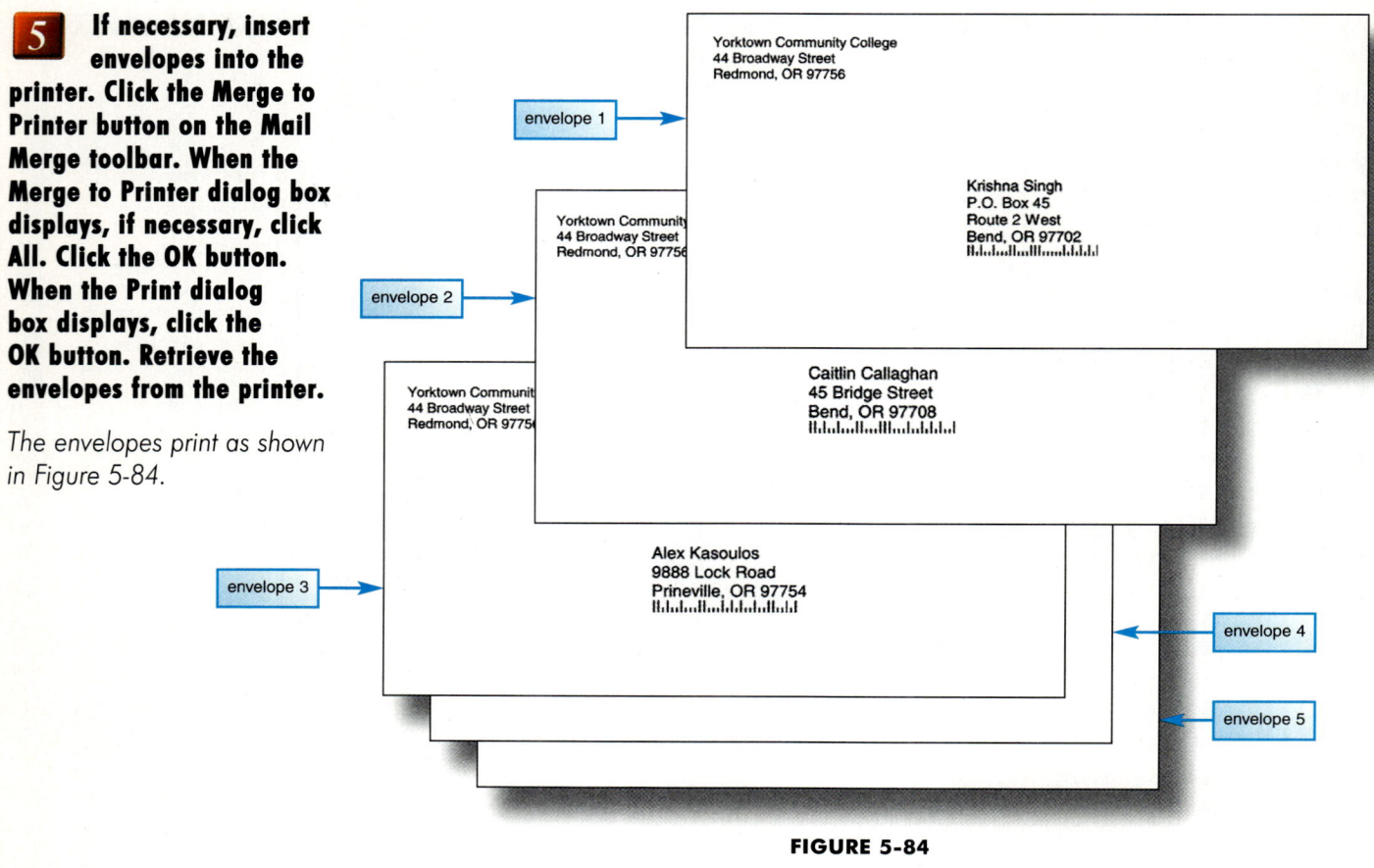

FIGURE 5-84

Saving the Envelopes

Perform the following steps to save the envelope main document.

TO SAVE THE ENVELOPE MAIN DOCUMENT

1. Insert your floppy disk into drive A.
2. Click the Save button on the Standard toolbar.
3. Type the file name `Graduation Envelopes` in the File name text box. Do not press the ENTER key after typing the file name.
4. If necessary, click the Save in box arrow, click 3½ Floppy (A:), and then double-click the Graduation folder.
5. Click the Save button in the Save As dialog box.

Word saves the document with the file name, Graduation Envelopes, in the Graduation folder on the floppy disk on drive A.

Merging All Data Records to a Directory

You may want to print the data records in the data source. Recall that the data source is saved as a Microsoft Access database table. Thus, you cannot open the data source in Word. To view the data source, click the Mail Merge Recipients button on the Mail Merge toolbar. One way to print the contents of the data source is to merge all data records in the data source into a single document, called a **directory**, instead of merging to a separate document for each data record.

Perform the following steps to merge the data records in the data source into a directory. Instead of using the Mail Merge Wizard, you will use the buttons on the Mail Merge toolbar to perform this merge.

Steps: To Merge to a Directory

1 **Click the New Blank Document button on the Standard toolbar. Click the Main document setup button on the Mail Merge toolbar. When the Main Document Type dialog box displays, click Directory and then point to the OK button.**

Word displays the Main Document Type dialog box (Figure 5-85).

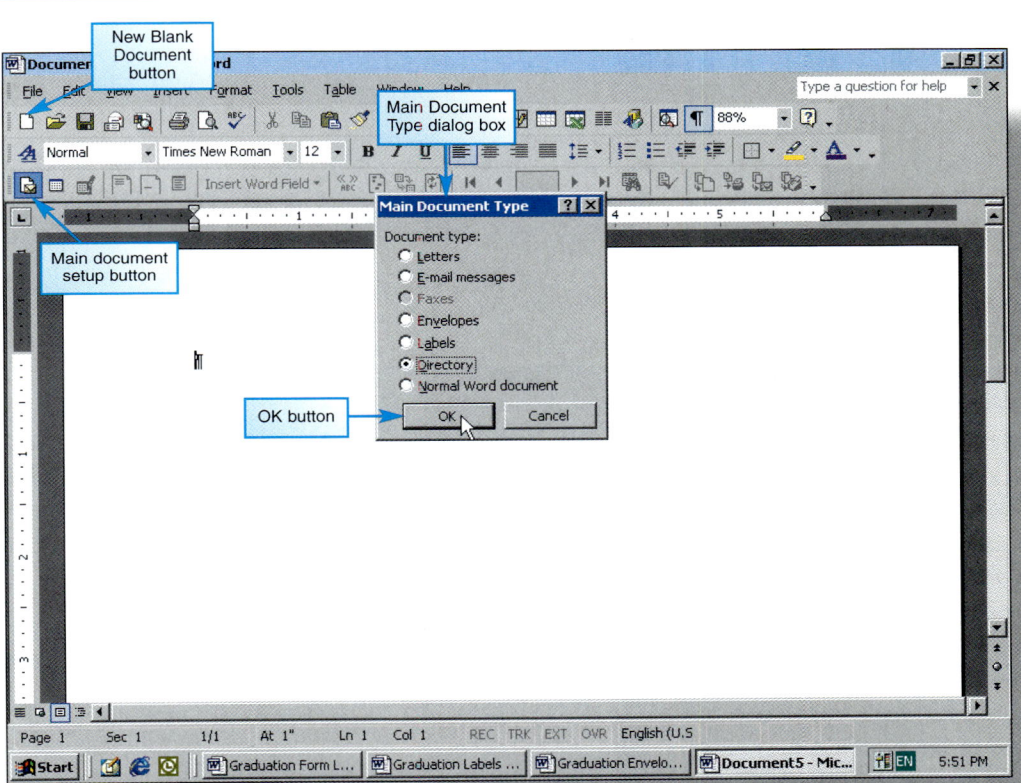

FIGURE 5-85

2 Click the OK button. Click the Open Data Source button on the Mail Merge toolbar. When the Select Data Source dialog box displays, if necessary, click the Look in box arrow, click 3½ Floppy (A:), and then double-click the Graduation folder. Click the file name, Graduate List, and then point to the Open button in the Select Data Source dialog box.

Word displays the Select Data Source dialog box (Figure 5-86). You use the existing data source, Graduate List, to create the directory.

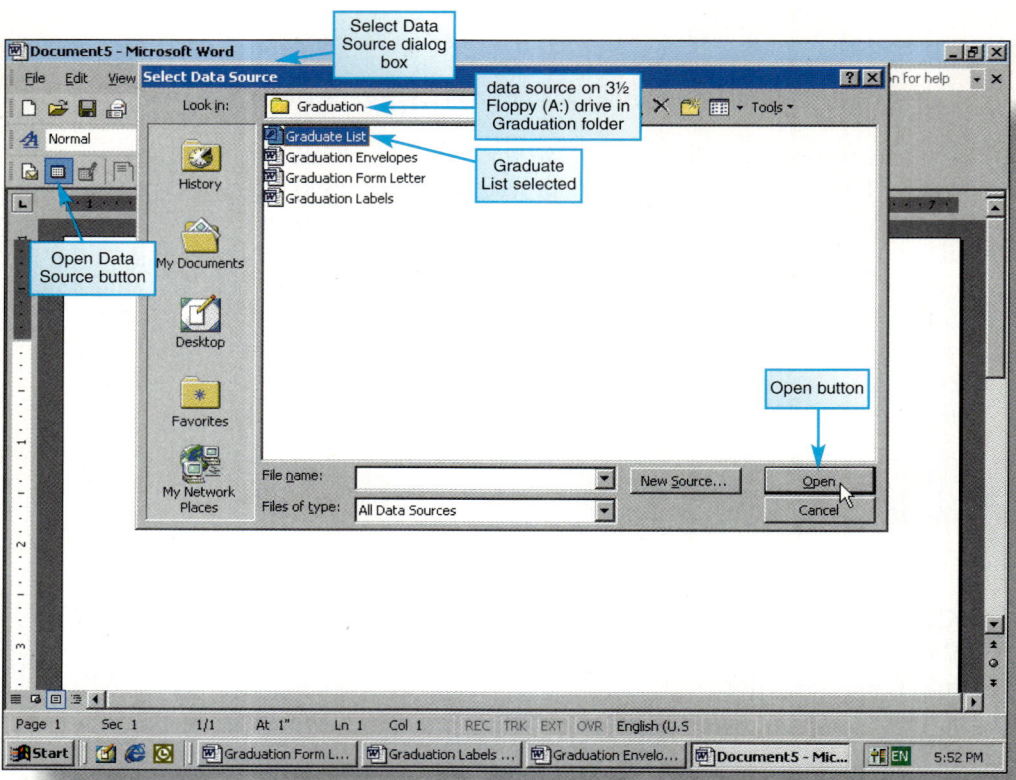

FIGURE 5-86

3 Click the Open button in the Select Data Source dialog box. Click the Insert Merge Fields button on the Mail Merge toolbar. When the Insert Merge Field dialog box displays, click First Name in the Fields list and then click the Insert button. Repeat for each remaining field in the Fields list. Point to the Close button in the Insert Merge Field dialog box (Figure 5-87).

4 Click the Close button.

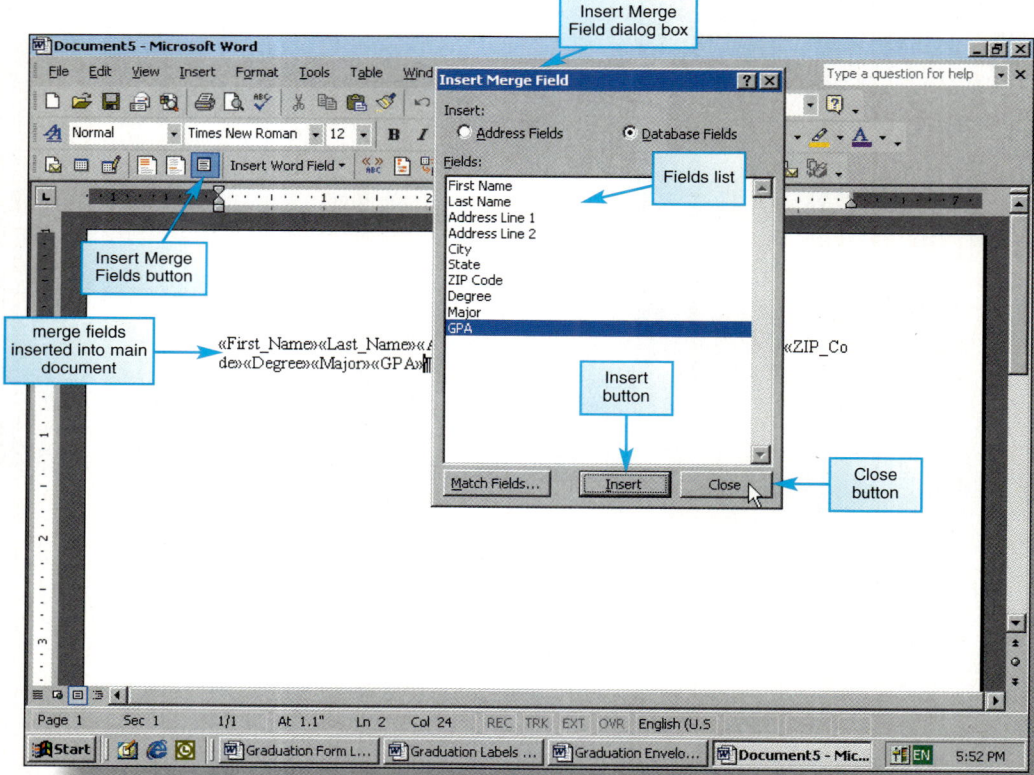

FIGURE 5-87

Merging All Data Records to a Directory • WD 5.65

You want the directory to be in a table form. That is, you want each data record to be in a single row and each merge field to be in a column. To convert the text to a table, you must separate the merge fields so Word knows where one column ends and the next begins. Thus, you will press the ENTER key between each merge field.

Perform the following steps to convert the text containing the merge fields to a table.

Steps: To Convert Text to a Table

1 **Position the insertion point between the First_Name and Last_Name merge fields. Press the ENTER key. Repeat for each merge field in the document. Click Edit on the menu bar and then click Select All to select the entire document. Click Table on the menu bar, point to Convert, and then point to Text to Table.**

Word places each merge field on a separate line, inserting the paragraph mark symbol after each merge field (Figure 5-88).

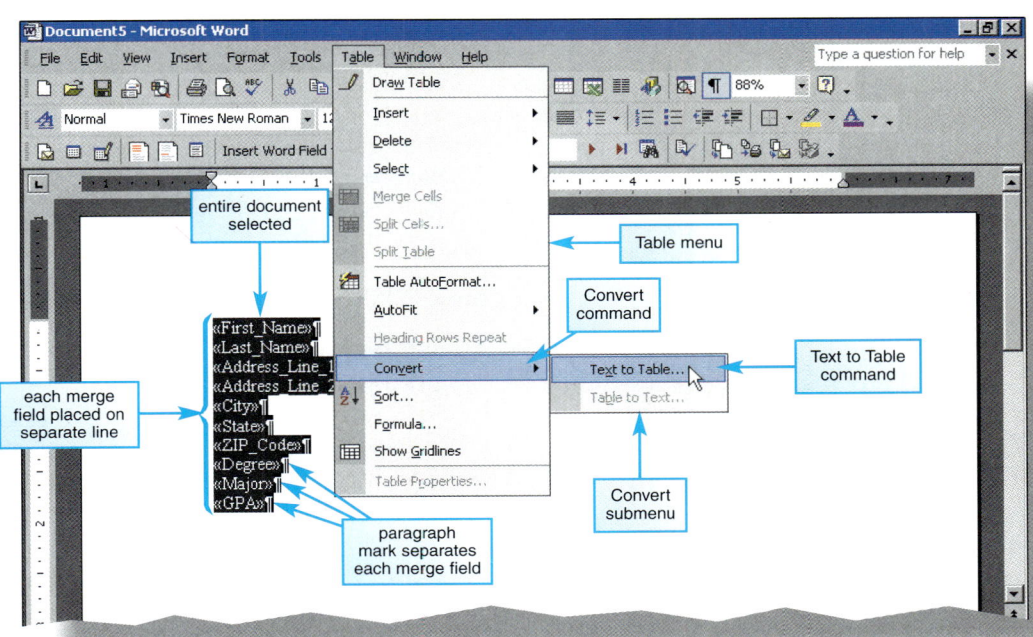

FIGURE 5-88

2 **Click Text to Table. Type 10 in the Number of columns text box and then point to the OK button.**

Word displays the Convert Text to Table dialog box (Figure 5-89).

3 **Click the OK button.**

Word converts the text of merge fields to a table (shown in Figure 5-91 on page WD 5.67). Each merge field is in its own column.

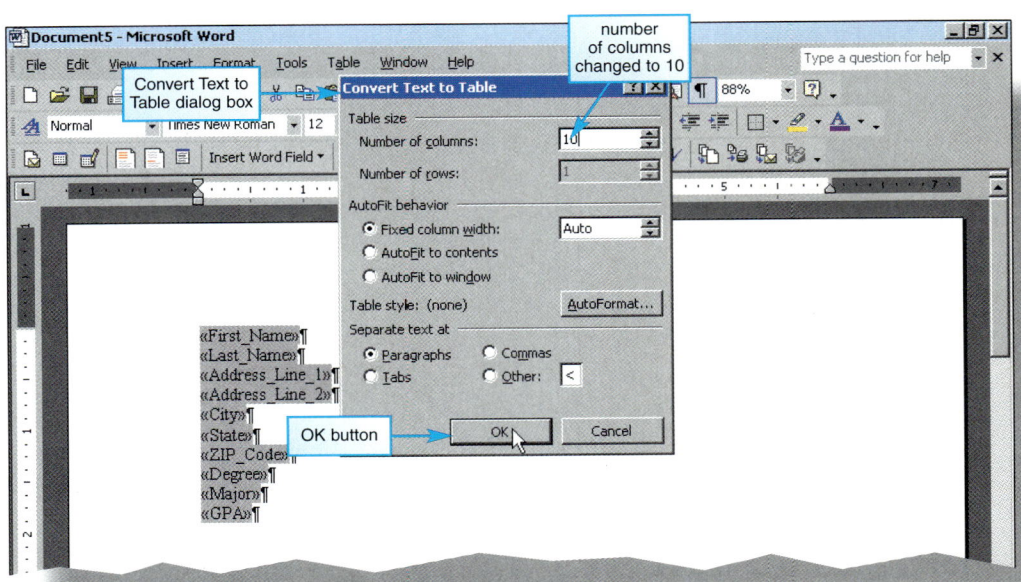

FIGURE 5-89

The table is too wide to fit on a piece of paper in **portrait orientation**; that is, with the short edge of the paper at the top. You can instruct Word to print a document in **landscape orientation** so the long edge of the paper is at the top. Perform the following steps to change the orientation of the document from portrait to landscape.

Steps: To Change Page Orientation

1 Click File on the menu bar and then click Page Setup. When the Page Setup dialog box displays, if necessary, click the Margins tab. Click Landscape in the Orientation area and then point to the OK button.

Word displays the Page Setup dialog box (Figure 5-90).

2 Click the OK button. Click the Zoom box arrow on the Standard toolbar and then click Page Width.

Word changes the print orientation to landscape (shown in Figure 5-91). With the zoom set to page width, the entire page displays in the document window.

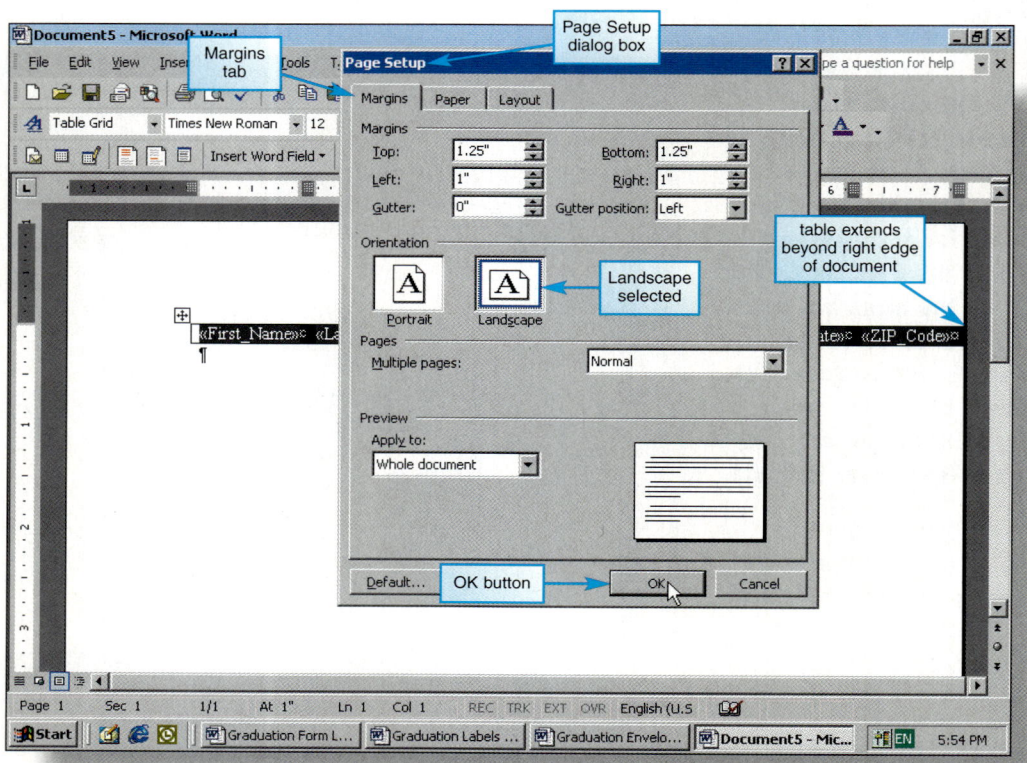

FIGURE 5-90

Other Ways

1. In Voice Command mode, say "File, Page Setup, Landscape, OK"

The next step is to merge the data records in the data source into the directory in a new document window, as described in the following steps.

TO MERGE TO A NEW DOCUMENT WINDOW

1 Click the Merge to New Document button on the Mail Merge taskbar.

2 When Word displays the Merge to New Document dialog box, if necessary, click All. Point to the OK button (Figure 5-91).

3 Click the OK button.

Word merges the data records into a single document in a new document window (shown in Figure 5-92 on page WD 5.68).

Merging All Data Records to a Directory • WD 5.67

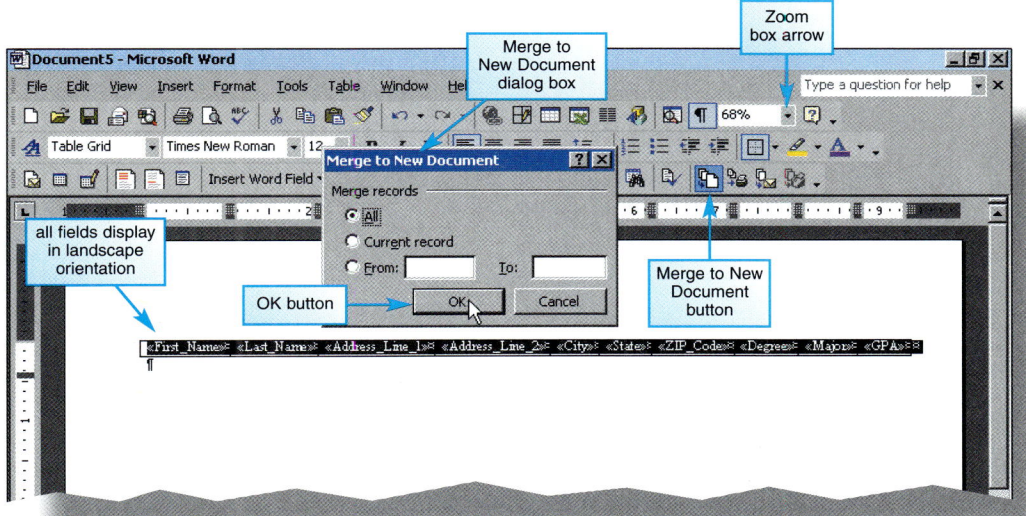

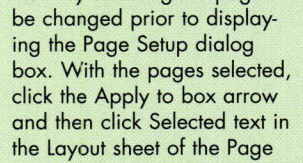

Page Orientation

You can change the page orientation for part of a document by selecting the pages to be changed prior to displaying the Page Setup dialog box. With the pages selected, click the Apply to box arrow and then click Selected text in the Layout sheet of the Page Setup dialog box. Word inserts a section break before and after the selected pages.

FIGURE 5-91

As discussed in earlier projects, you can add rows to tables, increase table widths, and use the Table AutoFormat command to format a table. Perform the following steps to format the table containing the records from the data source.

TO MODIFY AND FORMAT A TABLE

1. Click in the upper-left cell of the table. Click Table on the menu bar, point to Insert, and then click Rows Above.

2. Click in the left cell of the new row. Type `First Name` and then press the TAB key. Type `Last Name` and then press the TAB key. Type `Address Line 1` and then press the TAB key. Type `Address Line 2` and then press the TAB key. Type `City` and then press the TAB key. Type `State` and then press the TAB key. Type `ZIP Code` and then press the TAB key. Type `Degree` and then press the TAB key. Type `Major` and then press the TAB key. Type `GPA` as the last entry in the row.

3. With the insertion point somewhere in the table, click Table on the menu bar and then click Table AutoFormat.

4. When the Table AutoFormat dialog box displays, scroll through the Table styles list and then click Table Grid 4. Be sure only the Heading rows check box contains a check mark. All other check boxes should be cleared. Click the Apply button.

5. Point in the table and then click the table move handle in the upper-left corner of the table to select the table. Click the Outside Border button on the Formatting toolbar to place an outside border on the table. (If the face of the button does not display an outside border, click the Border button arrow and then click Outside Border.) Click anywhere to remove the selection.

6. Double-click the column border between the Address Line 1 and Address Line 2 columns to display all Address Line 1 data on a single line. Double-click the column border between the Address Line 2 and City columns to display all Address Line 2 data on a single line. Double-click the column border between the Major and GPA columns to display all Degree data on a single line. Repeat as necessary until each record displays on a single row.

The directory containing all records in the data source is formatted, as shown in Figure 5-92 on the next page.

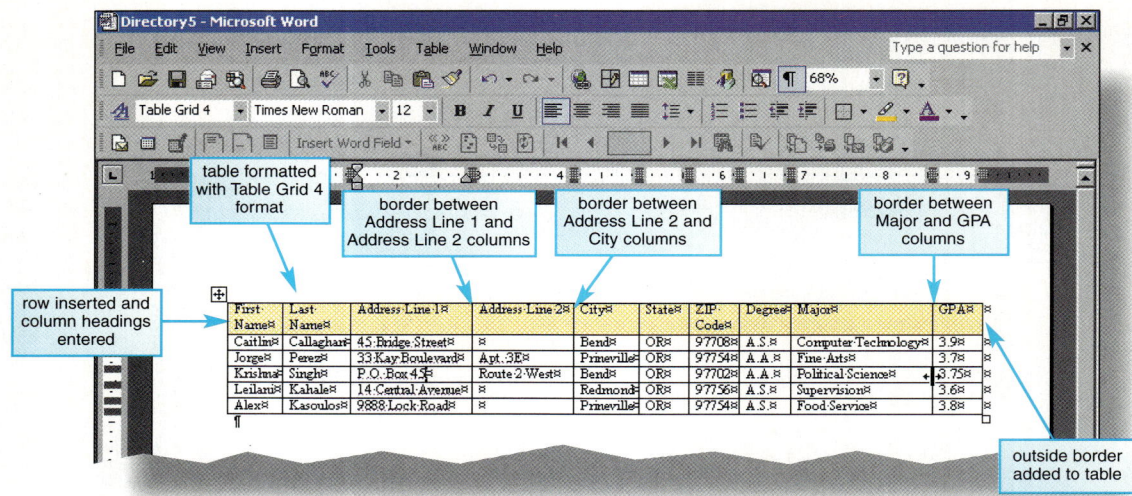

FIGURE 5-92

Perform the following step to sort the table by the ZIP Code column.

Steps To Sort a Table

1 **If the Tables and Borders toolbar does not display on the screen, click the Tables and Borders button on the Standard toolbar. If the Draw Table button is selected on the Tables and Borders toolbar, click it to deselect it. Position the insertion point somewhere in the ZIP Code column and then click the Sort Ascending button on the Tables and Borders toolbar.**

Word sorts the records in the table in ascending (smallest to largest) ZIP code order (Figure 5-93).

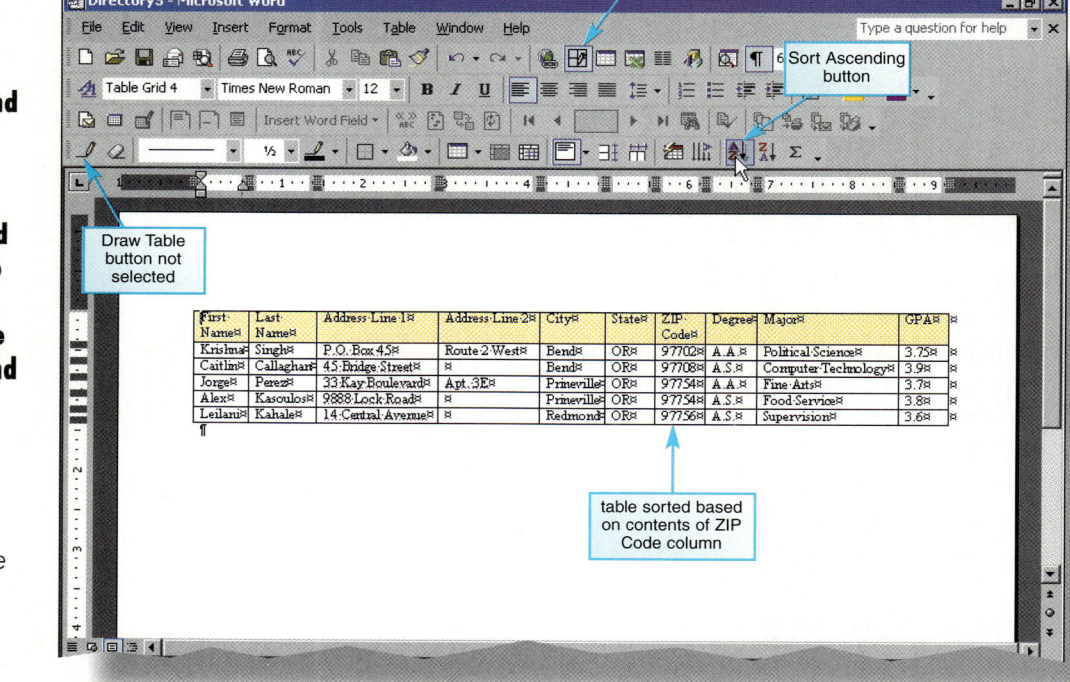

FIGURE 5-93

Other Ways

1. On Table menu click Sort, click Sort by box arrow, click column to sort, click OK button

To print the directory, perform the following step.

TO PRINT A DOCUMENT

1. Click the Print button on the Standard toolbar.

Word prints the document in landscape orientation (shown in Figure 5-22 on page WD 5.22).

As an alternative to merging to a directory, if you are familiar with Microsoft Access, you can open and print the data source in Access.

Saving the Directory

Perform the following steps to save the directory.

TO SAVE THE DIRECTORY

1. Insert your floppy disk into drive A.
2. Click the Save button on the Standard toolbar.
3. Type the file name Graduation Directory in the File name text box. Do not press the ENTER key after typing the file name.
4. If necessary, click the Save in box arrow, click 3½ Floppy (A:), and then double-click the Graduation folder.
5. Click the Save button in the Save As dialog box.

Word saves the document with the file name, Graduation Directory, in the Graduation folder on the floppy disk on drive A.

Closing All Open Word Documents and Quitting Word

You currently have five files open: Graduation Form Letters, Graduation Mailing Labels, Graduation Envelopes, Graduation Directory, and Document5. Instead of closing each file individually, you can close all open files at once, as shown in the steps on the next page.

Microsoft Certification

The Microsoft Office User Specialist (MOUS) Certification program provides an opportunity for you to obtain a valuable industry credential — proof that you have the Word 2002 skills required by employers. For more information, see Appendix E or visit the Shelly Cashman Series MOUS Web page at scsite.com/offxp/cert.htm.

Closing Form Letters

Word always asks if you want to save changes when you close a main document, even if you just saved the document. If you are sure that no additional changes were made to the document, click the No button; otherwise, click the Yes button - just to be safe.

Quick Reference

For a table that lists how to complete tasks covered in this book using the mouse, menu, shortcut menu, and keyboard, see the Quick Reference Summary at the back of this book or visit the Shelly Cashman Series Office XP Web page (scsite.com/offxp/qr.htm) and then click Microsoft Word 2002.

WD 5.70 • Project 5 • Generating Form Letters, Mailing Labels, Envelopes, and Directories   Microsoft **Word 2002**

Steps To Close All Open Word Documents

1 Press and hold the SHIFT key. While holding the SHIFT key, click File on the menu bar. Release the SHIFT key. Point to Close All on the File menu.

Word displays a Close All command, instead of a Close command, on the File menu because you pressed the SHIFT key when you clicked the menu name (Figure 5-94).

2 Click Close All. If a Microsoft Word dialog box displays, click the Yes button to save any changes made to the Graduation Form Letters, Graduation Mailing Labels, Graduation Envelopes, and Graduation Directory files. For the Document5 file, click the No button.

Word closes all open documents.

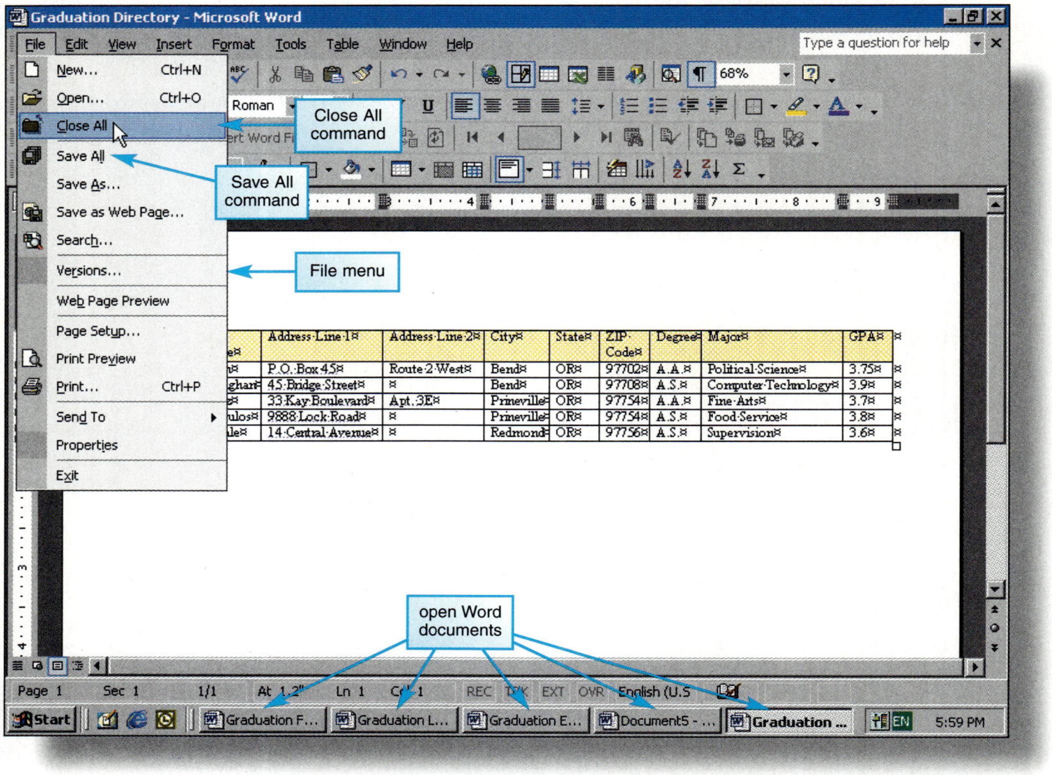

FIGURE 5-94

Notice the Save command also changes to a Save All command (Figure 5-94) when you SHIFT+click File on the menu bar. The **Save All command** saves all open documents at once.

Project 5 now is complete. Follow this step to quit Word.

TO QUIT WORD

1 Click the Close button in the Word window.

The Word window closes.

CASE PERSPECTIVE SUMMARY

You insert the form letters into the preaddressed envelopes, seal them, and apply necessary postage. Then, you take the envelopes to the post office to expedite delivery of the letters.

Your supervisor asks you to begin preparing another form letter that outlines details of the upcoming graduation ceremony. The letter should provide an in-depth explanation about the rehearsal, caps and gowns, announcements, and tickets. This task will be easier because the data source and mailing labels already are done. All you need to do is compose the form letter for the mail merge.

Project Summary

Project 5 introduced you to creating and printing form letters and addressing corresponding mailing labels and envelopes. First, you used a letter template to begin creating the main document for the form letter and then created a data source. Next, you entered graphics, text, and merge fields, and an IF field into the main document for the form letter. The form letter also included an outline numbered list. You learned how to merge and print all the records in the data source, as well as only records that meet a certain criterion. You also learned how to sort the data source records. You addressed mailing labels and envelopes to accompany the form letters. Finally, you merged all data records into a directory and printed the resulting directory.

What You Should Know

Having completed this project, you should now be able to perform the following tasks:

- Add Text to an AutoShape *(WD 5.15)*
- Address and Print Envelopes Using an Existing Data Source *(WD 5.60)*
- Address and Print Mailing Labels Using an Existing Data Source *(WD 5.54)*
- Apply a Paragraph Style *(WD 5.42)*
- Begin Typing the Body of the Form Letter *(WD 5.33)*
- Change Page Orientation *(WD 5.66)*
- Change Paragraph Formatting *(WD 5.19)*
- Change the Font Size of Text *(WD 5.44)*
- Close All Open Word Documents *(WD 5.70)*
- Convert Text to a Table *(WD 5.65)*
- Create a Folder while Saving *(WD 5.21)*
- Create an Outline Numbered List *(WD 5.38)*
- Display a Field Code *(WD 5.45)*
- Display Formatting Marks *(WD 5.07)*
- Edit a Field *(WD 5.30)*
- Edit the GreetingLine Merge Field *(WD 5.32)*
- Enter a Paragraph of Text *(WD 5.38)*
- Enter More Records *(WD 5.27)*
- Enter More Text *(WD 5.42)*
- Format a Drawing Canvas *(WD 5.18)*
- Format an AutoShape *(WD 5.14)*
- Insert an AutoShape *(WD 5.12)*
- Insert an IF Field into the Main Document *(WD 5.36)*
- Insert Merge Fields into the Main Document *(WD 5.34)*
- Merge the Form Letters to the Printer *(WD 5.48)*
- Merge to a Directory *(WD 5.63)*
- Merge to a New Document Window *(WD 5.66)*
- Modify and Format a Table *(WD 5.67)*
- Print a Document *(WD 5.69)*
- Print Field Codes in the Main Document *(WD 5.46)*
- Quit Word *(WD 5.70)*
- Remove a Merge Condition *(WD 5.51)*
- Reset Menus and Toolbars *(WD 5.06)*
- Resize the Drawing Canvas *(WD 5.17)*
- Save a Document Again *(WD 5.45)*
- Save the Data Source when Prompted by the Mail Merge Wizard *(WD 5.28)*
- Save the Directory *(WD 5.69)*
- Save the Envelope Main Document *(WD 5.62)*
- Save the Mailing Label Main Document *(WD 5.59)*
- Select and Replace More Placeholder Text *(WD 5.43)*
- Select Records to Merge *(WD 5.49)*
- Sort the Data Records *(WD 5.52)*
- Sort a Table *(WD 5.68)*
- Start and Customize Word *(WD 5.06)*
- Turn Field Codes Off for Printing *(WD 5.47)*
- Type a New Data Source *(WD 5.23)*
- Use a Template as the Main Document in a Mail Merge *(WD 5.08)*
- View Merged Data in the Main Document *(WD 5.53)*
- Zoom Text Width *(WD 5.07)*

Learn It Online

Instructions: To complete the Learn It Online exercises, start your browser, click the Address bar, and then enter scsite.com/offxp/exs.htm. When the Office XP Learn It Online page displays, follow the instructions in the exercises below.

1 Project Reinforcement

TF, MC, and SA Below Word Project 5, click the Project Reinforcement link. Print the quiz by clicking Print on the File menu. Answer each question. Write your first and last name at the top of each page, and then hand in the printout to your instructor.

2 Flash Cards

Below Word Project 5, click the Flash Cards link. When Flash Cards displays, read the instructions. Type 20 (or a number specified by your instructor) in the Number of Playing Cards text box, type your name in the Name text box, and then click the Flip Card button. When the flash card displays, read the question and then click the Answer box arrow to select an answer. Flip through Flash Cards. Click Print on the File menu to print the last flash card if your score is 15 (75%) correct or greater and then hand it in to your instructor. If your score is less than 15 (75%) correct, then redo this exercise by clicking the Replay button.

3 Practice Test

Below Word Project 5, click the Practice Test link. Answer each question, enter your first and last name at the bottom of the page, and then click the Grade Test button. When the graded practice test displays on your screen, click Print on the File menu to print a hard copy. Continue to take practice tests until you score 80% or better. Hand in a printout of the final practice test to your instructor.

4 Who Wants to Be a Computer Genius?

Below Word Project 5, click the Computer Genius link. Read the instructions, enter your first and last name at the bottom of the page, and then click the Play button. Hand in your score to your instructor.

5 Wheel of Terms

Below Word Project 5, click the Wheel of Terms link. Read the instructions, and then enter your first and last name and your school name. Click the Play button. Hand in your score to your instructor.

6 Crossword Puzzle Challenge

Below Word Project 5, click the Crossword Puzzle Challenge link. Read the instructions, and then enter your first and last name. Click the Play button. Work the crossword puzzle. When you are finished, click the Submit button. When the crossword puzzle redisplays, click the Print button. Hand in the printout.

7 Tips and Tricks

Below Word Project 5, click the Tips and Tricks link. Click a topic that pertains to Project 5. Right-click the information and then click Print on the shortcut menu. Construct a brief example of what the information relates to in Word to confirm you understand how to use the tip or trick. Hand in the example and printed information.

8 Newsgroups

Below Word Project 5, click the Newsgroups link. Click a topic that pertains to Project 5. Print three comments. Hand in the comments to your instructor.

9 Expanding Your Horizons

Below Word Project 5, click the Articles for Microsoft Word link. Click a topic that pertains to Project 5. Print the information. Construct a brief example of what the information relates to in Word to confirm you understand the contents of the article. Hand in the example and printed information to your instructor.

10 Search Sleuth

Below Word Project 5, click the Search Sleuth link. To search for a term that pertains to this project, select a term below the Project 5 title and then use the Google search engine at google.com (or any major search engine) to display and print two Web pages that present information on the term. Hand in the printouts to your instructor.

Apply Your Knowledge

1 Working with a Form Letter

Instructions: Start Word. Open the document, Wireless World Form Letter, on the Data Disk. If you did not download the Data Disk, see the inside back cover for instructions for downloading the Data Disk or see your instructor.

The document is a main document for Wireless World (Figure 5-95). You are to print the form letter with field codes displaying and then without field codes, add a record to the data source, and then merge the form letters to a file.

Perform the following tasks:

1. Click Tools on the menu bar and then click Options. When the Options dialog box displays, if necessary, click the Print tab. Click Field codes to select the check box and then click the OK button. Click the Print button on the Standard toolbar.

2. Click Tools on the menu bar and then click Options. When the Options dialog box displays, if necessary, click the Print tab. Click Field codes to remove the check mark from the check box and then click the OK button. Click the Print button on the Standard toolbar.

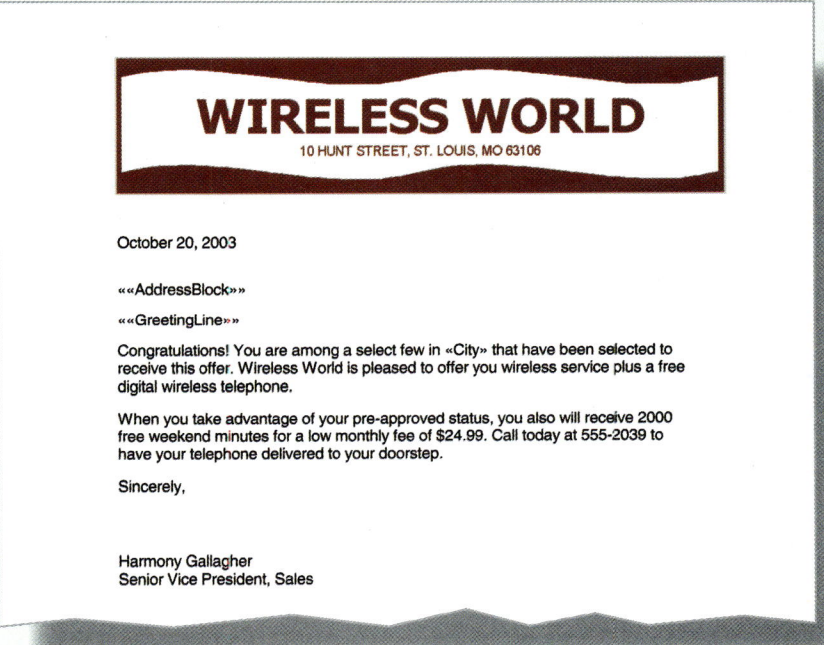

FIGURE 5-95

3. If the Mail Merge toolbar is not displaying on the screen, click Tools on the menu bar, point to Letters and Mailings, and then click Show Mail Merge Toolbar. Click the Mail Merge Recipients button on the Mail Merge toolbar. Click the Edit button in the Mail Merge Recipients dialog box. Add a record to the data source that contains your personal information; type Y in the Previous Customer field. Click the Close button in the dialog box.

4. Click the Last Name field name in the Mail Merge Recipients dialog box to sort the data source by last names. Click the OK button to close the dialog box.

5. Click the Merge to New Document button on the Mail Merge toolbar. When the Merge to New Document dialog box displays, click All and then click the OK button. If Word displays a dialog box about locked fields, click the OK button. Click the Print button on the Standard toolbar to print the letters in the document window. Click the Save button. Save the merged documents with the file name, Wireless World Merged Letters. Click File on the menu bar and then click the Close button.

6. Hold down the SHIFT key while clicking File on the menu bar. Click Close All.

In the Lab

1 Creating a Form Letter, Data Source, Mailing Labels, and Directory

Problem: Hope Kraliki, the manager of client services at Arrow Insurance, has asked you to send a letter to all current customers, informing them of the insurance company's new telephone number. You decide to use a form letter (Figure 5-96a).

Instructions:

1. Begin the mail merge process by clicking Tools on the menu bar, pointing to Letters and Mailings, and then clicking Mail Merge Wizard. Use the Elegant Merge Letter template to create a form letter. Close the Mail Merge task pane.

2. Replace the placeholder text at the top of the letterhead with the left-right arrow AutoShape. Add the text and formatting to the AutoShape as shown in Figure 5-96a.

3. Use the Reveal Formatting task pane to insert 24 points above the date line.

4. Restart the Mail Merge Wizard. Type a new data source using the data shown in Figure 5-96b. Delete fields not used, and add a field called Type of Insurance. Save the data source with the file name, Arrow Insurance Customers, in a folder called Arrow Insurance. *Hint*: You will need to create the folder while saving. Close the Mail Merge task pane.

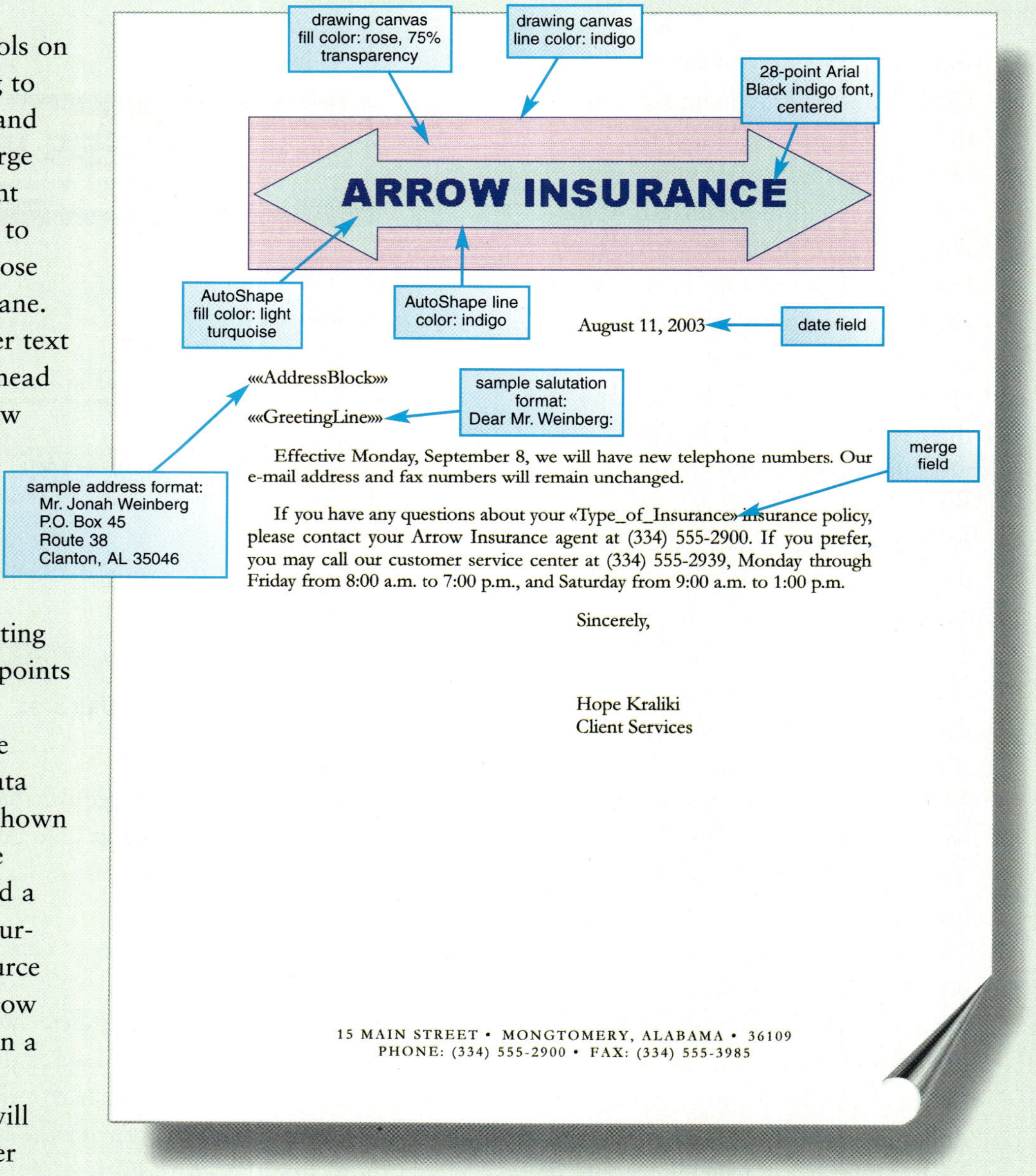

FIGURE 5-96a

In the Lab

Title	First Name	Last Name	Address Line 1	Address Line 2	City	State	ZIP Code	Type of Insurance
Mr.	Jonah	Weinberg	P.O. Box 45	Route 38	Clanton	AL	35046	auto
Mr.	Adrian	Valesquez	15 Duluth Street		Prattville	AL	36068	auto
Ms.	Chalandra	Obi	5576 Grove Lane	Apt. 7	Union Springs	AL	36089	life
Mrs.	Shannon	Murray	33099 Clark Street		Montgomery	AL	36109	health
Dr.	Fredrick	Houck	394 Front Drive		Auburn	AL	36830	liability

FIGURE 5-96b

5. Save the main document for the form letter with the file name, Arrow Insurance Form Letter, in the folder called Arrow Insurance. Compose the form letter for the main document as shown in Figure 5-96a. Edit the GreetingLine field so it ends with a colon, instead of a comma. Insert the merge field, type of insurance, in the first sentence of the second paragraph of the body of the letter. Resize the body of the letter to 14 point.

6. Save the main document for the form letter again. Print the main document twice: once with field codes displaying and once without field codes.

7. Merge and print the form letters.

8. In a new document window, address mailing labels using the same data source you used for the form letters. Put bar codes on the mailing labels. Save the mailing labels with the name, Arrow Insurance Mailing Labels, in the Arrow Insurance folder. Print the mailing labels.

9. If your printer allows, in a new document window, address envelopes using the same data source you used for the form letters. Put bar codes on the envelopes. Save the envelopes with the file name, Arrow Insurance Envelopes, in the folder called Arrow Insurance. Print the envelopes.

10. In a new document window, merge all data records in the data source to a directory. Insert all merge fields into the document. Convert the list of fields to a Word table (the table will have nine columns). Change the page layout to landscape orientation. Merge the directory layout to a new document window. Add a row to the top of the table and insert field names into the empty cells. Format the data source using the Table Grid 4 format in the Table AutoFormat dialog box (apply special formats only to the heading row). Resize the columns so each data record displays on a single row. Place a border around the entire table. Sort the table by the ZIP Code field. Save the directory with the name, Arrow Insurance Directory, in the folder called Arrow Insurance. Print the directory (shown in Figure 5-96b).

In the Lab

2 Creating a Form Letter with an IF Field and an Outline Numbered List

Problem: As the computer specialist at Citizens Broadcasting Network, the owner has asked you to send a letter to all members, requesting their donation for this year's membership drive. You have decided to use a form letter (Figure 5-97a). For members that reside in the west, you print the address of P.O. Box 11235 in the last line of the letter; for members that reside in the east, you print the address of P.O. Box 11278 in the last line of the letter.

Instructions:

1. Begin the mail merge process by clicking Tools on the menu bar, pointing to Letters and Mailings, and then clicking Mail Merge Wizard. Use the Elegant Merge Letter template to create a form letter. Close the Mail Merge task pane.

2. Replace the placeholder text at the top of the letterhead with the horizontal scroll AutoShape. Add the text and formatting to the AutoShape as shown in Figure 5-97a.

3. Use the Reveal Formatting task pane to insert 18 points above the date line. Edit the date field so it displays in the format: day month year.

4. Restart the Mail Merge Wizard. Type a new data source using the data shown in Figure 5-97b. Delete fields not used and add two fields: Region and Previous Donation. Save the data source with the file name, Citizen Members, in a folder called Citizens. *Hint*: You will need to create the folder while saving. Close the Mail Merge task pane.

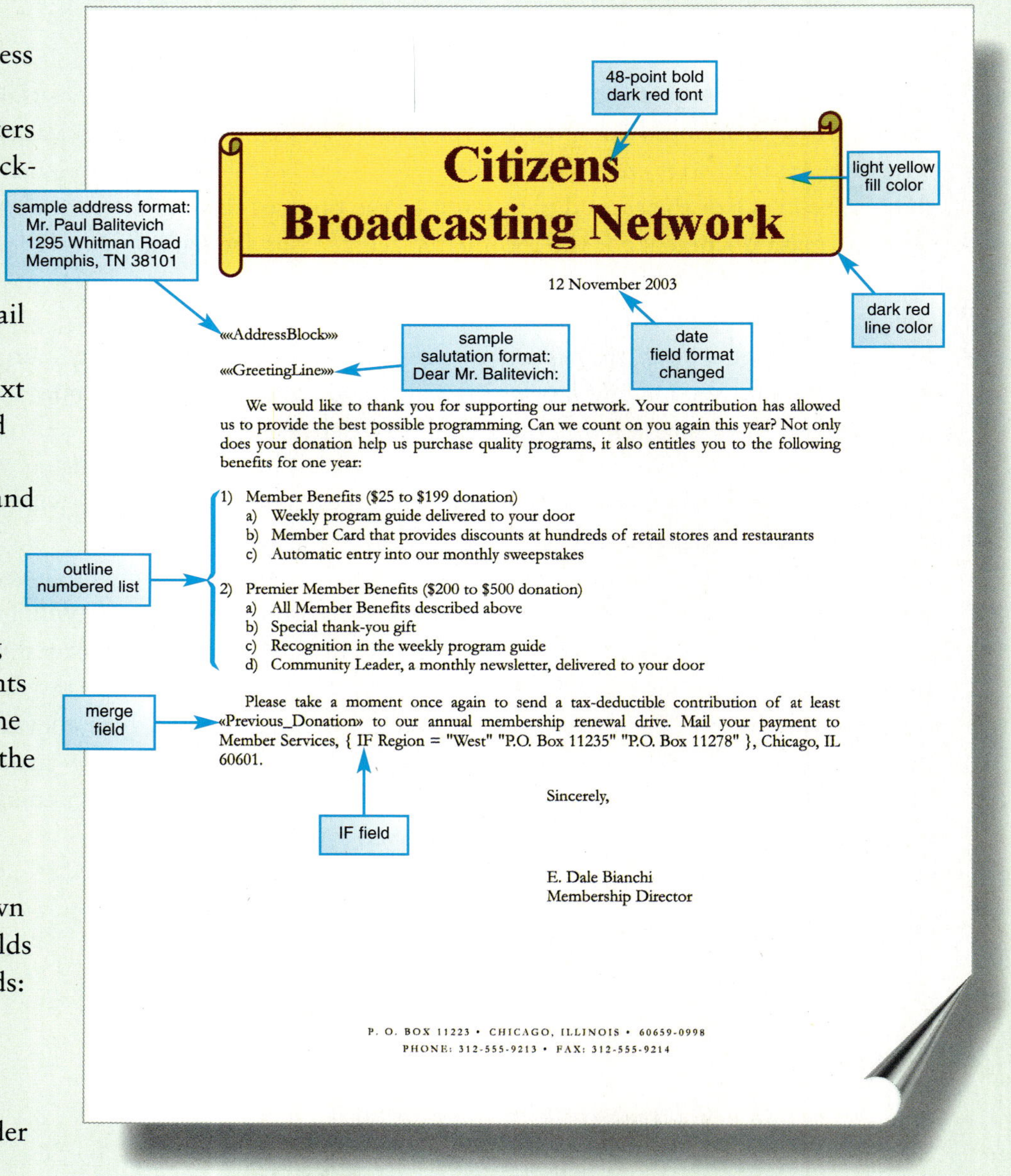

FIGURE 5-97a

In the Lab

Title	First Name	Last Name	Address Line 1	Address Line 2	City	State	ZIP Code	Region	Previous Donation
Mr.	Paul	Balitevich	1295 Whitman Road		Memphis	TN	38101	East	$150
Mrs.	Doris	Goldman	P.O. Box 158	2298 Elm Street	Dallas	TX	75201	West	$200
Mr.	Marcus	Green	22 Fifth Avenue		Anaheim	CA	92805	West	$125
Dr.	Jesse	Martinez	105 Lincoln Avenue		Chicago	IL	60601	East	$100
Ms.	Donna	Vandenburg	1029 Wolf Avenue	Apt. 9B	Boston	MA	02142	East	$75

FIGURE 5-97b

5. Save the main document for the form letter with the file name, Citizens Form Letter, in the folder called Citizens. Compose the main document for the form letter as shown in Figure 5-97a. Edit the GreetingLine merge field so it ends with a colon instead of a comma. Be sure to clear formatting before starting the outline numbered list. Apply the Body Text paragraph style to the paragraphs below the outline numbered list. The IF field tests if Region is equal to West; if it is, then print the text, P.O. Box 11235; otherwise print the text, P.O. Box 11278. Resize the body of the letter to 12 point.

6. Save the main document for the form letter again. Print the main document twice: once with field codes displaying and once without field codes.

7. Merge and print the form letters.

8. In a new document window, address mailing labels using the same data source you used for the form letters. Put bar codes on the mailing labels. Save the mailing labels with the file name, Citizens Mailing Labels, in the Citizens folder. Print the mailing labels.

9. If your printer allows, in a new document window, address envelopes using the same data source you used for the form letters. Put bar codes on the envelopes. Save the envelopes with the file name, Citizens Envelopes, in the folder called Citizens. Print the envelopes.

10. In a new document window, merge all data records in the data source to a directory. Insert all merge fields into the document. Convert the list of fields to a Word table (the table will have 10 columns). Change the page layout to landscape orientation. Merge the directory layout to a new document window. Add a row to the top of the table and insert field names into the empty cells. Format the data source using the Table Grid 4 format in the Table AutoFormat dialog box (apply special formats only to the heading row). Resize the columns so each data record displays on a single row. Place a border around the entire table. Sort the table by the Last Name field. Save the directory with the file name, Citizens Directory, in the folder called Citizens. Print the directory (shown in Figure 5-97b).

In the Lab

3 Designing a Data Source, Form Letter, and Mailing Labels from Sample Memos

Problem: The student services manager at Reeder College would like to schedule an advisor meeting before spring advising begins. Two separate session times will be scheduled: advisors of business majors will meet on Monday, October 13, and advisors of liberal arts majors will meet on Tuesday, October 14. Sample drafted memos for each type of advisor are shown in Figures 5-98a and 5-98b.

Instructions:

1. Decide which fields should be in the data source. Write the field names down on a piece of paper.
2. Begin the mail merge process by clicking Tools on the menu bar, pointing to Letters and Mailings, and then clicking Mail Merge Wizard. Use the Professional Memo template to create a form letter for the memorandums. Close the Mail Merge task pane.
3. Restart the Mail Merge Wizard. Type a new data source that contains five records. Two of the advisors may be the ones shown in the memos in Figures 5-98a and 5-98b. Save the data source with the file name, Reeder College Advisors, in a folder called Reeder. Close the Mail Merge task pane.

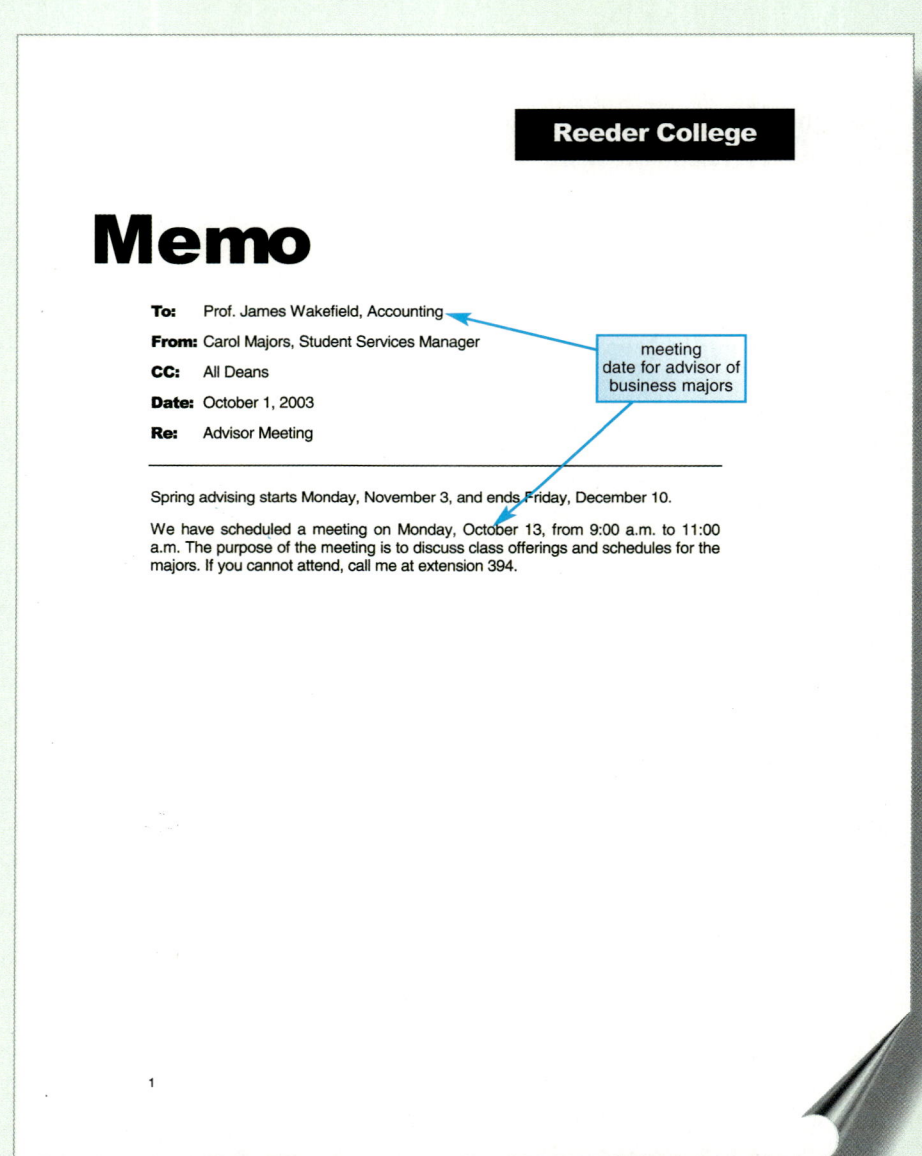

FIGURE 5-98a

In the Lab

4. Save the main document for the form letter with the file name, Reeder College Form Letter. Enter the text of the main document for the form letter shown in Figure 5-98. The IF field tests if Major is equal to Business; if it is, then print the text, Monday, October 13; otherwise print the text, Tuesday, October 14. Resize the contents of the memorandum to 11 point.
5. Print the main document twice, once with field codes displaying and once without field codes.
6. Merge and print the form letters.
7. In a new document window, address mailing labels using the same data source you used for the form letters. Save the mailing labels with the file name, Reeder College Mailing Labels, in the folder called Reeder. Print the mailing labels.

FIGURE 5-98b

Cases and Places

The difficulty of these case studies varies:
▶ are the least difficult; ▶▶ are more difficult; and ▶▶▶ are the most difficult.

1 ▶ You are unit assistant for the Lucky Stars youth group. Letters must be sent to all parents informing them of the summer camp sessions. Create a form letter using the following information: In a 16-point star AutoShape at the top of the letter: Lucky Stars; Address: 1177 Route 52, Brandon, FL 33509; Telephone: (813) 555-6654; Fax: (813) 555-6655. Create the data source shown in Figure 5-99. Use elegant merge letter for the main document for the form letter. Edit the date field so it shows the day of the week in addition to the month day and year. A sample salutation is as follows: To the Parents of Meena. First paragraph: The Lucky Stars summer youth camp at Lake Shawnee Camp is ready for your «Class». All cabins have been paneled, facilities have new water lines, the pool has been repaired, and the cafeteria has 50 new tables. Camp looks better than ever! Create an outline numbered list for the following list items: Starling Camps (grades 1 through 8) – June 1 to June 7, June 22 to June 28, and July 13 to July 19; Star Camps (grades 9 through 12) – June 8 to June 14, June 29 to July 5, and July 20 to July 26; Family Camps – June 15 to June 21, July 6 to July 12, July 27 to August 2. Last paragraph: If you would like to sign up for a session, call the coordinator of Lake Shawnee Camp at 555-0291. Use your name in the signature block. Sort the data source by the ZIP code field. Then, address and print accompanying labels or envelopes for the form letters. Save all documents in a folder called Lucky Stars.

First Name	Last Name	Address Line 1	Address Line 2	City	State	ZIP Code	Class
Meena	Dyrez	4938 Plaza Drive		Dover	FL	33527	Star
Tamara	Jacobsen	P.O. Box 53	7787 Highway 36	Mango	FL	33550	Star
Kaden	O'Malley	Nine Randolph Street		Brandon	FL	33509	Starling
Shaun	Studer	54 Center Street	Apt. 10	Dover	FL	33527	Starling
Jodi	Valesquez	14 Kearms Street		Mango	FL	33550	Star

FIGURE 5-99

2 ▶▶ You are hosting a holiday party on Saturday, December 8. The party will begin at 5:00 p.m. All guests are to bring an appetizer, side dish, or dessert that will serve at least 15 people. You will provide the main dish — turkey on the grill. The grab bag limit is $20 for adults and $10 for children. Anyone with questions should contact you. Create a form letter announcing the holiday party. Place the text, Holiday Party!, at the top of the letter in an AutoShape. Obtain the names and addresses of five of your friends or family members and use them as records in the data source. Then, address accompanying labels or envelopes for the form letters. Save all documents in a folder called Holiday Party.

3 ▶▶ The student government association at your school will be holding its sixth annual car wash on October 18 and October 19 from 8:00 a.m. to 5:00 p.m. each day in the library parking lot. Create a form letter requesting volunteers to wash cars, collect money, and donate supplies for the car wash. Be sure the top of the form letter has an AutoShape with appropriate text. Obtain the names and addresses of five of your classmates and use them as records in the data source. Then, address accompanying labels or envelopes for the form letters. Save all documents in a folder called Car Wash.

Cases and Places

4 ▶▶▶ You currently are seeking an employment position in your field of study. You already have prepared a resume and would like to send it to a group of potential employers. You decide to design a cover letter to send along with the resume. Obtain a recent newspaper and cut out three classified advertisements pertaining to your field of study. Locate two job advertisements on the Internet. Create the cover letter for your resume as a form letter. Be sure the cover letter contains your name, address, and telephone number. The data source should contain potential employers' names, addresses, and position being sought. Use the information in the classified ads from newspapers and the Internet for the data source. Then, address accompanying labels or envelopes for the cover letters. Turn in the want ads with your printouts.

5 ▶▶▶ If Microsoft Excel is installed on your system, you can use it to create a table and then use that table as the data source in a mail merge document. In Word, use Help to determine how to set up a data source in Excel. Start Excel and then create the table in Project 5 (Figure 5-22 on page WD 5.22) as an Excel worksheet. You may need to use Help in Excel to assist you in the procedure for creating and saving a worksheet in the proper format for a mail merge. Exit Excel. Start Word. Begin the mail merge process as discussed in Project 5. When specifying the data source, change the file type to Excel Files then click the workbook name of the file you created in Excel. Merge the form letter in Project 5 so it uses the fields in the Excel workbook. Then, address accompanying labels or envelopes for the cover letters.

6 ▶▶▶ If Microsoft Access is installed on your system, you can use it to view and print the contents of a data source created in Word. Start Access. In Access, use Help to assist you in the procedure for opening, viewing, and printing a database table. Open the table used in the Apply Your Knowledge exercise on page 5.73. The table is called Wireless World List. Open, view, and print the database table in Access. Quit Access

Microsoft Word 2002

PROJECT 6

Creating a Professional Newsletter

O B J E C T I V E S

You will have mastered the material in this project when you can:

- Understand desktop publishing terminology
- Create a WordArt drawing object
- Format a WordArt drawing object
- Add ruling lines above and below paragraphs
- Insert a symbol into a document
- Insert and format a floating graphic
- Format a document into multiple columns
- Justify a paragraph
- Format a character as a drop cap
- Insert a column break
- Place a vertical rule between columns
- Insert and format a text box
- Shade a paragraph
- Size and position a text box
- Use the Paste Special command to link items in a document
- Balance columns
- Insert and format a diagram
- Use the Format Painter button
- Add a page border
- Highlight text
- Animate text
- Search for a file
- Insert, view, and edit comments
- Compare and merge documents

Progressive Message Systems

From Post Office Stones to Contemporary Newsletters

In 1773, British nautical explorer Captain James Cook, lost sight of his sister ship, the Adventure, while sailing to New Zealand. After searching for this ship along the New Zealand coast without success, he left messages behind in bottles buried in the camps where he and his crew had come ashore. Earlier, in 1501, a sea captain set sail from Portugal on a lengthy voyage of unknown destination. Wishing to send news of his travels back home, he went ashore on the southern tip of Africa to deposit a letter, wrapped in pitch-covered canvas, under a stone. A message on the stone requested that whoever found his letter, forward it to his homeland. The tradition of the post office stone was created. Sea captains on their way to Europe — even bitter enemies of the writers — would pick up the letters and deliver them. This may have been the first example of a global newsletter messenger service.

Humankind always has thirsted for information about news and events. Native Americans used smoke signals to convey news. Africans used drums. Some say Australian aborigines developed telepathic powers. The Spanish Conquistadors scratched their news onto Inscription Rock in New Mexico. Armies of old relied on mirrors and semaphores. Then as technology progressed, the means of delivery grew more sophisticated, evolving from Pony Express and telegraph to modern fiber-optic cables, microwaves, and satellite relays.

Newsletters likewise have evolved into highly specialized vehicles that number in the thousands, addressing everything from astrology to investments to medicine to zoology.

No matter what the association, cause, or subject, a newsletter for it is likely to exist. Besides the blizzard of hardcopy newsletters delivered by mail everyday, e-mail and web sites reach millions more.

A good reason for the explosive growth of newsletters is that they get results. To unite people, organize an activity, persuade, or simply to pour out one's feelings, an attractive, well-written newsletter can boost sales, promote morale, raise money, or send your personal news to friends during the holiday season.

Snappy content, however, is not good enough. To reach out and seize someone's attention, newsletters must be more than merely attractive. Your newsletter must make a statement, provide appeal, and elicit interest.

In Word 2002, you have the ideal partner for creating eye-catching, dynamic newsletters. Word lets you produce crisp banner headlines; create WordArt drawing objects; manipulate columns, fonts, and blocks of copy at will; insert pictures into documents; link another document to the newsletter, then spice the whole thing with graphics and borders. Once you have the newsletter just right, word also provides the capability of merging names and addresses from a separate database, such as a student organization, your clients, or your family and friends. You also can e-mail the newsletter to others for approval before making many copies for distribution.

Early ship captains had to rely on chance that someone would find their messages in buried bottles or under stones. Once you complete your professional looking newsletter using Word's desktop publishing features, you have the advantage of being certain people will have access to it via the Internet or the postal system.

Microsoft Word 2002

Creating a Professional Newsletter

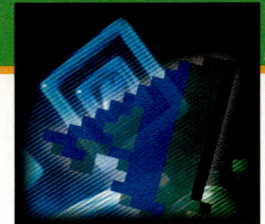

PROJECT 6

CASE PERSPECTIVE

As a member of the Briar Hills chapter of the Patriots of America (POA), you are required to serve on one committee. This year, you chose the Correspondence Committee because you are majoring in Office Automation. Your responsibility is to prepare the monthly newsletter, called the *Patriot Journal*. Each issue of the *Patriot Journal* contains a feature article and announcements. This month's feature article will cover a recent grave marking of Michael Bauer, a Revolutionary War patriot. You plan to create the article as a Word document. The article will give a background on the life of Michael Bauer, discuss how his grave was located, and then give an account of the ceremony. The announcements will inform members of an upcoming luncheon, remind them of Patriot Week, and inform them of the new POA saver card.

After you create the article, Gloria Fleck, regent of Briar Hills POA chapter, will review it. Then, you will insert the Word document into your newsletter. Your task now is to design the newsletter so the feature article spans the first two columns of page one and then continues on page two. The announcements should be located in the third column of page one of the newsletter.

Introduction

Professional looking documents, such as newsletters and brochures, often are created using desktop publishing software. With desktop publishing software, you can divide a document into multiple columns, wrap text around diagrams and other objects, change fonts and font sizes, add color and lines, and so on, to create an attention-grabbing document. A traditionally held opinion of desktop publishing software, such as Adobe PageMaker or QuarkXpress, is that it enables you to open an existing word processing document and enhance it through formatting not provided in your word processing software. Word, however, provides many of the formatting features that you would find in a desktop publishing package. Thus, you can create eye-catching newsletters and brochures directly within Word.

Project Six — Newsletter

Project 6 uses Word to produce the newsletter shown in Figure 6-1. The newsletter is a monthly publication for members of Patriots of America. Notice that it incorporates the desktop publishing features of Word. The body of each page of the newsletter is divided into three columns. A variety of fonts, font sizes, and colors add visual appeal to the document. The first page has text wrapped around a pull-quote and the second page has text wrapped around a diagram. Horizontal and vertical lines separate distinct areas of the newsletter, including a page border around the perimeter of each page.

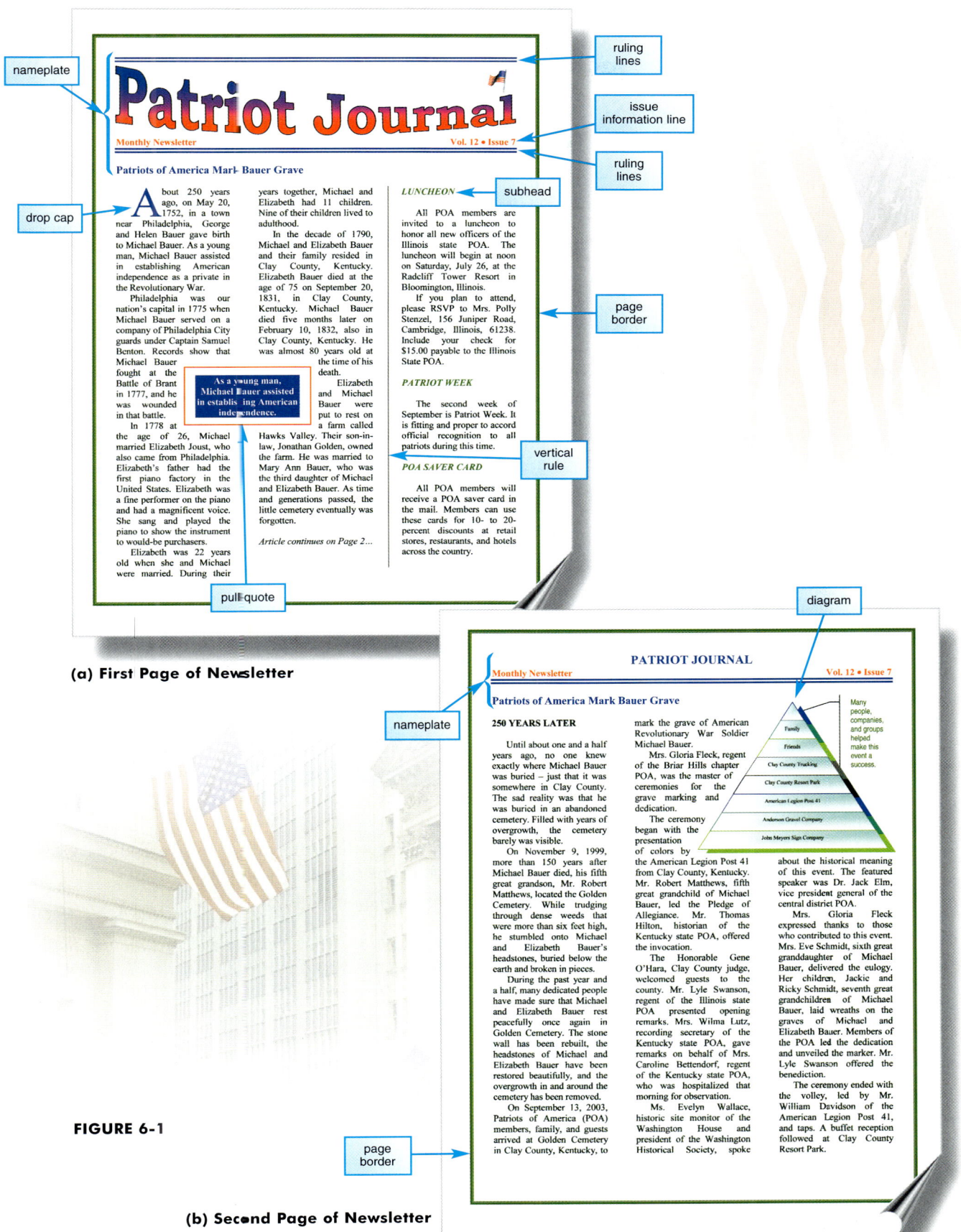

FIGURE 6-1

(a) First Page of Newsletter

(b) Second Page of Newsletter

More About

Desktop Publishing

For more information on desktop publishing, visit the Word 2002 More About Web page (www.scsite.com/wd2002/more.htm) and then click Desktop Publishing.

Desktop Publishing Terminology

As you create professional looking newsletters and brochures, you should understand several desktop publishing terms. In Project 6 (Figure 6-1 on the previous page), the **nameplate**, or **banner**, is the top portion of the newsletter above the three columns. The nameplate on the first page is more graphical than the one on the second page. A nameplate usually contains the name of the newsletter and the **issue information line**. The horizontal lines in the nameplate are called **rules**, or **ruling lines**.

Within the body of the newsletter, a heading, such as LUNCHEON, is called a **subhead**. The vertical line dividing the second and third columns on the first page of the newsletter is a **vertical rule**.

The first page of the newsletter contains a pull-quote (Figure 6-1a). A **pull-quote** is text that is *pulled*, or copied, from the text of the document and given graphical emphasis so it stands apart and grasps the reader's attention.

The text that wraps around an object, such as the pull-quote or the diagram, is referred to as **wrap-around text**. The space between the object and the text is called the **run-around**.

This project involves several steps requiring you to drag the mouse. Thus, you may want to cancel an action if you drag to the wrong location. Remember that you always can click the Undo button on the Standard toolbar to cancel your most recent action.

Starting Word

Perform the following steps to start Word, or ask your instructor how to start Word for your system.

TO START AND CUSTOMIZE WORD

1. Click the Start button on the Windows taskbar, point to Programs on the Start menu, and then click Microsoft Word on the Programs submenu.
2. If the Word window is not maximized, double-click its title bar to maximize it.
3. If the Language bar displays on the screen, click its Minimize button.
4. If the New Document task pane displays in the Word window, click the Show at startup check box to remove the check mark and then click the Close button in the upper-right corner of the task pane title bar.
5. If the toolbars display positioned on the same row, click the Toolbar Options button and then click Show Buttons on Two Rows.
6. Click View on the menu bar and then click Print Layout.

Word starts. After a few moments, an empty document titled Document1 displays in the Word window. You use print layout view in this project because the newsletter contains columns and a diagram. The Print Layout View button on the horizontal scroll bar is selected (shown in Figure 6-3 on page WD 6.09).

Resetting Menus and Toolbars

To set the menus and toolbars so they appear exactly as shown in this book, reset your menus and toolbars as outlined in Appendix D or follow these steps.

TO RESET MENUS AND TOOLBARS

1. Click the Toolbar Options button on the Standard toolbar and then point to Add or Remove Buttons. Point to Standard on the Add or Remove Buttons submenu. Scroll to and then click Reset Toolbar on the Standard submenu.
2. Click the Toolbar Options button on the Formatting toolbar and then point to Add or Remove Buttons. Point to Formatting on the Add or Remove Buttons submenu. Scroll to and then click Reset Toolbar on the Formatting submenu.
3. Click the Toolbar Options button on the Standard toolbar and then point to Add or Remove Buttons. Click Customize on the Add or Remove Buttons submenu.
4. When the Customize dialog box displays, if necessary, click the Options tab and then click the Reset my usage data button. When the Microsoft Word dialog box displays, click the Yes button. Click the Close button in the Customize dialog box.

Word resets the menus and toolbars.

Displaying Formatting Marks

It is helpful to display formatting marks that indicate where in the document you pressed the ENTER key, SPACEBAR, and other keys. Perform the following step to display formatting marks.

TO DISPLAY FORMATTING MARKS

1. If the Show/Hide ¶ button on the Standard toolbar is not selected already, click it.

Word displays formatting marks in the document window, and the Show/Hide ¶ button on the Standard toolbar is selected (shown in Figure 6-3 on page WD 6.09).

Changing All Margin Settings

Word is preset to use standard 8.5-by-11-inch paper, with 1.25-inch left and right margins and 1-inch top and bottom margins. For the newsletter in this project, you want all margins (left, right, top, and bottom) to be .75 inches.

Perform the following steps to change margin settings.

TO CHANGE ALL MARGIN SETTINGS

1. Click File on the menu bar and then click Page Setup.
2. When the Page Setup dialog box displays, if necessary, click the Margins tab. Type .75 in the Top text box and then press the TAB key.
3. Type .75 in the Bottom text box and then press the TAB key.
4. Type .75 in the Left text box and then press the TAB key.
5. Type .75 in the Right text box and then point to the OK button (Figure 6-2 on the next page).
6. Click the OK button to change the margin settings for this document.

Depending on the printer you are using, you may need to set the margins differently for this project.

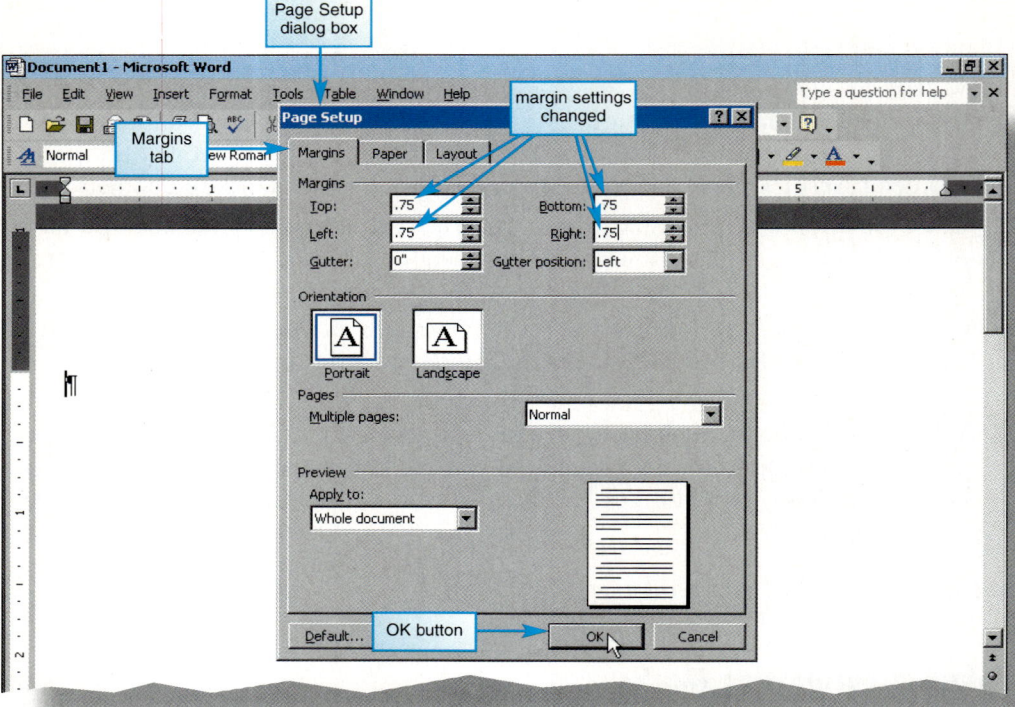

FIGURE 6-2

Zooming Text Width

When you **zoom text width** in print layout view, Word displays the text on the screen as large as possible without extending the right margin beyond the right edge of the document window. Perform these steps to zoom text width.

TO ZOOM TEXT WIDTH

1. Click the Zoom box arrow on the Standard toolbar.
2. Click Text Width.

Word computes the zoom percentage and displays it in the Zoom box (shown in Figure 6-3). Your percentage may be different depending on your computer.

Nameplates

The nameplate should contain, at a minimum, the title and date of the newsletter. The title should be displayed in as large a font size as possible. You also may include a logo in the nameplate. Many nameplates include a headline outlining the function of the newsletter. Some nameplates also include a short table of contents.

Creating the Nameplate

The nameplate on the first page of this newsletter consists of the information above the multiple columns (Figure 6-1a on page WD 6.05). In this project, the nameplate includes the newsletter title, Patriot Journal, the issue information line, and the title of the feature article. The steps on the following pages illustrate how to create the nameplate for the first page of the newsletter in this project.

Inserting a WordArt Drawing Object

In Project 5, you added an AutoShape drawing object to a document. Recall that a **drawing object** is a graphic you create using Word. You can create another type of drawing object with **WordArt**, which enables you to create special effects such as shadowed, rotated, stretched, skewed, and wavy text.

On the first page of the newsletter in this project, the newsletter name, Patriot Journal, is a WordArt drawing object. Perform the following steps to insert a WordArt drawing object.

Steps: To Insert a WordArt Drawing Object

1 If the Drawing toolbar does not display in the Word window, click the Drawing button on the Standard toolbar. Point to the Insert WordArt button on the Drawing toolbar (Figure 6-3).

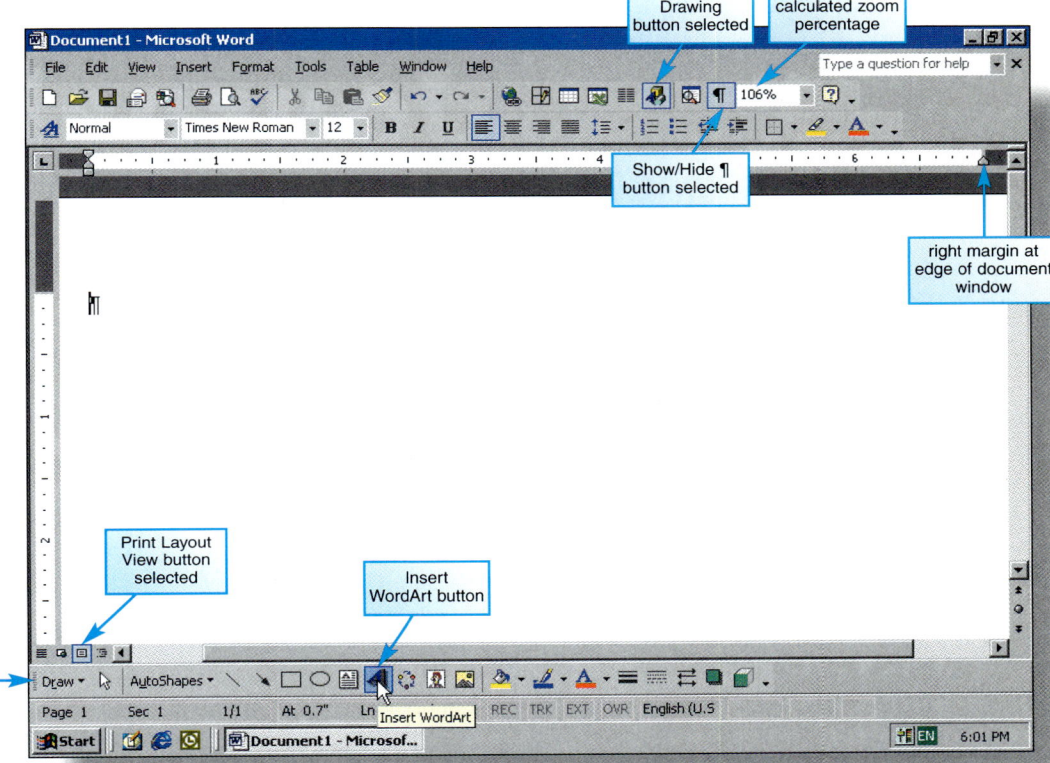

FIGURE 6-3

2 Click the Insert WordArt button. When the WordArt Gallery dialog box displays, if necessary, click the style in the upper-left corner and then point to the OK button.

The WordArt Gallery dialog box displays (Figure 6-4). You will add your own special text effects. Thus, the style in the upper-left corner is selected.

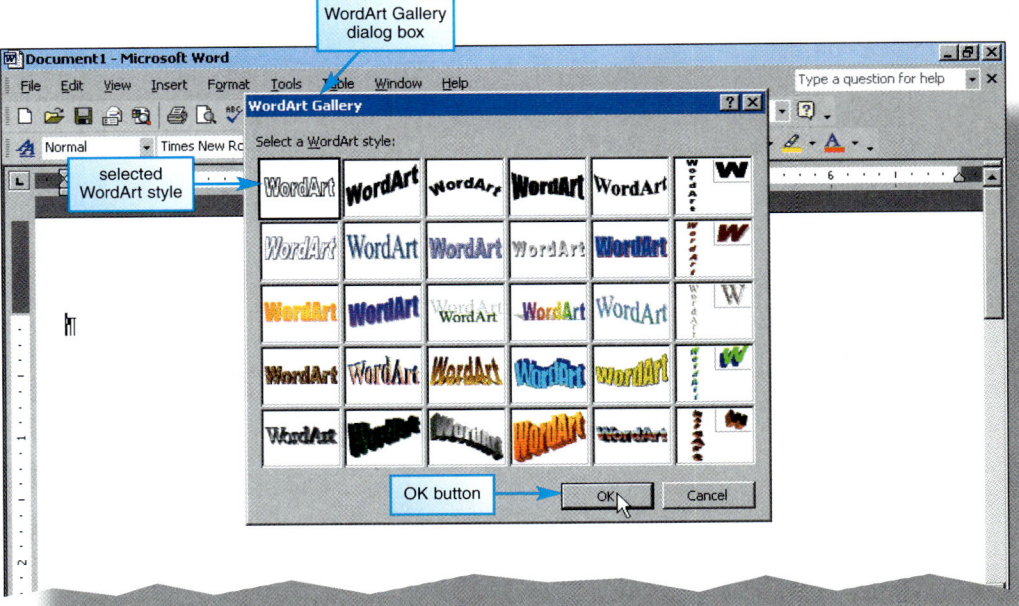

FIGURE 6-4

3 **Click the OK button. When the Edit WordArt Text dialog box displays, type** Patriot Journal **and then click the Font box arrow in the dialog box. Scroll to and then click Bookman Old Style, or a similar font. Click the Size box arrow in the dialog box, scroll to and then click 72. Click the Bold button in the dialog box. Point to the OK button.**

The Edit WordArt Text dialog box displays (Figure 6-5). In this dialog box, you enter the WordArt text and change its font, font size, and font style.

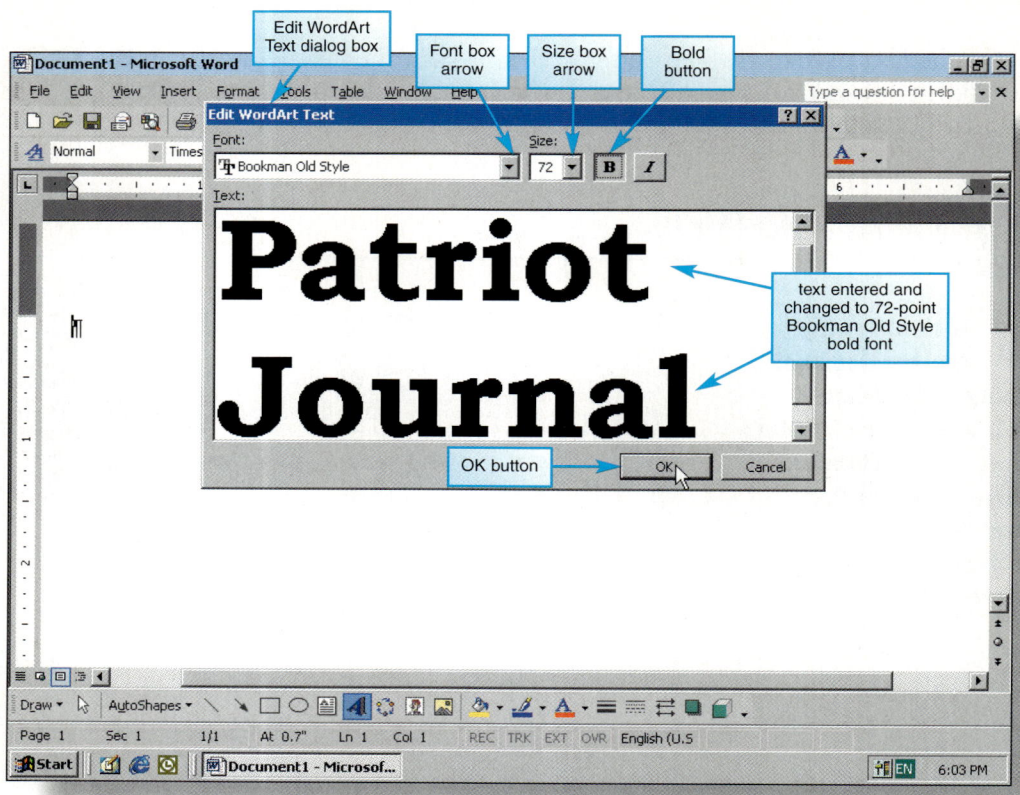

FIGURE 6-5

4 **Click the OK button. Click the WordArt object to select it. If the WordArt toolbar does not display on your screen, right-click the WordArt drawing object and then click Show WordArt Toolbar.**

A WordArt drawing object displays selected in the document window (Figure 6-6). When a WordArt drawing object is selected, the WordArt toolbar displays in the Word window.

Other Ways

1. On Insert menu point to Picture, click WordArt on Picture submenu
2. In Voice Command mode, say "Insert, Picture, WordArt"

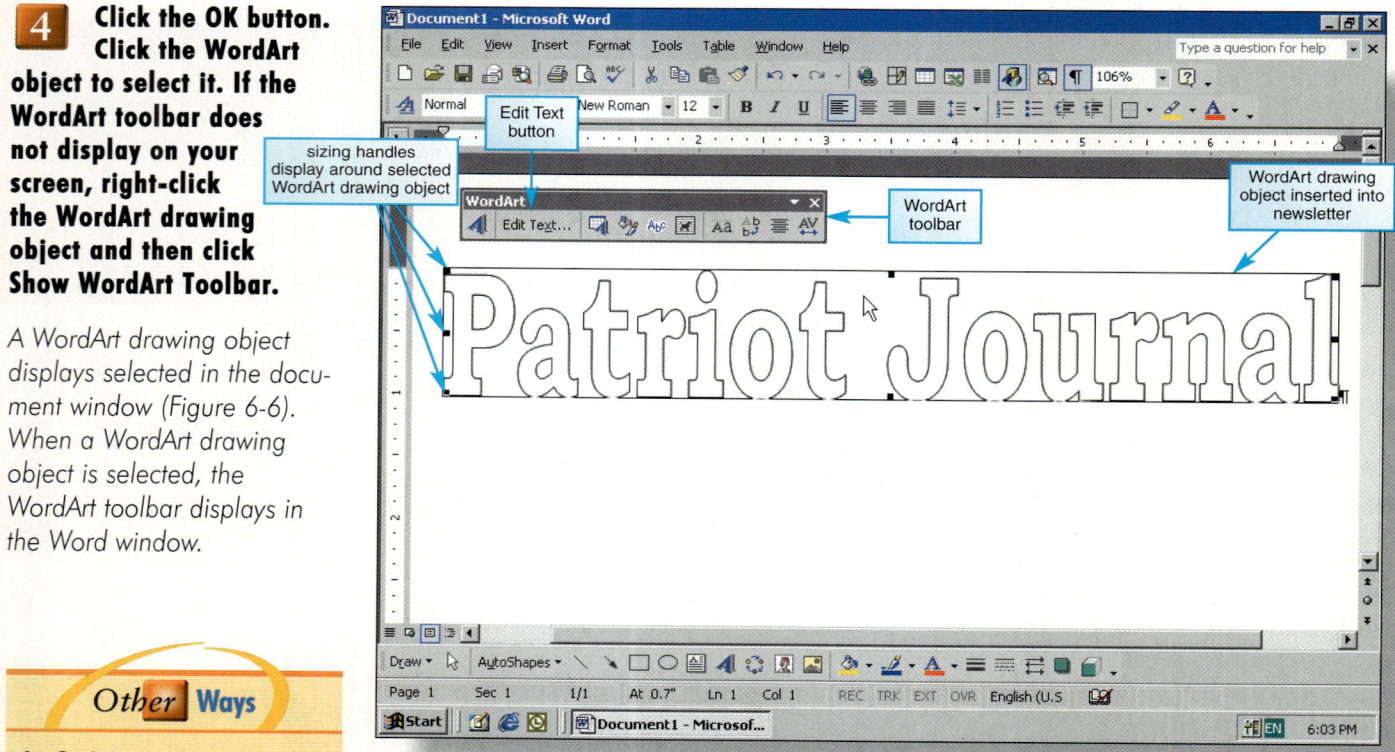

FIGURE 6-6

If a WordArt drawing object is too wide, you can decrease its font size or you can reduce its width. To change the size (width and height) of a WordArt drawing object, drag its sizing handles, just as you resize any other graphic. If, for some reason, you wanted to delete the WordArt drawing object, you could right-click it and then click Cut on the shortcut menu, or click it and then press the DELETE key.

To change the WordArt text, its font, its font size, or its font style, display the Edit WordArt Text dialog box (Figure 6-5) by clicking the Edit Text button on the WordArt toolbar.

Formatting a WordArt Drawing Object

You want to change the size and color of the WordArt drawing object. It should be slightly taller and display a blue to red gradient color effect. **Gradient** colors blend into one another. Thus, a blue color at the top of the characters should blend into a red color at the bottom of the characters. To make these formatting changes, you use the Format WordArt dialog box.

Perform the following steps to resize and change the color of the WordArt drawing object.

WordArt Drawing Objects

Keep in mind that WordArt drawing objects are not treated as Word text. Thus, if you misspell the contents of a WordArt drawing object and then spell check the document, Word will not flag a misspelled word(s) in the WordArt drawing object.

Steps To Format a WordArt Drawing Object

1 **Click the Format WordArt button on the WordArt toolbar. When the Format WordArt dialog box displays, if necessary, click the Size tab. In the Size and rotate area, select the text in the Height text box and then type** `1.3` **as the new height. If necessary, type** `7` **as the width. Point to the Colors and Lines tab.**

Word displays the Format WordArt dialog box (Figure 6-7).

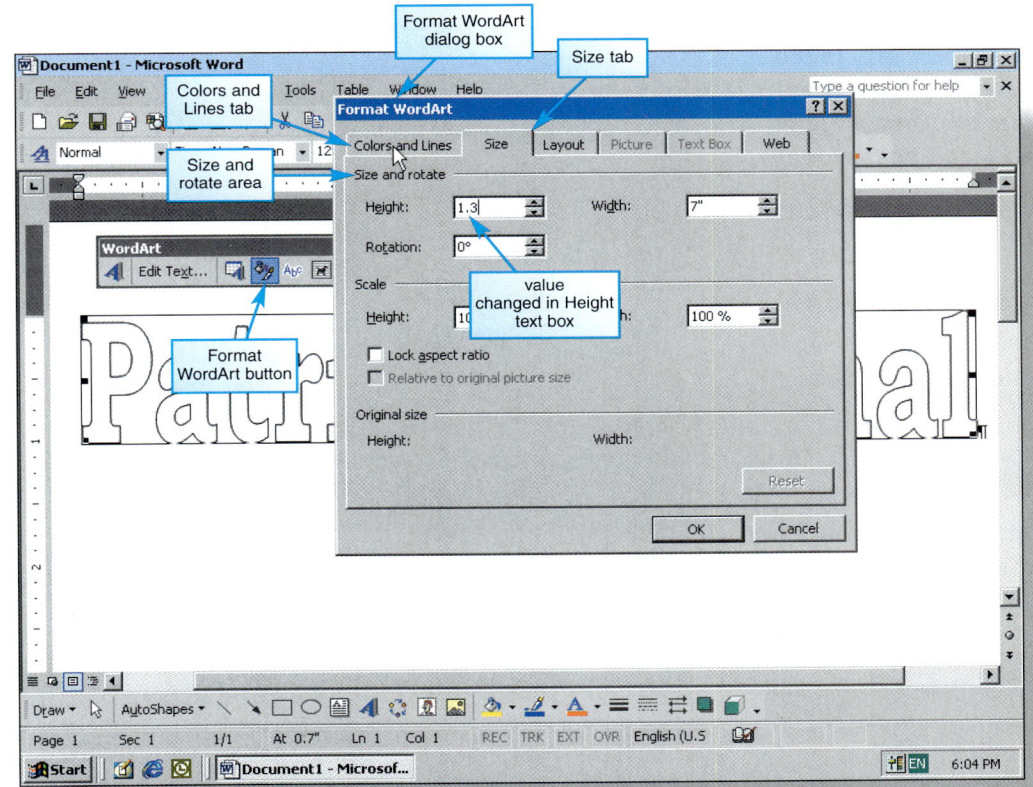

FIGURE 6-7

2 **Click the Colors and Lines tab. In the Fill area, click the Color box arrow and then point to the Fill Effects button.**

Word displays the Colors and Lines sheet in the Format WordArt dialog box (Figure 6-8). You can add a gradient color effect through the Fill Effects button.

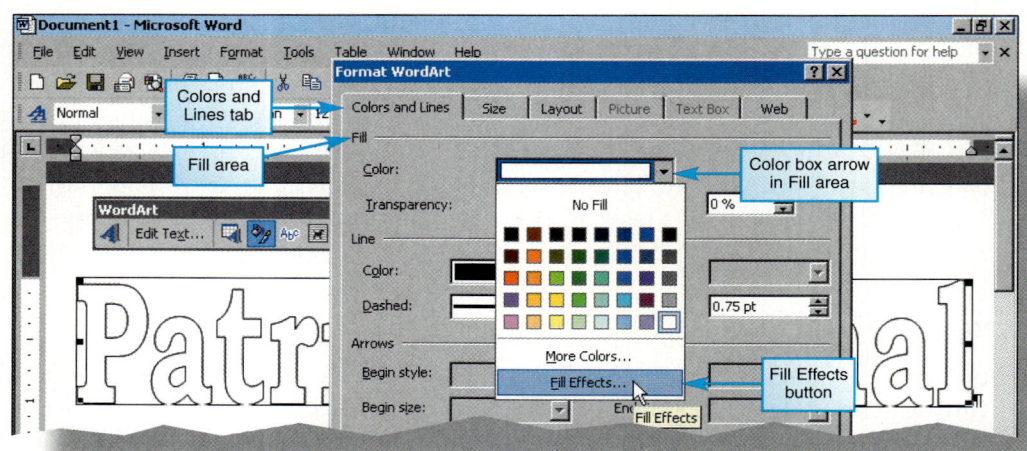

FIGURE 6-8

3 **Click the Fill Effects button. When the Fill Effects dialog box displays, if necessary, click the Gradient tab. In the Colors area, click Two colors and then point to the Color 1 box arrow.**

Word displays the Fill Effects dialog box (Figure 6-9). When you use two colors for a drawing object, Word uses a gradient effect to blend them into one another.

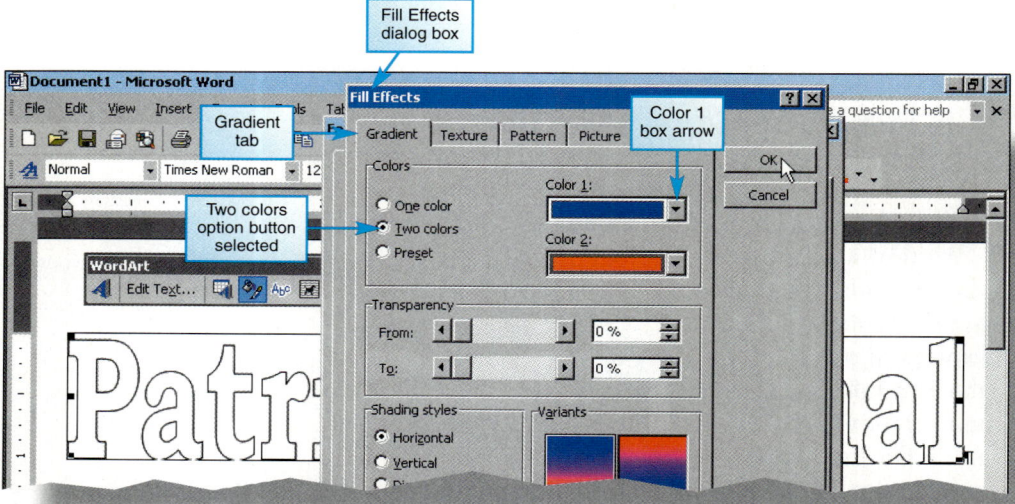

FIGURE 6-9

4 **Click the Color 1 box arrow and then click Blue. Click the Color 2 box arrow and then click Red. Point to the OK button.**

The selected colors for the WordArt object display in the Sample box (Figure 6-10). The default gradient shading style is horizontal, with color 1 blending downward into color 2.

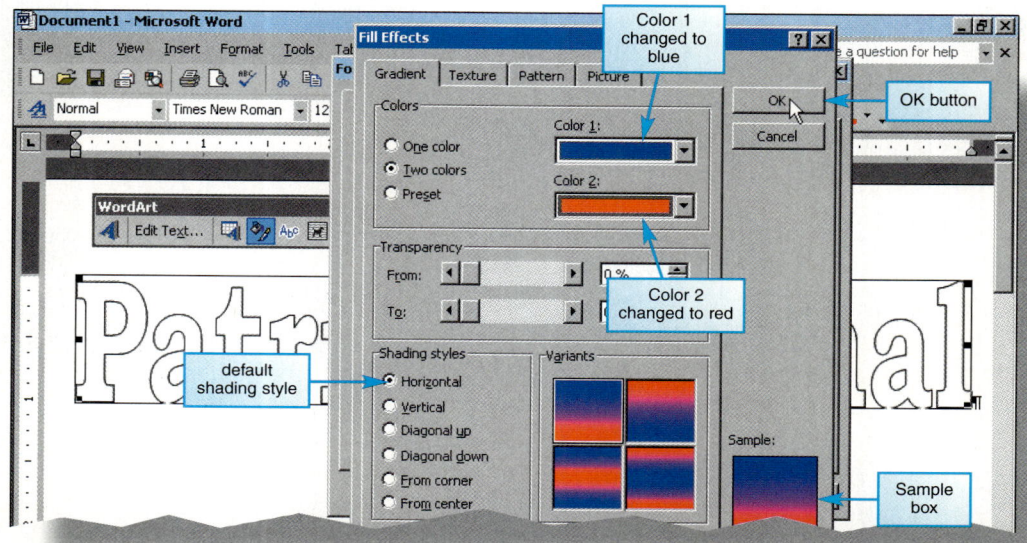

FIGURE 6-10

5 **Click the OK button. Click the OK button in the Format WordArt dialog box.**

Word changes the colors of the WordArt object (Figure 6-11).

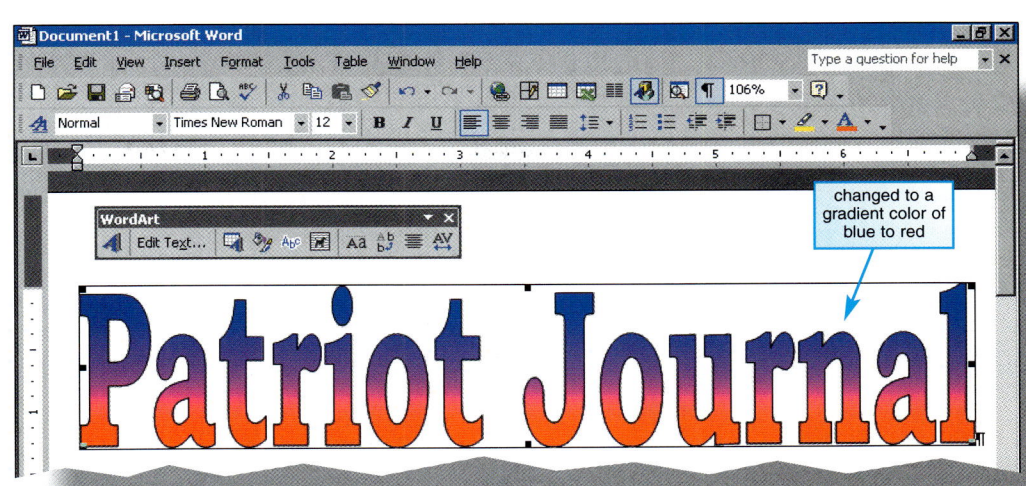

FIGURE 6-11

Changing the WordArt Shape

Word provides a variety of shapes to make your WordArt drawing object more interesting. Perform the following steps to change the WordArt drawing object to a curve down shape.

> **Other Ways**
> 1. On Format menu click WordArt, change desired options, click OK button
> 2. Right-click WordArt object, click Format WordArt on shortcut menu, change desired options, click OK button
> 3. In Voice Command mode, say "Format, WordArt, [select options], OK"

Steps To Change the Shape of a WordArt Drawing Object

1 **Click the WordArt Shape button on the WordArt toolbar. Point to Curve Down.**

Word displays a graphical list of available shapes (Figure 6-12). When you click a shape, the WordArt drawing object forms itself into the selected shape.

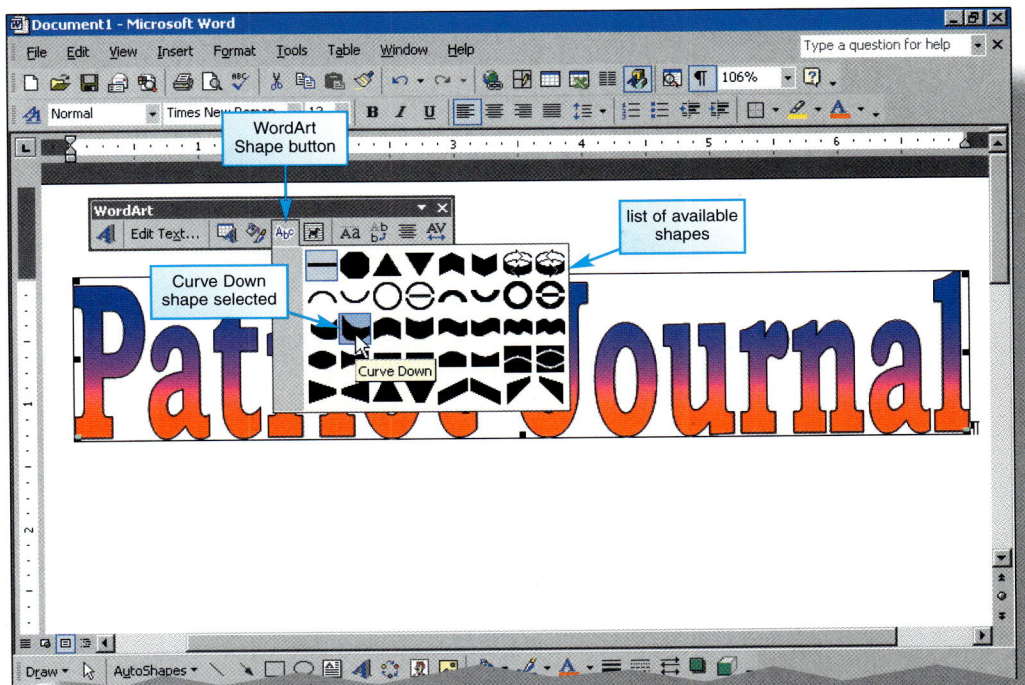

FIGURE 6-12

2 Click Curve Down. Click the paragraph mark to the right of the WordArt text.

The newsletter title displays in a curve down shape (Figure 6-13). The WordArt drawing object no longer is selected. Thus, the WordArt toolbar no longer displays in the Word window.

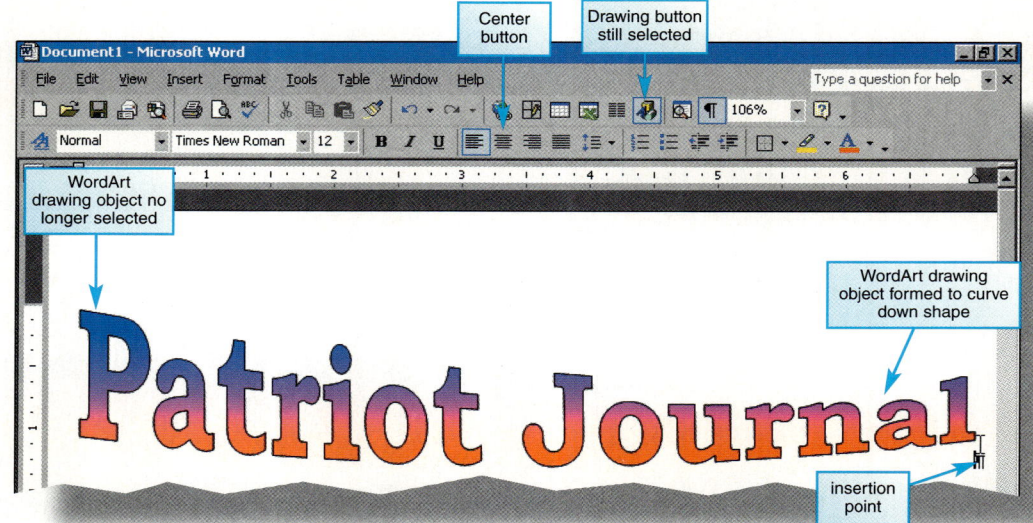

FIGURE 6-13

Leave the Drawing toolbar displaying in the Word window, because you will use it again later in this project.

Perform the following step to center the WordArt drawing object.

TO CENTER THE NEWSLETTER TITLE

1 Click the Center button on the Formatting toolbar.

Word centers the WordArt drawing object between the left and right margins (shown in Figure 6-14).

The next step is to add ruling lines above the newsletter title.

Adding Ruling Lines

In Word, you use borders to create **ruling lines**. As discussed in previous projects, Word can place borders on any edge of a paragraph(s), that is, the top, bottom, left, or right edges.

Perform the following steps to place ruling lines above the newsletter title.

TO USE BORDERS TO ADD RULING LINES

1 If the Tables and Borders toolbar does not display on the screen, click the Tables and Borders button on the Standard toolbar. Click the Line Style box arrow on the Tables and Borders toolbar and then click the first set of double lines in the list.

2 Click the Line Weight box arrow on the Tables and Borders toolbar and then click 2 ¼ pt.

3 Click the Border Color button on the Tables and Borders toolbar and then click Blue.

4 Click the Border button arrow on the Tables and Borders toolbar and then click Top Border.

The newsletter title and Tables and Borders toolbar display as shown in Figure 6-14.

When you press the ENTER key at the end of the newsletter title to advance the insertion point to the next line, Word carries forward formatting. You do not want the paragraphs and characters on line 2 to have the same formatting as line 1. Instead, you clear formatting so the characters on line 2 use the Normal style.

Perform the following steps to clear formatting.

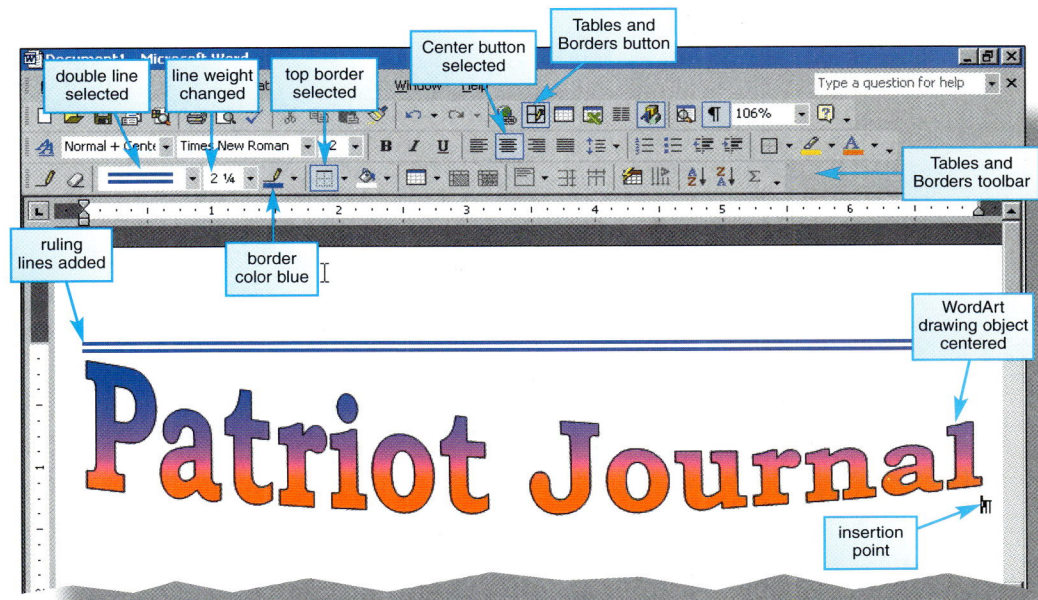

FIGURE 6-14

TO CLEAR FORMATTING

1. With the insertion point positioned at the end of line 1 (shown in Figure 6-14), press the ENTER key.
2. Click the Style box arrow on the Formatting toolbar and then point to Clear Formatting (Figure 6-15).
3. Click Clear Formatting.

Word applies the Normal style to the location of the insertion point.

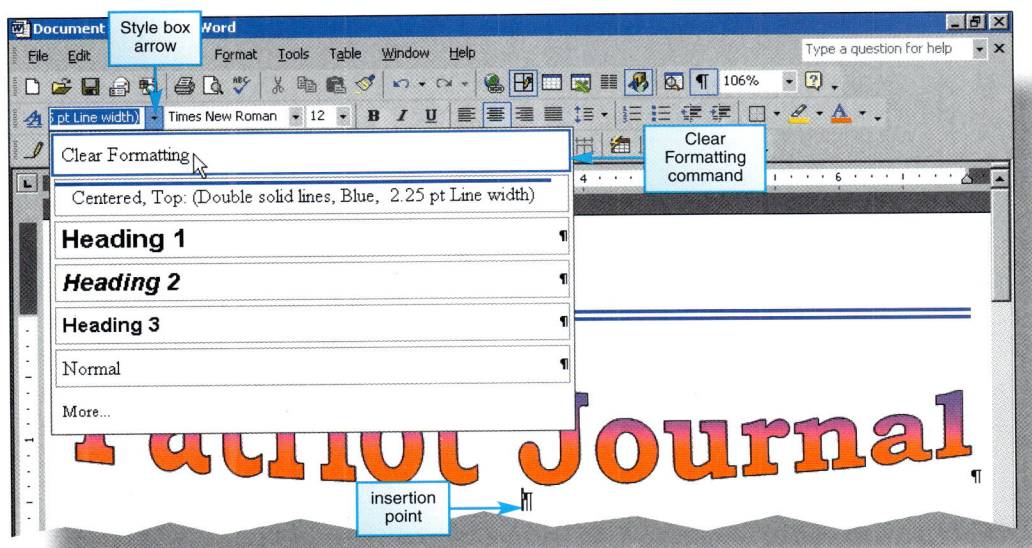

FIGURE 6-15

Depending on your installation of Word, the Normal style might be a different font or font size.

The next step is to enter the issue information line in the nameplate of the newsletter.

Inserting Special Characters

In addition to symbols, you can insert special characters including a variety of dashes, hyphens, spaces, apostrophes, and quotation marks through the Symbol dialog box. Click Insert on the menu bar, click Symbol, click the Special Characters tab, click the desired character in the Character list, click the Insert button, and then click the Close button.

Inserting Symbols

The issue information line in this newsletter contains the text, Monthly Newsletter, at the left margin and the volume and issue number at the right margin. As discussed previously, a paragraph cannot be formatted as both left-aligned and right-aligned. To place text at the right margin of a left-aligned paragraph, set a tab stop at the right margin.

In this newsletter, between the volume number and issue number is a large round dot. This special symbol is not on the keyboard. You insert dots and other symbols, such as letters in the Greek alphabet and mathematical characters, using the Symbol dialog box.

The following steps explain how to enter the text in the issue information line. First, you enter text at the left margin and set a right-aligned tab stop at the right margin. Then, you enter the text at the right margin, placing a dot symbol between the volume and issue numbers.

TO SET A RIGHT-ALIGNED TAB STOP

1. Click the Bold button on the Formatting toolbar. Click the Font Color button arrow on the Formatting toolbar and then click Red. Type `Monthly Newsletter` on line 2 of the newsletter.

2. Click Format on the menu bar and then click Tabs. When the Tabs dialog box displays, type 7 in the Tab stop position text box and then click Right in the Alignment area. Click the Set button (Figure 6-16).

3. Click the OK button.

After clicking the OK button, Word places a right-aligned tab stop at the right margin (shown in Figure 6-17).

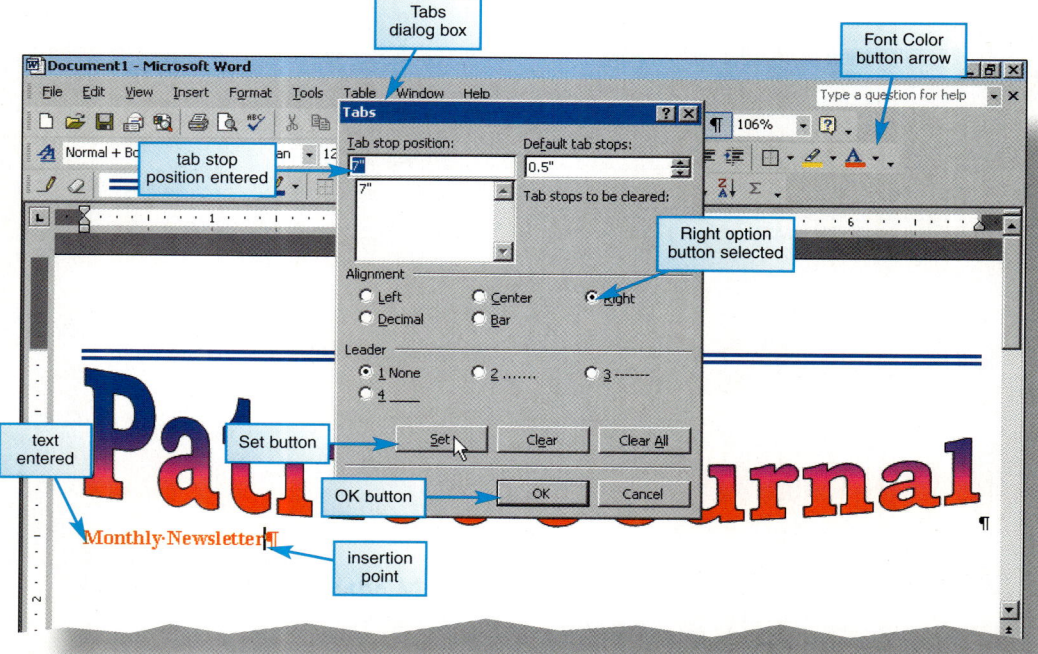

FIGURE 6-16

Perform the following steps to insert a symbol into a document.

Steps To Insert a Symbol

1 Press the TAB key. Type `Vol. 12` and then press the SPACEBAR. Click Insert on the menu bar and then point to Symbol.

The volume number displays at the right margin (Figure 6-17). Notice the right tab marker is positioned directly on top of the right margin on the ruler.

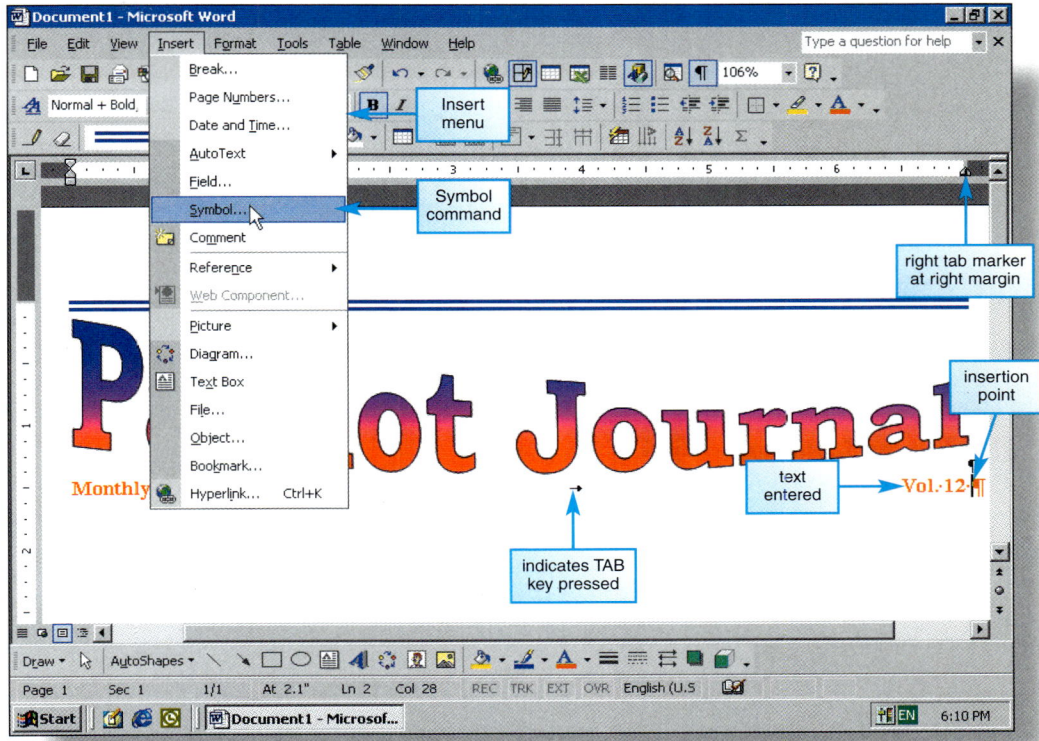

FIGURE 6-17

2 Click Symbol. When Word displays the Symbol dialog box, if necessary, click the Symbols tab. If necessary, click the Font box arrow in the Symbol dialog box, scroll to and then click Symbol. Scroll to and then click the dot symbol. Click the Insert button.

Word displays the Symbol dialog box (Figure 6-18). The dot symbol displays in the document to the left of the insertion point because you clicked the Insert button. At this point, you can insert additional symbols or close the Symbol dialog box.

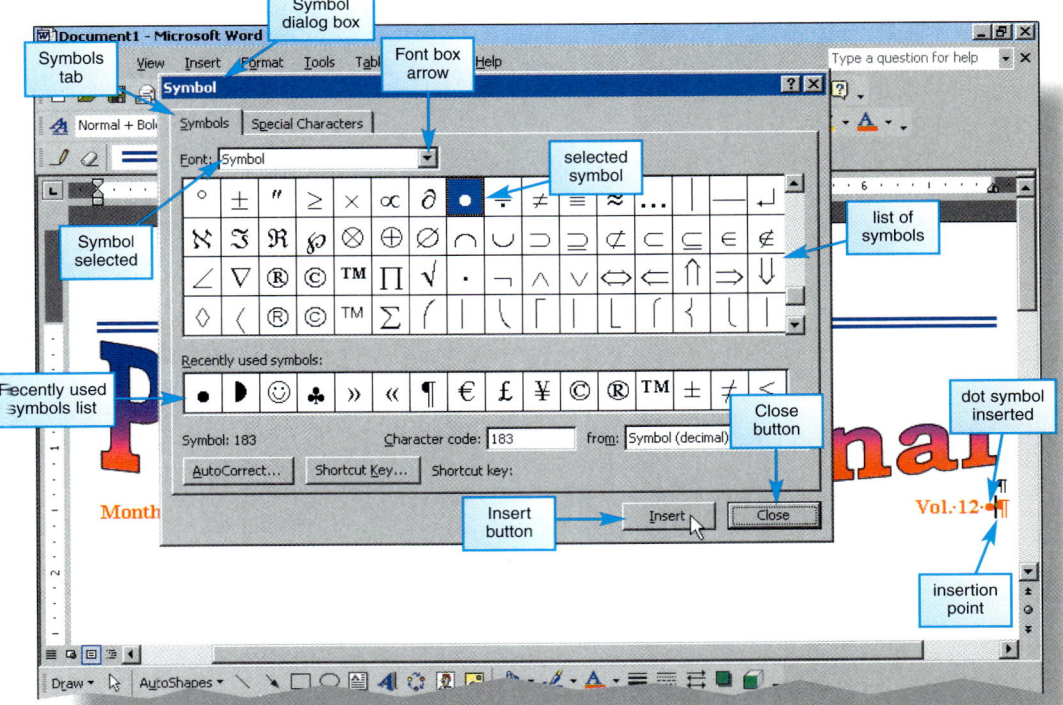

FIGURE 6-18

3 **Click the Close button in the Symbol dialog box. Press the SPACEBAR. Type** Issue 7 **and then click the Border button arrow on the Tables and Borders toolbar. Click Bottom Border.**

The issue information line is complete (Figure 6-19). Word uses the previously defined line style (double lines), line weight (2 ¼ point), and color (blue) for the bottom border.

4 **Click the Tables and Borders button on the Standard toolbar to remove the Tables and Borders toolbar from the screen.**

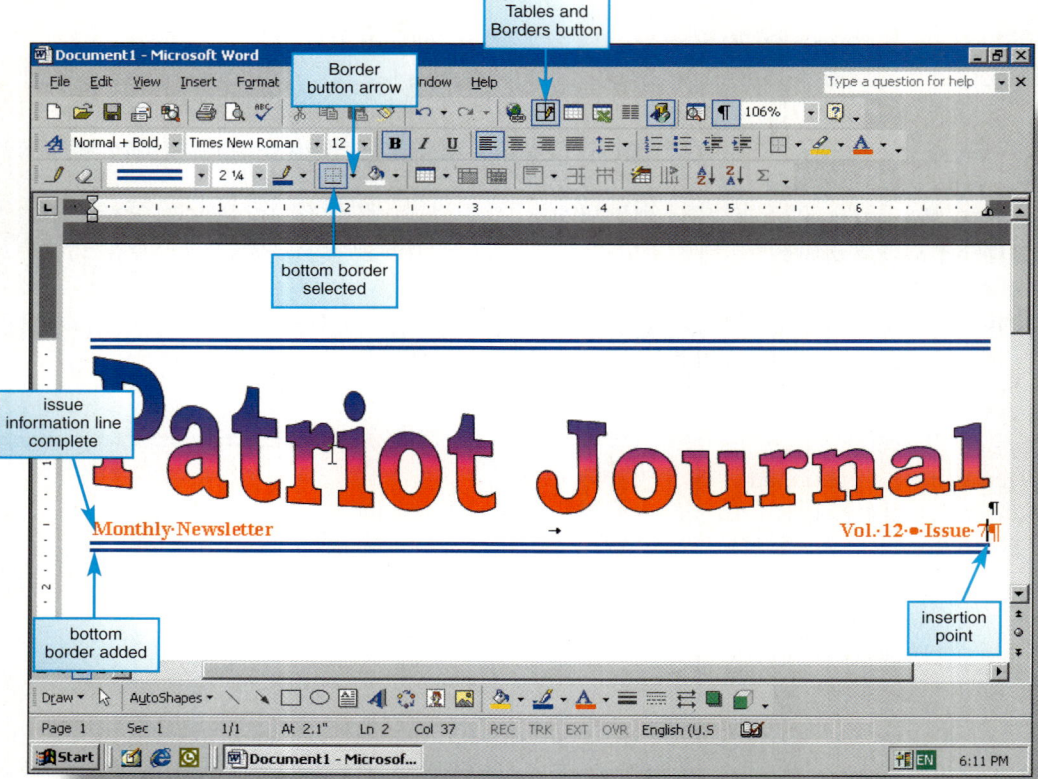

FIGURE 6-19

1. Press ALT+0 (zero) and then with the NUM LOCK key on, use numeric keypad to type ANSI character code for symbol
2. In Voice Command mode, say "Insert, Symbol, [select symbol], Insert, Close"

When you insert a symbol, Word places it in the Recently used symbols list in the Symbol dialog box (Figure 6-18 on the previous page).

You also can insert ANSI (American National Standards Institute) characters into a document by entering the ANSI code directly into the document. The **ANSI characters** are a predefined set of characters, including both characters on the keyboard and special characters, such as the dot symbol. To enter the ANSI code, make sure the NUM LOCK key on the numeric keypad is on. Press and hold the ALT key and then type the numeral zero followed by the ANSI code for the symbol. You must use the numeric keypad when entering the ANSI code. For a complete list of ANSI codes, see your Microsoft Windows documentation.

The next step is to insert an American flag Web clip art image into the nameplate.

Inserting and Formatting a Floating Graphic

When you insert a clip art image into a paragraph in a document, Word inserts the picture as an inline object. An **inline object** is an object that is part of a paragraph. With inline objects, you change the location of the object by setting paragraph options, such as centered, right-aligned, and so on.

In many cases, you want more flexibility in positioning graphics. That is, you want to position a graphic at a specific location in a document. To do this, the object must be floating. A **floating object** is an object that can be positioned at a specific location in a document or in a layer over or behind text in a document. You can position a floating object anywhere on the page.

In this project, for example, you want an American flag graphic to be positioned in the upper-right corner of the nameplate on the newsletter. Perform the following steps to insert a clip art image and then change it from an inline object to a floating object.

> **Note:** The following steps assume your computer is connected to the Internet. If it is not, go directly to the shaded steps at the top of the next page that are titled TO INSERT A GRAPHIC FILE FROM THE DATA DISK.

Designing Newsletters

For more information on designing newsletters, visit the Word 2002 More About Web page (www.scsite.com/wd2002/more.htm) and then click Designing Newsletters.

TO INSERT CLIP ART FROM THE WEB

1. Click Insert on the menu bar, point to Picture, and then click Clip Art on the Picture submenu.

2. In the Insert Clip Art task pane, drag through any text in the Search text text box to select the text. Type American flag and then press the ENTER key.

3. Point to the clip that matches the one shown in Figure 6-20 and then click the box arrow that displays to the right of the clip. (If the clip does not display in the task pane, click the Close button on the Insert Clip Art task pane to close the task pane and then proceed to the shaded steps at the top of the next page.)

4. Click Insert on the menu bar and then click the Close button on the Insert Clip Art task pane title bar. If necessary, scroll to display the image in the document window.

5. Reduce the size of the graphic to about one-quarter its original size by dragging a corner sizing handle inward so the size of the graphic resembles the one shown in Figure 6-20.

Word inserts and resizes the American flag graphic at the location of the insertion point (Figure 6-20). The graphic is an inline object, that is, part of the current paragraph.

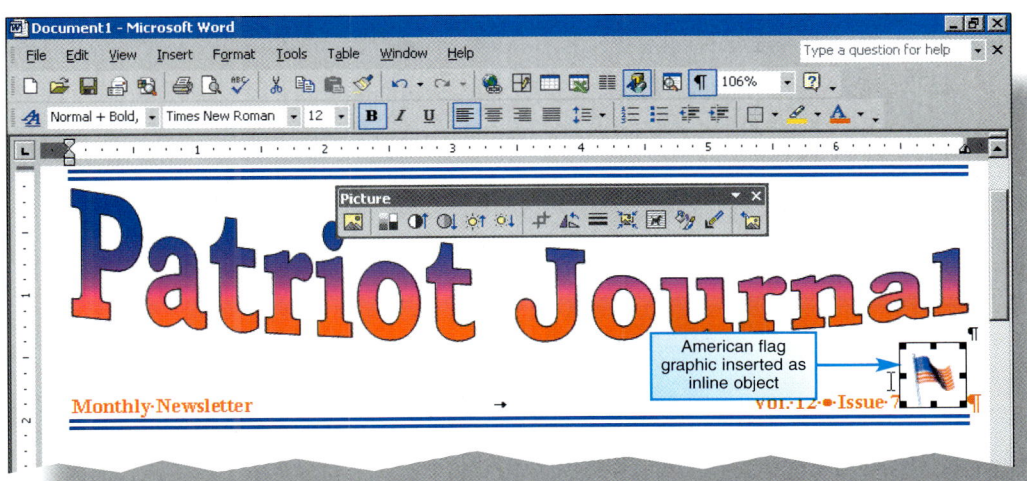

FIGURE 6-20

If you do not have access to the Web, you can insert the clip art file into the Word document from the Data Disk, as described in the steps on the next page. If you did not download the Data Disk, see the inside back cover for instructions for downloading the Data Disk or see your instructor.

Inserting Graphics

If you have a scanned image or photograph on disk that you would like to insert into a document, you would follow the steps to the right to insert the graphic file into the document.

TO INSERT A GRAPHIC FILE FROM THE DATA DISK

1. Click Insert on the menu bar, point to Picture, and then click From File.

2. Insert the Data Disk into drive A. When the Insert Picture dialog box displays, click the Look in box arrow and then click 3½ Floppy (A:). Click the file name j0178291 and then click the Insert button.

3. Reduce the size of the graphic to about one-quarter its original size by dragging a corner sizing handle inward so the size of the graphic resembles the one shown in Figure 6-20 on the previous page.

Word inserts and resizes the American flag graphic at the location of the insertion point (shown in Figure 6-20). The graphic is an inline object, that is, part of the current paragraph.

Depending on the location of your insertion point, the American flag graphic may be in a different position.

Perform the following steps to change the American flag graphic from inline to floating.

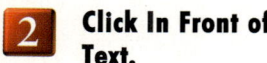 **To Format a Graphic as Floating**

 In the document window, click the graphic to select it. If the Picture toolbar does not display, right-click the graphic and then click Show Picture Toolbar on the shortcut menu. Click the Text Wrapping button on the Picture toolbar and then point to In Front of Text.

Notice that a selected inline object has small squares as sizing handles (Figure 6-21).

 Click In Front of Text.

Word changes the format of the graphic from inline to floating (Figure 6-22). You can position a floating object anywhere in the document. The sizing handles on a floating object display as small circles.

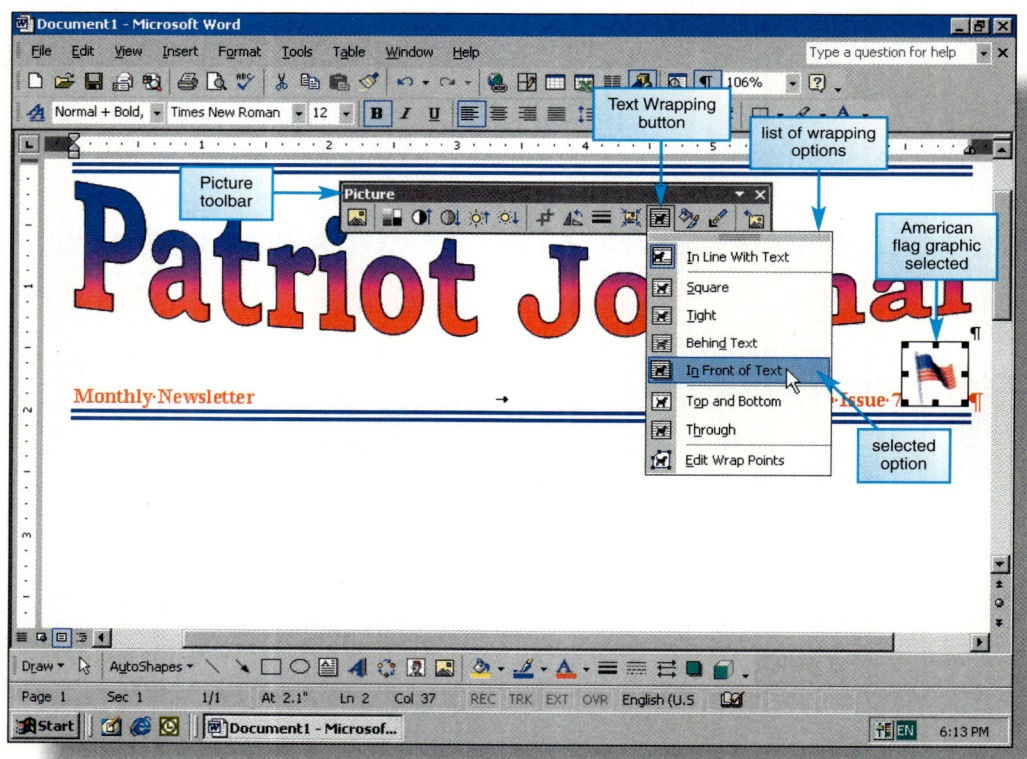

FIGURE 6-21

3 If necessary, scroll up to display the entire nameplate. Point to the middle of the graphic and when the mouse pointer has a four-headed arrow attached to it, drag the graphic to the location shown in Figure 6-22.

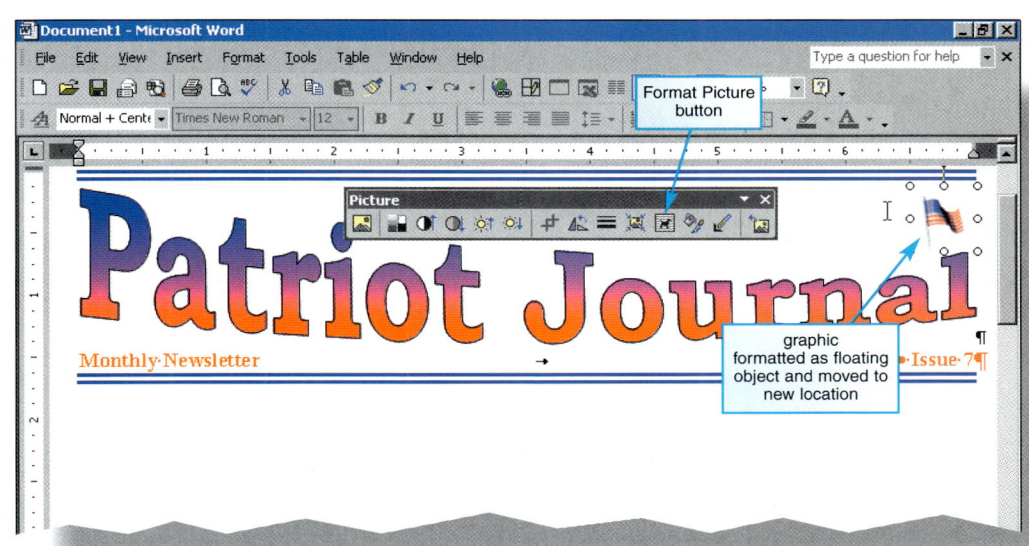

FIGURE 6-22

To place an object behind text, instead of in front of text, select the Behind Text wrapping style (Figure 6-21). You also can change the order of an object by right-clicking the object, pointing to Order on the shortcut menu, and then clicking the desired location for the currently selected object.

The next step is to flip the American flag graphic so the flag flies toward the left instead of toward the right. Perform the following steps to flip a graphic horizontally.

Other Ways

1. Click Format Picture button on Picture toolbar, click Layout tab, click In front of text, click OK button
2. On Format menu click Picture, click Layout tab, click In front of text, click OK button
3. In Voice Command mode, say "Format, Picture, Layout, In front of text, OK"

Steps: To Flip a Graphic

1 With the graphic still selected, click the Draw button on the Drawing toolbar. Point to Rotate or Flip on the Draw menu and then point to Flip Horizontal on the Rotate or Flip submenu.

Word displays the Draw menu above the Draw button (Figure 6-23).

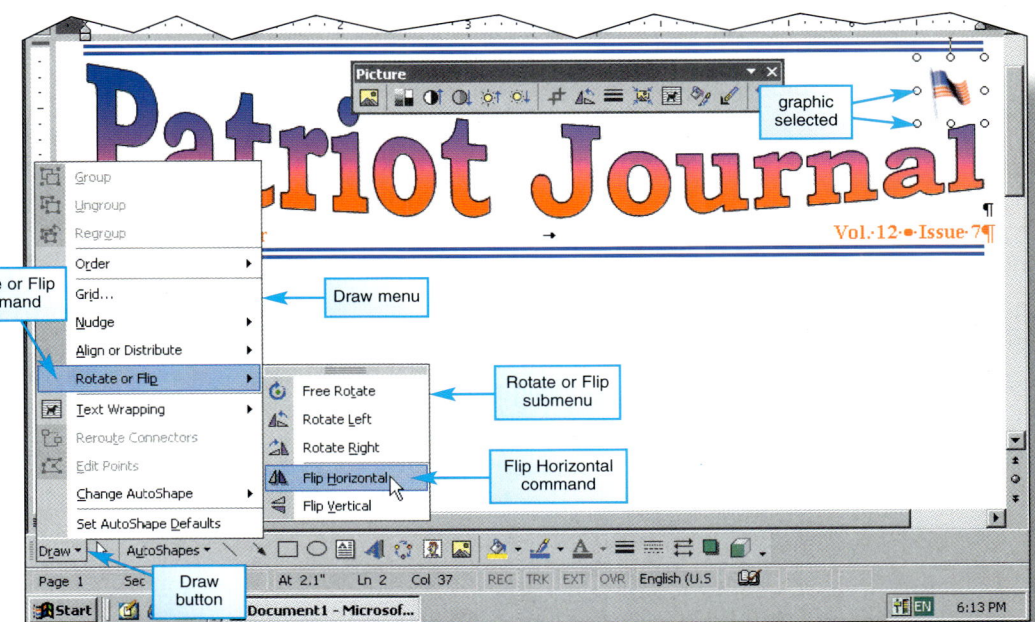

FIGURE 6-23

2 **Click Flip Horizontal. Click at the end of the issue information line.**

Word flips the graphic to display its mirror image (Figure 6-24).

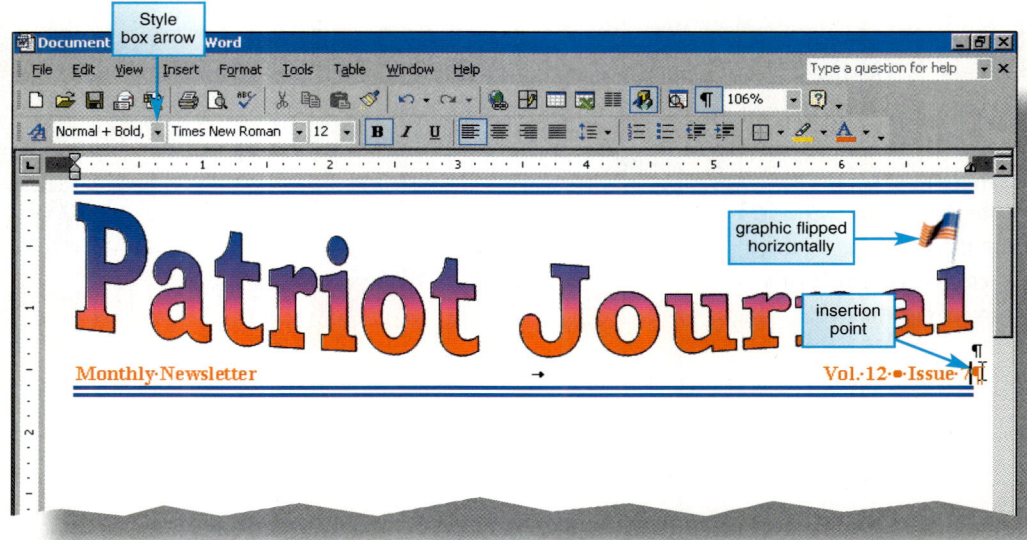

FIGURE 6-24

Other Ways

1. With Drawing toolbar displaying, in Voice Command mode, say "Draw, Flip or Rotate, Flip Horizontal"

The insertion point is at the end of the issue information line, which has a bottom border. As mentioned earlier, when you press the ENTER key in a bordered paragraph, Word carries forward the border to the next paragraph. Thus, after you press the ENTER key, you should clear formatting to format the new paragraph to the Normal style.

Perform the following steps to clear formatting.

TO CLEAR FORMATTING

1 With the insertion point positioned at the end of the issue information line (shown in Figure 6-24), press the ENTER key.

2 With the insertion point on line 3, click the Style box arrow on the Formatting toolbar and then click Clear Formatting.

Word applies the Normal style to the location of the insertion point.

One blank line below the bottom border is the name of the feature article, Patriots of America Mark Bauer Grave, in 14-point Times New Roman bold blue font. Perform the following steps to enter this text and then clear formatting on the line below the text.

Fonts

For more information on fonts, visit the Word 2002 More About Web page (www.scsite.com/wd2002/more.htm) and then click Fonts.

TO ENTER TEXT

1 With the insertion point on line 3, press the ENTER key.

2 Click the Font Size box arrow on the Formatting toolbar and then click 14. Click the Bold button on the Formatting toolbar. Click the Font Color button arrow and then click Blue.

3 Type `Patriots of America Mark Bauer Grave` and then press the ENTER key.

4 Click the Style box arrow on the Formatting toolbar and then click Clear Formatting.

The article title is entered (Figure 6-25). The paragraph at the location of the insertion point is returned to the Normal style.

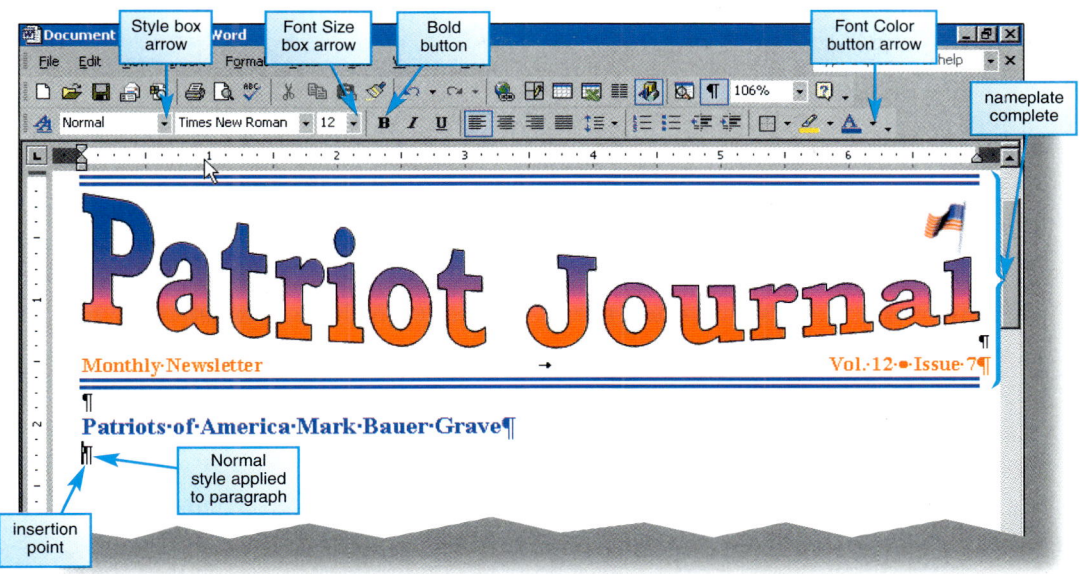

FIGURE 6-25

Saving the Newsletter

You have made several changes to this newsletter. Thus, you should save it, as described in the following steps.

TO SAVE THE NEWSLETTER

1. Insert a floppy disk into drive A.
2. Click the Save button on the Standard toolbar.
3. Type `Patriot Journal Newsletter` in the File name text box. Do not press the ENTER key.
4. Click the Save in box arrow and then click 3½ Floppy (A:).
5. Click the Save button in the Save As dialog box.

Word saves the document on a floppy disk in drive A with the file name, Patriot Journal Newsletter (shown in Figure 6-26 on the next page).

The nameplate for the newsletter is complete. The next step is to format the first page of the body of the newsletter.

Formatting the First Page of the Body of the Newsletter

The body of the newsletter in this project is divided into three columns (Figure 6-1a on page WD 6.05). The characters in the paragraphs are aligned on both the right and left edges — similar to newspaper columns. The first letter in the first paragraph is much larger than the rest of the characters in the paragraph. A vertical rule separates the second and third columns. The steps on the following pages illustrate how to format the first page of the body of the newsletter using these desktop publishing features.

Newspaper-Style Columns

Narrow columns generally are easier to read than wide ones. Columns, however, can be too narrow. Try to have between five and fifteen words per line. To do this, you may need to adjust the column width, the font size, or the leading. Leading is the line spacing, which can be adjusted through the Paragraph dialog box in Word.

Formatting a Document into Multiple Columns

The text in **snaking columns**, or newspaper-style columns, flows from the bottom of one column to the top of the next. The body of the newsletter in this project uses snaking columns.

When you begin a document in Word, it has one column. You can divide a portion of a document or the entire document into multiple columns. Within each column, you can type, modify, or format text.

To divide a portion of a document into multiple columns, you use section breaks. That is, Word requires that a new section be created each time you alter the number of columns in a document. Thus, if a document has a nameplate (one column) followed by an article of three columns followed by an article of two columns, then the document would be divided into a total of three sections.

In this project, the nameplate is one column and the body of the newsletter is three columns. Thus, you must insert a continuous section break below the nameplate. The term, continuous, means you want the new section to occur on the same page as the previous section.

Perform the following steps to divide the body of the newsletter into three columns.

Steps: To Insert a Continuous Section Break

1 With the insertion point on line 5 (shown in Figure 6-25 on the previous page), press the ENTER key. Click Insert on the menu bar and then click Break. When the Break dialog box displays, click Continuous in the Section break types area. Point to the OK button.

Word displays the Break dialog box (Figure 6-26). Continuous means you want the new section on the same page as the previous section.

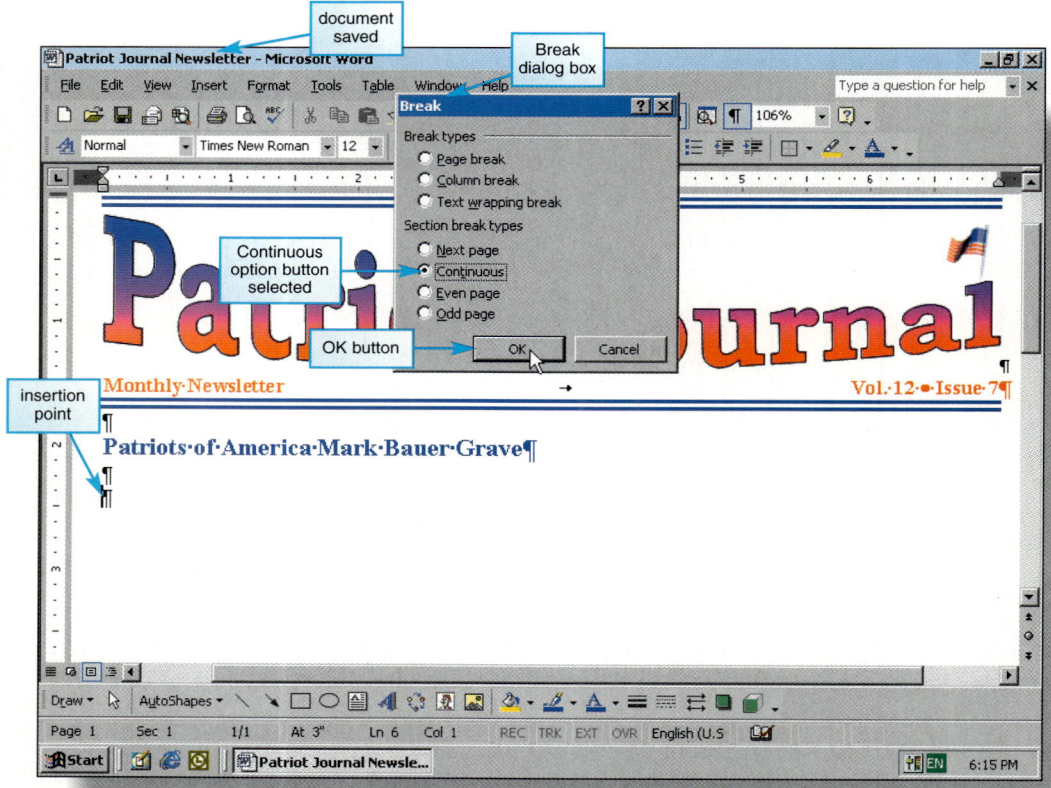

FIGURE 6-26

Formatting the First Page of the Body of the Newsletter • WD 6.25

2 **Click the OK button.**

Word inserts a continuous section break above the insertion point (Figure 6-27). The insertion point now is located in section 2.

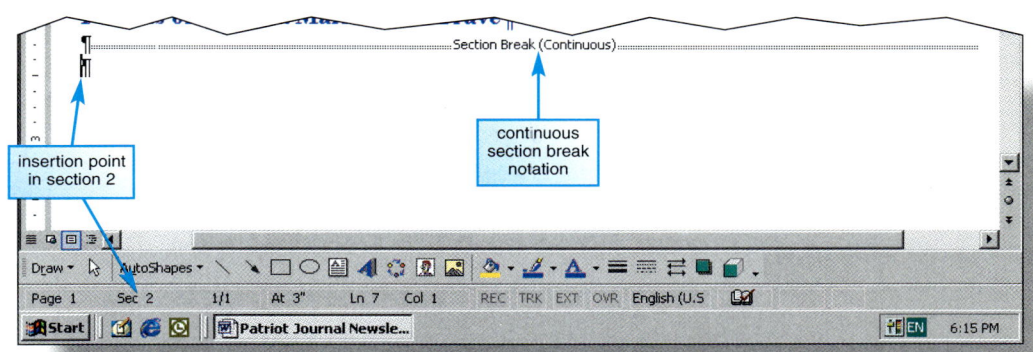

FIGURE 6-27

The document now has two sections. The nameplate is in the first section, and the insertion point is in the second section. The second section is to be formatted to three columns. Thus, perform the following steps to format the second section in the document to three columns.

1. In Voice Command mode, say "Insert, Break, Continuous, OK"

Steps To Change the Number of Columns

1 **If necessary, scroll down. Be sure the insertion point is in section 2. Point to the Columns button on the Standard toolbar (Figure 6-28).**

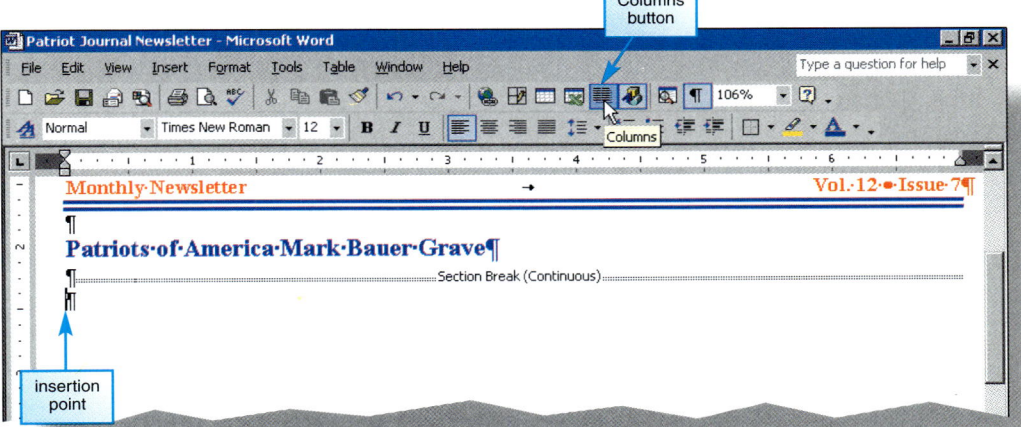

FIGURE 6-28

2 **Click the Columns button. Point to the third column in the columns list.**

Word displays a columns list graphic below the Columns button (Figure 6-29).

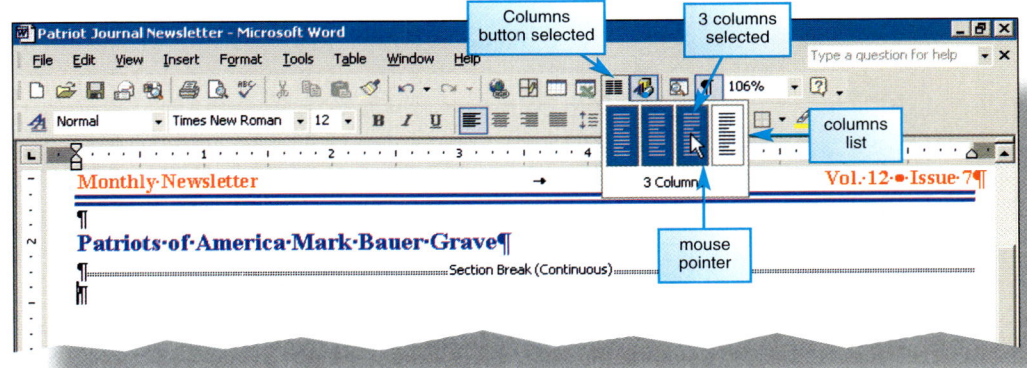

FIGURE 6-29

3 | **Click the third column in the list.**

Word divides the section containing the insertion point into three evenly sized and spaced columns (Figure 6-30). Notice that the ruler indicates the width of each column.

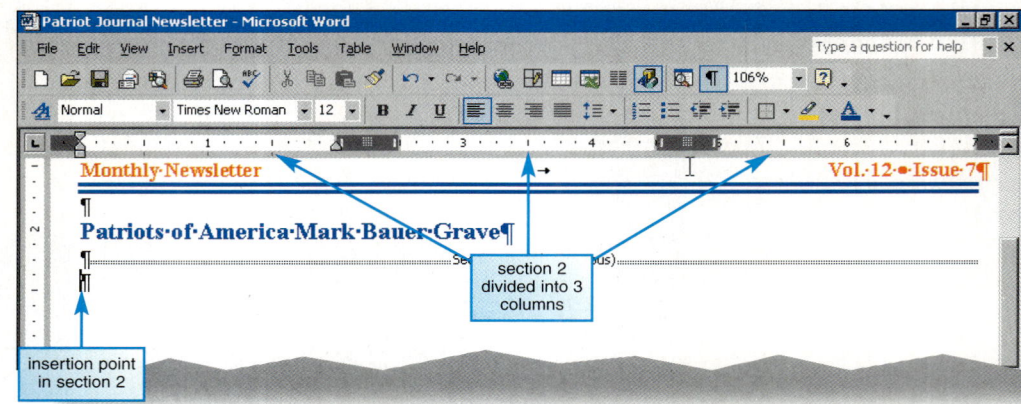

FIGURE 6-30

Other Ways

1. On Format menu click Columns, click desired number of columns in Presets area, click OK button
2. In Voice Command mode, say "Format, Columns, [select number of columns], OK"

When you use the Columns button to change the number of columns, Word creates columns of equal width. You can create columns of unequal width by clicking the Columns command on the Format menu.

Justifying a Paragraph

The text in the paragraphs of the body of the newsletter is **justified**, which means that the left and right margins are aligned, like the edges of newspaper columns. The first line of each paragraph is indented .25 inches. Perform the following steps to enter the first paragraph of the feature article using justified alignment.

Steps **To Justify a Paragraph**

1 | **Drag the First Line Indent marker in the first column on the ruler to the .25" mark. Point to the Justify button on the Formatting toolbar (Figure 6-31).**

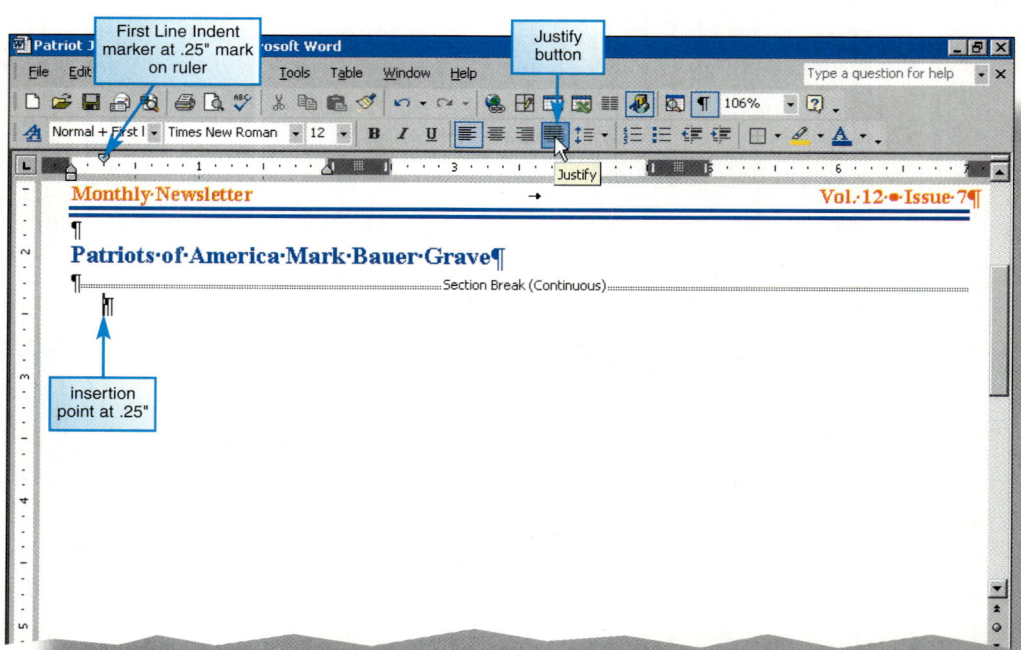

FIGURE 6-31

Formatting the First Page of the Body of the Newsletter • WD 6.27

2 Click the Justify button. Type the first paragraph of the feature article as shown in Figure 6-32. Press the ENTER key.

Word aligns both the left and right edges of the paragraph (Figure 6-32). Notice that Word places extra space between some words when text uses the justified format.

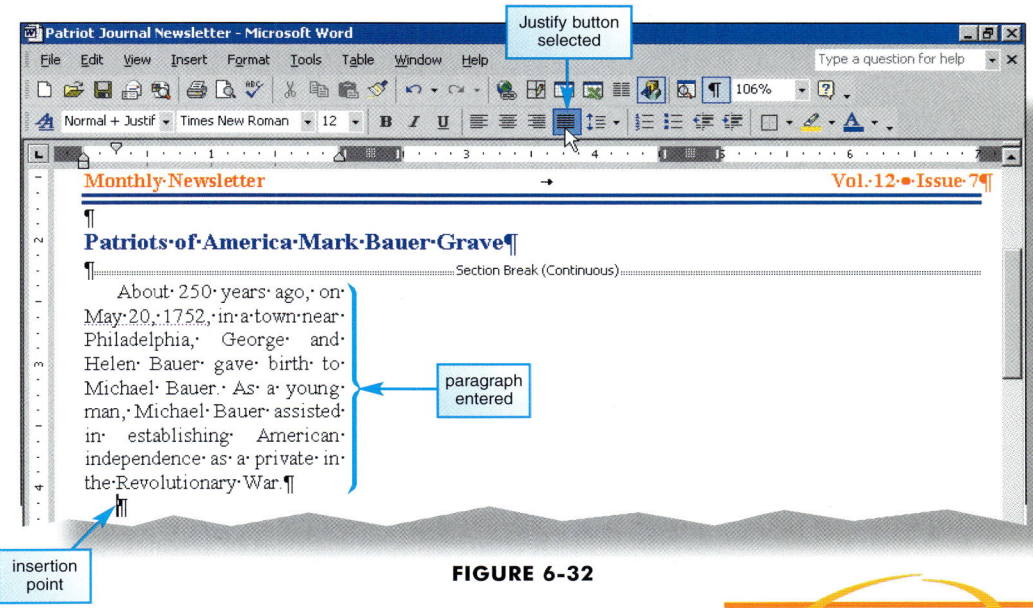

FIGURE 6-32

Other Ways

1. On Format menu click Paragraph, click Indents and Spacing tab, click Alignment box arrow, click Justified, click OK button
2. Press CTRL+J
3. In Voice Command mode, say "Justify"

Inserting the Remainder of the Feature Article

Instead of typing the rest of the feature article into the newsletter for this project, you will insert a file named Grave Marking Article into the newsletter. This file, which contains the remainder of the feature article, is located on the Data Disk. If you did not download the Data Disk, see the inside back cover for instructions for downloading the Data Disk or see your instructor.

Perform the following steps to insert the Grave Marking Article file into the newsletter.

 To Insert a File into the Newsletter

1 If necessary, insert the Data Disk into drive A. Click Insert on the menu bar and then click File. If necessary, click the Look in box arrow and then click 3½ Floppy (A:). Click Grave Marking Article and then point to the Insert button.

Word displays the Insert File dialog box (Figure 6-33). The selected file will be inserted at the location of the insertion point in the document.

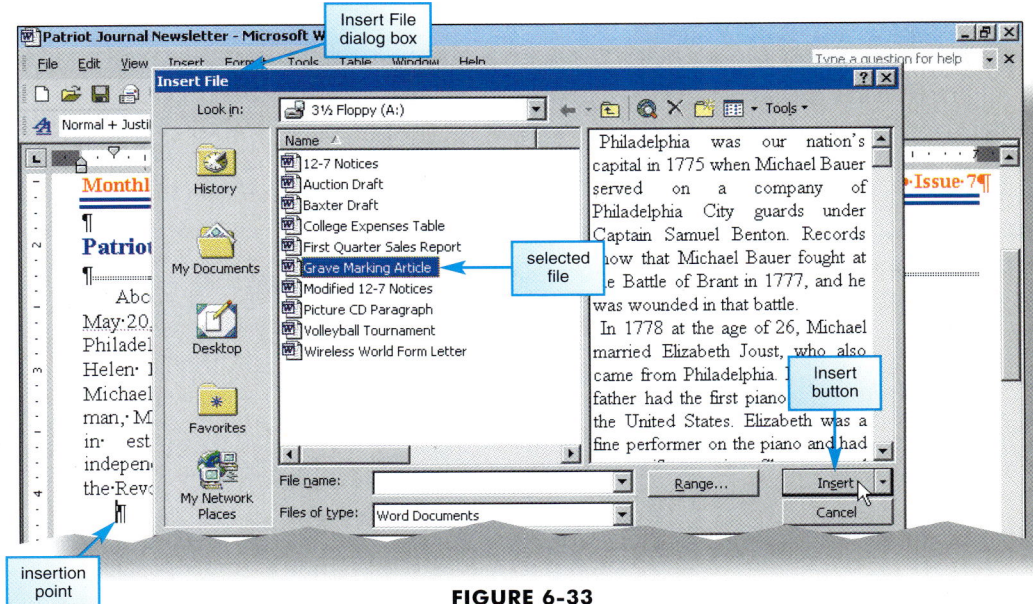

FIGURE 6-33

2 **Click the Insert button.**

Word inserts the file, Grave Marking Article, into the file Patriot Journal Newsletter at the location of the insertion point (Figure 6-34). The text automatically is formatted into columns.

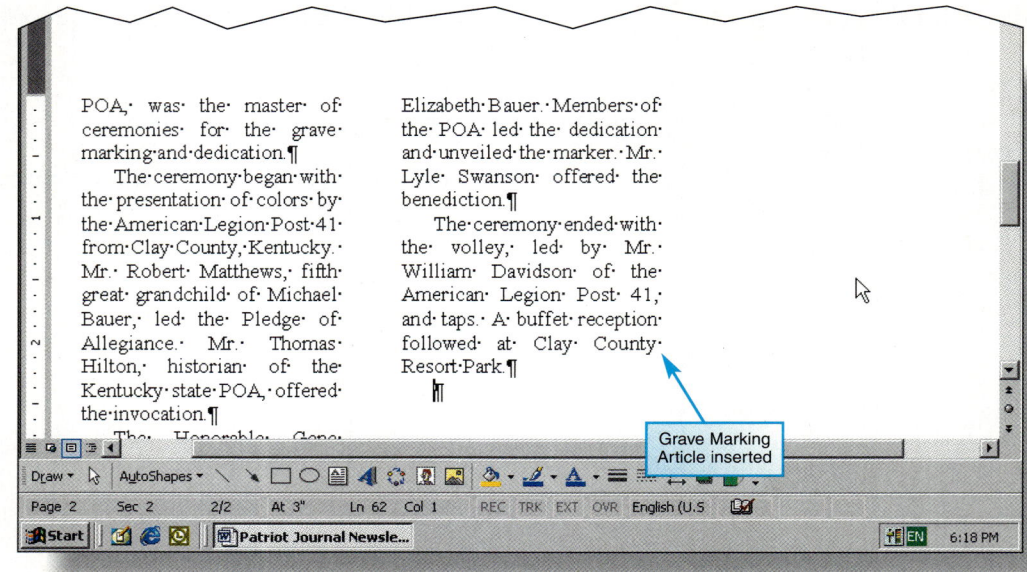

FIGURE 6-34

Other Ways

1. In Voice Command mode, say "Insert, File, [select file], Insert"

Formatting a Letter as a Drop Cap

You can format the first character in a paragraph to be a **drop cap**, which is a large, dropped capital letter. That is, a drop cap is larger than the rest of the characters in the paragraph. The text in the paragraph then wraps around the drop cap.

Perform the following steps to create a drop cap in the first paragraph of the feature article in the newsletter.

Steps To Format a Letter as a Drop Cap

1 **Press CTRL+HOME to scroll to the top of the document. Scroll down and then click anywhere in the first paragraph of the feature article. Click Format on the menu bar and then point to Drop Cap.**

The insertion point is in the first paragraph of the feature article (Figure 6-35).

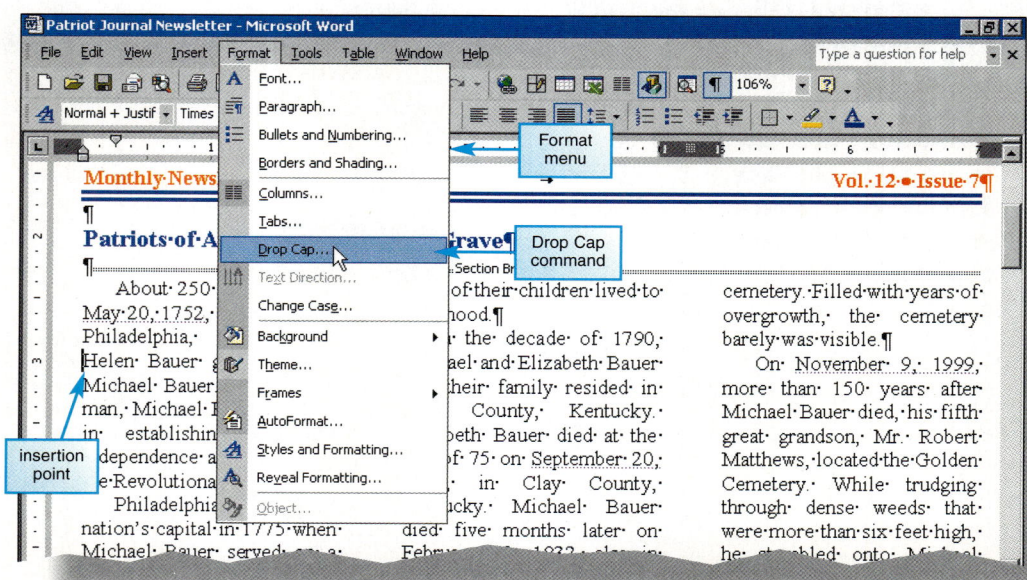

FIGURE 6-35

2 **Click Drop Cap. When the Drop Cap dialog box displays, click Dropped in the Position area. Point to the OK button.**

Word displays the Drop Cap dialog box (Figure 6-36).

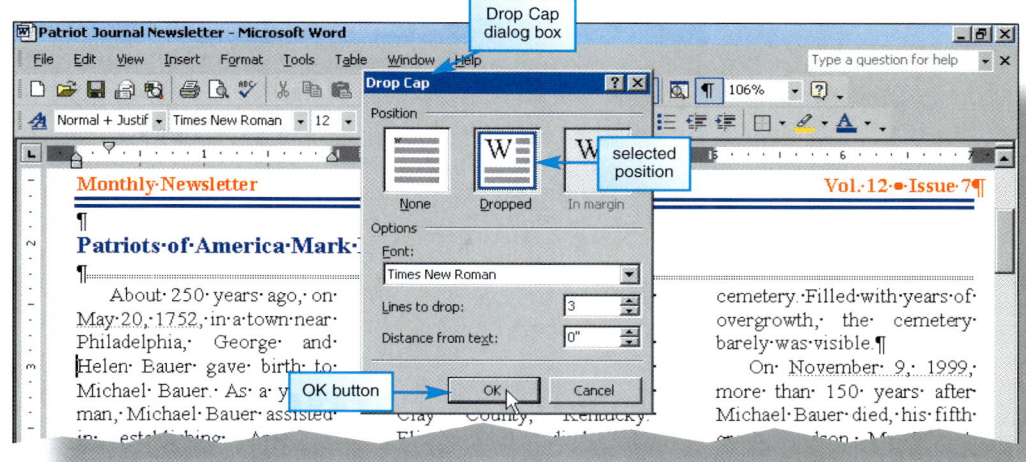

FIGURE 6-36

3 **Click the OK button. Word drops the letter A in the word, About, and wraps subsequent text around the drop cap (Figure 6-37).**

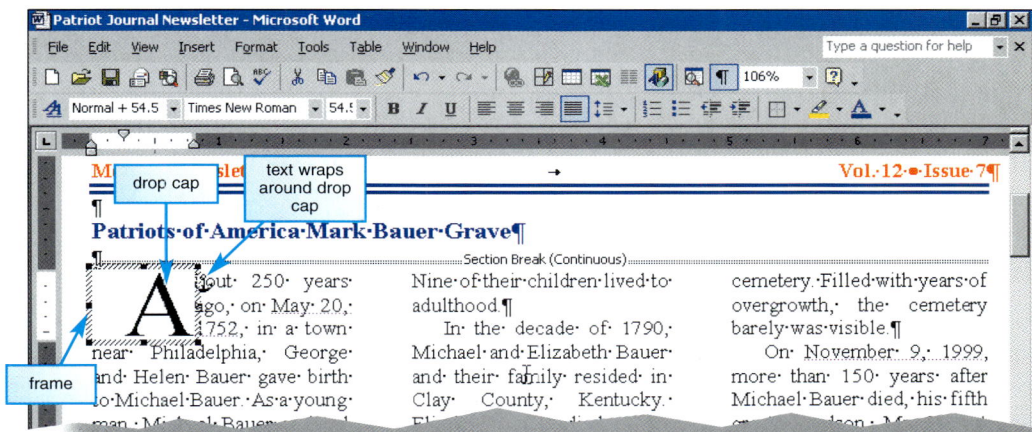

FIGURE 6-37

1. In Voice Command mode, say "Format, Drop Cap, Dropped, OK"

Drop Caps

A drop cap often is used to mark the beginning of an article. To format the entire first word as a drop cap, select the word. An alternative to a drop cap is a stick-up cap, which extends into the left margin, instead of sinking into the first few lines of the text. To insert a stick-up cap, click In margin in the Drop Cap dialog box.

When you drop cap a letter, Word places a frame around it. A **frame** is a container for text that allows you to position the text anywhere on the page. As illustrated in the previous steps, Word can format a frame so that text wraps around it.

To remove the frame from displaying in the document window, simply click outside the frame to display the insertion point elsewhere in the document.

The next step is to insert a column break before the subhead, 250 YEARS LATER.

Inserting a Column Break

Notice in Figure 6-1a on page WD 6.05 that the third column on the first page of the newsletter is not a continuation of the feature article. The third column contains several member announcements. The feature article continues on the second page of the newsletter (Figure 6-1b). In order for the member announcements to display in the third column, insert a **column break** at the bottom of the second column.

Before inserting the column break, you first must insert a next page section break at the bottom of the second column so that the remainder of the feature article moves to the second page. Then, insert a column break at the bottom of the second column so the announcements always display in the third column.

Perform the following steps to insert a next page section break at the bottom of the second column.

Steps: To Insert a Next Page Section Break

1 Scroll through the document to display the bottom of the second column of the first page in the document window. Click to the left of the 2 in the 250 YEARS LATER subhead. Click Insert on the menu bar and then click Break. When the Break dialog box displays, click Next page in the Section break types area. Point to the OK button.

The insertion point is at the beginning of the 250 YEARS LATER subhead (Figure 6-38).

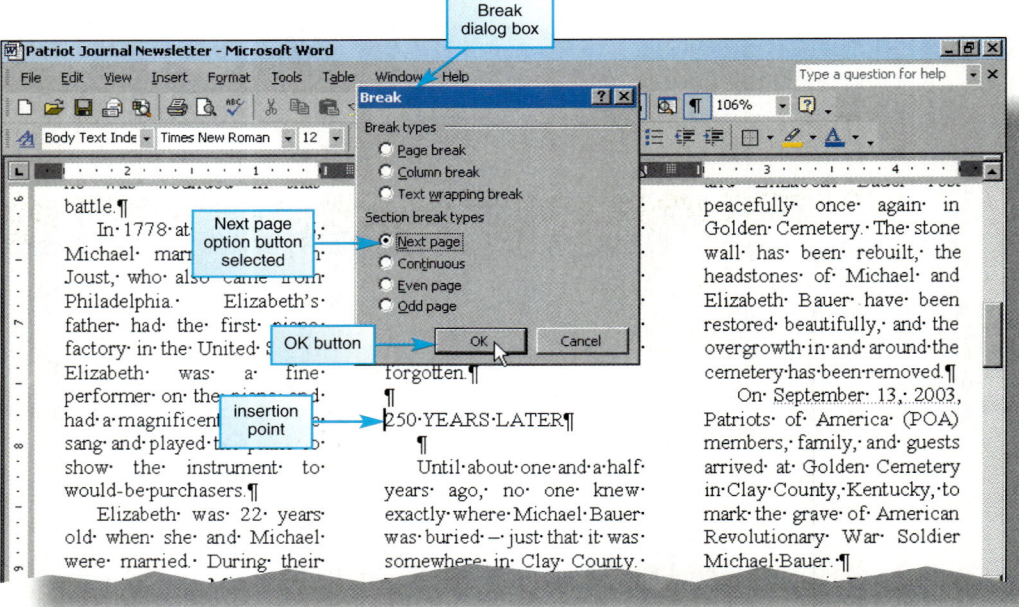

FIGURE 6-38

2 Click the OK button.

Word inserts a section break at the location of the insertion point (Figure 6-39). The remainder of the article displays on page 2 of the document because a next page section break includes a page break. On page 1, the bottom of the second column and the entire third column are empty.

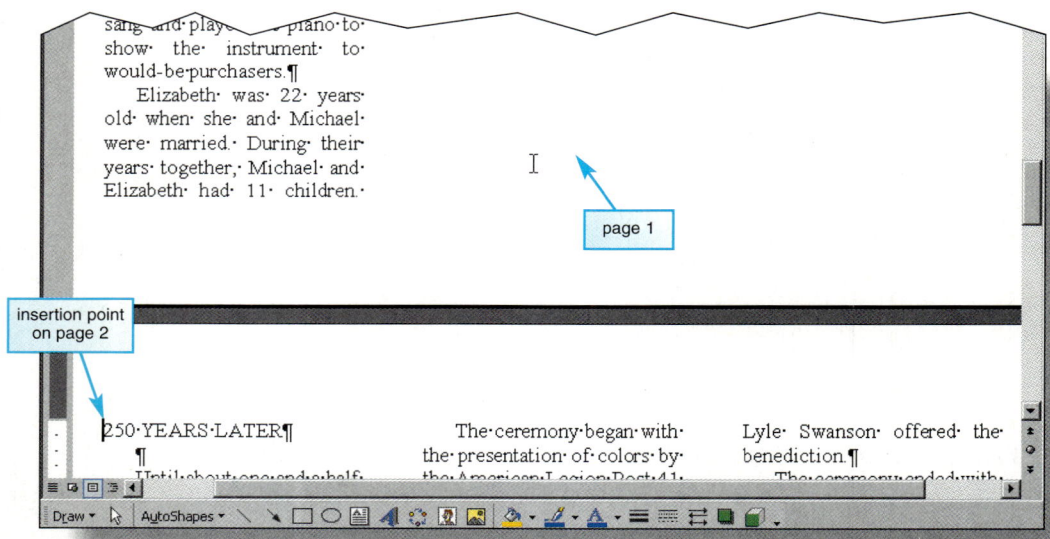

FIGURE 6-39

You want the member announcements to begin at the top of the third column, even though a small amount of room is available at the bottom of the second column. To move the insertion point to the top of the third column, insert a column break at the end of the text in the second column.

Perform the following steps to insert a column break.

Steps: To Insert a Column Break

1 Scroll up to display the bottom of the second column of the first page of the newsletter and then position the insertion point at the beginning of the line containing the next page section break notation. Press the ENTER key twice. Press the UP ARROW key. Press CTRL+I to turn on italics. Type `Article continues on Page 2...` and then press CTRL+I again to turn off italics. Press the ENTER key. Click Insert on the menu bar and then click Break. When the Break dialog box displays, click Column break in the Break types area. Point to the OK button (Figure 6-40).

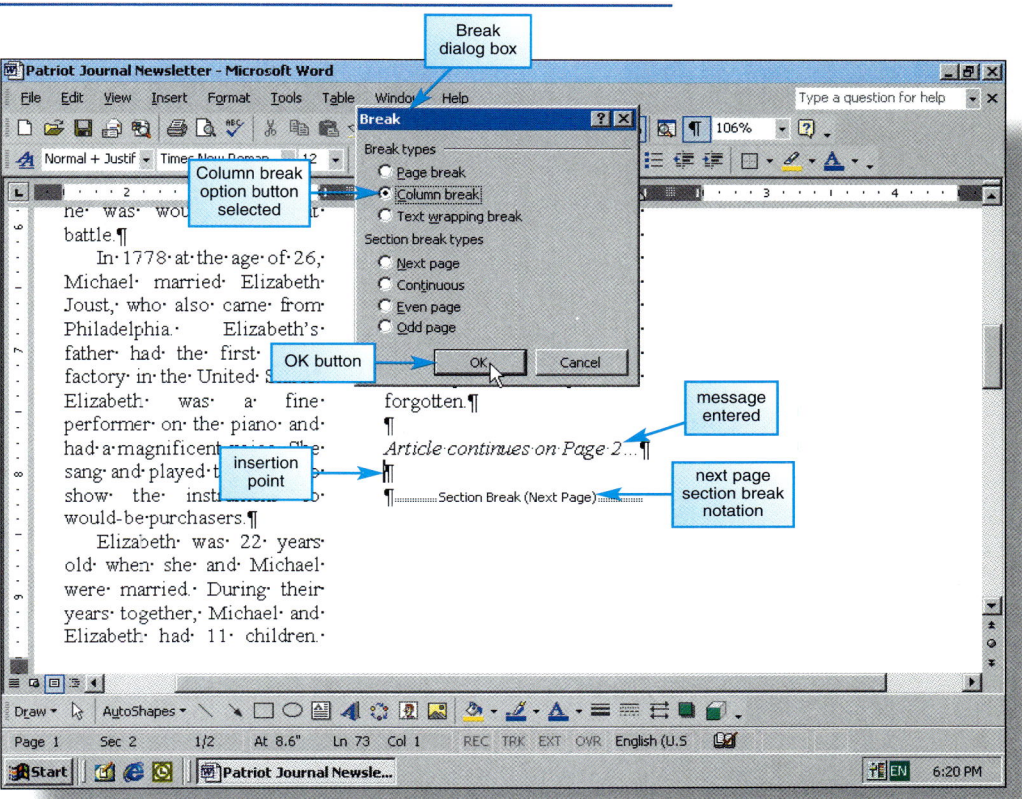

FIGURE 6-40

2 Click the OK button.

Word inserts a column break at the bottom of the second column and places the insertion point at the top of the third column (Figure 6-41).

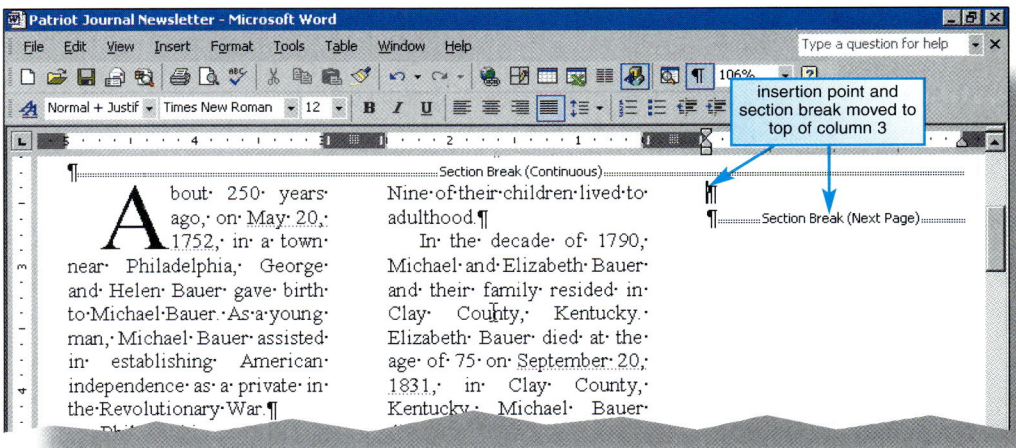

FIGURE 6-41

Jump Lines

An article that spans multiple pages should contain a jump or jump line, which informs the reader where to look for the rest of the article or story. The message on the first page is called a jump-to line, and a jump-from line marks the beginning of the continuation. The alignment of the jump-to and jump-from lines should be the same.

Perform the following step to save the newsletter again.

TO SAVE A DOCUMENT

 With the disk containing the newsletter file in drive A, click the Save button on the Standard toolbar.

Word saves the document again with the file name, Patriot Journal Newsletter.

To eliminate having to enter the entire third column of announcements into the newsletter, you insert the file named 12-7 Notices into the third column of the newsletter. This file contains the three announcements: the first about a luncheon, the second about Patriot Week, and the third about the POA saver card.

The 12-7 Notices file is located on the Data Disk. If you did not download the Data Disk, see the inside back cover for instructions for downloading the Data Disk or see your instructor.

Perform the following steps to insert the 12-7 Notices file into the newsletter.

TO INSERT A FILE INTO A COLUMN OF THE NEWSLETTER

1. If necessary, insert the Data Disk into drive A. With the insertion point at the top of the third column, click Insert on the menu bar and then click File.
2. When the Insert File dialog box displays, if necessary, click the Look in box arrow and then click 3½ Floppy (A:). Click the file name, 12-7 Notices.
3. Click the Insert button.

Word inserts the file 12-7 Notices into the third column of the newsletter (shown in Figure 6-42).

Perform the following step to display the entire page in the document window so you can see the layout of the first page of the newsletter thus far.

TO ZOOM WHOLE PAGE

 Click the Zoom box arrow on the Standard toolbar and then click Whole Page.

Word displays the first page of the newsletter in reduced form so that the entire page displays in the document window (Figure 6-42).

Justification

The paragraphs within the columns of a newsletter very often are justified; that is, flush at both left and right margins. This alignment often causes rivers, which are large gaps between words. One solution is to rearrange the words or add additional words to minimize the rivers. Another solution, not quite as common, is to use left-aligned text.

Formatting the First Page of the Body of the Newsletter • **WD 6.33**

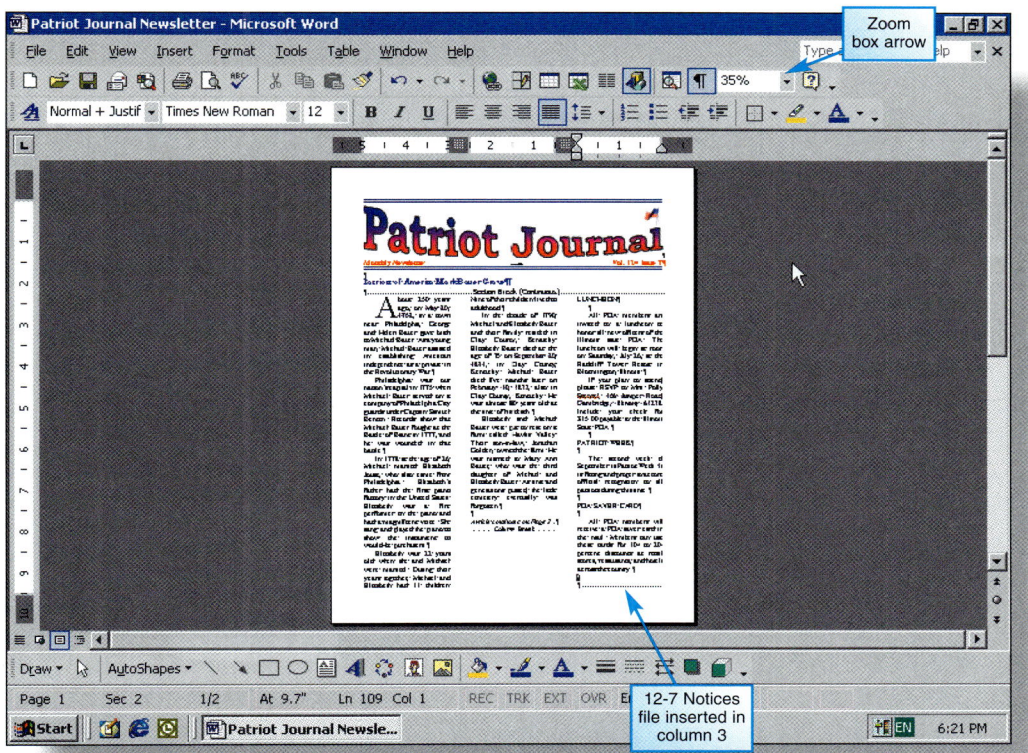

FIGURE 6-42

Perform the following step to return the zoom to text width.

TO ZOOM TEXT WIDTH

1 Click the Zoom box arrow on the Standard toolbar and then click Text Width.

Word extends the right margin to the right edge of the document window.

Adding a Vertical Rule Between Columns

In newsletters, you often see a vertical rule separating columns. With Word, you can place a vertical rule between *all* columns by clicking the Columns command on the Format menu and then clicking the Line between check box.

In this project, you want a vertical rule between only the second and third columns. To do this, place a left border spaced several points from the text. A point is approximately 1/72 of an inch.

Perform the steps on the next page to place a vertical rule between the second and third columns of the newsletter.

Column Breaks

A column break displays on the screen with the words Column Break separated by a thinly dotted horizontal line. The figure to the left shows the column break notation at the bottom of the second column. To remove a column break, select it and then click the Cut button on the Standard toolbar or press the DELETE key.

Vertical Rules

A vertical rule is used to guide the reader through the newsletter. If a multi-column newsletter contains a single article, place a vertical rule between every column. If different columns present different articles, place a vertical rule between each article.

Steps To Place a Vertical Rule between Columns

1 On the first page of the newsletter, drag the mouse from the top of the third column down to the bottom of the third column. Click Format on the menu bar and then point to Borders and Shading.

Word selects the entire third column of page 1 in the newsletter (Figure 6-43).

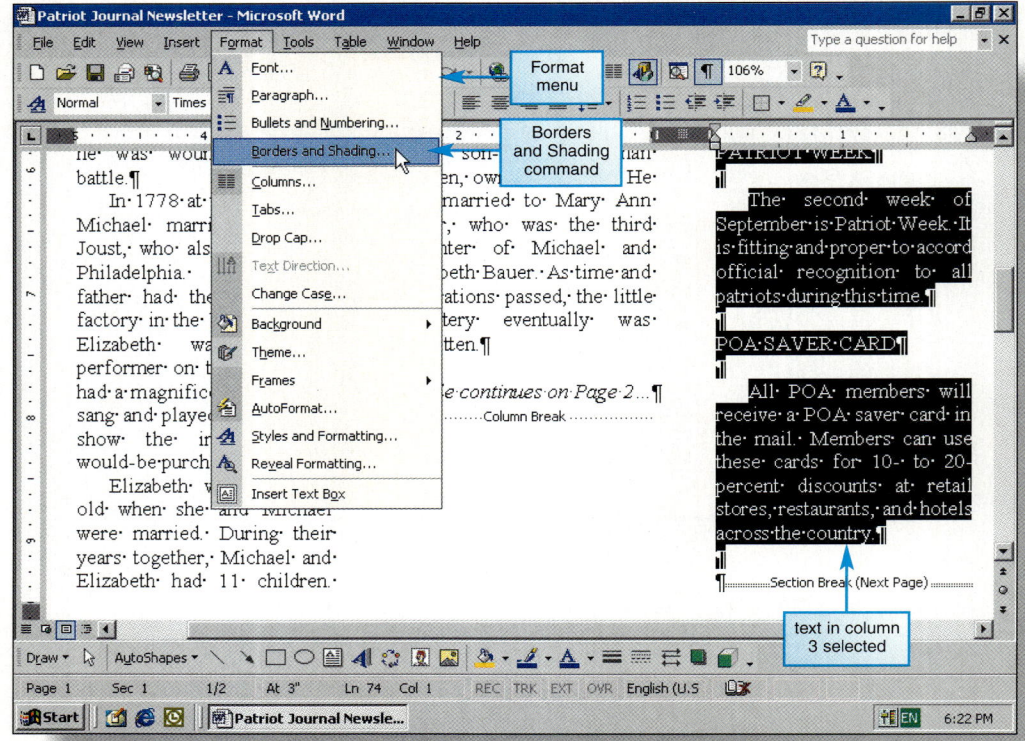

FIGURE 6-43

2 Click Borders and Shading. When the Borders and Shading dialog box displays, if necessary, click the Borders tab. Click the Left Border button in the Preview area. Point to the Options button.

Word displays the Borders and Shading dialog box (Figure 6-44). The border diagram graphically shows the selected borders.

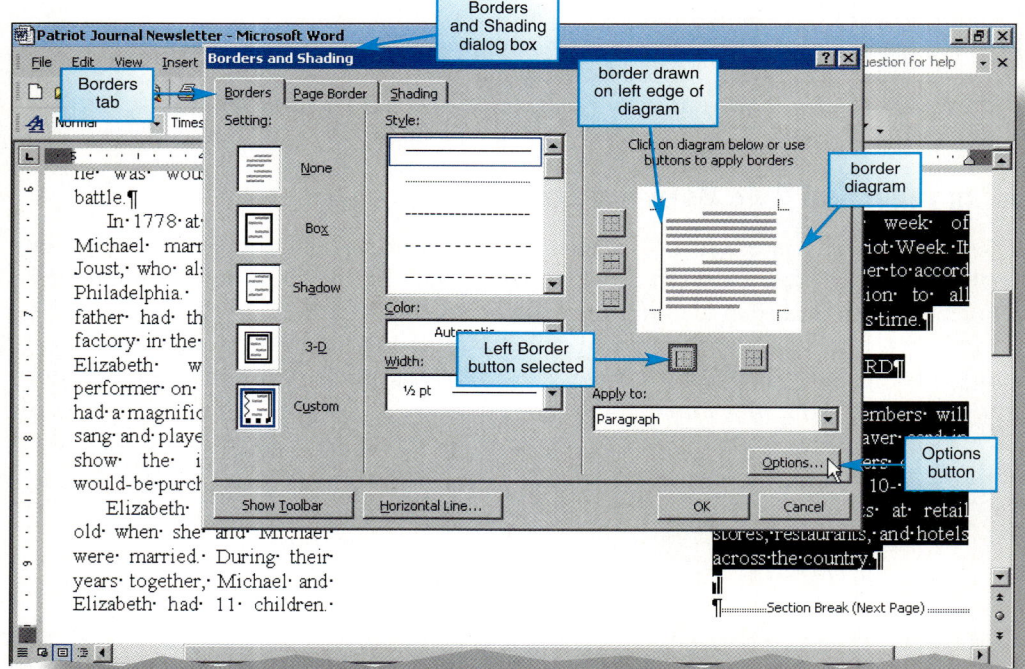

FIGURE 6-44

Formatting the First Page of the Body of the Newsletter • WD 6.35

3 **Click the Options button. When the Border and Shading Options dialog box displays, change the Left text box to 15 pt. Point to the OK button.**

The Preview area shows the border positioned 15 points from the left edge of the paragraph (Figure 6-45).

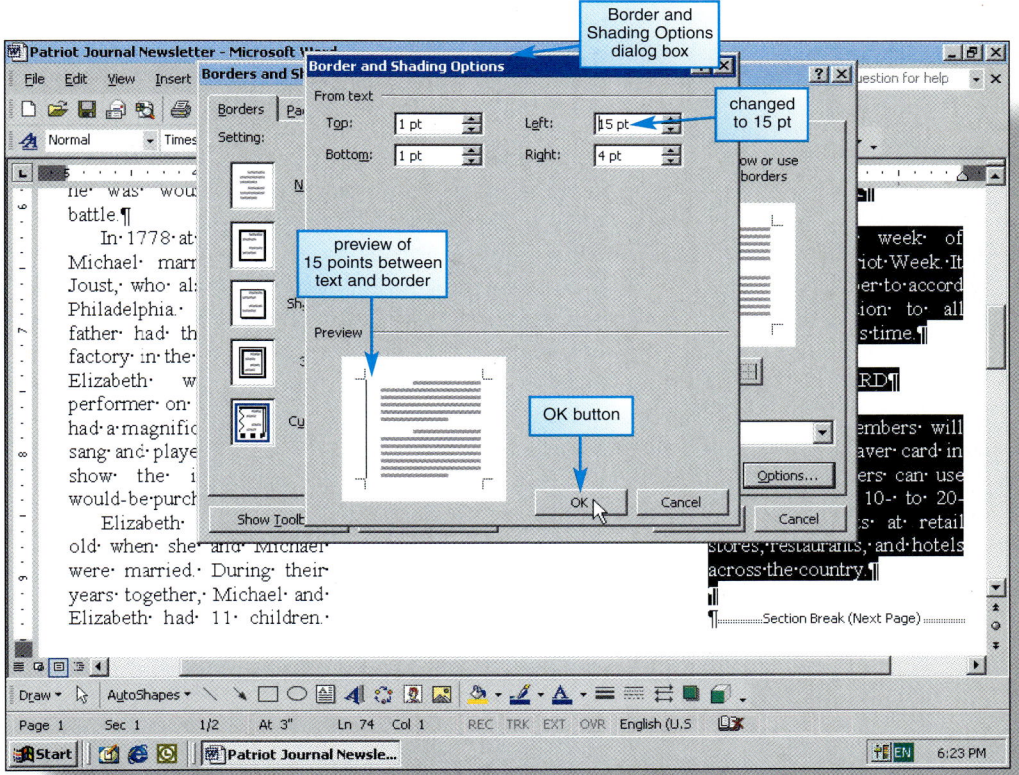

FIGURE 6-45

4 **Click the OK button. When the Borders and Shading dialog box is visible again, click its OK button. Click in the document to remove the selection from the third column.**

Word draws a border positioned 15 points from the left edge of the text in the third column (Figure 6-46). The border displays as a vertical rule between the second and third columns of the newsletter.

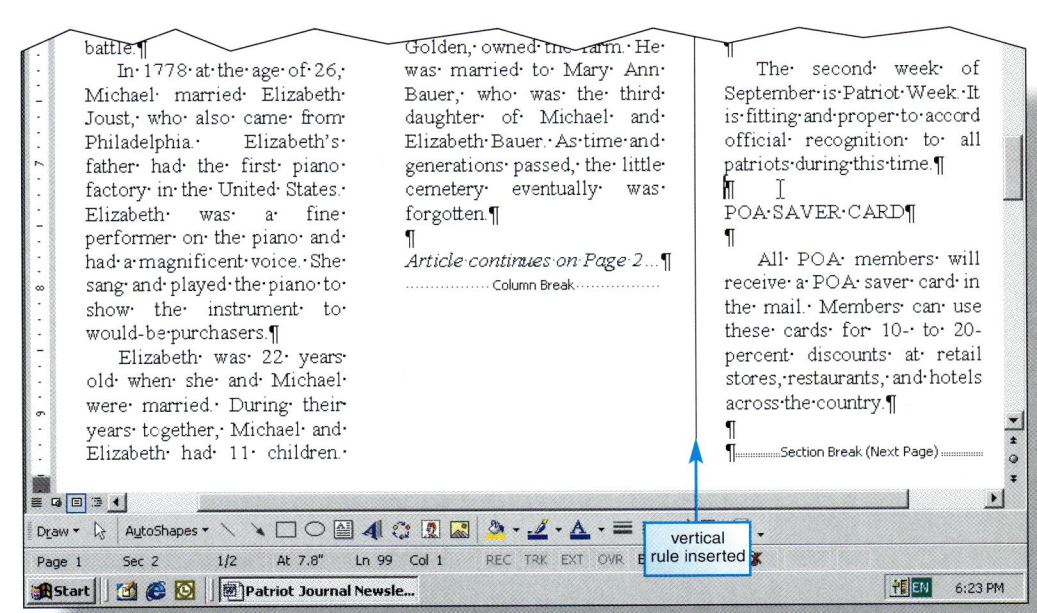

FIGURE 6-46

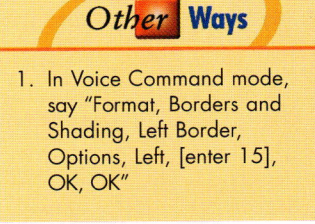

1. In Voice Command mode, say "Format, Borders and Shading, Left Border, Options, Left, [enter 15], OK, OK"

Pull-Quotes

Because of their bold emphasis, pull-quotes should be used sparingly in a newsletter. Pull-quotes are useful for breaking the monotony of long columns of text. Typically, quotation marks are used only if you are quoting someone directly. If you use quotation marks, use curly (or smart) quotation marks instead of straight quotation marks.

Creating a Pull-Quote

A pull-quote is text pulled, or copied, from the text of the document and given graphical emphasis so it stands apart and grasps the reader's attention. The newsletter in this project has a pull-quote on the first page between the first and second columns (Figure 6-1a on page WD 6.05).

To create a pull-quote, copy the text in the existing document to the Clipboard and then paste it into a column of the newsletter. To position the text between columns, place a text box around it. A text box, like a frame, is a container for text that allows you to position the text anywhere on the page. The difference between a text box and a frame is that a text box has more graphical formatting options than does a frame.

The steps on the following pages discuss how to create the pull-quote shown in Figure 6-1a.

Inserting a Text Box

The first step in creating the pull-quote is to copy the text to be used in the pull-quote and then insert a text box around it, as shown in the following steps.

Steps To Insert a Text Box

1 Scroll to display the first paragraph in the newsletter that contains the drop cap and then select the following text: **As a young man, Michael Bauer assisted in establishing American independence.** With the text selected, click the Copy button on the Standard toolbar.

The text for the pull-quote is selected (Figure 6-47).

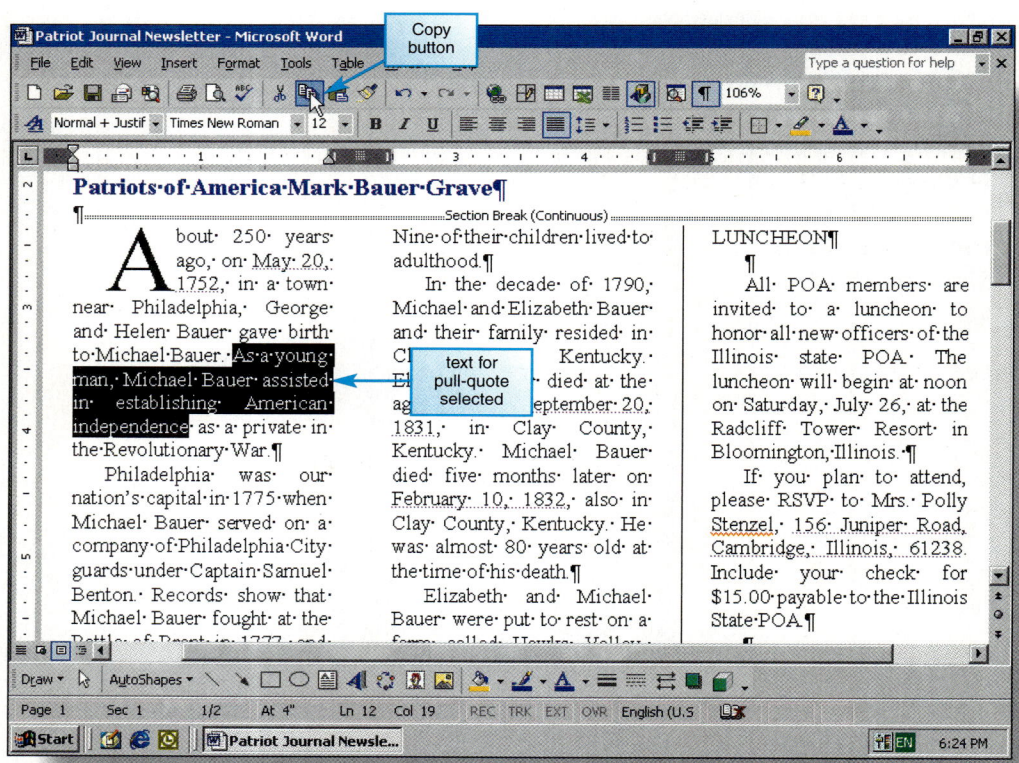

FIGURE 6-47

2 **Click at the end of the first paragraph that contains the drop cap and then click the Paste button on the Standard toolbar. Type a period (.) at the end of the pasted text. Select the entire sentence to be in the pull-quote. Point to the Text Box button on the Drawing toolbar (Figure 6-48).**

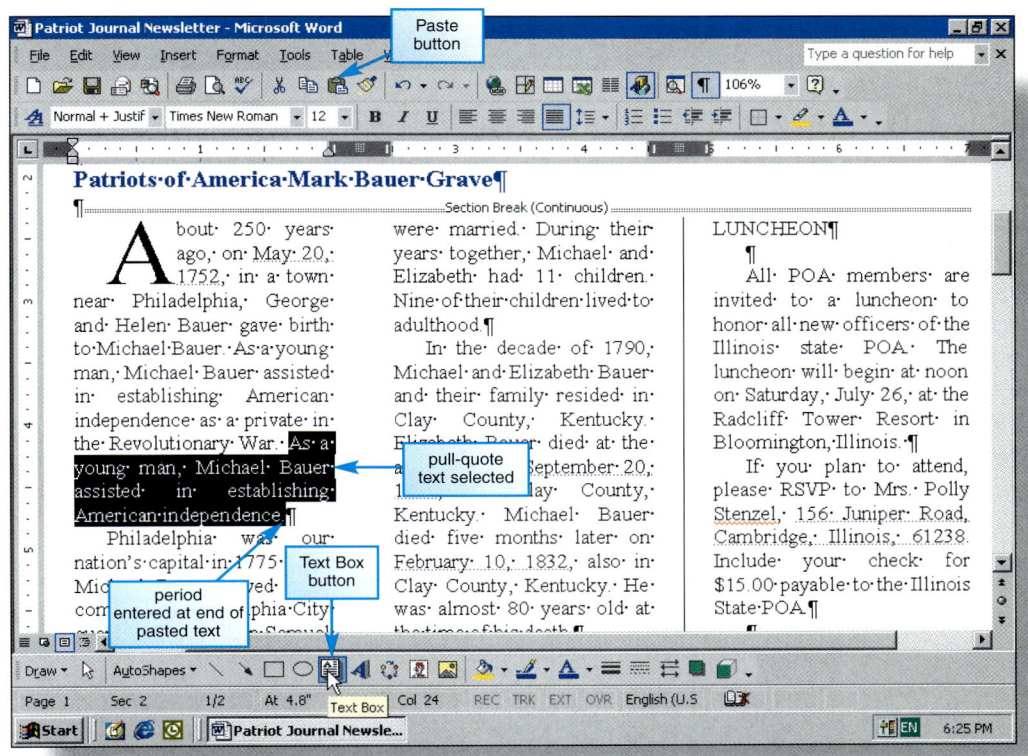

FIGURE 6-48

3 **Click the Text Box button.**

Word places a text box around the pull-quote (Figure 6-49). The pull-quote now may be positioned anywhere on the page.

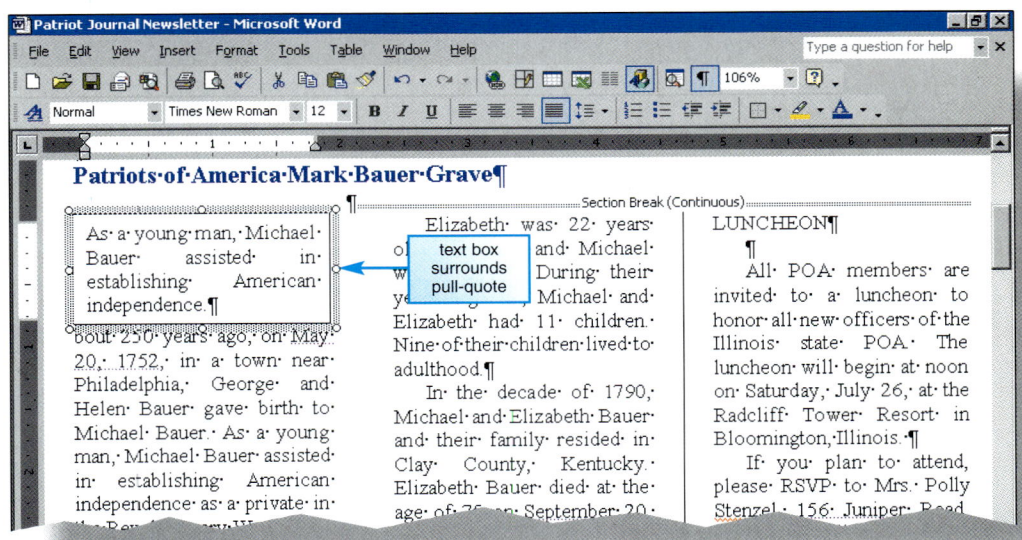

FIGURE 6-49

Depending on your printer, the text in the text box may wrap differently than shown in Figure 6-49.

The next step in formatting the pull-quote is to change the color and increase the weight of the text box, as described in the steps on the next page.

1. On Insert menu click Text Box
2. In Voice Command mode, say "Insert, Text Box"

Steps To Format a Text Box

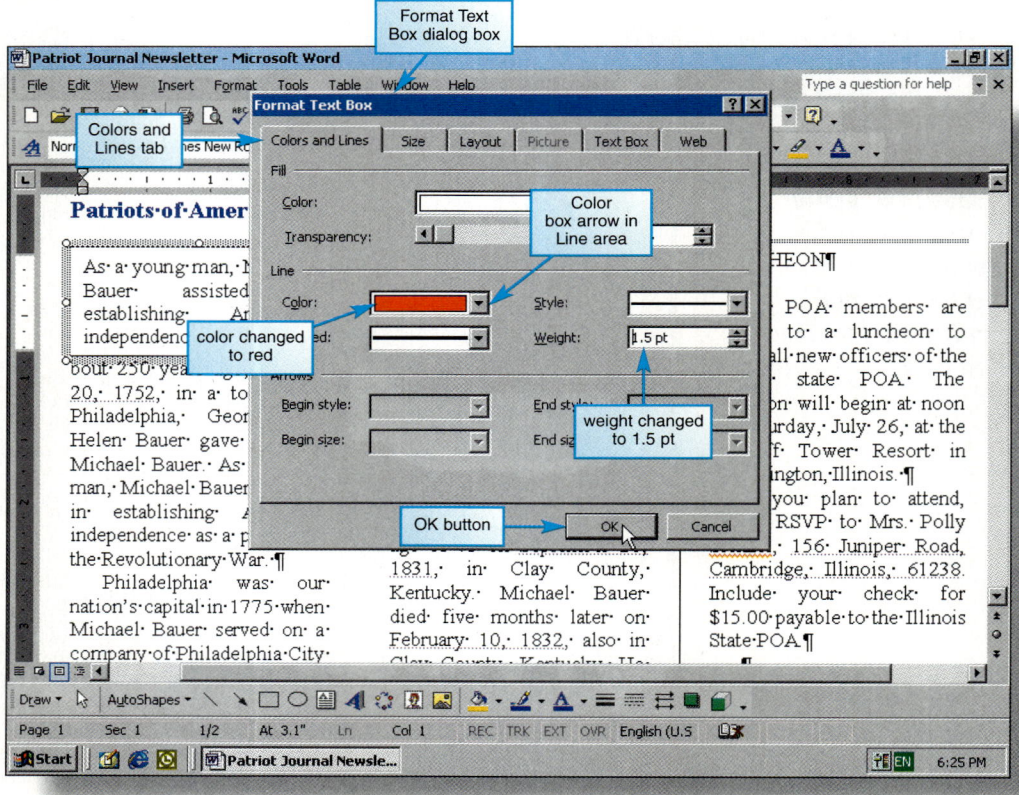

FIGURE 6-50

1 Point to an edge of the text box and double-click when the mouse pointer has a four-headed arrow attached to it. When the Format Text Box dialog box displays, if necessary, click the Colors and Lines tab. In the Line area, click the Color box arrow and then click Red. Change the Weight to 1.5 pt and then point to the OK button.

Word displays the Format Text Box dialog box (Figure 6-50).

2 Click the OK button.

Word formats the text box to a 1.5-point red line (shown in Figure 6-51).

1. On Format menu click Text Box
2. Right-click edge of text box, click Format Text Box on shortcut menu
3. In Voice Command mode, say "Format, Text Box"

The next step is to bold the characters and center the text in the pull-quote, as described in the following steps.

TO BOLD AND CENTER TEXT

1 Drag through the pull-quote text to select it.

2 Click the Bold button on the Formatting toolbar.

3 Click the Center button on the Formatting toolbar.

4 Click inside the pull-quote text to remove the selection.

Word bolds and centers the characters in the pull-quote (Figure 6-51).

Creating a Pull-Quote • WD 6.39

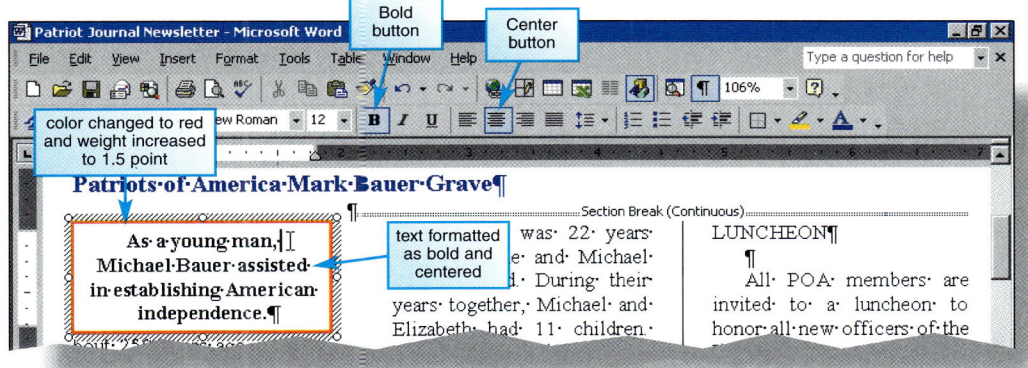

FIGURE 6-51

You want more space between the pull-quote in the text box and the text box itself. Perform the following steps to increase the left and right indentation and the spacing above and below the paragraph in the text box.

Steps To Change Paragraph Indentation and Spacing

1 **Right-click the pull-quote text and then click Paragraph on the shortcut menu. When the Paragraph dialog box displays, if necessary, click the Indents and Spacing tab. In the Indentation area, change the Left and Right text boxes to 0.1". In the Spacing area, change Before and After text boxes to 6 pt. Point to the OK button.**

Word displays the Paragraph dialog box (Figure 6-52). The Left and Right text boxes control the amount of space on the left and right edges of the paragraph. The Before and After text boxes control the amount of space above and below a paragraph.

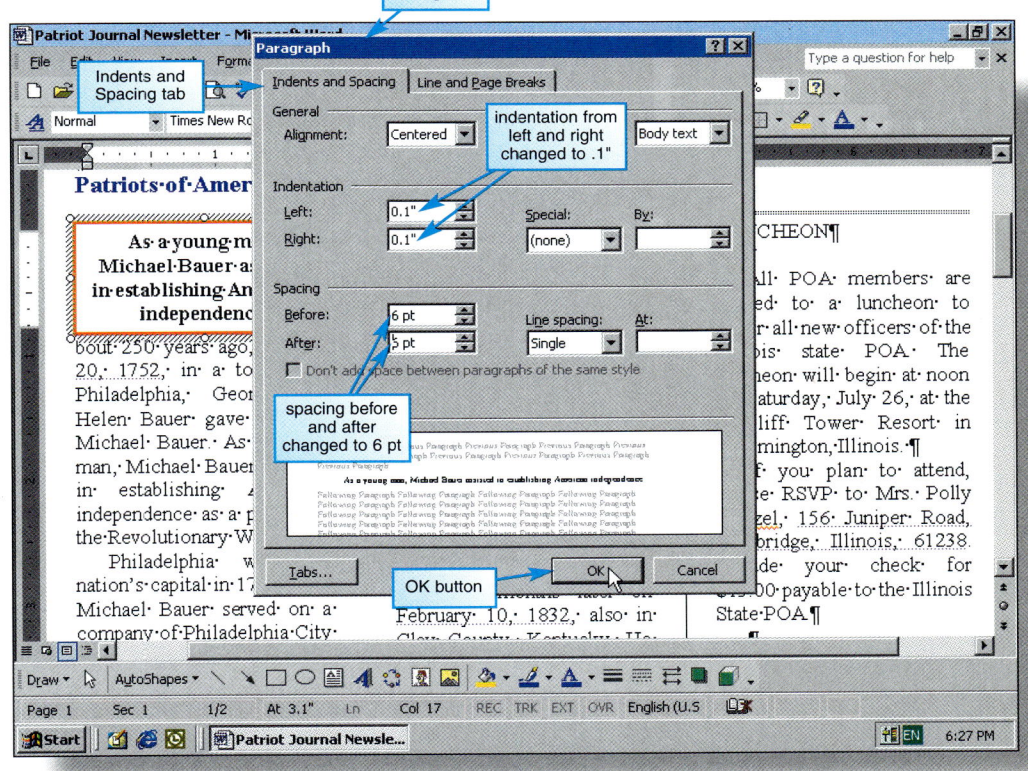

FIGURE 6-52

2 **Click the OK button.**

Word changes the paragraph indentation and spacing (shown in Figure 6-53 on the next page).

The next step in formatting the pull-quote is to shade the pull-quote paragraph blue, as shown in the following steps.

Steps: To Shade a Paragraph

1 If necessary, click in the pull-quote paragraph to position the insertion point in the pull-quote. Click Format on the menu bar and then click Borders and Shading. When the Borders and Shading dialog box displays, if necessary, click the Shading tab. In the Fill area, click Blue. Point to the OK button.

Word displays the Borders and Shading dialog box (Figure 6-53).

2 Click the OK button.

Word shades the paragraph blue (shown in Figure 6-54).

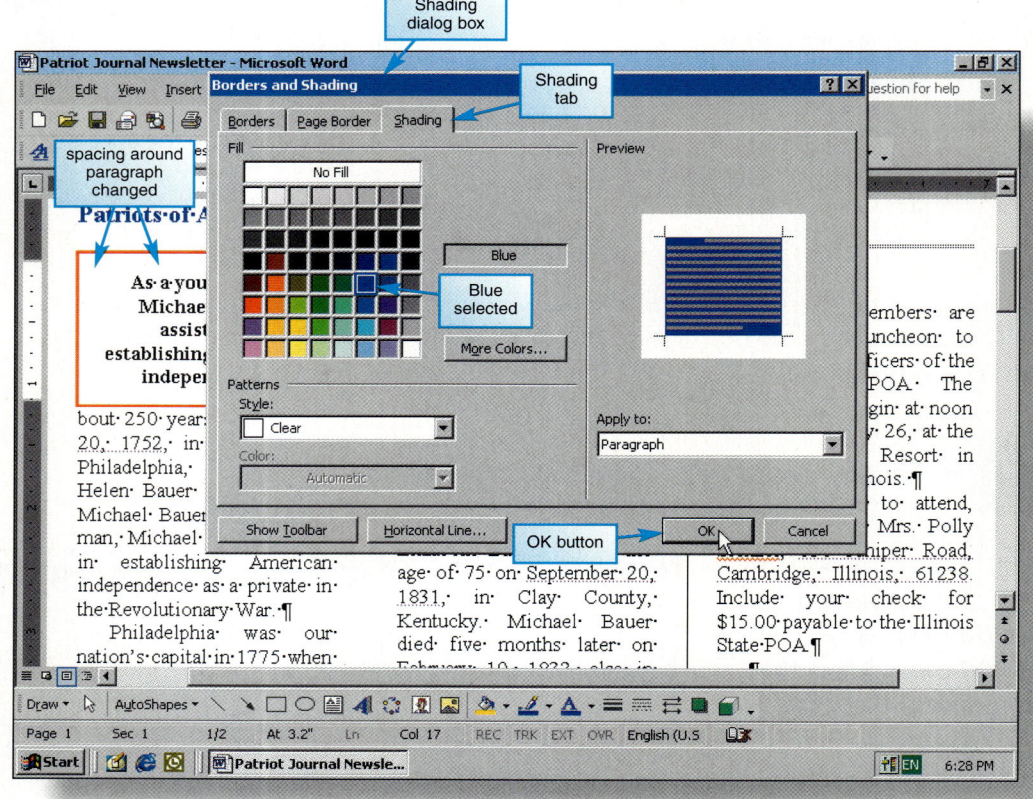

FIGURE 6-53

Other Ways

1. Click Shading Color button on Tables and Borders toolbar, click color
2. In Voice Command mode, say "Format, Borders and Shading, Shading, [select color], OK"

The characters in the paragraph currently are black, which is difficult to read on a blue background. Thus, change the color of the characters to white.

TO CHANGE THE COLOR OF CHARACTERS

1 Drag through the pull-quote text to select it.

2 Click the Font Color button arrow on the Formatting toolbar and then click White.

3 Click outside the selection to remove the highlight.

Word changes the color of the characters in the pull-quote to white (shown in Figure 6-54).

The next step in formatting the pull-quote is to resize it, as described in the following steps.

TO RESIZE A TEXT BOX

1. Click the edge of the text box to select it.

2. Drag the right-middle sizing handle to the right slightly to make the pull-quote a little wider so the pull-quote text looks more balanced.

3. Drag the bottom-middle sizing handle down a bit to make the space below the shading and the red border look the same as the space above the shading. You may need to move the bottom-middle sizing handle up and down a couple of times to readjust the paragraph shading properly.

The text box is resized (shown in Figure 6-54).

The final step is to position the pull-quote between the first and second columns of the newsletter, as shown in the following steps.

Steps: To Position a Text Box

1. **If necessary, click the edge of the text box to select it. Point to the text box.**

The mouse pointer has a four-headed arrow attached to it when positioned on the edge of a text box (Figure 6-54).

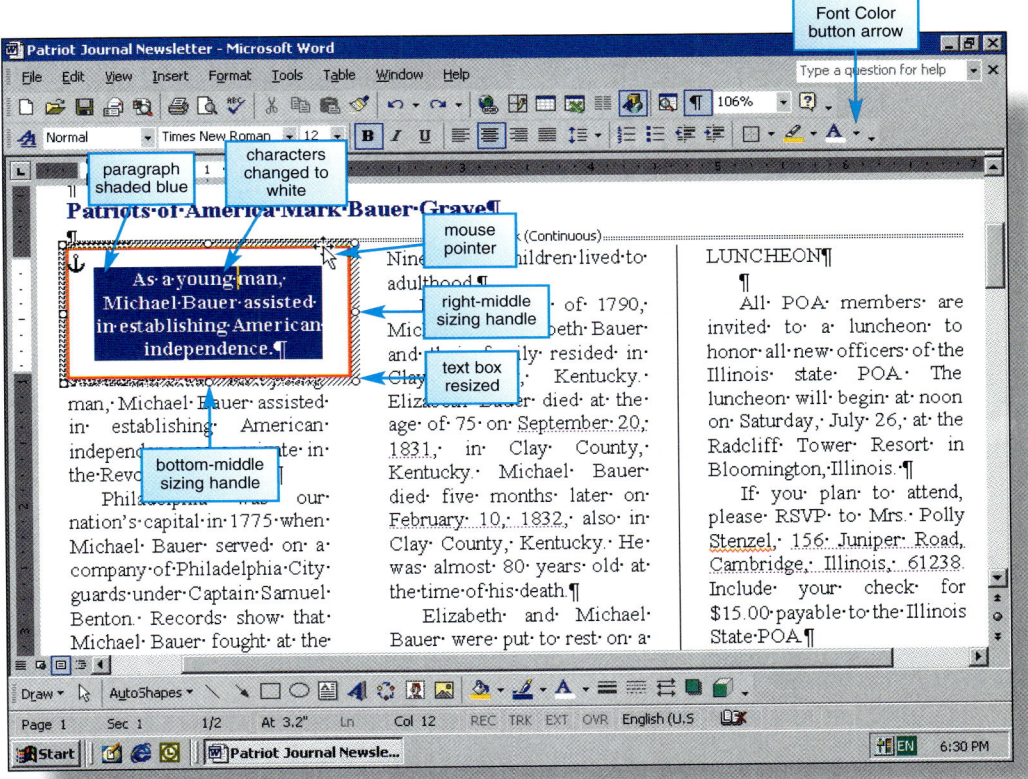

FIGURE 6-54

 **Drag the text box to its new location** (Figure 6-55). You may need to drag the text box a couple of times to position it similarly to this figure. When you drag the text box, if it drags in ¼ inch increments, click the Draw button on the Drawing toolbar, click Grid, remove the check mark from the Snap objects to grid check box, and then click the OK button. Click outside the text box to remove the selection.

The pull-quote is complete (Figure 6-55). Depending on your printer, your wordwrap around the text box may occur in different locations.

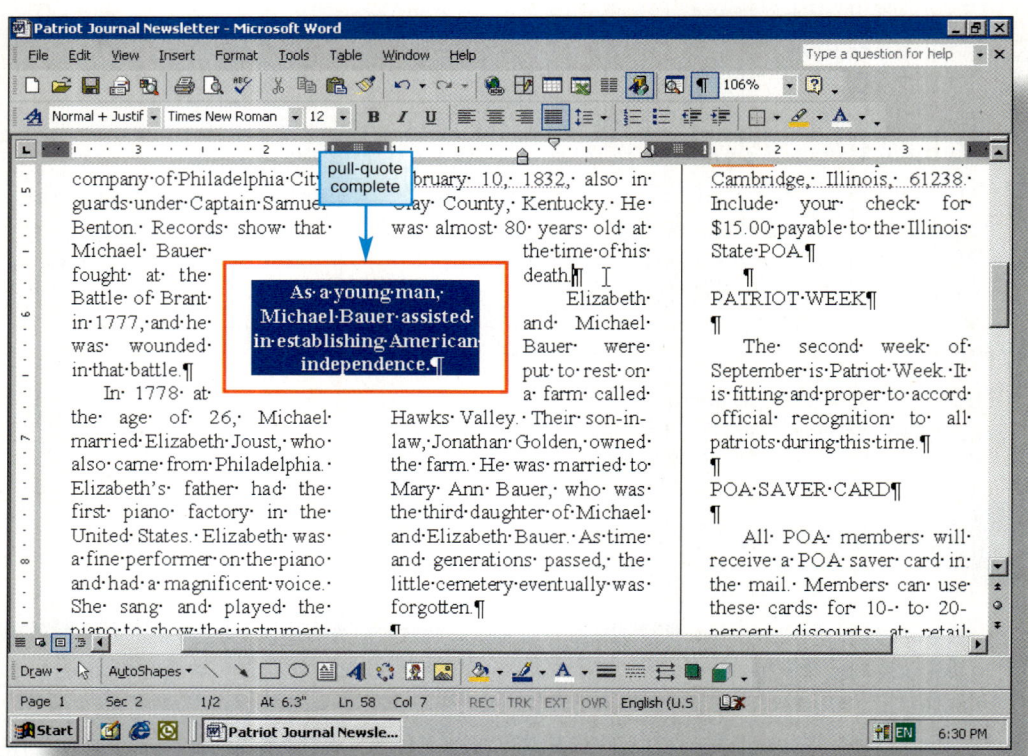

FIGURE 6-55

More About

Moving Text Boxes

To move a text box using the keyboard, select the text box and then press the ARROW keys on the keyboard. For example, each time you press the DOWN ARROW key, the selected text box moves down one line.

Perform the following step to save the document again.

TO SAVE A DOCUMENT

 With the disk containing the newsletter file in drive A, click the Save button on the Standard toolbar.

Word saves the document again with the file name, Patriot Journal Newsletter.

The first page of the newsletter is finished, with the exception of the page border and subhead colors, which will be added later in this project.

Formatting the Second Page of the Newsletter

The second page of the newsletter (Figure 6-1b on page WD 6.05) continues the feature article that began in the first two columns on the first page. The nameplate on the second page is simpler than the one on the first page of the newsletter. In addition to the text in the feature article, page two contains a diagram. The following pages illustrate how to format the second page of the newsletter in this project.

Changing Column Formatting

The document currently is formatted into three columns. The nameplate at the top of the second page, however, should be in a single column. The next step, then, is to change the number of columns at the top of the second page from three to one.

As discussed earlier in this project, Word requires a new section each time you change the number of columns in a document. Thus, you first will insert a continuous section break and then format the section to one column so you can enter the newsletter title.

Perform the following steps to format and enter the newsletter title on the second page of the newsletter.

Steps: To Change Column Formatting

1 Scroll through the document and then position the mouse pointer at the upper-left corner of the second page of the newsletter. Click Insert on the menu bar and then click Break. When the Break dialog box displays, click Continuous in the Section break types area. Point to the OK button.

Word displays the Break dialog box (Figure 6-56). A continuous section break will place the nameplate on the same physical page as the three columns of the continued feature article.

2 Click the OK button.

Word inserts a continuous section break above the insertion point.

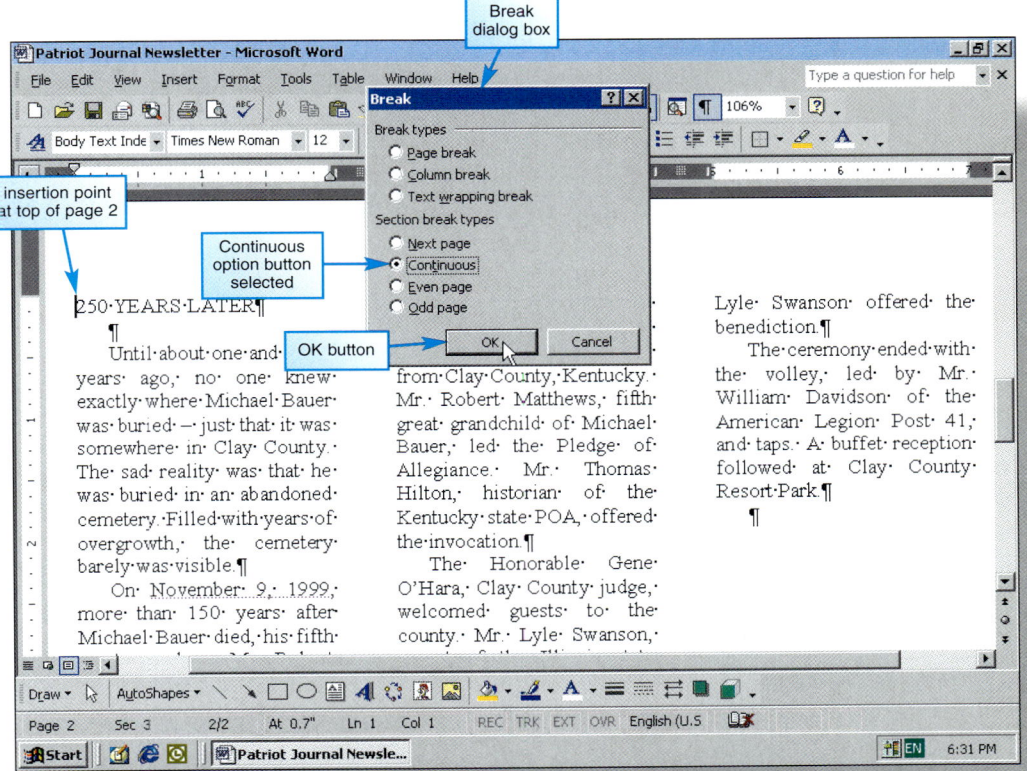

FIGURE 6-56

3 Press the UP ARROW key to position the insertion point in section 3 to the left of the section break notation. Click the Columns button on the Standard toolbar. Point to the first column in the columns list.

Word displays the columns list (Figure 6-57).

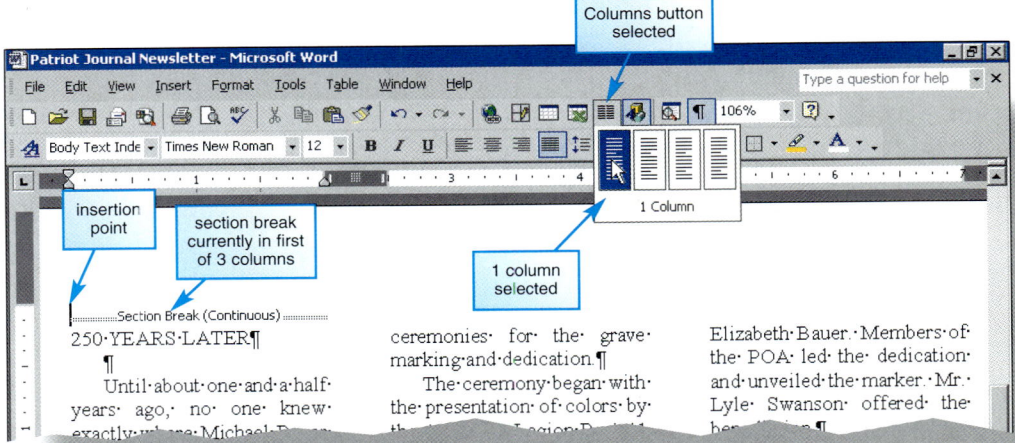

FIGURE 6-57

4 **Click the first column in the columns list.**

Word formats the current section to one column (Figure 6-58). The section break now extends from the left margin to the right margin.

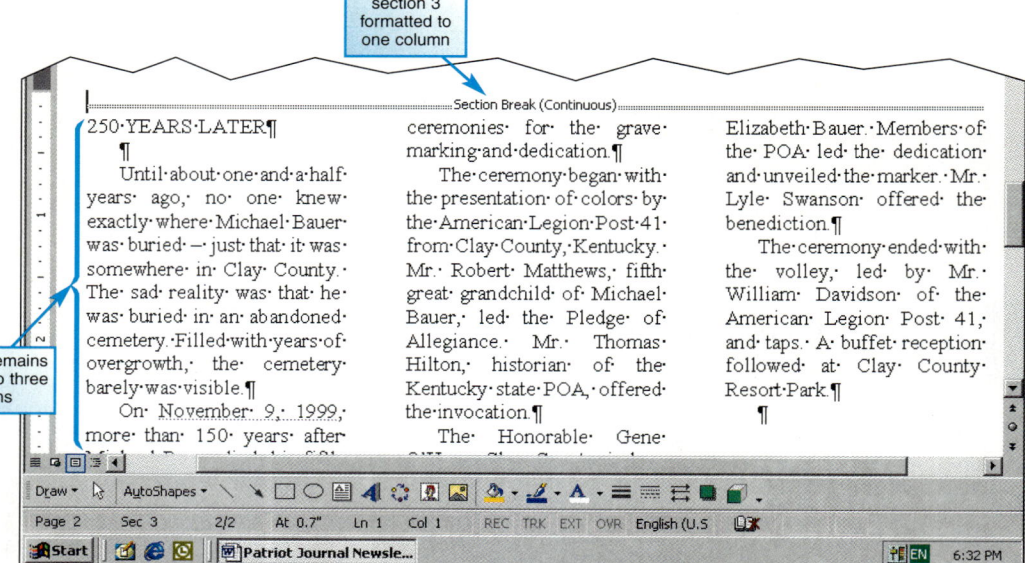

FIGURE 6-58

More About

Columns

If you already have typed text and would like it to be formatted in a different number of columns, select the text, click the Columns button on the Standard toolbar, and then click the number of columns desired in the columns list. Word automatically creates a new section for the newly formatted columns.

Perform the following steps to enter the newsletter title at the top of the second page in section 3.

TO FORMAT AND ENTER TEXT

1 With the insertion point in section 3 to the left of the section break notation, press the ENTER key twice. Press the UP ARROW key.

2 Click the Font Size box arrow on the Formatting toolbar and then click 16. Click the Bold button on the Formatting toolbar. Click the Center button on the Formatting toolbar. Click the Font Color button arrow and then click Blue.

3 Type PATRIOT JOURNAL and then press the ENTER key.

4 Click the Style box arrow on the Formatting toolbar and then click Clear Formatting.

The title is formatted and entered at the top of the second page of the newsletter (Figure 6-59).

More About

Inner Page Nameplates

The top of the inner pages of the newsletter may or may not have a nameplate. If you choose to create one for your inner pages, it should not be the same as, or compete with, the one on the first page. Inner page nameplates usually contain only a portion of the nameplate from the first page of a newsletter.

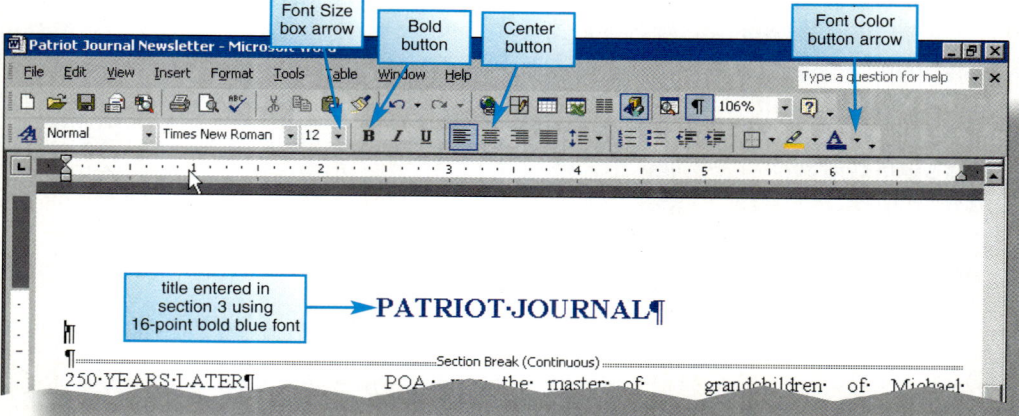

FIGURE 6-59

Using the Paste Special Command to Link Text

The rest of the nameplate on the second page is identical to the nameplate on the first page. That is, the issue information line displays below the newsletter title. A double line displays below the issue information line. Then, the title of the feature article displays one blank line below the bottom border. Thus, you will copy these lines of text from the nameplate on the first page and then paste it onto the second page.

The item you are copying is called the **source object**. The item you paste is called the **destination object**. Thus, the source object is the bottom part of the nameplate on the first page, and the destination object will be the bottom part of the nameplate on the second page of the newsletter.

Instead of using the Paste button to paste the source object to the destination object, you will use the Paste Special command. The **Paste Special command** allows you to link the pasted (destination) object to the copied (source) object. The advantage of linking these objects together is that if the source object ever changes, the destination object also will change automatically. That is, if you change the bottom part of the nameplate on page 1, the bottom part of the nameplate on page 2 also will change.

Perform the following steps to link a copied item.

Links

If you wanted to modify the location of the source file in a link or remove a link while leaving the source text in the destination document, click the link, click Edit on the menu bar and then click Links to display the Links dialog box. Follow the instructions in the dialog box to remove or modify the link.

To Link a Copied Item

1 Press CTRL+HOME to position the insertion point at the top of page 1. If necessary, scroll down. Drag through lines 2, 3, and 4 in the nameplate. Click the Copy button on the Standard toolbar.

The second, third, and fourth lines on the first page of the newsletter are copied to the Clipboard (Figure 6-60).

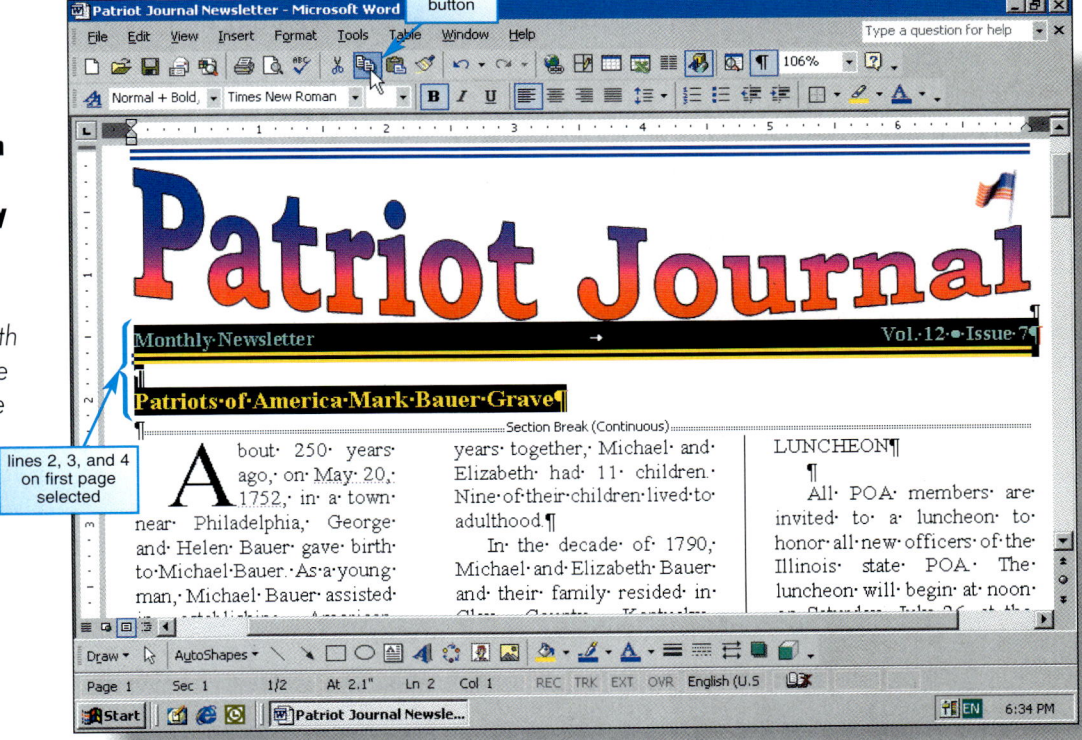

FIGURE 6-60

2 Press SHIFT+F5 to reposition the insertion point on line 2 of the second page of the newsletter. Click Edit on the menu bar and then point to Paste Special.

Recall that pressing SHIFT+F5 repositions the insertion point at your last editing location (Figure 6-61).

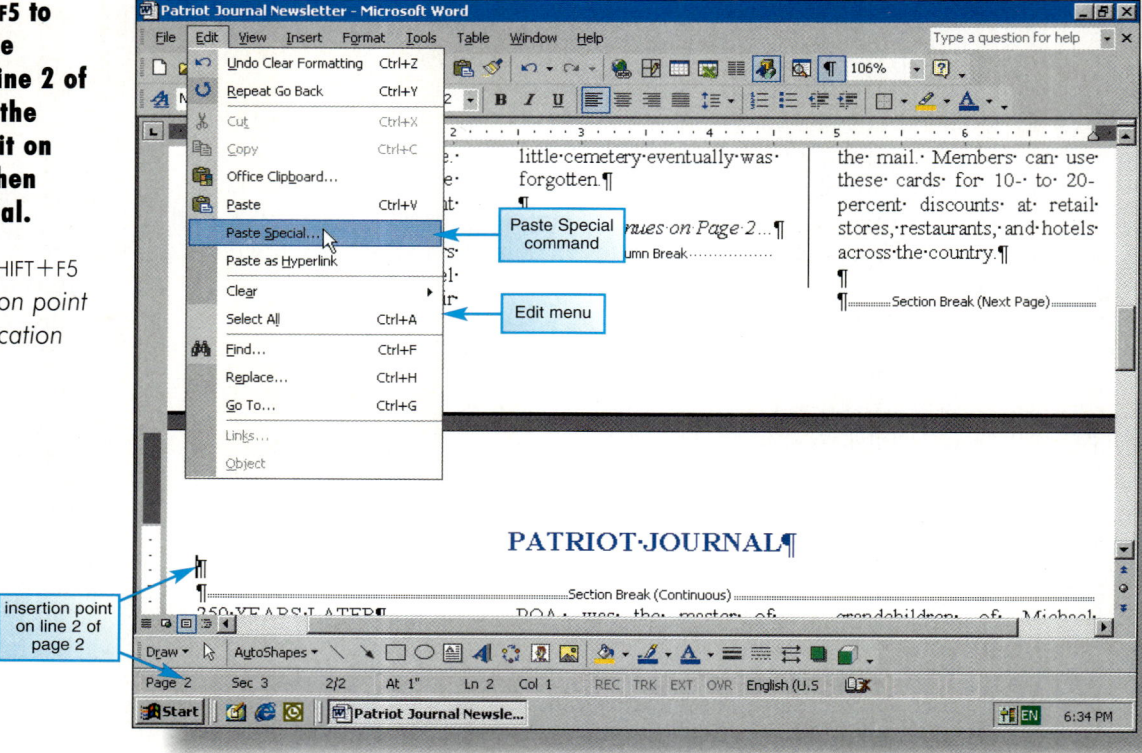

FIGURE 6-61

3 Click Paste Special. When the Paste Special dialog box displays, click Paste link. Click Formatted Text (RTF) in the As list and then point to the OK button.

Word displays the Paste Special dialog box (Figure 6-62).

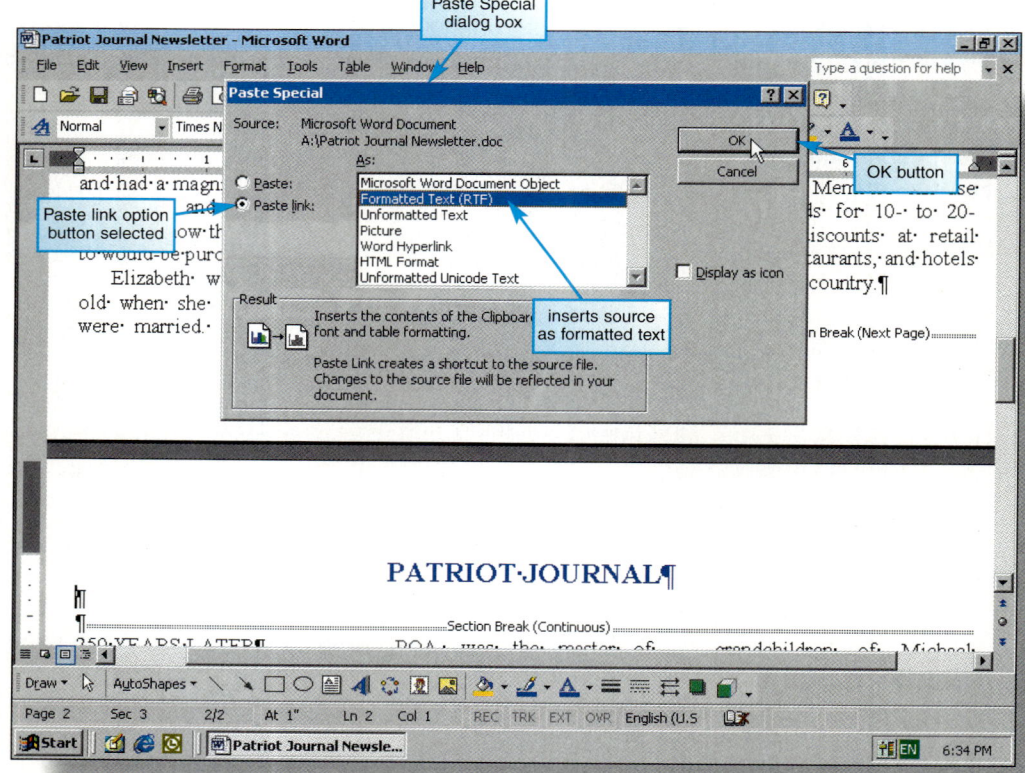

FIGURE 6-62

4 **Click the OK button. Press the DELETE key to delete the extra paragraph mark between the nameplate and the continuous section break on the second page.**

Word pastes the copied object at the location of the insertion point (Figure 6-63).

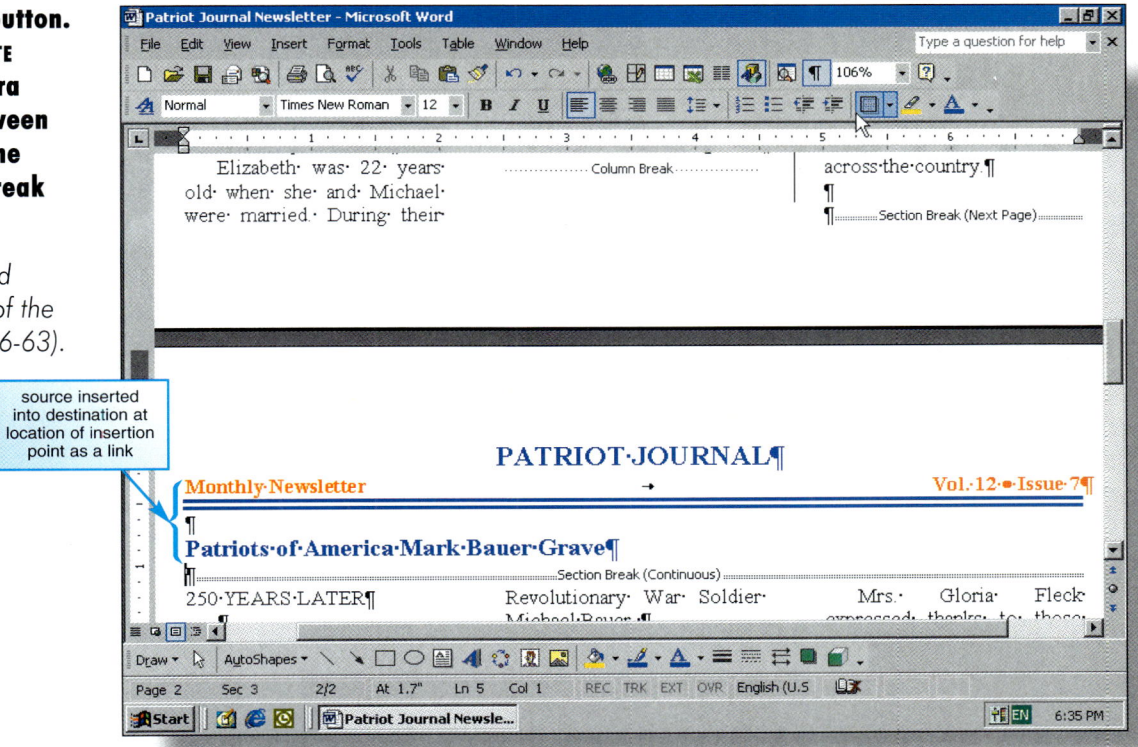

FIGURE 6-63

1. In Voice Command mode, say "Edit, Paste Special, Paste link, [select Formatted Text (RTF)], OK"

If a link, for some reason, is not updated automatically, click the link and then press the F9 key to update it manually. When you click in the link, it displays shaded in gray. This shading does not print; it helps you identify this item as a link.

Perform the next step to bold the subhead, 250 YEARS LATER.

TO BOLD TEXT

1 Click to the left of the line, 250 YEARS LATER, to select it.

2 Click the Bold button on the Formatting toolbar.

Word bolds the subhead, 250 YEARS LATER.

Subheads

A subhead should have emphasis in the body of the newsletter, but it should not compete with the text in the nameplate. In general, subheads should be one or two points larger than the body text. Usually subheads are bold, especially if they are the same font size as the body text.

Balancing Columns

Currently, the text on the second page of the newsletter completely fills up the first and second columns and spills into a portion of the third column. You would like the text in the three columns to consume the same amount of vertical space. That is, the three columns should be balanced.

To balance columns, you insert a continuous section break at the end of the text, as shown in the steps on the next page.

Steps: To Balance Columns

1 Scroll to the bottom of the text in the third column on the second page of the newsletter and then click the paragraph mark below the text. Click Insert on the menu bar and then click Break. When the Break dialog box displays, click Continuous in the Section break types area. Point to the OK button.

Word displays the Break dialog box (Figure 6-64).

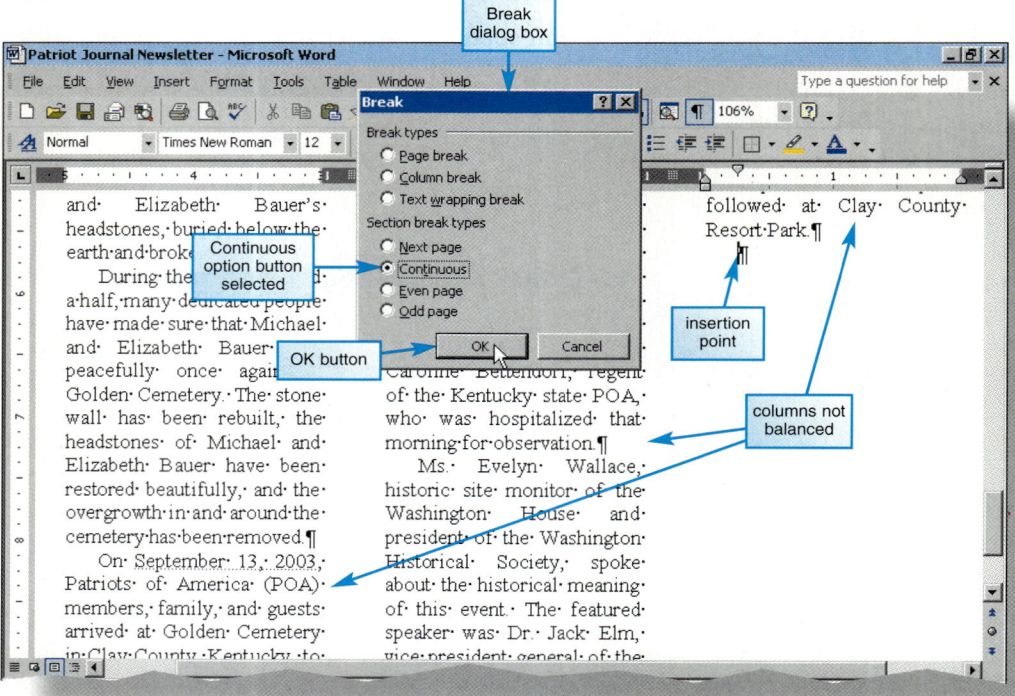

FIGURE 6-64

2 Click the OK button.

Word inserts a continuous section break, which balances the columns on the second page of the newsletter (Figure 6-65).

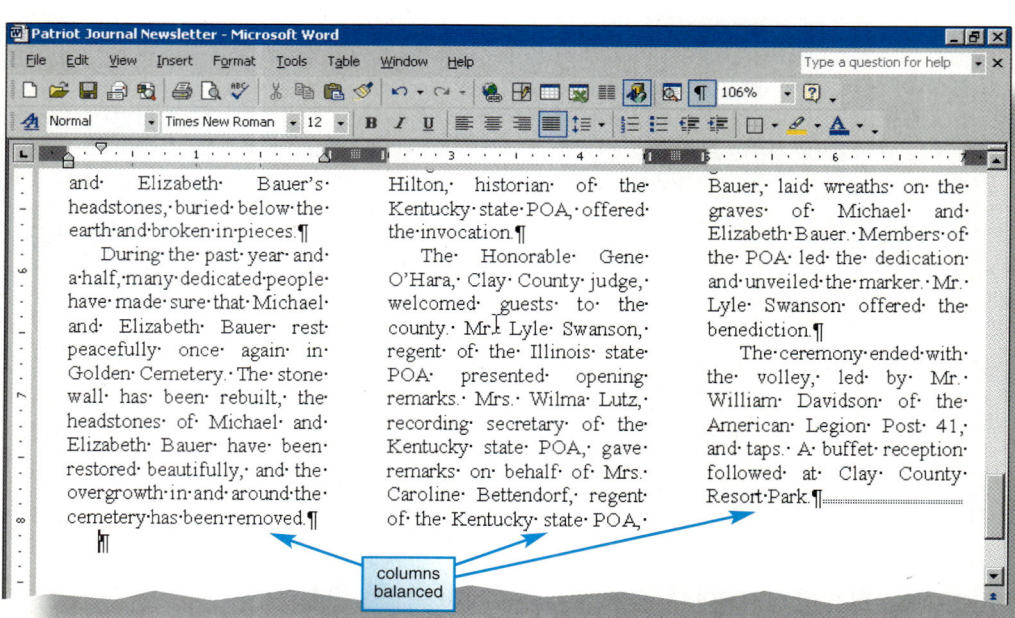

FIGURE 6-65

1. In Voice Command mode, say, "Insert, Break, Continuous, OK"

Perform the following step to save the document again.

TO SAVE A DOCUMENT

1 With the disk containing the newsletter file in drive A, click the Save button on the Standard toolbar.

Word saves the document again with the file name, Patriot Journal Newsletter.

The next step is to insert a diagram between the second and third columns on the second page of the newsletter.

Inserting a Diagram

In Word, you can insert an organization chart and five other types of diagrams in your documents: cycle, pyramid, radial, venn, and target. Table 6-1 on the next page briefly describes the purpose of each of these diagrams.

When working with these diagrams, it is best to insert the diagram in a single column layout so that you easily can see all its components. At this point in the newsletter, the number of columns is three. Thus, you will open a new document window, which has one column, insert and format the diagram, and then copy it to the newsletter.

Perform the following steps to insert a pyramid diagram into a new document window.

Steps To Insert a Diagram

1 **Click the New Blank Document button on the Standard toolbar. When Word displays a blank document window, click the Insert Diagram or Organization Chart button on the Drawing toolbar. When the Diagram Gallery dialog box displays, click the pyramid diagram and then point to the OK button.**

Word displays the Diagram Gallery dialog box in a new document window (Figure 6-66).

2 **Click the OK button.**

Word inserts a pyramid diagram in the document window (shown in Figure 6-67 on the next page). The Diagram toolbar displays on the screen.

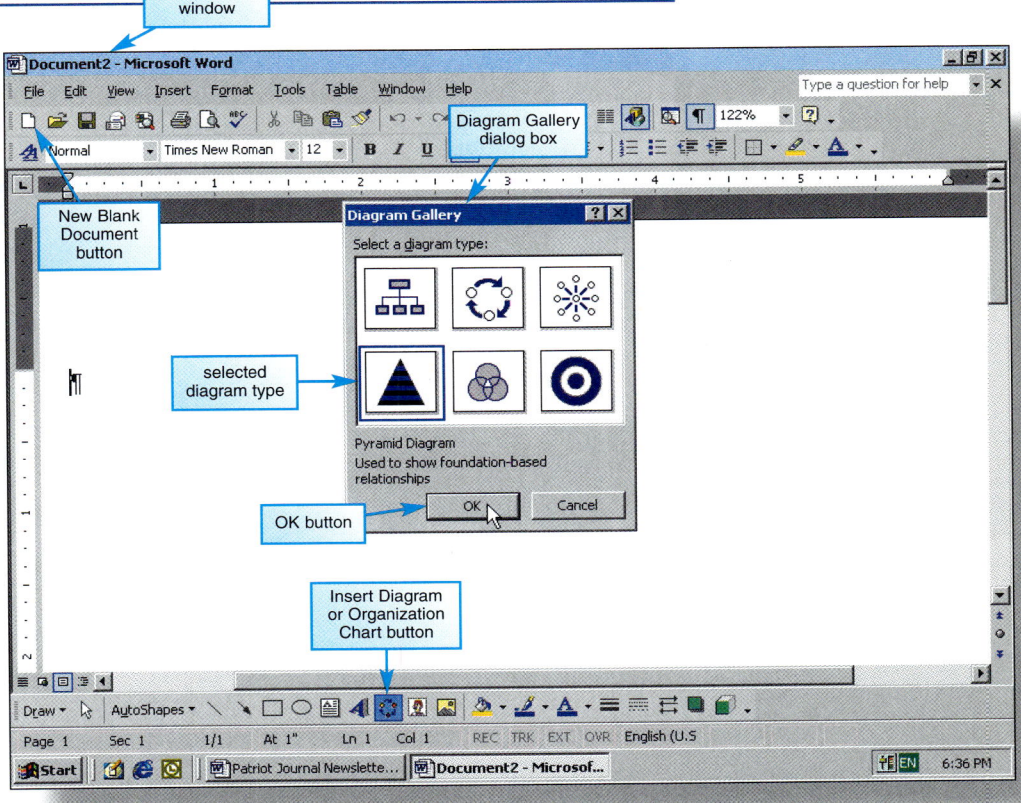

FIGURE 6-66

Table 6-1	Word Diagrams
DIAGRAM TYPE	PURPOSE
Cycle	Shows a process with continuous steps that form a loop
Organization	Shows hierarchical relationships
Pyramid	Shows items that relate to one another
Radial	Shows elements that relate to a central item
Venn	Shows overlapping items
Target	Shows steps toward a goal

The entire pyramid does not fit in the document window. Perform the following steps to change the zoom percentage so more of the pyramid displays.

TO ZOOM TO A PERCENTAGE

1. Click the Zoom box arrow on the Standard toolbar.
2. Click 75%.
3. If necessary, scroll up or down so the entire pyramid displays in the document window.

By changing the zoom percentage to 75%, more of the pyramid displays in the document window (Figure 6-67).

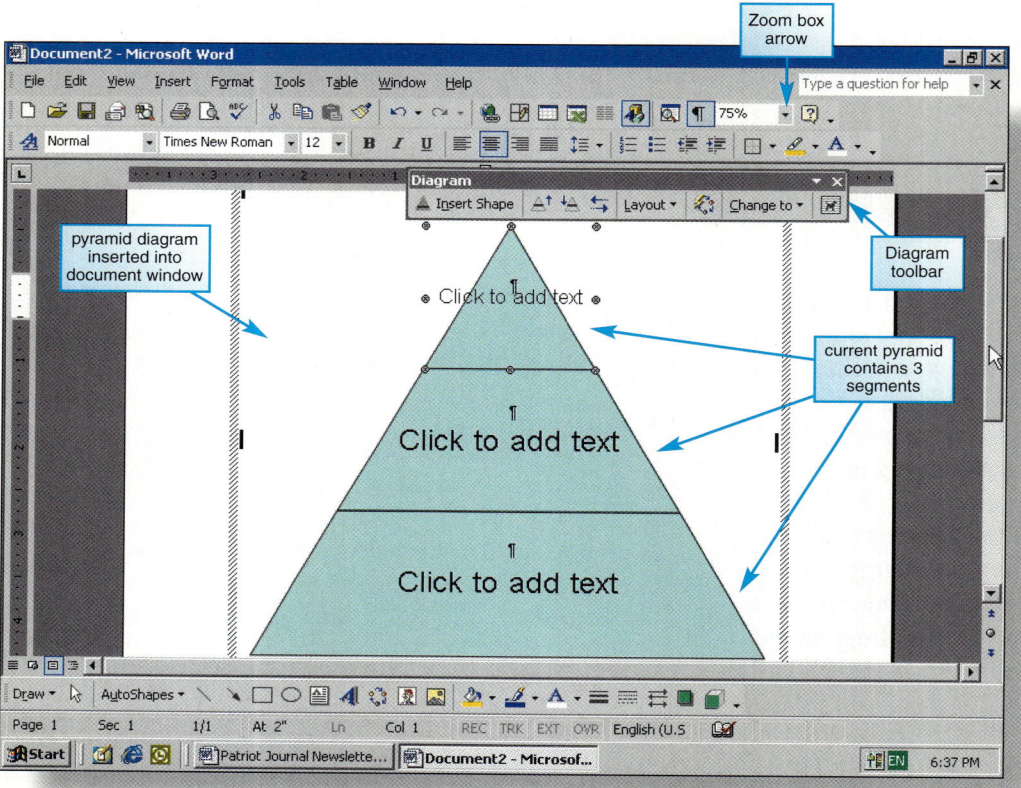

FIGURE 6-67

Diagram Segment Color

To change the fill color in a diagram segment, click the segment, click the Fill Color button arrow on the Drawing toolbar, and then click the desired color. To remove a fill color, click the Fill Color button arrow on the Drawing toolbar and then click No Fill.

The pyramid diagram in this newsletter is to contain a total of eight segments (Figure 6-1b on page 6.05). The current pyramid diagram contains only three segments. Thus, the next step is to add five more segments to the diagram. Perform the following step to add segments to a diagram.

Steps: To Add Segments to a Diagram

1 **With the diagram selected, click the Insert Shape button on the Diagram toolbar five times.**

Word adds five segments to the diagram (Figure 6-68).

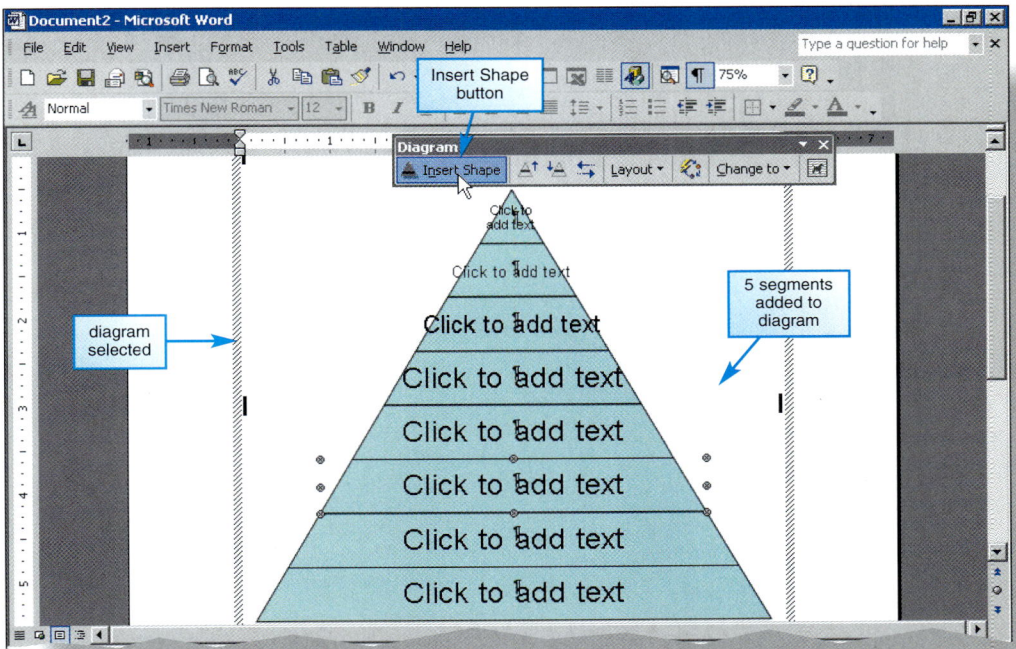

FIGURE 6-68

Other Ways

1. Right-click edge of segment, click Insert Shape on shortcut menu
2. With Diagram toolbar displaying, in Voice Command mode, say "Insert Shape"

If you add too many segments to a diagram, you can remove a segment. Simply click the edges of a segment to select it and then click the Cut button on the Standard toolbar or press the DELETE key.

The next step is to add text to the diagram. In this project, the top segment does not contain any text. You do not want it, however, to contain the placeholder text, Click to add text. Thus, to delete the placeholder text, you will select it and then press the SPACEBAR.

Perform the following steps to add text to the segments of the diagram.

Steps: To Add Text to a Diagram

1 **Click in the bottom (eighth) segment in the pyramid to select it. Type** John Meyers Sign Company **as the segment text.**

Word selects and adds text to the bottom segment (Figure 6-69).

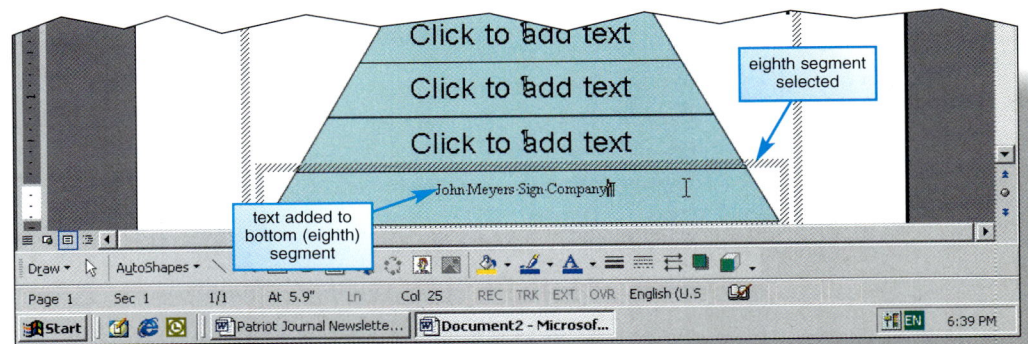

FIGURE 6-69

2 **Click the seventh segment. Type** Anderson Gravel Company **and then click the sixth segment. Type** American Legion Post 41 **and then click the fifth segment. Type** Clay County Resort Park **and then click the fourth segment. Type** Clay County Trucking **and then click the third segment. Type** Friends **and then click the second segment. Type** Family **and then click the first (top) segment. Press the SPACEBAR.**

The text is added to the diagram (Figure 6-70).

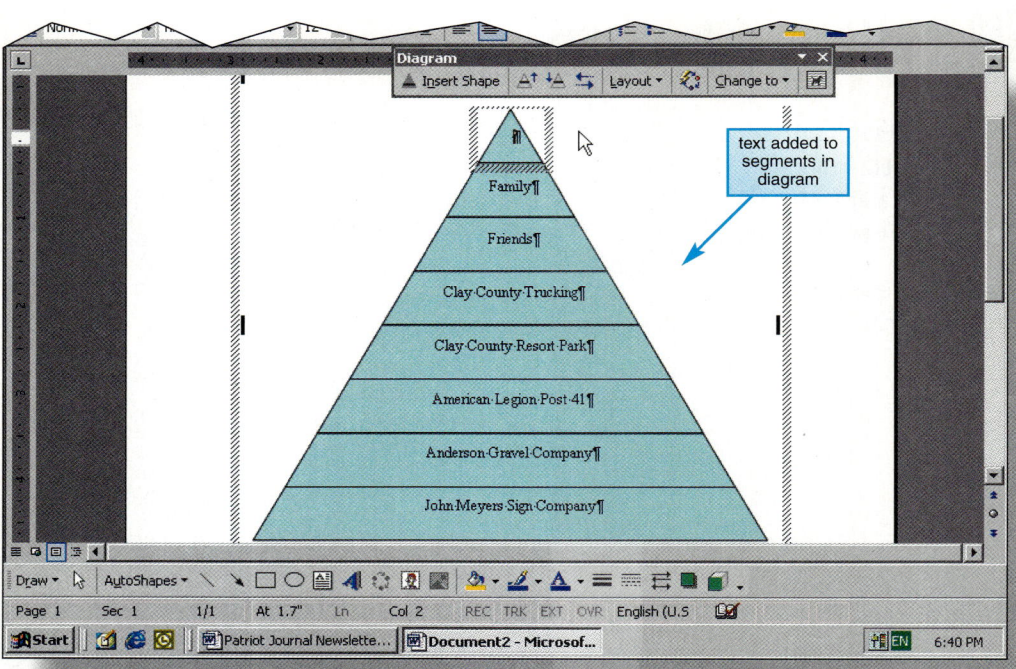

FIGURE 6-70

The next step is to format the diagram using one of the built-in AutoFormat styles, as shown in the following steps.

Steps To AutoFormat a Diagram

1 **Click the AutoFormat button on the Diagram toolbar. When the Diagram Style Gallery dialog box displays, click Square Shadows in the Select a Diagram Style list and then point to the Apply button.**

Word displays the Diagram Style Gallery dialog box (Figure 6-71). The selected style will be applied to the diagram in the document window.

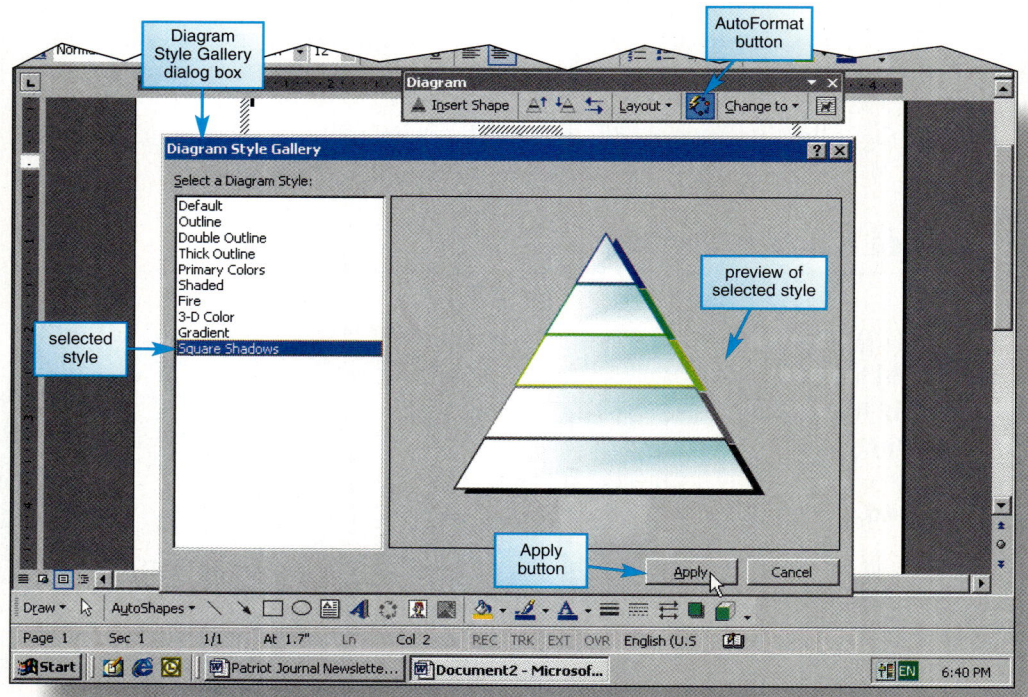

FIGURE 6-71

2 **Click the Apply button.**

Word applies the square shadows style to the diagram (Figure 6-72).

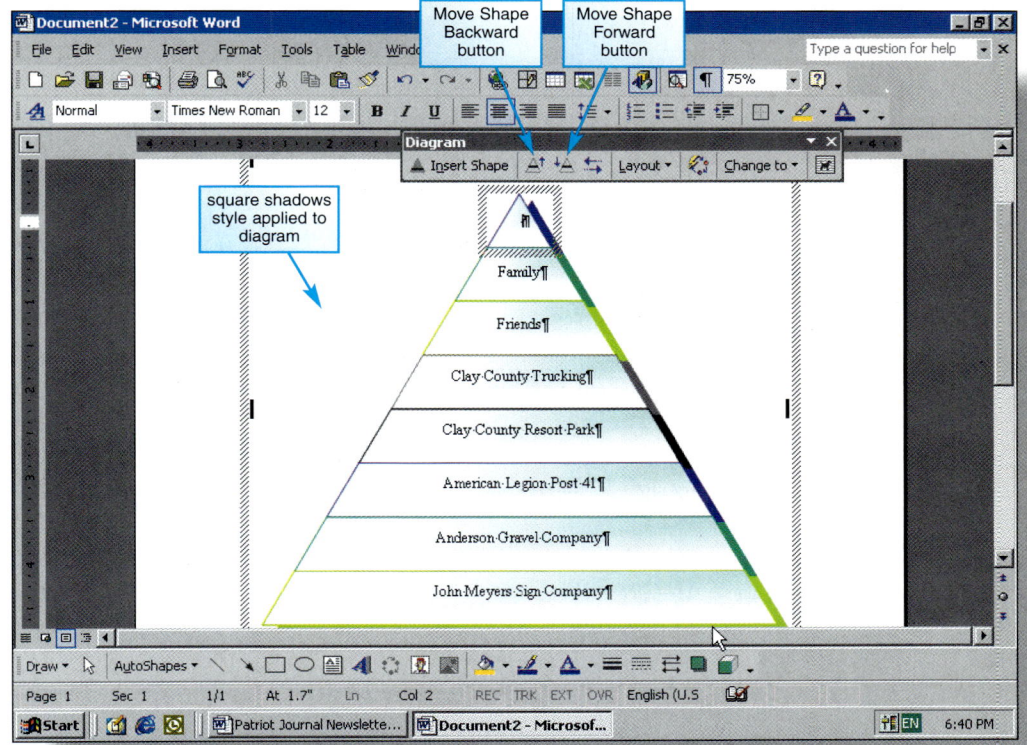

FIGURE 6-72

The next step is to reduce the size of the diagram so it will fit in the upper-right corner of the second page of the newsletter. You resize a diagram the same as any other graphic object. That is, you can drag its sizing handles or enter exact measurements into the Format Dialog box.

This diagram should be 3.2 inches tall and 3.5 inches wide. Perform the following steps to enter these measurements into the Format Diagram dialog box to resize the diagram.

TO RESIZE A DIAGRAM

1. Point to the frame surrounding the diagram and double-click when the mouse pointer has a four-headed arrow attached to it. When the Format Diagram dialog box displays, if necessary, click the Size tab. Click the Lock aspect ratio check box to remove the check mark. In the Size and rotate area, type 3.2 in the Height text box and then type 3.5 in the Width text box. (Figure 6-73 on the next page).
2. Click the OK button.

Word resizes the diagram (shown in Figure 6-74 on page WD 6.55).

Moving Diagram Segments

To move a segment of a diagram, select the segment and then click either the Move Shape Forward button or the Move Shape Backward button on the Diagram toolbar. For example, each time you click the Move Shape Forward button, the selected segment moves down one position in the diagram.

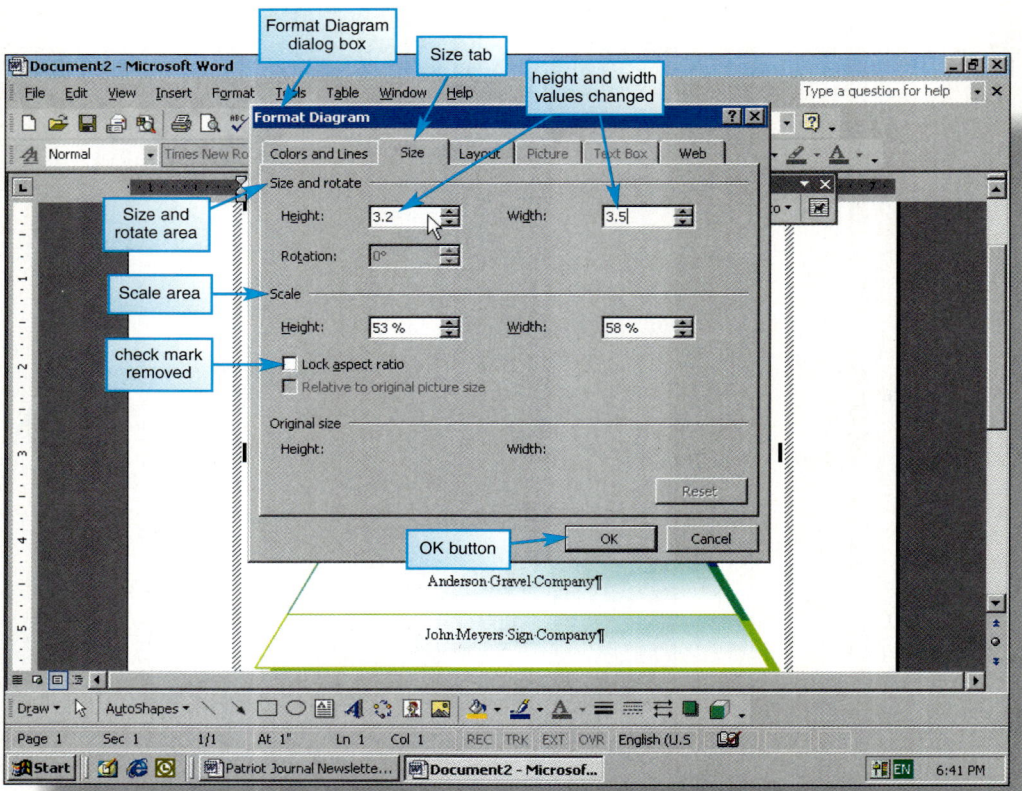

FIGURE 6-73

Notice in Figure 6-73 in the Scale area of the Format Diagram dialog box that the height and width percentages differ. When the Lock aspect ratio check box contains a check mark, Word keeps these values the same to maintain the proportions of the graphic. Thus, if you type height and width values in the Size and rotate area that distort these proportions, Word readjusts your entries. If you want the percentages to differ, remove the check mark from the Lock aspect ratio check box so Word will allow the proportions to vary.

The diagram now is too small to read. Perform the following steps to zoom text width.

TO ZOOM TEXT WIDTH

1 Click the Zoom box arrow on the Standard toolbar.

2 Click Text Width.

When you zoom text width, the text in the diagram is readable (shown in Figure 6-74).

As shown in Figure 6-1b on page 6.05, the diagram is to have a callout attached to its upper-right edge. A callout is a type of AutoShape. Recall in Project 5 you added a banner AutoShape to a document. Perform the following steps to add and format a callout AutoShape to the diagram.

Formatting the Second Page of the Newsletter • WD 6.55

 To Add and Format a Callout AutoShape

1 **Click the AutoShapes button on the Drawing toolbar. Point to Callouts and then point to Line Callout 3 (Accent Bar), as shown in Figure 6-74.**

2 **Click Line Callout 3 (Accent Bar). Position the crosshair mouse pointer directly above the pyramid and then click.**

Word adds a callout shape to the diagram. You need to resize and move the callout so it does not cover the pyramid.

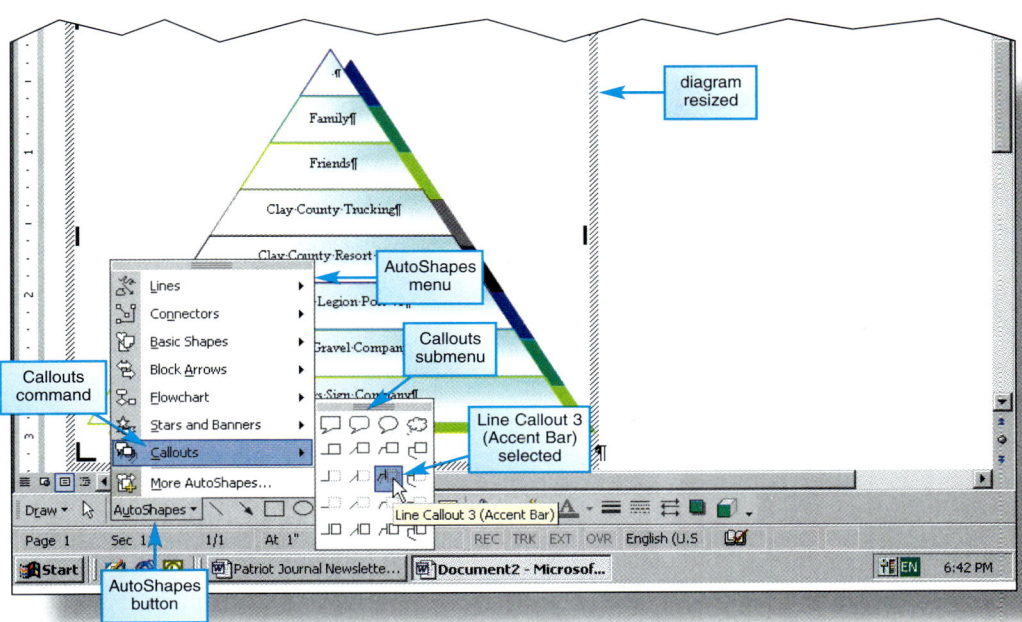

FIGURE 6-74

3 **Point to the edge of the callout and double-click when the mouse pointer has a four-headed arrow attached to it. When the Format AutoShape dialog box displays, if necessary, click the Size tab. In the Size and rotate area, type 2.1 in the Height text box and then type .8 in the Width text box. Point to the OK button.**

Word displays the Format AutoShape dialog box (Figure 6-75).

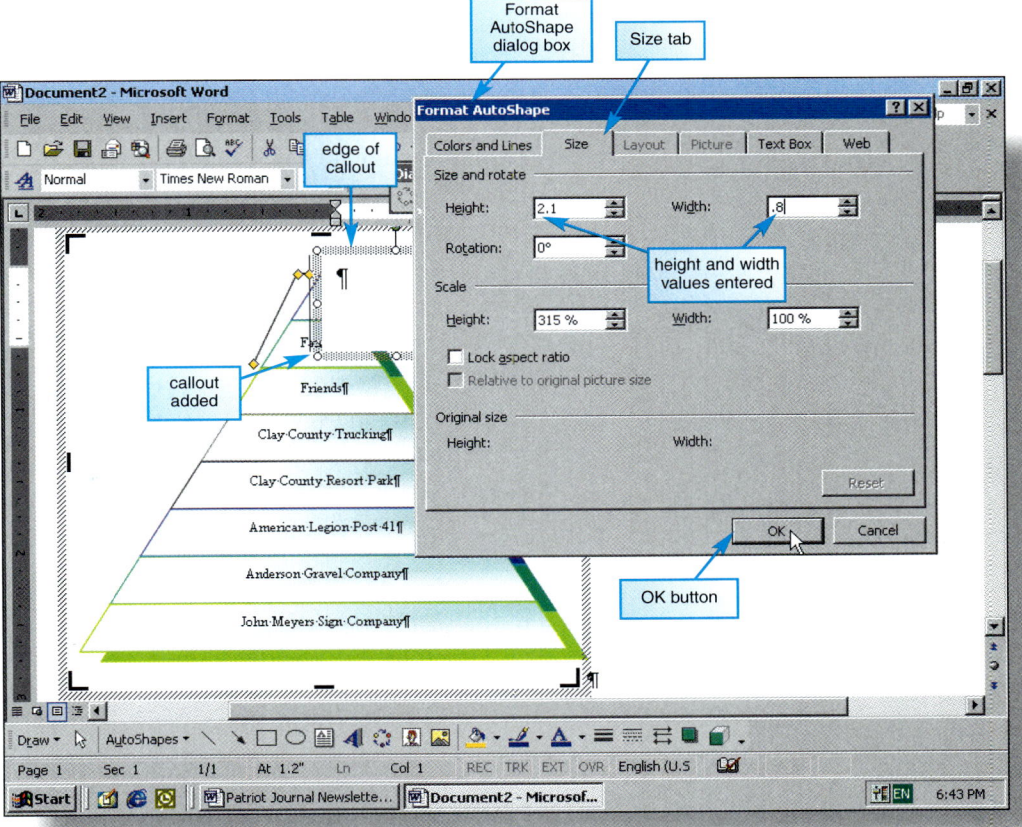

FIGURE 6-75

4 **Click the OK button.**

Word resizes the AutoShape.

5 **Drag the AutoShape up and to the right so it is located similarly to Figure 6-76. Drag the move handle (the yellow diamond) at the end of the connecting line to position it on the top section of the pyramid.**

Word displays the AutoShape to the right of the pyramid (Figure 6-76).

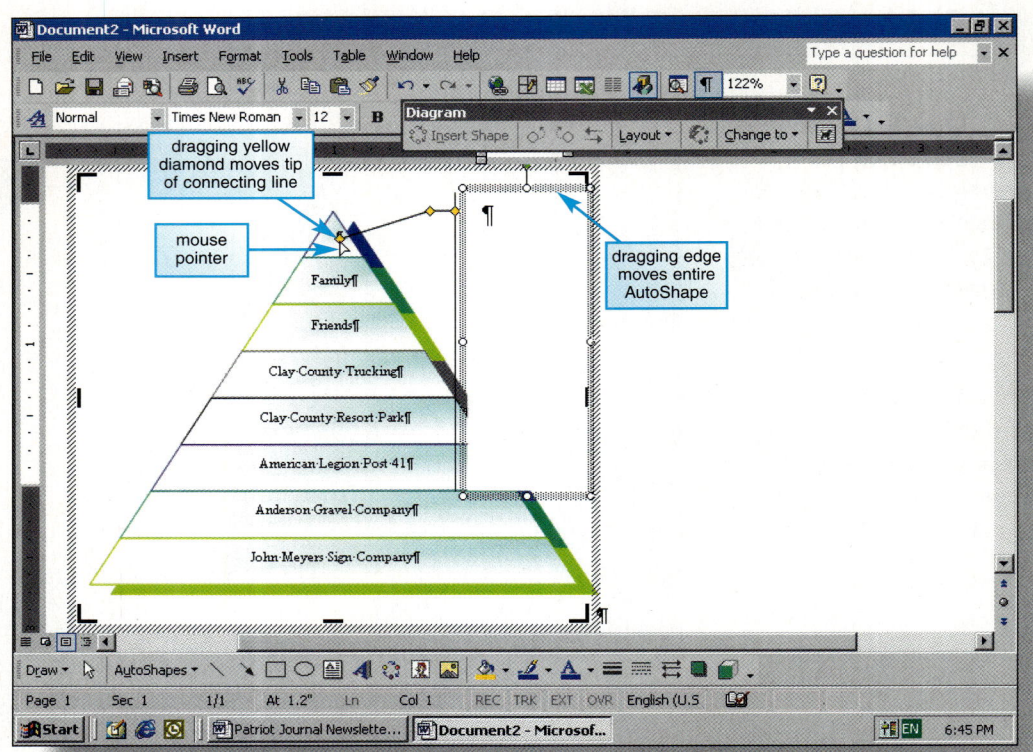

FIGURE 6-76

Perform the following steps to add text to the AutoShape.

TO ADD TEXT TO AN AUTOSHAPE

1 If necessary, drag the Diagram toolbar so it does not cover the Formatting toolbar. Click the paragraph mark in the AutoShape. Click the Font box arrow on the Formatting toolbar and then click Arial Narrow. Click the Font Size box arrow on the Formatting toolbar and then click 10. Click the Font Color button arrow on the Formatting toolbar and then click Green.

2 Type `Many people, companies, and groups helped make this event a success.`

The text is entered in the AutoShape (shown in Figure 6-77).

Currently, the AutoShape is positioned on top of the pyramid diagram. With the AutoShape in the top layer, notice it covers part of the pyramid. Thus, you want to move the AutoShape behind the diagram. To do this, you use the Order command, as shown in the following steps.

Steps To Reorder Graphic Objects

1 Right-click an edge of the callout AutoShape. Point to Order on the shortcut menu and then point to Send to Back on the Order submenu (Figure 6-77).

2 Click Send to Back.

Word places the AutoShape behind the pyramid (shown in Figure 6-78 on the next page). The AutoShape no longer covers part of the pyramid.

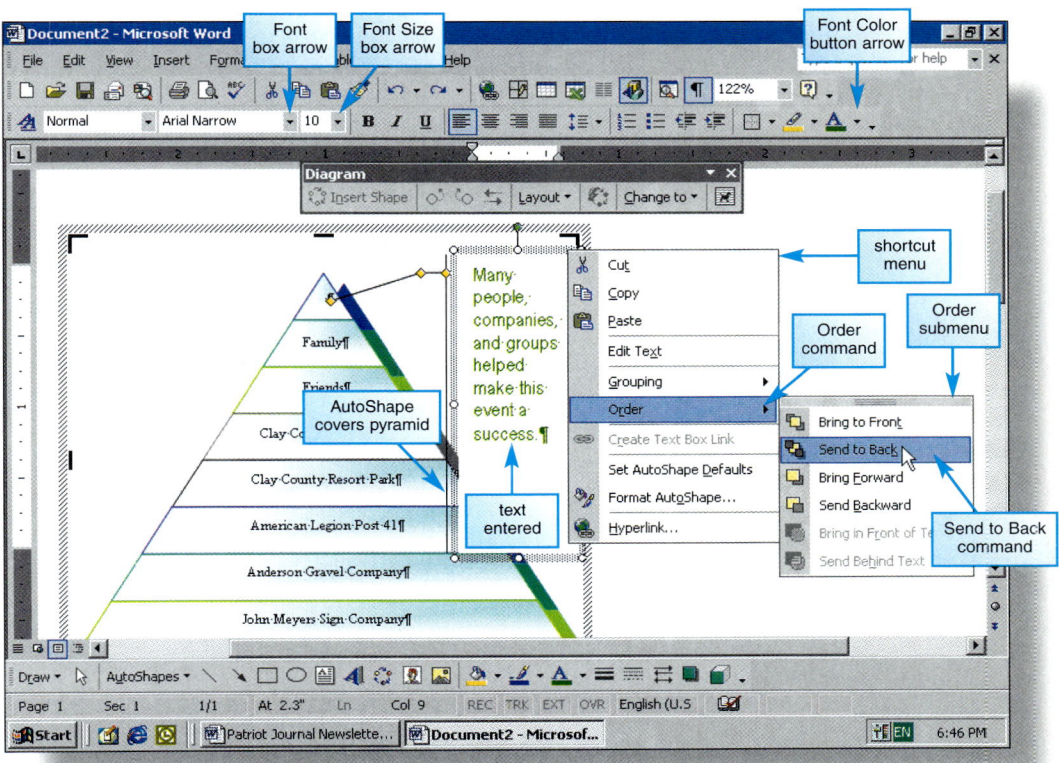

FIGURE 6-77

You want text in the newsletter to wrap around the diagram. Thus, the next step is to change the graphic from inline to floating, as described in the following steps.

TO FORMAT A GRAPHIC AS FLOATING

1 Click the frame around the diagram to select the diagram.

2 Click the Text Wrapping button on the Diagram toolbar and then click Square.

The diagram is formatted to a square wrapping style. This format will become apparent when you copy the diagram into the newsletter.

The diagram is finished. The next step is to copy it from this document window and then paste it into the newsletter. Perform the steps on the next page to copy and paste the diagram.

Other Ways

1. Click Draw button on Drawing toolbar, point to Order on Drawing menu, click Send to Back
2. With Drawing toolbar displaying, in Voice Command mode, say "Draw, Order, Send to Back"

More About

Grouping Graphics

You can group multiple graphic objects together so they become one single object. To do this, select the first object by clicking it and then select an additional object by holding down the CTRL key while clicking it. With all objects selected, click the Draw button on the Drawing toolbar and then click Group.

Steps   To Copy and Paste a Diagram

1 With the diagram still selected, click the Copy button on the Standard toolbar (Figure 6-78).

Word copies the diagram to the Clipboard.

2 Click File on the menu bar and then click Close. When the dialog box displays asking if you want to save the document, click the No button (unless you want to save the diagram by itself).

Word closes the file containing the diagram. It is not necessary to save the file, because the diagram already is on the Clipboard.

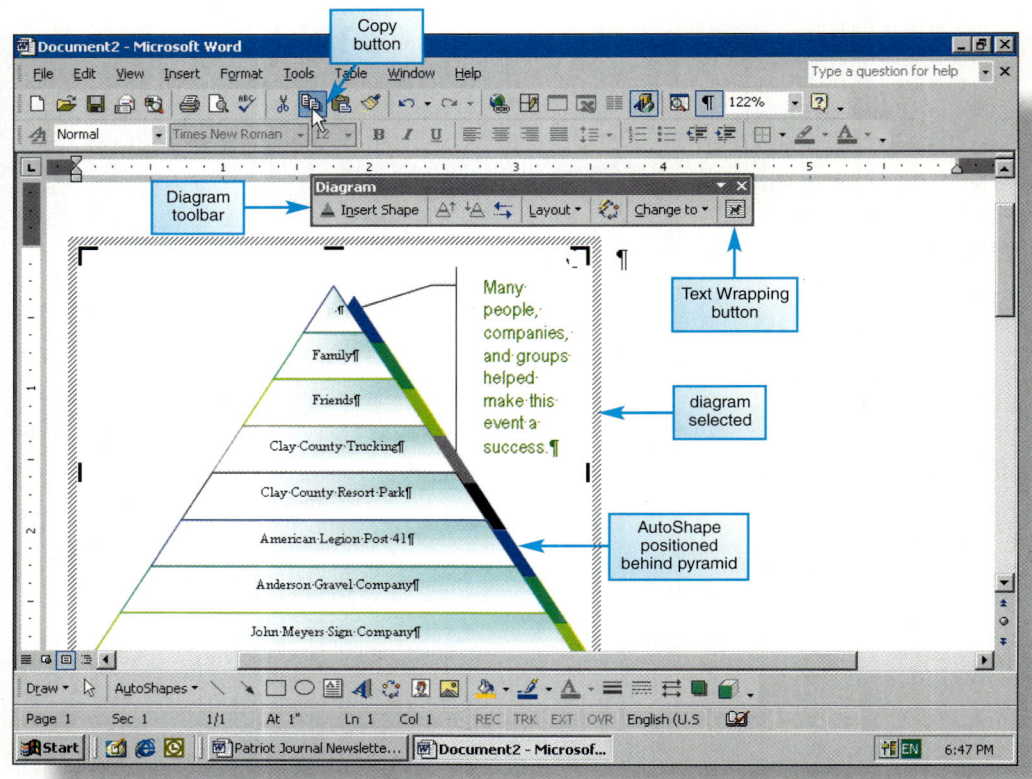

FIGURE 6-78

3 When the newsletter document window redisplays, scroll to display the top of the second page of the newsletter. Right-click at the end of the first paragraph in the second column. Point to Paste on the shortcut menu (Figure 6-79).

4 Click Paste.

Word pastes the diagram from the Clipboard into the document at the location of the insertion point.

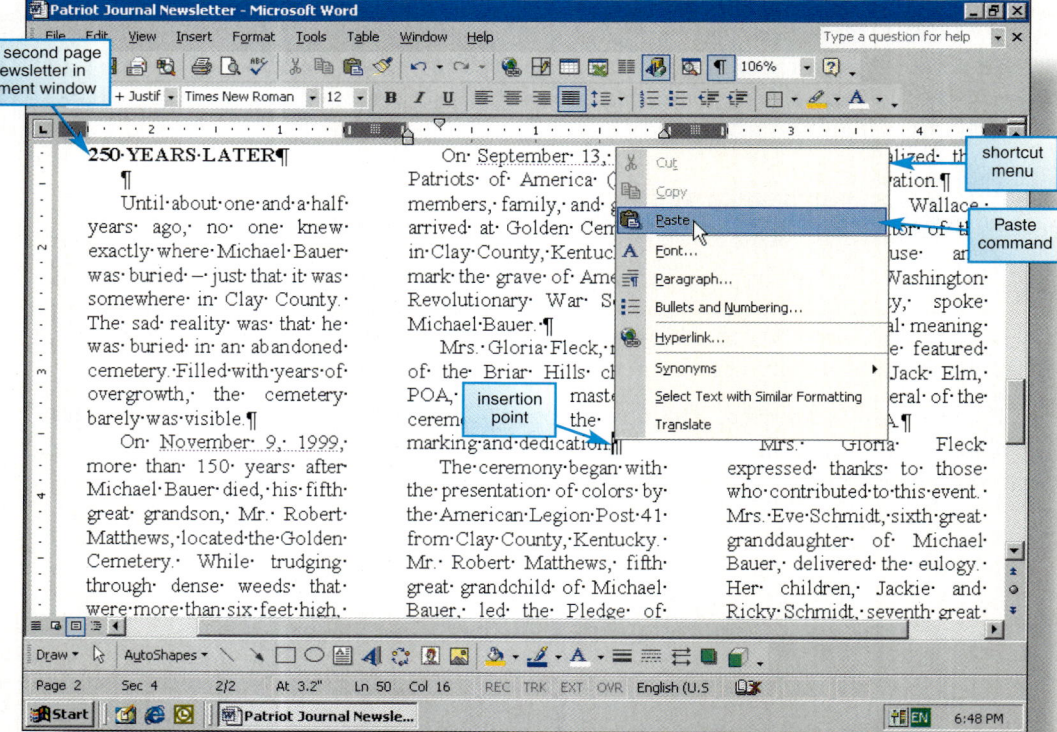

FIGURE 6-79

5 **Point to the frame on the diagram and when the mouse has a four-headed arrow attached to it, drag the diagram to the desired location. You may have to drag the graphic a couple of times to position it similarly to Figure 6-80.**

Depending on the printer you are using, the wordwrap around the diagram may occur in different locations (Figure 6-80).

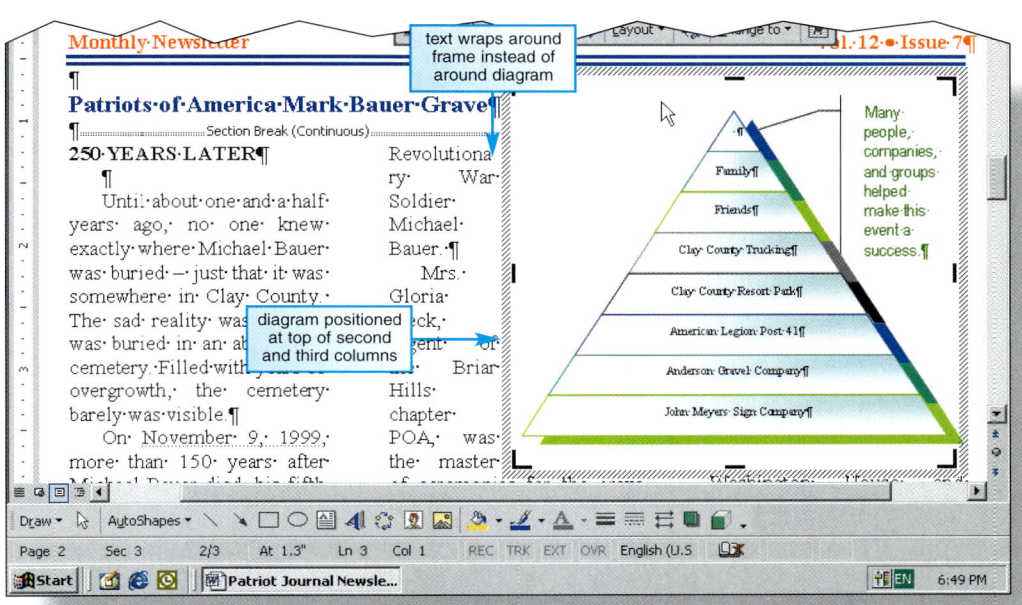

FIGURE 6-80

Notice in Figure 6-80 that the text in column two wraps around the frame, instead of the diagram because earlier you set the wrapping style to Square. To wrap the text around the diagram, change the wrapping style to Edit Wrap Points, as described in the following steps.

Steps To Change a Graphic's Wrapping Style

1 **With the diagram still selected, click the Text Wrapping button on the Diagram toolbar and then point to Edit Wrap Points (Figure 6-81).**

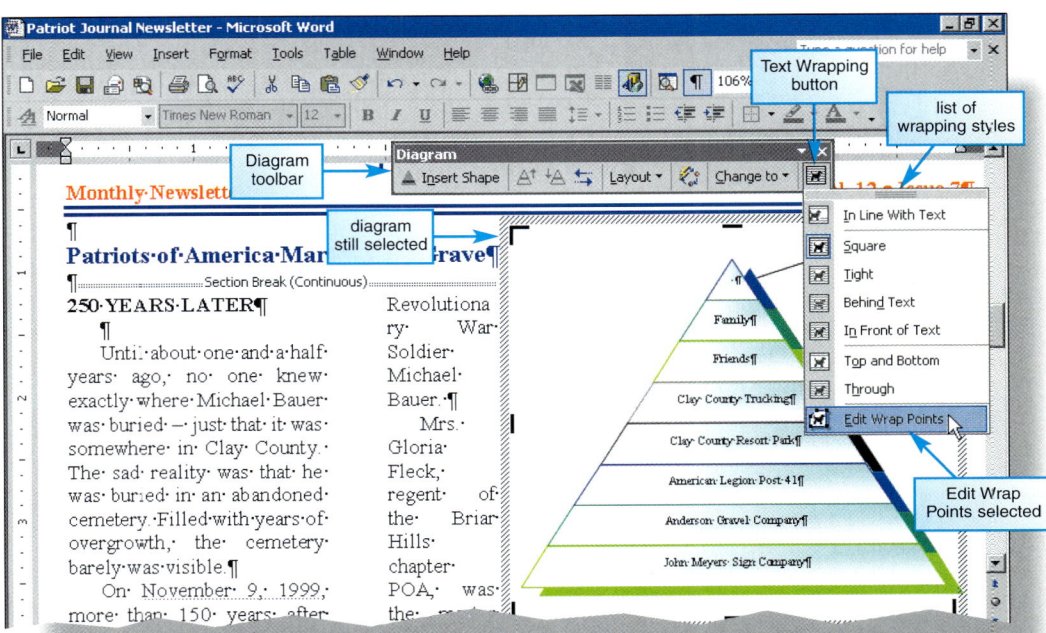

FIGURE 6-81

2 **Click Edit Wrap Points. Click outside the diagram to remove the selection. If the text does not wrap around the diagram properly, drag the text frame until you are satisfied with the wrap. If necessary, you can resize the diagram.**

Word wraps the text around the diagram, instead of around the diagram's frame (Figure 6-82).

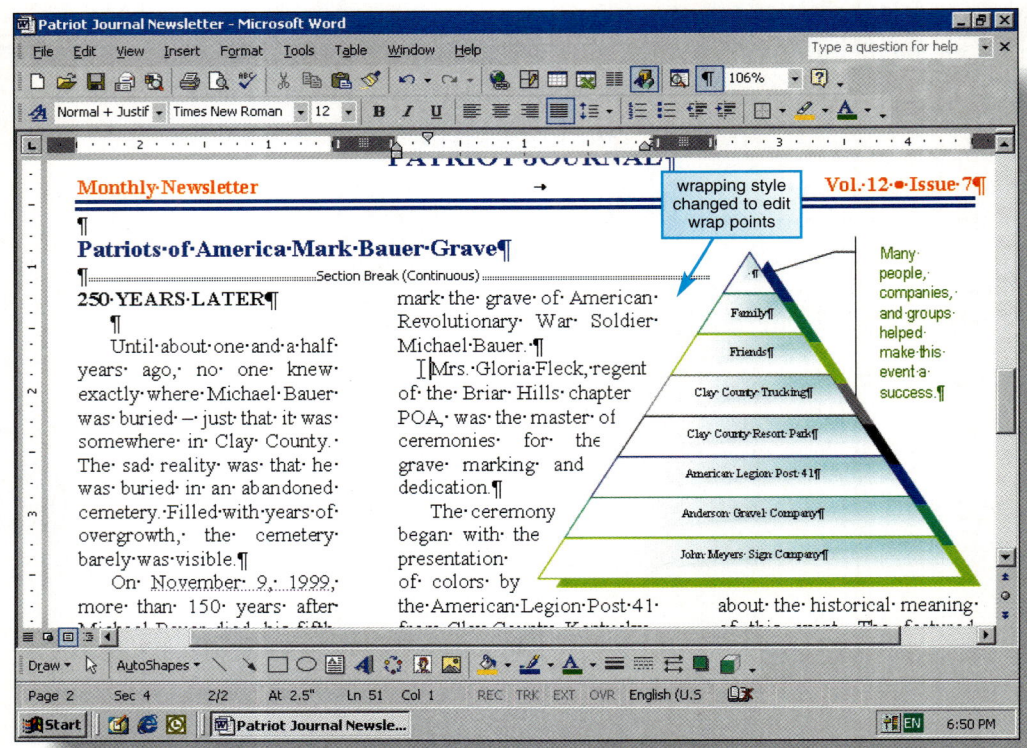

FIGURE 6-82

The text that wraps around the diagram is called wrap-around text. The space between the picture and the wrap-around text is called the run-around.

Perform the following step to save the document again.

TO SAVE A DOCUMENT

 With the disk containing the newsletter file in drive A, click the Save button on the Standard toolbar.

Word saves the document again with the file name, Patriot Journal Newsletter.

Enhancing the Newsletter with Color and a Page Border

You already have added color to many of the characters and lines in the newsletter in this project. You also want to color all of the subheads and add a border around each page of the newsletter. The following pages illustrate these tasks.

The first step is to color the drop cap, as described in the following steps.

Run-Around

The run-around, which is the space between the diagram and the text, should be at least 1/8" and should be the same for all graphics in the newsletter. Adjust the run-around of a selected graphic by clicking the Format Picture button on the Picture toolbar or double-clicking the frame surrounding a diagram, clicking the Layout tab, clicking the Advanced button, adjusting the Distance from text text boxes, and then clicking the OK button.

TO COLOR THE DROP CAP

1. Scroll to the top of the newsletter and then select the drop cap by double-clicking it.
2. Click the Font Color button arrow on the Formatting toolbar and then click Blue.

Word changes the color of the drop cap to blue (shown in Figure 6-83).

Using the Format Painter Button

Recall that subheads, such as LUNCHEON and PATRIOT WEEK, are internal headings placed throughout the body of a newsletter. Currently, all characters in the subheads are capitalized. You also want all of the subheads bold, italicized, and green.

Instead of selecting each subhead one at a time and then formatting it to bold, italics, and green, you can format the first subhead and then copy its formatting to the other subheads. To copy formatting, use the Format Painter button on the Standard toolbar, as shown in the following steps.

More About

Color

Avoid using light colors, like yellow, orange, or light green for text, because these colors are difficult to read. If you do not have a color printer, still change the colors because the colors will print in shades of black and gray. These shades add variety to your newsletter.

Steps: To Use the Format Painter Button

1 Double-click the LUNCHEON heading to select it. Click the Bold button on the Formatting toolbar. Click the Italic button on the Formatting toolbar. Click the Font Color button arrow on the Formatting toolbar and then click Green. Click in the LUNCHEON subhead to position the insertion point in the subhead. Double-click the Format Painter button on the Standard toolbar. Move the mouse pointer into the document window.

Word attaches a paintbrush to the mouse pointer when the Format Painter button is selected (Figure 6-83). The format painter has copied the bold, italic, green format.

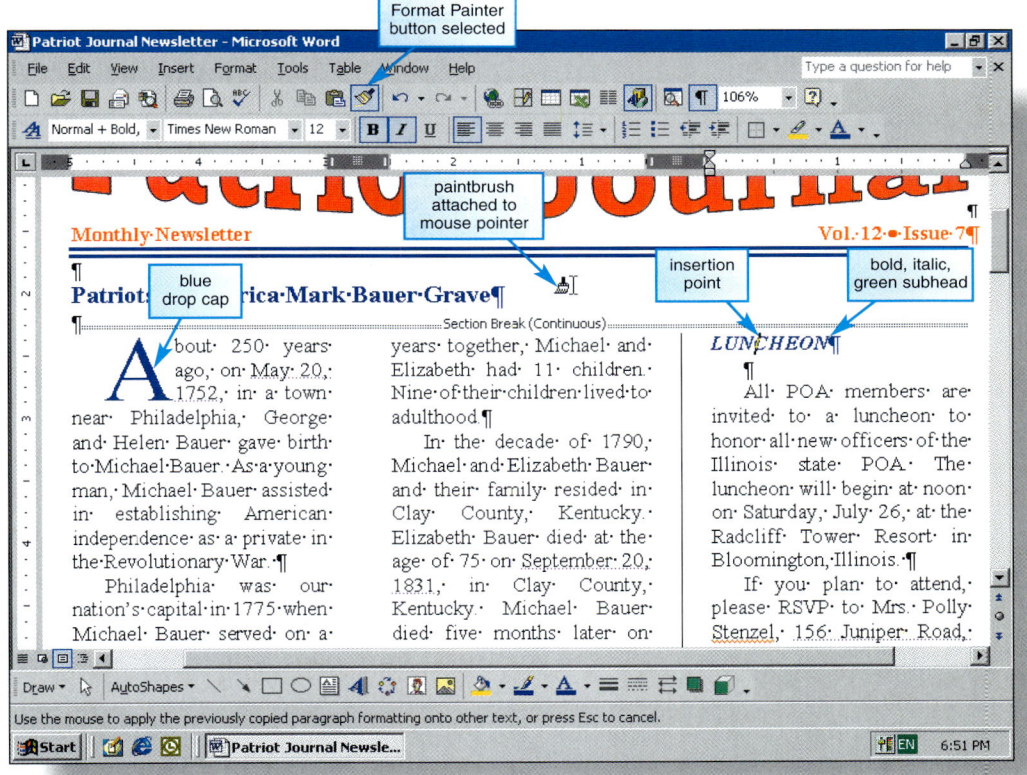

FIGURE 6-83

2 Scroll through the newsletter to the next subhead, PATRIOT WEEK. Select the subhead by clicking to its left. Scroll through the newsletter to the next subhead, POA SAVER CARD. Select the subhead by clicking to its left. Click the Format Painter button on the Standard toolbar to turn it off. Click outside the selection to remove the highlight.

Word copies the bold, italic, green font to the subheads (Figure 6-84).

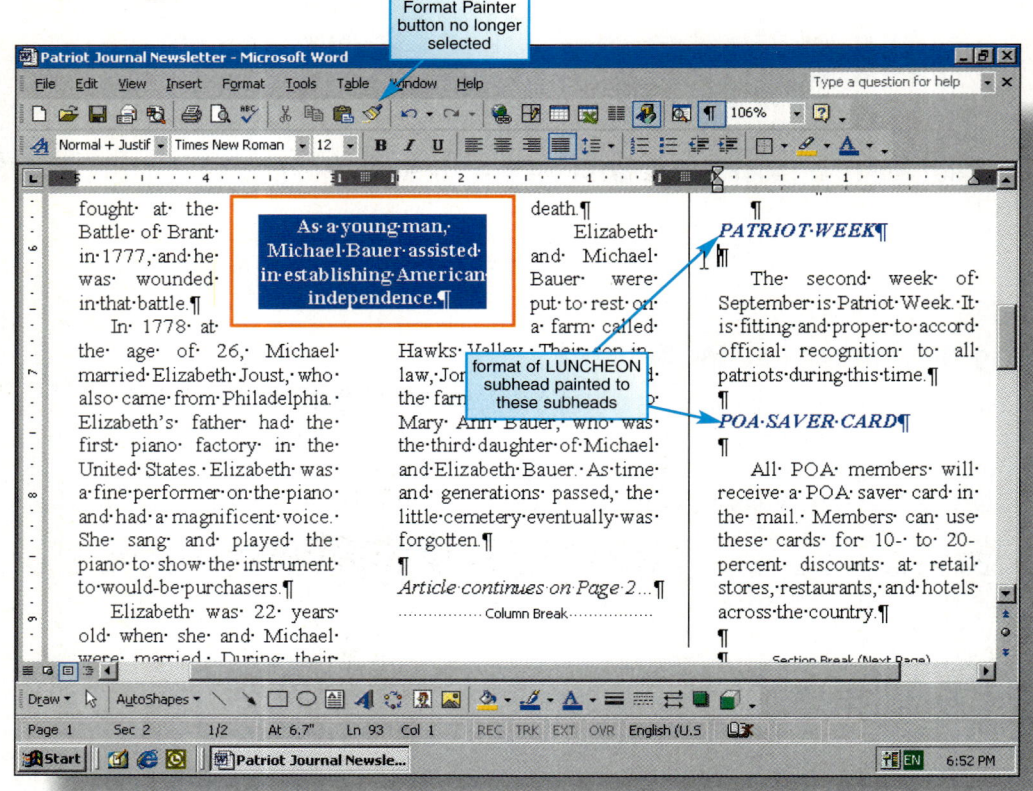

FIGURE 6-84

If you want to copy formatting to just one location in a document, click the Format Painter button, instead of double-clicking it. When you click the Format Painter button, it copies formatting to the next item you select and then immediately turns off the format painter.

The next step in enhancing the newsletter is to add a border around each page.

Adding a Page Border

In this and previous projects, you have added borders to the edges of a paragraph(s). In Word, you also can add a border around the perimeter of an entire page. Page borders add professionalism to your documents. Perform the following steps to add a green page border to the pages of the newsletter.

Page Borders

To place an artistic border around a page, such as trees or balloons, click the Art box arrow in the Page Border sheet in the Borders and Shading dialog box (Figure 6-85), click the desired artistic border, and then click the OK button. To place a border around just a certain page in a document, you must place that page in a separate section and then instruct Word to place the border in just that section.

Enhancing the Newsletter with Color and a Page Border • WD 6.63

Steps To Add a Page Border

1 **Click Format on the menu bar and then click Borders and Shading. When the Borders and Shading dialog box displays, if necessary, click the Page Border tab. Click Box in the Setting area. Scroll through the Style list and click the style shown in Figure 6-85. Click the Color box arrow and then click Green. Point to the OK button.**

Word displays the Borders and Shading dialog box (Figure 6-85). The page border is set to a 3-point green box.

2 **Click the OK button.**

Word places a page border on each page of the newsletter (shown in Figure 6-86 on the next page).

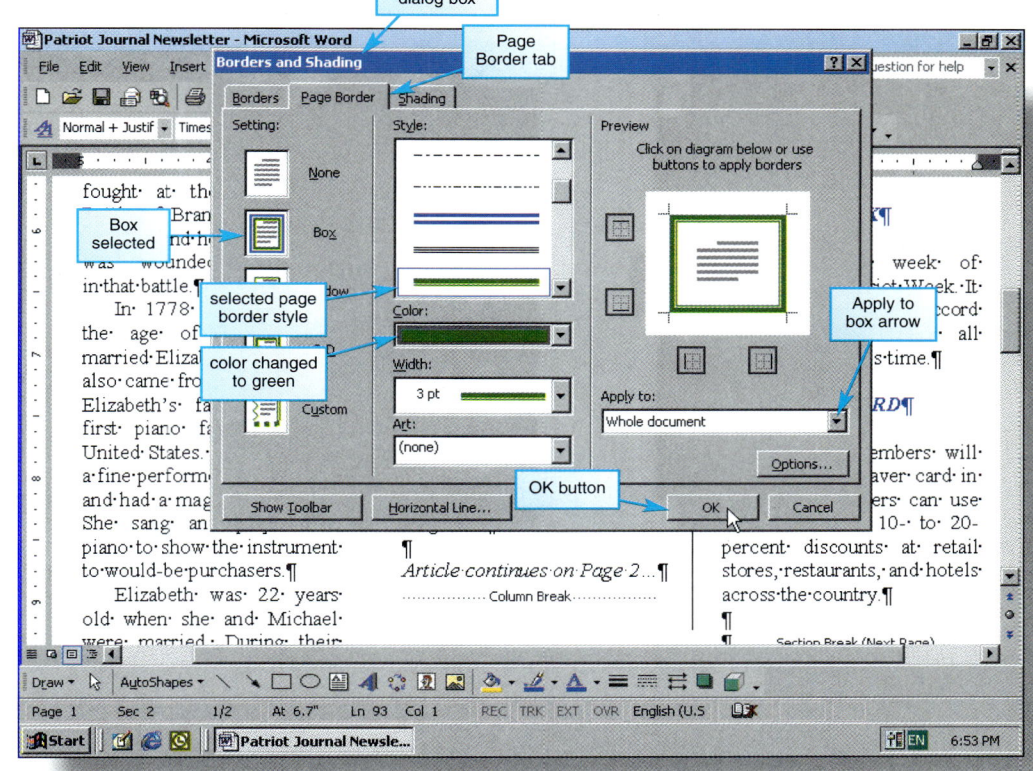

FIGURE 6-85

To see the borders on the newsletter, display both pages in the document window, as described in the following step.

TO ZOOM TWO PAGES

1 Click the Zoom box arrow on the Standard toolbar and then click Two Pages.

Word displays the pages of the newsletter in reduced form so that two pages display in the document window (Figure 6-86).

1. In Voice Command mode, say "Format, Borders and Shading, Page Border, [select settings], OK"

Page Borders

You can use the Apply to box arrow in the Page Border sheet to specify which sections/pages Word should apply the page border. For example, to apply the border to just the first page of the document, click the Apply to box arrow and then click This Section – First page only.

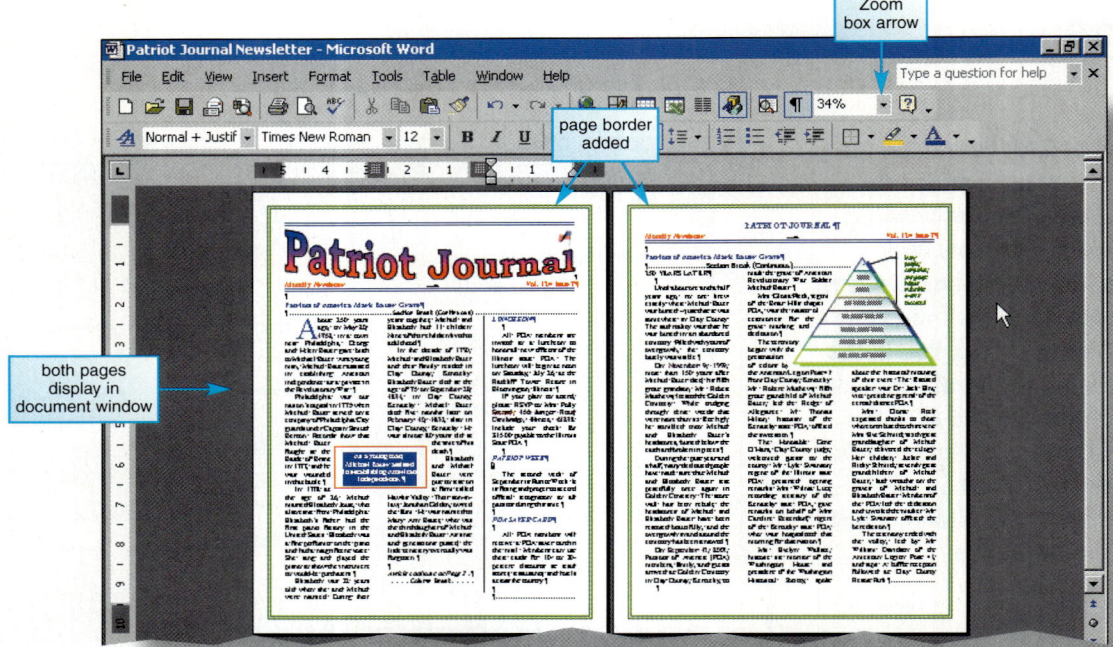

FIGURE 6-86

Perform the following step to return the display to zoom text width.

TO ZOOM TEXT WIDTH

1 Click the Zoom box arrow on the Standard toolbar and then click Text Width.

Word extends the right margin to the right edge of the document window.

The newsletter now is complete. You should save the document again and print it, as described in the following series of steps.

TO SAVE A DOCUMENT

1 With the disk containing the newsletter file in drive A, click the Save button on the Standard toolbar.

Word saves the document again with the file name, Patriot Journal Newsletter.

TO PRINT A DOCUMENT

1 Click the Print button on the Standard toolbar.

The printed newsletter is shown in Figure 6-1 on page WD 6.05.

Enhancing a Document for Online Viewing

Often you want to send documents to others online. For example, you may e-mail the Patriot Journal Newsletter instead of sending it via the postal service. Word provides some additional features for online documents. These include highlighted and animated text. The following pages illustrate each of these features.

Printing

If you want to save ink, print faster, or decrease printer overrun errors, print a draft. Click File on the menu bar, click Print, click the Options button, place a check mark in the Draft output check box, and then click the OK button in each dialog box.

Highlighting Text

Highlighting alerts a reader to online text's importance, much like a highlight marker does in a textbook. The following steps illustrate how to highlight text yellow.

Steps: To Highlight Text

1 Press CTRL+HOME. If necessary, scroll down. Drag through the feature article title, Patriots of America Mark Bauer Grave, to select it. Click the Highlight button arrow on the Formatting toolbar and then point to Yellow.

Word displays a variety of highlight color options (Figure 6-87).

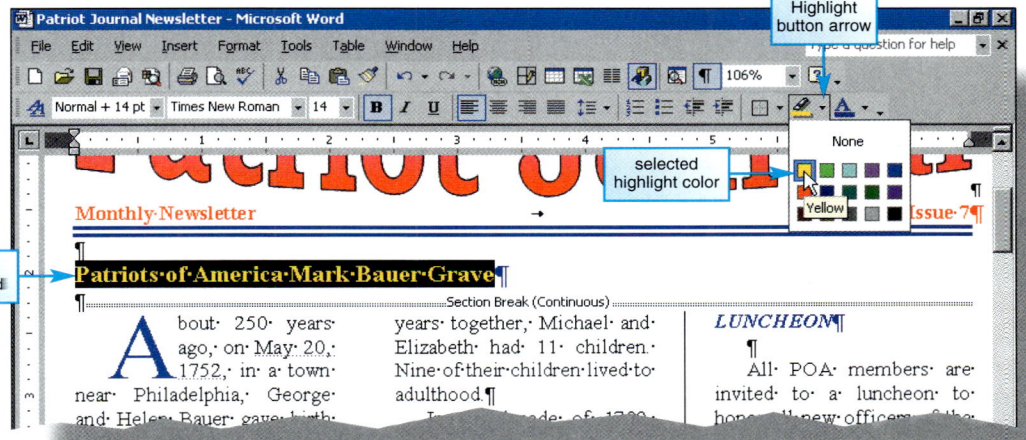

FIGURE 6-87

2 Click Yellow.

Word highlights the selection yellow (Figure 6-88).

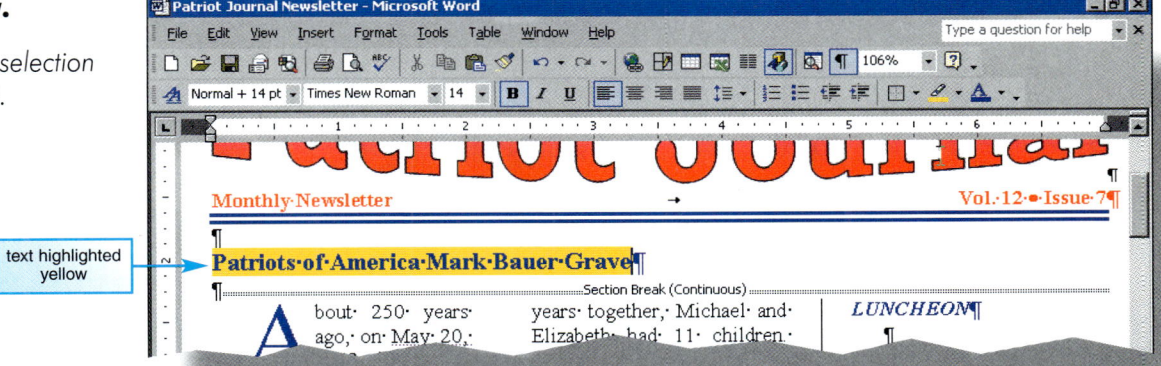

FIGURE 6-88

Other Ways

1. In Voice Command mode, say "Highlight, Yellow"

Notice in Figure 6-87 that Word provides a variety of colors for highlighting text. If the Highlight button already displays your desired highlight color on its face, you simply can click the Highlight button, instead of clicking the Highlight button arrow. If you wanted to remove a highlight, you would select the highlighted text, click the Highlight button arrow, and then click None.

If you scroll down to the second page of the newsletter, you will notice that the feature article title on the second page also is highlighted. Word automatically highlighted this text because earlier in this project you linked the nameplate on the second page to the nameplate on the first page.

Animating Text

When you **animate text**, it has the appearance of motion. To animate text in Word, you select it and then apply one of the predefined text effects in the Text Effects sheet in the Font dialog box.

In this newsletter, you want to apply the Marching Red Ants text effect to the words, Monthly Newsletter, in the issue information line. Once applied, the text will have a moving red dashed rectangle around it.

Perform the following steps to animate the words, Monthly Newsletter, in the issue information line.

Steps: To Animate Text

1 Drag through the text to animate it (in this case, Monthly Newsletter). Right-click the selected text and then click Font on the shortcut menu. When the Font dialog box displays, if necessary, click the Text Effects tab. Click Marching Red Ants in the Animations list. Point to the OK button.

Word displays the Font dialog box (Figure 6-89). The Preview area shows a sample of the selected animation.

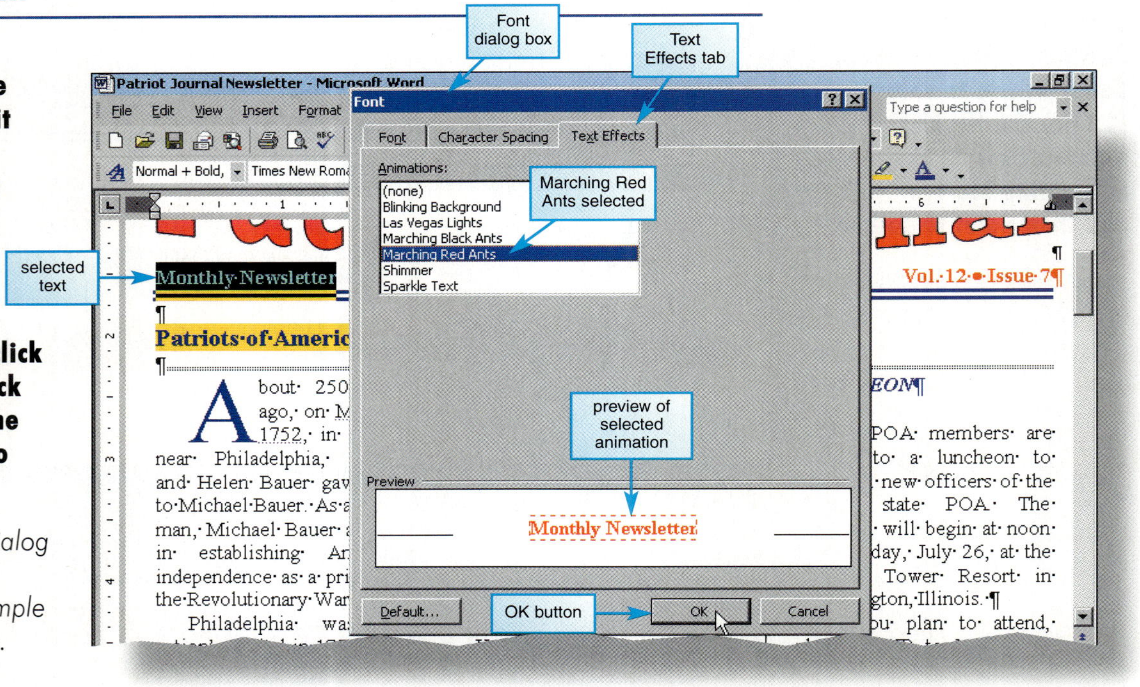

FIGURE 6-89

2 Click the OK button. Click outside the selected text.

Word applies the selected animation to the text (Figure 6-90).

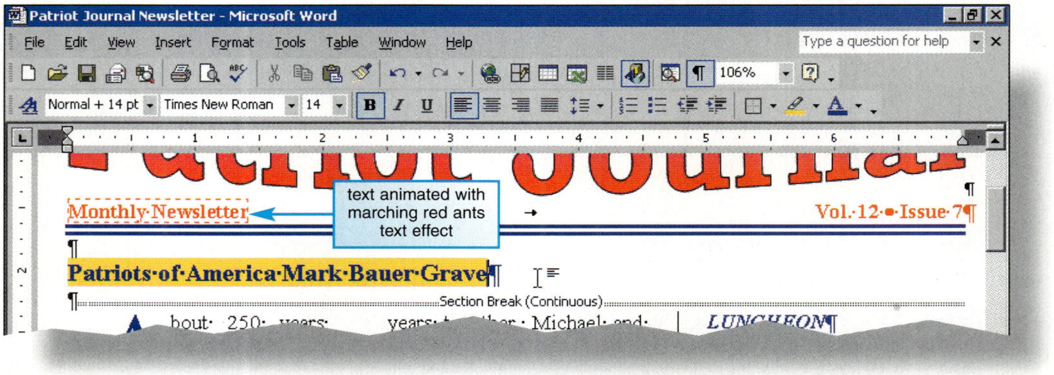

FIGURE 6-90

Other Ways

1. In Voice Command mode, say "Font, Format, Text Effects, [select desired animation], OK"

If you wanted to remove animation from text, you would select the text, right-click the selection, click Font on the shortcut menu, click the Text Effects tab, click (none) in the Animations list, and then click the OK button.

If you print a document that contains animated text, the animations do not show on the hard copy; instead the text prints as regular text. Thus, animations are designed specifically for documents that will be viewed online.

Collaborating with Others on a Document

When working on longer documents, such as the newsletter in this project, you may find that others contribute to parts of the document. Word provides several tools to assist you with working with others, or **collaborating**, on a document. The following sections describe some of these tools.

Searching for Files

Assume that after writing the 12-7 Notices file, you want to e-mail it to your regent for her review. To do this, you must know the name of the file. Assume you have forgotten the file name. Word provides a Search button that searches the contents of files based on a phrase you enter. You know that the file contains the text, POA SAVER CARD. Thus, you will search for this phrase.

Steps   To Search for a File

1 **Click the Search button on the Standard toolbar. When Word displays the Basic Search task pane, click the Search text text box and then type** POA SAVER CARD **as the Search text. Point to the Search button in the Basic Search task pane.**

Word displays the Basic Search task pane (Figure 6-91).

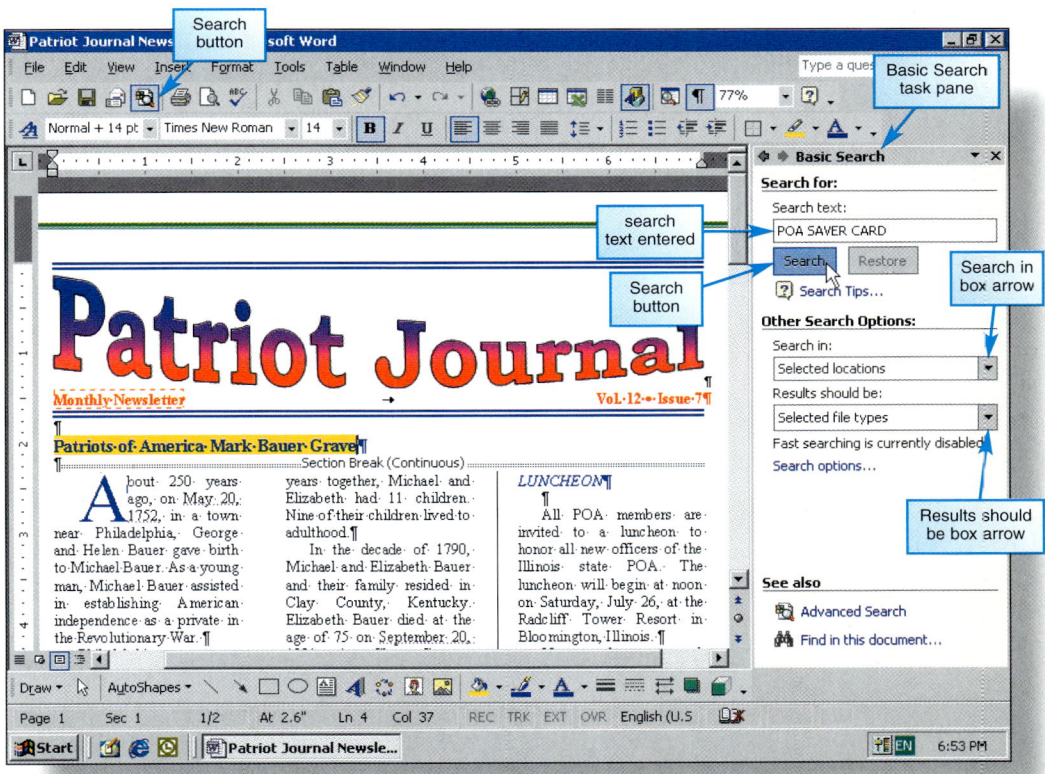

FIGURE 6-91

2 **Be sure the Data Disk is in drive A. Click the Search button.**

Word searches all drives on your computer and after a few seconds, displays all Office files containing the text you entered in the Search text text box. Your list may differ.

3 **Point to 12-7 Notices and then click the box arrow to its right. Point to Edit with Microsoft Word.**

A list of files that contain the text, POA SAVER CARD, displays in the Search Results task pane (Figure 6-92). You can open one of these files directly from the task pane.

4 **Click Edit with Microsoft Word. Click the Close button in the Search Results task pane.**

The file 12-7 Notices opens in a Word window (shown in Figure 6-93).

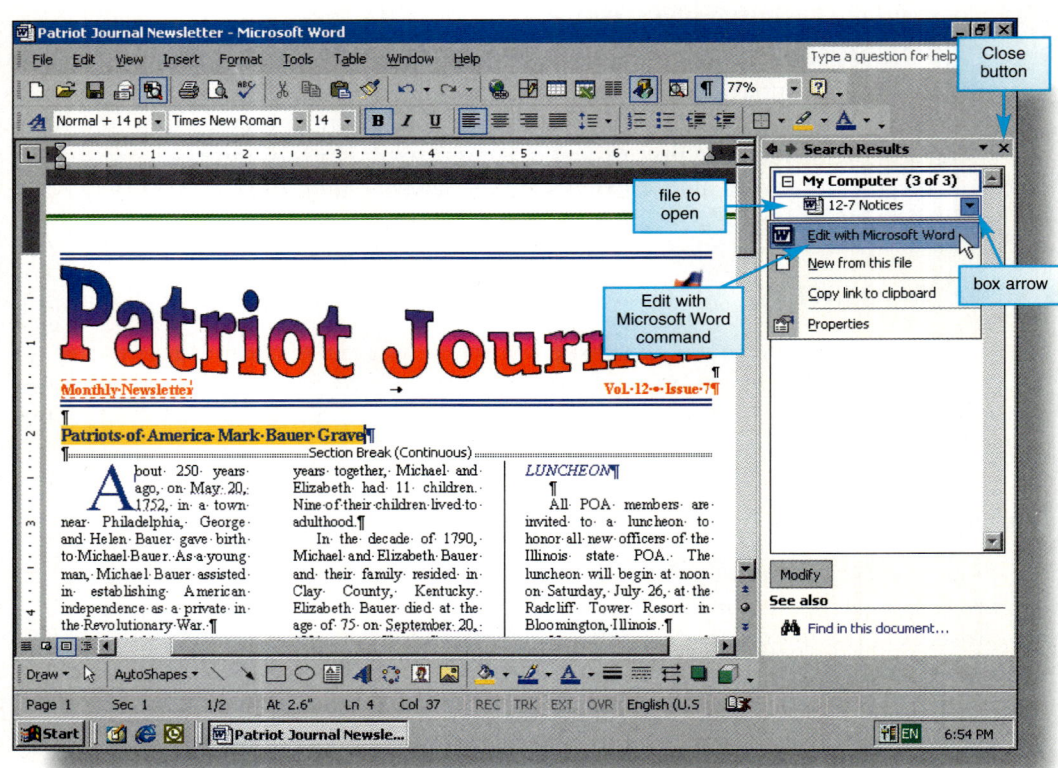

FIGURE 6-92

To narrow the drives searched, click the Search in box arrow in the Basic Search task pane (Figure 6-91 on the previous page) and remove the check mark from any drive you do not want searched. To narrow the types of files searched, click the Results should be box arrow in the Basic Search task pane and remove the check mark from any file type you do not want searched.

Inserting, Viewing, and Editing Comments

Now that you have located the file, you can e-mail it to your regent. Before doing this, you want to add a comment to the document. A **comment**, or annotation, is a note inserted into a document that does not affect the text of the document. In this file, you want to verify that the cost of the luncheon is $15.00. Perform the following steps to insert a comment into a document.

Steps: To Insert a Comment

1 Select the text on which you wish to comment (in this case, $15.00). Click Insert on the menu bar and then point to Comment (Figure 6-93).

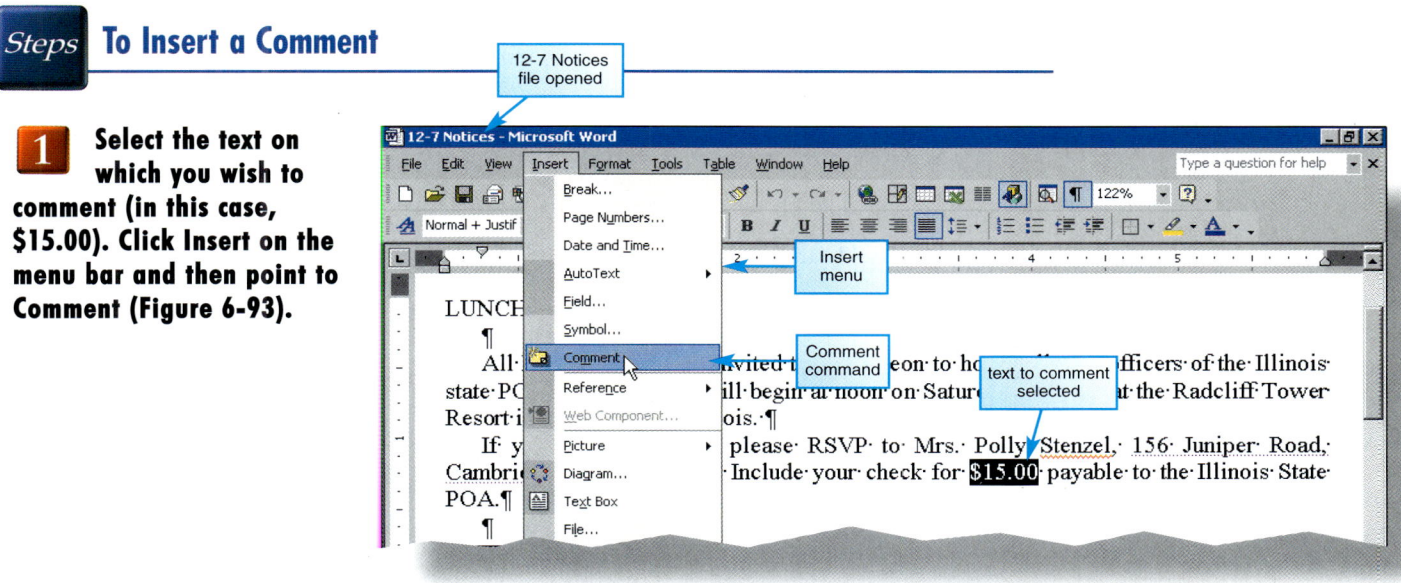

FIGURE 6-93

2 Click Comment. When Word displays a comment balloon, type `Please verify cost of luncheon.`

Word displays a **comment balloon**, into which you enter a comment (Figure 6-94). The Reviewing toolbar displays on the screen.

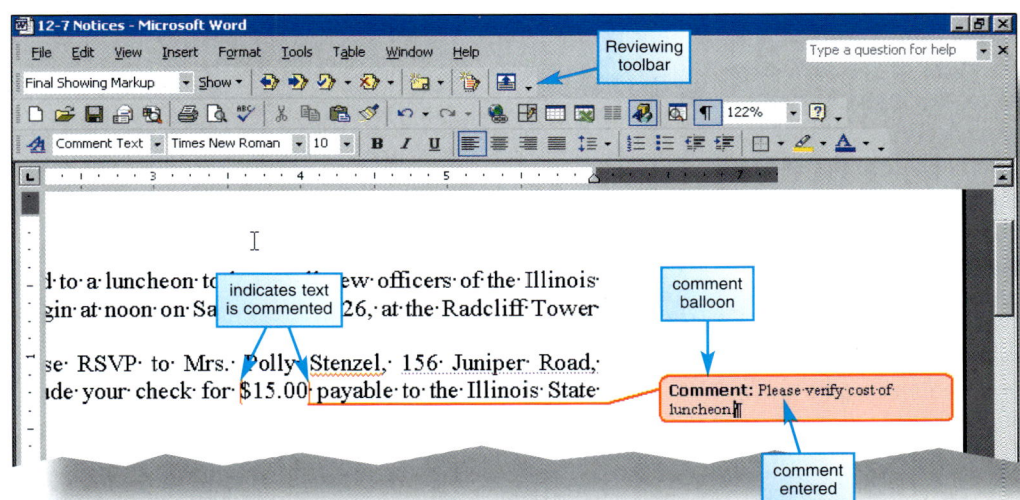

FIGURE 6-94

The comment now is part of the document. To keep the original file intact, save the commented file with a new file name, as described in the following steps.

TO SAVE A FILE WITH A NEW FILE NAME

1 Insert a floppy disk in drive A. Click File on the menu bar and then click Save As.

2 Type `Commented 12-7 Notices` in the File name text box. Do not press the ENTER key.

3 If necessary, click the Save in box arrow and then click 3½ Floppy (A:).

4 Click the Save button in the Save As dialog box.

Word saves the document on a floppy disk in drive A with the file name, Commented 12-7 Notices.

Comments

If you point to the comment, the name of the author of the comment displays in a ScreenTip. If the comment balloon does not display, click View on the menu bar and then click Markup.

Perform the following step to close the file.

TO CLOSE A FILE

1. Click File on the menu bar and then click Close.

Word closes the file.

Assume you e-mail the file to your regent for her review. When she opens it, she reads the comment and replies to it.

Steps: To View and Edit a Comment

1 **Open the file Commented 12-7 Notices. If the screen is in Normal view, click the Print Layout view button on the horizontal scroll bar. If the comment does not display to the right of the text, click View on the menu bar and then click Markup. Reduce the zoom percentage in the Zoom box so you can see the entire comment, as well as the document.**

Word displays the comment balloon to the right of the commented text (Figure 6-95).

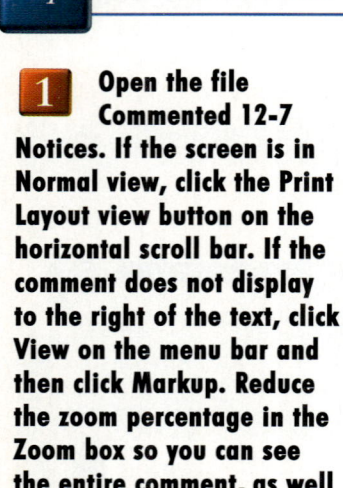

FIGURE 6-95

2 **Click at the end of the text in the comment balloon. With the insertion point at the end of the comment, press the ENTER key twice. Type** You are correct. The price is $15.00. **Click the Save button on the Standard toolbar.**

The comment is edited (Figure 6-96). The revised file is saved again.

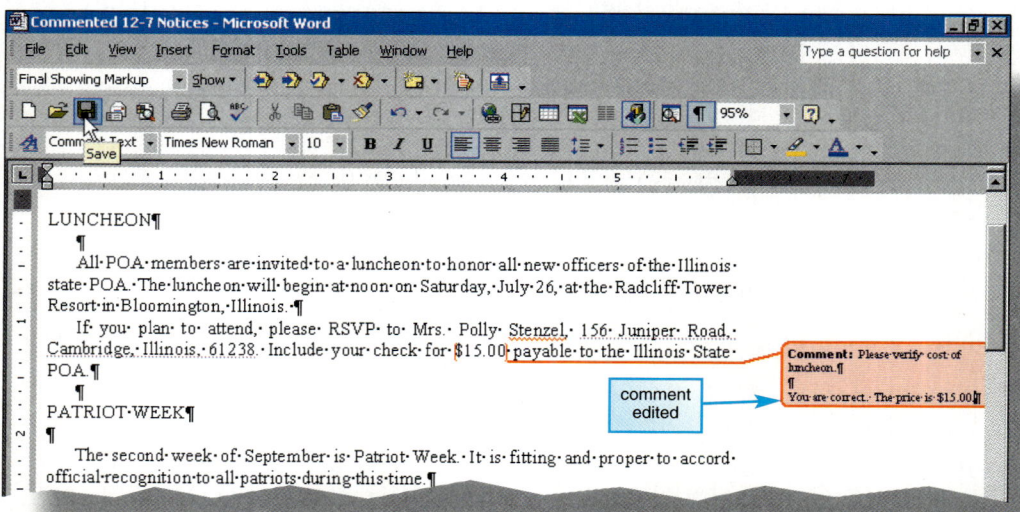

FIGURE 6-96

Collaborating with Others on a Document • WD 6.71

Your regent makes one additional change to the document, closes the file, and sends it back to you. Perform the following step to close the file.

TO CLOSE A FILE

1. Click File on the menu bar and then click Close.

Word closes the Commented 12-7 Notices file.

When you receive the file back from your regent, you read and then delete her comment. To delete a comment, right-click the comment and then click Delete on the shortcut menu; or click in the comment and click the Reject Change/Delete Comment button on the Reviewing toolbar.

Voice Comments

If your computer is equipped with a sound card and a microphone, you can record a voice comment into a document. Click the New Comment box arrow on the Reviewing toolbar, click Voice Comment, and then record the comment.

Comparing and Merging Documents

Recall that your regent indicated that she made a change to the document, but you cannot locate the change. With Word, you can compare two documents to each other so you easily can see any differences between the two files.

When merging, you have three merge choices: Merge, which merges into the document being opened; Merge into current document, which merges into the already opened document; or Merge into new document, which does not affect either document. The safest alternative is the last one, Merge into new document.

Perform the following steps to compare and merge documents into a new document.

 To Compare and Merge Documents

1. **Open the 12-7 Notices file. Click Tools on the menu bar and then point to Compare and Merge Documents (Figure 6-97).**

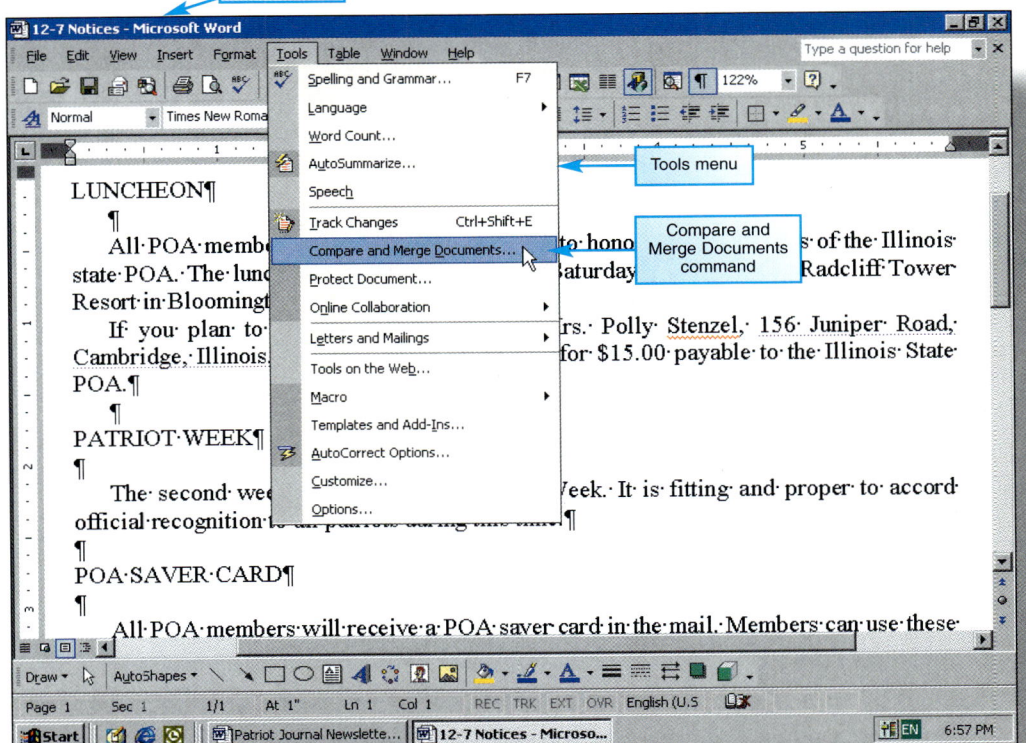

FIGURE 6-97

2 **Click Compare and Merge Documents. When the Compare and Merge Documents dialog box displays, if necessary, click the Look in box arrow and then click 3½ Floppy (A:). Click the file, Modified 12-7 Notices. Click the Merge button arrow and then point to Merge into new document.**

Word displays the Compare and Merge Documents dialog box (Figure 6-98).

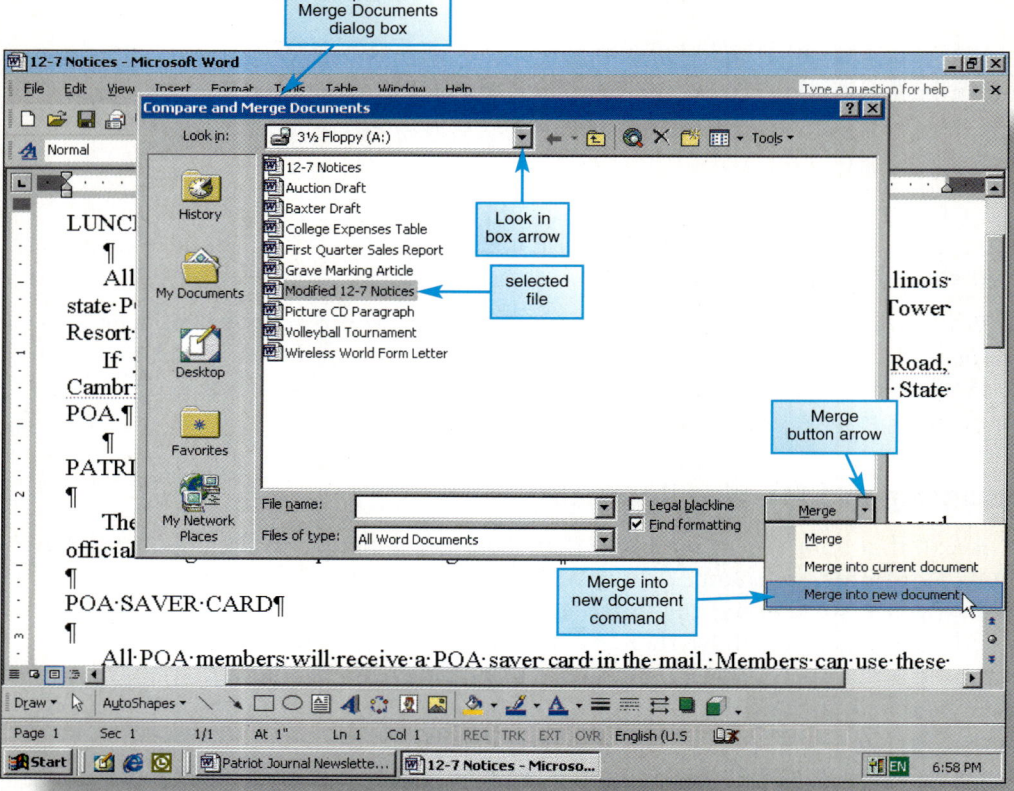

FIGURE 6-98

3 **Click Merge into new document. If necessary, scroll so the text and comment display in the document window.**

Word displays the change made to the document (Figure 6-99).

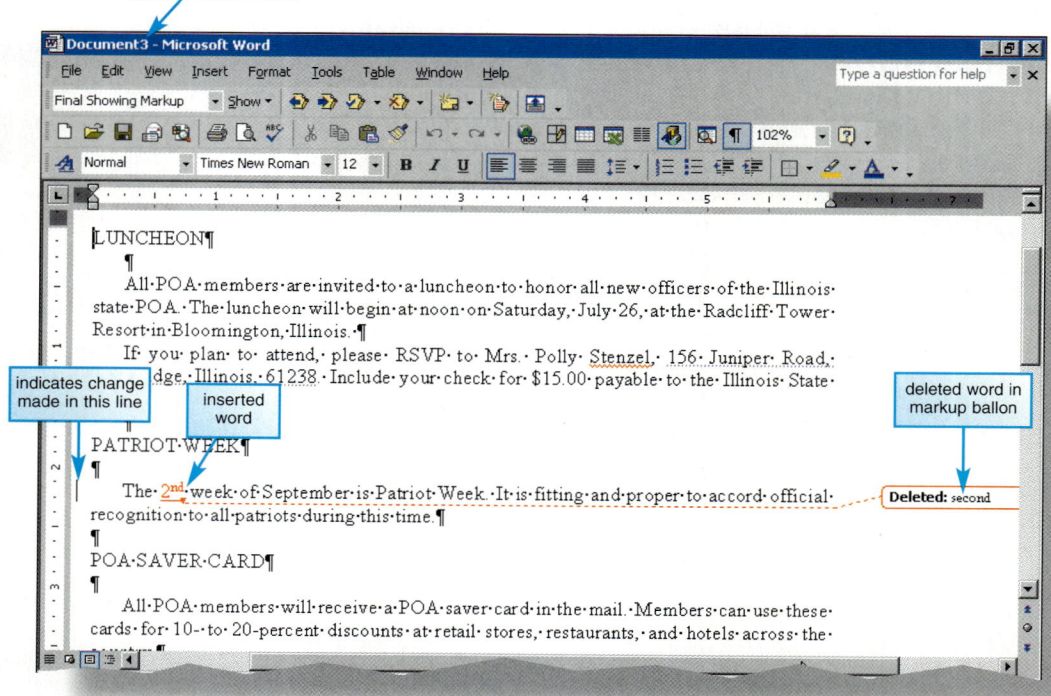

FIGURE 6-99

Your regent deleted the word, second, and replaced it with 2nd. Word shows the deleted text in a **markup balloon** to the right and shows the inserted text directly in the document. Both changes are in a different color so you can identify them easily.

After checking with a friend who is an administrative assistant, you decide to leave the word, second, as is. It is correct spelled out.

You now are finished with this project. Perform the following step to quit Word.

TO QUIT WORD

 Click File on the menu bar and then click Exit. Click No to any dialog boxes that Word displays.

The Word window closes.

Quick Reference

For a table that lists how to complete tasks covered in this book using the mouse, menu, shortcut menu, and keyboard, see the Quick Reference Summary at the back of this book or visit the Shelly Cashman Series Office XP Web page (scsite.com/offxp/qr.htm) and then click Microsoft Word 2002.

CASE PERSPECTIVE SUMMARY

Upon completion, you e-mail the entire newsletter to Gloria Fleck, regent of the Briar Hills POA chapter, for her review. She thinks it looks great and gives you approval to distribute.

You print the newsletter on a color printer and send the color printout to a local print shop to have 750 copies made. While the copies are being made, you ask Gloria if she has e-mail addresses of members. She does. You decide to add online enhancements, such as highlighted and animated text, to the newsletter and e-mail the online version to those members with e-mail addresses.

Project Summary

Project 6 introduced you to creating a professional looking newsletter using Word's desktop publishing features. You created a nameplate using a WordArt drawing object. You formatted the body of the newsletter into three columns and added a vertical rule between the second and third columns. You linked one section of the document to another. You created and formatted a pull-quote, inserted and formatted a diagram, and learned how to move these graphical objects between columns. You used the Format Painter button and added a page border to the newsletter. Finally, you learned how to highlight text and animate text; insert, view, and edit comments; and compare and merge documents.

Microsoft Certification

The Microsoft Office User Specialist (MOUS) Certification program provides an opportunity for you to obtain a valuable industry credential — proof that you have the Word 2002 skills required by employers. For more information, see Appendix E or visit the Shelly Cashman Series MOUS Web page at scsite.com/offxp/cert.htm.

What You Should Know

Having completed this project, you should now be able to perform the following tasks:

- Add a Page Border *(WD 6.63)*
- Add and Format a Callout AutoShape *(WD 6.55)*
- Add Segments to a Diagram *(WD 6.51)*
- Add Text to a Diagram *(WD 6.51)*
- Add Text to an AutoShape *(WD 6.56)*
- Animate Text *(WD 6.66)*
- AutoFormat a Diagram *(WD 6.52)*
- Balance Columns *(WD 6.48)*
- Bold and Center Text *(WD 6.38)*
- Bold Text *(WD 6.47)*
- Center the Newsletter Title *(WD 6.14)*
- Change a Graphic's Wrapping Style *(WD 6.59)*
- Change All Margin Settings *(WD 6.07)*
- Change Column Formatting *(WD 6.43)*
- Change Paragraph Indentation and Spacing *(WD 6.39)*
- Change the Color of Characters *(WD 6.40)*
- Change the Number of Columns *(WD 6.25)*
- Change the Shape of a WordArt Drawing Object *(WD 6.13)*
- Clear Formatting *(WD 6.15, WD 6.22)*
- Close a File *(WD 6.70, WD 6.71)*
- Color the Drop Cap *(WD 6.61)*
- Compare and Merge Documents *(WD 6.71)*
- Copy and Paste a Diagram *(WD 6.58)*
- Display Formatting Marks *(WD 6.07)*
- Enter Text *(WD 6.22)*
- Flip a Graphic *(WD 6.21)*
- Format a Graphic as Floating *(WD 6.57, WD 6.20)*
- Format a Letter as a Drop Cap *(WD 6.28)*
- Format a Text Box *(WD 6.38)*
- Format a WordArt Drawing Object *(WD 6.11)*
- Format and Enter Text *(WD 6.44)*
- Highlight Text *(WD 6.65)*
- Insert a Column Break *(WD 6.31)*
- Insert a Comment *(WD 6.69)*
- Insert a Continuous Section Break *(WD 6.24)*
- Insert a Diagram *(WD 6.49)*
- Insert a File into a Column of the Newsletter *(WD 6.32)*
- Insert a File into the Newsletter *(WD 6.27)*
- Insert a Graphic File from the Data Disk *(WD 6.20)*
- Insert a Next Page Section Break *(WD 6.30)*
- Insert a Symbol *(WD 6.17)*
- Insert a Text Box *(WD 6.36)*
- Insert a WordArt Drawing Object *(WD 6.09)*
- Insert Clip Art from the Web *(WD 6.19)*
- Justify a Paragraph *(WD 6.26)*
- Link a Copied Item *(WD 6.45)*
- Place a Vertical Rule between Columns *(WD 6.34)*
- Position a Text Box *(WD 6.41)*
- Print a Document *(WD 6.64)*
- Quit Word *(WD 6.73)*
- Reorder Graphic Objects *(WD 6.57)*
- Reset Menus and Toolbars *(WD 6.07)*
- Resize a Diagram *(WD 6.53)*
- Resize a Text Box *(WD 6.41)*
- Save a Document *(WD 6.32, WD 6.42, WD 6.49, WD 6.60, WD 6.64)*
- Save a File with a New File Name *(WD 6.69)*
- Save the Newsletter *(WD 6.23)*
- Search for a File *(WD 6.67)*
- Set a Right-Aligned Tab Stop *(WD 6.16)*
- Shade a Paragraph *(WD 6.40)*
- Start and Customize Word *(WD 6.06)*
- Use Borders to Add Ruling Lines *(WD 6.14)*
- Use the Format Painter Button *(WD 6.61)*
- View and Edit a Comment *(WD 6.70)*
- Zoom Text Width *(WD 6.08, WD 6.33, WD 6.54, WD 6.64)*
- Zoom to a Percentage *(WD 6.50)*
- Zoom Two Pages *(WD 6.63)*
- Zoom Whole Page *(WD 6.32)*

Learn It Online

Instructions: To complete the Learn It Online exercises, start your browser, click the Address bar, and then enter scsite.com/offxp/exs.htm. When the Office XP Learn It Online page displays, follow the instructions in the exercises below.

1 Project Reinforcement TF, MC, and SA

Below Word Project 6, click the Project Reinforcement link. Print the quiz by clicking Print on the File menu. Answer each question. Write your first and last name at the top of each page, and then hand in the printout to your instructor.

2 Flash Cards

Below Word Project 6, click the Flash Cards link. When Flash Cards displays, read the instructions. Type 20 (or a number specified by your instructor) in the Number of Playing Cards text box, type your name in the Name text box, and then click the Flip Card button. When the flash card displays, read the question and then click the Answer box arrow to select an answer. Flip through Flash Cards. Click Print on the File menu to print the last flash card if your score is 15 (75%) correct or greater and then hand it in to your instructor. If your score is less than 15 (75%) correct, then redo this exercise by clicking the Replay button.

3 Practice Test

Below Word Project 6, click the Practice Test link. Answer each question, enter your first and last name at the bottom of the page, and then click the Grade Test button. When the graded practice test displays on your screen, click Print on the File menu to print a hard copy. Continue to take practice tests until you score 80% or better. Hand in a printout of the final practice test to your instructor.

4 Who Wants to Be a Computer Genius?

Below Word Project 6, click the Computer Genius link. Read the instructions, enter your first and last name at the bottom of the page, and then click the Play button. Hand in your score to your instructor.

5 Wheel of Terms

Below Word Project 6, click the Wheel of Terms link. Read the instructions, and then enter your first and last name and your school name. Click the Play button. Hand in your score to your instructor.

6 Crossword Puzzle Challenge

Below Word Project 6, click the Crossword Puzzle Challenge link. Read the instructions, and then enter your first and last name. Click the Play button. Work the crossword puzzle. When you are finished, click the Submit button. When the crossword puzzle redisplays, click the Print button. Hand in the printout.

7 Tips and Tricks

Below Word Project 6, click the Tips and Tricks link. Click a topic that pertains to Project 6. Right-click the information and then click Print on the shortcut menu. Construct a brief example of what the information relates to in Word to confirm you understand how to use the tip or trick. Hand in the example and printed information.

8 Newsgroups

Below Word Project 6, click the Newsgroups link. Click a topic that pertains to Project 6. Print three comments. Hand in the comments to your instructor.

9 Expanding Your Horizons

Below Word Project 6, click the Articles for Microsoft Word link. Click a topic that pertains to Project 6. Print the information. Construct a brief example of what the information relates to in Word to confirm you understand the contents of the article. Hand in the example and printed information to your instructor.

10 Search Sleuth

Below Word Project 6, click the Search Sleuth link. To search for a term that pertains to this project, select a term below the Project 6 title and then use the Google search engine at google.com (or any major search engine) to display and print two Web pages that present information on the term. Hand in the printouts to your instructor.

Apply Your Knowledge

1 Commenting and Merging Documents

Instructions: Start Word. Open the document, Computing Careers Draft, on the Data Disk. If you did not download the Data Disk, see the inside back cover for instructions for downloading the Data Disk or see your instructor.

Performing the steps below, you are to work with comments and merge the document to another document.

Perform the following tasks:

1. Click View on the menu bar and then click Print Layout. If the comment does not display in the document window, click View on the menu bar and then click Markup. If the comment still does not display, click the Show button on the Reviewing toolbar and then click Comments.
2. Read the comment and follow its instruction. Remove the comment by right-clicking it and then clicking Delete Comment on the shortcut menu.
3. Drag through the text, U.S. Department of Labor's Bureau of Labor Statistics recently reported, to select it. Click Insert on the menu bar and then click Comment. Type `Can we get a copy of this report?`
4. Click File on the menu bar and then click Print. Click the Print what box arrow and then click Document showing markup. Click the OK button to print the document with comments.
5. Click in the comment you just inserted. Edit it so it reads: How much would it cost to get a copy of this report?
6. Click File on the menu bar and then click Print. Click the Print what box arrow and then click Document showing markup. Click the OK button to print the document with comments.
7. Remove the comment by right-clicking it and then clicking Delete Comment on the shortcut menu.
8. Save the revised file with the file name, Computing Careers Revised (Figure 6-100).
9. Click Tools on the menu bar and then click Compare and Merge Documents. When the Compare and Merge Documents dialog box displays, if necessary, click the Look in box arrow and then click 3½ Floppy (A:). Click Computing Careers Modified. Click the Merge button arrow and then click Merge into new document.
10. Save the new file with the file name, Merged Computing Careers.
11. Click File on the menu bar and then click Print. Click the Print what box arrow and then click Document showing markup. Click the OK button to print the document with markup.

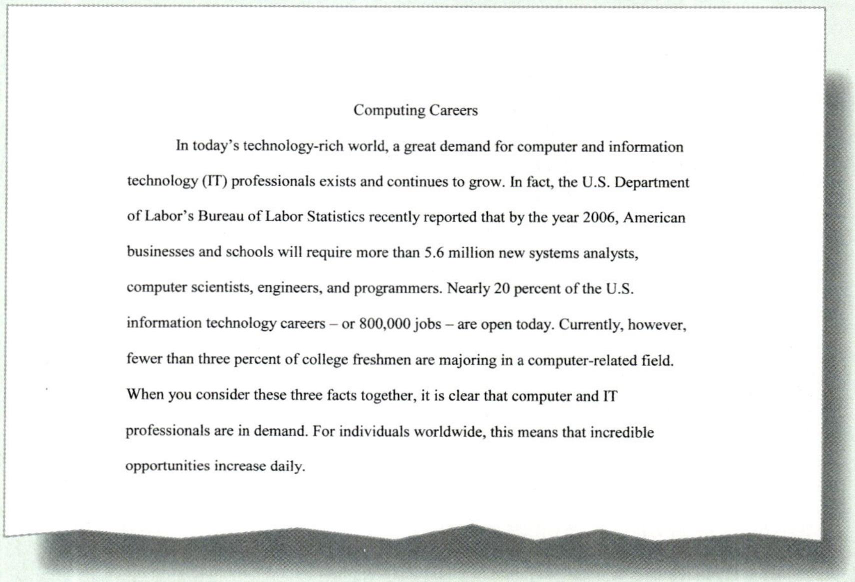

Computing Careers

In today's technology-rich world, a great demand for computer and information technology (IT) professionals exists and continues to grow. In fact, the U.S. Department of Labor's Bureau of Labor Statistics recently reported that by the year 2006, American businesses and schools will require more than 5.6 million new systems analysts, computer scientists, engineers, and programmers. Nearly 20 percent of the U.S. information technology careers – or 800,000 jobs – are open today. Currently, however, fewer than three percent of college freshmen are majoring in a computer-related field. When you consider these three facts together, it is clear that computer and IT professionals are in demand. For individuals worldwide, this means that incredible opportunities increase daily.

FIGURE 6-100

In the Lab

1 Creating a Newsletter with a Pull-Quote and an Article on File

Problem: You are an editor of the newsletter, *Health News*. The next edition is due out in one week. This issue's article will discuss computers and health risks (Figure 6-101). The newsletter also includes a pull-quote. The text for the feature article is on the Data Disk. If you did not download the Data Disk, see the inside back cover for instructions for downloading the Data Disk or see your instructor.

Instructions:

1. Change all margins to .75 inches. Depending on your printer, you may need different margin settings.
2. Create the nameplate using the formats identified in Figure 6-101. Create a continuous section break below the nameplate. Format section 2 to three columns.
3. Insert the Computer Health Risk Article on the Data Disk into section 2 below the nameplate.
4. Format the newsletter according to Figure 6-101. Use the Format Painter button to automate some of your formatting tasks.
5. Insert a continuous section break at the end of the document to balance the columns.
6. The text for the pull-quote is in the first paragraph of the article. Copy the text and then insert it into a text box. Change the line color to dark red, and the line weight to 1½ point. Format the characters in the pull-quote to bold, green font. Format the paragraph of the pull-quote to have a 6-point space above and below the paragraph and a 0.1" space to its left and right. Shade the paragraph light yellow. Position the text box as shown in Figure 6-101.
7. Save the document with Health News Newsletter as the file name. Print the newsletter.

FIGURE 6-101

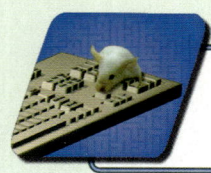

In the Lab

2 Creating a Newsletter with a Diagram and an Article on File

Problem: You are responsible for the monthly preparation of *Living with Computers*, a newsletter for subscribers to your company's Internet service. The next edition, due out in two weeks, is to discuss how to maintain a computer (Figure 6-102). This article already has been prepared and is on the Data Disk. If you did not download the Data Disk, see the inside back cover for instructions for downloading the Data Disk or see your instructor. You need to create the diagram.

Instructions:

1. Change all margins to .75 inch. Depending on your printer, you may need different margin settings.
2. Create the nameplate using the formats identified in Figure 6-102. Create a continuous section break below the nameplate. The clip art is located in the Clip Organizer. Change its wrapping style to In front of text. Format section 2 to two columns.
3. Insert the Maintaining a Computer Article on the Data Disk into section 2 below the nameplate.
4. Format the newsletter according to Figure 6-102. Use the Format Painter button to format the subheads. Insert a continuous section break at the end of the document to balance the columns. Create the pyramid diagram shown in Figure 6-102 in a separate document window. Change its height to 4 inches and its width to 3.8 inches. AutoFormat it to the double outline style. Change its wrapping style to square. Copy and paste it into the newsletter. Change its wrapping style to edit wrap points.
5. Save the document using Living with Computers Newsletter as the file name. Print the newsletter.

FIGURE 6-102

In the Lab

3 Creating a Newsletter from Scratch

Problem: You work part-time for Winfield Zoo, which publishes a newsletter for members of the zoo. Figure 6-103 shows the contents of the next issue.

Instructions:

1. Change all margins to .75 inches. Depending on your printer, you may need different margin settings.
2. Create the nameplate using the formats identified in Figure 6-103. **Hint:** Use the Shadow Style button on the Drawing toolbar to apply the shadow effect to the WordArt object in the nameplate. Create a continuous section break below the nameplate. Format section 2 to three columns.
3. Enter the text into section two using justified paragraph formatting. Insert the polar bear picture into the newsletter. The picture is located on the Data Disk. If you did not download the Data Disk, see the inside back cover for instructions for downloading the Data Disk or see your instructor. **Hint:** Search for the phrase, insert a picture, for help on inserting a picture. Use the Format Picture toolbar to add a green border around the picture. Add a text box below the picture as shown in Figure 6-103. Group the text box and the picture together. **Hint:** Use Help to learn about grouping objects.
4. Insert a continuous section break at the end of the third column in section 2. Format section 3 to one column. Create the table as shown at the bottom of the newsletter.
5. Format the newsletter according to Figure 6-103. Place a vertical rule between all columns in section 2. Use the Line between check box in the Columns dialog box (Format menu) to do this. Use the Format Painter button to automate some of your formatting tasks.
6. Save the document with Winfield Zoo Newsletter as the file name. Print the newsletter.

FIGURE 6-103

Cases and Places

The difficulty of these case studies varies:
▶ are the least difficult; ▶▶ are more difficult; and ▶▶▶ are the most difficult.

1 ▶ As your final project in CIS 144, you have been assigned the task of creating page WD 5.71 in this textbook. The page contains many desktop publishing elements: drop caps in the Project Summary and What You Should Know subheads, a variety of font sizes and font color, and balanced columns in the What You Should Know section. You may need to resize and move the drop cap frame so it aligns properly with the subheads. To display the half moon bullets, click the Customize button in the Bullets and Numbering dialog box. Click the Bullet button in the dialog box to locate the half moon bullet, and click the Font button in the dialog box to change the bullet color. Apply the Marching Red Ants effect to the Project Summary and What You Should Know headings. Highlight the sentence below the What You Should Know heading. Print the document. Change the layout of the What You Should Know section from 2 to 3 columns. Print the document.

2 ▶▶ You are an editor of *Health News*, a one-page newsletter published by the hospital at which you work. Last month's edition is shown in Figure 6-101 on page WD 6.77. The next edition is due out in three weeks. Your assignment is to decide on a feature article for the next edition of the *Health News* newsletter. Use your personal experiences as the basis for your feature article. Your article could address any health-related item. The newsletter should contain a pull-quote of the article. Enhance the newsletter with WordArt, color, ruling lines, and a page border using colors different from those used in Figure 6-101.

3 ▶▶ You are responsible for the monthly preparation of *Living with Computers*, a one-page newsletter for subscribers to the Internet service at which you work. Last month's edition is shown in Figure 6-102 on page WD 6.78. The next edition is due out in three weeks. Your assignment is to decide on a feature article for the next edition of the newsletter. The feature article should address some aspect of computers. Use your personal experiences as the basis for your feature article. The newsletter should contain an appropriate diagram. Enhance the newsletter with WordArt, color, ruling lines, and a page border using colors different from those used in Figure 6-102.

4 ▶▶▶ You are a member of a movie review club. Because you have a background in desktop publishing, you prepare the monthly two-page newsletter for club members. Your assignment is to design the newsletter and develop the next issue. The newsletter should have a feature article and some announcements for club members. Your feature article could discuss/review one or more recent movies. The feature article should span both pages of the newsletter, and club announcements should be on the first page of the newsletter. Use the Paste Special command to copy and then paste link some lines of the nameplate on page 1 to page 2. Enhance the newsletter with WordArt, color, shading, ruling lines, and a page border. Use an appropriate graphic, a diagram, and a pull-quote in the newsletter.

Microsoft Word 2002

Merging Form Letters to E-Mail Addresses Using an Outlook Contacts List

CASE PERSPECTIVE

In Project 5, you created form letters notifying upcoming graduates of general graduation procedures (see Figure 5-1 on page WD 5.05). Having completed these letters, you mention to your supervisor, Elizabeth Pulaski, that the form letters also can be e-mailed using Word — if you have e-mail addresses. Elizabeth contacts the admissions department and requests a list of student e-mail addresses. The admissions department sends an Outlook contacts list that contains the graduating student names and postal addresses, as well as e-mail addresses.

Word can use an Outlook contact list as a data source, providing the fields are set up to match the form letter fields. The admissions department added the Degree, Major, and GPA fields using the Outlook field names of User_Field_1, User_Field_2, and User_Field_3, respectively. You will modify the form letter so it references these field names.

To complete this Integration Feature, you will need the main document for the form letters created in Project 5. (If you did not create the form letters, see your instructor for a copy.)

Introduction

As discussed in Project 5, the basic content of a group of **form letters** is similar; however, items such as name, address, city, state, and ZIP code change from one letter to the next. Thus, form letters are personalized to the addressee.

The process of generating form letters involves creating a main document for the form letters and a data source, and then merging the two into a series of individual letters. In Project 5, you used the Mail Merge Wizard to create a new data source. Word saved this data source as an Access database table. In addition to Microsoft Access database tables, you can use an existing Microsoft Outlook contacts list, Microsoft Excel worksheet, Microsoft Word table, or a text file as the data source for form letters.

In this Integration Feature, you open the Graduation Form Letter main document file (Figure 1a on the next page). Then, you specify that you will use an Outlook contacts list (Figure 1b on the next page) as the data source. The Outlook contacts list for this project, which contains e-mail addresses, is located in an Outlook data file on the Data Disk. You will open the Outlook data file in Outlook and then merge data from the Outlook contacts list into the main document, Graduation Form Letter.

In Project 5, you learned that you can send merged documents to the printer or to a new document window. In this Integration Feature, you send the merged documents to e-mail addresses. This merge process creates a separate e-mail message for each person in the Outlook contacts list. Figure 1c on the next page shows the five e-mail messages created by this merge.

WDI 1.02 • Feature • Merging Form Letters to E-Mail Addresses Using an Outlook Contacts List

Microsoft Word 2002

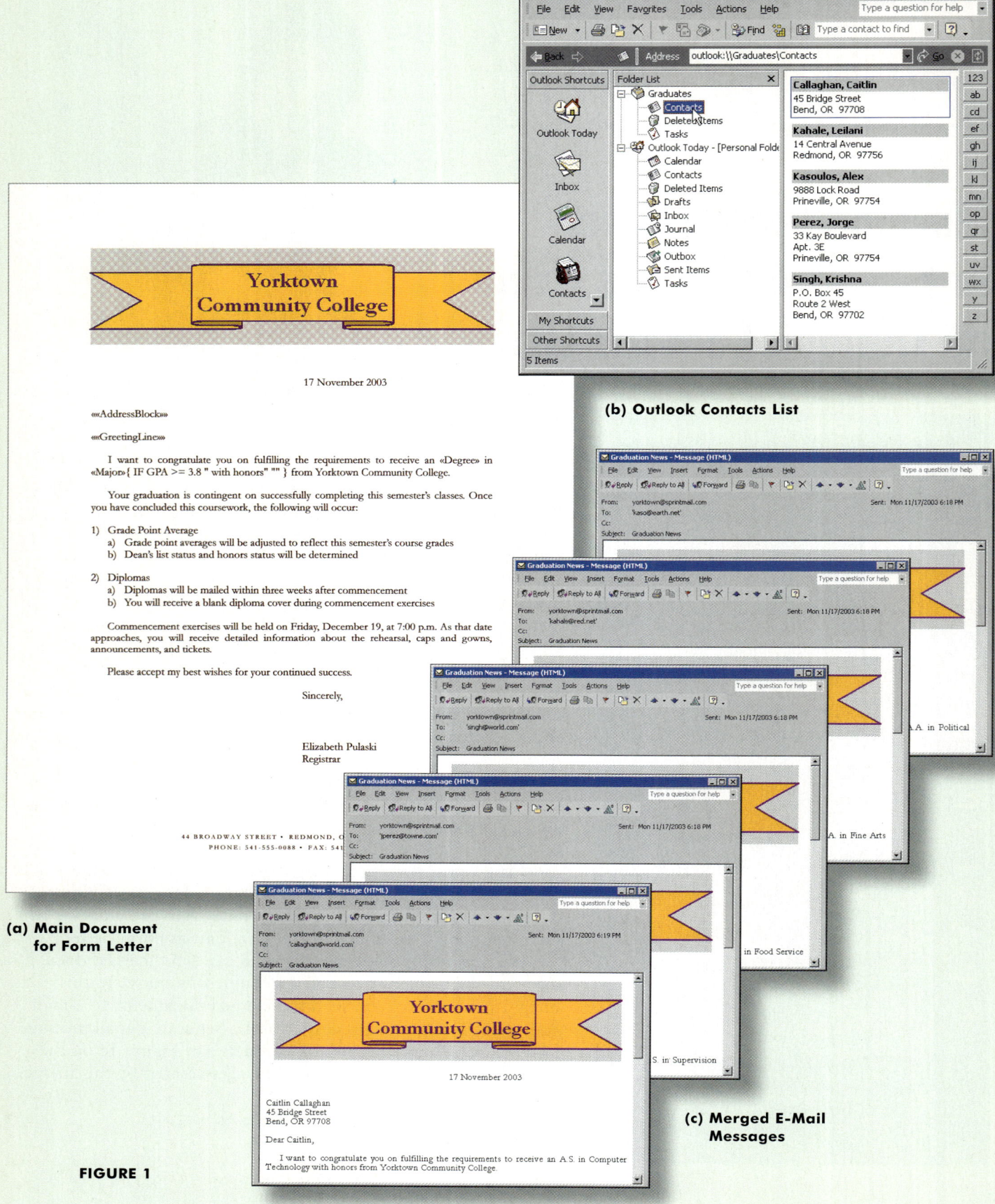

(a) Main Document for Form Letter

(b) Outlook Contacts List

(c) Merged E-Mail Messages

FIGURE 1

Introduction • WDI 1.03

Opening an Outlook Data File

In Outlook, a **contact** is a person about whom you have saved data such as first name, last name, postal address, and e-mail address. A **contacts list** is the collection of all your Outlook contacts. Outlook stores a contacts list in a **Contacts folder**, also called an **address book**. The contacts list for this project is located in an Outlook data file on the Data Disk. Thus, the first step in this project is to open the Outlook data file in Outlook so the Outlook contacts list is available for the merge. If you did not download the Data Disk, see the inside back cover for instructions for downloading the Data Disk or see your instructor.

Perform the following steps to open the Outlook data file.

More About

Mailing Lists

For more information on mailing lists available for purchase or download, visit the Word 2002 More About Web page (www.scsite.com/wd2002/more.htm) and then click Mailing Lists.

Steps To Open an Outlook Data File

1 **Click the Start button on the Windows taskbar, point to Programs on the Start menu, and then click Microsoft Outlook on the Programs submenu. If the Outlook window is not maximized, double-click its title bar to maximize it. If the Folder List does not display, click View on the menu bar and then click Folder List. Click File on the menu bar, point to Open, and then point to Outlook Data File on the Open submenu.**

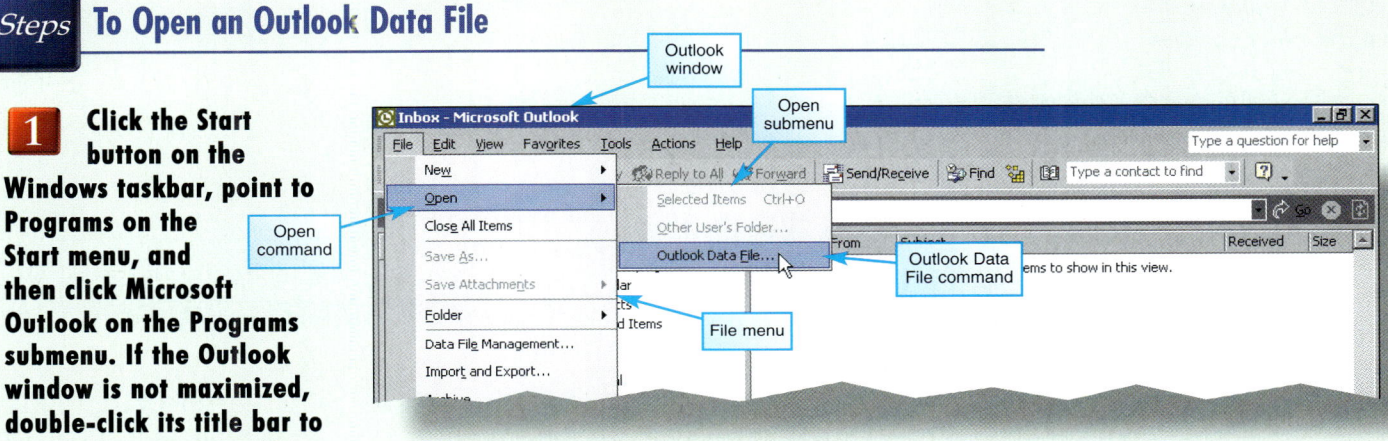

FIGURE 2

Outlook starts (Figure 2). Depending on previous settings, your Outlook window may differ.

2 **Click Outlook Data File. If necessary, insert the Data Disk into drive A. When the Open Outlook Data File dialog box displays, click the Look in box arrow and then click 3½ Floppy (A:). Click the file name Graduates and then point to the OK button.**

Outlook displays the Open Outlook Data File dialog box (Figure 3).

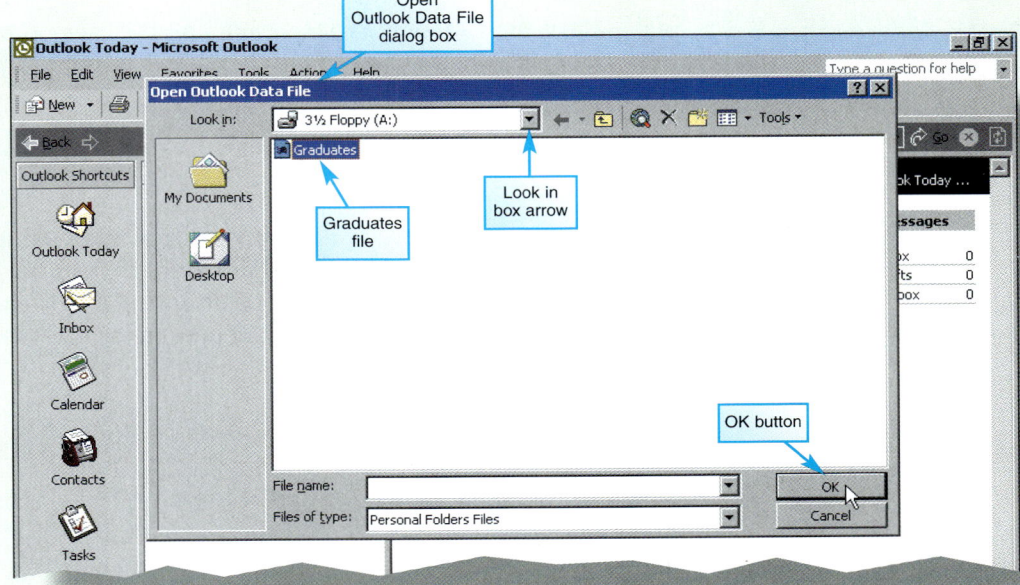

FIGURE 3

3 Click the OK button. When the Graduates folder displays in the Folder List, click the plus sign (+) to the left of the folder name to expand the folder. Click the Contacts folder in the Graduates folder.

Outlook opens the Outlook data file and displays the Graduates folder in the Folder List (Figure 4). The Contacts folder contains the same five student data records used in Project 5. The plus sign changes to a minus sign (–) when a folder is expanded.

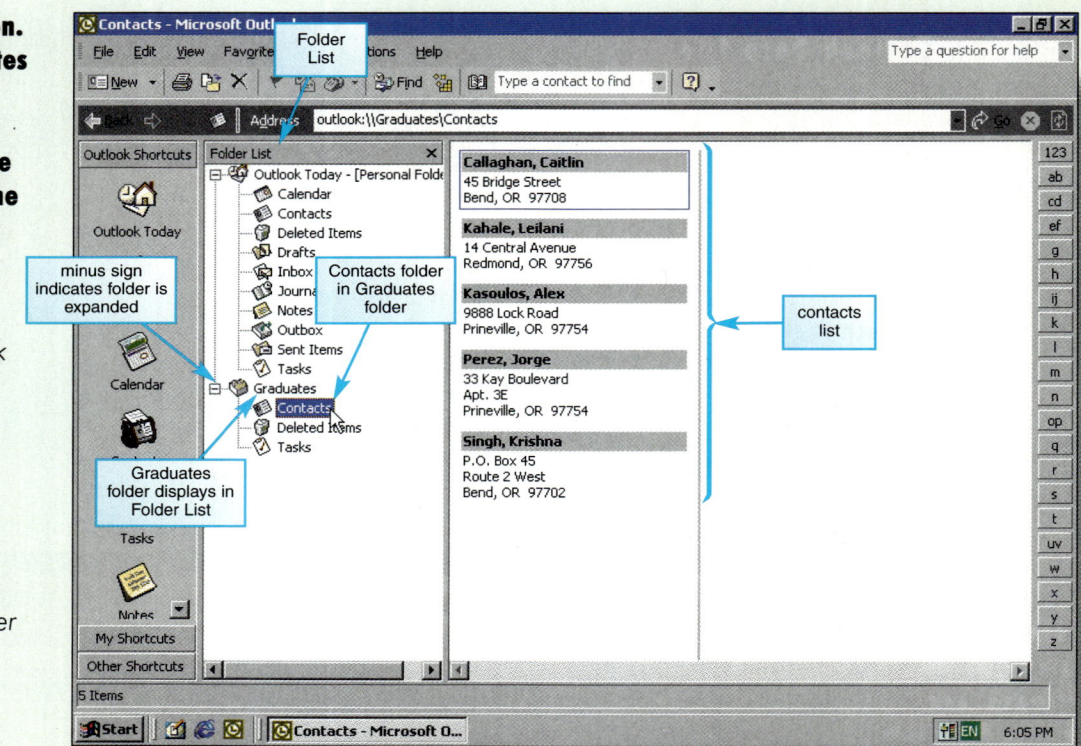

FIGURE 4

Perform the following steps to verify the Contacts folder is available for a mail merge.

TO CHECK A CONTACTS FOLDER'S SETTINGS

1 Right-click the Contacts folder in the Graduates folder and then click Properties on the shortcut menu.

2 When the Contacts Properties dialog box displays, click the Outlook Address Book tab. Be sure that a check mark is in the Show this folder as an e-mail address book check box.

3 Click the OK button.

With this check box selected, Word can access the contents of the Contacts folder.

In addition to the fields used in Project 5, each student in the Outlook contacts list also has an e-mail address. Recall from Project 5 that the data source contained a Degree, Major, and GPA field. In Outlook, the field names for each of these fields are User_Field_1, User_Field_2, and User_Field_3, respectively.

Changing the Data Source in a Form Letter

Currently, the data source for the Graduation Form Letter is an Access database table that you saved in a file named, Graduate List. The data source in this Integration Feature should be an Outlook contacts list.

Perform the following steps to change the data source designation to an Outlook contacts list.

More About

Outlook Data Sources

Instead of starting the mail merge in Word, you can start it in Outlook. To begin the process in Outlook, display and select a contacts list in the Outlook window, click Tools on the menu bar and then click Mail Merge. For help using this Outlook feature, type mail merge in the Ask a question box.

Steps — To Change a Data Source Designation

1 Start Word and then open the file named, Graduation Form Letter, created in Project 5. Click Tools on the menu bar, point to Letters and Mailings, and then click Mail Merge Wizard. When the Mail Merge task pane displays, if necessary, click Next or Previous at the bottom of the task pane to display Step 3 of 6 in the Mail Merge Wizard. Click Select from Outlook contacts in the Select recipients area and then point to Choose Contacts Folder.

Word displays Step 3 of 6 in the Mail Merge Wizard (Figure 5).

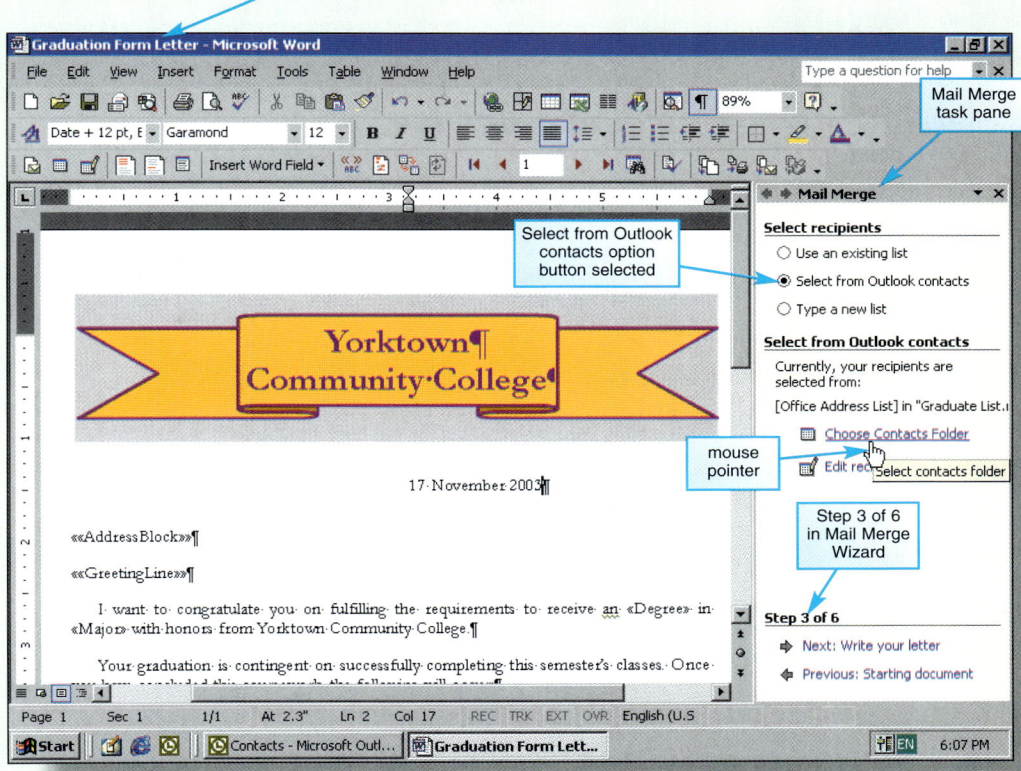

FIGURE 5

2 Click Choose Contacts Folder. If a Choose Profile dialog box displays, click the OK button. When the Select Contact List folder dialog box displays, click the folder name with the description, Graduates, and then point to the OK button.

Word displays the Select Contact List folder dialog box (Figure 6).

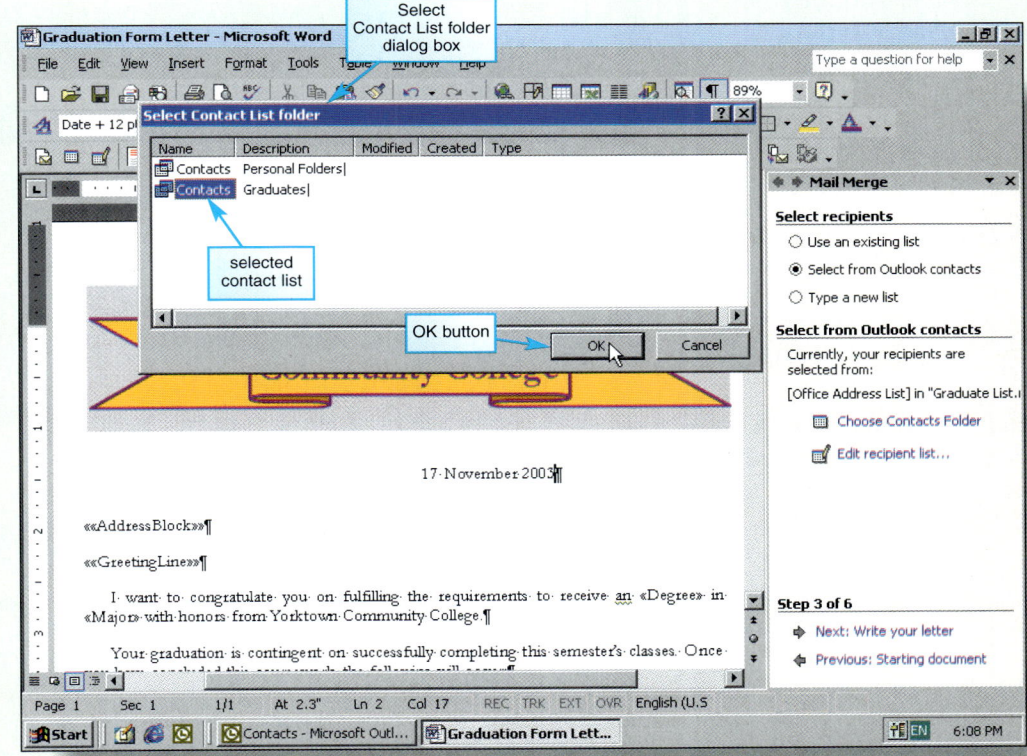

FIGURE 6

3 **Click the OK button. When Word displays the Invalid Merge Field dialog box, click the box arrow, scroll to and then click User_Field_3. Point to the OK button.**

Word displays the Invalid Merge Field dialog box (Figure 7). The field name for the GPA field is called User_Field_3 in the Outlook contacts list. Thus, you change the field name in this dialog box.

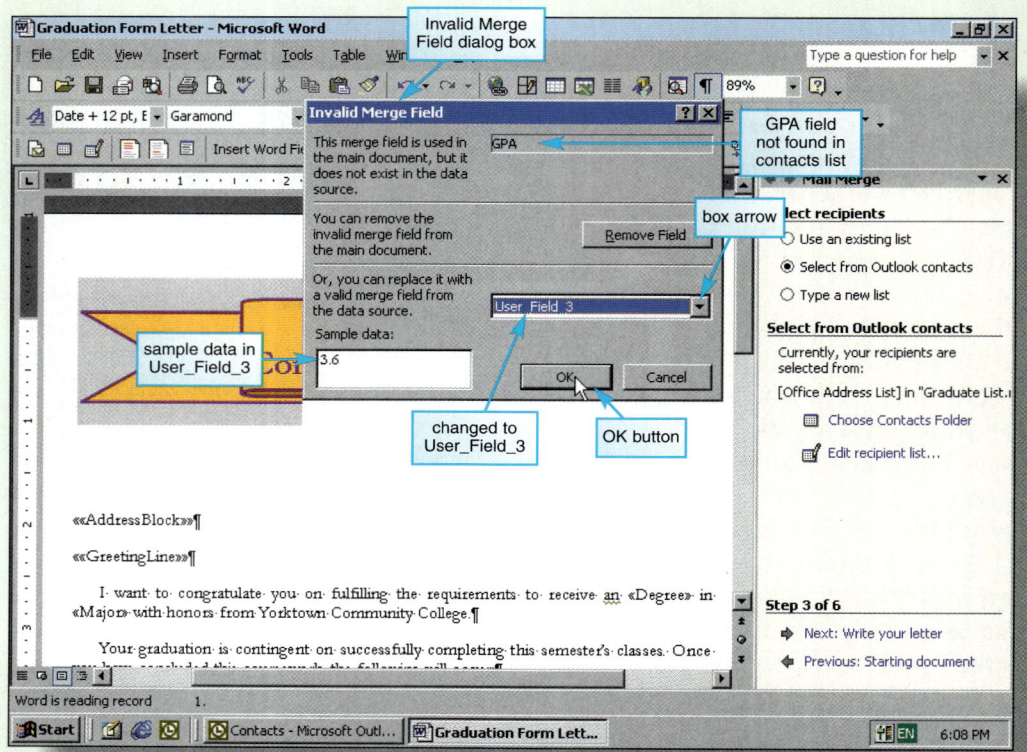

FIGURE 7

4 **Click the OK button. When Word displays the Mail Merge Recipients dialog box, point to the OK button.**

Word displays the Mail Merge Recipients dialog box, which shows all data in the Outlook contacts list (Figure 8).

5 **Click the OK button. Click the Close button on the Mail Merge task pane to close the task pane.**

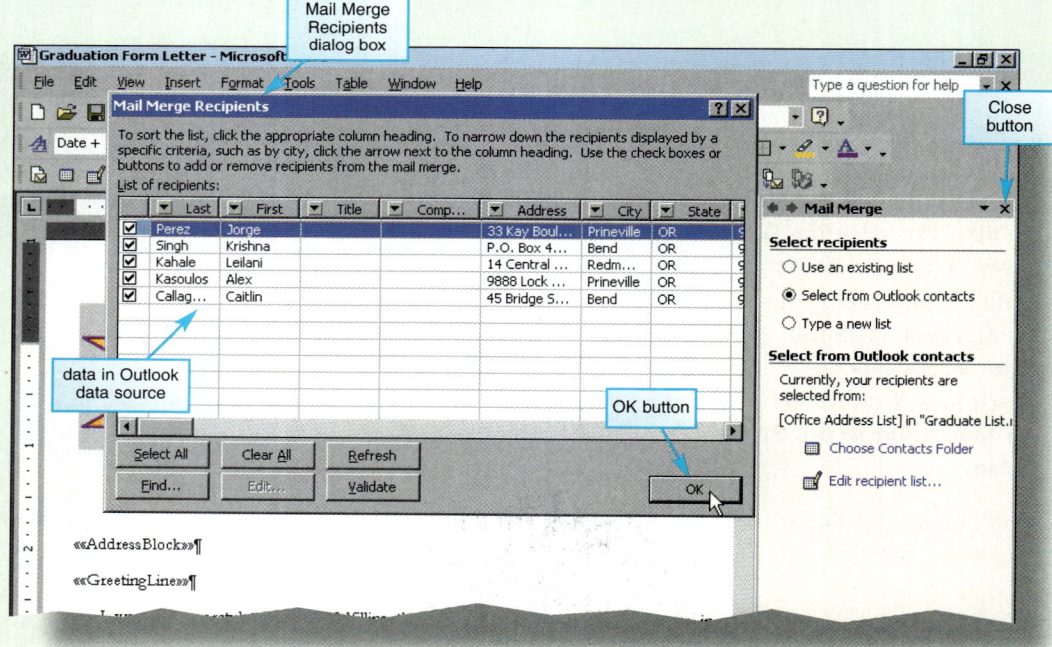

FIGURE 8

The Outlook data source now is the data source for the form letter. To maintain the original form letter with the Word table as the data source, save this form letter with a new file name, as described in the following steps.

TO SAVE THE FORM LETTER WITH A NEW FILE NAME

1. Insert your floppy disk into drive A.
2. Click File on the menu bar and then click Save As.
3. Type the file name `Graduate Form Letter Revised` in the File name text box. Do not press the ENTER key.
4. If necessary, click the Save in box arrow and then click 3½ Floppy (A:).
5. Click the Save button in the Save As dialog box.

Word saves the form letter on a floppy disk in drive A with the file name, Graduate Form Letter Revised (shown in Figure 9).

In the previous steps, Word flagged the GPA field in the form letter because the Outlook data source did not have a field called GPA. In Outlook, the GPA field is called User_Field_3. The form letter also contains a Degree field and a Major field, which have different names in the Outlook contacts list. The Degree field is called User_Field_1, and the Major field is called User_Field_2. Thus, you need to change these field name references for the Degree and Major field.

Perform the following steps to check for and fix any errors in the form letter.

Steps — To Check for Errors in the Main Document

1 If the Mail Merge toolbar does not display on the screen, click Tools on the menu bar, point to Letter and Mailings, and then click Show Mail Merge Toolbar. Click the Check for Errors button on the Mail Merge toolbar. When the Checking and Reporting Errors dialog box displays, click Complete the merge, pausing to report each error as it occurs. Point to the OK button.

Word displays the Checking and Reporting Errors dialog box (Figure 9).

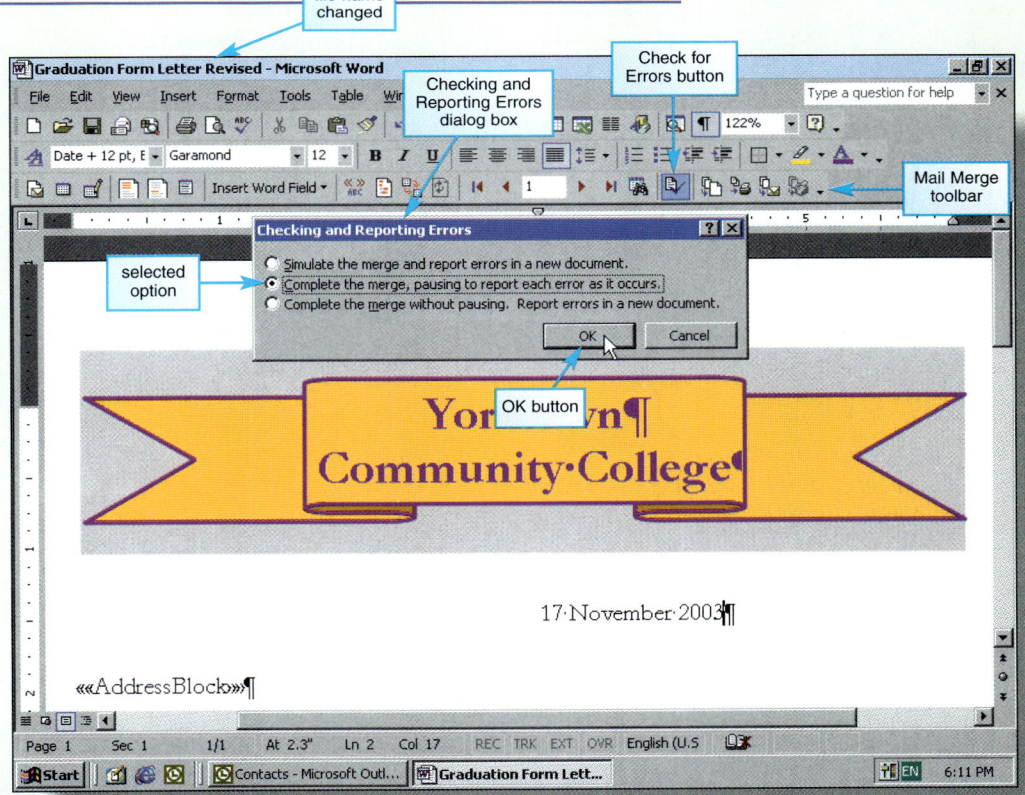

FIGURE 9

2 Click the OK button. When the Invalid Merge Field dialog box displays, click the box arrow, scroll to and then click User_Field_1. Point to the OK button.

Word displays the Invalid Merge Field dialog box (Figure 10). The field name for the Degree field is called User_Field_1 in the Outlook contacts list. Thus, you change the field name in this dialog box.

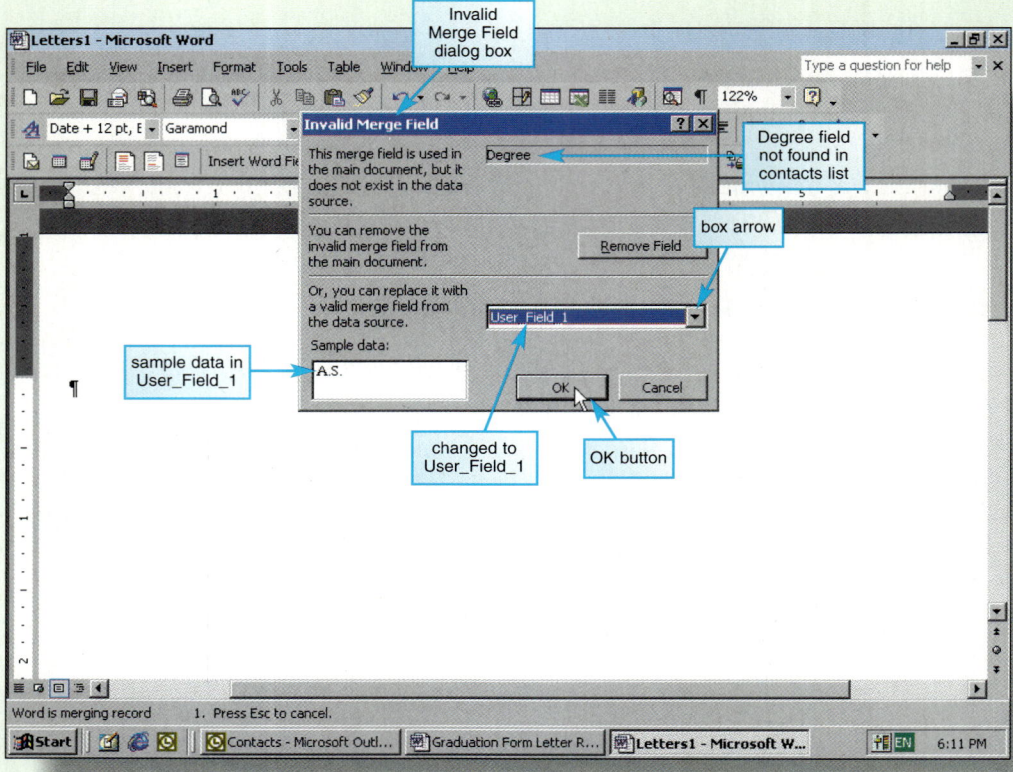

FIGURE 10

3 Click the OK button. When the next Invalid Merge Field dialog box displays, click the box arrow, scroll to and then click User_Field_2. Point to the OK button.

Word displays the Invalid Merge Field dialog box again (Figure 11). The field name for the Major field is called User_Field_2 in the Outlook contacts list.

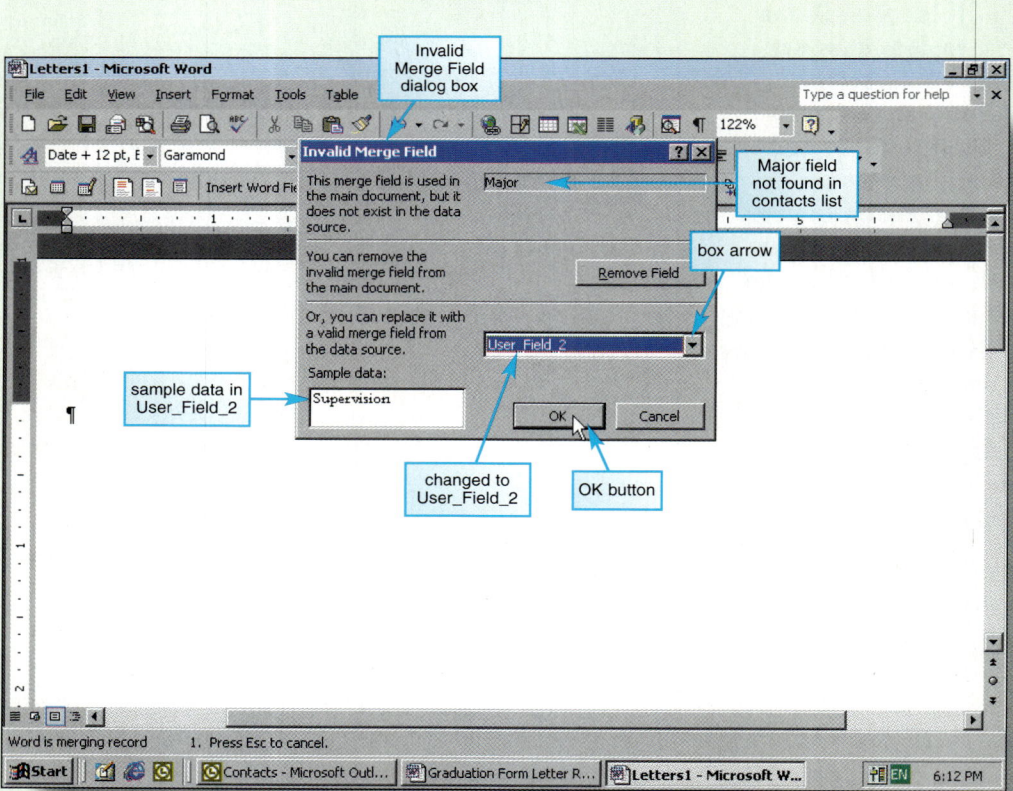

FIGURE 11

4 **Click the OK button. If Word displays a message about locked fields, click the OK button. When Word merges the form letters to a new document window, click File on the menu bar and then click Close. When Word displays a dialog box asking if you want to save changes, point to the No button.**

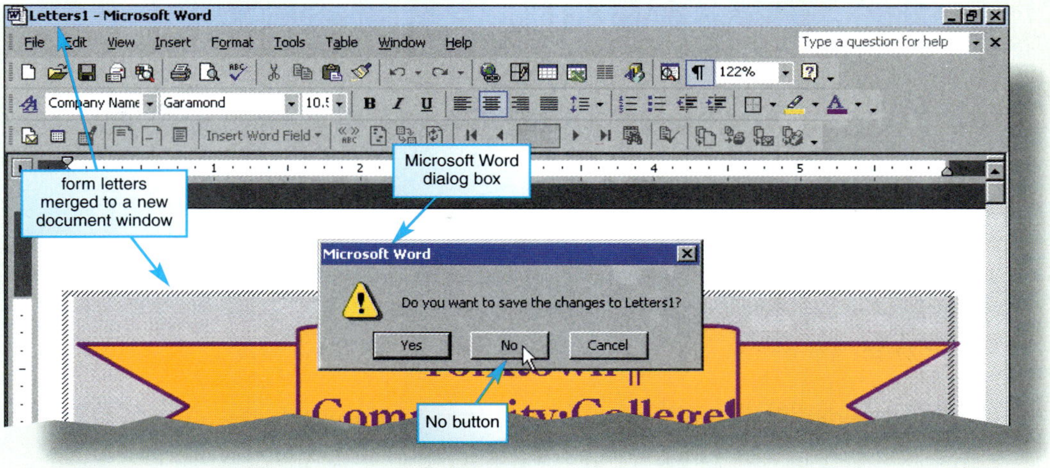

Word fixes all errors and merges the form letters to a new document window (Figure 12). You do not want to save the form letters in this document window.

FIGURE 12

5 **Click the No button.**

Word redisplays the main document window. The Degree and Major fields have been replaced with the field names, User_Field_1 and User_Field_2, respectively (shown in Figure 13 on the next page).

Perform the following step to save the revised form letter again.

TO SAVE A DOCUMENT AGAIN

1 Click the Save button on the Standard toolbar.

Word saves the main document for the form letter with the same name, Graduation Form Letter Revised.

The next step is to merge the form letters to the e-mail addresses specified in the Email Address field of the Outlook contacts list.

Merging to E-Mail Addresses

When you merge to e-mail addresses, you can instruct Word to insert the merged document in an HTML format, as plain text, or as an attachment. The HTML format converts the document to an HTML (Web page) format and displays the document in its entirety in the body of the e-mail message. Plain text removes any graphics and formatting and displays the unformatted document in its entirety in the body of the e-mail message. With an attachment, the Word document is attached to each e-mail message. When the users receive the e-mail message, they must open the attachment before they can read the message. In this feature, you want to use the HTML format.

Perform the steps on the next page to merge the form letters to e-mail addresses, sending each merged document in HTML format. If you are not connected to the Internet, Outlook places the messages in your outbox so you can send them later.

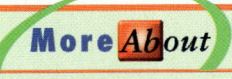

E-Mail Addresses

To merge only those records that contain an e-mail address, click the Mail Merge Recipients button on the Mail Merge toolbar. When the Mail Merge Recipients dialog box displays, scroll to display the e-mail address field, click the arrow to the left of the e-mail address field, click (Nonblanks) in the list, and then click the OK button.

Steps To Merge to E-Mail Addresses

 Click the Merge to E-mail button on the Mail Merge toolbar. When the Merge to E-mail dialog box displays, type Graduation News **in the Subject line text box, and then point to the OK button.**

Word displays the Merge to E-mail dialog box (Figure 13). HTML is the default mail format.

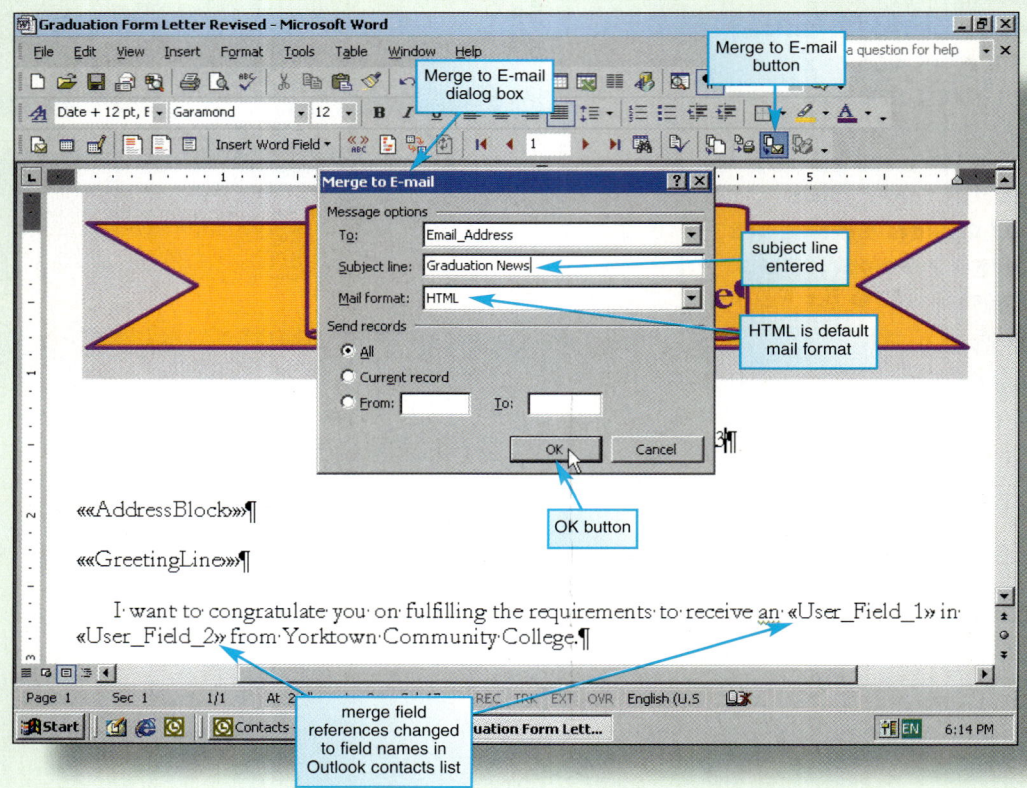

FIGURE 13

 Click the OK button. If Word displays a message about locked fields, click the OK button. If Outlook displays dialog boxes asking if you want to allow access to e-mail addresses, click the Yes button in each dialog box.

Word merges the form letters and distributes them as e-mail messages (shown in Figure 1c on page WDI 1.02).

The next steps consist of saving the main document again, quitting Word, and then removing the Graduates data file from Outlook.

TO SAVE THE MAIN DOCUMENT AGAIN

 Click the Save button on the Standard toolbar.

Word saves the form letters with the file name, Graduation Form Letters Revised, on a disk in drive A.

TO QUIT WORD

 Click the Close button at the right edge of Word's title bar.

The Word window closes.

Perform the following steps to remove the Graduates data file from Outlook.

Steps **To Remove an Outlook Data File**

1 **In the Outlook window, click File on the menu bar and then point to Data File Management (Figure 14).**

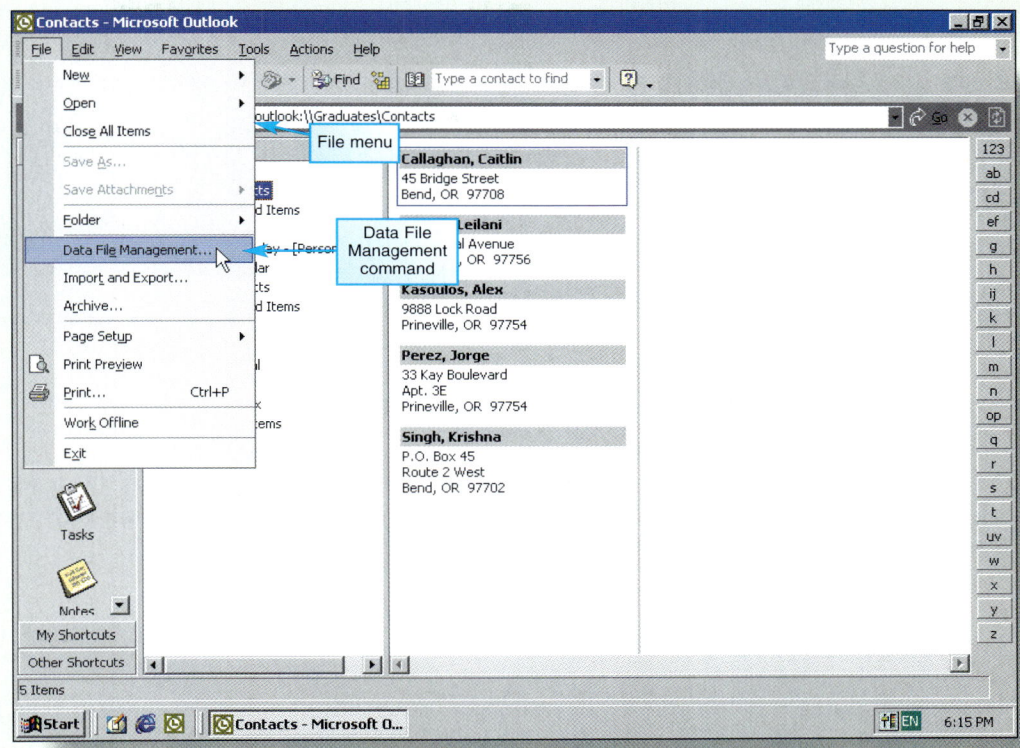

FIGURE 14

2 **When the Outlook Data Files dialog box displays, click Graduates in the list and then click the Remove button. When the Microsoft Outlook dialog box displays, point to the Yes button.**

Outlook displays a list of its data files (Figure 15).

3 **Click the Yes button. Click the Close button to close the Outlook Data Files dialog box.**

Outlook removes the Graduates data file from the list.

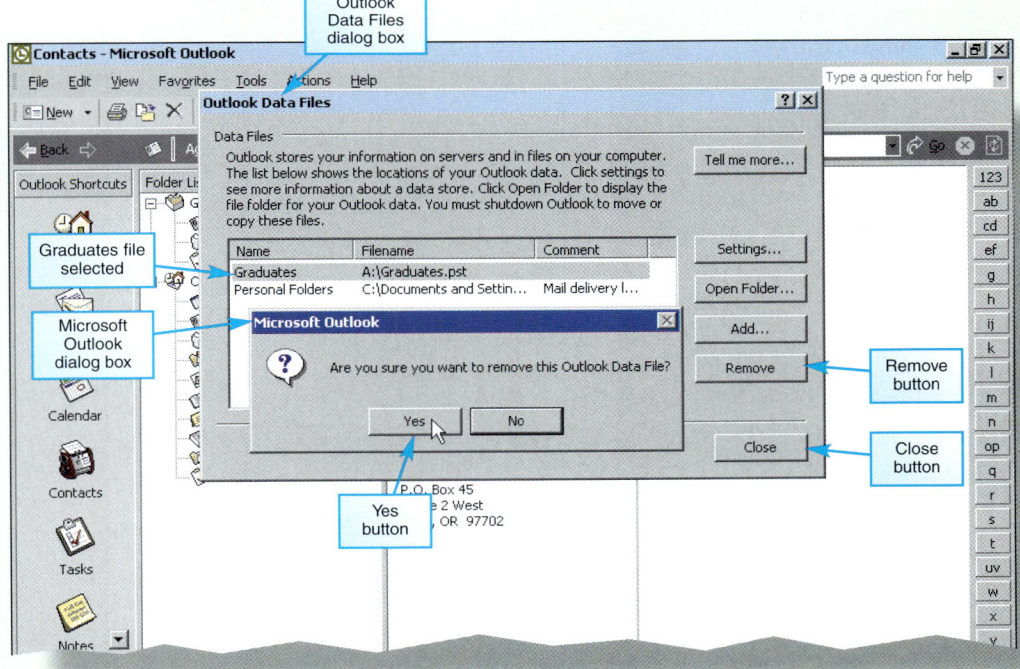

FIGURE 15

TO QUIT OUTLOOK

 Click the Close button at the right edge of Outlook's title bar.

The Outlook window closes.

CASE PERSPECTIVE SUMMARY

To verify that the merge worked correctly, Elizabeth added her own personal information as a contact in the Outlook contacts list — which means she should have an e-mail message with the subject of Graduation News in her inbox. Elizabeth starts Outlook and checks her messages. The e-mail message is there!

Elizabeth is amazed at how easy it is to distribute form letters to e-mail addresses. She is impressed with your work!

Integration Feature Summary

This Integration Feature introduced you to specifying an existing Outlook contacts list as a data source. You modified the existing data source and updated field names before performing the merge. You also learned how to merge documents and distribute them to e-mail addresses.

What You Should Know

Having completed this Integration Feature, you now should be able to perform the following tasks:

- Change a Data Source Designation *(WDI 1.05)*
- Check for Errors in the Main Document *(WDI 1.07)*
- Merge to E-Mail Addresses *(WDI 1.10)*
- Open an Outlook Data File *(WDI 1.03)*
- Quit Outlook *(WDI 1.12)*
- Quit Word *(WDI 1.10)*
- Remove an Outlook Data File *(WDI 1.11)*
- Save a Document Again *(WDI 1.09)*
- Save the Form Letter with a New File Name *(WDI 1.07)*
- Save the Main Document Again *(WDI 1.10)*

More About

Microsoft Certification

The Microsoft Office User Specialist (MOUS) Certification program provides an opportunity for you to obtain a valuable industry credential — proof that you have the Word 2002 skills required by employers. For more information, see Appendix E or visit the Shelly Cashman Series MOUS Web page at scsite.com/offxp/cert.htm.

More About

Quick Reference

For a table that lists how to complete tasks covered in this book using the mouse, menu, shortcut menu, and keyboard, see the Quick Reference Summary at the back of this book or visit the Shelly Cashman Series Office XP Web page (scsite.com/offxp/qr.htm) and then click Microsoft Word 2002.

In the Lab

1 Using an Outlook Contacts List as the Data Source for a Merge

Problem: Harmony Gallagher, senior vice president of sales at Wireless World, has an Outlook contacts list that she would like you to merge with the form letter shown in Figure 5-95 on page WD 5.73 in Project 5.

Instructions:

1. Open the document, Wireless World Form Letter, on the Data Disk. If you did not download the Data Disk, see the inside back cover for instructions for downloading the Data Disk or see your instructor.
2. In Outlook, open the Outlook data file named, Wireless.
3. In Word, use the Mail Merge Wizard to specify the data source as the Outlook contacts list. The Contacts Folder description is Wireless. The field name in Outlook for the Previous_Customer field is User_Field_1.
4. Save the main document using the file name, Wireless World Form Letter Revised.
5. Merge the form letters to the printer.

2 Distributing Form Letters to E-Mail Addresses

Problem: You created the form letter shown in Figure 5-96a on page WD 5.74 in Project 5. You decide to modify the data source to include e-mail addresses and then distribute the form letters to the e-mail addresses.

Instructions:

1. Open the Arrow Insurance Form Letter shown in Figure 5-96a. (If you did not create the form letter, see your instructor for a copy.)
2. Click the Mail Merge Recipients button on the Mail Merge toolbar and then click the Edit button in the Mail Merge Recipients dialog box. Add a new field, called E-mail Address, to the data source by clicking the Customize button in the dialog box. Enter the following e-mail addresses: valesquez@world.com, obi@earth.net, weinberg@clanton.net, murray@earth.net, houck@world.com. Add another record to the data source containing your personal information.
3. Merge the form letters to the e-mail addresses in HTML format. Print the e-mail message that is delivered to your inbox.
4. Save the main document using Arrow Insurance Form Letter Revised as the file name.

In the Lab

3 Creating an Outlook Contacts List and Merging It to E-Mail Addresses

Problem: Dale Bianchi, membership director of Citizens Broadcasting Network, would like you to create an Outlook contacts list and then merge it with the form letter shown in Figure 5-97a on page WD 5.76 in Project 5.

Instructions:

1. Start Outlook. Create an Outlook contacts list that contains the records shown in Figure 5-97b on page WD 5.77 in Project 5. Add an E-mail Address field with suitable e-mail addresses. Add yourself as a contact. You may need to use Help in Outlook to assist you in the procedure for adding contacts.
2. Start Word. Open the document, Citizens Form Letter, from your floppy disk. (If you did not create the form letter, see your instructor for a copy.)
3. In Word, use the Mail Merge Wizard to specify the data source as the Outlook contacts list you created in Step 1.
4. Merge the form letters to the e-mail addresses in HTML format. Print the e-mail message that is delivered to your inbox.
5. Save the main document using Citizens Form Letter Revised as the file name.

Microsoft Word 2002

PROJECT 7

Creating an Online Form

You will have mastered the material in this project when you can:

OBJECTIVES

- Design an online form
- Create a document template
- Highlight text
- Insert a table into a form
- Insert a text form field into a form
- Insert a drop-down form field into a form
- Insert a check box into a form
- Format form fields
- Use the Format Painter button
- Add Help text to form fields
- Insert and format a rectangle drawing object
- Animate text
- Protect a form
- Open a new document based on a template
- Fill out a form
- Save data on a form in a text file
- Modify the location of workgroup templates

Microsoft **Word 2002**

Virtual Shoppers
Find the Perfect Fit

Today's virtual individual enjoys the convenience of Internet shopping; communicating with friends, family, and colleagues via e-mail; researching information for school projects and work assignments; and participating in a myriad of other online activities.

No other facet of the Internet has garnered more interest than e-commerce. With hundreds of e-consumers attracted to the vast numbers of sales channels from e-retail to e-financial, sales are in the billions of dollars. Buying online is a bit more complicated, however, when it comes to purchasing clothing. Without the ability to try on the selected garments, how can you be sure of the fit?

This logistical problem can be frustrating to shoppers who are expected to spend $13 billion online for apparel by 2003.

Lands' End has come up with a solution to these virtual shopping woes. This Wisconsin-based direct merchant of traditional, casual clothes has developed Your Personal Model, a personalized 3-D representation of female customers that selects the most flattering clothes for their figures, suggests specific outfits for various occasions, and provides an online dressing room to try on the garments.

Shoppers begin their Your Personal Model shopping adventure by answering several questions regarding their physical features, such as specific skin tones, face shapes, hairstyles, and hair colors. They save their profiles for future shopping sprees, and proceed to the Welcome Page.

At this point, their models appear along with custom outfits designed for their bodies and for their lifestyles. The site may make suggestions for specific occasions such as gray Chinos and a beige sweater set for a casual workplace and a simple black knit dress for an informal weekend party.

The next step is to take these garments to The Dressing Room. There, the shoppers can view the particular clothes on their models. The site gives advice on choosing the proper size and then places the items in the customers' virtual shopping carts.

Ordering is easy. If they use Your Personal Model, the contents of their shopping carts display automatically in an order form.

Gary C. Comer, an avid sailor and advertising copywriter, founded Lands' End in 1961 in Chicago to sell sailing equipment and hardware via a catalog. In the 1970s, the company's focus switched to clothing. Today, Lands' End is the second largest apparel mail-order company with sales of more than $1.37 billion to its 6.1 million customers. The Lands' End Web site (www.landsend.com) was unveiled in 1995 and receives 15 million visitors yearly.

Internet shopping has created an important focus for the use of forms and online communication. In Project 7, you will develop a form by creating a template in Word 2002. The form will be structured as a survey in order to gather information and opinions from Web customers of Brim's Blooming Boutique. Survey information will provide an assessment of order types, customer satisfaction, and online convenience. As a result of the survey, changes may be implemented and successes enhanced.

With increasingly more people using computers in the home, school, and workplace, the use of well-thought-out online forms provides the ability to complete successfully many aspects of course work, vocational activities, and personal interests.

Microsoft Word 2002

Creating an Online Form

PROJECT 7

CASE PERSPECTIVE

For the past two years, Brim's Blooming Boutique has allowed customers to order flowers, plants, teddy bears, fruit baskets, and other gifts through its Web site. The number of customers placing orders online is growing rapidly. Carol Brim, the owner of Brim's Blooming Boutique, believes the Web site is easy to use. She wants to be sure, however, that customers have the same opinion. Carol knows that a satisfied customer is one who will return for more business.

Today, you receive a call from Carol, who is Aunt Carol to you. She knows you are majoring in Office Automation at school and wonders if you could create a survey to e-mail to all Web customers. The survey should ask for the customer's name, an opinion of the Web site navigation, the time it takes to shop, and the type of orders placed on the Web. You welcome the opportunity to help Aunt Carol. Designing and distributing the surveys will be fun. Once the completed surveys are returned, you will tabulate the responses and print them in a report for your favorite aunt.

Introduction

During your personal and professional life, you undoubtedly have filled out countless forms. Whether a federal tax form, a time card, an application, an order, a deposit slip, or a survey, a form is designed to collect information. In the past, forms were printed; that is, you received the form on a piece of paper, filled it in with a pen or pencil, and then returned it manually.

Today, people are concerned with using resources efficiently. To minimize waste of paper, save the world's trees, improve office efficiency, and improve access to data, many businesses attempt to become a paperless office. Thus, the online form has emerged. With an **online form**, you access the form using your computer, fill it out using the computer, and then return it via the computer. You may access the form at a Web site, on your company's intranet, or from your inbox if you receive it via e-mail.

Not only does an online form reduce the need for paper, it saves the time spent duplicating a form and distributing it. With more and more people owning a home computer, online forms have become a popular means of collecting personal information, as well. In Word, you easily can create an online form for distribution electronically, which then can be filled in using Word.

Project Seven — Online Form

Project 7 uses Word to create the online form shown in Figure 7-1. The form is a survey e-mailed to all Web customers of Brim's Blooming Boutique. Upon receipt of the form, customers fill it in, save it, and then e-mail it back to the boutique. Figure 7-1a shows how the form displays on a customer's screen initially (as a blank form); Figure 7-1b shows the form partially filled in by one customer; and Figure 7-1c shows how the customer filled in the entire form.

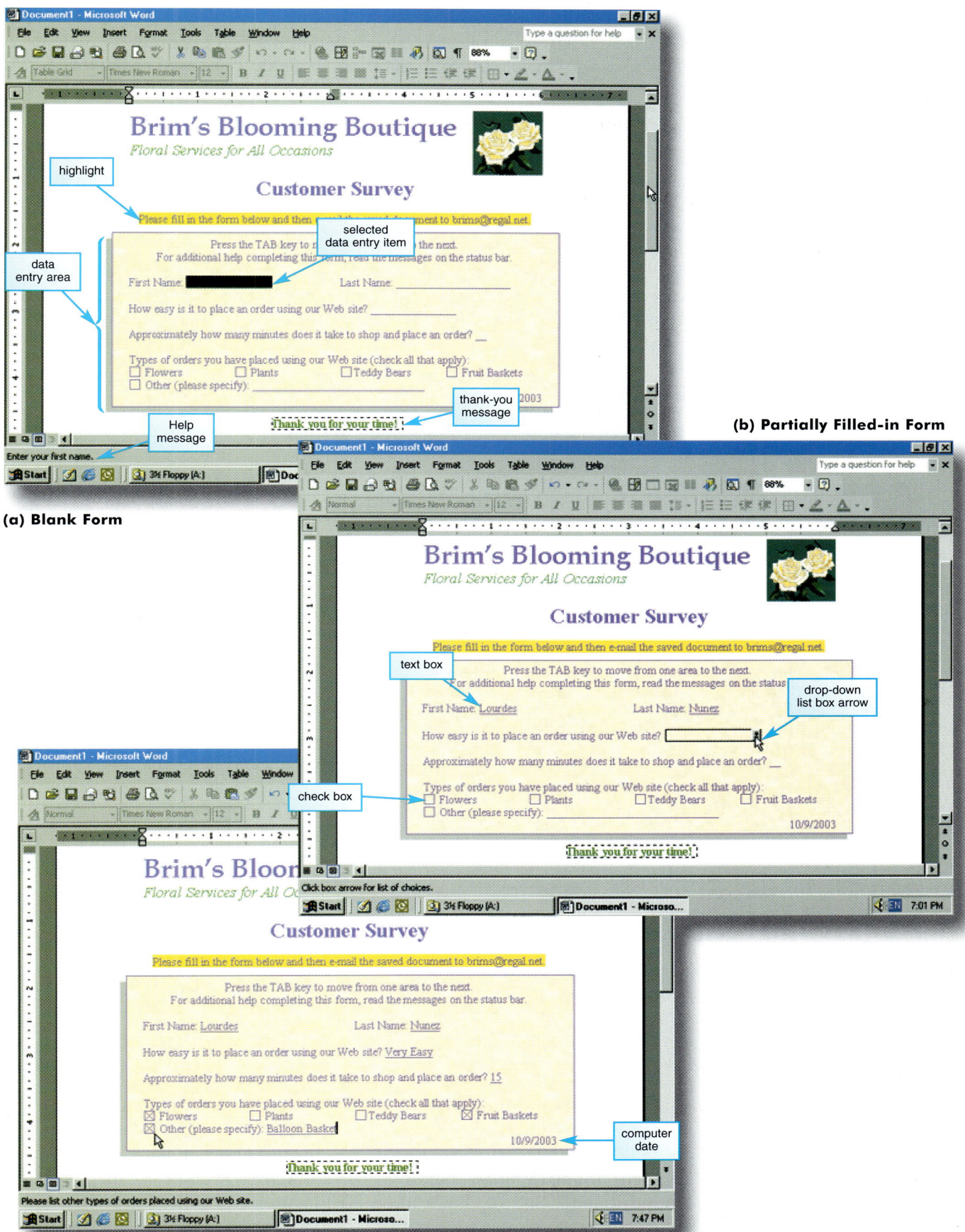

FIGURE 7-1

More About

Online Forms

For a sample online form on the Web, visit the Word 2002 More About Web page (www.scsite.com/wd2002/more.htm) and then click Sample Online Form.

The form is designed so it fits completely within the Word window — without a user having to scroll while filling in the form. The **data entry area** of the form is enclosed by a rectangle that is shaded in beige. The rectangle has a shadow on its left and bottom edges. The line above the data entry area is highlighted in yellow to draw the user's attention to the message. The thank-you message below the data entry area is surrounded by a moving rectangle.

The data entry area of the form contains four text boxes (First Name, Last Name, number of minutes, and Other), one drop-down list box (ease of use), and five check boxes (Flowers, Plants, Teddy Bears, Fruit Baskets, and Other). As a user presses the TAB key to move the selection from one data entry item to the next, the status bar displays a brief Help message that is related to the location of the selection. Note that in Word the drop-down list box does not display the box arrow until you tab to the drop-down list box. The date in the lower-right corner of the data entry area is the date from the computer on which the form is being displayed.

Starting Word

Follow these steps to start Word or ask your instructor how to start Word for your system.

TO START AND CUSTOMIZE WORD

1. Click the Start button on the Windows taskbar, point to Programs on the Start menu, and then click Microsoft Word on the Programs submenu.
2. If the Word window is not maximized, double-click its title bar to maximize it.
3. If the Language bar displays on the screen, click its Minimize button.
4. If the New Document task pane displays in the Word window, click the Show at startup check box to remove the check mark and then click the Close button in the upper-right corner of the task pane title bar.
5. If the toolbars display positioned on the same row, click the Toolbar Options button and then click Show Buttons on Two Rows.
6. If your screen differs from Figure 7-3 on page WD 7.09, click View on the menu bar and then click Print Layout.

Word starts. After a few moments, an empty document titled Document1 displays in the Word window (shown in Figure 7-3).

More About

Fields

For more information about fields, visit the Word 2002 More About Web page (www.scsite.com/wd2002/more.htm) and then click Fields.

Resetting Menus and Toolbars

To set the menus and toolbars so they appear exactly as shown in this book, you should reset your menus and toolbars as outlined in Appendix D or follow these steps.

TO RESET MENUS AND TOOLBARS

1. Click the Toolbar Options button on the Standard toolbar and then point to Add or Remove Buttons. Point to Standard on the Add or Remove Buttons submenu. Scroll to and then click Reset Toolbar on the Standard submenu.
2. Click the Toolbar Options button on the Formatting toolbar and then point to Add or Remove Buttons. Point to Formatting on the Add or Remove Buttons submenu. Scroll to and then click Reset Toolbar on the Formatting submenu.

3. Click the Toolbar Options button on the Standard toolbar and then point to Add or Remove Buttons. Click Customize on the Add or Remove Buttons submenu.

4. When the Customize dialog box displays, if necessary, click the Options tab and then click the Reset my usage data button. When the Microsoft Word dialog box displays, click the Yes button. Click the Close button in the Customize dialog box.

Word resets the menus and toolbars.

Displaying Formatting Marks

It is helpful to display formatting marks that indicate where in the document you pressed the ENTER key, SPACEBAR, and other keys. Perform the following step to display formatting marks.

TO DISPLAY FORMATTING MARKS

1. If the Show/Hide ¶ button on the Standard toolbar is not selected already, click it.

Word displays formatting marks in the document window, and the Show/Hide ¶ button on the Standard toolbar is selected (shown in Figure 7-3 on page WD 7.09).

Zooming Page Width

When you zoom page width, Word displays the page on the screen as large as possible in print layout view. Perform the following steps to zoom page width.

TO ZOOM PAGE WIDTH

1. Click the Zoom box arrow on the Standard toolbar.
2. Click Page Width in the Zoom list.

Word computes the zoom percentage and displays it in the Zoom box (shown in Figure 7-3). Your percentage may be different depending on your computer.

Designing an Online Form

To minimize the time spent creating a form on the computer, you should sketch it on a piece of paper first. A design for the online form in this project is shown in Figure 7-2 on the next page.

During the **form design**, you should create a well-thought-out draft of the form that attempts to include all essential form elements. These elements include the form's title, placement of text and graphics, instructions for users of the form, and field specifications. A **field** is a placeholder for data. A **field specification** defines characteristics of a field such as the field's type, length, format, and a list of possible values that may be entered into the field. Many designers place Xs in fields where a user will be allowed to enter any type of character, and 9s in fields where a user will be allowed to enter numbers only. For example, in Figure 7-2, a user can enter up to 15 of any type of character in the First Name text box and up to two numbers in the number of minutes text box.

Forms

Both Microsoft Word and Microsoft Access allow you to create forms and templates that contain complex formatting, pictures, check boxes, drop-down lists, or text areas. You can assign specific data types, formatting, and default text. You also can set conditions for adding data to a form, include macros that run automatically, and provide Help messages that make it easier for others to complete a form. Both programs allow you to create forms for online use, as well as forms to print on paper.

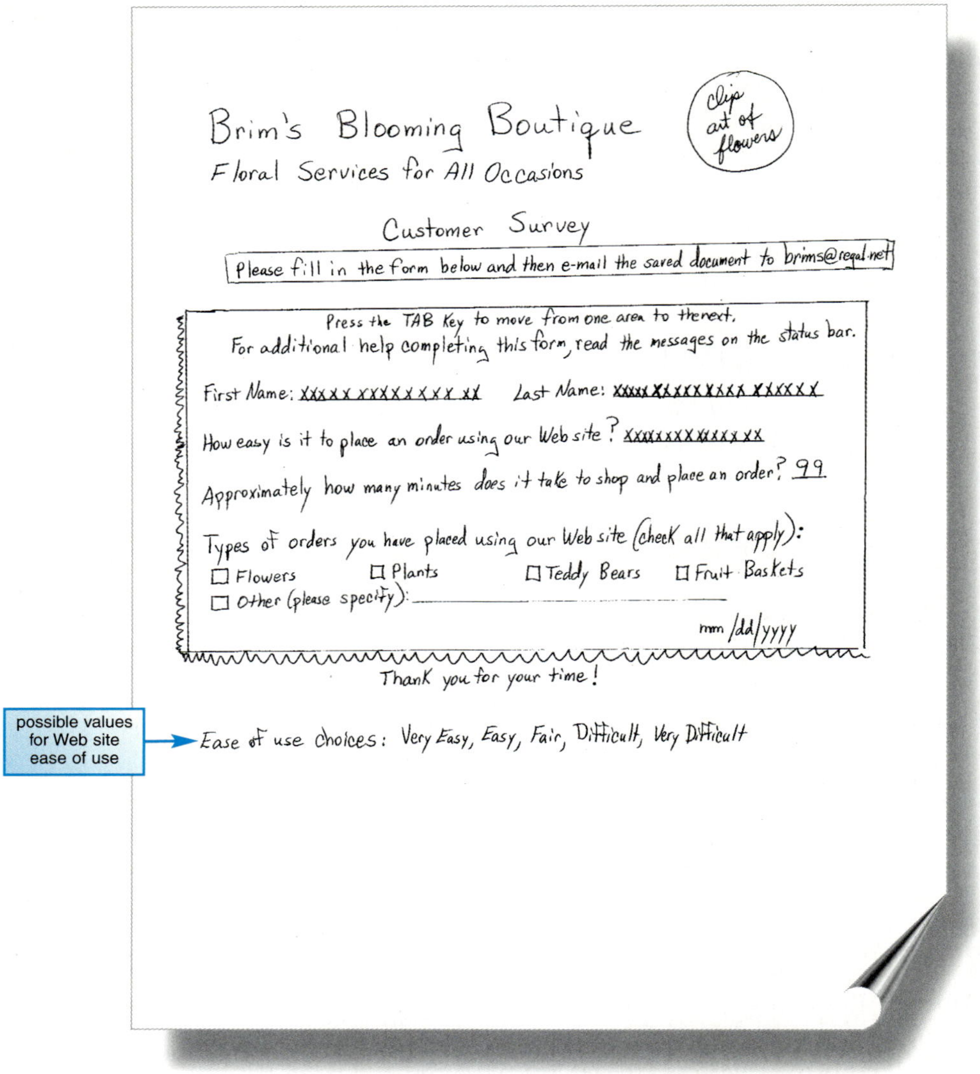

FIGURE 7-2

(handwritten draft annotations:)
- Brim's Blooming Boutique
- Floral Services for All Occasions
- clip art of flowers
- Customer Survey
- Please fill in the form below and then e-mail the saved document to brims@regal.net
- Press the TAB key to move from one area to the next.
- For additional help completing this form, read the messages on the status bar.
- First Name: XXXXX XXXXXXXX XX   Last Name: XXXXX XXXXXXXXX XXXXXX
- How easy is it to place an order using our Web site? XXXXXXXXXXXXX XX
- Approximately how many minutes does it take to shop and place an order? 99
- Types of orders you have placed using our Web site (check all that apply):
- ☐ Flowers   ☐ Plants   ☐ Teddy Bears   ☐ Fruit Baskets
- ☐ Other (please specify): _____
- mm/dd/yyyy
- Thank you for your time!

possible values for Web site ease of use → Ease of use choices: Very Easy, Easy, Fair, Difficult, Very Difficult

With this draft of the form in hand, the next step is to create the form in Word.

Creating an Online Form

The process of creating an online form begins with creating a template. Next, you insert and format any text, graphics, and fields where data is to be entered on the form. Finally, before you save the form for electronic distribution, you protect it. With a **protected form**, users can enter data only where you have placed form fields; that is, they will not be able to modify any other items on the form. Many menu commands and toolbar buttons are dimmed, and thus unavailable, in a protected form. The steps on the following pages illustrate how to create an online form.

Creating a Template

A **template** is a file that contains the definition of the appearance of a Word document, including items such as default font, font size, margin settings, and line spacing; available styles; and even placement of text. Every Word document you

---

More About

Protected Forms

If you open an existing form that has been protected, Word will not allow you to modify the form's appearance until you unprotect it. To unprotect a document, click Tools on the menu bar and then click Unprotect Document. If the form has been password-protected, you will be asked to enter a password when you invoke the Unprotect Document command.

create is based on a template. When you select Blank Document in the New Document task pane or when you click the New Blank Document button on the Standard toolbar, Word creates a document based on the Normal template. Word also provides other templates for more specific types of documents such as memos, letters, and fax cover sheets. Creating a document based on these templates can improve your productivity because Word has defined much of the document's appearance for you.

If you create and save an online form as a Word document that is based on the Normal template, users will be required to open that Word document to display the form on the screen. Next, they will fill in the form. Then, to preserve the content of the original form, they will have to save the form with a new file name. If they accidentally click the Save button on the Standard toolbar, Word will replace the original blank form with a filled-in form.

If you create and save the online form as a **document template** instead, users will open a new document window that is based on that template. This displays the form on the screen as a brand new Word document; that is, the document does not have a file name. Thus, the user fills in the form and then simply saves it. By using a template for the form, the original form remains intact when the user clicks the Save button.

Perform the following steps to create a document template to be used for the online form and then save the template with the name Brim's Survey.

Templates

Most documents have a file name and a three-character file extension. When a file extension displays, it is separated from the file name with a period. The extension, sometimes called the file type, often is assigned by an application, which helps Windows open the file with the correct software. For example, a Word document has an extension of doc, and a Word template has an extension of dot. Thus, a file named Finance Report.doc is a Word document, and a file named Learning Survey.dot is a Word template.

To Create a Document Template

1 **Click File on the menu bar and then click New. When the New Document task pane displays, click General Templates. When the Templates dialog box displays, if necessary, click the General tab. Click the Blank Document icon and then click Template in the Create New area. Point to the OK button.**

Word displays the Templates dialog box (Figure 7-3). The Template option button instructs Word to create a new template, instead of a new Word document.

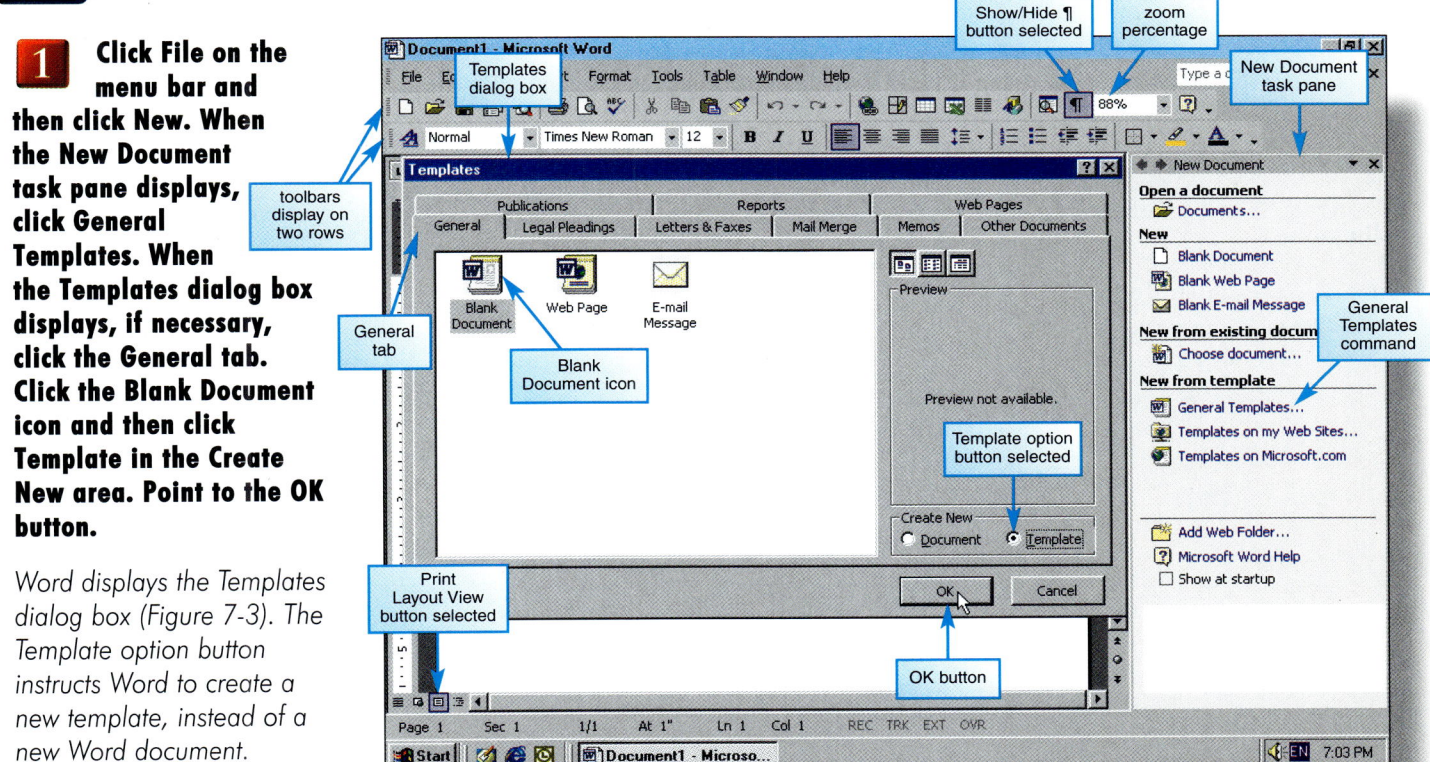

FIGURE 7-3

 **Click the OK button.**

Word displays a blank template titled Template1 in the Word window (Figure 7-4).

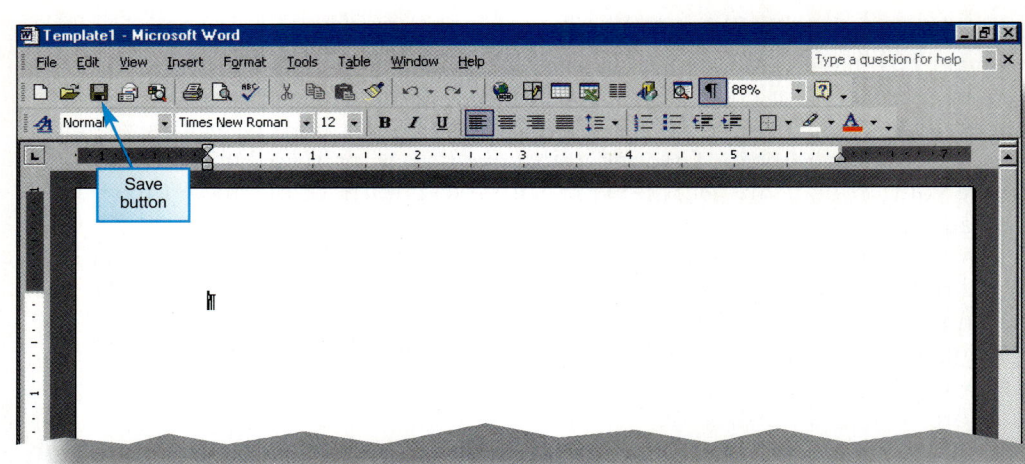

FIGURE 7-4

With a disk in drive A, click the Save button on the Standard toolbar. Type Brim's Survey **in the File name text box. If necessary, click the Save in box arrow and then click 3½ Floppy (A:). Point to the Save button in the Save As dialog box.**

Word displays the Save As dialog box with Document Template listed in the Save as type box (Figure 7-5).

Click the Save button in the Save As dialog box.

Word saves the template on the floppy disk in drive A with the file name, Brim's Survey (shown in Figure 7-6).

Other Ways

1. Click Start button on Windows taskbar, click New Office Document, click General tab, double-click Blank Document icon
2. Right-click Start button on Windows taskbar, click Open, double-click New Office Document, click General tab, double-click Blank Document icon
3. With task pane displaying, in Voice Command mode, say "General Templates, General, [select Blank Document icon], OK"

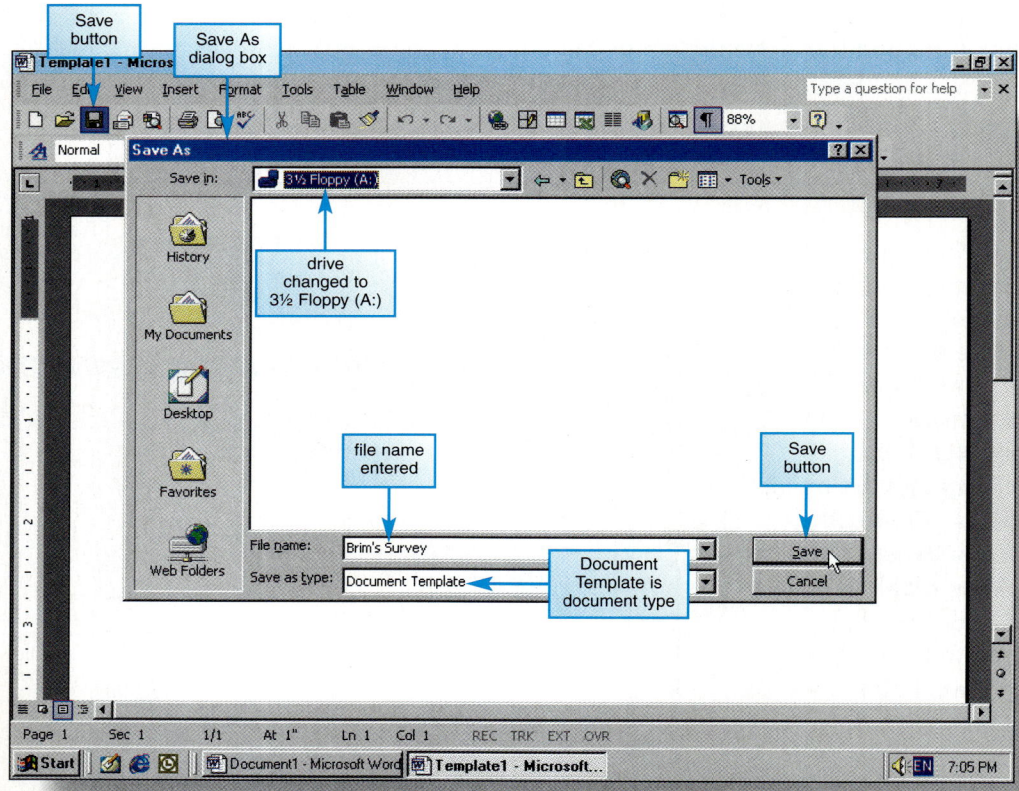

FIGURE 7-5

The next step in creating the online form is to enter the text, graphics, and fields into the template. Perform the following steps to format and enter the boutique name, business tag line, and survey title.

TO ENTER AND FORMAT TEXT

1. Click the Font box arrow on the Formatting toolbar, scroll to and then click Book Antiqua. Click the Font Size box arrow on the Formatting toolbar and then click 28. Click the Font Color button arrow on the Formatting toolbar and then click Violet. Press CTRL+B to turn on bold formatting. Type Brim's Blooming Boutique and then press CTRL+B to turn off bold formatting. Press the ENTER key.

2. Click the Font box arrow on the Formatting toolbar and then click Times New Roman. Click the Font Size box arrow on the Formatting toolbar and then click 16. Click the Font Color button arrow on the Formatting toolbar and then click Sea Green. Press CTRL+I to turn on italic formatting. Type Floral Services for All Occasions and then press CTRL+I to turn off italic formatting. Press the ENTER key twice.

3. Click the Font Size box arrow on the Formatting toolbar and then click 22. Click the Font Color button arrow on the Formatting toolbar and then click Violet. Press CTRL+B to turn on bold formatting. Press CTRL+E to center the paragraph. Type Customer Survey and then press CTRL+B to turn off bold formatting. Press the ENTER key.

The boutique name, business tag line, and survey title display as shown in Figure 7-6.

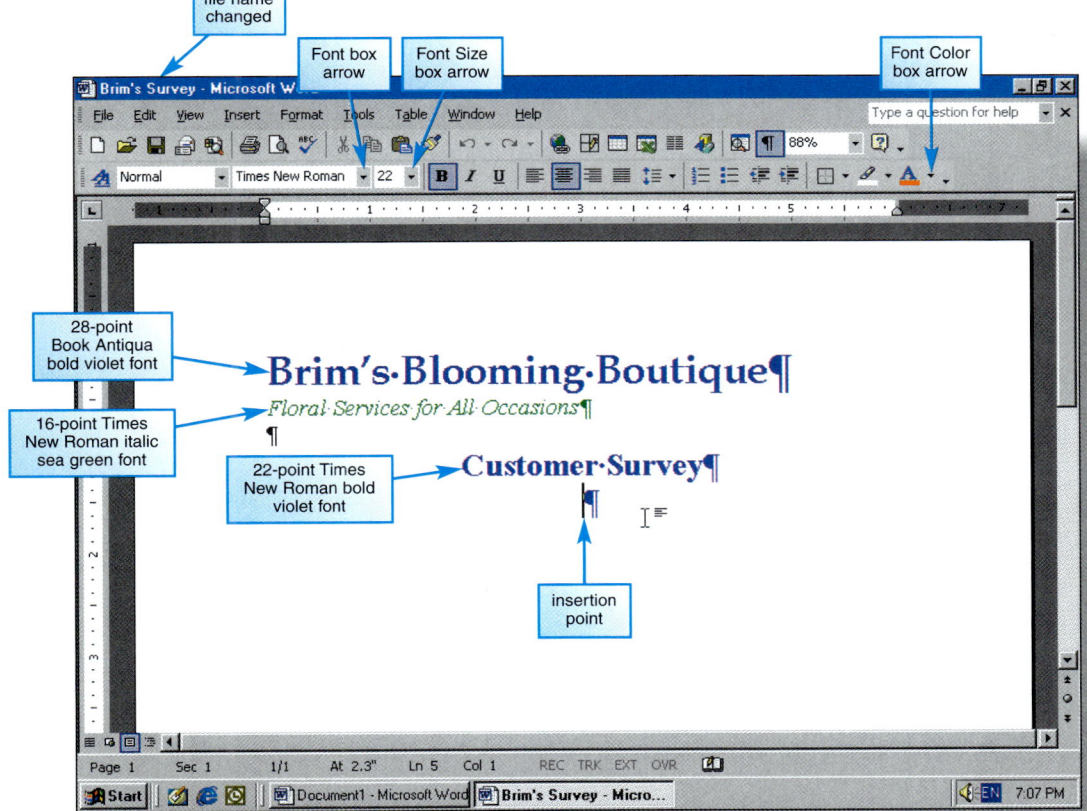

FIGURE 7-6

The next step is to insert the clip art of the flowers. Word inserts clip art as an inline graphic; that is, part of the current paragraph. You want to position the image of the flowers to the right of the boutique name (Figure 7-1 on page WD 7.05). Thus, the graphic needs to be a floating graphic instead of an inline graphic. Also, the graphic is too large for this form. Thus, after you insert the graphic you will reduce its size and change its wrapping style to Square, as described in the following steps.

TO INSERT AND FORMAT CLIP ART

1. With the insertion point on line 5, click Insert on the menu bar, point to Picture, and then click Clip Art. When the Insert Clip Art task pane displays, drag through any text in the Search text text box. Type flowers and then press the ENTER key.

2. Point to the clip of the flowers that matches the one shown in Figure 7-7. Click the box arrow that displays to the right of the clip and then click Insert on the menu. Click the Close button on the Insert Clip Art task pane title bar.

3. Double-click the graphic. When the Format Picture dialog box displays, if necessary, click the Size tab. Change the Height and Width in the Scale area to 50%.

4. Click the Layout tab and then click Square in the Wrapping style area. Click the OK button. Drag the flowers graphic to the right of the boutique name as shown in Figure 7-7.

5. Position the insertion point on the paragraph mark on line 5.

The graphic displays on the form, as shown in Figure 7-7.

More About

Designing Questionnaires

For more information on how to design a good questionnaire, visit the Word 2002 More About Web page (www.scsite.com/wd2002/more.htm) and then click Designing Questionnaires.

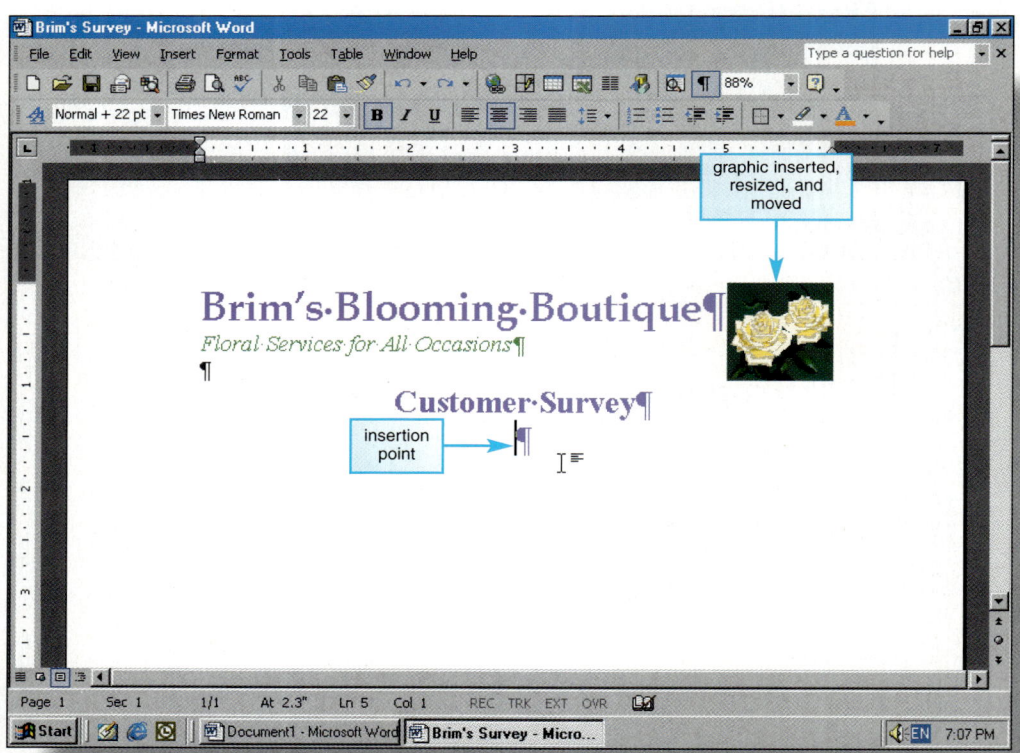

FIGURE 7-7

The next step is to enter the instructions and then highlight them in yellow.

Highlighting Text

You **highlight** text in an online document to alert the reader to the text's importance, much like a highlight marker does in a book. You want to draw attention to the instructions that specify where to mail the completed form. Thus, you highlight this line.

Perform the following steps to highlight text in a document.

Removing Highlights

To remove all highlights from a document, click Edit on the menu bar, click Select All, click the Highlight button arrow, and then click None. To remove an individual highlight, select the text from which you wish to remove the highlight, click the Highlight button arrow, and then click None.

Steps: To Highlight Text

1 Click the Font Size box arrow on the Formatting toolbar and then click 12. Click the Font Color button arrow on the Formatting toolbar and then click Automatic. Press the ENTER key. Type `Please fill in the form below and then e-mail the saved document to brims@regal.net.` Press the ENTER key. Right-click the hyperlink and then click Remove Hyperlink on the shortcut menu. If the Highlight button on the Formatting toolbar displays yellow on its face, click the Highlight button; otherwise, click the Highlight button arrow and then click Yellow. Position the mouse pointer in the document window.

The Highlight button is selected and displays yellow on its face (Figure 7-8). The mouse pointer displays as an I-beam with a highlighter attached to it.

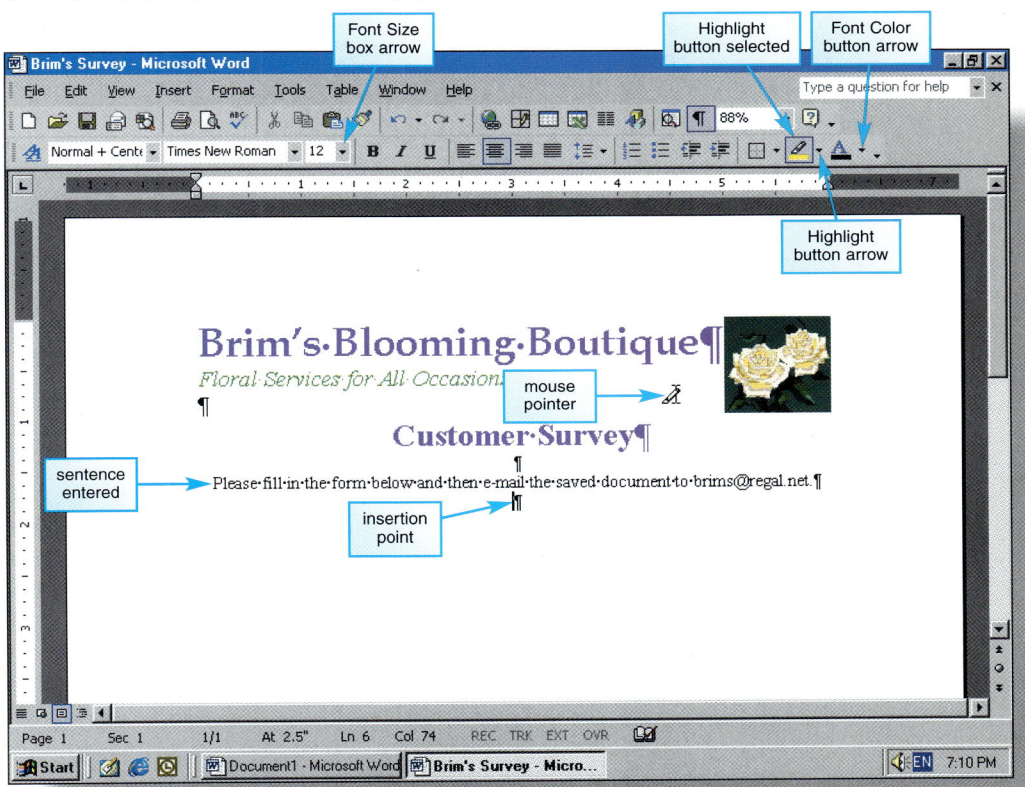

FIGURE 7-8

2 Click to the left of the sentence or drag through the sentence to highlight it.

Word highlights the selected text in yellow (Figure 7-9). The Highlight button remains selected.

3 Click the Highlight button on the Formatting toolbar to turn highlighting off (shown in Figure 7-10).

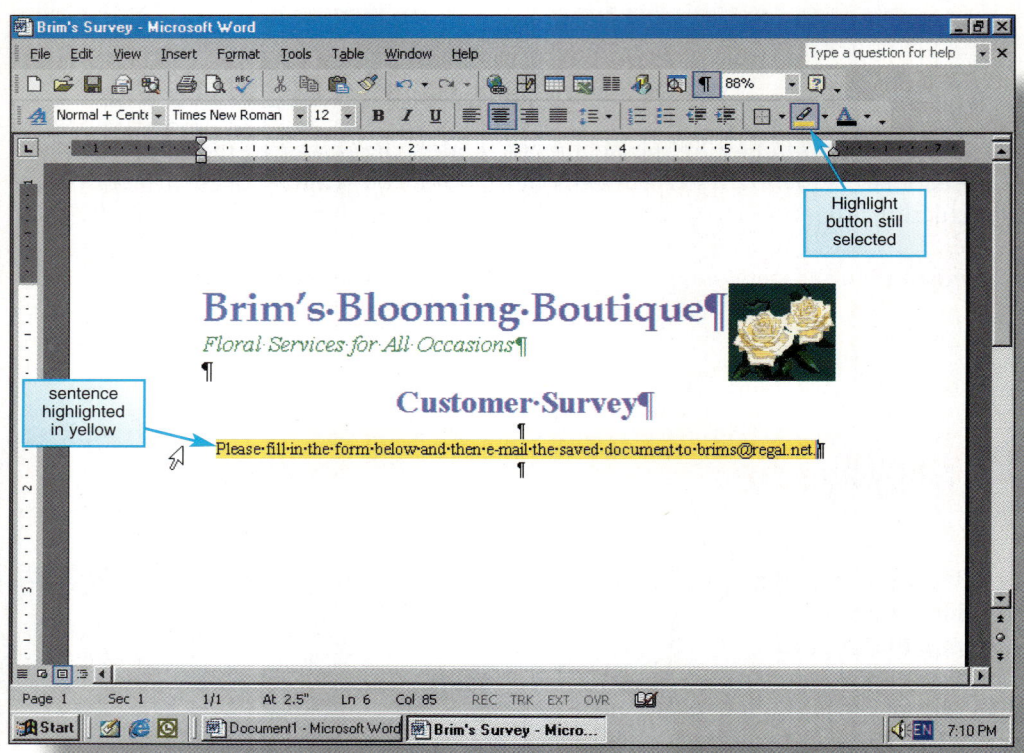

FIGURE 7-9

1. In Voice Command mode, say "Highlight, [select text], Highlight"

When the Highlight button is selected, you can continue to select text to be highlighted. The highlighter remains active until you click the Highlight button or press the ESC key to turn it off.

Word provides a variety of highlighter colors. To change the color, click the Highlight button arrow and then click the desired color.

The next step is to enter the instructions for filling in the data entry area of the form, as described in the following steps.

TO ENTER TEXT

1 Position the insertion point on the paragraph mark below the highlighted text and then press the ENTER key.

2 Click the Font Color box arrow and then click Violet. Type `Press the TAB key to move from one area to the next.` Press the ENTER key.

3 Type `For additional help completing this form, read the messages on the status bar.` Press the ENTER key twice.

4 Press CTRL+L to left-align the current paragraph.

The data entry area instructions are entered (shown in Figure 7-11 on page WD 7.16).

The next step is to insert a table to hold the fields in the data entry area of the form.

Creating an Online Form • WD 7.15

Inserting a Table into a Form

The first line of data entry in the form consists of the First Name text box, which begins at the left margin, and the Last Name text box, which begins at the center point. Although you could set tab stops to align the data in a form, it is easier to insert a table. For example, the first line could be a 1 × 2 table; that is, a table with one row and two columns. By inserting a 1 × 2 table, Word automatically positions the second column at the center point. Using tables in forms also keeps the data entered within the same region of the form, in case the user enters data that wraps to the next line on the screen.

When you insert a table, Word automatically surrounds it with a border. You do not want borders on tables in forms. Perform the following steps to enter a 1 × 2 table into the form and then remove its border.

Using Tables in Forms

At first glance, it might seem easier to set a tab stop wherever you would like a form field to display. Actually, it can become a complex task. Consider a row with three form fields. To space them evenly you must calculate where each tab stop should begin based on the width of the page and the margins. If you insert a 1 x 3 table instead, Word automatically calculates the size of three evenly spaced columns.

Steps: To Insert a Borderless Table into a Form

1 If the Forms toolbar does not display on the screen, click View on the menu bar, point to Toolbars, and then click Forms. If necessary, scroll up so that the boutique name is positioned at the top of the document window. With the insertion point on line 11, click the Insert Table button on the Forms toolbar. Point to the cell in the first row and second column of the grid.

Word displays a grid to define the dimension of the desired table (Figure 7-10). Word will insert the table immediately above the insertion point.

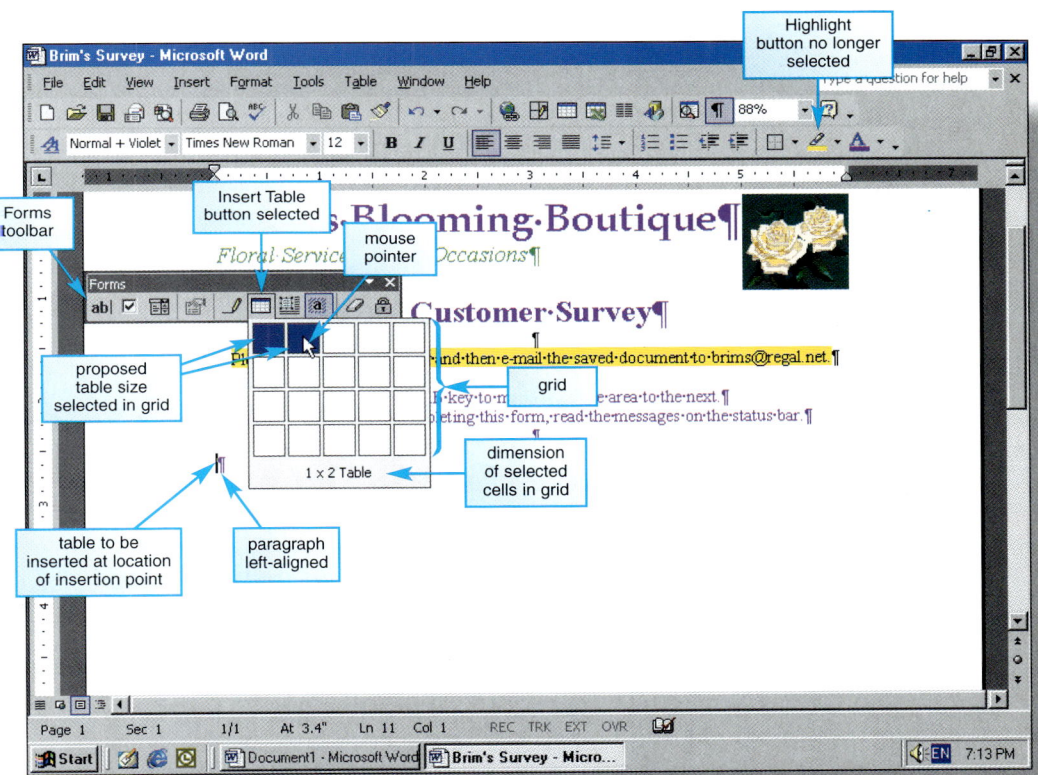

FIGURE 7-10

2 Click the cell in the first row and second column of the grid.

Word inserts an empty 1 × 2 table into the form. The insertion point is in the first cell (row 1 and column 1) of the table (shown in Figure 7-11 on the next page).

3 **When the table displays, point to the first cell and then, when the table move handle displays, click the table move handle to select the table. Click the Border button arrow on the Formatting toolbar and then point to No Border on the border palette.**

Word displays a list of border types on the border palette (Figure 7-11). The table is selected in the document.

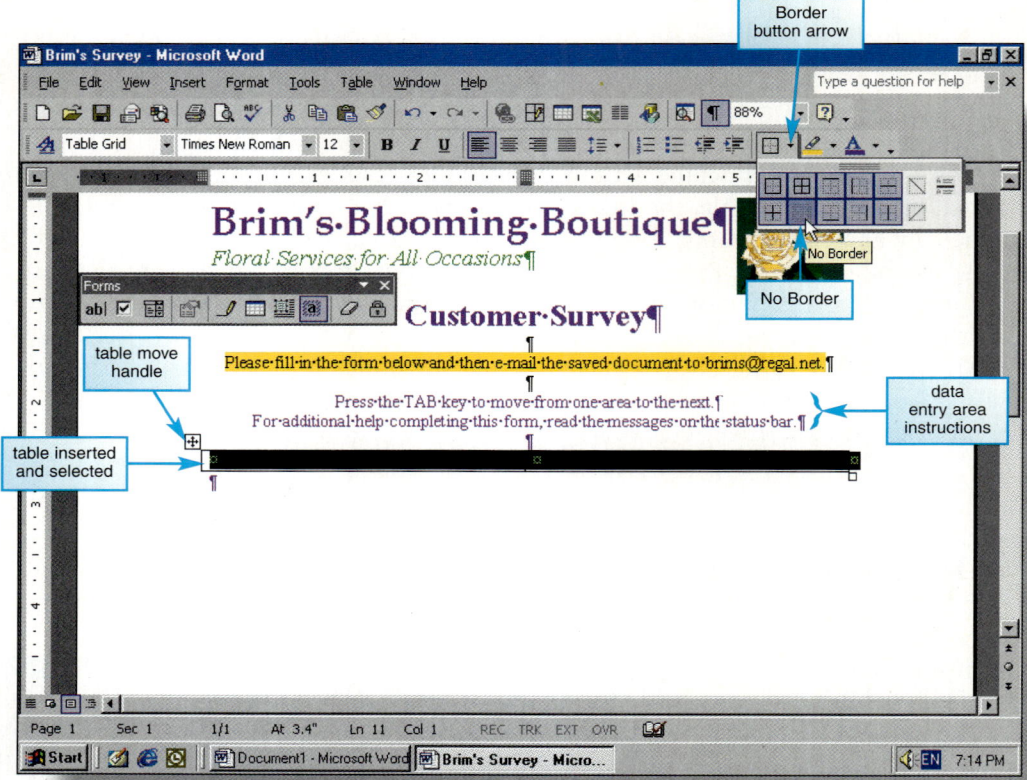

FIGURE 7-11

4 **Click No Border. Click in the first cell of the table to remove the selection. If your screen does not display end-of-cell marks, click the Show/Hide ¶ button on the Standard toolbar. If your table displays gridlines, click Table on the menu bar and then click Hide Gridlines.**

Word removes the border from the cells in the table (Figure 7-12). Only the end-of-row and end-of-cell marks display in the document window to identify cells in the table.

Other Ways

1. Click Insert Table button on Standard toolbar, click grid
2. On Table menu point to Insert, click Table, enter number of columns, enter number of rows, click OK button
3. In Voice Command mode, say "Table, Insert, Table, [enter number of columns and rows], OK"

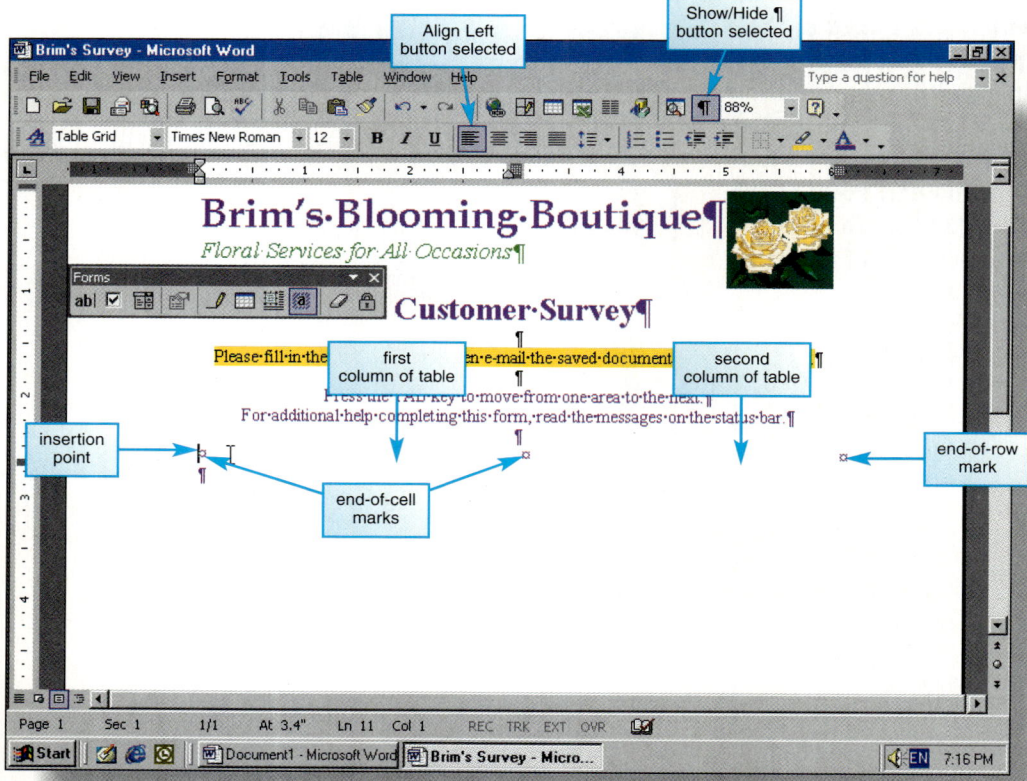

FIGURE 7-12

Each row of a table has an end-of-row mark, and each cell has an end-of-cell mark. The end-of-cell marks in Figure 7-12 are left-aligned because the cells are formatted as left-aligned. The data you enter within a cell wordwraps in that cell just as text does between the margins of a document. To place data into a cell, click the cell and then type. To advance rightward from one cell to the next, press the TAB key.

The next step is to enter fields into the cells of the table.

Inserting a Text Form Field that Accepts any Text

The first item that users enter on the Customer Survey is their first name. The field caption text, First Name, is to display to the left of a text box. A **field caption** is the text on the screen that informs the user what to enter into the field. Often a colon or some other character follows a field caption to separate the field caption from a text box or other data entry field.

To place a text box in the document, you insert a text form field. A **text form field** allows users to enter letters, numbers, and other characters into the field.

Perform the following steps to insert the field caption and the text form field into the first cell of the table.

> **More About**
>
> **Gridlines**
>
> If you want to see the table gridlines while developing a form, click Table on the menu bar and then click Show Gridlines. Gridlines are formatting marks that do not print. They are designed to help users easily identify table cells, rows, and columns.

Steps To Insert a Text Form Field

1 With the insertion point in the first cell of the table as shown in Figure 7-12, type First Name and then press the COLON (:) key. Press the SPACEBAR. Point to the Text Form Field button on the Forms toolbar.

Word places the field caption into the first cell of the table (Figure 7-13).

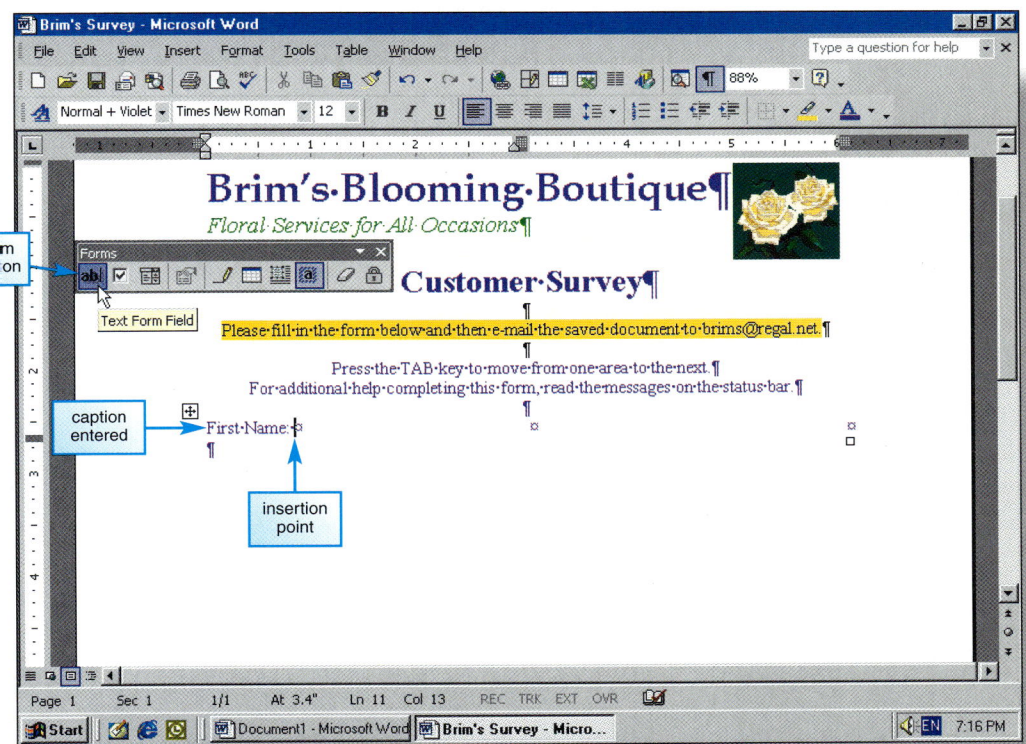

FIGURE 7-13

2 **Click the Text Form Field button. If the form field does not display shaded in gray, click the Form Field Shading button on the Forms toolbar.**

Word inserts a text form field at the location of the insertion point (Figure 7-14). The form field displays shaded in gray.

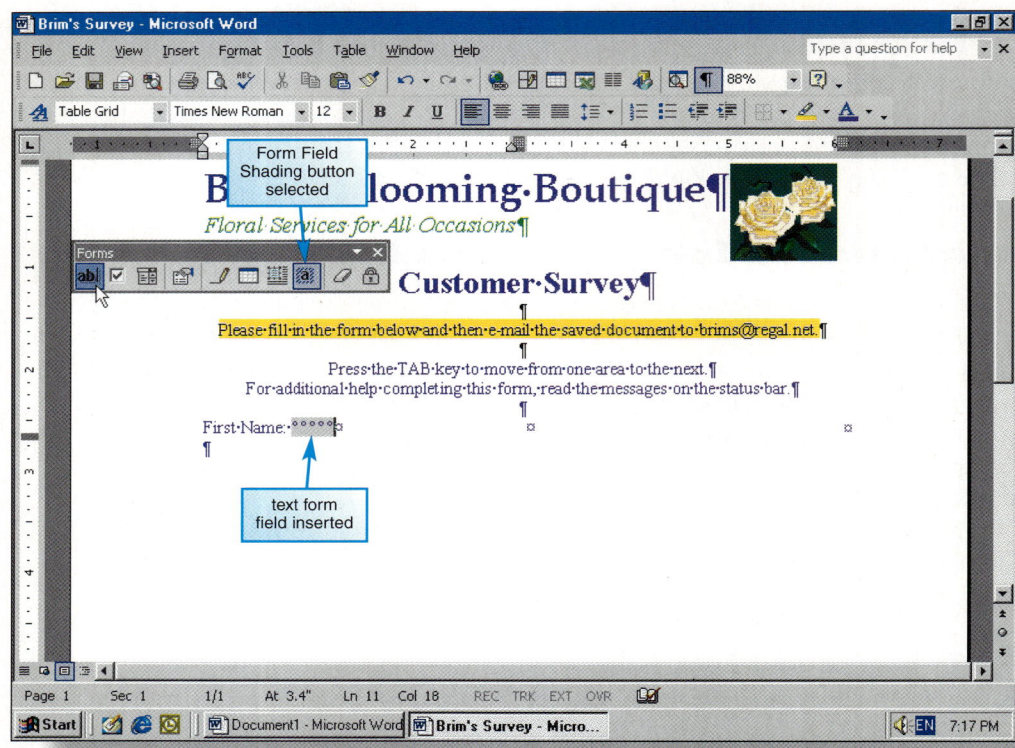

FIGURE 7-14

1. With Forms toolbar displaying, in Voice Command mode, say "Text Form Field" or say "Edit Box"

Field Lengths

The standard width for a first name field is 15 characters. Even though it may not accommodate all people, most businesses allow that much room in their files, mailing labels, and forms. The standard width for last name gradually is increasing. The Internal Revenue Service will increase its last name field width to 25 characters with the 2003 tax season, to accommodate the longer hyphenated names that are becoming so popular.

The text form field inserted by Word is five characters wide. You change its width, along with other characteristics of the form field, through the Text Form Field Options dialog box (Figure 7-15). You display this dialog box by double-clicking the text form field.

When this form displays on the screen initially (as a blank form), you want the text form fields to display an underline that signifies the data entry area. The text displayed initially in a field is called the **default text**. Thus, the default text for the text form fields on the Customer Survey is an underline.

You want to limit a user's entry for the first name to 15 characters. Thus, the underline should consume 15 spaces. You also want the first letter of each word that a user enters into the First Name text form field to be capitalized.

Perform the following steps to set the text form field for the first name so it displays 15 underscores as default text, to limit the user's entry to 15 characters, and to capitalize the first letter of each word the user enters.

Steps To Specify Text Form Field Options

1 Double-click the text form field (shown in Figure 7-14). When Word displays the Text Form Field Options dialog box, press the UNDERSCORE (_) key 15 times in the Default text text box. Double-click the Maximum length text box and then type 15 as the length. Click the Text format box arrow and then click First capital. Point to the OK button.

Word displays the Text Form Field Options dialog box (Figure 7-15).

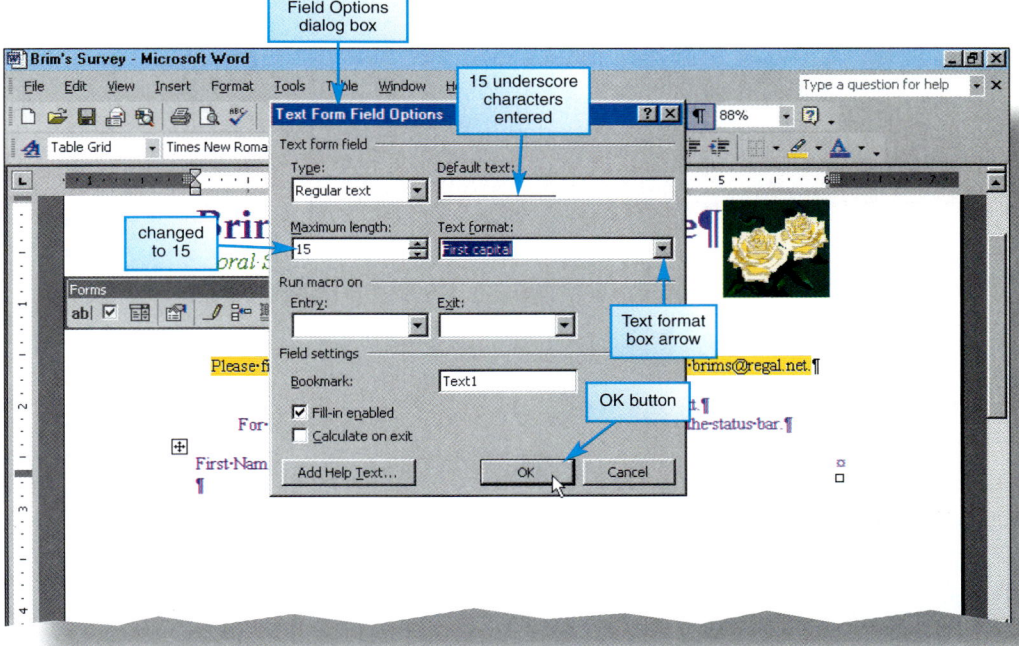

FIGURE 7-15

2 Click the OK button. Press the TAB key to move the insertion point to the beginning of the next cell in the table.

The text form field options are set (Figure 7-16).

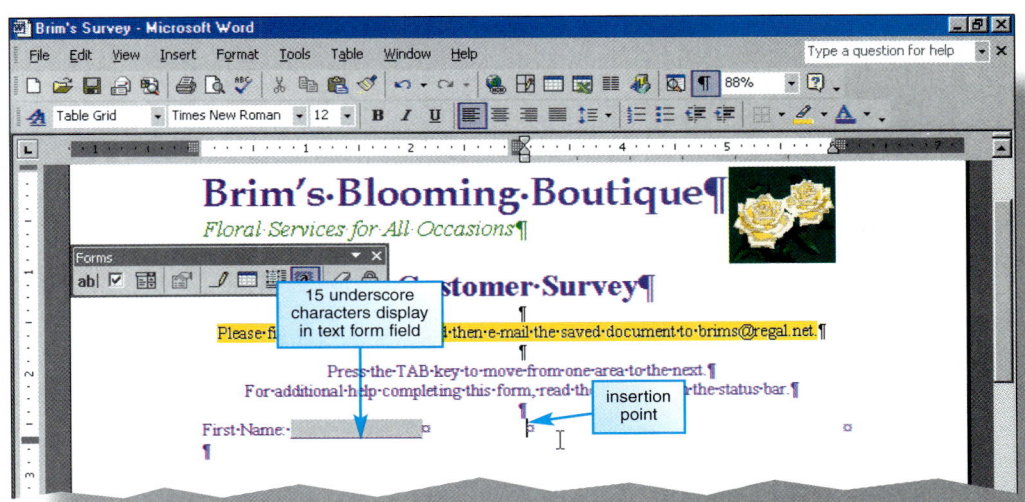

FIGURE 7-16

When you click the Text format box arrow in the Text Form Field Options dialog box (Figure 7-15), four choices display: Uppercase, Lowercase, First capital, and Title case. If you select one of these options, Word displays a user's entry according to your selection — after the user presses the TAB key to advance out of the form field. Table 7-1 on the next page illustrates how each option displays text that a user enters into the form field.

1. Click Form Field Options button on Forms toolbar
2. Right-click form field, click Properties on shortcut menu
3. With Forms toolbar displaying, in Voice Command mode, say "Form Field Options" or say "Properties"

Table 7-1	Text Formats for Text Form Fields
TEXT FORMAT	EXAMPLE
Uppercase	ALL LETTERS IN ALL WORDS ARE CAPITALIZED.
Lowercase	all letters in all words display as lowercase letters.
First capital	The first letter of the first word is capitalized.
Title case	The First Letter Of Every Word Is Capitalized.

The next form field to enter into the Customer Survey is the last name. The only difference between the options for the form fields for the last name and first name is that the last name allows up to 20 characters, instead of 15. Perform the following steps to insert and specify options for another text form field.

TO INSERT AND SPECIFY OPTIONS FOR A TEXT FORM FIELD

1. With the insertion point at the beginning of the second cell of the table, type Last Name and then press the COLON key. Press the SPACEBAR.

2. Click the Text Form Field button on the Forms toolbar.

3. Double-click the text form field for the last name. When Word displays the Text Form Field Options dialog box, press the UNDERSCORE key 20 times in the Default text text box. Double-click the Maximum length text box and then type 20 as the length. Click the Text format box arrow and then click First capital. Point to the OK button (Figure 7-17).

4. Click the OK button.

Word displays the form field for the last name according to the settings in the Text Form Field Options dialog box (shown in Figure 7-18).

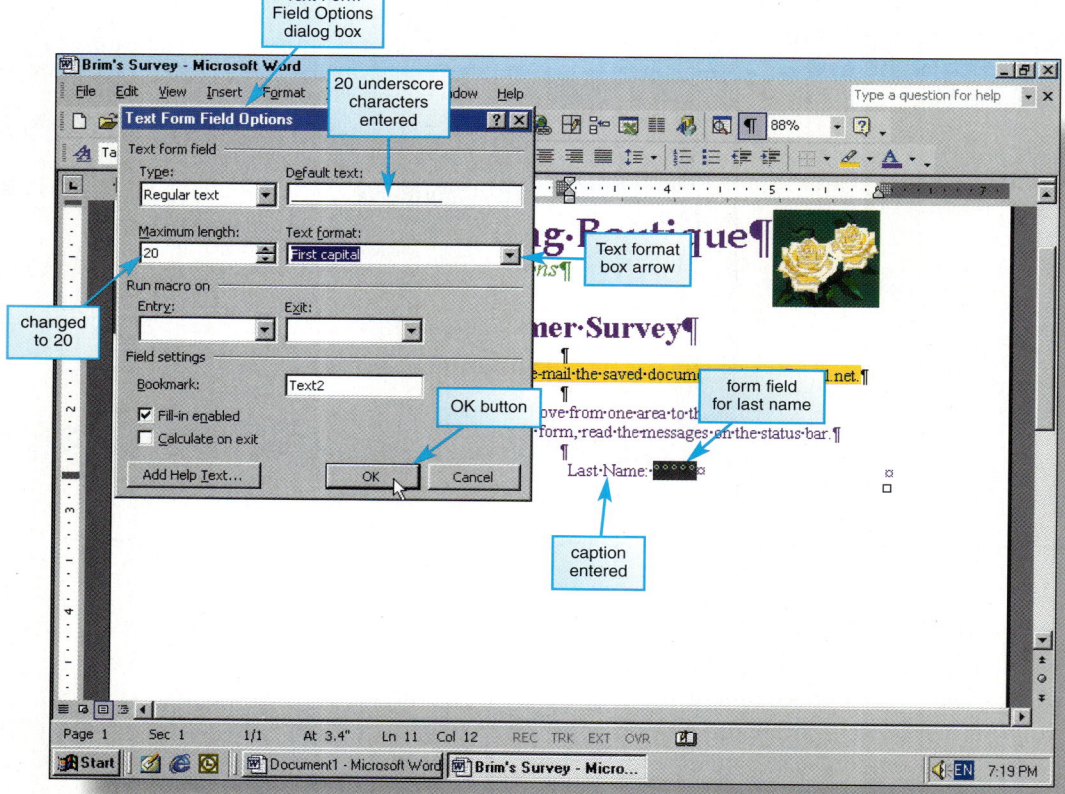

FIGURE 7-17

The next step in creating the Customer Survey is to insert a drop-down form field.

Inserting a Drop-Down Form Field

You use a **drop-down form field** when you want to present a set of choices to a user in the form of a drop-down list box. To view the set of choices, the user clicks an arrow that displays at the right edge of the form field, which displays a list box (Figure 7-1b on page WD 7.05). In this online form, the drop-down form field to be inserted is to contain the customer's opinion on how easy the Web site is to use. The valid choices to be presented to the user are Very Easy, Easy, Fair, Difficult, and Very Difficult.

Perform the following steps to insert a drop-down form field into the Customer Survey.

 To Insert a Drop-Down Form Field

1 **Click the paragraph mark below the table to position the insertion point below the First Name caption and then press the ENTER key. Type** How easy is it to place an order using our Web site? **and then press the SPACEBAR. Point to the Drop-Down Form Field button on the Forms toolbar.**

Word displays the field caption (Figure 7-18).

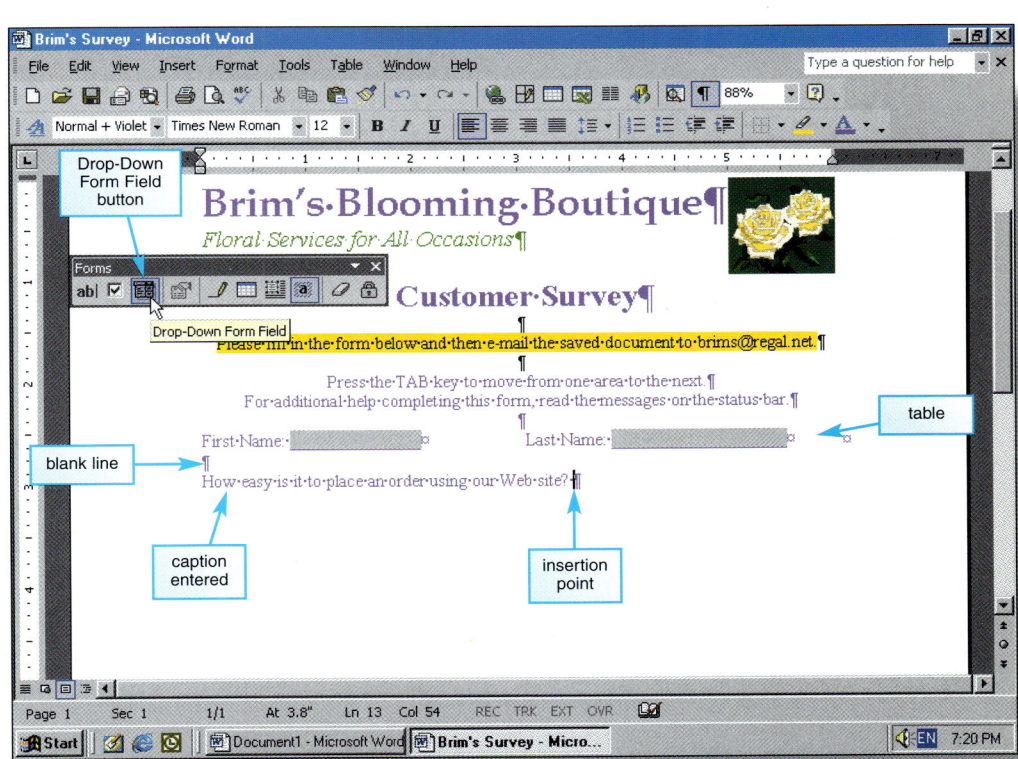

FIGURE 7-18

2 **Click the Drop-Down Form Field button.**

Word inserts a drop-down form field at the location of the insertion point (Figure 7-19). The form field displays shaded in gray.

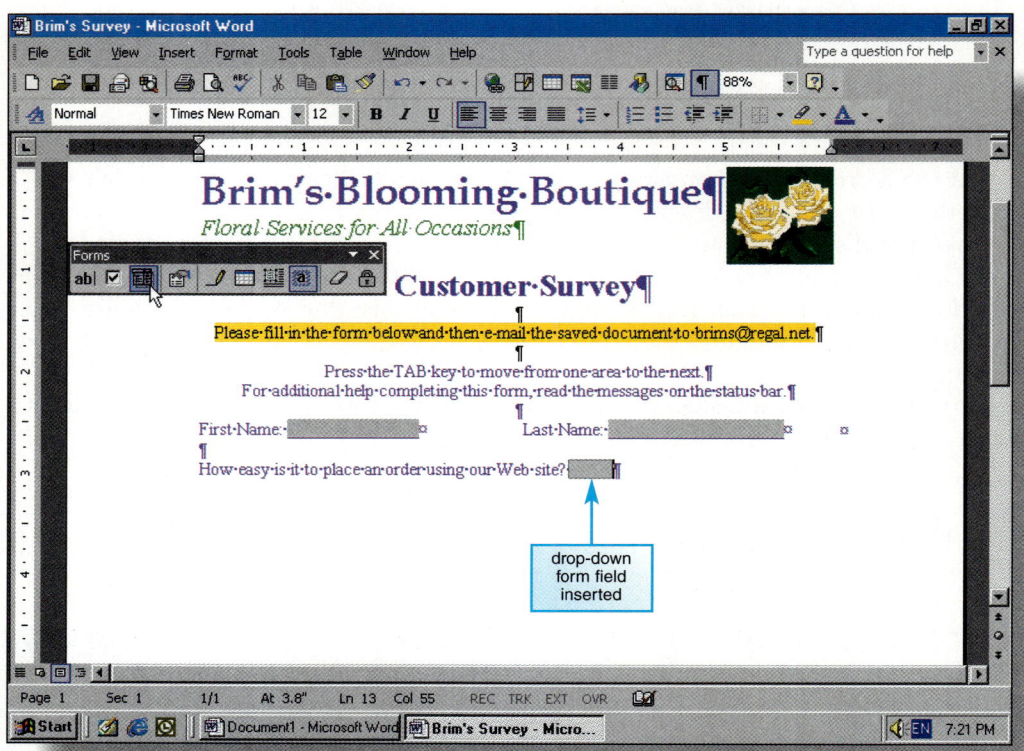

FIGURE 7-19

Other Ways

1. With Forms toolbar displaying, in Voice Command mode, say "Combo Box" or say "Drop-Down Form Field"

Recall that when the form displays on the screen initially (as a blank form), underscore characters should display where the text form fields are located. Similarly, the drop-down form field should display underscore characters when the form initially displays on the screen. This will help the user identify all the data entry areas.

In the text form field, you entered underscore characters as the default text. With a drop-down form field, Word displays the first item in the list on a blank form. Thus, you will enter 15 underscore characters as the first list item.

The drop-down form field initially is five characters wide. As you enter items into the drop-down list, Word increases the width of the form field to accommodate the item with the largest number of characters.

Perform the following steps to specify options for the drop-down form field.

More About

Drop-Down Form Fields

Instead of clicking the Add button in the Drop-Down Form Field Options dialog box (as shown in Figure 7-20) to move an item from the Drop-down item text box to the Items in drop-down list box, you can press the ENTER key.

Creating an Online Form • WD 7.23

Steps To Specify Drop-Down Form Field Options

1 **Double-click the drop-down form field. When Word displays the Drop-Down Form Field Options dialog box, press the UNDERSCORE key 15 times in the Drop-down item text box and then point to the Add button.**

Word displays the Drop-Down Form Field Options dialog box (Figure 7-20).

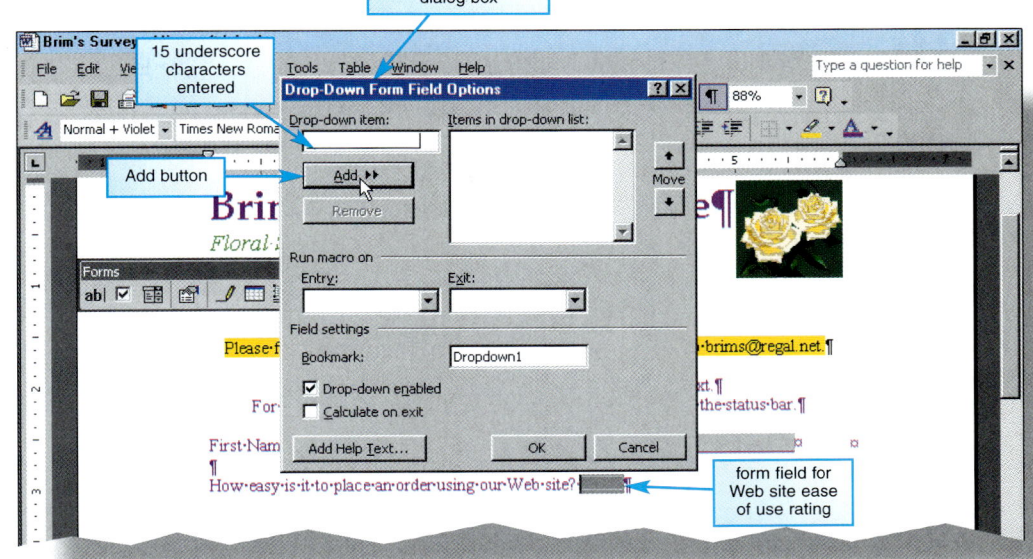

FIGURE 7-20

2 **Click the Add button.**

Word places the 15 underscore characters as the first item in the Items in drop-down list list (Figure 7-21). The Drop-down item text box now is empty, awaiting the next entry.

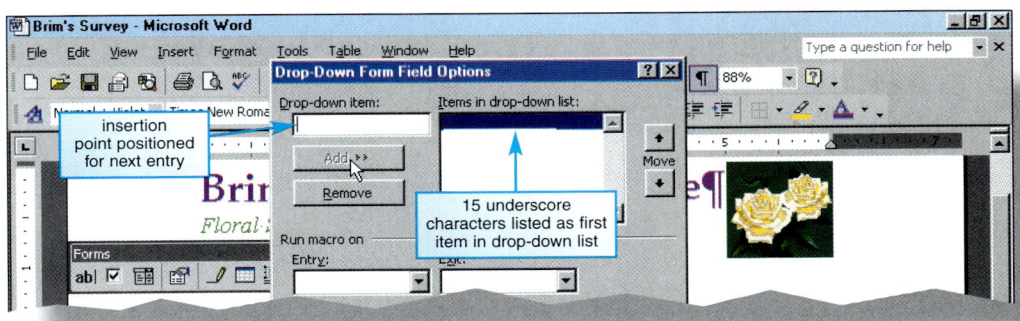

FIGURE 7-21

3 **With the insertion point positioned in the Drop-down item text box, type** Very Easy **and then click the Add button. Type** Easy **and then click the Add button. Type** Fair **and then click the Add button. Type** Difficult **and then click the Add button. Type** Very Difficult **and then click the Add button. Point to the OK button.**

The items in the drop-down list are entered (Figure 7-22).

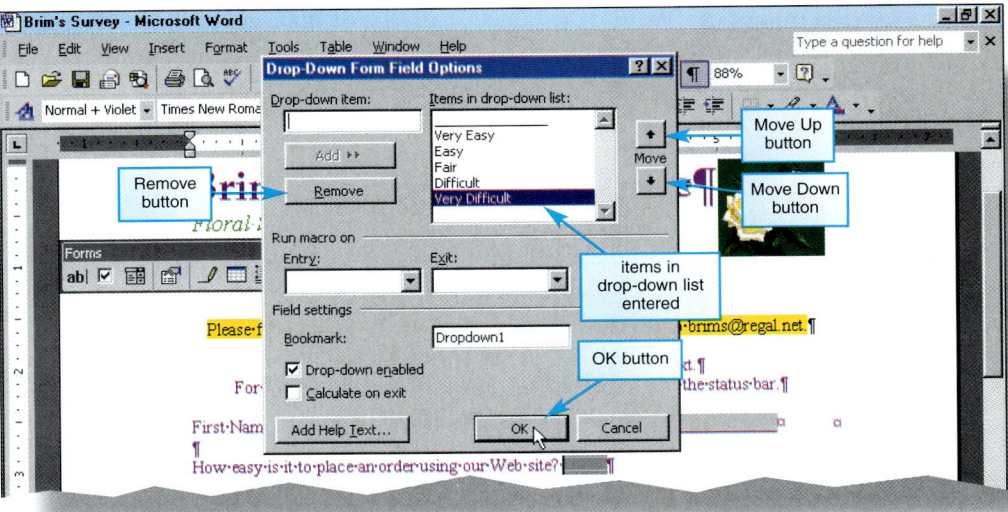

FIGURE 7-22

4 **Click the OK button. Press the END key to move the insertion point to the end of the line. Press the ENTER key twice.**

The list for the drop-down form field is defined (Figure 7-23). When you fill in the form, a box arrow will display at the right edge of the drop-down form field.

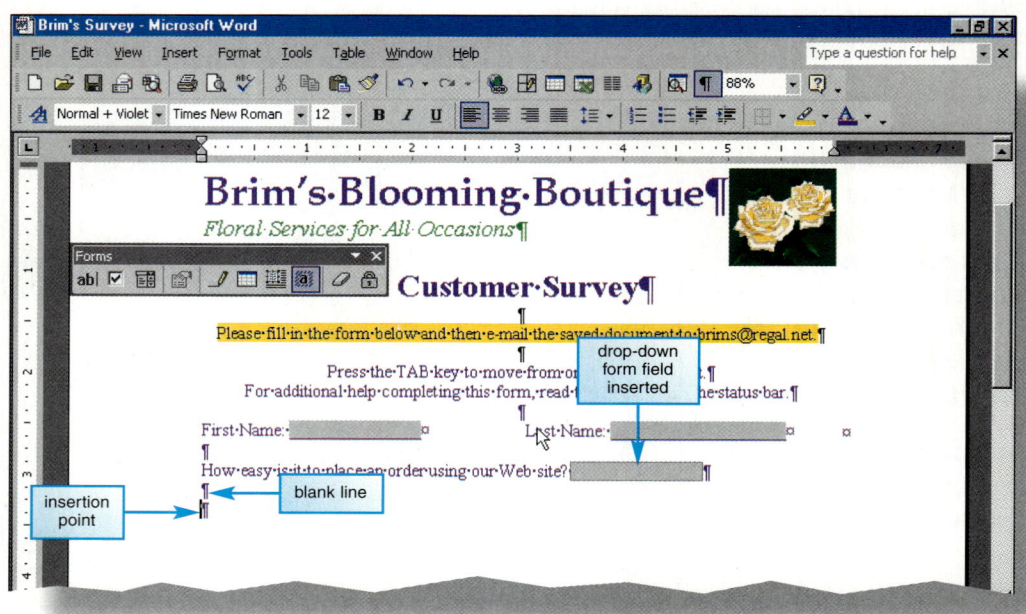

FIGURE 7-23

Other Ways

1. Click Form Field Options button on Forms toolbar
2. Right-click form field, click Properties on shortcut menu
3. With Forms toolbar displaying, in Voice Command mode, say "Form Field Options" or say "Properties"

Instead of clicking the Add button (Figure 7-20 on the previous page) to move items from the Drop-down item text box to the Items in drop-down list, you can press the ENTER key. This alternative method is used later in this project.

Notice in Figure 7-23 that the 15 underscore characters do not display on the screen yet. Word displays the first item in the drop-down list on the screen when you protect the form, which you will do later in this project.

After you enter items in a list box, if you want to modify their order, or add or delete one or more items, you would display the Drop-Down Form Field Options dialog box (Figure 7-22 on the previous page) by double-clicking the drop-down form field. To add more items, simply enter the text in the Drop-down item text box and then click the OK button. To remove an item, click it in the Items in drop-down list list and then click the Remove button. To reorder the list, click an item in the Items in drop-down list list and then click the Move Up button or Move Down button to move the item up or down one position each time you click the appropriate button.

The next step is to insert a text form field that requires a number.

Inserting a Text Form Field that Requires a Number

The next form field to be entered into the Customer Survey is for the approximate number of minutes a user spends shopping and placing an order. Most users easily would complete an order in fewer than 100 minutes. Thus, a two-digit input area is sufficient. You, therefore, will instruct Word to display two underscore characters when the form initially displays on the screen (as a blank form).

Valid minutes entered will vary greatly, but all minutes entered should be numeric. If you ultimately will be analyzing the data entered in a form with another type of software package such as a database, you do not want non-numeric data in fields that require numeric entries. To address this problem, Word can convert a non-numeric entry such as ABC to a zero.

Perform the following steps to insert and format this text form field.

Text Form Field Types

When you click the Type box arrow in the Text Form Field Options dialog box (shown in Figure 7-24), you have six options: Regular text, Number, Date, Current date, Current time, and Calculations. Regular text accepts any keyboard character. Number requires a numeric entry. Date requires a valid date. The last three options display the system date, the system time, or the result of a calculation, and do not allow a user to change the resulting displayed value.

TO INSERT AND SPECIFY OPTIONS FOR A TEXT FORM FIELD

1. With the insertion point positioned two lines below the previous entry, as shown in Figure 7-23, type Approximately how many minutes does it take to shop and place an order? and then press the SPACEBAR.

2. Click the Text Form Field button on the Forms toolbar.

3. Double-click the newly inserted text form field for the number of minutes. When Word displays the Text Form Field Options dialog box, click the Type box arrow and then click Number. Press the TAB key to position the insertion point in the Maximum length text box and then type 2 as the length. Press the TAB key to position the insertion point in the Default number text box and then press the UNDERSCORE key two times. Point to the OK button (Figure 7-24).

4. Click the OK button.

Word displays the text form field for the number of minutes according to the settings in the Text Form Field Options dialog box (shown in Figure 7-25 on the next page).

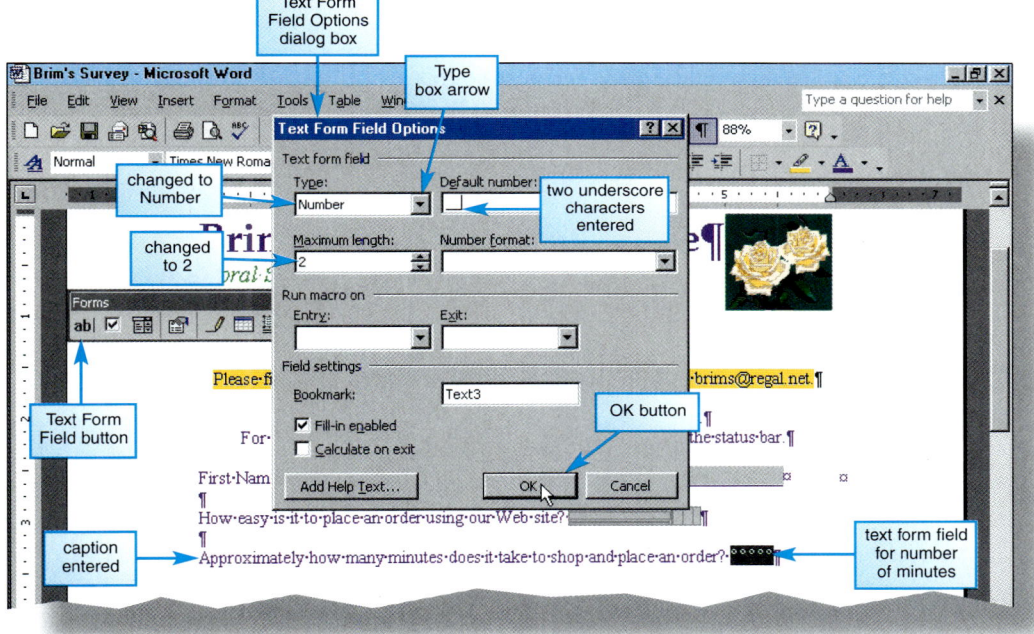

FIGURE 7-24

By changing the Type box to Number (Figure 7-24), Word will convert any non-numeric entry in this form field to a zero. Other valid text form field types are discussed later in this project.

The next step is to enter the check boxes into the Customer Survey.

Inserting a Check Box

The bottom of the data entry area of the Customer Survey contains five check boxes, one each for Flowers, Plants, Teddy Bears, Fruit Baskets, and Other. The Other check box also has a text form field to its right, which allows a user to explain further. Above the check boxes is a line of instructions pertaining to the check boxes. The following pages explain how to enter this section of the form.

The first step is to enter the line of text containing instructions for the check boxes. Perform the steps on the next page to enter this line of text.

Check Boxes

If you want an X to display in a check box when the form initially displays on the screen (as a blank form), double-click the check box form field. When the Check Box Form Field Options dialog box displays, click Checked in the Default value area, and then click the OK button.

TO ENTER TEXT

1 Press the END key to move the insertion point to the end of the line. Press the ENTER key twice. Type `Types of orders you have placed using our Web site (check all that apply)` and then press the COLON key.

2 Press the ENTER key.

The instructions for the check boxes display (shown in Figure 7-25).

You want four check boxes to display horizontally below the check box instructions. To do this and align the check boxes evenly across the line, insert a 1 × 4 borderless table; that is, a table with one row and four columns. Perform the following steps to insert a 1 × 4 table into the form.

TO INSERT A BORDERLESS TABLE INTO A FORM

1 With the insertion point on the paragraph mark below the check box instructions, click the Insert Table button on the Forms toolbar and then point to the cell in the first row and fourth column of the grid (Figure 7-25).

2 Click the cell in the first row and fourth column of the grid.

3 When the table displays, point to the first cell and then, when the table move handle displays, click the table move handle to select the table. Click the Border button arrow on the Formatting toolbar and then click No Border on the border palette.

4 Click in the first cell of the table.

Word inserts a 1 × 4 borderless table at the location of the insertion point (shown in Figure 7-26).

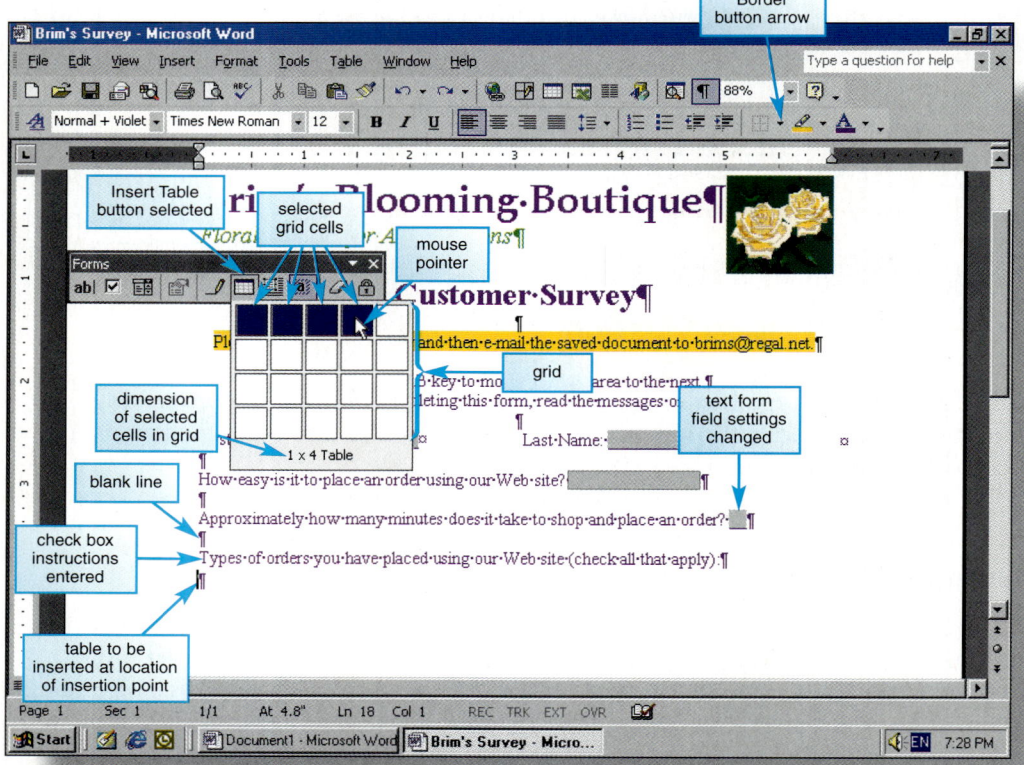

FIGURE 7-25

Creating an Online Form • WD 7.27

The next step is to insert the first check box into the first cell of the table as shown in the following steps.

To Insert a Check Box

1 **With the insertion point in the first cell of the table, point to the Check Box Form Field button on the Forms toolbar (Figure 7-26).**

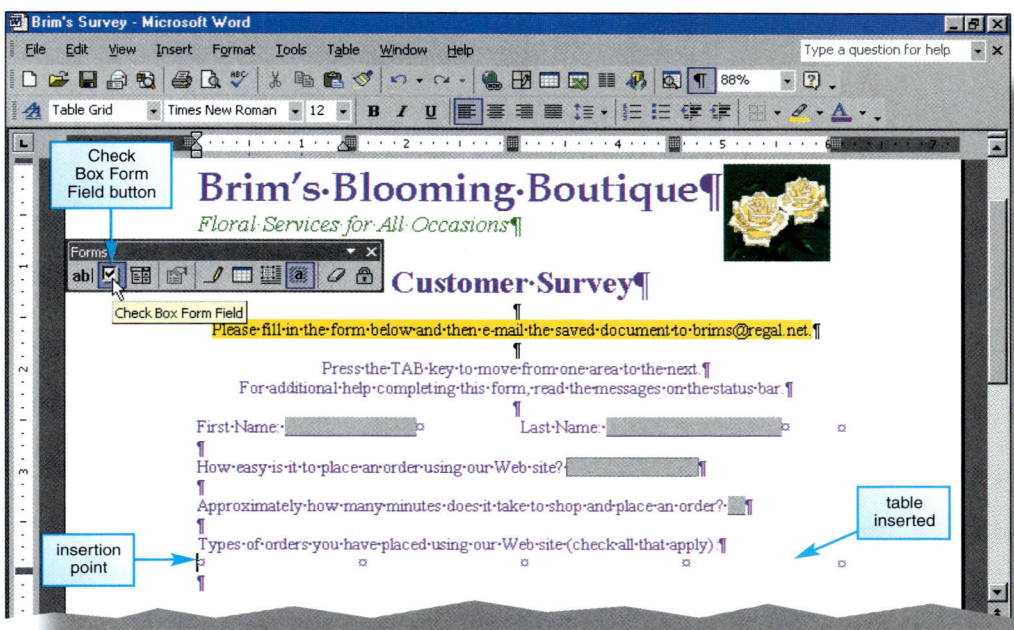

FIGURE 7-26

2 **Click the Check Box Form Field button. Press the SPACEBAR. Type** Flowers **and then press the TAB key.**

Word inserts a check box form field followed by its caption in the first cell of the table (Figure 7-27).

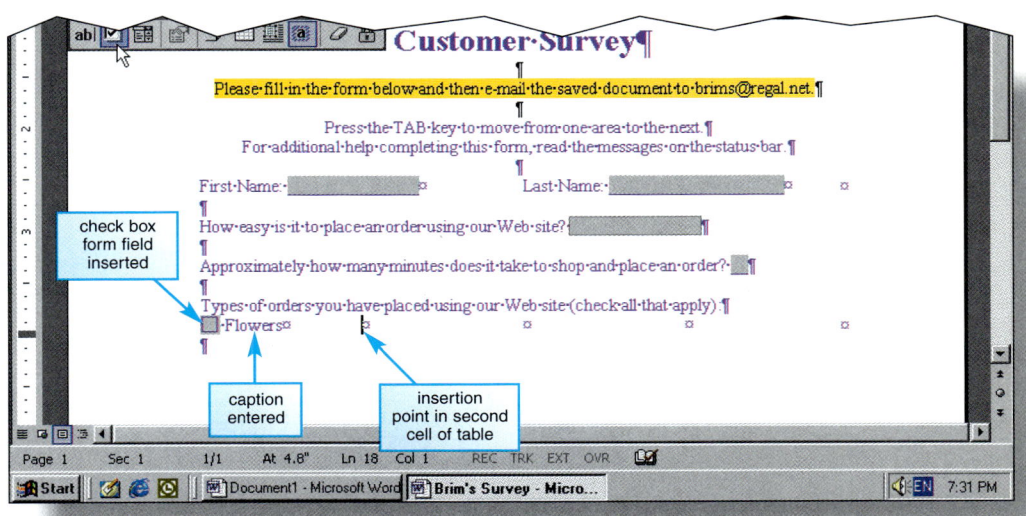

FIGURE 7-27

Other Ways

1. With Forms toolbar displaying, in Voice Command mode, say "Check Box"

The next step is to enter the remaining check box fields in the form, as described in the following steps.

TO INSERT ADDITIONAL CHECK BOX FORM FIELDS

1. With the insertion point in the second cell of the table, click the Check Box Form Field button on the Forms toolbar. Press the SPACEBAR. Type Plants and then press the TAB key.

2. With the insertion point in the third cell of the table, click the Check Box Form Field button on the Forms toolbar. Press the SPACEBAR. Type Teddy Bears and then press the TAB key.

3. With the insertion point in the fourth cell of the table, click the Check Box Form Field button on the Forms toolbar. Press the SPACEBAR. Type Fruit Baskets and then click the paragraph mark below the table.

4. With the insertion point below the table, click the Check Box Form Field button on the Forms toolbar. Press the SPACEBAR. Type Other (please specify) and then press the COLON key. Press the SPACEBAR.

The check box form fields are inserted (Figure 7-28).

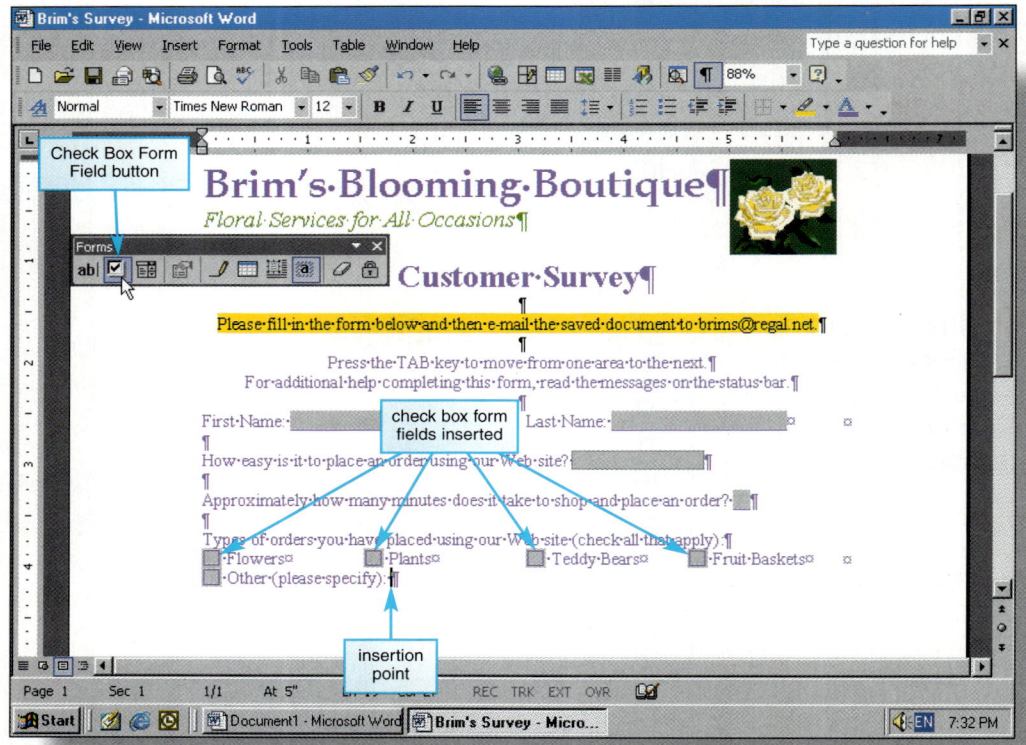

FIGURE 7-28

If users select the check box with the Other caption, you want them to explain the other type of order they placed using the Web site. To allow this, you insert a text form field as described in the following steps.

TO INSERT AND SPECIFY OPTIONS FOR A TEXT FORM FIELD

1. Click the Text Form Field button on the Forms toolbar.
2. Double-click the text form field for Other (please specify). When Word displays the Text Form Field Options dialog box, press the UNDERSCORE key 30 times in the Default text text box. Point to the OK button (Figure 7-29).
3. Click the OK button.

Word displays the text form field for the other types of orders according to the settings in the Text Form Field Options dialog box.

Text Form Fields

If the Maximum length box is set to Unlimited, as shown in Figure 7-29, the user can enter a maximum of 255 characters into the text box.

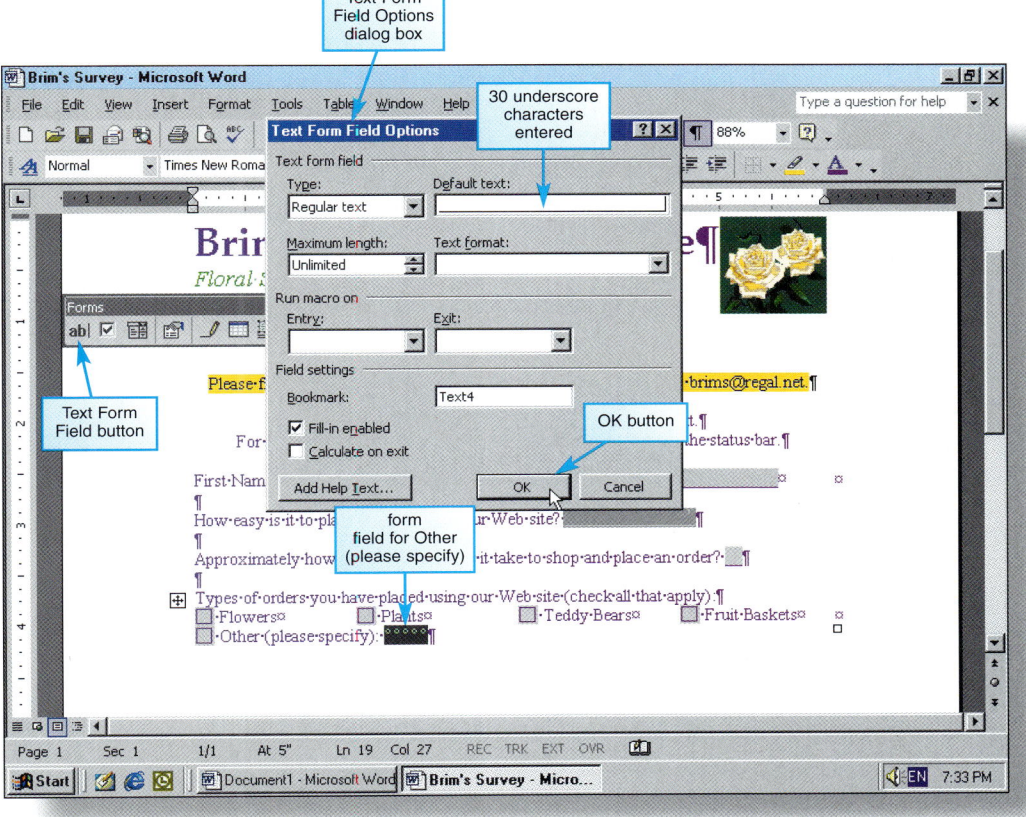

FIGURE 7-29

The next step is to display the current date on the form.

Inserting a Text Form Field that Displays the Current Date

The next form field to be entered into the Customer Survey is the current date. You do not want the user to enter the date; instead, you simply want the current date to display on the form. When a user fills in and e-mails the completed form, the date the user completed the form will display automatically.

You could insert the current date as a field by clicking Insert on the menu bar and then clicking Date and Time. If, however, you plan to analyze the data later using a database or some other software and you want the current date to be part of the data saved with the form, then you must insert a text form field that displays the current date. Perform the steps on the next page to insert and specify options for this text form field as the current date.

Steps: To Insert and Specify Options for a Text Form Field as the Current Date

1 Click at the end of the last text form field entered and then press the ENTER key. Press CTRL+R to right-align the paragraph. Click the Text Form Field button on the Forms toolbar. Double-click the new text form field that displays. When Word displays the Text Form Field Options dialog box, click the Type box arrow and then click Current date. Click the Date format box arrow and then click M/d/yyyy. Point to the OK button (Figure 7-30).

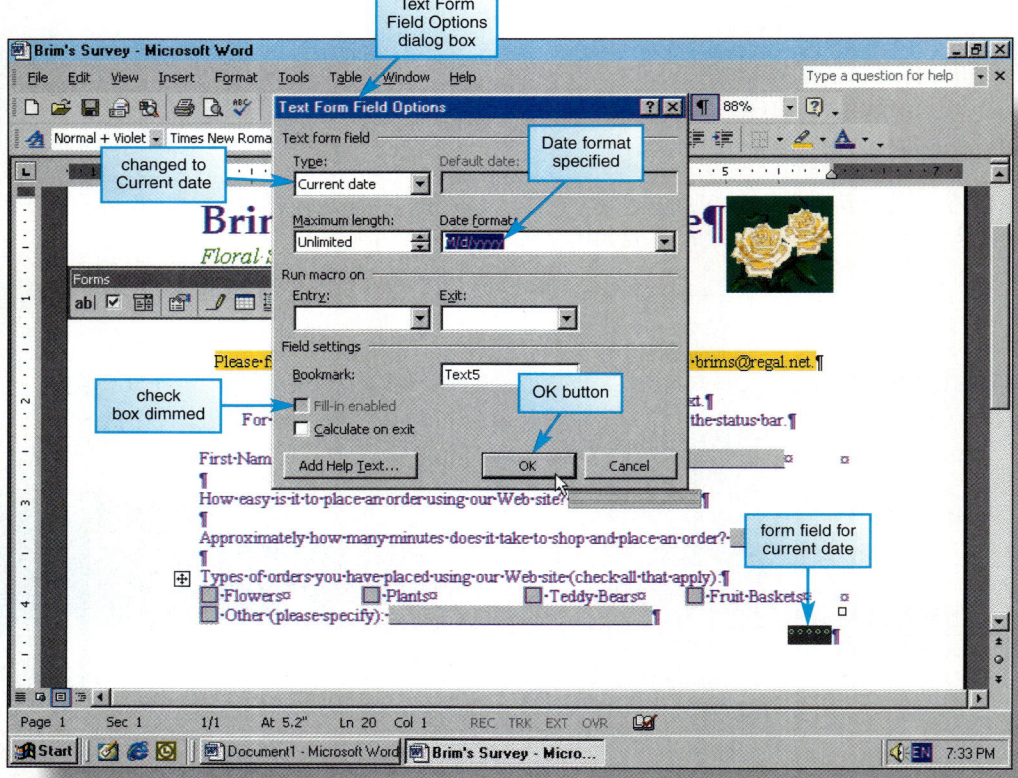

FIGURE 7-30

2 Click the OK button. Click outside the field to remove the selection.

Word displays the current date in the form field (Figure 7-31). Your date displayed will be different.

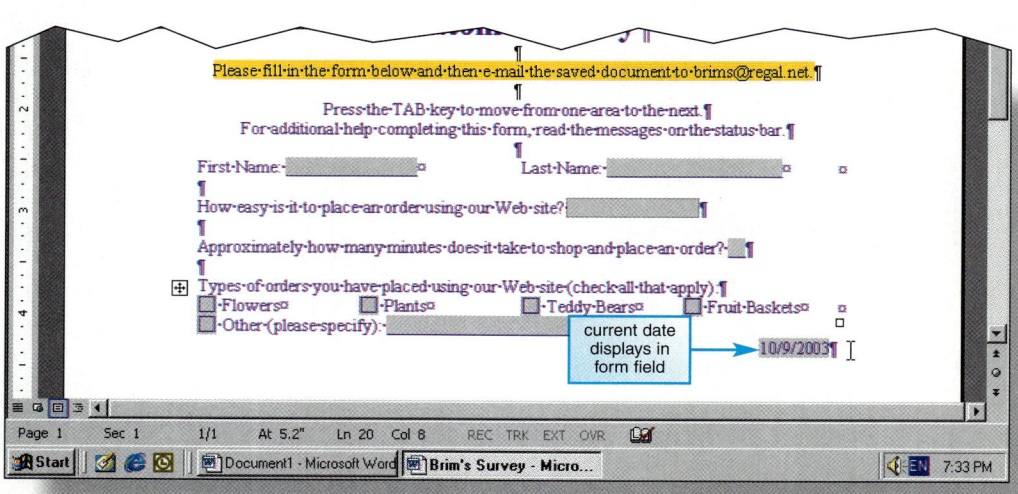

FIGURE 7-31

Other Ways

1. With the Forms toolbar displaying, in Voice Command mode, say "Text Form Field" or say "Edit Box"

Notice in the Text Form Field Options dialog box shown in Figure 7-30 that the Fill-in enabled check box in the Field settings area is dimmed. Word automatically dims this check box when you select Current date as the field type. When this check box is dimmed, a user is not allowed to modify the contents of the field when it displays on the screen. If you want a user to enter a date, you would select Date in the Type list instead of Current date.

Two other options in the Type list that also dim the Fill-in enabled check box are Current time and Calculation. That is, if you select Current time as the field type, Word displays the current time on the screen – so a user cannot change the time displayed. If you select Calculation as the field type, Word displays the result of a formula you enter.

The next step is to format the data entry fields.

Formatting Form Fields

As users enter data into the text form fields and the drop-down form field on the form, you want the characters they type to be underlined in violet. Word prevents users from formatting data they enter into form fields. Thus, specify any desired field formatting to fields on the form template. To format a field, select the field and then format it as you do any other text. In this case, you use the Font dialog box to specify an underline color.

Perform the following steps to underline the field for the first name in violet.

Date and Time

If a text form field type has been changed to Current date (Figure 7-30) or Current time and you intend to print the form, you should ensure that the date and time are current, or updated, before printing. To do this, click Tools on the menu bar, click Options, click the Print tab, place a check mark in the Update fields check box, and then click the OK button.

Steps: To Underline in Color

1 Click the text form field for the first name to select it. Right-click the selection and then point to Font on the shortcut menu (Figure 7-32).

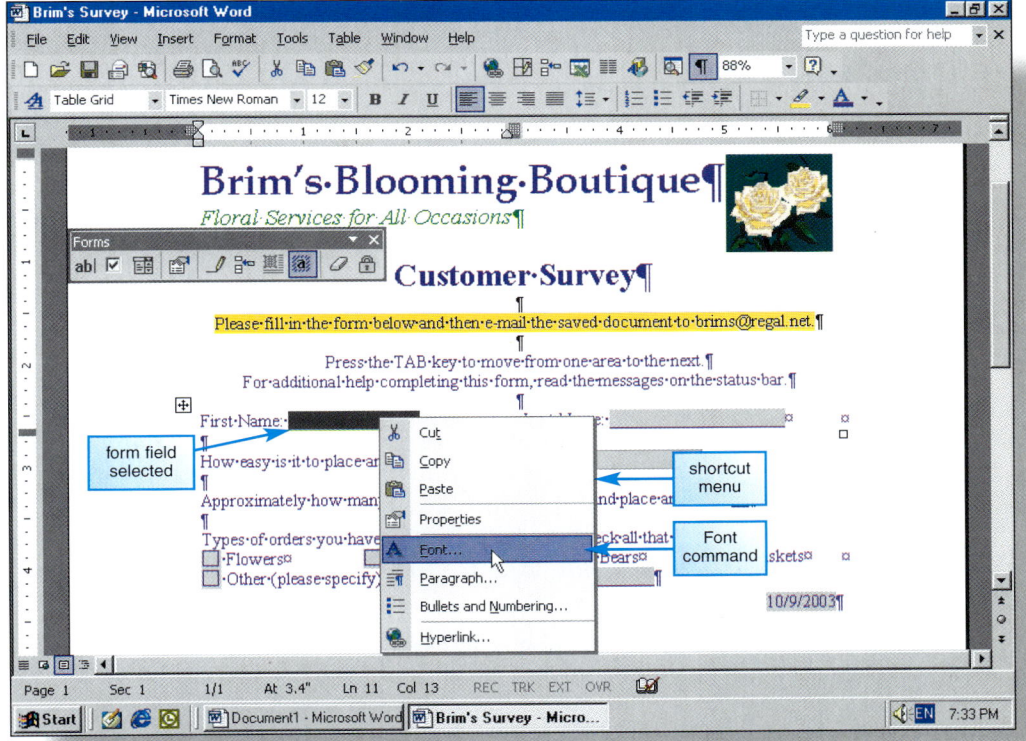

FIGURE 7-32

Click Font. When the Font dialog box displays, if necessary, click the Font tab. Click the Underline style box arrow and then click the first underline in the list. Click the Underline color box arrow and then click Violet. Point to the OK button.

Word displays the Font dialog box (Figure 7-33).

 Click the OK button.

Word formats the data entry for the field to 12-point Times New Roman underlined violet font (shown in Figure 7-34).

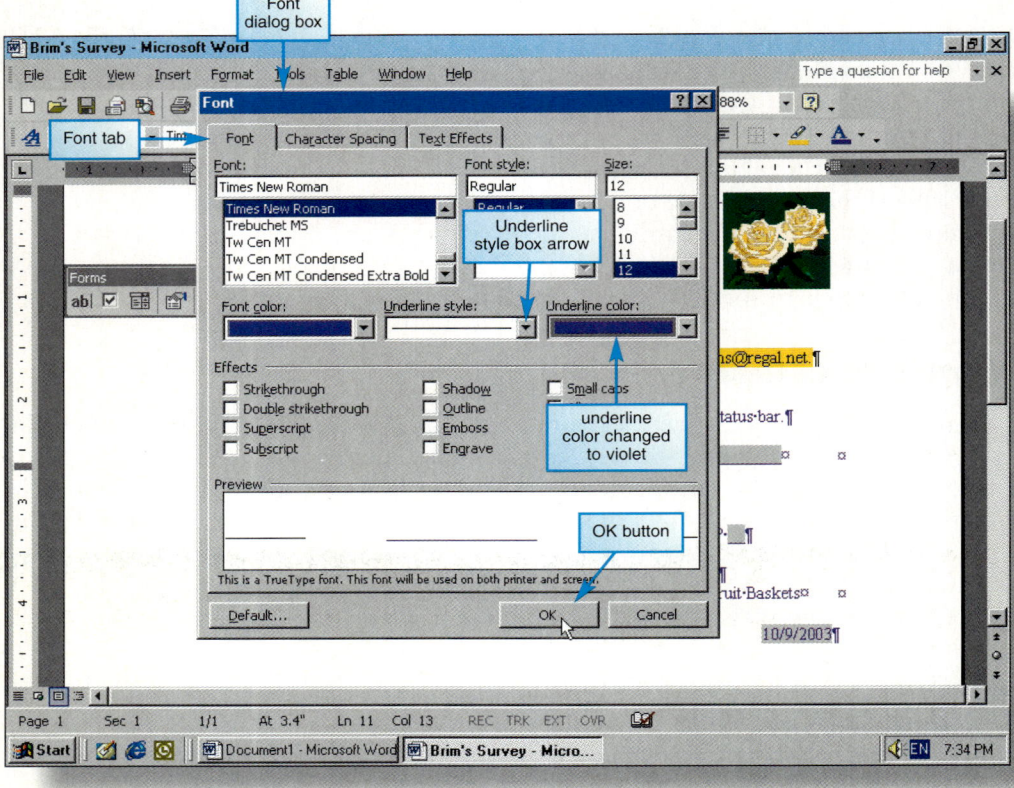

FIGURE 7-33

Other Ways

1. On Format menu click Font, click Font tab, select desired underline style, select desired underline color, click OK button
2. In Voice Command mode, say "Format, Font, Font, [select underline style and color], OK"

More About

Copying Formatting

If you want to copy paragraph formatting, such as alignment and line spacing, select the paragraph mark at the end of the paragraph prior to clicking the Format Painter button. If you want to copy just character formatting, such as fonts and font sizes, do not select the paragraph mark.

Earlier you set the text form fields to display an underline when the form displays initially on the screen (as a blank form). Thus, you will not notice a change to the First Name text form field after formatting it. The formatting options will take effect when you enter data into the form.

The next step is to copy this formatting to the other data entry fields on the screen.

Using the Format Painter Button

Instead of selecting each form field one at a time and then formatting it with the violet underline, you will copy the format assigned to the form field for the first name to the other text form fields and the drop-down form field.

To copy formats from one form field to another, select the form field from which you wish to copy formatting, click the Format Painter button on the Standard toolbar to copy the selected form field's formatting specifications, and then select the form field to which you wish to copy the formatting. To select a text form field, simply click it or drag through it. To select a drop-down form field, drag through it.

In this project, you are to copy formats from one form field to multiple form fields. Thus, you double-click the Format Painter button so that the format painter remains active until you turn it off, as shown in the following steps.

Steps To Use the Format Painter Button

1 With the text form field for the first name selected, double-click the Format Painter button on the Standard toolbar. Move the mouse pointer into the document window.

Word attaches a paintbrush to the mouse pointer when the Format Painter button is selected (Figure 7-34). The 12-point Times New Roman underlined violet font has been copied by the format painter.

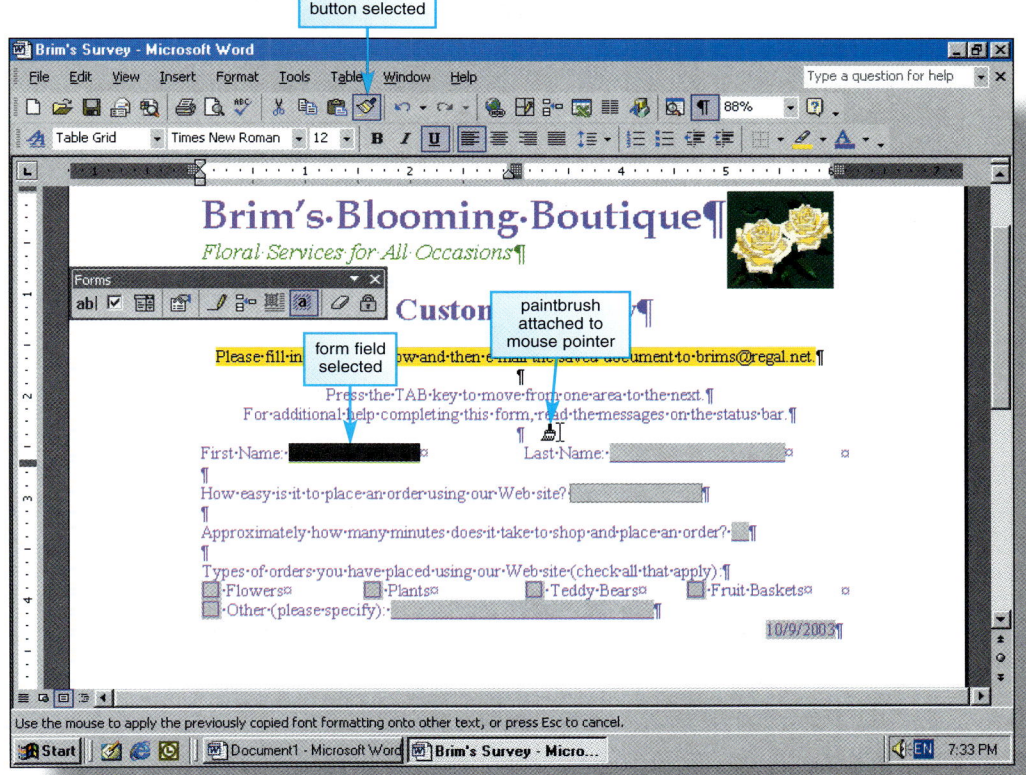

FIGURE 7-34

2 Click the text form field for the last name.

Word copies the 12-point Times New Roman underlined violet font to the text form field for the last name (Figure 7-35). The last name field is selected, and the format painter remains active, allowing you to select more fields to which you wish to copy the format.

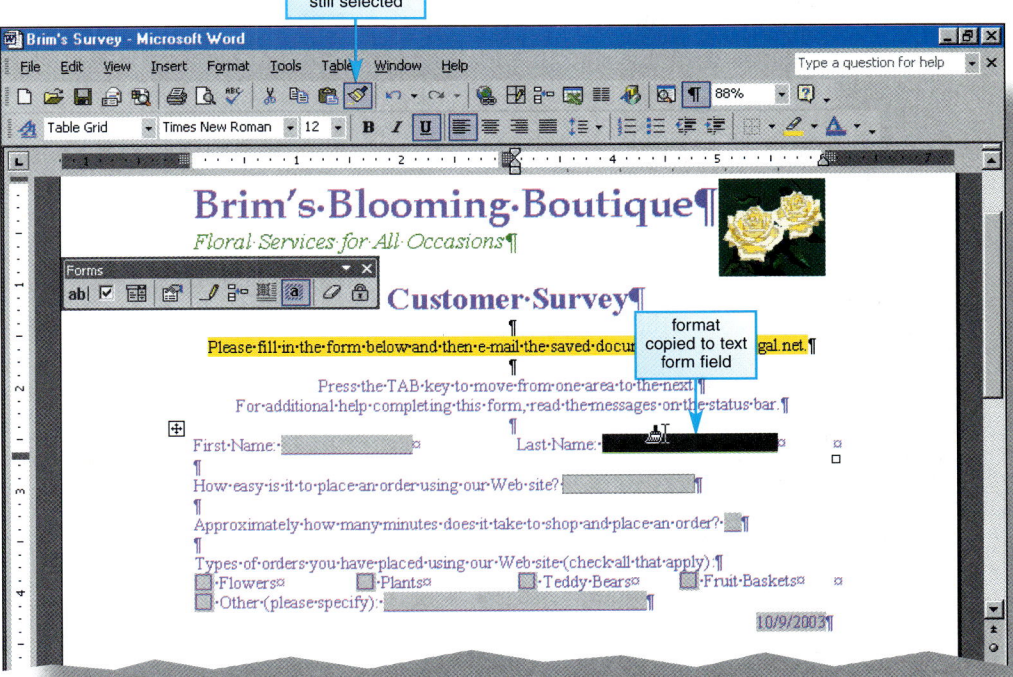

FIGURE 7-35

 **3** Drag through the ease of use drop-down form field. Click the text form field for the number of minutes. Click the text form field for Other (please specify). Click the Format Painter button on the Standard toolbar to turn off the format painter. Move the mouse pointer into the document window.

The format in the text form field for the first name is copied to all other text form fields and to the drop-down form field (Figure 7-36). The Format Painter button no longer is selected.

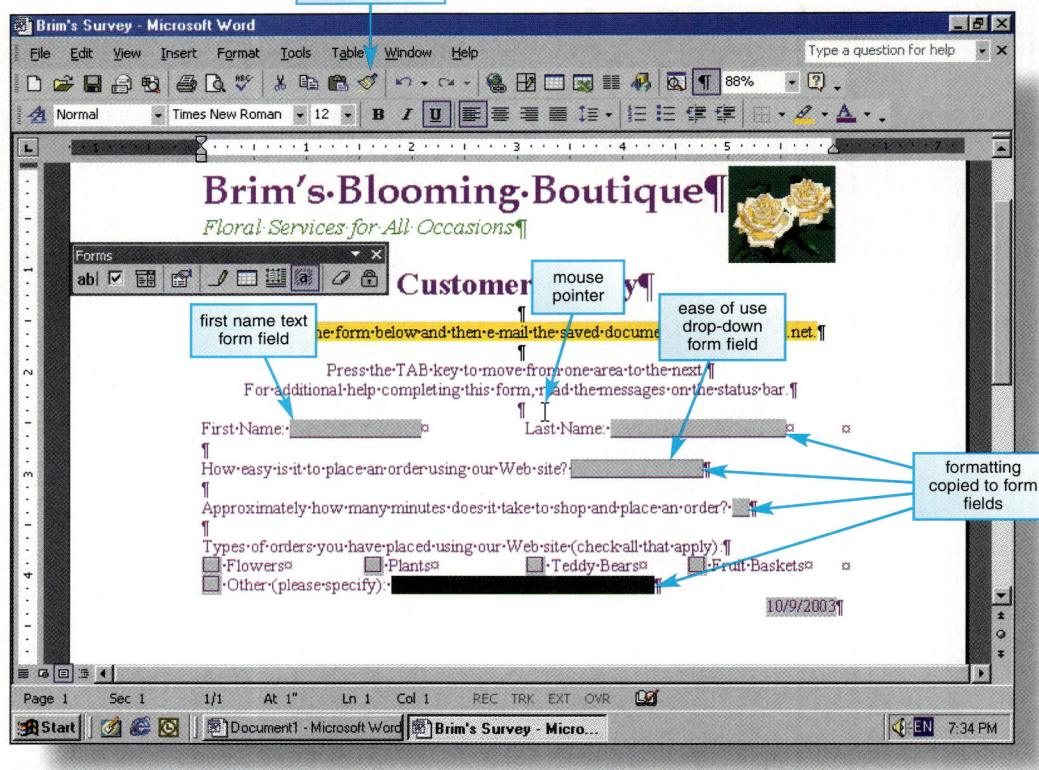

FIGURE 7-36

Other Ways

1. In Voice Command mode, say "[select text to copy from], Format Painter, [select text to copy formatting to]"

More About

Help Text

When you enter Help text to display on the status bar, you are limited to 138 characters. You can create longer Help text, up to 255 characters, for those that display in a dialog box when the user presses the F1 key. A good practice is to provide users as much help as possible; thus, you may wish to create both status bar Help text and dialog box Help text.

The next step is to add help for users to the form.

Adding Help Text to Form Fields

As users enter data into form fields, they may have a question about the purpose or function of a particular field. Thus, Word provides two Help mechanisms by which you can assist users during their data entry process. You can display a Help message on the status bar that relates to the current data entry field and/or you can display a Help dialog box when a user presses the F1 key. In this project, you want to display brief Help messages on the status bar as a user moves from form field to form field.

Perform the following steps to display a Help message on the status bar when the user is entering the first name.

Creating an Online Form • WD 7.35

Steps **To Add Help Text to a Form Field**

1 **Double-click the text form field for the first name (shown in Figure 7-36). When the Text Form Field Options dialog box displays, point to the Add Help Text button (Figure 7-37).**

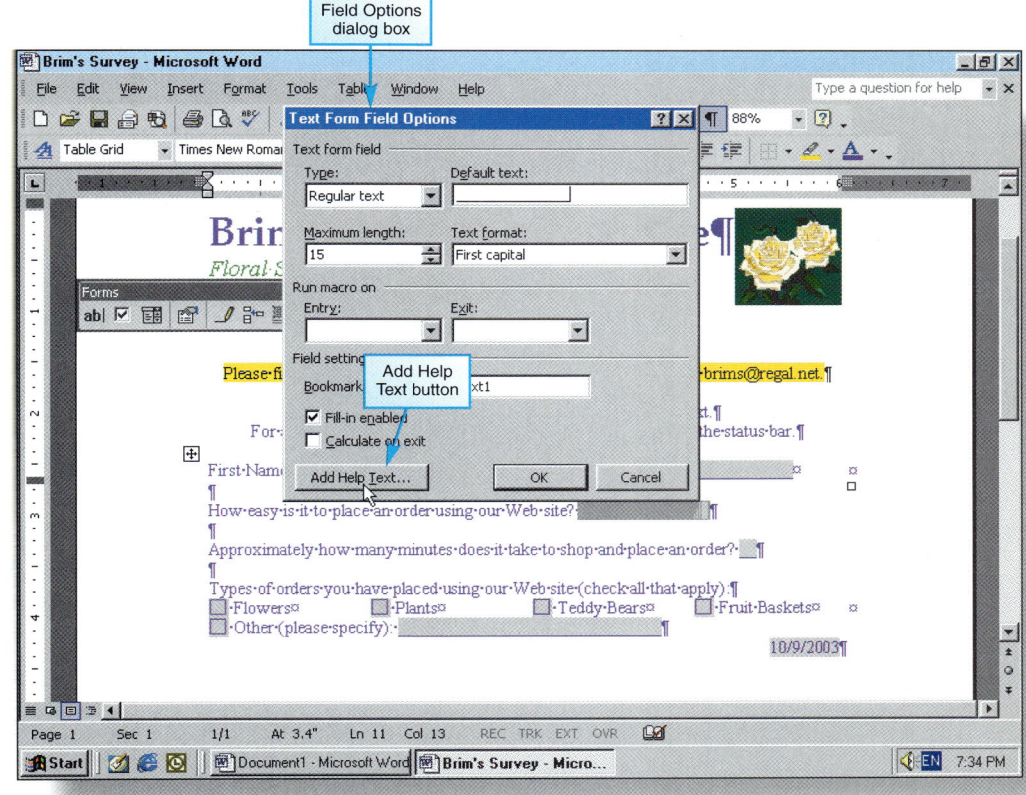

FIGURE 7-37

2 **Click the Add Help Text button. When the Form Field Help Text dialog box displays, if necessary, click the Status Bar tab. Click Type your own. Type** Enter your first name. **Point to the OK button.**

Word displays the Form Field Help Text dialog box (Figure 7-38).

3 **Click the OK button. Click the OK button in the Text Form Field Options dialog box.**

The Help text is entered for the first name text form field.

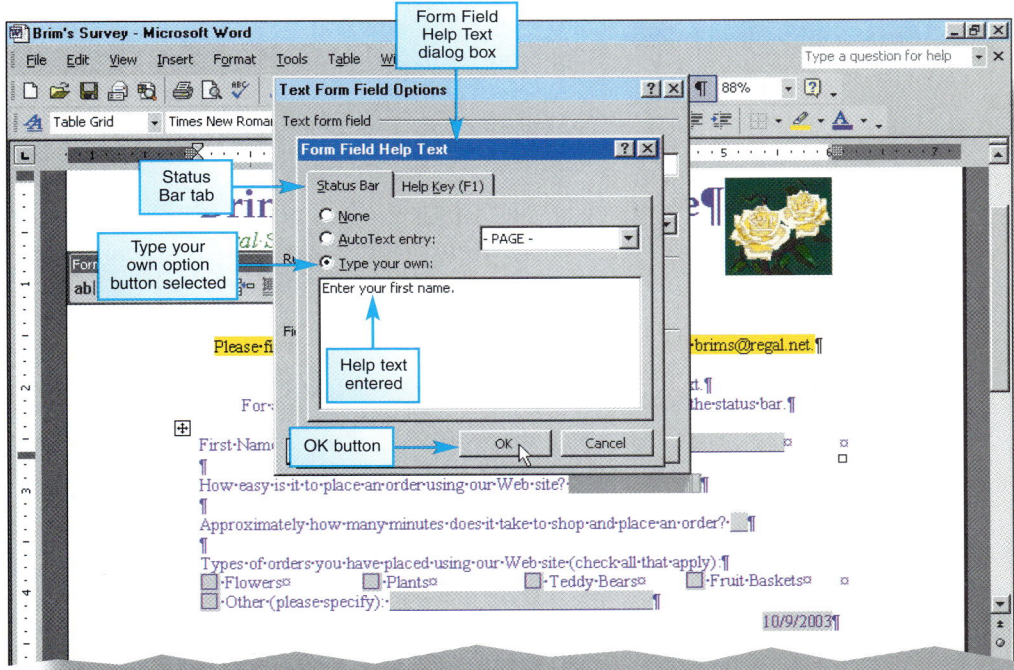

FIGURE 7-38

The F1 Key

If you want to enter Help text in a dialog box that displays when a user presses the F1 key, click the Help Key (F1) tab in the Form Field Help Text dialog box (shown in Figure 7-38 on the previous page). You enter Help text in the Help Key (F1) sheet in the same manner as in the Status Bar sheet.

The Help text does not display on the status bar until you protect the form, which you will do later in this project. At that time, you will enter data into the form and see the Help text display on the status bar.

The next step is to enter the Help text for the remaining form fields in the form. You repeat the procedure on the previous page for each data entry field on the form. The Help text for each field on the Customer Survey is shown in Table 7-2.

Table 7-2	Help Text for Fields on the Form	
FIELD	**FIELD TYPE**	**HELP TEXT TO DISPLAY ON STATUS BAR**
First Name	Text Form Field	Enter your first name.
Last Name	Text Form Field	Enter your last name.
ease of use	Drop-Down Form Field	Click box arrow for list of choices.
number of minutes	Text Form Field	Enter minutes in numbers.
Flowers	Check Box Form Field	Click check box to select or deselect.
Plants	Check Box Form Field	Click check box to select or deselect.
Teddy Bears	Check Box Form Field	Click check box to select or deselect.
Fruit Baskets	Check Box Form Field	Click check box to select or deselect.
Other (please specify)	Check Box Form Field	Click check box to select or deselect.
Other (please specify)	Text Form Field	Please list other types of orders placed using our Web site.

The following steps describe how to add the Help text shown in Table 7-2.

TO ADD MORE HELP TEXT

1. Double-click the text form field for the last name.

2. Click the Add Help Text button in the Text Form Field Options dialog box. When the Form Field Help Text dialog box displays, if necessary, click the Status Bar tab. Click Type your own. Type `Enter your last name`. Click the OK button. Click the OK button in the Text Form Field Options dialog box.

3. Double-click the ease of use drop-down form field.

4. Click the Add Help Text button in the Drop-Down Form Field Options dialog box. When the Form Field Help Text dialog box displays, if necessary, click the Status Bar tab. Click Type your own. Type `Click box arrow for list of choices`. Click the OK button. Click the OK button in the Drop-Down Form Field Options dialog box.

5. Double-click the text form field for the number of minutes.

6. Click the Add Help Text button in the Text Form Field Options dialog box. When the Form Field Help Text dialog box displays, if necessary, click the Status Bar tab. Click Type your own. Type `Enter minutes in numbers`. Click the OK button. Click the OK button in the Text Form Field Options dialog box.

7. Double-click the check box form field for Flowers.

8. Click the Add Help Text button in the Check Box Form Field Options dialog box. When the Form Field Help Text dialog box displays, if necessary, click the Status Bar tab. Click Type your own. Type `Click check box to select or deselect`. Click the OK button. Click the OK button in the Check Box Form Field Options dialog box.

9. Double-click the check box form field for Plants. Repeat Step 8.

10. Double-click the check box form field for Teddy Bears. Repeat Step 8.
11. Double-click the check box form field for Fruit Baskets. Repeat Step 8.
12. Double-click the check box form field for Other (please specify). Repeat Step 8.
13. Double-click the text form field for Other (please specify).
14. Click the Add Help Text button in the Text Form Field Options dialog box. When the Form Field Help Text dialog box displays, if necessary, click the Status Bar tab. Click Type your own. Type `Please list other types of orders placed using our Web site`. Click the OK button. Click the OK button in the Text Form Field Options dialog box.
15. Click outside the selected text to remove the selection.

Help text is entered for all data entry fields according to Table 7-2.

If you would like to change the Help text for any of the form fields, simply double-click the form field and then click the Add Help Text button in the dialog box. When the Form Field Help Text dialog box displays, if necessary, click the Status Bar tab. Make any necessary changes to the existing Help text and then click the OK button in the dialog boxes.

The next step is to remove the form field shading.

Removing Form Field Shading

The fields on the form currently are shaded (Figure 7-39). During the design of a form, it is helpful to display field shading so you easily can identify the fields. You do not want the fields to be shaded, however, when a user is entering data into a form. Thus, perform the following steps to remove form field shading.

Form Field Shading

If you print a form that displays form field shading, the shading will not print. To add shading to a field on a printed form, you must select the form field, click the Shading Color button arrow on the Tables and Borders toolbar, and then click the desired shading color. Likewise, if you want a border surrounding a field, select the form field, click the Border button arrow on the Tables and Borders toolbar, and then click the Outside Border button.

To Remove Form Field Shading

 **Point to the Form Field Shading button on the Forms toolbar (Figure 7-39).**

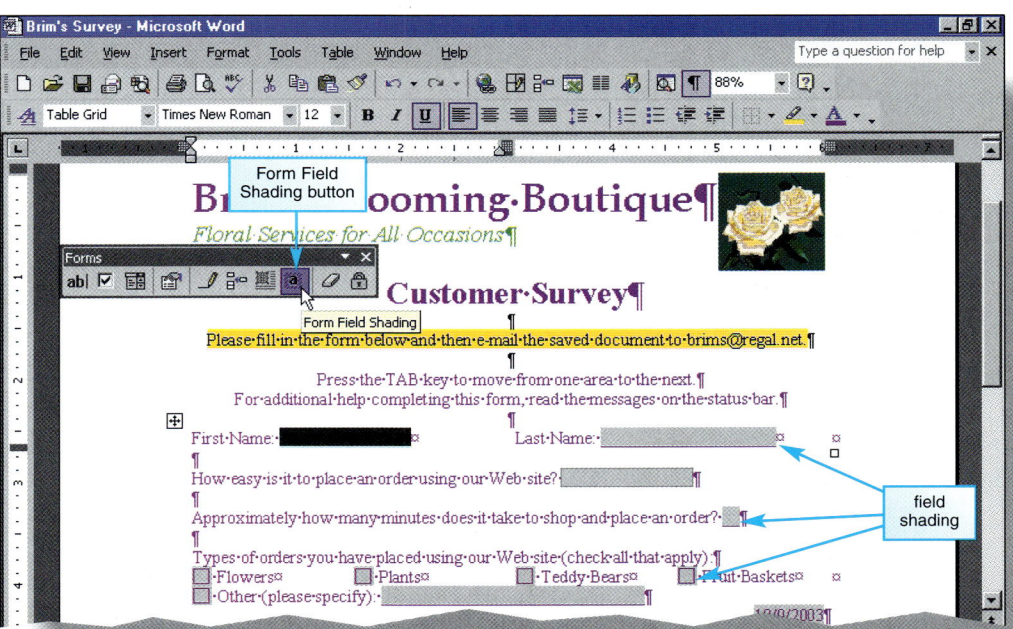

FIGURE 7-39

 **Click the Form Field Shading button.**

Word removes the shading from the form fields (Figure 7-40).

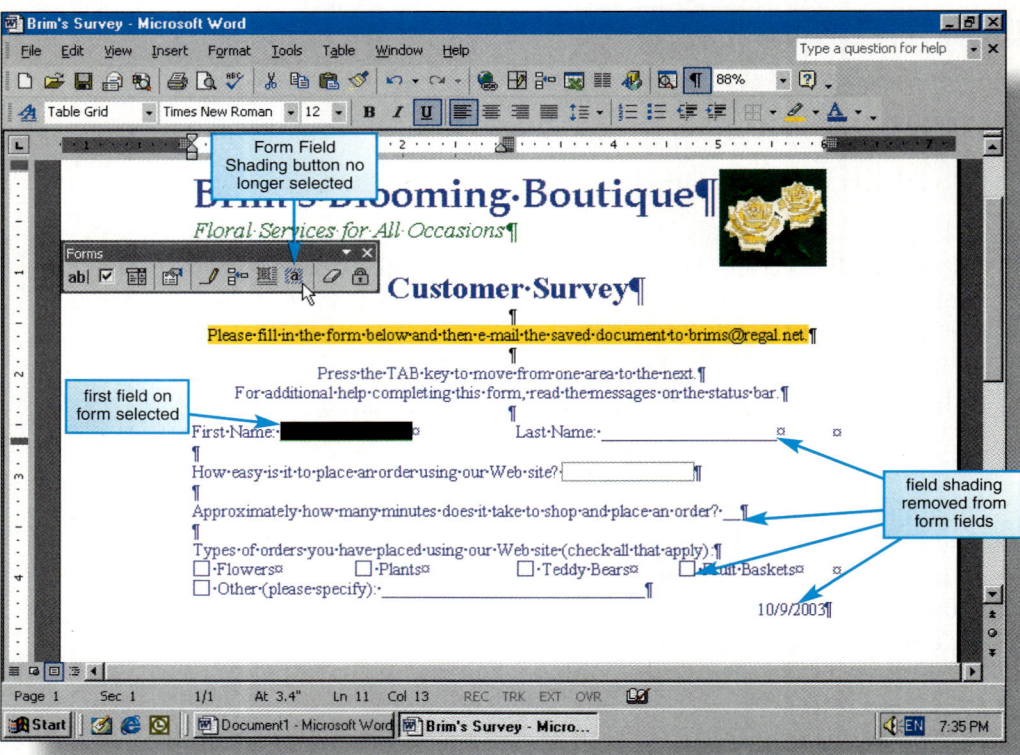

FIGURE 7-40

Other Ways

1. In Voice Command mode, say "Form Field Shading"

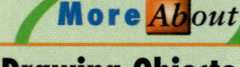

Drawing Objects

To change the color of a drawing object, click the Line Color button arrow on the Drawing toolbar and then click the desired color. To add a shadow to a drawing object, click the Shadow Style button on the Drawing toolbar and then click the desired shadow. To add a 3-D effect to a drawing object, click the 3-D Style button on the Drawing toolbar and then click the desired effect.

The next step is to emphasize the data entry area of the form.

Inserting and Formatting a Rectangle Drawing Object

The data entry area of the form includes all the form fields into which a user enters data. You want to call attention to this area of the form. Thus, you decide to place a rectangle around the data entry area, fill the rectangle with a texture, change the line color of the rectangle, and add a shadow to the rectangle. In Word, a rectangle is a type of drawing object.

The following pages explain how to insert and format a rectangle drawing object.

Steps: To Draw a Rectangle

1 **Click at the end of the form, positioning the insertion point after the date field. If the Drawing toolbar does not display on the screen, click the Drawing button on the Standard toolbar. Point to the Rectangle button on the Drawing toolbar (Figure 7-41).**

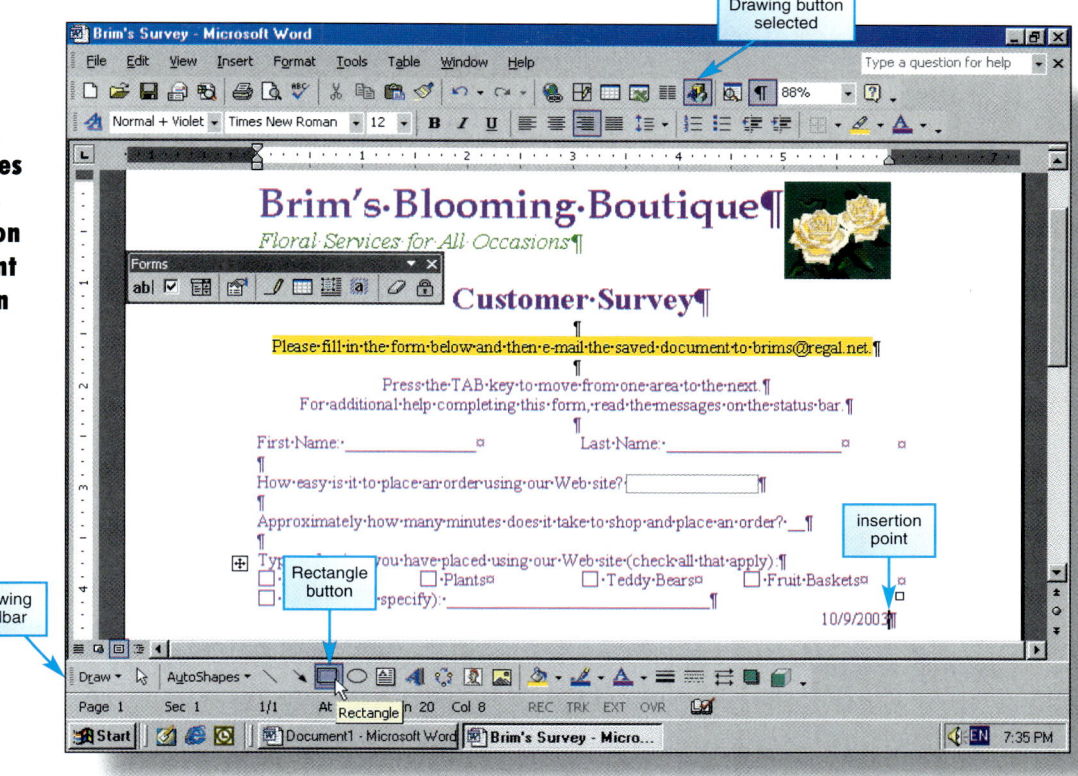

FIGURE 7-41

2 **Click the Rectangle button. When Word inserts the drawing canvas, scroll above the drawing canvas to display the form fields completely. Position the crosshair mouse pointer as shown in Figure 7-42.**

Word displays the mouse pointer as a crosshair, which you drag to form the size of the rectangle. Recall that the drawing canvas is a container that helps you resize and arrange shapes on the page. You do not want the AutoShape on the drawing canvas.

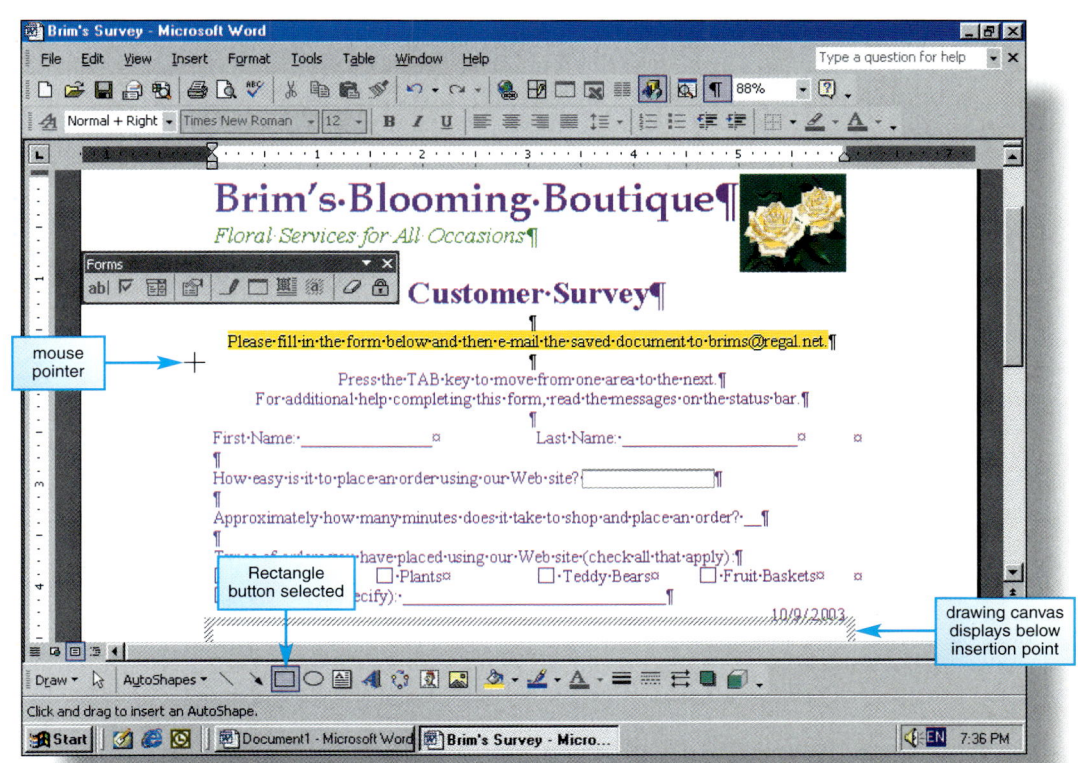

FIGURE 7-42

3 Drag the mouse pointer downward and rightward to form a rectangle as shown in Figure 7-43.

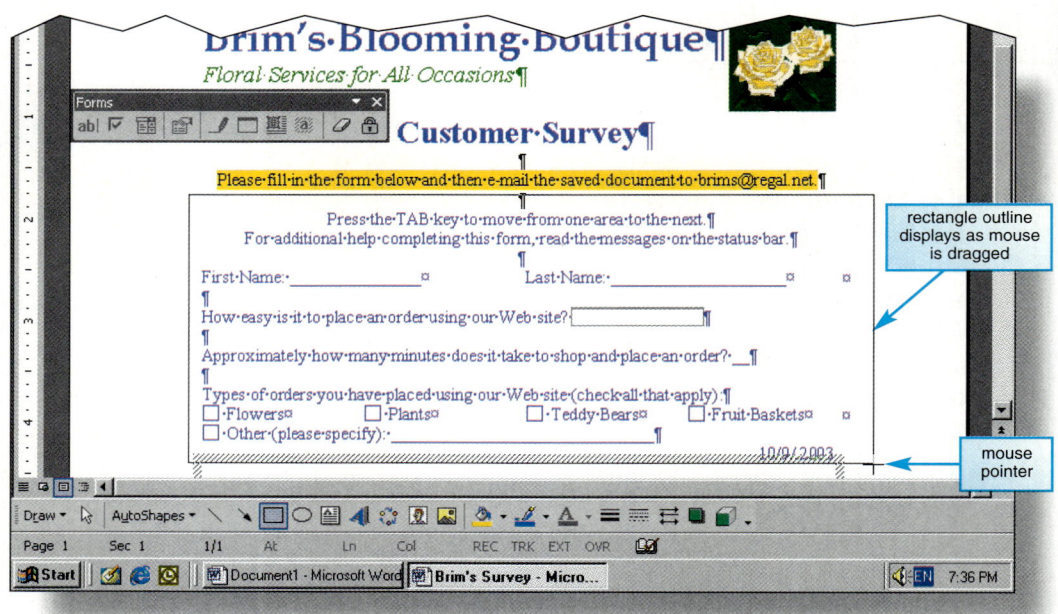

FIGURE 7-43

4 Release the mouse button. If Word positions the form text below the rectangle, click Format on the menu bar, click AutoShape, click the Layout tab, click In front of text, and then click the OK button. If you need to resize the rectangle after it is drawn, simply drag the sizing handles.

When you release the mouse button, Word positions the rectangle on top of the text, thus hiding the data entry area from view (Figure 7-44). Once the rectangle is drawn, Word removes the drawing canvas from the screen.

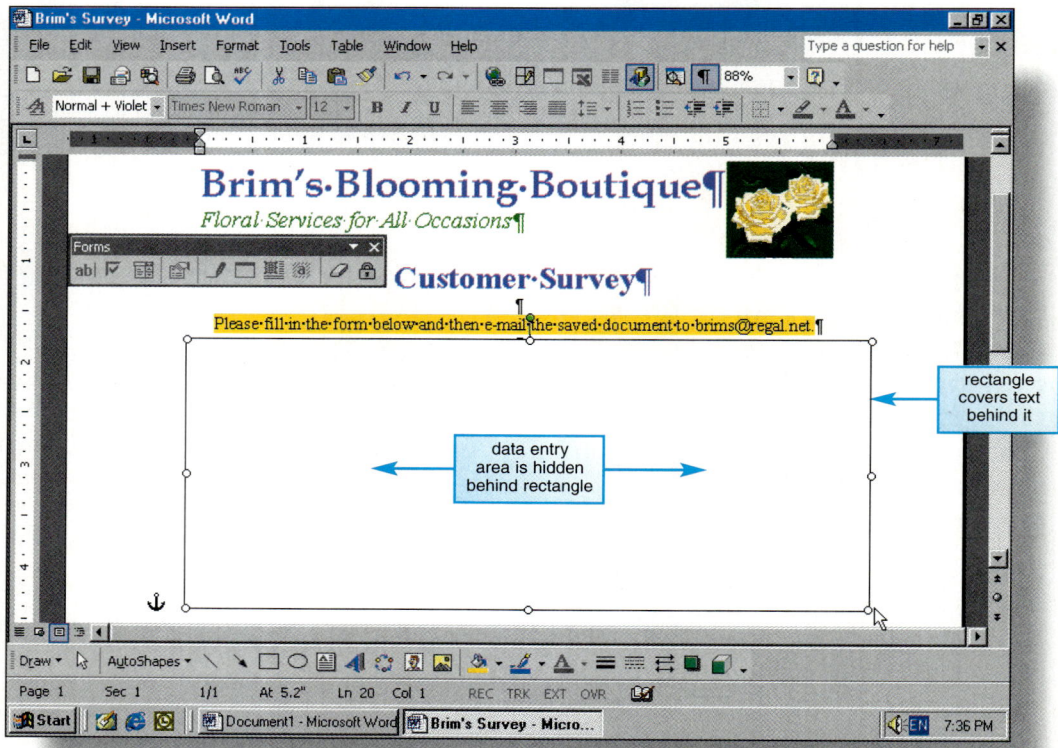

FIGURE 7-44

Other Ways

1. With Drawing toolbar displaying, in Voice Command mode, say "Rectangle, [draw rectangle]"

When you insert a drawing object into a document, Word initially places the drawing object in front of, or on top of, any text behind it. You can change the stacking order of the drawing object so that it displays behind the text, as shown in the following steps.

Steps To Send a Drawing Object behind Text

1 Point to the edge of the drawing object (in this case, the rectangle) until the mouse pointer displays a four-headed arrow and then right-click. Point to Order on the shortcut menu and then point to Send Behind Text (Figure 7-45).

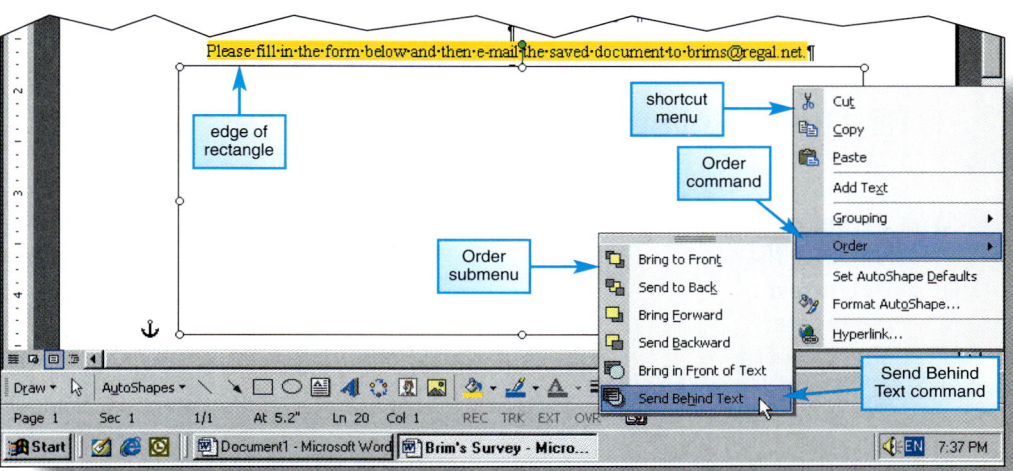

FIGURE 7-45

2 Click Send Behind Text.

Word positions the rectangle drawing object behind the text (Figure 7-46). The data entry area is visible again.

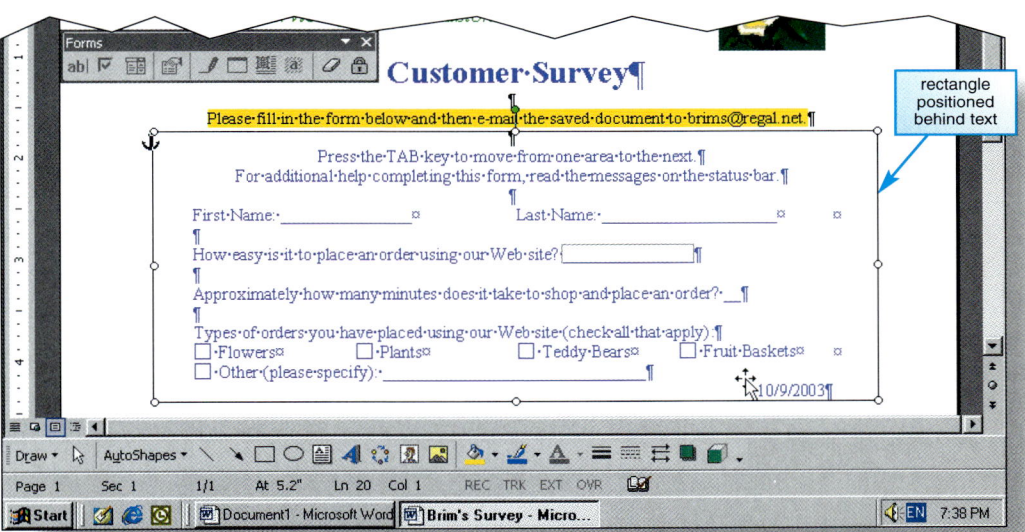

FIGURE 7-46

If you want to bring the drawing object on top of the text again, right-click one of its edges, point to Order on the shortcut menu, and then click Bring in Front of Text (Figure 7-45).

If you have multiple graphics displaying on the screen and would like them to overlap, you can change their stacking order by right-clicking the graphic to reorder, pointing to Order on the shortcut menu, and then clicking one of the first four commands on the Order submenu (Figure 7-45). The Bring to Front command displays the selected object at the top of the stack, and the Send to Back command displays the selected object at the bottom of the stack. The Bring Forward and Send Backward commands each move the drawing object forward or backward one layer in the stack.

Other Ways

1. Click drawing object, on Format menu click AutoShape, click Layout tab, click Behind text, click OK button
2. With drawing object selected, in Voice Command mode, say "Format, AutoShape, Layout, Behind text, OK"

The next step is to fill the inside of the rectangle. In Word, you can **fill**, or paint, the inside of a drawing object with a color or with an effect. **Fill effects** include gradient (two-toned) colors, textures, patterns, and pictures. Perform the following steps to format the drawing object, in this case the rectangle, using a texture fill effect.

Steps To Fill a Drawing Object with a Texture

1 **With the rectangle selected, click the Fill Color button arrow on the Drawing toolbar and then point to the Fill Effects button.**

The available predefined fill colors display, as well as the More Fill Colors and Fill Effects buttons (Figure 7-47).

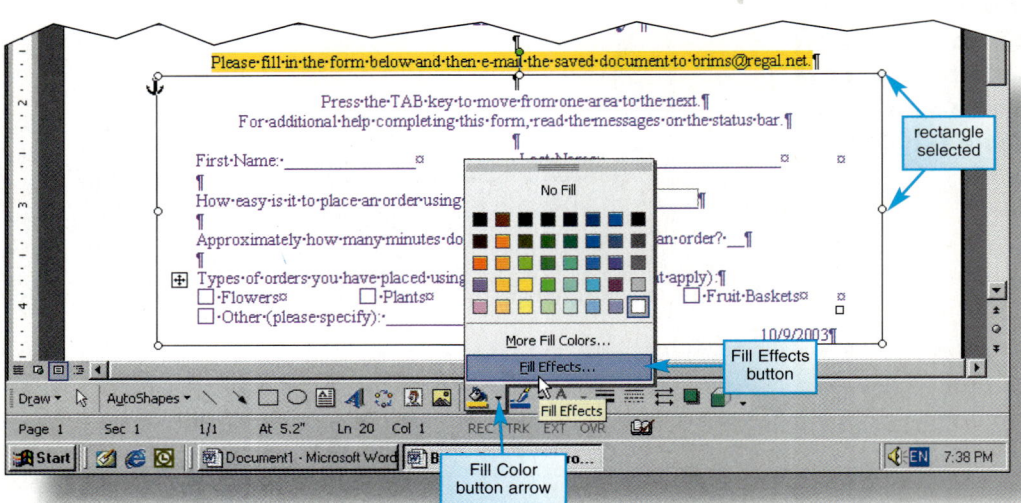

FIGURE 7-47

2 **Click the Fill Effects button. When the Fill Effects dialog box displays, if necessary, click the Texture tab. Click the third texture in the first row, Parchment, in the list of textures and then point to the OK button.**

Word displays the Fill Effects dialog box (Figure 7-48). The selected texture name displays below the textures.

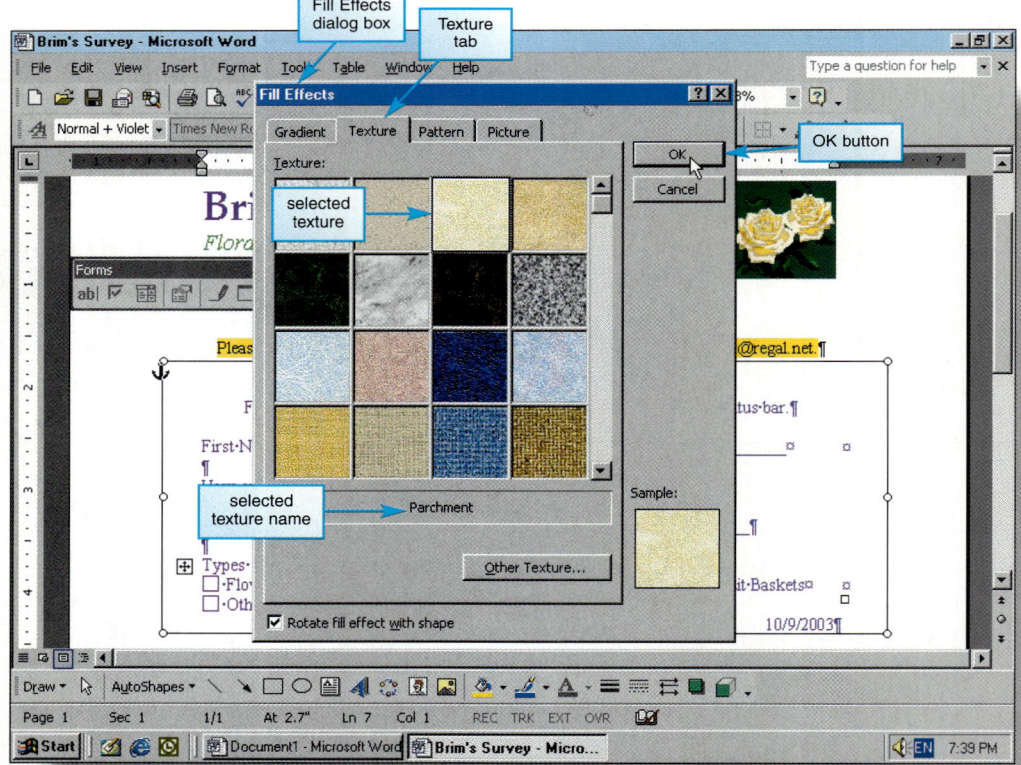

FIGURE 7-48

Creating an Online Form • WD 7.43

3 **Click the OK button.**

Word fills the rectangle with the Parchment texture (Figure 7-49).

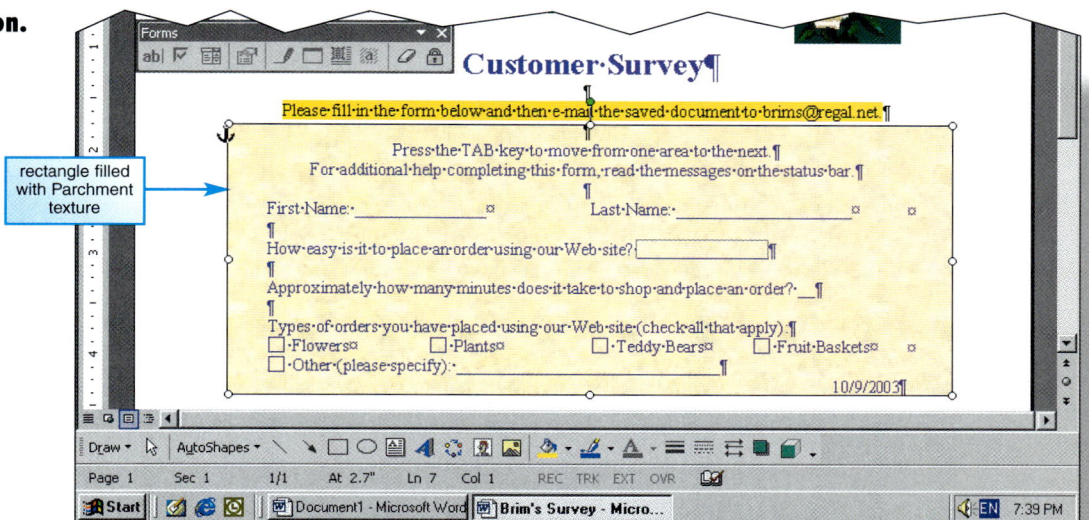

FIGURE 7-49

Other Ways

1. With drawing object selected, in Voice Command mode, say "Format, AutoShape, Colors and Lines, Fill Color, Fill Effects, Texture, [select desired texture], OK, OK"

The next step is to change the line color of the rectangle from the default color, black, to violet, which matches the color of the text. Perform the following steps to change the line color of the rectangle drawing object.

Steps To Change the Line Color of a Drawing Object

1 **With the rectangle selected, click the Line Color button arrow on the Drawing toolbar and then point to Violet.**

The available predefined line colors display, as well as the More Line Colors and Patterned Lines buttons (Figure 7-50).

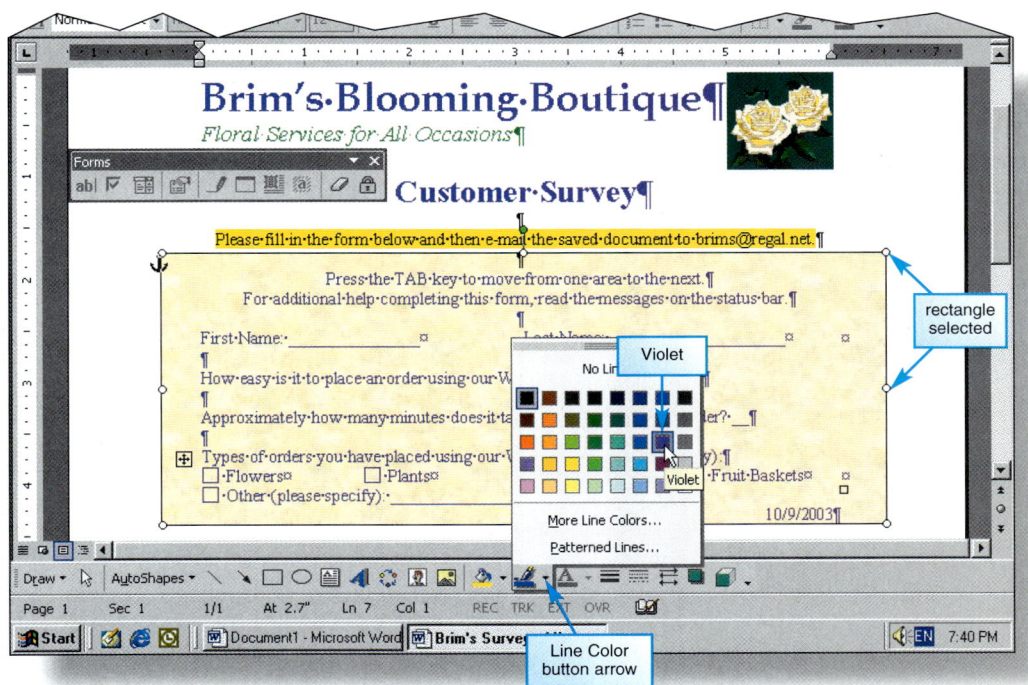

FIGURE 7-50

WD 7.44 • Project 7 • Creating an Online Form

2 Click Violet.

Word changes the rectangle's line color to violet (Figure 7-51).

Other Ways

1. Select drawing object, click AutoShape on Format menu, click Colors and Lines tab, click Color button arrow in Line area, click desired color, click OK button
2. Right-click edge of drawing object, click Format AutoShape on shortcut menu, click Colors and Lines tab, click Color button arrow in Line area, click desired color, click OK button
3. With drawing object selected, in Voice Command mode, say "Format, AutoShape, Colors and Lines, Line Color, [select color], OK"

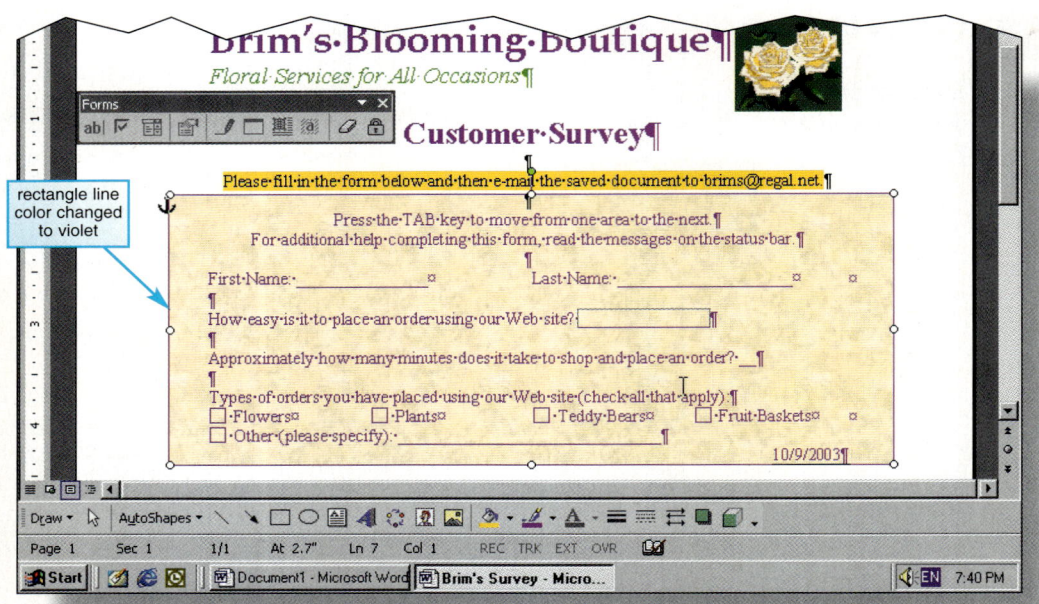

FIGURE 7-51

The next step is to add a shadow to the drawing object (in this case, the rectangle), as shown in the following steps.

Steps To Add a Shadow to a Drawing Object

1 With the rectangle selected, click the Shadow Style button on the Drawing toolbar. Point to Shadow Style 5.

The available predefined shadow styles display, as well as the Shadow Settings button (Figure 7-52).

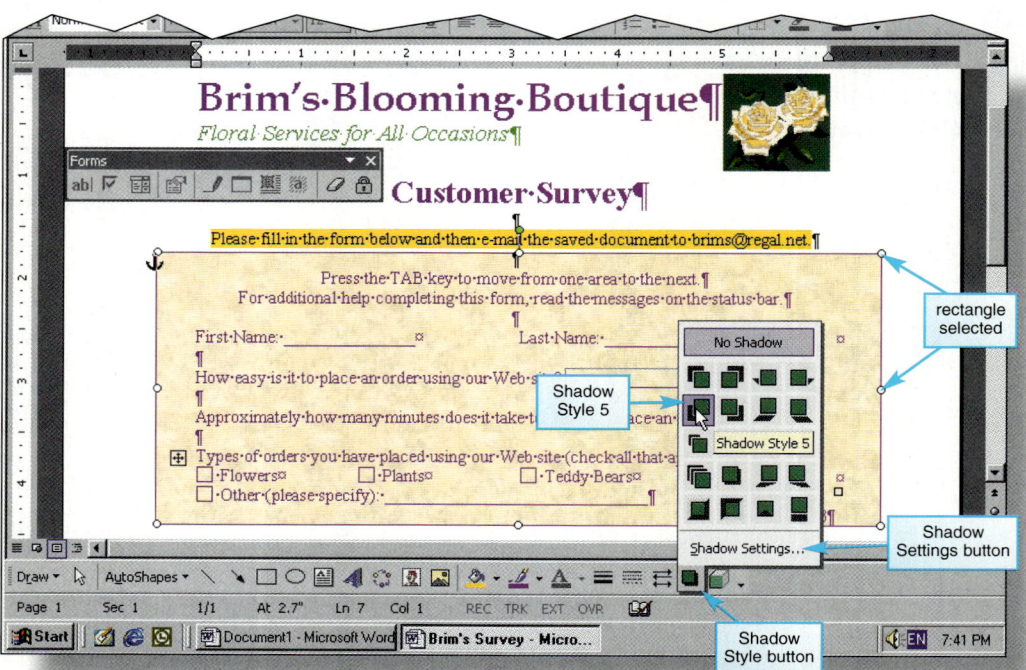

FIGURE 7-52

2 **Click Shadow Style 5. Click the Drawing button on the Standard toolbar to remove the Drawing toolbar. Click inside the selected rectangle to remove the selection. If necessary, scroll up to position the boutique name at the top of the document window.**

Word adds a shadow to the left and bottom of the rectangle (Figure 7-53). Turning off the Drawing toolbar allows you to see the entire form on the screen.

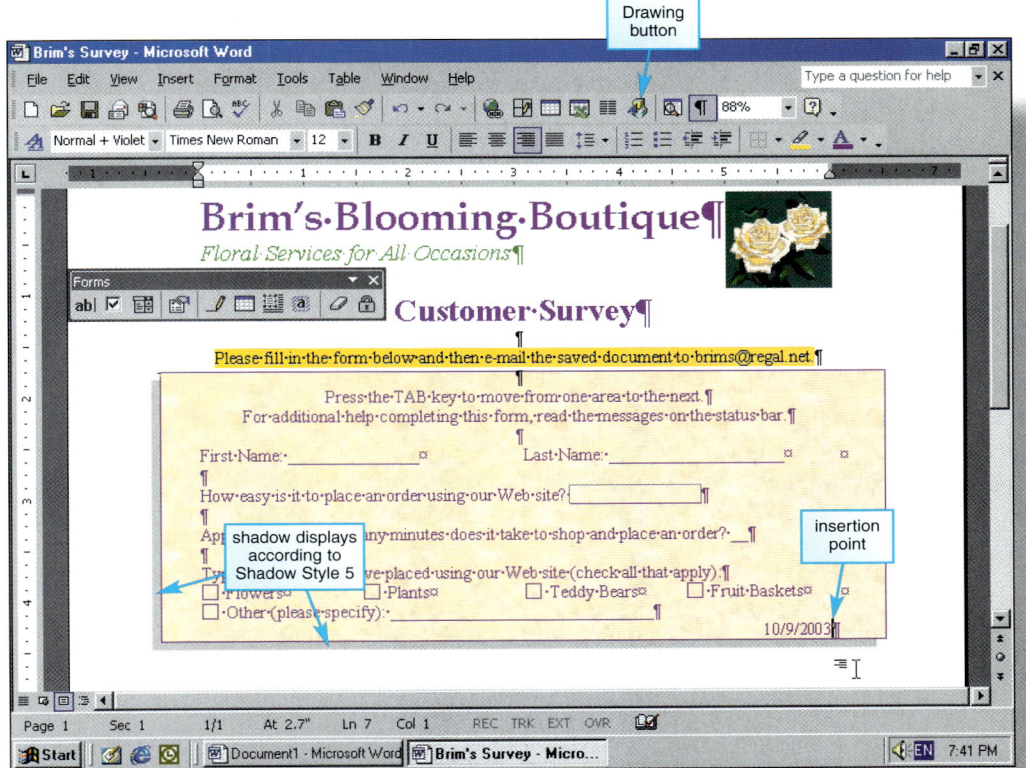

FIGURE 7-53

When clicked, the Shadow Settings button (Figure 7-52) displays the Shadow Settings toolbar. If you want Word to display a wider or narrower shadow, you may move the shadow up, down, left, or right, by clicking any of the four Nudge Shadow buttons on the Shadow Settings toolbar to create the effect you want. Each time you click Nudge Shadow, the shadow moves one point in the specified direction.

The next step is to enter and format the thank-you message below the data entry area.

Animating Text

In an online document, you can animate text in order to draw the reader's attention to it. When you **animate text**, it has the appearance of motion. To animate text in Word, you select it and then apply one of the predefined text effects in the Font dialog box.

For this form, you want the thank-you message below the data entry area to have a moving black rectangle around it, which is called the Marching Black Ants animation in the Font dialog box. Perform the steps on the next page to animate the thank-you message on the online form.

Other Ways

1. With Drawing toolbar displaying, in Voice Command mode, say "Shadow Style, [select shadow style]"

More About

Animated Text

Animated text can distract readers; thus, you should use it sparingly. If a reader wants to hide animated text, he or she can click Tools on the menu bar, click Options, click the View tab, remove the check mark from the Animated text check box, and then click the OK button. Animated text does not print on a hard copy.

Steps To Animate Text

1 **Position the insertion point at the end of the current date in the data entry area and then press the ENTER key twice. Click the Font Color button arrow on the Formatting toolbar and then click Sea Green. Press CTRL+E to center the paragraph and then type** Thank you for your time!

The thank-you message displays below the data entry area (Figure 7-54).

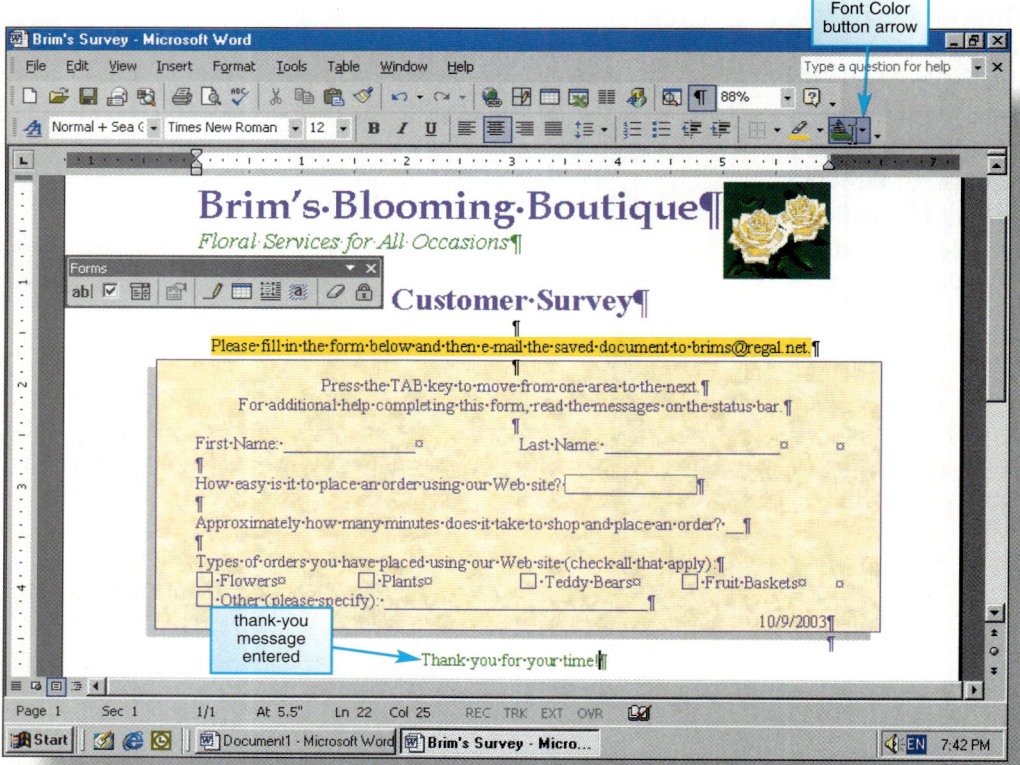

FIGURE 7-54

2 **Select the sentence just entered. Right-click the selection and then click Font on the shortcut menu. When the Font dialog box displays, if necessary, click the Text Effects tab. Click Marching Black Ants in the Animations list. Point to the OK button.**

Word displays the Font dialog box (Figure 7-55). The Preview area shows a sample of the selected animation.

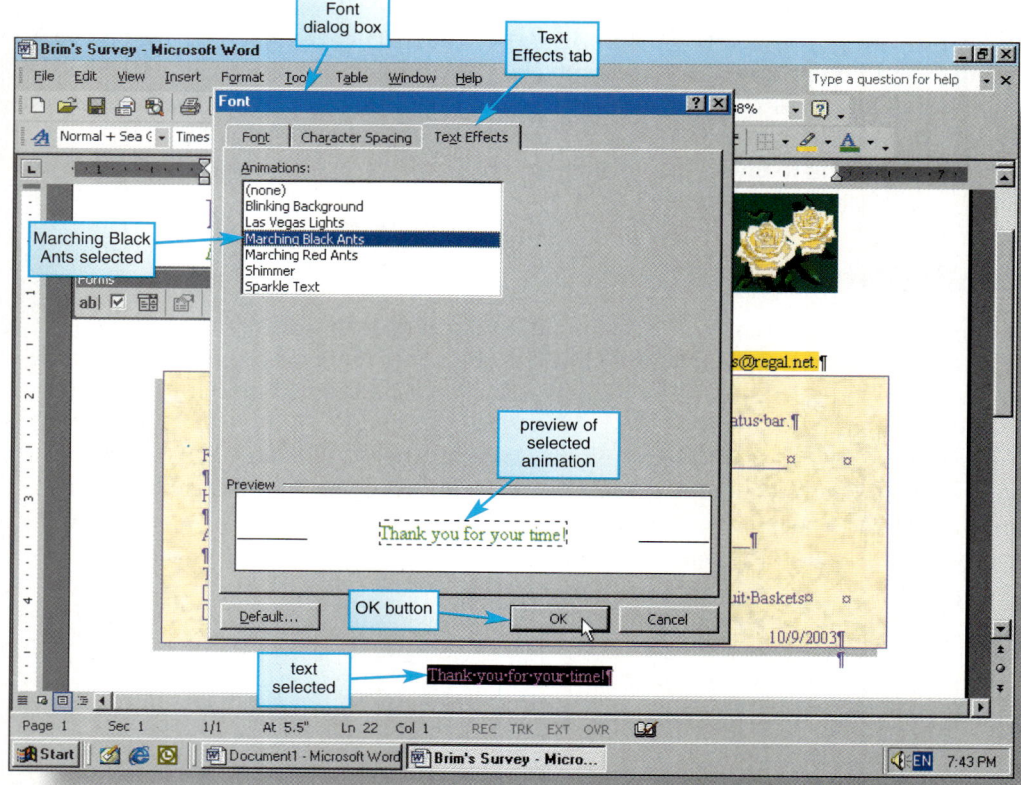

FIGURE 7-55

Creating an Online Form • WD 7.47

3 Click the OK button. Click outside the selected text to remove the selection.

Word applies the animation to the selected text (Figure 7-56).

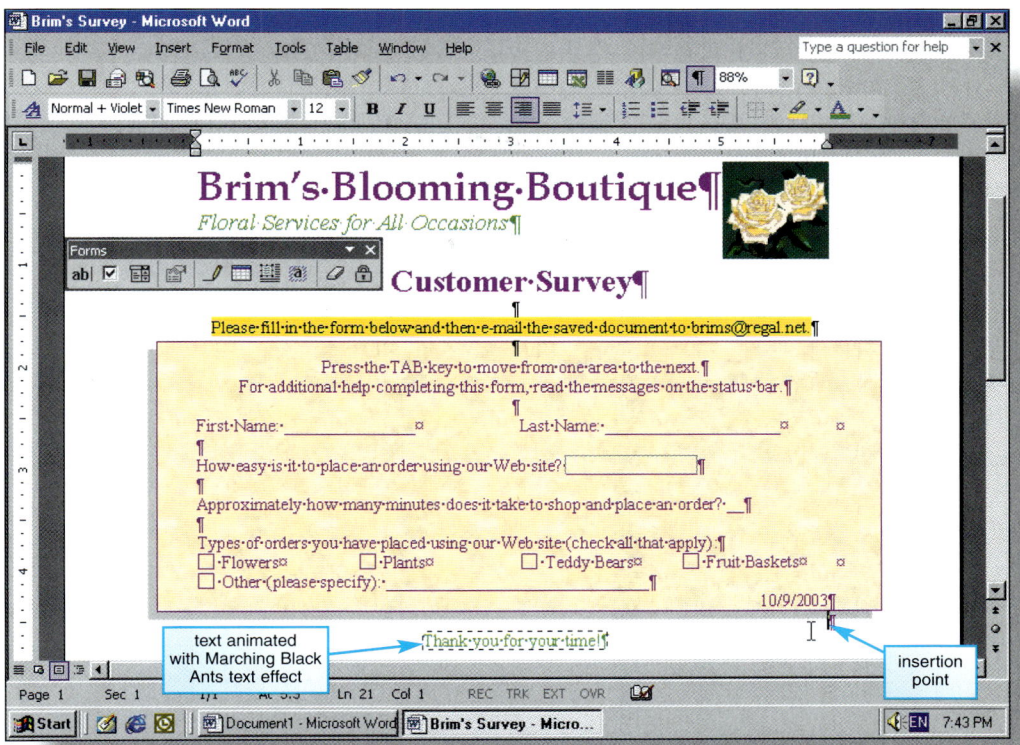

FIGURE 7-56

If you want to remove an animation from text, select the text, right-click the selection, click Font on the shortcut menu, click the Text Effects tab, click (none) in the Animations list, and then click the OK button.

If you print a document that contains animated text, the animations do not show on the hard copy; instead, the text prints as regular text. Thus, animations are designed specifically for documents that will be viewed online.

The next step in this project is to protect the Customer Survey.

Protecting a Form

It is crucial that you protect a form before making it available to users. When you **protect a form**, you are allowing users to enter data only in designated areas — specifically, the form fields that are enabled.

Perform the steps on the next page to protect the Customer Survey.

Other Ways

1. Select text, click Font on Format menu, click Text Effects tab, click desired animation, click OK button
2. In Voice Command mode, say "Format, Font, Text Effects, [select desired animation], OK"

More About

Protecting Forms

If you want only authorized users to be able to unprotect a form, you should password-protect the form. To do this, click Tools on the menu bar, click Protect Document, click Forms in the Protect document for area, type the password in the Password (optional) text box, and then click the OK button. Then, reenter the password in the Confirm Password dialog box.

Steps To Protect a Form

1 Point to the Protect Form button on the Forms toolbar (Figure 7-57).

2 Click the Protect Form button. Remove the Forms toolbar from the screen by clicking its Close button.

Word protects the form and then selects the first form field on the form (shown in Figure 7-58).

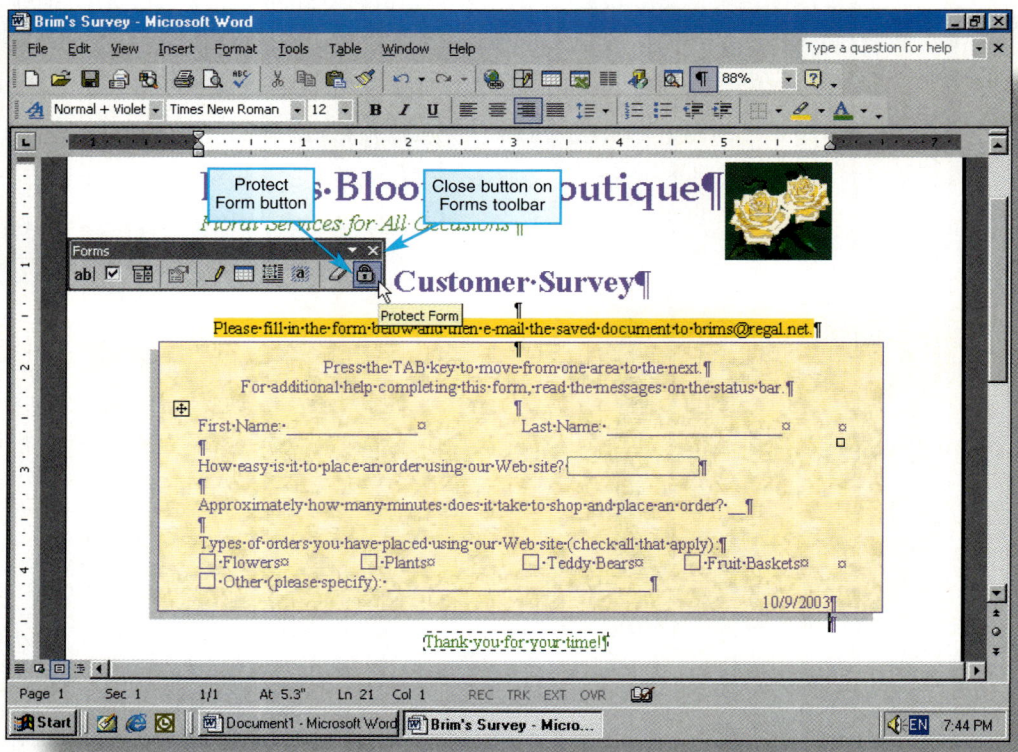

FIGURE 7-57

1. On Tools menu click Protect Document, click Forms, click OK button
2. In Voice Command mode, say "Protect Form"

When the form is protected, the selection displays in the first form field. To advance to the next form field, press the TAB key. To move to a previous form field, press SHIFT+TAB. You will enter data into this form later in the project.

The next step is to turn off the display of formatting marks. You do not want them on the form when a user opens it. Perform the following step to hide formatting marks.

TO HIDE FORMATTING MARKS

1 If the Show/Hide ¶ button on the Standard toolbar is selected, click it.

Word hides the formatting marks (Figure 7-58).

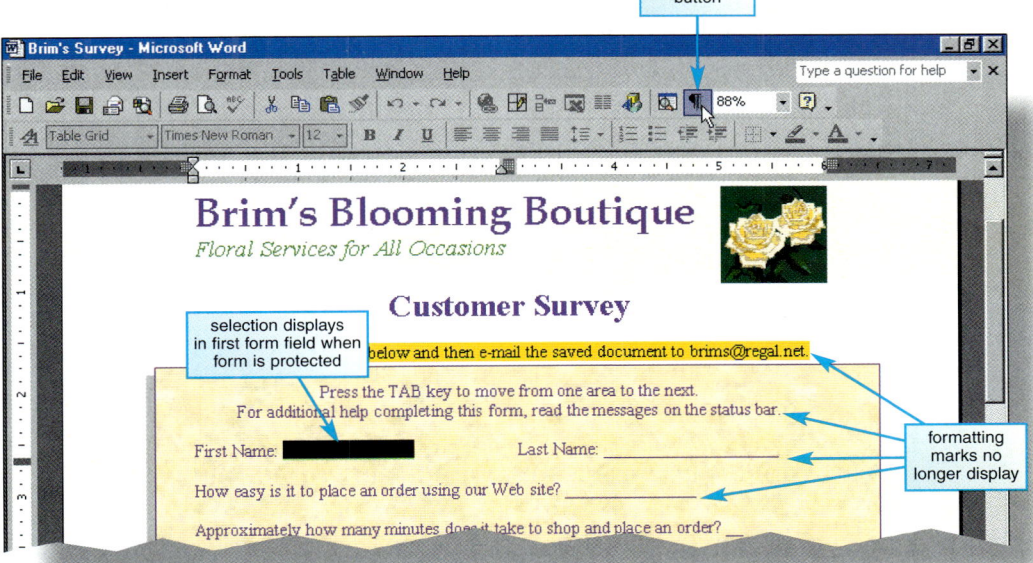

FIGURE 7-58

The online form template for this project now is complete. Perform the following steps to save it again and then quit Word.

TO SAVE THE DOCUMENT AGAIN

1. Click the Save button on the Standard toolbar.

Word saves the template with the same file name, Brim's Survey.

TO QUIT WORD

1. Click File on the menu bar and then click Exit.

The Word window closes.

Working with an Online Form

Once you have created a template, you then can make it available to users. Users do not open templates with the Open button on the Standard toolbar in Word. A developer of a template uses the Open button to open the template so it can be modified. A user, by contrast, starts a new Word document that is based on the template. That is, when a user accesses a template, the title bar displays the default file name, Document1 (or a similar name). Instead of the Word window being blank, however, it contains text and formatting associated with the template that the user accesses. For example, Word provides a variety of templates such as those for memos, letters, fax cover sheets, and resumes. If a user accesses a memo template, Word displays the contents of a basic memo in a new document window.

When you save the template to a disk in drive A, as instructed earlier in this project, a user can access your template through the My Computer window or Windows Explorer. Perform the steps on the next page to display a new Word document window that is based on the Brim's Survey template.

Web Forms

Online forms frequently are used on Web pages to collect and provide data. For example, you might create a form on a Web page that allows users to search a database you have stored on a Web server or collect data from visitors. A Web form typically contains a Submit button to send the information back to the host computer. The Submit button and other Web form controls are available on the Web Tools toolbar.

Steps: To Access a Template through Windows Explorer

1 Right-click the My Computer icon on the Windows desktop and then click Explore on the shortcut menu. When the Explorer window opens, if necessary, double-click its title bar to maximize the window. Click the Address text box to select it. Type `a:` and then press the ENTER key.

The Explorer window opens (Figure 7-59). Notice the icon for the Brim's Survey template has a small yellow bar at its top. Your Explorer window may display differently.

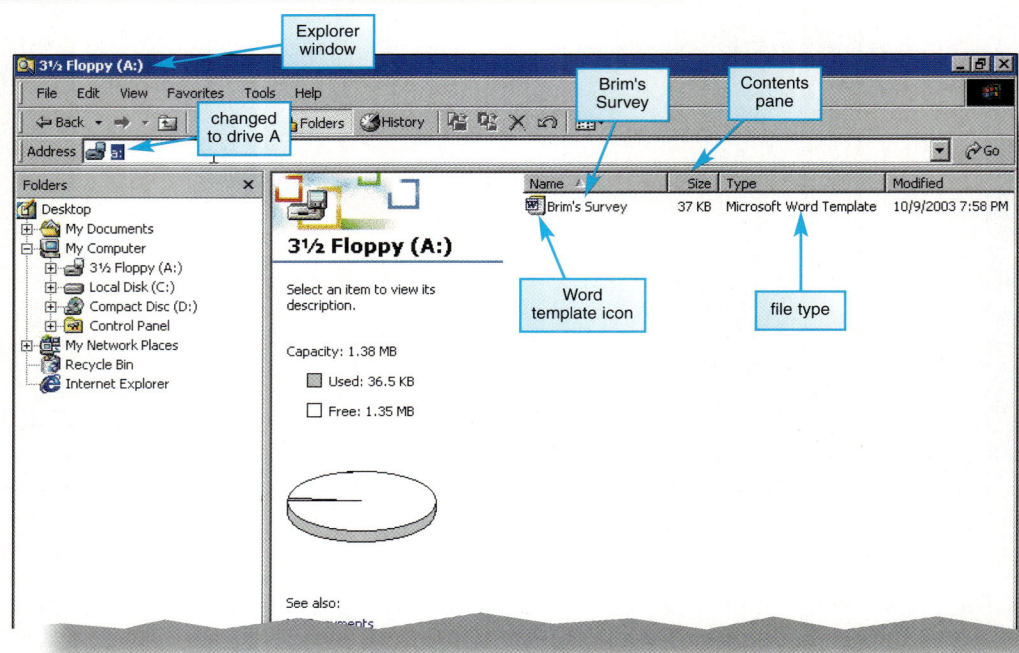

FIGURE 7-59

2 Double-click the Brim's Survey icon in the Contents pane. When Word starts, if necessary, maximize the Word window. If the Show/Hide ¶ button on the Standard toolbar is selected, click it. Zoom to Page Width. If gridlines display, click Table on the menu bar and then click Hide Gridlines. Scroll down so the entire form displays in the Word window.

Windows starts Word and displays a new document window that is based on the contents of the Brim's Survey template (Figure 7-60). The selection displays in the first form field, ready for a user's data entry. The corresponding Help message displays on the status bar.

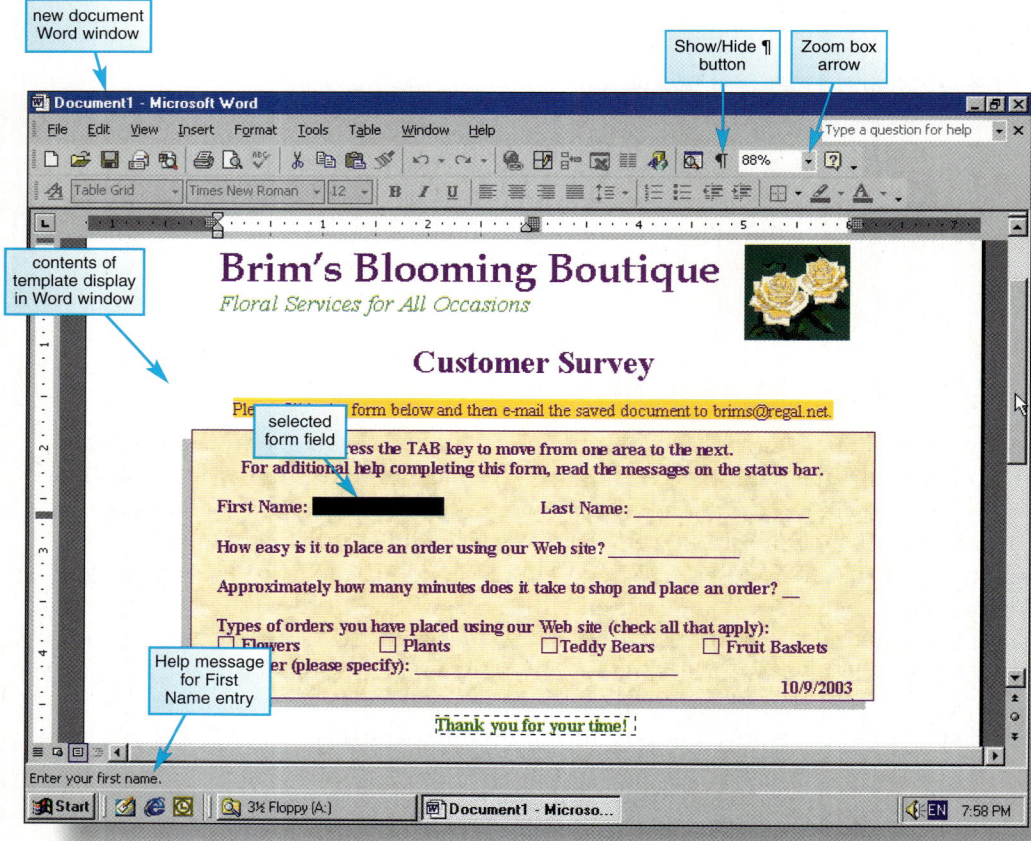

FIGURE 7-60

The next step is to enter data into the form. To advance to the next form field, a user presses the TAB key. To move to a previous form field, a user presses SHIFT+TAB. As a user tabs from one form field to the next, the status bar displays the Help messages related to the current field.

Perform the following steps to fill out the Customer Survey.

Steps: To Fill Out a Form

 With the First Name form field selected, type Lourdes **and then press the TAB key. Type** Nunez **in the Last Name form field. Press the TAB key to select the ease of use form field and display its box arrow. Click the box arrow and then point to Very Easy.**

The drop-down list displays (Figure 7-61).

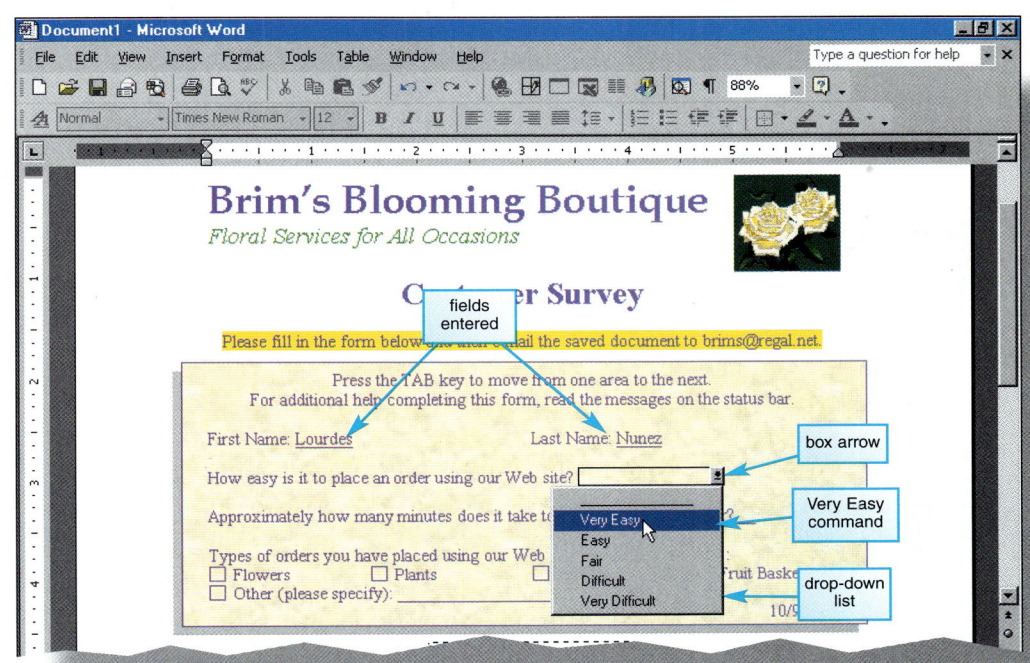

FIGURE 7-61

2 **Click Very Easy and then press the TAB key. Type** 15 **in the number of minutes text box. Press the TAB key. Click the following check boxes: Flowers, Fruit Baskets, and Other. Press the TAB key. Type** Balloon Basket **in the Other text box.**

The form is filled in (Figure 7-62). Notice that the text box and drop-down list box entries are underlined in violet.

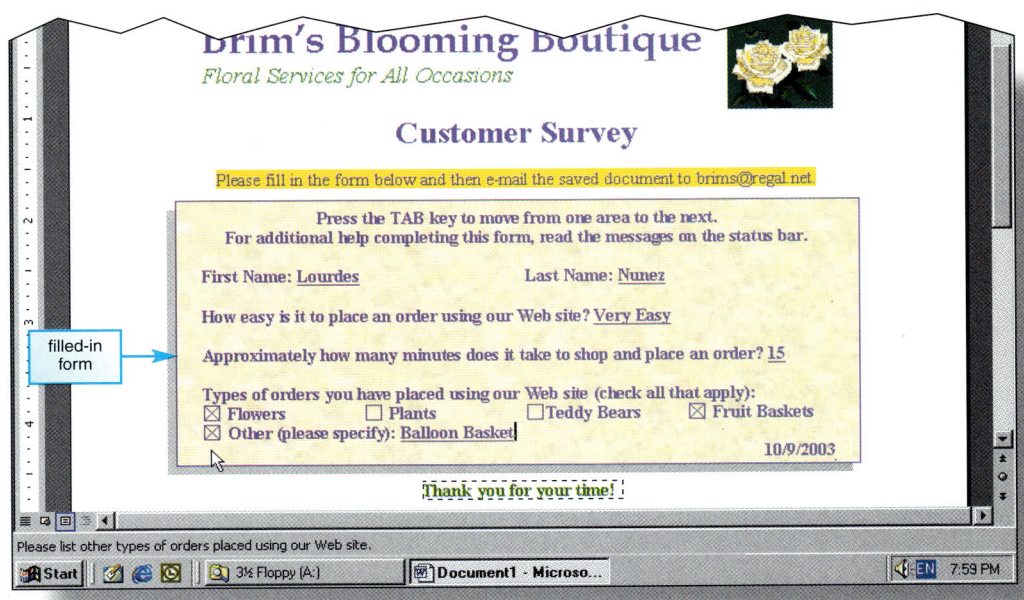

FIGURE 7-62

With the form filled in, a user can save it by clicking the Save button on the Standard toolbar. By basing the new document on a template, the blank Customer Survey remains unchanged because users are saving a new document instead of saving a modification to the survey. Perform the following steps to save the document that contains your responses.

TO SAVE A DOCUMENT

1. With a floppy disk in drive A, click the Save button on the Standard toolbar.
2. Type Nunez Form in the File name text box.
3. If necessary, click the Save in box arrow and then click 3½ Floppy (A:).
4. Click the Save button in the Save As dialog box.

Word saves the document with the file name, Nunez Form, on a disk in drive A (shown in Figure 7-64).

You can print the document as you print any other document. Keep in mind, however, that the colors used were designed for viewing online. Thus, different color schemes would have been selected if the form had been designed for a printout. Perform the following step to print the filled-in form.

TO PRINT A FORM

1. Click the Print button on the Standard toolbar.

Word prints the form (Figure 7-63). Notice the animation on the thank-you message does not print.

> **More About**
>
> **Printing**
>
> If you want to save ink, print faster, or decrease printer overrun errors, print a draft. Click File on the menu bar and then click Print. Click the Options button, place a check mark in the Draft output check box, and then click the OK button in each dialog box.

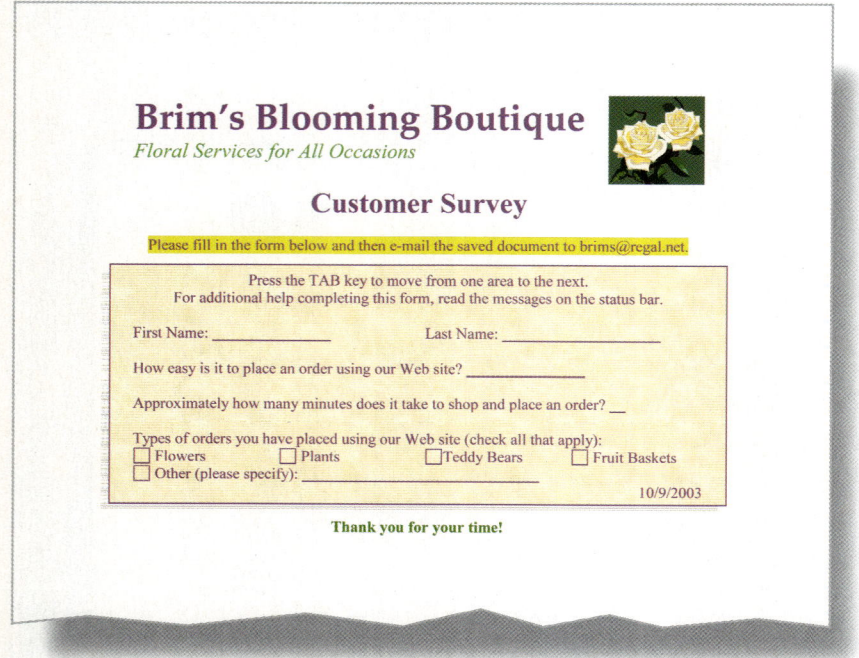

FIGURE 7-63

Saving Data on the Form

You may wish to gather the responses from the completed surveys and analyze them. Depending on the number of forms completed, tabulating the data manually could be a time-consuming and monumental task. One alternative is to use database software, such as Access, to assist you in analyzing the responses. To do this, you must save the data on each survey in a manner that will be recognized by the database software.

Word provides a means through the Save As dialog box to save the data in a comma-delimited text file so that it can be recognized by database software packages. A **comma-delimited text file** is a file that separates each data item with a comma and places quotation marks around text data items. Figure 7-69 on page WD 7.56 shows an example of a comma-delimited text file.

Perform the following steps to save the data from the form in a text file.

Steps: To Save Form Data in a Text File

1 Click File on the menu bar and then click Save As. When the Save As dialog box displays, click the Tools button and then point to Save Options.

Word displays the Save As dialog box (Figure 7-64).

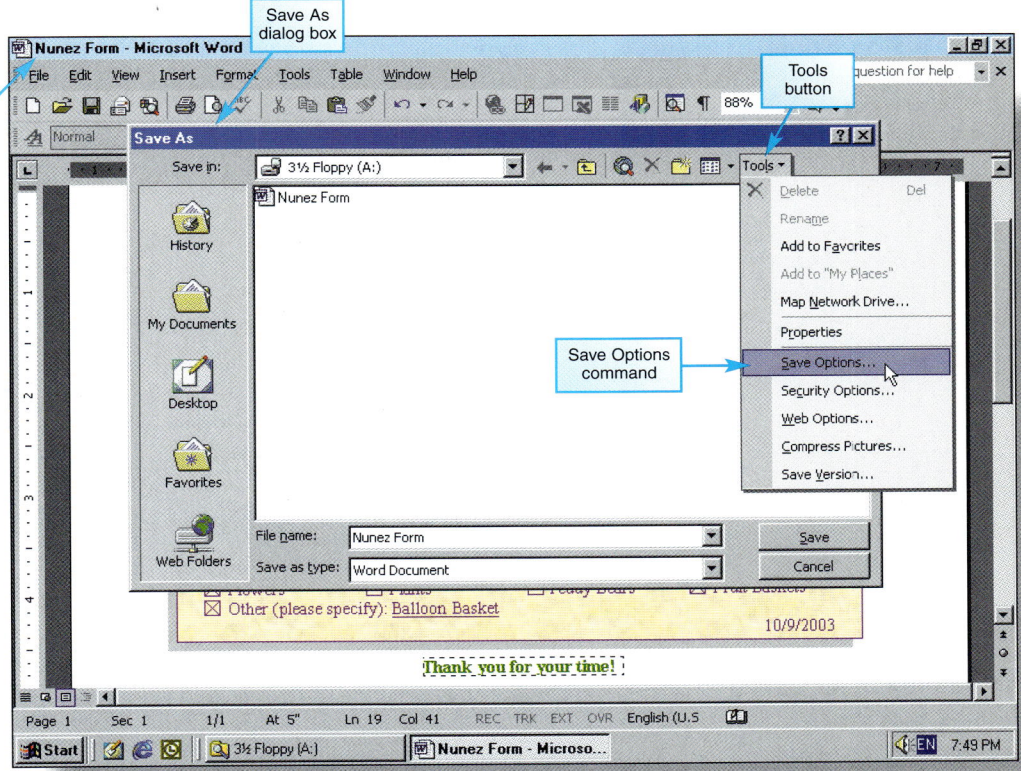

FIGURE 7-64

2 Click Save Options. When the Save dialog box displays, place a check mark in the Save data only for forms check box and then point to the OK button.

Word displays the Save dialog box (Figure 7-65).

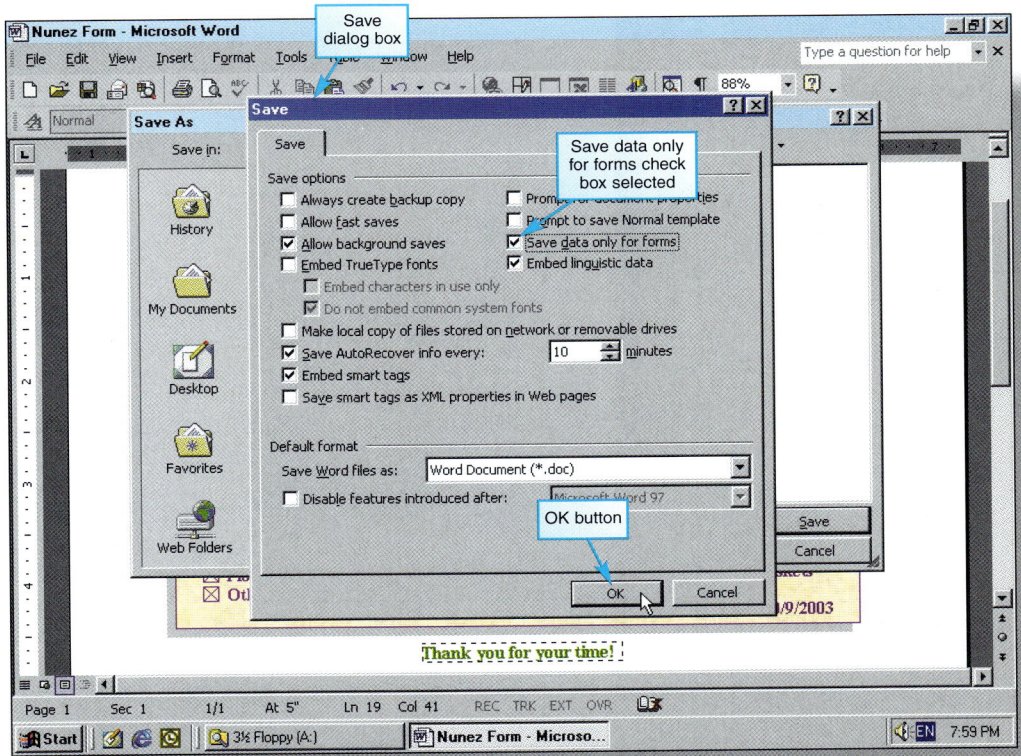

FIGURE 7-65

WD 7.54 • Project 7 • Creating an Online Form

3 **Click the OK button. When the Save As dialog box is visible again, point to its Save button.**

Word changes the document type in the Save as type box to Plain Text (Figure 7-66).

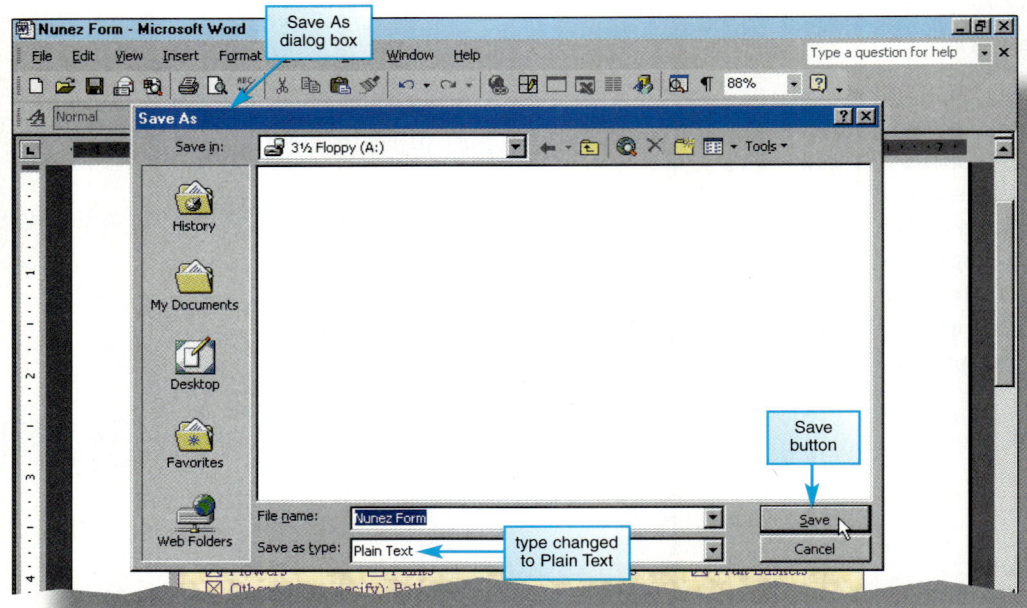

FIGURE 7-66

4 **Click the Save button in the Save As dialog box. When Word displays the File Conversion - Nunez Form dialog box, point to the OK button.**

The File Conversion - Nunez Form dialog box displays, indicating that some formatting may be lost (Figure 7-67).

5 **Click the OK button.**

Word saves the data on the form in a text file called, Nunez Form, without formatting.

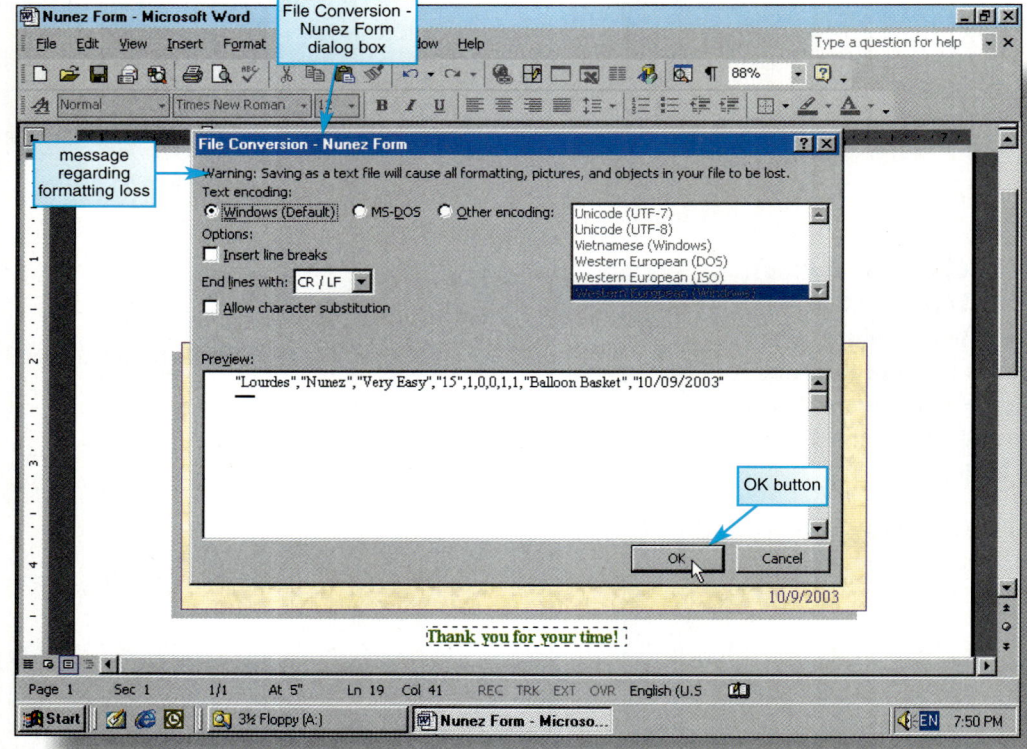

FIGURE 7-67

1. In Voice Command mode, say "Tools, Options, Save, Save data only for forms, OK, File, Save copy As, Save"

After you save the data to a text file, you should remove the check mark from the Save data only for forms check box so that Word will save the entire form the next time you save the document.

Perform the following steps to uncheck the Save data only for forms check box.

TO UNCHECK THE SAVE DATA ONLY FOR FORMS CHECK BOX

1. Click Tools on the menu bar and then click Options. When the Options dialog box displays, click the Save tab.
2. Click the Save data only for forms check box to remove the check mark. Click the OK button.

In the future, the entire form will be saved.

If you wanted to view the contents of the text file, you could open it in Word by performing the following steps.

Microsoft Access 2002

For more information on features of Access in analyzing data, visit the Word 2002 More About Web page (www.scsite.com/wd2002/more.htm) and then click Microsoft Access 2002.

Steps: To Open a Text File in Word

1. **Click the Open button on the Standard toolbar. When the Open dialog box displays, if necessary, click the Files of type box arrow and then click All Files. Click the text file called Nunez Form in the list and then point to the Open button in the dialog box.**

Word displays the Open dialog box (Figure 7-68). The icon for a text file looks like a piece of paper with writing on it. Depending on previous settings, your screen may not show a preview of the file.

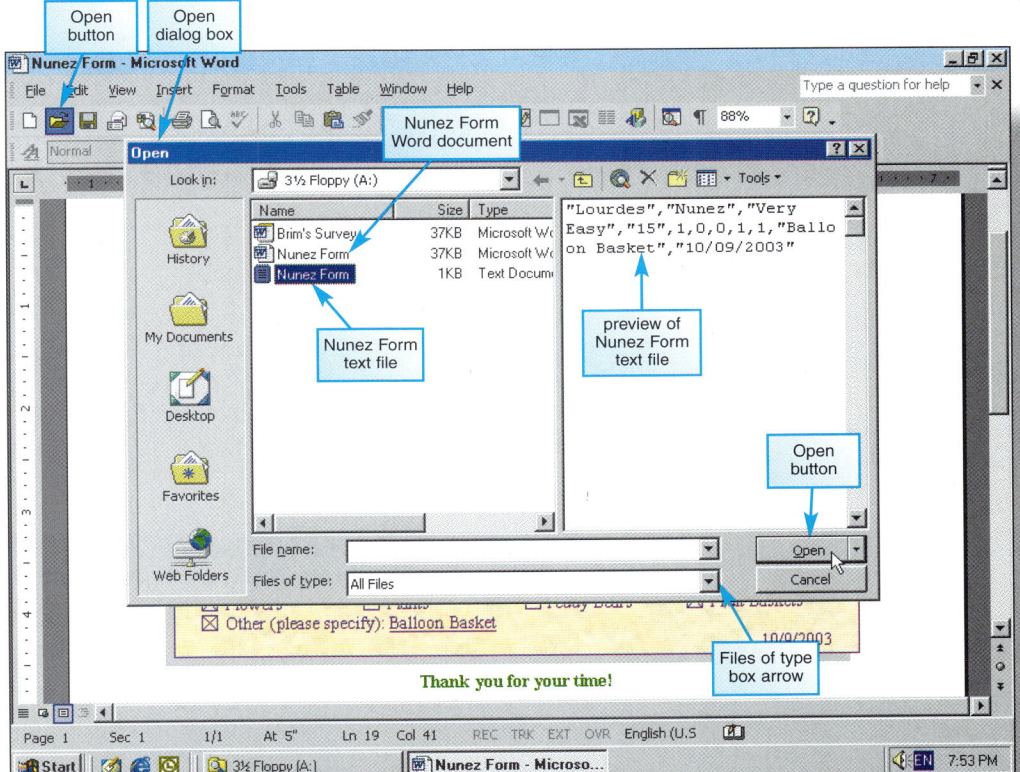

FIGURE 7-68

 **Click the Open button in the Open dialog box.**

The text file displays in the Word window (Figure 7-69).

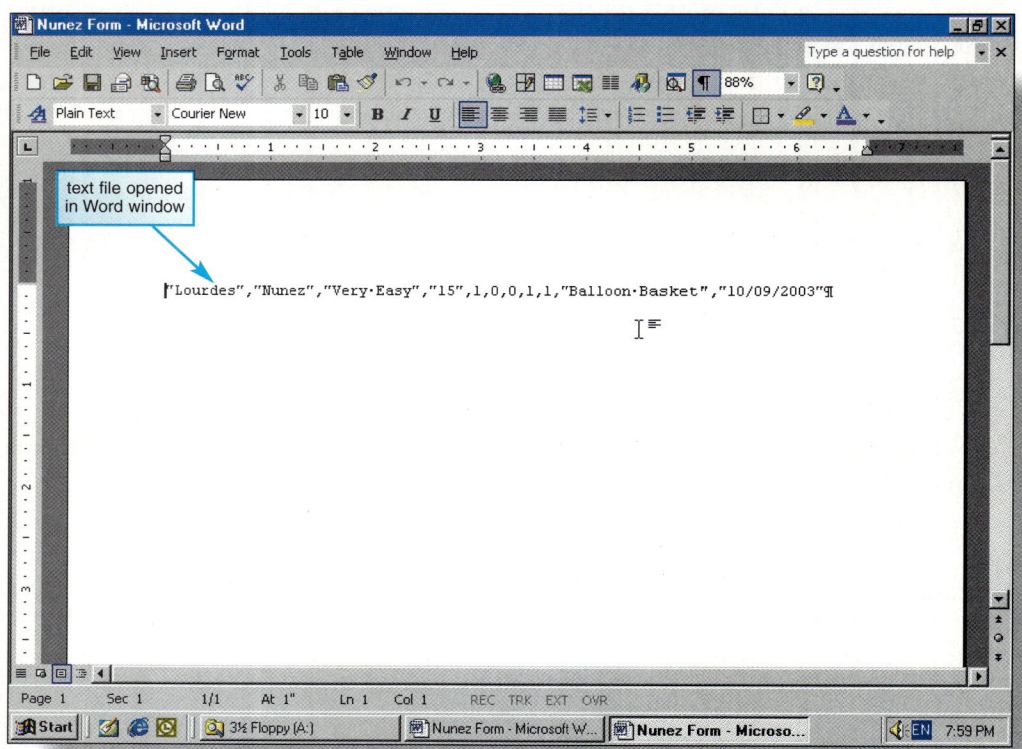

FIGURE 7-69

Other Ways

1. On File menu click Open, click Files of type box arrow, click All Files, double-click text file name
2. In Voice Command mode, say "File, Open, Files of type, All Files, [select file name], OK"

You also can display a text file in a text editor such as Notepad. To print the text file, click the Print button on the Standard toolbar.

Notice that the text file lists all data from the form fields, separating each form field with a comma. All text form fields and drop-down list form field entries are surrounded with quotation marks. Table 7-3 shows the form field and the corresponding entry in the text file.

Table 7-3 Mapping of Form Fields to Contents of Text File

FORM FIELD	FORM FIELD TYPE	TEXT FILE ENTRY
First Name	Text	"Lourdes"
Last Name	Text	"Nunez"
Ease of use	Drop-Down List	"Very Easy"
Number of minutes	Text	"15"
Flowers	Check Box	1
Plants	Check Box	0
Teddy Bears	Check Box	0
Fruit Baskets	Check Box	1
Other	Check Box	1
Other	Text	"Balloon Basket"
Date		"10/09/2003"

For the check boxes, a value of 1 (one) indicates that the user selected the check box, and a value of 0 (zero) indicates that a user did not select the check box. The text file is ready to be imported into a database table.

Perform the following step to close the window displaying the text file.

TO CLOSE A WINDOW

1 Click File on the menu bar and then click Close.

Word closes the window displaying the text file.

Working with Templates

If you want to modify the template, open it by clicking the Open button on the Standard toolbar, clicking the template name, and then clicking the Open button in the dialog box. Then, you must unprotect the form by clicking the Protect Form button on the Forms toolbar or by clicking Tools on the menu bar and then clicking Unprotect Document.

When you created the template in this project, you saved it on a floppy disk in drive A. In environments other than an academic setting, you would not save the template on a floppy disk. Instead, you would save it in the Templates folder, which is the folder Word initially displays in the Save As dialog box for a document template file type. When you save a template in the Templates folder, Word places an icon for the template in the General sheet in the Templates dialog box. Thus, to open a new Word document that is based on a template that has been saved in the Templates folder, you click File on the menu bar, and then click New. When the New Document task pane displays, click General Templates, and then, in the General sheet, double-click the template icon. Figure 7-70 shows the template icon for Brim's Survey in the General sheet in the Templates dialog box.

The Templates Folder

If you want a template to display in a tabbed sheet other than the General Sheet, save the template in the appropriate subfolder of the Templates folder. If you wish to create a custom tabbed sheet, create a new subfolder in the Templates folder. The subfolder name will be the name of the tabbed sheet.

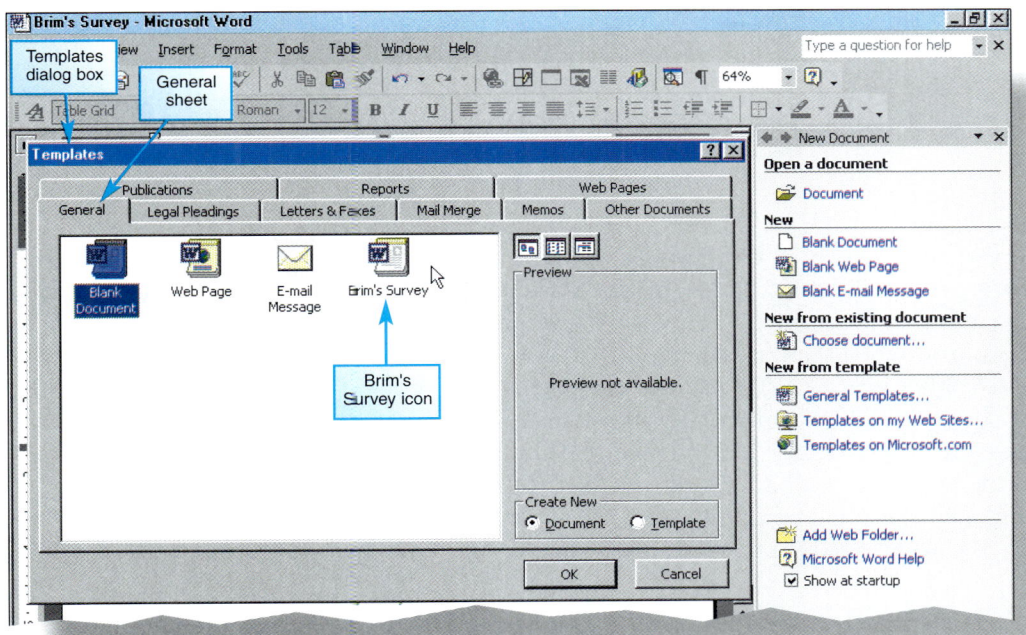

FIGURE 7-70

You also can make templates available on a network so others can share them. These templates, called **workgroup templates**, typically are stored on the network server by the network administrator as read-only files, which prevents users from inadvertently modifying them. You can change the location of workgroup templates in the Options dialog box (Figure 7-71) by clicking Tools on the menu bar, clicking Options, clicking the File Locations tab, clicking Workgroup templates in the File types list, and then clicking the Modify button. Locate the folder assigned to workgroup templates (as specified by the network administrator), and then click the OK button. With the workgroup template location specified, these templates also display in the General sheet in the Templates dialog box.

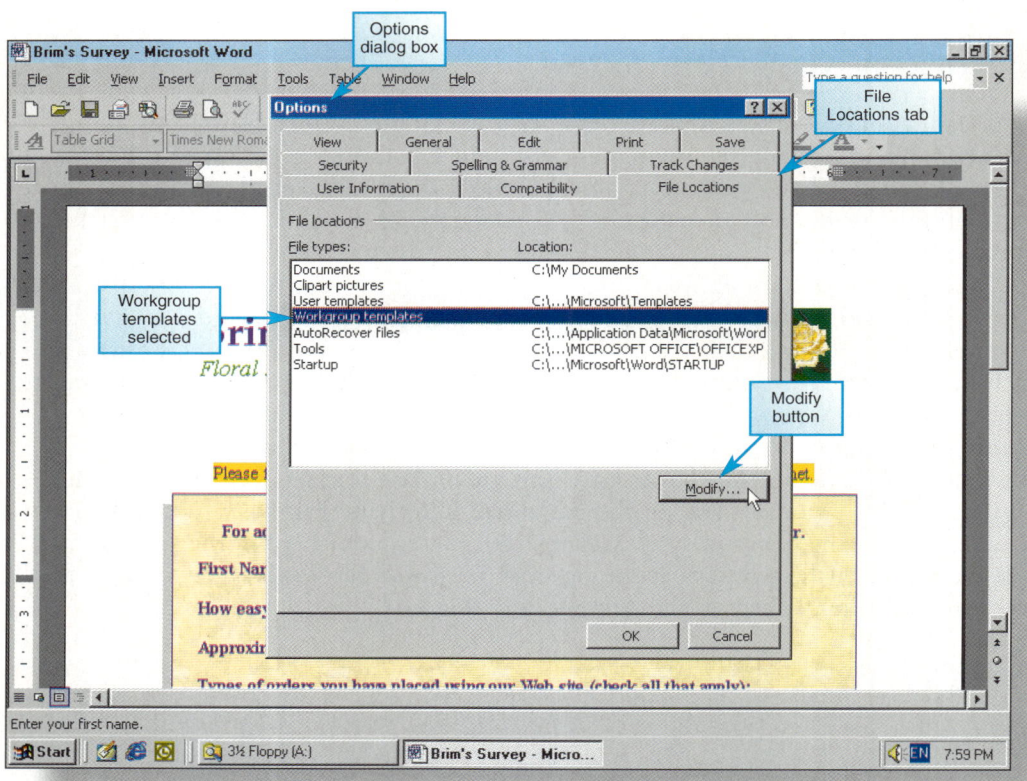

FIGURE 7-71

Quick Reference

For a table that lists how to complete tasks covered in this book using the mouse, menu, shortcut menu, and keyboard, see the Quick Reference Summary at the back of this book or visit the Shelly Cashman Series Office XP Web page (scsite.com/offxp/qr.htm) and then click Microsoft Word 2002.

Notice that the Options dialog box also lists locations of other files accessed by Word. Although you can change any of these locations through the Modify button, use caution when doing so because Word may not be able to access these types of files if you move their location.

Another way to share a form template is to e-mail it. You might want to e-mail the form template to co-workers for editing or collaboration, or you might e-mail a survey to respondents. To send a form template via e-mail, click the E-mail button on the Standard toolbar. Fill in the To, Subject, and Introduction text boxes, and then click the Send a Copy button. Your computer must be connected to the Internet for the following steps to work properly.

TO E-MAIL A FORM

1. With the filled-in Customer Survey displaying, click the E-mail button on the Standard toolbar.
2. Type your instructor's e-mail address in the To text box if your instructor gives you permission to do so. Type `Customer Survey` in the Subject text box. If an Introduction text box displays, type `Attached is the Customer Survey Form Template` in the Introduction text box.
3. If instructed to do so, click the Send a Copy button; otherwise, if you want to cancel the e-mail operation, click the E-mail button again.

The form template is e-mailed to the recipient named in the To text box.

The final steps are to quit Word and close Windows Explorer.

TO QUIT WORD

1. Click File on the menu bar and then click Exit.

The Word window closes.

TO CLOSE WINDOWS EXPLORER

1. Click the Close button on the Exploring - 3½ Floppy (A:) window's title bar.

The Explorer window closes, and the desktop displays.

CASE PERSPECTIVE SUMMARY

You e-mail the Customer Survey to 100 customers who have placed recent orders. Of the 100, you receive 61 completed forms. You decide to use Access to analyze the customer responses. Thus, you save each completed form as a text file.

You create an Access database that contains a table named Brim's Survey Results. The table contains one field for each form field on the survey. After you import the data from each text file into the table, you create a report that lists the total number of customers that selected each option on the form. From this report, you create an average customer response list for Aunt Carol at Brim's Blooming Boutique.

Project Summary

Project 7 introduced you to creating an online form. You created a document template as the basis for the form. Then, you added text form fields, a drop-down list form field, and check boxes to the form. You added Help text to each of these form fields. On the form, you also highlighted text, animated text, and added a rectangle drawing object around the data entry area. After you protected the form, you opened a new document based on the template and filled out the form. You also learned how to save the data on a form in a text file and how to modify the location of workgroup templates.

What You Should Know

Having completed this project, you should now be able to perform the following tasks:

- Access a Template through Windows Explorer *(WD 7.50)*
- Add a Shadow to a Drawing Object *(WD 7.44)*
- Add Help Text to a Form Field *(WD 7.35)*
- Add More Help Text *(WD 7.36)*
- Animate Text *(WD 7.46)*
- Change the Line Color of a Drawing Object *(WD 7.43)*
- Close a Window *(WD 7.57)*
- Close Windows Explorer *(WD 7.59)*
- Create a Document Template *(WD 7.09)*
- Display Formatting Marks *(WD 7.07)*
- Draw a Rectangle *(WD 7.39)*
- E-Mail a Form *(WD 7.59)*
- Enter and Format Text *(WD 7.11)*
- Enter Text *(WD 7.14, WD 7.26)*
- Fill a Drawing Object with a Texture *(WD 7.42)*
- Fill Out a Form *(WD 7.51)*
- Hide Formatting Marks *(WD 7.48)*
- Highlight Text *(WD 7.13)*
- Insert a Borderless Table into a Form *(WD 7.15, WD 7.26)*
- Insert a Check Box *(WD 7.27)*
- Insert a Drop-Down Form Field *(WD 7.21)*
- Insert a Text Form Field *(WD 7.17)*
- Insert Additional Check Box Form Fields *(WD 7.28)*
- Insert and Format Clip Art *(WD 7.12)*
- Insert and Specify Options for a Text Form Field *(WD 7.20, WD 7.25, WD 7.29)*
- Insert and Specify Options for a Text Form Field as the Current Date *(WD 7.30)*
- Open a Text File in Word *(WD 7.50)*
- Print a Form *(WD 7.52)*
- Protect a Form *(WD 7.48)*
- Quit Word *(WD 7.49, WD 7.59)*
- Remove Form Field Shading *(WD 7.37)*
- Reset Menus and Toolbars *(WD 7.06)*
- Save a Document *(WD 7.52)*
- Save Form Data in a Text File *(WD 7.53)*
- Save the Document Again *(WD 7.49)*
- Send a Drawing Object behind Text *(WD 7.41)*
- Specify Drop-Down Form Field Options *(WD 7.23)*
- Specify Text Form Field Options *(WD 7.19)*
- Start and Customize Word *(WD 7.06)*
- Uncheck the Save Data Only for Forms Check Box *(WD 7.55)*
- Underline in Color *(WD 7.31)*
- Use the Format Painter Button *(WD 7.33)*
- Zoom Page Width *(WD 7.07)*

More About

Microsoft Certification

The Microsoft Office User Specialist (MOUS) Certification program provides an opportunity for you to obtain a valuable industry credential — proof that you have the Word 2002 skills required by employers. For more information, see Appendix E or visit the Shelly Cashman Series MOUS Web page at scsite.com/offxp/cert.htm.

Learn It Online

Instructions: To complete the Learn It Online exercises, start your browser, click the Address bar, and then enter scsite.com/offxp/exs.htm. When the Office XP Learn It Online page displays, follow the instructions in the exercises below.

1 Project Reinforcement

TF, MC, and SA Below Word Project 7, click the Project Reinforcement link. Print the quiz by clicking Print on the File menu. Answer each question. Write your first and last name at the top of each page, and then hand in the printout to your instructor.

2 Flash Cards

Below Word Project 7, click the Flash Cards link. When Flash Cards displays, read the instructions. Type 20 (or a number specified by your instructor) in the Number of Playing Cards text box, type your name in the Name text box, and then click the Flip Card button. When the flash card displays, read the question and then click the Answer box arrow to select an answer. Flip through Flash Cards. Click Print on the File menu to print the last flash card if your score is 15 (75%) correct or greater and then hand it in to your instructor. If your score is less than 15 (75%) correct, then redo this exercise by clicking the Replay button.

3 Practice Test

Below Word Project 7, click the Practice Test link. Answer each question, enter your first and last name at the bottom of the page, and then click the Grade Test button. When the graded practice test displays on your screen, click Print on the File menu to print a hard copy. Continue to take practice tests until you score 80% or better. Hand in a printout of the final practice test to your instructor.

4 Who Wants to Be a Computer Genius?

Below Word Project 7, click the Computer Genius link. Read the instructions, enter your first and last name at the bottom of the page, and then click the Play button. Hand in your score to your instructor.

5 Wheel of Terms

Below Word Project 7, click the Wheel of Terms link. Read the instructions, and then enter your first and last name and your school name. Click the Play button. Hand in your score to your instructor.

6 Crossword Puzzle Challenge

Below Word Project 7, click the Crossword Puzzle Challenge link. Read the instructions, and then enter your first and last name. Click the Play button. Work the crossword puzzle. When you are finished, click the Submit button. When the crossword puzzle redisplays, click the Print button. Hand in the printout.

7 Tips and Tricks

Below Word Project 7, click the Tips and Tricks link. Click a topic that pertains to Project 7. Right-click the information and then click Print on the shortcut menu. Construct a brief example of what the information relates to in Word to confirm you understand how to use the tip or trick. Hand in the example and printed information.

8 Newsgroups

Below Word Project 7, click the Newsgroups link. Click a topic that pertains to Project 7. Print three comments. Hand in the comments to your instructor.

9 Expanding Your Horizons

Below Word Project 7, click the Articles for Microsoft Word link. Click a topic that pertains to Project 7. Print the information. Construct a brief example of what the information relates to in Word to confirm you understand the contents of the article. Hand in the example and printed information to your instructor.

10 Search Sleuth

Below Word Project 7, click the Search Sleuth link. To search for a term that pertains to this project, select a term below the Project 7 title and then use the Google search engine at google.com (or any major search engine) to display and print two Web pages that present information on the term. Hand in the printouts to your instructor.

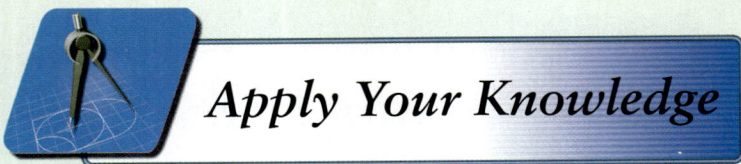

Apply Your Knowledge

1 Filling Out a Form

Instructions: In this assignment, you access a template through Windows Explorer. As shown in Figure 7-72, the template contains an online form. You are to fill in the form, save it, and print it. The template is located on the Data Disk. If you did not download the Data Disk, see the inside backcover for instructions for downloading the Data Disk or see your instructor.

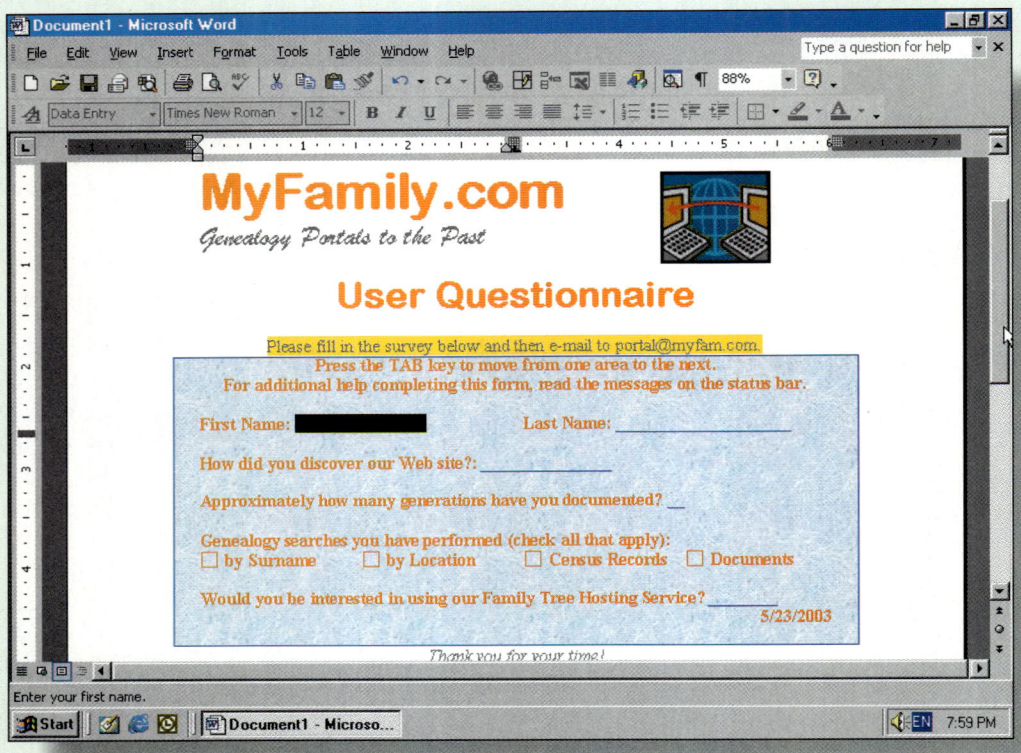

FIGURE 7-72

Perform the following steps.
1. Right-click the My Computer icon on the Windows desktop and then click Explore on the shortcut menu. When the Exploring window displays, click the Address text box to select it. With the Data Disk in drive A, type `a:` and then press the ENTER key. Double-click the MyFamily Questionnaire icon in the Contents pane.
2. When Word displays a new document based on the MyFamily Questionnaire template, scroll down so the entire form fits in the Word window. If the Show/Hide ¶ button on the Standard toolbar is selected, click it.
3. With the First Name text box selected, type `Marsha` and then press the TAB key.
4. With the Last Name text box selected, type `Louks` and then press the TAB key.
5. With the drop-down list box selected, click the box arrow. Click Search Engine in the How did you discover our Web site? drop-down list. Press the TAB key.
6. Type `5` in response to Approximately how many generations have you documented? Press the TAB key.
7. Place an X in the by Surname and Census Records check boxes by clicking them. Press the TAB key twice.

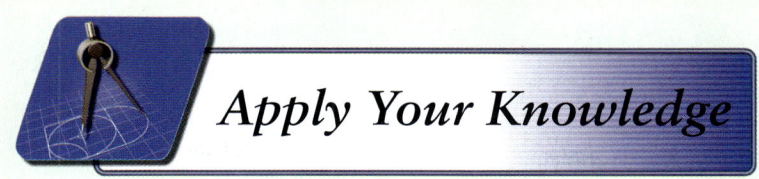

Apply Your Knowledge

8. With the drop-down list box selected, click the box arrow. Click Yes in the Would you be interested in using our Family Tree Hosting Service? drop-down list.
9. Save the file with the name Louks Form. Print the form.
10. Click File on the menu bar and then click Save As. When the Save As dialog box displays, click the Tools button and then click Save Options. When the Save dialog box displays, place a check mark in the Save data only for forms check box and then click the OK button. Click the Save button in the Save As dialog box. When Word displays the File Conversion dialog box, click the OK button.
11. Click Tools on the menu bar and then click Options. When the Options dialog box displays, click the Save tab. Click the Save data only for forms check box to remove the check mark. Click the OK button.
12. Click the Open button on the Standard toolbar. When the Open dialog box displays, click the Files of type box arrow and then click All Files. Click the text file called Louks Form in the list and then click the Open button in the dialog box. Print the text file.

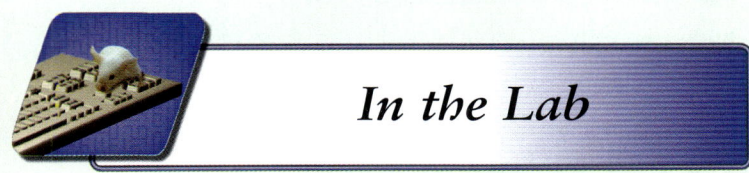

1 Creating an Online Form with a Texture Fill Effect

Problem: You work part-time for Web Management, a company specializing in hosting Web pages and wireless connections. Recently, Web Management has begun to offer customers a user portal, which is a highly-personalized browser interface, complete with free e-mail, file storage, and worldwide access. Your supervisor has asked you to prepare an online survey for Web customers. The survey should obtain the following information from the customer: first name, last name, whether they currently use a portal, the average time it takes for them to log on from home, and the kinds of services they think a portal should provide. You prepare the online form shown in Figure 7-73 on the next page.

Instructions:
1. Create a template called Portal Questionnaire for the online form.
2. Enter and format the company name, clip art, business tag line, and form title as shown in Figure 7-73.
3. Enter the form instructions and highlight them in yellow.
4. Enter the instructions in the data entry area, form field captions, and form fields as shown in Figure 7-73. First Name and Last Name are text form fields. Do you currently use a personal portal on the Internet? is a drop-down form field with these choices: Yes, No, and Uncertain. The Average time it takes you to log onto the Web from Home (in minutes) is a text field requiring numeric input. The choices below What services do you think a portal should offer? are check boxes. *Hint:* use a 2 × 3 borderless table. The Other check box also has a text form field to its right for further explanation. When the form initially displays on the screen as a blank form, the text form fields and drop-down form field should display underlines in dark blue.

(continued)

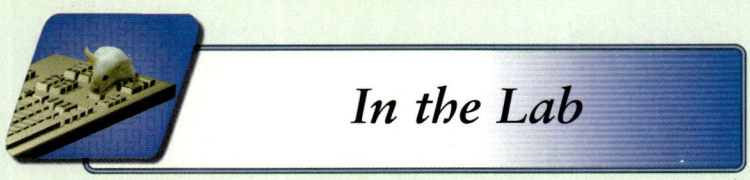

In the Lab

Creating an Online Form with a Texture Fill Effect *(continued)*

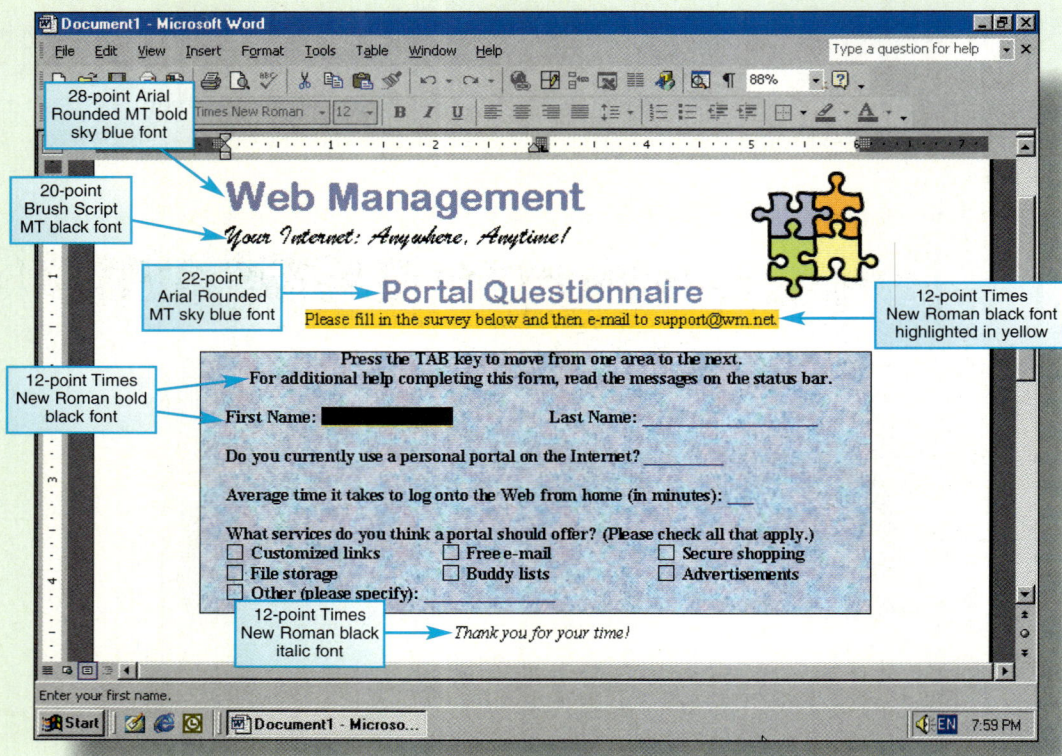

FIGURE 7-73

5. Enter the thank-you message as shown in Figure 7-73.
6. Insert a rectangle drawing object around the data entry area. Fill the rectangle drawing object with the Bouquet texture.
7. Add Help text to all the form fields.
8. Check the spelling of the form. Protect the form. Save the form again. Print the blank form.
9. Access the template through Windows Explorer. Fill out the form. Save the filled-out form. Print the filled-out form.

2 Creating an Online Form with a Gradient Fill Effect and Nudged Shadow

Problem: You work part-time for College Technical Support Services at Montgomery Community College. Your supervisor has asked you to prepare an online survey to be distributed to students who use the lab. The survey should obtain the following information from the students: first name, last name, how they would rate the computers, average time they have to wait to find an open station, and the types of computer applications they use. You prepare the online form shown in Figure 7-74.

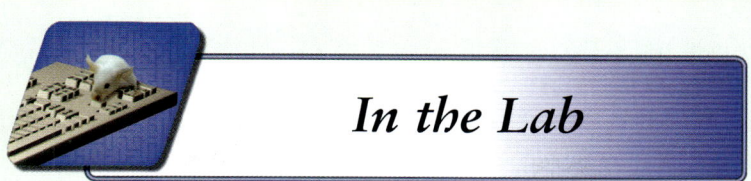
In the Lab

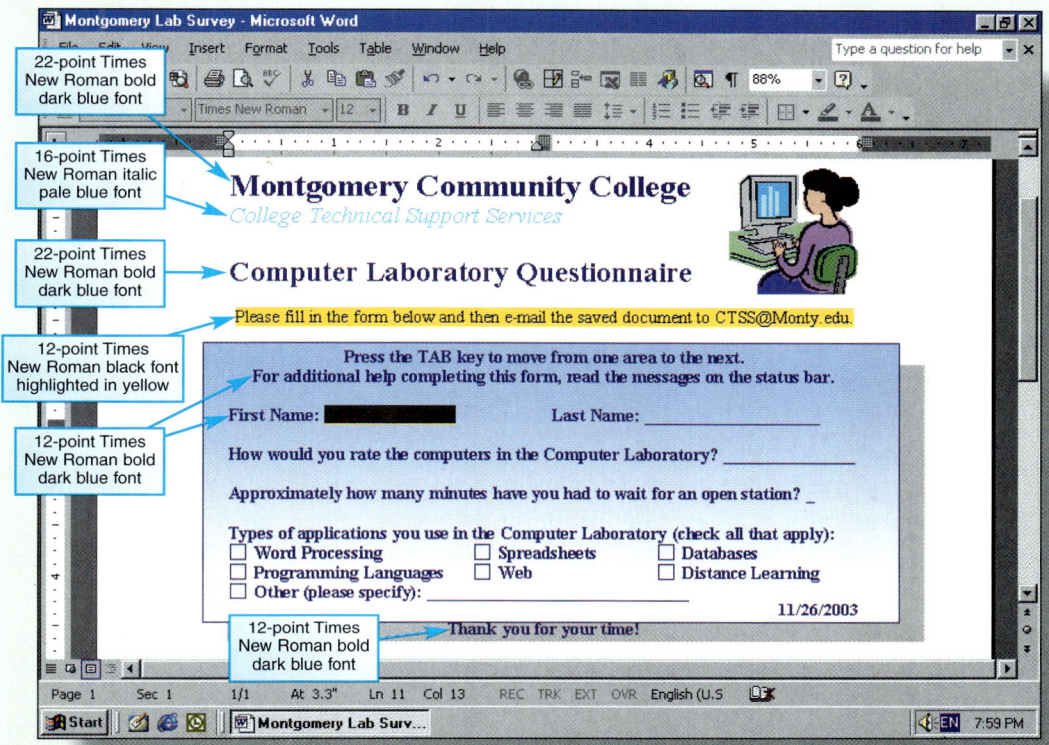

FIGURE 7-74

Instructions:

1. Create a template called Montgomery Lab Survey for the online form.
2. Enter and format the college name, department name, clip art, and form title as shown in Figure 7-74.
3. Enter the form instructions and highlight them in yellow.
4. Enter the instructions in the data entry area, form field captions, and form fields as shown in Figure 7-74. First Name and Last Name are text form fields. Rating the computers is a drop-down form field with these choices: Excellent, Good, Fair, Poor, No Opinion. The number of minutes students have to wait is a text form field that allows only a numeric entry. The types of applications are check boxes. The Other field is both a check box and a text form field. When the form initially displays on the screen as a blank form, the text form fields and drop-down form field should display underlines in dark blue.
5. Enter the thank-you message as shown in Figure 7-74.
6. Insert a rectangle drawing object around the data entry area. Change the rectangle line color to dark blue. Fill the rectangle with a two-color gradient of light blue to white. *Hint:* Click the Gradient tab in the Fill Effects dialog box.
7. Add Shadow Style 6 to the rectangle. With the rectangle selected, click the Shadow Style button, and then click Shadow settings. Click the Nudge Shadow Down button several times, so that the thank-you message displays in the rectangle's shadow. Click the Nudge Shadow Right button approximately the same number of times to even out the shadow on both the right and the bottom.

(continued)

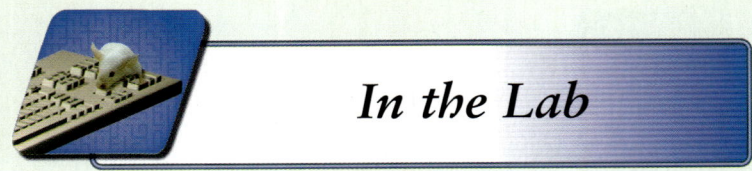

In the Lab

Creating an Online Form with a Gradient Fill Effect and Nudged Shadow *(continued)*

8. Add Help text to all the form fields.
9. Check the spelling of the form. Protect the form. Save the form again. Print the blank form.
10. Access the template through Windows Explorer. Fill out the form. Save and then print the filled-out form.
11. E-mail the template to your instructor, if your instructor gives you permission to do so.

3 Creating an Online Form with a Pattern Fill Effect

Problem: A new K&F Premier Movie Theater has opened in your town and you have been hired to help with public relations. Your supervisor has asked you to prepare an online survey asking Backstage Pass holders for their opinions on the recent premier. The survey should obtain the following information from the attendees: first name, last name, age group of viewer, opinion rating of the movie, other movies they have seen at this K&F theater, and whether or not they would recommend the movie to friends. You prepare the online form shown in Figure 7-75.

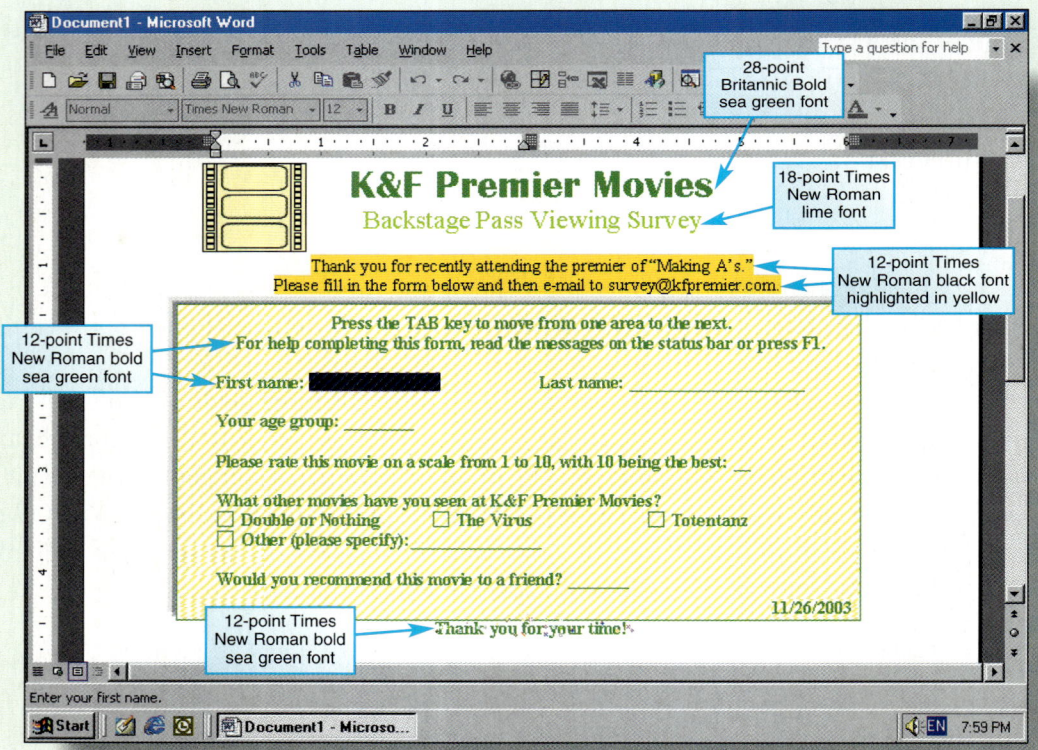

FIGURE 7-75

In the Lab

Instructions:

1. Create a template called Premier Movie Feedback for the online form.
2. Enter and format the company name, clip art, and form title as shown in Figure 7-75.
3. Enter the form instructions and highlight them in yellow.
4. Enter the instructions in the data entry area, form field captions, and form fields as shown in Figure 7-75. First name and Last name are text form fields. The age group should be a drop-down form field with these choices: 18-30, 31-49, 50-65, 66 or older. The rating is a text form field requiring a numeric entry. Other movies they have seen include three choices of movies as check boxes. Other is a check box followed by a text form field. The question, Would you recommend this movie to a friend? is followed by a drop-down form field containing the choices, Yes, No, and Unsure. The current date is a text form field. When the form initially displays on the screen as a blank form, the text form fields and drop-down form fields should display underlines in sea green.
5. Enter the thank-you message as shown in Figure 7-75. Animate the message using Sparkle Text.
6. Insert a rectangle drawing object around the data entry area. Change the rectangle line color to Sea Green. Fill the rectangle with a Wide upward diagonal pattern that has a foreground color of yellow. *Hint:* Click the Gradient tab in the Fill Effects dialog box. Add a shadow to the rectangle using Shadow Style 13.
7. Add Help text to all the form fields. The Help should display on the status bar, as well as when the user presses the F1 key.
8. Check the spelling of the form. Protect the form. Save the form again. Print the blank form.
9. Access the template through Windows Explorer. Fill out the form. Save the filled-out form. Print the filled-out form.
10. If you have access to a Web server or FTP site, save the template to the server or site (see Appendix C for instructions). Access the template from the Web site or FTP site.

Cases and Places

The difficulty of these case studies varies:
▶ are the least difficult; ▶▶ are more difficult; and ▶▶▶ are the most difficult.

1 ▶ You and a friend are starting a desktop publishing service, which includes products such as stationery, business and greeting cards, business forms, newsletters, and brochures. You decide to send a survey to all your friends (at least those with e-mail addresses) asking the types of products that might interest them. The top of the survey should list the name of your new company, Publisher It Here, along with the title of the survey, Customer Preference Survey. Insert an appropriate graphic of a computer from the Clip Organizer. Immediately above the data entry area, the following sentence should be highlighted: Please fill in the form below and then e-mail the saved document to survey@pih.com. The data entry area contains the following two sentences of instructions: Press the TAB key to move from one area to the next. For help completing this form, read the messages on the status bar or press the F1 key. The data entry area should request the customer's first name and last name. Display check boxes for the types of publications in which they might be interested (from list above and a check box for Other with a text box for users to enter other types of publications). Include a numeric data field for the maximum price they would be willing to pay for a personalized greeting card, and a drop-down list (Yes, No, Unsure) asking if they would buy supplies such as greeting cards over the Web. The form should contain the current date as a form field. The data entry area should be surrounded by a rectangle filled in with an appropriate fill effect. Below the form, place an animated thank-you message. All data entry fields should have Help text that displays on the status bar, as well as when the user presses the F1 key. Use the concepts and techniques presented in this project to create and format this online form.

2 ▶▶ As a student worker in the Computer Technology department at your school, you have been asked to send a survey to all students requesting feedback on the Distance Learning courses. Because each DL student on campus has an e-mail account, you decide to send an online form. The form should contain text boxes for the name of the online class they chose, their expected grade for the course, and the name of the teacher. Include drop-down list boxes asking the students the browser they use and the speed of their modem. Include check boxes for the type of equipment they needed for the course, such as scanner, microphone, fax machine, video camera, or other. The form should contain the current date as a form field. Use the concepts and techniques presented in this project to create and format the online form. Be sure to include an appropriate graphic from the Clip Organizer. If you have access to a Web server or FTP site, save the template to the server or site (see Appendix C for instructions). Access the template from the Web site or FTP site.

3 ▶▶ As a part-time assistant for your school's bookstore, you have been asked to send a survey to all customers requesting their opinion of the online order process. You decide to send an online form because each student has an e-mail account. The form should ask for customer opinions and preferences on various aspects of the bookstore's Web site. Enter user instructions. Use text boxes for items such as the name and class standing. Use a drop-down list for the time of day they usually shop with choices such as Morning, Afternoon, Evening, Late Night, Times Vary. Create check boxes to determine how students shop at the bookstore: Browse aisles, Order online, Mail order, and Other. Use the concepts and techniques presented in this project to create and format the online form. Be sure to include an appropriate graphic(s) from the Clip Organizer. E-mail the form template to your instructor, if your instructor gives you permission to do so.

Cases and Places

4 ▶▶ Many banks now offer Web Banking. Write a letter to a fictitious bank discussing the process of sending out Web site surveys to its customers. Suggest possible inclusions for text fields, drop-down lists, and check boxes. Use Microsoft Word Help to find information about automatic calculations and macros in forms. In your letter, list at least two ways the bank could use these form features. E-mail the letter to your instructor, if your instructor gives you permission to do so.

5 ▶▶▶ If Microsoft Access is installed on your computer, you can use it to create a database table and then use that table to analyze the data from Word forms. Your supervisor at Brim's Blooming Boutique would like to analyze the results of the surveys sent using Microsoft Access. To generate data for the database table, fill out the Project 7 Word form (Figure 7-1a on page WD 7.05) five times (acting as five separate customers) and save the form data for each filled-in form in a separate text file. Start Access. Click File on the menu bar and then click New. When the New File task pane displays, click Blank Database. Name the database, Brim's Customers. Click File on the menu bar, point to Get External Data, and then click Import. When the Import dialog box displays, change the file type to Text Files, locate the text file that contains one of the form's data, and then click the Import button. Use the Import Text Wizard to create a table for the form in Figure 7-1. Data in the text file is comma-delimited. Use field names that match the field captions on the form. Each form field, including the current date, should have a field name. When the Import Text Wizard prompts you, choose no primary key field. Name the table, Customer Survey Table. Repeat the process to import each of the remaining four text files into the existing table. After the table contains the five records, generate a report in Access that lists all the data collected from the forms.

6 ▶▶▶ If Microsoft Access is installed on your computer, you can use it to create a database table and then use that table to analyze the data from Word forms. Your supervisor at MyFamily.com would like to analyze the results of the surveys sent using Microsoft Access. To generate data for the database table, fill out the Apply Your Knowledge Exercise form (Figure 7-72 on page WD 7.62) five times (acting as five separate Web site visitors) and save the form data for each filled-in form in a separate text file. Start Access. Click File on the menu bar and then click New. When the New File task pane displays, click Blank Database. Name the database, MyFamily Customers. Click File on the menu bar, point to Get External Data, and then click Import. When the Import dialog box displays, change the file type to Text Files, locate the text file that contains one of the form's data, and then click the Import button. Use the Import Text Wizard to create a table for the form in Figure 7-72. Data in the text file is comma-delimited. Use field names that match the field captions on the form. Each form field, including the current date, should have a field name. When the Import Text Wizard prompts you, choose no primary key field. Name the table, Web Site Survey Table. Repeat the process to import each of the remaining four text files into the existing table. After the table contains the five records, generate a report in Access that lists all the data collected from the forms.

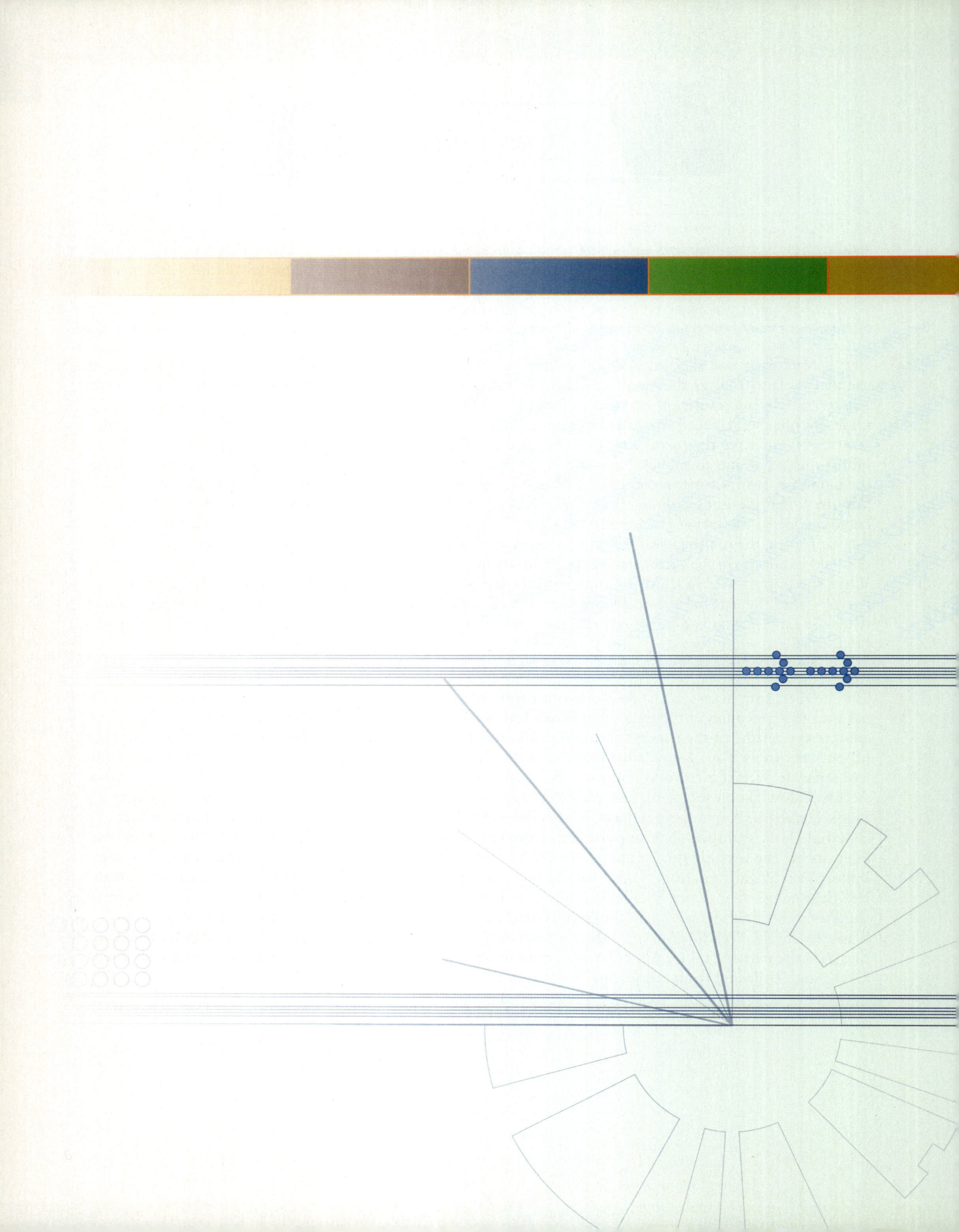

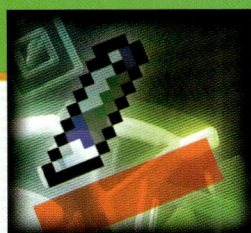

Microsoft Word 2002

PROJECT 8

Working With Macros and Visual Basic for Applications (VBA)

You will have mastered the material in this project when you can:

O B J E C T I V E S

- Unprotect a document
- Set a security level in Word
- Create a new style with a shortcut key
- Fill a drawing object with a gradient effect
- Add a 3-D effect to a drawing object
- Record and execute a macro
- Assign a macro to a toolbar button
- Record an automatic macro
- View a macro's VBA code
- Add comments to a macro's VBA code
- Modify a macro's VBA code
- Add code statements to a macro's VBA code
- Insert a VBA procedure
- Plan a VBA procedure
- Enter code statements in a VBA procedure
- Run a macro when a user exits a form field
- Insert an ActiveX control
- Format and set properties for an ActiveX control
- Write a VBA procedure for an ActiveX control
- Attach a digital signature

Microsoft **Word** 2002

The Financial Aid Process

1. Determine your estimated eligibility
2. Complete Application
3. Transmit on-line or mail form
4. Receive Federal Results
5. CSUF requests Documents
6. Take/Send Documents to Financial Aid
7. Wait patiently While Financial Aid Staff Review Files
8. Receive Award Letter
9. Sign and Return Award Letter

A Class Act
Broadening Educational Opportunities

Some of the United States' more prestigious universities owe their beginnings to a brilliant piece of federal legislature signed into law by President Abraham Lincoln on July 2, 1862. The Morrill Act, otherwise known as the Land-Grant College Act of 1862, was introduced by Justin Morrill of Vermont, who had been working to pass it since 1857. The Act provided funding for institutions of higher learning in each state. Ever since colonial times, basic education had been an important principle of American democratic thinking. By the 1860s, higher education was becoming more accessible, and educators and politicians desired to make some sort of advanced education available to all young Americans.

The act gave every state that had remained in the Union, a grant of 30,000 acres of public land for every member of its congressional delegation. Even the smallest state received 90,000 acres due to the fact that under the Constitution, every state had at least two senators and one representative. The states were directed to sell this land, using the proceeds to establish colleges in engineering, agriculture, and military science. More than 70 land grant colleges were established under the original Morrill Act.

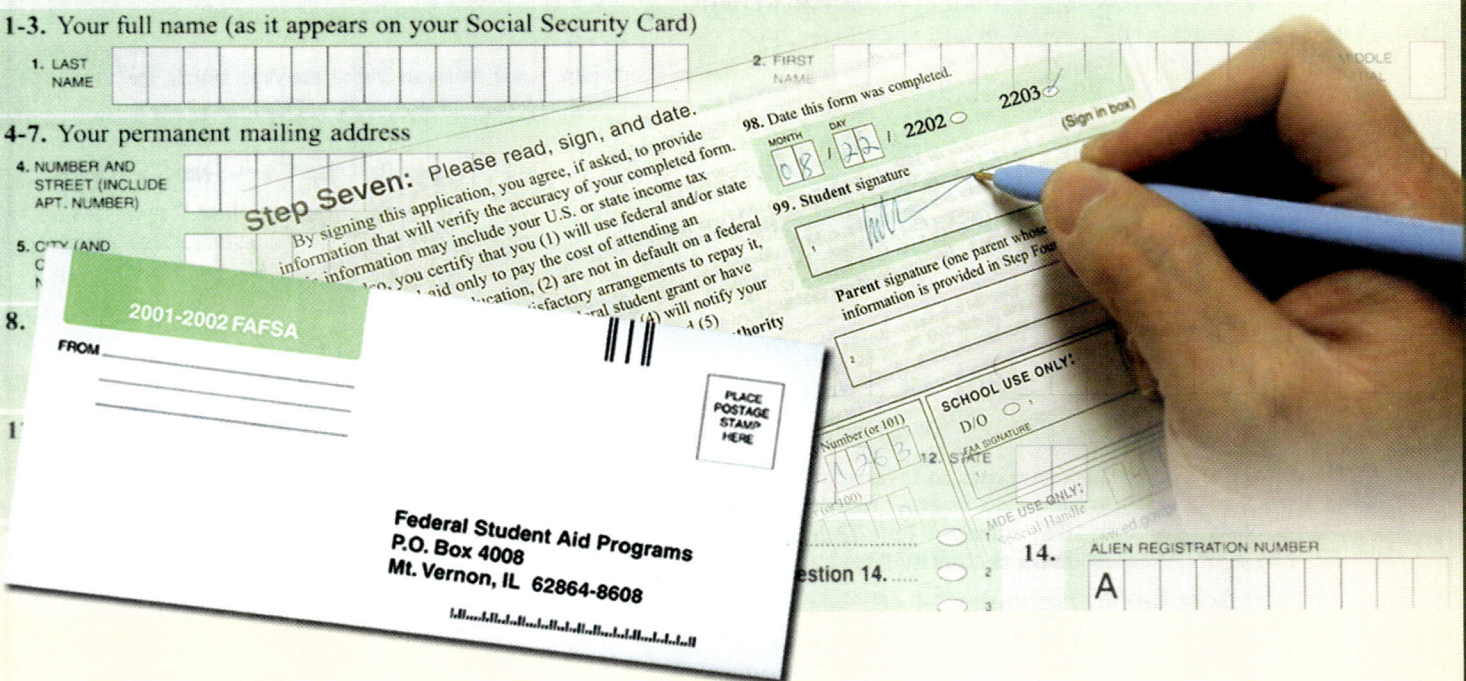

A second act in 1890 extended the land grant provisions to include the sixteen southern states.

Purdue University, one of the original land-grant colleges, began classes on September 16, 1874 with six instructors and 39 students. Five years earlier, the Indiana assembly accepted $150,000 from Lafayette civic leader, John Purdue, $50,000 from Tippecanoe County, and 100 acres of land from local citizens. In appreciation, the legislators decided that the university should be located in West Lafayette and named Purdue University.

Today, Purdue's buildings dwarf the original three structures. Current semester enrollment is more than 37,700, and graduates number more than 410,000, accounting for Purdue's reputation as one of America's top universities. Applying to Purdue is made more convenient by using the online forms available on Purdue's Web site (purdue.edu).

Semester fees and tuition for full-time enrollment grow at an exponential rate. The price tag for attending Purdue and similar universities may be financially out of reach for many potential students. Fortunately, Purdue and other colleges work with the U.S. Department of Education to help fund students' education through the Student Financial Assistance Program, the largest source of student aid in America. The Free Application for Federal Student Aid (FAFSA) offers online application forms for grants, loans, and work-study assistance. These online forms are crisp, clear, and convenient.

To make online forms viable, the designers must fine-tune them until they are practical, easy-to-use, and eye-catching. Similarly in this project, you will improve upon the online form created in Project 7, allowing you to produce a more efficient and visually pleasing form.

The importance of the land grant colleges cannot be overemphasized. Although originally slated as agricultural and technical schools, many of them grew into large universities, which over the years have educated millions of individuals. Submitting applications to these colleges and universities and applying for student loans, is made convenient through the use of the Internet and online forms.

Microsoft Word 2002

Working with Macros and Visual Basic for Applications (VBA)

PROJECT 8

CASE PERSPECTIVE

You recently designed the online survey for the owner of Brim's Blooming Boutique, who happens to be your Aunt Carol. Before showing your aunt the form, you decide to show it to your Web Page Design instructor for his opinion. He has several suggestions for improving the form.

First, he suggests changing the color scheme and graphics on the form. Second, the form should display without formatting marks showing and be positioned properly in the Word window without the user having to scroll. Third, if a user enters a letter or other nonnumeric value into the number of minutes text box, the form should display an error message. Fourth, if a user enters text into the Other text box, the form automatically should place an X in the Other check box. Finally, he suggests you add a button to the Standard toolbar that instructs Word to save only the data when you save the form. This button will save you many extra steps in analyzing customer responses.

To complete this project, you will need the online form template created in Project 7. (If you did not create the template, see your instructor for a copy.)

Introduction

When you issue an instruction to Word by clicking a button or a command, Word must have a step-by-step description of the task to be accomplished. For example, when you click the Print button on the Standard toolbar, Word follows a precise set of steps to print your document. In Word, this precise step-by-step series of instructions is called a **procedure**. A procedure also is referred to as a **program** or **code**.

The process of writing a procedure is called **computer programming**. Every Word command on a menu and button on a toolbar has a corresponding procedure that executes when you click the command or button. **Execute** means that the computer carries out the step-by-step instructions. In a Windows environment, an event causes the instructions associated with a task to be executed. An **event** is an action such as clicking a button, clicking a command, dragging a scroll box, or right-clicking selected text.

Although Word has many toolbar buttons and menu commands, it does not include a command or button for every possible task. Thus, Microsoft has included with Word a powerful programming language called Visual Basic for Applications. The **Visual Basic for Applications** (**VBA**) programming language allows you to customize and extend the capabilities of Word.

Project Eight — Working with Macros and Visual Basic for Applications

In this project, you improve upon the online form created in Project 7 (shown in Figure 7-1 on page WD 7.05). Figure 8-1a shows the revised blank form, in which the fonts, font sizes, graphic, highlight color, and fill effect in the drawing object are changed. Figure 8-1b shows an error message box that displays if

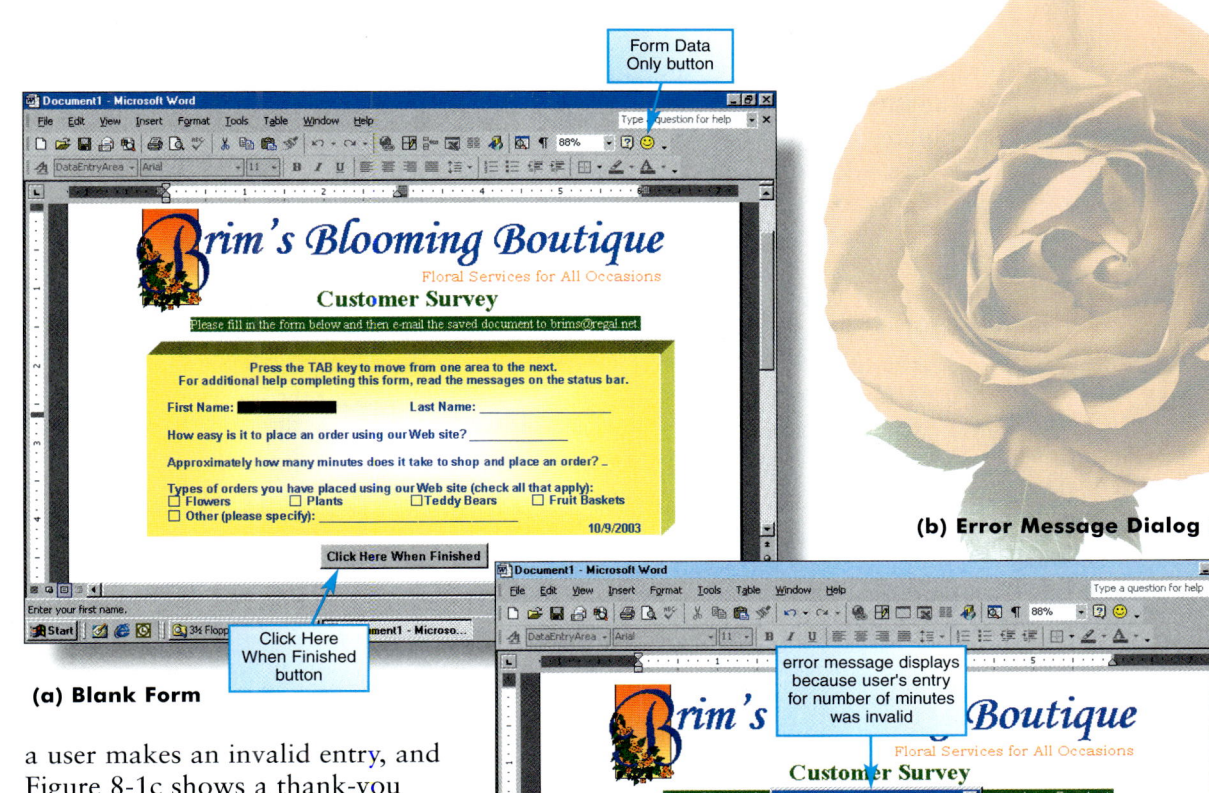

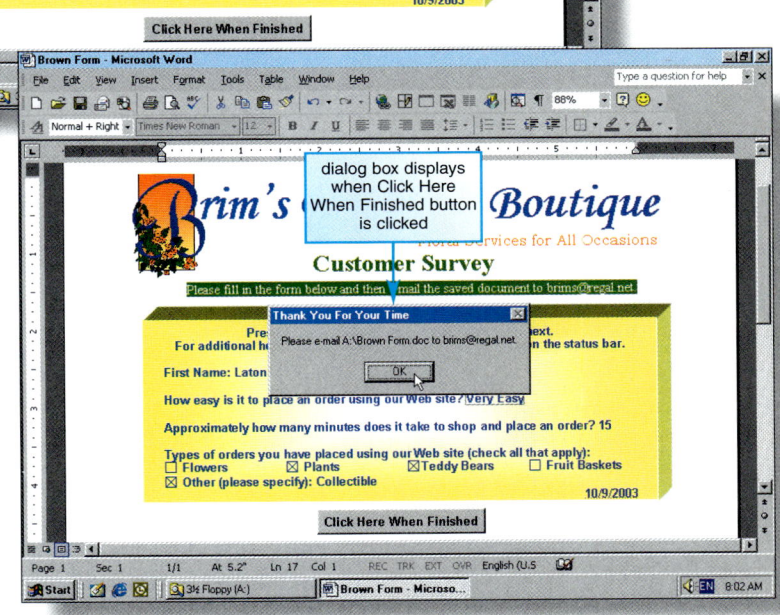

(a) Blank Form

(b) Error Message Dialog Box

(c) Thank-You Message Dialog Box

FIGURE 8-1

a user makes an invalid entry, and Figure 8-1c shows a thank-you message box that displays when the user clicks the button at the bottom of the form.

Four macros are saved with the template file so that they can be used while the template, or a document based on the template, displays in the Word window. A **macro** is a procedure made up of VBA code. The four macros are designed to make the form more efficient:

1. The first macro places a check mark in the Save data only for forms check box in the Save sheet in the Options dialog box. With this check box selected, the next time you click the Save button, Word will save the form data in a comma-delimited text file. Additionally, the Standard toolbar contains a new button called the Form Data Only button (Figure 8-1a). When you click the Form Data Only button or press ALT+D (the shortcut key assigned to the button), Word places a check mark in the Save data only for forms check box in the Save sheet in the Options dialog box.

WD 8.05

2. The second macro controls how the form initially displays on the screen (as a blank form). When a user starts a new Word document that is based on the form template, Word zooms page width, scrolls down six lines, hides gridlines, and hides formatting marks.
3. The third macro displays an error message if the user leaves the number of minutes text box blank or enters a nonnumeric entry in the text box. Figure 8-1b on the previous page displays the error message.
4. The fourth macro performs three actions when the user clicks the Click Here When Finished button:
   a. If the user entered text in the Other text box, then Word places an X in the Other check box (just in case the user left it blank).
   b. The Save As dialog box displays so the user can assign a file name to the filled-in form.
   c. A thank-you message box displays on the screen that informs the user what file should be e-mailed back to the boutique. Figure 8-1c on the previous page displays the thank-you message box for a filled-in form.

Figure 8-2 shows the VBA code for these macros. Code such as this, often is called a computer program.

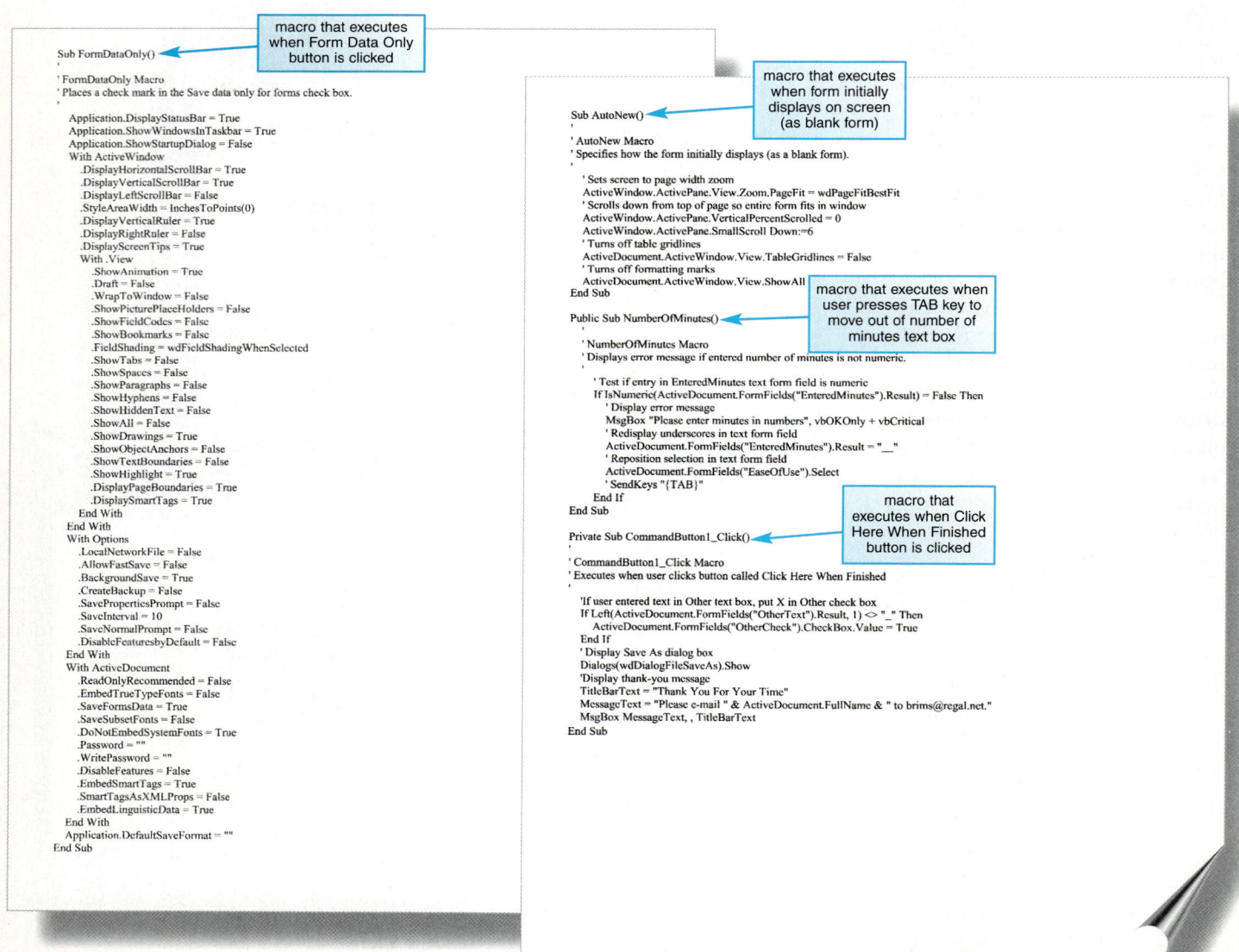

FIGURE 8-2

Starting Word and Opening an Office Document

The first step in this project is to open the template for the online form that was created in Project 7 so that you can modify it. (If you did not create the template, see your instructor for a copy.) Perform the following steps to start Word and then open the Brim's Survey file.

TO START AND CUSTOMIZE WORD AND OPEN AN OFFICE DOCUMENT

1. Click the Start button on the Windows taskbar, point to Programs on the Start menu, and then click Microsoft Word on the Programs submenu.
2. If the Word window is not maximized, double-click its title bar to maximize it.
3. If the Language bar displays on the screen, click its Minimize button.
4. If the New Document task pane displays in the Word window, click the Show at startup check box to remove the check mark and then click the Close button in the upper-right corner of the task pane title bar.
5. If the toolbars display positioned on the same row, click the Toolbar Options button and then click Show Buttons on Two Rows.
6. Click View on the menu bar and then click Print Layout.
7. With the disk containing the Brim's Survey template file in drive A, click File on the menu bar and then click Open. When the Open dialog box displays, if necessary, click the Look in box arrow and then click 3½ Floppy (A:). Click the Files of type box arrow and then click Document Templates.
8. Double-click the template named, Brim's Survey. Scroll down so the entire form displays in the Word window.

Online Forms

For a sample online form on the Web, visit the Word 2002 More About Web page (scsite.com/wd2002/more.htm) and then click Sample Online Form.

The online form titled, Brim's Survey, displays in the Word window.

Because this project uses floating graphics, you will use print layout view. Thus, the Print Layout View button on the horizontal scroll bar is selected.

Saving the Document with a New File Name

To preserve the contents of the Brim's Survey template file created in Project 7, save a copy of it with a new file name as described in the following steps.

TO SAVE A DOCUMENT WITH A NEW FILE NAME

1. With a floppy disk in drive A, click File on the menu bar and then click Save As.
2. Type Brim's New Survey in the File name text box. Do not press the ENTER key.
3. Click the Save as type box arrow and then click Document Template. If necessary, click the Save in box arrow and then click 3½ Floppy (A:).
4. Click the Save button in the Save As dialog box.

Word saves the document on a floppy disk in drive A with the new file name, Brim's New Survey (shown in Figure 8-3 on the next page).

Unprotecting a Document

The template for the Customer Survey online form is protected. When a document is **protected**, users cannot modify it in any manner — except for entering values into form fields placed on the form. Thus, before you can modify the online form, you must unprotect the form, as described in the following steps.

TO UNPROTECT A DOCUMENT

1. Click Tools on the menu bar and then point to Unprotect Document (Figure 8-3).
2. Click Unprotect Document.

Word unprotects the Brim's New Survey template.

Unprotecting Documents

If Word requests a password when you attempt to unprotect a document, you must enter a password in order to unprotect and then change the document. If you do not know the password, you cannot change the look of the form; you can enter data into its form fields, however.

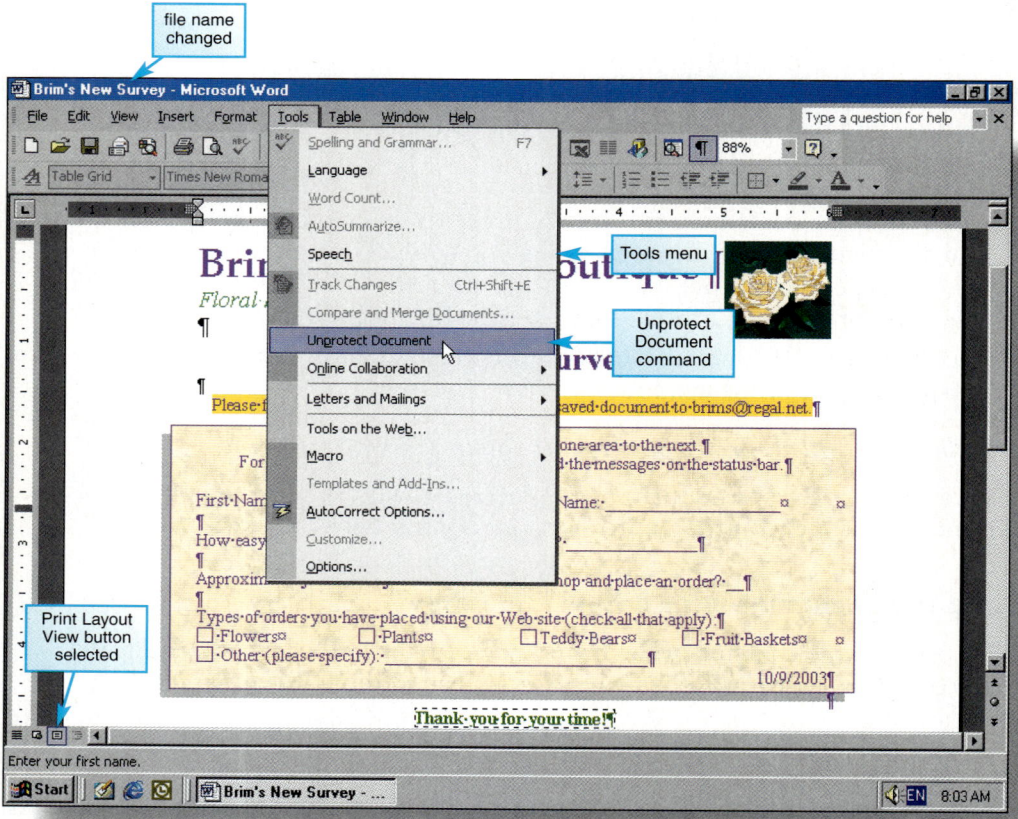

FIGURE 8-3

With the template unprotected, you can change its contents. Later in this project, after you have completed the modifications, you will protect the document again.

Resetting Menus and Toolbars

To set the menus and toolbars so they appear exactly as shown in this book, reset your menus and toolbars as outlined in Appendix D or follow these steps.

TO RESET MENUS AND TOOLBARS

1. Click the Toolbar Options button on the Standard toolbar and then point to Add or Remove Buttons. Point to Standard on the Add or Remove Buttons submenu. Scroll to and then click Reset Toolbar on the Standard submenu.
2. Click the Toolbar Options button on the Formatting toolbar and then point to Add or Remove Buttons. Point to Formatting on the Add or Remove Buttons submenu. Scroll to and then click Reset Toolbar on the Formatting submenu.
3. Click the Toolbar Options button on the Standard toolbar and then point to Add or Remove Buttons. Click Customize on the Add or Remove Buttons submenu.
4. When the Customize dialog box displays, if necessary, click the Options tab and then click the Reset my usage data button. When the Microsoft Word dialog box displays, click the Yes button. Click the Close button in the Customize dialog box.

Word resets the menus and toolbars.

Displaying Formatting Marks

It is helpful to display formatting marks that indicate where in the document you pressed the ENTER key, SPACEBAR, and other keys. Perform the following step to display formatting marks.

TO DISPLAY FORMATTING MARKS

1. If the Show/Hide ¶ button on the Standard toolbar is not selected already, click it.

Word displays formatting marks in the document window, and the Show/Hide ¶ button on the Standard toolbar is selected (shown in Figure 8-4 on the next page).

Zooming Page Width

When you zoom page width, Word displays the page on the screen as large as possible in print layout view. Perform the following steps to zoom page width.

TO ZOOM PAGE WIDTH

1. Click the Zoom box arrow on the Standard toolbar.
2. Click Page Width.

Word computes the zoom percentage and displays it in the Zoom box (shown in Figure 8-4). Your percentage may be different depending on your computer.

Setting a Security Level in Word

A **computer virus** is a potentially damaging computer program designed to affect, or infect, your computer negatively by altering the way it works without your knowledge or permission. Currently, more than 53,000 known computer viruses exist and an estimated six new viruses are discovered each day. The increased use of networks, the Internet, and e-mail has accelerated the spread of computer viruses.

Viruses

For more information about viruses, visit the Word 2002 More About Web page (scsite.com/wd2002/more.htm) and then click Viruses.

Macro Security

All templates, add-ins, and macros shipped with Office XP are digitally signed by Microsoft. If you add Microsoft to your list of trusted sources for one of these installed files, all subsequent interaction with these files will not display security dialog boxes.

To combat this evil, most computer users run antivirus programs that search for viruses and destroy them before they ever have a chance to infect the computer. Macros are a known carrier of viruses, because of the ease with which a person can write code for a macro. For this reason, you can reduce the chance your computer will be infected with a macro virus by setting a **security level** in Word. These security levels allow you to enable or disable macros. An enabled macro is a macro that Word will execute, and a **disabled macro** is a macro that is unavailable to Word. Table 8-1 summarizes the three available security levels in Word.

Table 8-1	Word Security Levels
SECURITY LEVEL	**CONDITION**
High	Word will execute only macros that are digitally signed. All other macros are disabled when the document is opened.
Medium	Upon opening a document that contains macros from an unknown source, Word displays a dialog box asking if you wish to enable the macros.
Low	Word turns off macro virus protection. The document is opened with all macros enabled, including those from unknown sources.

If Word security is set to high and you attach a macro to a document, Word will disable that macro when you open the document. Because you will be creating macros in this project, you should ensure that your security level is set to medium. Thus, each time you open this Word document or any other document that contains a macro from an unknown source, Word displays a dialog box warning that a macro is attached and allows you to enable or disable the macros. If you are confident of the source (author) of the document and macros, you should click the Enable Macros button in the dialog box. If you are uncertain about the reliability of the source of the document and macros, you should click the Disable Macros button.

Perform the following steps to set Word's security level to medium.

Steps: To Set a Security Level in Word

1 Click Tools on the menu bar, point to Macro, and then point to Security on the Macro submenu (Figure 8-4).

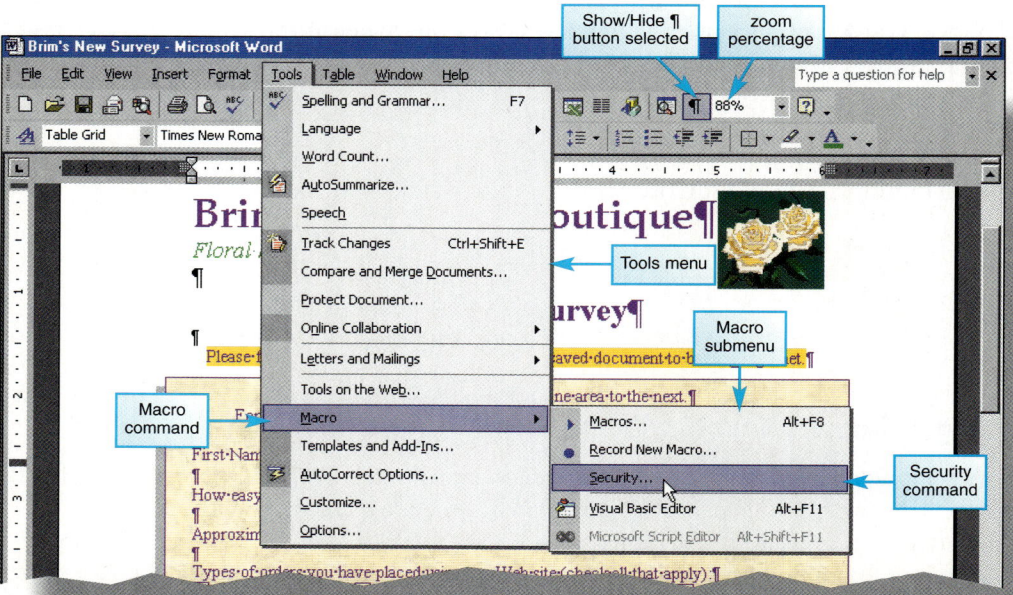

FIGURE 8-4

2 **Click Security. When the Security dialog box displays, if necessary, click the Security Level tab. Click Medium and then point to the OK button.**

Word displays the Security dialog box (Figure 8-5). The Medium option button is selected.

3 **Click the OK button.**

Word sets its security level to medium.

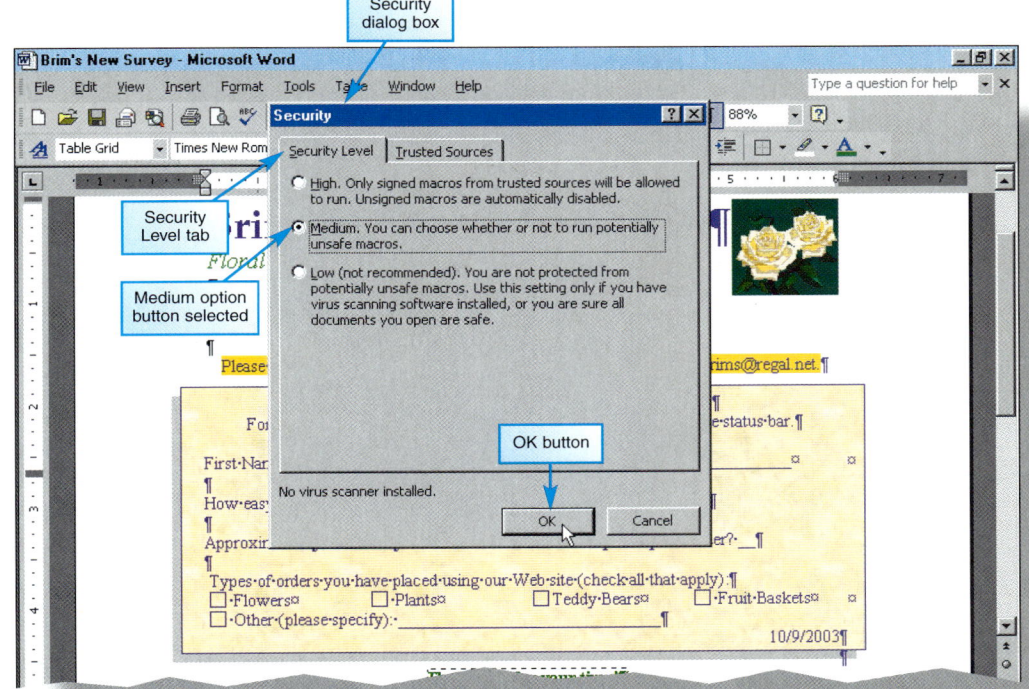

FIGURE 8-5

The next time you open a document that contains a macro from an unauthorized source, Word will ask if you wish to enable or disable the macro.

Modifying a Form

As suggested by your instructor, you will change the look of the Customer Survey. You will change the graphic, insert the headings into a text box, and then modify the fonts, font colors, font sizes, and alignment. You also will change the highlight color and the fill inside the rectangle drawing object. The following pages discuss how you modify the online form.

Modifying the Graphic

The first step in modifying the online form is to remove the existing graphic of the flowers and insert a new decorative graphic of the letter B to replace the first letter in Brim's. The new clip art image is available on the Web. If you do not have access to the Web, you may insert the graphic from a file on the Data Disk that accompanies this book. First, you will reduce the size of the inserted image. Then, you will change it from an inline object to a floating object. Finally, you will move the graphic to the left of the boutique name to use it as the first letter of the company name.

Perform the steps on the next page to delete the graphic on the form, insert a clip art image from the Web into the Word document, and then modify the graphic.

1. In Voice Command mode, say "Tools, Macro, Security, Medium, OK"

Macro Viruses

If Word's security level is set to low, Word does not warn you that a file contains a macro, thus leaving your computer open for macro viruses. A macro virus is a type of computer virus that is stored in a macro within a file, template, or add-in. If Word's security level is set to medium, Word warns you before opening a document containing a macro. For the best protection against macro viruses, purchase and install specialized antivirus software. For more information about using antivirus software, visit the Word 2002 More About Web Page (scsite.com/wd2002/more.htm) and then click Antivirus Software.

Note: The following steps assume your computer is connected to the Internet. If it is not, go directly to the shaded steps at the top of page WD 8.13.

TO CHANGE THE GRAPHIC

1. Click the graphic of the flowers to select it. Press the DELETE key.

2. Position the insertion point on the first line of the form, immediately to the left of the capital letter B. Click Insert on the menu bar, point to Picture, and then click Clip Art on the Picture submenu. In the Insert Clip Art task pane, drag through any text in the Search text text box to select the text. Type b and then press the ENTER key.

3. When Word displays thumbnails of clips that match the description, point to the clip shown in Figure 8-6. The globe icon in the lower-left corner of a thumbnail indicates the clip art is located on the Web.

4. Click the box arrow that displays to the right of the clip. Click Insert on the menu and then click the Close button in the Insert Clip Art task pane title bar.

5. When the graphic displays in the document, double-click the graphic. When the Format Picture dialog box displays, if necessary, click the Size tab. Change the height and width values in the Scale area to 58%.

6. Click the Layout tab and then click Square. Click the OK button.

7. Drag the graphic to the left so it is aligned approximately with the left side of the rectangle below it, as shown in Figure 8-6.

8. Click outside the graphic to deselect it. If necessary, drag the scroll box on the vertical scroll bar to display the entire form in the document window.

The graphic is resized and positioned as shown in Figure 8-6.

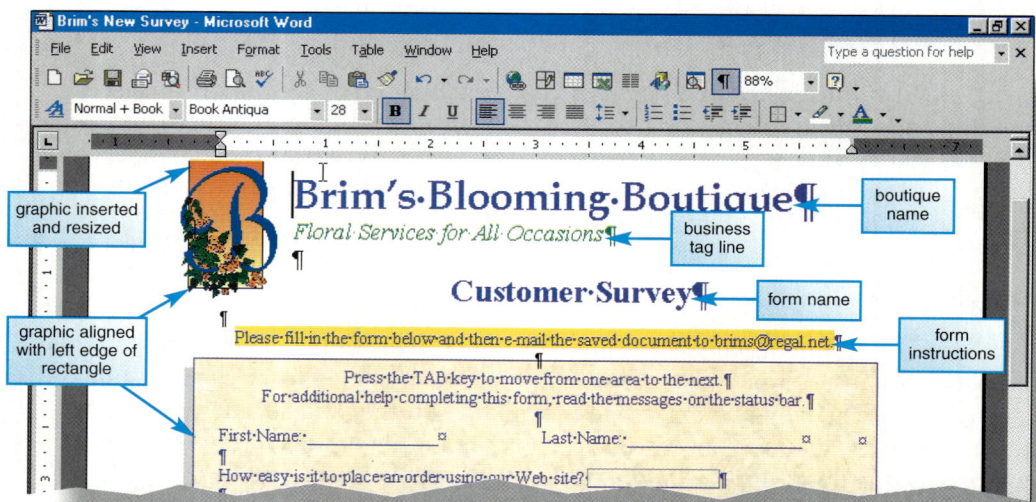

FIGURE 8-6

If you do not have access to the Web, you can insert the clip art file into the Word document from the Data Disk, as described in the following steps. If you did not download the Data Disk, see the inside back cover for instructions for downloading the Data Disk or see your instructor.

TO INSERT A GRAPHIC FILE FROM THE DATA DISK

1. With the insertion point at the beginning of the form, click Insert on the menu bar, point to Picture, and then click From File.
2. Insert the Data Disk into drive A. When the Insert Picture dialog box displays, click the Look in box arrow and then click 3½ Floppy (A:). Click the file name, letterB, and then click the Insert button.
3. When the graphic displays in the document, double-click the graphic. When the Format Picture dialog box displays, if necessary, click the Size tab. Change the height and width values in the Scale area to 58%.
4. Click the Layout tab and then click Square. Click the OK button.
5. Drag the graphic to the left so it approximately is aligned with the left side of the rectangle below it, as shown in Figure 8-6.
6. Click outside the graphic to deselect it.

Word inserts the clip into your document and resizes it (shown in Figure 8-6).

The next step in modifying the Customer Survey is to insert the boutique name, business tag line, and form name (Figure 8-6) into a text box and then change the alignment, font, font style, font size, and font color.

Inserting a Text Box and Formatting Text

To use the new graphical B as the first letter in Brim's Blooming Boutique, you need to delete the letter B and then move the text close to the graphic. Inserting the text into a text box allows you to move the text closer to the graphic. Perform the following steps to delete the letter B, and then insert and format the text box.

TO INSERT AND FORMAT A TEXT BOX

1. Select the first letter of Brim's and then press the DELETE key to remove the capital B. Press the DOWN ARROW key to position the insertion point on line 2. If necessary, right-click the green wavy underline below rim's and then click Ignore Once on the shortcut menu.
2. On the third line, delete the paragraph mark to remove the blank line. Also, delete the paragraph mark below the text, Customer Survey, to remove that blank line.
3. Select the first three lines of text that include the boutique name, the business tag line, and the form name. If the Drawing toolbar does not display on the screen, click the Drawing button on the Standard toolbar to display the Drawing toolbar. Click the Text Box button on the Drawing toolbar to place a text box around the selected text. (You will fix the cluttered appearance next.)
4. Click the Fill Color button arrow on the Drawing toolbar and then click No Fill. Click the Line Color button arrow on the Drawing toolbar and then click No Line.
5. Drag the text box to the right so that no text overlaps the graphic. Drag the right-middle sizing handle of the text box to approximately the 6 inch mark on the horizontal ruler, as shown in Figure 8-7 on the next page. If the form instructions line that is highlighted yellow below the text box wraps to a second line, drag the bottom-middle sizing handle on the text box down until the instructions display on a single line. You may need to move the text box around a bit to make your screen look like Figure 8-7.

Text Boxes

Text boxes and frames are both containers for text that can be positioned on a page and then sized. Earlier versions of Word used frames to wrap text around a graphic. With Word 2002, you can use text boxes to manipulate text and take advantage of new graphical effects. Text boxes provide nearly all the advantages of frames, plus they provide many additional advantages. You can use the Drawing toolbar to enhance text boxes with effects such as fill color - just as you can with any other drawing object.

6. Click the Drawing button on the Standard toolbar to remove the Drawing toolbar from the screen. Scroll as necessary to display the entire form.

Word inserts and formats the text box.

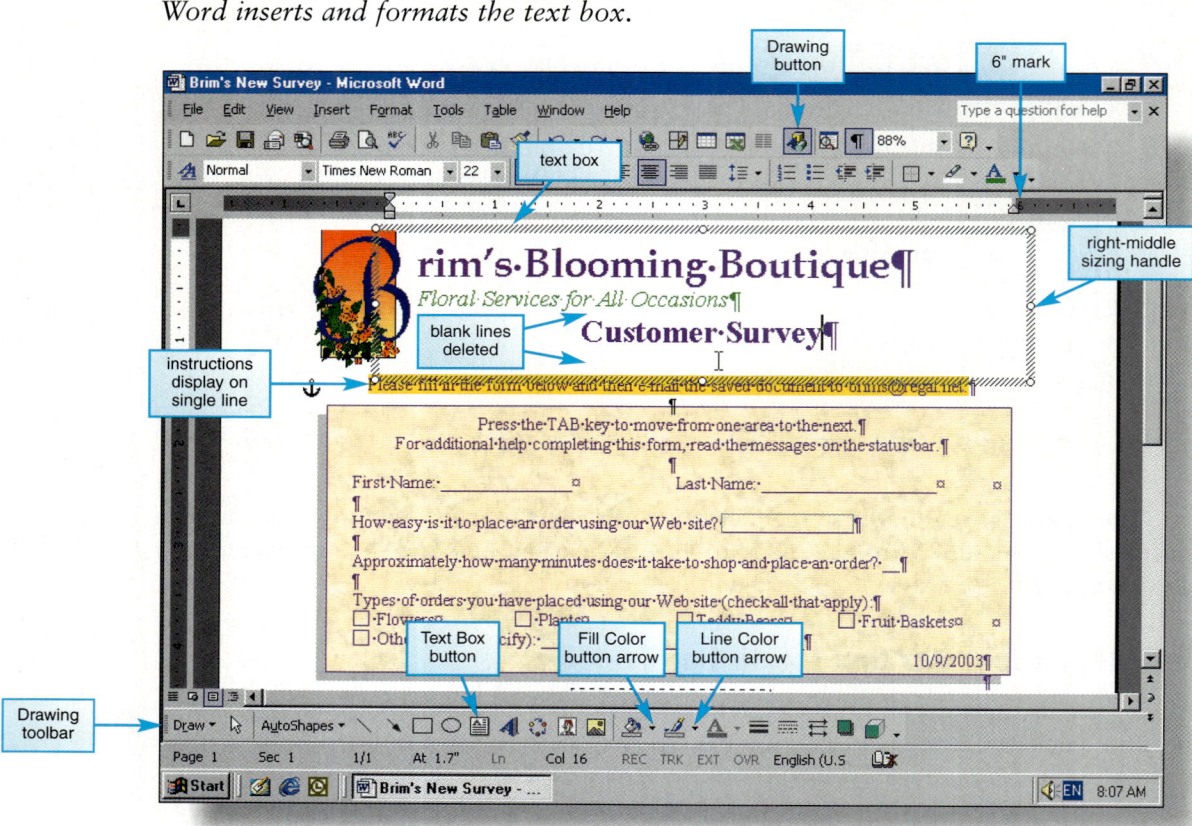

FIGURE 8-7

The next step is to format the text in the text box, as described in the steps below.

TO FORMAT TEXT IN A TEXT BOX

1. Select the first line of text in the text box, rim's Blooming Boutique. Click the Font box arrow on the Formatting toolbar. Scroll to and then click Monotype Corsiva. Click the Font Size box arrow on the Formatting toolbar. Scroll to and then click 48. Click the Font Color button arrow on the Formatting toolbar and then click Indigo.

2. Click the Align Right button on the Formatting toolbar to right-align the first line in the text box. If necessary, drag the left-middle sizing handle on the text box to the left so the entire company name displays on a single line.

3. Select the second line of text in the text box, which contains the business tag line: Floral Services for All Occasions. Click the Font box arrow on the Formatting toolbar. Scroll to and then click Bookman Old Style. Click the Font Size box on the Formatting toolbar and then click 14. Click the Italic button on the Formatting toolbar to turn off italic formatting. Click the Font Color button arrow on the Formatting toolbar and then click Orange.

4. Click the Align Right button on the Formatting toolbar to right-align the second line of text in the text box.

5. Select the third line of text in the text box, which contains the form name, Customer Survey. Click the Font Color button arrow on the Formatting toolbar and then click Green.
6. If necessary, drag the Left Indent marker on the horizontal ruler one-half inch to the left to center the form name above the rectangle.
7. If necessary, drag the text box closer to the graphic to facilitate reading the decorative B as the first letter in the boutique name.

The boutique name, business tag line, and form name display as shown in Figure 8-8.

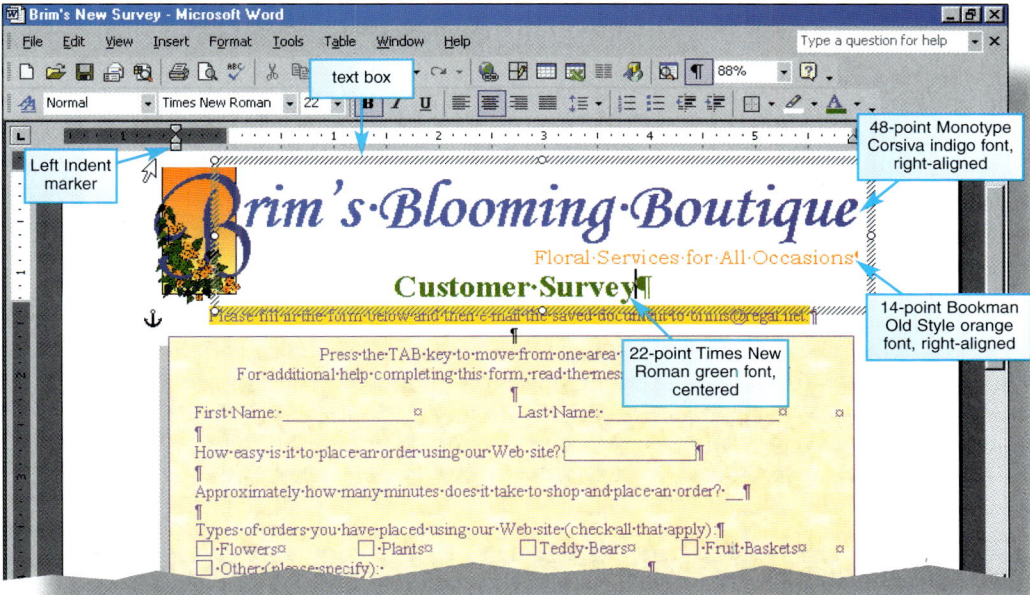

FIGURE 8-8

The next step is to format the form instructions. You will change the highlight color of the form instructions from yellow to green and then change the font color to white. You will right-align the text and then insert a blank line below the instructions in preparation for changes to the rectangle.

TO FORMAT THE FORM INSTRUCTIONS

1. Select the form instructions that currently are highlighted in yellow.
2. Click the Highlight button arrow on the Formatting toolbar and then click Green.
3. Click the Font Color button arrow on the Formatting toolbar and then click White.
4. Click the Center button on the Formatting toolbar.
5. Click the blank line below the instructions. Press the ENTER key to create a second blank line.

Word changes the highlight on the form instructions from yellow to green (Figure 8-9 on the next page). The font color changes to white, and the line is centered. Two blank lines display below the instructions.

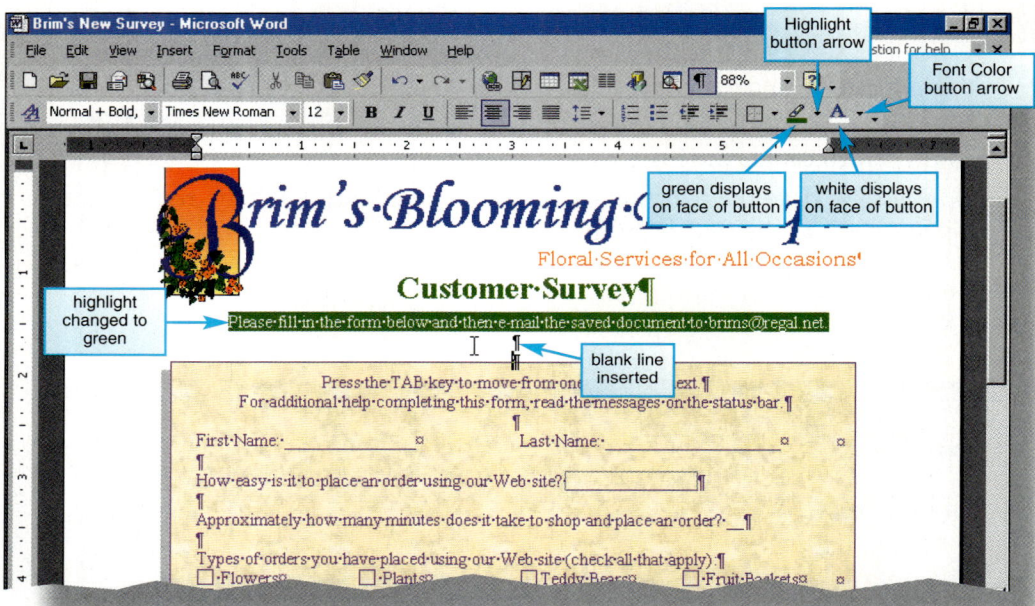

FIGURE 8-9

If your computer displays a red wavy underline below the e-mail address, right-click the e-mail address and then click Ignore Once on the shortcut menu. If your computer is set to change the formatting of e-mail addresses automatically, your display may differ.

The next step is to change the format of the text in the data entry area.

Creating a New Style with a Shortcut Key

All text in the data entry area should be formatted to 11-point Arial bold indigo font. You could select each text item in the data entry area, one at a time, and change its font to Arial, its font size to 11, its font style to bold, and its font color to indigo. A timesaving alternative, however, is to use a style. A **style** is a customized format that you can apply to text. Although Word has many built-in styles, none of them is an 11-point Arial bold indigo font. You can create your own new style, however, and then apply this style to the text in the data entry area of the form.

Word has two types of styles: character and paragraph. A **character style** defines attributes for selected text, such as font, font size, and font style. A **paragraph style** defines formatting for a paragraph, such as line spacing, text alignment, and borders. Paragraph styles can include a character style definition. In the data entry area of this form, you want to change text to 11-point Arial bold indigo font. Thus, you will create a character style.

Recall that shortcut keys are one or more keys you press on the keyboard to complete a task. Rather than selecting the newly created character style from a long list, using a keystroke combination gives you the advantage of not having to move your hands away from the keyboard to position the mouse on a different part of the screen and clicking and scrolling to locate the desired style. You can customize shortcut keys in Word by assigning the keystrokes to commands that do not have them already, removing shortcut keys that you do not want, or returning to the default shortcut key settings at anytime.

Perform the following steps to create a new character style, called DataEntryArea, which formats selected text to 11-point Arial bold indigo font. You will assign the shortcut, ALT+C, to the new character style.

Creating Styles

To create a character style, click the New Style button in the Styles and Formatting task pane. When the New Style dialog box displays, click the Style type box arrow and then click Character. To create a paragraph style, click the Style type box arrow in the New Style dialog box and then click Paragraph. If you accidentally create a paragraph style rather than a character style, all current paragraph formatting will be applied to the selected text. In the case of Figure 8-10 for example, a paragraph style would include the centered format.

Modifying a Form • WD 8.17

Steps To Create a Style That Has a Shortcut Key

1 Click the Styles and Formatting button on the Formatting toolbar. When the Styles and Formatting task pane displays, point to the New Style button.

Word displays the Styles and Formatting task pane (Figure 8-10). Your list of formats may be different.

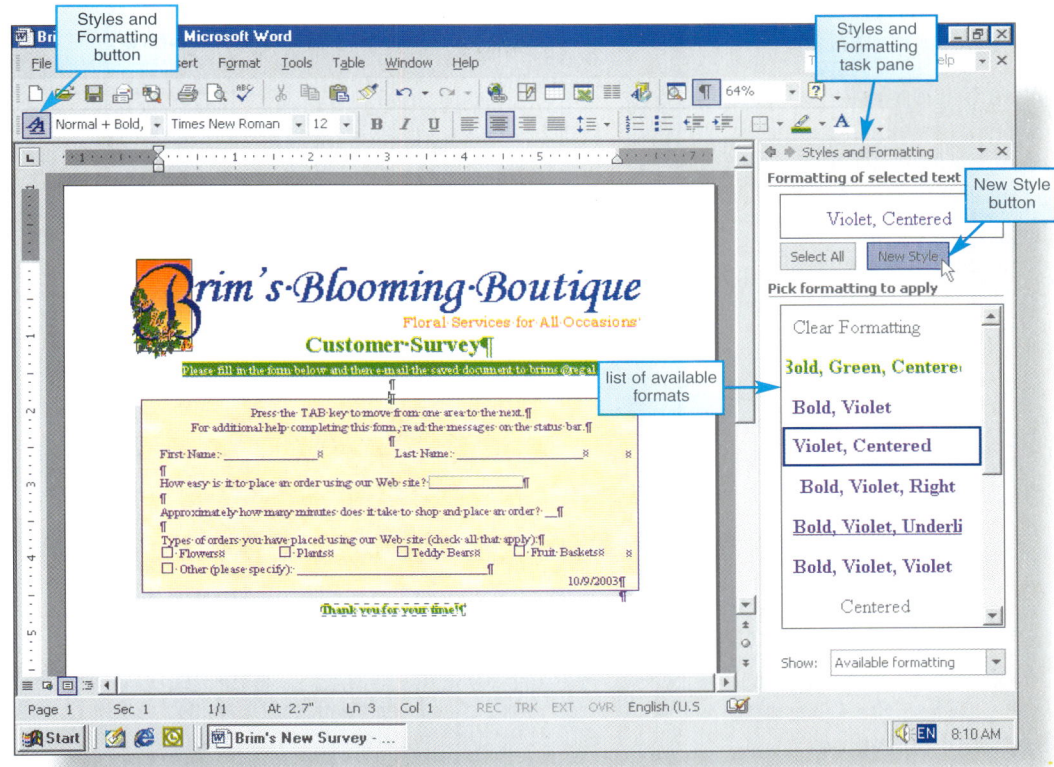

FIGURE 8-10

2 Click the New Style button. When the New Style dialog box displays, type `DataEntryArea` in the Name text box. Click the Style type box arrow and then click Character. In the Formatting area, click the Font box arrow and then click Arial; click the Font Size box arrow and then click 11; click the Bold button; click the Font Color button arrow and then click Indigo. Point to the Format button.

Word displays the New Style dialog box (Figure 8-11).

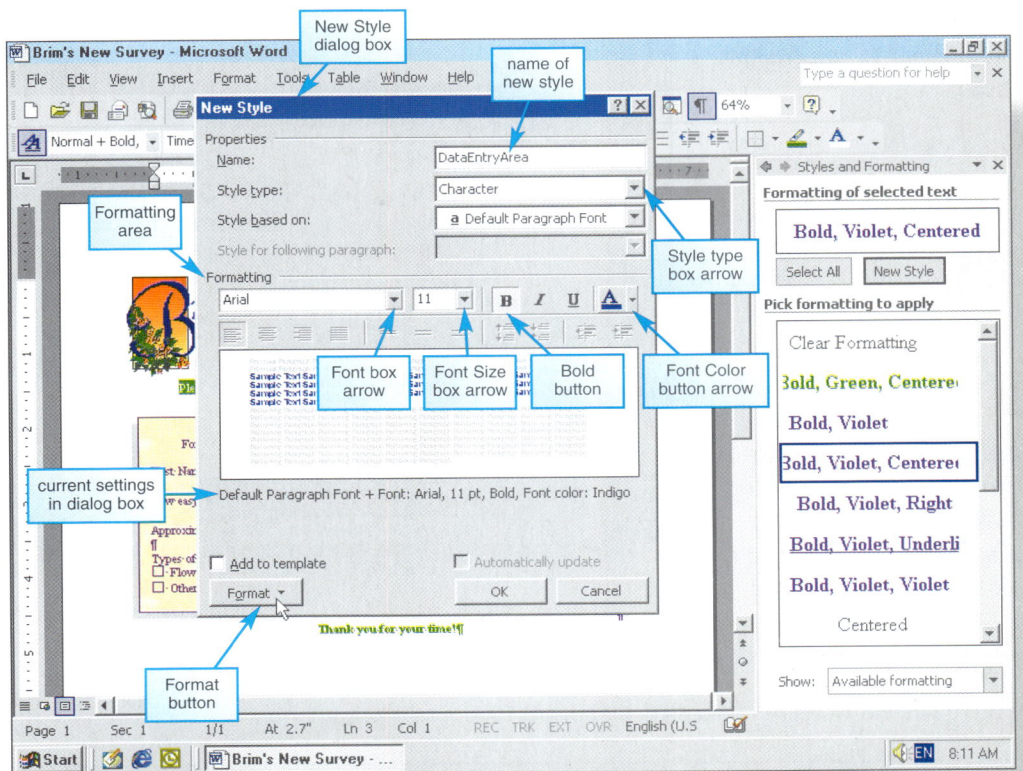

FIGURE 8-11

WD 8.18 • Project 8 • Working with Macros and Visual Basic for Applications (VBA)

3 **Click the Format button and then point to Shortcut key on the Format menu.**

Word displays a list of available formatting commands above or below the Format button (Figure 8-12). Some commands are dimmed because they relate to paragraph styles.

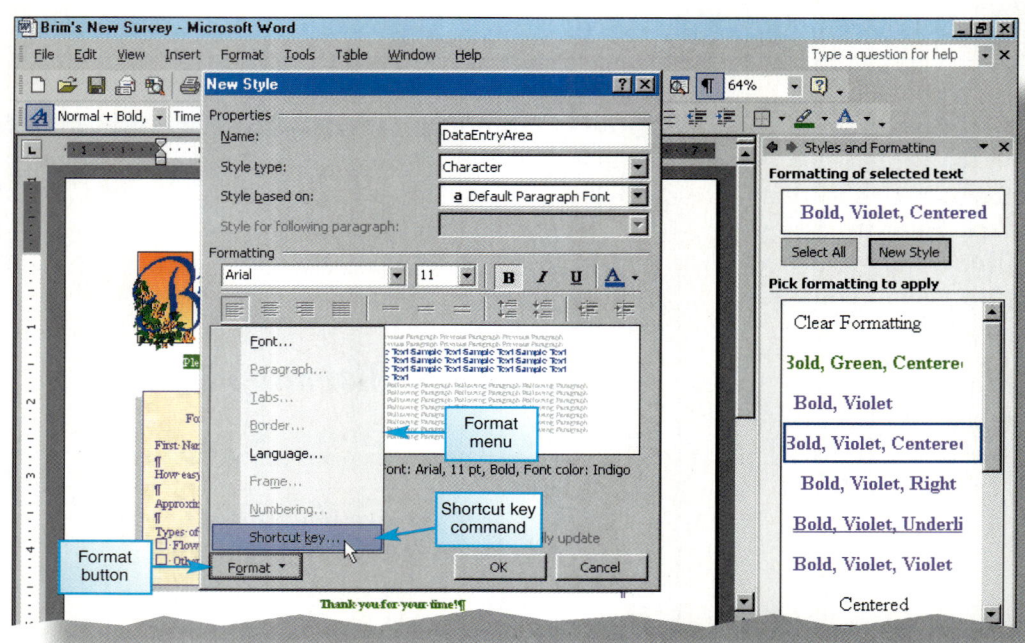

FIGURE 8-12

4 **Click Shortcut key. When the Customize Keyboard dialog box displays, press ALT+C. If necessary, click the Save changes in box arrow and then click Brim's New Survey. Point to the Assign button.**

Word displays the Customize Keyboard dialog box (Figure 8-13). The characters you pressed, ALT+C, display in the Press new shortcut key text box.

5 **Click the Assign button. Click the Close button to close the Customize Keyboard dialog box. When the New Style dialog box is visible again, click the OK button. Click the Close button in the Styles and Formatting task pane title bar.**

Word creates the DataEntryArea style along with its shortcut key, ALT+C.

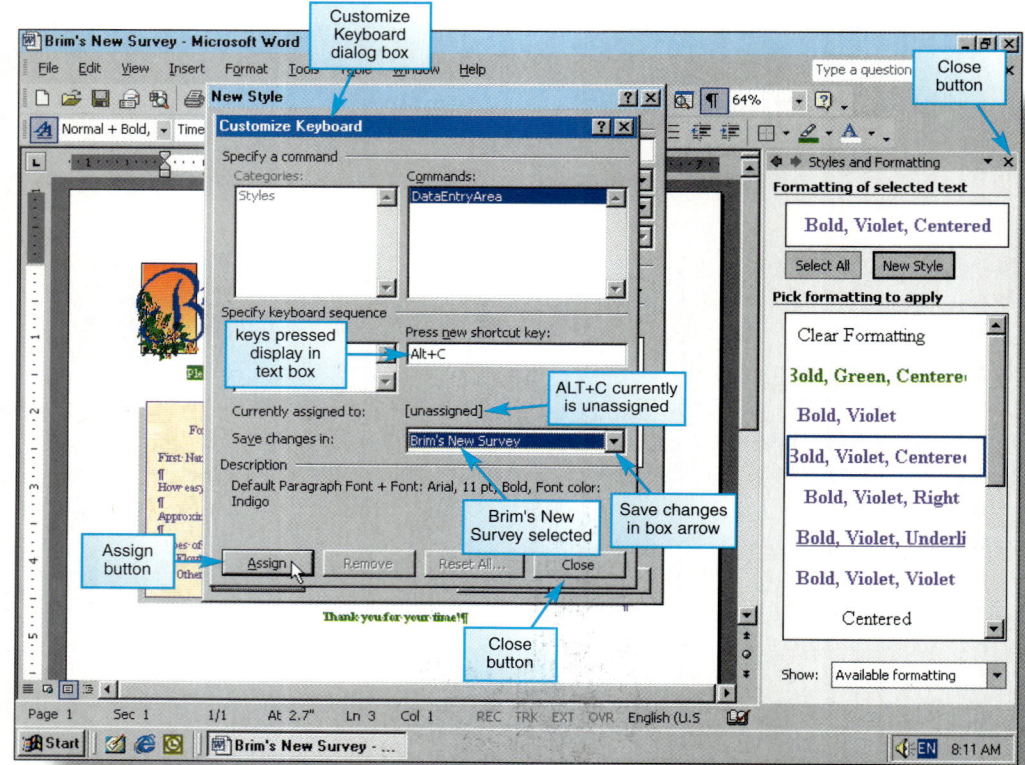

FIGURE 8-13

To apply a character style, select the text to be formatted and then apply the style. To apply a paragraph style, you do not need to select text before applying the style — simply click in the paragraph to be formatted and then apply the style.

In the previous steps, you created a shortcut key of ALT+C for the DataEntryArea style. Instead of using the Style box on the Formatting toolbar to apply the DataEntryArea style to text in the data entry area of the Customer Survey, you will use the shortcut key. Perform the following step to apply a style using a shortcut key.

Applying Styles

If you click the Style box arrow on the Formatting toolbar to apply styles, paragraph style names display a proofreader's paragraph mark, and character style names display an underlined letter a.

Steps: To Apply a Style Using a Shortcut Key

 If necessary, scroll to display the entire form in the document window. Drag through all of the text within the rectangle to select it and then press ALT+C. Click outside the selected text to remove the selection.

All of the text within the rectangle now is formatted with the new style; that is, 11-point Arial bold indigo font (Figure 8-14).

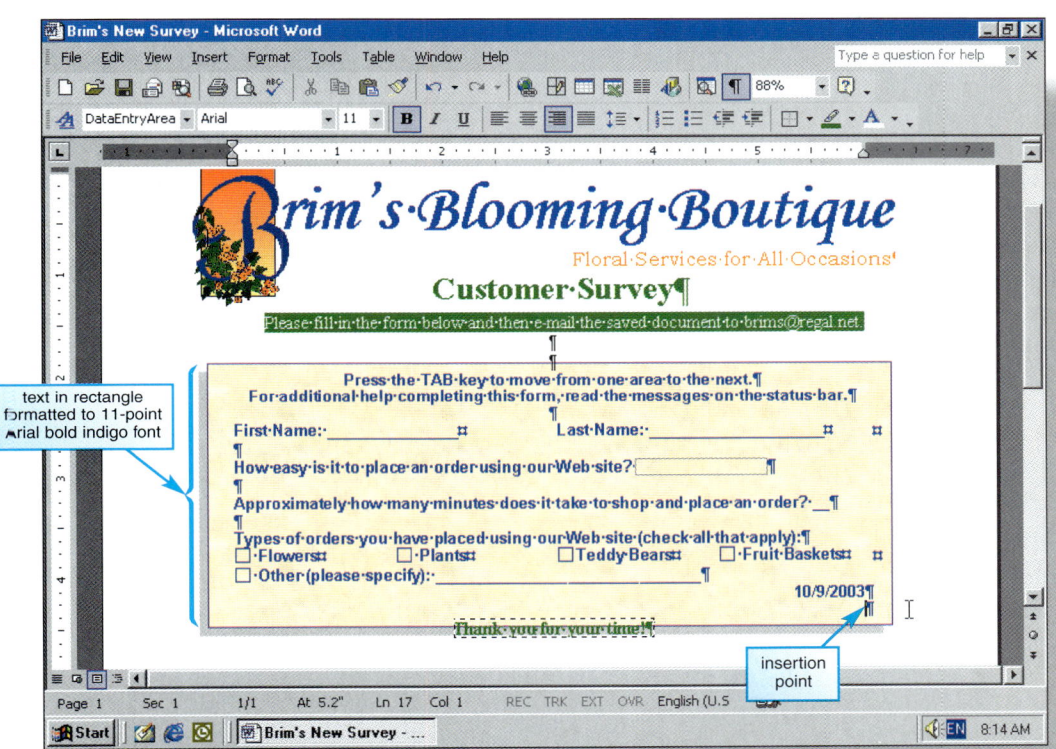

FIGURE 8-14

The next step is to add a gradient fill effect to the rectangle.

Filling a Drawing Object with a Gradient Effect

The data entry area in the form is surrounded with a rectangle drawing object, which currently is filled with the parchment texture. Other available fill effects include solid colors, gradient colors, patterns, and pictures. This project requires a gradient fill effect in the rectangle drawing object. **Gradient** means a gradual progression of colors and shades, usually from one color to another color, or from one shade to another shade of the same color.

Perform the steps on the next page to fill the rectangle drawing object with a gradient fill effect.

Other Ways

1. Click Style box arrow on Formatting toolbar, click style name
2. On Format menu click Styles and Formatting, click style name
3. In Voice Command mode, say "Format, Styles, [style name]"

Steps To Fill a Drawing Object with a Gradient Fill Effect

 Select the rectangle by pointing to an edge of the rectangle and clicking when the mouse pointer has a four-headed arrow attached to it. If the Drawing toolbar does not display on your screen, click the Drawing button on the Standard toolbar. Click the Fill Color button arrow on the Drawing toolbar and then click the Fill Effects button. When the Fill Effects dialog box displays, if necessary, click the Gradient tab. In the Colors area, click Two colors. Click the Color 1 box arrow and then click Light Yellow. Click the Color 2 box arrow and then click White. In the Shading styles area, click From center. In the Variants area, click the variant on the right. Point to the OK button.

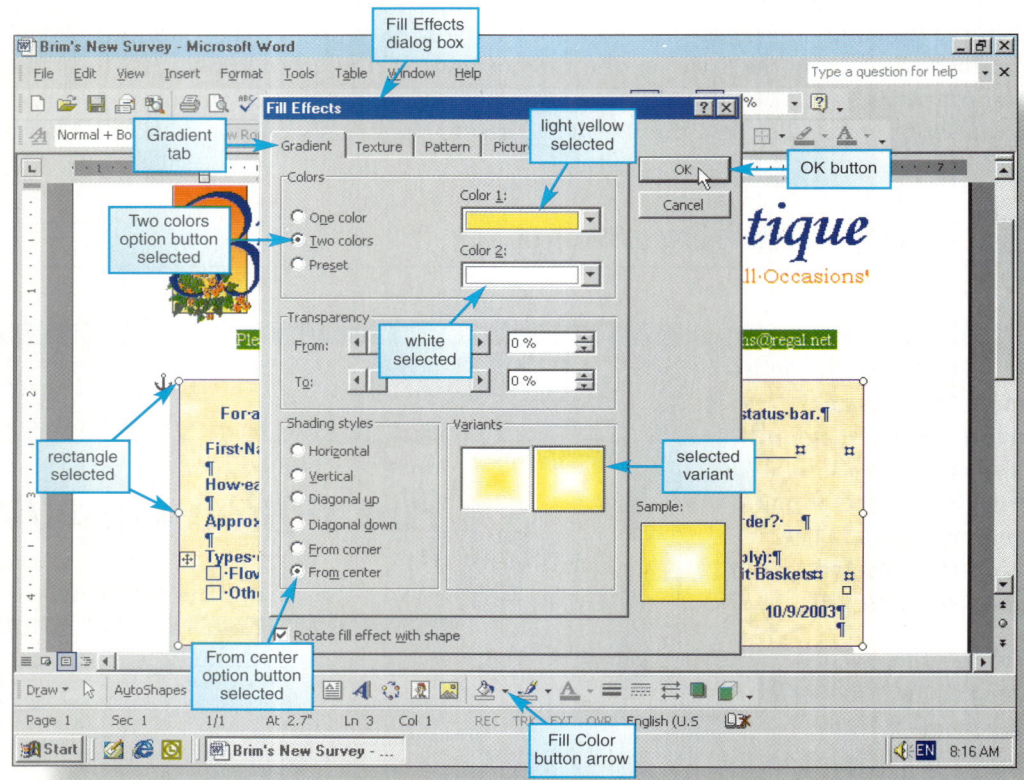

The Fill Effects dialog box displays (Figure 8-15).

FIGURE 8-15

Click the OK button.

Word fills the rectangle with the light yellow and white gradient effect (Figure 8-16).

Other Ways

1. Right-click edge of drawing object, click Format AutoShape on shortcut menu, click Colors and Lines tab, click Color button arrow in Fill area, click Fill Effects button, click Gradient tab
2. Select drawing object, click AutoShape on Format menu, click Colors and Lines tab, click Fill Color button arrow, click Fill Effects button, click Gradient tab

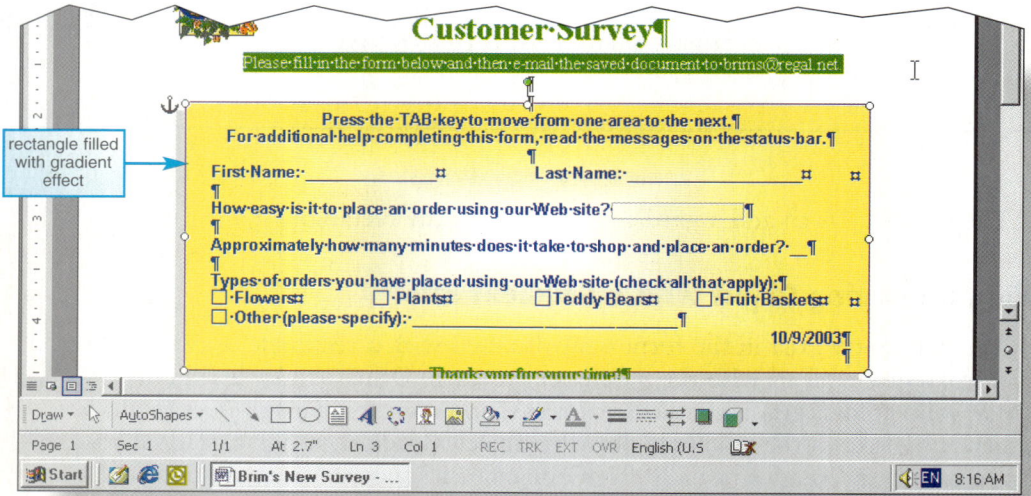

FIGURE 8-16

Notice in Figure 8-16 that the gradient fill is white in the center and gradually fills the entire drawing object to a solid yellow at the edges. This is because you selected From center in the Gradient sheet in the Fill Effects dialog box (Figure 8-15).

The next step is to add a 3-D effect to the rectangle drawing object.

Adding a 3-D Effect to a Drawing Object

You can add a 3-D effect to a drawing object by using the 3-D button on the Drawing toolbar. Adding a **3-D effect** changes the depth of the drawing object, its shadow color, the angle, the direction of lighting, and the surface reflection. When you add a 3-D effect, Word removes any previously applied shadow. Perform the following steps to add a 3-D effect to the rectangle drawing object that surrounds the data entry area of the Customer Survey.

3-D Effects

You can change the color, rotation, depth, lighting, or texture of a 3-D effect by using the 3-D Settings toolbar. To display this toolbar, click the 3-D button on the Drawing toolbar and then click the 3-D Settings button in the list.

 To Add a 3-D Effect

1 **With the rectangle still selected, click the 3-D Style button on the Drawing toolbar and then point to 3-D Style 1 (Figure 8-17).**

2 **Click 3-D Style 1.**

Word adds the 3-D Style 1 effect to the rectangle drawing object (shown in Figure 8-18 on the next page).

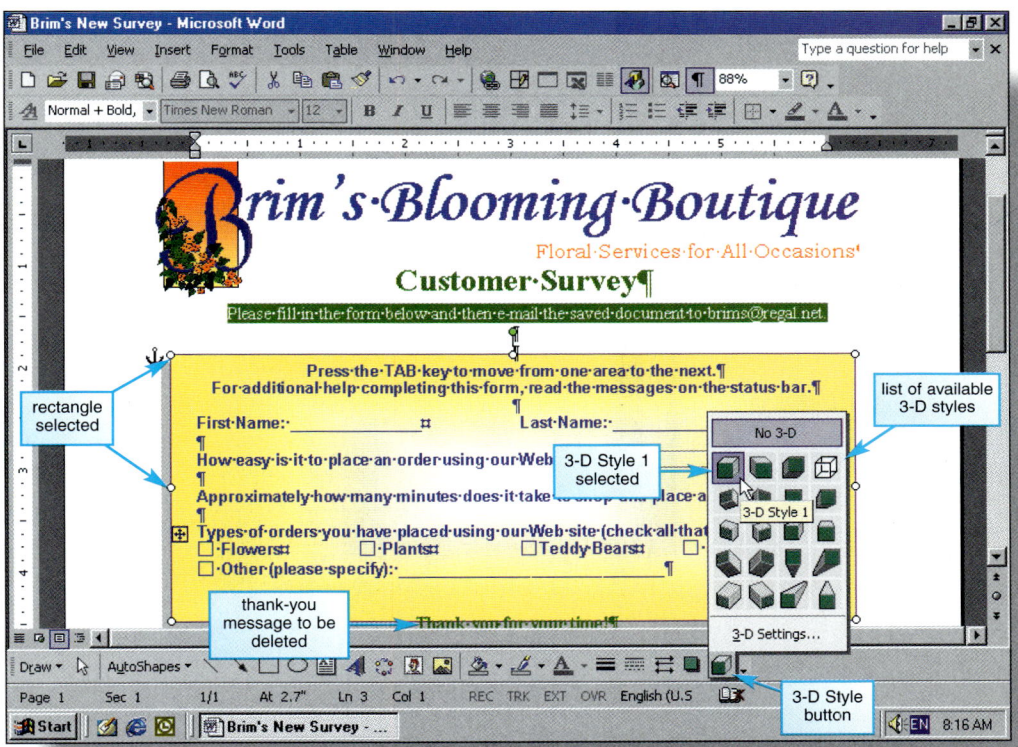

FIGURE 8-17

1. In Voice Command mode, say "3 D Style, [style name]"

The final step in modifying the form is to delete the thank-you message and resize the rectangle.

TO DELETE THE THANK-YOU MESSAGE AND RESIZE THE RECTANGLE

1. Select the line below the data entry area that contains the thank-you message and then press the DELETE key.
2. Point to an edge of the rectangle and click when the mouse pointer has a four-headed arrow attached to it. Drag the bottom-middle sizing handle on the rectangle up until the bottom of the rectangle is immediately below the date.
3. Click the Drawing button on the Standard toolbar to remove the Drawing toolbar from the screen. Scroll as necessary to display the entire form in the document window.

The online form displays as shown in Figure 8-18.

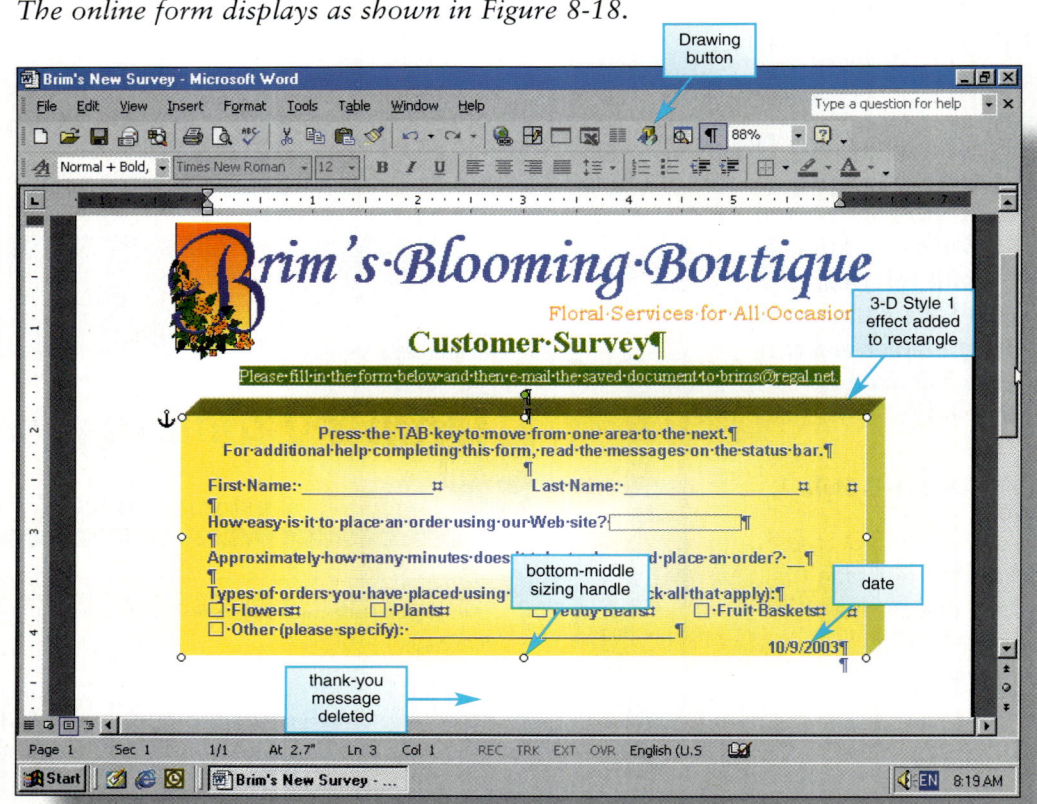

FIGURE 8-18

Because you have performed many formatting tasks thus far, perform the following step to save the form again.

TO SAVE A DOCUMENT

1. Click the Save button on the Standard toolbar.

Word saves the Brim's New Survey document on a floppy disk in drive A.

Using a Macro to Automate a Task

As previously discussed, a macro consists of a series of Word commands or instructions that are grouped together as a single command. This single command is a convenient way to automate a difficult or lengthy task. Macros often are used for formatting or editing activities, to combine multiple commands into a single command, or to select an option in a dialog box with a single keystroke.

To create a macro, you can use the macro recorder or the Visual Basic Editor. The following pages discuss how to use the macro recorder to create a macro. Later in this project, you use the Visual Basic Editor to create a macro.

Recording and Executing a Macro

When you receive filled-in forms from users, your next step will be to analyze the data on the forms. Often, you want to use database software, such as Access, to assist you in analyzing the responses on the forms. As discussed in Project 7, you must save the data on each survey in a comma-delimited text file so that Access can use the data. To do this, you must place a check mark in the Save data only for forms check box in the Save sheet in the Options dialog box — prior to clicking the Save button on the Standard toolbar.

If you receive 70 completed forms, you will be performing the following steps 70 times: click Tools on the menu bar, click Options, click the Save tab, place a check mark in the Save data only for forms check box, and then click the OK button. A timesaving alternative is to create a macro that places the check mark in the check box. Then, you simply execute the macro and click the Save button. Thus, the purpose of the first macro you create in this project is to select an option in a dialog box.

Word has a **macro recorder** that creates a macro automatically based on a series of actions you perform while it is recording. The macro recorder is similar to a video camera in that it records all actions you perform on a document during a period of time. Once you turn on the macro recorder, it records your activities; when you are finished recording activities, turn off the macro recorder to stop the recording. After you have recorded a macro, you can **execute the macro**, or play it back, anytime you want to perform that same set of actions.

To create the macro that will place a check mark in the Save data only for forms check box, you will follow this sequence of steps:

1. Start the macro recorder and specify options about the macro.
2. Place a check mark in the Save data only for forms check box in the Save sheet in the Options dialog box.
3. Stop the macro recorder.

The impressive feature of the macro recorder is that you actually step through the task as you create the macro — allowing you to see exactly what the macro will do before you use it.

When you first create the macro, you have to name it. The name for this macro is FormDataOnly. **Macro names** can be up to 255 characters long; they can contain numbers, letters, and underscores; they cannot contain spaces or other punctuation.

Earlier in this project, you assigned a shortcut key to a style. Likewise, you can assign a shortcut key to a macro, which allows you to run the macro by using its name or by pressing the shortcut key. Perform the steps on the next page to record the macro and assign ALT+D as its shortcut key.

More About

Naming Macros

If you give a new macro the same name as an existing built-in command in Microsoft Word, the new macro actions will replace the existing actions. Thus, you should be careful not to name a macro FileSave or after any other menu commands. To view a list of built-in macros in Word, point to Macro on the Tools menu, and then click Macros. Click the Macros in box arrow and then click Word Commands.

Steps: To Record a Macro and Assign It a Shortcut Key

1 **Double-click the REC status indicator on the status bar. When the Record Macro dialog box displays, type** `FormDataOnly` **in the Macro name text box. Click the Store macro in box arrow and then click Documents Based On Brim's New Survey. Select the text in the Description text box and then type** `Places a check mark in the Save data only for forms check box.` **Point to the Keyboard button.**

Word displays the Record Macro dialog box (Figure 8-19).

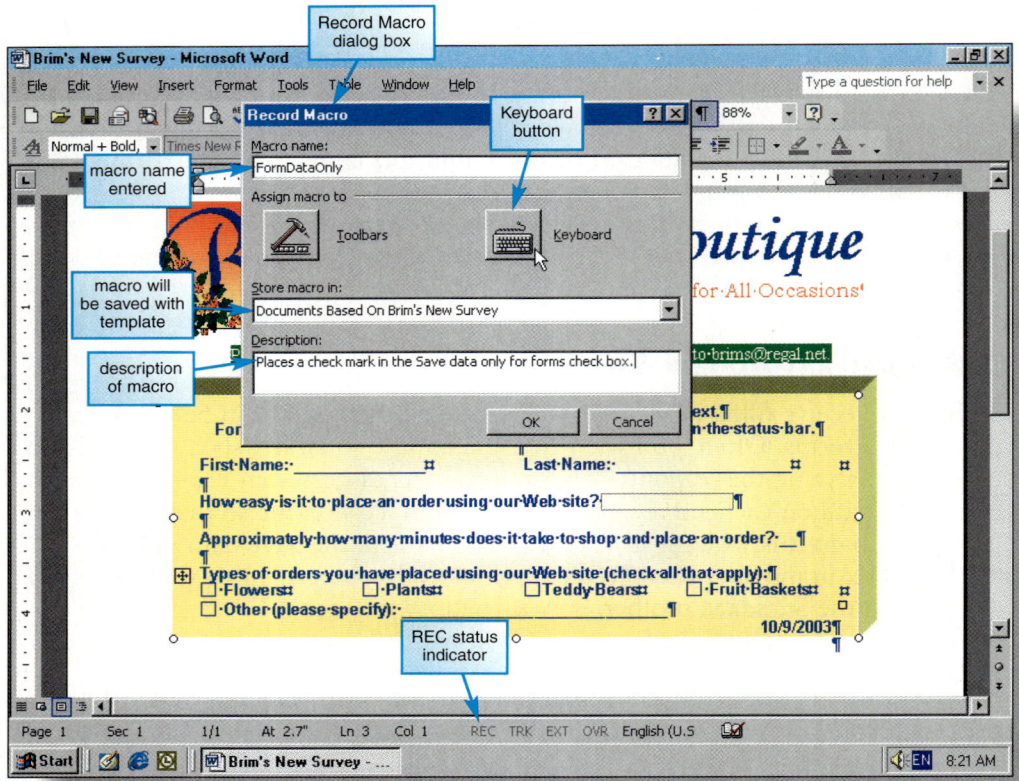

FIGURE 8-19

2 **Click the Keyboard button. When the Customize Keyboard dialog box displays, press ALT+D. Point to the Assign button.**

Word displays the Customize Keyboard dialog box (Figure 8-20). The characters you pressed, ALT+D, display in the Press new shortcut key text box.

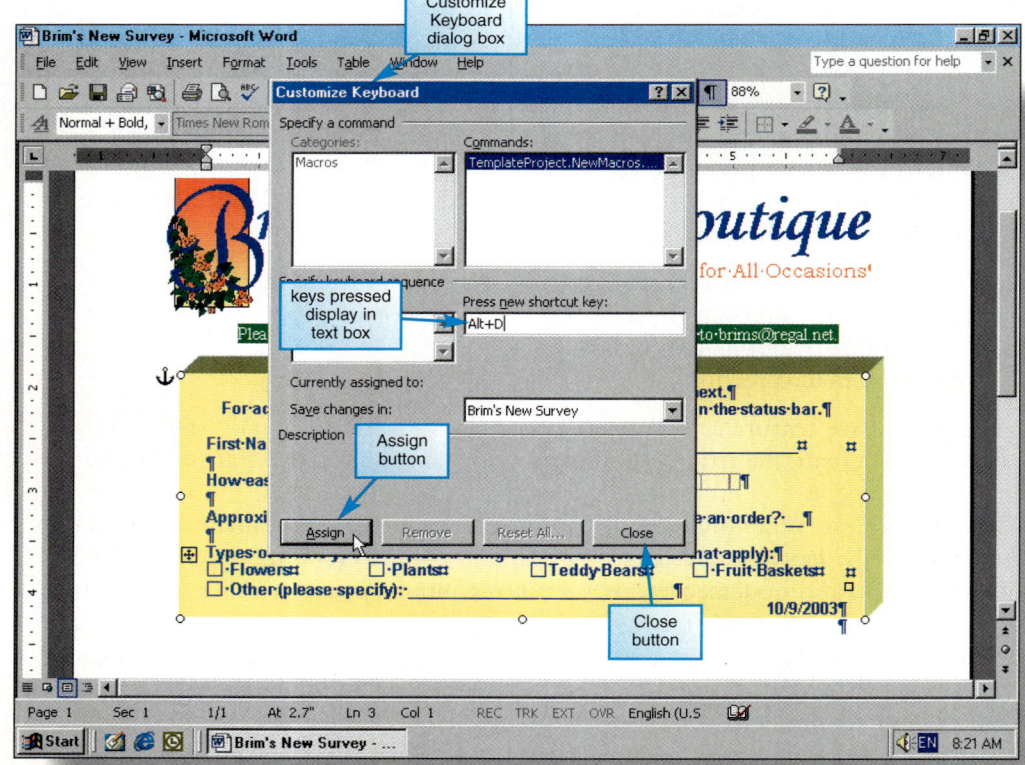

FIGURE 8-20

Using a Macro to Automate a Task • WD 8.25

3 **Click the Assign button. Click the Close button in the Customize Keyboard dialog box.**

Word assigns the shortcut key, ALT+D, to the FormDataOnly macro, closes the Customize Keyboard and Record Macro dialog boxes, darkens the REC status indicator on the status bar, and then displays the Stop Recording toolbar in the document window (Figure 8-21). The mouse pointer displays with a tape icon to remind you that you are recording. Any task you do will be part of the macro. When you are finished recording the macro, you will click the Stop Recording button on the Stop Recording toolbar.

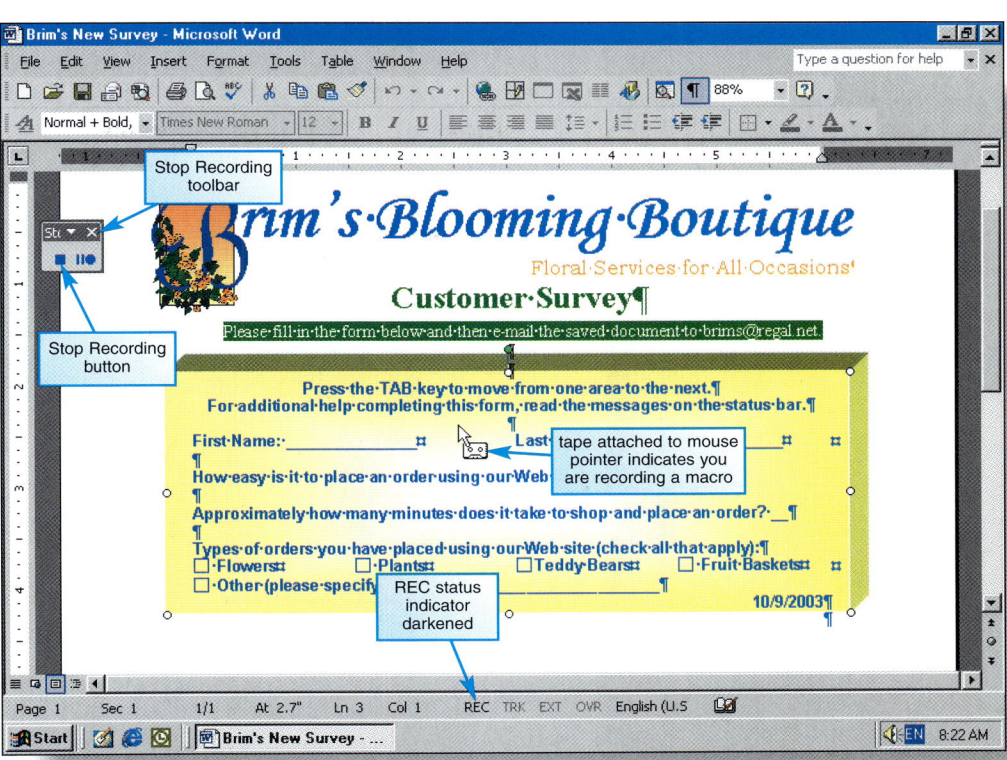

FIGURE 8-21

4 **Click Tools on the menu bar and then point to Options.**

When you are recording a macro and the mouse pointer is in a menu or pointing to a toolbar button, the tape icon does not display next to the pointer (Figure 8-22).

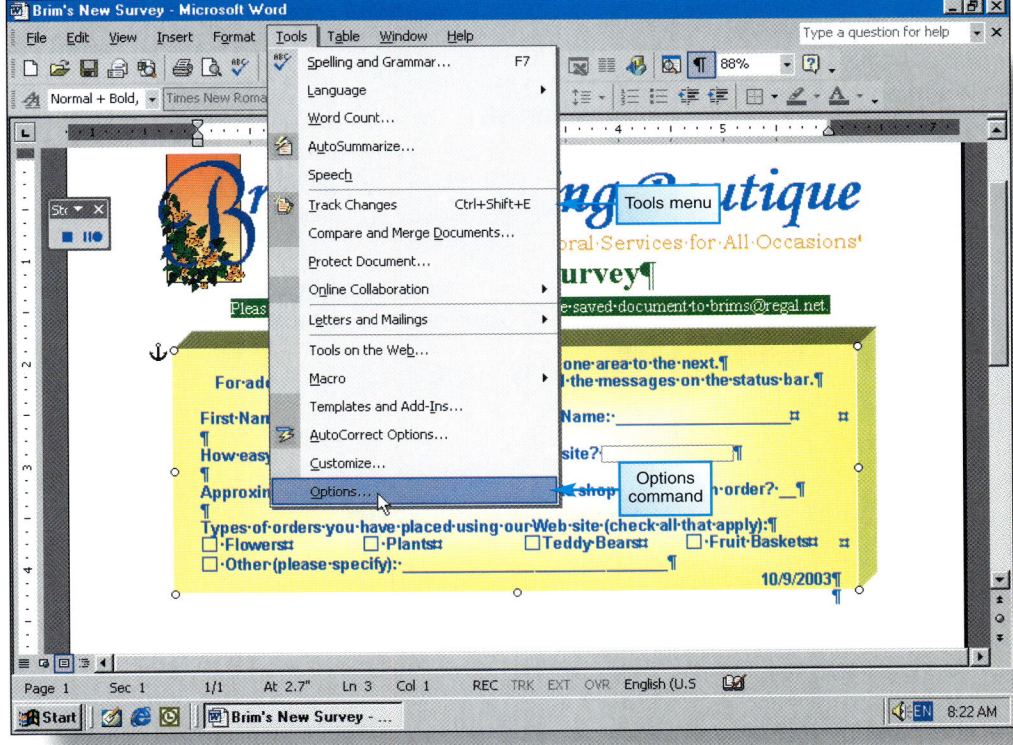

FIGURE 8-22

5 **Click Options. When the Options dialog box displays, if necessary, click the Save tab. Place a check mark in the Save data only for forms check box and then point to the OK button.**

The Options dialog box displays as shown in Figure 8-23.

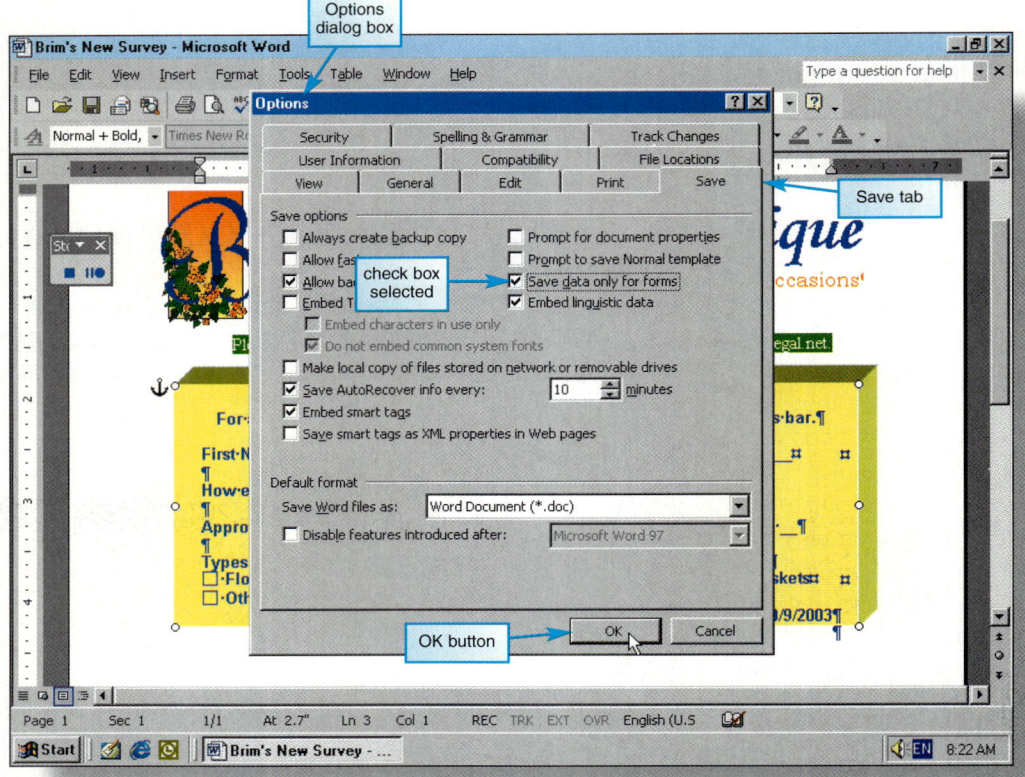

FIGURE 8-23

6 **Click the OK button. Point to the Stop Recording button on the Stop Recording toolbar (Figure 8-24).**

7 **Click the Stop Recording button.**

Word stops recording the keystrokes, closes the Stop Recording toolbar, and dims the REC status indicator on the status bar.

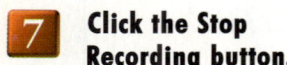
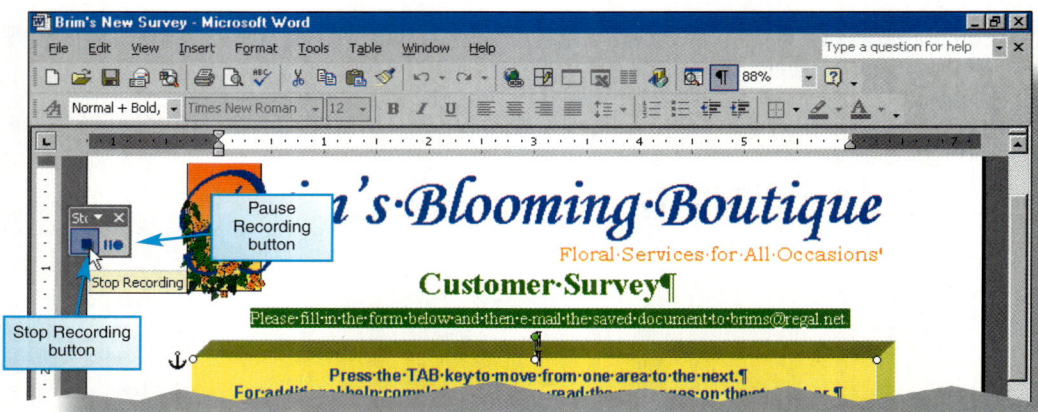

FIGURE 8-24

1. On Tools menu point to Macro, click Record New Macro, enter macro name, click Keyboard button, press shortcut keys, click Assign button, click Close button, record macro, click Stop Recording button on Stop Recording toolbar

2. In Voice Command mode, say "Tools, Macro, Record New Macro"

The menu commands, buttons, and options you clicked while the macro recorder was running are stored in the macro. If you recorded the wrong actions, delete the macro and record it again. You delete a macro by clicking Tools on the menu bar, pointing to Macro on the Tools menu, and then clicking Macros on the Macro submenu. When the Macro dialog box displays, click the name of the macro (FormDataOnly), click the Delete button, and then click the Yes button. Finally, record the macro again.

Using a Macro to Automate a Task • WD 8.27

If, while recording a macro, you want to perform some actions that should not be part of the macro, click the Pause Recording button on the Stop Recording toolbar (Figure 8-24) to suspend the macro recorder. The Pause Recording button changes to a Resume Recording button that you click when you want to continue recording.

In the Record Macro dialog box (Figure 8-19 on WD 8.24), you selected the location to store the macro in the Store macro in box. If you wanted a macro to be available to all documents you create that are based on the normal template, you would select All Documents (Normal.dot) in the Store macro in list. Most macros created with the macro recorder, however, are document specific, and thus are stored in the current template or document.

The next step is to execute, or run, the macro to ensure that it works. Recall that you assigned the shortcut key, ALT+D, to this macro. Perform the following steps to run the macro.

Macro Locations

In the Record Macro dialog box (Figure 8-19 on page WD 8.24), you indicate where Word should save the macro by selecting the appropriate location in the Store macro in list. When you store a macro with a document or a template, it is available only when the document or template is open. When you store a macro in All Documents (Normal.dot), the macro is always available in Word, regardless of the document you have open.

Steps To Run a Macro

1 Click Tools on the menu bar and then click Options. When the Options dialog box displays, if necessary, click the Save tab. Remove the check mark from the Save data only for forms check box and then click the OK button. Press ALT+D.

Word performs the instructions stored in the FormDataOnly macro.

2 To verify that the macro worked properly, display the Options dialog box by clicking Tools on the menu bar and then click Options. When the Options dialog box displays, if necessary, click the Save tab. Point to the OK button.

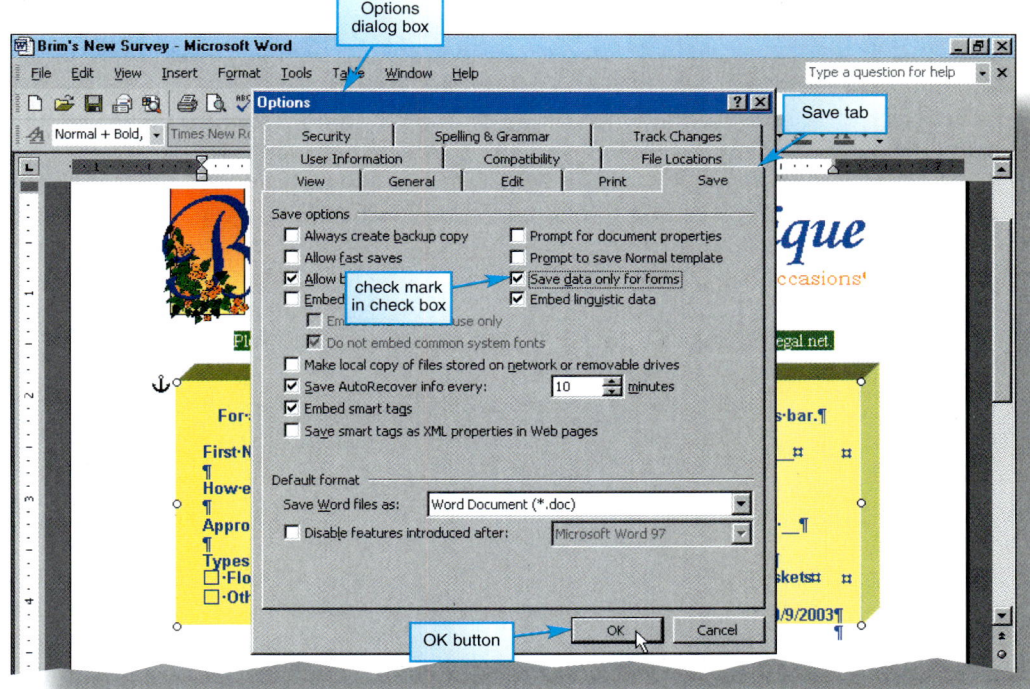

FIGURE 8-25

A check mark displays in the Save data only for forms check box, indicating that the macro executed properly (Figure 8-25).

3 Click the OK button.

1. On Tools menu point to Macro, click Macros, click macro name in Macro name list, click Run button
2. Press ALT+F8, click macro name in Macro name list, click Run button
3. In Voice Command mode, say, "Tools, Macro, [select macro], Run"

Customizing Word

In addition to customizing toolbars and their buttons, you can customize menus using the Customize dialog box. To add a command to a menu, for example, click Commands in the Categories list in the Commands sheet and then drag the desired command to the appropriate menu name.

You should remove the check mark from the Save data only for forms check box so that future saves will save the entire form.

TO UNCHECK THE SAVE DATA ONLY FOR FORMS CHECK BOX

1. Click Tools on the menu bar and then click Options. When the Options dialog box displays, if necessary, click the Save tab.

2. Remove the check mark from the Save data only for forms check box. Click the OK button.

Word removes the check mark from the Save data only for forms check box.

Assigning a Macro to a Toolbar Button

You can customize toolbars by adding buttons, deleting buttons, and changing the function or appearance of buttons. You also can assign a macro to a button. In this project, you want to create a toolbar button for the FormDataOnly macro so that instead of pressing the shortcut keys, you can click the button to place a check mark in the Save data only for forms check box in the Save sheet in the Options dialog box.

You customize a toolbar using the Customize command on the Tools menu. The key to understanding how to customize a toolbar is to recognize that when you have the Customize dialog box open, Word's toolbars and menus are in Edit mode. **Edit mode** allows you to modify the toolbars and menus.

Perform the following steps to assign the FormDataOnly macro to a new button on the Standard toolbar and then change the button image.

 To Customize a Toolbar

1. **Click Tools on the menu bar and then point to Customize (Figure 8-26).**

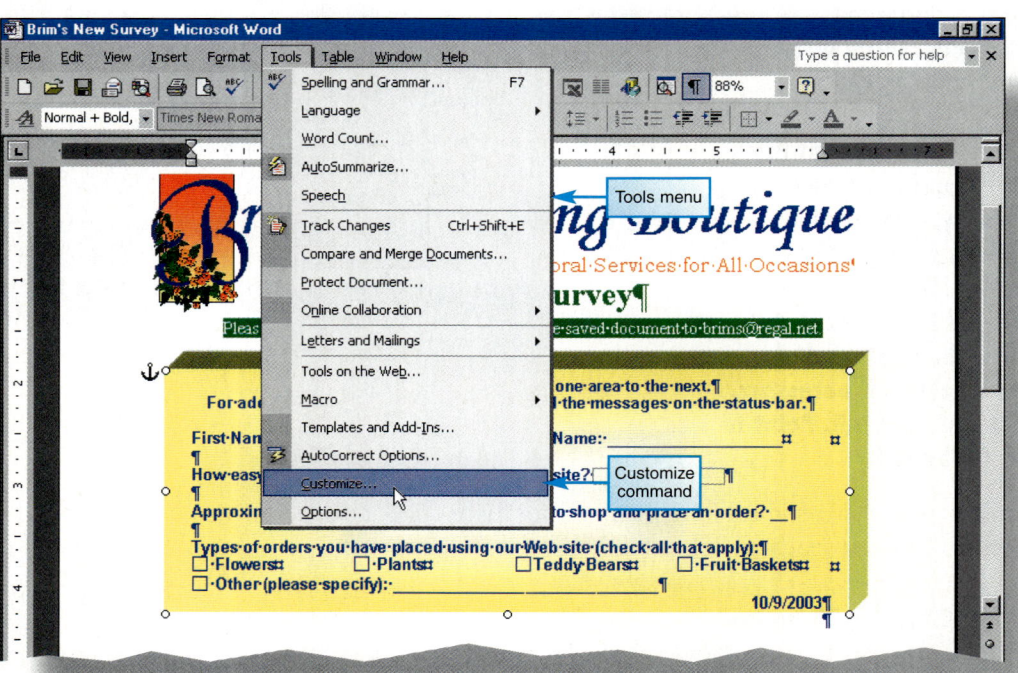

FIGURE 8-26

2 **Click Customize. When the Customize dialog box displays, if necessary, click the Commands tab. Scroll to and then click Macros in the Categories list. Click TemplateProject. NewMacros.FormDataOnly in the Commands list.**

The Customize dialog box displays (Figure 8-27).

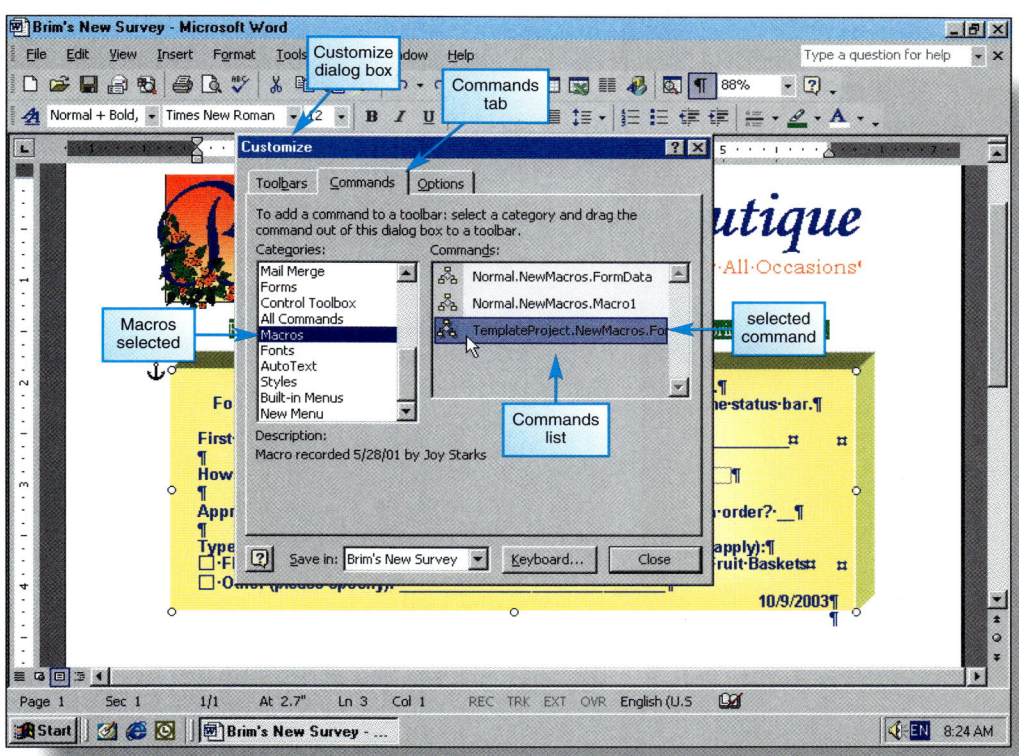

FIGURE 8-27

3 **Drag the selected command in the Commands list to the right of the Microsoft Word Help button on the Standard toolbar.**

A button containing the text, TemplateProject.NewMacros. FormDataOnly, displays next to the Microsoft Word Help button on the Standard toolbar (Figure 8-28). The toolbar may wrap to two lines because the button is so long. A thick border surrounds the new button indicating Word is in Edit mode.

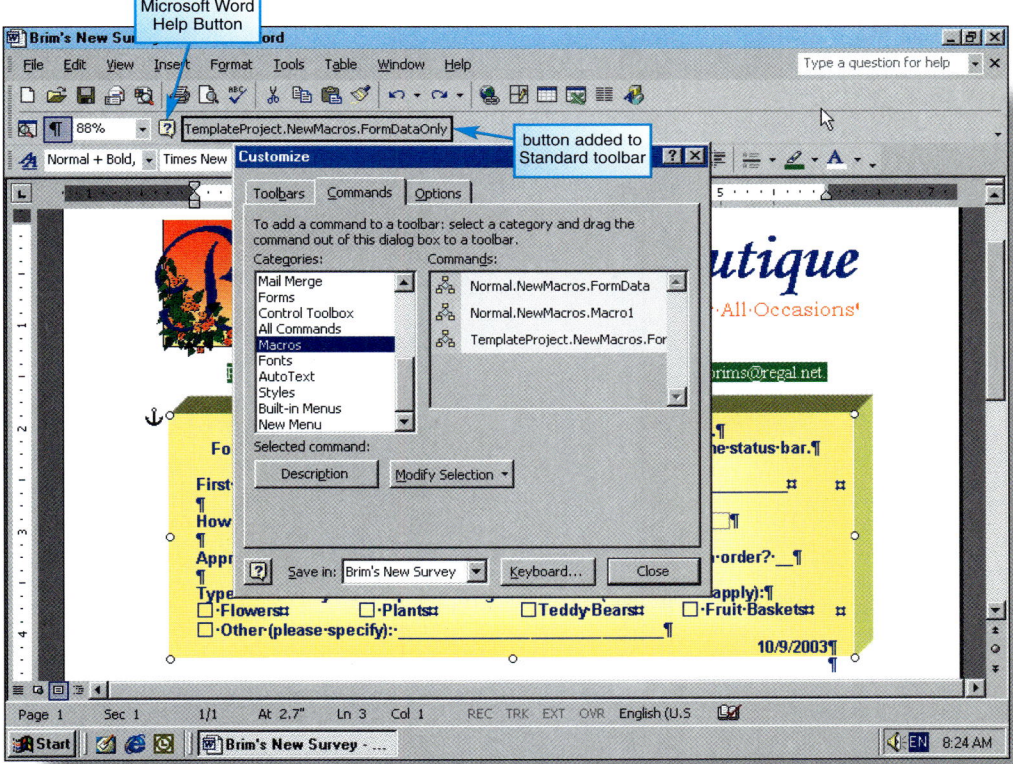

FIGURE 8-28

4 **Right-click the button just added to the Standard toolbar, point to Change Button Image on the shortcut menu, and then point to the smiley face image.**

Word displays a palette of button images from which you can select (Figure 8-29).

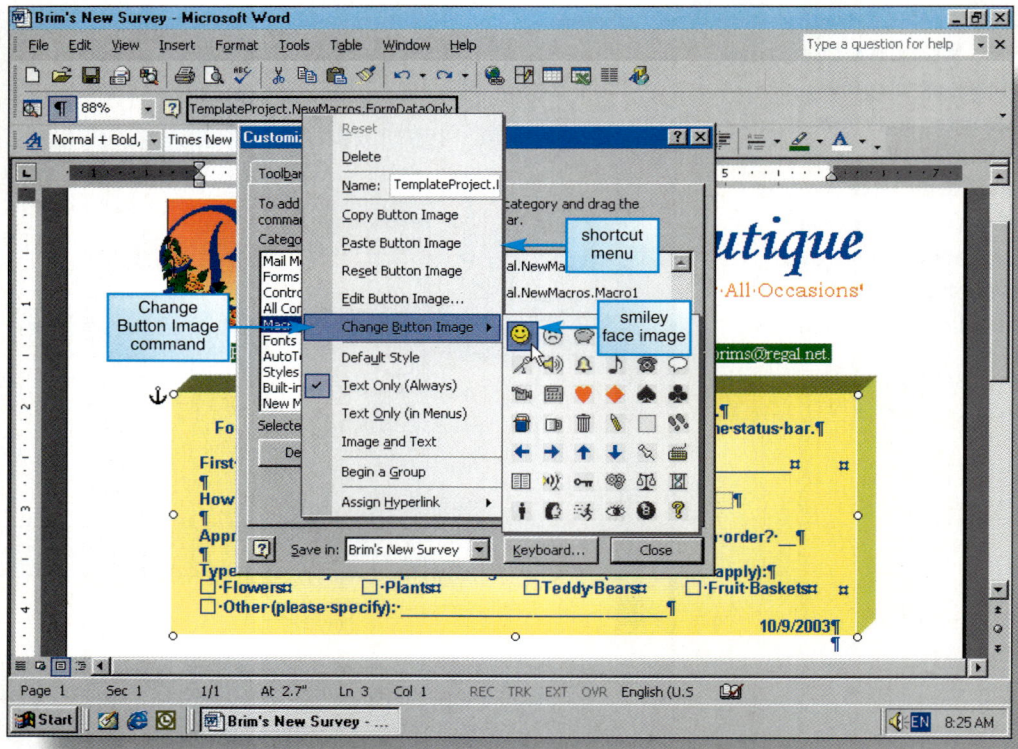

FIGURE 8-29

5 **Click the button with the smiley face image. Right-click the button just added to the Standard toolbar. Point to Text Only (in Menus) on the shortcut menu.**

Word places the smiley face image on the button (Figure 8-30).

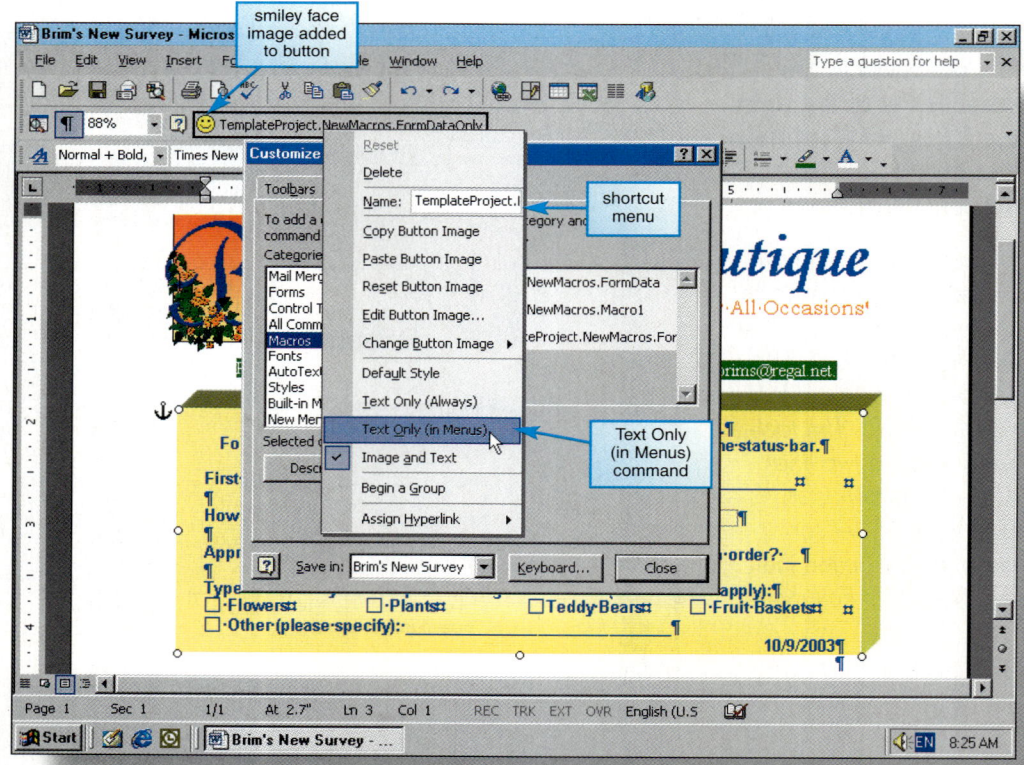

FIGURE 8-30

Using a Macro to Automate a Task • WD 8.31

6 **Click Text Only (in Menus). Point to the Close button in the Customize dialog box.**

The text, TemplateProject.NewMacros.FormDataOnly, no longer displays on the button (Figure 8-31). If you add the macro to a menu at a later time, the text will display in the menu.

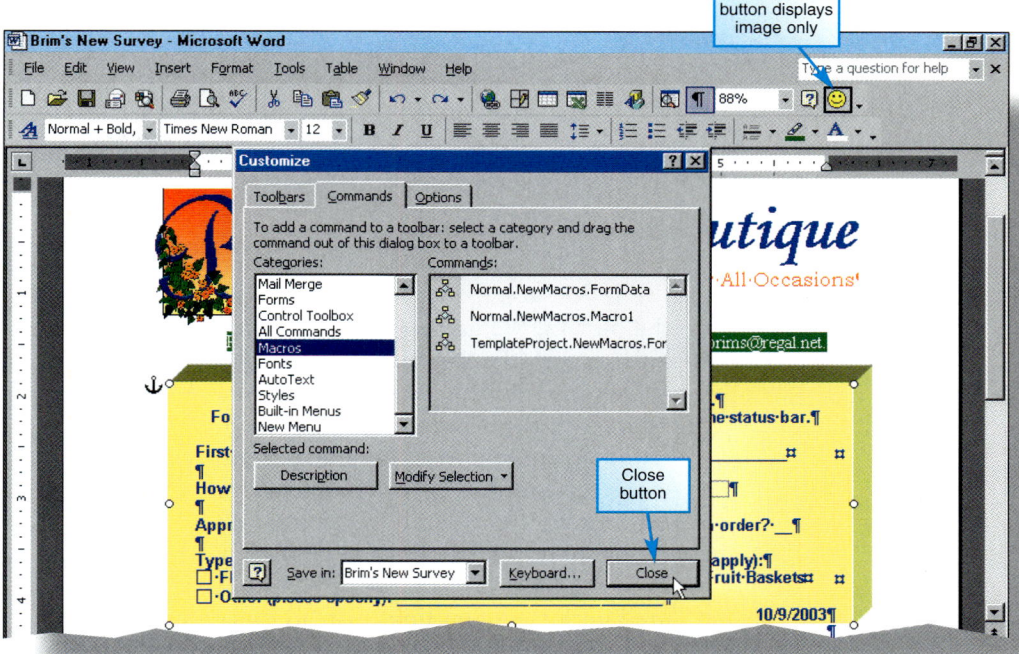

FIGURE 8-31

7 **Click the Close button in the Customize dialog box. Point to the Form Data Only button on the Standard toolbar.**

Word quits Edit mode. The Form Data Only button displays on the Standard toolbar with the ScreenTip, Form Data Only (Figure 8-32).

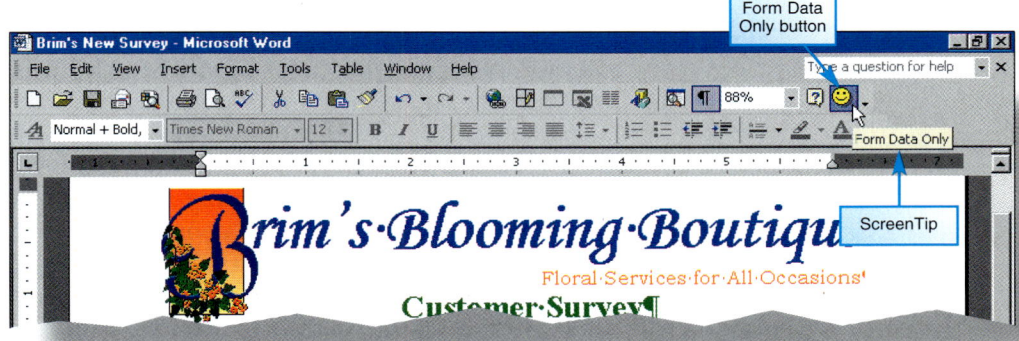

FIGURE 8-32

8 **Click the Form Data Only button on the Standard toolbar.**

Word places a check mark in the Save data only for forms check box in the Save sheet in the Options dialog box.

You can verify that the Form Data Only button works properly by clicking Tools on the menu bar, clicking Options, clicking the Save tab, and then confirming that a check mark displays in the Save data only for forms check box. You do not want the check mark in the check box now. Thus, remove the check mark as described in the steps on the next page.

Other Ways

1. On View menu click Toolbars, click Customize, click Commands tab
2. Right-click toolbar, click Customize on shortcut menu, click Commands tab
3. In Voice Command mode, say "View, Toolbars, Customize"

TO UNCHECK THE SAVE DATA ONLY FOR FORMS CHECK BOX

1 Click Tools on the menu bar and then click Options. When the Options dialog box displays, if necessary, click the Save tab.

2 Remove the check mark from the Save data only for forms check box. Click the OK button.

Word removes the check mark from the Save data only for forms check box.

If you wanted to assign a Web address to a button so that when the user clicks the button, the associated Web page displays on the screen, you would right-click the button with the Customize dialog box displaying as shown in Figure 8-30 on page WD 8.30, point to the Assign Hyperlink command, click Open, enter the Web address in the Assign Hyperlink dialog box, and then click the OK button.

You can add as many buttons as you want to a toolbar. You also can change the image on any button or change an existing button's function. For example, when in Edit mode (the Customize dialog box is active), you can right-click the Save button on the Standard toolbar and assign it a macro or a hyperlink. The next time you click the Save button, Word would execute the macro or start the application associated with the hyperlink, instead of saving a document.

As you add buttons, other buttons on the toolbar will be demoted to the More Buttons list. You also can create new toolbars. To create a new toolbar, click the Toolbars tab in the Customize dialog box and then click the New button.

To remove a button from a toolbar, while in Edit mode, right-click the button and then click Delete on the shortcut menu.

You reset the toolbars to their installation default by clicking the Toolbars tab in the Customize dialog box, selecting the toolbar name in the Toolbars list, and then clicking the Reset button. Each project in this book begins by resetting the toolbars because it is so easy to change the buttons on a toolbar.

You also can customize menus using a procedure similar to the one for customizing a toolbar. For example, to add a command to a menu, click a name in the Categories list in the Customize dialog box (Figure 8-27 on page WD 8.29) and drag the command name in the Commands list to the menu name on the menu bar. Then, when the menu displays, drag the command to the desired location in the menu list of commands. For additional information, see Appendix D.

Recording an Automatic Macro

In the previous section, you created a macro, assigned it a unique name (FormDataOnly), and then created a toolbar button that executed the macro. Word also has five prenamed macros, called **automatic macros**, which execute automatically when a certain event occurs. Table 8-2 lists the name and function of these automatic macros.

> **More About**
>
> **Automatic Macros**
>
> A document can contain only one AutoClose, AutoNew, and AutoOpen macro. The AutoExec and AutoExit macro, however, are not stored with the document; instead, they must be stored in the Normal template. Thus, only one AutoExec and only one AutoExit macro can exist for all Word documents.

Table 8-2	Automatic Macros
MACRO NAME	**RUNS**
AutoClose	When you close a document containing the macro
AutoExec	When you start Word
AutoExit	When you quit Word
AutoNew	When you create a new document based on a template containing the macro
AutoOpen	When you open a document containing the macro

The name you use for an automatic macro depends on when you want certain actions to occur. In this project, when a user creates a new Word document that is based on the Brim's New Survey template, you want the online form to display properly in the Word window. Thus, you will create an AutoNew macro using the macro recorder.

The form displays properly when the zoom is set to page width. Thus, you will record the steps to zoom to page width. Also, you want the entire form to display in the Word window so the user does not have to scroll to position the form. When you display the form in the Word window, the top of the form displays. Thus, you will go to the top of the page by dragging the scroll box to the top of the vertical scroll bar and then click the scroll arrow at the bottom of the vertical scroll bar several times to position the form properly.

Perform the following steps to create an AutoNew macro.

Steps: To Create an Automatic Macro

 Double-click the REC status indicator on the status bar. When the Record Macro dialog box displays, type AutoNew **in the Macro name text box. Click the Store macro in box arrow and then click Documents Based On Brim's New Survey. In the Description text box, type** Specifies how the form initially displays (as a blank form). **Point to the OK button.**

Word displays the Record Macro dialog box (Figure 8-33).

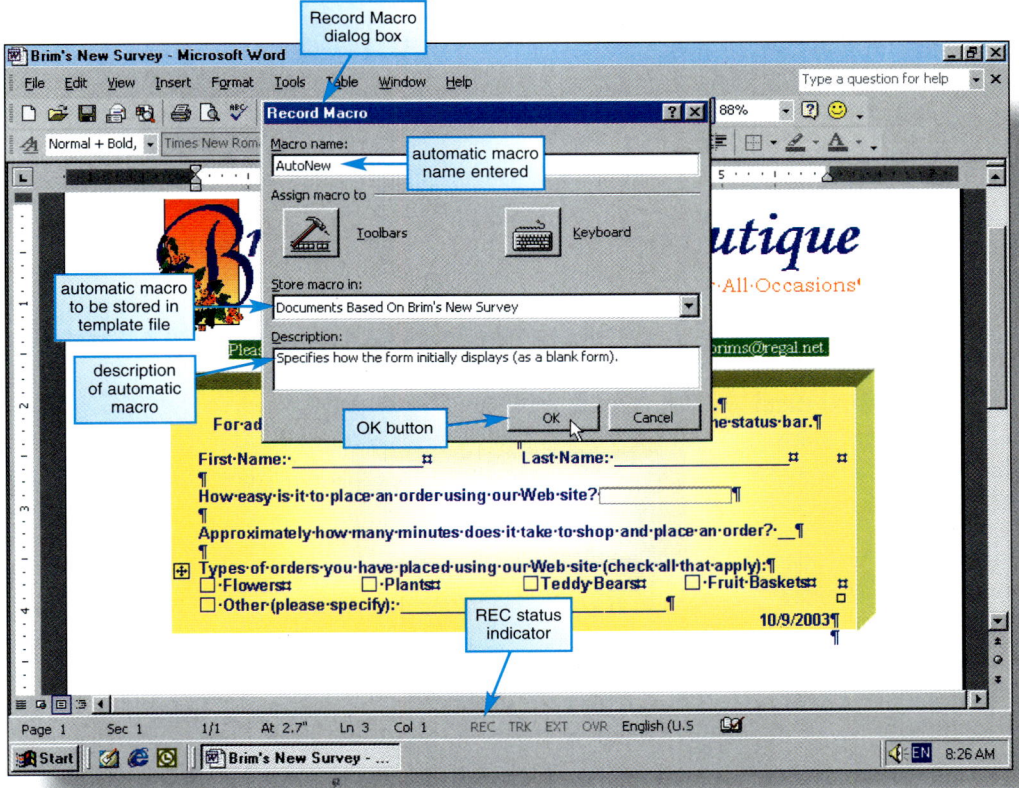

FIGURE 8-33

2 **Click the OK button.**

Word closes the Record Macro dialog box and then displays the Stop Recording toolbar in the document window.

3 **Click the Zoom box arrow and then point to Page Width.**

Recall that when you are recording a macro and the mouse pointer is in a menu or pointing to a toolbar button, the tape icon does not display next to the pointer (Figure 8-34).

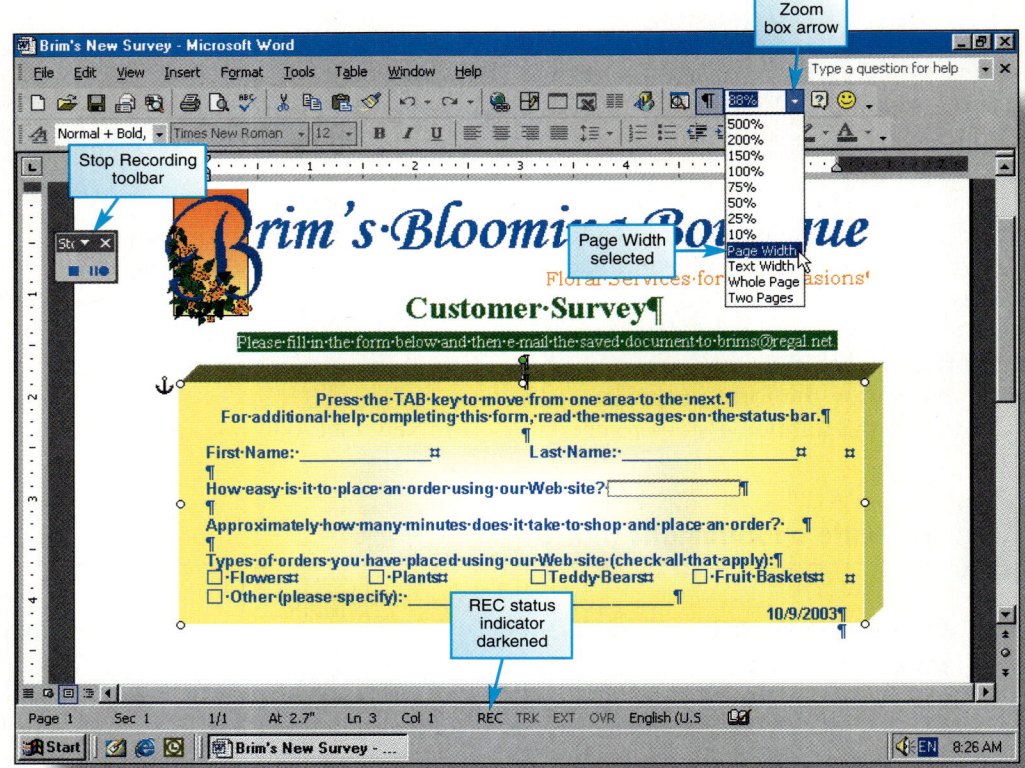

FIGURE 8-34

4 **Click Page Width. Drag the scroll box to the top of the vertical scroll bar. Point to the down scroll arrow on the vertical scroll bar.**

Word changes the zoom percentage and displays the top of the page in the document window (Figure 8-35).

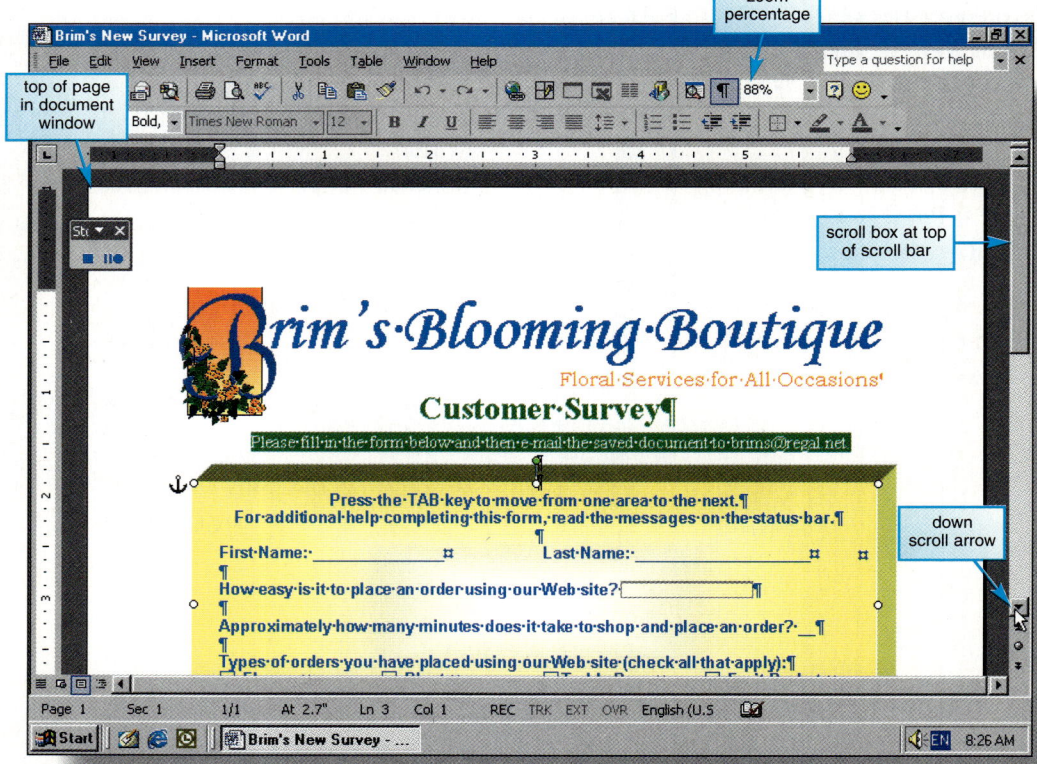

FIGURE 8-35

5 **Click the down scroll arrow on the vertical scroll bar five times. Point to the Stop Recording button on the Stop Recording toolbar.**

The online form displays as shown in Figure 8-36.

6 **Click the Stop Recording button.**

Word stops recording the keystrokes, closes the Stop Recording toolbar, and dims the REC status indicator on the status bar.

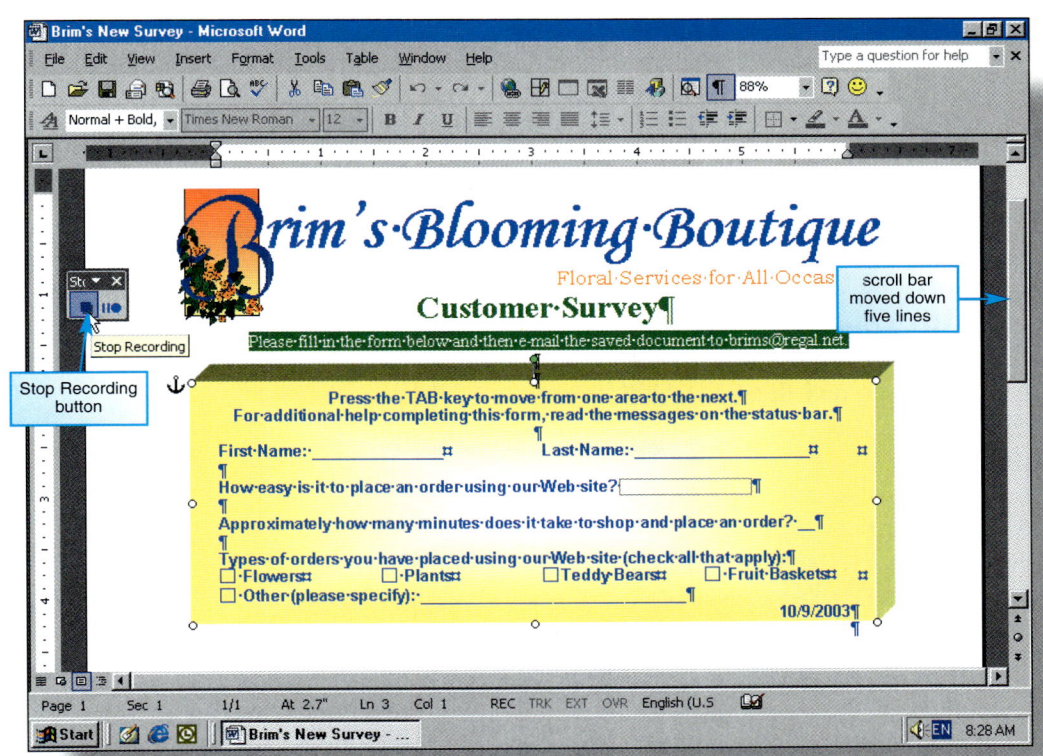

FIGURE 8-36

1. In Voice Command mode, say "Tools, Macro, Record New Macro"

Recording and Running Macros

If Word does not allow you to record or run a macro in a document, the document probably is marked as read-only. To record or run a macro in this document, save it with a new name using the Save As dialog box and then record or run the macro in the newly named document.

To test the automatic macro, you activate the event that causes the macro to execute. For example, the AutoNew macro runs whenever you create a new Word document that is based on the template. As discussed in Project 7, when you save a template to a disk in drive A, a user can create a Word document based on a template through the My Computer window or Windows Explorer.

Perform the steps on the next page to display a new Word document window that is based on the Brim's New Survey template.

Steps: To Test the AutoNew Macro

1 Click the Save button on the Standard toolbar. Click the Minimize button on the Word window title bar. When the Windows desktop displays, right-click the My Computer icon on the Windows desktop and then click Explore on the shortcut menu. When the Explorer window opens, click the Address text box to select it. Type a: and then press the ENTER key.

The Explorer window opens (Figure 8-37). Word still is running.

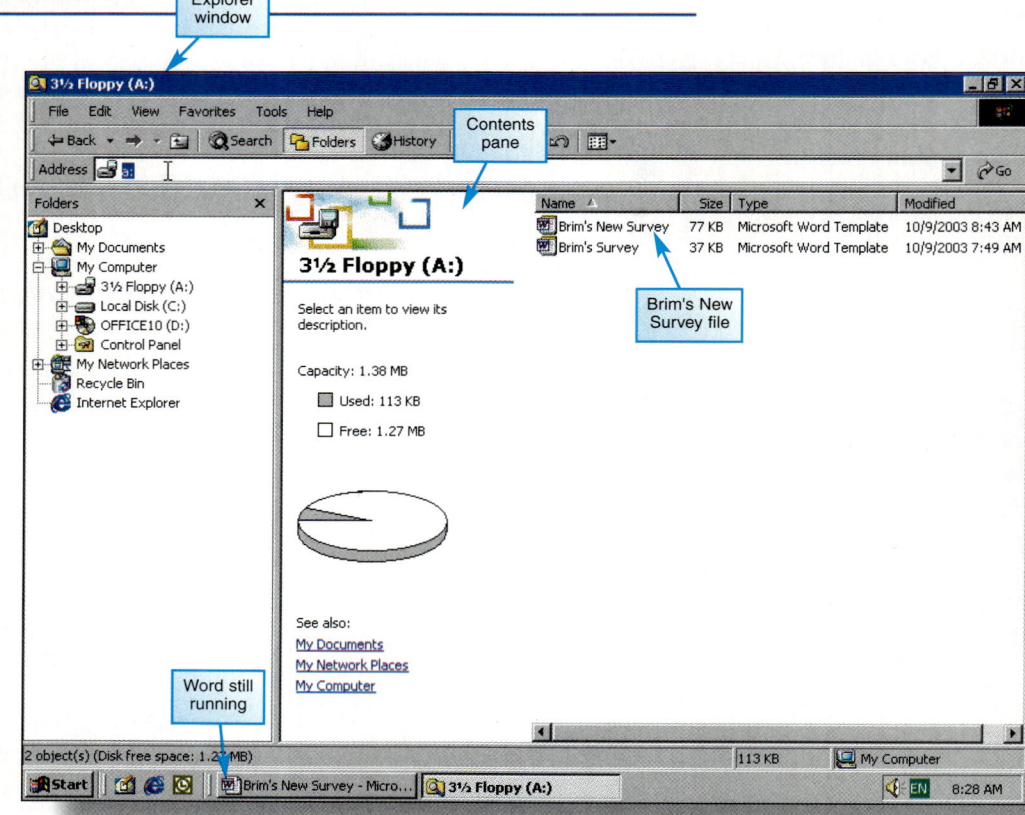

FIGURE 8-37

2 **Double-click the Brim's New Survey icon in the Contents pane.**

Word opens a new document window that is based on the contents of the Brim's New Survey (Figure 8-38). The zoom is set to page width, and the screen scrolls down five lines as instructed by the AutoNew macro.

3 **Click the Close button at the right edge of the Word title bar. If necessary, click the Brim's New Survey - Microsoft Word program button on the taskbar.**

The new document window closes. The Brim's New Survey template displays on the screen.

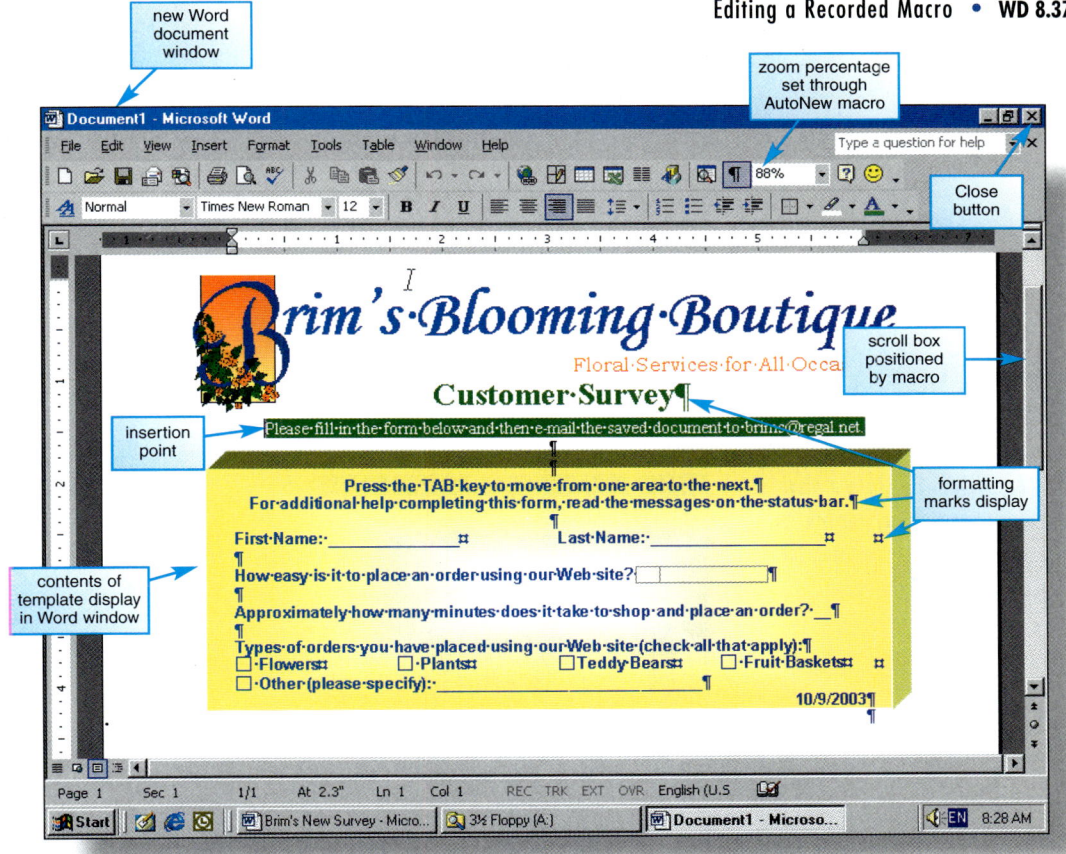

FIGURE 8-38

Notice in Figure 8-38 that the insertion point is at the beginning of the form instructions below the text box. Recall that when you make a form available for users to access, you first protect the form. Protecting a form places the selection in the first form field and allows users to access only the form fields. You did not protect the form yet because you are not finished modifying it. You simply tested the AutoNew macro to be sure it worked properly.

When testing the AutoNew macro, you noticed that the formatting marks displayed on the screen (Figure 8-38). You also noticed that the screen actually should scroll down one more line so it fits better in the Word window. Thus, you want to edit this macro.

Editing a Recorded Macro

The next step in this project is to edit the AutoNew macro. Word uses VBA to store a macro's instructions. Thus, to edit a recorded macro, you use the Visual Basic Editor. All Office applications use the Visual Basic Editor to enter, modify, and view VBA code associated with a document. The following pages explain how to use the Visual Basic Editor to view, enter, and modify VBA code.

Using VBA

For more information about using Visual Basic for Applications, visit the Word 2002 More About Web page (scsite.com/wd2002/more.htm) and then click Using VBA.

Viewing a Macro's VBA Code

As described earlier, a macro consists of VBA code, which the macro recorder automatically creates. You view the VBA code assigned to a macro through the Visual Basic Editor. Perform the following steps to view the VBA code associated with the AutoNew macro in the Customer Survey.

Steps: To View a Macro's VBA Code

1 Click Tools on the menu bar, point to Macro, and then point to Macros (Figure 8-39).

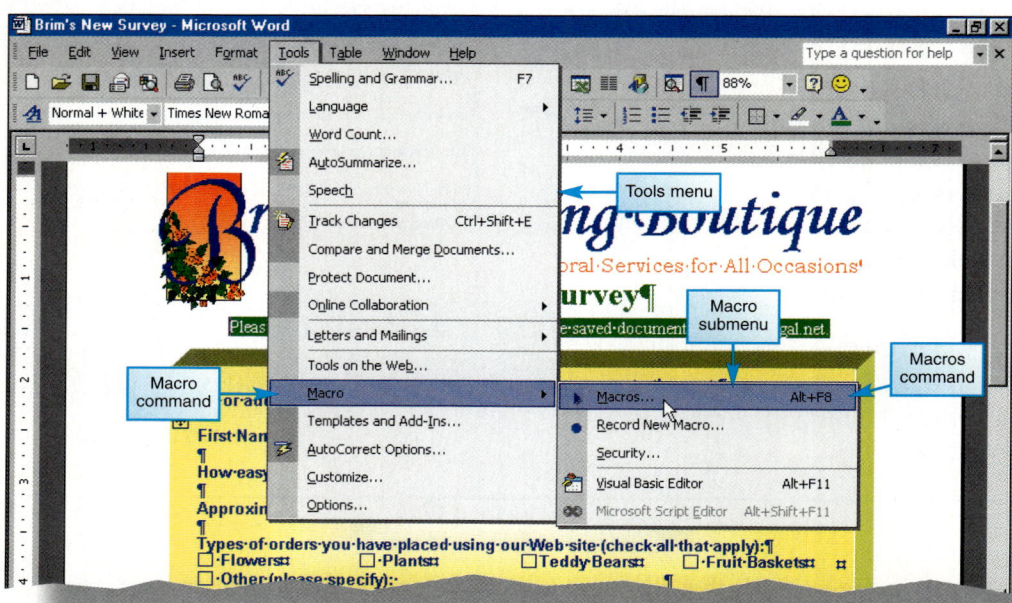

FIGURE 8-39

2 Click Macros. When the Macros dialog box displays, click the Macros in box arrow and then click Brim's New Survey (template). If necessary, click AutoNew in the Macro name list and then point to the Edit button.

The Macros dialog box displays (Figure 8-40).

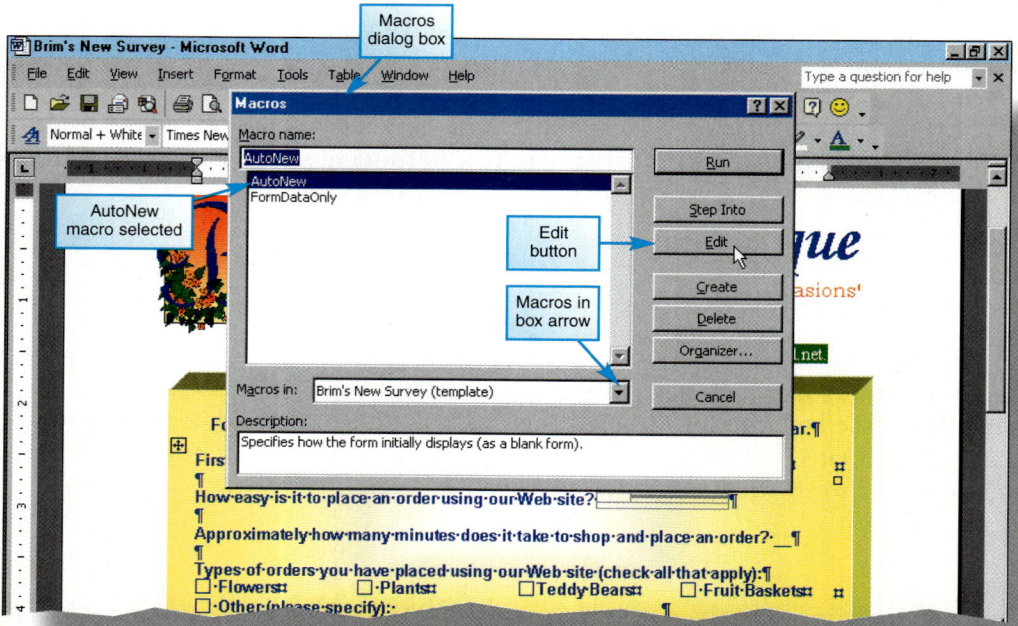

FIGURE 8-40

3 **Click the Edit button. If the Code window does not display, click View on the menu bar and then click Code. If the Project Explorer window displays, click its Close button. If the Properties window displays, click its Close button. If the Code window is not maximized, double-click its title bar.**

The Visual Basic Editor starts and displays the VBA code for the AutoNew macro in the Code window (Figure 8-41). Your screen may display differently depending on previous Visual Basic Editor settings.

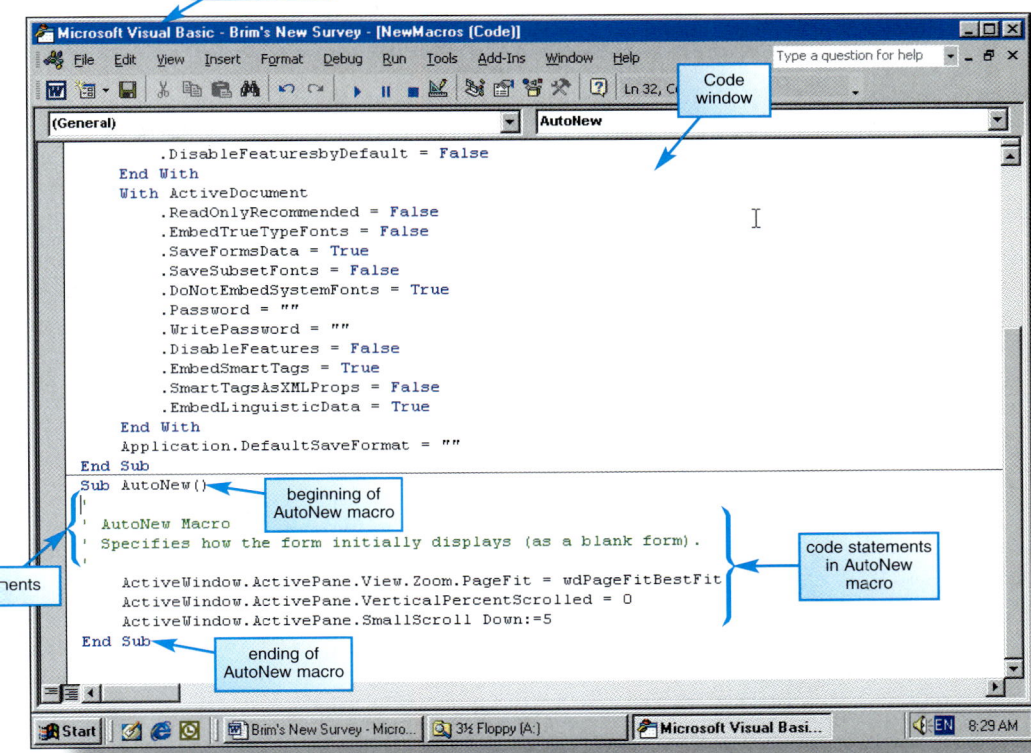

FIGURE 8-41

The named set of instructions associated with a macro is called a **procedure**. It is this set of instructions — beginning with the words Sub AutoNew in Figure 8-41 and continuing sequentially to the line with the words End Sub — that executes when you run the macro.

If you scroll up the Code window, you will see the code associated with the FormDataOnly macro. By scrolling through the two procedures of VBA code, you can see that the macro recorder generated many instructions.

The instructions within a procedure are called **code statements**. Each code statement can contain keywords, variables, constants, and operators. Table 8-3 on the next page explains the function of each of these elements of a code statement.

A procedure begins with a **Sub statement** and ends with an **End Sub statement**. As shown in Figure 8-41, the Sub statement is followed by the name of the procedure, which is the macro name (AutoNew). The parentheses following the macro name in the Sub statement are required. They indicate that arguments can be passed from one procedure to another. Passing arguments is beyond the scope of this project, but the parentheses still are required. The End Sub statement signifies the end of the procedure and returns control to Word. For clarity, code statement lines between the Sub statement and End Sub statement are indented four spaces.

Other Ways

1. On Tools menu point to Macro, click Visual Basic Editor, scroll to desired procedure
2. Press ALT+F11, scroll to desired procedure
3. In Voice Command mode, say "Tools, Macro, Visual Basic Editor"

Table 8-3 Elements of a Code Statement

CODE STATEMENT ELEMENT	DEFINITION	EXAMPLES
Keyword	Recognized by Visual Basic as part of its programming language. Keywords display in blue in the Code window.	Sub End Sub
Variable	An item whose value can be modified during program execution.	ActiveWindow.Active.Pane.SmallScroll TitleBar Text
Constant	An item whose value remains unchanged during program execution.	5
Operator	A symbol that indicates a specific action.	= +

Adding Comments to a Macro

Adding comments before and within a procedure helps you remember the purpose of the macro and its code statements at a later date. **Comments** begin with the word, Rem, or an apostrophe (') and display in green in the Code window. In Figure 8-41 on the previous page, for example, the macro recorder placed four comment lines below the Sub statement. These comments display the name of the macro and its description, as entered in the Record Macro dialog box. Comments have no effect on the execution of a procedure; they simply provide information about the procedure, such as its name and description.

The macro recorder, however, does not add comments to the executable code statements in the procedures. Any code statement that is not a comment is considered an **executable code statement**. The AutoNew procedure in Figure 8-41 contains three executable code statements. The first,

```
ActiveWindow.ActivePane.View.Zoom.PageFit = wdPageFitBestFit,
```

changes the zoom percentage to page width. The macro recorder generated this code statement when you clicked the Zoom box arrow on the Standard toolbar and then clicked Page Width.

The next two code statements scroll the screen downward five lines from the top of the page. The macro recorder generated these code statements when you dragged the scroll box to the top of the vertical scroll bar and then clicked the down scroll arrow on the vertical scroll bar five times.

You would like to enter comments that explain the purpose of executable code statements in the AutoNew procedure. You make changes such as these using the Visual Basic Editor. The Visual Basic Editor is a full-screen editor, which allows you to enter a procedure by typing lines of VBA code as if you were using word processing software. At the end of a line, you press the ENTER key or use the DOWN ARROW key to move to the next line. If you make a mistake in a code statement, you can use the ARROW keys and the DELETE or BACKSPACE keys to correct it. You also can move the insertion point to lines requiring corrections.

Perform the following steps to add comments above the executable code statements in the AutoNew procedure.

More About

VBA Statements

Instead of a long VBA statement on a single line, you can continue a VBA statement on the next line by placing an underscore character (_) at the end of the line to be continued and then pressing the ENTER key. To place multiple VBA statements on the same line, place a colon (:) between each statement.

Steps: To Add Comments to a Procedure

1 Click to the left of the letter A in the first code statement beginning with the word ActiveWindow in the AutoNew procedure and then press the ENTER key to add a blank line above the code statement. Press the UP ARROW key. Type `'Sets screen to page width zoom` and then press the DOWN ARROW key. Make sure you type the apostrophe at the beginning of the comment.

The first comment is entered and displays in green (Figure 8-42).

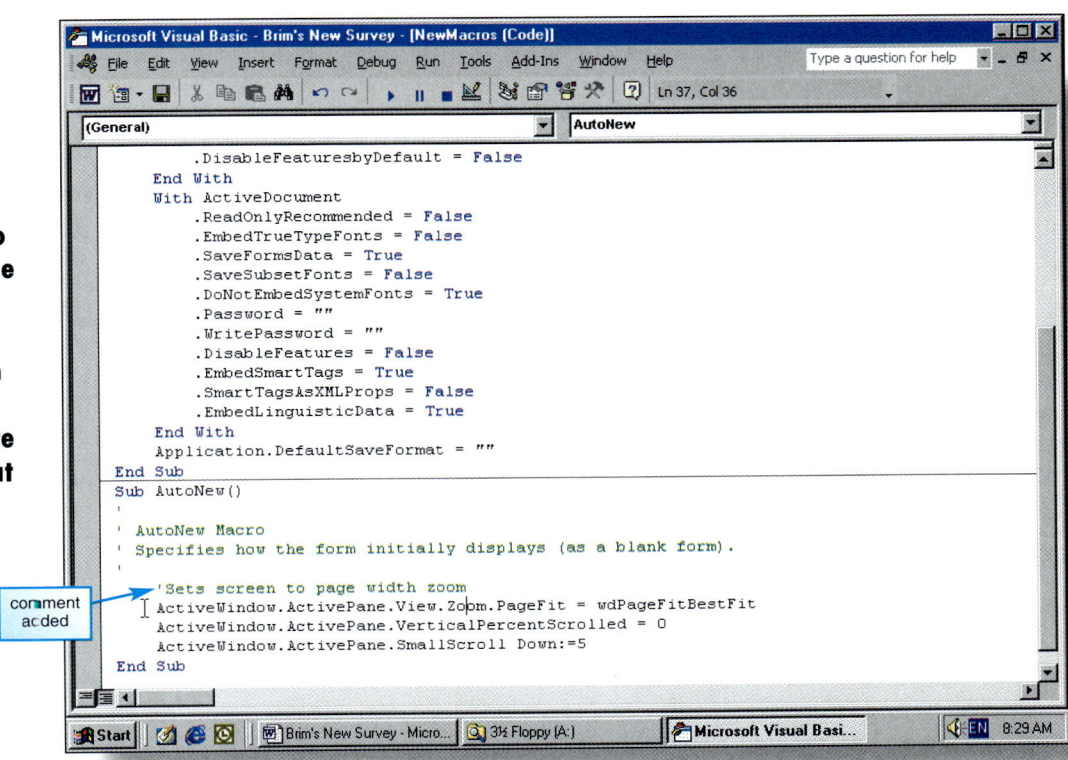

FIGURE 8-42

2 Click to the left of the letter A in the second code statement beginning with the word ActiveWindow and then press the ENTER key to add one blank line above the code statement. Press the UP ARROW key. Type `'Scrolls down from top of page so entire form fits in window` and then press the DOWN ARROW key. Make sure you type the apostrophe at the beginning of the comment.

The second comment is entered and displays in green (Figure 8-43).

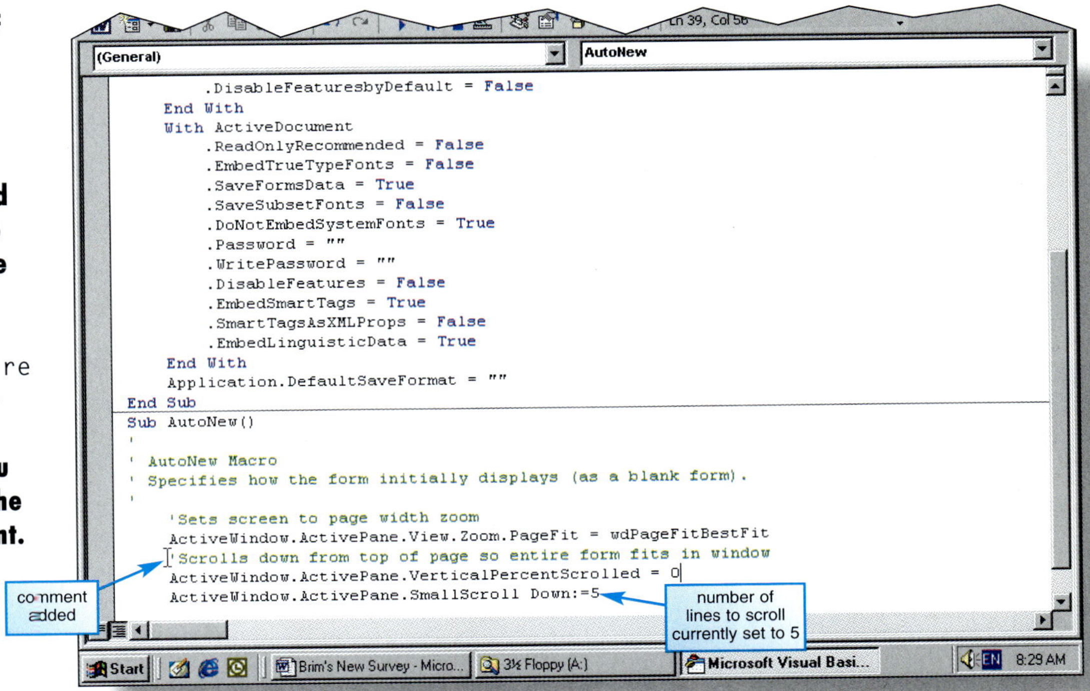

FIGURE 8-43

Modifying Existing Code in a Macro

The next step is to modify existing code in the AutoNew macro. Recall that when you tested the AutoNew macro, you noticed you should scroll down one more line so the boutique name displays closer to the top of the screen (shown in Figure 8-38 on page WD 8.37). Thus, you should change the 5 in the third executable code statement in the AutoNew procedure to a 6, as shown in the following step.

Steps: To Modify Existing Code

1. **Double-click the 5 at the end of the executable code statement above the End Sub statement. Type 6 as the new number of lines to scroll.**

   The code statement is modified (Figure 8-44).

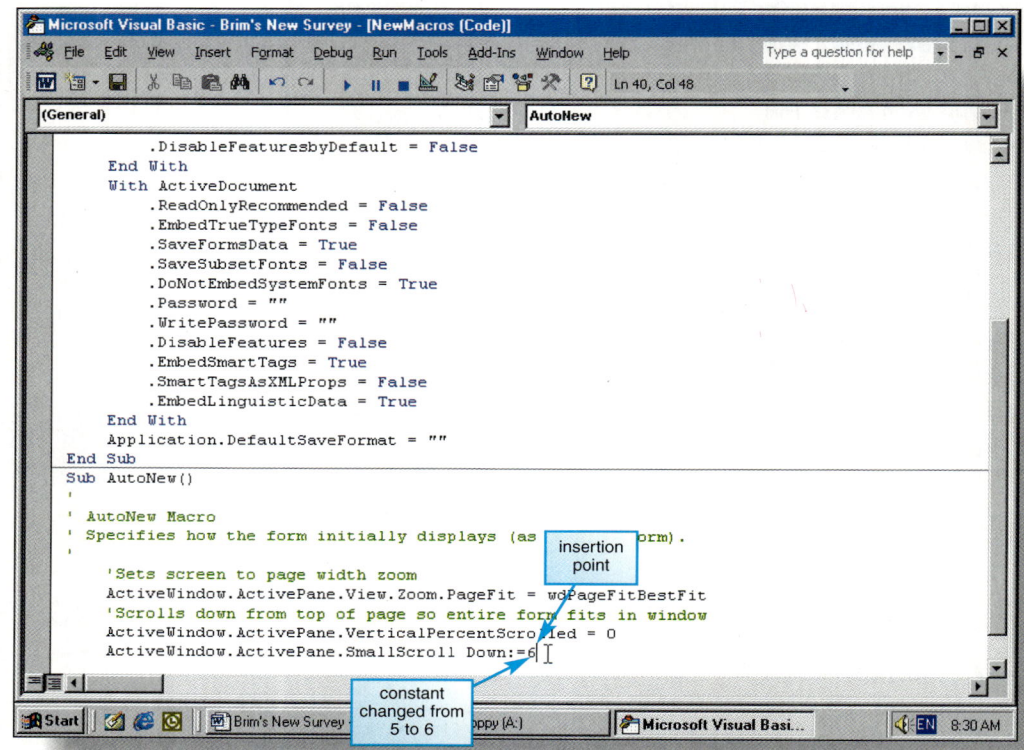

FIGURE 8-44

Table 8-4	Code Statements Added to AutoNew Procedure
ORDER	**CODE STATEMENT**
First new code statement	'Turns off table gridlines
Second new code statement	ActiveDocument.ActiveWindow.View.TableGridlines = False
Third new code statement	'Turns off formatting marks
Fourth new code statement	ActiveDocument.ActiveWindow.View.ShowAll = False

The next step is to add two more executable code statements to the AutoNew macro.

Entering Code Statements

In addition to changing the zoom to page width and scrolling down six lines, you would like to hide formatting marks and gridlines when a user initially displays this form (as a blank form). Thus, you will add two executable code statements, each preceded by a comment. Table 8-4 shows the code statements to be entered.

Perform the following step to add these code statements to the procedure.

Steps: To Add Code Statements to a Procedure

1 With the insertion point following the 6 as shown in Figure 8-44, press the ENTER key. Type the first new code statement shown in Table 8-4. Press the ENTER key. Enter the remaining three code statements shown in Table 8-4. Make sure you type an apostrophe at the beginning of both comment lines. Ignore any shortcut menus that display as you type.

The new code statements are entered into the AutoNew procedure (Figure 8-45).

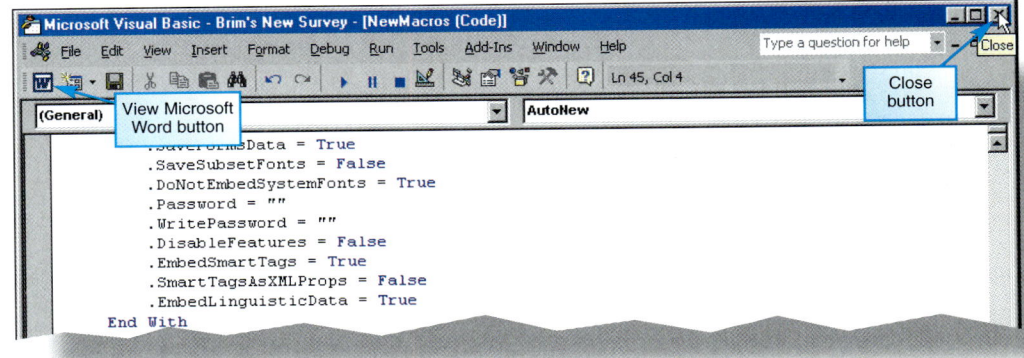

FIGURE 8-45

You could add many more statements to this procedure to ensure the initial screen displays properly. For example, you could close any open toolbars. For purposes of this project, you now are finished modifying the AutoNew macro. Thus, perform the following steps to quit the Visual Basic Editor and return control to Word.

Steps: To Quit the Visual Basic Editor

1 Point to the Close button on the right edge of the Microsoft Visual Basic title bar (Figure 8-46).

2 Click the Close button.

The Visual Basic Editor window closes and control returns to Word.

FIGURE 8-46

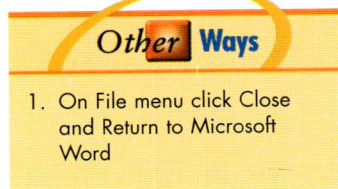

Other Ways

1. On File menu click Close and Return to Microsoft Word

Instead of closing the Visual Basic Editor, you can click the **View Microsoft Word button** on the Visual Basic toolbar (Figure 8-46 on the previous page) to minimize the Visual Basic Editor and return control to Word. If you plan to switch between Word and the Visual Basic Editor, then use the View Microsoft Word button; otherwise use the Close button.

Creating a Macro from Scratch Using VBA

The next macro to be created in this project is the one that displays an error message if the user enters a nonnumeric value in the number of minutes text box (shown in Figure 8-1b on page WD 8.05). The macro is to execute when the user presses the TAB key to move the insertion point out of the number of minutes text box. The following pages explain how to create this macro and attach it to the text form field for the number of minutes.

Modifying Form Field Options

The number of minutes text box is a text form field. To modify a text form field, you double-click the text form field to display the Text Form Field Options dialog box. Two changes are to be made in the dialog box: change the type and enter a bookmark.

In Project 7, you wanted only numbers to display in the text form field. Thus, you changed the text form field's type to Number. Doing so ensured that if a user entered a nonnumeric value in the text form field during data entry, the entry automatically was converted to a zero. In this project, you want to display an error message if the user enters a nonnumeric value. Thus, you must change the text form field's type back to Regular text so that you can display an error message if a user makes an incorrect entry.

You also want to change the bookmark for this text form field because you will be writing VBA code that references this text form field. A **bookmark** is an item in a document that you name for future reference. Currently, the bookmark is Text3, which is not very descriptive. A more meaningful bookmark would be EnteredMinutes. Notice this new bookmark does not have a space between the words, Entered and Minutes. This is because a bookmark cannot contain any spaces; a bookmark also must begin with a letter.

Perform the following steps to change the text form field type and edit the bookmark.

Bookmark Names

Each time you create a form field, Word assigns it a sequential default bookmark name. For example, the first text form field has a bookmark name of Text1, the second text form field has a bookmark name of Text2, the third text form field has a bookmark name of Text3, and so on.

Steps: To Change Options for a Text Form Field

1 Double-click the text form field for number of minutes. When the Text Form Field Options dialog box displays, point to the Type box arrow.

Word displays the Text Form Field Options dialog box (Figure 8-47).

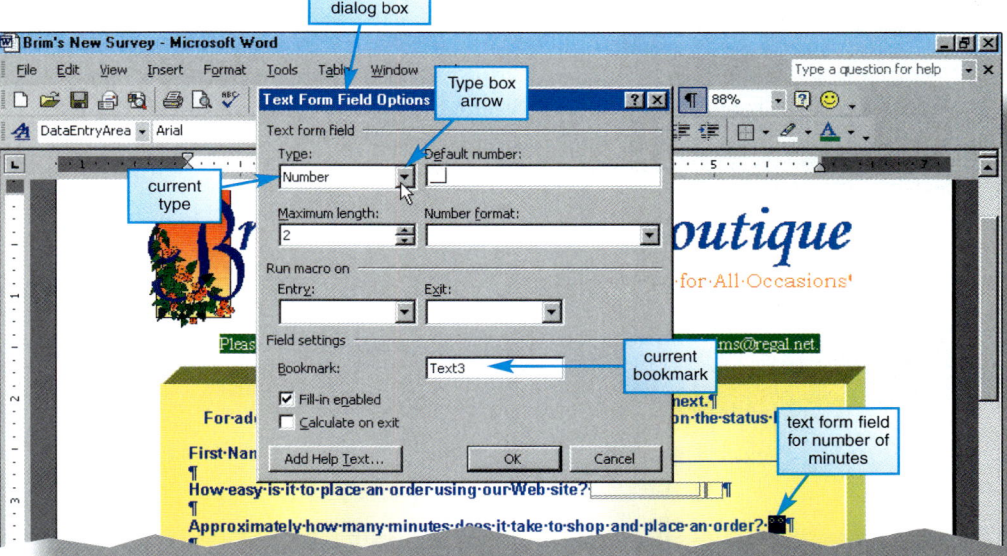

FIGURE 8-47

2 Click the Type box arrow and then click Regular text. Double-click the text in the Bookmark text box and then type EnteredMinutes as the new bookmark. Point to the OK button.

The form field options display as shown in Figure 8-48.

3 Click the OK button.

Word changes the form field options as specified in the Text Form Field Options dialog box.

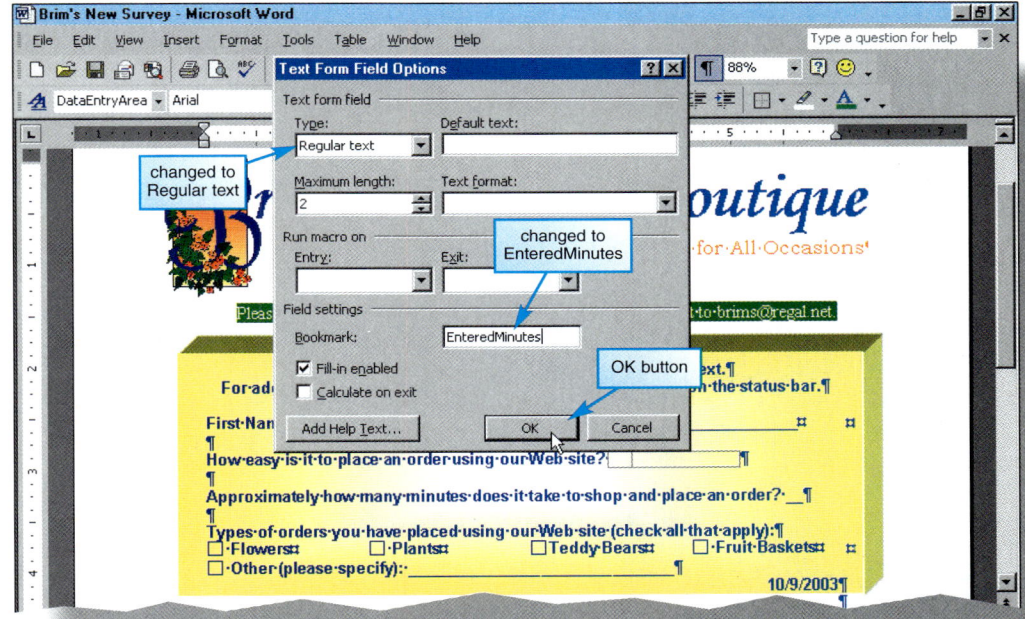

FIGURE 8-48

The next step is to change the bookmark for the drop-down form field for the ease of use from Dropdown3 to a more meaningful name, because this form field also will be referenced in the VBA code. Perform the steps on the next page to change the bookmark for the drop-down form field.

1. Click Form Field Options button on Forms toolbar
2. Right-click form field, click Properties on shortcut menu
3. With Forms toolbar displaying, in Voice Command mode, say "Form Field Options" or say "Properties"

TO CHANGE A BOOKMARK FOR A DROP-DOWN FORM FIELD

1 Double-click the drop-down form field for ease of use.

2 When the Drop-Down Form Field Options dialog box displays, double-click the text in the Bookmark text box and then type `EaseOfUse` as the new bookmark. Point to the OK button (Figure 8-49).

3 Click the OK button.

Word changes the form field options as specified in the Drop-Down Form Field Options dialog box.

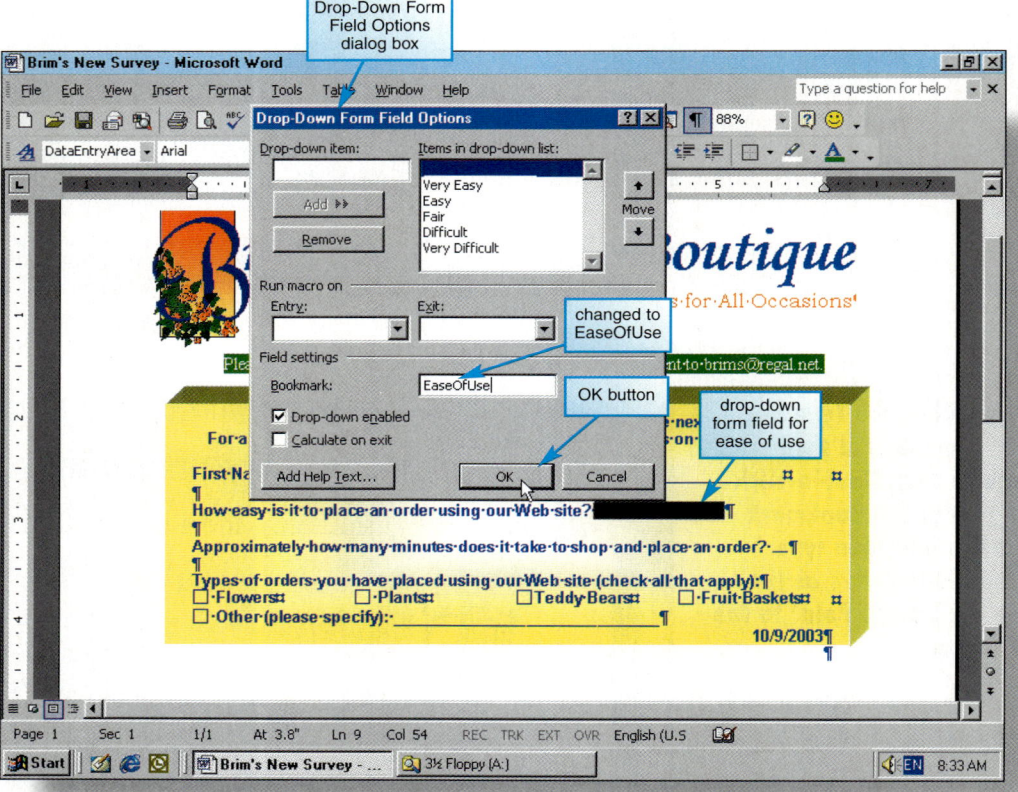

FIGURE 8-49

The next step is to insert a new procedure for the macro using the Visual Basic Editor.

Inserting a Procedure for the Macro

For the previous two macros, you used the macro recorder to create the macros, which generated corresponding VBA code from your actions. For this macro, you cannot record the displaying of the error message, because an error message for this text form field does not exist. Thus, you must write the VBA code for this macro using the Visual Basic Editor. To do this, you insert a procedure.

Perform the following steps to insert a new empty procedure named NumberOfMinutes.

Steps: To Insert a Visual Basic Procedure

1 Press ALT+F11 to open the Visual Basic Editor in a new window. If the Project Explorer displays, click its Close button. If the Properties window displays, click its Close button. If the Code window does not display, click View on the menu bar and then click Code. If necessary, maximize the Code window. Click the Insert UserForm button arrow and then point to Procedure.

The Visual Basic Editor displays as shown in Figure 8-50.

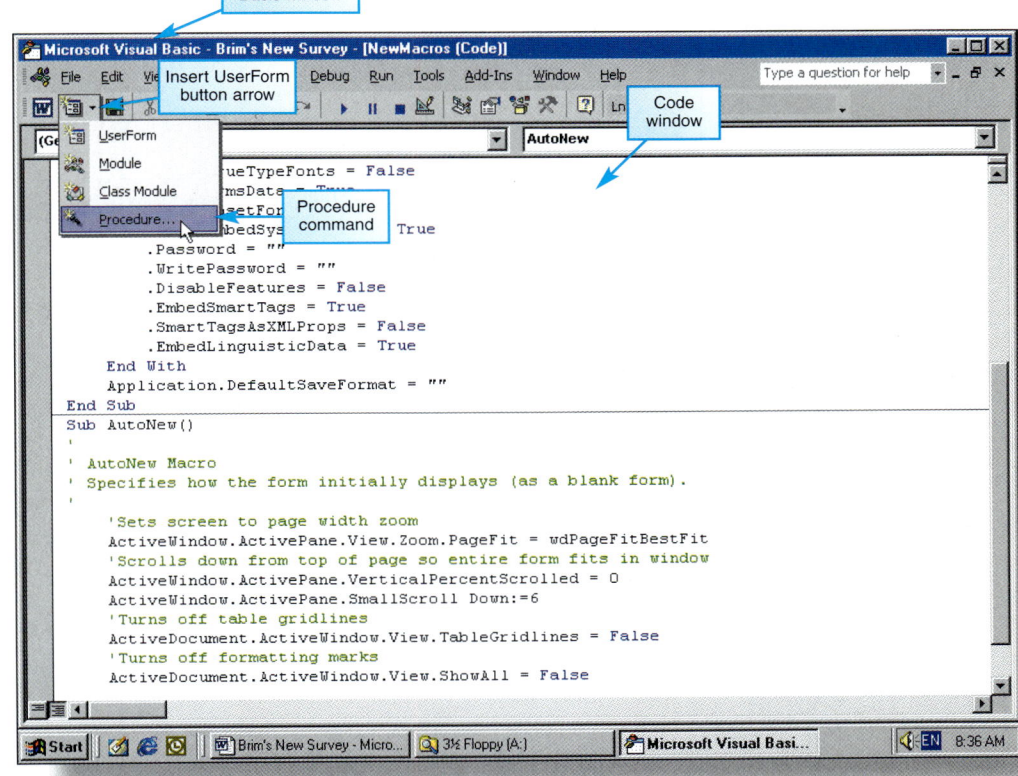

FIGURE 8-50

2 Click Procedure. When Word displays the Add Procedure dialog box, type NumberOfMinutes in the Name text box and then point to the OK button.

The Add Procedure dialog box displays (Figure 8-51).

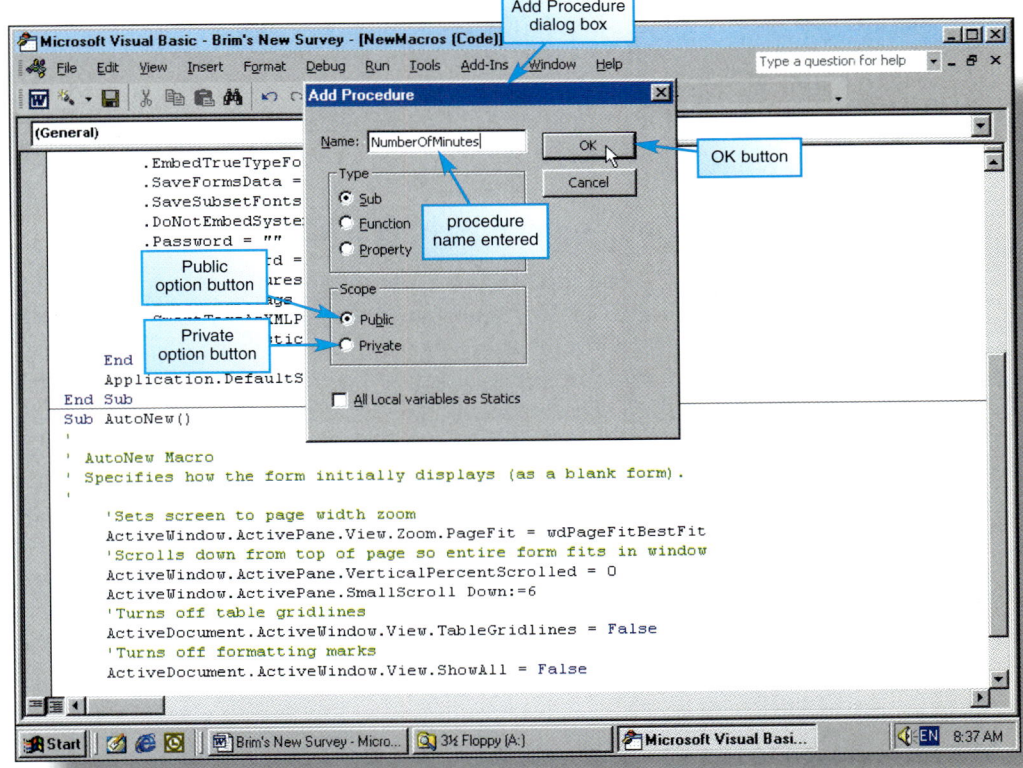

FIGURE 8-51

WD 8.48 • Project 8 • Working with Macros and Visual Basic for Applications (VBA)

| 3 | **Click the OK button.** |

A new procedure called NumberOfMinutes displays in the Code window (Figure 8-52).

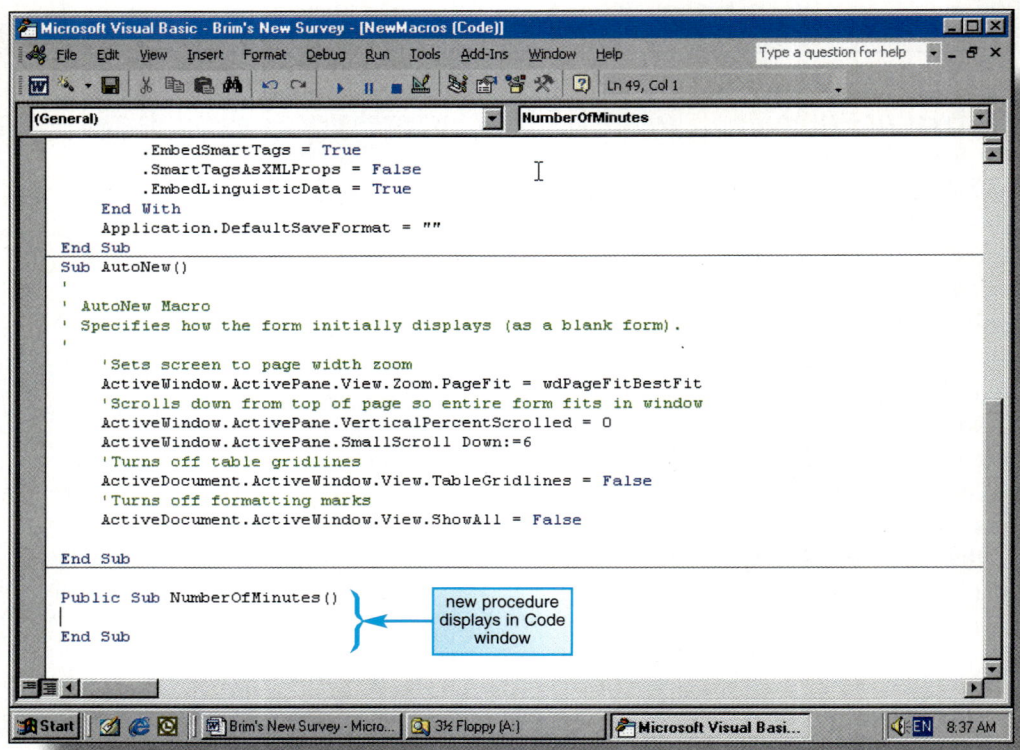

FIGURE 8-52

1. On Insert menu click Procedure, enter procedure name, click OK button
2. In Voice Command mode, say "Insert, Procedure"

Notice in Figure 8-52 that Sub and End Sub statements automatically are inserted into the procedure. The Sub statement, however, begins with the keyword Public, which means that this procedure can be executed from other documents or programs. Private, by contrast, means that the procedure can be executed only from this document. If you wanted a procedure to be private, you would click Private in the Scope area in the Add Procedure dialog box (Figure 8-51 on the previous page).

Planning and Writing a VBA Procedure

The next step is to write and then enter the code statements for the newly created NumberOfMinutes procedure. Before you write the statements, you should plan the procedure; that is, determine what tasks the procedure is to accomplish and the order in which the tasks should be executed. Planning the procedure is an extremely important activity because the order of statements determines the sequence of execution. If the order of statements is incorrect, the procedure will not execute properly.

Once you have planned the procedure thoroughly, the next step is to write the VBA code statements on paper similar to that shown in Table 8-5. Then, before entering the procedure, test it by putting yourself in the position of Word and stepping through the instructions one at a time. As you step through the procedure, think about how it affects the Word document. Testing a procedure before entering it is called **desk checking** and is an extremely important part of the development process.

Table 8-5 Code Statements for NumberOfMinutes Procedure

LINE	VBA CODE STATEMENT
1	`Public Sub NumberOfMinutes()`
2	`'`
3	`' NumberOfMinutes Macro`
4	`' Displays error message if entered number of minutes is not numeric.`
5	`'`
6	`    'Test if entry in EnteredMinutes text form field is numeric`
7	`    If IsNumeric(ActiveDocument.FormFields("EnteredMinutes").Result) = False Then`
8	`        'Display error message`
9	`        MsgBox "Please enter minutes in numbers", vbOKOnly + vbCritical`
10	`        'Redisplay underscores in text form field`
11	`        ActiveDocument.FormFields("EnteredMinutes").Result = "___"`
12	`        'Reposition selection in text form field`
13	`        ActiveDocument.FormFields("EaseOfUse").Select`
14	`        'SendKeys "{TAB}"`
15	`    End If`
16	`End Sub`

In the code statements shown in Table 8-5, lines 2, 3, 4, 5, 6, 8, 10, 12, and 14 are comments. Lines 1 and 16 contain the Sub and End Sub statements that were inserted automatically when you created the procedure. Line 7 is the first executable code statement. It is called an If...Then statement because it executes the line(s) of code up to the End If statement if the result of a condition is true. The condition in line 7 is IsNumeric(ActiveDocument.FormFields("EnteredMinutes").Result) = False. In nonprogramming terms, this condition is testing whether the user entered a number in the EnteredMinutes form field. (Recall that earlier in this project, you changed the bookmark for this form field to EnteredMinutes.) If not, then the statements up to the End If statement will be executed. If the user did enter a number, then the statements up to the End If statement are not executed and control returns to Word.

If the user entered a nonnumeric value in the EnteredMinutes form field, the next executable code statement is in line 9, which uses the MsgBox keyword to display a message box on the screen. The text inside the quotation marks displays inside the message box; vbOKOnly places an OK button in the message box, and vbCritical places an icon of an X in the dialog box. Table 8-6 lists the types of icons that can display in a message box.

After a user reads the message in the message box and clicks the OK button, the next executable code statement is in line 11, which replaces the user's invalid entry with underscore characters. Then, line 13 positions the selection in the EaseOfUse drop-down form field. Some later versions of Word may need line 14, which presses the TAB key so that the selection is positioned in the EnteredMinutes text form field — ready for the user to make another entry in the number of minutes text box. Currently the line is commented; that is, it begins with an apostrophe so VBA ignores the command. Later in the project, when you execute the macro, if the selection does not display in the number of minutes text form field, remove the apostrophe.

Having desk checked the code statements on paper, you now are ready to enter them into the Visual Basic Editor. Perform the steps on the next page to enter the code statements into the NumberOfMinutes procedure.

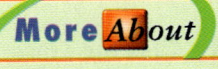

More About

InputBox

A MsgBox displays a message and one or more buttons that the user can click. If you would like the user to enter information that you can use in the VBA procedure, you should display an InputBox. An InputBox displays a message, a text box, and one or more buttons that the user can click. If the user clicks the OK button, the entered text is saved for use later in the procedure.

Table 8-6 Types of Icons for a Message Box

ICON	VISUAL BASIC CONSTANT
Letter X	vbCritical
Question mark	vbQuestion
Exclamation point	vbExclamation
Information symbol	vbInformation

Steps: To Enter the NumberOfMinutes Procedure

1 With the insertion point on the blank line between the Sub and End Sub statements in the Code window, type the code statements shown in lines 2 through 15 in Table 8-5 on the previous page. Make sure you enter an apostrophe at the beginning of each comment line. For clarity, indent code statements as shown in Table 8-5.

The NumberOfMinutes procedure is entered (Figure 8-53).

2 Verify your code statements by comparing them to Figure 8-53.

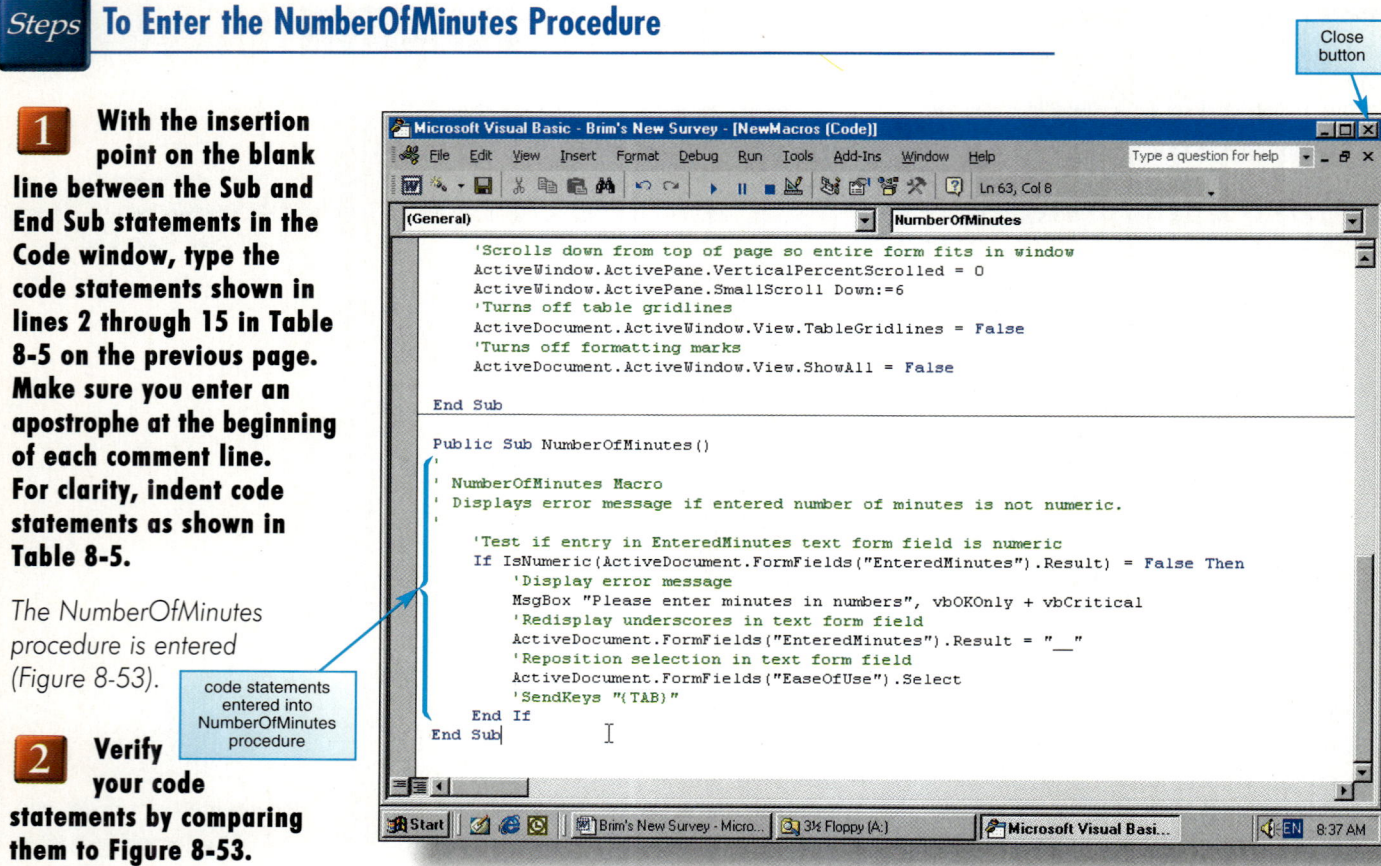

code statements entered into NumberOfMinutes procedure

FIGURE 8-53

3 Click the Close button on the right edge of the Microsoft Visual Basic title bar to return to the template.

The Microsoft Visual Basic window closes and control returns to Word.

The next step is to attach this procedure for the macro to the text form field for the number of minutes.

Running a Macro When a User Exits a Form Field

The NumberOfMinutes macro that you just created in the Visual Basic Editor should execute whenever a user presses the TAB key to move the insertion point out of the number of minutes text form field. That is, pressing the TAB key out of the number of minutes text form field is the event that is to trigger execution of the procedure. With respect to form fields, Word allows you to execute a macro under these two circumstances: (1) when the user enters a form field, and (2) when the user exits the form field. You specify when the macro should run through the Text Form Field Options dialog box. Perform the following steps to instruct Word to execute the NumberOfMinutes macro when a user exits the text form field for the number of minutes.

Steps To Run a Macro When a User Exits a Form Field

 Double-click the text form field for the number of minutes. When the Text Form Field Options dialog box displays, click the Exit box arrow, and then click NumberOfMinutes. Point to the OK button.

Word displays the Text Form Field Options dialog box (Figure 8-54). The selected macro name displays in the Exit box.

 Click the OK button.

The form field options are set as specified in the Text Form Field Options dialog box.

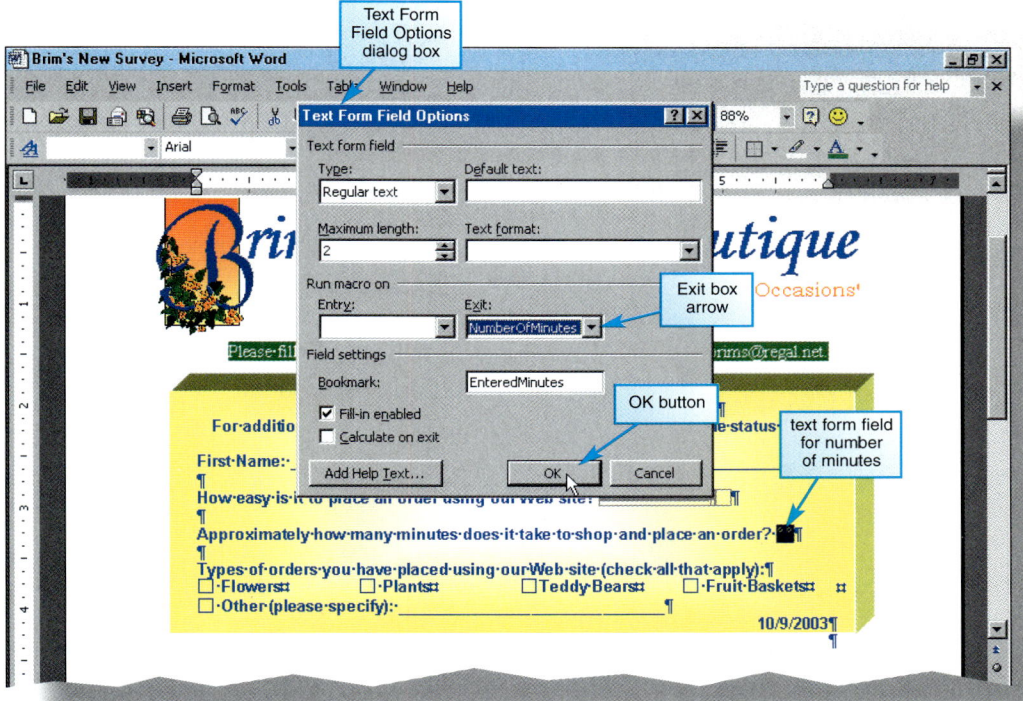

FIGURE 8-54

When you click the Entry or Exit box arrow in the Run macro on area in the Text Form Field Options dialog box, Word displays all available macros. You can select any one macro to run when the user enters or exits each form field in the form.

The NumberOfMinutes macro is complete. You will test this macro at the end of this project, after you create the next VBA procedure.

Adding an ActiveX Control to a Form

In addition to the form fields available on the Forms toolbar, you can insert an ActiveX control on a Word form. An **ActiveX control** is an object, such as a button or check box, which can be included in a form to be published on the World Wide Web. The major difference between a form field and an ActiveX control is that form fields require the use of Word, whereas ActiveX controls do not. Thus, if you intend to create a Web page form, you should place ActiveX controls on the form instead of form fields.

ActiveX controls have the appearance and functionality of Windows controls. For example, the check box ActiveX control displays like any check box in any Windows dialog box. A check box form field, by contrast, has an appearance unique to Word. That is, it displays an X (instead of a check mark). Users that are familiar with Windows applications will find it easier to work with ActiveX controls than working with form fields. With form fields, a user has to press the TAB key to move the insertion point from one form field to another. With an ActiveX control, the user can click in the form field or press the TAB key to move to it.

ActiveX

For more information about ActiveX, visit the Word More About Web page (scsite.com/wd2002/more.htm) and then click ActiveX.

Adding an ActiveX control to a form involves four major activities: insert the ActiveX control, set properties of the ActiveX control, format the ActiveX control, and write the macro for the ActiveX control using VBA. Word refers to the time in which you perform these four activities as **design mode**. When you run the form (fill it in) as a user does, by contrast, you are in **run mode**. The following pages explain how to add an ActiveX control to an online form.

Inserting an ActiveX Control

For this form, you would like to insert a command button that users click when they are finished filling in the form. When they click the button, three actions should occur:

1. If the user entered text in the Other text box, then Word places an X in the Other check box (in case the user forgot to place an X in the check box).
2. Word displays the Save As dialog box so the user can assign a file name to the filled-in form.
3. Word displays a thank-you message box on the screen.

To insert an ActiveX control, such as a command button, you use the Control Toolbox toolbar. Perform the following steps to insert an ActiveX control command button on the online form.

Steps: To Insert an ActiveX Control

1 If the Control Toolbox toolbar does not display on the screen already, click View on the menu bar, point to Toolbars, and then click Control Toolbox. Click the paragraph mark at the end of the form and then press the ENTER key. Center the paragraph mark. Position the insertion point on the centered paragraph mark below the data entry area. Point to the Command Button button on the Control Toolbox toolbar (Figure 8-55).

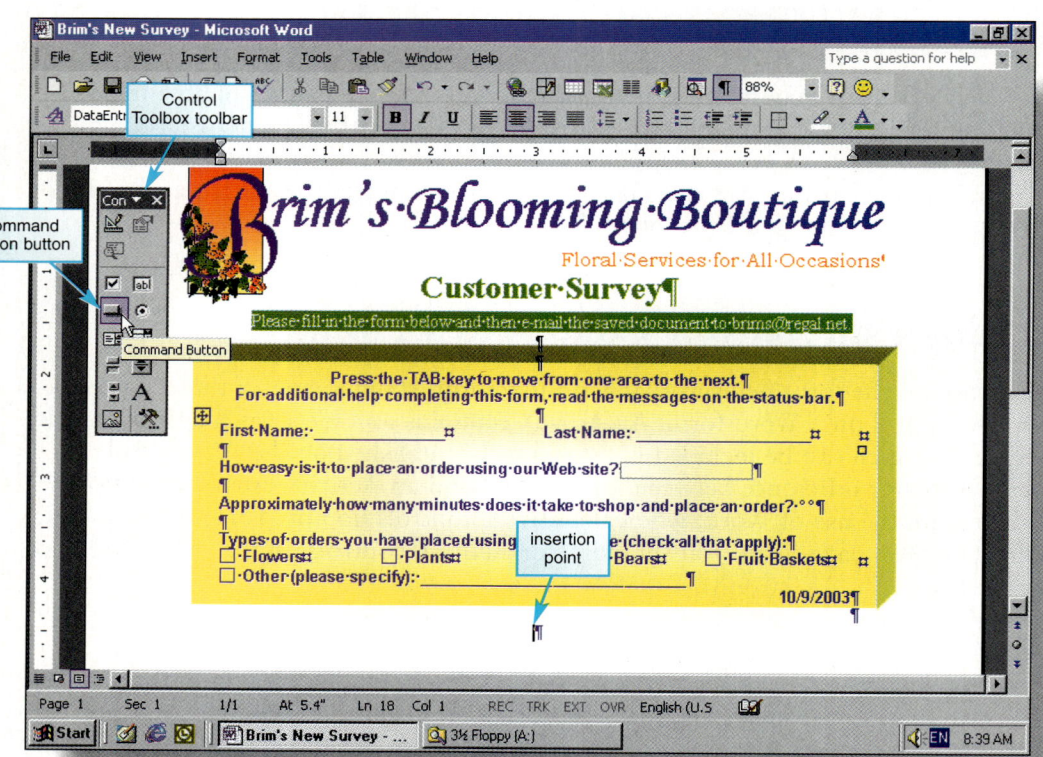

FIGURE 8-55

2 **Click the Command Button button.**

Word inserts a standard-sized command button at the location of the insertion point and switches to design mode (Figure 8-56). The text CommandButton1 partially displays on the face of the button. The button is selected and is surrounded by sizing handles.

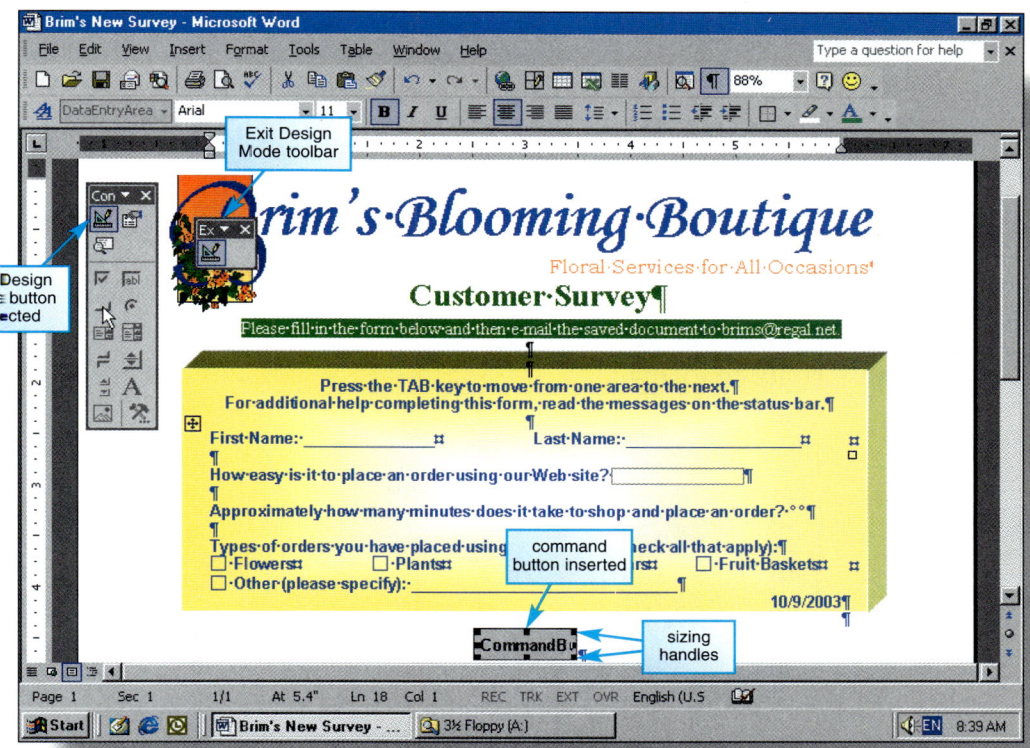

FIGURE 8-56

When you click a button on the Control Toolbox toolbar, Word automatically switches to design mode, changes the Design Mode button on the Control Toolbox toolbar to an Exit Design Mode button, and selects the Exit Design Mode button. Word also may display an Exit Design Mode toolbar. The Control Toolbox toolbar buttons are summarized in Table 8-7 on the next page.

The next step is to set the properties of the ActiveX control.

Setting Properties of an ActiveX Control

In Word, a command button ActiveX control has 20 different properties (shown in Figure 8-58 on page WD 8.55), such as the caption (the words on the face of the button), background color, foreground color, height, width, font, and so on. After you insert a command button into a form, you can change any one of the 20 properties to improve the button's appearance and modify its function. For this command button, you are to change its caption to the text, Click Here When Finished.

Other Ways

1. Click Design Mode button on Visual Basic toolbar
2. In Voice Command mode, say "Command Button"

More About

VBA Help

For help with VBA, code statements, and properties, type VBA help in the Ask a question box and then press the ENTER key. When the topics display, click Get Help for Visual Basic for Applications in Word.

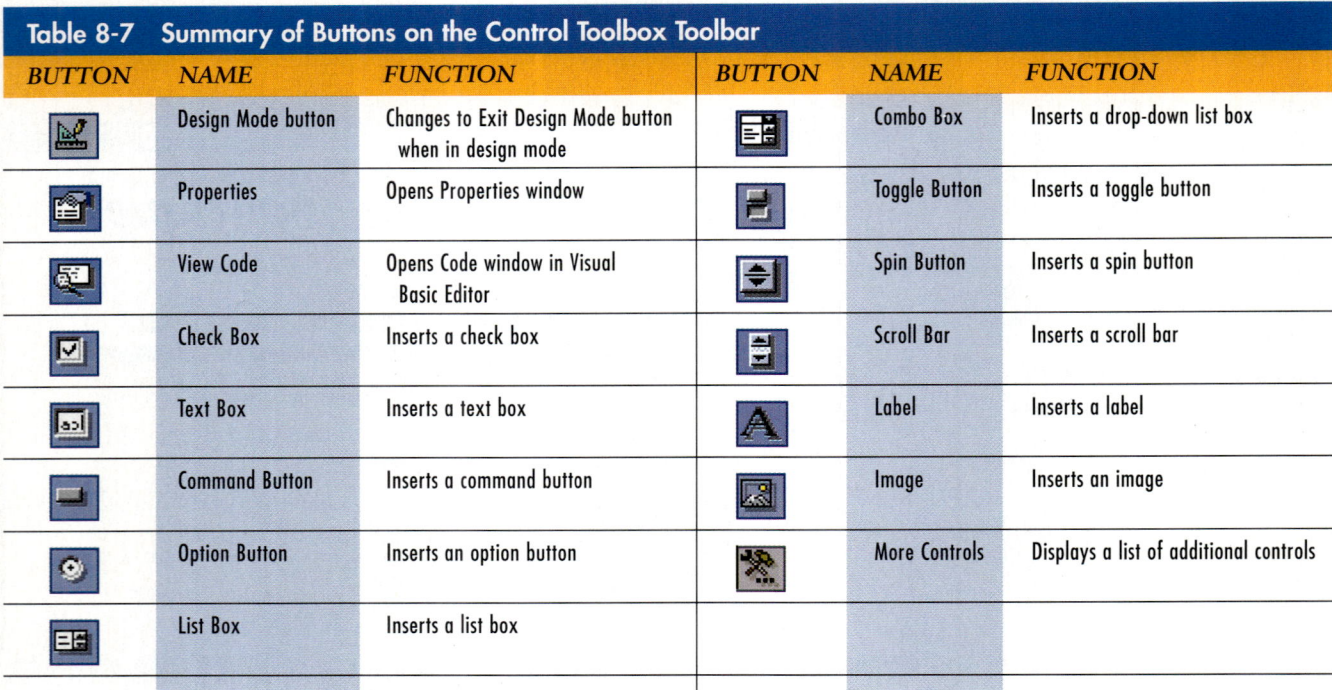

Table 8-7 Summary of Buttons on the Control Toolbox Toolbar

BUTTON	NAME	FUNCTION	BUTTON	NAME	FUNCTION
	Design Mode button	Changes to Exit Design Mode button when in design mode		Combo Box	Inserts a drop-down list box
	Properties	Opens Properties window		Toggle Button	Inserts a toggle button
	View Code	Opens Code window in Visual Basic Editor		Spin Button	Inserts a spin button
	Check Box	Inserts a check box		Scroll Bar	Inserts a scroll bar
	Text Box	Inserts a text box		Label	Inserts a label
	Command Button	Inserts a command button		Image	Inserts an image
	Option Button	Inserts an option button		More Controls	Displays a list of additional controls
	List Box	Inserts a list box			

Perform the following steps to change the Caption property of an ActiveX control.

Steps: To Set Properties of an ActiveX Control

 With the command button selected and Word in design mode, point to the Properties button on the Control Toolbox toolbar (Figure 8-57).

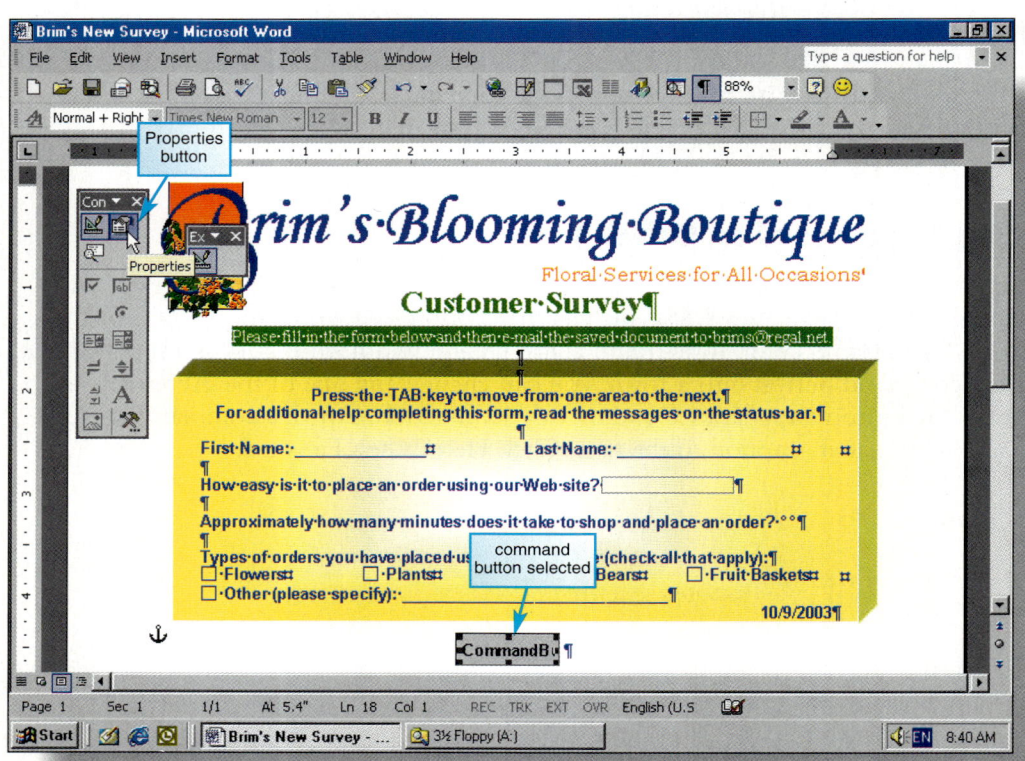

FIGURE 8-57

2 **Click the Properties button. When the Properties window opens, if necessary, click the Properties box arrow and then click CommandButton1 in the list. If necessary, click the Alphabetic tab. In the list, click Caption in the left column and then double-click CommandButton1 in the right column.**

The Property names display on the left, and the data for each property displays on the right (Figure 8-58).

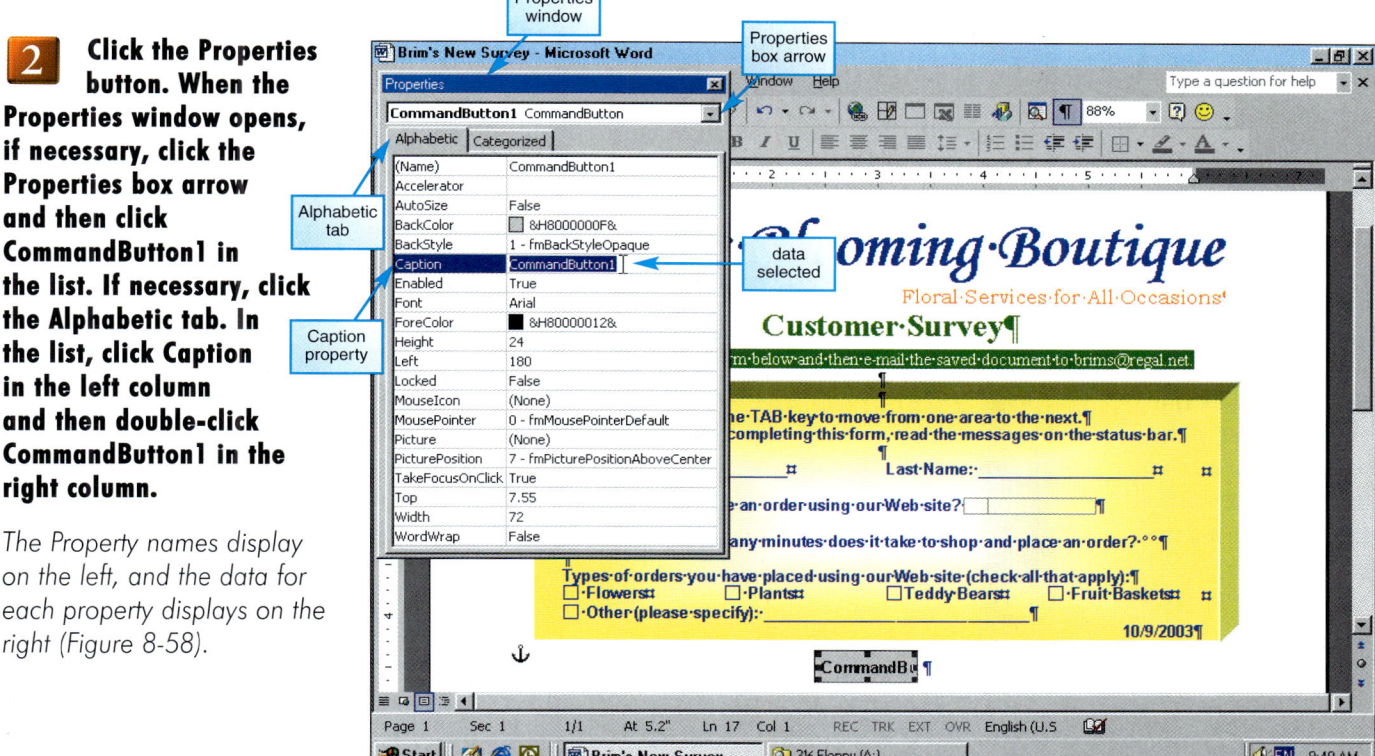

FIGURE 8-58

3 **Type** Click Here When Finished **as the new caption. Point to the Close button on the Properties window title bar.**

The Caption property is changed (Figure 8-59).

4 **Click the Close button on the Properties window title bar.**

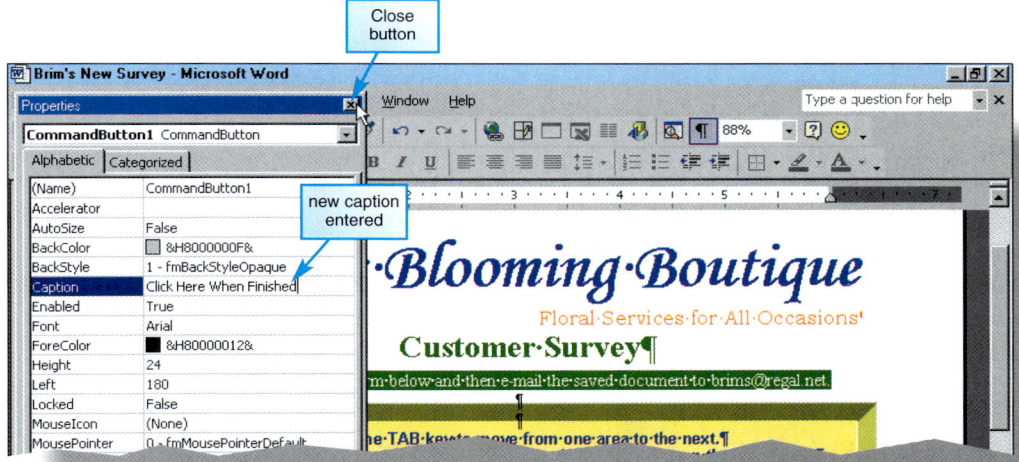

FIGURE 8-59

The Properties window (Figure 8-58) has two tabs, Alphabetic and Categorized. The **Alphabetic sheet** displays the properties in alphabetical order. The **Categorized sheet** displays the properties by subject, such as appearance, behavior, font, and miscellaneous.

The next step is to format the ActiveX control so it is a floating object and then resize it. You resize an ActiveX control the same way you resize any other object — by dragging its sizing handles.

1. In design mode, right-click control, click Properties on shortcut menu
2. Click Properties Window button on toolbar when Visual Basic Editor is active
3. In Voice Command mode, say "Properties"

Formatting the ActiveX Control

Word inserts the command button as an inline object; that is, part of the current paragraph. You want the command button to be a floating object so that you can position it anywhere on the form. Thus, perform the following steps to convert the command button from inline to floating.

Steps: To Format the ActiveX Control

1 Right-click the command button just inserted and then point to Format Control on the shortcut menu (Figure 8-60).

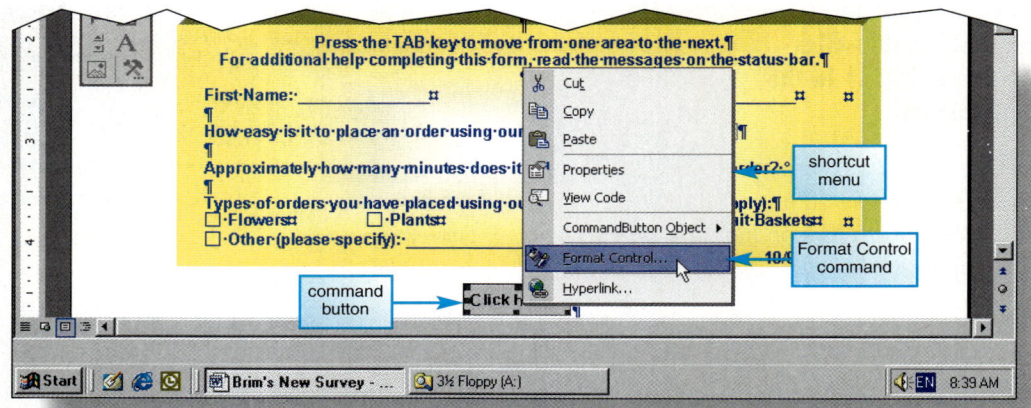

FIGURE 8-60

2 Click Format Control. When the Format Object dialog box displays, if necessary, click the Layout tab. Click Square in the Wrapping style area. Click Center in the Horizontal alignment area. Point to the OK button.

Word displays the Format Object dialog box (Figure 8-61). A square wrapping style changes an object to floating.

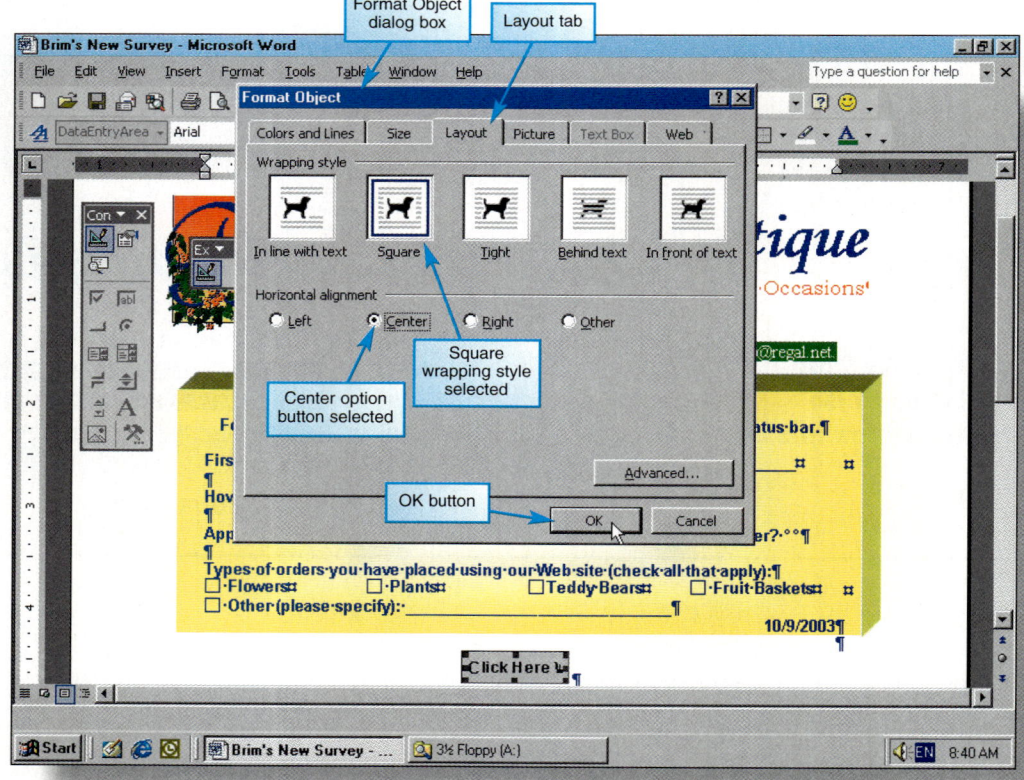

FIGURE 8-61

3 **Click the OK button. If necessary, drag the right-middle sizing handle to display the entire caption. Drag the control so that approximately one-quarter inch displays between the top of the command button and the bottom of the data entry area.**

The command button is positioned as shown in Figure 8-62.

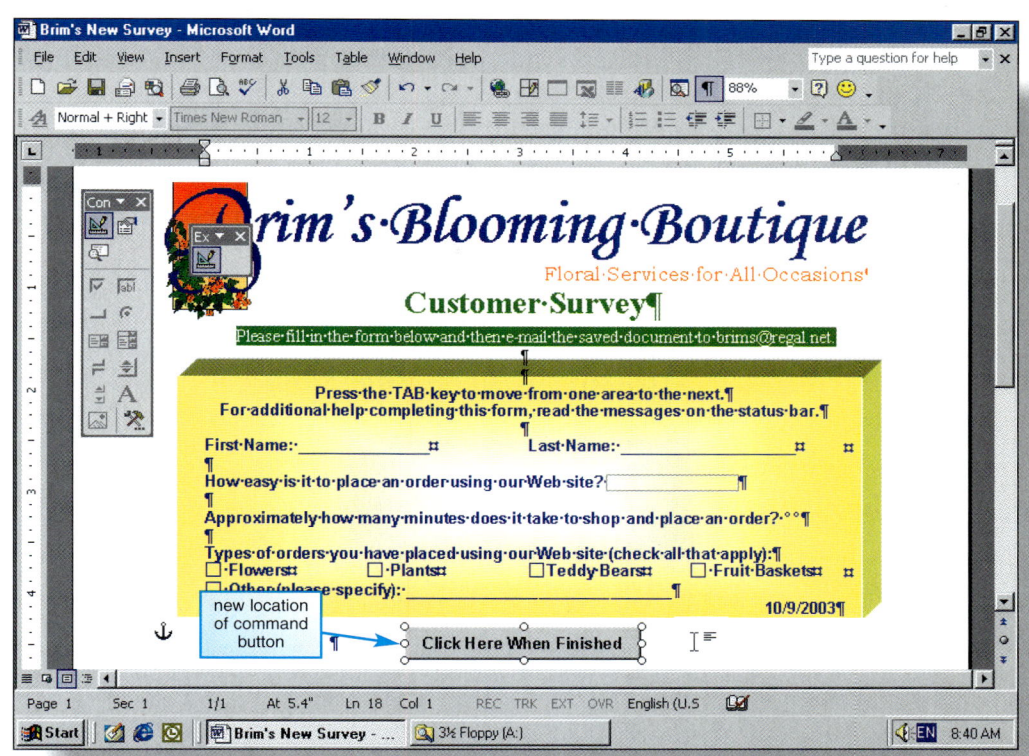

FIGURE 8-62

Writing the Macro for the ActiveX Control

The next step is to write and then enter the procedure for the macro that will execute when a user clicks the Click Here When Finished button. Clicking the button is the event that triggers execution of the macro.

As mentioned earlier, you should plan a procedure by writing its VBA code on paper similar to that shown in Table 8-8 on the next page. Then, before entering the procedure into the computer, desk check it.

Notice in line 1 that the name of the procedure in the Sub statement is CommandButton1_Click, which Word determines from the name of the button (shown in Figure 8-64 on page WD 8.59), and the event that causes the procedure to execute (Click).

The first executable code statement is an If…Then statement in line 7. This statement tests if the user entered text in the Other text box, which will have a bookmark of OtherText. If it does, then line 8 instructs Word to place an X in the Other check box, which will have a bookmark of OtherCheck; otherwise, Word skips lines 8 and 9 and then proceeds to line 10.

The next executable code statement is in line 11, which displays the Save As dialog box on the screen — allowing the user to save the form. Finally, line 15 displays a message box that contains two variables. The first is for the message text, which is defined in line 14; and the second is for the title bar text, which is defined in line 13. Variables are used to define these elements of the message box, because the text for the title bar and message is so long.

As illustrated earlier in this project, you use the Visual Basic Editor to enter code statements into a procedure. With Word in design mode and the ActiveX control selected, you can click the View Code button on the Control Toolbox toolbar to display the control's procedure in the Code window of the Visual Basic Editor.

Table 8-8 Click Here When Finished Button Procedure

LINE	VBA CODE STATEMENT
1	`Private Sub CommandButton1_Click()`
2	`'`
3	`' CommandButton1_Click Macro`
4	`' Executes when user clicks button called Click Here When Finished.`
5	`'`
6	`    'If user entered text in Other text box, put X in Other check box`
7	`    If Left(ActiveDocument.FormFields("OtherText").Result, 1) <> "_" Then`
8	`        ActiveDocument.FormFields("OtherCheck").CheckBox.Value = True`
9	`    End If`
10	`    'Display Save As dialog box`
11	`    Dialogs(wdDialogFileSaveAs).Show`
12	`    'Display thank-you message`
13	`    TitleBarText = "Thank You For Your Time"`
14	`    MessageText = "Please e-mail " & ActiveDocument.FullName & " to brims@regal.net."`
15	`    MsgBox MessageText, , TitleBarText`
16	`End Sub`

The code statements in lines 7 and 8 use bookmarks that need to be defined. You enter a bookmark in the Form Field Options dialog box. Perform the following steps to change the default bookmarks for the Other check box form field and the Other text form field.

TO CHANGE BOOKMARKS FOR FORM FIELDS

1 Double-click the check box form field for Other (shown in Figure 8-63).

2 When the Check Box Form Field Options dialog box displays, double-click the text in the Bookmark text box and then type OtherCheck as the new bookmark. Click the OK button.

3 Double-click the text form field for Other (shown in Figure 8-63).

4 When the Text Form Field Options dialog box displays, double-click the text in the Bookmark text box and then type OtherText as the new bookmark. Click the OK button.

Word changes form field options as specified in the Form Field Options dialog boxes.

Perform the following steps to enter the code statements for the procedure for the macro that will execute when a user clicks the Click Here When Finished button.

Adding an ActiveX Control to a Form • WD 8.59

 Steps   To Enter the Click Here When Finished Button Procedure

1 With Word in design mode, click the **Click Here When Finished** button and then point to the **View Code** button on the Control Toolbox toolbar (Figure 8-63).

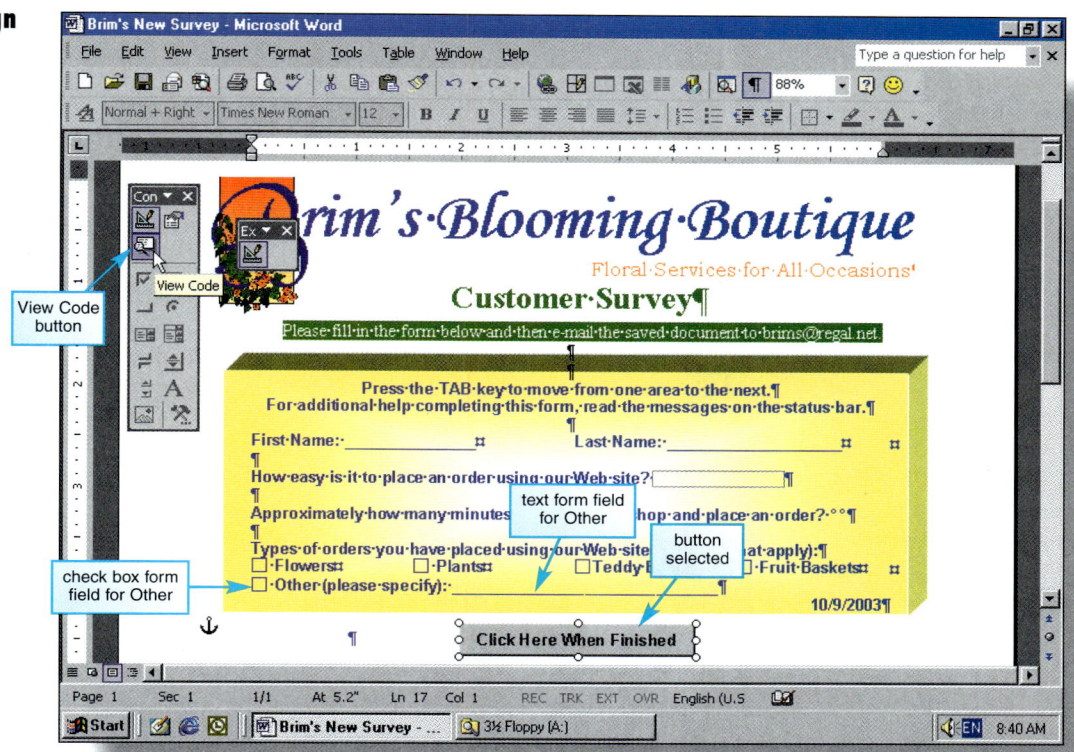

FIGURE 8-63

2 Click the **View Code** button. If the Project Explorer window opens, click its Close button. When the Visual Basic Editor window opens, if necessary, double-click the Code window title bar to maximize the window.

Word starts the Visual Basic Editor and opens the Microsoft Visual Basic window (Figure 8-64). The Visual Basic Editor automatically inserts the Sub and End Sub statements and positions the insertion point between the two statements.

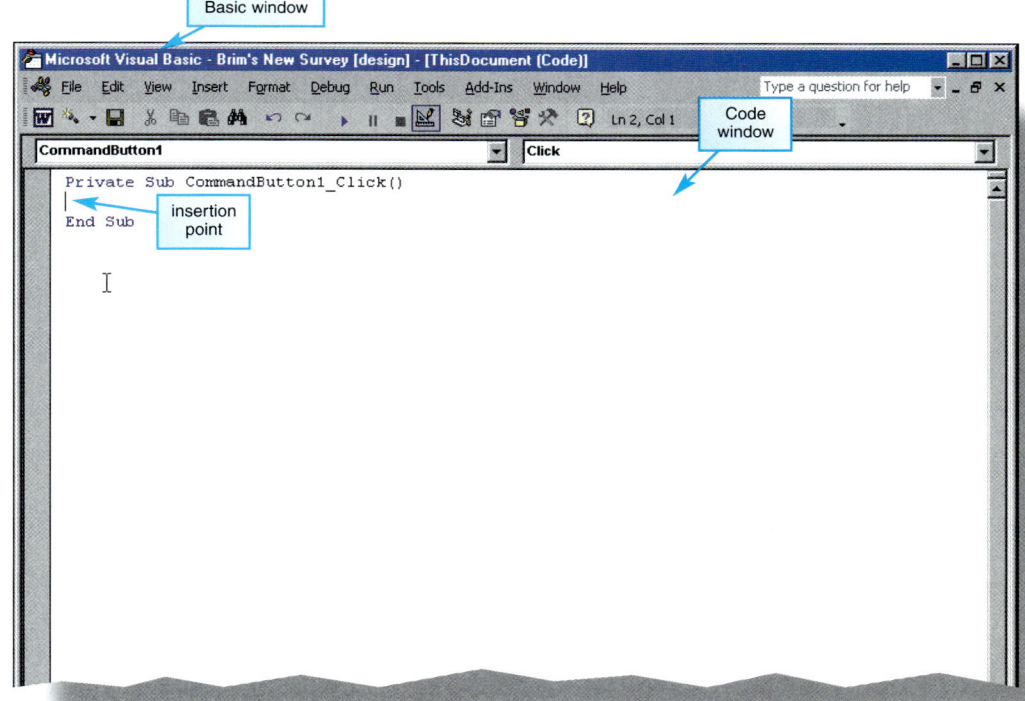

FIGURE 8-64

3 With the insertion point on the blank line between the Sub and End Sub statements in the Code window, type the code statements shown in lines 2 through 15 in Table 8-8 on page WD 8.58. Make sure you type an apostrophe at the beginning of each comment line. For clarity, indent the code statements as shown in Table 8-8.

The command button procedure is complete (Figure 8-65).

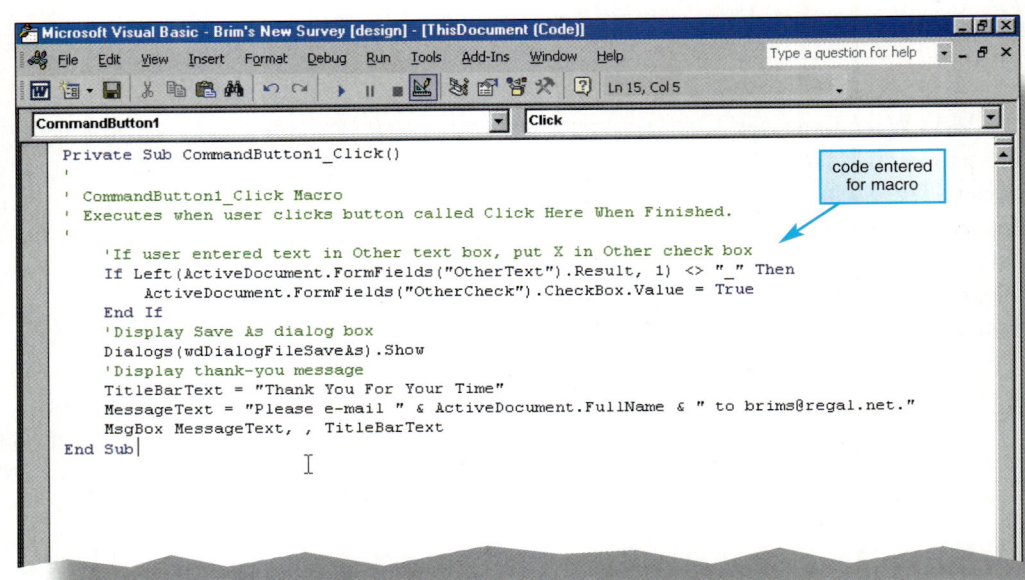

FIGURE 8-65

4 Verify your code statements by comparing them to Figure 8-65.

5 Click the Close button on the right edge of the Microsoft Visual Basic title bar to return to the online form. Point to the Exit Design Mode button on the Control Toolbox toolbar.

The online form displays as shown in Figure 8-66.

6 Click the Exit Design Mode button. Click the Close button on the Control Toolbox toolbar title bar.

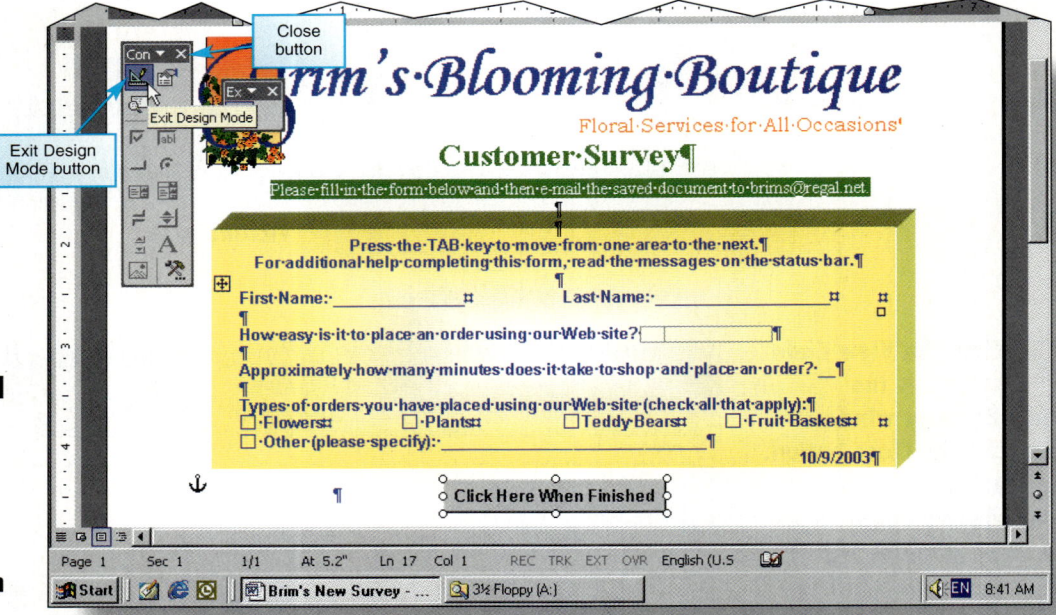

FIGURE 8-66

Word returns to run mode, which means if you click the Click Here When Finished button, Word will execute the associated macro.

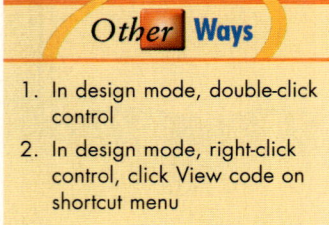

1. In design mode, double-click control
2. In design mode, right-click control, click View code on shortcut menu

More About Visual Basic for Applications

Visual Basic for Applications uses many more statements than those presented in this project. These statements, however, should help you understand the basic composition of a Visual Basic statement. For example, the code statement in line 11 of Table 8-8 on page WD 8.58 that displays the Save As dialog box includes a period. The entry on the left side of the period tells Word which object you want to affect (in this case, the dialog box). An object can be a document, a form field, a bookmark, a dialog box, a button, or any other control on a form. The entry on the right side of the period tells Word what you want to do to the object (in this case, display it).

Earlier you were shown how to change an object's properties using the Properties window (Figure 8-58 on page WD 8.55). This code statement from the NumberOfMinutes macro changed an object's property during execution of a procedure:

```
ActiveDocument.ActiveWindow.View.TableGridlines = False
```

This statement changes the TableGridlines property of the View object in the ActiveWindow object in the ActiveDocument object to false; that is, it hides table gridlines. An equal sign in a code statement instructs Word to make an assignment to a property, variable, or other object. In the previous code statement, the TableGridlines property was set to False.

Now that you have completed the macros, you once again should protect the form and save it, as shown in the following steps.

Web Forms

If you intend to publish a form on the World Wide Web, you should limit ActiveX controls to the standard HTML controls, which include the following: check box, drop-down list box, text box, submit and reset password, option button, list box, text area, submit with image, and hidden.

TO PROTECT THE FORM

1. Click Tools on the menu bar and then click Protect Document.
2. When the Protect Document dialog box displays, click Forms in the Protect document for area, and then click the OK button.

Word protects the form.

Protecting Documents

To protect a document so users cannot enter comments or track their changes (discussed in Project 9), click the Comments or Tracked Changes options button in the Protect Document dialog box.

TO SAVE A DOCUMENT

1. Click the Save button on the Standard toolbar.

Word saves the template with the same file name, Brim's New Survey.

Printing

If you want to print a form and wish to save ink, print faster, or minimize printer overrun errors, print a draft. Click File on the menu bar, click Print, click the Options button, place a check mark in the Draft output check box, and then click the OK button in each dialog box.

Testing the Online Form

The modifications and macros for the Brim's New Survey file are complete. You now are ready to test the form.

Perform the steps on the next page to test the form.

Steps: To Test the Form

 **Click the Explorer program button on the taskbar to display Windows Explorer and then double-click the Brim's New Survey icon in the Contents pane to display a new Word document based on the contents of the Customer Survey. If Word displays a Security Warning dialog box, click the Enable Macros button.**

As instructed by the AutoNew macro, the Word document zooms page width, scrolls down six lines, hides table gridlines, and hides formatting marks (Figure 8-67).

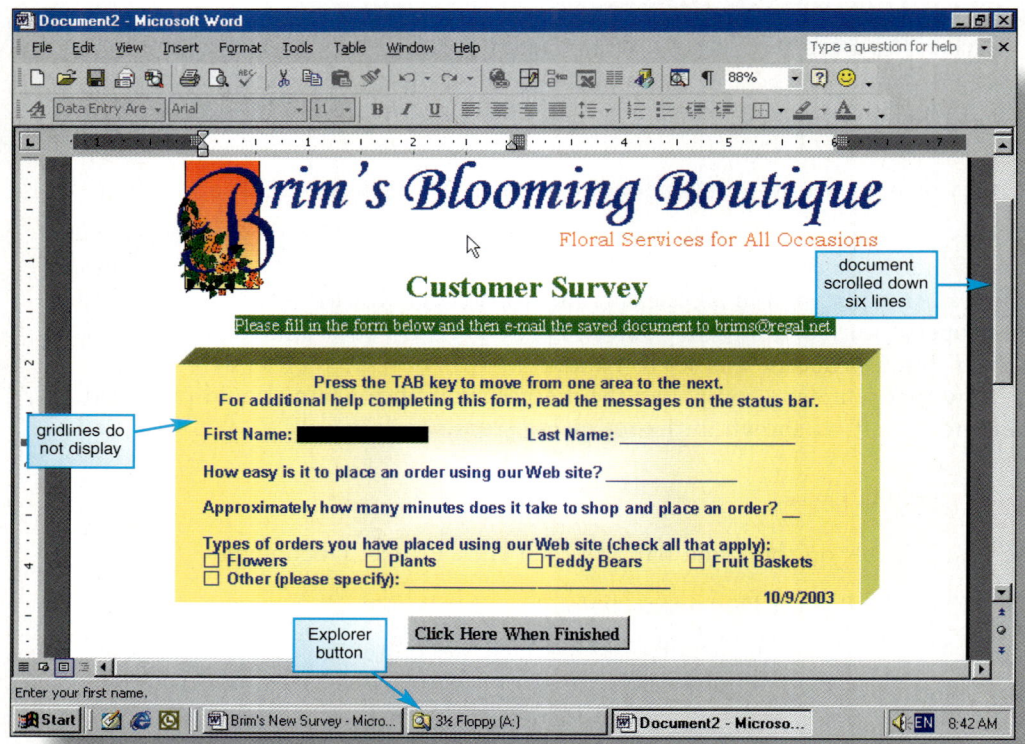

FIGURE 8-67

2 With the selection in the First Name text box, type Latonia and then press the TAB key. Type Brown in the Last Name text box. Press the TAB key to select the ease of use drop-down list box and display its box arrow. Click the ease of use box arrow and then click Very Easy. Press the TAB key. Type ab in the number of minutes text box. Press the TAB key. When the error message displays, point to the OK button.

As instructed by the NumberOfMinutes macro, an error message displays (Figure 8-68).

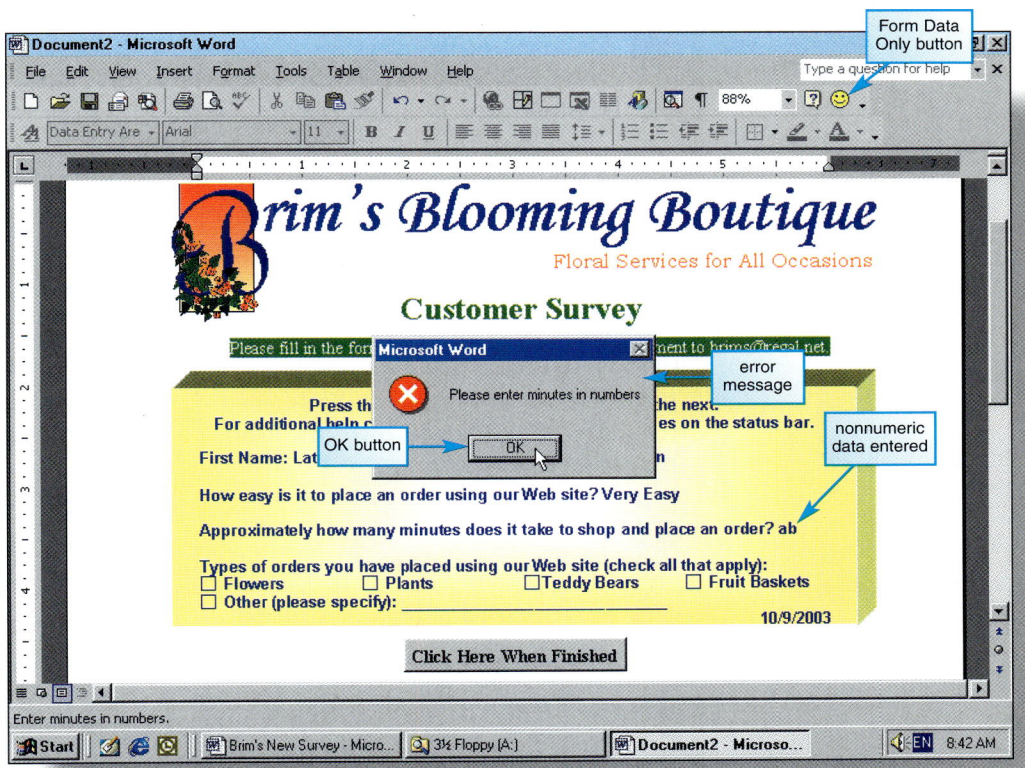

FIGURE 8-68

3 Click the OK button in the message box. Type 15 in the number of minutes text box. Press the TAB key. Click the following check boxes: Plants and Teddy Bears. Press the TAB key three times to position the selection in the Other text box. Type Collectible in the Other text box.

The data is entered.

To finish testing the online form, you will test the form's command button as well as the Form Data Only button in the Standard toolbar.

TO FINISH TESTING THE ONLINE FORM

1. Click the Click Here When Finished button.

2. As defined by the CommandButton1_Click procedure, Word displays the Save As dialog box. Change the Save in location to 3½ Floppy (A:). Type Brown Form in the File name text box and then click the Save button in the Save As dialog box.

3. When the save process is complete, the CommandButton1_Click procedure then displays a thank-you message box that indicates the name and location of the file the user should e-mail back to the boutique (shown in Figure 8-1c on page WD 8.05).

4. Click the OK button in the message box. Notice that Word placed an X in the Other check box.

5 Assume you are the person tabulating the form results at the boutique and just received the Brown Form. Click the Form Data Only button on the Standard toolbar, which instructs Word to place a check mark in the Save form data only check box in the Options dialog box. Click File on the menu bar and then click Save Copy As. If necessary, type `Brown Form` in the File name text box and then click the Save button to save the document as a text file.

6 When Word displays a file conversion warning message, click the OK button in the dialog box.

You have tested all aspects of the form. If a Word or Visual Basic error message displayed while you tested the form, make necessary corrections and then retest the form. To do this, close the Word window displaying the Brown Form. Unprotect the template. Make the corrections. Protect the template again. Save the template again. Retest the form. Repeat this procedure until the form displays as intended.

The next step is to close the Brown Form file and then close Windows Explorer.

TO CLOSE A FILE

1 Click File on the menu bar and then click Close. If a Word dialog box displays asking to save the changes, click the No button.

Word closes the Brown Form file.

TO CLOSE WINDOWS EXPLORER

1 Click the Close button on the Explorer window's title bar.

Windows Explorer closes.

Certified Digital Signatures

Several companies provide authenticated, certified digital signatures via the Web. For more information about digital signatures, visit the Word 2002 More About Web Page (scsite.com/wd2002/more.htm) and then click Certified Digital Signatures.

Digital Signatures

Some users prefer to attach a digital signature to verify the authenticity of a document. A **digital signature** is an electronic, encrypted, and secure stamp of authentication on a document. This signature confirms that the file originated from the signer (file developer) and that it has not been altered.

A digital signature references a digital certificate. A **digital certificate** is an attachment to a file, macro project, or e-mail message that vouches for its authenticity, provides secure encryption, or supplies a verifiable signature. Many users who receive online forms enable the macros based on whether they are digitally signed by a developer on the user's list of trusted sources.

You can obtain a digital certificate from a commercial **certification authority**, from your network administrator, or you can create a digital signature yourself. A digital certificate you create yourself is not issued by a formal certification authority. Thus, signed macros using such a certificate are referred to as **self-signed projects**. Certificates you create yourself are considered unauthenticated and still will generate a warning when opened if the security level is set to high or medium. Many users, however, consider self-signed projects safer to open than those with no certificates at all.

Attaching a Digital Signature to a File

A **file digital signature** is a digital signature that displays when you e-mail a document from Word. Word will display the digital signature whenever the document is opened. In the following steps, you will digitally sign a file from the Data Disk that accompanies this book. If you did not download the Data Disk, see the inside back cover for instructions for downloading the Data Disk or see your instructor.

Perform the following steps to open the file from the Data Disk and then save it with a new name.

Digital Signatures

When you attach a digital signature to a macro project, Word will display the digital signature when the user of the file is asked to enable macros. When you modify code in a signed macro project, its digital signature usually is removed. For this reason, you should digitally sign macros only after your solution has been saved, tested, and is ready for distribution.

TO OPEN A FILE FROM THE DATA DISK AND SAVE IT WITH A NEW NAME

1. With the Data Disk in drive A, click the Open button on the Standard toolbar.
2. When the Open dialog box displays, click 3½ Floppy (A:) in the Look in list. When the list of files displays, double-click the MyFamily Questionnaire icon in the Contents pane.
3. When the file displays, click the Zoom box arrow and then click Page Width. Scroll down so the complete form displays on the screen.
4. Click Tools on the menu bar and then click Unprotect Document.
5. Click File on the menu bar and then click Save As.
6. When the Save As dialog box displays, if necessary, click 3½ Floppy (A:) in the Look in list. Type Revised Questionnaire in the File name text box and then click the Save button in the Save As dialog box.

The file is saved on the floppy disk with the name, Revised Questionnaire.

Perform the following steps to digitally sign the file.

 **To Digitally Sign a File**

1. **Click Tools on the menu bar, and then click Options. When the Options dialog box displays, if necessary, click the Security tab. Point to the Digital Signatures button.**

The Security sheet displays options for passwords and protection, as well as digital signatures (Figure 8-69).

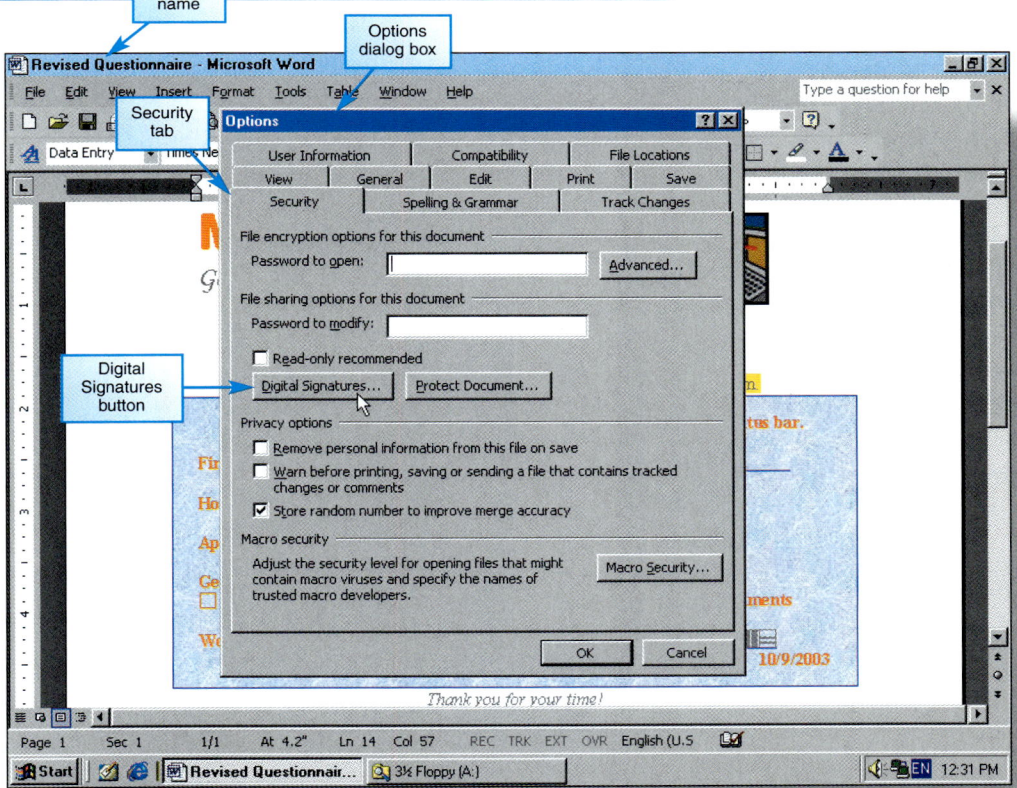

FIGURE 8-69

2 Click the Digital Signatures button. When the Digital Signature dialog box displays, point to the Add button.

Your Signer list may display previous certificates (Figure 8-70).

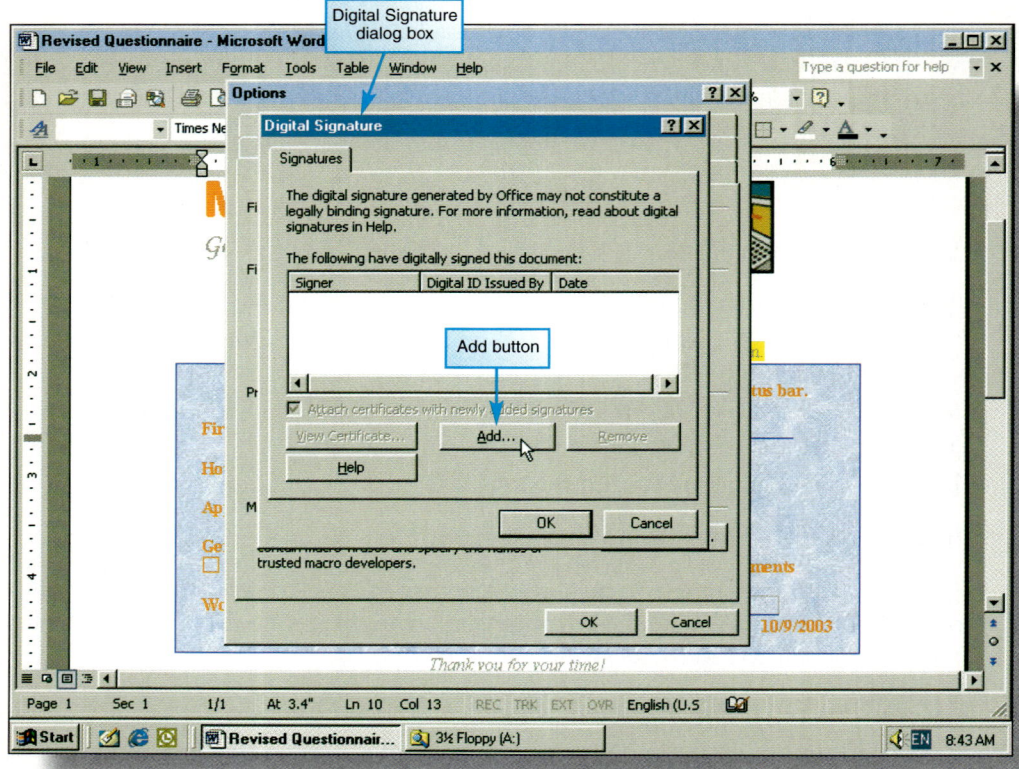

FIGURE 8-70

3 Click the Add button. If Word displays a dialog box, warning you about fonts, text, or pictures, click the Yes button. When the Select Certificate dialog box displays, click the certificate you wish to add and then point to the OK button. If your computer does not display any certificates, click the Cancel button in each dialog box and skip Step 4.

The boutique's certificate displays (Figure 8-71). Your display may differ.

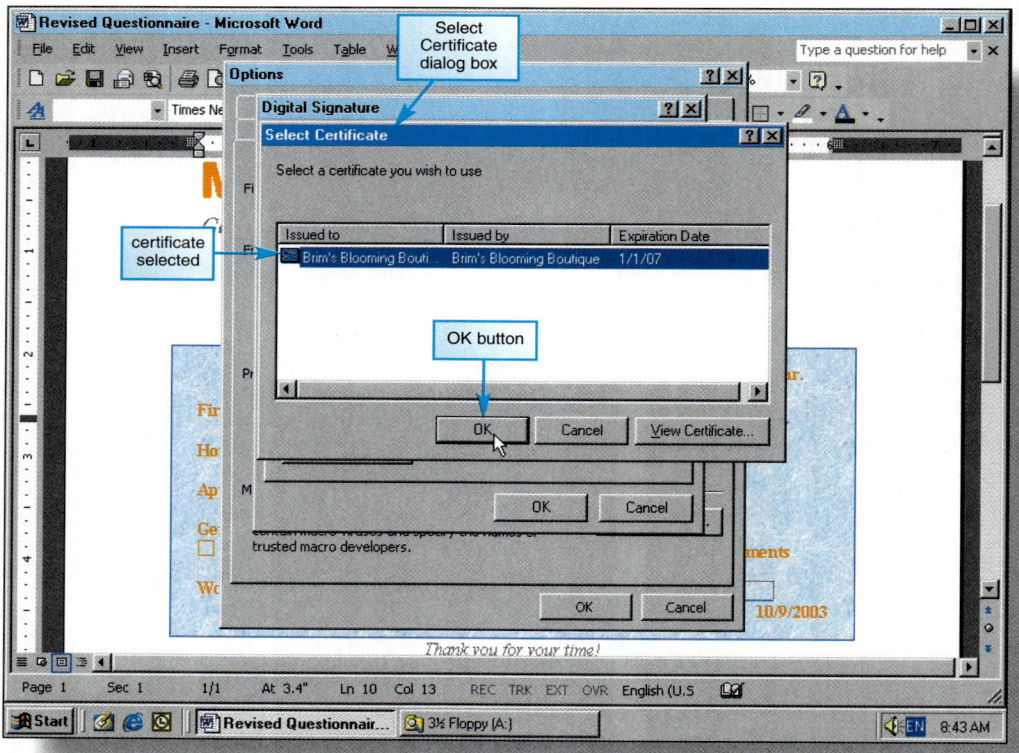

FIGURE 8-71

4 **Click the OK button. When the Digital Signature dialog box is visible again, click the OK button. When the Options dialog box is visible again, click the OK button.**

A certificate icon displays on the status bar, and the title bar displays (Signed) after the file name (Figure 8-72).

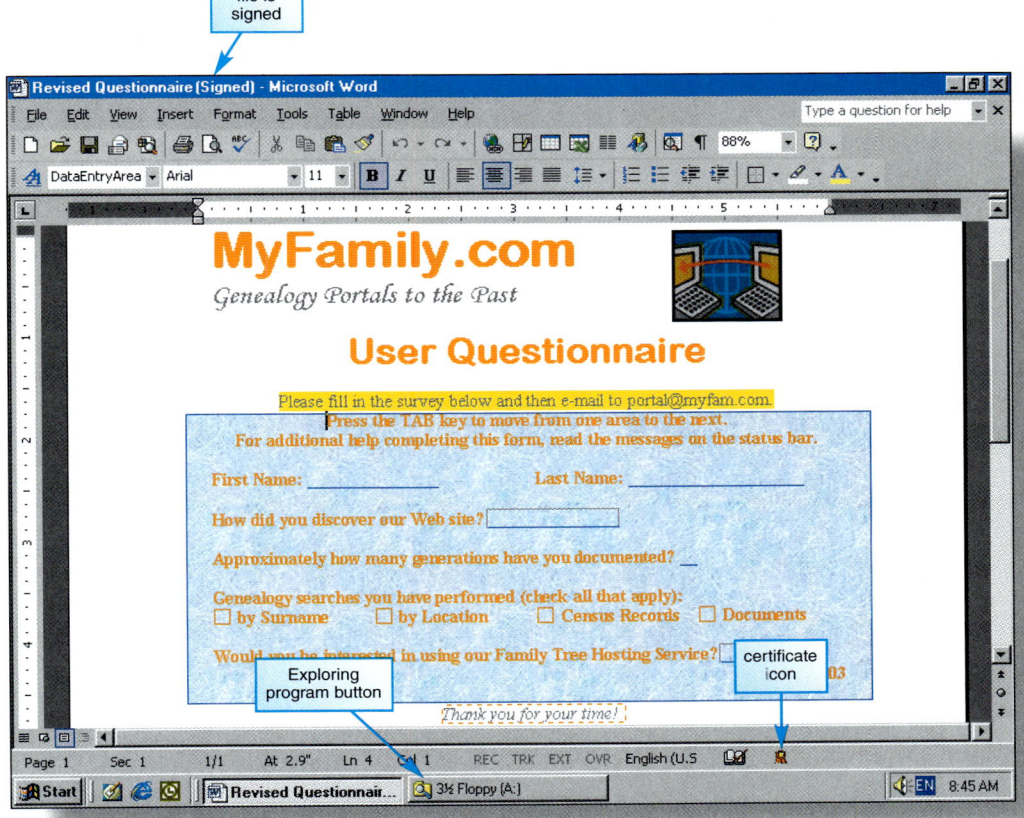

FIGURE 8-72

When you open a digitally signed document, Word displays a message announcing the signature on the status bar while the file opens. Once the file is opened, Word displays a certification icon on the status bar. You can double-click the icon to find out who digitally signed the document. The word, (Signed), also displays on the title bar, indicating the document is digitally signed.

If you do not have any digital certificates on your computer, you can create one by running a program named **Selfcert.exe** that is supplied with your Office program. Be aware that running this program multiple times can create duplicate digital signatures on the computer. You cannot remove duplicate digital signatures using Word.

You are finished with the form. Perform the following step to quit Word and close Windows Explorer.

TO QUIT WORD

1 Click File on the menu bar and then click Exit.

The Word window closes.

Self Certification

Microsoft Office XP uses Microsoft Authenticode technology to enable you to sign a file or a macro project digitally by using a digital certificate. The Selfcert.exe program is supplied with Office XP. The certificate used to create this signature confirms that the macro or document originated from the signer, and the signature confirms that it has not been altered.

Copying, Renaming, and Deleting Macros

You may find it necessary to copy a macro, rename a macro, or delete a macro. Macros cannot be copied or renamed from Word; instead, you must use the Visual Basic Editor. You can, however, delete a macro from Word.

Quick Reference

For a table that lists how to complete tasks covered in this book using the mouse, menu, shortcut menu, and keyboard see the Quick Reference Summary at the back of this book or visit the Shelly Cashman Series Office XP Web page (scsite.com/offxp/qr.htm) and then click Microsoft Word 2002.

Microsoft Certification

The Microsoft Office User Specialist (MOUS) Certification program provides an opportunity for you to obtain a valuable industry credential — proof that you have the Word 2002 skills required by employers. For more information, see Appendix E or visit the Shelly Cashman Series MOUSE Web page at scsite.com/offxp/cert.htm.

TO COPY A MACRO

1. Click Tools on the menu bar, point to Macro, and then click Macros on the Macro submenu. When the Macros dialog box displays, click the macro name to copy, and then click the Edit button to start the Visual Basic Editor and display the macro in the Code window.
2. Select all the text in the macro's VBA procedure; that is, drag from the Sub statement to the End Sub statement (including the Sub and End Sub statements).
3. Click Edit on the menu bar and then click Copy.
4. Position the insertion point in the destination area. Click Edit on the menu bar and then click Paste.

You can paste a macro into the same document or a different document.

TO RENAME A MACRO

1. Click Tools on the menu bar, point to Macro, and then click Macros on the Macro submenu. When the Macros dialog box displays, click the macro name to be renamed, and then click the Edit button to start the Visual Basic Editor and display the macro in the Code window.
2. Select the macro name following the keyword Sub at the beginning of the macro's procedure and then type a new macro name.

The macro will be renamed in the Macros dialog box.

TO DELETE A MACRO

1. Click Tools on the menu bar, point to Macro, and then click Macros on the Macro submenu.
2. When the Macros dialog box displays, click the macro name to be deleted, and then click the Delete button.
3. Click the Yes button in the Microsoft Word dialog box.

CASE PERSPECTIVE SUMMARY

Before showing the modified Brim's New Survey to your aunt, you decide to have two of your fellow students test it to be sure it works properly. They find one error. You unprotect the template, fix the error, protect the form again, and then test it one final time, just to be sure the error is fixed. Then, you e-mail the Customer Survey to Aunt Carol for her review. She is quite pleased with the results. Realizing the power of macros and Visual Basic for Applications, she asks you to train three members of her staff on how to create macros and VBA procedures in Word.

Project Summary

Project 8 introduced you to working with macros and Visual Basic for Applications (VBA). You modified the template for the online form created in Project 7. To change its appearance, you inserted a graphic from the Web, changed the text by creating and applying a new style, filled the drawing object with a gradient effect, and then added a 3-D effect to the rectangle drawing object. Then, you created a macro using the macro recorder and assigned the macro to a toolbar button. Next, you recorded an automatic macro. You viewed the macro's code using the Visual Basic Editor and added comments and code statements to the macro. You created another macro that executed when the user exits a form field. After inserting an ActiveX control, you set its properties, formatted it, and wrote a VBA procedure for it. Finally, you attached a digital signature.

What You Should Know

Having completed this project, you should now be able to perform the following tasks:

- Add a 3-D Effect *(WD 8.21)*
- Add Code Statements to a Procedure *(WD 8.43)*
- Add Comments to a Procedure *(WD 8.41)*
- Apply a Style Using a Shortcut Key *(WD 8.19)*
- Change a Bookmark for a Drop-Down Form Field *(WD 8.46)*
- Change Bookmarks for Form Fields *(WD 8.58)*
- Change the Graphic *(WD 8.12)*
- Change Options for a Text Form Field *(WD 8.45)*
- Close a File *(WD 8.64)*
- Close Windows Explorer *(WD 8.64)*
- Copy a Macro *(WD 8.68)*
- Create a Style That Has a Shortcut Key *(WD 8.17)*
- Create an Automatic Macro *(WD 8.33)*
- Customize a Toolbar *(WD 8.28)*
- Delete a Macro *(WD 8.68)*
- Delete the Thank-You Message and Resize the Rectangle *(WD 8.21)*
- Digitally Sign a File *(WD 8.65)*
- Display Formatting Marks *(WD 8.09)*
- Enter the Click Here When Finished Button Procedure *(WD 8.59)*
- Enter the NumberOfMinutes Procedure *(WD 8.50)*
- Fill a Drawing Object with a Gradient Fill Effect *(WD 8.20)*
- Finish Testing the Online Form *(WD 8.63)*
- Format Text in a Text Box *(WD 8.14)*
- Format the ActiveX Control *(WD 8.56)*
- Format the Form Instructions *(WD 8.15)*
- Insert a Graphic File from the Data Disk *(WD 8.13)*
- Insert a Visual Basic Procedure *(WD 8.47)*
- Insert an ActiveX Control *(WD 8.52)*
- Insert and Format a Text Box *(WD 8.13)*
- Modify Existing Code *(WD 8.42)*
- Open a File from the Data Disk and Save It with a New Name *(WD 8.65)*
- Protect the Form *(WD 8.61)*
- Quit the Visual Basic Editor *(WD 8.43)*
- Quit Word *(WD 8.67)*
- Record a Macro and Assign It a Shortcut Key *(WD 8.24)*
- Rename a Macro *(WD 8.68)*
- Reset Menus and Toolbars *(WD 8.09)*
- Run a Macro *(WD 8.27)*
- Run a Macro When a User Exits a Form Field *(WD 8.51)*
- Save a Document *(WD 8.22, WD 8.61)*
- Save a Document with a New File Name *(WD 8.07)*
- Set a Security Level in Word *(WD 8.10)*
- Set Properties of an ActiveX Control *(WD 8.54)*
- Start and Customize Word and Open an Office Document *(WD 8.07)*
- Test the AutoNew Macro *(WD 8.36)*
- Test the Form *(WD 8.62)*
- Uncheck the Save Data Only for Forms Check Box *(WD 8.28, WD 8.32)*
- Unprotect a Document *(WD 8.08)*
- View a Macro's VBA Code *(WD 8.38)*
- Zoom Page Width *(WD 8.09)*

Learn It Online

Instructions: To complete exercises 1 through 6, start your browser, click the Address bar, and then enter scsite.com/offxp/exs.htm. When the Office XP Learn It Online page displays, follow the instructions in the exercises.

1 Project Reinforcement TF, MC, and SA

Below Word Project 8, click the Project Reinforcement link. Print the quiz by clicking Print on the File menu. Answer each question. Write your first and last name at the top of each page, and then hand in the printout to your instructor.

2 Flash Cards

Below Word Project 8, click the Flash Cards link. When Flash Cards displays, read the instructions. Type 20 (or a number specified by your instructor) in the Number of Playing Cards text box, type your name in the Name text box, and then click the Flip Card button. When the flash card displays, read the question and then click the Answer box arrow to select an answer. Flip through Flash Cards. Click Print on the File menu to print the last flash card if your score is 15 (75%) correct or greater and then hand it in to your instructor. If your score is less than 15 (75%) correct, then redo this exercise by clicking the Replay button.

3 Practice Test

Below Word Project 8, click the Practice Test link. Answer each question, enter your first and last name at the bottom of the page, and then click the Grade Test button. When the graded practice test displays on your screen, click Print on the File menu to print a hard copy. Continue to take practice tests until you score 80% or better. Hand in a printout of the final practice test to your instructor.

4 Who Wants to Be a Computer Genius?

Below Word Project 8, click the Computer Genius link. Read the instructions, enter your first and last name at the bottom of the page, and then click the Play button. Hand in your score to your instructor.

5 Wheel of Terms

Below Word Project 8, click the Wheel of Terms link. Read the instructions, and then enter your first and last name and your school name. Click the Play button. Hand in your score to your instructor.

6 Crossword Puzzle Challenge

Below Word Project 8, click the Crossword Puzzle Challenge link. Read the instructions, and then enter your first and last name. Click the Play button. Work the crossword puzzle. When you are finished, click the Submit button. When the crossword puzzle redisplays, click the Print button. Hand in the printout.

7 Tips and Tricks

Below Word Project 8, click the Tips and Tricks link. Click a topic that pertains to Project 8. Right-click the information and then click Print on the shortcut menu. Construct a brief example of what the information relates to in Word to confirm you understand how to use the tip or trick. Hand in the example and printed information.

8 Newsgroups

Below Word Project 8, click the Newsgroups link. Click a topic that pertains to Project 8. Print three comments. Hand in the comments to your instructor.

9 Expanding Your Horizons

Below Word Project 8, click the Articles for Microsoft Word link. Click a topic that pertains to Project 8. Print the information. Construct a brief example of what the information relates to in Word to confirm you understand the contents of the article. Hand in the example and printed information to your instructor.

10 Search Sleuth

Below Word Project 8, click the Search Sleuth link. To search for a term that pertains to this project, select a term below the Project 8 title and then use the Google search engine at google.com (or any major search engine) to display and print two Web pages that present information on the term. Hand in the printouts to your instructor.

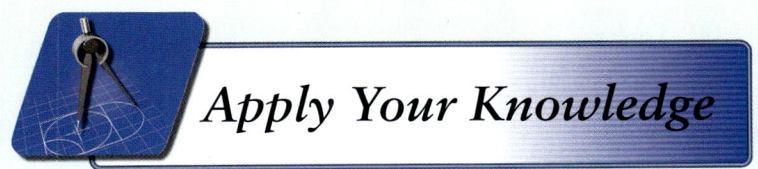

Apply Your Knowledge

1 Debugging VBA Code

Instructions: In this assignment, you access a template through Windows Explorer. As shown in Figure 8-73, the template contains an online form. The form contains two macros: one that executes when you initially display the form on the screen, and another that executes when you click the command button at the bottom of the screen. Each macro contains one coding error. You are to test the code by filling in the form. Then, correct the Visual Basic errors as they display on the screen.

The template is located on the Data Disk. If you did not download the Data Disk, see the inside back cover for instructions for downloading the Data Disk or see your instructor.

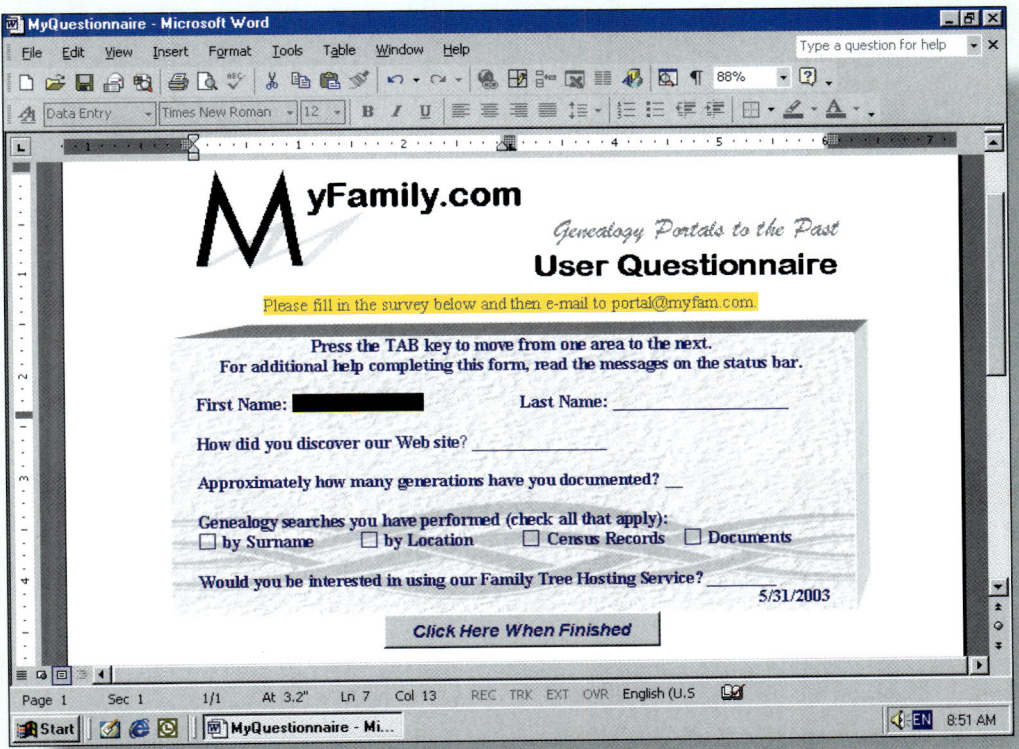

FIGURE 8-73

(continued)

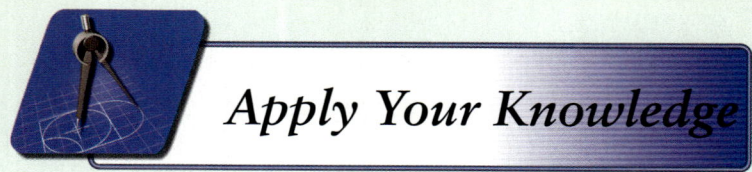

Apply Your Knowledge

Debugging VBA Code *(continued)*

Perform the following tasks:

1. Right-click the My Computer icon on the Windows desktop and then click Explore on the shortcut menu. When the Explorer window opens, click the Address text box to select it. With the Data Disk in drive A, type a: and then press the ENTER key. Double-click the MyQuestionnaire icon in the contents pane to display a new document based on the MyQuestionnaire template.
2. When Word displays a dialog box about macros, click the Enable Macros button.
3. When a Microsoft Visual Basic error message displays, click its OK button. If necessary, maximize the Microsoft Visual Basic window. Notice the text, .ZoomPageFit =, is highlighted because Visual Basic did not recognize it. The text should say, .Zoom.PageFit = (it is missing the period). Click the selected text and insert the period between the letters m and P. Then, click the Continue button on the Visual Basic Standard toolbar. Close the Microsoft Visual Basic window by clicking its Close button.
4. With the selection in the First Name text box, type Heinz and then press the TAB key.
5. With the selection in the Last Name text box, type Dortmund and then press the TAB key.
6. With the selection in the drop-down list box, click the box arrow. Click Search Engine in the drop-down list. Press the TAB key.
7. Type 12 in response to Approximately how many generations have you documented? Press the TAB key.
8. Place an X in each of the check boxes by clicking them. Press the TAB key.
9. With the selection on the drop-down list box at the bottom of the form, click the box arrow and then click Yes.
10. Click the Click Here When Finished button. When the Microsoft Visual Basic error message displays, click the OK button. If necessary, click the Microsoft Visual Basic - MyQuestionnaire program button on the taskbar to display the Visual Basic Editor. Notice the code statement that displays the Save As dialog box is highlighted as an error. To the right of the text, Dialogs(wdDialogFileSaveAs)., the word, Show, is missing. Type the word Show after the period. Click the Continue button on the Visual Basic Standard toolbar.
11. Type Dortmund Form in the Save As dialog box, change the Save in location to drive A, and then click the Save button in the Save As dialog box. When Word asks if you want to save changes to the template, click the No button. Click the OK button in the Thank You For Your Time message box.
12. Print the filled-in form.
13. Press ALT+F11. In the Microsoft Visual Basic window, click File on the menu bar and then click Print. When the Print dialog box displays, click Current Project and then click the OK button.

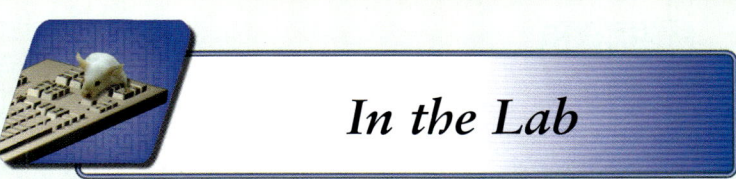

In the Lab

1 Creating an Automatic Macro for an Online Form

Problem: You created the online form shown in Figure 7-73 on page WD 7.64 for Web Management. Your supervisor has asked you to change its appearance and create a macro for the form so it displays properly on the screen when a user first displays it (as a blank form). You modify the form so it looks like the one shown in Figure 8-74.

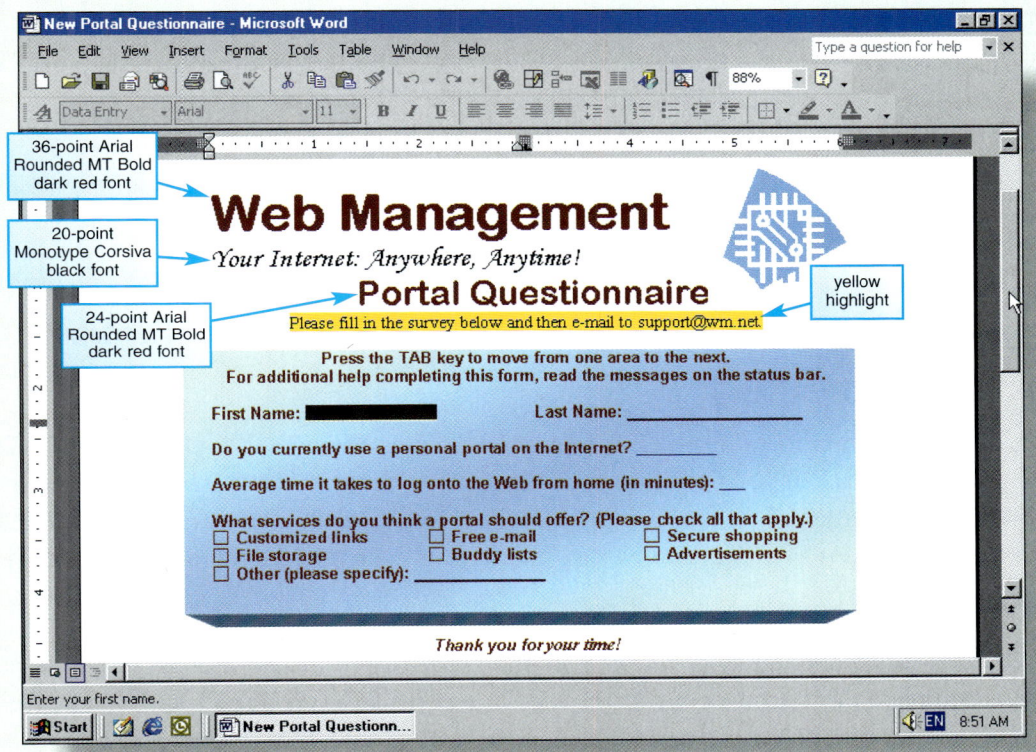

FIGURE 8-74

Instructions:

1. Open the template called Portal Questionnaire that you created in Lab 1 of Project 7 on page WD 7.64. Save the survey with a new file name of New Portal Questionnaire. If you did not complete this lab, see your instructor for a copy.
2. Modify the formats of the company name, business tag line, form title, form instructions, and thank-you message as shown in Figure 8-74. Remove the current clip art and insert the one shown in Figure 8-74. Resize the clip art image to 60 percent of its original size.
3. Change the fill effect in the rectangle drawing object to a two-tone gradient with pale blue and light turquoise. Choose the Diagonal up Shading Style and the lower-right Variant. Add the 3-D effect called 3-D Style 7.

(continued)

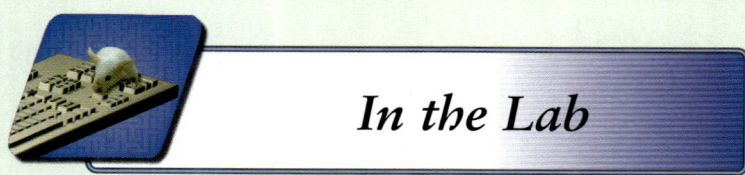

Creating an Automatic Macro for an Online Form (continued)

4. Create a new character style called DataEntryArea that is formatted with an 11-point Arial bold black font. Assign a shortcut key of ALT+D. Apply the style to all text in the data entry area.
5. Create an automatic macro called AutoNew using the macro recorder. The macro should change the zoom to page width and scroll down so the entire form fits in the document window. Run the macro to be sure it works.
6. Modify (edit) the macro in the Visual Basic Editor so that it also hides formatting marks and table gridlines. Also, modify the number of lines it scrolls down, if necessary. Run the macro again.
7. Print the Visual Basic code for the macro (in the Visual Basic Editor window, click File on the menu bar, click Print, click Current Project, click the OK button).
8. Protect the form. Save the form. Print the blank form.
9. Access the template through Windows Explorer. Fill in the form. Save the filled-in form. Print the filled-in form.

2 Creating an Online Form with an Automatic Macro, ActiveX Control, and Digital Signature

Problem: You created the online form shown in Figure 7-74 on page WD 7.65 for Montgomery Community College. Your supervisor has asked you to change its appearance, create a macro for the form so it displays properly on the screen when a user first displays it (as a blank form), and add a button that automatically displays the Save As dialog box for the user. You modify the form so it looks like the one shown in Figure 8-75.

Instructions:

1. Open the template called Montgomery Lab Survey that you created in Lab 2 of Project 7 on page WD 7.65. If you did not complete this lab, see your instructor for a copy. Save the survey with a new file name of ML Survey.
2. Remove the current clip art and insert a decorative M graphic from the Web as shown in Figure 8-75. If you do not have access to the Web, the graphic is on the Data Disk in a file called letterM. Resize the graphic to 45 percent of its original size. Delete the M in Montgomery and insert the first three lines of text into a text box. Modify the formats of the college name, form title, and form instructions as shown in Figure 8-75. Left-align the college name. Reposition it, if necessary.
3. Change the fill effect in the rectangle drawing object to the parchment texture. Add the 3-D effect called 3-D Style 19.
4. Create a new character style called DataEntryArea that is formatted with an 11-point Arial bold green font. Assign a shortcut key of ALT+D. Apply the style to all text in the data entry area.
5. Create an automatic macro called AutoNew using the macro recorder. The macro should change the zoom percentage to page width and scroll down so the entire form fits in the document window. Run the macro to be sure it works.
6. Modify (edit) the macro in the Visual Basic Editor so that it also hides formatting marks and table gridlines. Also, modify the number of lines it scrolls down, if necessary. Run the macro again.

In the Lab

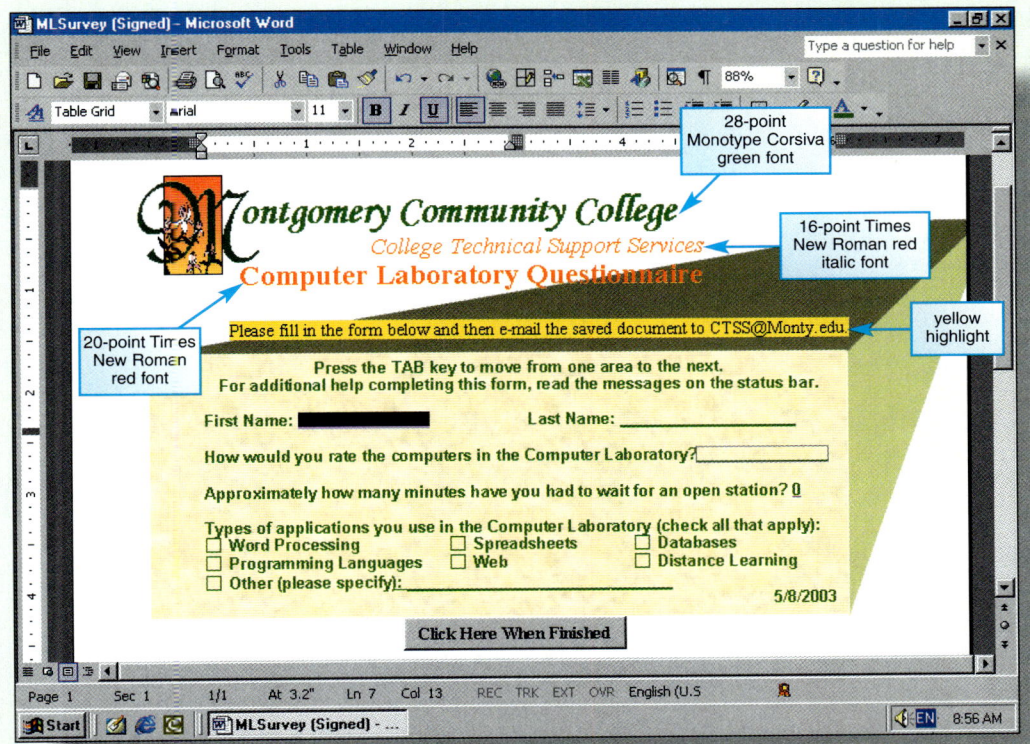

FIGURE 8-75

7. Remove the thank-you message line. Insert a command button ActiveX control. Format the command button as a floating object. Change its caption property to the text, Click Here When Finished. Change its Font property to 12-point Times New Roman bold font. Resize the button so the entire caption displays. Add code to the button so that when the user clicks the button it displays the Save As dialog box and displays a thank-you message.
8. Print the Visual Basic code for the macros (in the Visual Basic Editor window, click File on the menu bar, click Print, click Current Project, click the OK button).
9. Protect the form. Save the form. Print the blank form.
10. Attach a digital signature to the form.
11. Access the template through Windows Explorer. Fill in the form. Save the filled-in form. Print the filled-in form.

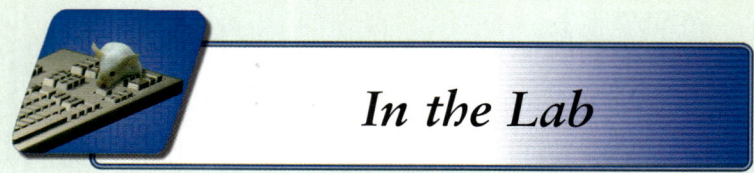

In the Lab

3 Creating an Automatic Macro, Data Entry Macros, and ActiveX Control for an Online Form

Problem: You created the online form shown in Figure 7-75 on page WD 7.66 for K&F Premier Movies. Your supervisor has asked you to change its appearance, create a macro for the form so it displays properly on the screen when a user first displays it (as a blank form), and create a macro that displays an error message when the user leaves the numeric rating field blank or enters a nonnumeric entry. Add a button that automatically displays the Save As dialog box for the user, and create a macro and corresponding button on the toolbar that places a check mark in the Save form data only check box. You modify the form so it looks like the one shown in Figure 8-76.

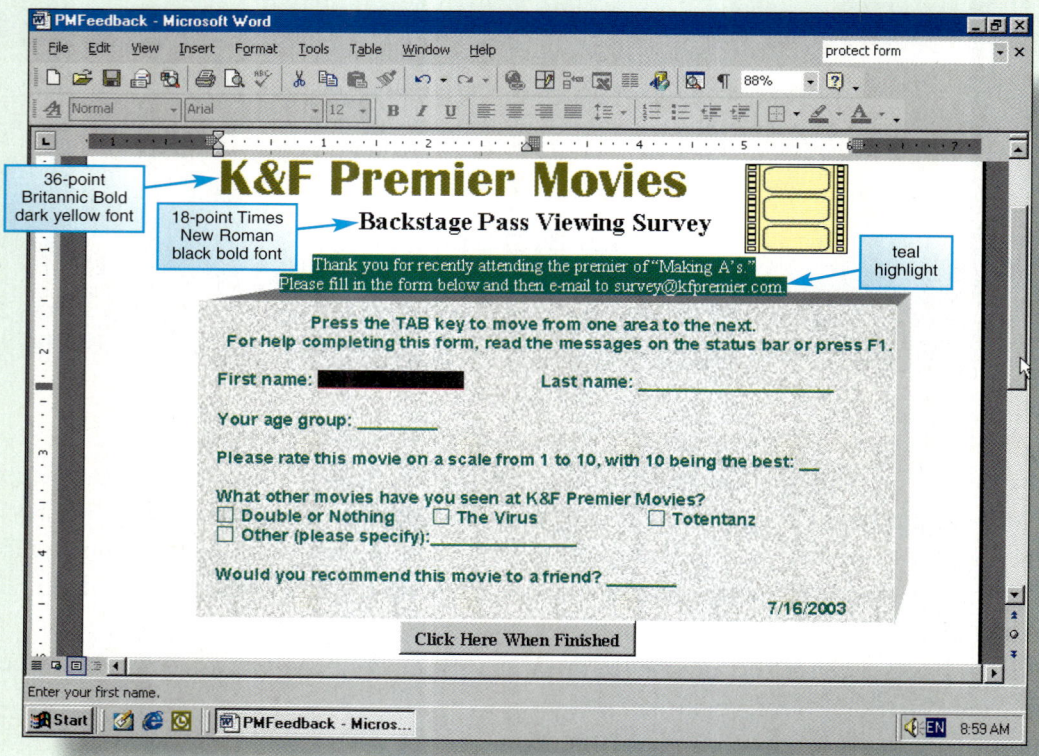

FIGURE 8-76

Instructions:

1. Open the template called Premier Movie Feedback that you created in Lab 3 of Project 7 on page WD 7.66. If you did not complete this lab, see your instructor for a copy. Save the survey with a new file name of PM Feedback.
2. Modify the formats of the company name, form title, and form instructions as shown in Figure 8-76. Move the current clip art to the right of the title as shown in Figure 8-76. Left-align the company name. Reposition it, if necessary.

In the Lab

3. Change the fill effect in the rectangle drawing object to the newsprint texture. Add the 3-D effect called 3-D Style 11.
4. Create a new character style called DataEntryArea that is formatted with a 12-point Arial bold teal font. Assign a shortcut key of ALT+D. Apply the style to all text in the data entry area.
5. Create an automatic macro called AutoNew using the macro recorder. The macro should change the zoom percentage to page width and scroll down so the entire form fits in the document window. Run the macro to be sure it works.
6. Modify (edit) the macro in the Visual Basic Editor so that it also hides formatting marks and table gridlines. Also, modify the number of lines it scrolls down, if necessary. Run the macro again.
7. Create a macro that displays an error message when the user exits the rating field if the user leaves the entry blank or enters a nonnumeric entry.
8. Remove the thank-you message line. Insert a command button ActiveX control. Format the command button as a floating object. Change its caption property to the text, Click Here When Finished. If necessary, change its Font property to 12-point Times New Roman bold font. Resize the button so the entire caption displays. Add code to the button so that when the user clicks the button, it displays the Save As dialog box and displays a thank-you message.
9. Record a macro that places a check mark in the Save data only for forms check box in the Save sheet in the Options dialog box. Create a toolbar button for this macro; use the image of a coffee cup for the button. Also, add a command to the Tools menu for this macro. (For information on adding commands to menus, also see Appendix D.)
10. Copy the AutoNew macro to a macro called TestMacro. Change the TestMacro name to the name MacroTest.
11. Print the Visual Basic code for the macros (in the Visual Basic Editor window, click File on the menu bar, click Print, click Current Project, and then click the OK button).
12. Delete the macro called MacroTest.
13. Delete the coffee cup button from the toolbar. Delete the macro command from the Tools menu.
14. Protect the form. Save the form. Print the blank form.
15. Access the template through Windows Explorer. Fill in the form. Save and then print the filled-in form.

Cases and Places

The difficulty of these case studies varies:
▶ are the least difficult; ▶▶ are more difficult; and ▶▶▶ are the most difficult.

1 ▶ You created the online form for the desktop publishing service that was defined in Cases and Places Assignment 1 in Project 7 on page WD 7.68. You decide to change its appearance; that is, change its fonts, font sizes, fill effects, colors, and clip art, and use a graphic from the Web in the company name. You also decide that the form should include the following:
 1. When the form initially displays on the screen (as a blank document), Word zooms page width, scrolls down to display the entire form in the Word window, hides formatting marks, and hides gridlines.
 2. If the user leaves the text box containing the price they would be willing to pay for a card blank or enters a nonnumeric entry, an error message should display.
 3. The form should contain a Click Here When Finished button that when clicked does the following:
    a. If the user entered text in the Other text box, then Word places an X in the Other check box (just in case the user left it blank).
    b. The Save As dialog box displays so the user can assign a file name to the filled-in form.
    c. A thank-you message displays on the screen that informs the user what file should be e-mailed back to the service.

2 ▶▶ You created the survey for the Computer Technology Department at your school that was defined in Cases and Places Assignment 2 in Project 7 on page WD 7.68. The department chair has asked you to change the survey's appearance (all fonts, font sizes, colors, graphics, and fill effects), create a macro for the form so it displays properly on the screen when a user first displays it (as a blank form), and add a button that when clicked automatically displays the Save As dialog box for the user and then displays a thank-you message. Use the concepts and techniques presented in this project to modify the online form. Attach a digital signature to the document.

3 ▶▶ You created the survey for your school's bookstore that was defined in Cases and Places Assignment 3 in Project 7 on page WD 7.68. The director of the bookstore has asked you to change the survey's appearance (use a text box and change all fonts, font sizes, colors, graphics, and fill effects), create a macro for the form so it displays properly on the screen when a user first displays it (as a blank form), and add a button that when clicked automatically displays the Save As dialog box for the user and then displays a thank-you message. Use the concepts and techniques presented in this project to modify the online form. Be sure to use a different graphic from the Clip Organizer or from the Web.

Cases and Places

4 ▶▶ Search the Web for companies that certify digital signatures, such as VeriSign, Inc. Use Word to create a list of companies you find, the kinds of information they require their customers to submit, and the cost. Search each certification company's Web site for customers they have certified in the past, and list two for each company. Ask an IT professional at your school or place of employment if he or she can provide you with an internal certificate. Write a paragraph describing what you learned. Finally, write a paragraph describing your definition of trusted sources, based on your research. Save the report and then attach a digital certificate to it. E-mail the report to your instructor, if your instructor gives you permission to do so.

5 ▶▶▶ An Internet Service Provider's online survey asks business users what percentage of their business comes via Web-based technologies. These business users are asked to enter a decimal percentage rate for that percentage; however, many users enter a whole number, such as 7, instead of a decimal, such as .07. Write the code, including appropriate comments, for a macro that tests the field for a numeric value greater than 1 and then converts it to a decimal by multiplying it by .01. Use the concepts and techniques presented in this project to write an If…Then statement to test the field's value. Then, use Microsoft Word Help to look up automatic calculations and assign a new value to form fields.

6 ▶▶▶ The owner of Brim's Blooming Boutique would like to publish the Customer Survey (Figure 8-1 on page WD 8.05) on the Web. Thus, all of the form fields must be changed to ActiveX controls; that is, you have to delete the Word form fields and insert similar ActiveX controls. Also, she would like every text box and drop-down list box to display an error message if the user leaves the entry blank, which means you will write a VBA procedure for each of the objects. Use the concepts and techniques presented in this project to modify the online form.

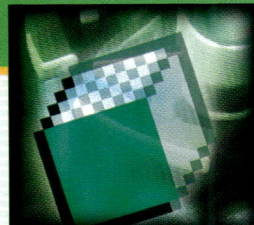

Microsoft Word 2002

PROJECT 9

Working with a Master Document, an Index, and a Table of Contents

OBJECTIVES

You will have mastered the material in this project when you can:

- Insert, modify, review, and delete comments
- Track changes in a document
- Save multiple versions of a document
- Accept and reject tracked changes
- Add and modify a caption
- Create a cross-reference
- Mark index entries
- Password-protect a document
- Work with a master document and subdocuments
- Create and modify an outline
- Insert and format a diagram
- Create a table of figures
- Build and modify an index
- Create and modify a table of contents
- Add a bookmark
- Create alternating headers
- Set a gutter margin
- Use the Document Map

Microsoft **Word 2002**

Smooth Styles
Penning the Perfect Paper

Does this scenario sound somewhat familiar? Your English instructor has announced that 90 percent of your semester grade will be based on three assigned research papers. The topics she has selected, however, sound unfamiliar. You need not panic. Researching the subjects on the Internet most likely will provide you with numerous relevant sites. Additionally, a variety of style guidelines from a number of established documentation sources are available that can assist you in composing your reports. In Project 9, you will use Word 2002 to produce a reference document titled, Discovering Your Computer, containing multiple pages, a table of contents, a table of figures, and an index.

After selecting a topic, the work begins: researching your subject, finding reference materials, taking notes, and outlining. Then, you write a series of drafts, check language and style, rewrite the final paper, and maybe more than once! To ensure that the reader of your paper can navigate easily, you need a table of contents and an index. It is a good habit to verify your references and make certain that all of your sources are given the appropriate credit. The citation procedure may seem tedious, but it is the way your readers know how to find additional information on the subjects and the way you ethically give credit to the individuals who have researched these topics before you.

Finally, you must consider the type of binding. You do not want your hard work misplaced or lost. Although folders or

other kinds of binders are a nice final addition, some instructors have certain preferences for handing in your completed work, and you always should be aware of their requirements.

In academia, three major style systems for writers of research and scientific papers generally are recognized. Scholars in the humanities use The Modern Language Association (MLA). The MLA style is organized in the *MLA Handbook for Writers of Research Papers*. Researchers in the social sciences use another popular style developed by the American Psychological Association (APA). The APA style is documented in the *Publication Manual of the American Psychological Association*. The third style is the number system used by the Council of Biology Editors (CBE). The CBE manual, *Scientific Style and Format*, describes the citation-sequence system and the name-year system used by writers in the applied sciences.

Writers also consult other style handbooks such as *The Chicago Manual of Style,* the *American Chemical Society Handbook for Authors,* the *Microsoft Manual of Style for Technical Writers,* and others.

Teams of instructors and scholars develop the style guidelines in each of these major publications. The *MLA Handbook,* for example, originated in 1951 for MLA members, and later was expanded to become a guide for undergraduates. Subsequent revisions are published on a regular basis. The MLA makes the guide available on the Internet, which includes up-to-date conventions for documenting sources on the World Wide Web. You can visit MLA online (www.mla.org).

Because style systems frequently are revised, it is essential to utilize the latest revision. Fortunately, many of the major documentation sources can be accessed on the Web, providing direction on formatting headings, works cited, tables, statistics, and more. For additional information, visit the Word 2002 More About Web page (scsite.com/wd2002/more.htm).

Microsoft Word 2002

Working with a Master Document, an Index, and a Table of Contents

PROJECT 9

CASE PERSPECTIVE

As a public service, the Clark County Public Library develops and prints multipage documents that contain information it feels may be helpful to community members. One of its series, titled Discovering Your Computer, presents a brief overview of some aspect of computers.

Keith Bettenhaus, library director, included a public opinion survey about the Discovering Your Computer series in its last pamphlet. Comments were very positive. Suggestions were made, however, that the documents could be more organized including items such as a table of contents and index, and be made available online.

Employees in the technical services department assemble these documents, with assistance from employees in other departments. For example, the office automation staff assists with the content for the Discovering Your Computer series. In coordinating all the comments and edits of these documents, Keith has noticed much inefficiency. As a part-time computer specialist in the technical services department for the library, you have been assigned the task of redesigning the production of these documents.

Introduction

During the course of your academic studies and professional endeavors, you may find it necessary to compose a document that is many pages in length or even one that is hundreds of pages. When composing a long document, you must ensure that the document is organized so a reader easily can locate material within the document. Sometimes a document of this nature is called a **reference document**.

By placing a table of contents at the beginning of the document and an index at the end, you help a reader navigate through a long document. If a document contains several illustrations, each illustration should have a caption. In addition, the illustrations could be listed in a table, called a table of figures, which identifies the location of each figure in the document. For long documents that will be viewed online, you should incorporate hyperlinks so a user can click the link to jump from one portion of the document to another.

Project Nine — Master Document, Index, and Table of Contents

Project 9 uses Word to produce the reference document shown in Figure 9-1. The document, called Discovering Your Computer, is a public information guide that is distributed by the Clark County Public Library to interested employees and patrons. Notice that the inner margin between facing pages has extra space to allow duplicated copies of the document to be bound — without the binding covering the words.

PROJECT 9

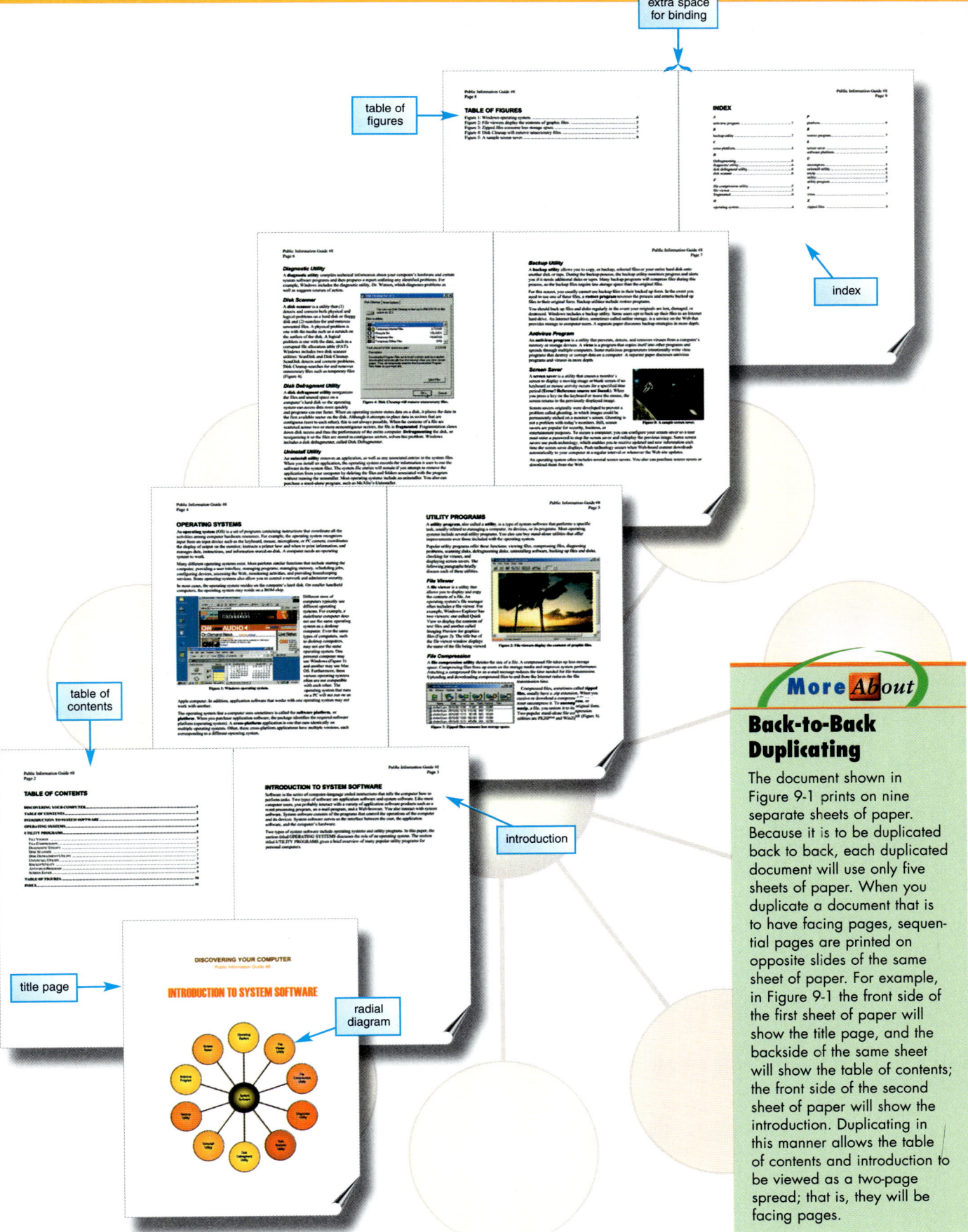

FIGURE 9-1

More About

Back-to-Back Duplicating

The document shown in Figure 9-1 prints on nine separate sheets of paper. Because it is to be duplicated back to back, each duplicated document will use only five sheets of paper. When you duplicate a document that is to have facing pages, sequential pages are printed on opposite slides of the same sheet of paper. For example, in Figure 9-1 the front side of the first sheet of paper will show the title page, and the backside of the same sheet will show the table of contents; the front side of the second sheet of paper will show the introduction. Duplicating in this manner allows the table of contents and introduction to be viewed as a two-page spread; that is, they will be facing pages.

WD 9.05

The Discovering Your Computer public information guide document begins with a title page. The radial diagram on the title page is designed to entice the recipient to open the document and read it. Next is the table of contents, followed by an introduction. The document then discusses two topics: operating systems and utility programs. At the end of the document is a table of figures and an index to assist readers in locating information. A miniature version of the Discovering Your Computer public information guide document is shown in Figure 9-1 on the previous page; for a more readable view, visit scsite.com/wd2002/project9.htm.

You have asked employees in the office automation area to write the content for the operating systems and utility programs sections of the document and then e-mail the files to you for inclusion in the Discovering Your Computer public information guide document. You already have received the completed Utility Programs section, which now is ready to include in the Discovering Your Computer public information guide document.

Joy, an office automation specialist, has written a first draft of the Operating Systems section and e-mailed it to her supervisor Keith, and her co-workers Anita, Donna, and Patti, for review. After Joy receives it back from them, she will make any necessary adjustments to the document and then e-mail it to you.

You will incorporate the two completed files, Operating Systems and Utility Programs, into a single file and create a title page, table of contents, introduction, table of figures, and index so the document is organized.

The following pages explain how the Operating Systems section of the document is reviewed and modified and how you assemble the final document. For purposes of this project, certain files that are e-mailed to various people or departments are included on the Data Disk. If you did not download the Data Disk, see the inside back cover for instructions for downloading the Data Disk or see your instructor.

More About

Reference Documents

For a sample reference document on the Web that contains elements commonly found in long documents, visit the Word 2002 More About Web page (scsite.com/wd2002/more.htm) and then click Sample Reference Document.

Starting Word

Follow these steps to start Word or ask your instructor how to start Word for your system.

TO START AND CUSTOMIZE WORD

1. Click the Start button on the Windows taskbar, point to Programs on the Start menu, and then click Microsoft Word on the Programs submenu.
2. If the Word window is not maximized, double-click its title bar to maximize it.
3. If the Language bar displays on the screen, click its Minimize button.
4. If the New Document task pane displays in the Word window, click the Show at startup check box to remove the check mark and then click the Close button in the upper-right corner of the task pane title bar.
5. If the toolbars display positioned on the same row, click the Toolbar Options button and then click Show Buttons on Two Rows.
6. Click View on the menu bar and then click Print Layout.

Word starts. After a few moments, an empty document titled Document1 displays in the Word window.

Resetting Menus and Toolbars

To set the menus and toolbars so they appear exactly as shown in this book, reset your menus and toolbars as outlined in Appendix D or follow these steps.

TO RESET MENUS AND TOOLBARS

1. Click the Toolbar Options button on the Standard toolbar and then point to Add or Remove Buttons. Point to Standard on the Add or Remove Buttons submenu. Scroll to and then click Reset Toolbar on the Standard submenu.
2. Click the Toolbar Options button on the Formatting toolbar and then point to Add or Remove Buttons. Point to Formatting on the Add or Remove Buttons submenu. Scroll to and then click Reset Toolbar on the Formatting submenu.
3. Click the Toolbar Options button on the Standard toolbar and then point to Add or Remove Buttons. Click Customize on the Add or Remove Buttons submenu.
4. When the Customize dialog box displays, if necessary, click the Options tab and then click the Reset my usage data button. When the Microsoft Word dialog box displays, click the Yes button. Click the Close button in the Customize dialog box.

Word resets the menus and toolbars.

Displaying Formatting Marks

Recall that it is helpful to display formatting marks that indicate where in the document you pressed the ENTER key, SPACEBAR, and other keys. Perform the following step to display formatting marks.

TO DISPLAY FORMATTING MARKS

1. If the Show/Hide ¶ button on the Standard toolbar is not selected already, click it.

Word displays formatting marks in the document window, and the Show/Hide ¶ button on the Standard toolbar is selected (shown in Figure 9-2 on the next page).

Zooming Page Width

When you zoom page width, Word displays the page on the screen as large as possible in print layout view. Perform the following steps to zoom page width.

TO ZOOM PAGE WIDTH

1. Click the Zoom box arrow on the Standard toolbar.
2. Click Page Width in the Zoom list.

Word computes the zoom percentage and displays it in the Zoom box (shown in Figure 9-2). Your percentage may be different.

Reviewing a Document

Reviewing a document is one of the collaborative tools provided in Word. One person creates the document; other people make changes to the same document. Those changes then display on the screen with options for reviewers to accept or reject them. For demonstration purposes, this project illustrates how both an originator (author) and a reviewer work with a document.

The following pages illustrate the reviewing features of Word.

E-Mailing a Document for Review

The first step in e-mailing a document for review is to open it. Joy has written a first draft of the Operating Systems section of the Discovering Your Computer public information guide document. She is ready to e-mail this draft to her supervisor, Keith, for review.

For this project, the Operating Systems Draft file that Keith is to review is located on the Data Disk. If you did not download the Data Disk, see the inside back cover for instructions for downloading the Data Disk or see your instructor.

Open the Operating Systems Draft file, as described in the following steps.

> **More About**
>
> **Proofreading Marks**
>
> For more information on marks and abbreviations used by proofreaders, visit the Word 2002 More About Web page (scsite.com/wd2002/more.htm) and then click Proofreading Marks.

Steps: To Open and E-Mail a Document for Review

1 Click the Open button on the Standard toolbar. When the Open dialog box displays, click the Look in box arrow and then click 3½ Floppy (A:). Click Operating Systems Draft in the list and then click the Open button in the dialog box. When the Operating System Draft file displays in the document window, click File on the menu bar, point to Send To, and then point to Mail Recipient (for Review) on the Send To submenu (Figure 9-2).

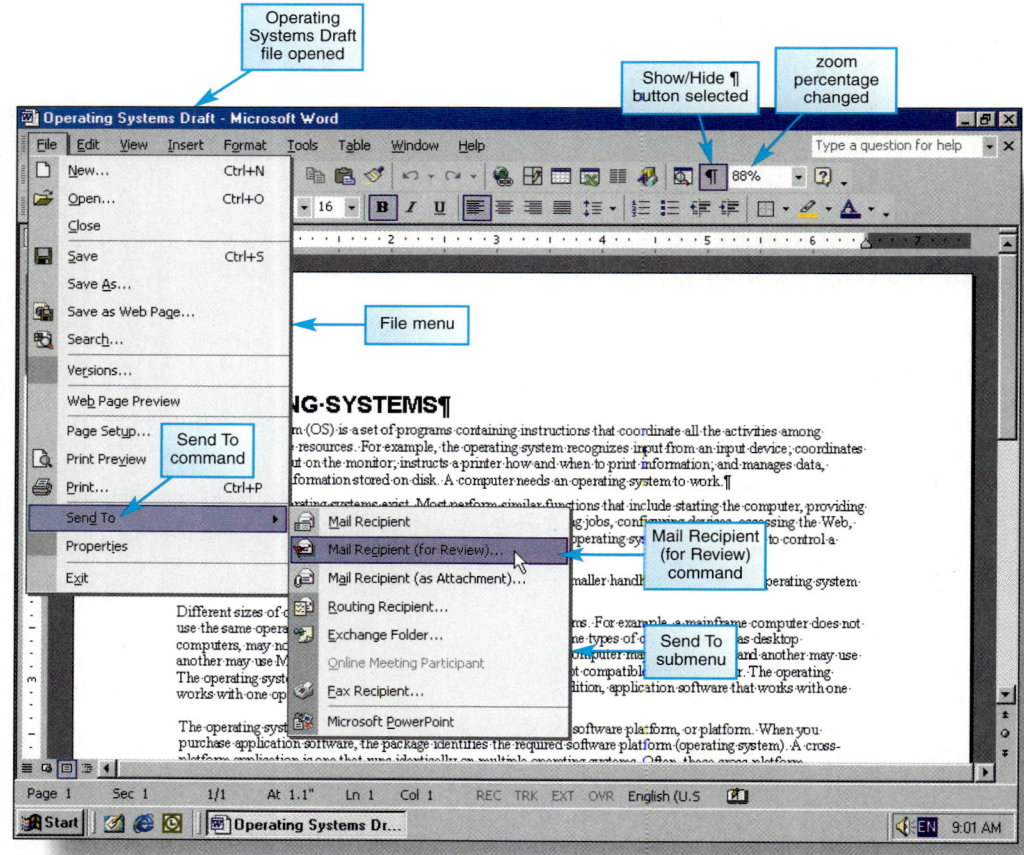

FIGURE 9-2

2 **Click Mail Recipient (for Review). When the Please review 'Operating Systems Draft' window displays, type your e-mail address in the To text box, or type an address provided by your instructor. Point to the Send button.**

Word displays the Please review 'Operating Systems Draft' window for the mail message (Figure 9-3). Notice the mail message automatically displays a message in the Subject text box and includes the Operating Systems Draft file as an attachment.

3 **Click the Send button, if directed to do so by your instructor.**

Word sends the document shown in Figure 9-4a on the next page to the named recipient in the To text box. The Reviewing toolbar also may automatically display in the Word window (shown in Figure 9-5 on page WD 9.11).

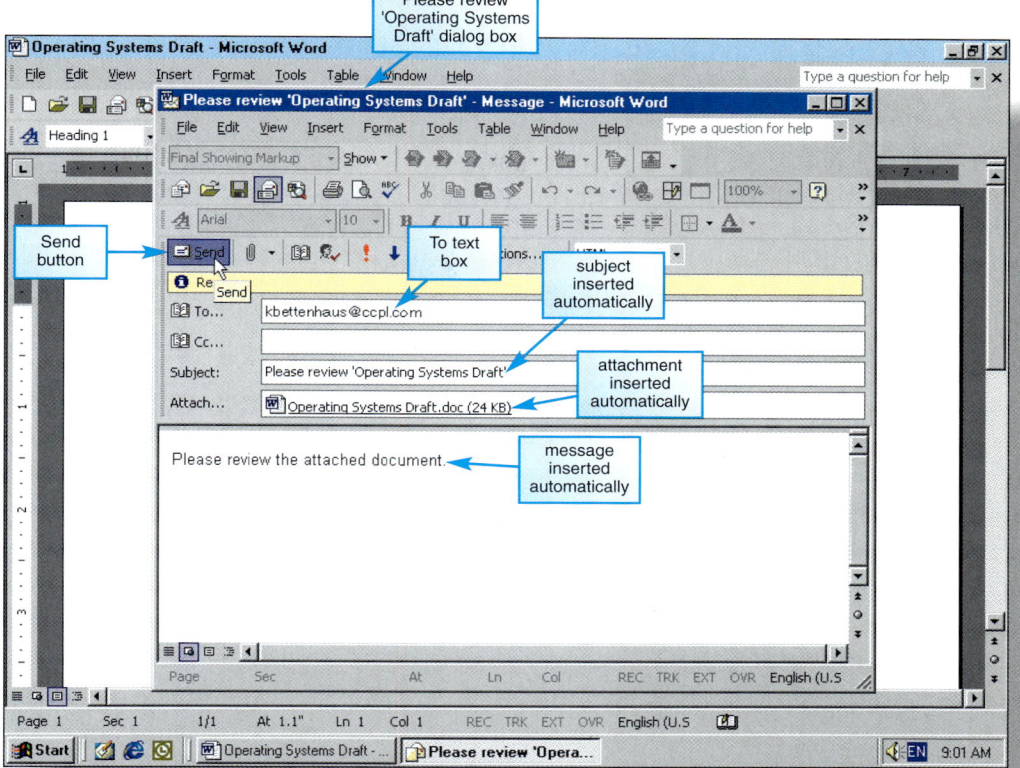

FIGURE 9-3

Other Ways

1. In Exploring window, right-click file, point to Send To on shortcut menu, click Mail Recipient on Send To submenu
2. In Voice Command mode, say "File, Send To, Mail Recipient for Review, [enter e-mail address], Send"

When a reviewer receives a document e-mailed for review, the subject line in the e-mail program shows the name of the attached file and a paper clip displays to denote the attachment. The reviewer simply double-clicks the document attachment in the mail message to start the application and open the document.

Reviewing the Document

After reading through the Operating Systems Draft file, Keith has some suggested changes. Keith could print a copy of the document and write his suggested changes using proofreader's revision marks, as shown in Figure 9-4a. Instead of writing his suggestions on the printed draft copy, however, Keith plans to use Word's **change-tracking feature** and enter his suggested changes directly into the document. Then, Joy can choose to accept or reject each of the changes online. As a comparison, Figure 9-4b on the next page shows the final copy of the Operating Systems file, after Joy reviews the changes suggested by Keith and modifies the document accordingly. When comparing Figures 9-4a and 9-4b, notice that Joy makes most of the changes suggested by Keith.

(a) Draft of Operating Systems File with Suggested Changes

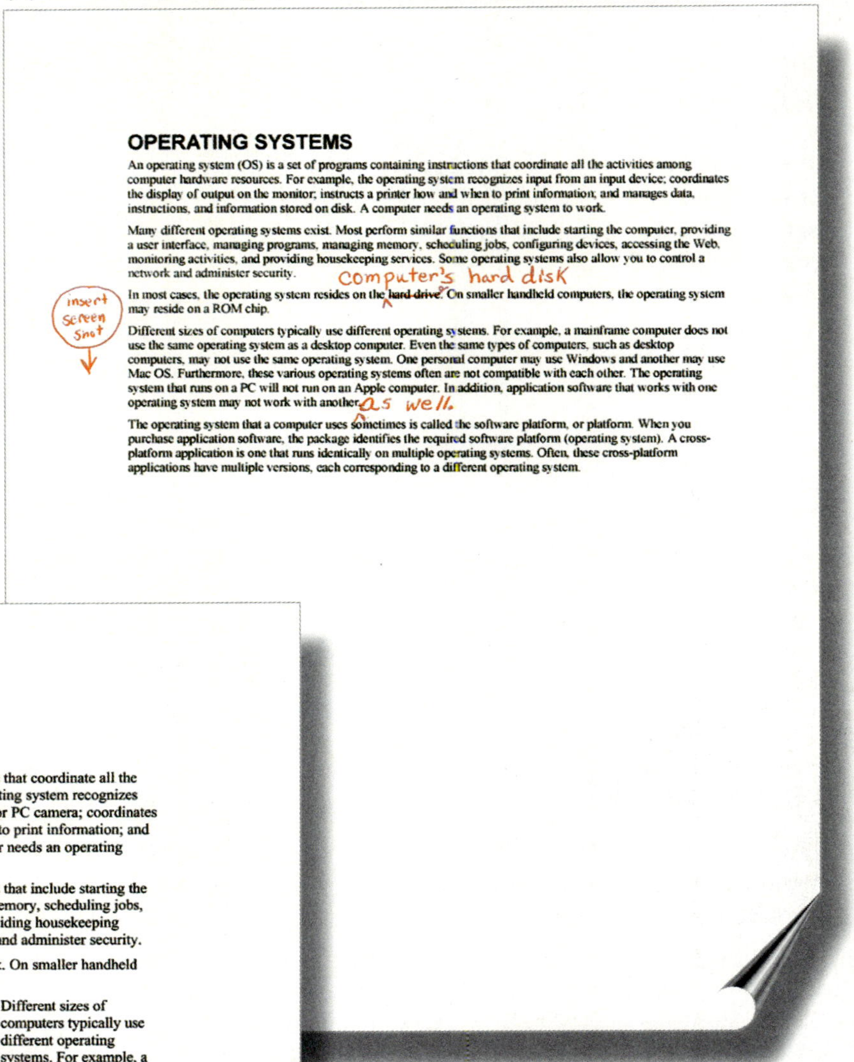

OPERATING SYSTEMS

An operating system (OS) is a set of programs containing instructions that coordinate all the activities among computer hardware resources. For example, the operating system recognizes input from an input device; coordinates the display of output on the monitor; instructs a printer how and when to print information; and manages data, instructions, and information stored on disk. A computer needs an operating system to work.

Many different operating systems exist. Most perform similar functions that include starting the computer, providing a user interface, managing programs, managing memory, scheduling jobs, configuring devices, accessing the Web, monitoring activities, and providing housekeeping services. Some operating systems also allow you to control a network and administer security.

In most cases, the operating system resides on the ~~hard drive~~ *computer's hard disk*. On smaller handheld computers, the operating system may reside on a ROM chip.

insert screen shot ↓

Different sizes of computers typically use different operating systems. For example, a mainframe computer does not use the same operating system as a desktop computer. Even the same types of computers, such as desktop computers, may not use the same operating system. One personal computer may use Windows and another may use Mac OS. Furthermore, these various operating systems often are not compatible with each other. The operating system that runs on a PC will not run on an Apple computer. In addition, application software that works with one operating system may not work with another *as well*.

The operating system that a computer uses sometimes is called the software platform, or platform. When you purchase application software, the package identifies the required software platform (operating system). A cross-platform application is one that runs identically on multiple operating systems. Often, these cross-platform applications have multiple versions, each corresponding to a different operating system.

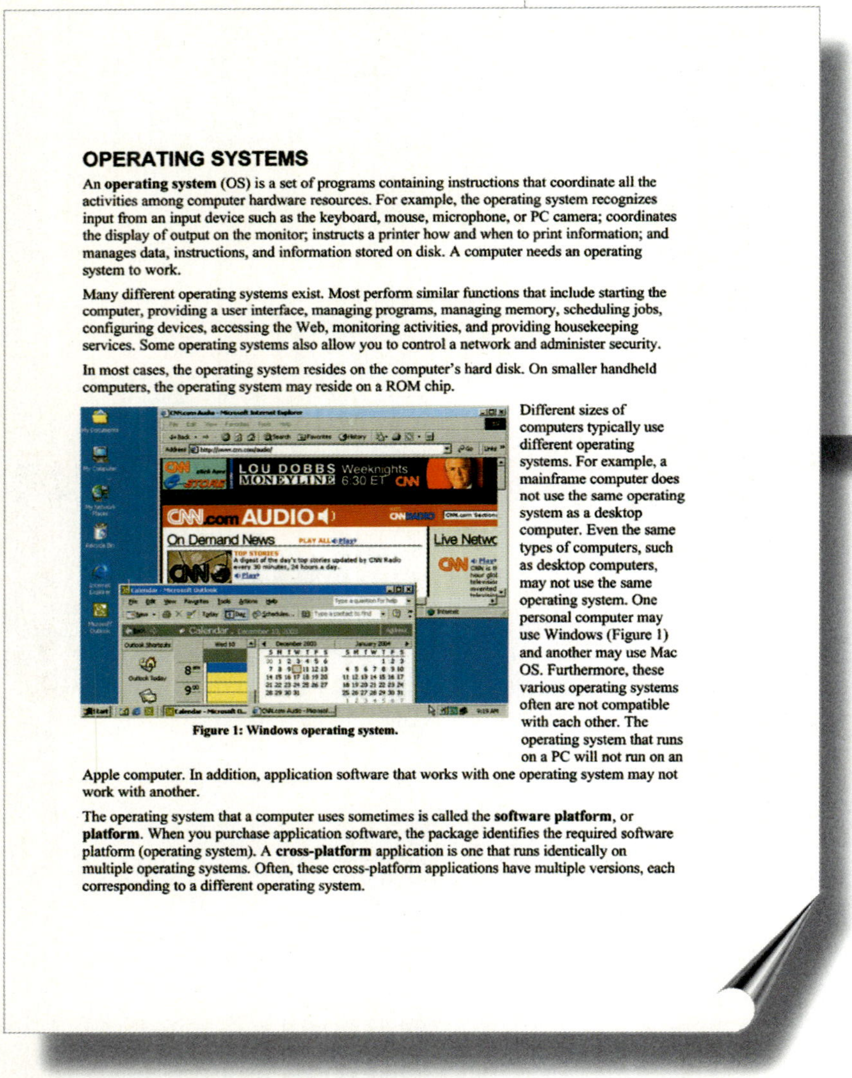

OPERATING SYSTEMS

An **operating system** (OS) is a set of programs containing instructions that coordinate all the activities among computer hardware resources. For example, the operating system recognizes input from an input device such as the keyboard, mouse, microphone, or PC camera; coordinates the display of output on the monitor; instructs a printer how and when to print information; and manages data, instructions, and information stored on disk. A computer needs an operating system to work.

Many different operating systems exist. Most perform similar functions that include starting the computer, providing a user interface, managing programs, managing memory, scheduling jobs, configuring devices, accessing the Web, monitoring activities, and providing housekeeping services. Some operating systems also allow you to control a network and administer security.

In most cases, the operating system resides on the computer's hard disk. On smaller handheld computers, the operating system may reside on a ROM chip.

Figure 1: Windows operating system.

Different sizes of computers typically use different operating systems. For example, a mainframe computer does not use the same operating system as a desktop computer. Even the same types of computers, such as desktop computers, may not use the same operating system. One personal computer may use Windows (Figure 1) and another may use Mac OS. Furthermore, these various operating systems often are not compatible with each other. The operating system that runs on a PC will not run on an Apple computer. In addition, application software that works with one operating system may not work with another.

The operating system that a computer uses sometimes is called the **software platform**, or **platform**. When you purchase application software, the package identifies the required software platform (operating system). A **cross-platform** application is one that runs identically on multiple operating systems. Often, these cross-platform applications have multiple versions, each corresponding to a different operating system.

(b) Final Version of Operating Systems File

FIGURE 9-4

Reviewing a Document • WD 9.11

Saving a Document with a New File Name

To preserve the contents of the original Operating Systems Draft file, save a copy of it with a new file name, as described in the following steps.

TO SAVE A DOCUMENT WITH A NEW FILE NAME

1. With a floppy disk in drive A, click File on the menu bar and then click Save As.
2. Type Operating Systems in the File name text box. Do not press the ENTER key.
3. If necessary, click the Save in box arrow and then click 3½ Floppy (A:).
4. Click the Save button in the Save As dialog box.

Word saves the document on a floppy disk in drive A with the file name, Operating Systems (shown in Figure 9-5).

Inserting Comments

A **comment**, or annotation, is a note inserted into a document that does not affect the text of the document. Reviewers often use comments to communicate suggestions, tips, and other messages to the author of a document. For example, Keith believes that the document would have more impact if it included a figure showing a screen shot of Windows. Perform the following steps, as a reviewer, to insert a comment of this nature into the document.

More About

Comments

If you have a pen-equipped computer, you can insert pen comments that become drawing objects in the document. Likewise, if your computer has a microphone and sound card, you can record voice comments that are attached to the document as recordings.

To Insert a Comment

1. Select the text on which you wish to comment (in this case, the word, Windows, in the fourth paragraph). Click Insert on the menu bar and then point to Comment (Figure 9-5).

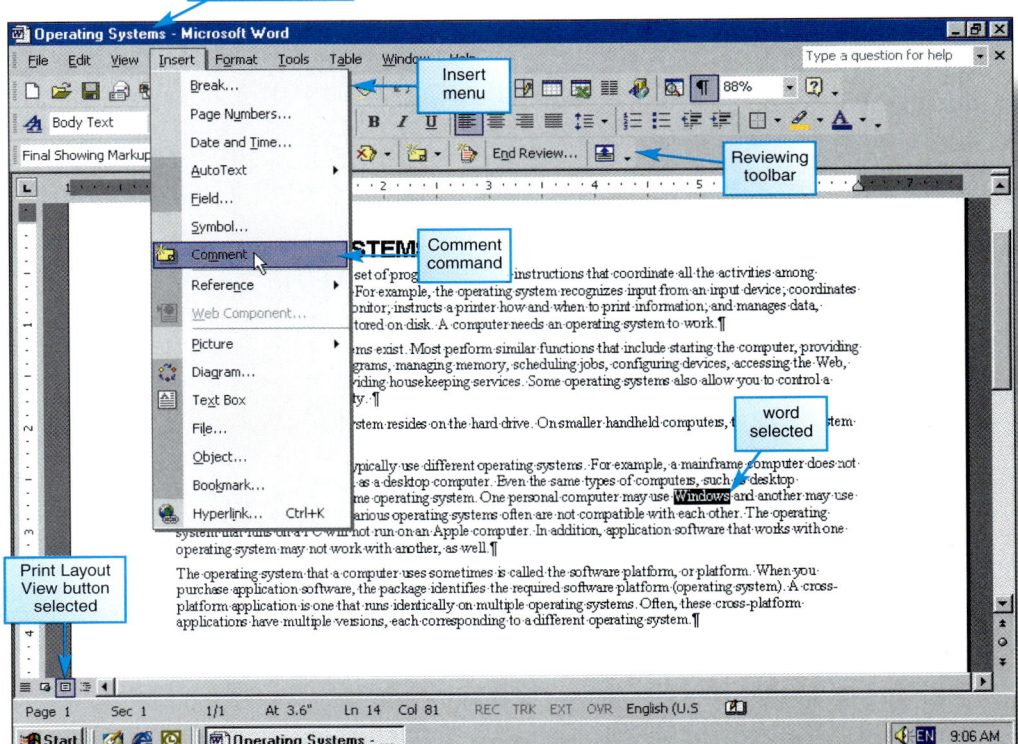

FIGURE 9-5

WD 9.12 • Project 9 • Working with a Master Document, an Index, and a Table of Contents

Microsoft **Word 2002**

2 **Click Comment. Click Zoom box arrow on the Standard toolbar and then click 100%. Click the right scroll arrow on the horizontal scroll bar to view completely the comment balloon.**

Word displays a *comment balloon* to the right of the text on the page and displays *comment marks* as parentheses around the selected text in the document window (Figure 9-6). The insertion point is positioned in the comment balloon to the right of the word, Comment.

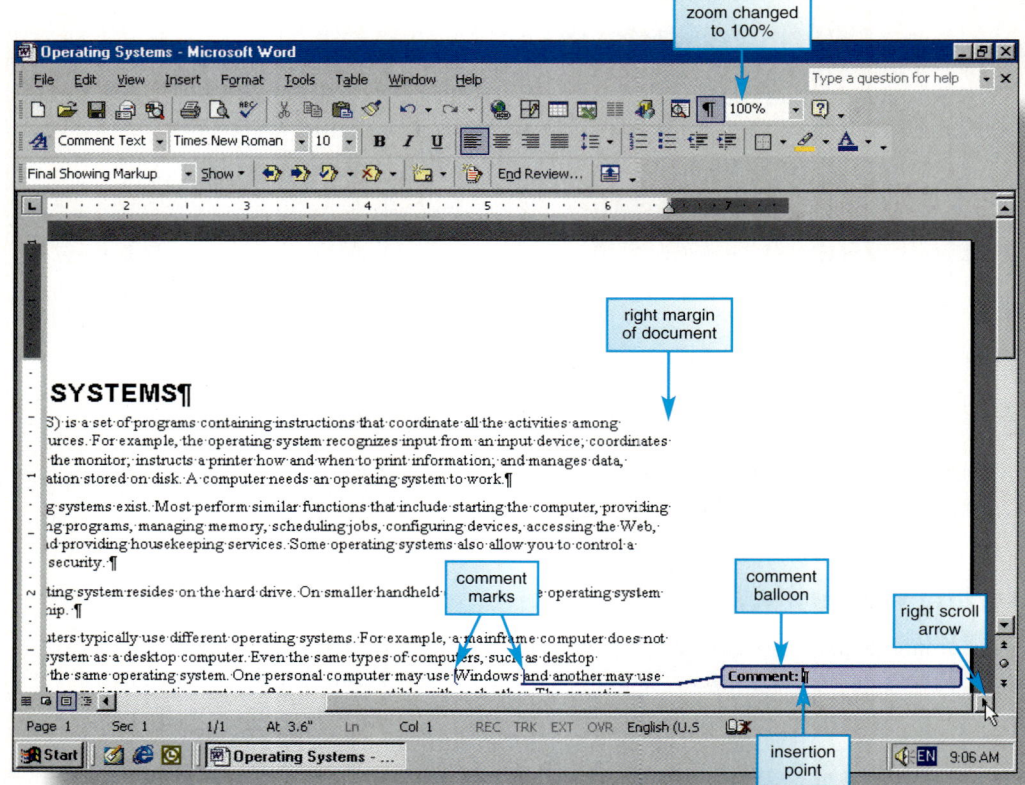

FIGURE 9-6

3 **Type** I suggest you insert a screen shot of the Windows desktop here to emphasize the importance of this topic. **Point to the comment mark (the parenthesis), inserted to the left of the word, Windows.**

Word displays a ScreenTip when you point to a comment mark (Figure 9-7). Your screen may scroll differently as you type comments.

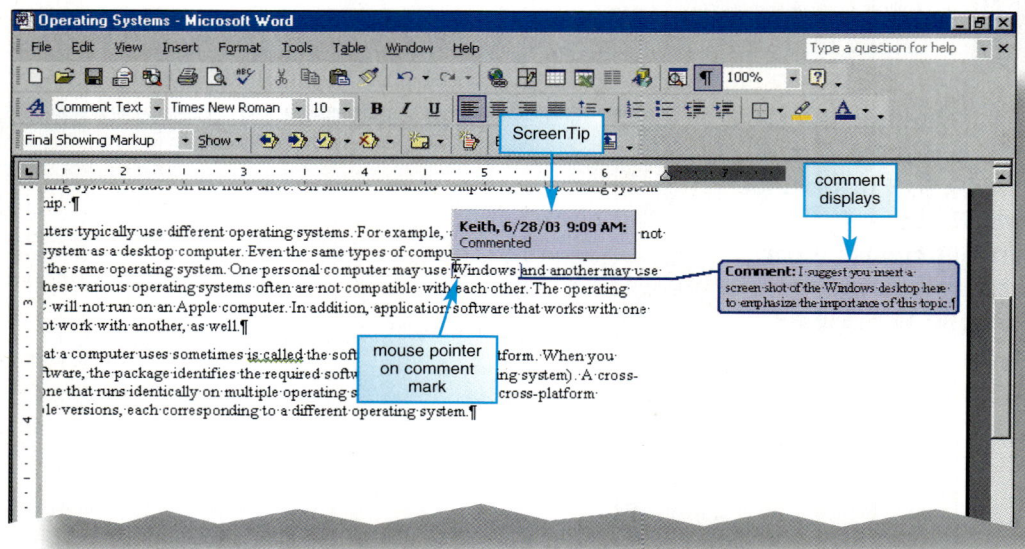

FIGURE 9-7

Other Ways

1. Click New Comment button on Reviewing toolbar
2. In Voice Command mode, say "Insert, Comment"

As with footnotes, if you point to the comment mark, Word displays the comment and the name of the comment's author above the comment mark as a ScreenTip. Comments display in comment balloons in both print layout and Web layout views.

Word uses predefined settings for the reviewer's name that display in the ScreenTip. If the name that displays is not correct, you can change it by clicking

Tools on the menu bar, clicking Options, clicking the User Information tab, and entering the correct name. In addition to the reviewer's name, each reviewer's comments are shaded in a different color to help you visually differentiate among multiple reviewers' comments.

Instead of selecting text on which you wish to comment (as shown in Step 1 on page WD 9.11), you simply can click at the location where you want to insert the comment. In this case, the comment marks (parenthesis) display side by side at the location of the insertion point.

Word always cannot display the complete text of a comment in the comment balloon. To see longer comments, to view comments in normal view, or to see items such as inserted or deleted graphics and text boxes, use the **Reviewing Pane**. Figure 9-8 shows the Reviewing Pane that contains the comment just added, as well as the changes to be made in the next series of steps.

To display the Reviewing Pane, click the Reviewing Pane button on the Reviewing toolbar or right-click the TRK status indicator on the status bar and then click Reviewing Pane on the shortcut menu. To close the Reviewing Pane, click the Reviewing Pane button on the Reviewing toolbar again.

Reviewing

To review just formatting changes, click the Show button on the Reviewing toolbar and then click Insertions and Deletions to remove the check mark. Click the Show button again and then click Comments to remove the check mark. To review changes made by a single person, click the Show button, point to Reviewers, and then click the reviewer name. Then, click the Next button on the Reviewing toolbar to view the changes.

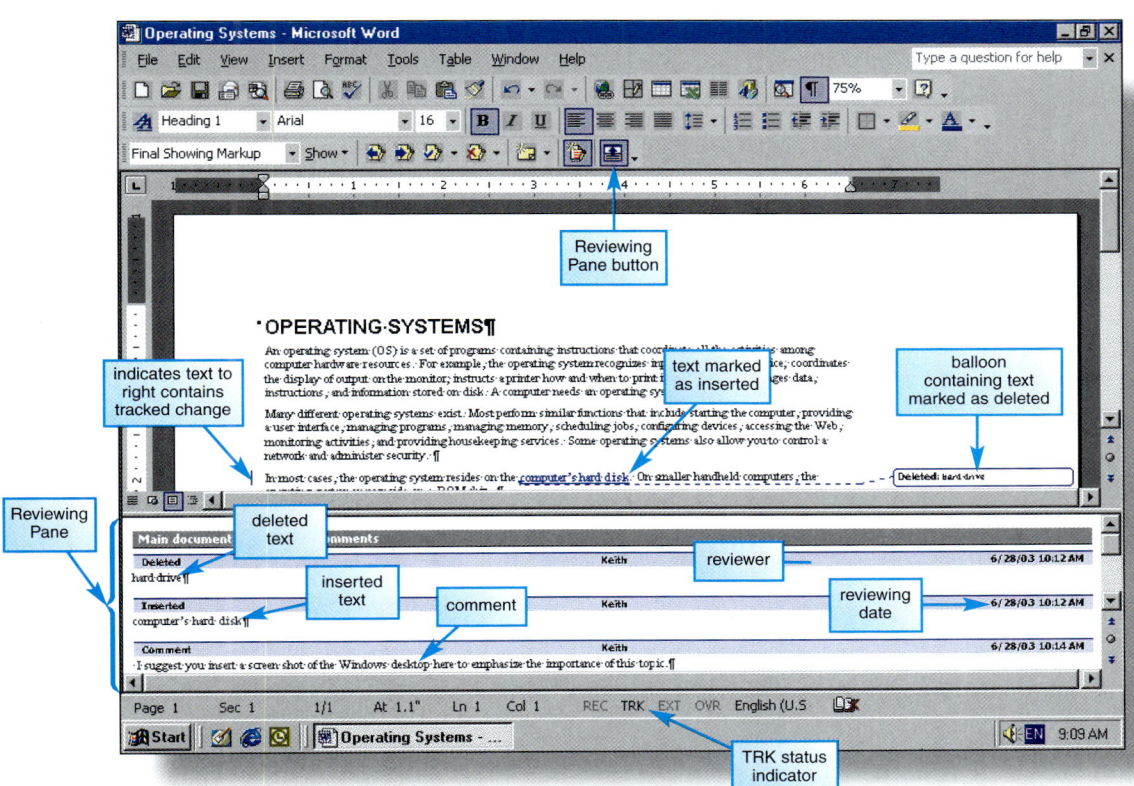

FIGURE 9-8

You modify comments by clicking inside the comment balloon and editing as you edit text in the document window. To edit comments in the Reviewing Pane, click the comment in the Reviewing Pane and then edit the comment as you would any Word text.

When you print a document with comments, Word by default, chooses the zoom percentage and page orientation to best display the comments in the printed document. If you want to print the comments only (without printing the document), click File on the menu bar, click Print, click the Print what box arrow, click List of markup, and then click the OK button. If you want to print the document without

The Reviewing Toolbar

To display the Reviewing toolbar, click View on the menu bar, point to Toolbars, and then click Reviewing. The Reviewing toolbar contains buttons that enable you to work with comments and tracked changes.

More About

Color of Tracked Changes

If multiple reviewers track changes to a document, the changes of each reviewer are marked in a different color. To change the color or other aspects of reviewer marks, right-click the TRK status indicator on the status bar, click Options on the shortcut menu, adjust settings in the Track Changes dialog box, and then click the OK button.

comments, click File on the menu bar, click Print, click the Print what box arrow, click Document, and then click the OK button.

The next step is to track changes while editing the document.

Tracking Changes

Keith has two suggested changes for the Operating Systems document: (1) in the third paragraph change the phrase, hard drive, to the phrase, computer's hard disk, and (2) insert the words, as well, at the end of the fourth paragraph. To track changes in a document, you turn on the change-tracking feature by double-clicking the TRK status indicator on the status bar. When you edit a document that has the change-tracking feature enabled, Word marks all text or graphics that you insert, delete, or modify and calls the revised version a **markup**. Thus, an author can identify the changes a reviewer has made by looking at the markup in the document. The author also has the ability to accept or reject any change that a reviewer has made to a document.

The following pages illustrate how a reviewer tracks changes to a document and then how the author (originator) reviews the tracked changes made to the document.

Steps To Track Changes

1 Press CTRL+HOME to position the insertion point at the beginning of the document. Double-click the TRK status indicator on the status bar.

Word darkens the characters in the TRK status indicator on the status bar (Figure 9-9).

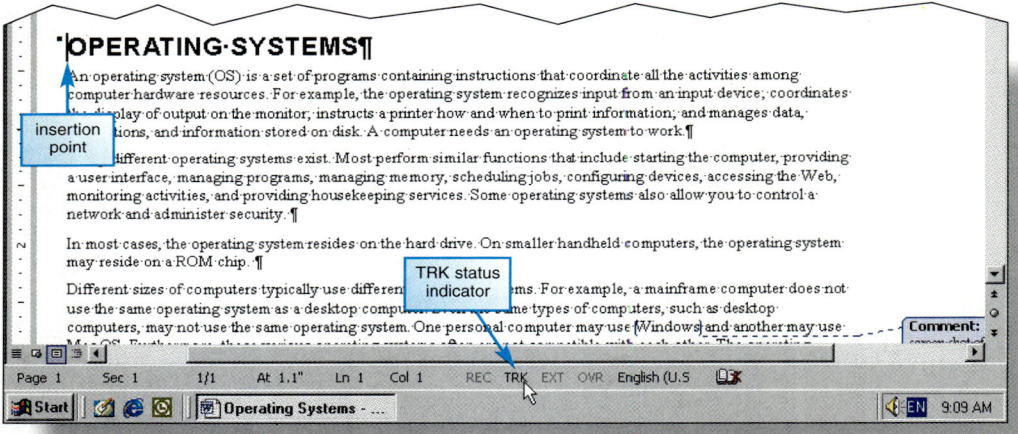

FIGURE 9-9

2 In the third paragraph, select the text, hard drive (Figure 9-10).

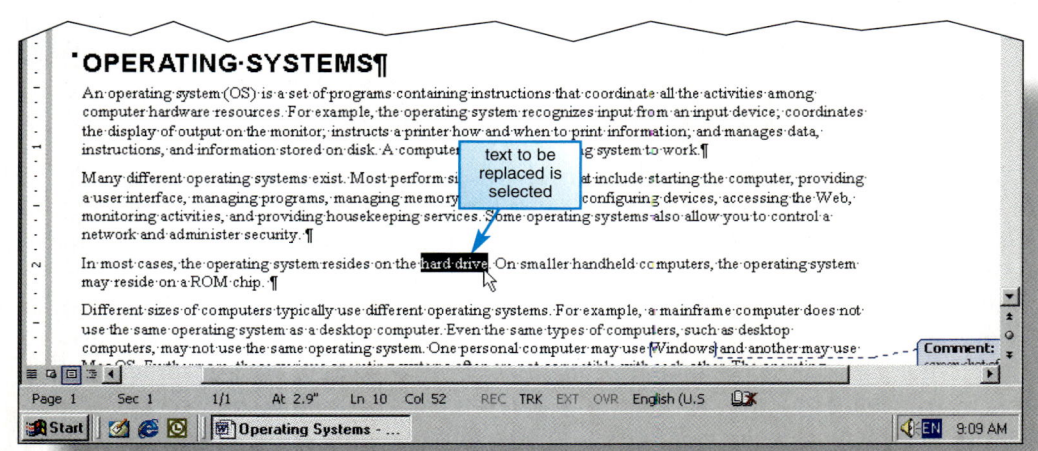

FIGURE 9-10

3 **With the text still selected, type** computer's hard disk **as the replacement text. Click the right scroll arrow to display the markup balloon.**

Word marks the selection, hard disk, as deleted, and marks the words, computer's hard disk, as inserted (Figure 9-11). Deleted text displays in a *markup balloon*, and inserted text displays in the document in color and underlined.

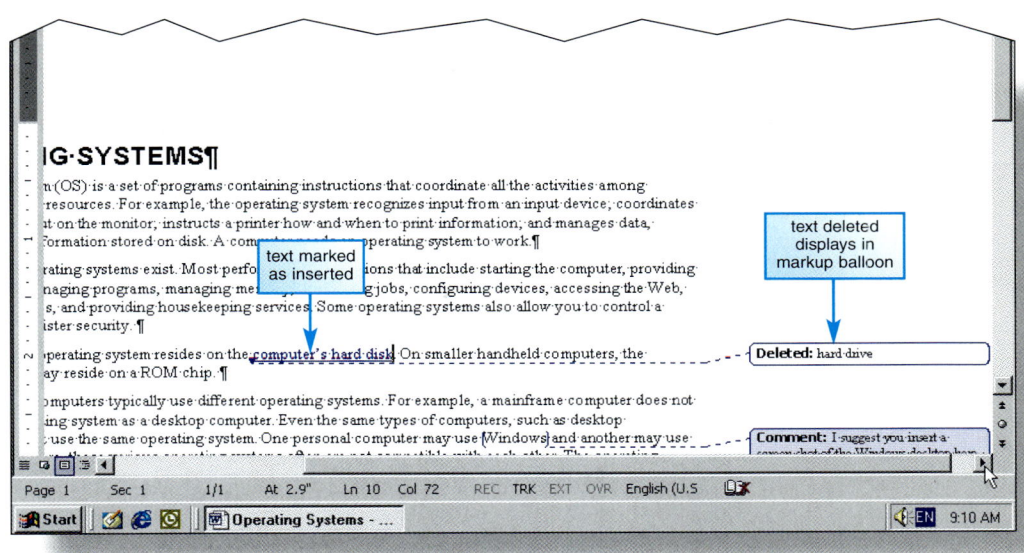

FIGURE 9-11

4 **Scroll down to display the end of the fourth paragraph. Click to the left of the period at the end of the last sentence in the paragraph. Press the SPACEBAR and then type** as well **at the end of the sentence.**

Word marks the inserted text, as well, as inserted (Figure 9-12). That is, it displays in color and underlined.

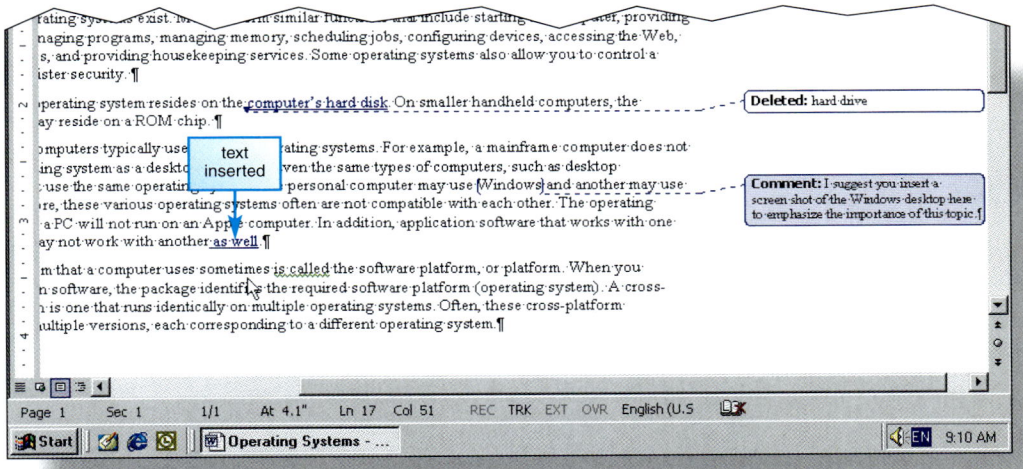

FIGURE 9-12

1. Click Track Changes button on Reviewing toolbar
2. On Tools menu click Track Changes
3. Press CTRL+SHIFT+E
4. In Voice Command mode, say "Tools, Track Changes"

    Tracked changes display in markup balloons in both print layout and Web layout views. These changes are called **revision marks**. In normal view, tracked changes display as **strikethroughs** for deleted text and underlined for inserted text. Word places a **changed line** (a vertical bar) at the left edge of each line that contains a tracked change. In any view, if you point to a tracked change, Word displays a ScreenTip that identifies the reviewer's name and the type of change made by that reviewer. As with comments, Microsoft Word cannot always display the complete text of a tracked change in a markup balloon. Use the Reviewing Pane to view longer revisions.

    The Reviewing toolbar contains buttons and boxes to view versions of documents; show specific kinds of changes or specific reviewers; review, accept, or delete each change in sequence; edit comments; and turn on or off review features. Figure 9-13 on the next page identifies each of these buttons and boxes.

    The next step is to turn off the change-tracking feature, as described in the step on the next page.

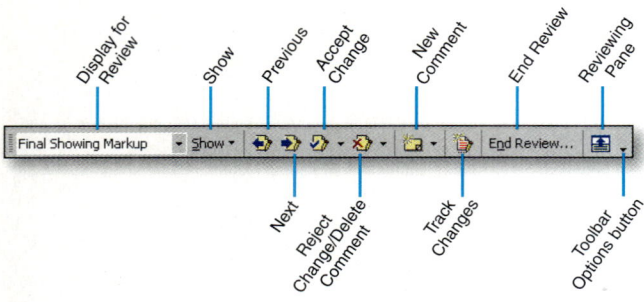

FIGURE 9-13

TO STOP TRACKING CHANGES

1 Double-click the TRK status indicator on the status bar.

Word dims the characters in the TRK status indicator on the status bar (shown in Figure 9-14).

Saving Multiple Versions of a Document

When Joy receives the reviewed document from Keith via e-mail, she wants to preserve a copy of the document that contains the tracked changes. Instead of saving it with a new file name, she opts to save a separate version of the document. Using the version feature saves disk space because Word saves only the changes among versions — as opposed to a complete copy of the file. The downside is that you cannot modify a version; you only can open and print versions.

When saving a **version** of a document, you insert a description of the version so you can identify it at a later time. The version represents the current state, or snapshot, of the document.

For purposes of this project, you will save a version of the Operating Systems document that is on your disk. Perform the following steps to save a version of a document.

Steps To Save a Version of a Document

1 Click File on the menu bar and then point to Versions (Figure 9-14).

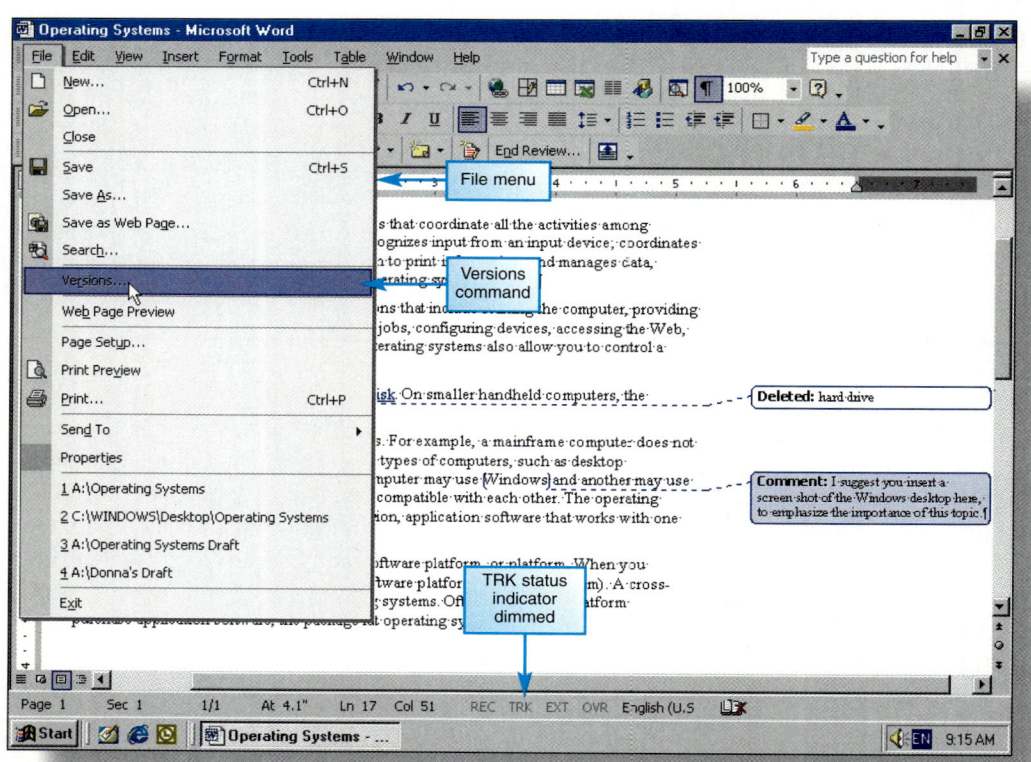

FIGURE 9-14

 **Click Versions. When the Versions in Operating Systems dialog box displays, click the Save Now button. When Word displays the Save Version dialog box, type** Contains comments and tracked changes from Keith. **Point to the OK button.**

Word displays the Versions in Operating Systems dialog box, followed by the Save Version dialog box (Figure 9-15).

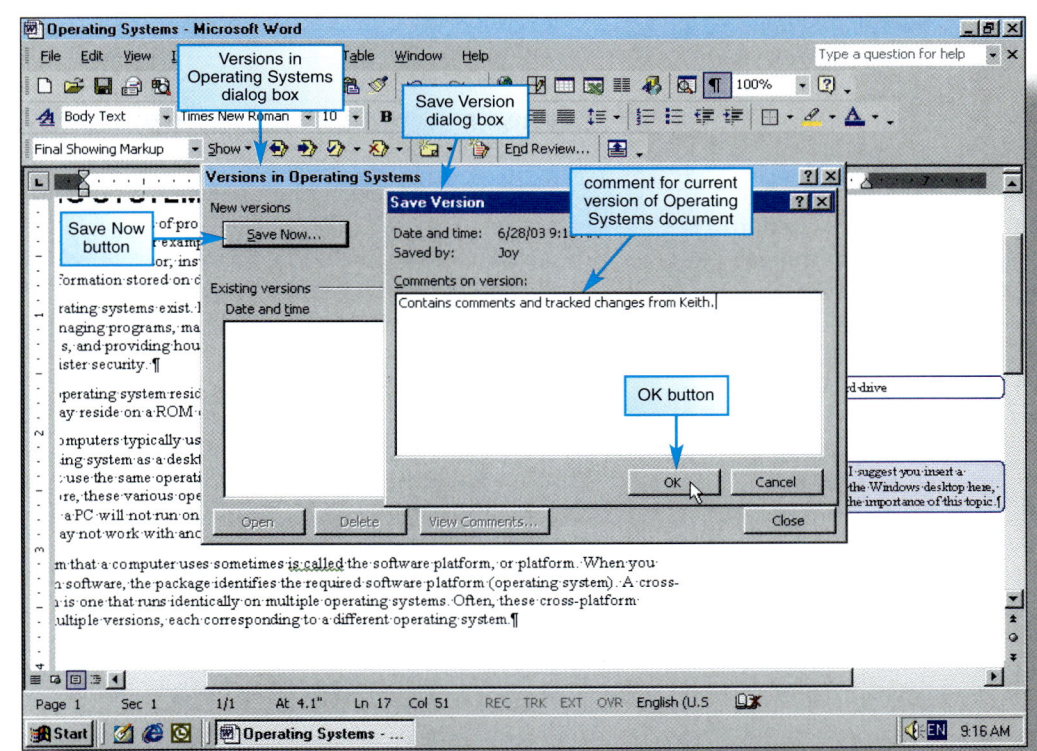

 **Click the OK button.**

Word saves the current state of the document along with the entered comment.

FIGURE 9-15

To open a previous version of a document, click File on the menu bar, click Versions, click the version you wish to open in the Existing versions list, and then click the Open button in the Versions in [file name] dialog box. If, for some reason, you wanted to edit a previous version of a document, you would open it and then save it with a new file name.

Reviewing Tracked Changes

Next, Joy would like to read the tracked changes and comments from Keith. She could scroll through the document and point to each markup to read it, but she might overlook one or more changes using this technique. A more efficient method is to use the Reviewing toolbar to review the changes and comments one at a time, deciding whether to accept, modify, or delete them. To do this, be sure the markups display on the screen. If they do not, click View on the menu bar and then click Markup.

Perform the steps on the next page to review the changes and comments from Keith.

Other Ways

1. In Voice Command mode, say "File, Versions, Save Now, [type comment], OK"

More About

Versions

To automatically save a version of a document when you close the document, click File on the menu bar, click Versions, place a check mark in the Automatically save a version on close check box, and then click the Close button.

Steps: To Review Tracked Changes

1 **Press CTRL+HOME to position the insertion point at the beginning of the document. Point to the Next button on the Reviewing toolbar.**

With the insertion point at the beginning of the document, the review of tracked changes and comments will begin at the top of the document (Figure 9-16).

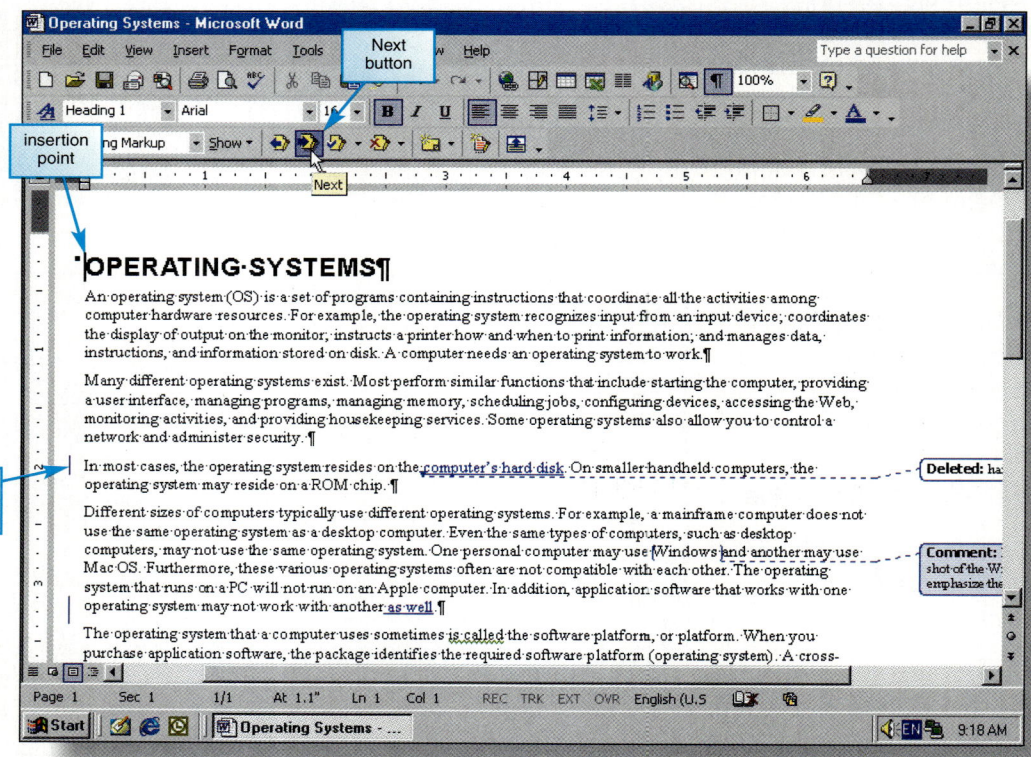

FIGURE 9-16

2 **Click the Next button. If necessary, click the right scroll arrow on the horizontal scroll bar so that the markup balloon is visible. Point to the Accept Change button on the Reviewing toolbar.**

Word selects the tracked change, which is the deleted text (Figure 9-17). You will accept this change.

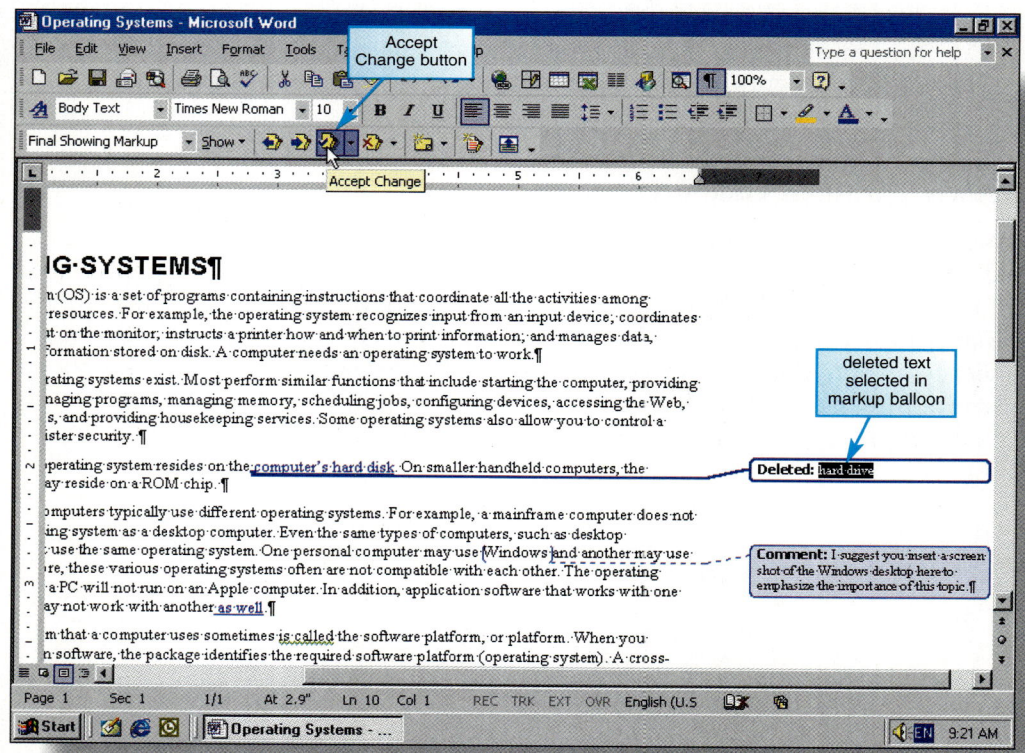

FIGURE 9-17

3 **Click the Accept Change button and then click the Next button on the Reviewing toolbar.**

Word accepts the deletion and selects the next change, the inserted text (Figure 9-18).

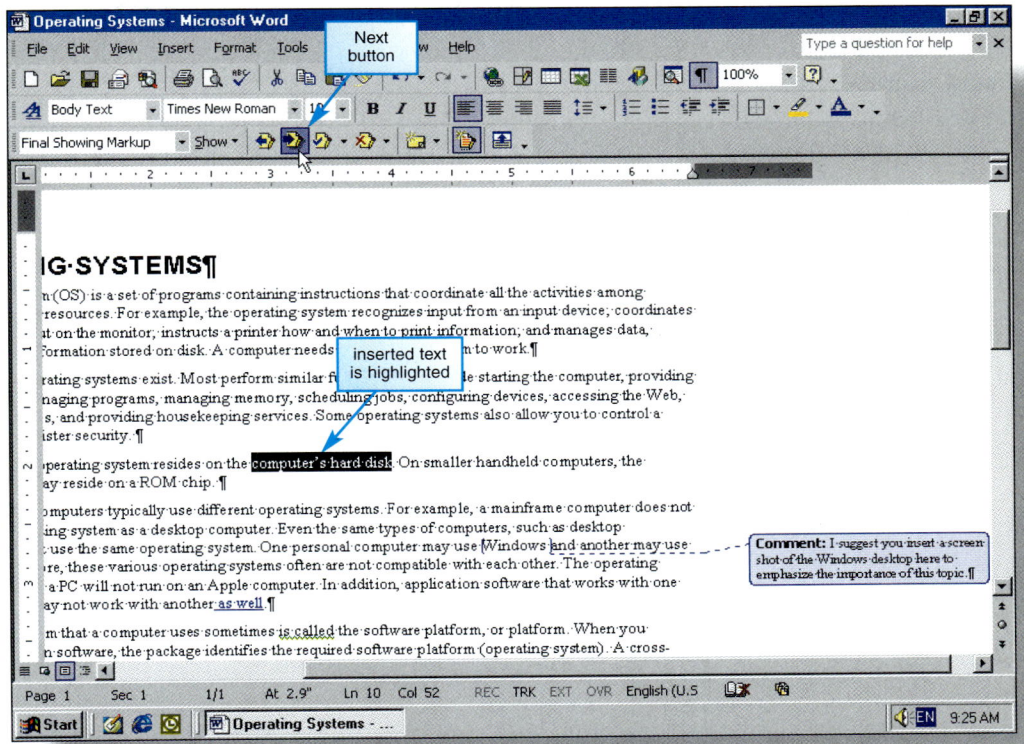

FIGURE 9-18

4 **Click the Accept Change button and then click the Next button on the Reviewing toolbar. When Word displays the insertion point in the comment balloon, point to the Reject Change/Delete Comment button on the Reviewing toolbar.**

The previous insertion is accepted, and now the comment is selected (Figure 9-19).

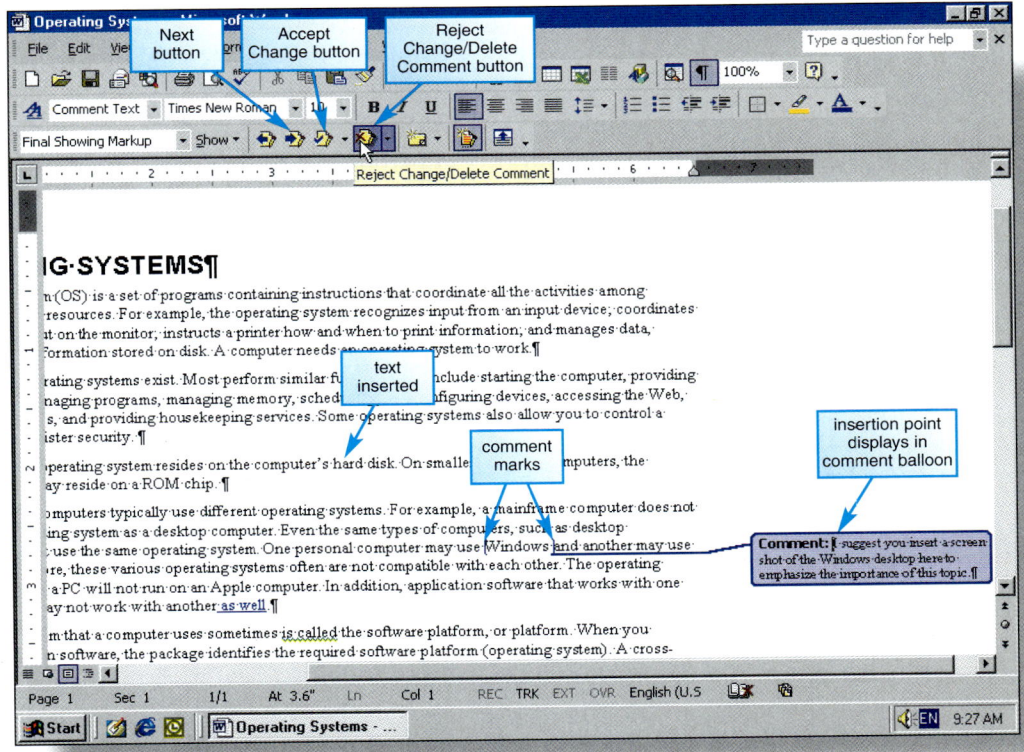

FIGURE 9-19

5 **Click the Reject Change/Delete Comment button. After Word deletes the comment, point to the Next button on the Reviewing toolbar again.**

Word deletes the comment balloon and the comment marks in the document (Figure 9-20).

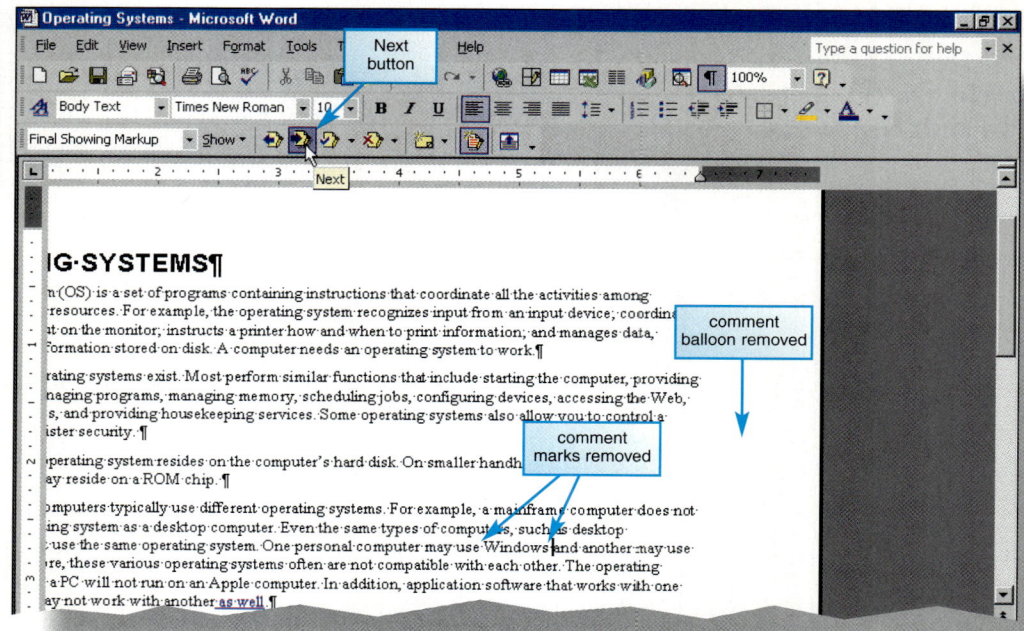

FIGURE 9-20

6 **Click the Next button. When Word selects the insertion of the words, as well, point to the Reject Change/Delete Comment button on the Reviewing toolbar.**

The words, as well, are selected (Figure 9-21). You do not want to accept this change because the words are unnecessary.

7 **Click the Reject Change/Delete Comment button.**

The review of tracked changes is complete.

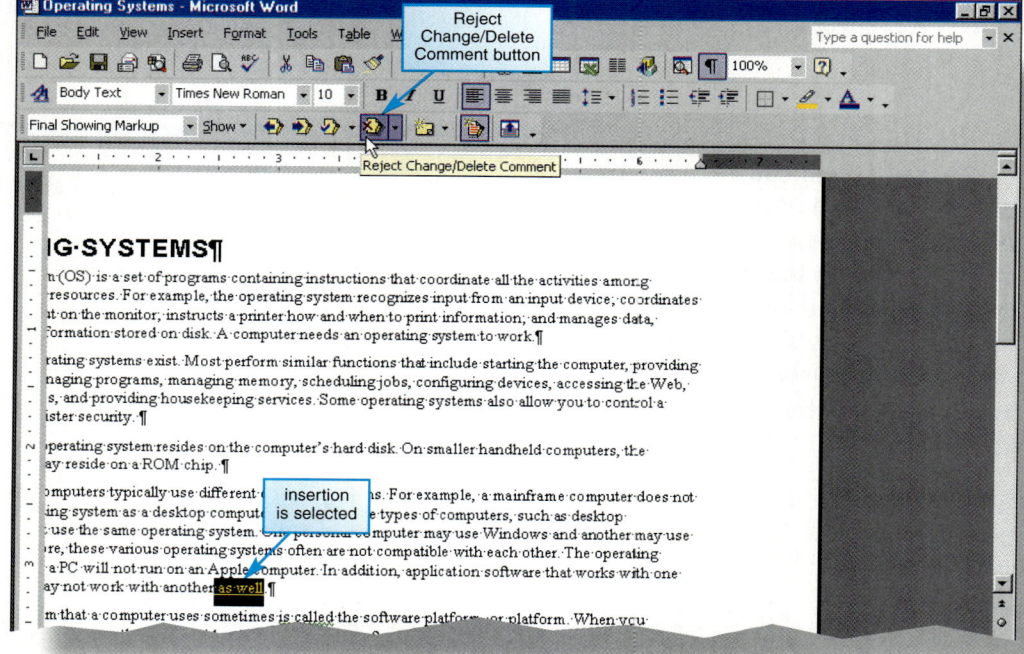

FIGURE 9-21

1. Scroll through document and right-click tracked change or comment reference mark
2. On File menu click Print, click Print what box arrow, click Document showing markup
3. In Voice Command mode, say "Track Changes"

You also may accept or reject a change or comment by right-clicking it. On the shortcut menu, choices display that allow you to accept or reject the changes.

If you are certain you plan to accept all changes in a document containing tracked changes, you can accept all the changes at once by clicking the Accept Change button arrow on the Reviewing toolbar and then clicking Accept All

Changes in Document. Likewise, you can click the Reject Change/Delete Comment button arrow on the Reviewing toolbar and then click Reject All Changes in Document or Delete All Comments in Document to reject all the changes or delete all the comments at once. If you click either of these commands by mistake, you can click the Undo button on the Standard toolbar to undo the action.

If you click the Next button and no tracked changes remain, a dialog box displays informing you the document contains no more changes. If this occurs, click the OK button.

To see how a document will look if you accept all the changes, without actually accepting them, click Markup on the View menu or click the Display for Review button on the Reviewing toolbar and then click Final. To print a hard copy that shows how the document will look if you accept all the changes, click Markup on the View menu so the tracked changes do not display, and then print in the usual manner.

More About

Displaying Comments

If a comment's text does not display in a ScreenTip when you point to the comment reference mark, click Tools on the menu bar, click Options, click the View tab, place a check mark in the ScreenTips check box, and then click the OK button.

Comparing and Merging Documents

When a document has multiple reviewers, you can use Word's Compare and Merge feature to compare any two documents. Word shows the differences among the documents as tracked changes that you can accept or reject. The changes display the reviewer's name in the ScreenTip.

Joy has sent the document to her co-workers, Anita, Donna, and Patti. You want to compare and merge each of the changed documents to Joy's document. Each co-worker's document is saved on the Data Disk that accompanies this book. If you did not download the Data Disk, see the inside back cover for instructions for downloading the Data Disk or see your instructor.

Perform the following steps to compare and merge documents.

Steps: To Compare and Merge Documents

1 Insert the Data Disk into drive A. With the Operating Systems document still displaying in the Word window, press CTRL+HOME to position the insertion point at the beginning of the document. Click the Zoom box arrow on the Standard toolbar and then click Page Width. Click Tools on the menu bar and then point to Compare and Merge Documents (Figure 9-22).

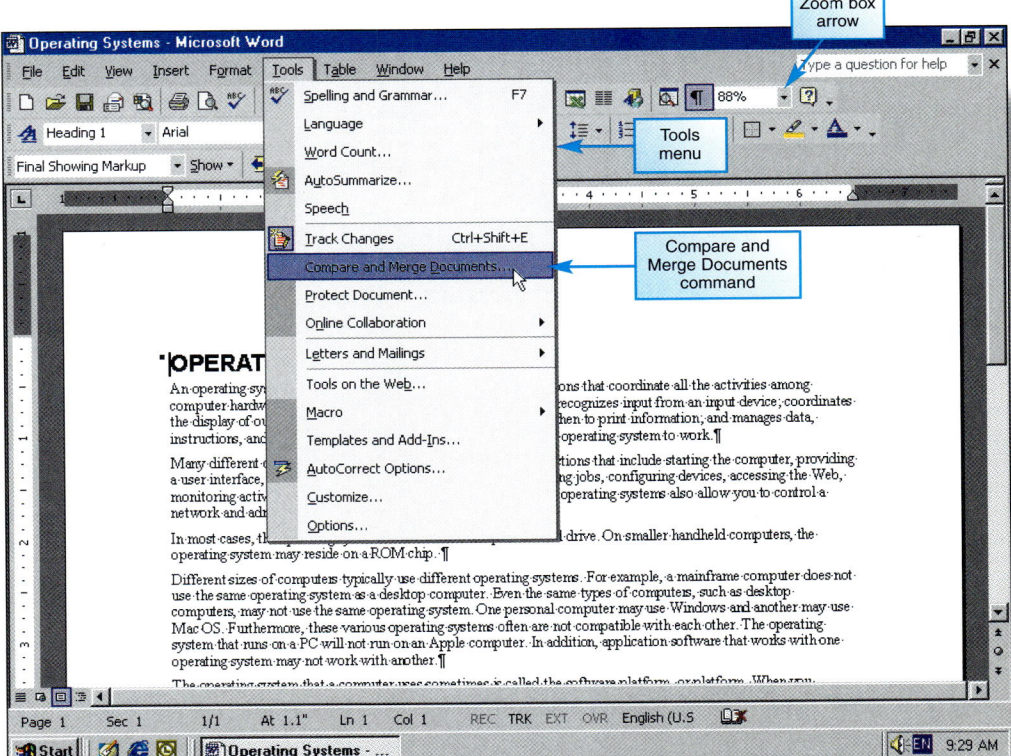

FIGURE 9-22

WD 9.22 • Project 9 • Working with a Master Document, an Index, and a Table of Contents

2 **Click Compare and Merge Documents. When the Compare and Merge Documents dialog box displays, if necessary click the Look in box arrow and then click 3½ Floppy (A:). Click Anita's Draft in the list. Click the Merge button arrow and then point to Merge into current document.**

The Merge menu displays three commands: Merge, Merge into current document, and Merge into new document (Figure 9-23).

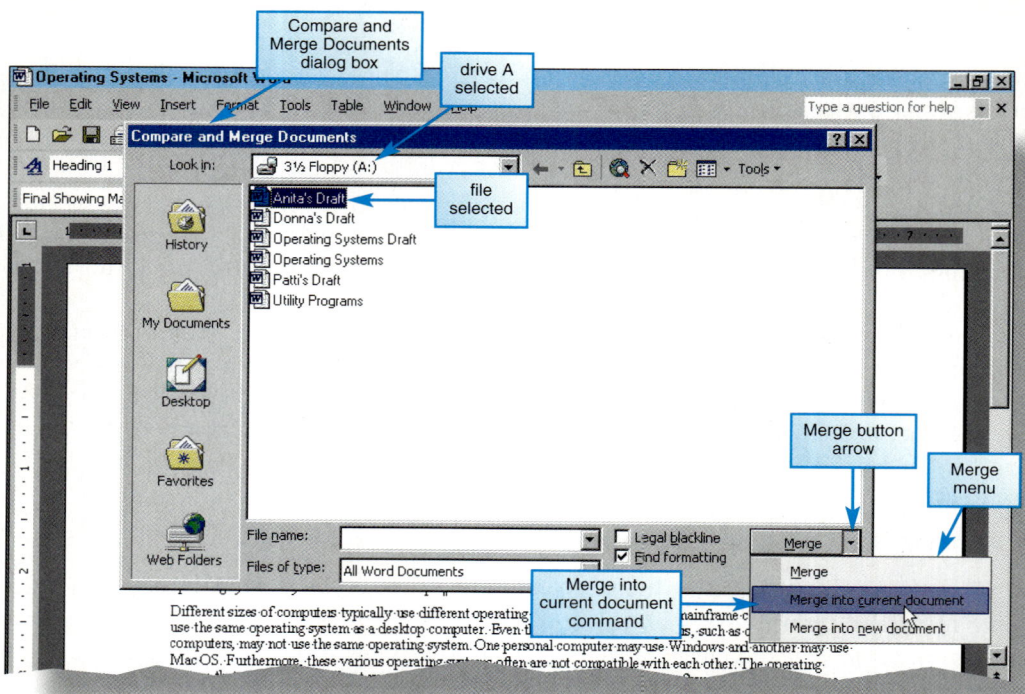

FIGURE 9-23

3 **Click Merge into current document. When the document again is visible, click the Next button on the Reviewing toolbar. When the first change displays, point to the Accept Change button on the Reviewing toolbar.**

You will accept the change (Figure 9-24).

4 **Click the Accept Change button. Click the Next button on the Reviewing toolbar. When Word displays a dialog box indicating the document contains no more tracked changes, click the OK button.**

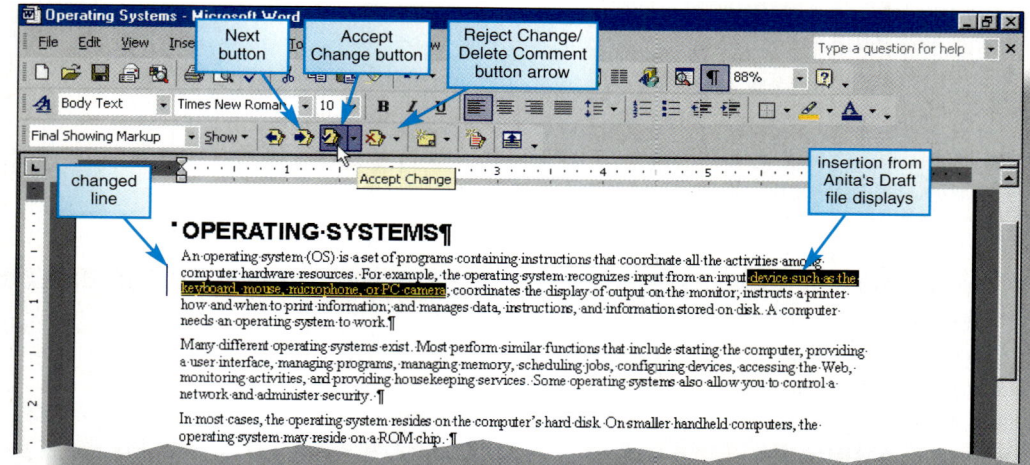

FIGURE 9-24

The merge contained only one change. Anita's change to the document has been made.

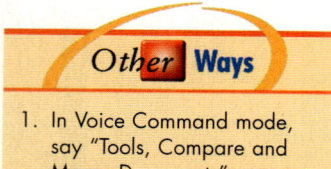

1. In Voice Command mode, say "Tools, Compare and Merge Documents"

Joy now will merge the other two drafts from her co-workers into the Operating Systems document. Perform the following steps to merge both documents into the current document and then review the changes. You will reject all the changes from the two drafts.

TO COMPARE AND MERGE, REJECTING CHANGES

1. With the Data Disk in drive A, click Tools on the menu bar and then click Compare and Merge Documents.

2. When the Compare and Merge Documents dialog box displays, if necessary click the Look in box arrow and then click 3½ Floppy (A:). Click Donna's Draft in the list. Click the Merge button arrow and then click Merge into current document.

3. Repeat Steps 1 and 2 to merge Patti's Draft from the Data Disk.

4. When the document again displays, read through all the tracked changes. Click the Reject Change/Delete Comment button arrow on the Reviewing toolbar and then click Reject All Changes in Document.

The document displays with no changes accepted from either the Donna's Draft or Patti's Draft files.

Even if a reviewer does not remember to use the change-tracking feature while editing a document, you can use Word's Compare and Merge feature to compare the reviewer's document to your original document. Word will track changes to display all differences between the two documents — which you can accept or reject later.

Because you now are finished tracking changes, you can hide the Reviewing toolbar, as shown in the following steps.

TO HIDE THE REVIEWING TOOLBAR

1. Right-click the Reviewing toolbar.

2. Click Reviewing on the shortcut menu.

Word hides the Reviewing toolbar. Thus, it no longer displays in the Word window.

Preparing a Document to Be Included in a Longer Document

Joy is not finished with the Operating Systems file yet. Based on the comment from Keith, Joy needs to include a screen shot of Windows. After the screen shot is inserted, she needs to add a figure caption to the graphic — because public information guide documents always have figure captions. Then, she will modify the text so it references the figure. The last page of all public information guide documents is an index, so Joy will mark any words in the Operating Systems document that should be listed in the index. As a precaution, she will ensure that single lines of any paragraph do not display by themselves on a page. Finally, Joy will save the document with a password, which will allow only authorized individuals to open and modify the file in the future.

The following pages outline these changes to the Operating Systems document. The final copy of the document is shown in Figure 9-4b on page WD 9.10.

Inserting and Formatting a Graphic

The graphic you will insert in the Operating Systems document is located on the Data Disk that accompanies this book. If you did not download the Data Disk, see the inside back cover for instructions for downloading the Data Disk or see your instructor. The graphic displays a screen shot of Windows. A **screen shot** is

Screen Shots

Many computer application programs exist to help capture screen images. For information on a screen capture program, visit the Word 2002 More About Web page (scsite.com/wd2002/more.htm) and then click Capture Screen Images.

a picture of the screen captured either by pressing the PRINT SCREEN key on the keyboard or by using special screen capturing software. You will insert the screen shot graphic, resize it, and then change it from an inline graphic to a floating graphic.

Perform the following steps to insert the screen shot graphic from the file on the Data Disk.

TO INSERT A GRAPHIC

1. Position the insertion point at the beginning of the fourth paragraph in the Operating Systems file. Click Insert on the menu bar, point to Picture, and then click From File on the Picture submenu.
2. When the Insert Picture dialog box displays, click the Look in box arrow and then click 3½ Floppy (A:).
3. Click Windows Screen Shot in the list of files and then click the Insert button.

Word inserts the screen shot graphic into the document.

You want the screen shot graphic to be smaller in the document. Thus, perform the following steps to resize the graphic.

TO RESIZE A GRAPHIC

1. Double-click the graphic.
2. When the Format Picture dialog box displays, click the Size tab. Change the height and width values in the Scale area to 55%.
3. Click the OK button.

Word reduces the size of the screen shot graphic to 55 percent of its original size (Figure 9-25).

Graphics

Two basic types of graphics that you can use to enhance your documents are drawing objects and pictures. Drawing objects include AutoShapes, diagrams, curves, lines, and WordArt drawing objects — all of which become part of your Word document. Pictures are graphics created from another file, which include bitmaps, scanned pictures, photographs, and clip art.

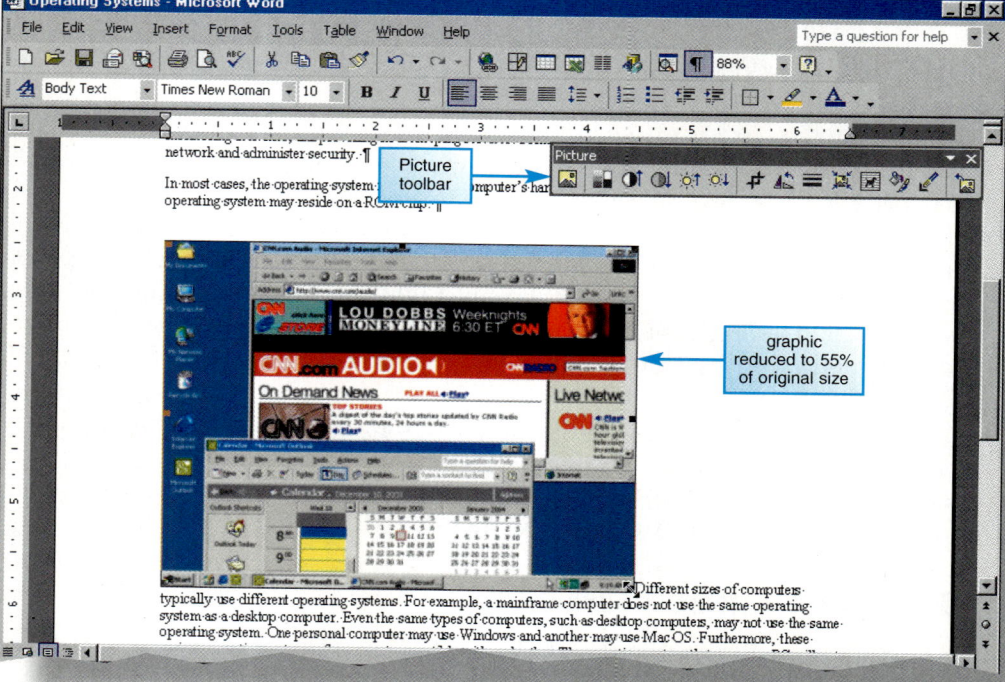

FIGURE 9-25

Notice in Figure 9-25 that the screen shot graphic is inline; that is, the graphic is part of the current paragraph. You want to position the graphic to the left of the paragraph and have the text wrap to the right of the graphic. Thus, the graphic needs to be a floating graphic instead of an inline graphic. To accomplish this, change the graphic's wrapping style to square, as shown in the following steps.

TO CHANGE AN INLINE GRAPHIC TO A FLOATING GRAPHIC

1. If the Picture toolbar does not display, right-click the graphic, and then click Show Picture Toolbar on the shortcut menu. With the graphic still selected, click the Text Wrapping button on the Picture toolbar and then point to Square (Figure 9-26).

2. Click Square.

3. If necessary, scroll down to display the graphic and then drag the graphic to the left of the paragraph to position the graphic as shown in Figure 9-27 on the next page.

Word converts the graphic from inline to floating so you can position it anywhere on the page.

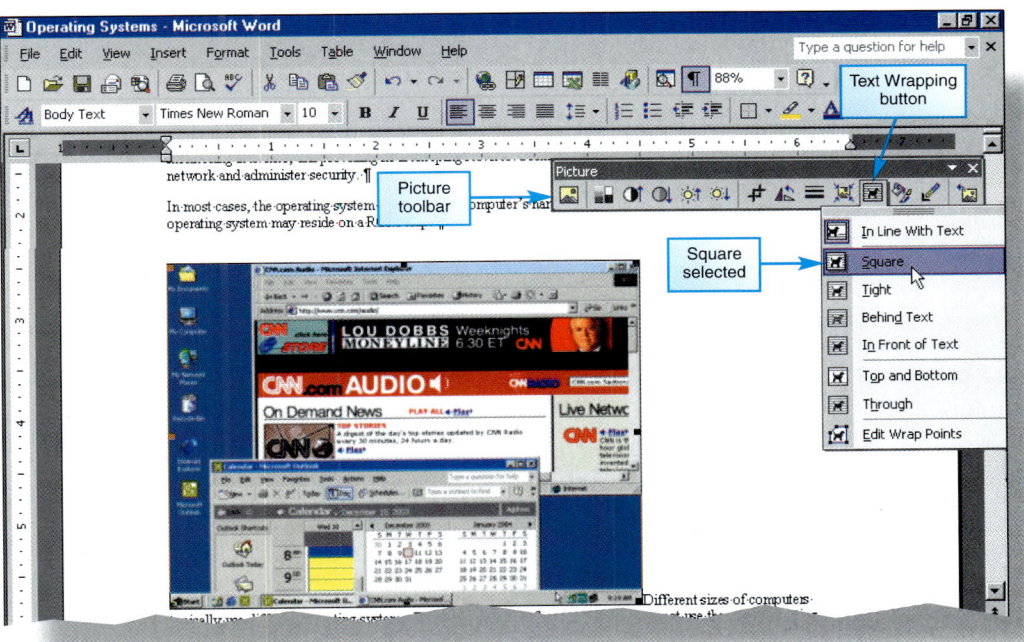

FIGURE 9-26

The next step is to add a caption to the graphic.

Adding a Caption

At the end of all public information guide documents is a table of figures, which lists all figures and their corresponding page numbers. Word generates this table of figures from the captions in the document. A **caption** is a numbered label, such as Figure 1, that you can add to a table, figure, equation, or other item. If you move, delete, or add captions in a document, Word renumbers remaining captions in the document automatically.

Perform the steps on the next page to add a caption to the graphic.

Editing Graphics

Use the Drawing toolbar to edit drawing objects using color, patterns, borders, and other effects. Use the Picture toolbar and color and shading buttons on the Drawing toolbar to edit pictures. In some cases, you must ungroup and convert a picture to a drawing object before you can use many of the other Drawing toolbar options.

Captions

If your caption displays with extra characters inside curly braces {}, Word is displaying field codes instead of field results. Press ALT+F9 to display the caption correctly as field results. If your caption prints field codes, click Tools on the menu bar, click Options, click the Print tab, remove the check mark from the Field codes check box, click the OK button, and then print the document again.

Steps: To Add a Caption

1 With the graphic still selected, click Insert on the menu bar, point to Reference, and then point to Caption on the Reference submenu (Figure 9-27).

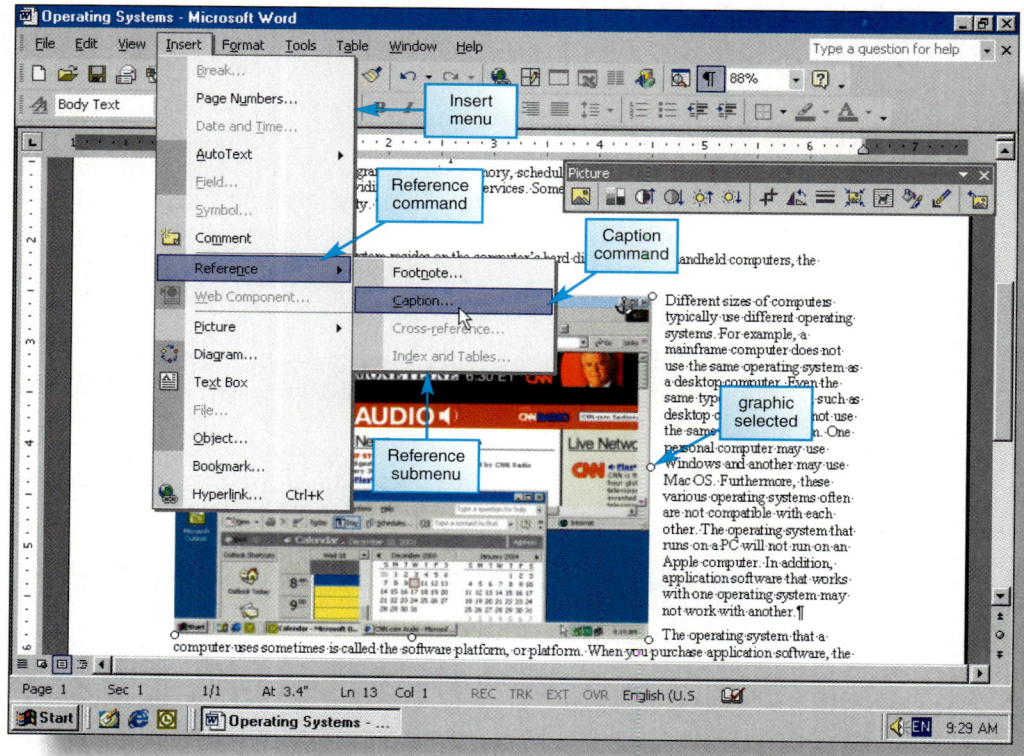

FIGURE 9-27

2 Click Caption. When the Caption dialog box displays, if necessary, click the Caption text box to position the insertion point after the text, Figure 1. Press the COLON (:) key and then press the SPACEBAR. Type Windows operating system. Point to the OK button.

Word displays the Caption dialog box (Figure 9-28). Word will position the caption for this figure below the graphic.

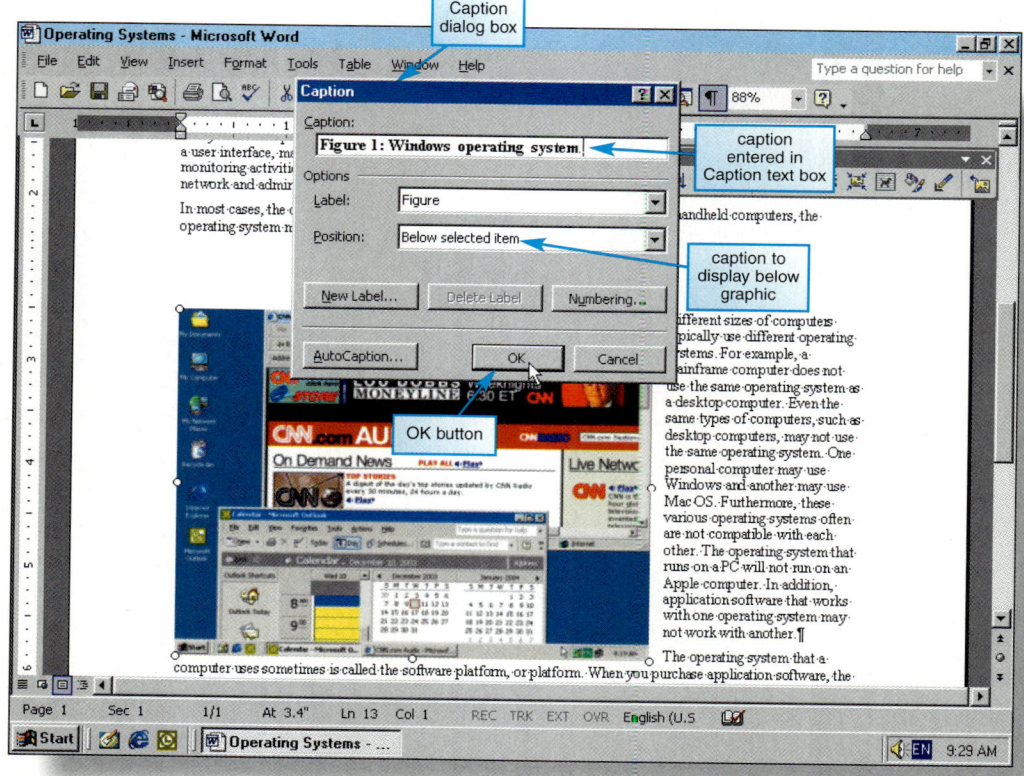

FIGURE 9-28

3 **Click the OK button.**

Word inserts the caption in a text box below the selected graphic (Figure 9-29).

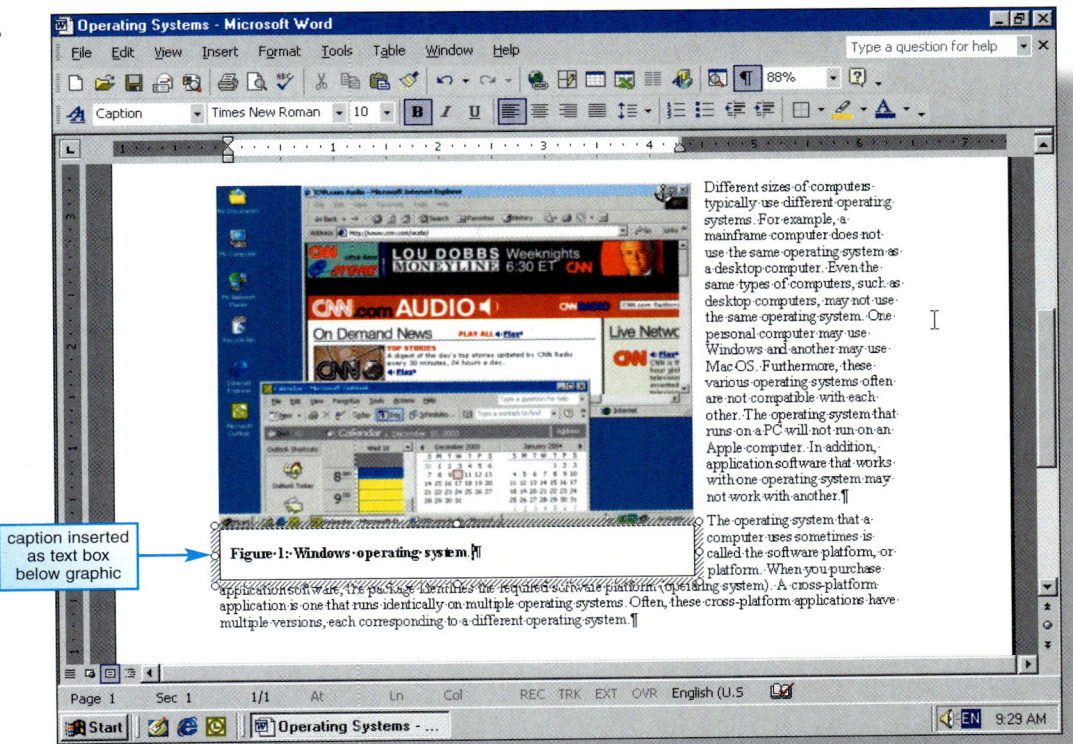

FIGURE 9-29

If, at a later time, you insert a new item with a caption, or move or delete items containing captions, Word automatically updates caption numbers throughout the document.

A caption contains a field. In Word, a **field** is a placeholder for data that you expect might change in a document. Examples of fields you have used in previous projects are page numbers, merge fields, IF fields, form fields, and the current date.

Because the caption number is a field, you update it using the same technique used to update a field. That is, to update all caption numbers, select the entire document and then press the F9 key or right-click the selection and then click Update Field on the shortcut menu. When you print a document, Word updates the caption numbers automatically, whether or not the document window displays the updated caption numbers.

When you add a caption to an inline graphic, the caption is not inserted in a text box. As just illustrated, however, the caption for a floating graphic is inserted in a text box. If you plan to generate a table of figures for a document, a caption cannot be in a text box. Instead, it must be in a frame. Perform the steps on the next page to convert the text box to a frame.

Other Ways

1. In Voice Command mode, say "Insert, Reference, Caption"

Steps To Convert a Text Box to a Frame

1 With the text box selected, click Format on the menu bar and then click Text Box. When the Format Text Box dialog box displays, click the Text Box tab and then point to the Convert to Frame button.

Word displays the Format Text Box dialog box (Figure 9-30).

2 Click the Convert to Frame button. When Word displays a dialog box indicating some formatting of the frame may be lost, click the OK button. If Word displays a dialog box asking if you want a Frame command on the Insert menu, click the Cancel button.

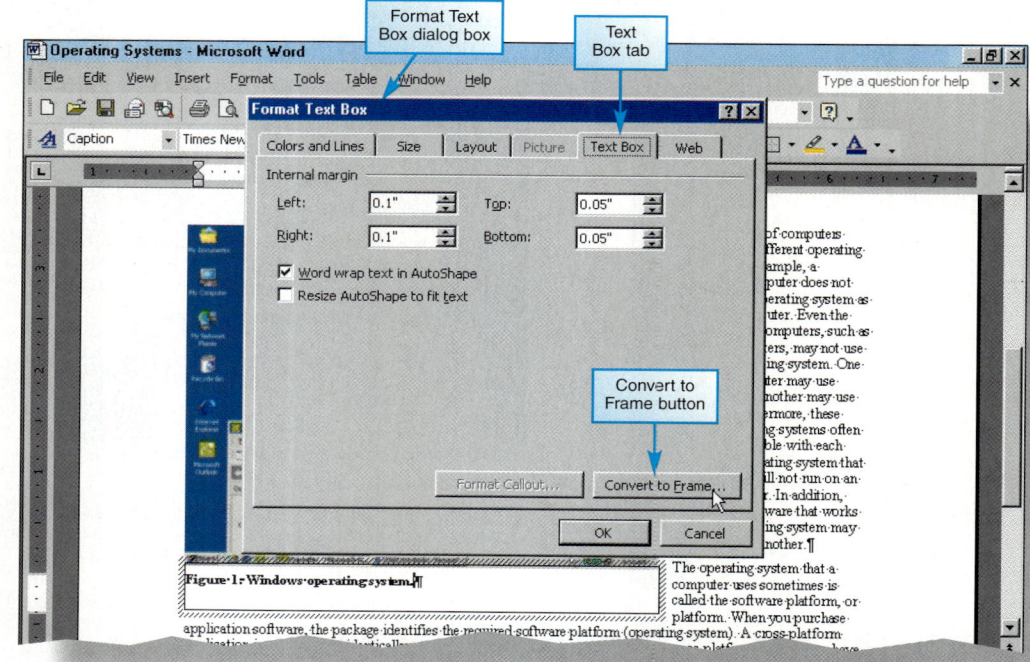

FIGURE 9-30

Word converts the text box to a frame. You did not format the text box; thus, you will not lose any formatting in the conversion from a text box to a frame.

Other Ways

1. Right-click text box, click Format Text Box on shortcut menu, click Text Box tab, click Convert to Frame button
2. In Voice Command mode, say "Format, Text Box, Text Box, Convert to Frame, OK"

Notice in Figure 9-29 on the previous page that the caption has a border around it. This is because Word automatically placed a border around the caption when it was a text box. You do not want the border around the caption. You also want to center the contents of the caption. Perform the following steps to modify the caption.

TO MODIFY THE CAPTION

1 With the caption frame selected, click the Border button arrow on the Formatting toolbar and then click No Border.

2 Click in the caption text and then click the Center button on the Formatting toolbar.

Word modifies the caption (shown in Figure 9-31).

The next step is to add a reference to the new figure in the document text.

Creating a Cross-Reference

In public information guide documents, the text always makes a specific reference to a figure and explains the contents of the figure. Thus, you want to enter a phrase into the document that refers to the figure of the screen shot graphic. Recall that the Operating Systems file will be inserted into a larger file. You do not know what the figure number of the graphic will be in the new document. In Word, you can create a **cross-reference**, which is a link to an item such as a heading, caption, or footnote in a document. By creating a cross-reference to the caption, the text that mentions the figure will update whenever the caption to the figure updates.

Perform the following steps to create a cross-reference.

Steps: To Create a Cross-Reference

1 **Position the insertion point so that it is immediately to the left of the text, and another may use, in the fourth paragraph. Press the LEFT PARENTHESIS (() key. Click Insert on the menu bar, point to Reference, and then point to Cross-reference on the Reference submenu (Figure 9-31).**

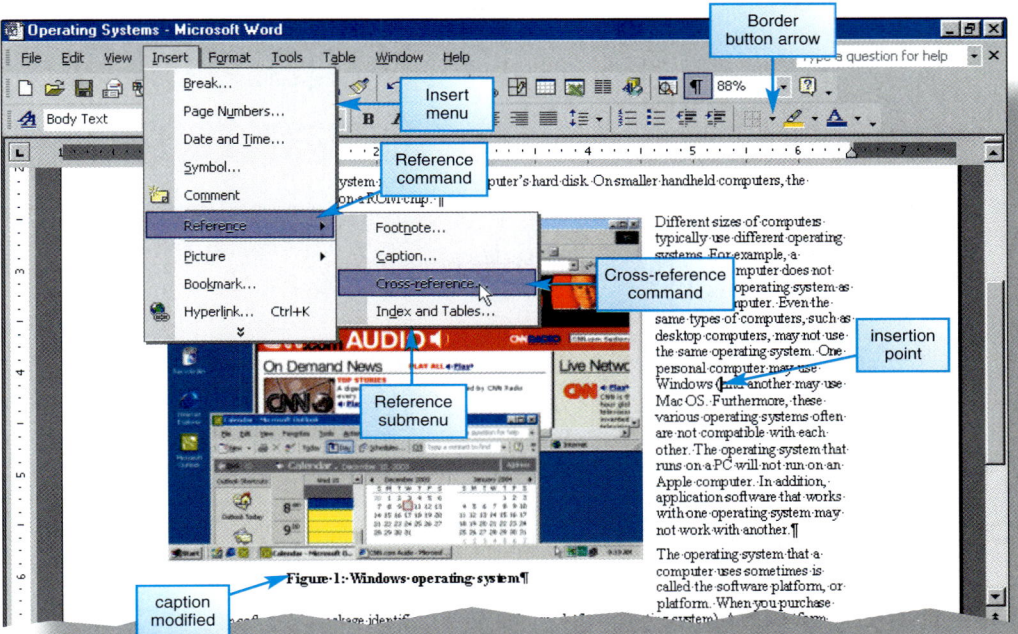

FIGURE 9-31

2 **Click Cross-reference. When the Cross-reference dialog box displays, click the Reference type box arrow and then click Figure. Click the Insert reference to box arrow and then click Only label and number. If the Insert as hyperlink check box contains a check mark, remove the check mark. Point to the Insert button.**

Word displays the Cross-reference dialog box (Figure 9-32). You want the text to display only the label (the word, Figure) and the label number (the figure number).

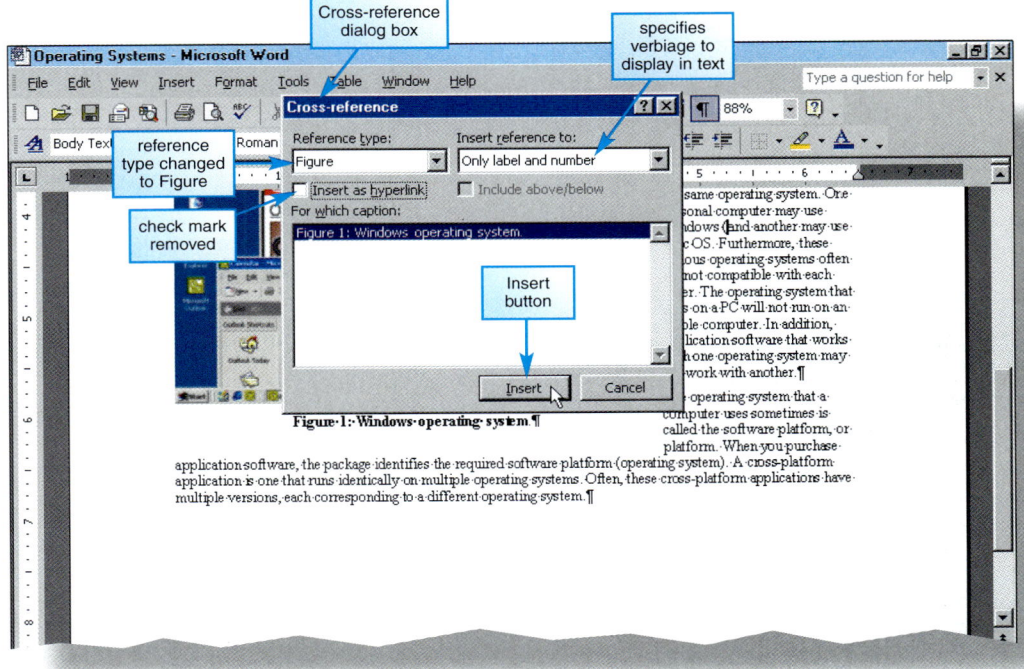

FIGURE 9-32

3 **Click the Insert button. Click the Close button in the Cross-reference dialog box. Press the RIGHT PARENTHESIS ()) key and then press the SPACEBAR.**

Word inserts the cross-reference to the figure into the document text (Figure 9-33). Because the figure number in the document is a field, Word may shade it gray — depending on your Word settings.

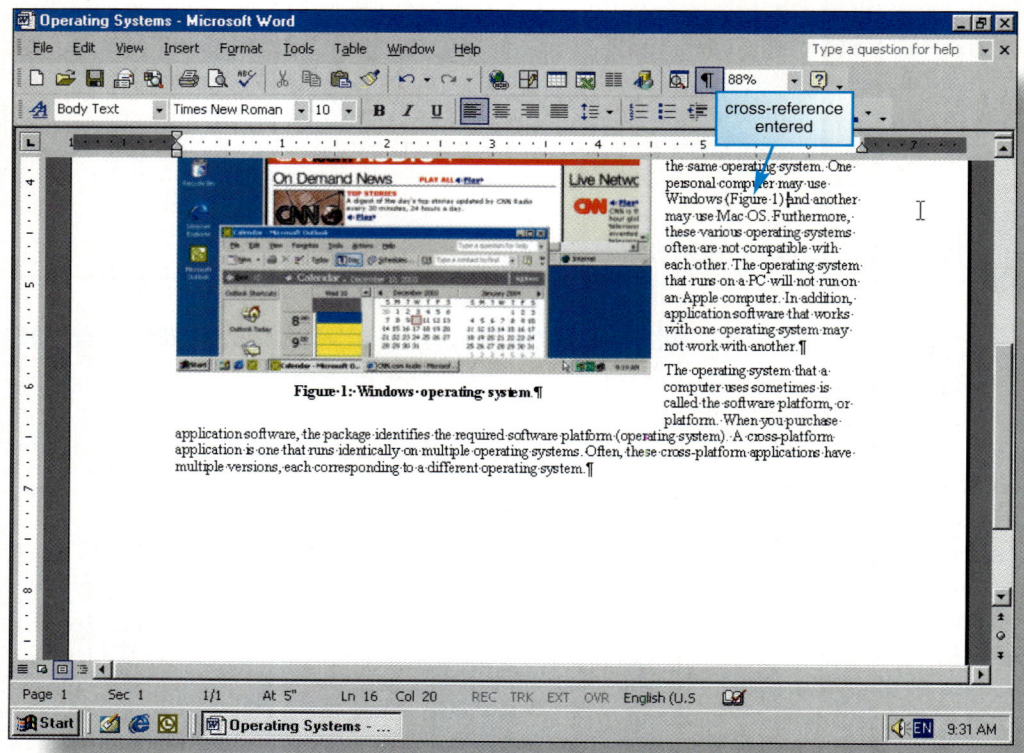

FIGURE 9-33

1. In Voice Command mode, say "Insert, Reference, Cross-reference"

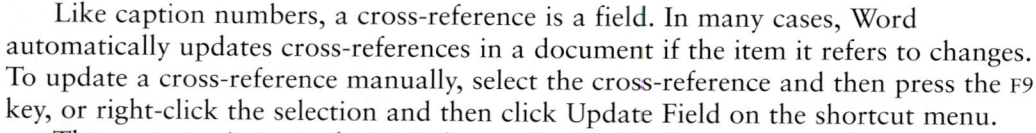

Like caption numbers, a cross-reference is a field. In many cases, Word automatically updates cross-references in a document if the item it refers to changes. To update a cross-reference manually, select the cross-reference and then press the F9 key, or right-click the selection and then click Update Field on the shortcut menu.

The next step is to mark any index entries in this document.

Marking Index Entries

At the end of all public information guide documents is an index, which lists important terms discussed in the document along with each term's corresponding page number. For Word to generate the index, you first must mark any item you wish to appear in the index. When you mark an index entry, Word creates a field that is used to build the index. The fields are hidden and display on the screen only when you are displaying formatting marks; that is, when the Show/Hide ¶ button on the Standard toolbar is selected.

In this document, you want the words, operating system, in the first sentence below the Operating Systems heading, to be marked as an index entry. To alert the reader that this term is in the index, you also bold it in the document. Perform the following steps to mark this index entry.

Cross-References

If your cross-reference displays odd characters inside curly braces {}, Word is displaying field codes instead of field results. Press ALT+F9 to display the cross-reference correctly. If your cross-reference prints field codes, click Tools on the menu bar, click Options, click the Print tab, remove the check mark from the Field codes check box, click the OK button, and then print the document again.

Steps: To Mark an Index Entry

1 Press CTRL+HOME to position the insertion point at the beginning of the document. Select the text you wish to appear in the index (the words, operating system, in this case). Press ALT+SHIFT+X. When the Mark Index Entry dialog box displays, point to the Mark button.

Word displays the Mark Index Entry dialog box (Figure 9-34).

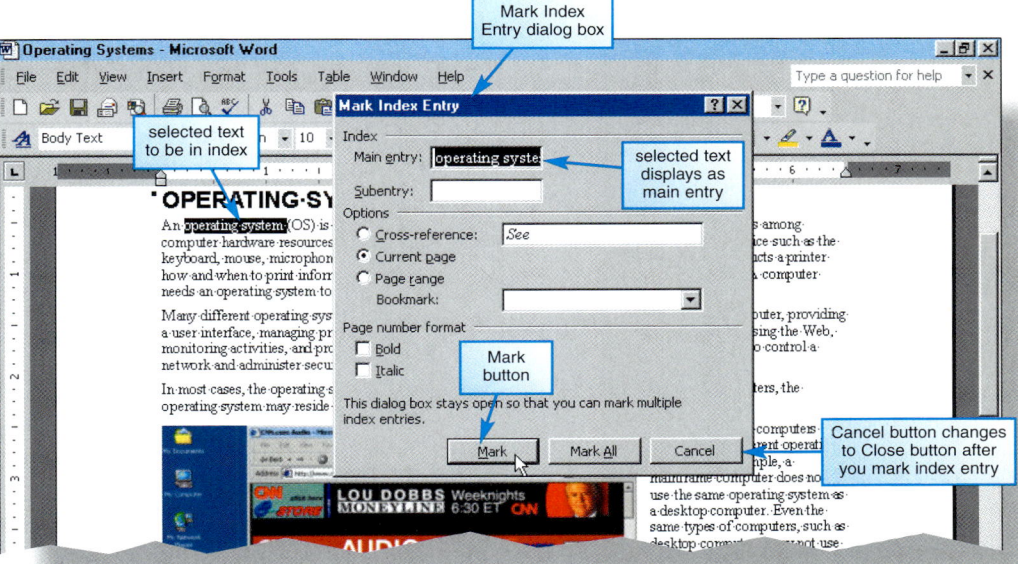

FIGURE 9-34

2 Click the Mark button. Click the Close button in the Mark Index Entry dialog box. Again, select the words, operating system, to the left of the left brace and then press CTRL+B to apply bold formatting.

Word inserts an index entry field into the document (Figure 9-35). These fields display on the screen only when the Show/Hide ¶ button on the Standard toolbar is selected.

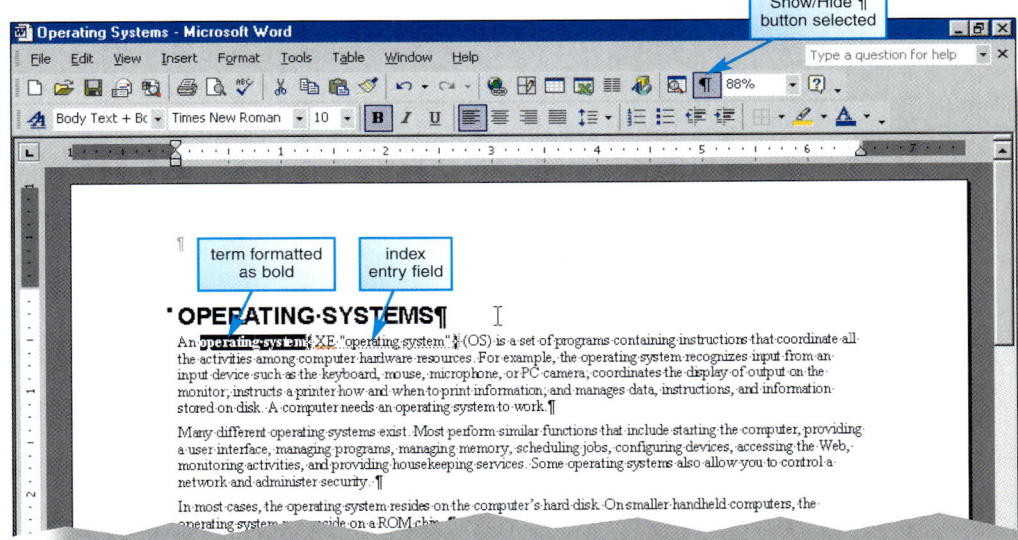

FIGURE 9-35

Word leaves the Mark Index Entry dialog box open until you close it, which allows you to mark multiple index entries without having to reopen the dialog box repeatedly. To mark multiple index entries, click in the document window, scroll to and select the next index entry, click the Main entry text box in the Mark Index Entry dialog box (shown in Figure 9-34), and then click the Mark button.

Perform the steps on the next page to mark more index entries and bold them.

Other Ways

1. Select text, on Insert menu point to Reference, click Index and Tables on Reference submenu, click Index tab, click Mark Entry button, click Mark button, click Close button
2. In Voice Command mode, say "Insert, Reference, Cross-reference"

TO MARK MORE INDEX ENTRIES AND BOLD THEM

1. Scroll to and then select the text, software platform, in the first sentence of the fifth paragraph.
2. Press ALT+SHIFT+X.
3. Click the Mark button. Click the Close button in the Mark Index Entry dialog box. Again, select the words, software platform, to the left of the left brace and then press CTRL+B to bold the words.
4. Repeat Steps 1, 2, and 3 for the word, platform, at the end of the same sentence.
5. Repeat Steps 1, 2, and 3 for the word, cross-platform, later in the same paragraph.

Word inserts index entry fields into the document. The terms display in bold.

Controlling Widows and Orphans

A **widow** is created when the last line of a paragraph displays by itself at the top of a page, and an **orphan** occurs when the first line of a paragraph displays by itself at the bottom of a page. Word, by default, prevents widows and orphans from occurring in a document.

Recall that the Operating Systems document will be incorporated into a larger document, the Discovering Your Computer public information guide document. Although the Operating Systems document fits on a single page now, Joy is unsure as to how the Operating Systems document will be inserted into the Discovering Your Computer public information guide document. Because she does not want the first or last line of a paragraph to display by itself on any page, Joy will ensure that widows and orphans cannot occur.

To verify that no one has changed the default setting, perform the following steps to ensure that widow and orphan lines cannot occur.

More About

Index Entries

Index entries may include a switch, which is a slash followed by a letter inserted after the field text. Switches include \b to apply bold formatting to the entry's page number, \f to define an entry type, \i to make the entry's page number italic, \r to insert a range of pages numbers, \t to insert specified text in place of a page number, and \y to specify that the subsequent text defines the yomi or pronunciation for the index entry. A colon in an index entry precedes a subentry keyword in the index.

To Verify the Widow and Orphan Setting

1 Press CTRL+HOME to position the insertion point at the beginning of the document. Press CTRL+A to select all the paragraphs in the document. Right-click the selection and then click Paragraph on the shortcut menu. When the Paragraph dialog box displays, click the Line and Page Breaks tab and then ensure that the Widow/Orphan control check box contains a check mark. Point to the OK button.

Word displays the Paragraph dialog box (Figure 9-36). A check mark displays in the Widow/Orphan control check box.

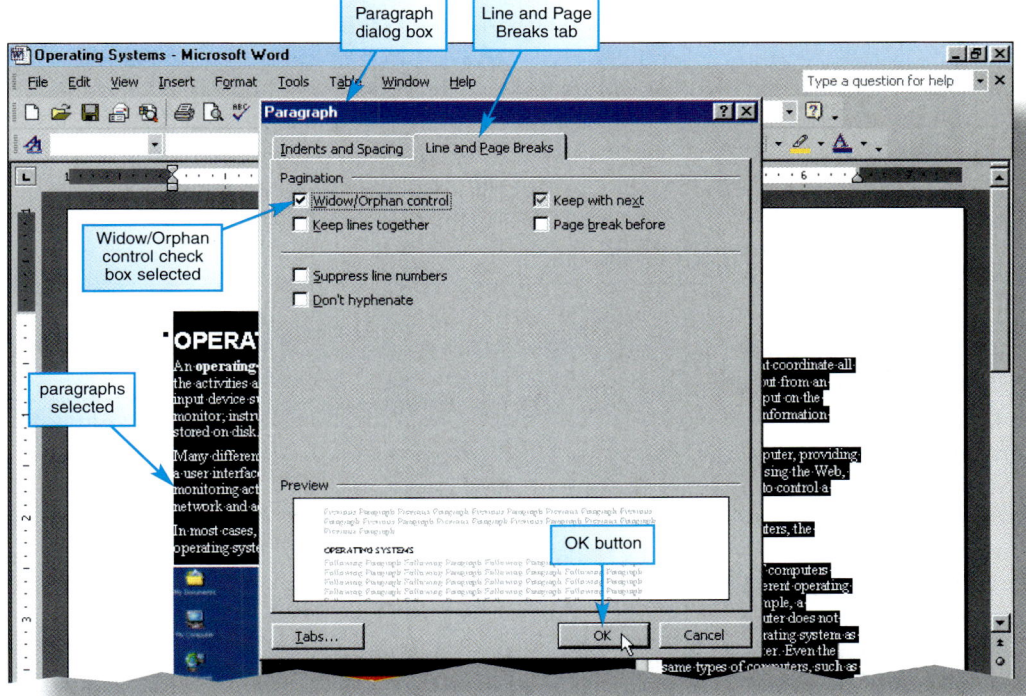

FIGURE 9-36

2 Click the OK button. Click anywhere in the document to remove the selection.

Word ensures that no widows or orphans can occur in this document.

Other Ways

1. On Format menu click Paragraph, click Line and Page Breaks tab, click Widow/Orphan control, click OK button
2. In Voice Command mode, say "Format, Paragraph, Line and Page Breaks, Widow/Orphan Control, OK"

The options in the Line and Page Breaks sheet in the Paragraph dialog box (Figure 9-36) are designed to provide you with options in how lines and paragraphs print. The Keep lines together check box can be used to ensure that a page break does not occur within a single paragraph, by positioning the insertion point in the appropriate paragraph and then selecting the check box. If you do not want a page break to occur between two paragraphs, click in the appropriate paragraph and then place a check mark in the Keep with next check box. Similarly, if you want a page break to occur immediately before a paragraph, place a check mark in the Page break before check box.

If, for some reason, you wanted to allow a widow or an orphan in a document, you would position the insertion point in the appropriate paragraph, display the Line and Page Breaks sheet in the Paragraph dialog box, and then remove the check mark from the Widow/Orphan control check box.

Password-Protecting a File

Joy is finished with the Operating Systems file and is ready to send it to Keith for inclusion in the Discovering Your Computer public information guide document. Keith, her supervisor, has specified that all incoming documents be password-protected. A **password-protected document** is a document that requires a password to open or modify it. Password protecting the document helps to ensure that the document has been modified by only authorized individuals.

In Word, a password may be up to 15 characters in length and can include letters, numbers, spaces, and symbols. Passwords are **case-sensitive**, which means that the password always must be entered in the same case in which it was saved. That is, if you enter a password in all uppercase letters, it must be entered in uppercase letters when the file is opened or modified.

Keith has suggested using the password, computer (in lowercase), for the file. Perform the following steps to password-protect the file.

Steps To Password-Protect a File

1 If necessary, insert the disk containing the Operating Systems file into drive A. Click File on the menu bar and then click Save As. When the Save As dialog box displays, if necessary, click the Save in box arrow and then click 3½ Floppy (A:). Click the Tools button and then point to Security Options.

Word displays the Save As dialog box (Figure 9-37).

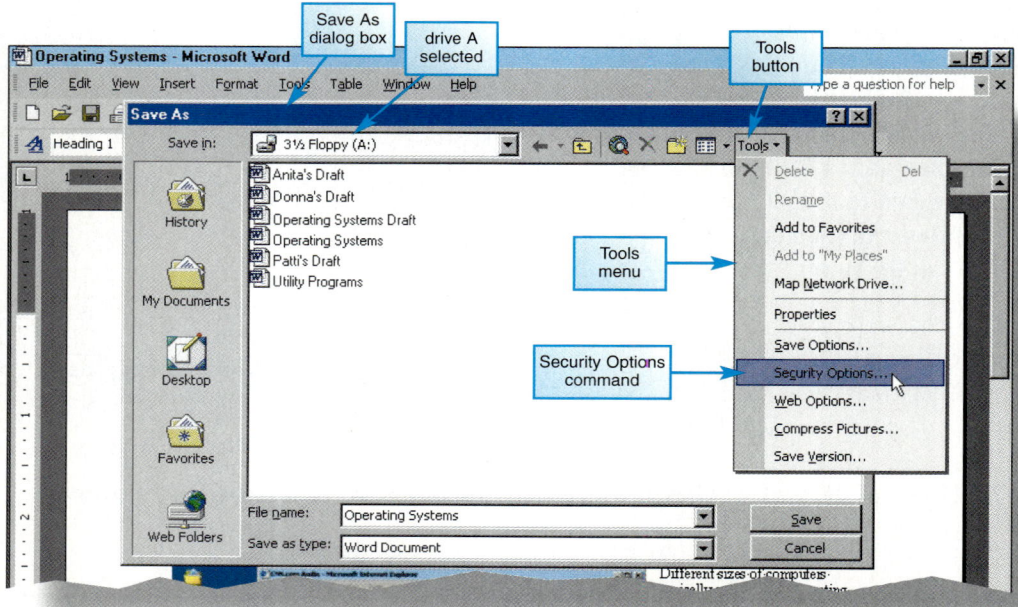

FIGURE 9-37

2 Click Security Options. When the Security dialog box displays, type computer in the Password to open text box. Point to the OK button.

Word displays the Security dialog box (Figure 9-38). When you type the password, computer, Word displays a series of asterisks (*) instead of the actual characters you type.

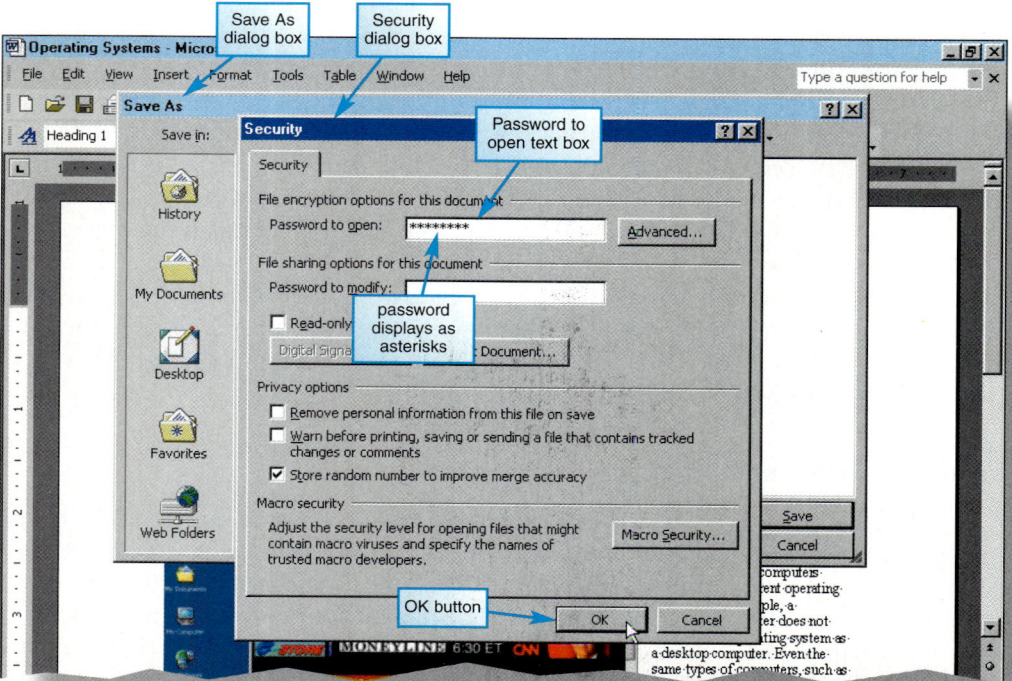

FIGURE 9-38

3 **Click the OK button. When Word displays the Confirm Password dialog box, type** computer **in the Reenter password to open text box. Point to the OK button in the Confirm Password dialog box.**

Word displays the Confirm Password dialog box (Figure 9-39). Again, the password displays as a series of asterisks (*) instead of the actual characters you type.

4 **Click the OK button. When the Save As dialog box is visible again, click its Save button.**

Word saves the document with the password, computer.

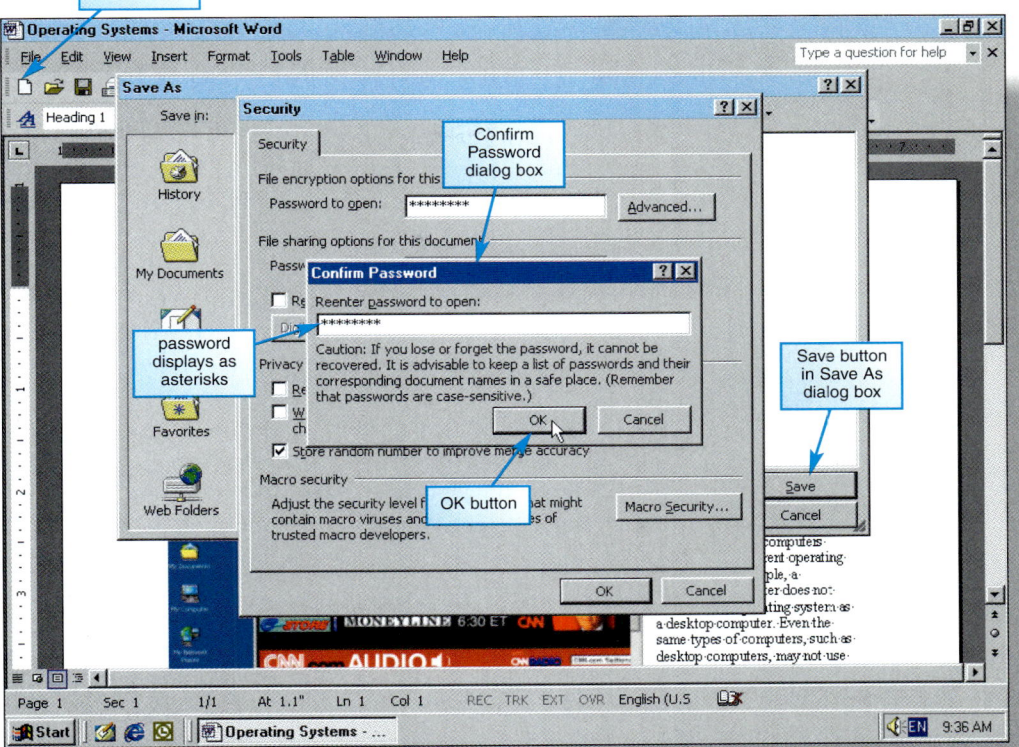

FIGURE 9-39

When someone attempts to open the document in the future, he or she will be prompted to enter the password.

The Operating Systems file is complete. Perform the following steps to close the file.

TO CLOSE THE DOCUMENT

1. Click File on the menu bar and then click Close.

2. If a Document1 program button displays on the taskbar, click it to display a blank document in the document window. If you do not have a Document1 button on the taskbar, click the New Blank Document button on the Standard toolbar.

Word closes the Operating Systems file and displays a blank document in the document window.

Joy e-mails the Operating Systems document to you for inclusion in the Discovering Your Computer public information guide document. For purposes of this project, you will use the document you just saved on your disk.

Other Ways

1. On Tools menu click Options, click Security tab, enter password, on File menu click Save As

2. In Voice Command mode, say "Tools, Options, Security, [type password], OK, File, Save As"

More About

Selecting Passwords

For more information on selecting good passwords, visit the Word 2002 More About Web page (scsite.com/wd2002/more.htm) and then click Selecting Passwords.

Master Documents

Master documents can be used when multiple people prepare different sections of a document or when a document contains separate elements such as the chapters in a book. If multiple people in a network need to work on the same document, divide the document into subdocuments and store the master document on the network server. Then, multiple users can work on different sections of the document simultaneously.

Outlines

If you wanted to rearrange the headings in an outline, for example move one up, you would drag its outline symbol in the direction you wanted to move it.

Working with a Master Document

When you are creating a document from a series of other documents, you may want to create a master document to organize all the documents. A **master document** is simply a document that contains other documents, which are called the **subdocuments**. In addition to subdocuments, a master document can contain its own text and graphics.

In this project, the master document file is named DC #8, which stands for Discovering Your Computer public information guide #8. The file DC #8 contains three subdocuments: an Introduction file, the Operating Systems file, and the Utility Programs file. The first has yet to be created, and the latter two (Operating Systems and Utility Programs) have been written by other individuals and e-mailed for inclusion in the DC #8 document. The master document also contains other items: a title page, a table of contents, a table of figures, and an index. The following pages illustrate how to create this master document and insert the necessary elements into the document to create the DC #8 document.

Creating an Outline

To create a master document, you must be in outline view. You then enter the headings of the document as an outline using Word's built-in heading styles. As discussed in previous projects, a style is a customized format that you can apply to text. Word has nine heading styles named Heading 1, Heading 2, and so on. Each contains different formatting that you can apply to headings in a document.

In an outline, the major heading displays at the left margin with each subordinate, or lower-level, heading indented. In Word, the built-in Heading 1 style displays at the left margin in outline view. Heading 2 style is indented, Heading 3 style is indented further, and so on.

You do not want to use a built-in heading style for the paragraphs of text within the document because when you create a table of contents, Word places all lines formatted using the built-in heading styles in the table of contents. Thus, the text below each heading is formatted using the Body Text style. By using styles in the document, all pages will be formatted similarly — even though various people create them.

The DC #8 document contains the following seven major headings: Discovering Your Computer, Table of Contents, Introduction to System Software, Operating Systems, Utility Programs, Table of Figures, and Index (shown in Figure 9-1 on page WD 9.05). Two of these headings (Operating Systems and Utility Programs) are not entered in the outline; instead, they are part of the subdocuments that you insert into the master document in the next section.

You want each heading to print at the top of a new page. You might want to format the pages within a heading differently from those pages in other headings. Thus, you will insert next page section breaks between each heading.

Perform the following steps to create an outline that contains headings to be used in the master document.

Steps: To Create an Outline

1 **With a new document window displaying, click the Outline View button on the horizontal scroll bar. If your screen does not display the Outlining toolbar, click View on the menu bar, point to Toolbars, and then click Outlining. If the three buttons identified on the Outlining toolbar in this figure are not selected on your screen, click the button(s).**

Word switches to outline view (Figure 9-40). An outline symbol displays to the left of each paragraph. You use outline symbols to rearrange text or display and hide text.

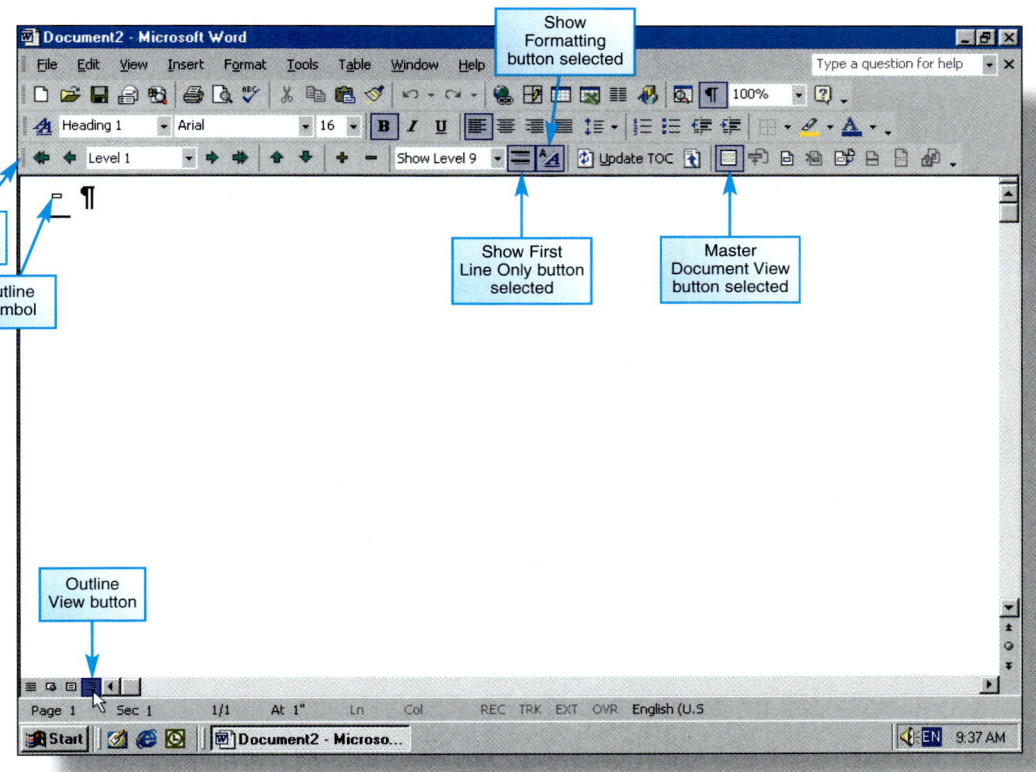

FIGURE 9-40

2 **Type DISCOVERING YOUR COMPUTER and then press the ENTER key.**

Word enters the first heading using the built-in Heading 1 style (Figure 9-41).

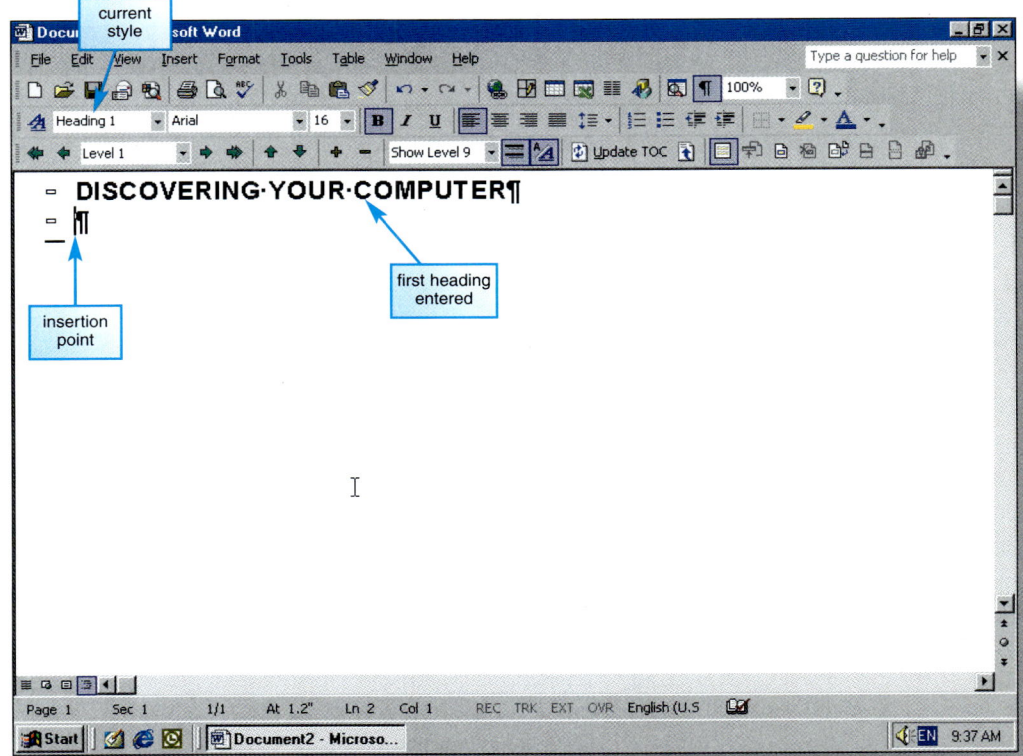

FIGURE 9-41

3 **Click Insert on the menu bar and then click Break. When the Break dialog box displays, click Next page in the Section break types area and then point to the OK button.**

The Break dialog box displays (Figure 9-42).

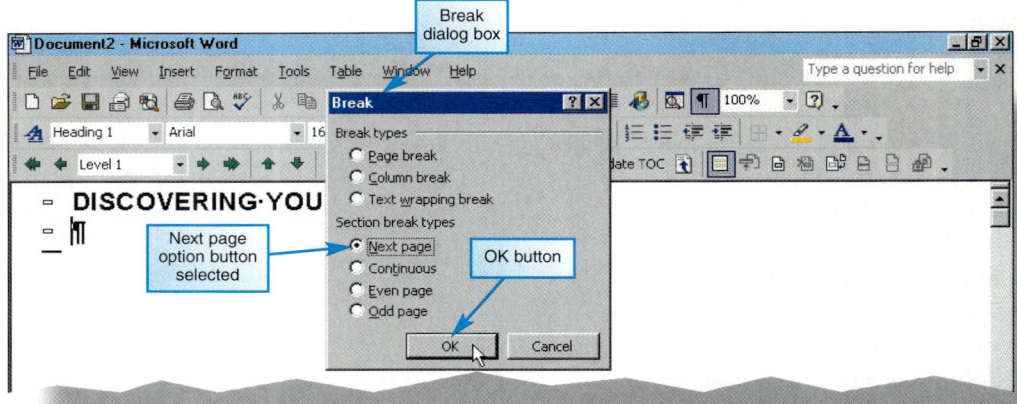

FIGURE 9-42

4 **Click the OK button. Type** TABLE OF CONTENTS **and then press the ENTER key.**

Word inserts a next page section break below the first heading (Figure 9-43). The new text also displays.

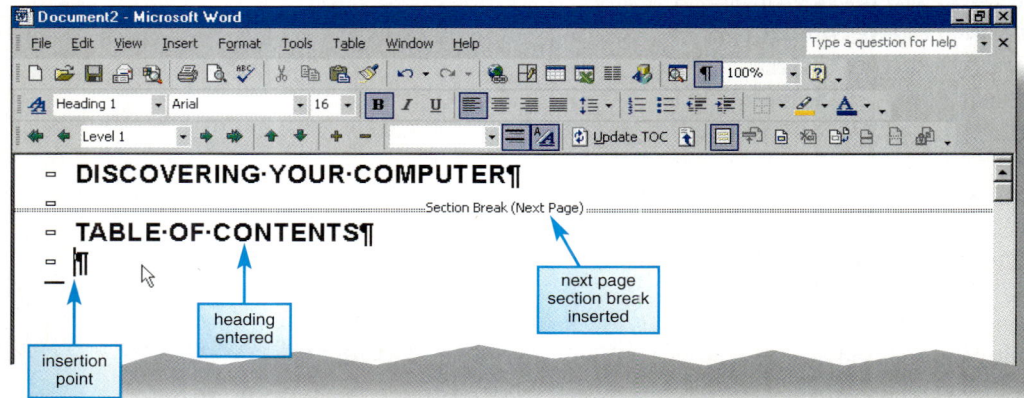

FIGURE 9-43

5 **Click Insert on the menu bar and then click Break. When the Break dialog box displays, click Next page in the Section break types area. Click the OK button.**

6 **Type** INTRODUCTION TO SYSTEM SOFTWARE **and then press the ENTER key. Repeat Step 5. Type** TABLE OF FIGURES **and then press the ENTER key. Repeat Step 5. Type** INDEX **and then press the ENTER key (Figure 9-44).**

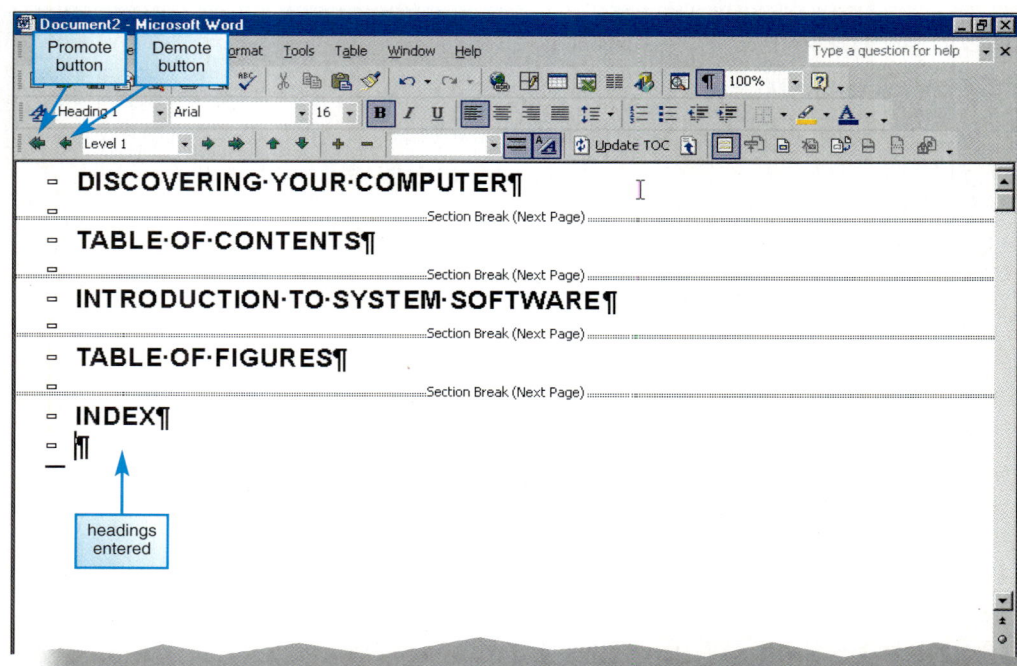

FIGURE 9-44

The Next Page section break between each heading will cause each heading to begin at the top of a new page.

The Outlining toolbar contains buttons and boxes for promoting and demoting items in the outline, changing the outline level, as well as buttons to update and display the table of contents. Figure 9-45 identifies the buttons and boxes on the Outlining toolbar.

The two other major headings, Operating Systems and Utility Programs, will be inserted as subdocuments, as discussed in the following pages. When you insert these files as subdocuments, the headings will become part of the outline.

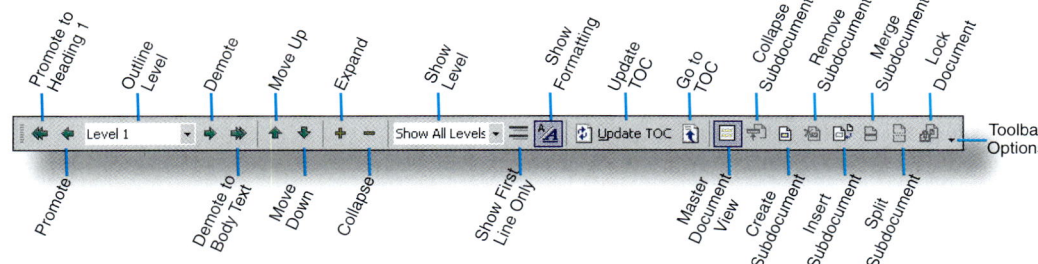

FIGURE 9-45

Inserting a Subdocument in a Master Document

The next step is to insert one of the subdocuments into the master document. Word places the first line of text in the subdocument at the first heading level because it is defined using the Heading 1 style. Nonheading text uses the Body Text style. Figure 9-46 shows the Operating Systems subdocument and identifies the styles used in the document.

The subdocument to be inserted is the Operating Systems file that you modified earlier in this project. Recall that you saved the document with the password, computer. Thus, you will enter that password when prompted by Word, as shown in the steps on the next page.

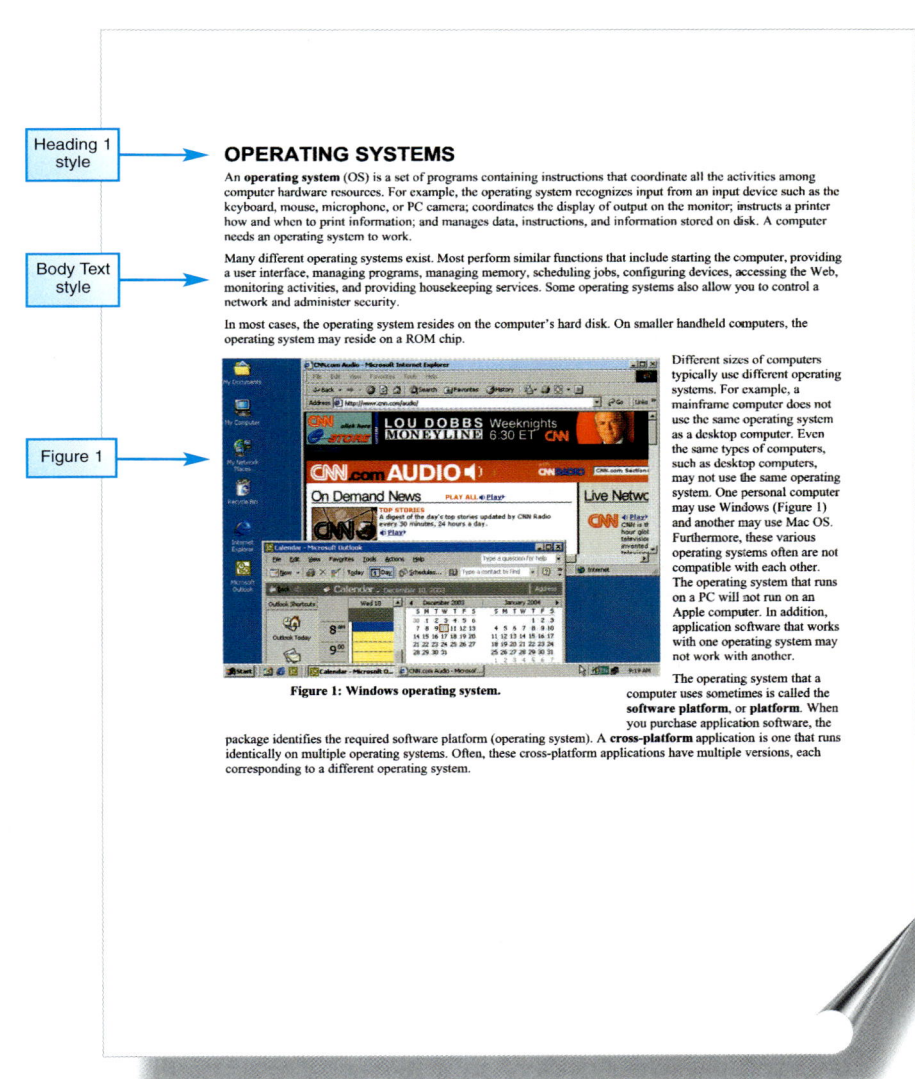

FIGURE 9-46

Steps: To Insert a Password-Protected File as a Subdocument

 If necessary, insert into drive A the floppy disk containing the Operating Systems file. Position the insertion point where you want to insert the subdocument (on the section break between the INTRODUCTION TO SYSTEM SOFTWARE and TABLE OF FIGURES headings). Click the Insert Subdocument button on the Outlining toolbar. When the Insert Subdocument dialog box displays, if necessary, click the Look in box arrow and then click 3½ Floppy (A:). Click the file name, Operating Systems, and then point to the Open button in the Insert Subdocument dialog box (Figure 9-47).

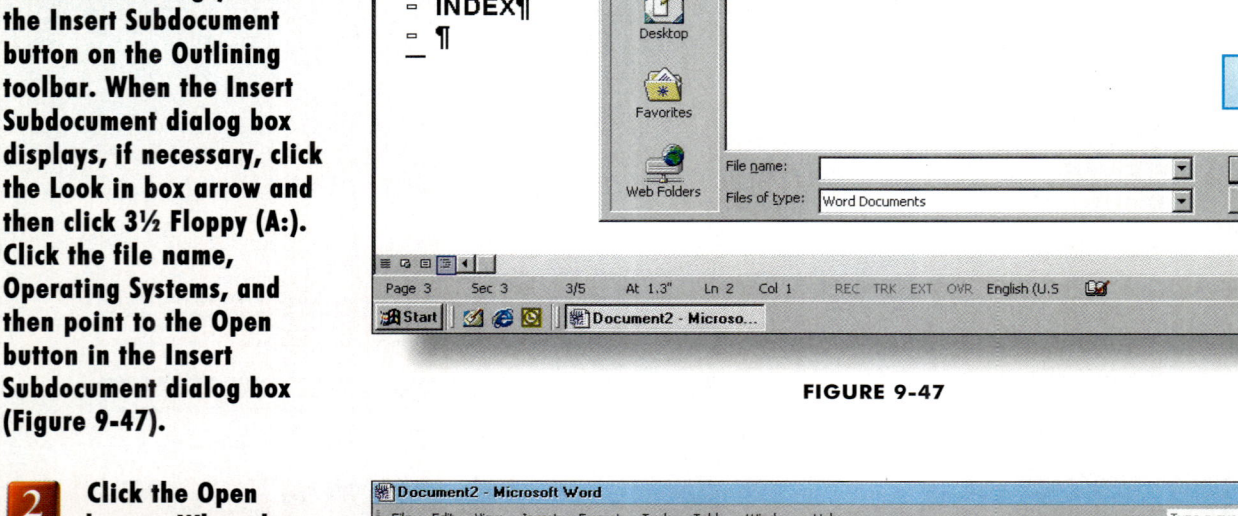

FIGURE 9-47

Click the Open button. When the Password dialog box displays, type computer **in the text box. Point to the OK button.**

Word displays the Password dialog box, which requests your password for the Operating Systems file (Figure 9-48). Asterisks display instead of the actual password characters.

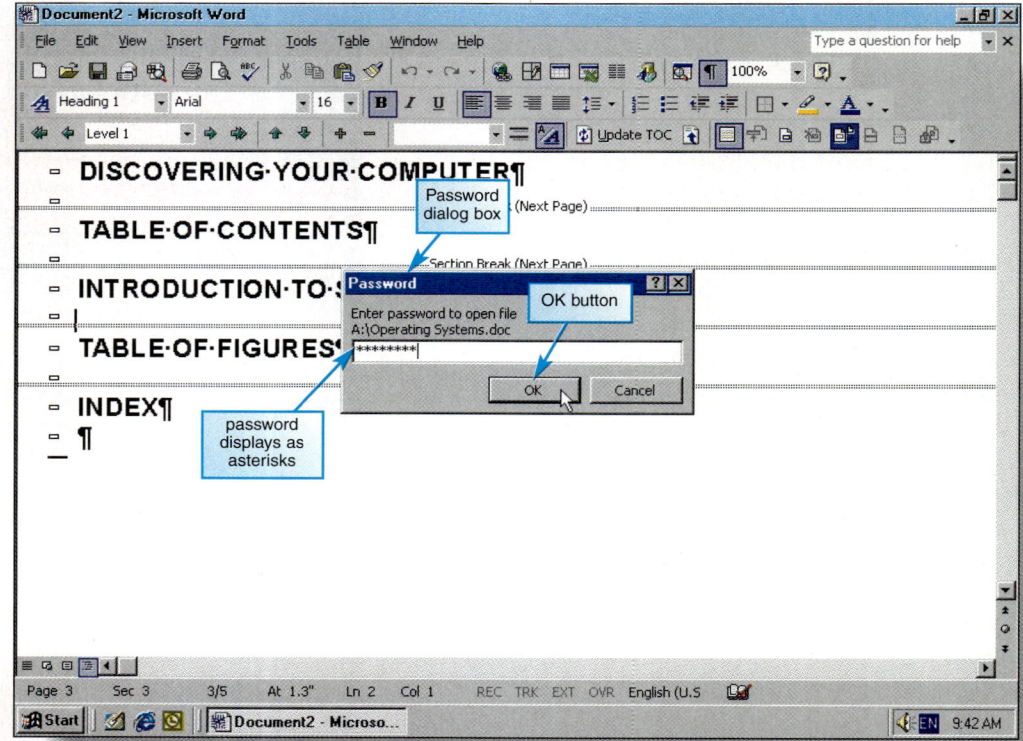

FIGURE 9-48

3 **Click the OK button.**

Word inserts the Operating Systems file into the document (Figure 9-49). Notice the document contains marked index entries. Only the first line of each paragraph displays because the Show First Line Only button on the Outlining toolbar is selected.

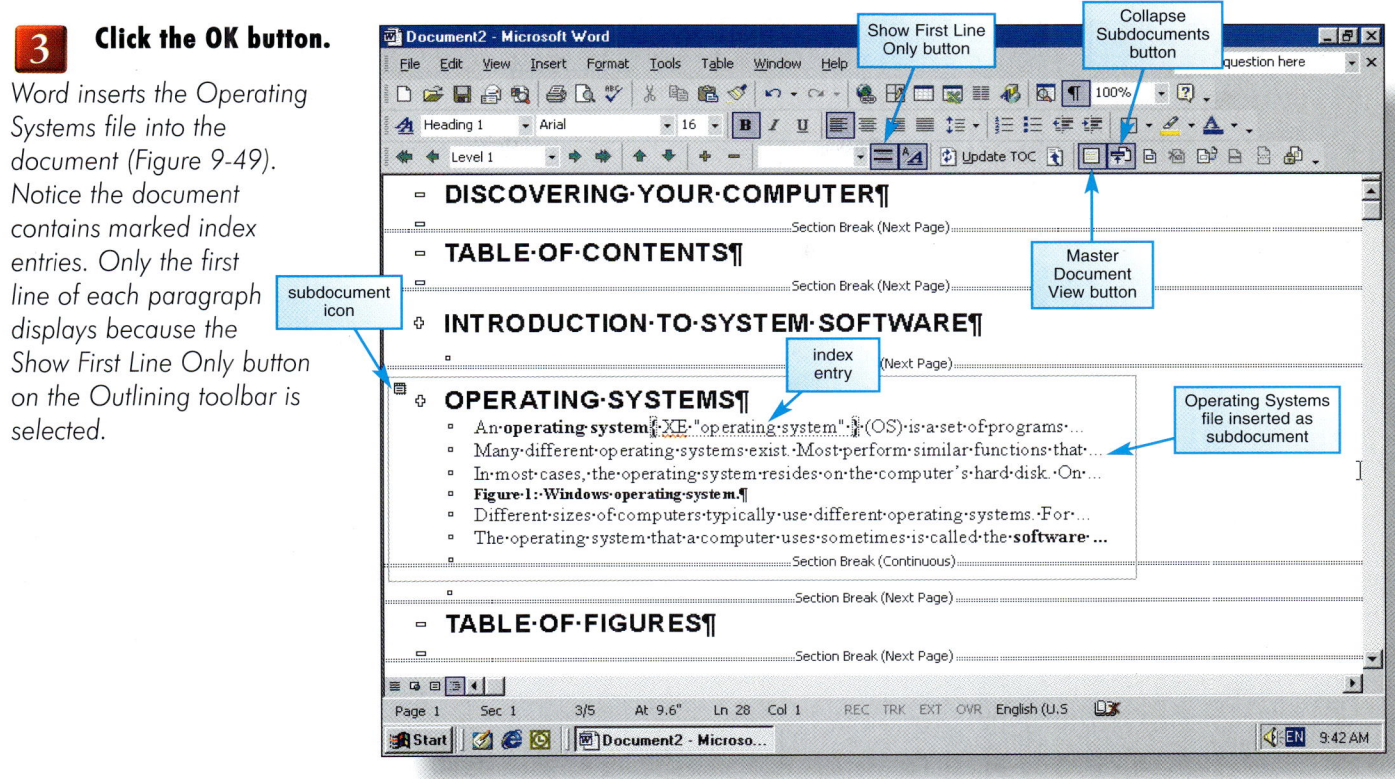

FIGURE 9-49

The next step is to insert another subdocument below the Operating Systems subdocument. The next subdocument to be inserted is named Utility Programs and is located on the Data Disk. If you did not download the Data Disk, see the inside back cover for instructions for downloading the Data Disk or see your instructor.

Perform the following steps to insert another subdocument.

TO INSERT ANOTHER SUBDOCUMENT

1. Insert the Data Disk into drive A. Scroll down and, if necessary, position the insertion point on the next page section break above the Table of Figures heading. Click the Insert Subdocument button on the Outlining toolbar.

2. When the Insert Subdocument dialog box displays, if necessary, click the Look in box arrow and then click 3½ Floppy (A:). Click the Utility Programs file name in the Look in list and then click the Open button in the Insert Subdocument dialog box.

3. Scroll up to display the top of the inserted subdocument.

Word inserts the Utility Programs file into the outline below the Operating Systems subdocument (Figure 9-50 on the next page).

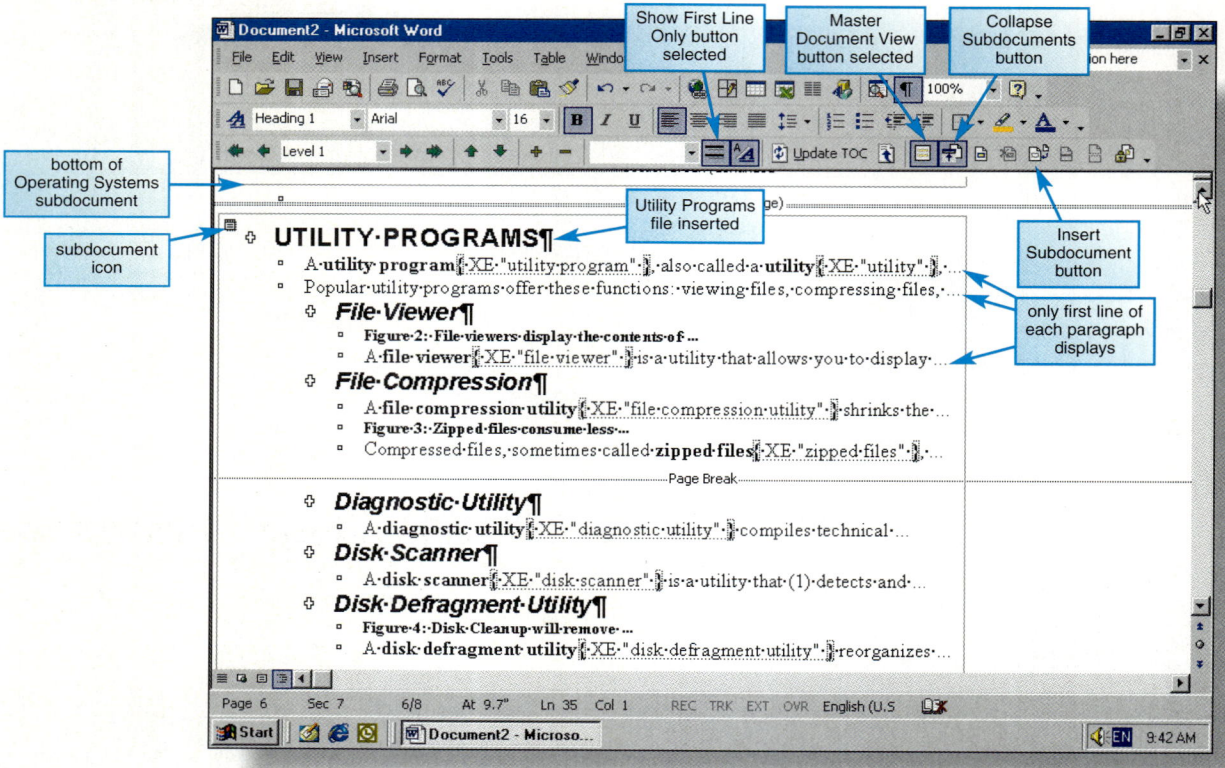

FIGURE 9-50

The inserted file shown in Figure 9-50 is the same document shown on pages 5, 6, and 7 in Figure 9-1 on page WD 9.05. Notice that in Figure 9-50 only the first line of each paragraph displays. This is because the Show First Line Only button on the Outlining toolbar is selected. If you wanted to display all lines in all paragraphs, you would click the Show First Line Only button so it is not selected.

The master document shown in Figure 9-50 is expanded. When in outline view, an expanded document is one that displays the contents of its subdocuments. A collapsed document, by contrast, displays subdocuments as hyperlinks; that is, instead of displaying the contents of the subdocuments, Word displays the name of the subdocuments in blue and underlined. Later in this project, you work with a collapsed document.

To collapse an expanded document and display subdocuments as hyperlinks, click the Collapse Subdocuments button on the Outlining toolbar. To expand subdocuments, click the Expand Subdocuments button on the Outlining toolbar.

You can open a subdocument in a separate document window and modify it. To open a collapsed subdocument, click the hyperlink. To open an expanded subdocument, double-click the subdocument icon (Figure 9-50) to the left of the document heading. If the subdocument icon does not display on the screen, click the Master Document View button on the Outlining toolbar. When you are finished working on a subdocument, close it and return to the master document by clicking File on the menu bar and then clicking Close.

You have performed several tasks. Thus, you should save the document as described in the following steps.

The Lock Icon

If a lock icon displays next to a subdocument's name, either the master document is collapsed or the subdocument is locked. If the master document is collapsed, simply click the Expand Subdocuments button on the Outlining toolbar. If the subdocument is locked, you will be able to open the subdocument but will not be able to modify it.

TO SAVE A DOCUMENT

1. With your floppy disk in drive A, click the Save button on the Standard toolbar.

2. Type DC #8 in the File name text box. Do not press the ENTER key after typing the file name.

3. If necessary, click the Save in box arrow and then click 3½ Floppy (A:). Click the Save button in the Save As dialog box. If a Microsoft Word dialog box displays, click the OK button.

Word saves the document on a floppy disk in drive A with the file name, DC #8 (shown in Figure 9-51).

When you save a master document, Word also saves the subdocument files on the disk. Thus, the DC #8 file, the Operating Systems file, and the Utility Programs file all are saved when you save the DC #8 file.

Creating a Subdocument from a Master Document

The next step is to create a new subdocument for the INTRODUCTION TO SYSTEM SOFTWARE section of the DC #8 document. Perform the following steps to create a subdocument.

> **More About**
>
> **Creating Subdocuments**
>
> If the Create Subdocument button is dimmed, you need to expand subdocuments by clicking the Expand Subdocuments button on the Outlining toolbar. Then, the Create Subdocument button should be available.

Steps: To Create a New Subdocument

1. Press CTRL+HOME. Point to the plus outline symbol to the left of the heading, INTRODUCTION TO SYSTEM SOFTWARE, and then click when the mouse pointer changes to a four-headed arrow to select the heading. Point to the Create Subdocument button on the Outlining toolbar (Figure 9-51).

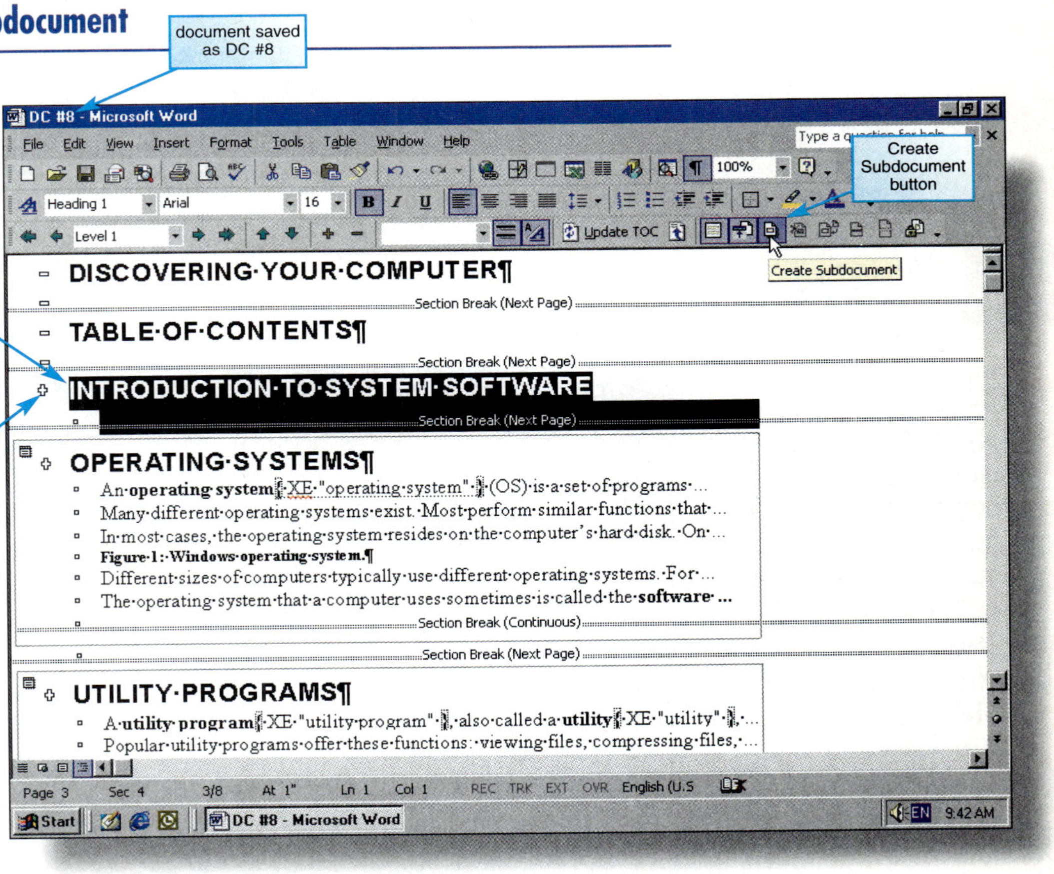

FIGURE 9-51

2 **Click the Create Subdocument button.**

Word creates a subdocument for the INTRODUCTION TO SYSTEM SOFTWARE heading (Figure 9-52). If Word places a continuous section break above or below the subdocument, do not remove this section break.

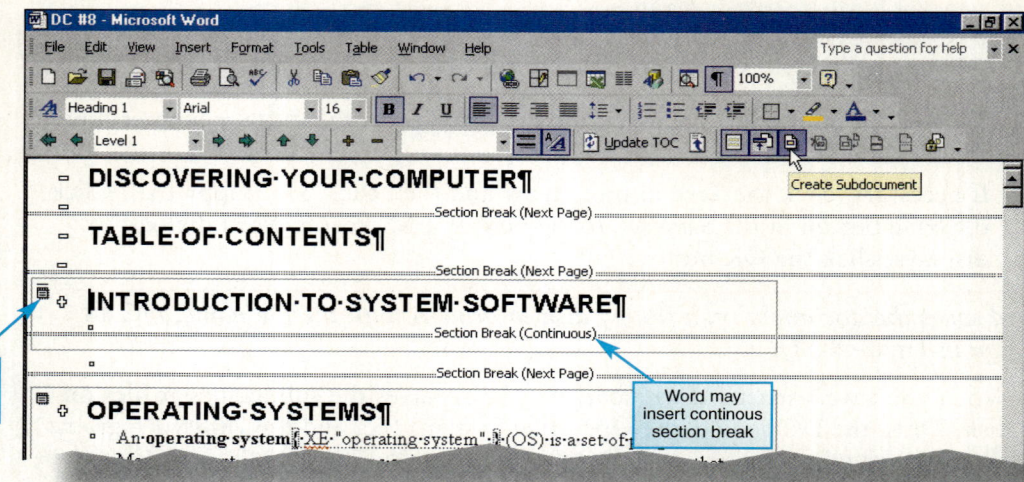

FIGURE 9-52

Other Ways

1. To create a subdocument, in Voice Command mode, say "Create Subdocument"

The next time you save the DC #8 document, Word will create another document called INTRODUCTION TO SYSTEM SOFTWARE on your disk.

Modifying an Outline

You would like to enter the text for the Introduction to System Software section of the document. The paragraphs of text in the Introduction to System Software section should not use a built-in heading style; instead, they should be formatted using the Body Text style. You can enter the text in outline view, as shown in the following steps.

Steps To Modify an Outline

1 **Position the insertion point immediately after the last E in the heading, INTRODUCTION TO SYSTEM SOFTWARE. Press the ENTER key twice and then press the UP ARROW key once, to position the insertion point on the blank line below the heading. Point to the Demote to Body Text button on the Outlining toolbar (Figure 9-53).**

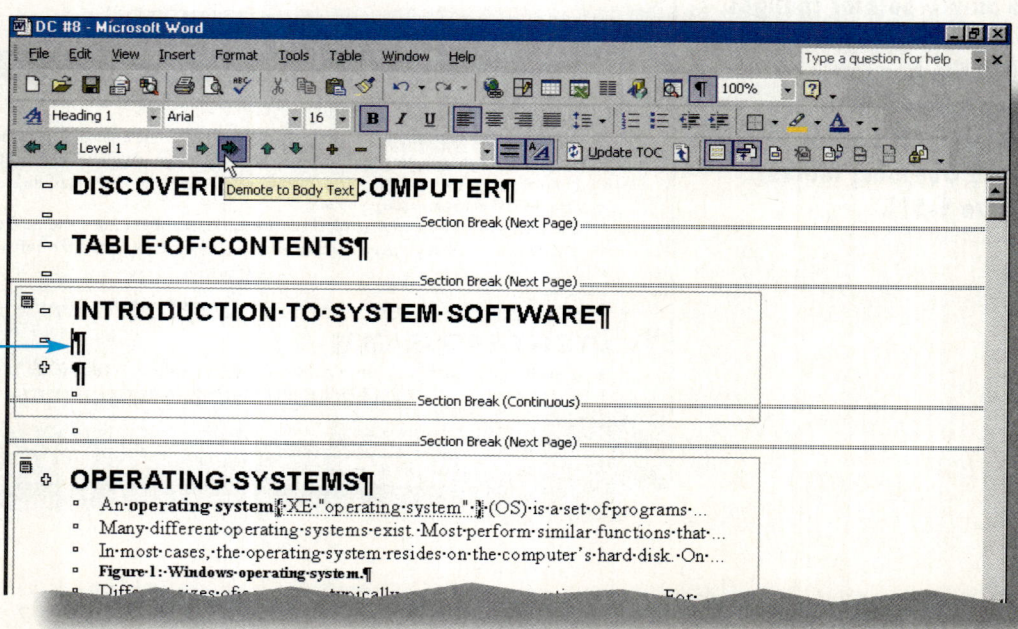

FIGURE 9-53

2 **Click the Demote to Body Text button.**

Word changes the style of the current line from Heading 1 to Body Text (Figure 9-54).

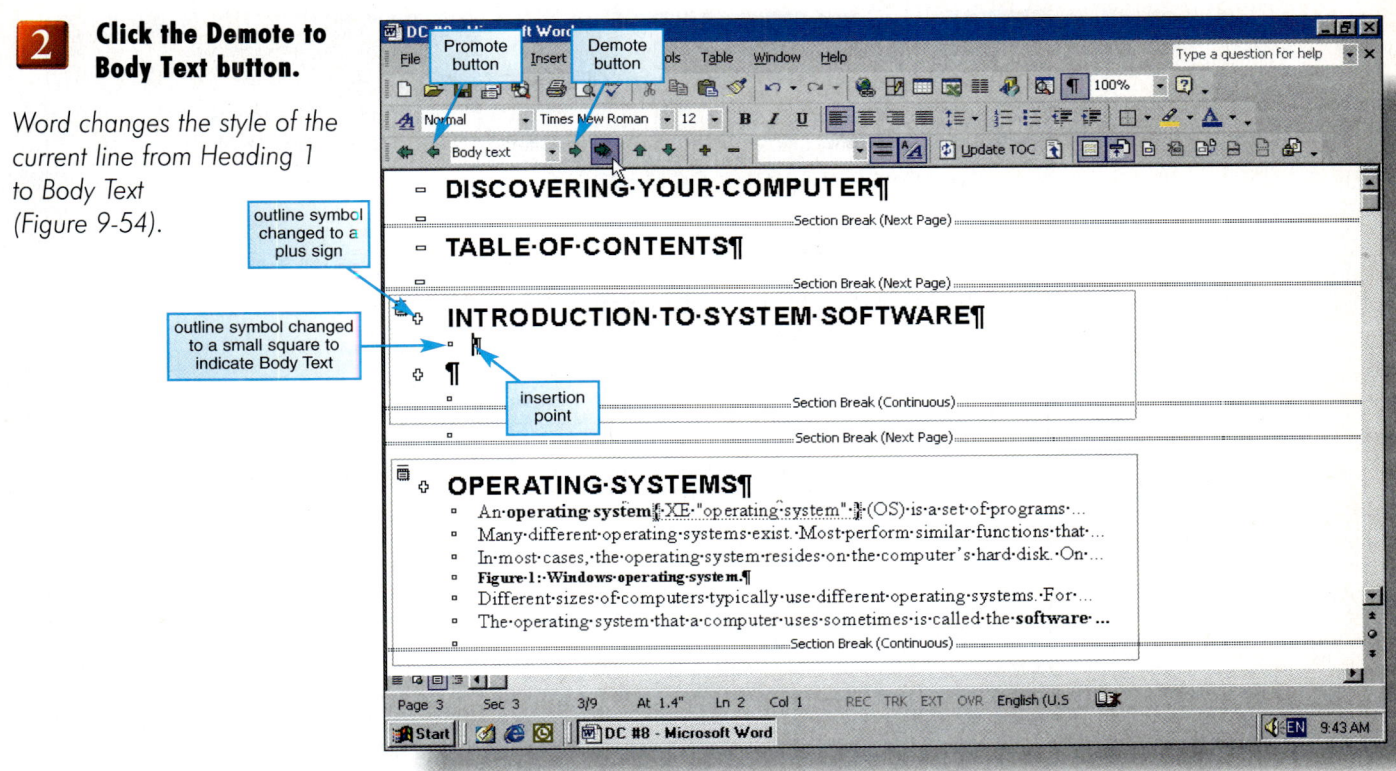

FIGURE 9-54

Notice in Figure 9-54 that the outline symbols changed. The outline symbol to the left of the INTRODUCTION TO SYSTEM SOFTWARE heading changed from a minus sign to a plus sign, indicating the heading has subordinate text. The outline symbol below the heading changed from a minus sign to a small square, indicating it is formatted using the Body Text style.

If you wanted to change a heading to a lower-level, or subordinate, heading style instead of to the Body Text style, such as for a subheading, you would press the TAB key or click the Demote button on the Outlining toolbar; or you can drag the outline symbol to the right. Likewise, to change a heading to a higher-level heading, you would press the SHIFT+TAB keys or click the Promote button on the Outlining toolbar (as you did previously); or you can drag the outline symbol to the left.

The next step is to enter the text of the introduction as described in the following steps.

TO ENTER BODY TEXT INTO AN OUTLINE

1. If the Show First Line Only button on the Outlining toolbar is selected, click it. Click the Style box arrow on the Formatting toolbar and then click Body Text.
2. With the insertion point on the line below the INTRODUCTION TO SYSTEM SOFTWARE heading (shown in Figure 9-54), type the first paragraph shown in Figure 9-55 on the next page. Press the ENTER key.
3. Type the second paragraph shown in Figure 9-55.

The INTRODUCTION TO SYSTEM SOFTWARE section is complete (Figure 9-55).

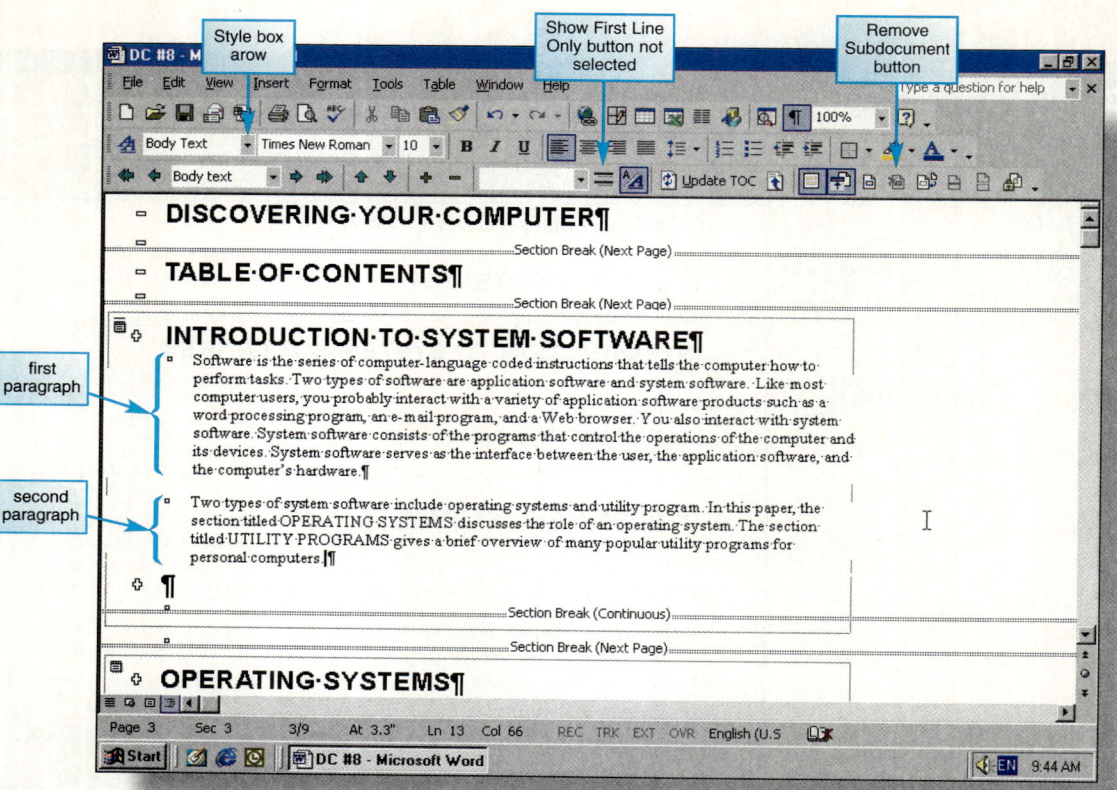

FIGURE 9-55

In outline view, text does not display formatted. Instead, each subheading is indented below the previous heading. Text formatted using the Body Text style, such as that shown in Figure 9-55, also displays indented. To display text properly formatted, switch to print layout view.

If, for some reason, you wanted to remove a subdocument from a master document, you would expand the subdocuments, click the subdocument icon to the left of the subdocument's first heading, and then press the DELETE key. Although Word removes the subdocument from the master document, the subdocument file remains on disk.

Occasionally, you may want to convert a subdocument to part of the master document — breaking the connection between the text in the master document and the subdocument. To do this, expand the subdocuments, click the subdocument icon, and then click the Remove Subdocument button on the Outlining toolbar.

Entering Text and Graphics as Part of the Master Document

The next step is to create the title page for the DC #8 document. The completed title page is shown in Figure 9-56. You decide not to create a subdocument for the title page; instead you will enter the text as part of the master document. The title page contains graphics. Thus, you will work in print layout view as opposed to outline view.

On the title page, you want only the first line of text (DISCOVERING YOUR COMPUTER) to show up in the table of contents. Thus, only the first line should be the Heading 1 style. The remaining lines will be formatted using the Body Text style. To be sure that all text below the Heading 1 style is formatted to the Body Text style, demote the blank line below the heading to body text as described in the following steps.

Outline View

When the Show First Line Only button on the Outline toolbar is selected, only the first line of each paragraph displays. When the button is not selected, all text associated with the paragraph displays.

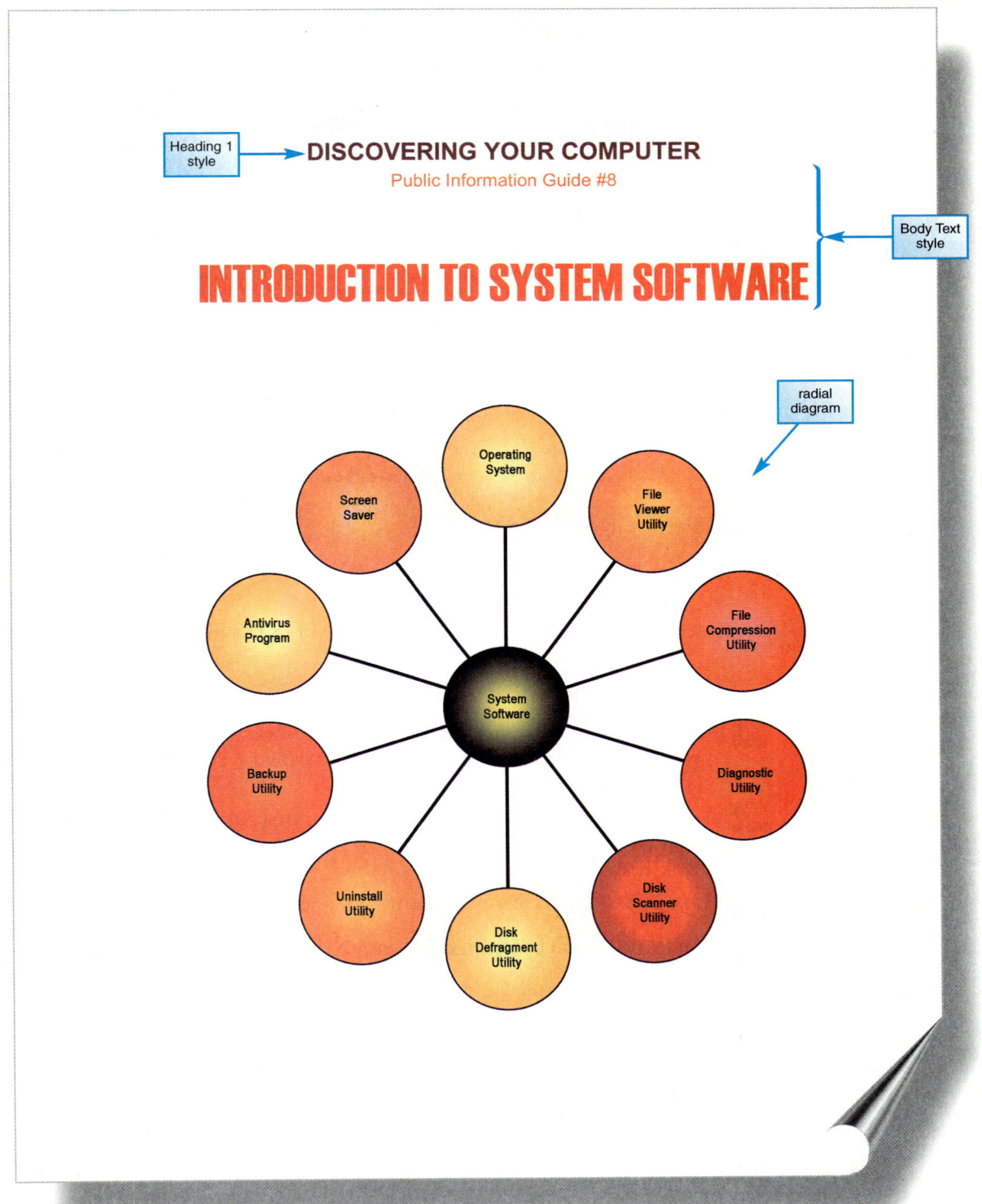

FIGURE 9-56

TO DEMOTE A LINE TO BODY TEXT

1 In outline view, position the insertion point on the section break below the DISCOVERING YOUR COMPUTER heading.

2 Click the Demote to Body Text button on the Outlining toolbar.

Word changes the current line from Heading 1 style to Body Text style (Figure 9-57 on the next page).

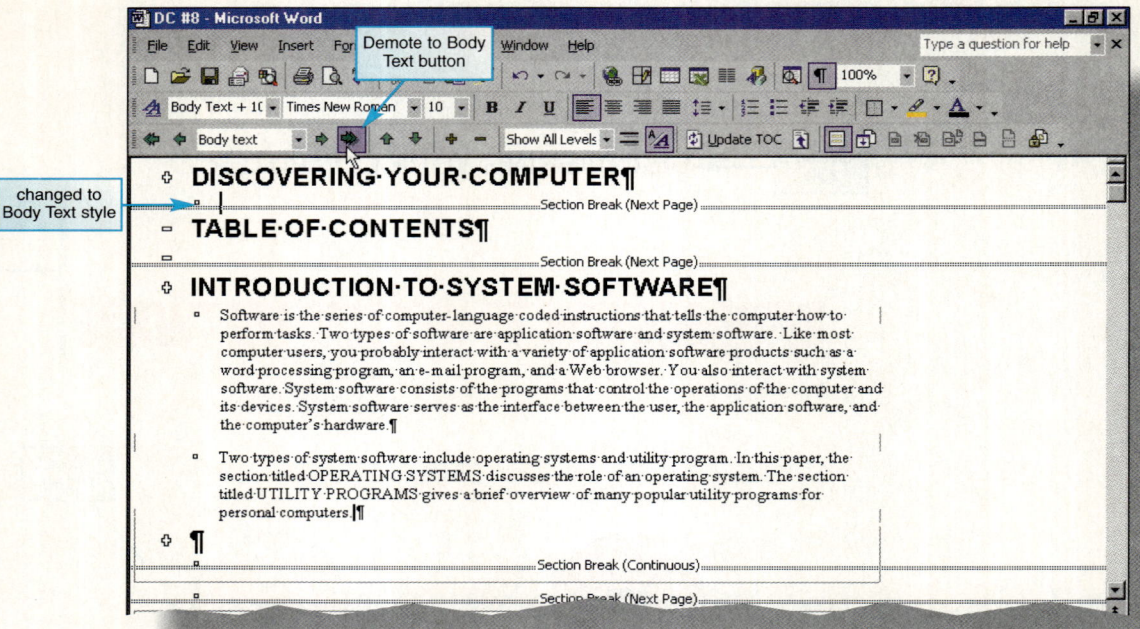

FIGURE 9-57

Enter the text for the title page as described in the following steps.

TO ENTER AND FORMAT TITLE PAGE TEXT

1. Click the Print Layout View button on the horizontal scroll bar to switch to print layout view. Click the Zoom box arrow on the Standard toolbar and then click Page Width.

2. With the insertion point at the end of the first line on the title page, press the ENTER key twice. Press the UP ARROW key to position the insertion point on the blank line.

3. Type `Public Information Guide #8` and then press the ENTER key.

4. Press CTRL+2 to change line spacing to double. Press the ENTER key.

5. Type `INTRODUCTION TO SYSTEM SOFTWARE` and then press the ENTER key.

6. Select all lines on the title page above the section break, including the blank lines, and then click the Center button on the Formatting toolbar.

7. Select the DISCOVERING YOUR COMPUTER line. Click the Font Color button arrow on the Formatting toolbar and then click Brown.

8. Select the Public Information Guide #8 line. Click the Font box arrow and then click Arial. If necessary, click the Font Size box arrow and then click 12. Click the Font Color button arrow and then click Orange.

9. Select the line, INTRODUCTION TO SYSTEM SOFTWARE. Click the Font box arrow and then click Haettenschweiler. Click the Font Size box arrow and then click 36. Click the Font Color button arrow and then click Red. Click to the left of the section break.

The title page displays as shown in Figure 9-58.

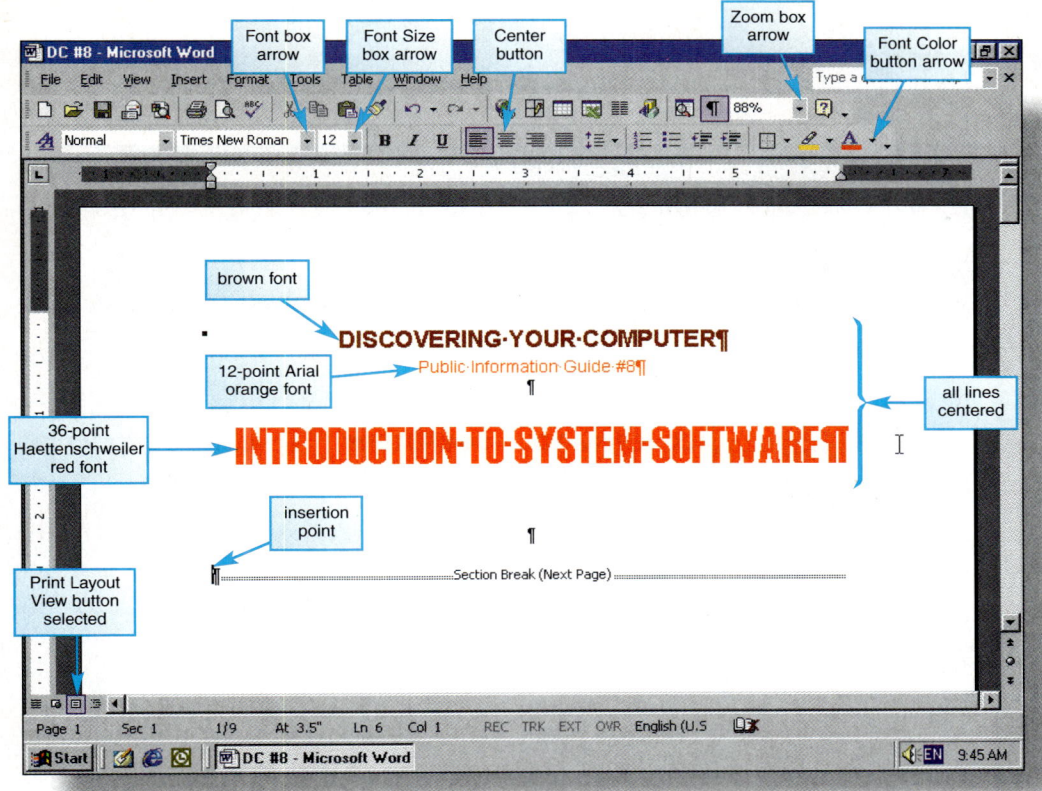

FIGURE 9-58

The next step is to add a radial diagram to the title page.

Inserting a Diagram

You can insert two types of graphics into a Word document: a picture and a drawing object. A **picture** is a graphic that was created in another program. Examples of pictures are scanned images, photographs, and clip art. A **drawing object** is a graphic that you create using Word. You can modify or enhance drawing objects using the Drawing toolbar. Examples of drawing objects include diagrams, AutoShapes, curves, lines, and WordArt.

In this project, you add a **diagram**, which is a predefined shape or shapes in Word. Word provides a Diagram Gallery (shown in Figure 9-60 on the next page) with diagrams such as organization charts, cycle diagrams, radial diagrams, pyramid diagrams, Venn diagrams, and target diagrams. Each diagram contains embedded text boxes with instructions that indicate where to click to add text. The DC #8 title page includes a radial diagram, which is used to show relationships of a core element. The core element, or main idea, displays in the middle of the diagram. Spokes lead outward to subtopics. Each element, or shape, may include text and formatting. The text for the core element and each subtopic in the project is listed in Table 9-1. The completed diagram is shown in Figure 9-56 on page WD 9.47.

Perform the steps on the next page to insert the radial diagram, format it, and then insert and format the text in each element.

Table 9-1 Radial Diagram Text	
ELEMENT (subtopic elements begin at the top and proceed clockwise)	**TEXT**
Center element	System Software
Element 1	Operating System
Element 2	File Viewer Utility
Element 3	File Compression Utility
Element 4	Diagnostic Utility
Element 5	Disk Scanner Utility
Element 6	Disk Defragment Utility
Element 7	Uninstall Utility
Element 8	Backup Utility
Element 9	Antivirus Program
Element 10	Screen Saver

WD 9.50 • Project 9 • Working with a Master Document, an Index, and a Table of Contents

Steps: To Insert and Format a Diagram

1 **With the insertion point positioned as shown in Figure 9-59, click Insert on the menu bar and then point to Diagram (Figure 9-59).**

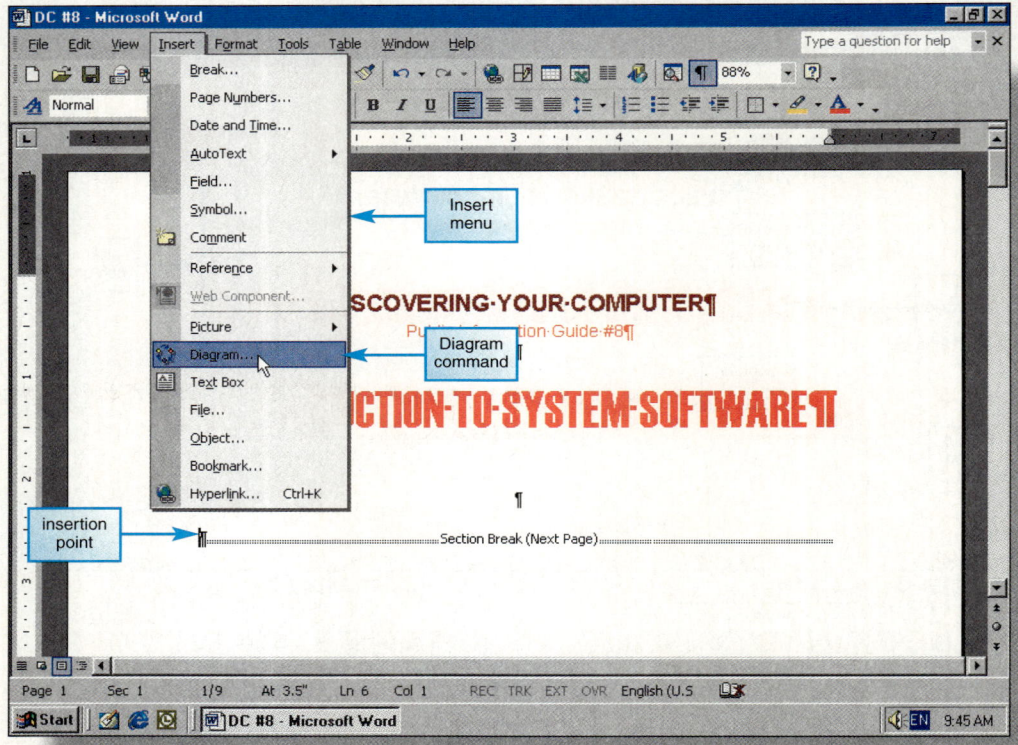

FIGURE 9-59

2 **Click Diagram. When the Diagram Gallery dialog box displays, click Radial Diagram and then point to the OK button.**

The Diagram Gallery dialog box displays a brief description of the selected diagram type (Figure 9-60).

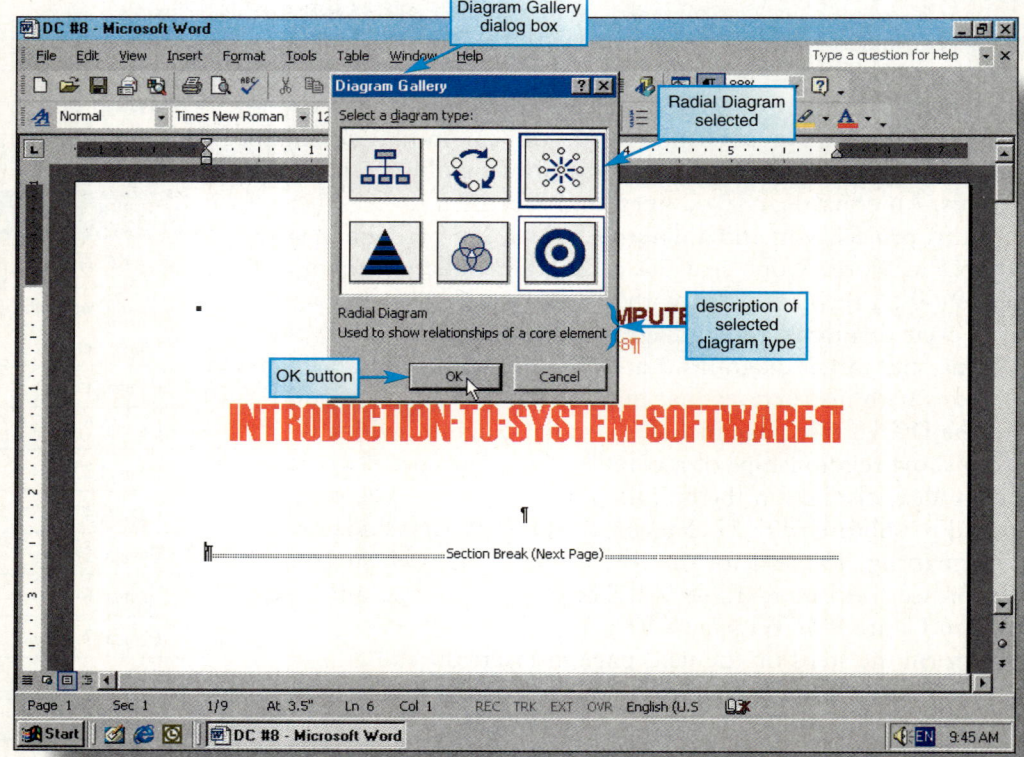

FIGURE 9-60

Working with a Master Document • WD 9.51

3 **Click the OK button. Point to the Insert Shape button on the Diagram toolbar.**

The radial diagram displays as an inline graphic with three spokes (Figure 9-61). Word automatically displays the drawing canvas, the Diagram toolbar, and the Drawing toolbar.

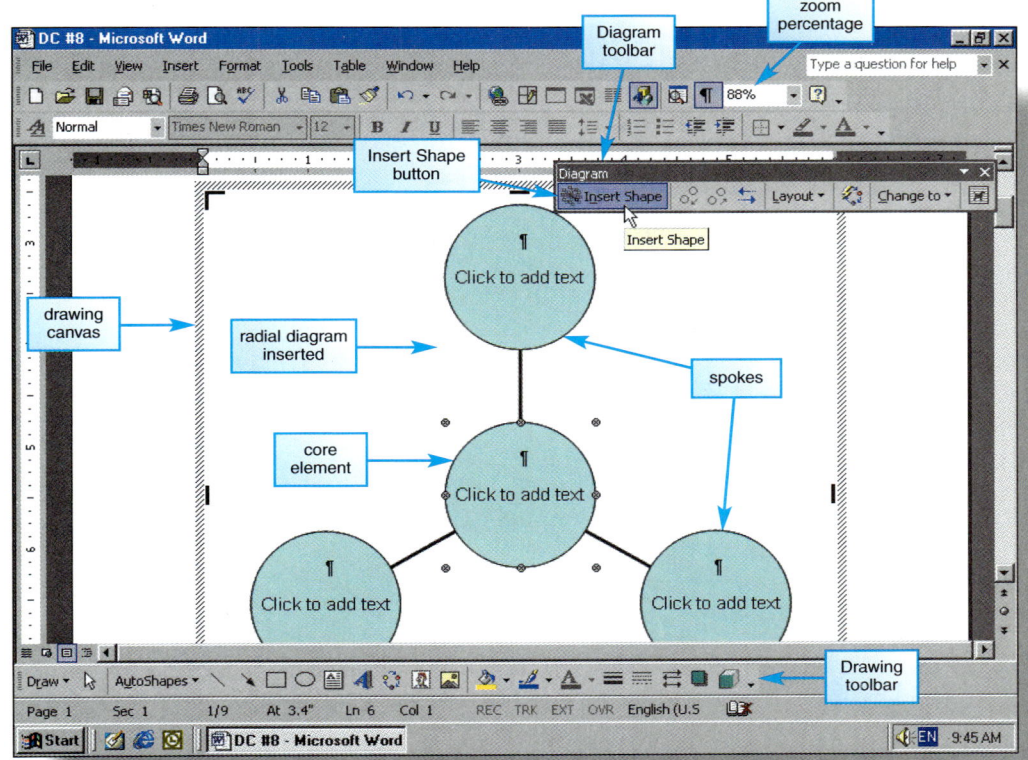

FIGURE 9-61

4 **Click the Insert Shape button seven times to create a total of ten spokes. Point to the AutoFormat button on the Diagram toolbar.**

As you insert more shapes or elements to a radial diagram, Word automatically resizes the diagram and spaces the elements evenly (Figure 9-62).

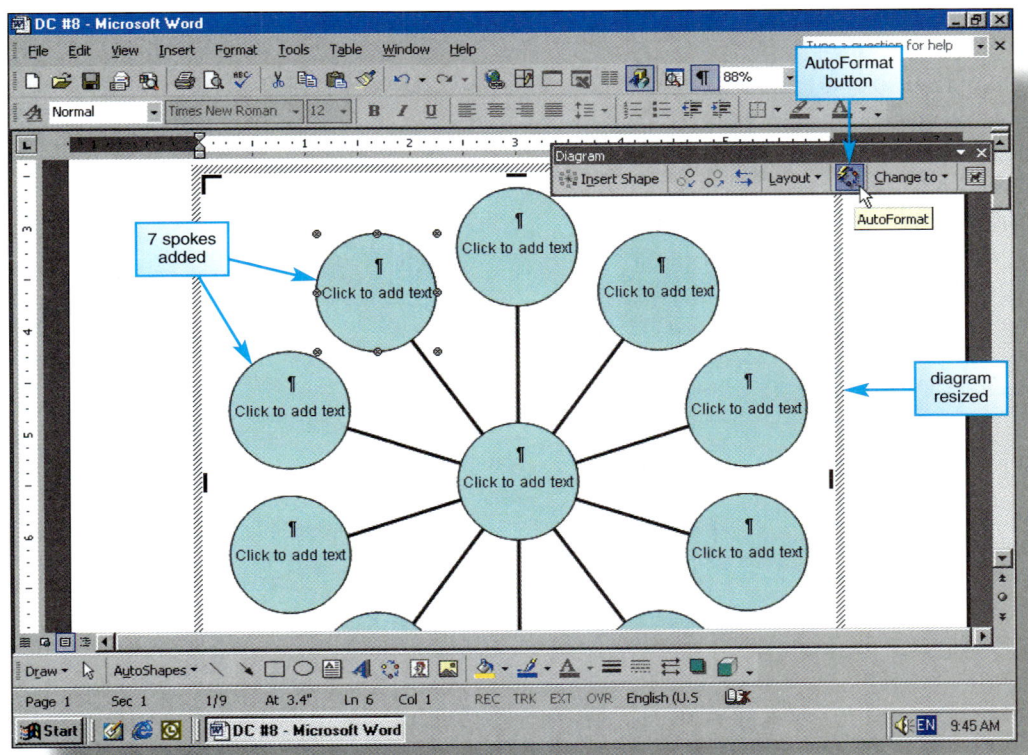

FIGURE 9-62

5 **Click the AutoFormat button. When the Diagram Style Gallery dialog box displays, click Fire in the Select a Diagram Style list and then point to the Apply button.**

The Select a Diagram Style list contains a variety of radial diagram styles (Figure 9-63). A preview of the selected style displays.

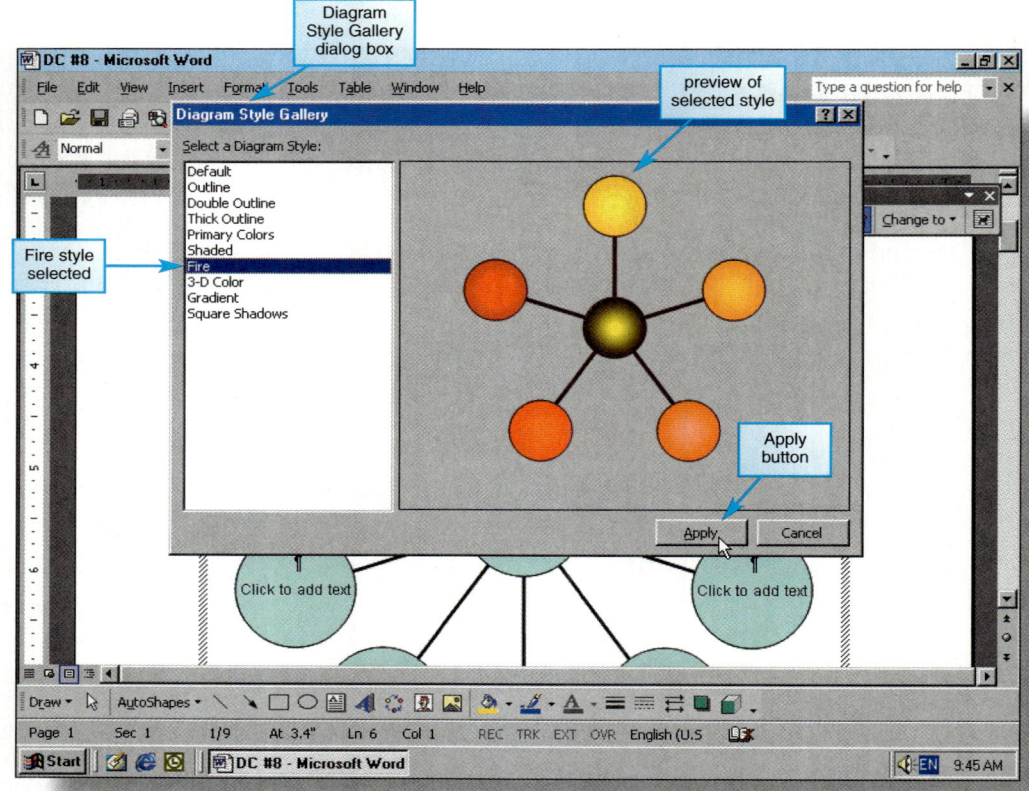

FIGURE 9-63

6 **Click the Apply button. Click the center circle to select it. Click the Font box arrow on the Formatting toolbar and then click Arial Narrow. Click the Bold button on the Formatting toolbar. When the insertion point displays, press the ENTER key. Type** System **and then press the ENTER key. Type** Software **to finish inserting the text.**

The text for the core element displays (Figure 9-64).

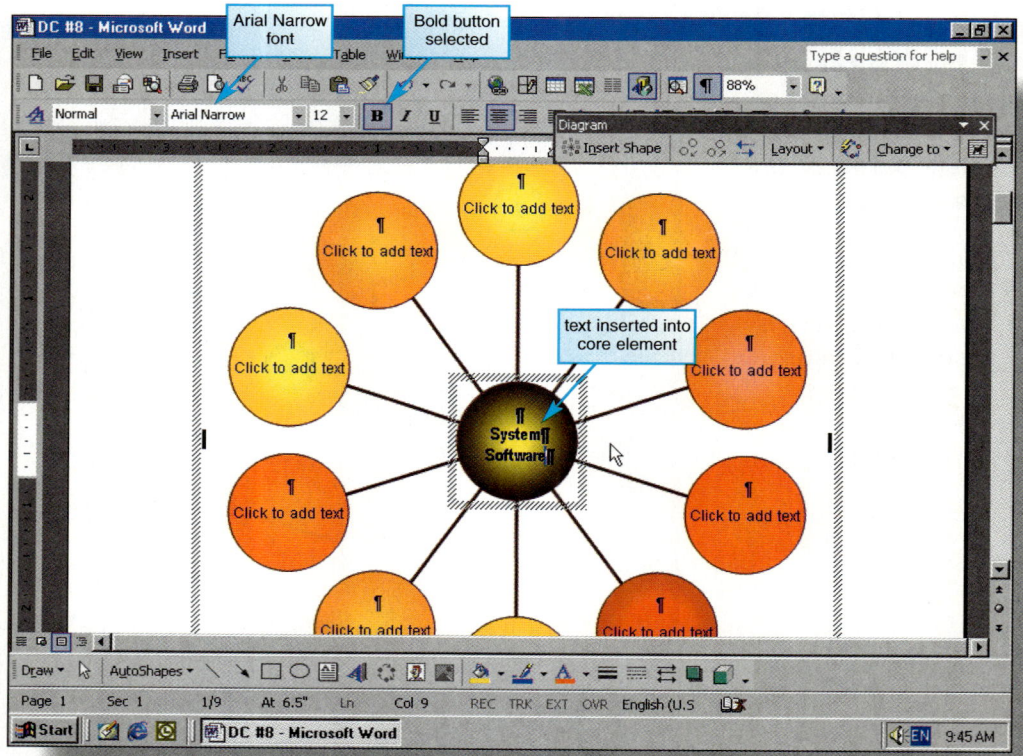

FIGURE 9-64

7 One at a time, beginning with the top center circle and moving clockwise, click each circle to add the text from Table 9-1 on page WD 9.49. In each circle, first press the ENTER key and then type the text, pressing the ENTER key between each word.

The completed text displays in each circle (Figure 9-65). Some words may wrap to two lines or only partially display. You will format the text in the next steps.

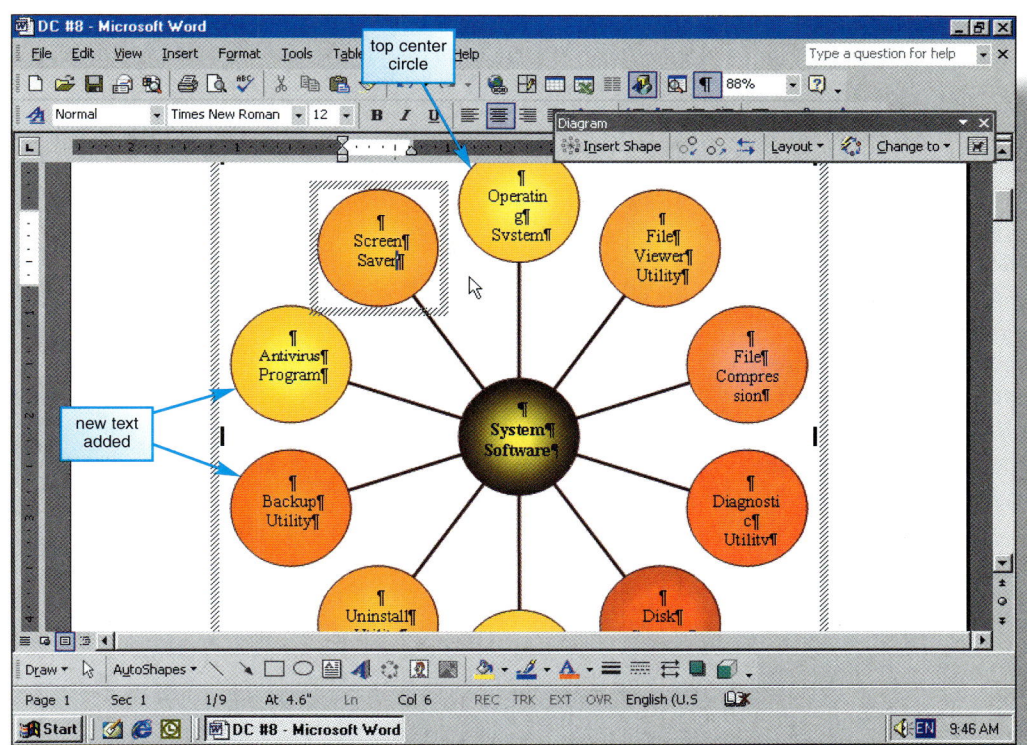

FIGURE 9-65

8 Drag through the text in the top center circle to select its text. Click the Font box arrow on the Formatting toolbar and then click Arial Narrow in the list. Click the Font Size box on the Formatting toolbar and then click 9 in the list. Click the Bold button on the Formatting toolbar. Double-click the Format Painter button on the Standard toolbar.

The text in the top-center circle is 9-point Arial Narrow bold font (Figure 9-66). You will copy the format of the text in this circle to the remaining circles in the diagram.

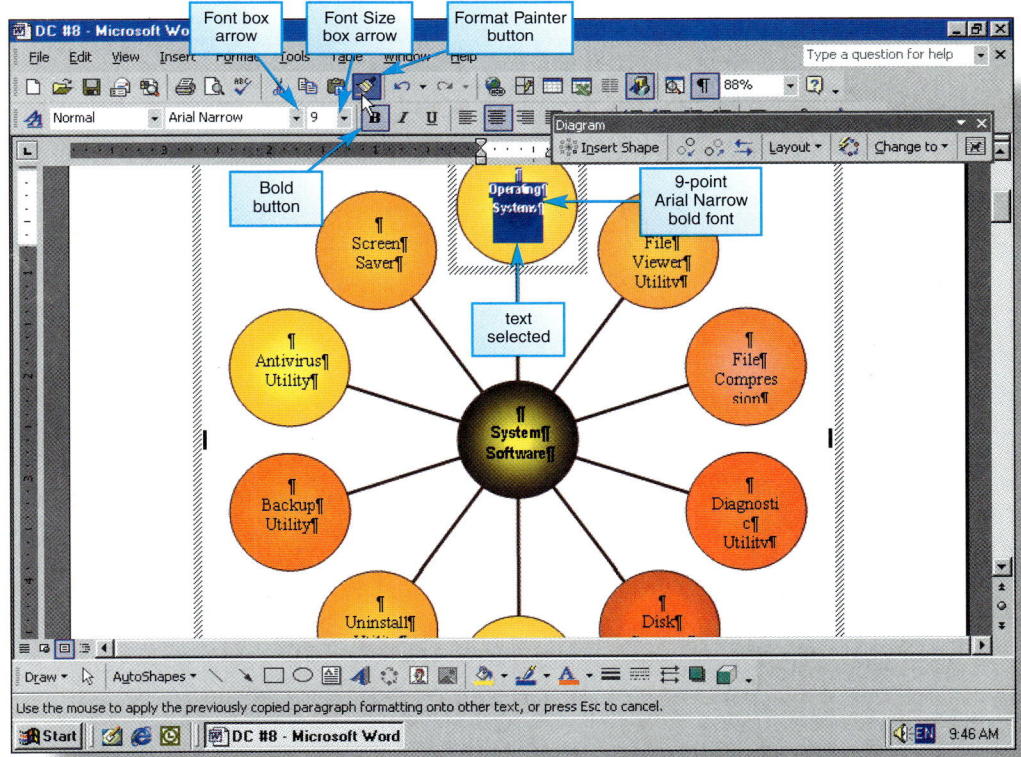

FIGURE 9-66

9 **Drag through the text in each of the remaining nine circles. When you have finished, click the Format Painter button on the Standard toolbar again to deselect it, and then click outside the drawing canvas, so the diagram no longer is selected. Click the Drawing button on the Standard toolbar to remove the Drawing toolbar from the screen.**

The formatting from the text in the top circle is applied to each of the remaining outer circles (Figure 9-67).

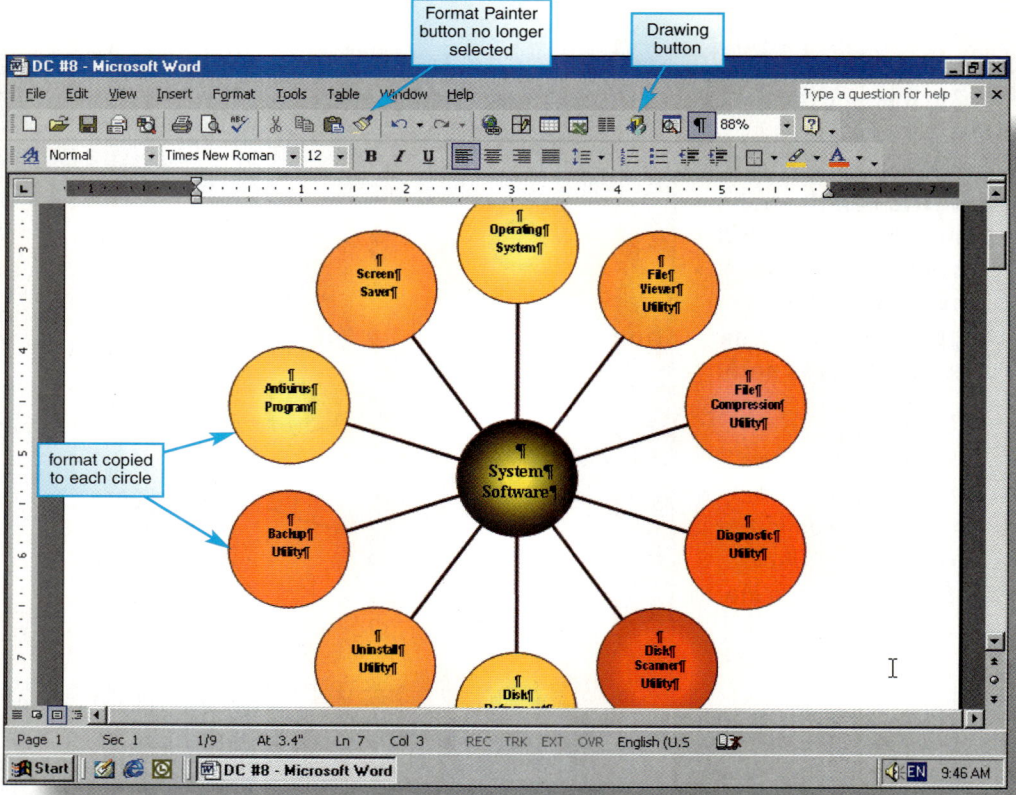

FIGURE 9-67

Other Ways

1. To format diagram, right-click diagram, click Format Diagram on shortcut menu
2. To insert diagram, in Voice Command mode, say "Insert, Diagram"

More About

Indexes and Tables

If your index, table of contents, or table of figures displays odd characters inside curly braces {}, then Word is displaying field codes instead of field results. Press ALT+F9 to display the index or table correctly. If your index or table prints field codes, click Tools on the menu bar, click Options, click the Print tab, remove the check mark from the Field codes check box, click the OK button, and then print the document again.

You formatted the diagram with a preset style named, Fire. Alternately, you can format the pieces of the diagram individually, adding color, changing line weights and style, or adding fills, textures, and backgrounds. To format an individual shape, click to select it and then use the Drawing toolbar to format it individually.

The Diagram toolbar, shown in Figure 9-61 on page WD 9.51, contains buttons to add elements or segments, move elements forward (clockwise) or backward (counterclockwise), format the layout, and wrap text.

The title page is complete. The next step is to create the table of figures for the DC #8 document.

Creating a Table of Figures

All public information guide documents have a table of figures following the text of the document. A **table of figures** is a list of all illustrations such as graphics, pictures, and tables in a document. Word creates the table of figures from the captions in the document. Perform the following steps to create a table of figures.

Working with a Master Document • WD 9.55

Steps: To Create a Table of Figures

1 If it is selected, click the Show/Hide ¶ button on the Standard toolbar to hide formatting marks. Scroll down to display the TABLE OF FIGURES heading. Position the insertion point at the end of the heading. Press the ENTER key. Click Insert on the menu bar, point to Reference and then point to Index and Tables on the Reference submenu (Figure 9-68).

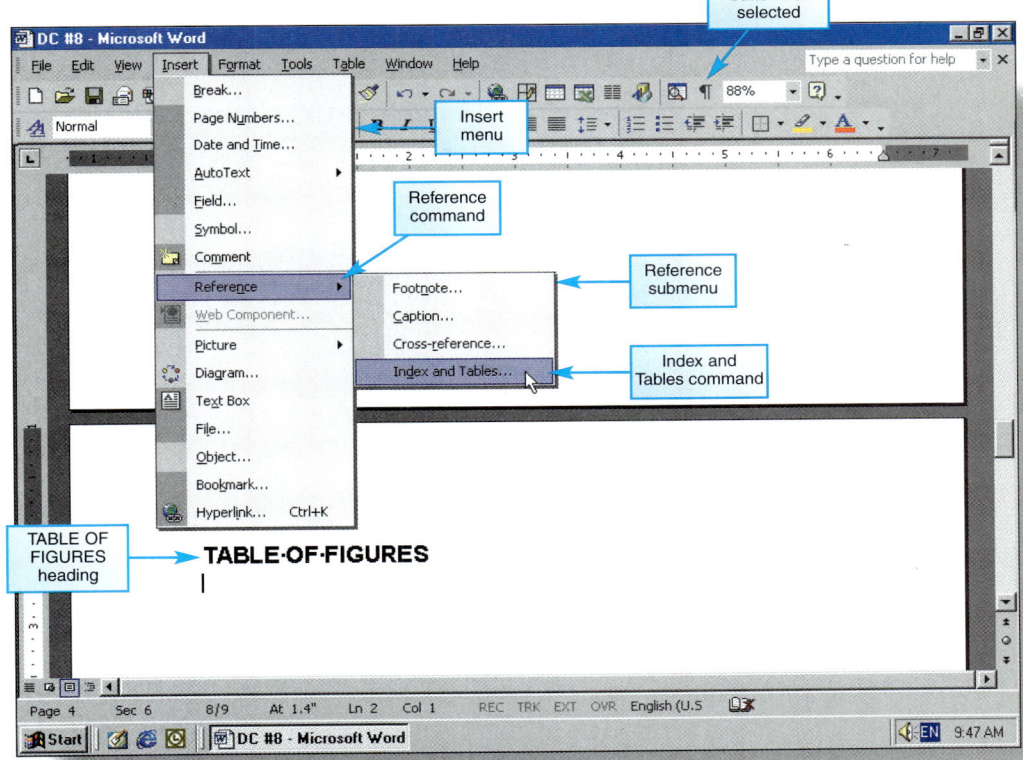

FIGURE 9-68

2 Click Index and Tables. If a Microsoft Word dialog box displays asking you to open the subdocuments, click the Yes button. When the Index and Tables dialog box displays, if necessary, click the Table of Figures tab. Be sure that all check boxes in the dialog box contain check marks. Point to the OK button.

Word displays the Table of Figures sheet in the Index and Tables dialog box (Figure 9-69).

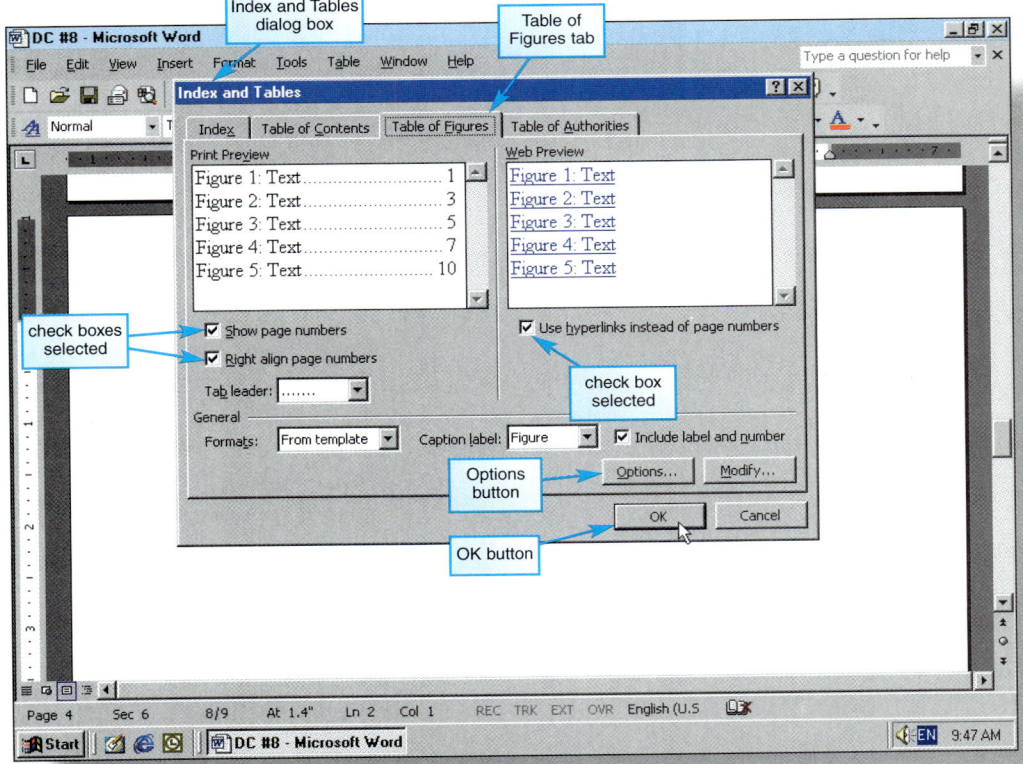

FIGURE 9-69

3 **Click the OK button.**

Word creates a table of figures at the location of the insertion point (Figure 9-70).

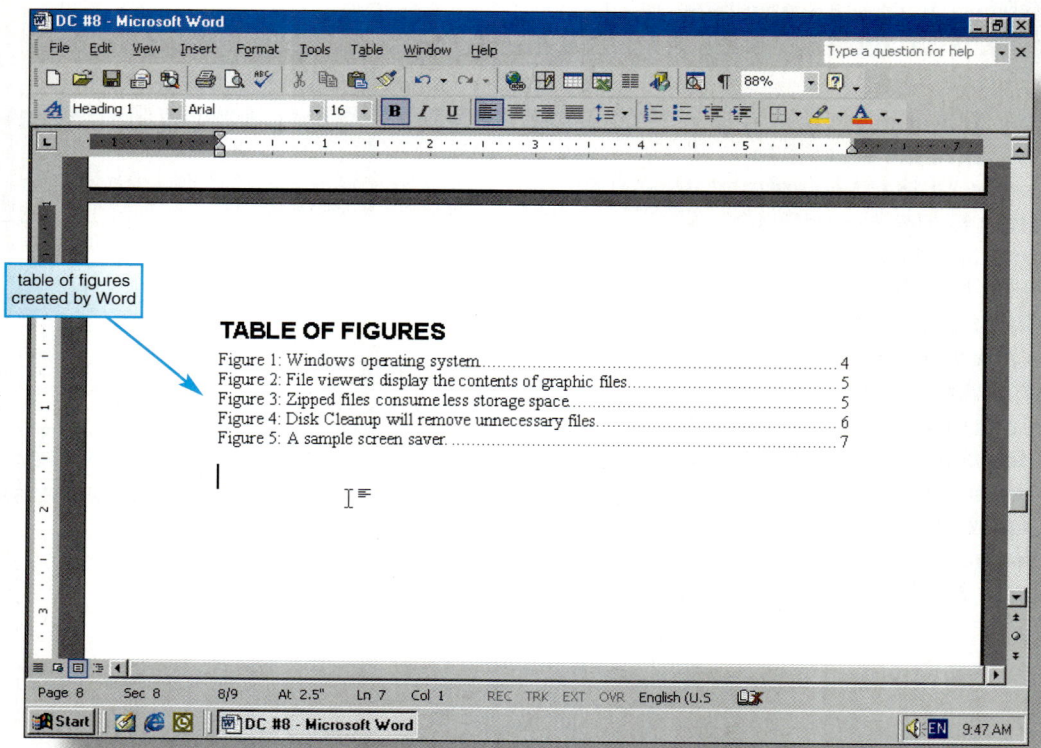

FIGURE 9-70

1. In Voice Command mode, say "Insert, Reference, Index and Tables"

Index Entries

Instead of marking index entries in a document, you can create a concordance file, which Word uses to mark index entries automatically. The concordance file contains two columns: (1) the first column identifies the text in the document you want Word to mark as an index entry, and (2) the second column lists the index entries to be generated from the text in the first column. To mark entries in the concordance file, click the AutoMark button in the Index and Tables dialog box.

When you modify captions in a document or move illustrations to a different location in the document, you will have to update the table of figures. To do this, click to the left of the table and then press the F9 key.

If you did not use captions to create labels for your illustrations in a document and would like Word to generate a table of figures, you can instruct Word to create the table using the built-in style you used for the captions. To do this, click the Options button in the Table of Figures sheet (Figure 9-69 on the previous page) to display the Table of Figures Options dialog box.

The next step is to build an index for the document.

Building an Index

As mentioned earlier in this project, public information guide documents end with an index, which lists important terms discussed in the document along with each term's corresponding page number. For Word to generate the index, you first must mark any item you wish to appear in the index. Earlier in this project, you marked an entry in the Operating Systems file. The Utility Programs file, which is located on the Data Disk, already has index entries marked.

Once all index entries are marked, you can have Word build the index from the index entry fields in the document. The index entry fields display on the screen when the Show/Hide ¶ button on the Standard toolbar is selected; that is, when you display formatting marks. Index entry field codes may alter the document pagination. Thus, you should hide field codes before building an index.

Perform the following steps to build an index.

Steps To Build an Index

1 Scroll down and click to the right of the INDEX heading and then press the ENTER key. If the Show/Hide ¶ button on the Standard toolbar is selected, click it. Click Insert on the menu bar, point to Reference, and then click Index and Tables on the Reference submenu. When the Index and Tables dialog box displays, if necessary, click the Index tab. Click the Formats box arrow. Scroll to and then click Formal. Point to the OK button.

Word displays the Index sheet in the Index and Tables dialog box (Figure 9-71). The Formats box contains a variety of available index styles.

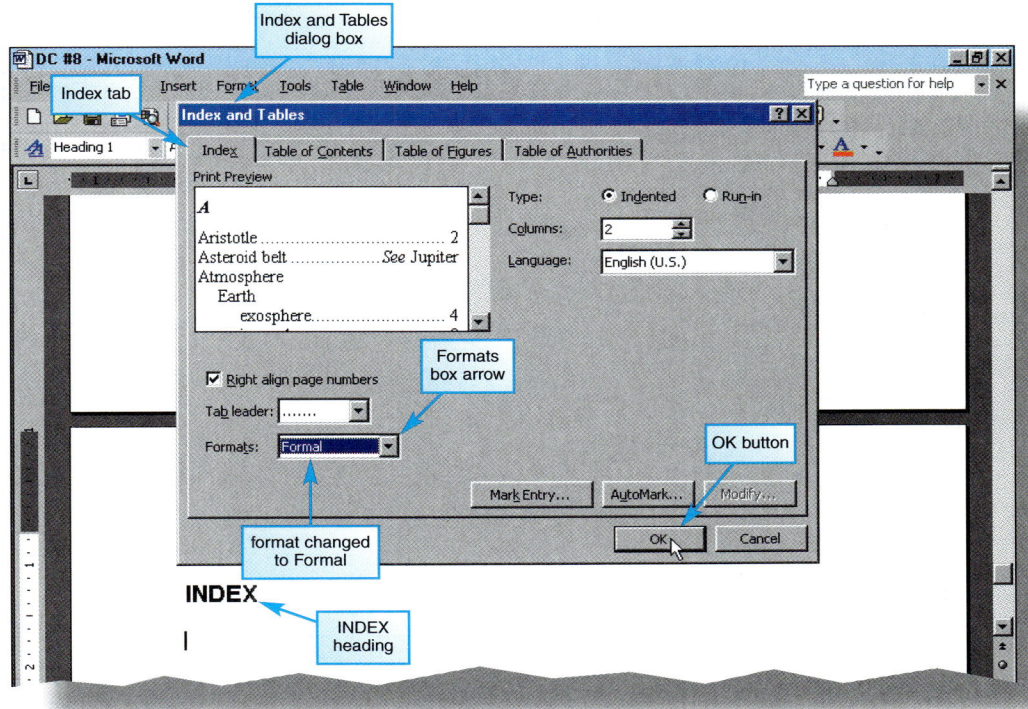

FIGURE 9-71

2 Click the OK button. If necessary, click outside the index to remove the selection.

Word creates a formal index at the location of the insertion point (Figure 9-72).

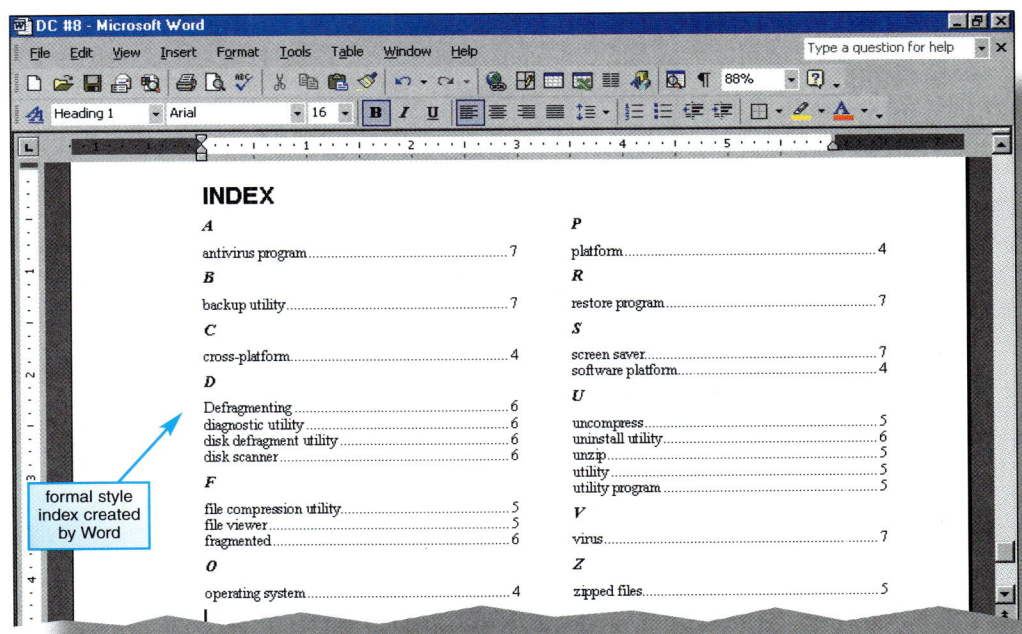

FIGURE 9-72

Other Ways

1. In Voice Command mode, say "Insert, Reference, Index and Tables"

To update an index, click to the left of the index to select it and then press the F9 key. To delete an index, click to the left of the index and then press SHIFT+F9 to display field codes. Drag through the entire field code, including the braces, and then press the DELETE key.

When you display the document on the screen, the index entries may still appear — even with the Show/Hide ¶ button not selected. If you want to remove them, click Tools on the menu bar, click Options, click the View tab, remove the check mark from the Hidden text check box, and then click the OK button.

The next step is to create the table of contents for the DC #8 document.

Creating a Table of Contents

A table of contents is a list of all headings in a document and their associated page numbers. When you use Word's built-in heading styles (for example, Heading 1), you can instruct Word to create a table of contents from these headings. In the DC #8 document, the heading of each section uses the Heading 1 style, and subheadings use the Heading 2 style. Thus, perform the following steps to create a table of contents from heading styles.

Modifying a Table of Contents

The table of contents that Word generates may contain a heading that you do not want. To remove a heading from the table of contents, you should change the style applied to the heading from a built-in heading to a non-heading style. Then, update the table of contents.

Steps: To Create a Table of Contents

1 Scroll up and click to the right of the TABLE OF CONTENTS heading. Press the ENTER key. Click Insert on the menu bar, point to Reference, and then click Index and Tables on the Reference submenu. When the Index and Tables dialog box displays, if necessary, click the Table of Contents tab. Click the Formats box arrow and then click Formal. Point to the OK button.

Word displays the Table of Contents sheet in the Index and Tables dialog box (Figure 9-73). The Formats list contains a variety of available table of contents styles.

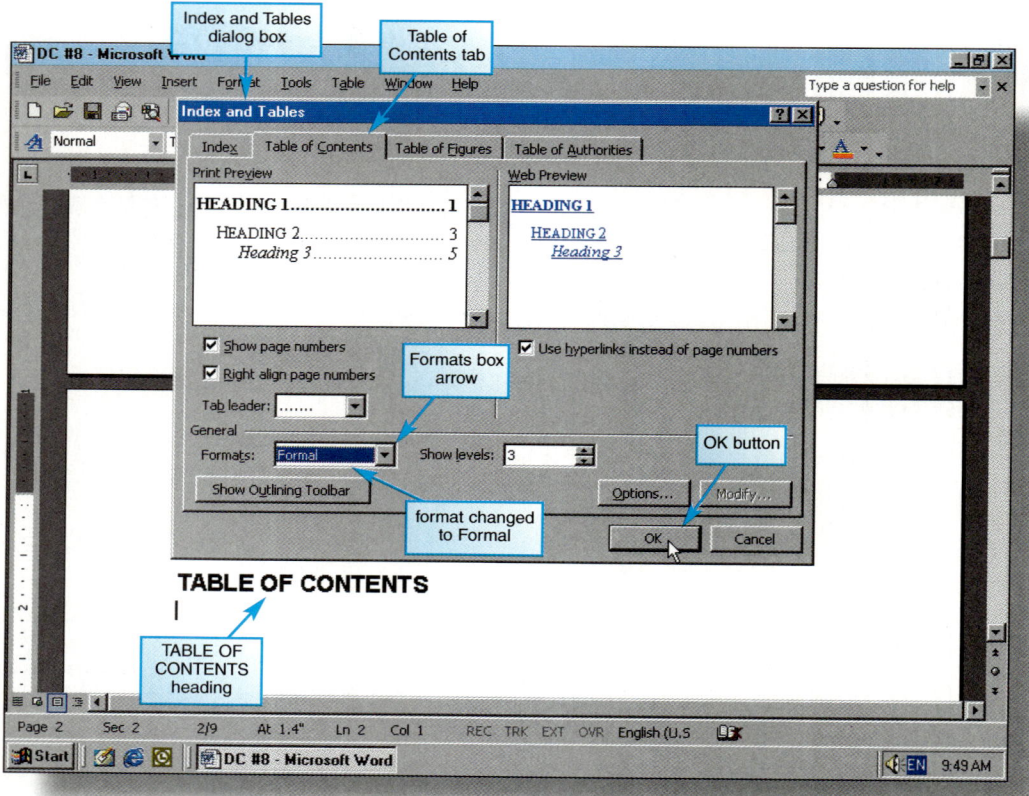

FIGURE 9-73

2 Click the OK button. If a dialog box displays asking if you want to replace the selected table of contents, click the No button.

Word creates a formal table of contents at the location of the insertion point (Figure 9-74).

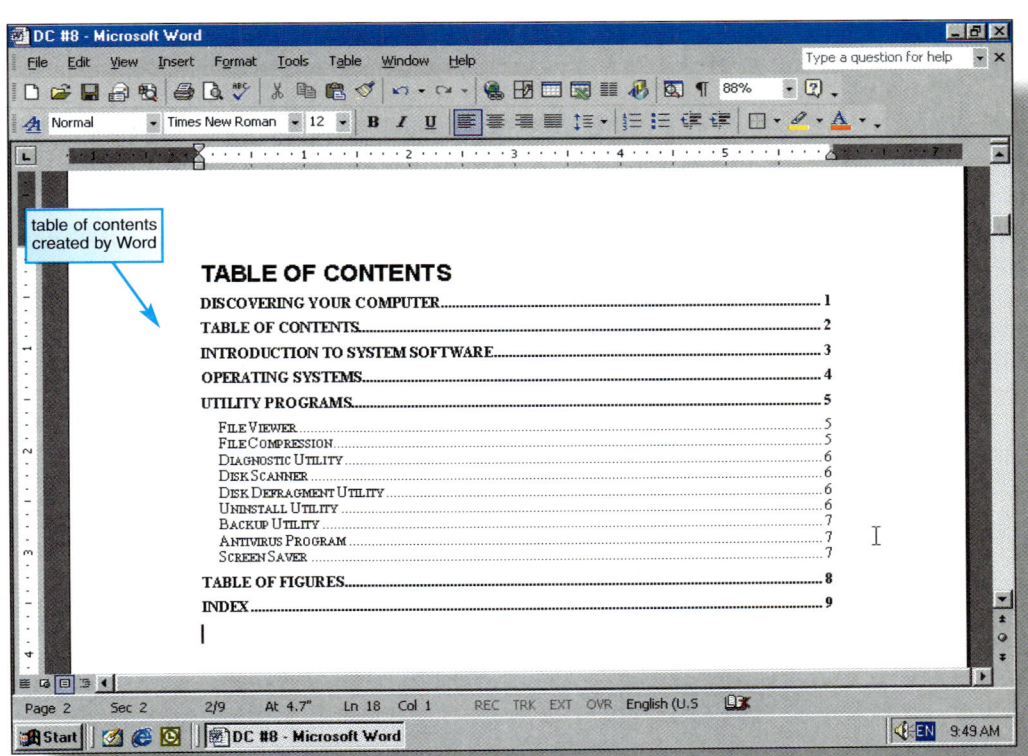

FIGURE 9-74

1. In Voice Command mode, say "Insert, Reference, Index and Tables"

When you change headings or text in a document, you should update its associated table of contents. To update a table of contents, click to the left of the table of contents to select it and then press the F9 key.

In a document that contains a table of contents or a table of figures, you can use these tables to navigate through a document. When you CTRL+click any of the entries in either table, Word displays the associated text or graphics in the document window. For example, if you CTRL+click Screen Saver in the table of contents, Word displays the page containing the Screen Saver section.

The next step is to add bookmarks to the document.

Adding Bookmarks

To further assist users in navigating through a document, you can add bookmarks. A bookmark is an item in a document that you name for future reference. For example, you could bookmark the two headings, Operating Systems and Utility Programs, so users easily could jump to these two areas of the document. Perform the steps on the next page to add these bookmarks.

Bookmarks

To show bookmarks in a document, click Tools on the menu bar, click Options, click the View tab, place a check mark in the Bookmarks check box, and then click the OK button. If your bookmark displays an error message, select the entire document and then press the F9 key to update the fields in the document.

Steps: To Add a Bookmark

1 Scroll to the Operating Systems heading in the document. Drag through the heading Operating Systems to select it. Click Insert on the menu bar and then point to Bookmark (Figure 9-75).

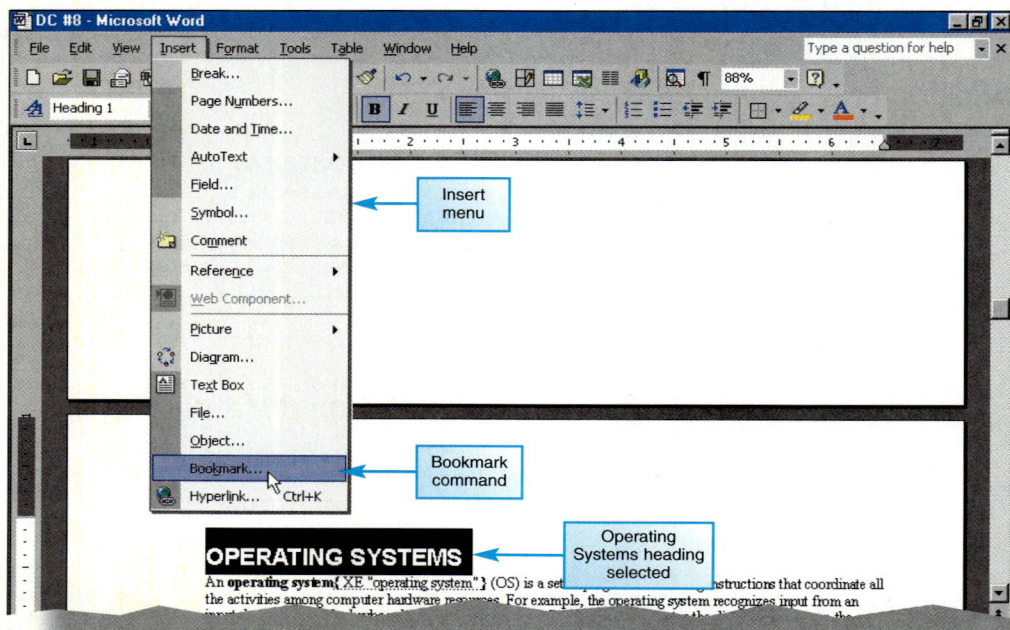

FIGURE 9-75

2 Click Bookmark. When the Bookmark dialog box displays, type `OperatingSystems` in the Bookmark name text box and then point to the Add button.

Word displays the Bookmark dialog box (Figure 9-76). Bookmark names can contain only letters, numbers, and the underscore character (_). They also must begin with a letter and contain no spaces.

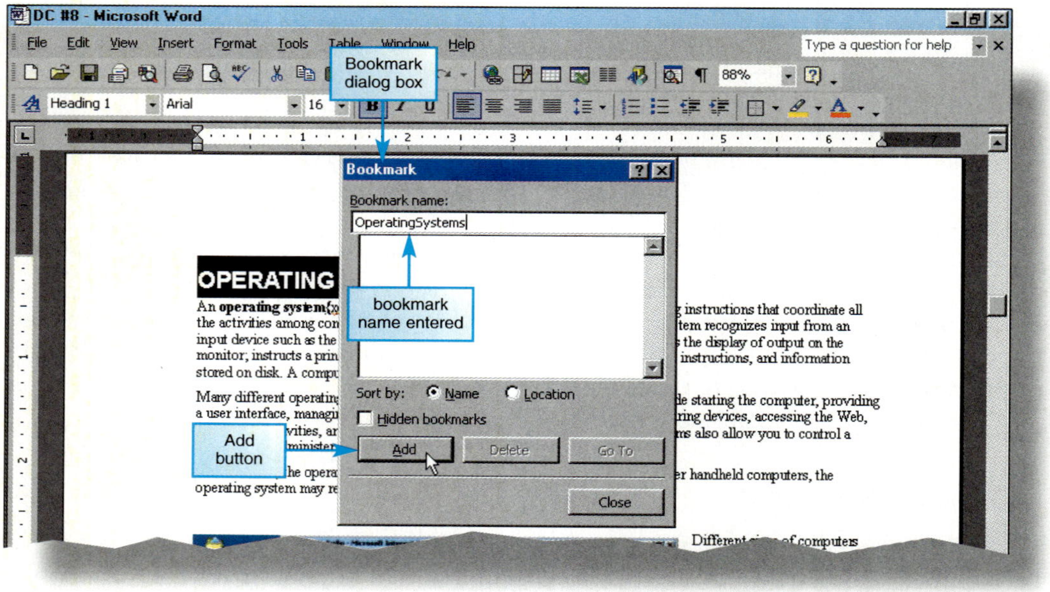

3 Click the Add button.

Word adds the bookmark name to the list of existing bookmarks for the document.

FIGURE 9-76

4 Repeat Steps 1 through 3 for the Utility Programs heading in the document, using the bookmark name of UtilityPrograms.

Other Ways

1. In Voice Command mode, say "Insert, Bookmark"

Once you have added bookmarks, you can jump to a bookmark by displaying the Bookmark dialog box (shown in Figure 9-76), clicking the bookmark name in the list, and then clicking the Go To button; or by pressing the F5 key to display the Go To dialog box, clicking bookmark in the list, selecting the bookmark name, and then clicking the Go To button.

The text of the document now is complete. The next step is to place a header on all pages of the document, except the title page.

Creating Alternating Headers and Footers

Public information guide documents are designed so that they can be duplicated back-to-back. That is, the document prints on nine separate pages. When you duplicate it, however, pages one and two are printed on opposite sides of the same sheet of paper. Thus, the nine page document when printed back-to-back only uses five sheets of paper.

In many books and documents that have facing pages, the page number is on the outside edges of the pages. In Word, you accomplish this task by specifying one type of header for even-numbered pages and another type of header for odd-numbered pages.

Perform the following steps to create alternating headers beginning with the second page of the document.

More About

Publishing and Graphic Arts Terms

For more information on terms used in publishing and graphic arts, visit the Word 2002 More About Web page (scsite.com/wd2002/more.htm) and then click Publishing and Graphic Arts Terms.

Steps To Create Alternating Headers

1 Position the insertion point in the Table of Contents heading (section 2 of the document). Click View on the menu bar and then click Header and Footer. Click the Page Setup button on the Header and Footer toolbar. When the Page Setup dialog box displays, if necessary, click the Layout tab. Click Different odd and even. Click the Apply to box arrow and then click This point forward. Point to the OK button.

Word displays the Page Setup dialog box (Figure 9-77).

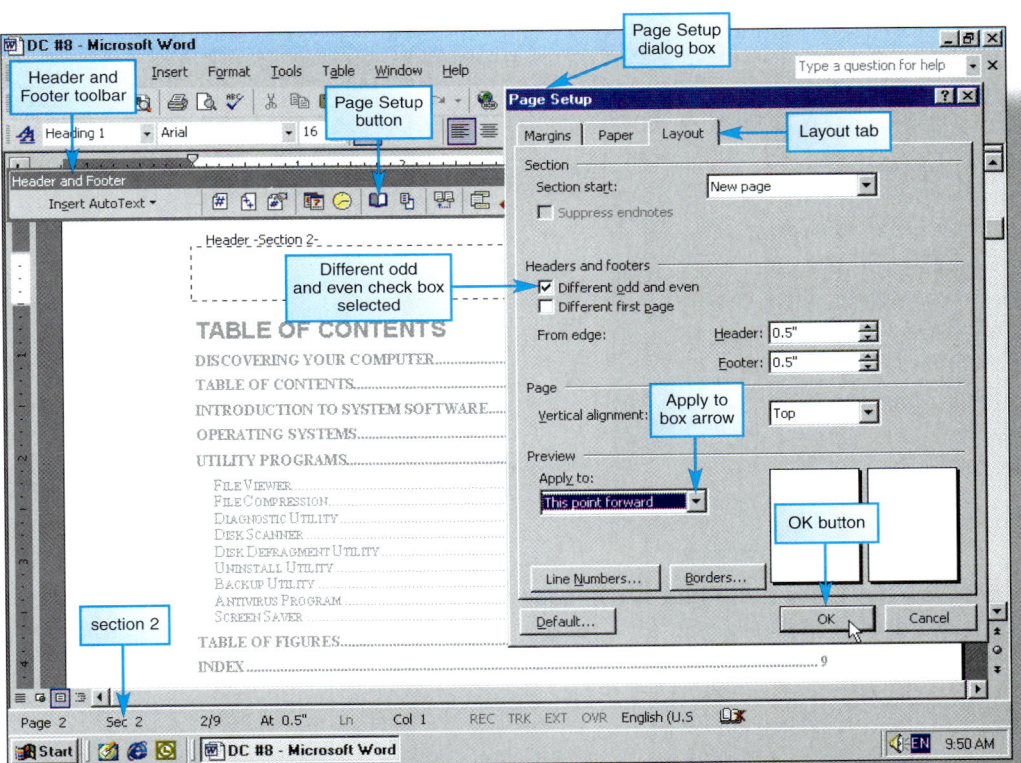

FIGURE 9-77

2 Click the OK button. If the Same as Previous button on the Header and Footer toolbar is selected, click it. Type Public Information Guide #8 and then press the ENTER key. Type Page and then press the SPACEBAR. Click the Insert Page Number button on the Header and Footer toolbar. Press the ENTER key. Point to the Show Next button on the Header and Footer toolbar.

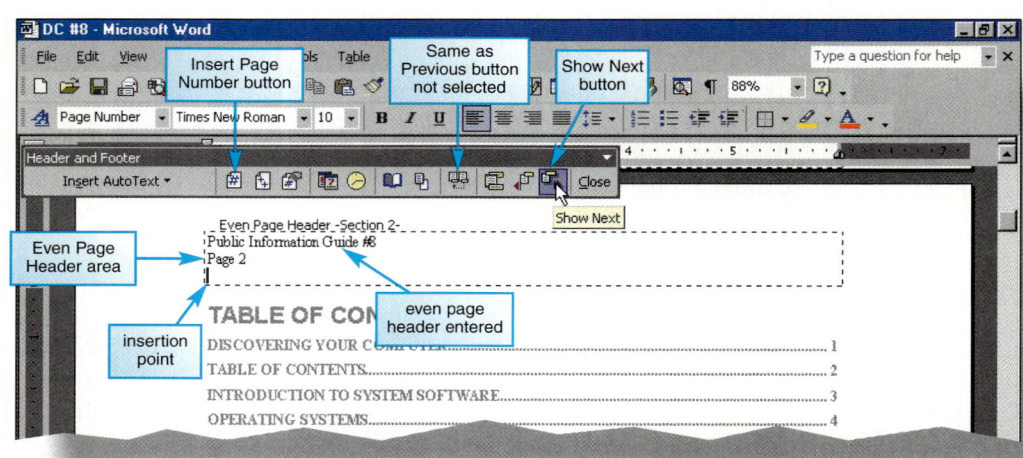

FIGURE 9-78

Word displays the Even Page Header area (Figure 9-78). You want text on even page numbers to be left-aligned and text on odd page numbers to be right-aligned. The Show Next button will display the Odd Page Header area.

3 Click the Show Next button. If the Same as Previous button on the Header and Footer toolbar is selected, click it. Click the Align Right button on the Formatting toolbar. Type Public Information Guide #8 and then press the ENTER key. Type Page and then press the SPACEBAR. Click the Insert Page Number button on the Header and Footer toolbar. Press the ENTER key.

The odd page header is complete (Figure 9-79).

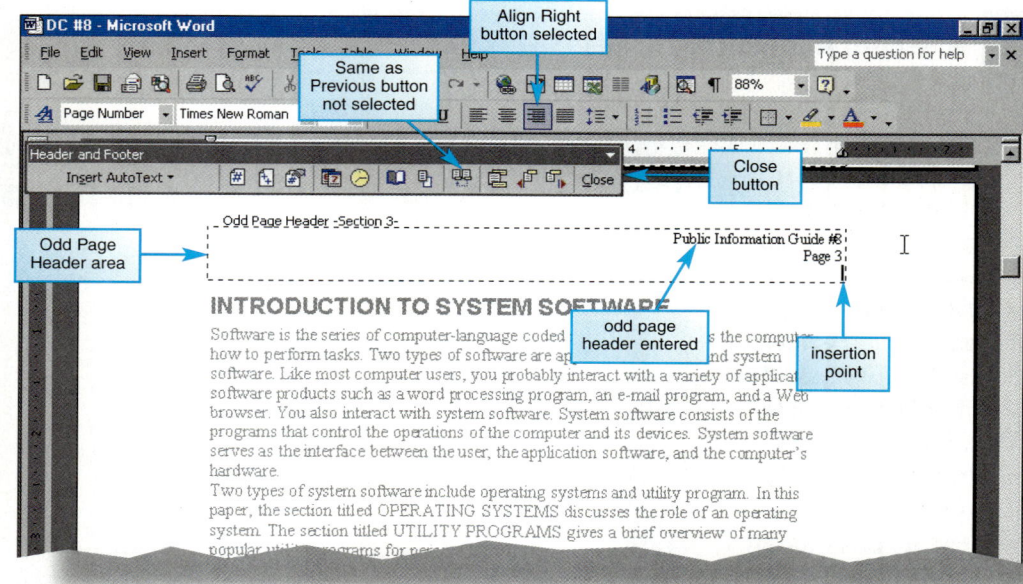

FIGURE 9-79

4 Click the Close button on the Header and Footer toolbar to remove the Header and Footer toolbar from the screen.

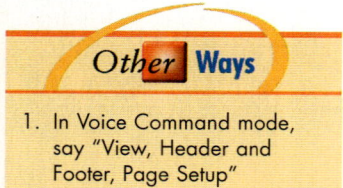

1. In Voice Command mode, say "View, Header and Footer, Page Setup"

To create alternating footers, follow the same basic procedure as you would to create alternating headers, except enter text in the footer area instead of the header area.

The next step is to set a gutter margin for the document.

Setting a Gutter Margin

Public information guide documents are designed so that the inner margin between facing pages has extra space to allow printed versions of the documents to be bound (such as stapled) — without the binding covering the words. This extra space in the inner margin is called the gutter margin.

Perform the following steps to set a three-quarter inch left and right margin and a one-half inch gutter margin.

Steps: To Set a Gutter Margin

  Click File on the menu bar and then click Page Setup. When the Page Setup dialog box displays, if necessary, click the Margins tab. Type .75 **in the Left text box,** .75 **in the Right text box, and** .5 **in the Gutter text box. Click the Apply to box arrow and then click Whole document. Point to the OK button.**

Word displays the Page Setup dialog box (Figure 9-80). The Preview area illustrates the position of the gutter margin.

Click the OK button.

Word sets the gutter margin for the entire document.

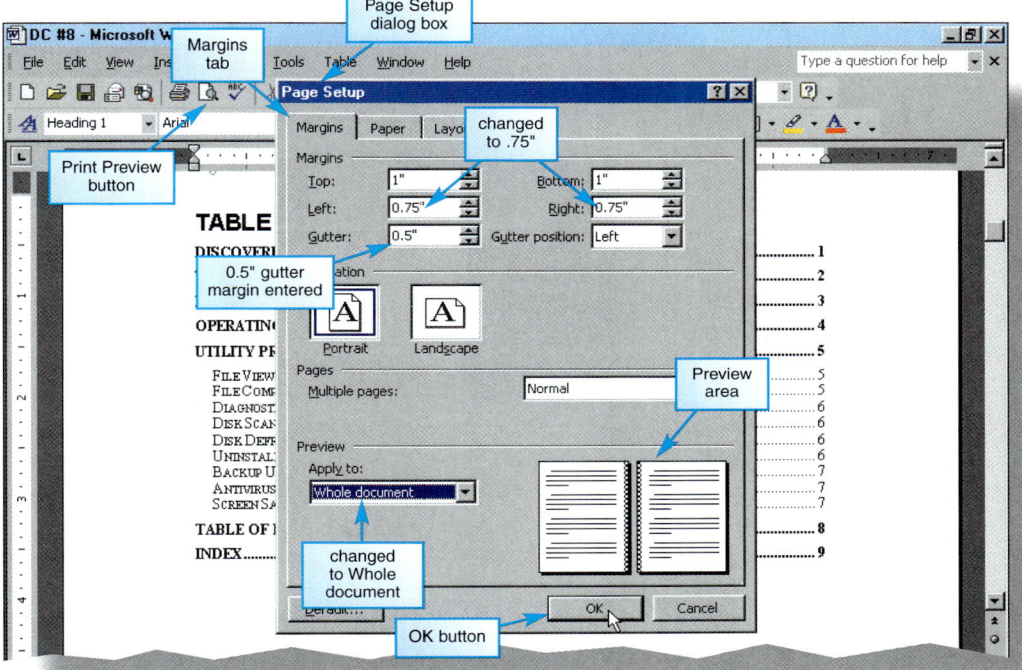

FIGURE 9-80

Other Ways

1. In Voice Command mode, say "File, Page Setup"

You notice that the Body Text style uses a 10-point font. You prefer a 12-point font. Perform the following steps to change the Body Text style from 10 to 12 point.

TO MODIFY A STYLE

1. Position the insertion point in the body text in the INTRODUCTION TO SYSTEM SOFTWARE section. Click the Styles and Formatting button on the Formatting toolbar to display the Styles and Formatting task pane.

2. Point to Body Text in the Styles and Formatting task pane and then click the box arrow that displays to the right of Body Text. Click Modify in the menu. When the Modify Style dialog box displays, if necessary, click the Font Size box arrow in the dialog box and then click 12. Click the OK button. Click the Close button on the Styles and Formatting task pane.

Word changes all text formatted using the Body Text style in the document from 10 to 12 point.

To view the layout of all the pages in the document, display all the pages in print preview as described in the following steps.

TO DISPLAY SEVERAL PAGES IN PRINT PREVIEW

1. Click the Print Preview button on the Standard toolbar.
2. Click the Multiple Pages button on the Print Preview toolbar. Click the right-bottom icon in the grid (when the description reads 2 x 6 pages) to display the pages in the Discovering Your Computer public information guide document as shown in Figure 9-81.
3. Click the Close button on the Print Preview toolbar.

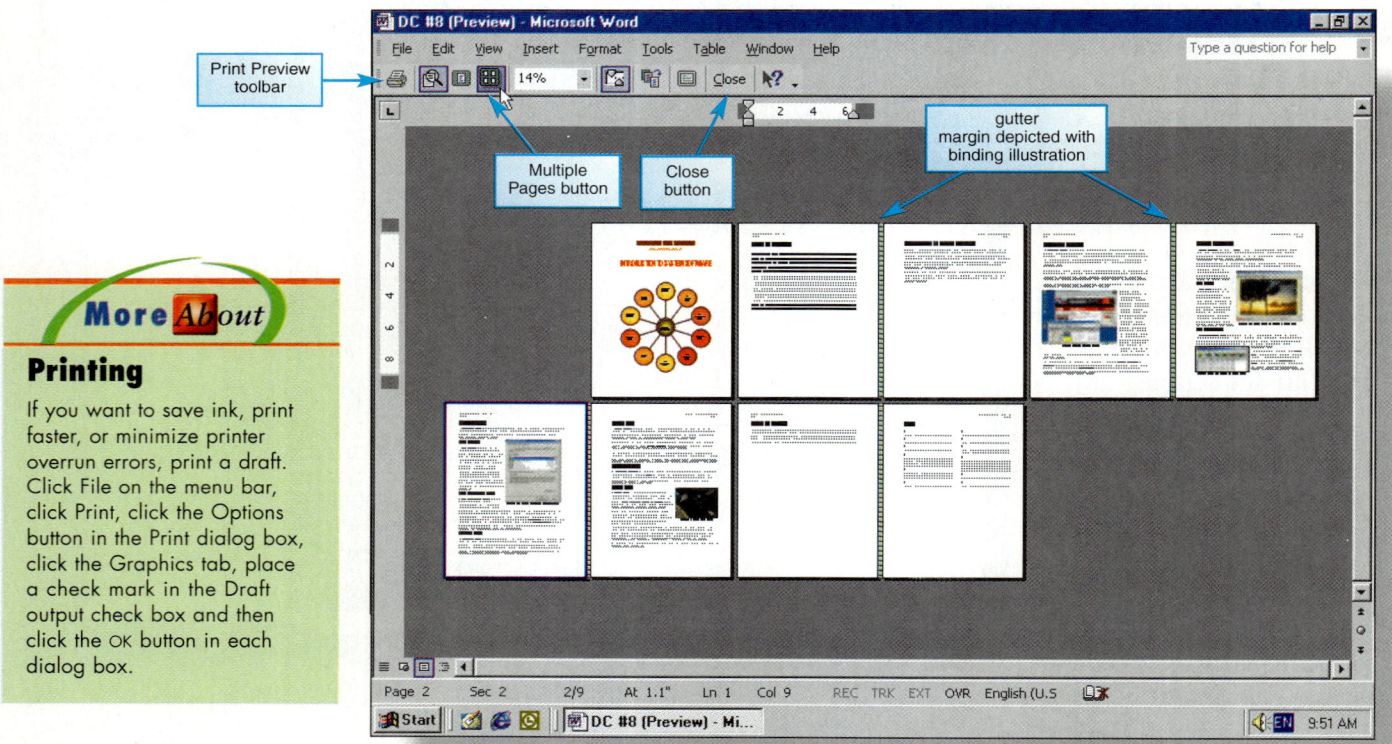

FIGURE 9-81

> **More About**
>
> **Printing**
>
> If you want to save ink, print faster, or minimize printer overrun errors, print a draft. Click File on the menu bar, click Print, click the Options button in the Print dialog box, click the Graphics tab, place a check mark in the Draft output check box and then click the OK button in each dialog box.

The reference master document for this project now is complete. Perform the following steps to save it again, print it, and then close the document.

TO SAVE AND PRINT THE DOCUMENT

1. Click the Save button on the Standard toolbar.
2. Click the Print button on the Standard toolbar.

Word saves the document with the same file name, DC #8. The completed document prints each page shown in Figure 9-1 on page WD 9.05 on a separate piece of paper.

TO CLOSE THE DOCUMENT

1. Click File on the menu bar and then click Close.

Opening a Master Document

You may wish to open a master document at a later date to edit or print its contents. When you open the master document, the subdocuments are collapsed; that is, the subdocuments display as hyperlinks. Thus, switch to outline view and expand the subdocuments, as shown in the following steps.

Steps: To Open a Master Document

1 **Open the DC #8 document. Click the Outline View button on the horizontal scroll bar. Be sure the Show/Hide ¶ button on the Standard toolbar is selected. Make sure the Show First Line Only button on the Outlining toolbar is not selected. Scroll down to display the hyperlinks. Point to the Expand Subdocuments button on the Outlining toolbar.**

Word displays the DC #8 document in outline view (Figure 9-82).

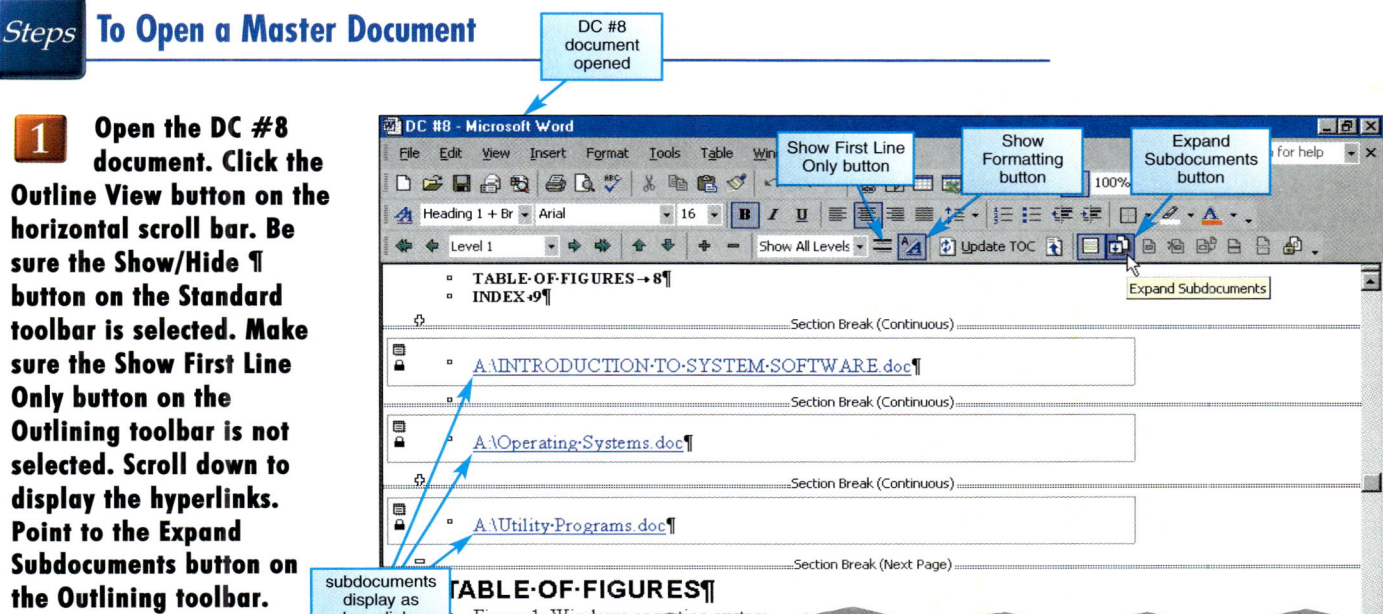

FIGURE 9-82

2 **Click the Expand Subdocuments button. When the Password dialog box displays, type** computer **and then click the OK button. Scroll down to display the subdocuments.**

Word displays the contents of the subdocuments in the master document (Figure 9-83).

3 **Click the Print Layout View button on the horizontal scroll bar.**

The master document is ready to be printed or modified.

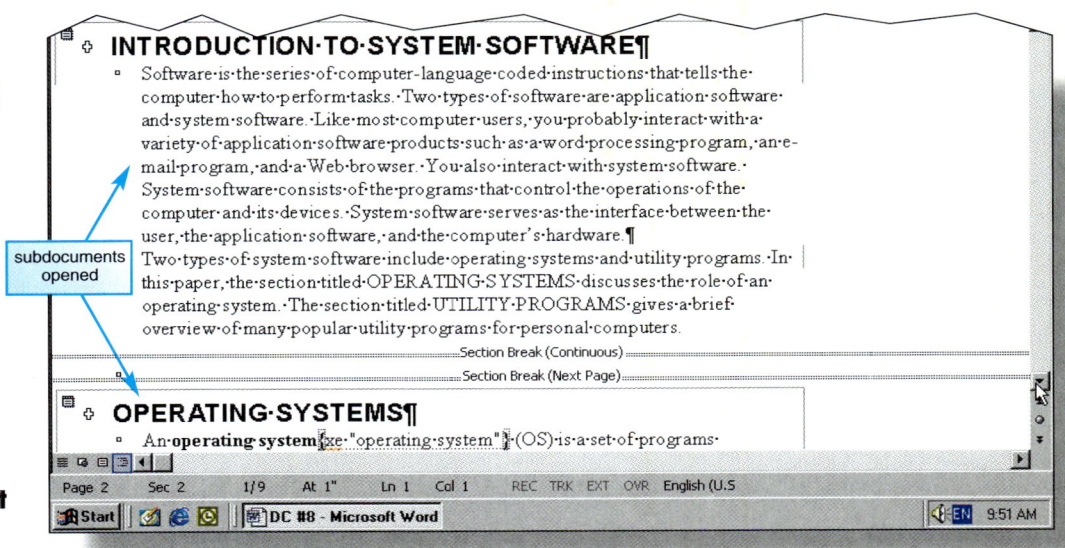

FIGURE 9-83

1. In Voice Command mode, say "File, Open, [select file], OK, Outline View"

Using the Document Map

When you use Word's built-in heading styles in a document, you can use the Document Map to navigate quickly through the document. The **Document Map** is a separate area at the left edge of the Word window that displays these headings in an outline format. When you click a heading in the Document Map, Word scrolls to and displays that heading in the document window.

Perform the following steps to use the Document Map.

Steps: To Use the Document Map

1 If the Show/Hide ¶ button on the Standard toolbar is selected, click it. Click the Document Map button on the Standard toolbar. Right-click the Document Map and then click All on the shortcut menu to ensure that all headings display.

Word displays the Document Map in a separate pane at the left edge of the Word window (Figure 9-84). The Document Map lists all headings that are formatted using Word's built-in heading styles. Your document map may show some blank lines between headings.

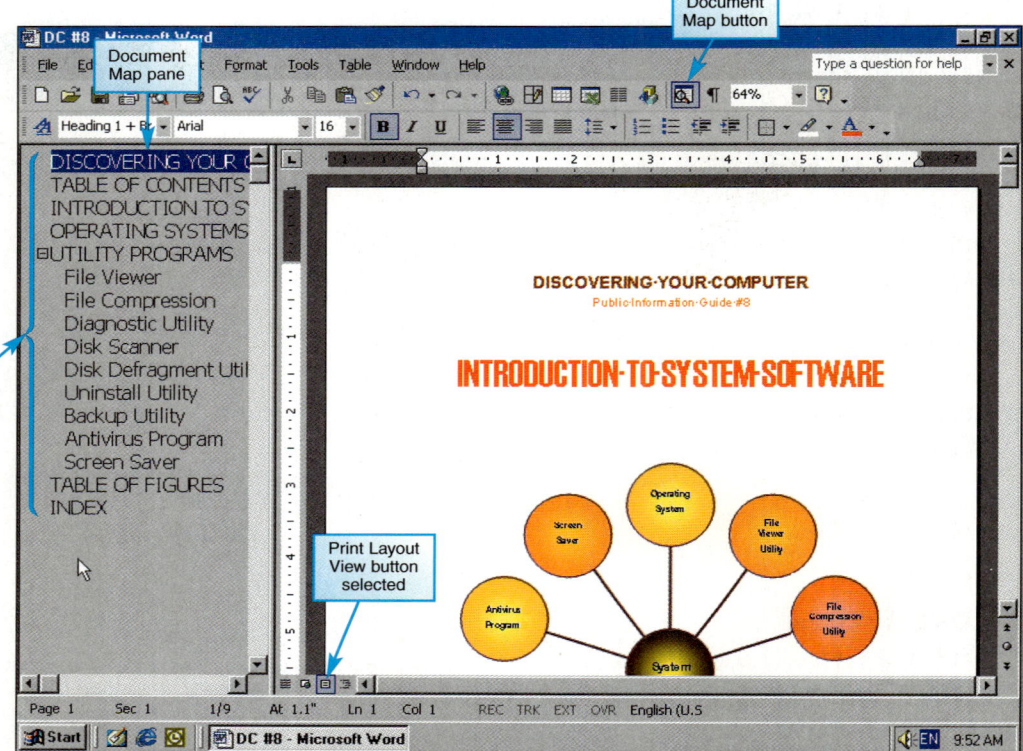

FIGURE 9-84

2 **Click TABLE OF CONTENTS in the Document Map pane.**

Word scrolls to and displays the TABLE OF CONTENTS heading at the top of the document window (Figure 9-85).

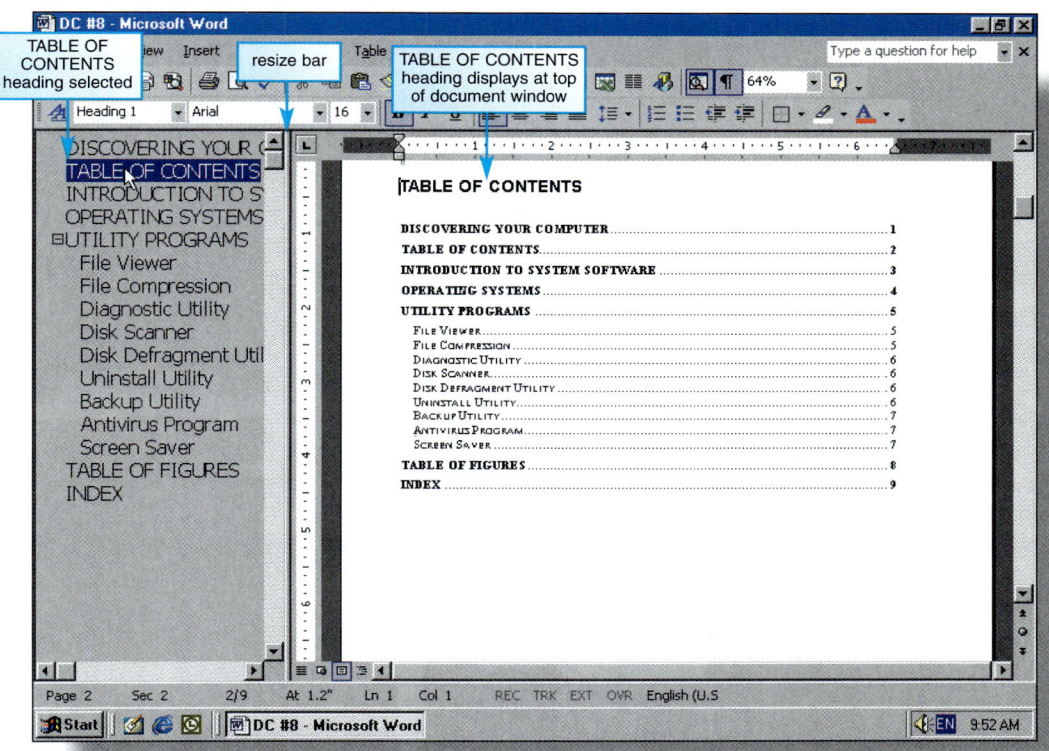

FIGURE 9-85

1. In Voice Command mode, say "Document Map"

Subdocuments

If you want to change the name of a subdocument, you cannot use Windows Explorer. Instead, display the document in outline view, click the Collapse Subdocuments button on the Outlining toolbar, and then click the hyperlink of the document to be renamed. When the subdocument displays in its own Word window, click File on the menu bar, click Save As, change the document name, and then click the Save button in the dialog box. Then, return to the master document by clicking File on the menu bar and then clicking Close.

To display any subheadings below a heading, click the plus sign (+) to the left of the heading. Likewise, to hide any subheadings, click the minus sign (–) to the left of the heading.

If a heading is too wide for the Document Map pane, you do not need to make the Document Map pane wider — simply point to the heading to display a ScreenTip that shows the complete title. You can change the width of the Document Map pane, however, by dragging the resize bar to the left or right.

Modifying the Table of Contents and Index

Assume you wanted to change the title of the TABLE OF CONTENTS to just the word, CONTENTS. Assume also that you want to change the index entry for cross-platform to the phrase, cross-platform application. After making these changes to the document, you must update the table of contents and the index as shown in the steps on the next page.

Steps: To Modify a Table of Contents and Index

1 Drag through the words, TABLE OF, in the TABLE OF CONTENTS heading and then press the DELETE key. Click the OPERATING SYSTEMS heading in the Document Map pane. Scroll to and then click immediately to the right of the m inside the braces containing the index entry for cross-platform. Press the SPACEBAR and then type `application` to modify the entry.

The document is modified (Figure 9-86).

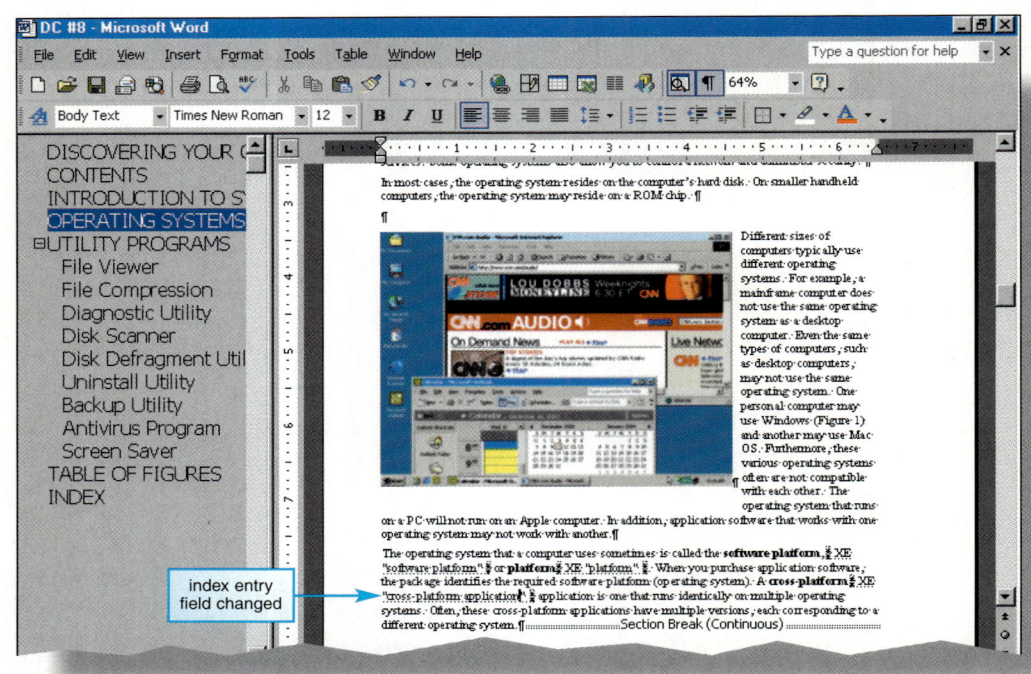

FIGURE 9-86

2 If the Show/Hide ¶ button on the Standard toolbar is selected, click it. In the Document Map pane, click CONTENTS and then click the contents listing in the document window to select the table. Press the F9 key. When the Update Table of Contents dialog box displays, click Update entire table and then point to the OK button.

Word displays the Update Table of Contents dialog box (Figure 9-87).

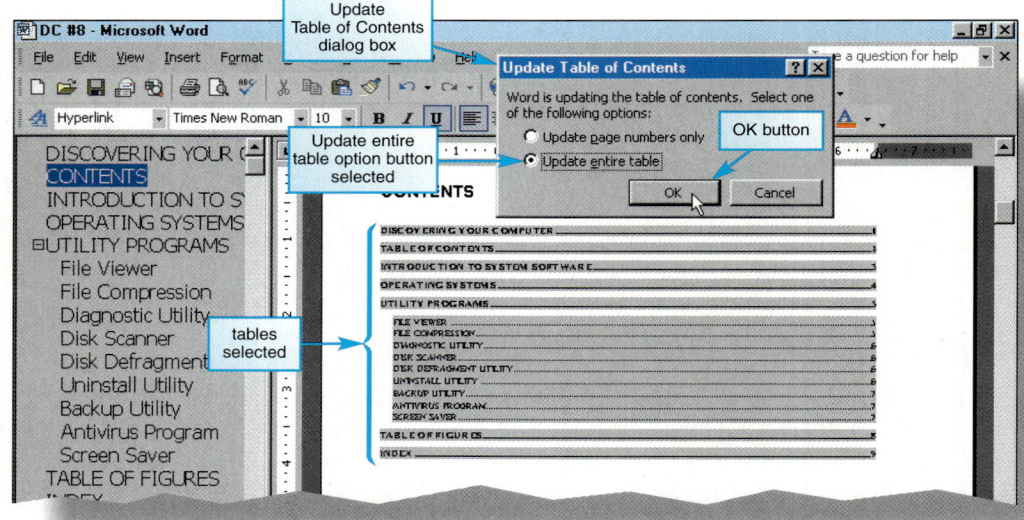

FIGURE 9-87

3 Click the OK button. Repeat Step 2, clicking INDEX in the Document Map pane. Word will update the index when you press the F9 key.

Word updates the index, changing the index entry from cross-platform to cross-platform application.

Other Ways

1. Click Update TOC button on Outlining toolbar
2. In Voice Command mode, say "Update Table of Contents"

By selecting the entire table of contents or index and then pressing the F9 key, you are instructing Word to update all fields in the document. If you want to update a single field, select it and then press the F9 key.

The next step is to hide the Document Map, as described in the following step.

TO HIDE THE DOCUMENT MAP

1. Click the Document Map button on the Standard toolbar.

Word removes the Document Map pane from the Word window.

You also can hide the Document Map by double-clicking the resize bar to its right (shown in Figure 9-85 on page WD 9.67).

You are finished modifying the document. Perform the following step to quit Word.

TO QUIT WORD

1. Click the Close button on the Word title bar. When Word displays a dialog box asking if you wish to save changes, click the No button.

The Word window closes.

Quick Reference

For a table that lists how to complete tasks covered in this book using the mouse, menu, shortcut menu, and keyboard, see the Quick Reference Summary at the back of this book or visit the Shelly Cashman Series Office XP Web page (scsite.com/offxp/qr.htm) and then click Microsoft Word 2002.

CASE PERSPECTIVE SUMMARY

You send the redesigned public information guide document to Keith for his approval. He is thrilled with the new design. The table of contents, table of figures, and index really organize the document for a reader. He gives you approval to duplicate and distribute the document.

Keith would like you to conduct training classes for company employees on the change-tracking features of Word. You send an e-mail announcing the schedule and topic of the training classes. Next, you write a set of instructions to distribute to each attendee at the training classes. Your first class is tomorrow — it will be nice to be on the other side of the podium!

Microsoft Certification

The Microsoft Office User Specialist (MOUS) Certification program provides an opportunity for you to obtain a valuable industry credential — proof that you have the Word 2002 skills required by employers. For more information, see Appendix E or visit the Shelly Cashman Series MOUS Web page at scsite.com/offxp/cert.htm.

Project Summary

Project 9 introduced you to creating a long document with a table of contents, a table of figures, and an index. You inserted, modified, reviewed, and deleted comments. You also tracked changes, and accepted and rejected the tracked changes. You learned how to save multiple versions of a document, add and modify a caption, insert a diagram, create a cross-reference, mark index entries, add a bookmark, verify the widow/orphan setting, password-protect a document, create alternating headers, and set a gutter margin. You also worked with master documents and subdocuments. Finally, you used the Document Map to navigate through the document.

What You Should Know

Having completed this project, you should now be able to perform the following tasks:

- Add a Bookmark *(WD 9.60)*
- Add a Caption *(WD 9.26)*
- Build an Index *(WD 9.57)*
- Change an Inline Graphic to a Floating Graphic *(WD 9.25)*
- Close the Document *(WD 9.35, WD 9.64)*
- Compare and Merge Documents *(WD 9.21)*
- Compare and Merge, Rejecting Changes *(WD 9.23)*
- Convert a Text Box to a Frame *(WD 9.28)*
- Create a Cross-Reference *(WD 9.29)*
- Create a New Subdocument *(WD 9.43)*
- Create a Table of Contents *(WD 9.58)*
- Create a Table of Figures *(WD 9.55)*
- Create Alternating Headers *(WD 9.61)*
- Create an Outline *(WD 9.37)*
- Demote a Line to Body Text *(WD 9.47)*
- Display Formatting Marks *(WD 9.07)*
- Display Several Pages in Print Preview *(WD 9.64)*
- Enter and Format Title Page Text *(WD 9.48)*
- Enter Body Text into an Outline *(WD 9.45)*
- Hide the Document Map *(WD 9.69)*
- Hide the Reviewing Toolbar *(WD 9.23)*
- Insert a Comment *(WD 9.11)*
- Insert a Graphic *(WD 9.24)*
- Insert a Password-Protected File as a Subdocument *(WD 9.40)*
- Insert and Format a Diagram *(WD 9.50)*
- Insert Another Subdocument *(WD 9.41)*
- Mark an Index Entry *(WD 9.31)*
- Mark More Index Entries and Bold Them *(WD 9.32)*
- Modify a Style *(WD 9.63)*
- Modify a Table of Contents and Index *(WD 9.68)*
- Modify an Outline *(WD 9.44)*
- Modify the Caption *(WD 9.28)*
- Open and E-Mail a Document for Review *(WD 9.08)*
- Open a Master Document *(WD 9.65)*
- Password-Protect a File *(WD 9.34)*
- Quit Word *(WD 9.69)*
- Reset Menus and Toolbars *(WD 9.07)*
- Resize a Graphic *(WD 9.24)*
- Review Tracked Changes *(WD 9.18)*
- Save a Document *(WD 9.43)*
- Save a Document with a New File Name *(WD 9.11)*
- Save a Version of a Document *(WD 9.16)*
- Save and Print the Document *(WD 9.64)*
- Set a Gutter Margin *(WD 9.63)*
- Start and Customize Word *(WD 9.06)*
- Stop Tracking Changes *(WD 9.16)*
- Track Changes *(WD 9.14)*
- Use the Document Map *(WD 9.66)*
- Verify the Widow and Orphan Setting *(WD 9.33)*
- Zoom Page Width *(WD 9.07)*

Learn It Online

Instructions: To complete the Learn It Online exercises, start your browser, click the Address bar, and then enter scsite.com/offxp/exs.htm. When the Office XP Learn It Online page displays, follow the instructions in the exercises below.

1 Project Reinforcement

TF, MC, and SA Below Word Project 9, click the Project Reinforcement link. Print the quiz by clicking Print on the File menu. Answer each question. Write your first and last name at the top of each page, and then hand in the printout to your instructor.

2 Flash Cards

Below Word Project 9, click the Flash Cards link. When Flash Cards displays, read the instructions. Type 20 (or a number specified by your instructor) in the Number of Playing Cards text box, type your name in the Name text box, and then click the Flip Card button. When the flash card displays, read the question and then click the Answer box arrow to select an answer. Flip through Flash Cards. Click Print on the File menu to print the last flash card if your score is 15 (75%) correct or greater and then hand it in to your instructor. If your score is less than 15 (75%) correct, then redo this exercise by clicking the Replay button.

3 Practice Test

Below Word Project 9, click the Practice Test link. Answer each question, enter your first and last name at the bottom of the page, and then click the Grade Test button. When the graded practice test displays on your screen, click Print on the File menu to print a hard copy. Continue to take practice tests until you score 80% or better. Hand in a printout of the final practice test to your instructor.

4 Who Wants to Be a Computer Genius?

Below Word Project 9, click the Computer Genius link. Read the instructions, enter your first and last name at the bottom of the page, and then click the Play button. Hand in your score to your instructor.

5 Wheel of Terms

Below Word Project 9, click the Wheel of Terms link. Read the instructions, and then enter your first and last name and your school name. Click the Play button. Hand in your score to your instructor.

6 Crossword Puzzle Challenge

Below Word Project 9, click the Crossword Puzzle Challenge link. Read the instructions, and then enter your first and last name. Click the Play button. Work the crossword puzzle. When you are finished, click the Submit button. When the crossword puzzle redisplays, click the Print button. Hand in the printout.

7 Tips and Tricks

Below Word Project 9, click the Tips and Tricks link. Click a topic that pertains to Project 9. Right-click the information and then click Print on the shortcut menu. Construct a brief example of what the information relates to in Word to confirm you understand how to use the tip or trick. Hand in the example and printed information.

8 Newsgroups

Below Word Project 9, click the Newsgroups link. Click a topic that pertains to Project 9. Print three comments. Hand in the comments to your instructor.

9 Expanding Your Horizons

Below Word Project 9, click the Articles for Microsoft Word link. Click a topic that pertains to Project 9. Print the information. Construct a brief example of what the information relates to in Word to confirm you understand the contents of the article. Hand in the example and printed information to your instructor.

10 Search Sleuth

Below Word Project 9, click the Search Sleuth link. To search for a term that pertains to this project, select a term below the Project 9 title and then use the Google search engine at google.com (or any major search engine) to display and print two Web pages that present information on the term. Hand in the printouts to your instructor.

WD 9.72 • Project 9 • Working with a Master Document, an Index, and a Table of Contents

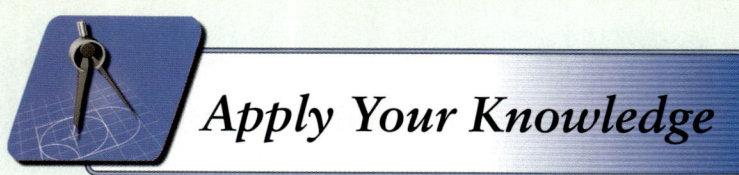

Apply Your Knowledge

1 Using Word's Change-Tracking Feature

Instructions: Start Word. Open the document, Client Server Concepts Draft, on the Data Disk. If you did not download the Data Disk, see the inside back cover for instructions for downloading the Data Disk or see your instructor.

As shown in Figure 9-88, the document contains reviewer's comments and tracked changes. You are to review and delete the comments and then accept or reject each of the tracked changes.

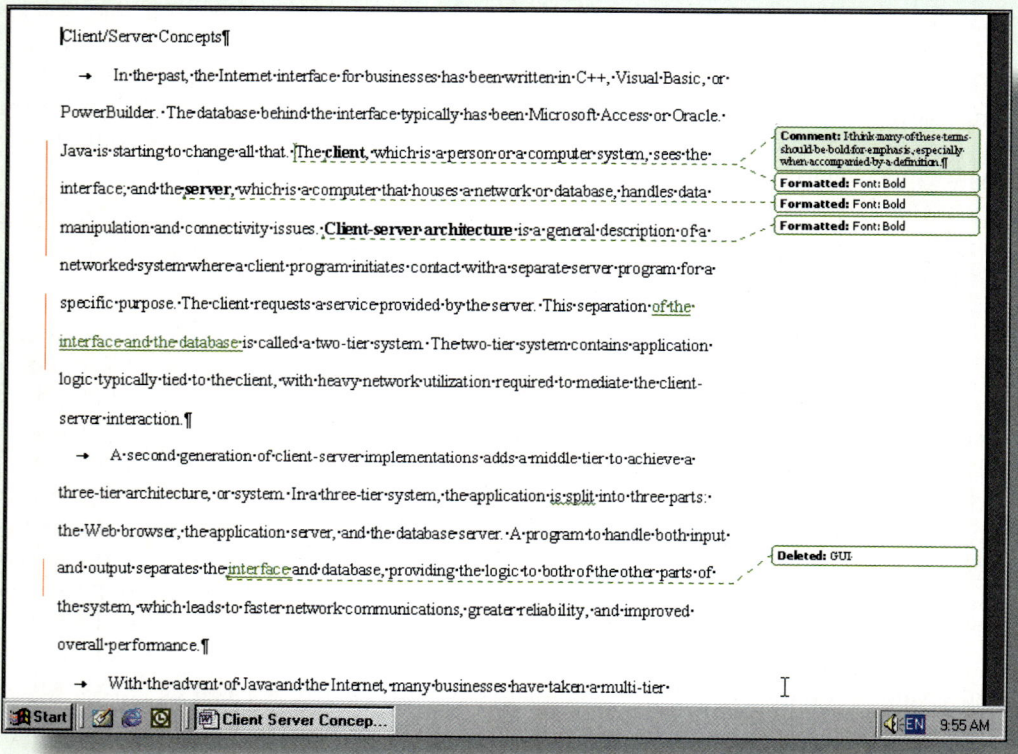

FIGURE 9-88

Perform the following tasks:
1. Click the Print Layout View button on the horizontal scroll bar. If the Reviewing toolbar does not display, click View on the menu bar, point to Toolbars, and then click Reviewing. If the TRK status indicator on the status bar displays darkened double-click it to dim it.
2. Click File on the menu bar, click Print, click the Print what box arrow, and then click Document showing markup in the list. Click the OK button to print the document with tracked changes and comments. Click File on the menu bar, click Print, click the Print what box arrow, and then click Document in the list. Click the OK button to print the document with all marked changes made.
3. Press CTRL+HOME. Click the Next button on the Reviewing toolbar. Read the comment. Right-click the comment balloon and then click Delete Comment on the shortcut menu to delete the comment.

Apply Your Knowledge

4. Click the Next button on the Reviewing toolbar. If necessary, scroll to display the markup balloon. Click the Accept Change button to accept the bold formatting.
5. Repeat Step 4 twice, to accept the next two formatting changes.
6. Click the Next button on the Reviewing toolbar. Click the Accept Change button to accept the insertion of the phrase (of the interface and the database).
7. Click the Next button. If necessary, scroll to display the markup balloon. Click the Accept Change button twice to accept the replacement of the word, GUI, with the word, interface.
8. Click the Next button on the Reviewing toolbar. If necessary, scroll to display the tracked change balloon. Click the Accept Change button to accept the insertion of the word, therefore.
9. Click the Next button on the Reviewing toolbar. If necessary, scroll to display the comment balloon. Read the comment. Right-click the comment balloon and then click Delete Comment on the shortcut menu. Right-click the inserted phrase (such as JavaScript or CGI) and then click Accept Insertion on the shortcut menu.
10. Click the Next button. Scroll, if necessary to display the tracked change balloon. Click the Reject Change/Delete Comment button to reject the insertion of the word, substantial.
11. At the end of the document, insert the following comment: Tracked changes accepted and rejected.
12. Save the reviewed document with the name, Client Server Concepts Revised. Print the document with comments.

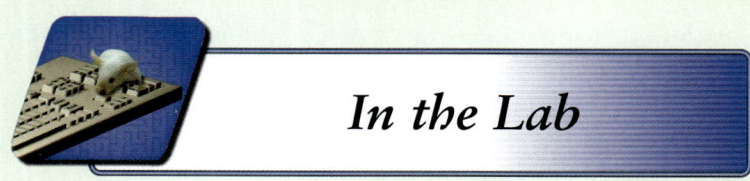

In the Lab

1 Working with a Master Document, Table of Contents, and Index

Problem: You are an editor for Dixon Publishing, a national company that publishes how-to manuals. You are to begin assembling Chapter 3 of a desktop publishing manual. You design chapters of the books as master documents and insert subdocuments as you receive chapter text from authors. You are responsible for inserting figure captions, creating the table of contents and index, and formatting the chapter. A miniature version of the Chapter 3 document is shown in Figure 9-89; for a more readable view, visit scsite.com/ wd2002/ project9.htm.

You just received the first subdocument for Chapter 3. Thus, you lay out the master document for the chapter. The subdocument used in this lab is on the Data Disk. If you did not download the Data Disk, see the inside back cover for instructions for downloading the Data Disk or see your instructor.

Instructions:

1. Open the document, Chapter 3 Creating Brochures Draft, from the Data Disk. Save the document with a new file name, Chapter 3 Creating Brochures.
2. If necessary, switch to print layout view. Add the following caption to the first figure: Page 1 of the Scholarship Brochure. Add the following caption to the second figure: Page 2 of the Scholarship Brochure.
3. Below the first graphic, the paragraph should end with the phrase, as shown in Figure 1, with the text Figure 1 being a cross-reference. Modify the sentence accordingly. Make a similar change to the text about the second figure.
4. Mark each bold term as an index entry.
5. Save the Chapter 3 Creating Brochures file again and then close the file.
6. Start a new Word document. Switch to outline view. Enter the following Heading 1 headings on separate lines of the outline: Chapter 3 — Creating Brochures, Table of Contents, and Index. Insert a next page section break between the headings.
7. Save the master document with the file name, Desktop Publishing. Between the Table of Contents and Index headings, insert the Chapter 3 Creating Brochures file as a subdocument.
8. If necessary, switch to print layout view. On page 1 (the title page) below the Chapter 3 — Creating Brochures heading, enter this line double-spaced in 20-point Times New Roman: Confidential Work in Progress. Below that text, insert a clip art image of a book. Below the graphic, enter these lines double-spaced in 20-point Times New Roman underlined: Authors: J. Reneau and M. Louks; Editor: D. Montgomery; Proofreader: B. Arslanian. On the next line, type Date to Film: 10/22/2003 and then press the ENTER key. Type Bound Book Date: 11/19/2003 as the last line. Center all text and graphics on the title page.
9. Build an index for the document. In the Index sheet, use the formal format for the index and place a check mark in the Right align page numbers check box. Remember to hide formatting marks prior to building the index.
10. Create a table of contents for the document. Use the Formal format.
11. Beginning on the second page (the table of contents), create a header as follows: print the words, Chapter 3 Page, followed by the page number at the right margin. The title page does not have a header. Note: Because you do not want facing pages in this document, you do not create alternating headers.
12. Change all margins to 1" with a gutter margin of .5". Be sure to change the Apply to box to Whole document.
13. Verify that the following headings begin on a new page: Table of Contents, Introduction, and Index. If any do not, insert a next page section break.
14. Because you modified the margins, update the table of contents and index.
15. Save the document again. Print the document. Staple the document along the gutter margin.

In the Lab

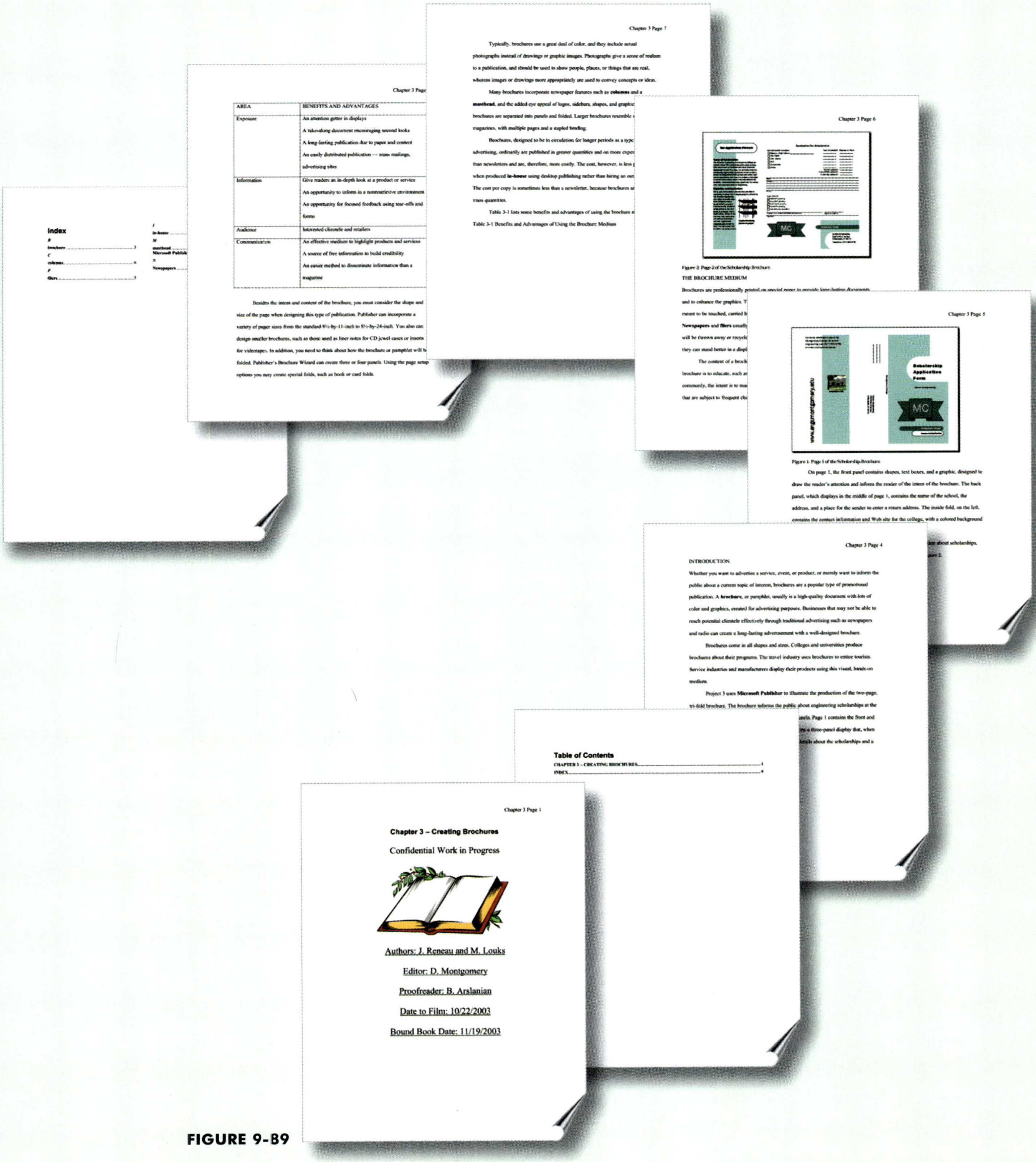

FIGURE 9-89

In the Lab

2 Working with Diagrams

Problem: As part of the statistics class you are taking, your instructor has asked you to prepare a report about various kinds of illustrative diagrams and how they help explain data. The title of your report is Showing Relationships through Diagrams. The report describes diagrams such as organization charts, cycle diagrams, radial diagrams, pyramid diagrams, Venn diagrams, and target diagrams. A miniature version of the Showing Relationships through Diagrams is shown in Figure 9-90 on page WD 9.77; for a more readable view, visit scsite.com/wd2002/project9.htm.

The Showing Relationships through Diagrams document is located on the Data Disk. If you did not download the Data Disk, see the inside back cover for instructions for downloading the Data Disk or see your instructor.

Instructions:

1. Open the document, Showing Relationships through Diagrams Draft, from the Data Disk. Save the document with a new file name, Showing Relationships through Diagrams.
2. Change all margins to 1" with a gutter margin of .5".
3. Insert right-aligned page numbers as a header on every page after the first.
4. You are to insert diagrams and captions in this document. Table 9-2 on the next page displays the types of diagrams and their captions. In the Showing Relationships through Diagrams document, below the paragraph in item number one, insert an organization chart with three tiers. *Hint*: To insert a new element into the diagram, click any element in the diagram to select it, and then click the Insert Shape button on the Organization Chart toolbar. The new element will be positioned below the selected element. Switch to print layout view. Add the following caption to the diagram: Figure 1: Organization charts show hierarchical relationships.
5. Insert the remaining diagrams in the corresponding paragraphs in the Showing Relationships through Diagrams document. Use a different AutoFormat for each one.

Table 9-2	Diagrams and Captions		
NUMBER	DIAGRAM	INSTRUCTIONS	CAPTION
1	organization chart	Create at least three tiers	Organization charts show hierarchical relationships
2	cycle diagram	Create at least four segments	Cycle diagrams show a process within a continual cycle
3	radial diagram	Create at least six spokes	Radial diagrams show relationships of a core element
4	pyramid diagram	Create at least four levels	Pyramid diagrams show foundation-based relationships
5	Venn diagram	Create at least three overlapping circles	Venn diagrams show areas of overlap between elements
6	target diagram	Create at least four rings or tracks	Target diagrams show steps toward a goal

6. Create a table of contents for the document. Use the Formal format.
7. Indent the left margin of each caption by .25" so that they align with the left edge of the figures. *Hint:* Click in the caption and then drag the Left Indent Marker on the ruler to the .25" mark.
8. At the end of the first paragraph on each page, add a sentence referencing the figure, such as: Figure 1 shows a sample organization chart. The text, Figure, (and its number) should be a cross-reference.
9. Add a bookmark to each caption with an appropriate name.

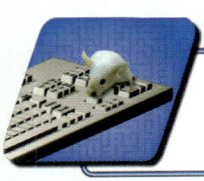

In the Lab

10. Verify that widows and orphans cannot occur.
11. Mark the following text as index entries: organization chart, cycle diagram, radial diagram, pyramid diagram, Venn diagram, and target diagram. You will find each phrase in the first sentence of each numbered paragraph. After marking the entries, bold them in the text.
12. Insert a page break at the end of the document. Change the style of the first line on the new page from List Number to Heading 1. On the new page, type the heading Index using the Heading 1 style. Below the heading, build an index for the document. Use the Formal format for the index. Remember to hide formatting marks prior to building the index.
13. Modify the document as follows: mark all figure captions as index entries.
14. Update the index. Remember to hide formatting marks prior to rebuilding the index.
15. Go to the bookmark using the Go To dialog box.
16. Save the document again. Print the document. Staple the document along the gutter margin.

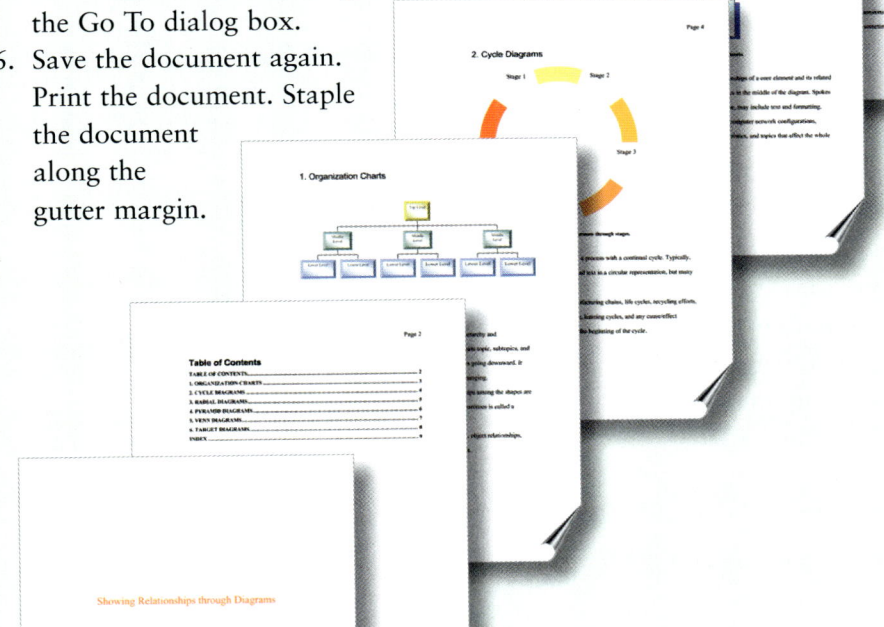

FIGURE 9-90

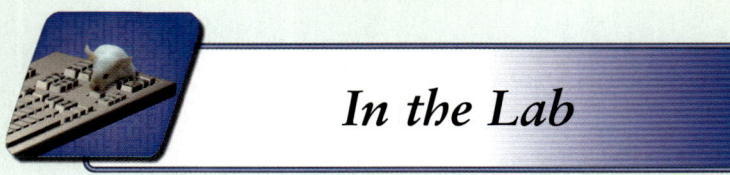

In the Lab

3 Working with a Master Document, Index, Tables of Figures and Contents, and Callouts

Problem: You are the computer technician at the Plattsburg Youth Center. The director of youth programs mentions to you that he constantly is receiving questions about using the computers in the lab. He wants you to create a series of instructional booklets for youths, similar to miniature user manuals, which explains various aspects of computers. The first one you create is titled, How to Use Windows Explorer. A miniature version of this document is shown in Figure 9-91; for a more readable view, visit scsite.com/wd2002/project9.htm.

You design the instructional booklet as a master document. You create one subdocument and insert an existing document as the other. The existing subdocument is on the Data Disk. If you did not download the Data Disk, see the inside back cover for instructions for downloading the Data Disk or see your instructor.

Instructions:

1. Open the document, How to Use Windows Explorer Draft, from the Data Disk. Save the document with a new file name, How to Use Windows Explorer.
2. Switch to print layout view. Add the following captions to the figures:
    Figure 1: Step 1 in Starting Windows Explorer
    Figure 2: Step 2 in Starting Windows Explorer
    Figure 3: Step 1 in Displaying the Contents of a Folder
    Figure 4: Step 2 in Displaying the Contents of a Folder
    Figure 5: Step 1 in Expanding a Folder
    Figure 6: Step 2 in Expanding a Folder
    Figure 7: Step 1 in Collapsing a Folder
    Figure 8: Step 2 in Collapsing a Folder
    Figure 9: Step 1 in Quitting Windows Explorer
3. Add a callout to each figure, except Figure 2, that identifies the mouse pointer in each figure. Use the Line 3 style of callout with each callout containing the text, mouse pointer.
4. Insert a cross-reference for each figure. Insert the cross-reference in the parentheses that end each sentence immediately above each figure. Insert only the word, Figure, and the figure number as the cross-reference. For cross-references in an italicized sentence, italicize the cross-reference (after inserting the cross-reference, select it and then italicize it).
5. In the section titled, The Exploring — My Computer Window, mark these words/phrases as index entries: menu bar, hierarchy, contents, folder, minus sign, subfolders, collapsing the folder, plus sign, expanding the folder, and status bar. Also, bold each of these words/phrases in the text. Mark each of the STEPS headings as index entries.
6. Save the How to Use Windows Explorer file again and then close the file.
7. Start a new Word document. Switch to outline view. Enter the following Heading 1 headings on separate lines of the outline: The Computer Basics Series, Table of Contents, Windows Explorer, Table of Figures, and Index. Insert a next page section break between each heading.
8. Save the master document with the file name, Windows Explorer. Between the Introduction and Table of Figures headings, insert the How to Use Windows Explorer file as a subdocument.

In the Lab

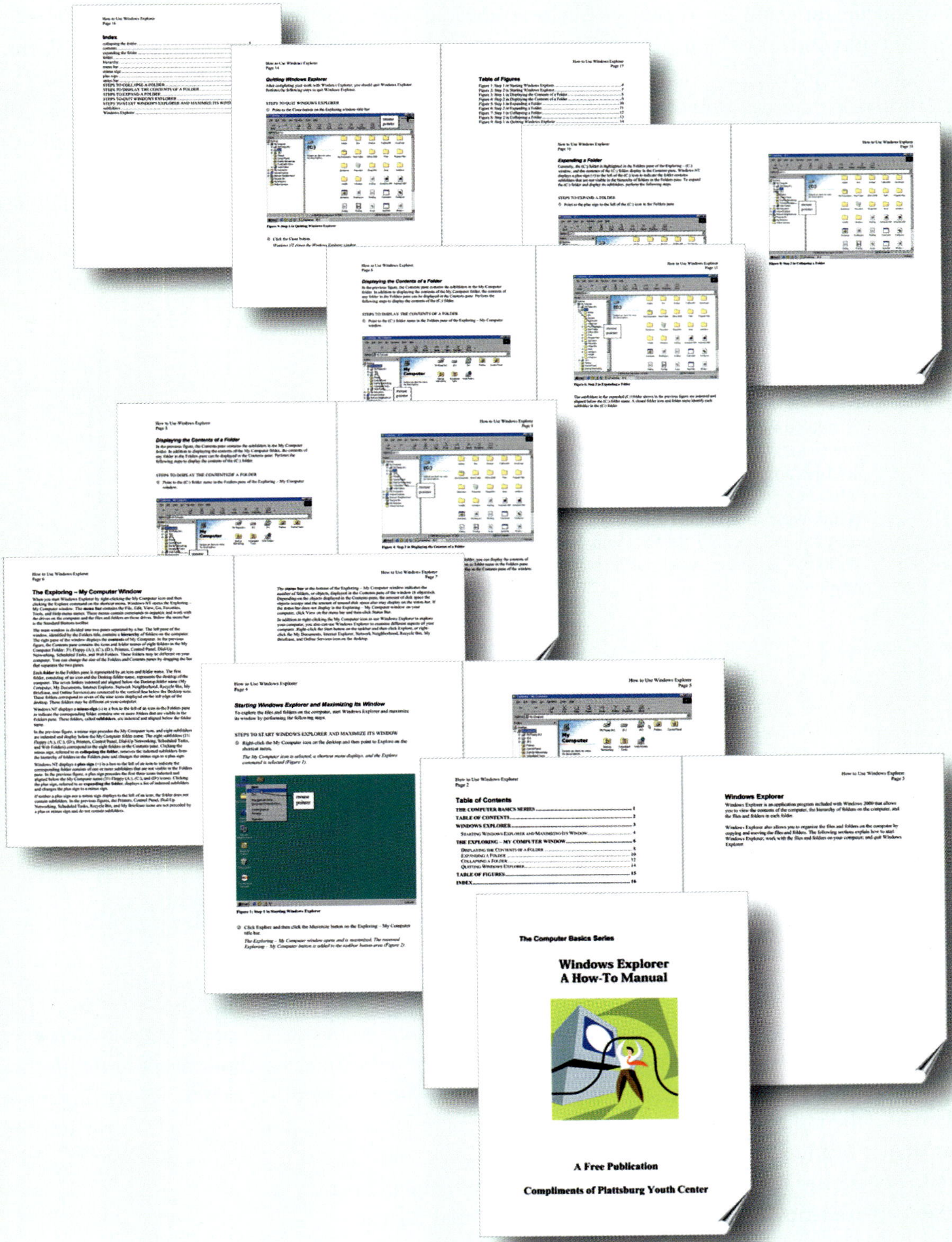

FIGURE 9-91

(continued)

In the Lab

9. Create a subdocument using the Windows Explorer heading. Using the Body Text style, enter the text for the two paragraphs shown in Figure 9-92 for the Windows Explorer section. In this section, mark the phrase, Windows Explorer, as an index entry. Also, bold the phrase.

10. On page 1 (the title page), double-spaced below the The Computer Basics Series heading, enter the following text in 28-point Rockwell bold font: Windows Explorer, A How-To Manual. Then, insert a clip art image of a computer. Use the keywords, computer cartoon, to locate the graphic. Enlarge the graphic. Below the graphic, enter these lines double-spaced in 24-point Times New Roman font: A Free Publication, Compliments of Plattsburg Youth Center. Center all text and graphics on the title page.

Windows Explorer

Windows Explorer is an application program included with Windows 2000 that allows you to view the contents of the computer, the hierarchy of folders on the computer, and the files and folders in each folder.

Windows Explorer also allows you to organize the files and folders on the computer by copying and moving the files and folders. The following sections explain how to start Windows Explorer; work with the files and folders on your computer; and quit Windows Explorer.

FIGURE 9-92

11. Build an index for the document that does not include the headings on the title page or the table of contents page. In the Index sheet, use the From template format for the index, place a check mark in the Right align page numbers check box, and change the number of columns to 1. Remember to hide formatting marks prior to building the index. *Hint*: To omit certain headings in the index, change the style of the heading to a style other than a heading style.

12. Create a table of figures for the document. Use the From template format.

13. Create a table of contents for the document. Use the Formal format.

In the Lab

14. Beginning on the second page (the table of contents), create alternating headings as follows: even-numbered pages should print at the left margin the words, How to Use Windows Explorer, on the first line and Page, followed by the page number on the second line. Odd-numbered pages should print the same text at the right margin. The title page does not have a header.
15. For the entire document, set the left and right margins to 1" and set a gutter margin of .5".
16. Verify that the following headings begin on a new page: Table of Contents, Windows Explorer, Starting Windows Explorer and Maximizing Its Window, The Exploring - My Computer Window, Table of Figures, and Index. If any do not, insert a next page section break.
17. Because margins have changed, update the fields, table of contents, and index by selecting the entire document and then pressing the F9 key.
18. Save the document again. Print the document. If you have access to a copy machine, duplicate the document back-to-back.

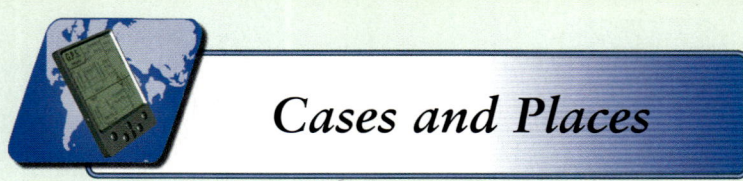

Cases and Places

The difficulty of these case studies varies:
▶ are the least difficult; ▶▶ are more difficult; and ▶▶▶ are the most difficult.

1 ▶ As editor for the school newspaper, you review all articles before they are published. One section of the newspaper spotlights a student of the week. For the next issue, the author has prepared an article about an interesting student and sent it to you for review. The article, named Jim Williamson Candidate, is located on the Data Disk. If you did not download the Data Disk, see the inside back cover for instructions for downloading the Data Disk or see your instructor. When you review the article, you find several areas where you wish to make changes and offer suggestions. You are to use Word's change-tracking feature to insert, delete, and replace text in the article. Make at least 10 changes to the article and add at least three comments. Print the article with tracked changes showing and without tracked changes showing. Also, print comments. Save the article containing the tracked changes as a version. Assume you are the author of the article and have received it back from the editor. Delete the comments and accept all the changes in the document. Obtain the tracked changes documents from three other students in your class. Compare and merge the documents from these students into your document. Save the merged document using the password, merge. If your instructor permits, e-mail the merged document for his or her review.

2 ▶ You are an editor for Dixon Publishing, a national company that publishes how-to manuals. The chapter you are working on is called Project 4. You design the chapters as master documents and insert subdocuments as you receive chapter text from authors. You are responsible for creating the table of contents and index and formatting the chapter. You just received the first subdocument for Project 4. The article, named Tracking Changes, is located on the Data Disk. If you did not download the Data Disk, see the inside back cover for instructions for downloading the Data Disk or see your instructor. Set up a master document that contains the following: title page, table of contents, reviewing a document file as a subdocument, table of figures, and index. Use the concepts and techniques presented in this project to format the document.

3 ▶▶ Your instructor in CIS 216 has distributed notes about object-oriented terminology and concepts. The notes are in a Word document named OO Terminology, which is located on the Data Disk. If you did not download the Data Disk, see the inside back cover for instructions for downloading the Data Disk or see your instructor. Your assignment is to insert a diagram that illustrates the relationship of object types, supertypes, and subtypes. Read the article and then choose an object with which you are familiar, such as a mode of transportation, an article of clothing, or a food item. Use a three-level organization chart available in the Diagram Gallery. Your diagram should have one element at the top, three in the second level, and six in the third level. To add a new element to the diagram, click any element in the diagram and then click Insert Shape on the Organization Chart toolbar to insert a new subelement. Place your object in the second level of the diagram and then fill in examples for each of the other elements. Choose an appropriate AutoFormat. Insert a caption below the chart and a reference to the figure in the text. Use the concepts and techniques presented in this project to format the document.

Cases and Places

4 ▶▶ As your final project in CIS 286, your instructor has asked you to prepare a master document that has at least one subdocument, a title page, a table of contents, a table of figures, and an index. The subdocument is to contain the text and figures on pages WD 9.36 through WD 9.38 in this project. To capture a screen shot, display the screen on your computer and then press the PRINT SCREEN key. To include the screen shot in your Word document, click the Paste button on the Standard toolbar in the Word window. Use the concepts and techniques presented in this project to format the document.

5 ▶▶▶ You are a trainer with the Computer Support Services at the college. Your supervisor has asked you to create a series of instructional booklets, similar to miniature user manuals, for lab assistants that explain the various aspects of computers. The first instructional booklet you prepared is shown in Figure 9-91 on page WD 9.79. Your assignment is to prepare the next instructional booklet for the lab assistants. Write the instructional booklet on a software application with which you are familiar and to which you have access. Use the software application's Help system, textbooks, and other instructional books for reference. The booklet is to be a how-to type of document that includes screen shots. To capture a screen shot, display the screen on your computer and then press the PRINT SCREEN key. To include the screen shot in your Word document, click the Paste button on the Standard toolbar in the Word window. The figures should contain captions. The document should contain the following sections: title page, table of contents, how-to discussion, table of figures, and index. Use the concepts and techniques presented in this project to format the document.

6 ▶▶▶ You are a student peer advisor for the School of Technology. Several students have asked you about MOUS (Microsoft Office User Specialist) certification. Because you also are interested in the MOUS certification, you decide to prepare a document outlining information about the exam (cost, description, how to prepare, where to take the exam, etc.). You obtain most of your information through links at the Shelly Cashman Series MOUS Web page at scsite.com/offxp/cert.htm. Because the document will be quite lengthy with many headings and subheadings, you organize it as a master document. In addition to information about MOUS, the document also contains the following: title page, table of contents, and index. Include at least one screen shot as a figure. To capture a screen shot, display the screen on your computer and then press the PRINT SCREEN key. To include the screen shot in your Word document, click the Paste button on the Standard toolbar in the Word window. All figures should contain captions. Use the concepts and techniques presented in this project to format the document.

Microsoft Word 2002

Linking an Excel Worksheet and Charting Its Data in Word

CASE PERSPECTIVE

At a recent faculty meeting of the computer information systems department at Edwards College, an agenda item about the recent fund-raising campaign led to a discussion about results of the campaign. The campaign raised money in four categories: scholarships, computer laboratories, faculty support, and curriculum development. Campaign donors selected a category to which they wished their money directed.

Faculty members were very interested in the results of the campaign. Specifically, they wanted to know the total number of donors, as well as the total amount pledged in each donation category. Jamie Daraska, department head, indicated she would contact the administrative affairs office for the exact numbers and then distribute the results in memo form to all department faculty.

One week later, Jamie received the figures from administrative affairs in an Excel worksheet. As her assistant, Jamie has asked you to create a memo that links the Excel worksheet to the memo. She also would like a chart of the Excel worksheet to show graphically the donation pledges by category.

Introduction

With Microsoft Office XP products, you can insert part or all of a document, called an **object**, created in one application into a document created in another application. For example, you could insert an Excel worksheet into a Word document. In this case, the Excel worksheet (the object) is called the **source document** (inserted from) and the Word document is called the **destination document** (inserted into). You can use one of three techniques to insert objects from one application to another: copy and paste, embed, or link.

When you copy an object by clicking the Copy button on the Standard toolbar and then paste it by clicking the Paste button on the Standard toolbar, the source document becomes part of the destination document. You edit a **pasted object** using editing features of the destination application. For example, an Excel worksheet would become a Word table that you can edit in Word.

Similarly, an embedded object becomes part of a destination document. The difference between an embedded object and a pasted object is that you edit the contents of an **embedded object** using the editing features of the source application. For example, an embedded Excel worksheet remains as an Excel worksheet in the Word document. To edit the worksheet in the Word document, double-click the worksheet to display Excel menus and toolbars in the Word window. If you edit the Excel worksheet by opening the worksheet from within Excel, however, the embedded object will not be updated in the Word document.

A **linked object**, by contrast, does not become a part of the destination document even though it appears to be a part of it. Rather, a connection is established between the source and destination documents so that when you open the destination document, the linked object displays as part of it. When you edit a linked object, the source application starts and opens the source document that contains the linked object. For example, a linked

Excel worksheet remains as an Excel worksheet. To edit the worksheet from the Word document, double-click the worksheet to start Excel and display the worksheet file in an Excel window. Unlike an embedded object, if you edit the Excel worksheet by opening it from Excel, the linked object will be updated in the Word document, too.

You would use the link method when the contents of an object are likely to change and you want to ensure that the most current version of the object displays in the source document. Another reason to link an object is if the object is large, such as a video clip or a sound clip.

As shown in Figure 1, this integration feature links an Excel worksheet to a Word document (a memo) and then links a Word chart to the Excel worksheet data. That is, the Excel worksheet is inserted into the Word document in the form of an Excel worksheet. Word also charts the data in the Excel worksheet. Because the data is inserted into the Word document as a link, anytime you open the memo in Word, the latest version of the Excel worksheet data displays in the memo. Figure 1a shows the memo draft (without any links to Excel); Figure 1b shows the Excel worksheet; and Figure 1c shows the final copy of the memo with links to the Excel worksheet and its data.

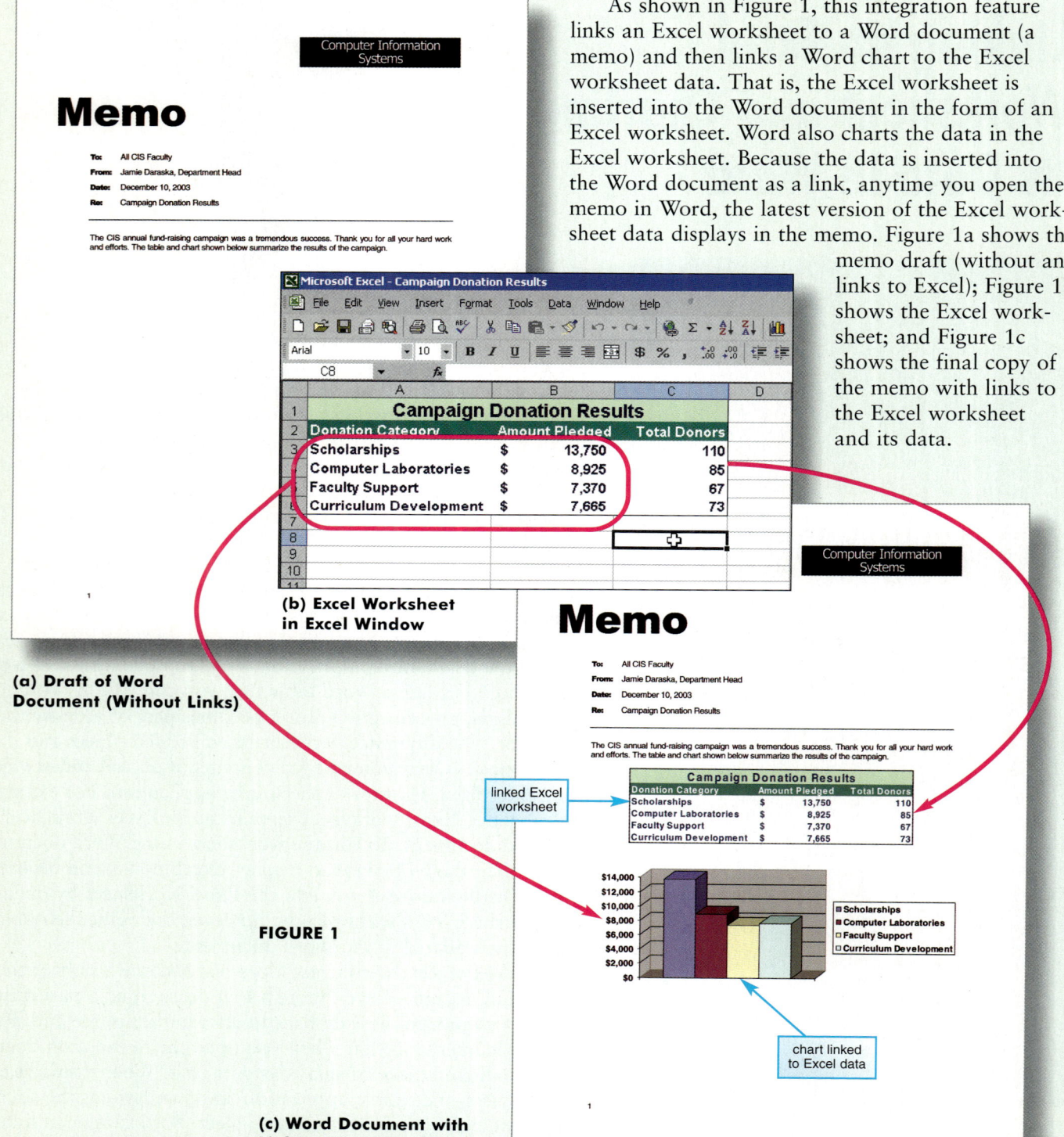

FIGURE 1

(a) Draft of Word Document (Without Links)

(b) Excel Worksheet in Excel Window

(c) Word Document with Links to Excel Worksheet

Starting Word and Opening a Document

The first step in this integration feature is to open the draft of the memo that is to include the linked worksheet data. The memo file, named Campaign Memo Draft, is located on the Data Disk. If you did not download the Data Disk, see the inside back cover for instructions for downloading the Data Disk or see your instructor.

Perform the following steps to open the memo.

TO START AND CUSTOMIZE WORD AND OPEN A DOCUMENT

1. Click the Start button on the Windows taskbar, point to Programs on the Start menu, and then click Microsoft Word on the Programs submenu.
2. If the Word window is not maximized, double-click its title bar to maximize it.
3. If the Language bar displays on the screen, click its Minimize button.
4. If the New Document task pane displays in the Word window, click the Show at startup check box to remove the check mark and then click the Close button in the upper-right corner of the task pane title bar.
5. If the toolbars display positioned on the same row, click the Toolbar Options button and then click Show Buttons on Two Rows. Reset the toolbars as described in Appendix D.
6. With the Data Disk in drive A, click the Open button on the Standard toolbar. When the Open dialog box displays, if necessary, click the Look in box arrow and then click 3½ Floppy (A:). Double-click the file named Campaign Memo Draft.
7. Click View on the menu bar and then click Print Layout. If the Show/Hide ¶ button on the Standard toolbar is not selected, click it.

Word starts and opens the Campaign Memo Draft file.

Office XP

For more information on the features of Microsoft Office XP, visit the Word 2002 More About Web page (scsite.com/wd2002/more.htm) and then click Microsoft Office XP Features.

Saving the Document with a New File Name

To preserve the contents of the original Campaign Memo Draft file, save a copy of it on the Data Disk with a new file name as described in the following steps.

TO PRESERVE THE CONTENTS OF AN ORIGINAL FILE

1. With the Data Disk in drive A, click File on the menu bar and then click Save As.
2. Type `Campaign Memo` in the File name text box. Do not press the ENTER key.
3. If necessary, click the Save in box arrow and then click 3½ Floppy (A:).
4. Click the Save button in the Save As dialog box.

Word saves the document on the Data Disk in drive A with a new file name of Campaign Memo (shown in Figure 2 on the next page).

Saving Linked Documents

When working with linked documents on floppy disks, both the source and destination documents must be saved on the same disk. If they reside on different disks, Word will display an error message indicating it cannot find the destination file when it attempts to save or open the source file.

Linking an Excel Worksheet

The next step in this integration feature is to insert the Excel worksheet (source document) in the Campaign Memo (destination document) as a linked object. The Excel worksheet (Campaign Donation Results) is located on the Data Disk.

WDI 2.04 • Integration Feature • Linking an Excel Worksheet and Charting Its Data in Word

Microsoft **Word 2002**

Perform the following steps to link the Excel worksheet to the Word document.

Steps To Link an Excel Worksheet to a Word Document

1 Position the insertion point on the paragraph mark at the end of the memo (below the paragraph of text). Click Insert on the menu bar and then point to Object (Figure 2).

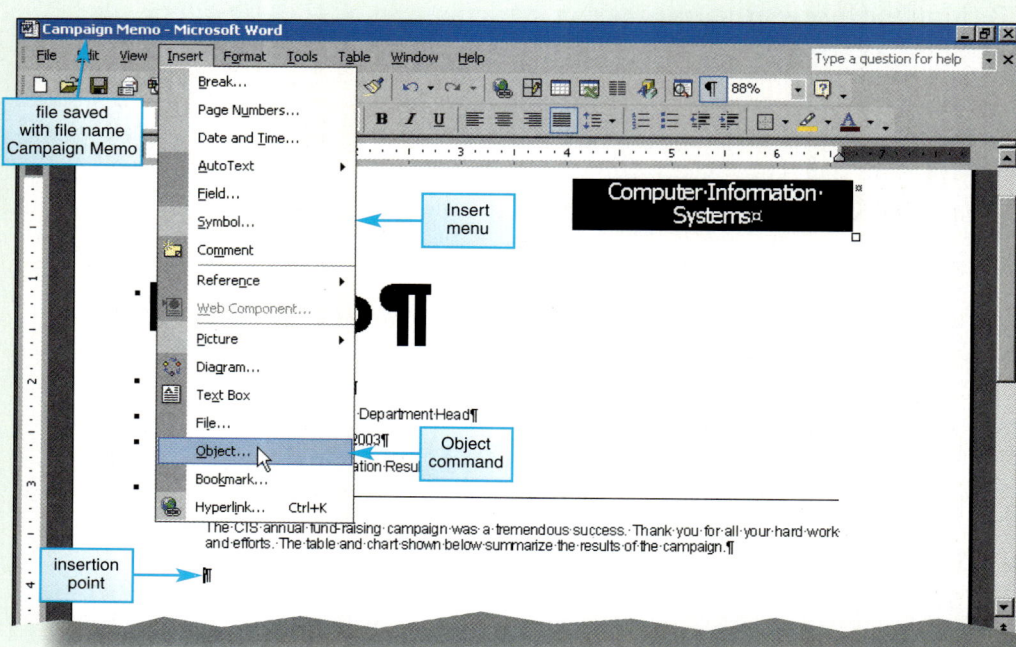

FIGURE 2

2 Click Object. When the Object dialog box displays, if necessary, click the Create from File tab. With the Data Disk in drive A, click the Browse button. When the Browse dialog box displays, locate on the Data Disk the Excel file called Campaign Donation Results. Click Campaign Donation Results in the list and then point to the Insert button in the Browse dialog box.

Word displays the Object dialog box and then the Browse dialog box (Figure 3).

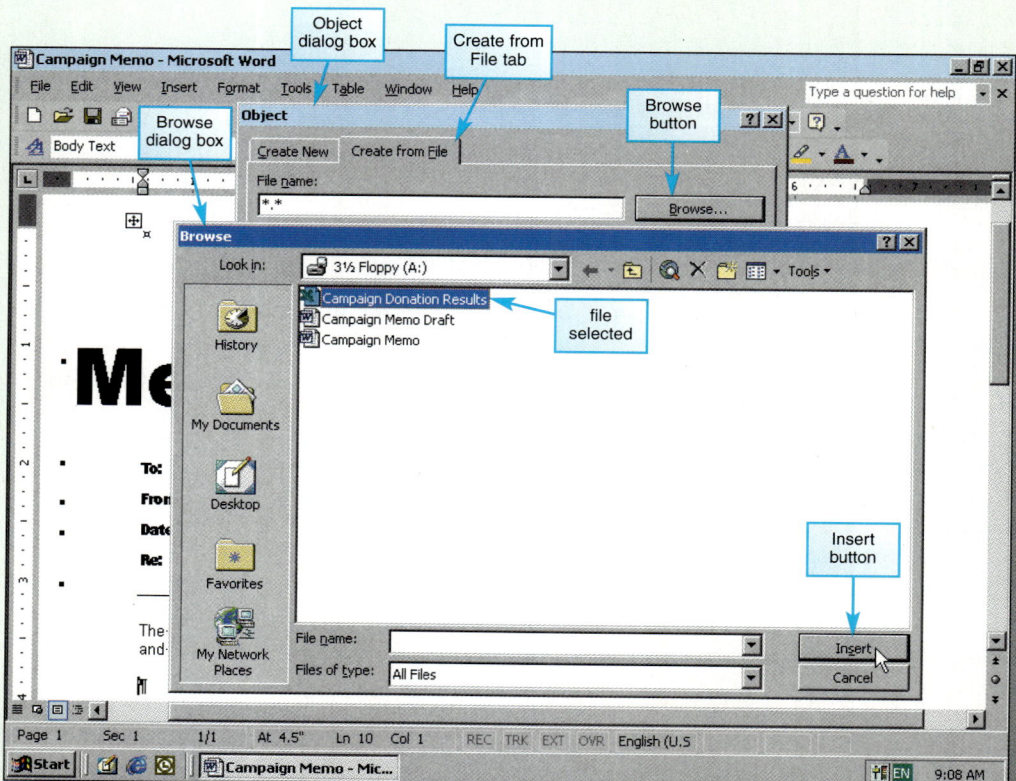

FIGURE 3

3 **Click the Insert button. When the Browse dialog box closes and the entire Object dialog box is visible again, place a check mark in the Link to file check box and then point to the OK button.**

The Object dialog box displays the name of the selected file in the File name text box (Figure 4). The xls following the file name, Campaign Donation Results, identifies the file as an Excel worksheet.

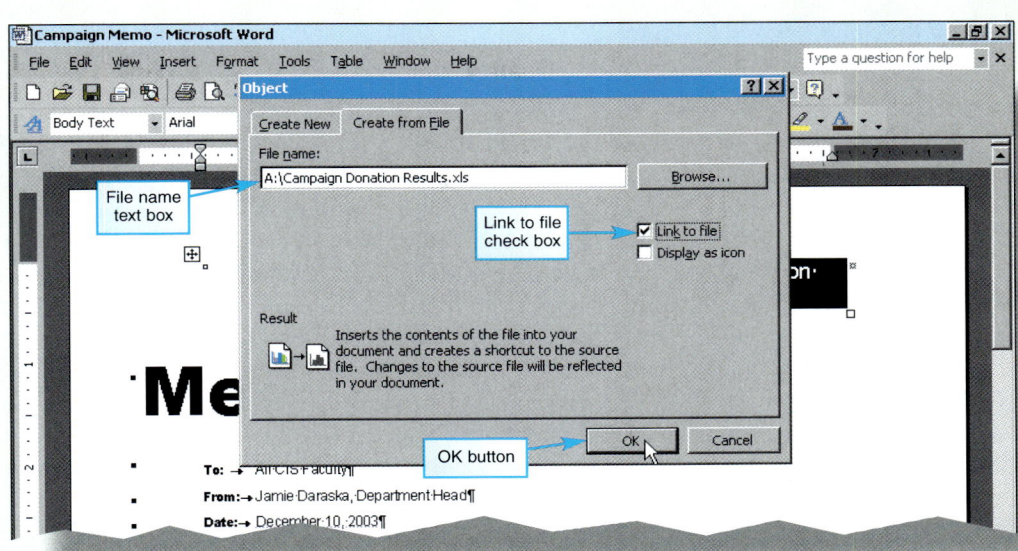

FIGURE 4

4 **Click the OK button. Click the Center button on the Formatting toolbar. If necessary, scroll down so the Excel table displays in the document window.**

Word inserts the Excel worksheet as a linked object at the location of the insertion point (Figure 5). The object is centered between the document margins.

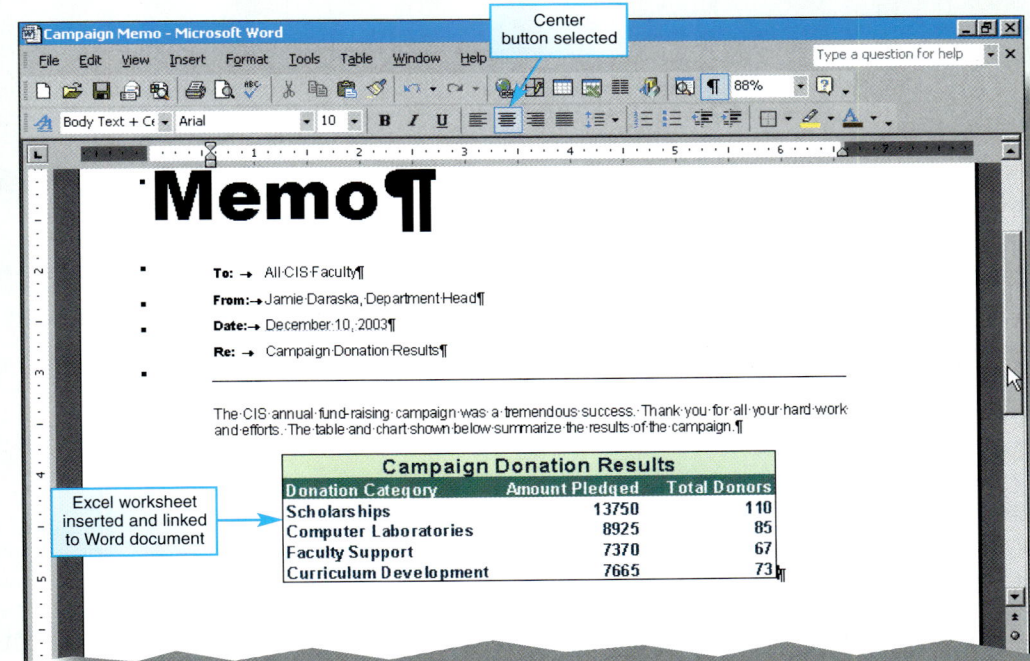

FIGURE 5

The Excel worksheet now is linked to the Word document. If you save the Word document and reopen it, the worksheet will display just as it does in Figure 5. If you wanted to delete the worksheet, you would select it and then press the DELETE key.

If you wanted to embed an Excel worksheet instead of link it, you would not place a check mark in the Link to file check box in the Object dialog box (Figure 4).

1. Copy object in source application to the Clipboard; in destination application, on Edit menu click Paste Special, click Paste link, click Microsoft Excel Worksheet Object, click OK button

Excel Worksheets

To insert a blank Excel worksheet into a Word document, click the Insert Microsoft Excel Worksheet button on the Standard toolbar and then click the grid at the location that represents the number of rows and columns to be in the worksheet. The menus and toolbars change to Excel menus and toolbars. To redisplay Word menus and toolbars, click outside the Excel worksheet in the Word document.

Creating a Chart from an Excel Worksheet

You easily can use Word to chart data through **Microsoft Graph 2002**, a charting application that is embedded in Word. Graph is an embedded application. Thus, it has its own menus and commands. With these commands, you can modify the appearance of the chart.

Graph can chart data in a Word table or it can chart data from another Office application, such as Excel. If you want Graph to chart data that is in a Word table, select the data to be charted prior to starting Graph, and then Graph automatically will chart the selected data.

To chart data from another application, such as Excel, start Graph without selecting any data. This causes Graph to create a sample chart with sample data. Then, you either copy and paste or link the data from another application to the sample chart.

In this integration feature, you want to link the Excel data to the chart in the Word document. Thus, you will start Graph and it will create a sample chart. Then, you will link the Excel data to the chart.

Perform the following steps to start Graph.

Steps: To Create a Sample Chart

1 **Position the insertion point on the paragraph mark to the right of the Excel worksheet in the Word document and then press the ENTER key. Click Insert on the menu bar, point to Picture, and then point to Chart on the Picture submenu (Figure 6).**

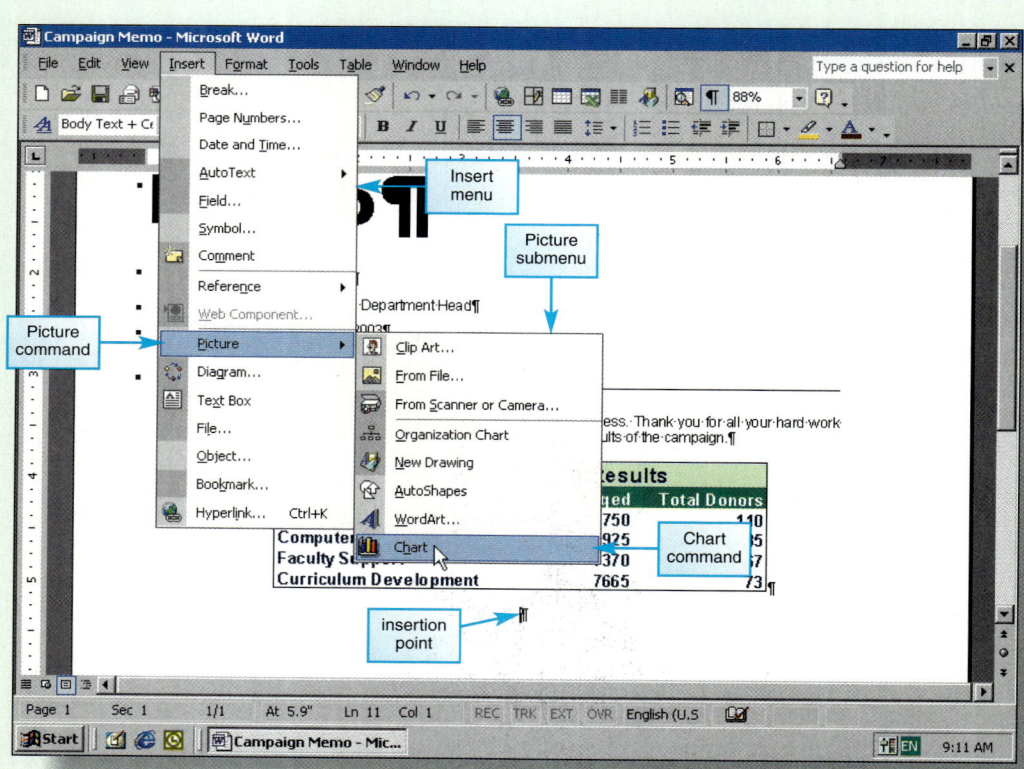

FIGURE 6

Creating a Chart from an Excel Worksheet • WDI 2.07

2 **Click Chart. If your screen does not display a Datasheet window, click the View Datasheet button on the Standard toolbar.**

Word starts the Microsoft Graph 2002 application (Figure 7). Graph creates a sample chart at the location of the insertion point and displays sample data in the Datasheet window.

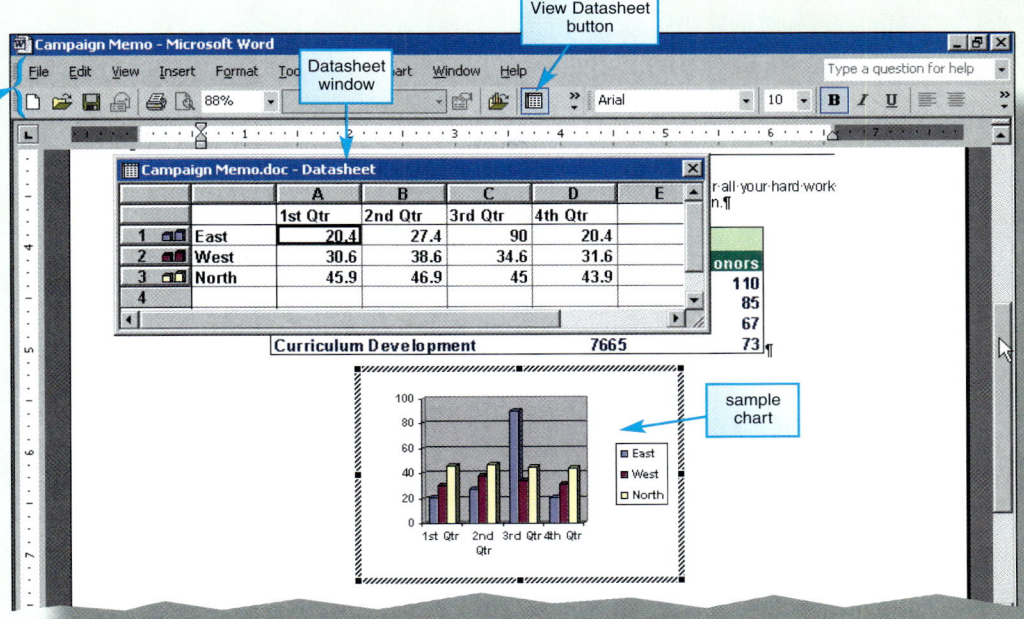

FIGURE 7

The menus on the menu bar and buttons on the toolbars change to Graph menus and toolbars. That is, the Graph program is running inside the Word program.

You can copy and paste data from an Excel worksheet into the sample chart or you can link the Excel data to the sample chart. In this integration feature, you link the data to the chart. To link the data, start Excel and display the workbook containing the worksheet data to be linked, copy the data in the worksheet to the Clipboard, and then use Graph's Paste Link command to link the data on the Clipboard to the Word document.

Thus, the first step in linking the data from the Excel worksheet to the Word chart is to open the Excel workbook that contains the worksheet data to be charted. The Excel workbook that contains the data to be linked to the chart is the Campaign Donation Results workbook file, which is located on the Data Disk.

Perform the following steps to start Excel and open a workbook.

TO START AND CUSTOMIZE EXCEL AND OPEN AN EXCEL WORKBOOK

1 Click the Start button on the Windows taskbar, point to Programs on the Start menu, and then click Microsoft Excel on the Programs submenu.

2 If the Excel window is not maximized, double-click its title bar to maximize it.

3 If the Language bar displays on the screen, click its Minimize button.

4 If the New Workbook task pane displays, click its Close button.

5 With the Data Disk in Drive A, click the Open button on the Standard toolbar. When the Open dialog box displays, if necessary, click the Look in box arrow and then click 3½ Floppy (A:). Double-click the Excel file named Campaign Donation Results.

6 Reset Excel toolbars as described in Appendix D.

Excel starts and displays the Campaign Donation Results file in the Excel window (shown in Figure 8 on the next page).

Other Ways

1. In Voice Command mode, say "Insert, Picture, Chart"

More About

Starting Excel

If a Word document that displays on the screen contains a linked Excel worksheet, you also can start Excel by double-clicking the Excel worksheet in the Word document. For example, if you double-click the Campaign Donation Results worksheet in the Word document, Excel starts and then displays the associated Excel workbook in an Excel window.

With both Word and Excel open, you can switch between the applications by clicking the appropriate program button on the taskbar.

Next, copy to the Clipboard the Excel data to be charted and then paste link it from the Clipboard to the chart, as shown in the following steps.

Steps To Chart Excel Data in Word

  In the Excel window, drag through cells in the range A3:B6 to select them. Click the Copy button on the Standard toolbar.

The Excel window is active (Figure 8). A marquee displays around the range A3:B6, which has been copied to the Clipboard.

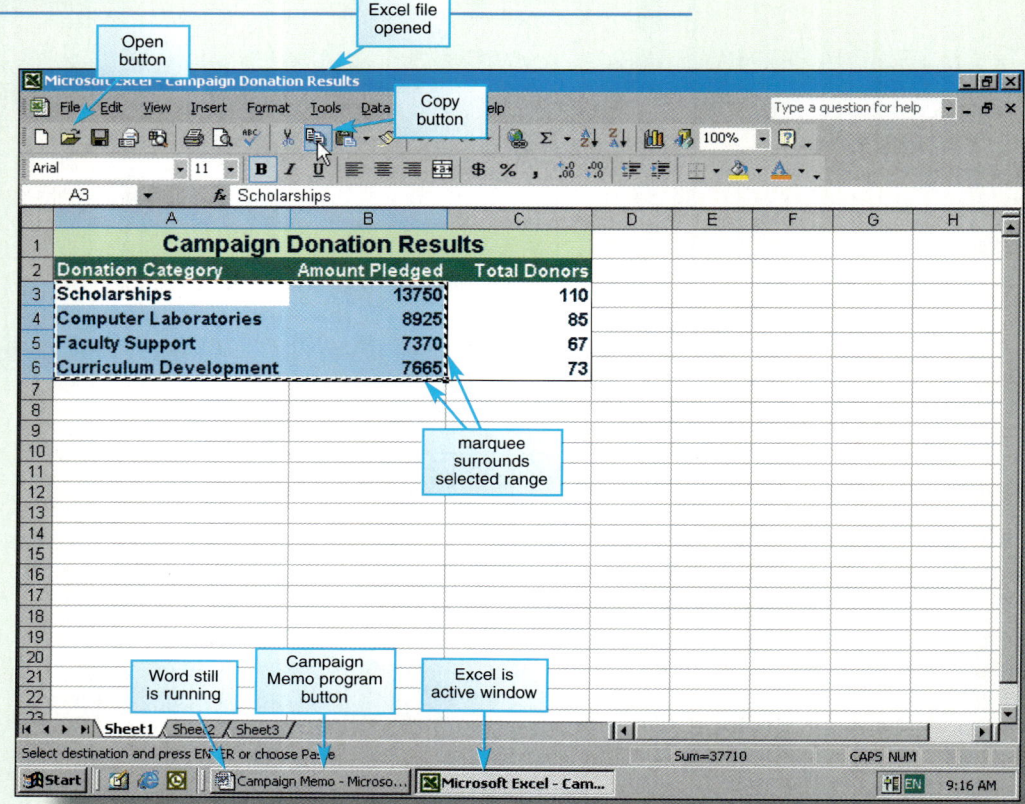

FIGURE 8

Creating a Chart from an Excel Worksheet • WDI 2.09

2 Click the Campaign Memo - Microsoft Word program button on the taskbar. Click anywhere in the Datasheet window. (If Graph is not active in the Word window, double-click the chart.) Click Edit on the menu bar and then point to Paste Link.

Graph still is active within Word (Figure 9).

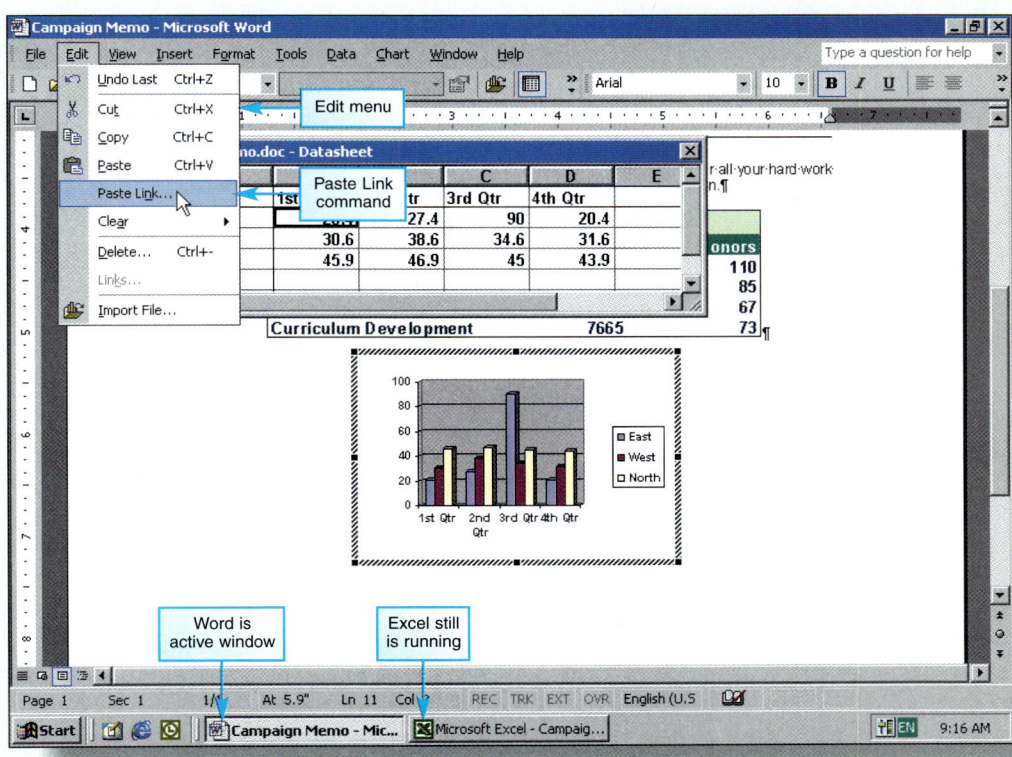

FIGURE 9

3 Click Paste Link. When Graph displays a dialog box indicating the linked data will replace existing data, click the OK button.

Graph copies the data from the Clipboard into the Datasheet window, replacing the sample data currently in the Datasheet window (Figure 10). Graph then charts the contents of the Datasheet window.

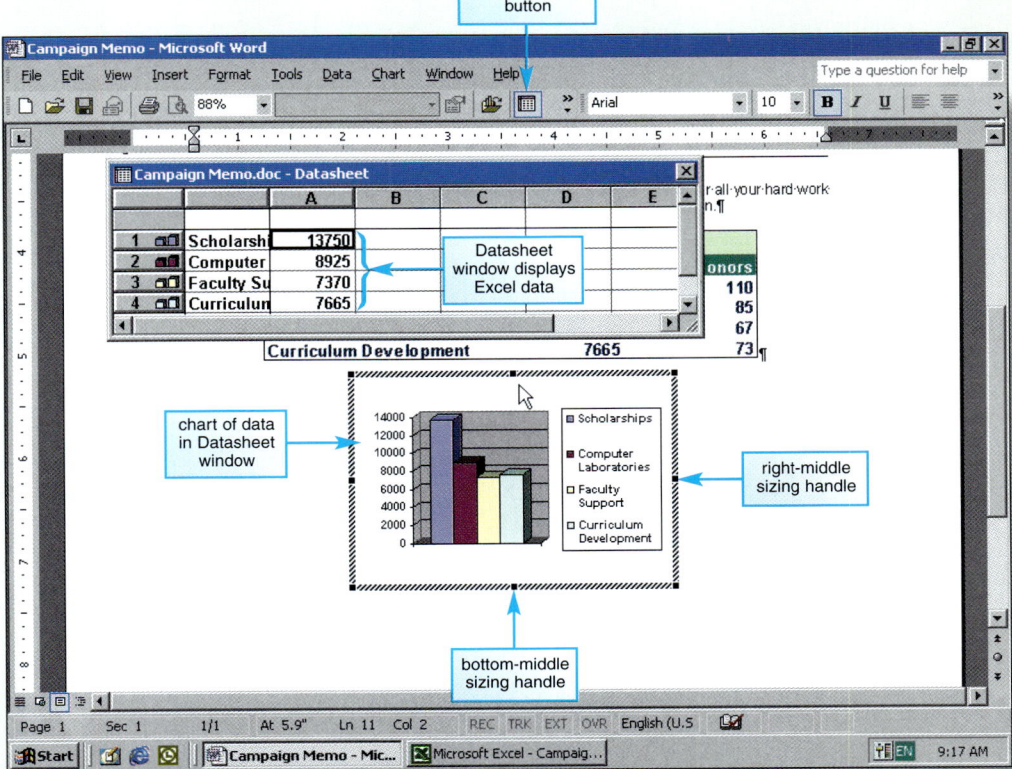

FIGURE 10

Graph charts the Excel data. The Excel data is linked to the chart. Thus, if you change any of the data in the Excel worksheet, it will be reflected in the chart.

If you wanted to copy and paste the chart data, instead of link it, you would not need to start Excel as described in the previous steps. After starting Graph, copy the Excel worksheet data by clicking Edit on the Graph menu bar, clicking Import File, locating the file name in the Import File dialog box, clicking the Open button in the Import File dialog box, clicking Entire sheet or entering the range in the Import File Options dialog box, and then clicking the OK button. When you use the Import File command to copy Excel worksheet data, the data in the chart will not be updated if the contents of the Excel worksheet change.

The next step is to format the chart. You want to make the size of the chart larger, as described in the following steps.

TO FORMAT THE CHART IN GRAPH

1. Click the View Datasheet button on the Standard toolbar to remove the Datasheet window from the screen.

2. Point to the bottom-middle sizing handle on the selection rectangle and drag it downward approximately one inch.

3. Point to the right-middle sizing handle on the selection rectangle that surrounds the chart and legend and drag it rightward until each item in the legend displays on a single line.

Graph resizes the chart.

You are finished modifying the chart. The next step is to exit Graph and return to Word.

TO EXIT GRAPH AND RETURN TO WORD

1. Click somewhere outside the chart.

Word closes the Graph application (Figure 11). Word's menus and toolbars redisplay below the title bar.

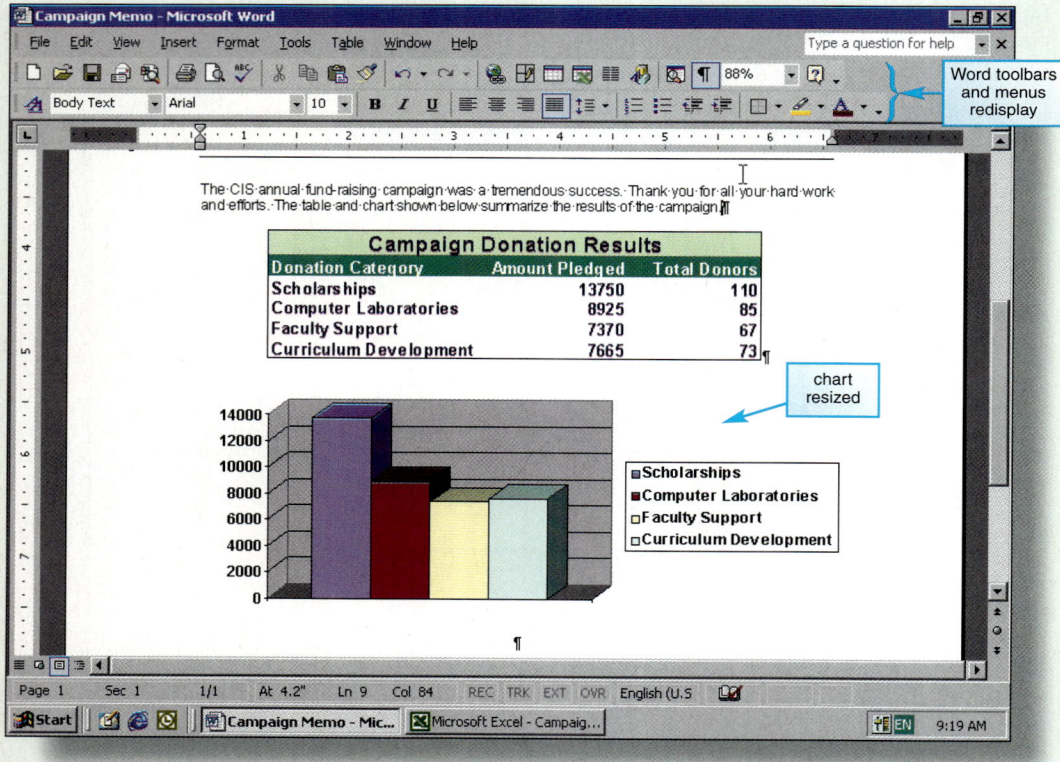

FIGURE 11

If, for some reason, you wanted to modify an existing chart in a document, you would double-click the chart to reopen the Microsoft Graph 2002 application. Then, you can make any necessary changes to the chart. When you are finished making changes to the chart, click anywhere outside the chart to return to Word.

You are finished with the memo. Save the document again, print it, and then quit Word as described in the following steps.

TO SAVE A DOCUMENT

1 With the Data Disk in drive A, click the Save button on the Standard toolbar.

Word saves the document on the Data Disk in drive A.

TO QUIT WORD

1 Click the Close button on Word's title bar.

The Word window closes.

> **More About**
>
> **Linking Excel Data**
>
> If you want to display a linked worksheet as an icon, instead of as the worksheet itself, do the following: copy the data to be linked in Excel, switch to Word, click Edit on the menu bar, click Paste Special, click Paste link, click the desired option in the As list, place a check mark in the Display as icon check box, and then click the OK button.

Editing a Linked Worksheet

At a later time, you may find it necessary to change the data in the Excel worksheet. Any changes you make to the Excel worksheet while in Excel will be reflected in the Excel table and chart in the Word document because the objects are linked.

Perform the following steps to change the format of the dollar amounts in the amount pledged cells to currency.

Steps To Edit a Linked Object

 With the Excel worksheet displaying on the screen, drag through cells B3:B6 to select them. Click the Currency Style button on the Formatting toolbar. Click the Decrease Decimal button on the Formatting toolbar twice.

The format of the numbers in cells B3:B6 changes from general to currency (Figure 12).

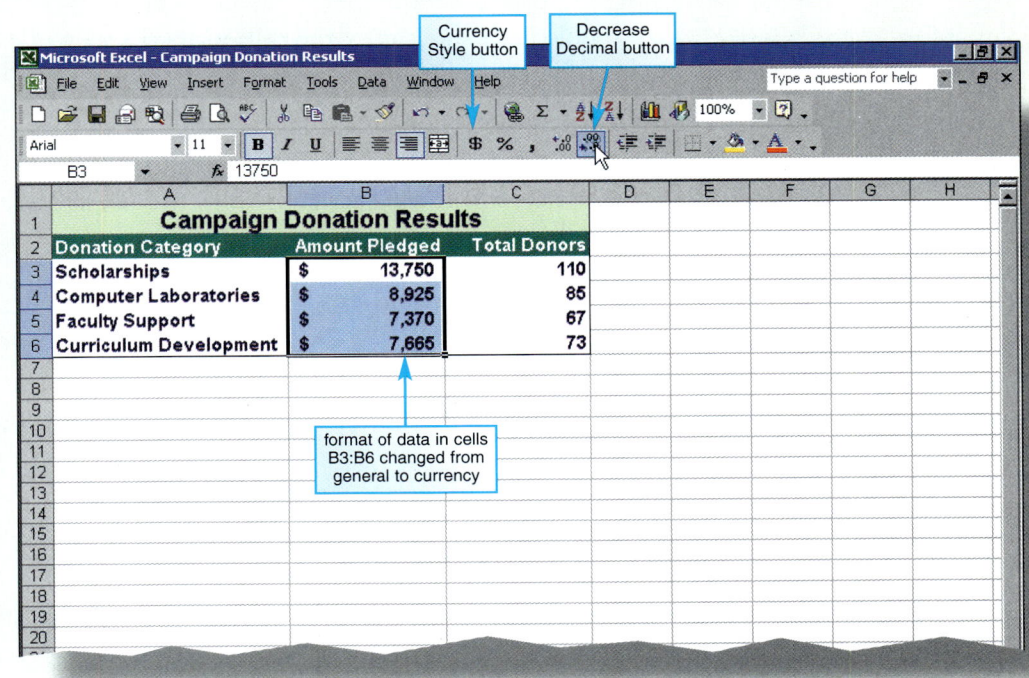

FIGURE 12

2 Click in cell C8 to remove the selection from the worksheet. Click the Save button on the Standard toolbar. Click the Close button at the right edge of Excel's title bar.

Excel saves the changes to the worksheet. The Excel window closes.

3 Start Word and then open the Campaign Memo document on the Data Disk. If the table does not display the updated data format, click it and then press the F9 key. If the chart does not display updated data, double-click the chart and then click outside the chart to exit Graph.

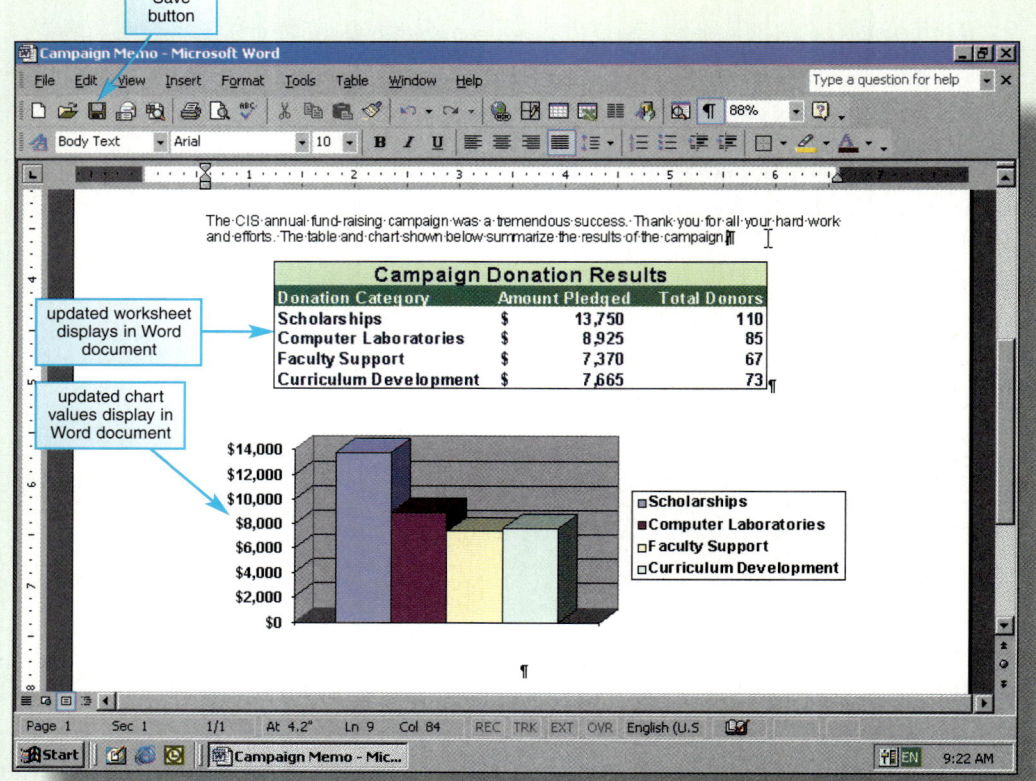

FIGURE 13

The Word document displays the updates to the Excel worksheet object and chart object (Figure 13).

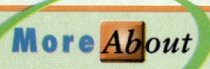

Linking Excel Worksheets

This project illustrated how to link an Excel worksheet and display it in a Word document as an Excel worksheet object. To display the linked worksheet as a Word document, follow these steps instead of the steps on pages WDI 2.04 and WDI 2.05: Click Insert on the menu bar and then click File. When the Insert dialog box displays, if necessary, click the Files of type box arrow and then click All Files. Click the Excel file name, click the Insert button arrow, and then click Insert as Link. Click the OK button when the Open Worksheet dialog box displays.

You also can edit any of the cells in the Excel worksheet (the object) while it displays as part of the Word document. To edit the worksheet, double-click it. If Excel is running already, the computer will switch to it and display the linked workbook in Excel. If Excel is not running, the system will start Excel automatically and then display the linked workbook in Excel.

Perform the following series of steps to save and print the Word document and then quit Word.

TO SAVE THE WORD DOCUMENT AGAIN

1 With the Data Disk in drive A, click the Save button on the Standard toolbar.

Word saves the revised Campaign Memo on a floppy disk in drive A.

TO PRINT A DOCUMENT

1 Click the Print button on the Standard toolbar.

Word prints the memo as shown in Figure 1c on page WDI 2.02.

TO QUIT WORD

1. Click the Close button at the right edge of Word's title bar.

The Word window closes.

CASE PERSPECTIVE SUMMARY

Jamie distributes the memo to the department faculty so they can review it prior to the department meeting. At the meeting, they quickly conclude from the memo that the majority of donors contributed to scholarships. Thus, they decide to post scholarship information in advisors' offices.

Two weeks later, the manager of administrative affairs asks Jamie how she included the table and chart in the memo. Jamie confesses that she did not compose the memo and directs him to you so that you can show him how to link documents between applications.

Integration Feature Summary

This Integration Feature introduced you to linking an Excel worksheet to a Word document. You also charted Excel data in Word using an embedded Microsoft Graph charting application. Then, you modified the linked worksheet to see the changes reflected in the Word document.

What You Should Know

Having completed this Integration Feature, you now should be able to perform the following tasks:

- Chart Excel Data in Word *(WDI 2.08)*
- Create a Sample Chart *(WDI 2.06)*
- Edit a Linked Object *(WDI 2.11)*
- Exit Graph and Return to Word *(WDI 2.10)*
- Format the Chart in Graph *(WDI 2.10)*
- Link an Excel Worksheet to a Word Document *(WDI 2.04)*
- Preserve the Contents of an Original File *(WDI 2.03)*
- Print a Document *(WDI 2.12)*
- Quit Word *(WDI 2.11, WDI 2.13)*
- Save a Document *(WDI 2.11)*
- Save the Word Document Again *(WDI 2.12)*
- Start and Customize Excel and Open an Excel Workbook *(WDI 2.07)*
- Start and Customize Word and Open a Document *(WDI 2.03)*

Quick Reference

For a table that lists how to complete tasks covered in this book using the mouse, menu, shortcut menu, and keyboard, see the Quick Reference Summary at the back of this book or visit the Shelly Cashman Series Office XP Web page (scsite.com/offxp/qr.htm) and then click Microsoft Access 2002.

Microsoft Certification

The Microsoft Office User Specialist (MOUS) Certification program provides an opportunity for you to obtain a valuable industry credential — proof that you have the Word 2002 skills required by employers. For more information, see Appendix E or visit the Shelly Cashman Series MOUS Web page at scsite.com/offxp/cert.htm.

In the Lab

1 Linking an Excel Table to a Word Document

Problem: Marty Yonkovich, director of admissions at River Community College, has created an Excel worksheet that lists the number of full-time and part-time students majoring in each department on campus. He would like you to prepare a memo that includes the Excel worksheet.

Instructions:

1. Create a memo using a memo template. Save the memo using the file name, Department Major Memo. The memo is to all department heads, from Marty Yonkovich, and should have a subject of Full-Time and Part-Time Student Distribution by Department. In the memo, type the following sentence: `The table shown below lists the total number of full-time and part-time students in each department on campus. Please call me if you have any questions.`
2. Link the Students by Major Excel worksheet, which is on the Data Disk to the Word memo file.
3. Save the Word memo file again.
4. Print the Word memo file.

2 Linking Data from an Excel Worksheet to a Word Chart

Problem: Marty Yonkovich, director of admissions at River Community College, has created an Excel worksheet that lists the number of full-time and part-time students majoring in each department on campus. He would like you to prepare a memo that includes a chart of the Excel worksheet data.

Instructions:

1. Create a memo using a memo template. Save the memo using the file name, Department Major Memo with Chart. The memo is to all department heads, from Marty Yonkovich, and should have a subject of Full-Time and Part-Time Student Distribution by Department. In the memo, type the following sentence: `The chart shown below shows the total number of full-time and part-time students in each department on campus. Please call me if you have any questions.`
2. Link the Students by Major Excel worksheet data, which is on the Data Disk, to a Word chart.
3. Save the Word memo file again.
4. Print the Word memo file.

3 Creating an Excel Worksheet and Linking It to a Word Document

Problem: Your science instructor, Mr. Edwards, has requested that you collect the daily high and low temperatures for a 10-day period and create an Excel worksheet that lists the data. Then, you are to prepare a memo that links the Excel worksheet to the memo and includes a chart of the Excel data.

Instructions: Create a memo to Mr. Edwards using a memo template. Explain the contents of the worksheet and chart in the memo. Link the Excel worksheet to the Word memo file. Link the Excel worksheet data to a Word chart. Save the Word memo file again. Print the Word memo file. Close Word. In Excel, change the high and low temperatures for two of the days. Open the Word memo file, be sure the linked table and chart data are updated, and then print the updated memo.

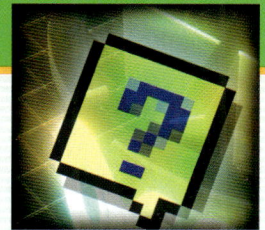

APPENDIX A
Microsoft Word Help System

Using the Word Help System

This appendix demonstrates how you can use the Word Help system to answer your questions. At anytime while you are using Word, you can interact with its Help system to display information on any Word topic. It is a complete reference manual at your fingertips.

As shown in Figure A-1, you can access Word's Help system in four primary ways:

1. Ask a Question box on the menu bar
2. Function key F1 on the keyboard
3. Microsoft Word Help command on the Help menu
4. Microsoft Word Help button on the Standard toolbar

If you use the Ask a Question box on the menu bar, Word responds by opening the Microsoft Word Help window, which gives you direct access to its Help system. If you use one of the other three ways to access Word's Help system, Word responds in one of two ways:

FIGURE A-1

1. If the Office Assistant is turned on, then the Office Assistant displays with a balloon (lower-right side in Figure A-1 on the previous page).
2. If the Office Assistant is turned off, then the Microsoft Word Help window displays (lower-left side in Figure A-1 on the previous page).

The best way to familiarize yourself with the Word Help system is to use it. The next several pages show examples of how to use the Help system. Following the examples are a set of exercises titled Use Help that will sharpen your Word Help system skills.

Ask a Question Box

The **Ask a Question box** on the right side of the menu bar lets you type questions in your own words, or you can type terms, such as template, smart tags, or speech. Word responds by displaying a list of topics related to the term(s) you entered. The following steps show how to use the Ask a Question box to obtain information about how smart tags work.

Steps: To Obtain Help Using the Ask a Question Box

 Type smart tags **in the Ask a Question box on the right side of the menu bar and then press the ENTER key. When the Ask a Question list displays, point to the About smart tags link.**

The Ask a Question list displays (Figure A-2). Clicking the See more link displays a new list of topics in the Ask a Question list. As you enter questions and terms in the Ask a Question box, Word adds them to its list. If you click the Ask a Question box arrow, a list of previously asked questions and terms will display.

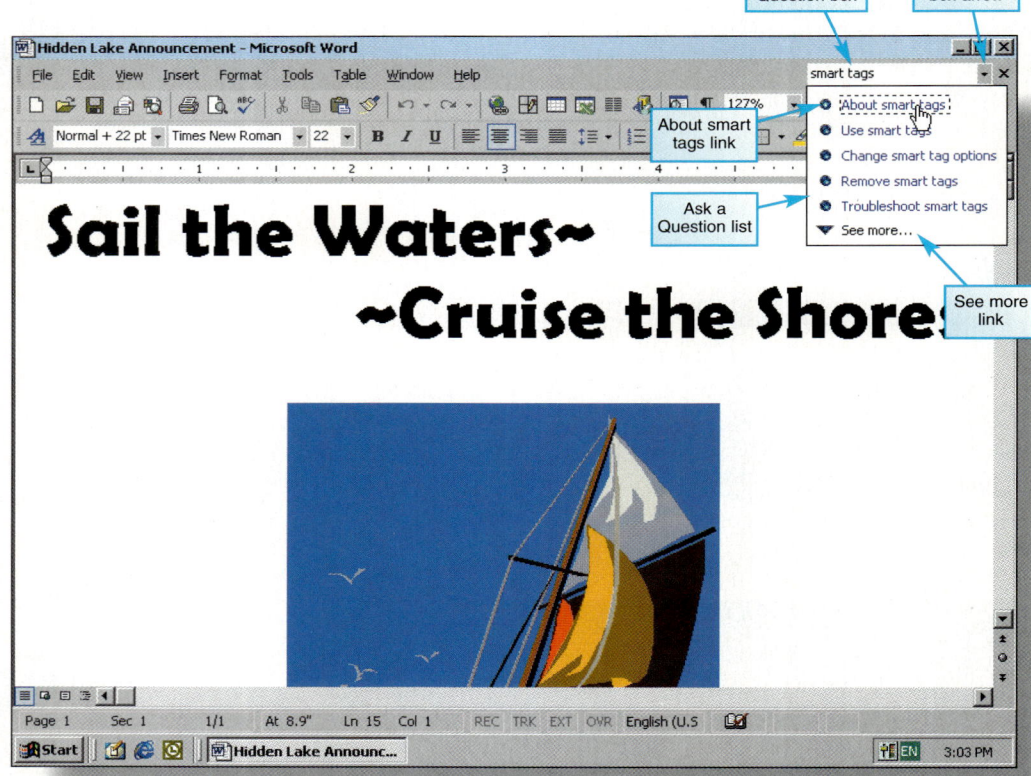

FIGURE A-2

2 Click About smart tags. When the Microsoft Word Help window displays, double-click its title bar to maximize it. If necessary, click the Contents tab.

Word displays and maximizes the Microsoft Word Help window (Figure A-3). A toolbar displays at the top of the window. The left side of the window contains the Contents, Answer Wizard, and Index tabs. The right side of the window contains the About smart tags topic.

3 Click the Close button on the Microsoft Word Help window title bar.

The Microsoft Word Help window closes and the document window is active.

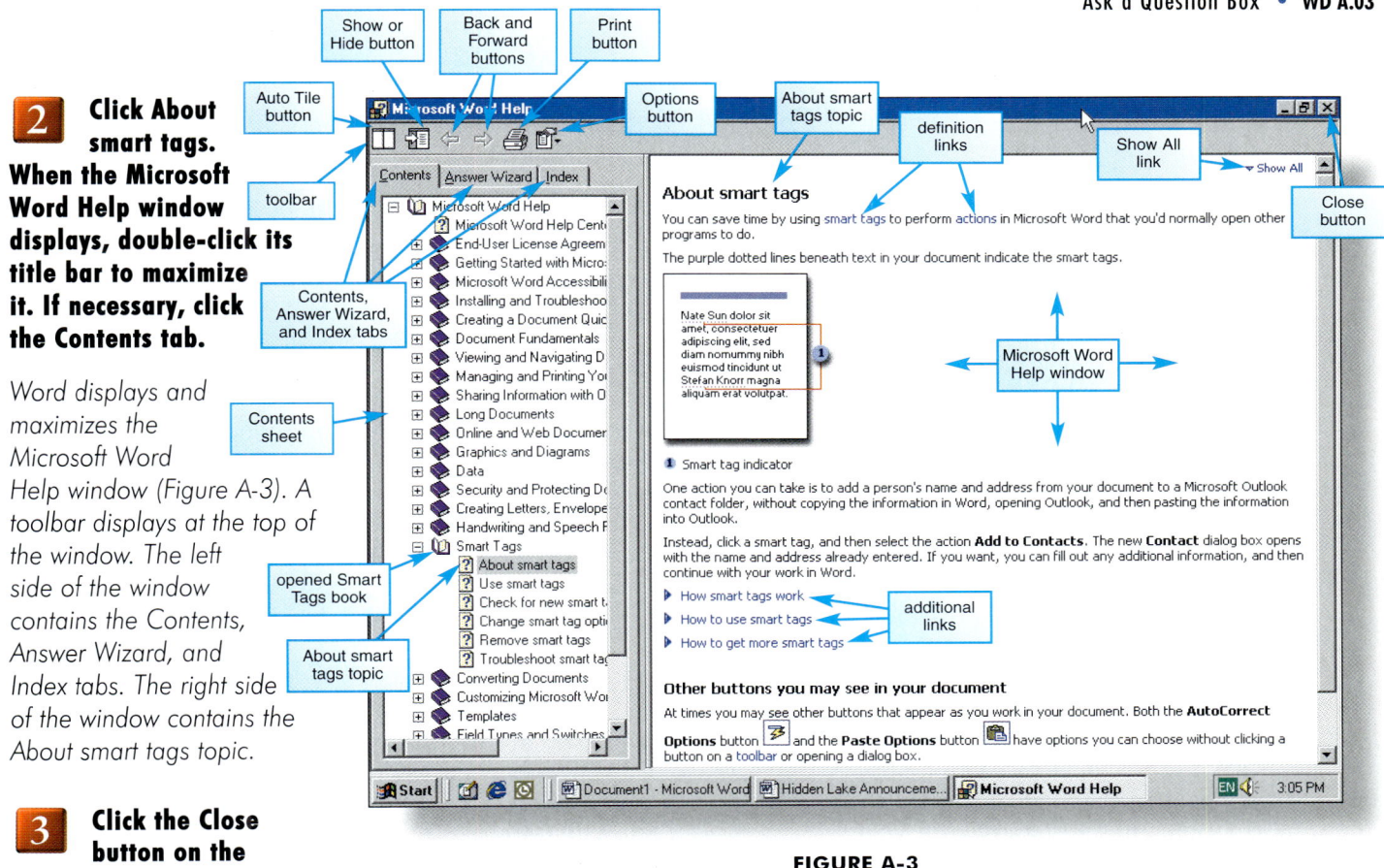

FIGURE A-3

The right side of the Microsoft Word Help window shown in Figure A-3 contains the About smart tags topic. The two links at the top of the window, smart tags and actions, display in blue font. Clicking either of these links displays a definition in green font following the link. Clicking again removes the definition. The How smart tags work link, How to use smart tags link, and How to get more smart tags link also display on the right side of the window. Clicking one of these links displays additional information about the link. Clicking again removes the information. Clicking the Show All link in the upper-right corner of the window causes the text associated with each link to display. In addition, the Hide All link replaces the Show All link.

If the Contents sheet is active on the left side of the Microsoft Word Help window, then Word opens the book that pertains to the topic for which you are requesting help. In this case, Word opens the Smart Tags book, which includes a list of topics related to smart tags. If you need additional information about the topic, you can click one of the topics listed below the Smart Tags book name.

The six buttons on the toolbar in the Microsoft Word Help window (Figure A-3) allow you to navigate through the Help system, change the display, and print the contents of the window. Table A-1 lists the function of each button on the toolbar.

Table A-1	Microsoft Word Help Toolbar Buttons	
BUTTON	NAME	FUNCTION
	Auto Tile	Tiles the Microsoft Word Help window and Microsoft Word window when the Microsoft Word Help window is maximized
or	Show or Hide	Displays or hides the Contents, Answer Wizard, and Index tabs
	Back	Displays the previous Help topic
	Forward	Displays the next Help topic
	Print	Prints the current Help topic
	Options	Displays a list of commands

The Office Assistant

The **Office Assistant** is an icon that displays in the Word window (shown in the lower-right side of Figure A-1 on page WD A.01) when it is turned on and not hidden. It has dual functions. First, it will respond in the same way the Ask a Question box does with a list of topics that relate to an entry you make in the text box at the bottom of the balloon. The entry can be in the form of a word, phrase, or question written as if you were talking. For example, if you want to learn more about saving a file, in the balloon text box, you can type any of the following terms or phrases: save, save a file, how do I save a file, or anything similar. The Office Assistant responds by displaying a list of topics from which you can choose. Once you choose a topic, it displays the corresponding information.

Second, the Office Assistant monitors your work and accumulates tips during a session on how you might increase your productivity and efficiency. You can view the tips at anytime. The accumulated tips display when you activate the Office Assistant balloon. Also, if at anytime you see a lightbulb above the Office Assistant, click it to display the most recent tip.

You may or may not want the Office Assistant to display on the screen at all times. You can hide it, and then show it at a later time. You may prefer not to use the Office Assistant at all. Thus, not only do you need to know how to show and hide the Office Assistant, but you also need to know how to turn the Office Assistant on and off.

Showing and Hiding the Office Assistant

When Word initially is installed, the Office Assistant may be off. You turn on the Office Assistant by clicking the **Show the Office Assistant command** on the Help menu. If the Office Assistant is on the screen and you want to hide it, you click the **Hide the Office Assistant command** on the Help menu. You also can right-click the Office Assistant to display its shortcut menu and then click the **Hide command** to hide it. You can move it to any location on the screen. You can click it to display the Office Assistant balloon, which allows you to request Help.

Turning the Office Assistant On and Off

The fact that the Office Assistant is hidden, does not mean it is turned off. To turn the Office Assistant off, it must be displaying in the Word window. You right-click it to display its shortcut menu (right side of Figure A-4). Next, click Options on the shortcut menu. When you click the **Options command**, the **Office Assistant dialog box** displays (left side of Figure A-4).

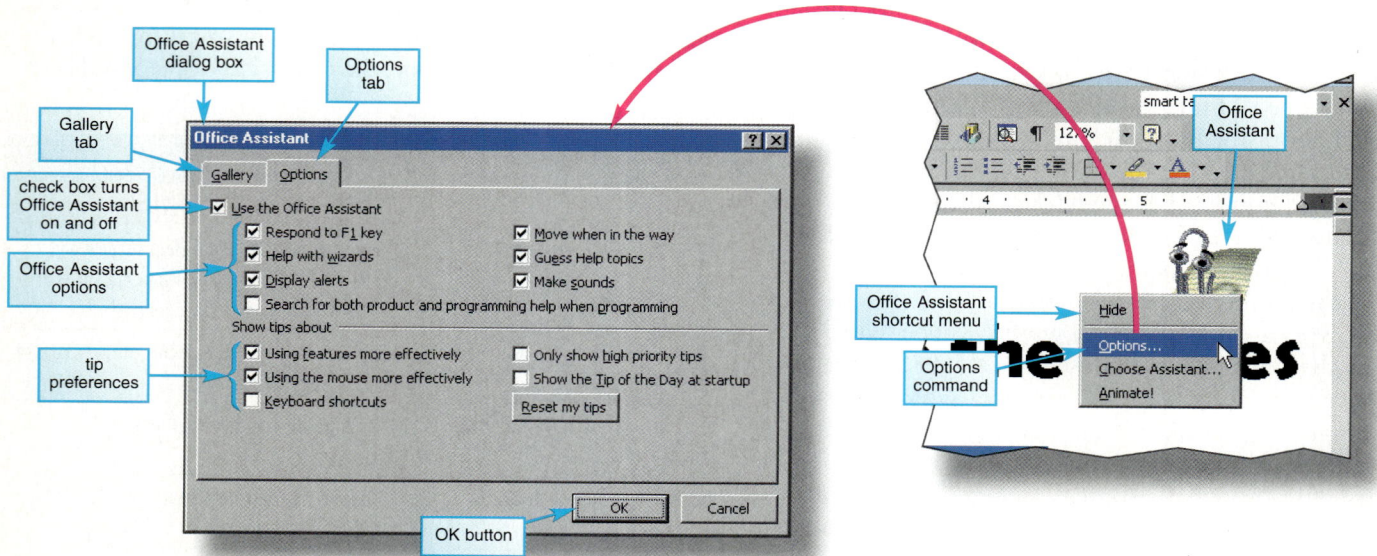

FIGURE A-4

In the **Options sheet** in the Office Assistant dialog box, the **Use the Office Assistant check box** at the top of the sheet determines whether the Office Assistant is on or off. To turn the Office Assistant off, remove the check mark from the Use the Office Assistant check box and then click the OK button. As shown in Figure A-1 on page WD A.01, if the Office Assistant is off when you invoke Help, then Word displays the Microsoft Word Help window instead of displaying the Office Assistant. To turn the Office Assistant on later, click the **Show the Office Assistant command** on the Help menu.

Through the Options command on the Office Assistant shortcut menu, you can change the look and feel of the Office Assistant. For example, you can hide the Office Assistant, turn the Office Assistant off, change the way it works, choose a different Office Assistant icon, or view an animation of the current one. These options also are available by clicking the **Options button** that displays in the Office Assistant balloon (Figure A-5).

The **Gallery sheet** (Figure A-4) in the Office Assistant dialog box allows you to change the appearance of the Office Assistant. The default is the paper clip (Clippit). You can change it to a bouncing red happy face (The Dot), a robot (F1), the Microsoft Office logo (Office Logo), a wizard (Merlin), the earth (Mother Nature), a cat (Links), or a dog (Rocky).

Using the Office Assistant

As indicated earlier, the Office Assistant allows you to enter a word, phrase, or question and then responds by displaying a list of topics from which you can choose to display Help. The following steps show how to use the Office Assistant to obtain Help on speech recognition.

Steps To Use the Office Assistant

1 **If the Office Assistant is not turned on, click Help on the menu bar and then click Show the Office Assistant. Click the Office Assistant. When the Office Assistant balloon displays, type** what is speech recognition **in the text box immediately above the Options button. Point to the Search button.**

The Office Assistant balloon displays and the question, what is speech recognition, displays in the text box (Figure A-5).

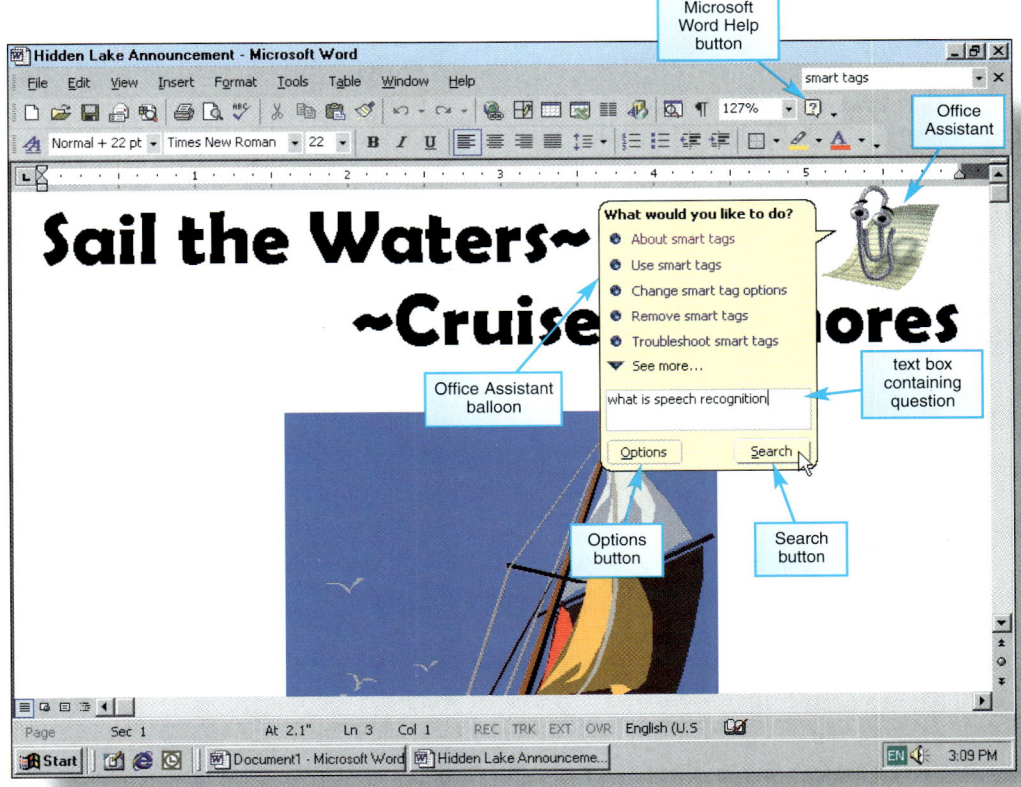

FIGURE A-5

WD A.06 • Appendix A • Microsoft Word Help System

2 **Click the Search button. When the Office Assistant balloon redisplays, point to the topic, About speech recognition.**

A list of links displays in the Office Assistant balloon (Figure A-6).

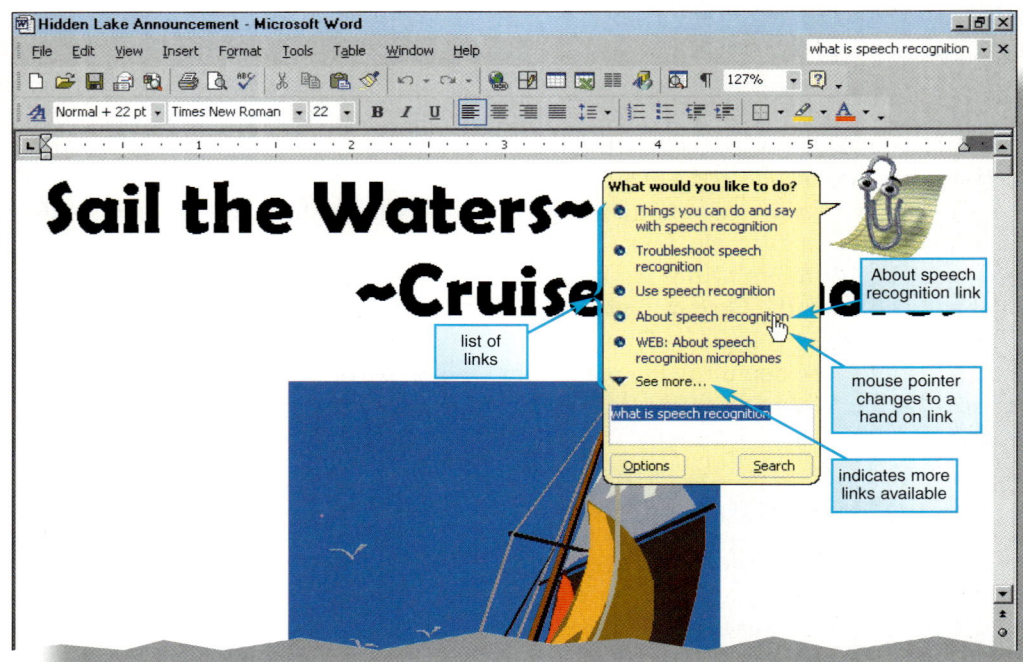

FIGURE A-6

3 **Click the topic, About speech recognition (Figure A-7). If necessary, move or hide the Office Assistant so you can view all of the text on the right side of the Microsoft Word Help window.**

The About speech recognition topic displays on the right side of the Microsoft Word Help window (Figure A-7). Clicking the Show All link in the upper-right corner of the window expands all links.

4 **Click the Close button on the Microsoft Word Help window title bar to close Help.**

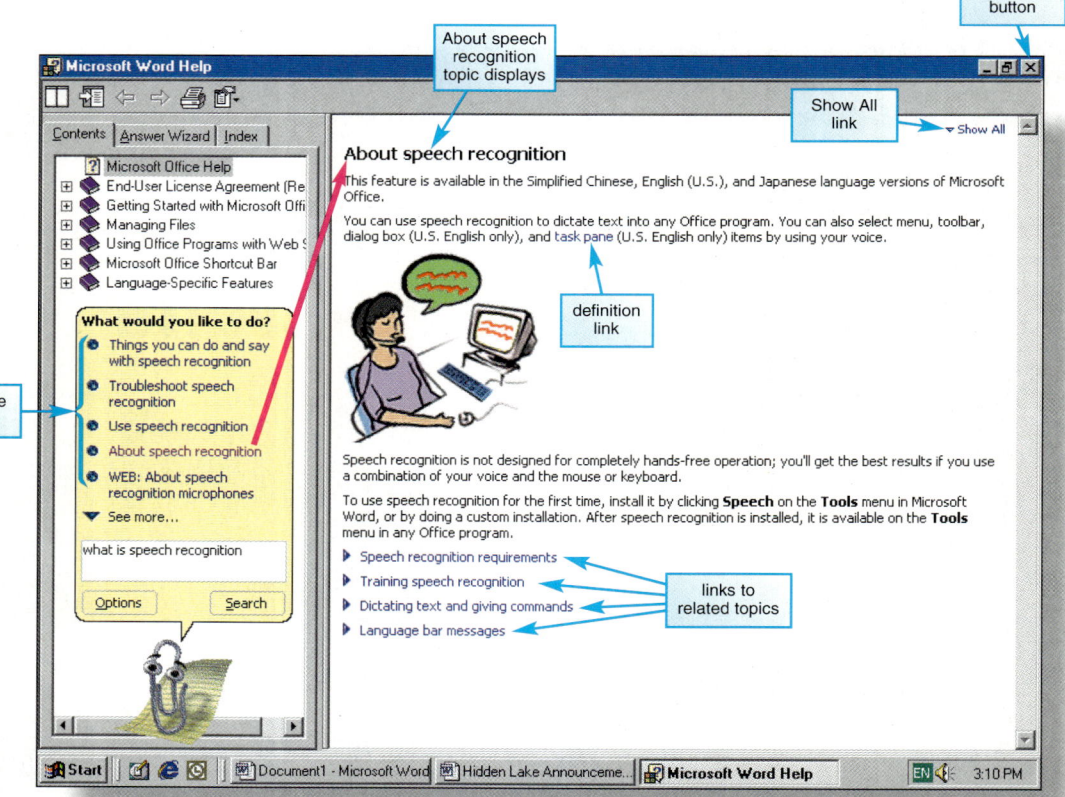

FIGURE A-7

The Microsoft Word Help Window

If the Office Assistant is turned off and you click the Microsoft Word Help button on the Standard toolbar, the Microsoft Word Help window displays (Figure A-8). The left side of this window contains three tabs: Contents, Answer Wizard, and Index. Each tab displays a sheet with powerful look-up capabilities.

Use the Contents sheet as you would a table of contents at the front of a book to look up Help. The Answer Wizard sheet answers your queries the same as the Office Assistant. You use the Index sheet in the same fashion as an index in a book to look up Help. Click the tabs to move from sheet to sheet.

Besides clicking the Microsoft Word Help button on the Standard toolbar, you also can click the Microsoft Word Help command on the Help menu, or press the F1 key to display the Microsoft Word Help window to gain access to the three sheets. To close the Microsoft Word Help window, click the Close button in the upper-right corner on the title bar.

Using the Contents Sheet

The **Contents sheet** is useful for displaying Help when you know the general category of the topic in question, but not the specifics. The following steps show how to use the Contents sheet to obtain information about handwriting recognition.

TO OBTAIN HELP USING THE CONTENTS SHEET

1. Click the Microsoft Word Help button on the Standard toolbar (shown in Figure A-5 on page WD A.05).

2. When the Microsoft Word Help window displays, double-click the title bar to maximize the window. If necessary, click the Show button to display the tabs.

3. Click the Contents tab. Double-click the Handwriting and Speech Recognition book in the Contents sheet. Double-click the Handwriting Recognition book.

4. Click the subtopic, About handwriting recognition, below the Handwriting Recognition book (Figure A-8).

5. Close the Microsoft Help window.

Word displays Help on the subtopic, About handwriting recognition (Figure A-8).

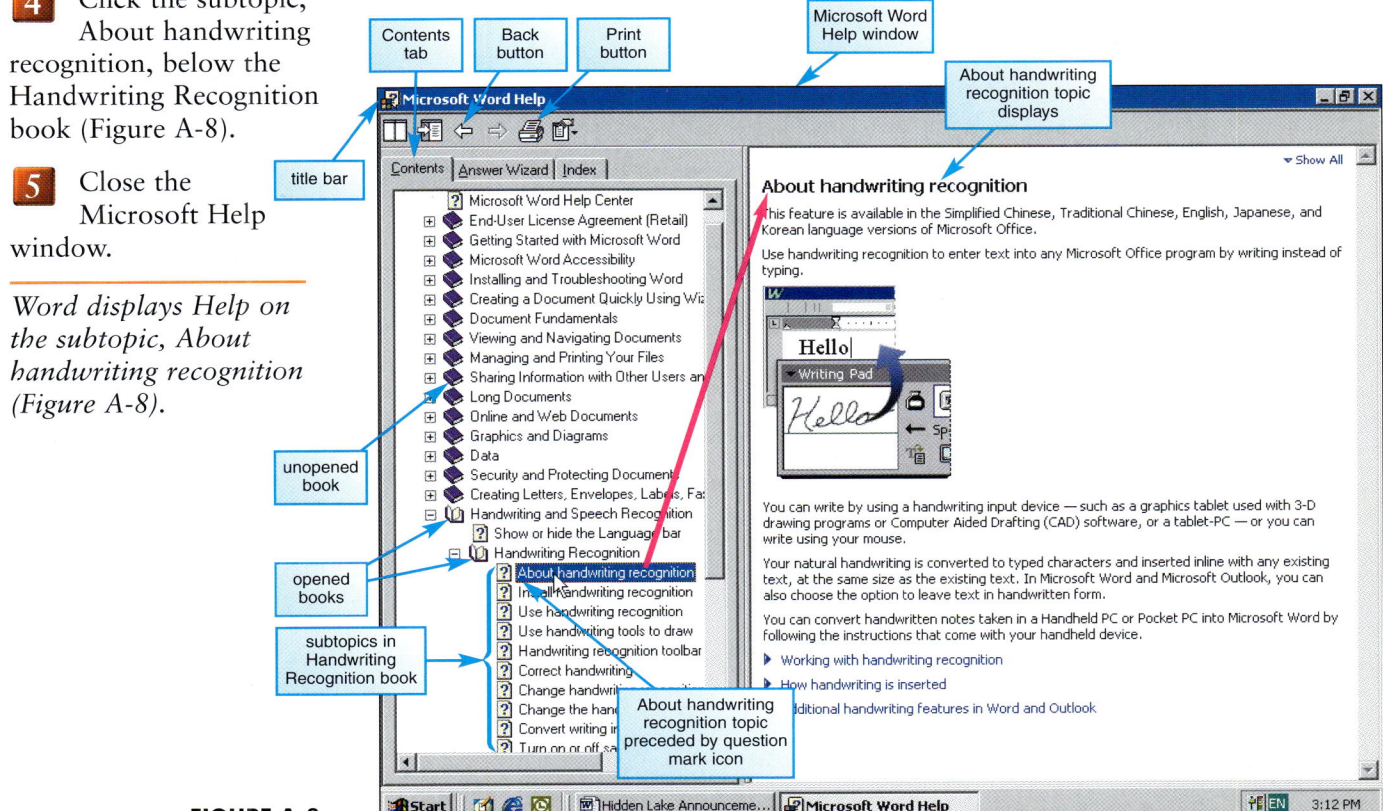

FIGURE A-8

Once the information on the subtopic displays, you can read it or you can click the Print button to obtain a printed copy. If you decide to click another subtopic on the left or a link on the right, you can get back to the Help page shown in Figure A-8 on the previous page by clicking the Back button.

Each topic in the Contents list is preceded by a book icon or question mark icon. A **book icon** indicates subtopics are available. A **question mark icon** means information on the topic will display if you double-click the title. The book icon opens when you double-click the book (or its title) or click the plus sign (+) to the left of the book icon.

Using the Answer Wizard Sheet

The **Answer Wizard sheet** works like the Office Assistant in that you enter a word, phrase, or question and it responds by listing topics from which you can choose to display Help. The following steps show how to use the Answer Wizard sheet to obtain Help on translating or looking up text in the dictionary of another language.

TO OBTAIN HELP USING THE ANSWER WIZARD SHEET

1. With the Office Assistant turned off, click the Microsoft Word Help button on the Standard toolbar (shown in Figure A-5 on page WD A.05).

2. When the Microsoft Word Help window displays, double-click the title bar to maximize the window. If necessary, click the Show button to display the tabs.

3. Click the Answer Wizard tab. Type translation in the What would you like to do? text box on the left side of the window. Click the Search button.

4. When a list of topics displays in the Select topic to display list, click Translate or look up text in the dictionary of another language (Figure A-9).

5. Close the Microsoft Help window.

Word displays Help on how to translate or look up text in the dictionary of a different language on the right side of the Microsoft Word Help window (Figure A-9).

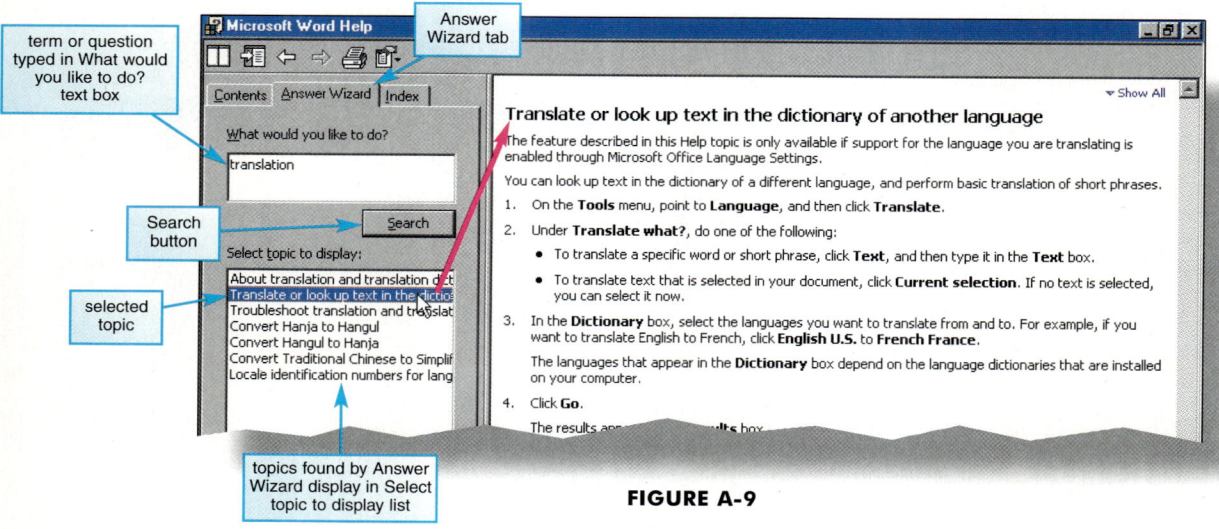

FIGURE A-9

If the topic, Translate or look up text in the dictionary of another language, does not include the information you are seeking, click another topic in the list. Continue to click topics until you find the desired information.

Using the Index Sheet

The third sheet in the Microsoft Word Help window is the Index sheet. Use the **Index sheet** to display Help when you know the keyword or the first few letters of the keyword you want to look up. The following steps show how to use the Index sheet to obtain Help on understanding the readability scores available to evaluate the reading level of a document.

TO OBTAIN HELP USING THE INDEX SHEET

1. With the Office Assistant turned off, click the Microsoft Word Help button on the Standard toolbar (shown in Figure A-5 on page WD A.05).

2. When the Microsoft Word Help window displays, double-click the title bar to maximize the window. If necessary, click the Show button to display the tabs.

3. Click the Index tab. Type `readability` in the Type keywords text box on the left side of the window. Click the Search button.

4. When a list of topics displays in the Choose a topic list, click Readability scores.

5. When the Readability scores topic displays on the right side of the window (Figure A-10), click the Show All link in the upper-right corner of the right side of the window.

Word displays information about readability scores and two links on the right side of the window (Figure A-10). Clicking the Show All link expands the two links and displays the Hide All link. As you type readability into the Type keywords box, Word recognizes and completes the word and automatically appends a semicolon to the keyword.

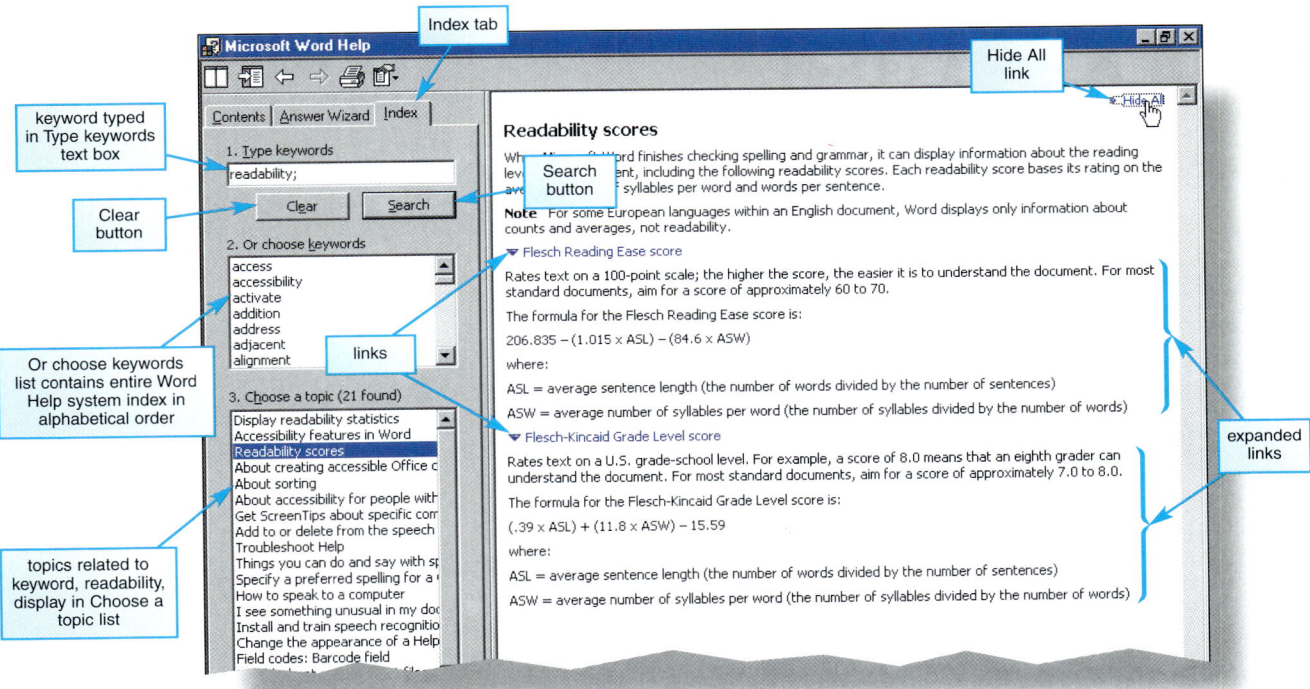

FIGURE A-10

An alternative to typing a keyword in the Type keywords text box is to scroll through the Or choose keywords list (the middle list on the left side of the window). When you locate the keyword you are searching for, double-click it to display Help on the topic. Also in the Or choose keywords list, the Word Help system displays other topics that relate to the new keyword. As you begin typing a new keyword in the Type keywords text box, Word jumps to that point in the middle list box. To begin a new search, click the Clear button.

What's This? Command and Question Mark Button

Use the What's This? command on the Help menu or the Question Mark button in a dialog box when you are not sure what an object on the screen is or what it does.

What's This? Command

You use the **What's This? command** on the Help menu to display a detailed ScreenTip. When you click this command, the mouse pointer changes to an arrow with a question mark. You then click any object on the screen, such as a button, to display the ScreenTip. For example, after you click the What's This? command on the Help menu and then click the Zoom box on the Standard toolbar, a description of the Zoom box displays (Figure A-11). You can print the ScreenTip by right-clicking it and then clicking Print Topic on the shortcut menu.

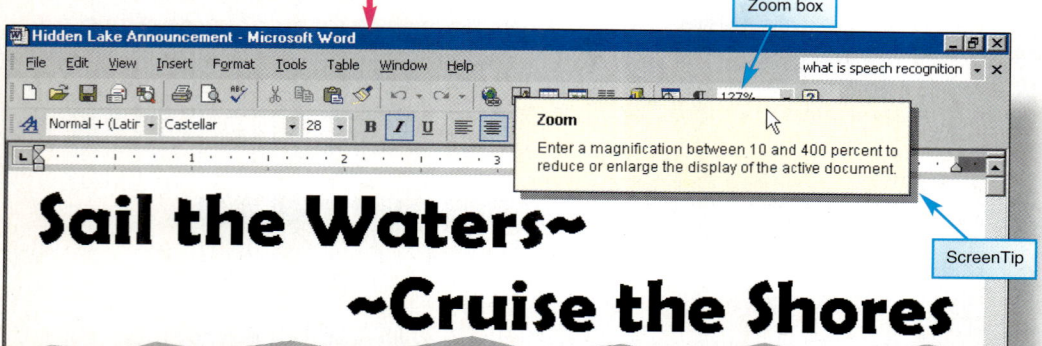

FIGURE A-11

Question Mark Button

Similarly to the What's This? command, the **Question Mark button** displays a ScreenTip. You use the Question Mark button with dialog boxes. It is located in the upper-right corner on the title bar of the dialog boxes, next to the Close button. For example, in Figure A-12, the Print dialog box displays on the screen. If you click the Question Mark button in the upper-right corner of the dialog box and then click the Print to file check box, an explanation of the Print to file check box displays in a ScreenTip. You can print the ScreenTip by right-clicking it and clicking Print Topic on the shortcut menu.

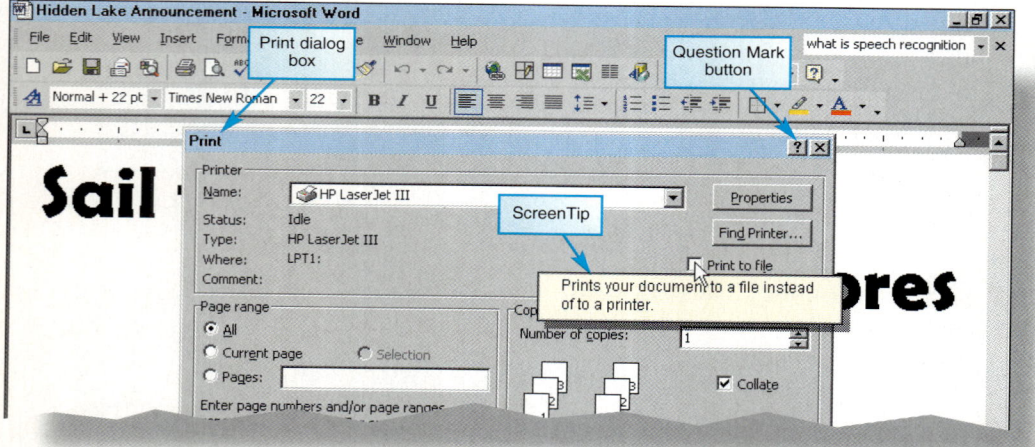

FIGURE A-12

If a dialog box does not include a Question Mark button, press SHIFT+F1. This combination of keys will change the mouse pointer to an arrow with a question mark. You then can click any object in the dialog box to display the ScreenTip.

Office on the Web Command

The **Office on the Web command** on the Help menu displays a Microsoft Web page containing up-to-date information on a variety of Office-related topics. To use this command, you must be connected to the Internet. When you invoke the Office on the Web command, the Assistance Center Home page displays. Read through the links that in general pertain to topics that relate to all Office XP topics. Scroll down and click the Word link in the Help By Product area to display the Assistance Center Word Help Articles Web page (Figure A-14). This Web page contains numerous helpful links related to Word.

Other Help Commands

Four additional commands available on the Help menu are Activate Product, WordPerfect Help, Detect and Repair, and About Microsoft Word. The WordPerfect Help command is available only if it was included as part of a custom installation of Word 2002.

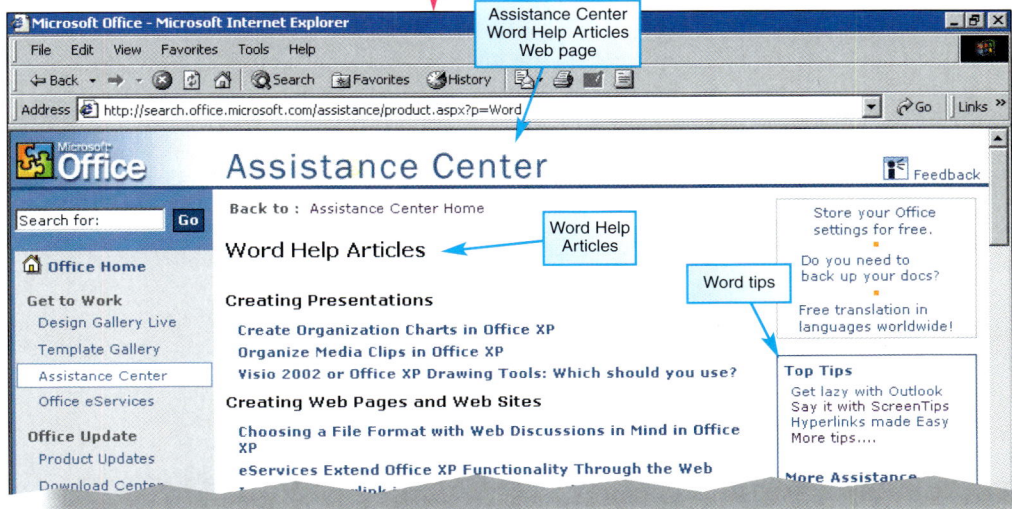

FIGURE A-14

Activate Product Command

The **Activate Product command** on the Help menu lets you activate your Microsoft Office subscription if you selected the Microsoft Office Subscription mode.

WordPerfect Help Command

The **WordPerfect Help command** on the Help menu offers assistance to WordPerfect users switching to Word. When you choose this command, Word displays the Help for WordPerfect Users dialog box. The instructions in the dialog box step the user through the appropriate selections.

Detect and Repair Command

Use the **Detect and Repair command** on the Help menu if Word is not running properly or if it is generating errors. When you invoke this command, the Detect and Repair dialog box displays. Click the Start button in the dialog box to initiate the detect and repair process.

About Microsoft Word Command

The **About Microsoft Word command** on the Help menu displays the About Microsoft Word dialog box. The dialog box lists the owner of the software and the product identification. You need to know the product identification if you call Microsoft for assistance. The three buttons below the OK button are the System Info button, Tech Support button, and Disabled Items button. The **System Info button** displays system information, including hardware resources, components, software environment, Internet Explorer 5, and Office XP applications. The **Tech Support button** displays technical assistance information. The **Disabled Items button** displays a list of items that were disabled because they prevented Word from functioning correctly.

Use Help

1 Using the Ask a Question Box

Instructions: Perform the following tasks using the Word Help system.

1. Click the Ask a Question box on the menu bar, and then type how do I add a bullet. Press the ENTER key.
2. Click Add bullets or numbering in the Ask a Question list. If the Word Help window is not maximized, double-click the Microsoft Word Help window title bar. Read and print the information. One at a time, click the three links on the right side of the window to learn about bullets. Print the information. Hand in the printouts to your instructor.
3. If necessary, click the Show button to display the tabs. Click the Contents tab to prepare for the next step. Click the Close button in the Microsoft Word Help window.
4. Click the Ask a Question box and then press the ENTER key. Click About bulleted lists in the Ask a Question box. When the Microsoft Word Help window displays, maximize the window. Read and print the information. Click the two links on the right side of the window. Print the information. Hand in the printouts to your instructor.

2 Expanding on the Word Help System Basics

Instructions: Use the Word Help system to understand the topics better and answer the questions listed below. Answer the questions on your own paper, or hand in the printed Help information to your instructor.

1. If the Office Assistant is on, right-click the Office Assistant. When the shortcut menu displays, click Options. Click Use the Office Assistant to remove the check mark, and then click the OK button.
2. Click the Microsoft Word Help button on the Standard toolbar. Maximize the Microsoft Word Help window. Click Getting Help on the right side of the window. Click the five links in the About getting help while you work topic. Print the information and hand in the printouts to your instructor. Close the Microsoft Word Help window.
3. Press the F1 key. Maximize the Microsoft Word Help window. Click the Answer Wizard tab. Type help in the What would you like to do? text box, and then click the Search button. Click Guidelines for searching Help. Click the four links on the right side of the window. Print the information and hand in the printouts to your instructor.
4. Click the Contents tab. Click the plus sign (+) to the left of the Document Fundamentals book. Click the plus sign (+) to the left of the Selecting Text and Graphics book. One at a time, click the three topics below the Selecting Text and Graphics book. Read and print each one. Close the Microsoft Word Help window. Hand in the printouts to your instructor.
5. Click Help on the menu bar and then click What's This? Click the E-mail button on the Standard toolbar. Right-click the ScreenTip, click Print Topic on the shortcut menu, and click the Print button. Click Format on the menu bar and then click Paragraph. When the Paragraph dialog box displays, click the Question Mark button on the title bar. Click the Special box. Right-click the ScreenTip, click Print Topic, and then click the Print button. Close the Paragraph dialog box and Microsoft Word window.

APPENDIX B

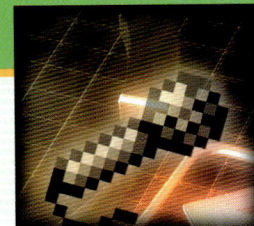

Speech and Handwriting Recognition

Introduction

This appendix discusses how you can create and modify documents using Office XP's new input technologies. Office XP provides a variety of **text services**, which enable you to speak commands and enter text in an application. The most common text service is the keyboard. Two new text services included with Office XP are speech recognition and handwriting recognition.

When Windows was installed on your computer, you specified a default language. For example, most users in the United States select English (United States) as the default language. Through text services, you can add more than 90 additional languages and varying dialects such as Basque, English (Zimbabwe), French (France), French (Canada), German (Germany), German (Austria), and Swahili. With multiple languages available, you can switch from one language to another while working in Word. If you change the language or dialect, then text services may change the functions of the keys on the keyboard, adjust speech recognition, and alter handwriting recognition.

The Language Bar

You know that text services are installed properly when the Language Indicator button displays by the clock in the tray status area on the Windows taskbar (Figure B-1a) or the Language bar displays on the screen (Figure B-1b or B-1c). If the Language Indicator button displays in the tray status area, click it, and then click the **Show the Language bar command** (Figure B-1a). The Language bar displays on the screen in the same location it displayed last time.

You can drag the Language bar to any location in the window by pointing to its move handle, which is the vertical line on its left side (Figure B-1b). When the mouse pointer changes to a four-headed arrow, drag the Language bar to the desired location.

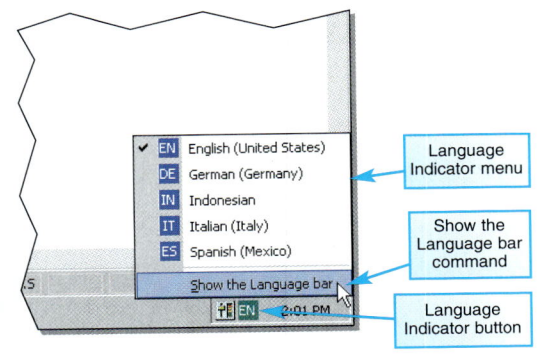

(a) **Language Indicator Button in Tray Status Area on Windows Taskbar and Its Menu**

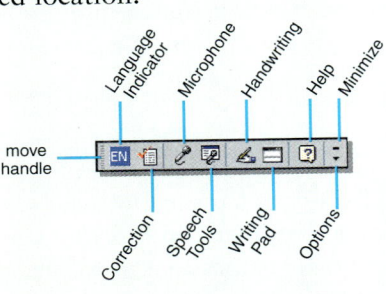

(b) **Language Bar with Text Labels Disabled**

(c) **Language Bar with Text Labels Enabled**

FIGURE B-1

If you are sure that one of the services was installed and neither the Language Indicator button nor the Language bar displays, then do the following:

1. Click Start on the Windows taskbar, point to Settings, click Control Panel, and then double-click the Text Services icon in the Control Panel window.
2. When the Text Services dialog box displays, click the Language Bar button, click the Show the Language bar on the desktop check box to select it, and then click the OK button in the Language Bar Settings dialog box.
3. Click the OK button in the Text Services dialog box.
4. Close the Control Panel window.

You can perform tasks related to text services by using the **Language bar**. The Language bar may display with just the icon on each button (Figure B-1b on the previous page) or it may display with text labels to the right of the icon on each button (Figure B-1c on the previous page). Changing the appearance of the Language bar will be discussed shortly.

Buttons on the Language Bar

The Language bar shown in Figure B-2a contains nine buttons. The number of buttons on your Language bar may be different. These buttons are used to select the language, customize the Language bar, control the microphone, control handwriting, and obtain help.

When you click the **Language Indicator button** on the far left side of the Language bar, the Language Indicator menu displays a list of the active languages (Figure B-2b) from which you can choose. When you select text and then click the **Correction button** (the second button from the left), a list of correction alternatives displays in the Word window (Figure B-2c). You can use the Correction button to correct both speech recognition and handwriting recognition errors. The **Microphone button**, the third button from the left, enables and disables the microphone. When the microphone is enabled, text services adds two buttons and a balloon to the Language toolbar (Figure B-2d). These additional buttons and the balloon will be discussed shortly.

The fourth button from the left on the Language bar is the Speech Tools button. The **Speech Tools button** displays a menu of commands (Figure B-2e) that allows you to hide or show the balloon on the Language bar; train the Speech Recognition service so that it can better interpret your voice; add and delete words from its dictionary, such as names and other words not understood easily; and change the user profile so more than one person can use the microphone on the same computer.

The fifth button from the left on the Language bar is the Handwriting button. The **Handwriting button** displays the **Handwriting menu** (Figure B-2f), which lets you choose the Writing Pad (Figure B-2g), Write Anywhere (Figure B-2h), the Drawing Pad (Figure B-2i), or the on-screen keyboard (Figure B-2j). The **On-Screen Symbol Keyboard command** on the Handwriting menu displays an on-screen keyboard that allows you to enter special symbols that are not available on the On-Screen Standard Keyboard. You can choose only one form of handwriting at a time.

The sixth button indicates which one of the handwriting forms is active. For example, in Figure B-1a on the previous page, the Writing Pad is active. The handwriting recognition capabilities of text services will be discussed shortly.

The seventh button from the left on the Language bar is the Help button. The **Help button** displays the Help menu. If you click the Language Bar Help command on the Help menu, the Language Bar Help window displays (Figure B-2k). On the far right of the Language bar are two buttons stacked above and below each other. The top button is the Minimize button and the bottom button is the Options button. The **Minimize button** minimizes (hides) the Language bar so that the Language Indicator button displays in the tray status area on the Windows taskbar. The next section discusses the Options button.

Customizing the Language Bar

The down arrow icon immediately below the Minimize button in Figure B-2a is called the Options button. The **Options button** displays a menu of text services options (Figure B-2l). You can use this menu to hide the Correction, Speech Tools, Handwriting, and Help buttons on the Language bar by clicking their names to remove the check mark to the left of each button. The Settings command on the Options menu displays a dialog box that lets you customize the Language bar. This command will be discussed shortly. The Restore Defaults command redisplays hidden buttons on the Language bar.

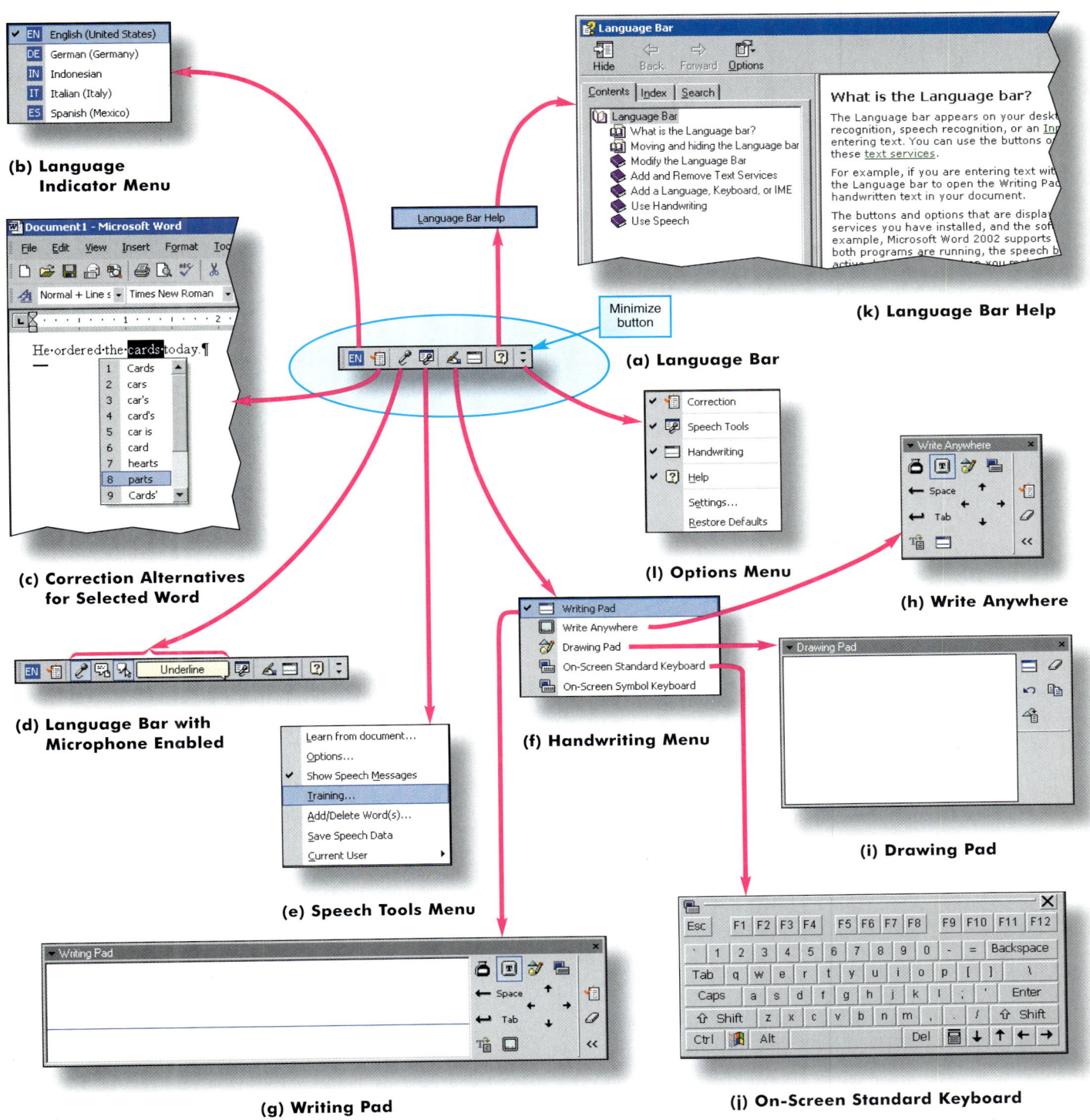

FIGURE B-2

If you right-click the Language bar, a shortcut menu displays (Figure B-3a on the next page). This shortcut menu lets you further customize the Language bar. The **Minimize command** on the shortcut menu minimizes the Language bar the same as the Minimize button on the Language bar. The **Transparency command** toggles the Language bar between being solid and transparent. You can see through a transparent Language bar (Figure B-3b). The **Text Labels command** toggles text labels on the Language bar on (Figure B-3c) and off (Figure B-3a). The **Additional icons in taskbar command** toggles between only showing the Language Indicator button in the tray status area and showing icons that represent the text services that are active (Figure B-3d).

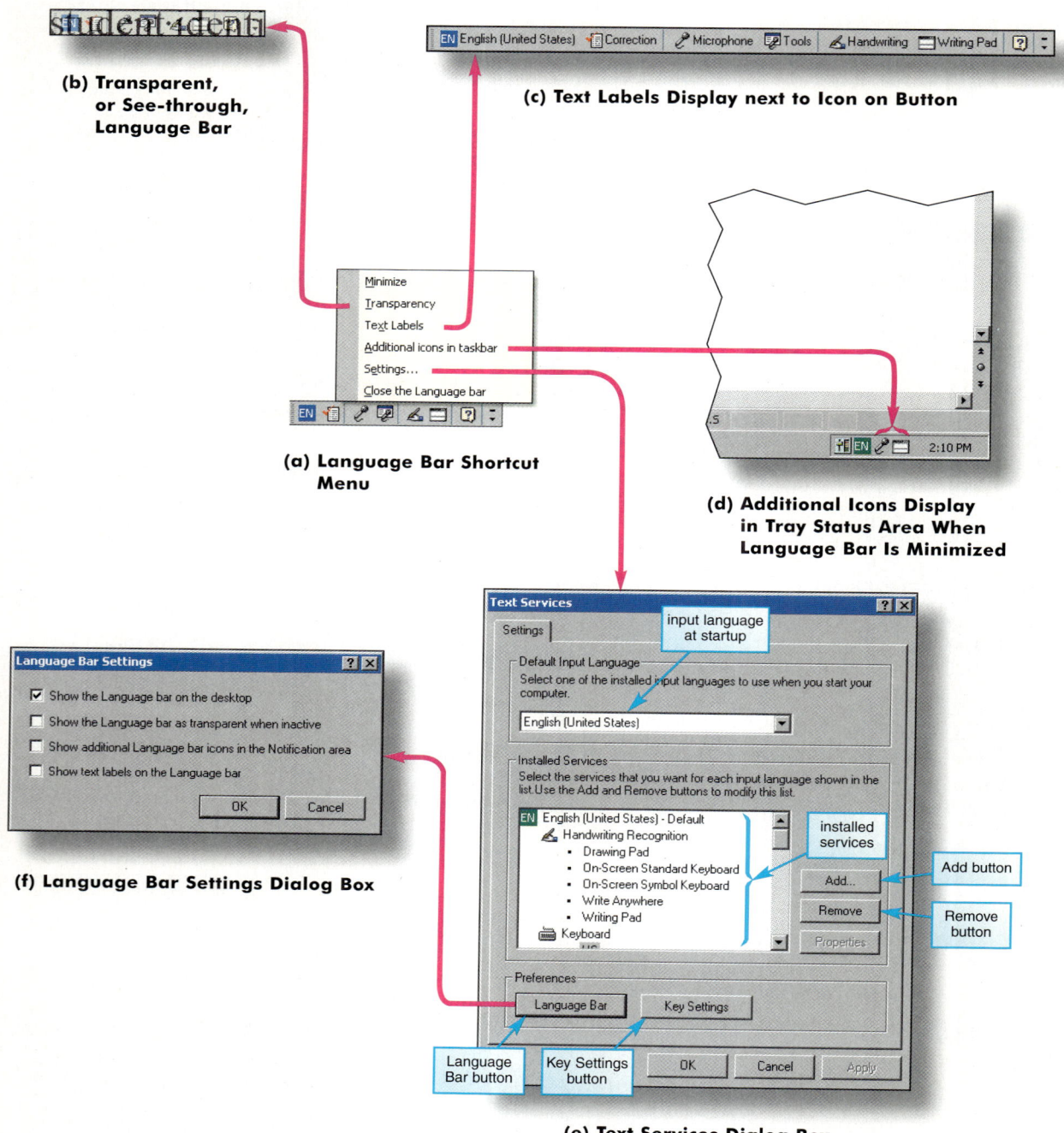

FIGURE B-3

The **Settings command** displays the Text Services dialog box (Figure B-3e). The **Text Services dialog box** allows you to select the language at startup; add and remove text services; modify keys on the keyboard; and modify the Language bar. If you want to remove any one of the entries in the Installed Services list, select the entry, and then click the Remove button. If you want to add a service, click the Add button. The Key Settings button allows you to modify the keyboard. If you click the **Language Bar button** in the Text Services dialog box, the **Language Bar Settings dialog box** displays (Figure B-3f). This dialog box contains Language bar options, some of which are the same as the commands on the Language bar shortcut menu described earlier.

The **Close the Language bar command** on the shortcut menu shown in Figure B-3a closes the Language bar and hides the Language Indicator button in the tray status area on the Windows taskbar. If you close the Language bar and want to redisplay it, follow the instructions at the top of page WD B.02.

Speech Recognition

The **Speech Recognition service** available with Office XP enables your computer to recognize human speech through a microphone. The microphone has two modes: dictation and voice command (Figure B-4). You switch between the two modes by clicking the Dictation button and the Voice Command button on the Language bar. These buttons display only when you turn on Speech Recognition by clicking the **Microphone button** on the Language bar (Figure B-5 on the next page). If you are using the Microphone button for the very first time in Word, it will require that you check your microphone settings and step through voice training before activating the Speech Recognition service.

The **Dictation button** places the microphone in Dictation mode. In **Dictation mode**, whatever you speak is entered as text at the location of the insertion point. The **Voice Command button** places the microphone in Voice Command mode. In **Voice Command mode**, whatever you speak is interpreted as a command. If you want to turn off the microphone, click the Microphone button on the Language bar or in Voice Command mode say, "Mic off" (pronounced mike off). It is important to remember that minimizing the Language bar does not turn off the microphone.

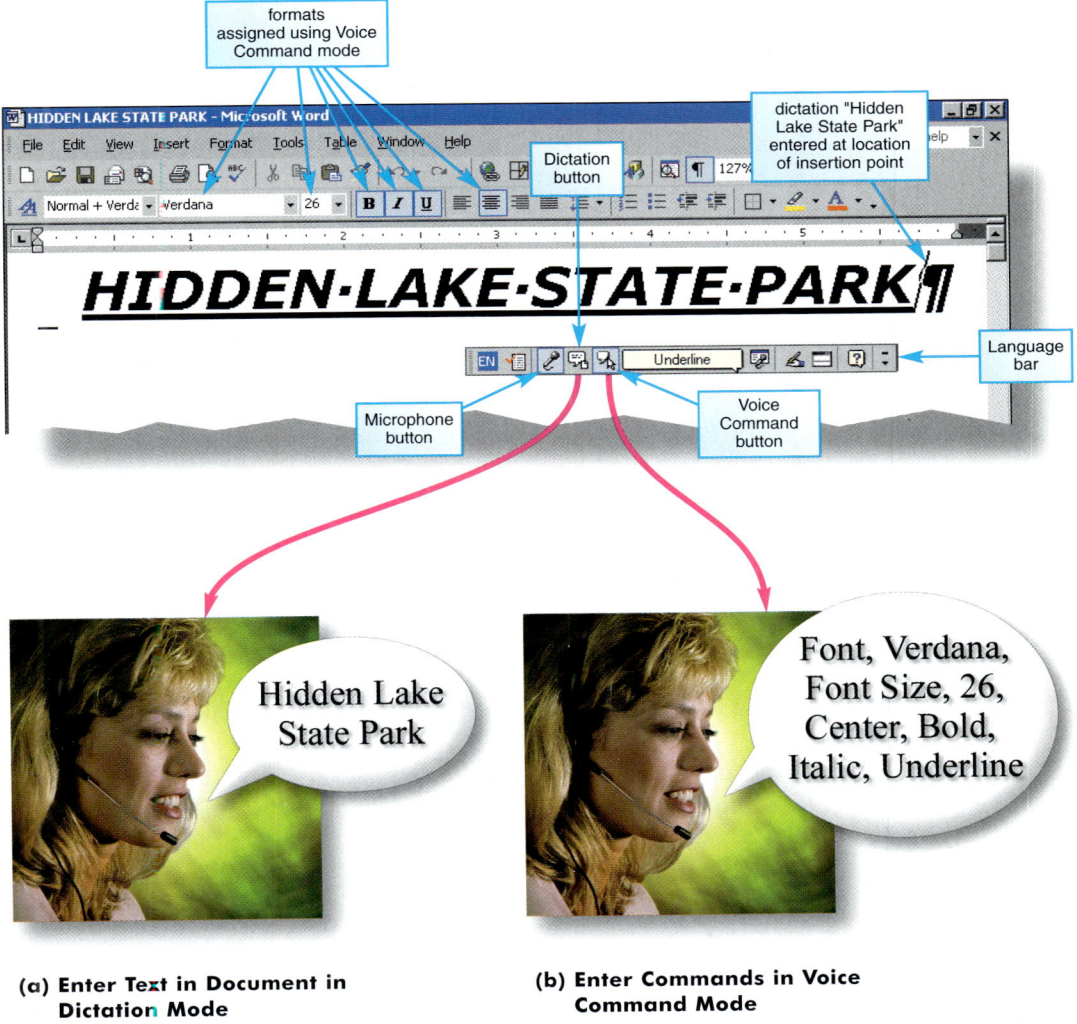

(a) Enter Text in Document in Dictation Mode

(b) Enter Commands in Voice Command Mode

FIGURE B-4

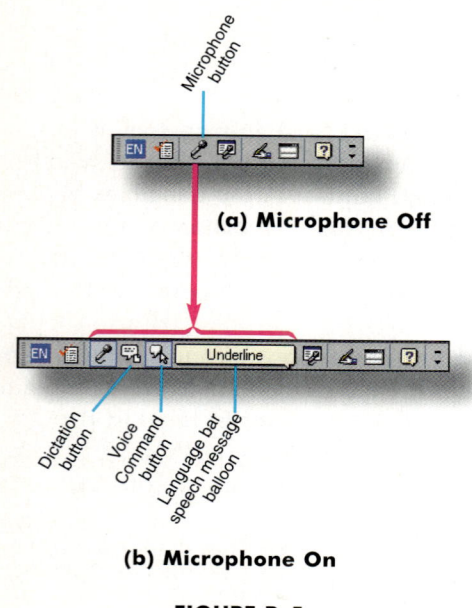

(a) Microphone Off

(b) Microphone On

FIGURE B-5

The **Language bar speech message balloon** shown in Figure B-5b displays messages that may offer help or hints. In Voice Command mode, the name of the last recognized command you said displays. If you use the mouse or keyboard instead of the microphone, a message will appear in the Language bar speech message balloon indicating the word you could say. In Dictation mode, the message, Dictating, usually displays. The Speech Recognition service, however, will display messages to inform you that you are talking too soft, too loud, too fast, or to ask you to repeat what you said by displaying, What was that?

Getting Started with Speech Recognition

For the microphone to function properly, you should follow these steps:

1. Make sure your computer meets the minimum requirements.
2. Install Speech Recognition.
3. Set up and position your microphone, preferably a close-talk headset with gain adjustment support.
4. Train the Speech Recognition service.

The following sections describe these steps in more detail.

SPEECH RECOGNITION SYSTEM REQUIREMENTS For Speech Recognition to work on your computer, it needs the following:

1. Microsoft Windows 98 or later or Microsoft Windows NT 4.0 or later
2. At least 128 MB RAM
3. 400 MHz or faster processor
4. Microphone and sound card

INSTALLING SPEECH RECOGNITION If Speech Recognition is not installed on your computer, start Microsoft Word and then click Speech on the Tools menu.

SET UP AND POSITION YOUR MICROPHONE Set up your microphone as follows:

1. Connect your microphone to the sound card in the back of the computer.
2. Position the microphone approximately one inch out from and to the side of your mouth. Position it so you are not breathing into it.
3. On the Language bar, click the Speech Tools button, and then click Options (Figure B-6a).
4. When the Speech Properties dialog box displays (Figure B-6b), if necessary, click the Speech Recognition tab.
5. Click the Configure Microphone button. Follow the Microphone Wizard directions as shown in Figures B-6c, B-6d, and B-6e. The Next button will remain dimmed in Figure B-6d until the volume meter consistently stays in the green area.
6. If someone else installed Speech Recognition, click the New button in the Speech Properties dialog box and enter your name and then click the Finish button. Click the Train Profile button and step through the Voice Training Wizard. The Voice Training Wizard will require that you enter your gender and age group. It then will step you through voice training.

You can adjust the microphone further by clicking the **Settings button** (Figure B-6b) in the Speech Properties dialog box. The Settings button displays the **Recognition Profile Settings dialog box** that allows you to adjust the pronunciation sensitivity and accuracy versus recognition response time.

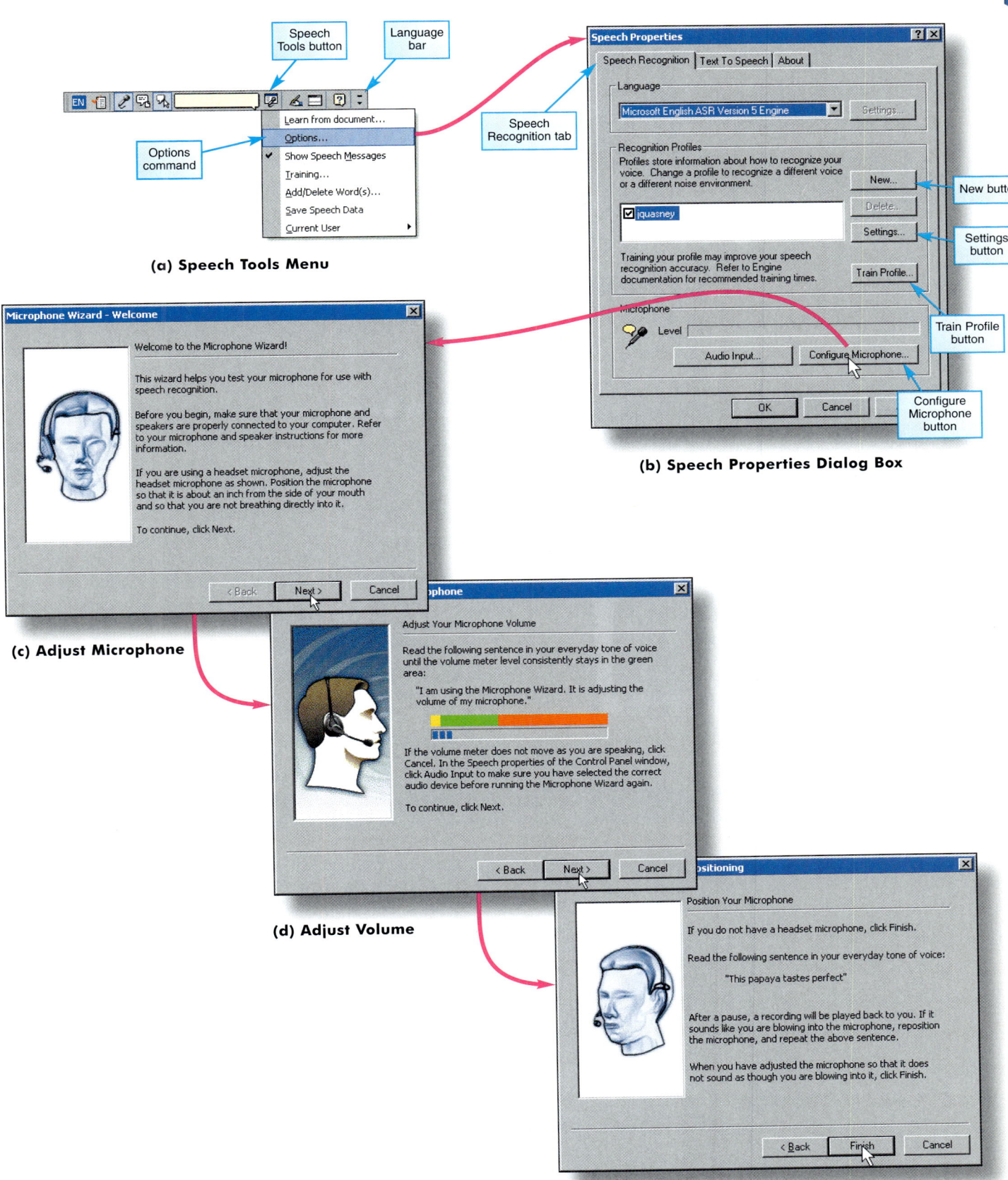

FIGURE B-6

TRAIN THE SPEECH RECOGNITION SERVICE The Speech Recognition service will understand most commands and some dictation without any training at all. It will recognize much more of what you speak, however, if you take the time to train it. After one training session, it will recognize 85 to 90 percent of your words. As you do more training, accuracy will rise to 95 percent. If you feel that too many mistakes are being made, then continue to train the service. The more training you do, the more accurately it will work for you. Follow these steps to train the Speech Recognition service:

1. Click the Speech Tools button on the Language bar and then click Training (Figure B-7a).
2. When the **Voice Training dialog box** displays (Figure B-7b), click one of the sessions and then click the Next button.
3. Complete the training session, which should take less than 15 minutes.

If you are serious about using a microphone to speak to your computer, you need to take the time to go through at least three of the eight training sessions listed in Figure B-7b.

Using Speech Recognition

Speech recognition lets you enter text into a document similarly to speaking into a tape recorder. Instead of typing, you can dictate text that you want to display in the document, and you can issue voice commands. In **Voice Command mode**, you can speak menu names, commands on menus, toolbar button names, and dialog box option buttons, check boxes, list boxes, and button names. Speech Recognition, however, is not a completely hands-free form of input. Speech recognition works best if you use a combination of your voice, the keyboard, and the mouse. You soon will discover that Dictation mode is far less accurate than Voice Command mode. Table B-1 lists some tips that will improve the Speech Recognition service's accuracy considerably.

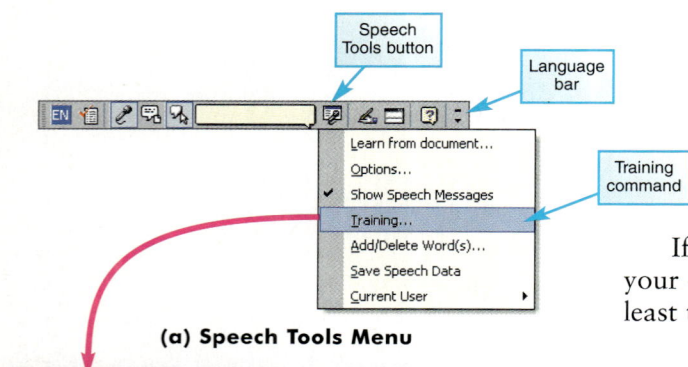

(a) Speech Tools Menu

(b) Voice Training Dialog Box

FIGURE B-7

Table B-1	Tips to Improve Speech Recognition
NUMBER	**TIP**
1	The microphone hears everything. Though the Speech Recognition service filters out background noise, it is recommended that you work in a quiet environment.
2	Try not to move the microphone around once it is adjusted.
3	Speak in a steady tone and speak clearly.
4	In Dictation mode, do not pause between words. A phrase is easier to interpret than a word. Sounding out syllables in a word will make it more difficult for the Speech Recognition service to interpret what you are saying.
5	If you speak too loudly or too softly, it makes it difficult for the Speech Recognition service to interpret what you said. Check the Language bar speech message balloon for an indication that you may be speaking too loudly or too softly.
6	If you experience problems after training, adjust the recognition options that control accuracy and rejection by clicking the Settings button shown in Figure B-6b on the previous page.
7	When you are finished using the microphone, turn it off by clicking the Microphone button on the Language bar or in Voice Command mode say, "Mic off." Leaving the microphone on is the same as leaning on the keyboard.
8	If the Speech Recognition service is having difficulty with unusual words, then add the words to its dictionary by using the Learn from document command or Add/Delete Word(s) command on the Speech Tools menu (Figure B-8a). The last names of individuals and the names of companies are good examples of the types of words you should add to the dictionary.
9	Training will improve accuracy; practice will improve confidence.

The last command on the Speech Tools menu is the Current User command (Figure B-8a). The **Current User command** is useful for multiple users who share a computer. It allows them to configure their own individual profiles, and then switch between users as they use the computer.

For additional information on the Speech Recognition service, click the Help button on the Standard toolbar, click the Answer Wizard tab, and search for the phrase, Speech Recognition.

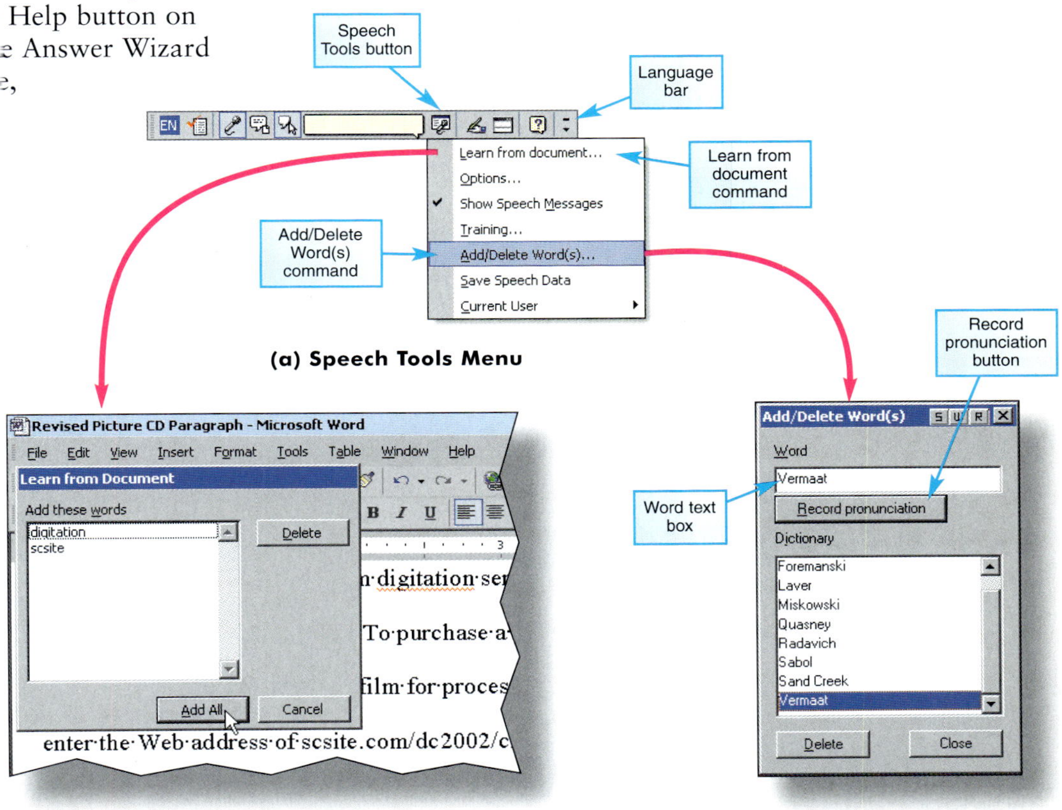

(a) Speech Tools Menu

(b) Learn from Document Dialog Box in Word Window

(c) Add/Delete Word(s) Dialog Box

FIGURE B-8

Handwriting Recognition

Using the Office XP handwriting recognition capabilities, you can enter text and numbers into Word by writing instead of typing. You can write using a special handwriting device that connects to your computer or you can write on the screen using your mouse. Four basic methods of handwriting are available by clicking the **Handwriting button** on the Language bar: Writing Pad, Write Anywhere, Drawing Pad, and On-Screen Keyboard. Although the on-screen keyboard does not involve handwriting recognition, it is part of the Handwriting menu and, therefore, will be discussed in this section.

If your Language bar does not include the Handwriting button (Figures B-1b or B-1c on page WD B.01), then for installation instructions click the Help button on the Standard toolbar, click the Answer Wizard tab, and search for the phrase Install Handwriting Recognition.

Writing Pad

To display the Writing Pad, click the Handwriting button on the Language bar and then click Writing Pad. The **Writing Pad** resembles a note pad with one or more lines on which you can use freehand to print or write in cursive. You can form letters on the line by moving the mouse while holding down the mouse button. With the **Text button** selected, the handwritten text is converted to typed characters and inserted into the document (Figure B-9a on the next page).

Consider the example in Figure B-9a. With the insertion point at the top of the document, the name, Millie, is written in cursive on the **Pen line** in the Writing Pad. As soon as the name is complete, the Handwriting Recognition service automatically converts the handwriting to typed characters and inserts the name into the document at the location of the insertion point.

With the **Ink button** selected, the text is inserted in handwritten form into the document. Once inserted, you can change the font size and color of the handwritten text (Figure B-9b).

To the right of the note pad is a rectangular toolbar. Use the buttons on this toolbar to adjust the Writing Pad, move the insertion point, and activate other handwriting applications.

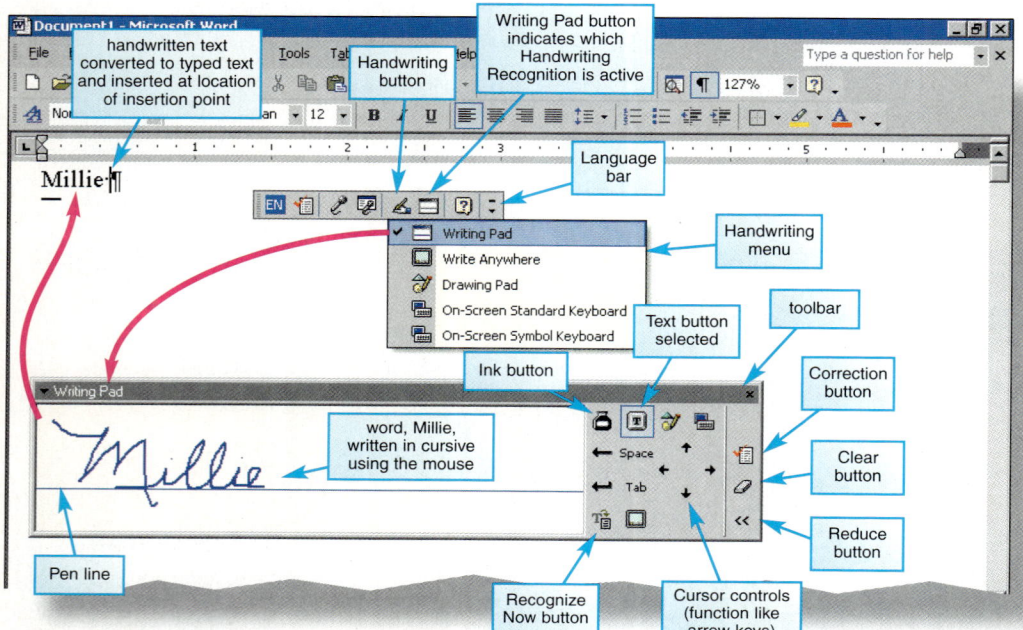

(a) Text Button Selected

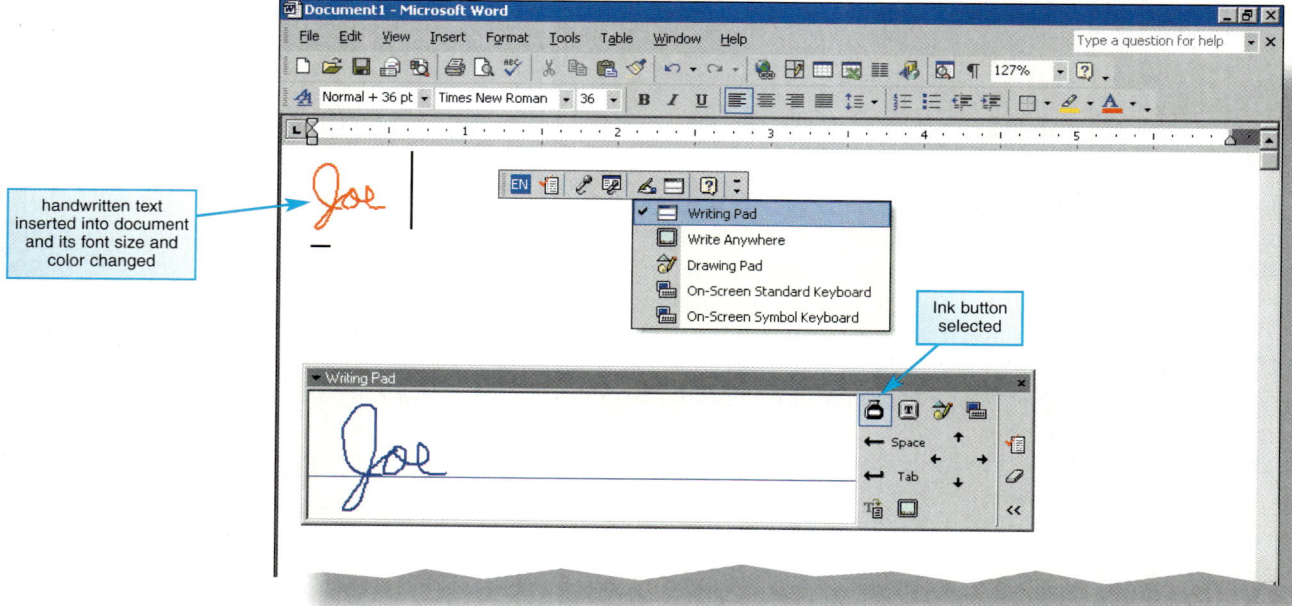

(b) Ink Button Selected

FIGURE B-9

You can customize the Writing Pad by clicking the **Options button** on the left side of the title bar and then clicking the Options command (Figure B-10a). Invoking the **Options command** causes the Handwriting Options dialog box to display. The **Handwriting Options dialog box** contains two sheets: Common and Writing Pad. The **Common sheet** lets you change the pen color and pen width, adjust recognition, and customize the toolbar area of the Writing Pad. The **Writing Pad sheet** allows you to change the background color and the number of lines that display in the Writing Pad. Both sheets contain a **Restore Default button** to restore the settings to what they were when the software was installed initially.

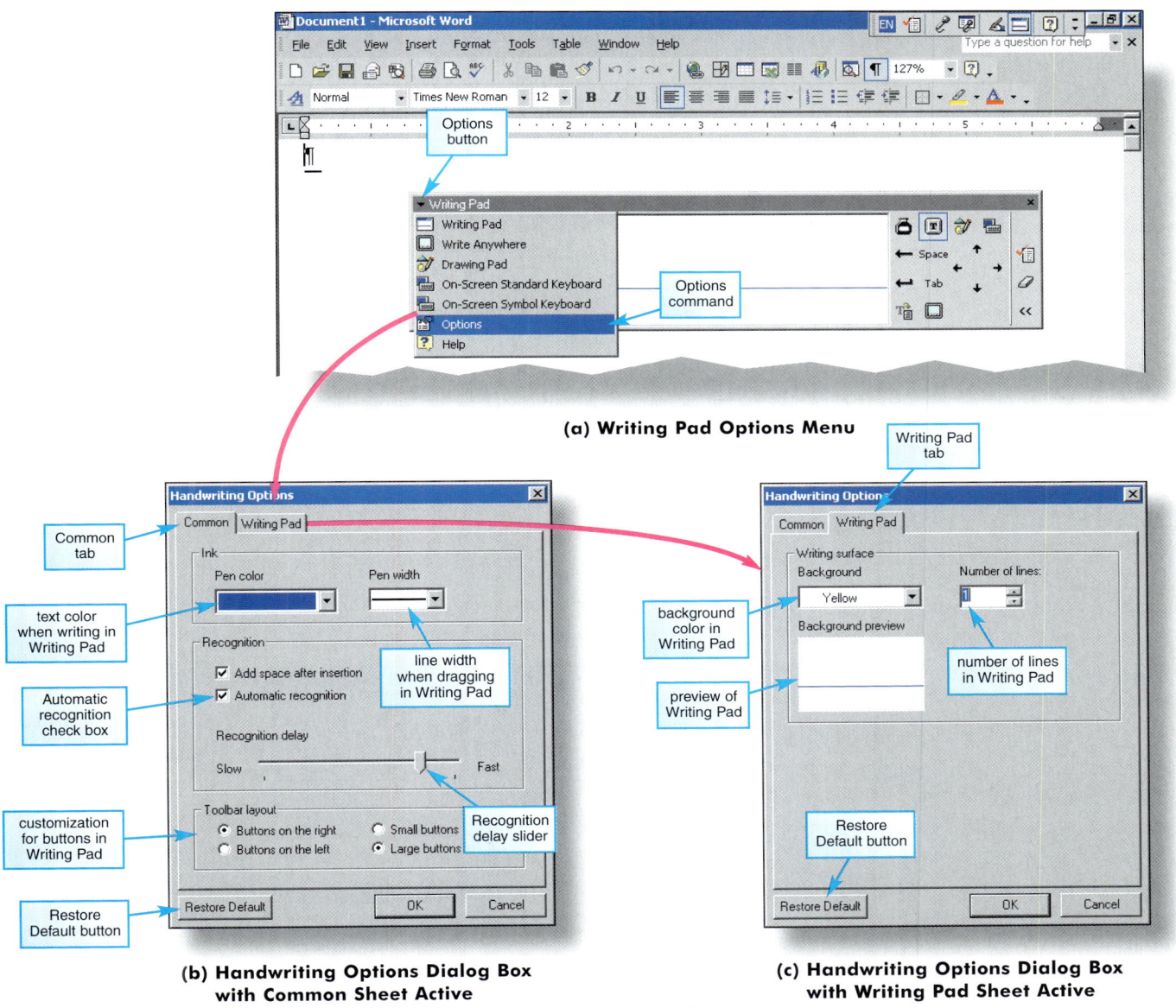

FIGURE B-10

When you first start using the Writing Pad, you may want to remove the check mark from the **Automatic recognition check box** in the Common sheet in the Handwriting Options dialog box (Figure B-10b). With the check mark removed, the Handwriting Recognition service will not interpret what you write in the Writing Pad until you click the **Recognize Now button** on the toolbar (Figure B-9). This allows you to pause and adjust your writing.

The best way to learn how to use the Writing Pad is to practice with it. Also, for more information, click the Help button on the Standard toolbar, click the Answer Wizard tab, and search for the phrase, Handwriting Recognition.

Write Anywhere

Rather than use a Writing Pad, you can write anywhere on the screen by invoking the **Write Anywhere command** on the Handwriting menu (Figure B-11) that displays when you click the Handwriting button on the Language bar. In this case, the entire window is your writing pad.

In Figure B-11, the word, Chip, is written in cursive using the mouse button. Shortly after you finish writing the word, the Handwriting Recognition service

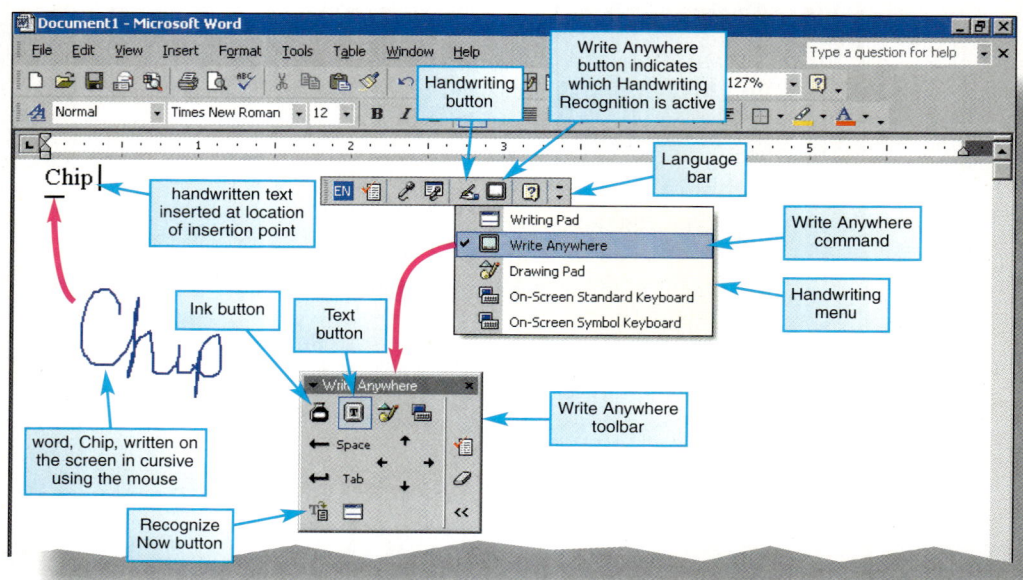

FIGURE B-11

interprets it, assigns it to the location of the insertion point in the document, and erases what you wrote. Similarly to the Writing Pad, Write Anywhere has both an Ink button and a Text button so you can insert either handwritten characters or have them converted to typed text.

It is recommended that when you first start using the Writing Anywhere service that you remove the check mark from the Automatic recognition check box in the Common sheet in the Handwriting Options dialog box (Figure B-10b on the previous page). With the check mark removed, the Handwriting Recognition service will not interpret what you write on the screen until you click the Recognize Now button on the toolbar (Figure B-11).

Write Anywhere is more difficult to use than the Writing Pad, because when you click the mouse button, Word may interpret the action as moving the insertion point rather than starting to write. For this reason, it is recommended that you use the Writing Pad.

Drawing Pad

To display the Drawing Pad, click the Handwriting button on the Language bar and then click Drawing Pad (Figure B-12). With the **Drawing Pad**, you can insert a freehand drawing or sketch into a Word document. To create the drawing, point in the Drawing Pad and move the mouse while holding down the mouse button.

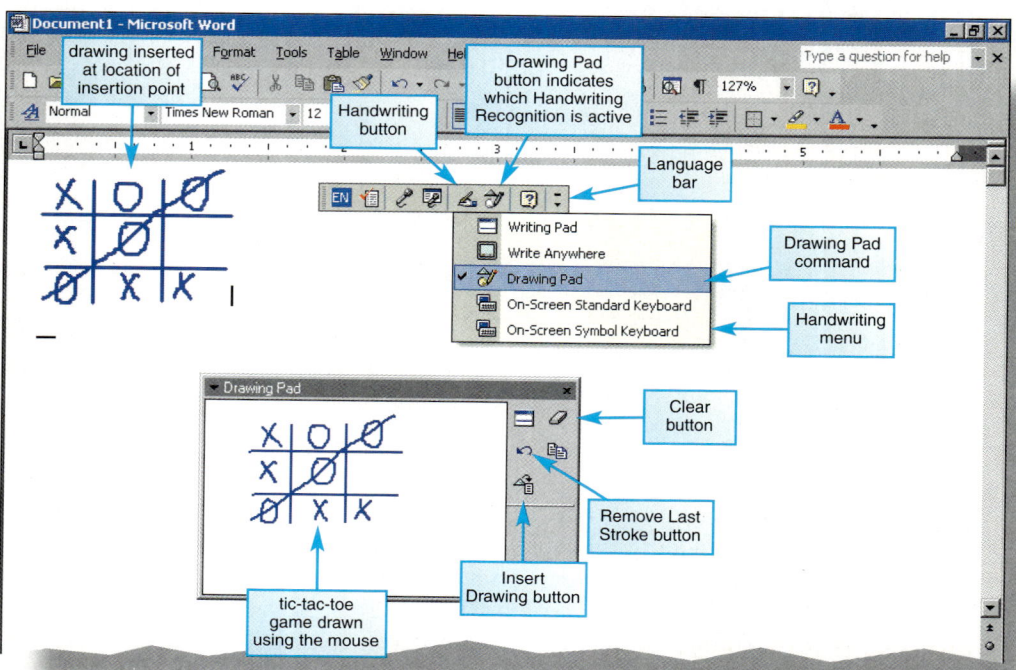

FIGURE B-12

In Figure B-12, the mouse button was used to draw a tic-tac-toe game in the Drawing Pad. To insert the drawing into the Word document at the location of the insertion point, click the Insert Drawing button on the rectangular toolbar to the right of the Drawing Pad. Other buttons on the toolbar allow you to erase a drawing, erase your last drawing stroke, copy the drawing to the Office Clipboard, or activate the Writing Pad.

You can customize the Drawing Pad by clicking the Options button on the left side of the title bar and then clicking the Options command (Figure B-13a). Invoking the **Options command** causes the Draw Options dialog box to display (Figure B-13b). The **Draw Options dialog box** lets you change the pen color and pen width and customize the toolbar area of the Drawing Pad. The dialog box also contains a Restore Default button that restores the settings to what they were when the software was installed initially.

The best way to learn how to use the Drawing Pad is to practice with it. Also, for more information, click the Help button on the Standard toolbar, click the Answer Wizard tab, and search for the phrase, Drawing Pad.

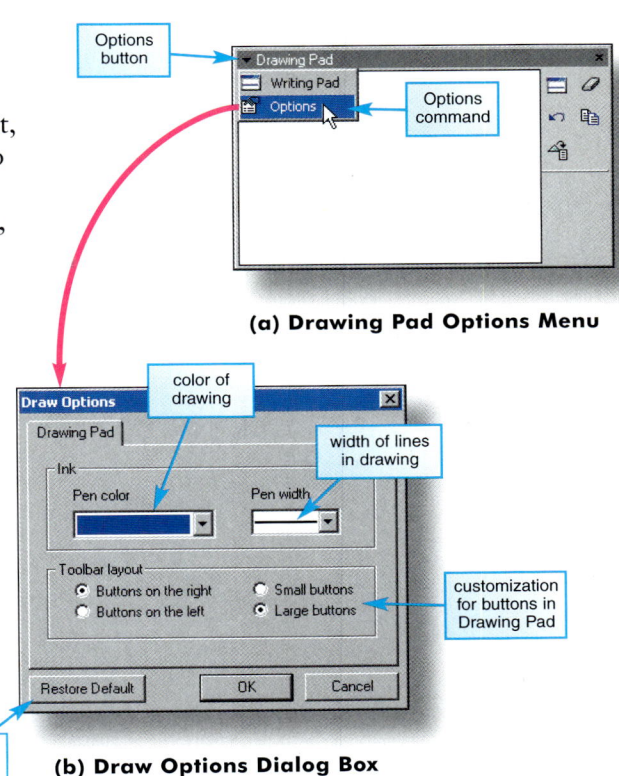

FIGURE B-13

On-Screen Keyboard

The **On-Screen Standard Keyboard command** on the Handwriting menu (Figure B-14) displays an on-screen keyboard. The **on-screen keyboard** lets you enter characters into a document by using your mouse to click the keys. The on-screen keyboard is similar to the type found on handheld computers.

The **On-Screen Symbol Keyboard command** on the Handwriting menu (Figure B-14) displays a special on-screen keyboard that allows you to enter symbols that are not on your keyboard, as well as Unicode characters. **Unicode characters** use a coding scheme capable of representing all the world's current languages.

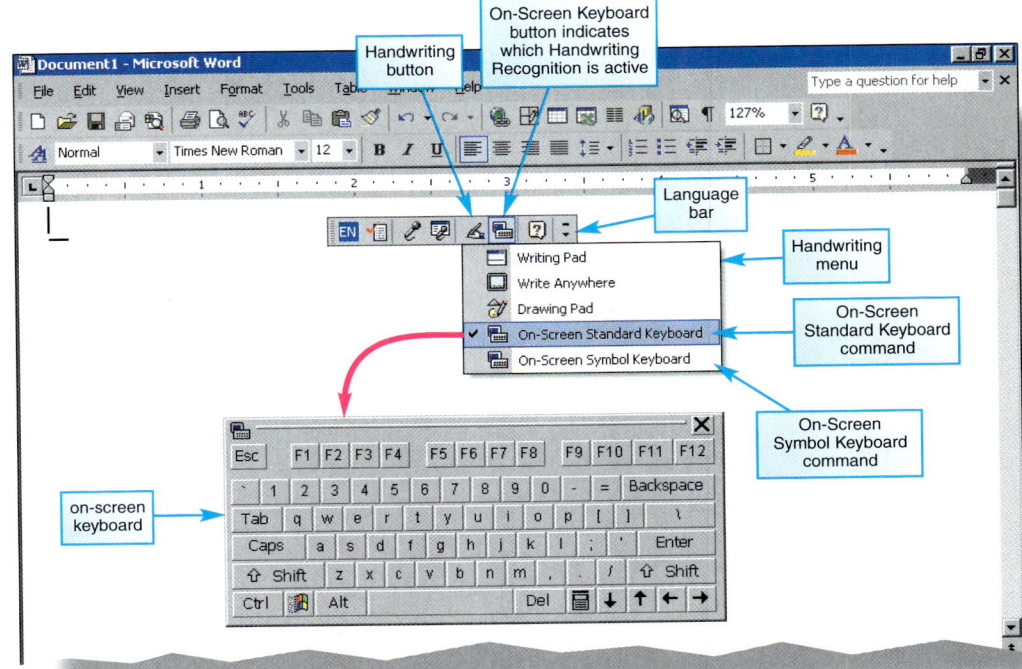

FIGURE B-14

APPENDIX C
Publishing Office Web Pages to a Web Server

With the Office applications, you use the Save as Web Page command on the File menu to save the Web page to a Web server using one of two techniques: Web folders or File Transfer Protocol. A **Web folder** is an Office shortcut to a Web server. **File Transfer Protocol** (**FTP**) is an Internet standard that allows computers to exchange files with other computers on the Internet.

You should contact your network system administrator or technical support staff at your ISP to determine if their Web server supports Web folders, FTP, or both, and to obtain necessary permissions to access the Web server. If you decide to publish Web pages using a Web folder, you must have the Office Server Extensions (OSE) installed on your computer.

Using Web Folders to Publish Office Web Pages

When publishing to a Web folder, someone first must create the Web folder before you can save to it. If you are granted permission to create a Web folder, you must obtain the URL of the Web server, a user name, and possibly a password that allows you to access the Web server. You also must decide on a name for the Web folder. Table C-1 explains how to create a Web folder.

Office adds the name of the Web folder to the list of current Web folders. You can save to this folder, open files in the folder, rename the folder, or perform any operations you would to a folder on your hard disk. You can use your Office program or Windows Explorer to access this folder. Table C-2 explains how to save to a Web folder.

Using FTP to Publish Office Web Pages

When publishing a Web page using FTP, you first must add the FTP location to your computer before you can save to it. An **FTP location**, also called an **FTP site**, is a collection of files that reside on an FTP server. In this case, the FTP server is the Web server.

To add an FTP location, you must obtain the name of the FTP site, which usually is the address (URL) of the FTP server, and a user name and a password that allows you to access the FTP server. You save and open the Web pages on the FTP server using the name of the FTP site. Table C-3 explains how to add an FTP site.

Office adds the name of the FTP site to the FTP locations list in the Save As and Open dialog boxes. You can open and save files using this list. Table C-4 explains how to save to an FTP location.

Table C-1 Creating a Web Folder
1. Click File on the menu bar and then click Save As (or Open).
2. When the Save As dialog box (or Open dialog box) displays, click My Network Places (or Web Folders) on the Places Bar. Double-click Add Network Place (or Add Web Folder).
3. When the Add Network Place Wizard dialog box displays, click the Create a new Network Place option button and then click the Next button. Type the URL of the Web server in the Folder location text box, enter the folder name you want to call the Web folder in the Folder name text box, and then click the Next button. Click Empty Web and then click the Finish button.
4. When the Enter Network Password dialog box displays, type the user name and, if necessary, the password in the respective text boxes and then click the OK button.
5. Close the Save As or the Open dialog box.

Table C-2 Saving to a Web Folder
1. Click File on the menu bar and then click Save As.
2. When the Save As dialog box displays, type the Web page file name in the File name text box. Do not press the ENTER key.
3. Click My Network Places on the Places Bar.
4. Double-click the Web folder name in the Save in list.
5. If the Enter Network Password dialog box displays, type the user name and password in the respective text boxes and then click the OK button.
6. Click the Save button in the Save As dialog box.

Table C-3 Adding an FTP Location
1. Click File on the menu bar and then click Save As (or Open).
2. In the Save As dialog box, click the Save in box arrow and then click Add/Modify FTP Locations in the Save in list; or in the Open dialog box, click the Look in box arrow and then click Add/Modify FTP Locations in the Look in list.
3. When the Add/Modify FTP Locations dialog box displays, type the name of the FTP site in the Name of FTP site text box. If the site allows anonymous logon, click Anonymous in the Log on as area; if you have a user name for the site, click User in the Log on as area and then enter the user name. Enter the password in the Password text box. Click the OK button.
4. Close the Save As or the Open dialog box.

Table C-4 Saving to an FTP Location
1. Click File on the menu bar and then click Save As.
2. When the Save As dialog box displays, type the Web page file name in the File name text box. Do not press the ENTER key.
3. Click the Save in box arrow and then click FTP Locations.
4. Double-click the name of the FTP site to which you wish to save.
5. When the FTP Log On dialog box displays, enter your user name and password and then click the OK button.
6. Click the Save button in the Save As dialog box.

APPENDIX D
Resetting the Word Toolbars and Menus

Word customization capabilities allow you to create custom toolbars by adding and deleting buttons and to personalize menus based on their usage. Each time you start Word, the toolbars and menus display using the same settings as the last time you used it. This appendix shows you how to reset the Standard and Formatting toolbars and menus to their installation settings.

Steps: To Reset the Standard and Formatting Toolbars

1 **Click the Toolbar Options button on the Standard toolbar and then point to Add or Remove Buttons on the Toolbar Options menu.**

The Toolbar Options menu and the Add or Remove Buttons submenu display (Figure D-1).

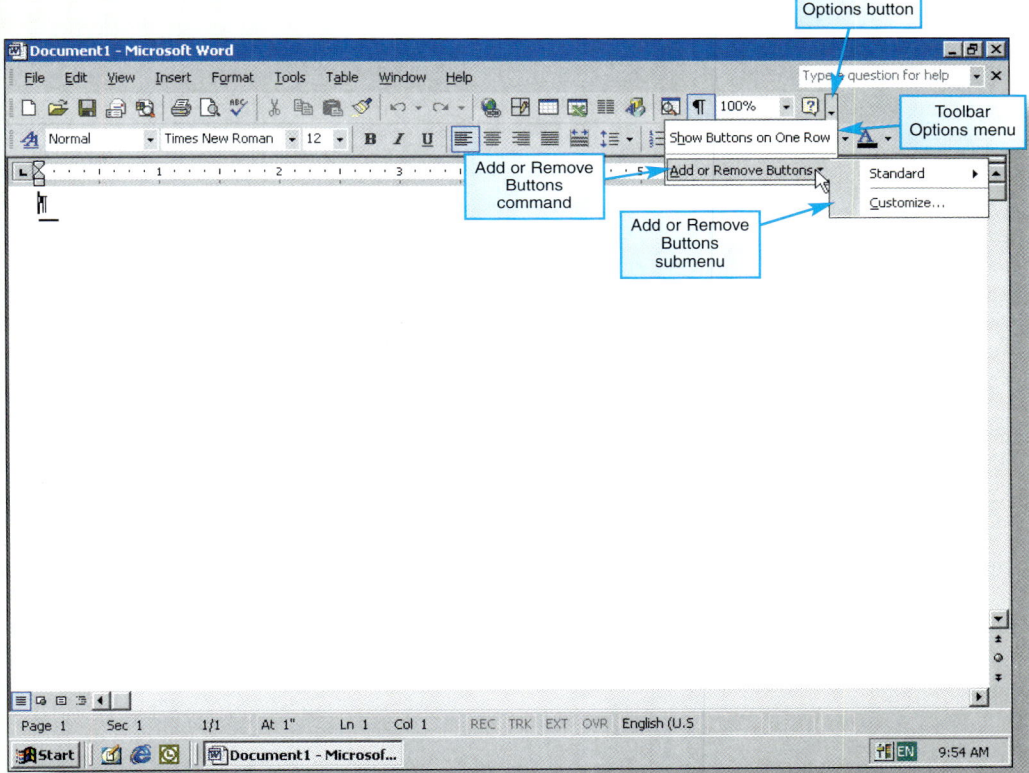

FIGURE D-1

WD D.01

2 **Point to Standard on the Add or Remove Buttons submenu. When the Standard submenu displays, scroll down and then point to Reset Toolbar.**

The Standard submenu displays indicating the buttons and boxes that display on the toolbar (Figure D-2). Clicking a button name with a check mark to the left of the name removes the check mark and then removes the button from the toolbar.

3 **Click Reset Toolbar.**

Word resets the Standard toolbar to its installation settings.

4 **Reset the Formatting toolbar by following Steps 1 through 3 and replacing any reference to the Standard toolbar with the Formatting toolbar.**

Other Ways

1. On View menu point to Toolbars, click Customize on Toolbars submenu, click Toolbars tab, click toolbar name, click Reset button, click OK button, click Close button
2. Right-click toolbar, click Customize, click Toolbars tab, click toolbar name, click Reset button, click OK button, click Close button
3. In Voice Command mode, say "View, Toolbars, Customize, Toolbars, [toolbar name], Reset, OK, Close"

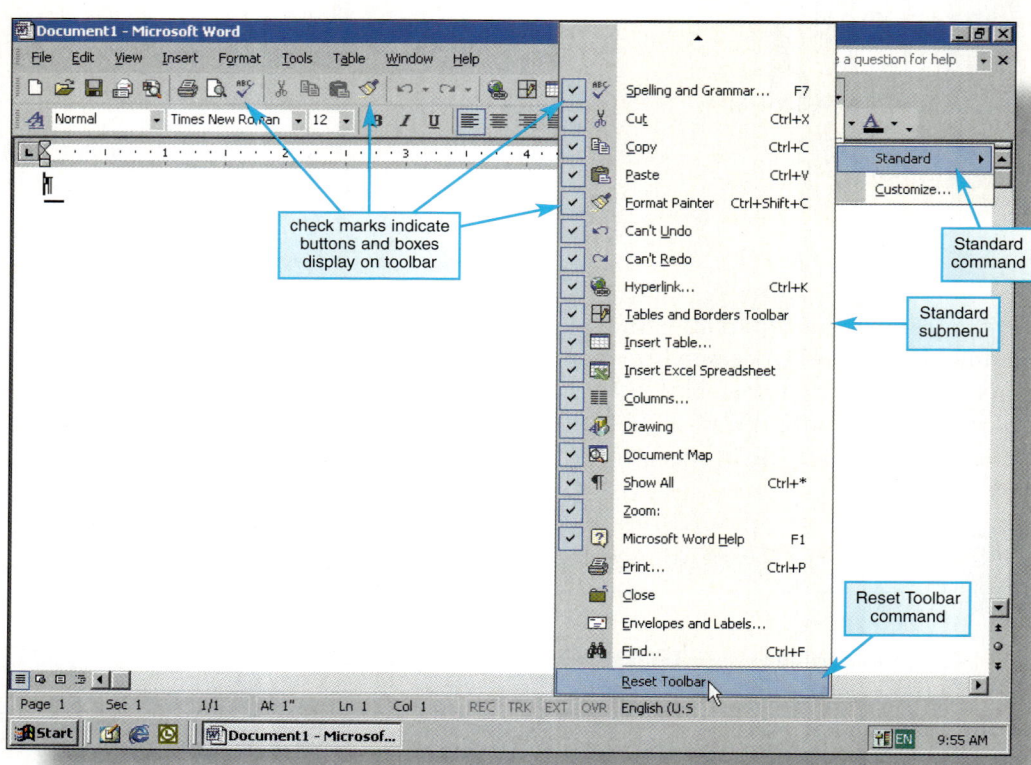

FIGURE D-2

Steps: To Reset Menus

1 **Click the Toolbar Options button on the Standard toolbar and then point to Add or Remove Buttons on the Toolbar Options menu. Point to Customize on the Add or Remove Buttons submenu.**

The Toolbar Options menu and the Add or Remove Buttons submenu display (Figure D-3).

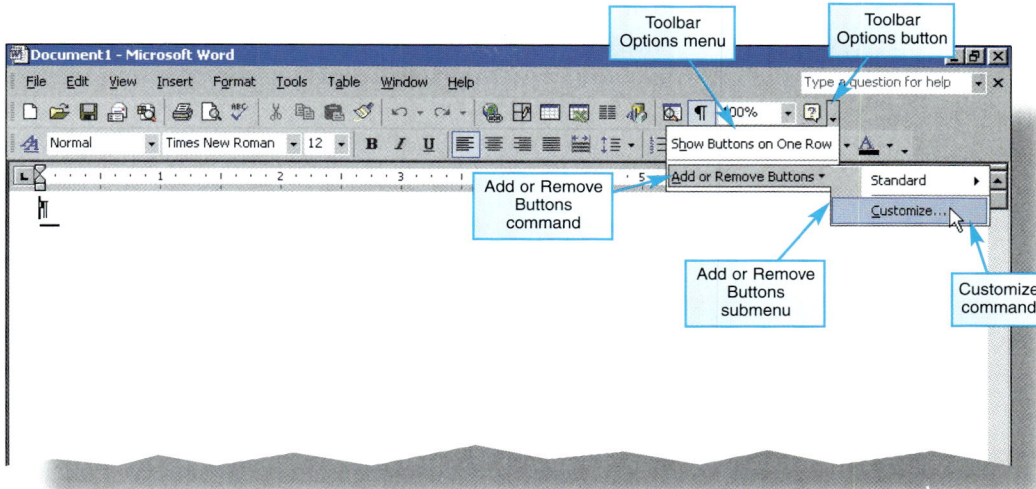

FIGURE D-3

2 **Click Customize. When the Customize dialog box displays, click the Options tab and then point to the Reset my usage data button.**

The Customize dialog box displays (Figure D-4). The *Customize dialog box* contains three tabbed sheets used for customizing the Word toolbars and menus.

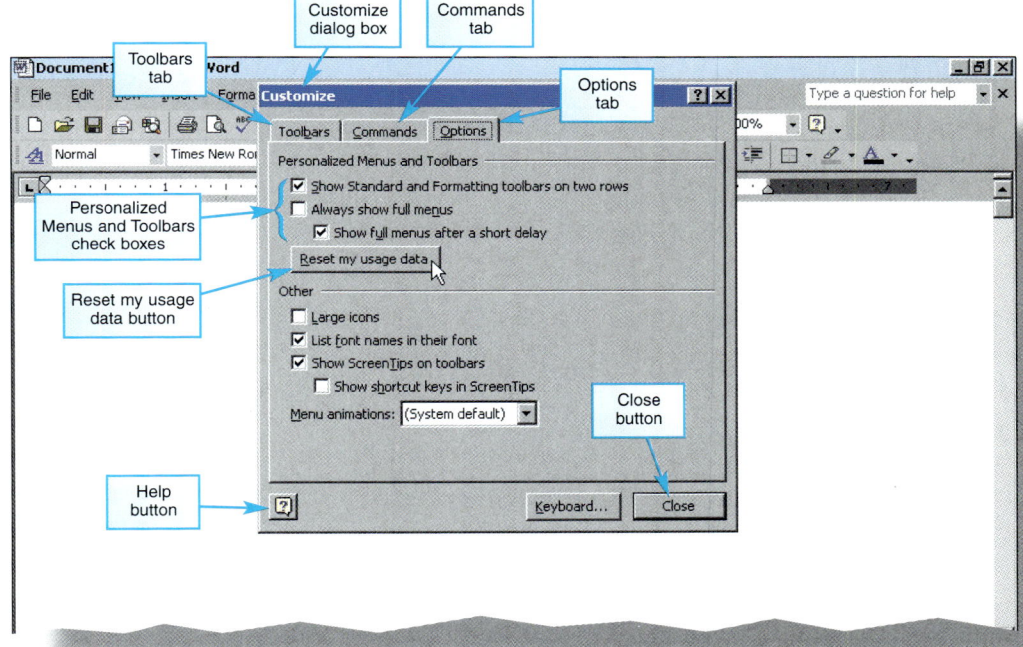

FIGURE D-3

3 **Click the Reset my usage data button. When the Microsoft Word dialog box displays, click the Yes button. Click the Close button in the Customize dialog box.**

Word resets the menus to the installation settings.

1. On View menu point to Toolbars, click Customize on Toolbars submenu, click Options tab, click Reset my usage data button, click Yes button, click Close button
2. In Voice Command mode, say "View, Toolbars, Customize, Options, Reset my usage data, Yes, Close"

In the Options sheet in the Customize dialog box shown in Figure D-4 on the previous page, you can turn off toolbars displaying on two rows and turn off short menus by removing the check marks from the two top check boxes. Click the Help button in the lower-left corner of the Customize dialog box to display Help topics that will assist you in customizing toolbars and menus.

Using the Commands sheet, you can add buttons to toolbars and commands to menus. Recall that the menu bar at the top of the Word window is a special toolbar. To add buttons, click the Commands tab in the Customize dialog box. Click a category name in the Categories list and then drag the command name in the Commands list to a toolbar. To add commands to a menu, click a category name in the Categories list, drag the command name in the Commands list to the menu name on the menu bar, and then, when the menu displays, drag the command to the desired location in the menu list of commands.

In the Toolbars sheet, you can add new toolbars and reset existing toolbars. If you add commands to menus as described in the previous paragraph and want to reset the menus to their default settings, do the following: (1) Click View on the menu bar and then point to Toolbars; (2) click Customize; (3) click the Toolbars tab; (4) click Menu Bar in the Toolbars list; (5) click the Reset button; (6) click the OK button; and then (7) click the Close button.

APPENDIX E
Microsoft Office User Specialist Certification Program

What Is MOUS Certification?

The Microsoft Office User Specialist (MOUS) Certification Program provides a framework for measuring your proficiency with the Microsoft Office XP applications, such as Word 2002, Excel 2002, Access 2002, PowerPoint 2002, Outlook 2002, and FrontPage 2002. The levels of certification are described in Table E-1.

Table E-1 Levels of MOUS Certification

LEVEL	DESCRIPTION	REQUIREMENTS	CREDENTIAL AWARDED
Expert	Indicates that you have a comprehensive understanding of the advanced features in a specific Microsoft Office XP application	Pass any ONE of the Expert exams: Microsoft Word 2002 Expert Microsoft Excel 2002 Expert Microsoft Access 2002 Expert Microsoft Outlook 2002 Expert Microsoft FrontPage 2002 Expert	Candidates will be awarded one certificate for each of the Expert exams they have passed: Microsoft Office User Specialist: Microsoft Word 2002 Expert Microsoft Office User Specialist: Microsoft Excel 2002 Expert Microsoft Office User Specialist: Microsoft Access 2002 Expert Microsoft Office User Specialist: Microsoft Outlook 2002 Expert Microsoft Office User Specialist: Microsoft FrontPage 2002 Expert
Core	Indicates that you have a comprehensive understanding of the core features in a specific Microsoft Office 2002 application	Pass any ONE of the Core exams: Microsoft Word 2002 Core Microsoft Excel 2002 Core Microsoft Access 2002 Core Microsoft Outlook 2002 Core Microsoft FrontPage 2002 Core	Candidates will be awarded one certificate for each of the Core exams they have passed: Microsoft Office User Specialist: Microsoft Word 2002 Microsoft Office User Specialist: Microsoft Excel 2002 Microsoft Office User Specialist: Microsoft Access 2002 Microsoft Office User Specialist: Microsoft Outlook 2002 Microsoft Office User Specialist: Microsoft FrontPage 2002
Comprehensive	Indicates that you have a comprehensive understanding of the features in Microsoft PowerPoint 2002	Pass the Microsoft PowerPoint 2002 Comprehensive Exam	Candidates will be awarded one certificate for the Microsoft PowerPoint 2002 Comprehensive exam passed.

Why Should You Get Certified?

Being a Microsoft Office User Specialist provides a valuable industry credential — proof that you have the Office XP applications skills required by employers. By passing one or more MOUS certification exams, you demonstrate your proficiency in a given Office XP application to employers. With over 100 million copies of Office in use around the world, Microsoft is targeting Office XP certification to a wide variety of companies. These companies include temporary employment agencies that want to prove the expertise of their workers, large corporations looking for a way to measure the skill set of employees, and training companies and educational institutions seeking Microsoft Office XP teachers with appropriate credentials.

The MOUS Exams

You pay $50 to $100 each time you take an exam, whether you pass or fail. The fee varies among testing centers. The Expert exams, which you can take up to 60 minutes to complete, consists of between 40 and 60 tasks that you perform online. The tasks require you to use the application just as you would in doing your job. The Core exams contain fewer tasks, and you will have slightly less time to complete them. The tasks you will perform differ on the two types of exams.

How Can You Prepare for the MOUS Exams?

The Shelly Cashman Series® offers several Microsoft-approved textbooks that cover the required objectives on the MOUS exams. For a listing of the textbooks, visit the Shelly Cashman Series MOUS site at scsite.com/offxp/cert.htm and click the link Shelly Cashman Series Office XP Microsoft-Approved MOUS Textbooks (Figure E-1). After using any of the books listed in an instructor-led course, you will be prepared to take the MOUS exam indicated.

How to Find an Authorized Testing Center

You can locate a testing center by calling 1-800-933-4493 in North America or visiting the Shelly Cashman Series MOUS site at scsite.com/offxp/cert.htm and then clicking the link Locate an Authorized Testing Center Near You (Figure E-1). At this Web site, you can look for testing centers around the world.

Shelly Cashman Series MOUS Web Page

The Shelly Cashman Series MOUS Web page (Figure E-1) has more than fifteen Web sites you can visit to obtain additional information on the MOUS Certification Program. The Web page (scsite.com/offxp/cert.htm) includes links to general information on certification, choosing an application for certification, preparing for the certification exam, and taking and passing the certification exam.

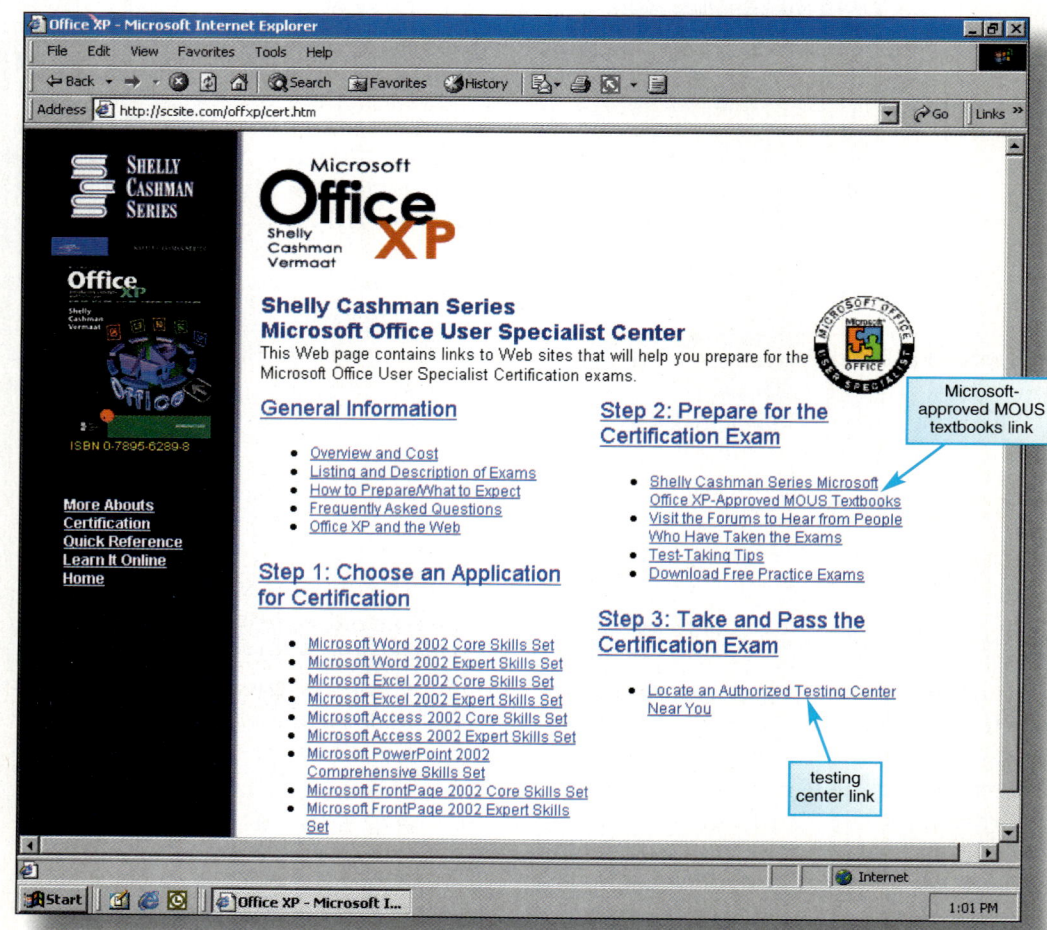

FIGURE E-1

Microsoft Office User Specialist Certification Map • WD E.03

APPENDIX E

Microsoft Word 2002 User Specialist Certification Core and Expert Maps

This book has been approved by Microsoft as courseware for the Microsoft Office User Specialist (MOUS) program. After completing the projects and exercises in this book, students will be prepared to take the Core-level and Expert-level Microsoft Office User Specialist Examinations for Microsoft Word 2002. Table E-2 lists the Microsoft Word 2002 Core Exam skill sets, activities, page numbers where the activities are demonstrated, and page numbers where the activities can be practiced. Table E-3 lists the Microsoft Word 2002 Expert Exam skill sets, activities, page numbers where the activities are demonstrated, and page numbers where the activities can be practiced.

Table E-2 Microsoft Word 2002 MOUS Core Skill Sets, Activities, and Locations in Book

SKILL SET	ACTIVITY	ACTIVITY DEMONSTRATED IN BOOK	ACTIVITY EXERCISE IN BOOK
I. Inserting and Modifying Text	A. Insert, modify, and move text and symbols	WD 1.21-26, WD 1.58, WD 2.20-24, WD 2.38-39, WD 2.46, WD 2.48-49, WD 3.19-20, WD 6.17-18, WD 6.36-37, WD 6.45-47	WD 1.64-65 (Steps 9, 13, 14), WD 2.57 (Steps 1-5), WD 2.59 (In the Lab 1 Step 2), WD 2.61-62 (In the Lab 2 Part 1 Step 2, Part 2 Step 4), WD 2.62-63 (In the Lab 3 Step 2), WD 3.64 (In the Lab 1 Step 2), WD 3.65 (In the Lab 2 Step 1), WD 6.77 (In the Lab 1 Steps 2, 6), WD 6.78 (In the Lab 2 Step 2), WD 6.79 (In the Lab 3 Step 2), WD 6.80 (Cases & Places 4)
	B. Apply and modify text formats	WD 1.20, WD 1.32, WD 1.35-36, WD 1.41, WD 1.43, WD 1.45, WD 3.28, WD 4.50-52, WD 6.28-29, WD 6.61-62	WD 1.66-67 (In the Lab 1 Steps 1, 5, 8-10), WD 1.67-68 (In the Lab 2 Steps 1, 5, 8-10), WD 1.68-69 (In the Lab 3 Steps 1, 5, 7, 9-10); WD 1.70-71 (Cases & Places 1-7), WD 2.57 (Apply Your Knowledge Steps 3, 7), WD 2.60-62 (In the Lab 2 Part 2 Steps 8-9), WD 3.65 (In the Lab 2 Step 1), WD 4.72-73 (In the Lab 1 Step 3a), WD 6.77 (In the Lab 1 Step 4), WD 6.78 (In the Lab 2 Step 4), WD 6.79 (In the Lab 3 Step 5)
	C. Correct spelling and grammar usage	WD 1.22, WD 1.27-29, WD 2.50-52	WD 1.64-65 (Apply Your Knowledge Steps 1-8), WD 1.66 (In the Lab 1 Step 3), WD 1.67-68 (In the Lab 2 Step 3), WD 1.68 (In the Lab 3 Step 3), WD 2.58-59 (In the Lab 1 Step 4), WD 2.60-61 (In the Lab 2 Step 4), WD 2.62 (In the Lab 3 Step 4)
	D. Apply font and text effects	WD 4.13-15, WD 4.38-39, WD 6.65-67	WD 4.72-73 (In the Lab 1), WD 4.74-75 (In the Lab 2), WD 4.76-78 (In the Lab 3), WD 6.80 (Cases & Places 1)
	E. Enter and format Date and Time	WD 3.43-44, WD 5.30-31	WD 3.65 (In the Lab 2 Step 2), WD 5.76-77 (In the Lab 2 Step 3), WD 5.80 (Cases & Places 1)
	F. Apply character styles		WD 5.76-77 (In the Lab 2 Step 3), WD 5.80 (Cases & Places 1) WD 4.72-73 (In the Lab 1 Step 3a)
II. Creating and Modifying Paragraphs	A. Modify paragraph formats	WD 1.32, WD 1.37-38, WD 2.10, WD 2.17, WD 2.18 Table 2-2, WD 2.19, WD 2.36-38, WD 3.21, WD 3.37-38, WD 4.08-11, WD 6.26-27, WD 6.34-35, WD 6.39-40	WD 1.66-67 (In the Lab 1 Steps 6-7, 11), WD 1.67-68 (In the Lab 2 Steps 6-7, 11), WD 1.68-69 (In the Lab 3 Steps 6-8, 11); WD 1.70-71 (Cases & Places 1-7), WD 2.58-59 (In the Lab 1 Step 1), WD 2.60-62 (In the Lab 2 Step 1), WD 2.62 (In the Lab 1 Step 1), WD 3.64 (In the Lab 1 Step 2) WD 3.65 (In the Lab 2 Step 1), WD 4.72-73 (In the Lab 1, Step 1), WD 4.74-75 (In the Lab 2 Step 1), WD 4.76-78, In the Lab 3 Step 1), WD 6.77 (In the Lab 1 Steps 1, 6), WD 6.79 (In the Lab 3 Steps 3, 5)
	B. Set and modify tabs	WD 3.30-32, WD 3.42-43	WD 3.65 (In the Lab 2 Step 2), WD 3.66 (Cases & Places 5)
	C. Apply bullet, outline, and numbering format to paragraphs	WD 3.54-56, WD 5.38-41	WD 1.68 (In the Lab 3 Step 8), WD 3.64 (In the Lab 1), WD 3.65 (In the Lab 2), WD 3.66 (Cases & Places 5), WD 5.76-77 (In the Lab 2 Step 5), WD 5.80 (Cases & Places 1), WD 5.80 (Cases & Places 1)
	D. Apply paragraph styles	WD 5.41-42	WD 5.76-77 (In the Lab 2 Step 5), WD 5.80 (Cases & Places 1)

Table E-2 Microsoft Word 2002 MOUS Core Skill Sets, Activities, and Locations in Book *(continued)*

SKILL SET	ACTIVITY	ACTIVITY DEMONSTRATED IN BOOK	ACTIVITY EXERCISE IN BOOK
III. Formatting Documents	A. Create and modify a header and a footer	WD 2.11-15, WD 4.29-32	WD 2.58-59 (In the Lab 1 Step 1), WD 2.60-62 (In the Lab 2 Step 1), WD 2.62-63 (In the Lab 3 Step 1), WD 4.76-78 (In the Lab 3 Steps 6-8), WD 4.79-80 (Cases & Places 5-6)
	B. Apply and modify column settings	WD 6.23-35, WD 6.43-44, WD 6.48, WD 6.59-60	WD 6.77 (In the Lab 1 Steps 2-5), WD 6.78 (In the Lab 2 Steps 2-4), WD 6.79 (In the Lab 3 Steps 2-5), WD 6.80 (Cases & Places 1-4)
	C. Modify document layout and Page Setup options	WD 2.08, WD 2.14, WD 2.33, WD 4.22, WD 4.29-30, WD 5.66, WD 6.30	WD 2.59 (In the Lab 1 Steps 1-2), WD 4.72-73 (In the Lab 1 Step 2), WD 4.74-75 (In the Lab 2 Step 2), WD 4.76-78 (In the Lab 3 Steps 2, 6), WD 5.74-75 (In the Lab 1 Step 10), WD 5.76-77 (In the Lab 2 Step 10), WD 6.80 (Cases & Places 4)
	D. Create and modify tables	WD 3.49-54, WD 4.32-37, WD 4.53-63, WD 5.67	WD 3.63 (Apply Your Knowledge Steps 1-8), WD 3.65 (In the Lab 2), WD 4.70-71 (Apply Your Knowledge Steps 1-14), WD 4.72-73 (In the Lab 1 Step 3b), WD 4.73-74 (In the Lab 2 Step 3), WD 4.76-78 (In the Lab 3 Steps 4-5), WD 4.79-80 (Cases & Places 1-6), WD 5.74-75 (In the Lab 1 Step 10), WD 5.76-77 (In the Lab 2 Step 10)
	E. Preview and Print documents, envelopes, and labels	WD 1.54-55, WD 3.25-26, WD 3.57-58, WD 4.65	WD 1.64-65 ((Apply Your Knowledge Step 16), WD 1.66-67 (In the Lab 1 Step 15), WD 1.67-68 (In the Lab 2 Steps 13, 15), WD 1.68-69 (In the Lab 3 Steps 13, 15), WD 3.64 (In the Lab 1 Step 5), WD 3.65 (In the Lab 2 Steps 5, 6)
IV. Managing Documents	A. Manage files and folders for documents	WD 5.20-21	WD 5.74-75 (In the Lab 1 Step 4), WD 5.76-77 (In the Lab 2 Step 4), WD 5.78-79 (In the Lab 3 Step 3), WD 5.80 (Cases & Places 1-3)
	B. Create documents using templates	WD 3.08-14, WDW 1.05-08, WD 5.08-10	WD 3.64 (In the Lab 1 Steps 1-2), WD 3.66 (Cases & Places 1-5), WDW 1.14 (In the Lab 2), WD 5.74-75 (In the Lab 1 Steps 1-2), WD 5.76-77 (In the Lab 2 Steps 1-2), WD 5.78-79 (In the Lab 3 Steps 1-2)
	C. Save documents using different names and file formats	WD 1.30, WD 1.53-54, WDW 1.03	WD 1.65 (Apply Your Knowledge Step 15), WD 1.66-67 (In the Lab 1 Steps 4, 14), WD 1.67-68 (In the Lab 2 Steps 4, 14), WD 1.68-69 (In the Lab 3 Steps 4, 14)
V. Working with Graphics	A. Insert images and graphics	WD 1.46-49, WD 5.11-19, WD 6.55-57	WD 1.66-67 (In the Lab 1 Step 12), WD 1.67-68 (In the Lab 2 Step 12), WD 1.68-69 (In the Lab 3 Steps 12 -13), WD 1.70-71 (Cases & Places 1-7), WD 5.74-75 (In the Lab 1 Step 2), WD 5.76-77 (In the Lab 2 Step 2), WD 5.80 (Cases & Places 1-3), WD 6.78 (In the Lab 2 Step 2), WD 6.79 (In the Lab 3 Step 3)
	B. Create and modify diagrams and charts	WD 4.39-45, WD 6.49-54, WD 6.59 -60	WD 4.74-75 (In the Lab 2 Step 3), WD 4.76-78 (In the Lab 3 Step 5), WD 4.79-80 (Cases & Places 2-6), WD 6.78 (In the Lab 2 Step 4)
VI. Workgroup Collaboration	A. Compare and Merge documents	WD 6.71-73	WD 6.76 (Apply Your Knowledge Step 9)
	B. Insert, view, and edit comments	WD 6.68-71	WD 6.76 (Apply Your Knowledge Steps 1-7)
	C. Convert documents into Web pages	WDW 1.03, WDW 1.11	WDW 1.14 (In the Lab 1), WDW 1.14 (In the Lab 2)

Table E-3 Microsoft Word 2002 MOUS Expert Skill Sets, Activities, and Locations in Book

SKILL SET	ACTIVITY	ACTIVITY DEMONSTRATED IN BOOK	ACTIVITY EXERCISE IN BOOK
I. Customizing Paragraphs	A. Control Pagination	WD 4.46-48, WD 9.32-33	WD 4.76-78 (In the Lab 3 Steps 5-6), WD 4.79-80 (Cases & Places 2-6), WD 9.81-82 (Cases and Places 1-6)
	B. Sort paragraphs in lists and tables	WD 2.41-42, WD 5.52, WD 5.68	WD 2.60-62 (In the Lab 2 Step 3), WD 5.73 (In the Lab Step 4), WD 5.74-75 (In the Lab 1 Step 10), WD 5.76-77 (In the Lab 2 Step 10), WD 5.80 (Cases & Places 1)
II. Formatting Documents	A. Create and format document sections	WD 3.39, WD 4.12, WD 4.18-20, WD 4.23, WD 4.66-67, WD 5.19-20, WD 9.61-63	WD 4.70-71 (Apply Your Knowledge Step 17), WD 4.72-73 (In the Lab 1 Step 2), WD 4.74-75 (In the Lab 2 Step 2), WD 4.76-78 (In the Lab 3 Steps 2, 14), WD 5.74-75 (In the Lab 1 Step 3), WD 5.76-77 (In the Lab Step 3), WD 9.73-75 (In the Lab 1 Step 12), WD 9.78-80 (In the Lab 3 Steps 14-15)
	B. Create and apply character and paragraph styles	WD 2.27-31, WD 4.50-53, WD 5.41-42, WD 8.17-19	WD 2.60-62 (In the Lab 2 Part 2 Step 8), WD 4.72-73 (In the Lab 1 Step 3a), WD 5.76-77 (In the Lab 2 Step 5), WD 5.80 (Cases & Places 1), WD 8.73-74 (In the Lab 1 Step 4), WD 8.74-75 (In the Lab 2 Step 4), WD 8.76-77 (In the Lab 3 Step 4), WD 9.75-76 (In the Lab 1 Step 11)
	C. Create and update document indexes, tables of contents, figures, and authorities	WD 9.26-28, WD 9.30-32, WD 9.54-59, WD 9.67-69	WD 9.73-75 (In the Lab 1 Steps 2, 4, 9, 10, 14), WD 9.75-77 (In the Lab 2 Steps 4, 6, 10-13), WD 9.78-80 (In the Lab 3 Steps 2, 5, 11-13, 17)
	D. Create cross-references	WD 9.28-30	WD 9.73-75 (In the Lab 1 Step 3), WD 9.75-77 (In the Lab 2 Step 8), WD 9.78-80 (In the Lab 3 Step 4)
	E. Add and revise endnotes and footnotes	WD 2.24-32	WD 2.60-63 (In the Lab 2 Part 1 Step 2, Part 2 Steps 3-4, 7-9), WD 3.62-63 (In the Lab 3 Steps 3- 4), WD 2.64 (Cases & Places 1-5)
	F. Create and manage master documents and subdocuments	WD 9.36-48, WD 9.64-65	WD 9.73-75 (In the Lab 1 Steps 6-8), WD 9.78-80 (In the Lab 3 Steps 7-10), WD 9.81 (Cases & Places 2, 4-6)
	G. Move within documents	WD 2.43-44, WD 9.59-61, WD 9.66-67, WD 9.69	WD 2.62 (In the Lab 2 Part 2 Step 4), WD 9.75-77 (In the Lab 2 Step 14), WD 9.81 (Cases & Places 2, 4-6)
	H. Create and modify forms using various form controls	WD 7.08-47	WD 7.63-64 (In the Lab 1), WD 7.64-66 (In the Lab 2), WD 7.66-67 (In the Lab 3), WD 7.68-69 (Cases & Places 1-3)
	I. Create forms and prepare forms for distribution	WD 7.47-48, WD 7.57-59, WD 8.08, WD 8.61	WD 7.63-64 (In the Lab 1 Steps 8-9), WD 7.64-66 (In the Lab 2 Steps 9-11), WD 7.66-67 (In the Lab 3 Steps 8-10), WD 7.68-69 (Cases & Places 1-3), WD 8.73-74 (In the Lab 1 Steps 8-9), WD 8.74-75 (In the Lab 2 Steps 9,11), WD 8.76-77 (In the Lab 3 Steps 14-15)
III. Customizing Tables	A. Use Excel data in tables	WDI 2.04-12	WDI 2.14 (In the Lab 1), WDI 2.14 (In the Lab 2), WDI 2.14 (In the Lab 3)
	B. Perform calculations in Word tables	WD 4.33-34, WD 4.61	WD 3.63 (Apply Your Knowledge Step 4), WD 4.70-71 (Apply Your Knowledge Steps 1, 4, 9-10), WD 4.76-78 (In the Lab 3 Step 7)
IV. Creating and Modifying Graphics	A. Create, modify, and position graphics	WD 1.50-53, WD 3.29-30, WD 4.16, WD 4.40-41, WD 4.54-57, WD 5.11-18, WD 6.09-14, WD 6.21-22, WD 6.36-38, WD 6.41, WD 6.49, WD 6.51-54, WD 6.55-57, WD 6.59-60, WD 7.38-41, WD 8.19-21, WD 9.49-54	WD 1.67-68 (In the Lab 2 Steps 12-13), WD 1.68-69 (In the Lab 3 Steps 12-13), WD 4.72-73 (In the Lab 1 Steps 1, 3b), WD 4.74-75 (In the Lab 2 Steps 1, 3), WD 4.76-78 (In the Lab 3 Steps 1, 4, 7), WD 5.74-75 (In the Lab 1 Step 2), WD 5.76-77 (In the Lab 2 Step 2), WD 5.80 (Cases & Places 1-3), WD 6.77 (In the Lab 1 Steps 1, 6), WD 6.78 (In the Lab 2 Steps 1-2, 4), WD 6.79 (In the Lab 3 Steps 1, 3), WD 7.63-64 (In the Lab 1 Step 6), WD 7.64-66 (In the Lab 2 Steps 6-7), WD 7.66-67 (In the Lab 3 Step 6), WD 7.68-69 (Cases & Places 1-3), WD 8.74-75 (In the Lab 2 Step 3), WD 8.76-77 (In the Lab 3 Step 3), WD 8.78-79 (Cases & Places 1-3), WD 9.75-77 (In the Lab 2 Steps 4-5), WD 9.81-82 (Cases & Places 4-6)
	B. Create and modify charts using data from other applications	WD 4.45 (More About Charts), WDI 2.06-12	WDI 2.14 (In the Lab 1), WDI 2.14 (In the Lab 2), WDI 2.14 (In the Lab 3)

Table E-3 Microsoft Word 2002 MOUS Expert Skill Sets, Activities, and Locations in Book (continued)

SKILL SET	ACTIVITY	ACTIVITY DEMONSTRATED IN BOOK	ACTIVITY EXERCISE IN BOOK
	C. Align text and graphics	WD 4.60, WD 4.62, WD 4.64-65, WD 6.11-13, WD 6.20-22, WD 6.28-29, WD 6.36-42, WD 6.55-57, WD 6.59-60 WD 7.41	WD 4.72-73 (In the Lab 1 Step 3b), WD 4.76-78 (In the Lab 3 Step 11), WD 4.79-80 (Cases & Places 2-6), WD 6.77 (In the Lab 1), WD 6.78 (In the Lab 2), WD 6.79 (In the Lab 3)
V. Customizing Word	A. Create, edit, and run macros	WD 8.23-27, WD 8.32-44, WD 8.46-50, WD 8.36-37, WD 8.51	WD 8.71-72 (Apply Your Knowledge), WD 8.73-74 (In the Lab 1 Steps 5-7), WD 8.74-75 (In the Lab 2 Steps 5-8), WD 8.76-77 (In the Lab 3 Steps 5-13), WD 8.78-79 (Cases & Places 1-3, 5-6)
	B. Customize menus and toolbars	WD 8.28-32	WD 8.76-77 (In the Lab 3 Steps 9, 13)
VI. Workgroup Collaboration	A. Track, accept, and reject changes to documents	WD 6.70, WD 9.11-23	WD 6.76 (Steps 2, 3, 5), WD 9.72-73 (Steps 1-12), WD 9.81-82 (Cases & Places 1)
	B. Merge input from several reviewers	WD 9.08-09, WD 9.21-23	WD 9.81-82 (Cases & Places 1)
	C. Insert and modify hyperlinks to other documents and Web pages	WD 2.39-40, WD 2.53, WD 3.40, WDW 1.04, WDW 1.10	WD 2.57 (Apply Your Knowledge Steps 6-7), WD 2.58-59 (In the Lab 1 Steps 3, 6), WD 2.60-61 (In the Lab 1 Part 1 Steps 3, 6), WD 2.65 (In the Lab 2 Step 2), WDW 1.14 (In the Lab 2)
	D. Create and edit Web documents in Word	WDW 1.12-13, Appendix C	WDW 1.14 (In the Lab 1), WDW 1.14 (In the Lab 2), WD 7.66-67 (In the Lab 3 Step 10), WD 7.68-69 (Cases & Places 2)
	E. Create document versions	WD 9.16-17	WD 9.81-82 (Cases & Places 1)
	F. Protect documents	WD 7.47-48, WD 8.08, WD 8.61, WD 9.33-35, WD 9.40	WD 7.63-64 (In the Lab 1 Step 8), WD 7.64-66 (In the Lab 2, Step 9), WD 7.66-67 (In the Lab 3 Step 8), WD 7.68-69 (Cases & Places 1-3), WD 8.73-74 (In the Lab 1 Step 8), WD 8.74-75 (In the Lab 2 Step 9), WD 8.76-77 (In the Lab 3 Step 14), WD 9.81-82 (Cases & Places 1-6)
	G. Define and modify default file locations for workgroup templates	WDW 1.09, WDW 1.12-13, WD 7.57-58	WDW 1.14 (In the Lab 2), WD 7.66-67 (In the Lab 3 Step 10), WD 7.68-69 (Cases & Places 2), WD 8.78-79 (Cases & Places 6)
	H. Attach digital signatures to documents	WD 8.64-67	WD 8.74-75 (In the Lab 2 Step 10), WD 8.78-79 (Cases & Places 2-4)
VII. Using Mail Merge	A. Merge letters with a Word, Excel, or Access data source	WD 5.07-53, WDI 1.07-10	WD 5.73 (Apply Your Knowledge Step 5), WD 5.74-75 (In the Lab 1), WD 5.76-77 (In the Lab 2), WD 5.78-79 (In the Lab 3), WD 5.80-81 (Cases & Places 1-5), WDI 1.13 (In the Lab 1), WDI 1.13 (In the Lab 2), WDI 1.14 (In the Lab 3)
	B. Merge labels with a Word, Excel, or Access data source	WD 5.54-59	WD 5.74-75 (In the Lab 1 Step 8), WD 5.76-77 (In the Lab 2 Step 8), WD 5.78-79 (In the Lab 3 Step 7), WD 5.80-81 (Cases & Places 1-5)
	C. Use Outlook data as mail merge data source	WDI 1.05-10	WDI 1.13 (In the Lab 1), WDI 1.14 (In the Lab 3)

Index

Abbreviations, AutoCorrect entries for, WD 2.24
Accepting tracked changes, WD 9.18, WD 9.20
Actions, undoing, WD 1.38, WD 1.58
Active document, WD 3.28
ActiveX control, **WD 8.51**
   adding to form, WD 8.51-60
   formatting, WD 8.55-56
   inserting, WD 8.52-53
   macro for, WD 8.57-60
   properties of, WD 8.53-54
   resizing, WD 8.55-56
Add a column, to table, **WD 4.33**
Add or Remove Buttons submenu, Standard command, WD 2.07
Add Pages panel (Web Page Wizard dialog box), **WDW 1.06**
Add rows, to table, WD 4.32-33
Add/Sort Headings panel (Resume Wizard dialog box), **WD 3.12**
Additions to documents, WD 1.57
Address book, **WDI 1.03**
Address panel (Resume Wizard dialog box), **WD 3.10**
Addresses, WD 3.39-40
   envelopes, WD 3.57, WD 5.59-62
   inside, WD 3.41, WD 3.44
   mailing labels, WD 3.58, WD 5.54-59
   Outlook, WDI 1.03
AddressBlock merge field, **WD 5.32**
Align Right button (Formatting toolbar), table cells, WD 4.36-37
Alignment
   clip art, WD 1.49
   data in cells, WD 4.59-62
   data in columns, WD 4.61-62
   end-of-cell marks, WD 4.56
   headers, WD 9.62
   paragraph, WD 1.36-37
   section, WD 4.23
   tab stop, WD 3.31, WD 3.43
   table, WD 3.53-54
   table cells, WD 4.36, WD 7.17
   text in text box, WD 8.14
   vertical, WD 4.19
Alphabetic sheet (Properties window), **WD 8.55**
Alternating headers and footers, WD 9.61-62
Animating text, **WD 6.66-67, WD 7.45**
Animation effects, WD 4.15
ANSI characters, **WD 6.18**
Antivirus programs, WD 8.10
APA (American Psychological Association) documentation style, **WD 2.04, WD 2.06, WD 2.15, WD 9.03**
Apostrophe ('), comments beginning with, WD 8.40, WD 8.41
Application, embedded, WDI 2.06
Applying styles, WD 2.30
   character style, WD 4.52, WD 8.19
   to form letter, WD 5.41-42
   paragraph style, WD 8.19
Ascending sort order, **WD 2.42**
Ask a Question box, **WD 1.59-61**
Asterisk (*), automatic bulleted list and, WD 3.54-55
Asterisk (*) wildcard character, WD 4.24
Attachment
   e-mailing document as, WD 2.54
   e-mailing document for review, WD 9.08-09
   security and, WD 8.09-10
Author references, MLA style for, WD 2.06
AutoComplete tip, **WD 2.16, WD 3.48**
AutoCorrect, **WD 2.20-24**
AutoCorrect command (Tools menu), WD 2.23
AutoCorrect entries, **WD 2.38-39**
AutoCorrect Options button, **WD 2.21-22**

AutoCorrect Options command (Tools menu)
   smart tags, WD 2.16, WD 2.21, WD 3.58
   spelling, WD 1.27
AutoFit command (Table menu), WD 3.52
AutoFormat, WD 4.35, WD 6.52-53
AutoFormat As You Type, WD 3.22-23
AutoFormat command (Tools menu), WD 3.22
AutoFormat style, for diagram, WD 6.52-53
Automatic macros, **WD 8.32-37**
Automatic page breaks, **WD 2.33-34**
AutoNew macro
   creating, WD 8.32-35
   editing, WD 8.37-44
   testing, WD 8.36-37
AutoShape, **WD 5.11-16**
   callout, WD 6.54-55
AutoShape command (Format menu), WD 5.15
AutoSum button (Tables and Borders toolbar), **WD 4.33**
AutoText command (Insert menu), WD 3.45
AutoText entry, **WD 3.44-46, WD 3.47-48, WD 3.56**

Back-to-back duplicating, WD 9.05, WD 9.61
Background command (Format menu), watermark, WD 4.64
Background Print icon, WD 1.14
Background repagination, **WD 2.33**
Background Save icon, WD 1.14
BACKSPACE key, correcting errors using, WD 1.58
Banner, **WD 6.06**
Bar code, **WD 5.54**
Blank document, opening new, WD 3.27
Blank lines
   above paragraph, WD 4.63
   demoting to body text, WD 9.46-47
   entering in document, WD 1.23
   inserting between chart and table, WD 4.46
   line spacing and, WD 2.10
Body, of research paper, WD 2.15-34
Body of newsletter, formatting, WD 6.23-35
Body text
   demoting line to, WD 9.46-47
   entering into outline, WD 9.45
Bold button (Formatting toolbar), WD 1.45
Bold text, WD 1.44-45
Bookmark, **WD 8.44, WD 8.58, WD 9.59-61**
   changing, for drop-down form field, WD 8.46
Bookmark command (Insert menu), WD 9.60
Border button (Formatting toolbar), WD 3.36, WD 4.10
Borders, **WD 3.35**
   adding to paragraph, WD 4.08
   bottom, for paragraph, WD 3.35-36
   caption, WD 9.27, WD 9.28
   chart, WD 4.46
   color, WD 4.09
   frame, WDW 1.08-09
   line weight, WD 4.09
   page, WD 6.62-63
   removing, WD 4.10
   ruling lines, WD 6.14-15
   table, WD 7.16
Borders and Shading command (Format menu)
   borders, WD 4.10, WD 4.11
   vertical rule, WD 6.34-35
Bottom border, for paragraph, WD 3.35-36
Bound documents, gutter margins and, WD 9.63

Break, WD 3.21-22
Break command (Insert menu)
   page break, WD 2.35
   next page section break, WD 4.22
Bring in Front of Text command (Order submenu), WD 7.41
Browse by Page command (Select Browse Object menu), WD 2.13, WD 2.43-44
Browser, WDW 1.11-13
Browser window, WD 2.53
Bullet, **WD 3.21, WD 4.48-49**
Bulleted list, **WD 3.21**
   adding automatically while typing, WD 3.54-55
   picture bullets, WD 4.48-49
Bullets and Numbering command (Format menu), WD 3.21
Bullets button (Formatting toolbar), WD 3.21
Business form letters, **WD 5.04**
Business letter, WD 3.06
   components of, WD 3.41
   form letters, WD 5.04
Buttons
   assigning macro to, WD 8.28-31
   assigning Web address to, WD 8.32
   smart tag, WD 3.58

Callout AutoShape, formatting, WD 6.54-55
Cancel printing, WD 1.55
Cap, drop, **WD 6.28-29**
Capitalization
   AutoCorrect and, WD 2.20, WD 2.24
   CAPS LOCK key and, WD 1.24
CAPS LOCK key, WD 1.24
Caption property, ActiveX control and, WD 8.53-54
Captions, **WD 9.25-28**
   cross-reference to, WD 9.29-31
   field, WD 7.17
   modifying, WD 9.56
   table of figures created from, WD 9.54
Case-sensitive, **WD 9.34**
Categorized sheet (Properties window), **WD 8.55**
Cells, in table, **WD 3.16-17, WD 3.50, WD 7.15-17**
   aligning data in, WD 4.59-62
   alignment of, WD 4.36
   formatting, WD 7.17
   merging, WD 4.61
   selecting, WD 4.56
   shading, WD 4.62
Center, optical, WD 1.49
Center button (Formatting toolbar)
   paragraph, WD 1.38, WD 1.39
   table, WD 3.54
Centered tab stop, WD 3.32
Centering
   caption contents, WD 9.28
   chart, WD 4.45
   page in Print Preview window, WD 3.26
   paragraph containing graphic, WD 1.49
   paragraph horizontally, **WD 1.38, WD 1.39**
   paragraph using shortcut keys, WD 2.17
   table, WD 3.53-54, WD 4.36
   title of works cited page, WD 2.36
   vertically on page, WD 4.18-19, WD 4.23
Certificate, digital, WD 8.64
Certification authority, **WD 8.64**
Certified digital signatures, WD 8.64
Change Text Direction button (Tables and Borders toolbar), WD 4.60
Changed line, **WD 9.15**
Change-tracking feature, **WD 9.09-21**
Character effects, WD 5.43
Character formatting, **WD 1.32, WD 1.34-36, WD 4.50**
Character styles, **WD 3.19, WD 4.50-51, WD 8.16-19**

Characters
   ANSI, WD 6.18
   finding special, WD 2.49
   leader, WD 3.30
   selecting to format, WD 1.33
   shortcut keys for formatting, WD 2.18
   tab, WD 3.32
Charts, table, WD 4.39-46
   changing type, WD 4.43-44
   creating from Excel worksheet, WDI 2.06-11
   Excel, displaying in Word document, WD 4.45
   formatting, WD 4.41-42, WD 4.45-46
   legend, WD 4.41-42
   resizing, WD 4.43
Check Box Form Field button (Forms toolbar), WD 7.27
Check boxes, WD 7.25-29
   Help text on, WD 7.36-37
Citations, for research paper, WD 2.04-06
Clear formatting, **WD 3.36-39**
Clearing formatting, WD 6.15
Click and Type, WD 2.13-14
Click and Type pointer, **WD 2.13**
Clip art, **WD 1.46**
   alignment of, WD 1.49
   animation, WD 4.15
   inserting from Web, WD 4.15-16
   inserting into Word document, WD 1.46-53
   online form, WD 8.11-12
   resizing using sizing handles, WD 1.50-53
   searching for, WD 1.47
   template, WD 7.12
Clipboard, **WD 2.44**
Close All command (File menu), WD 5.70
Close button (title bar), WD 1.55
Close command (File menu), WD 1.58
Closing
   note pane, WD 2.31
   Word document, WD 1.58
Code, **WD 8.04, WD 8.37-44**
Code statements, **WD 8.39**
   adding, WD 8.42-43
   entering in procedure, WD 8.58
   executable, WD 8.40, WD 8.57
Collaborating on document, **WD 6.67-73**
Collapsed document, WD 9.42, WD 9.65
Collecting and pasting, items from Clipboard, **WD 1.32-35**
Colon (:), in index entry, WD 9.31
Color
   border, WD 4.09
   gradient, WD 6.11-12
   highlighting, WD 6.65, WD 7.13
   newsletter, WD 6.60-62
   printing, WD 4.26
   pull-quote, WD 6.40
   text form field, WD 7.31
   underline, in text form field, WD 7.31-32
   WordArt drawing object, WD 6.11-12
Color schemes, WDW 1.08
Column boundary, **WD 3.52**
Column break, newsletter, **WD 6.29-32**
Columns, newsletter
   balancing, WD 6.47-48
   changing formatting, WD 6.42-43
   snaking, WD 6.24-25
   vertical rule separating, WD 6.33-34
Columns, table, WD 3.16, WD 3.17, WD 3.49
   adding, WD 4.33, WD 7.15-17
   alignment of data in, WD 4.61-62
   charting, WD 4.39-40
   deleting from table, WD 4.33
   distributing evenly, WD 4.58
   drawing in table, WD 4.55-56
   resizing, WD 3.51-52
   summing, WD 4.33-34
   width, WD 4.61

I.01

Comma-delimited text file, **WD 7.52**
Command button, ActiveX control for, WD 8.52-53
Command Button button (Control Toolbox toolbar), WD 8.52-53
Commands
 dimmed, WD 1.15
 hidden, WD 1.15
 speaking, WD 1.17
 undoing, WD 1.38, WD 1.58
Comment balloon, **WD 9.12**
Comment command (Insert menu), WD 9.11
Comment marks, **WD 9.12**
Comments, **WD 6.68**, **WD 9.11-14**
 displaying, WD 9.21
 inserting, WD 6.68-69
 macro, WD 8.40-41
 reviewing, WD 9.18-20
Compare and Merge Documents command (Tools menu), WD 6.71, WD 9.21-22
Comparison operator, in condition, WD 5.35
Complimentary close, business letter, **WD 3.41**
Computer programming, **WD 8.04**
Concordance file, WD 9.56
Conditions, printing text in form letter and, **WD 5.35**, WD 5.51
Contacts folder, **WDI 1.03**
Contacts list, **WDI 1.03**
Continuous section break, inserting in newsletter, WD 6.24, WD 6.47-48
Control Toolbox toolbar, WD 8.52
 buttons on, WD 8.54
Copied item, linking, WD 6.45-47
Copy button (Standard toolbar), items between documents, WD 3.33-34
Copying
 CTRL key used in, WD 2.47
 Excel data to be charted, WDI 2.08
 formats from one form field to another, WD 7.32
 items using Office Clipboard, WD 3.32-35
 macros, WD 8.67-68
 object, WDI 2.01
 paragraph formatting, WD 7.32
 text, WD 2.44
Correcting errors, WD 1.21, WD 1.57-58
 AutoCorrect used for, WD 2.20-23
 grammar and spelling at same time, WD 2.50-52
Council of Biology Editors (CBE) style, WD 9.03
Cover letter, **WD 3.04**, **WD 3.41**
 creating, WD 3.41-57
 envelope and mailing label for, WD 3.57-58
 letterhead for, WD 3.27-40
Create Subdocument button (Outlining toolbar), WD 9.43
Cross-reference, **WD 9.29-31**
CTRL key
 copying item using, WD 2.47
 navigating hyperlinks using, WD 2.53
 selecting text using, WD 2.44-45
Current date, text form field for, WD 7.29-31
Custom tab stop, **WD 3.30-31**
Customize command (Tools menu), toolbars, WD 8.28
Customizing
 menus, WD 8.28, WD 8.32
 toolbars, WD 2.07, WD 8.28
 Word, WD 1.09-12
Cut button (Standard toolbar)
 footnote, WD 2.32
 moving text using, WD 2.46
Cutting, **WD 2.44**, WD 2.46

Data entry area, online form, **WD 7.06**
Data field, **WD 5.22**
Data records, **WD 5.21**
 merging all to directory, WD 5.63-66

selecting to merge and print, WD 5.49-50
 sorting to merge and print, WD 5.52-53
Data source, **WD 5.06**
 changing, WDI 1.04-05
 creating, WD 5.21-30
 merging main document with, WD 5.48
 Outlook, WDI 1.03
Datasheet, **WD 4.41**
Datasheet window, **WD 4.41**, WDI 2.07-09
Date
 current, inserting in document, WD 3.43-44
 current, text form field for, WD 7.29-31
Date line, business letter, **WD 3.41**, WD 3.42-44
Decimal-aligned tab stop, WD 3.32
Default, **WD 1.19**
 margin settings, WD 2.07
 text in form fields, **WD 7.18**
DELETE key, correcting errors using, WD 1.58
Deleting, WD 1.57
 columns from table, **WD 4.33**
 footnote, WD 2.31
 macro, WD 8.26, WD 8.67-68
 manual page break, WD 2.35
 rows from table, **WD 4.33**
 text from existing document, WD 1.58
Demoting line, to body text, WD 9.46-47
Descending sort order, **WD 2.42**
Design Mode button (Control Toolbox toolbar), WD 8.53
Designing online form, WD 7.07-08
Desk checking, **WD 8.48**
Desktop publishing terminology, WD 6.06
Destination document, **WDI 2.01**
 inserting source document as linked object in, WDI 2.03-04
Destination object, **WD 6.45**
Diagram, **WD 9.49-54**
 adding text to, WD 6.51-52
 AutoFormat, WD 6.52-53
 inserting in newsletter, WD 6.49-50
Diagram command (Insert menu), WD 9.50
Dictating text, WD 1.17
Dictionary, WD 1.27
Digital certificate, **WD 8.64**
Digital signature, **WD 8.64-67**
Dimension, table, **WD 3.49**
Dimmed commands, **WD 1.15**
Directory, merging all data records to, **WD 5.63-66**
Disabled macro, **WD 8.10**
Display Map command (Smart Tag Actions menu), WD 3.59
Displaying
 bookmarks, WD 9.59
 comments, WD 9.21
 end-of-cell marks, WD 7.16
 field codes, WD 5.45-46
 formatting marks, WD 1.23-24
 gridlines, WD 3.17
 header area, WD 2.12
 horizontal ruler, WD 2.18
 markups, WD 9.17
 Reviewing Pane, WD 9.13
 ruler, WD 1.13
 smart tags, WD 2.16, WD 2.21
 subheadings, WD 9.67
 table gridlines, WD 7.17
 task panes, WD 1.49
 toolbar, WD 1.50, WD 7.15
 toolbar buttons, WD 1.11, WD 1.16
Distribute Columns Evenly button (Tables and Borders toolbar), WD 4.58
Distribute Rows Evenly button (Tables and Borders toolbar), WD 4.57
Docked toolbar, **WD 1.17**, **WD 2.13**

Document Map, **WD 9.66-67**
Document window, **WD 1.12-14**
Documents
 active, WD 3.28
 announcement, WD 1.06-62
 bookmarks, WD 9.59-61
 changes made to, WD 1.57-58
 closing, WD 1.58
 collaboration on, WD 6.67-73
 collapsed, WD 9.42, WD 9.65
 comparing and merging, WD 6.71, WD 9.21-22
 deleting text from, WD 1.58
 digital signature, WD 8.64-67
 entering text, WD 1.21-29
 expanded, WD 9.42
 inserting clip art into, WD 1.46-53
 inserting existing into open document, WD 4.21-26
 inserting text into, WD 1.58
 letterhead, WD 3.27-40
 linking Excel worksheet to, WDI 2.02, WDI 2.03-05
 multiple versions of, WD 9.16-17
 online form, WD 7.04-59
 online viewing, WD 6.64-67
 opening, WD 1.55-57
 opening previous version of, WD 9.17
 password-protected, WD 9.33-35, WD 9.40
 preparing to include in longer document, WD 9.23-35
 printing, WD 1.54-55
 protected, WD 7.08, WD 8.37
 reviewing, WD 9.08-23
 saving, WD 1.29-32
 saving all open, WD 5.70
 saving as Web page, WDW 1.03-04
 saving with new file name, WD 4.26, WD 9.11
 section, WD 4.21-22
 switching from one open to another, WD 3.32
 template, WD 7.08-10
 version of, WD 9.16
 Web page, WDW 1.01-14
Documentation styles, for research papers, WD 2.04
Double-click, Click and Type using, WD 2.13-14
Double-space, WD 2.06, **WD 2.10**
 footnote, WD 2.29
Draft, printing, WD 3.25
Drag/dragging
 moving text using, WD 2.46
 moving toolbar by, WD 2.13
Drag-and-drop editing, **WD 2.44**, WD 2.45-47
Draw menu, Rotate or Flip command, WD 6.21
Draw Table button (Tables and Borders toolbar), **WD 4.53-54**
Draw Table feature, **WD 4.53-54**
Drawing, WD 4.53, WD 8.13
Drawing canvas, **WD 5.11**, WD 5.16-20
Drawing object, **WD 5.11**, **WD 6.08**, **WD 9.49**
 diagram, WD 9.49-54
 filling with gradient effect, WD 8.19-21
 filling with texture, WD 7.42-43
 line color, WD 7.43-44
 pen comments as, WD 9.11
 rectangle, WD 7.38-45
 shadow, WD 7.44-45
 stacking order, WD 7.40-41
 3-D effect, WD 8.21
Drawing toolbar, WD 9.49
Drop cap, **WD 6.28-29**
Drop-down form field, **WD 7.21**
 changing bookmark for, WD 8.46
 inserting, WD 7.21-24
Drop-Down Form Field button (Forms toolbar), WD 7.21
Duplicating, back-to-back, WD 9.05, WD 9.61

Edit menu
 Go To command, WD 2.44
 Paste Link command, WDI 2.09
 Paste Special command, linking text, WD 6.45-47
 Repeat command, WD 1.39
 Replace command, WD 2.49
 Undo command, WD 1.39
Edit mode, **WD 8.28**, WD 8.29
Editing
 change-tracking and, WD 9.14
 comments, WD 9.13
 drag-and-drop, WD 2.44, WD 2.45-47
 embedded object, WDI 2.01
 fields, WD 5.30-31
 footnote, WD 2.32
 graphic, WD 9.25
 hyperlink, WDW 1.10
 linked object, WDI 2.01
 linked worksheet, WDI 2.11-12
 merge fields, WD 5.32
 recorded macro, WD 8.37-44
 records, WD 5.29
 research paper, WD 2.44-52
 Web page from browser, WDW 1.12-13
E-mail
 document for review, WD 9.08-09
 file digital signature and, WD 8.64-65
 form template, WD 7.58-59
 reference document, WD 9.08-09
 research paper, WD 2.54
E-mail addresses
 formatting as hyperlink, WDW 1.04
 merging to, WDI 1.09-10
 removing hyperlink autoformat from, WD 3.39-40
E-Mail button (Standard toolbar), WD 2.54, WD 7.58-59
Embedded, **WDI 2.01**, WDI 2.06
End mark, **WD 1.13**
End Sub statement, **WD 8.39**
Endnote, **WD 2.24**
End-of-cell mark, **WD 3.16**, WD 7.16
 alignment of, WD 4.56
End-of-row mark, WD 7.16, WD 7.17
ENTER key
 AutoComplete and, WD 2.16
 bulleted list and, WD 3.21
 blank line created using, WD 1.23, WD 1.24, WD 1.25
 paragraph formatting and, WD 2.20, WD 2.38
Envelopes, addressing and printing, WD 3.57-58, WD 5.59-62
Eraser button (Tables and orders toolbar), **WD 4.56**
Essential business letter elements, **WD 3.41**
Excel chart, displaying in Word document, WD 4.45
Excel worksheet
 creating chart from, WDI 2.06-11
 linking to Word document, WDI 2.02, WDI 2.03-05
Executable code statement, **WD 8.40**, WD 8.57
 modifying, WD 8.42
Execute, **WD 8.04**
Execute the macro, **WD 8.23-28**
 when user exits form field, WD 8.50-51
Exit command (File menu), WD 1.55
Expand Subdocuments button (Outlining toolbar), WD 9.65
Expanded document, WD 9.42
Explanatory notes, MLA style for, WD 2.06, WD 2.24
Expression, in condition, WD 5.35

False text, **WD 5.35**
Field caption, **WD 7.17**
Field codes, WD 5.35, **WD 5.45**, WD 9.25
 displaying, WD 5.45-46
 index and, WD 9.56
 printing, WD 5.46-47

turning off, WD 4.29
Field name, **WD 5.22**
Field results, **WD 5.45**, WD 9.25
Field specification, **WD 7.07**
Fields, **WD 5.30, WD 9.27**
   caption, WD 9.27
   cross-reference, WD 9.29-30
   default text in, WD 7.18
   index entry, WD 9.56
   inserting in main document, WD 5.32-33
   inserting text form, WD 7.17-20, WD 7.24-25
   modifying, WD 5.30-31
   online form and, **WD 7.07**
Figures, WD 9.29-31
File command (Insert menu)
   newsletter, WD 6.27
   Word document into open document, WD 4.24-25
File digital signature **WD 8.64-65**
File extension, WD 7.09
File menu
   Close command, WD 1.58
   Close All command, WD 5.70
   Exit command, WD 1.55
   New command, letterhead file, WD 3.27
   New command, templates, WD 7.09, WD 7.57
   New command, Web page template, WDW 1.05
   opening file using, WD 1.55
   Page Setup command, margins, WD 2.08, WD 6.07
   Page Setup command, page orientation, WD 2.09, WD 5.66
   Page Setup command, vertical alignment, WD 4.19, WD 4.23
   Print command, WD 1.54
   Print command, drafts, WD 3.25
   Print command, field codes, WD 5.46
   Print command, page number options, WD 4.29
   Print command, specific pages, WD 4.26
   Print Preview command, WD 3.26
   Properties command, document statistics, WD 2.33
   Save All command, WD 5.70
   Save As command, WD 1.32, WD 1.54, WD 4.26
   Save As command, digital signature, WD 8.65
   Save As command, online form data, WD 7.53
   Save As command, passwords, WD 9.34
   Save as Web Page command, WDW 1.03
   Save command, WD 1.53
   Send To command, e-mailing document as attachment, WD 2.54, WD 9.08-09
   Versions command, WD 9.16
   Web Page Preview command, WDW 1.11
File name, WD 1.29, WD 1.31
   saving document with new, WD 4.26, WD 9.11
   saving existing document with same, WD 1.53-54
Files
   attaching digital signature to, WD 8.64-65
   clip art, WD 4.17, WD 8.12
   comma-delimited text, WD 7.52
   concordance, WD 9.56
   importing Excel data for chart, WDI 2.10
   inserting in newsletter, WD 6.27-28
   inserting subdocument, WD 9.40-42
   master document, WD 9.36
   opening using wildcard characters, WD 4.24
   Outlook, WDI 1.03
   password-protected, WD 9.33-35
   preview of, WD 4.24

searching for, WD 6.67
security and, WD 8.10, WD 8.64, WD 9.33-35
types, WD 7.09
Fill color, WD 7.42, WD 8.13
Fill Color button arrow (Drawing toolbar), WD 7.42, WD 8.20
Fill effects, WD 7.42, WD 8.19-21
Finding and replacing text, WD 2.48-49
Finding, WD 4.24, WD 2.49
Finish panel (Resume Wizard dialog box), **WD 3.13**
First Line Indent marker, **WD 2.18-19**
First Record button (Mail Merge toolbar), **WD 5.53**
First-line indent, **WD 2.18-19**
   centering chart and, WD 4.45, WD 4.46
   footnote, WD 2.27, WD 2.29-30
   justifying paragraph, WD 6.26
Flipping graphic, WD 6.21-22
Floating graphic
   changing inline graphic to, WD 9.25
   formatting, WD 6.57
   inserting, WD 6.18-19
Floating object, **WD 6.18-21**
Floating toolbar, **WD 1.17, WD 1.50**, WD 2.13
Folder, **WD 1.30, WD 5.20-21**
Font, **WD 1.19**
   changing, WD 1.36, WD 1.40
   footnotes, WD 2.27
   spacing and, WD 1.33
   text box, WD 8.15
Font box arrow (Formatting toolbar), WD 1.36
Font color
   letterhead, WD 3.28-29, WD 3.35
   text box for online form, WD 8.15
Font Color button arrow (Formatting toolbar), letterhead, WD 3.28-29
Font command (Format menu)
   bold, WD 1.45
   color, WD 3.29
   font size, WD 1.20
   font style, WD 1.36
   italics, WD 1.41
   superscript, WD 4.38
   underline, WD 1.43
Font command (shortcut menu)
   animated text, WD 7.46
   shadow, WD 4.13
   text form field, WD 7.31
Font dialog box, WD 1.40
   formatting characters using, WD 4.12-13
Font size, **WD 1.19**
   changing, WD 1.20, WD 1.34-35, WD 1.40
   footnotes, WD 2.27, WD 2.29
   letterhead, WD 3.35
Font Size box arrow (Formatting toolbar), WD 1.35
Footers, **WD 2.11, WD 4.29**
   alternating, WD 9.62
   creating different from previous section footer, WD 4.30-31
Footnote, in research paper, **WD 2.24-32**
   deleting, WD 2.31
   editing, WD 2.32
   formatting, WD 2.27-28
   moving, WD 2.32
   style, WD 2.27-30
Footnote Text style, WD 2.27-28
Form Data Only button, adding to toolbar, WD 8.28-31
Form design, **WD 7.07**
Form Field Shading button (Forms toolbar), WD 7.18, WD 7.37
Form fields
   bookmarks for, WD 8.44, WD 8.58
   check box, WD 7.25-29
   drop-down, WD 7.21-24
   formatting, WD 7.31-34
   Help text, WD 7.34-37
   moving from one to another, WD 8.51
   modifying using VBA, WD 8.44-45

moving to, WD 7.48, WD 7.51
rectangle around, WD 7.38-45
removing shading, WD 7.37
running macro when user exits, WD 8.50-51
shading, WD 7.18, WD 7.37
Form letters, WD 5.04-71, **WDI 1.01-12**
AutoShapes in, WD 5.11-16
changing data source, WDI 1.04-05
data source, WD 5.06, WD 5.21-30
directory as table, WD 5.65-68
envelopes for, WD 5.59-62
mailing labels for, WD 5.54-59
main document for, WD 5.06, WD 5.07-10, WD 5.30-47
merging documents, WD 5.48
Outlook data source, WDI 1.03
printing, WD 5.48
printing text in using IF field, WD 5.35
template, WD 5.08-10
Format menu
   AutoShape command, WD 5.15
   Background command, watermark, WD 4.64
   Borders and Shading command, border, WD 4.10, WD 4.11
   Borders and Shading command, vertical rule, WD 6.34-35
   Bullets and Numbering command, bulleted list, WD 3.21
   Bullets and Numbering command, outline numbered list, WD 5.41
   Drawing Canvas command, WD 5.17
   Font command, bold, WD 1.45
   Font command, color, WD 3.29
   Font command, font size, WD 1.20
   Font command, font style, WD 1.36
   Font command, italics, WD 1.41
   Font command, superscript, WD 4.38
   Font command, underline, WD 1.43
   Paragraph command, alignment, WD 1.37
   Paragraph command, centering, WD 1.38
   Paragraph command, hanging indent, WD 2.37
   Paragraph command, left indent, WD 2.20
   Paragraph command, line spacing, WD 2.11
   Picture command, size, WD 1.52
   Reveal Formatting command, WD 2.36, WD 4.66-67
   Tabs command, WD 3.31, WD 3.42
   Text Box command, WD 6.38
   Text Box command, converting text box to frame, WD 9.28
   WordArt command, WD 6.13
Format Page Number button (Header and Footer toolbar), WD 4.30
Format Painter button, WD 6.61-62, WD 7.32-33
Format Picture button (Picture toolbar), WD 1.52-53
Formatting
   AutoFormat, WD 3.22-23
   AutoShape, WD 5.13-14
   ActiveX control, WD 8.55-56
   body of newsletter, WD 6.23-35
   callout AutoShape, WD 6.54-55
   character, WD 1.32, WD 1.34-36, WD 4.12-13
   chart, WD 4.41-42, WD 4.45-46
   chart in Graph, WDI 2.10
   clearing, WD 3.36-39, WD 6.15
   clearing for style, WD 4.12, WD 4.15
   Click and Type and, WD 2.13
   date and time, WD 3.44
   diagram, WD 6.52-53, WD 9.51-54
   Drawing Canvas, WD 5.17-19
   drop cap, WD 6.28-29
   e-mail address as hyperlink, WDW 1.04
   ENTER key and, WD 2.20, WD 2.38
   finding, WD 2.49
   footnote, WD 2.27-28

form fields, WD 7.31-34
graphic, WD 9.23-24
graphic as floating, WD 6.20-21
highlight text, WD 7.13
hyperlinks, WD 2.39-40
legend, WD 4.42
letterhead, WD 3.35-36
line spacing, WD 2.10-11
nonadjacent characters, WD 4.37-38
online form instructions, WD 8.15
paragraphs, WD 1.32-34, WD 1.36-38
research paper, WD 2.07-34
Resume Wizard and, WD 3.08
revealing, WD 2.36, WD 4.66-67
second page of newsletter, WD 6.42-60
section, WD 4.21-22, WD 4.24
shortcut keys for, WD 2.16-17
table, WD 4.34-39, WD 4.59-60
table cells, WD 7.17
template and, WD 3.04, WD 7.08, WD 7.11, WD 7.12
template clip art, WD 7.12
template text, WD 7.11
text box text, WD 8.14-15
text entered in form fields, WD 7.19-20
text following chart, WD 4.46-47
title page, WD 4.07, WD 9.48
titles of works, WD 2.06
WordArt drawing object, WD 6.11-12
Formatting marks, **WD 1.23**
   displaying, WD 1.23-24
Formatting toolbar, **WD 1.15-17**
   resetting, WD 2.07
Forms, WD 8.26, WD 8.27
Forms toolbar, WD 7.15
Formula command (Table menu), WD 4.34
Frame, **WDW 1.01, WD 5.12, WD 5.43**
   caption, in WD 9.27-28
   converting text box to, WD 9.27-28
   resizing, WDW 1.08-09
Frame border, **WDW 1.08-09**
Frames page, **WDW 1.01**
FTP location, WDW 1.02
Full menu, **WD 1.14**

Go To command (Edit menu), WD 2.44
Go to Record text box (mail merge), WD 5.53
Gradient, **WD 6.11, WD 8.19**
Grammar
   AutoCorrect and, WD 2.20
   checking with spelling, WD 2.50-52
   proofing for errors, WD 2.42
Graphics, **WD 1.46**
   adding caption to, WD 9.25-27
   centering paragraph containing, WD 1.49
   editing, WD 9.25
   entering as part of master document, WD 9.46-48
   flipping, WD 6.21-22
   floating, WD 6.18-19, WD 6.57
   formatting, WD 9.23-24
   grouping, WD 6.57
   inline, adding caption to, WD 9.25-27
   inline, changing to floating, WD 9.25
   inserting, WD 3.29, WD 9.23-24
   letterhead, WD 3.28-29
   proportions of, WD 1.52, WD 1.53
   online form, WD 8.11-12
   resizing, WD 1.50-53, WD 3.29, WD 9.24
   screen shot, WD 9.23-24
   wrapping style, WD 6.59
GreetingLine merge field, **WD 5.32**
Gridlines (table), **WD 3.17, WD 7.17**
Grouping graphics, WD 6.57
Gutter margin, WD 9.63

Handwriting recognition, WD 1.17-18
Hanging indent, **WD 2.36-37**
Hanging Indent marker, **WD 2.36-37**
Hard copy, **WD 1.54**

Hard page break, WD 2.35
Header, **WD 2.11, WD 4.29**
  alternating, WD 9.61-62
  creating different from previous section header, WD 4.29
  numbering pages using, WD 2.11-15
  page numbers in alternating, WD 9.62
  viewing, WD 2.12-13, WD 2.15
Header and Footer command (View menu)
Header and Footer command (View menu)
  alternating headers, WD 9.61
  creating different header from previous section header, WD 4.29
  creating header, WD 2.12
Header and Footer toolbar, WD 2.12-13, WD 4.29
Header area, displaying, WD 2.12
Header record, **WD 5.21**
Heading styles
  changing heading to lower- or higher-level, WD 9.45
  Document Map and, WD 9.66-67
  master document headings as outline using, WD 9.36, WD 9.37
Headings
  bookmarks, WD 9.59, WD 9.60
  changing to lower- or higher-level heading style, WD 9.45
  Document Map, WD 9.66-67
  entering as outline for master document, WD 9.36-39
  printing, WD 9.36
  resume, WD 3.11-12
  table of contents, WD 9.58-59
Health, of wrist, WD 1.27
Help, WD 1.59-61
  categories of, WD 1.61
  Media Gallery, WD 1.46
  online, WD 1.59
  shortcut keys and, WD 2.16
  Visual Basic for Applications, WD 8.53
  wizards and, WD 3.09
Help message, for online form, WD 7.50
Help text, adding to form fields, WD 7.34-37
Hidden command, **WD 1.15**
Hide Gridlines command (Table menu), **WD 3.17**
Hiding
  animated text, WD 7.45
  gridlines, WD 3.17
  subheadings, WD 9.67
  white space, WD 3.15
Highlight, **WD 7.13**
Highlight button (Formatting toolbar), WD 7.13
Highlighting text, WDW 1.09, WD 6.65, WD 7.13
Horizontal line, WDW 1.10, WD 4.55
Horizontal ruler, **WD 1.13, WD 1.18**
  changing margin settings using, WD 2.07
  displaying, WD 2.18
  indent markers on, WD 2.18-19, WD 2.36-37
  tab stop settings, WD 3.30, WD 3.42-43
Horizontally centering text, WD 1.38, WD 1.39
HTML format, WDI 1.09
HTML Source command (View menu), WDW 1.11
Hyperlink, **WD 2.39**
  adding to Web page, WDW 1.10
  assigning button for, WD 8.32
  converting to regular address, WD 3.39-40
  converting Web addresses to, WD 2.39-40
  editing, WDW 1.10
  formatting e-mail address as, WDW 1.04
  formatting for research paper, WD 2.06

navigating, WD 2.39, WD 2.53
subdocuments displayed as, WD 9.42
testing, WDW 1.12
works cited page, WD 2.39-40
Hyphen, nonbreaking, WD 3.45

If...Then:, **WD 5.35**, WD 8.57
If...Then...Else:, **WD 5.35**, WD 5.37
Illustration, moving, WD 9.56
Importing Excel data for chart, WDI 2.10
Indentation
  hanging, WD 2.36-37
  left marker, WD 2.18, WD 2.37
  MLA style, WD 2.06, WD 2.18
  outline, WD 9.36
  text box, WD 8.15
  wrap text and, WD 2.38
Index, WD 9.04
  building, WD 9.56-58
  concordance file and, WD 9.56
  marking entries, WD 9.30-31
  modifying, WD 9.67-69
Inline graphic, WD 9.25-27
Inline object, **WD 6.18**
  command button as, WD 8.56
InputBox, WD 8.49
Insert command (Table menu), WD 7.16
Insert Clip Art task pane, WD 1.47-49, WD 4.15
Insert command (Table menu), WD 3.50
Insert Hyperlink button (Standard toolbar), WD 2.40
Insert menu
  AutoText command, WD 3.45
  Bookmark command, WD 9.60
  Break command, next page section break, WD 4.22, WD 9.38
  Break command, page break, WD 2.35
  Comment command, WD 9.11
  Date and Time command, WD 3.43
  Diagram command, WD 9.50
  File command, newsletter, WD 6.27
  File command, Word document into open document, WD 4.24-25
  Object command, chart, WDI 2.04
  Object command, graph, WD 4.41
  Page Numbers command, WD 2.15
  Picture command, chart, WD 4.40-41, WDI 2.06
  Picture command, clip art from Media Gallery, WD 1.46-47
  Picture command, clip art from Web, WD 4.16
  Picture command, graphic in letterhead, WD 3.28-29
  Picture command, screen shot, WD 9.24
  Picture command, WordArt, WD 6.10
  Procedure command, WD 8.48
  Reference command, captions, WD 9.26
  Reference command, cross-reference, WD 9.29
  Reference command, footnote, WD 2.25
  Reference command, index, WD 9.31, WD 9.57
  Reference command, table of contents, WD 9.58
  Reference command, table of figures, WD 9.55
  Symbol command, WD 2.38
  Symbol command, nonbreaking space, WD 3.47
  Text Box command, WD 6.37
Insert mode, **WD 1.58**
Insert Page Number button (Header and Footer toolbar), WD 2.14
Insert Subdocument button (Outlining toolbar), WD 9.40
Insert Table button (Forms toolbar), WD 7.15
Insert Table button (Standard toolbar), WD 3.49-50, WD 4.32

Insert WordArt button (Drawing toolbar), WD 6.09
Inserting
  ActiveX control, WD 8.52-53
  AutoText entry, WD 3.44, WD 3.47-48
  bookmarks, WD 9.59-61
  check boxes in online form, WD 7.25-29
  clip art from Media Gallery, WD 1.46
  clip art from Web, WD 4.15-16
  column break, WD 6.29-32
  comments, WD 6.68-69, WD 9.11-14
  continuous section break, WD 6.24, WD 6.47-48
  current date, WD 3.43
  diagram in newsletter, WD 6.49-51
  diagram in reference document, WD 9.49-54
  document into another document, WDI 2.01
  drop-down form field, WD 7.21
  empty Word table, WD 3.49
  existing document into open document, WD 4.21-26
  fields in main document, WD 5.32-33
  file into newsletter, WD 6.27-28
  floating graphic, WD 6.18-19
  footnotes, WD 2.24-25
  graphic for letterhead, WD 3.28-29
  graphic for online form, WD 8.12
  graphic screen shot for reference document, WD 9.23-24
  IF field into main document, WD 5.35-37
  linked object, WDI 2.03-05
  manual page break, WD 2.35
  merge fields in main document, WD 5.34
  next page section break, WD 6.30-31
  nonbreaking space, WD 3.45-46
  page number in header, WD 2.14
  page number in section, WD 4.29-30
  procedure for macro, WD 8.46-47
  rectangle drawing object on online form, WD 7.38-40
  section break, WD 4.21-22
  subdocument in master document, WD 9.39-42
  symbols automatically, WD 2.38-39
  symbols in newsletter, WD 6.16-18
  table into online form, WD 7.15-17
  table of contents, WD 9.58
  text box for newsletter, WD 6.36-37
  text box for online form, WD 8.13-14
  text form field for numbers, WD 7.24-25
  text form field for text, WD 7.17-20
  text into existing document, WD 1.58
  WordArt drawing object, WD 6.08-09
Insertion point, **WD 1.13, WD 1.21**
  bulleted list and, WD 3.21, WD 3.56
  captions, WD 9.26
  chart, WDI 2.06
  clip art and, WD 1.46
  comment balloon, WD 9.12
  cross-reference, WD 9.29
  drag-and-drop editing and, WD 2.46
  inserting file and, WD 4.25
  linked object, WDI 2.04
  note reference mark and, WD 2.26
  pasting from Office Clipboard and, WD 3.35
  positioned at top of document, WD 1.34
  scroll box and, WD 1.26
  section break, WD 4.22
  selecting sentence and, WD 2.45
  tab stops and, WD 3.31
  table, WD 3.17, WD 3.51, WD 4.32, WD 4.33, WD 7.15
Inside address, business letter, **WD 3.41**, WD 3.44
Internet Explorer, editing Web page from, WDW 1.12-13
Issue information line, **WD 6.06**, WD 6.16

Italic button (Formatting toolbar), WD 1.41
Italic text, WD 1.41
  titles of works, WD 2.06

Jump lines, WD 6.32
Jumping
  to bookmark, WD 9.61
  to Web address, **WD 2.39**, WD 2.53
Justify paragraphs, **WD 5.38**
Justifying paragraph, WD 6.26-27

Keyword, index, WD 9.31

Labels, mailing, WD 3.58, WD 5.54-59
Landscape orientation
  document, WD 2.09
  table, **WD 5.66**
Language, Word detecting, WD 1.14
Language bar, WD 1.08, WD 1.09, WD 1.10, **WD 1.17**
Language Indicator button (taskbar tray status area), WD 1.17
Laser printer, WD 3.57
Last Record button (Mail Merge toolbar), **WD 5.53**
Layout, alternating headers and, WD 9.61
Leader characters, WD 3.30
Left indent
  paragraph, WD 2.18, WD 2.37
  text box, WD 8.15
Left Indent marker, **WD 2.18, WD 2.37**
Left margin, note reference mark and, WD 2.26
Left tab icon, WD 3.42
Left-aligned, **WD 1.36**
  footnotes, WD 2.27
  paragraph, WD 1.36
  paragraph using shortcut keys, WD 2.17
  tab stop, WD 3.32
  table, WD 3.53
Legend, **WD 4.41-42**
Letter, drop cap, WD 6.28-29
Letters, business, WD 3.06
Letterhead
  components of, WD 3.40
  copying information from resume to, WD 3.32-35
  for cover letter, WD 3.27-40
  graphic for, WD 3.28-29
Letters and Mailing command (Tools menu)
  form letters, WD 5.08
  mailing labels, WD 3.57, WD 5.54-55
Line
  bottom border, WD 3.35-36
  separating sections of Web page, WDW 1.10
Line, of text
  blank, entering in document, WD 1.23
  selecting, WD 2.45
  selecting and formatting, WD 1.39-40
Line break, **WD 3.21-22**
  widows and orphans and, WD 9.33
Line break character, **WD 3.21**
Line color, for rectangle drawing object, WD 7.43-44
Line spacing, **WD 2.10**
  footnote, WD 2.29
  MLA style, WD 2.06, WD 2.10
Line Spacing button arrow (Formatting toolbar), WD 2.10
Line weight, border, WD 4.09
Lines of text, keeping together, WD 4.46-47
Linked object, **WDI 2.01**
  editing, WDI 2.11-12
Linking
  Excel data to Word chart, WDI 2.07
  Excel worksheet to Word document, WDI 2.02, WDI 2.03-05
  text using Paste Special command, WD 6.45-47
List, outline, WD 3.56
List styles, **WD 3.19**

Index • I.05

Macro command (Tools menu)
  deleting macro, WD 8.26
  running macro, WD 8.27
  security, WD 8.10
  viewing VBA code, WD 8.38
Macro names, **WD 8.23**, WD 8.24
Macro recorder, **WD 8.23-28**
Macros, WD 8.05, **WD 8.22-68**
  ActiveX control, WD 8.57-60
  assigning to toolbar button, WD 8.28-31
  automatic, WD 8.32-37
  AutoNew, WD 8.36-37
  comments, WD 8.40-41
  copying, WD 8.67-68
  creating from scratch, using VBA, WD 8.44-51
  deleting, WD 8.26, WD 8.67-68
  digital certificate and, WD 8.64
  disabled, WD 8.10
  editing recorded, WD 8.37-44
  executing, WD 8.23-28
  inserting procedure for, WD 8.46-50
  locations, WD 8.27
  modifying code in, WD 8.42
  pausing recording, WD 8.27
  recording, WD 8.23-28
  renaming, WD 8.67-68
  running, WD 8.27
  security and, WD 8.09-11
  self-signed projects, WD 8.64
  storing, WD 8.27
  viewing VBA code, WD 8.38-39
Mail merge
  main document, WD 5.06, WD 5.07-10
  selecting data records, WD 5.49-50
  sorting data records, WD 5.52-53
Mail Merge toolbar, **WD 5.07**, WD 5.29
Mail Merge Wizard, **WD 5.07**, WD 5.08-09
Mail Recipient, WD 9.08-09
Mailing labels, WD 3.58, WD 5.54-59
Main document, **WD 5.06**
  checking for errors in, WDI 1.06-07
  composing, WD 5.30-47
  field codes, WD 5.45-47
  identifying, WD 5.07-10
  inserting fields in, WD 5.32-33
  inserting IF field into, WD 5.35-37
  inserting merge fields in, WD 5.34
  merging with data source, WD 5.48
  viewing merged data in, WD 5.53
Manual page break, **WD 2.35**
Map, displaying using smart tag, WD 3.59-60
Margins
  alignment of text at, WD 1.36-37
  changing all settings, WD 6.07
  default settings, WD 2.07
  gutter, WD 9.63
  Left Indent marker used to change, WD 2.18
  MLA style, WD 2.06
  research paper, WD 2.06, WD 2.07-09
Mark Index entries, WD 9.30-31
Markup **WD 9.15**
Markup, **WD 9.14**, WD 9.17
Markup balloon, **WD 6.73**
Markup command (View menu), WD 9.17
Master document, **WD 9.36**
  creating subdocument from, WD 9.43-44
  entering text and graphics, WD 9.46-48
  heading styles, WD 9.36, WD 9.37
  inserting subdocument in, WD 9.39-42
  opening, WD 9.65
  removing subdocument from, WD 9.46
  saving, WD 9.43
  working with, WD 9.36-69
Media Gallery, **WD 1.46**
Menu, **WD 1.14**
  customizing, WD 8.28, WD 8.32

resetting, WD 1.17
Menu bar, **WD 1.14**
Merge Cells button (Tables and Borders toolbar), WD 4.61
Merge field characters, **WD 5.32**
Merge fields, **WD 5.32**
Merge into current document command (Merge menu), WD 9.22
Merge menu, WD 9.22
Merged data, viewing, WD 5.53
Merging, **WD 5.06**
  collaboration and, WD 6.71
  to e-mail addresses, WDI 1.09-10
  main document with data source, WD 5.48
  tracked changes and, WD 9.21-22
Message, business letter, **WD 3.41**
Message box, icons for, WD 8.49
Microsoft Authenticode technology, WD 8.67
Microsoft Graph 2002, **WD 4.39**, **WDI 2.06-11**
Microsoft IntelliMouse®, WD 3.17
Microsoft Office User Specialist (MOUS), WDW 1.12
Microsoft Office XP, WDI 2.03
Microsoft Word command (Start, Programs menu), WD 1.08
Microsoft Word Help button (Resume Wizard dialog box), **WD 3.09**
MLA (Modern Language Association of America) documentation style, **WD 2.04**, WD 2.06, WD 9.03
Modifications to documents, WD 1.57
Modified block style, **WD 3.41**, **WD 5.10**
More Buttons list, WD 8.32
Mouse
  scrolling with, WD 1.26
  selection techniques, WD 2.45
Mouse pointer, **WD 1.13**
  selecting sentence and, WD 2.45
Move handle, **WD 1.16**
  docked toolbar, WD 2.13
  table, WD 3.17, WD 7.16
Moving
  docked toolbar, WD 2.13
  footnote, WD 2.32
  illustration, WD 9.56
  legend, WD 4.41-42
  selected text, WD 2.46
  tab stop, WD 3.43
  table, WD 3.17, WD 7.16
  text, WD 2.44-47
  text box, WD 8.13
MsgBox, WD 8.49
Multiple versions of document, saving, WD 9.16-17
My Documents folder, WD 1.30

Nameplate, **WD 6.06**, WD 6.08-22
  inner page, WD 6.44
Names
  bookmark, WD 8.44
  macro, WD 8.23, WD 8.24, WD 8.67-68
  subdocuments, WD 9.67
Navigating hyperlink, WD 2.39, WD 2.53
Navigation panel (Web Page Wizard dialog box), **WDW 1.06**
Nested tables, WD 4.59
Network, templates available on, WD 7.58
New Blank Document button (Standard toolbar), WD 1.58, WD 3.27
New command (File menu)
  letterhead file, WD 3.27
  templates, WD 7.09, WD 7.57
  Web page template, WDW 1.05
New Document task pane, WD 1.09, WD 1.10
New document window, opening, WD 3.27
New Office Document command (Start button), WD 1.08
New style, creating, WD 8.16-19

New Web Page button (Standard toolbar), WDW 1.03, WDW 1.04
Newsletter, WD 6.04-74
  column break, WD 6.29-32
  diagram in, WD 6.49-51
  enhancing with color and page border, WD 6.60-64
  formatting body of, WD 6.23-35
  formatting second page of, WD 6.42-60
  inserting file into, WD 6.27-28
  inserting symbols, WD 6.16-18
  nameplate, WD 6.06, WD 6.08-22
  pull-quote, WD 6.06, WD 6.36-42
  ruling lines, WD 6.06, WD 6.14-15
  snaking columns, WD 6.24-25
Next page section break, WD 4.22, WD 6.30-31, WD 9.38
Next Record button (Mail Merge toolbar), **WD 5.53**
Nonbreaking hyphen, **WD 3.45**
Nonbreaking space, WD 3.45-46
Normal command (View menu)
  ruler display, WD 1.13, WD 2.07
Normal style, returning formatting to, WD 3.36-37
Normal template, WD 7.09
Normal view
  changing margins in, WD 2.07-09
  page breaks and, WD 2.33
Note pane, **WD 2.26**, WD 2.31
Note reference mark, **WD 2.24**, WD 2.26, WD 2.31
  MLA style for, **WD 2.06**
Note text, **WD 2.24**
Notes
  explanatory, WD 2.06, WD 2.24
  superscript and, WD 2.24, WD 2.26
  writing papers using, WD 2.15
Number
  caption, WD 9.25-27
  text form field for, WD 7.24-25
Numbered list
  adding automatically while typing, WD 3.56
  outline, WD 3.56, WD 5.38-41
Numbering
  note reference marks, WD 2.24

Object, **WDI 2.01**
  destination, WD 6.45
  drawing, WD 6.08
  embedded, WDI 2.01
  floating, WD 6.18-21
  inline, WD 6.18, WD 8.56
  linked, WDI 2.01
  pasted, WDI 2.01
  source, WD 6.45
Object command (Insert menu)
  chart, WD 2.04
  graph, WD 4.41
Office Assistant, WD 1.11
Office Clipboard, **WD 3.32-35**
Office Clipboard icon, WD 3.35
Office Speech Recognition software, WD 1.08, WD 1.09, **WD 1.17-18**
Online form, **WD 7.04-59**
  ActiveX control, WD 8.51-60
  animating text, WD 7.45-47
  check boxes on, WD 7.25-29
  creating, WD 7.08-49
  data entry area, WD 7.06
  designing, WD 7.07-08
  drop-down form field for, WD 7.21-24
  e-mailing, WD 7.58-59
  filling out, WD 7.51-52
  formatting form fields, WD 7.31-34
  formatting instructions, WD 8.15
  gradient effect, WD 8.19-21
  graphic on, WD 8.11-12
  Help message, WD 7.50
  Help text for form fields, WD 7.34-37
  highlighted text on, WD 7.13-14
  inserting table, WD 7.15-17
  inserting text box, WD 8.13-14
  inserting text form field that accepts any text, WD 7.17-20

modifying, WD 8.11-22
  opening, WD 7.55-56
  protected, WD 7.08, WD 7.47-48, WD 8.09-11, WD 8.37
  recording and executing macro, WD 8.23-28
  rectangle drawing object on, WD 7.38-45
  resizing rectangle, WD 8.22
  saving, WD 7.52
  saving data on, WD 7.52-54
  sharing, WD 7.58-59
  template for, WD 7.08-13
  testing, WD 8.61-63
  text form field for current date, WD 7.29-31
  text form fields for numbers, WD 7.24-25
  text form fields for text, WD 7.17-20
  3-D effect, WD 8.21
  working with, WD 7.49-57
Online Help, WD 1.59
Online viewing, enhancing document for, WD 6.64-67
Open button (Standard toolbar), WD 1.57
Open documents, saving all, WD 5.70
Open Office Document command (Start menu), WD 1.56
Opening
  files using wildcard characters, WD 4.24
  master document, WD 9.65
  new document window, WD 3.27
  online form, WD 7.55-56
  Outlook data file, WDI 1.03
  previous version of document, WD 9.17
  subdocument, WD 9.42
  template, WD 7.49, WD 7.50, WD 7.57
  text file, WD 7.55-56
  Word document, WD 1.55-57
Optional Headings panel (Resume Wizard dialog box), **WD 3.12**
Options command (Tools menu)
  drag-and-drop editing, WD 2.45
  file display, WD 1.55
  hiding animated text, WD 7.45
  passwords, WD 9.35
  saving data for forms, WD 8.25-26, WD 8.27
  white space, WD 3.15
Order command (shortcut menu), WD 7.41
Organize Pages panel (Web Page Wizard dialog box), **WDW 1.07**
Orphan, **WD 4.48**, **WD 9.32-33**
Outline
  Document Map, WD 9.66-67
  entering body text into, WD 9.45
  master document, WD 9.36-39
  modifying, WD 9.44-45
  numbered list, WD 3.56, **WD 5.38-41**
Outline numbered list, WD 3.56, **WD 5.38-41**
Outline view, WD 9.36-37, WD 9.42
Outline View button (horizontal scroll bar), WD 9.37
Outlining toolbar, WD 9.37, WD 9.39
Outlook data file, opening, WDI 1.03
Overtype mode, **WD 1.58**
OVR status indicator, **WD 1.58**

Page, browsing by, WD 2.13, WD 2.43-44
Page border, WD 6.62-63
Page breaks, WD 2.33-35
  preventing, WD 4.48
  widows and orphans and, WD 9.33
Page indicator (status bar), WD 2.44
Page numbers
  alternating headers and, WD 9.62
  entering using header, WD 2.11-15
  entering using Page Numbers command, WD 2.11
  inserting in section, WD 4.29-30
  MLA style, WD 2.06

research paper, WD 2.11-15
table of contents for reference document, WD 9.58-59
Page Numbers command (Insert menu), WD 2.15
Page orientation, WD 5.66
Page Setup command (File menu)
  margins, WD 2.08
  orientation, WD 2.09
  page orientation, WD 5.66
  vertical alignment, WD 4.19, WD 4.23
Page width, zooming, WD 1.18-19, WD 2.09
Pages, back-to-back duplicating and, WD 9.05, WD 9.61
Pagination, index entry field codes and, WD 9.56
Panel names, wizard dialog box and, **WD 3.08**
Paper size, margins settings for, WD 2.07
Paragraph
  alignment, WD 1.36-37
  beginning new, WD 1.25
  blank line above, WD 4.63
  bold text in, WD 1.44-45
  border, WD 4.08
  bottom border, WD 3.35-36
  centering, WD 1.38
  centering using shortcut keys, WD 2.17
  centering, with graphic, WD 1.49
  formatting, WD 1.32-34, WD 1.36-38
  italic text in, WD 1.41
  justifying, WD 6.26-27
  keeping lines together, WD 4.46-47
  orphan, WD 9.32
  selecting, WD 2.45
  selecting to format, WD 1.33-34
  shading, WD 4.11
  shortcut keys for formatting, WD 2.18
  sorting, WD 2.41-42
  underlined text in, WD 1.43
  widow, WD 9.32
Paragraph command (Format menu)
  alignment, WD 1.37
  centering, WD 1.38
  hanging indent, WD 2.37
  indentation, WD 2.20
  line spacing, WD 2.11
Paragraph formatting, **WD 1.32-34**, WD 1.36-38
Paragraph mark, copying paragraph formatting by selecting, WD 7.32
Paragraph styles, **WD 3.19, WD 8.16**
  applying to form letter, WD 5.41-42
  applying to online form, WD 8.19
Parentheses, code statements and, WD 8.39
Parenthetical citations, in research paper, **WD 2.06**
Password-protected document, **WD 9.33**
  online form, WD 7.47-48
  reference document, WD 9.33-35, WD 9.40
Paste button (Standard toolbar), WD 2.32, WD 2.46
Paste Link command (Edit menu), WDI 2.09
Paste Options button, **WD 2.47**
Paste Options menu, WD 2.47
Paste Special command (Edit menu), linking text, **WD 6.45-47**
Pasted object, **WDI 2.01**
Pasting, **WD 2.44**
  from Clipboard, **WD 1.32**, WD 1.35-37
  Excel data to be charted, WDI 2.09
  link, WD 6.45, WDI 2.01, WDI 2.09
Pen comments, WD 9.11
Period (.), number of spaces after, WD 1.33
Personal form letters, **WD 5.04**
Personalizing
  cover letter, WD 3.27
  resume, WD 3.16-26

Picture, **WD 5.11**, WD 9.24, **WD 9.49**
Picture bullets, WD 4.48-49
Picture command (Insert menu),
  chart, WD 4.40-41, WDI 2.06
  clip art from Web, WD 4.16
  screen shot, WD 9.24
  size, WD 1.52
  WordArt, WD 6.10
Picture toolbar, WD 1.50, WD 1.52
Placeholder, WD 7.07
  text, **WD 3.19, WD 5.10,** WD 5.12
Planning proposal, **WD 4.04**
Point (font size measurement), **WD 1.20**
Portrait orientation
  document, WD 2.09
  table, **WD 5.66**
Positioning text box, WD 6.41-42
POSTNET (POSTal Numeric Encoding Technique) delivery-point bar code, **WD 5.54**
Preview, WDW 1.11, **WD 4.24**
Previous Record button (Mail Merge toolbar), **WD 5.53**
Print button (Print Preview toolbar), WD 3.26
Print button (Standard toolbar), WD 1.54
Print command (File menu), WD 1.54
  drafts, WD 3.25
  field codes, WD 5.46
  page number options, WD 4.29
  specific pages, WD 4.26
Print layout view, **WD 2.13, WD 3.14**
  changing margins in, WD 2.07, WD 2.09
  footnote in, WD 2.31
  header in, WD 2.12-15
  resume in, WD 3.14
Print Layout View button, WD 2.13, **WD 3.14**
Print preview, **WD 3.25**
  centering page in window, WD 3.26
  displaying several pages in, WD 9.64
  footnote in, WD 2.31
  header in, WD 2.13, WD 2.15
  resume, WD 3.25-26
Print Preview button (Standard toolbar), WD 1.55, WD 3.25
Print Preview command (File menu), WD 3.26
Printer, WD 1.54, WD 3.57
Printing, WD 1.54-55
  back-to-back duplicating, WD 9.05, WD 9.61
  bound documents and, WD 9.63
  canceling, WD 1.55
  colors, WD 4.26
  comments, WD 9.13
  drafts, WD 3.25, WD 3.25
  envelopes, WD 3.57, WD 5.59-62
  field codes, WD 5.46-47
  form letter, WD 5.48
  gutter margins and, WD 9.63
  headings, WD 9.36
  mailing labels, WD 5.58-59
  orientation, WD 2.09, WD 5.66
  page number options, WD 4.29
  resume in print preview, WD 3.25
  shortcut keys list, WD 2.16
  specific pages, WD 4.26
  wordwrap and, WD 1.25
Printout, **WD 1.54**
Private keyword, procedure and, WD 8.48
Procedure, **WD 8.04, WD 8.39**
  adding code statements to, WD 8.42-43
  adding comments to, WD 8.40-41
  entering code statements in, WD 8.58
  inserting for macro, WD 8.46-50
  planning and writing, WD 8.48-50
  private, WD 8.48
  public, WD 8.48
  testing, WD 8.48
Procedure command (Insert menu), WD 8.48
Professional resume, WD 3.10

Program, WD 8.04
Program buttons, on taskbar, WD 3.28
Programs submenu (Start menu), Microsoft Word command, WD 1.08
Proofreading, **WD 2.42-44**, WD 3.56
Properties, ActiveX control, WD 8.53-54
Properties button (Control Toolbox toolbar), WD 8.54
Properties command (File menu), document statistics, WD 2.33
Properties window, WD 8.55
Proposals, types of, WD 4.04
Protect Document command (Tools menu), online form, WD 7.47, WD 7.48, WD 7.57
Protect Forms button (Forms toolbar), WD 7.48, WD 7.57
Protected document
  macros and, WD 8.09-11
  online form, WD 7.08, WD 7.47-48, WD 8.09-11, WD 8.37
  password and, WD 9.33-35, WD 9.40
  removing protection, WD 7.08
Protected form, **WD 7.08**, WD 7.47-48, WD 8.09-11, WD 8.37
Public keyword, procedure and, WD 8.48
Publishing to Internet, **WDW 1.02,** WDW 1.13
Pull-quote, **WD 6.06**, WD 6.36-42
Pyramid diagram, WD 6.50-51

Question mark (?) wildcard character, WD 4.24
Questionnaires, designing, WD 7.12
Quitting
  Visual Basic Editor, WD 8.43
  Word, WD 1.55

Radial diagram, WD 9.49-54
REC status indicator (record macro), WD 8.24
Recorded macro
  automatic macros, WD 8.32-37
  creating, WD 8.23-28
  editing, WD 8.37-44
Records, **WD 5.21-27,** WD 5.29
Recount button (Count toolbar), WD 2.34
Rectangle (online form)
  filling with texture, WD 7.42-43
  inserting and formatting, WD 7.38-45
  line color, WD 7.43-44
  resizing, WD 8.22
Rectangle button (Drawing toolbar), online form, WD 7.39
Redo button (Standard toolbar), **WD 1.38-39**
Reference command (Insert menu)
  captions, WD 9.26
  cross-reference, WD 9.29
  footnote, WD 2.25
  index, WD 9.31, WD 9.57
  table of contents, WD 9.58
  table of figures, WD 9.55
Reference document, **WD 9.04-69**
  alternating headers and footers, WD 9.61-62
  bookmarks, WD 9.59-61
  captions, WD 9.25-28
  cross-references, WD 9.29-31
  diagram in, WD 9.49-54
  gutter margin, WD 9.63
  index, WD 9.04, WD 9.30-32, WD 9.56-58, WD 9.67-69
  orphans, WD 9.32-33
  table of contents, WD 9.04, WD 9.58-59, WD 9.67-69
  table of figures, WD 9.04, WD 9.25, WD 9.54-56
  title page, WD 9.46-48
  widows, WD 9.32-33
References
  MLA style for, WD 2.06
  resume, WD 3.24

Rejecting tracked changes, WD 9.19, WD 9.21
Rem, comments beginning with, WD 8.40
Remove Hyperlink command (shortcut menu), WD 3.40
Removing
  borders, WD 4.10, WD 9.28
  document protection, WD 7.08
  form field shading, WD 7.37
  hyperlink from address, WD 3.40
  selection, WD 1.45
  subdocument from master document, WD 9.46
  table line, WD 4.56
  text animation, WD 7.47
Repeat command (Edit menu), **WD 1.39**
Replace command (Edit menu), WD 2.49
Replacing placeholder text, WD 3.19-20
Research paper, WD 2.04-55
  body of, WD 2.15-34
  documentation styles, WD 2.04-06
  e-mailing, WD 2.54
  footnotes in, WD 2.24-32
  formatting, WD 2.07-34
  indenting paragraphs, WD 2.06, WD 2.18-20
  line spacing, WD 2.06, WD 2.10-11
  margins, WD 2.06, WD 2.07-09
  page breaks, WD 2.33-34
  proofing, WD 2.42-44
  revising, WD 2.44-52
  saving, WD 2.18
  works cited in, WD 2.06, WD 2.35-42
Research proposal, **WD 4.04**
Reset Toolbar command (Standard submenu), WD 2.07
Resetting menus and toolbars, WD 2.07
Resizing
  ActiveX control, WD 8.55-56
  chart, WD 4.43
  diagram, WD 6.53
  graphic, **WD 1.50-53,** WD 3.29, WD 9.24
  table columns, WD 3.51-52
  text box, WD 5.16
  Web page frame, WDW 1.08-09
  WordArt drawing object, WD 6.11
Resolution, printer, WD 1.54
Resume, **WD 3.04**
  AutoFormat, WD 3.22-24
  contents, WD 3.16
  copying information to letterhead from, WD 3.32-35
  creating using Resume Wizard, WD 3.08-14
  envelope and mailing label for, WD 3.57-58
  personalizing, WD 3.16-26
  saving as Web page, WDW 1.01-14
  viewing and printing, WD 3.25-26
Resume Wizard, **WD 3.08-14**
Reveal Formatting command (Format menu), WD 2.36, WD 4.66-67
Reviewing document, **WD 9.08-23**
  comments, WD 9.11-14
  tracked changes, WD 9.17-21
Reviewing Pane, **WD 9.13**
Reviewing toolbar, WD 9.13, WD 9.15, WD 9.17, WD 9.18-19
Revising research paper, WD 2.44-52
Revision marks, **WD 9.15**
Right margin, page number at, WD 2.12
Right-aligned, **WD 1.37, WD 2.12**
  header, WD 2.12, WD 2.13
  tab stop, WD 3.32, WD 6.16
Rotate or Flip command (Draw menu), WD 6.21
Row boundary, **WD 3.52**
Rows (table), WD 3.16, WD 3.17, WD 3.49
  adding, WD 4.32-33, WD 7.15
  charting, WD 4.39-40

deleting, WD 4.33
distributing evenly, WD 4.57
drawing in table, WD 4.55-56
summing, WD 4.33-34
Ruler
 changing margin settings using, WD 2.07, WD 2.09
 displaying or hiding, WD 1.13
 table and, WD 3.17
 vertical, WD 1.13, WD 3.14
Ruler command (View menu), WD 1.13
Ruler command (View menu), WD 2.18
Rules, **WD 6.06**
 vertical, WD 6.06, WD 6.33-34
Ruling lines, **WD 6.06, WD 6.14-15**
Run-around, **WD 6.06**, WD 6.60
Running macro, WD 8.27
 when user exits form field, WD 8.50-51

Sales proposal, **WD 4.04-68**
 chart, WD 4.39-46
 inserting existing document into open document, WD 4.21-26
 table, WD 4.32-40
 title page, WD 4.07-20
 watermark, WD 4.64-65
Salutation, business letter, **WD 3.41,** WD 3.46-47
Save All command (File menu), **WD 5.70**
Save As command (File menu), WD 4.26
 digital signature, WD 8.65
 document with new file name, WD 1.32, WD 1.54
 online form data, WD 7.53
 passwords, WD 9.34
Save as Web Page command (File menu), WDW 1.03
Save button (Standard toolbar), WD 1.29-32, WD 1.53
Save command (File menu), WD 1.53
Saving
 active document with new file name, WD 4.26
 all open documents, WD 5.70
 creating folder while, WD 5.20-21
 data for forms, WD 8.26, WD 8.27
 data source, WD 5.28
 document, WD 1.29-32
 document as Web page, WDW 1.03-04
 document with new file name, WD 9.11
 existing document with same file name, WD 1.53-54
 letterhead as template, WD 3.41
 linked documents, WDI 2.03
 master document, WD 9.43
 multiple versions of document, WD 9.16-17
 online form data, WD 7.52-54
 research paper, WD 2.18
 template, WD 7.10, WD 7.49, WD 7.57
Screen shot, **WD 9.23-24**
ScreenTip, **WD 1.11**, WD 1.15
Scroll bars, **WD 1.13**
Scroll box, **WD 1.13, WD 1.26**
Scrolling, WD 1.26-27, WD 1.41-42
Scrolls, **WD 1.26**
Search button (Standard toolbar), WD 6.67
Searching, WD 1.47, WD 6.67
Section, **WD 4.21**
 alignment, WD 4.23
 inserting page number in, WD 4.29-30
Section break, **WD 4.21-22**
 continuous, WD 6.24, WD 6.47-48
 next page, WD 6.30-31, WD 9.38
Section footer, creating footer different from previous, WD 4.30-31
Section header, creating header different from previous, WD 4.29
Security
 digital signature and, WD 8.64-67

macros and, WD 8.09-11
online form, WD 7.47-48, WD 8.09-11
passwords, WD 9.33-35, WD 9.40
setting level, WD 8.09-10
viruses and, WD 8.09-10
Security level, **WD 8.10**
Select, **WD 1.33**
Select Browse Object button (vertical scroll bar)
 browsing by page, WD 2.13, WD 2.43-44
 finding and replacing text, WD 2.49
 finding text, WD 2.49
Select Browse Object menu, Browse by Page command, WD 2.13
Selected text, **WD 1.33**
Selecting, **WD 1.33**
 cells in Word table, WD 3.16
 chart, WD 4.45
 data records to merge and print, WD 5.49-50
 group of words, WD 1.44
 line of text and formatting, WD 1.39-40
 paragraphs to format, WD 1.33-34
 placeholder text, WD 3.19-20
 rows and column to chart, WD 4.39-40
 nonadjacent text, WD 4.37-38
 sentence, WD 2.44-45
 table, WD 7.16
 table items, WD 3.53
 table text, WD 4.56
 techniques for, WD 2.45
 word, WD 1.42-43
Selection, removing, WD 1.45
Selection rectangles, **WD 1.50**
Selfcert.exe, digital signature and, **WD 8.67**
Self-signed projects, **WD 8.64**
Send a Copy button, WD 2.54
Send Behind Text command (Order submenu), WD 7.41
Send To command (File menu), e-mailing document as attachment, WD 2.54, WD 9.08-09
Sentence, selecting, WD 2.44-45
Shading
 form field, WD 7.18, WD 7.37
 paragraph, WD 4.11
 pull-quote, WD 6.40
 removing from form field, WD 7.37
 table cells, WD 4.62
Shading Color button arrow (Tables and Borders toolbar), WD 4.11
Shadow, WD 4.12-13, WD 7.44-45
Shadow Style button (Drawing toolbar), WD 7.44
Shape, WD 9.51, WD 9.54
 WordArt drawing object, WD 6.13-14
Short menu, **WD 1.14**, WD 1.15
Shortcut keys, **WD 2.16-17**
 creating style that has, WD 8.16-19
Shortcut menu, WD 1.14
Show First Line Only button (Outlining toolbar), WD 9.42
Show Gridlines command (Table menu), WD 7.17
Show Gridlines command (Table menu), **WD 3.17**
Show/Hide ¶ button (Standard toolbar), WD 1.24, WD 2.07, WD 7.16
Signature, digital, WD 8.64-67
Signature block, business letter, **WD 3.41**
Sizing handles, **WD 1.50**, WD 4.45
Smart tag, WD 2.16, WD 2.21, **WD 2.47-48, WD 3.58-60**
Smart Tag Actions button, WD 2.47-48, WD 3.59
Smart Tag Actions menu, WD 2.48
 Display Map command, WD 3.59
Snaking columns, **WD 6.24-25**
Soft page breaks, **WD 2.33**
Sort command (Table menu), WD 2.41

Sorting
 data records to merge and print, WD 5.52-53
 paragraphs, WD 2.41-42
 table of addresses, WD 5.68
Source document, **WDI 2.01**
 inserting in destination document as linked object, WDI 2.03-04
Source object, **WD 6.45**
Sources, citing, WD 2.04-06
Space
 nonbreaking, WD 3.45-46
 white, WD 3.15
SPACEBAR, pressing after period, WD 1.33
Spaces, number after period, WD 1.33
Spacing, fonts and, WD 1.33
Special characters, finding, WD 2.49
Speech recognition, WD 1.08-09, WD 1.17-18
Spelling, WD 1.05
 AutoCorrect and, WD 2.20-23
 checking while typing, WD 1.27-29
 checking with grammar, WD 2.50-52
 proofing for errors, WD 2.42
Spelling and Grammar button (Standard toolbar), WD 2.51
Spelling and Grammar command (Tools menu), WD 2.52
Spelling and Grammar Status icon, WD 1.14, **WD 1.22,** WD 1.27-28
Standard command (Add or Remove Buttons submenu), WD 2.07
Standard Headings panel (Resume Wizard dialog box), **WD 3.11**
Standard toolbar, **WD 1.15-17**
 adding button to, WD 8.28-31
 resetting, WD 2.07
Start menu, WD 1.08, WD 1.56
Start panel (Resume Wizard dialog box), **WD 3.09**
Starting Word, WD 1.07-09
Status bar, **WD 1.13,** WD 1.21
 Help text on, WD 7.34
 page indicator on, WD 2.44
 Status indicators, WD 1.13-14
Strikethroughs, **WD 9.15**
Style box (Formatting toolbar), WD 2.2, WD 3.197
 clearing formatting and, WD 4.12, WD 4.15
Style command (shortcut menu), footnote, WD 2.28
Style panel (Resume Wizard dialog box), **WD 3.10**
Styles, **WD 2.27, WD 3.18, WD 8.16**
 applying, WD 2.30
 business letter, WD 3.41
 character, WD 3.19, **WD 4.50-51,** WD 8.16-18
 clear formatting, WD 3.39, WD 4.12, WD 4.15
 creating character, WD 4.50-51
 creating that has shortcut key, WD 8.16-19
 footnote, WD 2.27-30
 Formatting toolbar and, WD 3.19
 list, WD 3.19
 modifying, WD 2.27-30
 paragraph, WD 3.19, WD 8.16
 resume, WD 3.10
 table, WD 3.19
 template and, WD 7.08
 types of, WD 3.19, WD 5.42
 writing, WD 9.02-03
Style box arrow (Formatting toolbar), applying styles using, WD 8.19
Styles and Formatting button (Formatting toolbar), WD 2.30, WD 3.19, WD 3.39, WD 8.17
Styles and Formatting task pane, **WD 3.19, WD 8.17-18**
Sub statement, **WD 8.39**
Subdocuments, **WD 9.36**
 collapsed, WD 9.42
 creating from master document, WD 9.43-44

inserting in master document, WD 9.39-42
names, WD 9.67
removing from master document, WD 9.46
Subhead, **WD 6.06,** WD 6.47
Subheadings, displaying or hiding, WD 9.67
Submenu, **WD 1.14**
Summing table contents, WD 4.33-34
Superscript, **WD 2.24,** WD 2.26, WD 4.38
Switch, index entries including, WD 9.31
Switch Between Header and Footer button (Header and Footer toolbar), WD 4.31
Symbol command (Insert menu)
 inserting symbol automatically, WD 2.38
 nonbreaking space, WD 3.47
Synonym, **WD 2.50**
Symbols
 bullet, WD 4.48
 inserting automatically, WD 2.38-39
 inserting in newsletter, WD 6.16-18

Tab alignment, WD 3.32, WD 3.43, WD 6.16
Tab character, **WD 3.32,** WD 3.53
TAB key, WD 2.20, WD 3.50, WD 3.53
Tab stop, **WD 3.30**
 alignment of, WD 3.32, WD 3.43, WD 6.16
 custom, WD 3.30-31
 right-aligned, WD 6.16
 setting using ruler, WD 3.42-43
Table AutoFormat button (Tables and Borders toolbar), WD 4.35
Table AutoFormat command (Table menu), WD 4.35
Table menu
 AutoFit command, WD 3.52
 Formula command, WD 4.34
 Hide Gridlines command, WD 3.17
 Insert command, WD 3.50, WD 7.16
 Show Gridlines command, WD 3.17, WD 7.17
 Sort command, WD 2.41
 Table AutoFormat command, WD 4.35
Table move handle, **WD 3.17**
Table of contents, **WD 9.04,** WD 9.58-59, WD 9.67-69
Table of figures, WD 9.04, **WD 9.54-56**
 captions and, WD 9.25
Table resize handle, **WD 3.52**
Table styles, **WD 3.19**
Tables, **WD 3.16-17**
 adding rows and columns to, WD 4.32-33
 alignment, WD 3.53-54, WD 4.36
 centering, WD 4.36
 charting, WD 4.39-46, WDI 2.06
 check box in, WD 7.26-27
 creating with Insert Table button, WD 3.49-50
 dimension of, WD 3.49
 directories as, WD 5.65-68
 drawing, WD 4.53-64
 entering data in, WD 3.50-51, WD 4.58-59
 formatting, WD 4.34-39, WD 4.59-60
 gridlines, WD 3.17, WD 7.17
 inserting into online form, WD 7.15-17
 keeping together, WD 4.46
 move handle, WD 3.17
 nested, WD 4.59
 resizing columns, WD 3.51-52
 sales proposal, WD 4.32-40
 selecting, WD 7.16
 selecting text, WD 4.56
 sorting addresses, WD 5.68
 summing contents, WD 4.33-34
 wrapping text, WD 4.56

Tables and Borders button (Standard toolbar), **WD 4.08**
Tables and Borders toolbar, **WD 4.08**
Tabs command (Format menu), WD 3.31, WD 3.42
Task Pane command (View menu), WD 1.49
 resume, WD 3.14
 Web page, WDW 1.08
Task panes, **WD 1.09**, **WD 1.10**
 Word, displaying, WD 1.49
Taskbar, program buttons on, WD 3.14, WD 3.28
Template, **WD 3.04**, **WD 5.08**, **WD 7.08**
 creating for online form, WD 7.08-13
 e-mailing, WD 7.58-59
 entering and formatting clip art, WD 7.12
 entering and formatting text, WD 7.11
 main document in mail merge, WD 5.08-10
 modifying, WD 7.57
 normal, WD 7.09
 opening, WD 7.49, WD 7.50, WD 7.57
 resume and, WD 3.08-09
 saving, WD 7.10, WD 7.49, WD 7.57
 saving letterhead as, WD 3.41
 Web page, WDW 1.05
 workgroup, WD 7.58
Testing
 AutoNew macro, WD 8.36-37
 online form, WD 8.61-63
 procedure, WD 8.48
Text
 adding to AutoShape, WD 5.15-16, WD 6.56
 animated, WD 4.15, WD 6.66-67, WD 7.45-47
 AutoText entry for, WD 3.44-46, WD 3.47-48
 default, in form fields, WD 7.18
 diagram, WD 6.51-52, WD 9.52-53
 entering as part of master document, WD 9.46-48
 entering in Word document, WD 1.21-29
 false, WD 5.35
 finding and replacing, WD 2.48-49
 footer, WD 2.11
 formatting nonadjacent, WD 4.37-38
 header, WD 2.11-15
 highlighting, WDW 1.09, WD 6.65, WD 7.13
 keeping together lines of, WD 4.46-47
 linking text using Paste Special command, WD 6.45-47
 moving, WD 2.44-47
 note, WD 2.24
 selecting, WD 2.44-45
 selecting table, WD 4.56
 selecting to format, WD 1.33
 sorting, WD 2.41-42
 template, WD 7.11
 true, WD 5.35
 WordArt object, WD 6.10
 wrap-around, WD 6.06
Text box
 converting to frame, WD 9.27-28
 inserting in newsletter, WD 6.36-40
 resizing, WD 5.16
Text boxes (online form), WD 7.15
 formatting text for, WD 8.14-15
 inserting, WD 8.13-14
 text form field for, WD 7.17-20
Text Box command (Format menu), WD 6.38
 converting text box to frame, WD 9.28
Text Box command (Insert menu), WD 6.37
Text file, WD 7.52, WD 7.55-56
Text form field, **WD 7.17**
 current date, WD 7.29-31
 formatting, WD 7.31-32
 Help text on, WD 7.34-36
 inserting, WD 7.17-18

modifying using VBA, WD 8.44-45
number of characters in, WD 7.19
for numbers, WD 7.24-25
running macro when user exits, WD 8.50-51
for text, WD 7.17-20
text formats for, WD 7.19-20
types, WD 7.24
Text Form Field button (Forms toolbar), WD 7.17
Text wrapping, WD 4.56, WD 9.25
Text Wrapping button (Picture toolbar), WD 9.25
Texture, drawing object, WD 7.42
Theme, **WDW 1.08**
Thesaurus, **WD 2.50**
3-D effect, **WD 8.21**
3-D Style button (Drawing toolbar), WD 8.21
Thumbnails, **WD 4.15**
Tick marks, horizontal ruler, **WD 3.30**
Tilde (~) key, WD 1.21
Title
 newsletter, WD 6.06, WD 6.08-22
 research paper, WD 2.06
Title and Location panel (Web Page Wizard dialog box), **WDW 1.05**
Titles of works, formatting for research paper, WD 2.06
Title page, WD 4.07-20
 APA style and, WD 2.16
 for reference document, WD 9.46-48
Toolbar Options button (Standard toolbar), resetting toolbars, WD 2.07
Toolbar Options list, WD 1.11, WD 1.16
Toolbars, **WD 1.15**
 assigning macro to button on, WD 8.28-31
 displaying, WD 1.50, WD 7.15
 displaying buttons on, WD 1.11, WD 1.16
 docked, WD 1.17, WD 2.13
 floating, WD 1.17, WD 1.50, WD 2.13
 More Buttons list, WD 8.32
 resetting, WD 1.17, WD 2.07
 toggle buttons, WD 1.41
Toolbars command (View menu), WD 1.50, WD 8.31
Tools menu
 AutoCorrect command, WD 2.23
 AutoCorrect Options command, smart tags, WD 2.16, WD 2.21, smart tags, WD 3.58
 AutoCorrect Options command, spelling, WD 1.27
 AutoFormat command, WD 3.22
 Compare and Merge Documents command, WD 6.71, WD 9.21-22
 Customize command, toolbars, WD 8.28
 Letters and Mailing command, form letters, WD 5.08
 Letters and Mailings command, mailing labels, WD 3.57, WD 5.54-55
 Macro command, security, WD 8.10
 Macro command, viewing VBA code, WD 8.38
 Options command, bookmarks, WD 9.59
 Options command, drag-and-drop editing, WD 2.45
 Options command, file display, WD 1.55
 Options command, hiding animated text, WD 7.45
 Options command, passwords, WD 9.35
 Options command, saving data for forms, WD 8.25-26, WD 8.27
 Options command, white space, WD 3.15
 Protect Document command, online form, WD 7.47, WD 7.48, WD 7.57

Speech command, WD 1.18
Spelling and Grammar command, WD 2.52
Track Changes command, WD 9.15
Unprotect Document command, WD 7.08
Word Count command, WD 2.32
Track Changes command (Tools menu), WD 9.15
TRK status indicator (track changes), WD 9.14
True text, **WD 5.35**

Underline, WD 1.43, WD 7.31-32
 hyperlink citations, WD 2.06
Underline button (Formatting toolbar), WD 1.43
Underscore characters
 in drop-down form field, WD 7.22
 in text form fields WD 7.18-19
Undo
 action, WD 1.38-39, WD 1.58
 AutoCorrect entry, WD 2.21
Undo button (Standard toolbar), **WD 1.38-39**, **WD 1.58**
Undo button arrow (Standard toolbar), WD 1.39
Undo command (Edit menu), WD 1.39
Unprotect Document command (Tools menu), WD 7.08
Updating, WD 5.30, WD 6.47

Version of document, **WD 9.16**
Versions command (File menu), WD 9.16
Vertical alignment
 of cell data, WD 4.59-60
 centering on page, WD 1.39, WD 4.18-19, WD 4.23
Vertical line, drawing table using, WD 4.55
Vertical rule, **WD 6.06**
 separating columns, WD 6.33-34
Vertical ruler, WD 1.13, WD 3.14
 changing margin settings using, WD 2.07
Vertically centering text, WD 1.39, WD 4.18-19, WD 4.23
View menu
 Header and Footer command, WD 2.12, WD 4.29, WD 9.61
 HTML Source command, WDW 1.11
 Markup command, WD 9.17
 Normal command, Normal view, WD 2.07
 Normal command, ruler display, WD 1.13
 Ruler command, WD 1.13, WD 2.18
 Task Pane command, WD 1.49
 Task Pane command, resume, WD 3.14
 Task Pane command, Web page, WDW 1.08
 Toolbars command, WD 1.50, WD 8.31
 Zoom command, WD 1.19, WD 3.18
View Microsoft Word button (Visual Basic toolbar), **WD 8.44**
Viewing
 document online, WD 6.64-67
 footnote, WD 2.31
 header, WD 2.12-13, WD 2.15
 macro's VBA code, WD 8.38-39
 merged data, WD 5.53
 Web page in default browser, WDW 1.11
Virus, macros and, **WD 8.09-10**
Visual Basic Editor, WD 8.37-44
 entering code statements in procedure, WD 8.58
Visual Basic for Applications (VBA), **WD 8.04**
 creating macro from scratch using, WD 8.44-51
 editing macros and, WD 8.37-44
 help with, WD 8.53
 macros and, WD 8.05
 modifying code, WD 8.42

planning and writing procedure, WD 8.48-50
viewing macro's code, WD 8.38-39
Visual Theme panel (Web Page Wizard dialog box), **WDW 1.08**

Watermark, **WD 4.64-65**
Web, inserting clip art from, WD 4.15-16
Web addresses
 assigning to button, WD 8.32
 converting to hyperlinks, WD 2.39-40
Web folder, WDW 1.02
Web layout view, WDW 1.03
Web Layout View button, WDW 1.03
Web page
 adding link to, WDW 1.10
 button to connect to, WD 8.32
 creating using Web Page Wizard, WDW 1.04-08
 creating using Word, WDW 1.01-14
 editing from browser, WDW 1.12-13
 form on, WD 7.49
 HTML source code for, WDW 1.11
 lines separating sections of, WDW 1.10
 modifying, WDW 1.08-11
 saving resume as, WDW 1.01-14
 saving Word document as, WDW 1.03-04
 viewing in default browser, WDW 1.11
Web page authoring, **WDW 1.01**, **WDW 1.03**
Web Page Preview command (File menu), **WDW 1.11**
Web Page Wizard, WDW 1.01, **WDW 1.04-08**
Web sites, formatting for research paper, WD 2.06
White space, hiding, WD 3.15
Widow, **WD 4.48**, **WD 9.32-33**
Wildcard characters, WD 4.24
Windows Clipboard, WD 3.32
Windows screen resolution, WD 1.18
Windows taskbar, WD 1.08
Wizard, **WD 3.04**
Word 2002, **WD 1.06**
 customizing, WD 1.09-12
 quitting, WD 1.55
 starting, WD 1.07-09
Word count, WD 2.32-33, WD 2.34
Word Help system, **WD 1.59-61**
Word window, WD 1.08-09, WD 1.11, **WD 1.12-19**
 note pane in, WD 2.26
WordArt, for newsletter nameplate, **WD 6.08-14**
WordArt command (Format menu), WD 6.13
Words
 selecting, WD 1.42-43, WD 2.45
 selecting group of, WD 1.44
Wordwrap, **WD 1.25**
Workgroup templates, **WD 7.58**
Works cited, in research paper, **WD 2.06**, **WD 2.35-42**
Works cited page, **WD 2.34-42**
Wrap text, indents and, WD 2.38
Wrap-around text, **WD 6.06**
Wrapping style, graphic, WD 6.59
Wrist injury, WD 1.27

X, displaying in check box, WD 7.25

ZIP code, WD 5.54
Zoom a percentage, WD 6.50
Zoom box arrow (Standard toolbar), WD 2.09, WD 3.18
Zoom command (View menu), WD 1.19, WD 3.18
Zoom page width, **WD 1.18-19**, **WD 2.09**
Zoom percentage, WD 1.18
Zoom text width, **WD 3.17-18**, **WD 5.07**, **WD 6.08**
Zoom whole page, WD 4.18, WD 6.32

Microsoft WORD 2002 Quick Reference Summary

In Microsoft Word 2002, you can accomplish a task in a number of ways. The following table provides a quick reference to each task presented in this textbook. The first column identifies the task. The second column indicates the page number on which the task is discussed in the book. The subsequent four columns list the different ways the task in column one can be carried out. You can invoke the commands listed in the MOUSE, MENU BAR, and SHORTCUT MENU columns using Voice commands.

Microsoft Word 2002 Quick Reference Summary

TASK	PAGE NUMBER	MOUSE	MENU BAR	SHORTCUT MENU	KEYBOARD SHORTCUT
1.5 Line Spacing	WD 2.18		Format | Paragraph | Indents and Spacing tab	Paragraph | Indents and Spacing tab	CTRL+5
ActiveX Control, Format	WD 8.56		Format | Control	Format | Control	
ActiveX Control, Insert	WD 8.52	Desired button on Control Toolbox toolbar			
ActiveX Control, Set Properties	WD 8.54	Properties button on Control Toolbox toolbar		Properties	
ActiveX Control, Write Code	WD 8.59	View Code button on Control Toolbox toolbar		View Code	
Animate Text	WD 6.66		Format | Font | Text Effects tab	Font | Text Effects tab	
AutoCorrect Entry, Create	WD 2.23		Tools | AutoCorrect Options | AutoCorrect tab		
AutoCorrect Options	WD 2.22	AutoCorrect Options button			
AutoShape, Add Text	WD 5.15			Add Text	
AutoShape, Format	WD 5.14	Double-click inside AutoShape	Format | AutoShape	Format AutoShape	
AutoShape, Insert	WD 5.12	AutoShapes button on Drawing toolbar	Insert | Picture | AutoShapes		
AutoText Entry, Create	WD 3.45		Insert | AutoText | New		ALT+F3
AutoText Entry, Insert	WD 3.47		Insert | AutoText		Type entry, then F3
Blank Line Above Paragraph	WD 2.18		Format | Paragraph | Indents and Spacing tab	Paragraph | Indents and Spacing tab	CTRL+0
Bold	WD 1.45	Bold button on Formatting toolbar	Format | Font | Font tab	Font | Font tab	CTRL+B
Bookmark, Add	WD 9.60		Insert | Bookmark		
Bookmark, Go To	WD 9.61	Select Browse Object button on vertical scroll bar	Edit | Go To		CTRL+G
Border, Bottom	WD 3.38	Border button arrow on Formatting toolbar	Format | Borders and Shading | Borders tab		
Border, Page	WD 6.63		Format | Borders and Shading | Page Border tab	Borders and Shading | Page Border tab	
Bulleted List	WD 3.54	Bullets button on Formatting toolbar	Format | Bullets and Numbering | Bulleted tab	Bullets and Numbering | Bulleted tab	* and then space followed by text, then ENTER
Capitalize Letters	WD 2.18		Format | Font | Font tab	Font | Font tab	CTRL+SHIFT+A
Caption, Add	WD 9.26		Insert | Caption		
Caption, Update Caption Number	WD 9.27			Update Field	F9

QR.01

Microsoft Word 2002 Quick Reference Summary (continued)

TASK	PAGE NUMBER	MOUSE	MENU BAR	SHORTCUT MENU	KEYBOARD SHORTCUT
Case of Letters	WD 2.18				SHIFT+F3
Center	WD 1.38	Center button on Formatting toolbar	Format | Paragraph | Indents and Spacing tab	Paragraph | Indents and Spacing tab	CTRL+E
Center Text Vertically	WD 4.19		File | Page Setup | Layout tab		
Character Formatting, Remove	WD 2.18		Format | Font | Font tab	Font | Font tab	CTRL+SPACEBAR
Character Style, Apply	WD 4.52	Style box arrow on Formatting toolbar	Format | Styles and Formatting		
Character Style, Create	WD 4.51	Styles and Formatting button on Formatting toolbar	Format | Styles and Formatting		
Chart, Change Chart Type	WD 4.43		Chart | Chart Type	Right-click chart, Chart Type	
Chart, Move Legend	WD 4.42		Select legend, Format | Selected Legend | Placement tab	Right-click legend, Format Legend | Placement tab	
Chart, Resize	WD 4.43	Drag sizing handles			
Chart Table	WD 4.40		Insert | Picture | Chart		
Clip Art, Insert	WD 1.46		Insert | Picture | Clip Art		
Clip Art, Insert from Web	WD 4.16		Insert | Picture | Clip Art		
Close All Open Documents	WD 5.70		SHIFT+File | Close All		
Close Document	WD 1.58	Close button on menu bar	File | Close		CTRL+W
Color Characters	WD 3.28	Font Color button arrow on Formatting toolbar	Format | Font | Font tab	Font | Font tab	
Column Break, Insert	WD 6.31		Insert | Break		CTRL+SHIFT+ENTER
Columns	WD 6.25	Columns button on Standard toolbar	Format | Columns		
Columns, Balance	WD 6.48		Insert | Break		
Columns, Format	WD 6.25		Format | Columns		
Comment, Delete	WD 9.18	Reject Change/Delete Comment button on Reviewing toolbar		Right-click comment reference mark in document window, click Delete Comment	
Comment, Insert	WD 6.69 WD 9.11	New Comment button on Reviewing toolbar	Insert | Comment		
Comment, Modify	WD 9.13	Double-click comment reference mark in document window	View | Comments	Right-click comment reference mark in document window, click Edit Comment	
Comment, Print	WD 9.13		File | Print | Options button		
Comment, Review	WD 9.18	Next button on Reviewing toolbar			
Compare and Merge Documents	WD 6.71 WD 9.21		Tools | Compare and Merge Documents		
Copy (Collect Items)	WD 3.33	Copy button on Standard toolbar	Edit | Copy	Copy	CTRL+C
Cross-Reference, Create	WD 9.29		Insert | Reference | Cross-reference		
Count Words	WD 2.32	Recount button on Word Count toolbar	Tools | Word Count		
Data Source, Change Designation	WDI 1.05	Open Data Source button on Mail Merge toolbar	Tools | Letters and Mailings | Mail Merge Wizard		
Data Source, Type New	WD 5.23	Mail Merge Recipients button on Mail Merge toolbar	Tools | Letters and Mailings | Mail Merge Wizard		
Date, Insert	WD 3.43		Insert | Date and Time		
Delete (Cut) Text	WD 1.54	Cut button on Standard toolbar	Edit | Cut	Cut	CTRL+X
Demote List Item	WD 3.56	Decrease Indent button on Formatting toolbar			

Microsoft Word 2002 Quick Reference Summary

TASK	PAGE NUMBER	MOUSE	MENU BAR	SHORTCUT MENU	KEYBOARD SHORTCUT
Diagram, Add Segments	WD 6.51	Insert Shape button on Diagram toolbar		Insert Shape	
Diagram, AutoFormat	WD 6.52	AutoFormat button on Diagram toolbar			
Diagram, Insert	WD 6.49	Insert Diagram or Organization Chart button on Drawing toolbar			
Digitally Sign a File	WD 8.65		Tools | Options | Security tab		
Distribute Columns Evenly	WD 4.57	Distribute Columns Evenly button on Tables and Borders toolbar	Table | AutoFit | Distribute Columns Evenly		
Distribute Rows Evenly	WD 4.57	Distribute Rows Evenly button on Tables and Borders toolbar	Table | AutoFit | Distribute Rows Evenly		
Document Map	WD 9.66	Document Map button on Standard toolbar			
Document Window, Open New	WD 3.27	New Blank Document button on Standard toolbar		File | New | Blank Document	CTRL+N
Double-Space Text	WD 2.09	Line Spacing button on Formatting toolbar	Format | Paragraph | Indents and Spacing tab	Paragraph | Indents and Spacing tab	CTRL+2
Double Strikethrough Characters	WD 4.15		Format | Font | Font tab	Font | Font tab	
Double-Underline	WD 2.18		Format | Font | Font tab	Font | Font tab	CTRL+SHIFT+D
Drawing Canvas, Format	WD 5.18	Double-click edge of drawing canvas	Format | Drawing Canvas	Format Drawing Canvas	
Drawing Canvas, Resize	WD 5.17	Drag sizing handles	Format | Drawing Canvas | Size tab	Format Drawing Canvas | Size tab	
Drawing Object, 3-D Effect	WD 8.21	3-D Style button on Drawing toolbar			
Drawing Object, Fill	WD 7.42	Fill Color button arrow on Drawing toolbar	Format | AutoShape | Colors and Lines tab	Format AutoShape | Colors and Lines tab	
Drawing Object, Line Color	WD 7.43	Line Color button on Drawing toolbar	Format | AutoShape | Colors and Lines tab	Format AutoShape | Colors and Lines tab	
Drawing Object, Order	WD 7.41	Draw button on Drawing toolbar, Order	Format | AutoShape | Layout tab	Order	
Drawing Object, Shadow	WD 7.44	Shadow Style button on Drawing toolbar			
Drop Cap	WD 6.28		Format | Drop Cap		
Edit Field	WD 5.31			Edit Field	
E-Mail Document	WD 2.54	E-mail button on Standard toolbar	File | Send to | Mail Recipient		
E-Mail Document for Review	WD 9.08		File | Send To | Mail Recipient (for Review)		
Emboss, Characters	WD 4.15		Format | Font | Font tab	Font | Font tab	
Engrave, Characters	WD 4.15		Format | Font | Font tab	Font | Font tab	
Envelope, Address	WD 3.57		Tools | Letters and Mailings | Envelopes and Labels | Envelopes tab		
Erase Table Lines	WD 4.56	Eraser button on Tables and Borders toolbar			
Field Code, Display	WD 5.45		Tools | Options | View tab	Toggle Field Codes	ALT+F9
Field Codes, Print	WD 5.46		Tools | Options | Print tab		
Find	WD 2.49	Select Browse Object button on vertical scroll bar	Edit | Find		CTRL+F
Find and Replace	WD 2.48	Double-click status bar to left of status indicators	Edit | Replace		CTRL+H
First-Line Indent	WD 2.19	Drag First Line Indent marker on ruler	Format | Paragraph | Indents and Spacing tab	Paragraph | Indents and Spacing tab	

Microsoft Word 2002 Quick Reference Summary (continued)

TASK	PAGE NUMBER	MOUSE	MENU BAR	SHORTCUT MENU	KEYBOARD SHORTCUT
Folder, Create	WD 5.21		File | Save As | Create New Folder button		CTRL+F12 | Create New Folder button
Font	WD 1.36	Font box arrow on Formatting toolbar	Format | Font | Font tab	Font | Font tab	CTRL+SHIFT+F
Font Size	WD 1.20	Font Size box arrow on Formatting toolbar	Format | Font | Font tab	Font | Font tab	CTRL+SHIFT+P
Footer	WD 4.31	Switch Between Header and Footer button on Header and Footer toolbar	View | Header and Footer		
Form, Add Help Text	WD 7.35	Double-click form field		Right-click form field, click Properties	
Form, Change Bookmark	WD 8.45	Double-click form field		Right-click form field, click Properties	
Form, Check Box Options	WD 7.25	Double-click check box form field		Right-click form field, click Properties	
Form, Drop-Down Form Field Options	WD 7.23	Double-click drop-down form field		Right-click form field, click Properties	
Form, Insert Check Box	WD 7.27	Check Box Form Field on Forms toolbar			
Form, Insert Drop-Down Form Field	WD 7.21	Drop-Down Form Field button on Forms toolbar			
Form, Insert Table	WD 7.15	Insert Table button on Forms toolbar	Table | Insert | Table		
Form, Insert Text Form Field	WD 7.17	Text Form Field button on Forms toolbar			
Form, Protect	WD 7.48	Protect Form button on Forms toolbar	Tools | Protect Document		
Form, Remove Field Shading	WD 7.37	Form Field Shading button on Forms toolbar			
Form, Save Data Only	WD 7.53		File | Save As | Tools | Save Options		
Form, Text Form Field Options	WD 7.19	Double-click text form field		Right-click form field, click Properties	
Format Characters, Font Dialog Box	WD 4.13		Format | Font| Font tab		
Format Painter	WD 6.61	Format Painter button on Standard toolbar			
Footnote, Create	WD 2.25		Insert | Reference | Footnote		
Footnote, Delete	WD 2.31	Delete note reference mark in document window			
Footnote, Edit	WD 2.32	Double-click note reference mark in document window	View | Footnotes		
Footnotes to Endnotes, Convert	WD 2.32		Insert | Reference | Footnote		
Formatting, Clear	WD 3.39	Styles and Formatting button on Formatting toolbar or Style box arrow on Formatting toolbar			CTRL+SPACEBAR; CTRL+Q
Formatting Marks	WD 1.24	Show/Hide ¶ button on Standard toolbar	Tools | Options | View tab		CTRL+SHIFT+*
Formatting, Reveal	WD 2.36	Other Task Panes button on open task pane	Format | Reveal Formatting		
Full Menu	WD 1.14	Double-click menu name	Click menu name, wait few seconds		
Go To	WD 2.42	Select Browse Object button on vertical scroll bar	Edit | Go To		CTRL+G
Graph, Exit and Return to Word	WD 4.44	Click anywhere outside chart			

Microsoft Word 2002 Quick Reference Summary

TASK	PAGE NUMBER	MOUSE	MENU BAR	SHORTCUT MENU	KEYBOARD SHORTCUT
Graphic, Convert to Floating	WD 6.20	Text Wrapping button on Picture toolbar	Format | Picture | Layout tab	Format Picture | Layout tab	
Graphic, Flip	WD 6.21	Draw button on Drawing toolbar			
Graphic Objects, Reorder	WD 6.57	Draw button on Drawing toolbar		Order	
GreetingLine Merge Field, Edit	WD 5.32			Edit Greeting Line	
Gridlines, Show	WD 7.17		Table | Show Gridlines		
Gutter Margin	WD 9.63		File | Page Setup | Margins tab		
Hanging Indent, Create	WD 2.37	Drag Hanging Indent marker on ruler	Format | Paragraph | Indents and Spacing tab	Paragraph | Indents and Spacing tab	CTRL+T
Hanging Indent, Remove	WD 2.18	Drag Hanging Indent marker on ruler	Format | Paragraph | Indents and Spacing tab	Paragraph | Indents and Spacing tab	CTRL+SHIFT+T
Header, Different from Previous	WD 4.29		View | Header and Footer		
Header, Display	WD 2.12		View | Header and Footer		
Headers, Alternating	WD 9.61	Page Setup button on Header and Footer toolbar	File | Page Setup | Layout tab		
Help	WD 1.59 and Appendix A	Microsoft Word Help button on Standard toolbar	Help | Microsoft Word Help		F1
Hidden Characters	WD 4.15		Format | Font | Font tab	Font | Font tab	
Highlight Text	WDW 1.09 WD 6.65	Highlight button on Formatting toolbar			
HTML Source	WDW 1.11		View | HTML Source		
Hyperlink, Convert to Regular Text	WD 3.40	AutoCorrect Options button | Undo Hyperlink		Remove Hyperlink	CTRL+Z
Hyperlink, Create	WD 2.40	Insert Hyperlink button on Standard toolbar		Hyperlink	Web address then ENTER or SPACEBAR
Hyperlink, Edit	WDW 1.10	Insert Hyperlink button on Standard toolbar		Hyperlink	
IF Field, Insert	WD 5.36	Insert Word Field button on Mail Merge toolbar	Insert | Field		
Indent, Decrease	WD 2.18	Decrease Indent button on Formatting toolbar	Format | Paragraph | Indents and Spacing tab	Paragraph | Indents and Spacing tab	CTRL+SHIFT+M
Indent, Increase	WD 2.18	Increase Indent button on Formatting toolbar	Format | Paragraph | Indents and Spacing tab	Paragraph | Indents and Spacing tab	CTRL+M
Index, Build	WD 9.57		Insert | Reference | Index and Tables | Index tab		
Index, Update	WD 9.67			Right-click selected index, click Update Field	Select index, F9
Index Entry, Mark	WD 9.31		Insert | Reference | Index and Tables | Index tab		ALT+SHIFT+X
Insert File	WD 4.24		Insert | File		
Italicize	WD 1.41	Italic button on Formatting toolbar	Format | Font | Font tab	Font | Font tab	CTRL+I
Justify Paragraph	WD 6.26	Justify button on Formatting toolbar	Format | Paragraph | Indents and Spacing tab	Paragraph | Indents and Spacing tab	CTRL+J
Keep Lines Together	WD 4.47		Format | Paragraph | Line and Page Breaks tab	Paragraph | Line and Page Breaks tab	
Language Bar	WD 1.18	Language Indicator button in tray	Tools | Speech		
Last Editing Location	WD 4.25				SHIFT+F5
Leader Characters	WD 3.30		Format | Tabs		
Left-Align	WD 2.17	Align Left button on Formatting toolbar	Format | Paragraph | Indents and Spacing tab	Paragraph | Indents and Spacing tab	CTRL+L

Microsoft Word 2002 Quick Reference Summary (continued)

TASK	PAGE NUMBER	MOUSE	MENU BAR	SHORTCUT MENU	KEYBOARD SHORTCUT
Line Break, Enter	WD 3.21				SHIFT+ENTER
Link Copied Excel Data to Word Chart	WDI 2.08		Edit	Paste Link		
Link Copied Item	WD 6.45		Edit	Paste Special		
Link Excel Worksheet	WDI 2.04		Insert	Object	Create from File tab		
List Item, Demote	WD 5.41	Increase Indent button on Formatting toolbar			SHIFT+TAB
List Item, Promote	WD 5.41	Decrease Indent button on Formatting toolbar			TAB
Macro, Copy	WD 8.68	In Visual Basic Editor, Copy button on Standard toolbar, then Paste button on Standard toolbar	In Visual Basic Editor, Edit	Copy; then Edit	Paste	In Visual Basic Editor, Copy then Paste	In Visual Basic Editor, CTRL+C then CTRL+V
Macro, Delete	WD 8.68		Tools	Macro	Macros		
Macro, Record	WD 8.24	Double-click REC status indicator on status bar	Tools	Macro	Record New Macro		
Macro, Run	WD 8.27	Run Macro button on Standard toolbar in Visual Basic Editor	Tools	Macro	Macros		ALT+F8
Macro, Run on Exit	WD 8.51	Double-click form field		Right-click form field, click Properties	
Macro, View VBA Code	WD 8.38		Tools	Macro	Macros		ALT+F11
Mail Merge, Directory	WD 5.63	Main document setup button on Mail Merge toolbar	Tools	Letters and Mailings	Mail Merge Wizard		
Mail Merge, Envelopes	WD 5.60	Main document setup button on Mail Merge toolbar	Tools	Letters and Mailings	Mail Merge Wizard		
Mail Merge, Mailing Labels	WD 5.54	Main document setup button on Mail Merge toolbar	Tools	Letters and Mailings	Mail Merge Wizard		
Mail Merge, Select Records	WD 5.49	Mail Merge Recipients button on Mail Merge toolbar			
Mail Merge, Sort Data Records	WD 5.52	Mail Merge Recipients button on Mail Merge toolbar			
Mail Merge Fields, Insert	WD 5.34	Insert Merge Field button on Mail Merge toolbar			
Mail Merge to New Document Window	WD 5.66	Merge to New Document button on Mail Merge toolbar			
Mail Merge to Printer	WD 5.48	Merge to Printer button on Mail Merge toolbar			
Mail Merged Data, View	WD 5.53	View Merged Data button on Mail Merge toolbar			
Mailing Label, Address	WD 3.58		Tools	Letters and Mailings	Envelopes and Labels	Labels tab		
Margins	WD 2.08	In print layout view, drag margin boundary on ruler	File	Page Setup	Margins tab		
Master Document, Open	WD 9.65	Open button on Standard toolbar, then Expand Subdocuments button on Outlining toolbar			
Menus and Toolbars, Reset	WD 2.07	Toolbar Options button on toolbar	Add or Remove Buttons	Customize	Options tab	View	Toolbars	Customize	Options tab		
Merge, Check for Errors	WDI 1.07	Check for Errors button on Mail Merge toolbar			
Merge to E-Mail Addresses	WDI 1.10	Merge to E-mail button on Mail Merge toolbar			
Move Selected Text	WD 2.46	Drag and drop	Edit	Cut; Edit	Paste	Cut; Paste	CTRL+X; CTRL+V
Nonbreaking Hyphen	WD 3.46		Insert	Symbol	Special Characters tab		CTRL+SHIFT+HYPHEN

Microsoft Word 2002 Quick Reference Summary

TASK	PAGE NUMBER	MOUSE	MENU BAR	SHORTCUT MENU	KEYBOARD SHORTCUT
Nonbreaking Space	WD 3.47		Insert	Symbol	Special Characters tab		CTRL+SHIFT+SPACEBAR
Note Pane, Close	WD 2.31	Close button in note pane			
Numbered List	WD 3.56	Numbering button on Formatting toolbar	Format	Bullets and Numbering	Numbered tab	Bullets and Numbering	Numbered tab	1. and then space followed by text, then ENTER
Office Clipboard Task Pane, Display	WD 3.33	Double-click Office Clipboard icon in tray	Edit	Office Clipboard		
Open Document	WD 1.56	Open button on Standard toolbar	File	Open		CTRL+O
Outline Numbered List	WD 5.38		Format	Bullets and Numbering	Outline Numbered tab	Bullets and Numbering	Outline Numbered tab	
Outline, Characters	WD 4.15		Format	Font	Font tab	Font	Font tab	
Outline, Create	WD 9.37	Outline View button on horizontal scroll bar	View	Outline		
Outline, Demote Heading	WD 9.45	Demote button on Outlining toolbar			TAB
Outline, Demote Heading to Body Text	WD 9.44	Demote to Body Text button on Outlining toolbar			TAB until style is Body Text
Outline, Promote Heading	WD 9.45	Promote button on Outlining toolbar			SHIFT+TAB
Outline, Show First Line of Paragraphs	WD 9.46	Show First Line Only button on Outlining toolbar			
Page Alignment	WD 4.23		File	Page Setup	Layout tab		
Page Break	WD 2.35		Insert	Break		CTRL+ENTER
Page Numbers, Insert	WD 2.14	Insert Page Number button on Header and Footer toolbar	Insert	Page Numbers		
Page Numbers, Modify	WD 4.30	Format Page Number button on Header and Footer toolbar	Insert	Page Numbers	Format button		
Page Orientation	WD 5.66		File	Page Setup	Paper Size tab		
Paragraph, Change Format	WD 5.19	Click link in Reveal Formatting task pane	Format	Paragraph	Indents and Spacing tab	Paragraph	Indents and Spacing tab	
Paragraph Formatting, Remove	WD 2.18		Format	Paragraph	Indents and Spacing tab	Paragraph	Indents and Spacing tab	CTRL+Q
Paragraph Style, Apply	WD 5.42	Style box arrow on Formatting toolbar	Format	Styles and Formatting		
Password-Protect File	WD 9.34		File	Save As	Tools	Security Options		
Paste	WD 3.35	Paste button on Standard toolbar or click icon in Office Clipboard gallery in Office Clipboard task pane	Edit	Paste	Paste	CTRL+V
Paste Options, Display Menu	WD 2.47	Paste Options button			
Picture Bullets	WD 4.48		Format	Bullets and Numbering	Bulleted tab	Bullets and Numbering	Bulleted tab	
Print Document	WD 1.54	Print button on Standard toolbar	File	Print		CTRL+P
Print Preview	WD 3.25	Print Preview button on Standard toolbar	File	Print Preview		CTRL+F2
Promote List Item	WD 3.56	Increase Indent button on Formatting toolbar			
Propagate Labels	WD 5.58	Propagate Labels button on Mail Merge toolbar	Tools	Letters and Mailings	Mail Wizard		
Quit Word	WD 1.55	Close button on title bar	File	Exit		ALT+F4
Rectangle, Draw	WD 7.39	Rectangle button on Drawing toolbar			

Microsoft Word 2002 Quick Reference Summary (continued)

TASK	PAGE NUMBER	MOUSE	MENU BAR	SHORTCUT MENU	KEYBOARD SHORTCUT
Redo Action	WD 1.39	Redo button on Standard toolbar	Edit | Redo		
Repeat Command	WD 1.39		Edit | Repeat		
Resize Graphic	WD 1.51	Drag sizing handle	Format | Picture | Size tab	Format Picture | Size tab	
Resize Graphic, Format Picture Dialog Box	WD 4.17	Double-click graphic	Format | Picture | Picture tab	Format Picture | Picture tab	
Restore Graphic	WD 1.53	Format Picture button on Picture toolbar	Format | Picture | Size tab	Format Picture | Size tab	
Resume Wizard	WD 3.07		File | New | General Templates | Other Documents tab		
Reveal Formatting	WD 4.66		Format | Reveal Formatting		
Reviewer Initials, Change	WD 9.13		Tools | Options | User Information tab		
Right-Align	WD 1.37	Align Right button on Formatting toolbar	Format | Paragraph | Indents and Spacing tab	Paragraph | Indents and Spacing tab	CTRL+R
Ruler, Show or Hide	WD 1.13		View | Ruler		
Save, All Open Documents	WD 5.70		SHIFT + File | Save All		
Save as Web Page	WDW 1.03		File | Save as Web Page		
Save Document - New Name	WD 1.54		File | Save As		F12
Save Document - Same Name	WD 1.53	Save button on Standard toolbar	File | Save		CTRL+S
Save New Document	WD 1.30	Save button on Standard toolbar	File | Save		CTRL+S
Save Version	WD 9.16		File | Versions		
Search for File	WD 6.67	Search button on Standard toolbar			
Section Break, Continuous	WD 6.24		Insert | Break		
Section Break, Next Page	WD 4.22		Insert | Break		
Security Level	WD 8.10		Tools | Macro | Security | Security Level tab		
Select Document	WD 2.45	Point to left and triple-click	Edit | Select All		CTRL+A
Select Graphic	WD 1.50	Click graphic			
Select Group of Words	WD 1.44	Drag through words			CTRL+SHIFT+RIGHT ARROW
Select Line	WD 1.40	Point to left of line and click			SHIFT+DOWN ARROW
Select Multiple Paragraphs	WD 1.34	Point to left of first paragraph and drag down			CTRL+SHIFT+DOWN ARROW
Select Nonadjacent Text	WD 4.37				CTRL, while selecting additional text
Select Paragraph	WD 2.45	Triple-click paragraph			
Select Sentence	WD 2.45	CTRL+click sentence			CTRL+SHIFT+RIGHT ARROW
Select Word	WD 1.42	Double-click word			CTRL+SHIFT+RIGHT ARROW
Shade Paragraph	WD 6.40	Shading Color button on Tables and Borders toolbar	Format | Borders and Shading | Shading tab	Borders and Shading | Shading tab	
Shadow, on Characters	WD 4.15		Format | Font | Font tab	Font | Font tab	
Single-Space	WD 4.58	Line Spacing button arrow on Formatting toolbar	Format | Paragraph | Indents and Spacing tab	Paragraph | Indents and Spacing tab	CTRL+1
Small Uppercase Letters	WD 2.18		Format | Font | Font tab	Font | Font tab	CTRL+SHIFT+K
Smart Tag Actions, Display Menu	WD 3.59	Point to smart tag indicator, click Smart Tag Actions button			
Sort Paragraphs	WD 2.41		Table | Sort		
Spelling and Grammar Check At Once	WD 2.51	Spelling and Grammar button on Standard toolbar	Tools | Spelling and Grammar	Spelling	F7
Spelling Check as You Type	WD 1.28	Double-click Spelling and Grammar Status icon on status bar		Right-click flagged word, click correct word on shortcut menu	

Microsoft Word 2002 Quick Reference Summary

TASK	PAGE NUMBER	MOUSE	MENU BAR	SHORTCUT MENU	KEYBOARD SHORTCUT
Strikethrough, characters	WD 4.15		Format | Font | Font tab	Font | Font tab	
Style, Create	WD 8.17	Styles and Formatting button on Formatting toolbar	Format | Styles and Formatting		
Style, Modify	WD 2.28	Styles and Formatting button on Formatting toolbar	Format | Styles and Formatting		
Styles and Formatting Task Pane, Display	WD 3.19	Styles and Formatting button on Formatting toolbar	View | Task Pane		
Subdocument, Break Connection	WD 9.46	Remove Subdocument icon on Outlining toolbar			
Subdocument, Create	WD 9.43	Create Subdocument button on Outlining toolbar			
Subdocument, Delete	WD 9.46	Click subdocument icon, press DELETE			
Subdocument, Insert	WD 9.40	Insert Subdocument button on Outlining toolbar			
Subdocuments, Collapse	WD 9.42	Collapse Subdocuments button on Outlining toolbar			
Subdocuments, Expand	WD 9.42	Expand Subdocuments button on Outlining toolbar			
Subscript	WD 2.18		Format | Font | Font tab	Font | Font tab	CTRL+=
Superscript	WD 2.18		Format | Font | Font tab	Font | Font tab	CTRL+SHIFT+PLUS SIGN
Switch to Open Document	WD 3.32	Program button on taskbar	Window | document name		
Symbol, Insert	WD 6.17		Insert | Symbol	ALT+0 (zero) then ANSI code on numeric keypad	
Synonym	WD 2.50		Tools | Language | Thesaurus	Synonyms | desired word	SHIFT+F7
Tab Stops, Set	WD 3.31	Click location on ruler	Format | Tabs		
Table, Add a Row	WD 4.32	Insert Table button arrow on Tables and Borders toolbar	Table | Insert | Rows Above or Rows Below	Right-click selected row, Insert Rows	TAB in lower-right cell
Table, Adjust Row Height	WD 4.61	Drag row border	Table | Table Properties | Row tab	Table Properties | Row tab	
Table, Align Cell Contents	WD 4.62	Align button arrow on Tables and Borders toolbar	Table | Table Properties | Cell tab	Table Properties | Cell tab	
Table, AutoFormat	WD 3.53 WD 4.35	Table AutoFormat button on Tables and Borders toolbar	Table | Table AutoFormat		
Table, Convert Text	WD 5.65		Table | Convert | Text to Table		
Table, Draw	WD 4.54	Tables and Borders button on Standard toolbar	Table | Draw Table		
Table, Insert Empty	WD 3.49	Insert Table button on Standard toolbar	Table | Insert | Table		
Table, Insert Row	WD 3.16		Table | Insert | Rows Above/Below	Right-click selected row; Insert Rows	
Table, Resize Column	WD 3.54	Drag column boundary	Table | Table Properties | Column tab	Table Properties | Column tab	
Table, Resize Column to Contents	WD 3.52	Double-click column boundary	Table | AutoFit | AutoFit to Contents	AutoFit | AutoFit to Contents	
Table, Right-Align Cell Contents	WD 4.36	Align Right button on Formatting toolbar	Format | Paragraph | Indents and Spacing tab		CTRL+R
Table, Rotate Cell Text	WD 4.60	Change Text Direction button on Tables and Borders toolbar	Format | Text Direction	Text Direction	
Table, Select	WD 3.53	Click table move handle	Table | Select | Table		ALT+5 (on numeric keypad)
Table, Select Cell	WD 3.53	Click left edge of cell			Press TAB
Table, Select Column	WD 3.53	Click top border of column			

Microsoft Word 2002 Quick Reference Summary (continued)

TASK	PAGE NUMBER	MOUSE	MENU BAR	SHORTCUT MENU	KEYBOARD SHORTCUT
Table, Select Multiple Cells	WD 3.53	Drag through cells			
Table, Select Row	WD 3.53	Click to left of row			
Table, Shade Cells	WD 4.62	Shading Color button arrow on Tables and Borders toolbar	Format | Borders and Shading | Shading tab	Borders and Shading | Shading tab	
Table, Sort	WD 5.68	Sort Ascending button on Tables and Borders toolbar	Table | Sort		
Table, Sum a Column	WD 4.34	AutoSum button on Tables and Borders toolbar	Table | Formula		
Table of Contents, Create	WD 9.58		Insert | Reference | Index and Tables | Table of Contents tab		
Table of Contents, Update	WD 9.67			Right-click selected table of contents, click Update Field	Select table of contents, F9
Table of Figures, Create	WD 9.55		Insert | Reference | Index and Tables | Table of Figures tab		
Task Pane, Close	WD 1.10	Close button on task pane	View | Task Pane		
Task Pane, Display Different	WD 1.49	Other Task Panes button on task pane			
Template, Create	WD 7.09		File | New | General Templates		
Template, Open	WD 3.41		File | New | General Templates		
Template, Use in Mail Merge	WD 5.08		Tools | Letters and Mailings | Mail Merge Wizard		
Text Box, Convert to a Frame	WD 9.28	Double-click text box	Format | Text Box	Format Text Box	
Text Box, Format	WD 6.38	Double-click text box	Format | Text Box	Format Text Box	
Text Box, Insert	WD 6.36	Text Box button on Drawing toolbar	Insert | Text Box		
Toolbar, Customize	WD 8.28		Tools | Customize	Customize	
Toolbar, Dock	WD 2.13	Drag toolbar to dock			
Toolbar, Float	WD 2.13	Double-click between two buttons or boxes on toolbar			
Toolbar, Show Entire	WD 1.16	Double-click move handle on toolbar			
Track Changes	WD 9.14	Double-click TRK status indicator on status bar	Tools | Track Changes		CTRL+SHIFT+E
Track Changes, Stop	WD 9.16	Double-click TRK status indicator on status bar	Tools | Track Changes		CTRL+SHIFT+E
Tracked Changes, Display	WD 9.14	Display for Review button arrow on Reviewing toolbar	View | Markup		
Tracked Changes, Review	WD 9.18	Click Next button on Reviewing toolbar		Right-click tracked change	
Underline	WD 1.43	Underline button on Formatting toolbar	Format | Font | Font tab	Font | Font tab	CTRL+U
Underline, in color	WD 7.31		Format | Font	Font	
Underline Words, not Spaces	WD 2.18		Format | Font | Font tab	Font | Font tab	CTRL+SHIFT+W
Undo Command or Action	WD 1.39	Undo button on Standard toolbar	Edit | Undo		CTRL+Z
Unprotect Document	WD 8.08	Protect Form button on Forms toolbar	Tools | Unprotect Document		
Vertical Rule	WD 6.34		Format | Borders and Shading | Borders tab		
Visual Basic Editor, Insert Procedure	WD 8.47	Insert UserForm button arrow on Standard toolbar	Insert | Procedure		

Microsoft Word 2002 Quick Reference Summary

TASK	PAGE NUMBER	MOUSE	MENU BAR	SHORTCUT MENU	KEYBOARD SHORTCUT
Visual Basic Editor, Quit	WD 8.43	Close button on title bar	File	Close and Return to Microsoft Word		ALT+Q
Watermark	WD 4.64		Format	Background	Printed Watermark		
Web Page Frame, Resize	WDW 1.09	Drag frame border	Format	Frames	Frame Properties	Frame tab		
Web Page, View	WDW 1.11		File	Web Page Preview		
Web Page Wizard	WDW 1.05		File	New	General Templates	Web Pages tab		
White Space, Hide or Show	WD 3.15	Hide or Show White Space button	Tools	Options	View tab		
Widow/Orphan Setting	WD 9.33		Format	Paragraph	Paragraph	
WordArt Drawing Object, Format	WD 6.11	Format WordArt button on WordArt toolbar	Format	WordArt	Format WordArt	
WordArt Drawing Object, Insert	WD 6.09	Insert WordArt button on Drawing toolbar	Insert	Picture	WordArt		
WordArt Drawing Object, Shape	WD 6.13	WordArt Shape button on WordArt toolbar			
Wrap Text Around Graphic	WD 6.59	Text Wrapping button Picture or Diagram toolbar	Format	Picture or Diagram	Layout tab	Format Picture or Format Diagram	Layout tab	
Zoom Page Width	WD 1.19	Zoom box arrow on Formatting toolbar	View	Zoom		
Zoom Text Width	WD 3.18	Zoom box arrow on Formatting toolbar	View	Zoom		
Zoom Whole Page	WD 6.32	Zoom box arrow on Formatting toolbar	View	Zoom		